CORPORATE AND WHITE COLLAR CRIME:
AN ANTHOLOGY

ANDERSON'S
Law School Publications

ADMINISTRATIVE LAW ANTHOLOGY
by Thomas O. Sargentich

ADMINISTRATIVE LAW: CASES AND MATERIALS
by Daniel J. Gifford

ADMIRALTY LAW ANTHOLOGY
by Robert M. Jarvis

APPELLATE ADVOCACY: PRINCIPLES AND PRACTICE (Second Edition)
Cases and Materials
by Ursula Bentele and Eve Cary

A CAPITAL PUNISHMENT ANTHOLOGY
by Victor L. Streib

CASES AND PROBLEMS IN CRIMINAL LAW (Second Edition)
by Myron Moskovitz

THE CITATION WORKBOOK
by Maria L. Ciampi, Rivka Widerman and Vicki Lutz

COMMERCIAL TRANSACTIONS: PROBLEMS AND MATERIALS
Vol. 1: Secured Transactions Under the UCC
Vol. 2: Sales Under the UCC and the CISG
Vol. 3: Negotiable Instruments Under the UCC and the CIBN
by Louis F. Del Duca, Egon Guttman and Alphonse M. Squillante

A CONSTITUTIONAL LAW ANTHOLOGY
by Michael J. Glennon

CONSTITUTIONAL TORTS
by Sheldon H. Nahmod, Michael L. Wells, and Thomas A. Eaton

CONTRACTS
Contemporary Cases, Comments, and Problems
by Michael L. Closen, Richard M. Perlmutter and Jeffrey D. Wittenberg

A CONTRACTS ANTHOLOGY
by Peter Linzer

CORPORATE AND WHITE COLLAR CRIME: AN ANTHOLOGY
by Leonard Orland

A CRIMINAL LAW ANTHOLOGY
by Arnold H. Loewy

CRIMINAL LAW: CASES AND MATERIALS
by Arnold H. Loewy

CRIMINAL PROCEDURE: TRIAL AND SENTENCING
by Arthur B. LaFrance and Arnold H. Loewy

ECONOMIC REGULATION
Cases and Materials
by Richard J. Pierce, Jr.

ELEMENTS OF LAW
by Eva H. Hanks, Michael E. Herz and Steven S. Nemerson

ENDING IT: DISPUTE RESOLUTION IN AMERICA
Descriptions, Examples, Cases and Questions
by Susan M. Leeson and Bryan M. Johnston

ENVIRONMENTAL LAW (Second Edition)
Vol. 1: Environmental Decisionmaking: NEPA and the Endangered Species Act
Vol. 2: Water Pollution; Vol. 3: Air Pollution; Vol. 4: Hazardous Wastes
by Jackson B. Battle, Mark Squillace, Maxine I. Lipeles and Robert L. Fischman

ENVIRONMENTAL PROTECTION AND JUSTICE
Readings and Commentary on Environmental Law and Practice
by Kenneth A. Manaster

Continued

CORPORATE AND WHITE COLLAR CRIME: AN ANTHOLOGY

EDITED BY
LEONARD ORLAND

Professor of Law
University of Connecticut
School of Law

ANDERSON PUBLISHING COMPANY

CORPORATE AND WHITE COLLAR CRIME: AN ANTHOLOGY

© 1995 by Anderson Publishing Co.

ISBN: 0-87084-870-4

Library of Congress Cataloging-in-Publication Data

Corporate and white collar crime : an anthology / [edited by] Leonard
   Orland.
        p.   cm.
      ISBN 0-8784-870-4
      1. White collar crimes – United States. 2. Commercial crimes –
United States. 3. Criminal liability of juristic persons – United States.
4. Corporation law – United States – Criminal provisions.
I. Orland, Leonard.
KF9350.A75C67   1995
345.73'0268 – dc20
[347.305268]

95-11892
CIP

TO

Louis B. Schwartz – formerly Benjamin Franklin Professor of Law at the University of Pennsylvania and now Professor of Law at the University of California, Hastings College of Law – who has been my mentor and friend for thirty-five years and a source of inspiration for me and for generations of lawyers and legal scholars.

Contents

PART II
PUNISHMENT

PART III
CRIMES

Preface

This volume collects and structures the principal corporate and white collar crime literature. Conceived as ancillary reading for corporate and white collar crime law school courses which utilize rapidly emerging innovative casebooks (e.g., N. Abrams and S. Beale, *Federal Criminal Law* (2d. Ed., 1993), K. Brickey, *Corporate and White Collar Crime* (1990), P. Bucy, *White Collar Crime* (1992) and H. First, *Business Crime* (1990)), the book may also inform graduate and professional school courses in criminology and business and provide an independent source for law school courses and seminars.

The legal profession, in recent years, has seen a comparable emergence of innovative treatises on corporate and white collar crime, e.g., S. Arkin, E. Dudley, M. Eisenstein, J. Rakoff, D. Re and J. Siffert, *Business Crime* (1994), K. Brickey, *Corporate Criminal Liability* (2d. Ed., 1992), O. Obermaier and R. Morvillo, *White Collar Crime* (2d. Ed., 1995), L. Orland and H.R. Tyler, Jr., *Corporate Crime Law Enforcement in America* (1987), R. Rakoff, L. Blumkin and R. Sauber, *Corporate Sentencing Guidelines* (1993), J. Villa, *Banking Crimes* (1987), and the Annual *White Collar Crime* National Institute Materials of the ABA Criminal Justice Section. Hopefully, a one volume collection of the principal corporate and white collar crime literature will supplement these treatises and constitute a useful deskbook for practicing lawyers, prosecutors and judges.

Part I, "Crime", collects the theoretical and policy literature on the problems associated with use of the criminal sanction to enforce economic norms, addresses the difficult conceptual problems of differentiating corporate crime from tort, assembles the sociological literature on white collar and corporate crime, beginning with Sutherland's classic work in 1940, and confronts the core question of the justification for corporate criminal liability. Part II, "Punishment", presents the economic, sociological and public policy literature of white collar and corporate punishment and considers the increasingly important practice of imposing ancillary sanctions in white collar crime cases. Part III, "Crimes", assembles the leading law review literature on principal corporate and white collar crimes – conspiracy, RICO, mail fraud, securities fraud, antitrust, tax fraud, money laundering and homicide.

I have followed conventional form in noting editorial deletions with one exception: all footnotes have been deleted without explicit notation.

Dean Hugh Macgill of the University of Connecticut Law School has provided strong and sustained institutional, financial and scholarly support.

I have also received substantial assistance and support from the libraries of Yale University and from the Institution for Social and Policy Studies of Yale University and from its former director, Professor Joseph LaPalambara. I would like to record by special thanks and appreciation for the support and technical assistance of Shoshanah Asnis in the downloading and electronic editing of materials from the WESTLAW and LEXIS data bases, to Mary Ann Potoniac and Cheryl DeFilippo for superb manuscript typing, to Scott Gottlieb for outstanding research assistance, and to Delia Roy, for overall wordprocessing supervision and final manuscript preparation and for years of ever cheerful and always supportive professional assistance. Without their generous assistance, this effort to harness the modern technologies of data retrieval and word processing to the task of manuscript preparation would not have been imaginable for those of us from the cut and paste era of typewriters, scissors and glue.

Part I

Crime

A. Business Crime

Henry A. Hart, Jr., *The Aims of the Criminal Law*, 23 Law & Contemp. Probs. 401–436 (1958)*

I

Introduction

In trying to formulate the aims of the criminal law, it is important to be aware both of the reasons for making the effort and of the nature of the problem it poses.

The statement has been made, as if in complaint, that "there is hardly a penal code that can be said to have a single basic principle running through it." But it needs to be clearly seen that this is simply a fact, and not a misfortune. A penal code that reflected only a single basic principle would be a very bad one. Social purposes can never be single or simple, or held unqualifiedly to the exclusion of all other social purposes; and an effort to make them so can result only in the sacrifice of other values which also are important. Thus, to take only one example, the purpose of preventing any particular kind of crime, or crimes generally, is qualified always by the purposes of avoiding the conviction of the innocent and of enhancing that sense of security throughout the society which is one of the prime functions of the manifold safeguards of American criminal procedure. And the same thing would be true even if the dominant purpose of the criminal law were thought to be the rehabilitation of offenders rather than the prevention of offenses.

Examination of the purposes commonly suggested for the criminal law will show that each of them is complex and that none may be thought of as wholly

excluding the others. Suppose, for example, that the deterrence of offenses is taken to be the chief end. It will still be necessary to recognize that the rehabilitation of offenders, the disablement of offenders, the sharpening of the community's sense of right and wrong, and the satisfaction of the community's sense of just retribution may all serve this end by contributing to an ultimate reduction in the number of crimes. Even socialized vengeance may be accorded a marginal role, if it is understood as the provision of an orderly alternative to mob violence.

The problem, accordingly, is one of the priority and relationship of purposes as well as of their legitimacy—of multi-valued rather than of single-valued thinking.

There is still another range of complications which are ignored if an effort is made to formulate any single "theory" or set of "principles" of criminal law. The purpose of having principles and theories is to help in organizing thought. In the law, the ultimate purpose of thought is to help in deciding upon a course of action. In the criminal law, as in all law, questions about the action to be taken do not present themselves for decision in an institutional vacuum. They arise rather in the context of some established and specific procedure of decision: in a constitutional convention; in a legislature; in a prosecuting attorney's office; in a court charged with the determination of guilt or innocence; in a sentencing court; before a parole board; and so on. This means that each agency of decision must take account always of its own place in the institutional system and of what is necessary to maintain the integrity and workability of the system as a whole. A complex of institutional ends must be served, in other words, as well as a complex of substantive social ends.

The principal levels of decision in the criminal law are numerous. The institutional considerations involved at the various levels differ so markedly that it seems worth while to discuss the question of aims

* Reprinted with permission.

separately, from the point of view of each of the major agencies of decision.

II
THE PERSPECTIVE OF CONSTITUTIONAL MAKERS

We can get our broadest view of the aims of the criminal law if we look at them from the point of view of the makers of a constitution—of those who are seeking to establish sound foundations for a tolerable and durable social order. From this point of view, these aims can be most readily seen, as they need to be seen, in their relation to the aims of the good society generally.

In this setting, the basic question emerges: Why should the good society make use of the method of the criminal law at all?

A. What the Method of the Criminal Law Is

The question posed raises preliminarily an even more fundamental inquiry: What do we mean by "crime" and "criminal"? Or, put more accurately, what should we understand to be "the method of the criminal law," the use of which is in question? This latter way of formulating the preliminary inquiry is more accurate, because it pictures the criminal law as a process, a way of doing something, which is what it is. A great deal of intellectual energy has been misspent in an effort to develop a concept of crime as "a natural and social phenomenon" abstracted from the functioning system of institutions which make use of the concept and give it impact and meaning. But the criminal law, like all law, is concerned with the pursuit of human purposes through the forms and modes of social organization, and it needs always to be thought about in that context as a method or process of doing something.

What then are the characteristics of this method?

1. The method operates by means of a series of directions, or commands, formulated in general terms, telling people what they must or must not do. Mostly, the commands of the criminal law are "must-nots," or prohibitions, which can be satisfied by inaction. "Do not murder, rape, or rob." But some of them are "musts," or affirmative requirements, which can be satisfied only by taking a specifically, or relatively specifically, described kind of action. "Support your wife and children," and "File your income tax return."

2. The commands are taken as valid and binding upon all those who fall within their terms when the time comes for complying with them, whether or not they have been formulated in advance in a single authoritative set of words. They speak to members of the community, in other words, in the community's behalf, with all the power and prestige of the community behind them.

3. The commands are subject to one or more sanctions for disobedience which the community is prepared to enforce.

Thus far, it will be noticed, nothing has been said about the criminal law which is not true also of a large part of the noncriminal, or civil, law. The law of torts, the law of contracts, and almost every other branch of private law that can be mentioned operate, too, with general directions prohibiting or requiring described types of conduct, and the community's tribunals enforce these commands. What, then, is distinctive about the method of the criminal law?

Can crimes be distinguished from civil wrongs on the ground that they constitute injuries to society generally which society is interested in preventing? The difficulty is that society is interested also in the due fulfillment of contracts and the avoidance of traffic accidents and most of the other stuff of civil litigation. The civil law is framed and interpreted and enforced with a constant eye to these social interests. Does the distinction lie in the fact that proceedings to enforce the criminal law are instituted by public officials rather than private complainants? The difficulty is that public officers may also bring many kinds of "civil" enforcement actions—for an injunction, for the recovery of a "civil" penalty, or even for the detention of the defendant by public authority. Is the distinction, then, in the peculiar character of what is done to people who are adjudged to be criminals? The difficulty is that, with the possible exception of death, exactly the same kinds of unpleasant consequences, objectively considered, can be and are visited upon unsuccessful defendants in civil proceedings.

If one were to judge from the notions apparently underlying many judicial opinions, and the overt language even of some of them, the solution of the puzzle is simply that a crime is anything which is *called* a crime, and a criminal penalty is simply the penalty provided for doing anything which has been given that name. So vacant a concept is a betrayal of intellectual bankruptcy. Certainly, it poses no intelligible issue for a constitution-maker concerned to decide whether to make use of "the method of the criminal law." Moreover, it is false to popular understanding, and false also to the understanding embodied in existing constitutions. By implicit assumptions that are more impressive than any explicit assertions, these constitutions proclaim that a conviction for crime is a distinctive and serious matter—a something, and not a nothing. What is that something?

4. What distinguishes a criminal from a civil sanction and all that distinguishes it, it is ventured, is the judgment of community condemnation which accompanies and justifies its imposition. As Professor Gardner wrote

not long ago, in a distinct but cognate connection.

The essence of punishment for moral delinquency lies in the criminal conviction itself. One may lose more money on the stock market than in a court-room; a prisoner of war camp may well provide a harsher environment that a state prison; death on the field of battle has the same physical characteristics as death by sentence of law. It is the expression of the community's hatred, fear, or contempt for the convict which alone characterizes physical hardship as punishment.

If this is what a "criminal" penalty is, then we can say readily enough what a "crime" is. It is not simply anything which a legislature chooses to call a "crime." It is not simply antisocial conduct which public officers are given a responsibility to suppress. It is not simply any conduct to which a legislature chooses to attach a "criminal" penalty. It is conduct which, if duly shown to have taken place, will incur a formal and solemn pronouncement of the moral condemnation of the community.

The method of criminal law, of course, involves something more than the threat (and, on due occasion, the expression) of community condemnation of antisocial conduct. It involves, in addition, the threat (and, on due occasion, the imposition) of unpleasant physical consequences, commonly called punishment. But if Professor Gardner is right, these added consequences take their character as punishment from the condemnation which precedes them and serves as the warrant for their infliction. Indeed, the condemnation plus the added consequences may well be considered, compendiously, as constituting the punishment. Otherwise, it would be necessary to think of a convicted criminal as going unpunished if the imposition or execution of his sentence is suspended. In traditional thought and speech, the ideas of crime and punishment have been inseparable; the consequences of conviction for crime have been described as a matter of course of "punishment." The Constitution of the United States and its amendments, for example, use this word or its verb form in relation to criminal offenses no less than six times. Today, "treatment" has become a fashionable euphemism for the older, ugly word. This bowdlerizing of the Constitution and of conventional speech may serve a useful purpose in discouraging unduly harsh sentences and emphasizing that punishment is not an end in itself. But to the extent that it dissociates the treatment of criminals from the social condemnation of their conduct which is implicit in their conviction, there is danger that it will confuse thought and do a disservice.

At least under existing law, there is a vital difference between the situation of a patient who has been committed to a mental hospital and the situation of an inmate of a state penitentiary. The core of the difference is precisely that the patient has not incurred the moral condemnation of his community, whereas the convict has. . . .

III
THE PERSPECTIVE OF THE LEGISLATURE

A legislature deals with crimes always in advance of their commission (assuming the existence of constitutional prohibitions or practices excluding ex post facto laws and bills of attainder). it deals with them not by condemnation and punishment, but only by threat of condemnation and punishment, *to be imposed always be other agencies.* It deals with them always by directions formulated in *general terms.* The primary parts of the directions have always to be interpreted and applied by the private persons – the potential offenders – to whom they are initially addressed. In the event of a breach or claim of breach, both the primary and the remedial parts must be interpreted and applied by the various officials – police, prosecuting attorneys, trial judges and jurors, appellate judges, and probation, prison, and parole authorities – responsible for their enforcement. The attitudes, capacities, and practical conditions of work of these officials often put severe limits upon the ability of the legislature to accomplish what it sets out to accomplish.

If the primary parts of a general direction are to work successfully in any particular instance, otherwise than by fortunate accident, four conditions have always to be satisfied: (1) the primary addressee who is supposed to conform his conduct to the direction must know (a) of its existence, and (b) of its content in relevant respects; (2) he must know about the circumstances of fact which make the abstract terms of the direction applicable in the particular instance; (3) he must be able to comply with it; and (4) he must be willing to do so.

The difficulties of satisfying these conditions vitally affect the fairness and often even the feasibility of the effort to control the behavior of large numbers of people by means of general directions, subject only to an after-the-event sanction. This is so even when the sanction is civil, such as a judgment for compensatory damages or restoration of benefits. But the difficulties are especially acute when the sanction is criminal. For then, something more is involved than the simply necessity of getting the direction complied with in a sufficient proportion of instances to keep it in good working order – that is, to maintain respect for it and to avoid arbitrary discrimination in singling out individual violators as subjects of enforcement proceedings. If what was said in part two is correct, it is necessary to be able to say in good conscience in *each* instance in which a criminal sanction is imposed for a violation of law that the violation was blameworthy and, hence, deserving of the moral condemnation of the community. This raises two closely related questions which lie at the heart of the problems of the criminal law; *First,* what are the ingredients of moral blameworthiness which warrant a judgment of community condemnation? *Second,* retracing the ground of part two, can the position be maintained that guilt in the sense of the criminal law is an individual matter and cannot justly be pronounced by the community if the individual's conduct affords no basis for a judgment of moral condemnation?

These questions present themselves in different guises in different types of criminal statutes. They can best be examined separately in relation to the various major types of purposes for which a legislature may seek to employ a criminal sanction.

A. The Statement of the Minimum Obligations of Responsible Citizenship: The Control of Purposeful Conduct

The core of a sound penal code in any view of the function of the criminal law is the statement of those minimum obligations of conduct which the conditions of community life impose upon every participating member if community life is to be maintained and to prosper—that is, of those obligations which result not from a discretionary and disputable judgment of the legislature, but from the objective facts of the interdependencies of the people who are living together in the community and of their awareness of the interdependencies.

In the mind of any legislator who recognizes this central and basic job as a distinct one and who is trying to do it faithfully and intelligently, a variety of aims will coalesce, to the point of becoming virtually indistinguishable. The inculcation of a sense of social responsibility throughout the society will be the dominant aim. But the stated obligations will, at the same time, represent desired standards of conduct and so will necessarily involve the aim of deterrence of undesired conduct. Since violators are to be condemned as defaulters in their duty to the community and treated accordingly, the aim can also be described as punitive. And if the conduct declared to be criminal does, indeed, evince a blameworthy lack of social responsibility, the declaration will also constitute an essential first step in identifying those members of the community whose behavior shows them to be in need of cure and rehabilitation, and this aim will likewise be included. So also, subordinately, will be the aim of temporary or permanent disablement of certain of the more serious offenders.

Returning now to the four conditions earlier stated for the successful operation of a general direction and to the problem of deciding when a failure of compliance due to a failure to satisfy one of the conditions is blameworthy, it will be seen that in this area of the criminal law, the difficulties are minimal, so long at least as the legislature is denouncing purposeful or knowing, as distinguished from reckless or merely negligent, conduct.

If the legislature does a sound job of reflecting community attitudes and needs, actual knowledge of the wrongfulness of the prohibited conduct will usually exist. Thus, almost everyone is aware that murder and forcible rape and the obvious forms of theft are wrong. But in any event, knowledge of wrongfulness can fairly be assumed. For any member of the community who does these things without knowing that they are criminal is blameworthy, as much for his lack of knowledge as for his actual conduct. This seems to be the essential rationale of the maxim, *Ignorantia legis neminem excusat,* which has been so much misunderstood and abused in relation to regulatory crimes, involving conduct which is not intrinsically wrongful.

Similarly, knowledge of the circumstances of fact which make the law's directions applicable will ordinarily exist when harms are inflicted or risks created of the elementary and obvious types sought to be prevented by these intrinsically wrongful crimes. But suppose that knowledge does not exist? The traditional criminal law, concerned almost exclusively with crimes of this kind, has ready to hand a solution in the traditional maxim that ignorance of fact excuses, as well as in cognate doctrines such as that of claim-of-right in the law of theft. If the legislature can depend upon the courts to read these doctrines into its enactments, the requisite of blameworthiness as an element of criminality will be respected.

Obligations of conduct fixed by a fair appraisal of the minimum requirements for the maintenance and fostering of community life will, by hypothesis, be obligations which normal members of the community will be *able* to comply with, given the necessary awareness of the circumstances of fact calling for compliance. But suppose that in a particular case, this ability does not exist? Again, the traditional law provides materials for solution of the problem when inability negatives blameworthiness; and the only question is whether the legislature can count upon the courts to make use of the materials. The materials include doctrines with respect to duress, as well as doctrines providing for the exculpation of those individuals who because of mental disease or defect are to be deemed incapable of acting as responsible, participating members of society.

There remains only the question of willingness to comply. In relation to directions which make a reasonably grounded appeal to the citizen's sense of responsibility as a citizen, this willingness is likely to be at a maximum. Individuals who are able but unwilling to comply with such directions are precisely the ones who ought to be condemned as criminals.

In the sphere of conduct which is intrinsically wrongful, the legislature's task is further simplified by its ability (or the ability which it is entitled to suppose it has) to rely upon the courts for the elaboration of detail and the solution of unanticipated or peripheral problems. Indeed, this was a body of law which was largely built up by English judges without benefit of acts of Parliament and which in this country required the intervention of the legislature, on its primary side, only to satisfy the theoretical and emotional appeal of the maxim, *Nullum crimen sine lege*. Despite the maxim, most American legislatures have been content to make use of familiar words and phrases of the common law, relying upon the courts to fill in their meaning, and even leaving whole areas of doctrine, such as criminal intent and various phases of justification, entirely to the courts. So long as the courts are faithful in their reflection of the community's understanding of what is morally blameworthy, judgments of conviction are not subject to the reproach of being, even in spirit, ex post facto.

B. The Statement of the Minimum Obligations of Responsible Citizenship: The Control of Reckless and Negligent Conduct

Special difficulties are presented when the criminal law undertakes to state an obligation of conduct in a way which requires an addressee, if he is to comply with it, to have a certain kind of general knowledge or experience, or to exercise a certain degree of skill and attention, or to make an appraisal of the probable consequences of what he does or omits to do with a certain degree of accuracy. When can a criminal sanction be properly authorized in cases in which the addressee fails in one or another of these respects and harm results or a risk is created because of his failure?

For example, one who undertakes to practice as a physician does not know that flannels saturated with kerosene will tend to produce severe burns if applied directly to the flesh of a patient. A foreman of a railroad section gang misreads a timetable and orders railroad tracks to be taken up for replacement just before a train is due. The owner of a night club fails to realize that the means of egress would be inadequate if a fire were to break out when the club was crowded. Upon precisely what kind of showing can a legislature justly provide that such people are to be condemned

and punished as criminals? If the legislature requires that an awareness of the risk be brought home to the actor and that the risk be one which, by the general standards of the community, is plainly excessive, a direction for criminal punishment creates no difficulty of principle, however trying may be the problems of application. For judgment about whether a given risk can justifiably be taken to promote a given end depends upon the evaluations implicit in community standards of right and wrong to which each member of the community can justly be expected to conform his conduct. If an individual knowingly takes a risk of a kind which the community condemns as plainly unjustifiable, then he is morally blameworthy and can properly be adjudged a criminal. He is criminally reckless in the traditional sense articulated with precision by the draftsmen of the American Law Institute's Model Penal Code.

This concept of criminal recklessness may well embrace not only situations in which the actor adverts directly to the possibility of the ultimate harm, but those in which he adverts only to his own deficiencies in appraising the possibility of harm or preventing it from coming to pass and to the possible consequences of *those* deficiencies. Thus, the doctor who swathes his patient with kerosene-soaked rags, without even suspecting what is going to happen, may, nevertheless, know that special knowledge and training is generally needed in order to treat patients safely and successfully and that he does not have that knowledge and training. In any such situation, if the actor knows of his deficiency and of the risk which such a deficiency creates, and if *that* risk is one which in community understanding is plainly unjustifiable, there is a basis for legislative condemnation of the conduct as criminally reckless.

Moreover, as considered more fully under the next subheading, if the actor knowingly goes counter to a valid legislative determination that the risk he is taking is excessive, even though he himself does not believe it to be, there is an independent basis for moral condemnation in this deliberate defiance of law.

The question remains whether simple unawareness of risk, without awareness of any deficiency preventing appreciation or avoidance of it and without any element of knowing disregard of a relevant legislative decision, can justly be declared to be culpable. The answer would seem clearly to be no, at least in those situations in which the actor lacks the ability either to refrain from the conduct which creates the risk or to correct the deficiency which makes engaging in the conduct dangerous, for otherwise, the third of the requisites above stated for the successful operation of a general direction is impossible to satisfy. But suppose the actor has this ability? Guilt would, then, seem to depend upon whether he has been put upon notice of his duty to use his ability to a degree which makes his unawareness of the duty, in the understanding of the community, genuinely blameworthy. In exceptional situations of elementary and obvious danger, the circumstances of fact of which the actor is conscious may be sufficient in themselves to give this notice. But this can be true only when the significance of the circumstances of fact would be apparent to one who shares the community's general sense of right and wrong. If this is not so—if appreciation of the significance of the facts depends upon knowledge of what happens to be written in the statute books—then, the problem becomes one of the nature and extent of the moral obligation to know what is so written, which is discussed under the next subheading.

Criminal punishment of merely negligent behavior is commonly justified not on the ground that violators can be said to be individually blameworthy, but on the ground that the threat of such punishment will help to teach people generally to be more careful. This proposes, as legitimate, an aim for the legislature which is drastically different from that of inculcating minimum standards of personal responsibility to society. The issue it raises are examined under the subheading after the next.

C. The Regulation of Conduct which Is Not Intrinsically Wrongful: Bases of Blameworthiness

The statute books of the forty-nine states and the United States are filled with enactments carrying a criminal sanction which are obviously motivated by other ends, primarily, than that of training for responsible citizenship. The legislature simply wants certain things done and certain other things not done because it believes that the doing or the not doing of them will secure some ultimate social advantage, and not at all because it thinks the immediate conduct involved is either rightful or wrongful in itself. It employs the threat of criminal condemnation and punishment as an especially forceful way of saying that it really wants to be obeyed, or else simply from lack of enough imagination to think of a more appropriate sanction. Such enactments present problems which neither the courts nor the legislature of this country have yet succeeded in thinking through.

When a legislature undertakes to prohibit or require conduct theretofore untouched by the criminal law, what considerations *ought* to guide it in deciding whether to declare that noncompliance with its direction shall be a crime?

1. If the legislature can, in good conscience, conclude that the new direction embodies standards of behavior which have to be observed, under existing social conditions, if social life is to be maintained, then the use of a criminal sanction raises no difficulty. Obviously, there is room for growth, as conditions and attitudes in society change, in the central body of law earlier discussed which undertakes to state the minimum obligations of responsible citizenship. Obviously also, the legislature is an appropriate agency to settle debatable questions about the appropriate extent of growth, whether or not it is desirable for courts to have a share in the process.

Statutes which make well-considered additions to the list of the citizen's basic obligations are not open to the objection of undue multiplication of crimes. Normal principles of culpability moreover, can properly apply to such offenses, and should apply. Absent exceptional circumstances, in other words, ignorance of the criminality of the conduct (act or omission) which is forbidden ought not to be a defense. *Per contra,* ignorance of the facts ought to be. And, of course, the usual defenses based on inability to comply should be available.

2. If the legislature cannot, in good conscience, regard conduct which it wishes to forbid as wrongful in itself, then it has always the option of declaring the conduct to be criminal only when the actor knows of its criminality or recklessly disregards the possibility that it is criminal. For knowing or reckless disregard of legal obligation affords an independent basis of blameworthiness justifying the actor's condemnation as a criminal, even when his conduct was not intrinsically antisocial. It is convenient to use the word "wilful" to describe this mode of culpability, although the term is by no means regularly so limited in conventional usage.

The inclusion in a new regulatory crime of the requirement of "wilfulness" avoids any difficulty of principle in the use of the criminal sanction—assuming that the requirement comprehends not only a culpable awareness (knowing or reckless) of the law, but a culpable awareness also of the facts making the law applicable, together with a sufficient ability to comply. The requirement, moreover, mitigates any objection on the score of undue multiplication of regulatory crimes, although it can hardly eliminate it entirely.

3. Under what, if any, circumstances may a legislature properly direct the conviction as a criminal of a person whose conduct is not wrongful in itself and who neither knows nor recklessly disregards the possibility that he is violating the law?

To engage knowingly or recklessly in conduct which is wrongful in itself and which has, in fact, been condemned as a crime is either to fail to comprehend the community's accepted moral values or else squarely to challenge them. The maxim, *Ignorantia legis neminem excusat,* expresses the wholly defensible and, indeed, essential principle that the action, in either event, is blameworthy. If, however, the criminal law adheres to this maxim when it moves from the condemnation of those things which are *mala in se* to the condemnation of those things which are merely *mala prohibita,* it necessarily shifts its ground from a demand that every responsible member of the community understand and respect the community's moral values to a demand that everyone know and understand what is written in the statute books. Such a demand is *toto coelo* different. In no respect is contemporary law subject to greater reproach than for its obtuseness to this fact.

Granting that blame may, in some circumstances, attach to an actor's antecedent failure to determine the legality of his conduct, it is, in any event, blame of a very distinctive kind.

a. The blame in such a case is largely unrelated, in gravity or any other respect, to the external conduct itself, or its consequences, for which the actor is purportedly convicted. Indeed, all such instances of conduct in ignorance of laws enjoining *mala prohibita* might well be thought of as constituting a single type of crime, if they constitute any kind of crime at all — the crime of ignorance of the statutes of their interpretation. Knowledge of the facts and ability to comply may be formal requisites of criminality, but in the absence of knowledge of the law, they are irrelevant, and willingness to comply remains untested. The whole weight of the law's efforts to achieve its purpose has to be carried, in the first instance, by the effort to get people to know and understand its requirements.

b. In such cases, the essential crime, if that is what it is, is always a crime of omission. If the purported crime is itself one of omission, as in the failure to take out a license, then the offense is doubly negative. As Professor Graham Hughes has recently abundantly demonstrated,

> . . . a penal policy of omissions and a criminal jurisprudence of offenses of omission are overdue. . . . [W]here inaction is evidently socially harmful, no good reason appears for shrinking from penal prohibition. Any penal policy, however, must be linked with a consciousness of the need to promulgate and publicize offenses of omission and a recognition by the judiciary that conventional attitudes to *mens rea,* particularly with respect to ignorance of the law, are not adequate tools to achieve justice for those accused of inaction.

Even when the nominal crime is one of commission rather than omission, the problem of promulgating and publicizing the offense, which Professor Hughes mentions, is likely to be serious if the nature of the affirmative conduct gives no warning of the possibility of an applicable criminal prohibition. But it is especially likely to be serious when the nominal crime is itself one of omission, for mere inaction often gives no such warning whatever.

c. The gist of a crime of statutory ignorance may lie not in the failure to inform oneself of the existence of an applicable statute, which is always in some sense a do-able thing if the statutes are published and there is a decent index to them, but in the failure to divine their meaning, which may be altogether non-do-able. All statutes are, of necessity, indeterminate in some of their applications. When a criminal enactment proscribes conduct which is *malum in se,* such as murder or manslaughter, however, the moral standards of the community are available always as a guide in the resolution of its indeterminacies, and there is a minimum of unfairness when doubt is resolved against a particular defendant. This guidance is missing when the proscribed conduct is merely *malum prohibitum.* The resolution of doubts must, thus, depend not upon a good human sense of moral values, but upon a sound grasp of technical doctrines and policies of statutory interpretation. Dean Pound has justly observed of American lawyers and judges that "we have no well-developed technique of developing legislative texts." To condemn a layman as blameworthy for a default of technical judgment in a matter which causes trouble even for professional judges is, in many cases, so manifestly beyond reason that courts have developed various makeshift devices to avoid condemnation in particular situations. And the draftsmen of the Model Penal Code have devised for such cases a generalized defense of limited scope. Until the nature and dimensions of the problem have been more fully perceived, however, no genuinely satisfactory solution can be reached.

d. No doubt there are situations in which one who engages in a particular course of conduct assumes an obligation, in general community understanding, to know about the law applicable to that kind of conduct. Sometimes, this may be true in areas of statutory law affecting people generally, such as motor vehicle laws. It is most likely to be true of laws applicable to particular occupations. One cannot say categorically, therefore, that ignorance of a law creating a merely statutory crime never affords a basic for moral condemnation. What can be said, in general terms, is that (1) the criminal law as a device for getting people to know about statutes and interpret them correctly is a device of dubious and largely unproved effectiveness; (2) the indiscriminate use of the device dilutes the force of the threat of community condemnation as a means of influencing conduct in other situations where the basis for moral condemnation is clear; (3) the loss to society from this dilution is always unnecessary, since the legislature has always the alternatives of either permitting a good faith belief in the legality of one's conduct to be pleaded and proved as a defense, or of providing a civil rather than a criminal sanction for nonwilful violations.

e. Under what, if any, circumstances may a legislature properly direct the conviction as a criminal of one who knows about the applicable law but who has been negligent, although not reckless, in ascertaining the facts which make the law applicable to his conduct—where the kind of conduct involved is morally neutral, both from the point of view of the actor and in actuality?

In the usual situation of assertedly criminal negligence earlier discussed, the harm caused or threatened by failure of advertence is one which it would be morally wrongful to cause advertently. The assertion of a duty of attention is, thus, strengthened by the gravity of the risks actually involved. In the situation now under discussion, the facts are morally neutral, even to one who knows about them, save for the existence of an applicable statute. Thus, the basis of blame, if any, is inattention to one's duty as a citizen to see that the law gets complied with in all the situations to which it is supposed to apply. For example, manufactured food becomes adulterated or misbranded within the meaning of a statute, but in a way which involves no danger to health.

Condemning a person for lack of ordinary care in ascertaining facts at least does not involve the offense to justice sometimes involved in the ignorance-of-interpretation-of-statute cases of condemning him for failure to do the impossible. But otherwise, most of the points just made about ignorance of regulatory law apply: (1) the basis of moral blame will usually be thin and may be virtually nonexistent; (2) the likelihood of substantial social gain in stimulating greater care is dubious; (3) the social cost is a weakening of the moral force and, hence, the effectiveness of the threat of criminal conviction; and (4) the cost is unnecessary, since the legislature has always the alternative of a civil sanction.

D. Strict Liability

A large body of modern law goes far beyond an insistence upon a duty of ordinary care in ascertaining facts, at the peril of being called a criminal. To an absolute duty to know about the existence of a regulatory statute and interpret it correctly, it adds an absolute duty to know about the facts. Thus, the porter who innocently carries the bag of a hotel guest not knowing that it contains a bottle of whisky is punished as a criminal for having transported intoxicating liquor. The corporation president who signs a registration statement for a proposed securities issue not knowing that his accountants have made a mistake is guilty of the crime of making a "false" representation to the state blue-sky commissioner. The president of a corporation whose employee introduces into interstate commerce a shipment of technically but harmlessly adulterated food is branded as a criminal solely because he was the president when the shipment was made. And so on, *ad* almost *infinitum.*

In all such cases, it is possible, of course, that a basis of blameworthiness might have been found in the particular facts. Perhaps the company presidents actually *were* culpably careless in their supervision. Conceivably, even, the porter was culpably remiss in failing to ask the traveler about the contents of his bag, or at least in failing to shake it to see if he could hear a gurgle. But these possibilities are irrelevant. For the statutes in question, as interpreted, do not require any such defaults to be proved against a defendant, nor even permit him to show the absence of such a default in defense. The offenses fall within "the numerous class in which diligence, actual knowledge and bad motives are immaterial. . . ." Thus, they squarely pose the question whether there can be any justification for condemning and punishing a human being as a criminal when he has done nothing which is blameworthy.

It is submitted that there can be no moral justification for this, and that there is not, indeed, even a rational, amoral justification.

1. People who do not know and cannot find out that they are supposed to comply with an applicable command are, by hypothesis, nondeterrable. So far as personal amenability to legal control is concerned, they stand in the same posture as the plainest lunatic under the *M'Naghten* test who "does not know the nature and quality of his act or, if he does know it, does not know that the act is wrong."

2. If it be said that most people will know of such commands and be able to comply with them, the answer, among others, is that nowhere else in the criminal law is the probable, or even the certain, guilt of nine men regarded as sufficient warrant for the conviction of a tenth. In the tradition of Anglo-American law, guilt of crime is personal. The main body of the criminal law, from the Constitution on down, makes sense on no other assumption.

3. If it be asserted that strict criminal liability is necessary in order to stimulate people to be diligent in learning the law and finding out when it applies,

the answer, among others, is that this is wholly unproved and prima facie improbable. Studies to test the relative effectiveness of strict criminal liability and well-designed civil penalties are lacking and badly needed. Until such studies are forthcoming, however, judgment can only take into account (a) the inherent unlikelihood that people's behavior will be significantly affected by commands that are not brought definitely to their attention: (b) the long-understood tendency of disproportionate penalties to promote disrespect rather than respect for law, unless they are rigorously and uniformly enforced; (c) the inherent difficulties of rigorous and uniform enforcement of strict criminal liability and the impressive evidence that it is, in fact, spottily and unevenly enforced; (d) the greater possibilities or flexible and imaginative adaptation of civil penalties to fit particular regulatory problems, the greater reasonableness of such penalties, and their more ready enforceability; and (e) most important of all, the shocking damage that is done to social morale by open and official admission that crime can be respectable and criminality a matter of ill chance, rather than blameworthy choice.

4. If it be urged that strict criminal liability is necessary in order to simplify the investigation and prosecution of violations of statutes designed to control mass conduct, the answer, among others, is that (a) maximizing compliance with law, rather than successful prosecution of violators, is the primary aim of any regulatory statute; (b) the convenience of investigators and prosecutors is not, in any event, the prime consideration in determining what conduct is criminal; (c) a prosecutor, as a matter of common knowledge, always assumes a heavier burden in trying to secure a criminal conviction than a civil judgment; (d) in most situations of attempted control of mass conduct, the technique of a first warning, followed by criminal prosecution only of knowing violators, has not only obvious, but proved superiority; and (e) the common-sense advantages of using the criminal sanction only against deliberate violators is confirmed by the policies which prosecutors themselves tend always to follow when they are free to make their own selection of cases to prosecute.

5. Moral, rather than crassly utilitarian, considerations re-enter the picture when the claim is made, as it sometimes is, that strict liability operates, in fact, only against people who are really blameworthy, because prosecutors only pick out the really guilty ones for criminal prosecution. This argument reasserts the traditional position that a criminal conviction imports moral condemnation. To this, it adds the arrogant assertion that it is proper to visit the moral condemnation of the community upon one of its members on the basis solely of the private judgment of his prosecutors.

Such a circumvention of the safeguards with which the law surrounds other determinations of criminality seems not only irrational, but immoral as well.

6. But moral considerations in a still larger dimension are the ultimately controlling ones. In its conventional and traditional applications, a criminal conviction carries with it an ineradicable connotation of moral condemnation and personal guilt. Society makes an essentially parasitic, and hence illegitimate, use of this instrument when it uses it as a means of deterrence (or compulsion) of conduct which is morally neutral. This would be true even if a statute were to be enacted proclaiming that no criminal conviction hereafter should ever be understood as casting any reflection on anybody. For statutes cannot change the meaning of words and make people stop thinking what they do think when they hear the words spoken. But it is doubly true – it is ten-fold, a hundred-fold, a thousandfold true – when society continues to insist that crimes *are* morally blameworthy and then tries to use the same epithet to describe conduct which is not.

7. To be sure, the traditional law recognizes gradations in the gravity of offenses, and so does the Constitution of the United States. But strict liability offenses have not been limited to the interpretively-developed constitutional category of "petty offenses," for which trial by jury is not required. They include even some crimes which the Constitution expressly recognizes as "infamous." Thus, the excuse of the Scotch servant girl for her illegitimate baby, that "It was only such a leetle one," is not open to modern legislatures. And since a crime remains a crime, just as a baby is unalterably a baby, it would not be a good excuse if it were. Especially is this so since the legislature could avoid the taint of illegitimacy, much more surely than the servant girl, by simply saying that the "crime" is not a crime, but only a civil violation. . . .

HERBERT L. PACKER, *The Businessman as Criminal, The Limits of the Criminal Sanction*, 354–363 (1968)*

There is a vast area of criminal proscription that

* Reprinted with permission from *The Limits of the Criminal Sanction* by Herbert L. Packer with the permission of the publishers, Stanford University Press. © 1968 by Herbert L. Packer.

does not deal with either of the two principal kinds of antisocial activity we have so far been discussing: on the one hand, gross and immediate injuries or threats of injury to the security of person and property; on the other, vice crime, i.e., consensual sexual misconduct, drug abuse, and gambling. This area of proscription deals with legitimate economic activity, which in an acquisitive society like ours is the principal form of behavior that brings people and institutions into contact with each other and with more or less coercive forms of social control. In terms of our broad categories of sanctioning modes, this is the domain of compensation and, increasingly, of regulation; but it is also the domain of punishment, although in an interstitial and ancillary way. The term "white-collar crime" partially defines the area in question. As introduced by the sociologist E.H. Sutherland, the term refers to crimes that persons of respectability and high social status commit in the course of their occupations. It is a sociological concept that cuts across legal categories, and it is admittedly imprecise as a definition of categories of crime. The proper function of the term is probably connotative rather than denotative. Nonetheless, it has some usefulness as a boundary-setting term.

Another boundary-setting term is "regulatory offenses." This refers to the vast and disorganized set of proscriptions that are used for the job of regulating the mode in which business enterprise by individuals and corporations is carried on. These regulations touch every aspect of business life. The food and drug laws control the quality and safety of what the consumer buys by means of detailed regulation of both the end products and the processes by which the products are manufactured and distributed. Labor laws regulate the hours and conditions of employment over a wide spectrum of concerns that ranges from preventing the exploitation of children to requiring adequate toilet facilities. Housing codes contain detailed prescriptions of minimum standards for space, lighting, ventilation, heating, and sanitation. The skills of practitioners of arts as diverse as medicine and plumbing are checked out and guaranteed through elaborate systems of occupational licensing. Much of the financing of business enterprise is regulated through securities laws. The health of the competitive economy is safeguarded by the antitrust laws. In each of these cases, and in many others as well, the system of sanctions includes reliance on the criminal sanction. In none is it the primary reliance, and this feature serves at once to distinguish this category of crime from the others we have been discussing. Our inquiry is into the general utility of ancillary reliance on the criminal sanction in the economic sphere.

This focus entitles us to lay aside forms of economic conduct that are primarily controlled by the criminal sanction, of which the prototypes are cheating and embezzlement. If I sell you a piece of glass on the representation that it is a diamond, I am guilty of fraud or, as it is technically known, obtaining by false pretenses. If I collect your rent and pocket the money, I am guilty of embezzlement. Now it is true that I may be subject to a wide variety of other sanctions in either of these two prototype cases, depending on how heavily regulated my particular line of business happens to be. These may include such things as compensatory or penal damages, administrative cease and desist orders, judicial injunctions, civil fines, and revocation of occupational licenses. These may in certain areas become so effective that the criminal sanction itself lapses into disuse. Usually, however, these other sanctions operate to control kinds of conduct that are not clearly criminal under general proscriptions of fraud or embezzlement. It may also be true that specific criminal proscriptions ancillary to other forms of economic regulation are most effective when they most closely resemble the prototype general offenses of fraud and embezzlement. We will return to that possibility when, later in the discussion, we compare tax fraud with criminal violation of the antitrust laws.

What, generally speaking, are the purposes for which we invoke the criminal sanction to deal with economic offenses? There is really only one. These proscriptions are uniquely deterrent in their trust. Through them we seek to maintain a high standard of conformity among those who might be tempted to further their own economic advantage by violating the law. These are, generally speaking, sanctions addressed to the law-abiding. The subsidiary goal of intimidation does not bulk large, partly because the criminal sanction is in fact invoked very infrequently against economic offenders and partly because once a man has been identified as an economic offender there is a range of other regulatory devices, as well as strong informal pressure, to prevent his repeating his offense. Incapacitation is not involved at all: we do not send a tax evader to jail to keep him during that period of time from engaging in continued tax evasion. And certainly no one would claim any rehabilitative effect from the imposition of criminal punishment on those pillars of the community who happen to get convicted of economic offenses. The case for this use of the criminal sanction rests squarely on deterrence.

The use of criminal sanctions in dealing with economic offenses could, if properly studied, be an excellent proving ground for deterrence theory. Unfortunately, our ignorance in this area is quite as profound as it is elsewhere in the study of sanctions. Consequently, we can do little more than speculate. There is much to be said in favor of a probable high deterrent efficacy for criminal punishment in the field of economic activity. People who value their standing in the community are likely to be especially sensitive to the stigma associated with a criminal conviction, as well as to the antecedent unpleasantnesses of the criminal process. Furthermore, the kind of conduct that runs afoul of economic regulation is neither happenstance nor impulsive: people who commit tax fraud, or conspire to rig prices, or knowingly sell adulterated foods have ample opportunity to calculate their courses of action, to weigh the risks against the advantages, and to take into account the possibility that their conduct will expose them to being branded as criminal. The other side of this coin is that it takes a substantial enforcement effort to make and keep the deterrent threat of the criminal sanction a potent one. It may be a close question whether the enforcement resources required to bring the threat up to its minimal level of credibility might not be better expended in noncriminal modes of regulation. Furthermore, there is the totally unexplored issue of what it takes to give the criminal sanction its bite when "respectable" offenders are involved. Is the fact of conviction enough? (Conversely, is the fact of accusation enough? If so, and especially if the conviction rate is not high, there may be a substantial question of fairness raised.) Or must there be a jail sentence? Must it actually be served, or is it enough that it be imposed? How important is publicity? Our information about this kind of issue is mere impression and anecdote.

Our comparative experience with federal criminal prosecutions in the tax fraud and in the antitrust fields may be instructive. For the past forty or more years, substantial felony penalties have been provided for federal income tax evasion. During most of that time, however, criminal enforcement was sporadic, being reserved essentially as an aid to the civil recovery of taxes due and as a means of prosecuting racketeers and other "public enemies" who were not otherwise easily within the reach of federal criminal law. Beginning in 1952 a new policy of across-the-board criminal enforcement was inaugurated by the Tax Division of the Department of Justice. Something on the order of six hundred to seven hundred criminal tax fraud cases are initiated each year, with a rate of conviction approaching 100 per cent and with about 40 per cent of those convicted receiving prison terms. Of course, nobody knows how effective this enforcement pattern has been in deterring potential violators. Common sense suggests, however, that it is more efficacious than is the case with criminal antitrust prosecutions. There are, to begin with, very few of these, since antitrust cases are invariably "big" cases. Twenty-five a year would be considered a lot. By no means all of these involve individual defendants. Of course, where only corporate defendants are charged or convicted, a fine is the only available sanction. The conviction rate is quite low, and prison sentences are remarkably rare. In fact, since the famous *Electrical Equipment* cases in 1960, in which seven corporate executives received and served jail sentences, no antitrust defendant has been imprisoned. In the flush of enthusiasm after that event, an official of the Antitrust Division wrote:" . . . similar sentences in a few cases each decade would almost cleanse our economy of the cancer of collusive price-fixing. . . ." Whether that prediction would have been accurate no one can say; its factual predicate has not occurred.

We do not know whether criminal enforcement of the tax fraud laws has been "more effective" than criminal enforcement of the antitrust laws. We have no measures of effectiveness. But let us draw the common sense inference that it has been, and speculate about why this should be presumptively so. First, and most obviously, there is a difference in the level of enforcement effort. Granted that tax fraud is a far more pervasive form of illegal activity than is collusive price-fixing, granted even that the ration of prosecutions to actual incidents may not be different, there is probably a minimum threshold of enforcement activity above which one must rise in order to have a significant deterrent impact. Next, there is the fact that tax fraud is far more closely analogous to well-established and well-understood patterns of criminal behavior than is price-fixing. Tax fraud may be viewed as a special kind of obtaining by false pretenses, or of embezzlement, or both. The taxpayer makes false representations, either by affirmative misstatement or by omission, about the extent of his income. Or he may breach his fiduciary responsibility to account to the government for its share of his income. However it is viewed, the wrongfulness of his conduct is easily understood. The point is underlined by the fact that lots of people go to jail for tax fraud, but the relationship is a reciprocal one. Would they go to jail in such large numbers if juries and judges were not persuaded that their conduct is deserving of criminal punishment? Antitrust defendants do not go to jail at least in part because judges and juries are not convinced that their conduct is morally bad. It is complicated conduct. Even when the fact of conspiracy is clear, with all the distinctive marks of concealment and the accompanying aura of wrongdoing, it is far from clear to all but the economically sophisticated what they are conspiring about and why it is so bad for them to be doing so. Their behavior is too close to the groove of what is accepted as conventional businessmen's activity for it to excite the sense of indignation and outrage that it takes for criminal sanctions to be unsparingly applied. We have seen over and over again that moral outrage ought not to be a sufficient condition for the imposition of criminal liability; this is one of the cases that should remind us that it is, after all, a necessary condition.

I mean to suggest that there is a complex and subtle relationship between the vigorous enforcement of a criminal prohibition and public acceptance of the propriety of employing criminal sanctions. It is by no means clear that we can persuade the public to view conduct as wrongful by making it criminal. Law, even criminal law, simply is not that potent a weapon of social control. Our experience with the use of the criminal sanction during the Prohibition period suggests that the reverse is true: far from stigmatizing hitherto morally neutral conduct as wrongful, the intensive application of the criminal sanction to such conduct has the effect of de-criminalizing the criminal law. If we make criminal that which people regard as acceptable, either nullification occurs or, more subtly, people's attitude toward the meaning of criminality undergoes a change.

There is, indeed, some reason to fear that sensitivity toward the criminal sanction has decreased as the formal apparatus of the criminal law has been called on to deal with a wide variety of morally neutral conduct. Typically, what takes place in these prosecutions is a compromise with the idea of criminality. The formal indications of criminality are all there, but the outcome is typically a fine, rather than an actual or even conditional sentence of imprisonment. One can observe a kind of trade-off at work in large areas of formally "criminal" enforcement of economic regulations. The conduct selected for treatment as criminal may be itself fairly trivial. Or, if it does carry a serious risk of harm, as in the adulteration or misbranding of drugs, the law may dispense with a showing that the violation occurred through any fault of the actor-through intentional, reckless, or even negligent conduct. In return, the penalties invoked are what one might call para-civil: they do not involve the distinctively criminal aspect of conditional or absolute loss of liberty. It is unclear what advantage enforcement derives from this kind of arrangement. It may be that the stigma of criminality is thereby somehow imposed on people who neither incurred the just condemnation of the criminal law nor suffered the ordinary penalties of that condemnation. We have no empirical basis, so far as I am aware, for knowing whether the advantage is real or apparent. What does seem clear is that it represents either an exercise in futility or the debasement of what should be the law's most powerful weapon.

I have not so far in these pages touched on some of the more technical problems that arise in the area of economic regulatory offenses, notably the question of corporate criminality. Economic enterprise is typically carried on through complex organizational structures. It is seldom easy to trace the threads of individual action and hence of individual responsibility through these structures. Often all that is patent will turn out to be the activity of some relatively low-placed member of the organization. The implication may be fairly strong that his activity was known to those in charge, but the fact of knowledge may be difficult to prove. Yet the criminal law does not ordinarily permit one person to be held criminally liable for the acts of another unless it can be shown that he aided in their commission or, at the very least, recklessly tolerated their commission by one whom he could have controlled, had he chosen to do so. There are two possible lines of solution. One is to relax the requirements for the imposition of vicarious liability. On the whole this has not been done with respect to serious offenses because of an understandable reluctance to expose a man to criminal punishment without convincing proof of personal guilt. The other course is to impose criminal liability on the corporation itself. This the law has regularly done, and we are now accustomed to seeing corporate entities convicted of committing crimes. Often, indeed, the corporation is convicted while individual defendants are acquitted, even where proof of individual guilt is strong. This differential treatment is often used as a justification for imposing criminal liability on corporations as well as on natural persons. The argument is, however, of questionable merit, because we have no way of knowing whether the individual defendants would have been acquitted in the absence of a convenient corporate scapegoat.

Of course, the only punishment that can be imposed on a corporation is a fine, apart from the stigma of conviction itself. How real that stigma is may be doubted. Sociologists of the Sutherland persuasion talk about corporate recidivists; but there is very little evidence to suggest that the stigma of criminality means anything very substantial in the life of a corporation. John Doe has friends and neighbors; a corporation has none. And the argument that the fact of criminal conviction may have an adverse effect on a corporation's economic position seems fanciful. A substantial proportion of America's 500 largest industrial concerns have been convicted of one or more economic regulatory offenses, but it has never been shown to make any difference to their economic position. The most famous corporate conviction in recent years was that of the General Electric Company and three other concerns in the *Electrical Equipment* cases. It is true that the price of G.E.'s stock declined following the conviction, but that was generally and, it seems, accurately attributed to the fear that substantial treble damage payments would have to be made to the many buyers of heavy electrical equipment who had been forced to pay higher than competitive prices as a result of the collusive price-fixing activities of G.D. and the other corporate defendants.

Given the difficulty of attributing guilt to individuals for corporate crime and the rather ineffective sanctions available against the corporation itself, one may well ask whether the present degree of reliance on the criminal sanction in the field of economic regulation may not be misplaced. Here again the question of alternatives presents itself, as it must always do in any examination of the usefulness of the criminal sanction. Where economic gain is the motive for the infraction and where the ability to impose significant economic deprivation on the offender exists, it may well be questioned whether the criminal sanction's contribution offers value equivalent to cost. To impose criminal standards of procedure and criminal criteria of proof for the end result of nothing more than a financial exaction may well be to pay a higher social cost than is necessary. Indeed, the conventional monetary fine structure of the criminal sanction may limit the deprivation far beyond what would be possible with a more flexible public or private damage action. There is also the possibility, exemplified in the enforcement of the antitrust laws, that extensive criminal prosecution simply diverts attention and resources away from the more fundamental task of assuring a competitive structure for industry. In this instance, as in others, the criminal sanction may be not only ineffective but diversionary. Its ready availability makes us less astute than we otherwise might be to devise sanctions that are better adapted to the exigencies of economic regulation than those to be found in the powerful, but limited and crude, repertory of the criminal sanction.

The problem may well be to devise sanctions that are not overly severe. Monetary exactions are presumably not too severe if some proportion is maintained between them and either the gain that has accrued or the loss that has been caused by the illegal activity in question. Forced dissolution, or "corporate capital punishment" is a remedy that might be reserved for repeated and flagrant instances of economic offenses. The concomitant for people might be a prohibition of continued work in certain lines. And then there is the unexploited sanction of publicity. If those who do business with the public were forced to expose the fact of their derelictions, through either labeling or advertising, a powerful deterrent to transgression might be added. Devices of this kind make conventional criminal sanctions pale by comparison. They suggest that thought needs to be given either to retreating from the criminal sanction in the economic regulatory sphere or to expanding its scope so as to achieve a better match between punishment and crime.

The doubts that I have raised about the use of criminal sanctions in the economic regulatory sphere are not by any means as all-encompassing as those that seem warranted in the realm of morals offenses. (There is, by the way, a certain affinity between the two. They are both economic at base and may perhaps both be characterized as exhibiting the wisdom of meddling as little as possible between willing buyers and sellers, assuming them to be reasonably well informed about what it is that they are bartering about.) It may be useful to summarize the several conditions which, to the extent that they obtain, conduce toward the prudent employment of criminal sanctions in the economic sphere. First, the actor should be a person who is clearly identifiable as the responsible party. Second, the nature of the conduct should be simple enough that it can be understood by a nonspecialized judge and jury. Third, it should be conduct that, when understood, will be viewed by a substantial segment of the community as wrongful – preferably wrongful because of its intrinsic nature, but as a minimum, wrongful if it is clear that the defendant knew or should have known that the was behaving contrary to an accepted standard. Finally, there should be some basis for believing that the enforcement of the economic regulation in question against this particular defendant is not arbitrary or discriminatory. If all of these conditions are met, it cannot be said that the invocation of the criminal sanction is unwise.

Edmund W. Kitch, *Economic Crime Theory*, 2 ENCYCLOPEDIA OF CRIME AND JUSTICE 670–678 (1983)*

INTRODUCTION

There is no generally accepted definition of the term *economic crime* and no distinct body of literature on the theory and practice of economic crime (Stearns; Elliott and Willingham, pp. 227-261). Economic crime might, for instance, be defined as crime undertaken for economic motives. So defined, it would

---

* "Economic Crime: Theory" by Edmund W. Kitch. Reprinted with permission of Simon & Schuster Macmillan from *Encyclopedia of Crime and Justice*, Sanford H. Kadish, Editor in Chief, Vol. 2 pp. 670-679. Copyright © 1983 by The Free Press.

sweep broadly across the field of crime from misdemeanor larceny to vast financial crimes, and from crimes of stealth to crimes of violence. The only crimes excluded by this definition are crimes undertaken for darker motives with no hope of economic gain. Such a definition would have its uses, for economic gain is doubtless an important motive in much criminal activity. It would tend, however, to make the discussion here nearly congruent with the subject of crime. For the purposes of this article, *economic crime* is defined as criminal activity with significant similarities to the economic activity of normal, noncriminal business.

There are two major styles of economic crime. The first consists of crimes committed by businessmen as an adjunct to their regular business activities. Businessmen's responsibilities give them the opportunity, for example, to commit embezzlement, to violate regulations directed at their area of business activity, or to evade the payment of taxes. This style of economic crime is often called white-collar crime. The second style of economic crime is the provision of illegal goods and services or the provision of goods and services in an illegal manner. Illegal provision of goods and services requires coordinated economic activity similar to that of normal business, but all of those engaged in it are involved in crime. The madam operating a brothel has many concerns identical to the manager of a resort hotel, and the distributor of marijuana must worry about the efficiency and reliability of his distribution system just as does a distributor of any other product. This type of economic crime is often called organized crime because the necessity of economic coordination outside the law leads to the formation of criminal groups with elaborate organizational customs and practices (Nelli).

Economic crime has three features that make it of special interest. First, the economic criminal adopts methods of operation that are difficult to distinguish from normal commercial behavior. Second, economic crime may involve the participation of economically successful individuals of otherwise upright community standing. Third, many economic crimes present special challenges to prosecutors, to the criminal justice system, and to civil liberties.

Some economic crimes are stunning in their size, complexity, and daring, and are accompanied by high living and a veneer of glamour. The intrigues and adventures of the large-scale economic criminal, often accompanied by spectacular financial collapses, are recounted at length in the nation's newspapers (Dunn; Moffitt).

The most important economic crime is the organized appropriation of goods and property by stealth or fraud.

Organized theft of goods from businesses requires elaborate organization for the conversion of those goods into cash. Such organized-theft rings can present a far larger threat to legitimate business than occasional and nonsystematic theft, because of the potentially large losses involved. Aside form the usual penalties for the conversion of property, the law attempts to control this activity by regulating the resale market for used property. Pawnshops are subject to licensing and inspection. The organized receiving of stolen property is itself a crime (Model Penal Code § 223.6).

Fraud crimes depend upon the perpetrator's persuading his victim that his objectives are normal and legitimate. Such frauds impose costs on all businesses, because they increase the amount of resources that investors and customers must devote to the activity of detecting and preventing fraud.

Another type of economic crime supports tax or regulatory objectives of the government. Thus, the government uses the threat of criminal punishment to reduce the gains from tax evasion, sale of illegal services or commodities, avoidance of restrictive licensing regimes, or entry into illegal business arrangements.

Economic crimes are often committed by individuals of high social and economic standing. This is the phenomenon of white-collar crime. At first blush, it may seem surprising because such individuals have advantageous alternative opportunities. Why do they engage in crime when they are already well paid and respected? The phenomenon is the result of several interacting factors.

First, individuals with a background in productive enterprise have a large comparative advantage in the commission of certain kinds of economic crime. In order to evade taxes, embezzle funds, or commit an antitrust violation, one must have the opportunity to pay taxes, handle frauds, or make business decisions. Many kinds of theft are facilitated by detailed knowledge of business practices and procedures that can be learned only through advanced education and participation in business affairs.

Second, government regulatory or tax regimes often create conditions that make their violation extraordinarily profitable. If the tax rate is high or the government is attempting to suppress a commodity or service in strong demand, the economic gains from thwarting the law become very large. The magnitude of this temptation may overcome normal inhibitions.

Third, the criminal conduct may be difficult to distinguish morally from legal activity. The sale of a commodity that is illegal may seem to the criminal little different from the sale of a legal commodity. Tax evasion may seem little different from tax avoidance. Finally, the frequency of detection and punishment of some economic crimes is low.

TYPES OF ECONOMIC CRIME

There are three major types of economic crime: property crimes, regulatory crimes, and tax crimes, the most complex of which are regulatory crimes.

Property crimes. Property crimes are acts that threaten property held by private persons or by the state. Theft statutes, which make criminal the taking of property, are the paradigm. The modern integrated theft offense was formulated and recommended by the American Law Institute in Article 223 of the Model Penal Code. The law previously made distinctions between numerous theft offenses according to the manner in which the property was taken and the nature of the property taken.

The integrated theft article of the Model Penal Code is supplemented by Article 224 on forgery and fraudulent practices, the scope of which suggests the range of stratagems available to the modern economic criminal. It prohibits forgery; the fraudulent destruction, removal, or concealment of recordable instruments; tampering with records; the passing of bad checks; the use of stolen or canceled credit cards; deceptive business practices; commercial bribery; the rigging of contests; the defrauding of secured creditors; fraud in insolvency; the receiving of deposits in a failing financial institution; the misapplication of entrusted property; and securing the execution of documents by deception.

Regulatory crimes. Regulatory crimes are actions that violate government regulations. One type of regulation limits the sale of certain kinds of services or commodities. This can be further subdivided into prohibition of the activity altogether, as in the ban on the sale of prostitution services or marijuana, and subjection of the activity to government licensing, as in the regulation of the sale of pharmaceutical drugs. Activities are chosen for licensing because they are thought to represent a special threat to the community at large if not properly conducted. By requiring licensing, the government, usually through an administrative agency, hopes to monitor and control the service or commodity being sold.

For example, the Securities Act of 1933, as amended, 15 U.S.C. §§ 77a-77aa (1976 & Supp. IV 1980) requires that public interstate securities issues be registered with the Securities and Exchange Commission (SEC) and that specified procedures be followed prior to their sale. The act reflects a congressional judgment that the issuance of securities is an activity particularly prone to large-scale fraud and that a system of licensing securities issues can reduce the incidence of fraud. Failure to comply with the statutory procedures is a crime. In the Securities Exchange Act of 1934, as amended, 15 U.S.C. §§ 77b-e, j, k, m,

o, s, and 78 a-kk (1976 & Supp. IV 1980), Congress extended this approach to the licensing of brokers and dealers in securities, and made engaging in these activities without SEC approval a crime. Congress hoped thereby to reduce the level of fraudulent activity by brokers and dealers in securities. However, although licensing statutes sometimes serve legitimate purposes, all too often they are passed and administered in order to protect the interests of those in a given business from the competition of newcomers.

Another type of regulatory crime is the violation of regulatory reporting statutes. In order to make regulation effective, the statutes require the regulated firms to provide extensive information to the regulatory officials. Failure to provide these reports, or the submission of false reports, is usually a crime.

Other regulatory statutes make criminal the operation of a commercial enterprise in a way that creates unreasonable risks to workers or consumers. The operation of an inherently unsafe workplace and the sale of adulterated foods are both made criminal in order to reduce the incidence of these harmful activities. In the United States, the prominent examples are the Federal Food, Drug and Cosmetic Act of 1938, as amended, 21 U.S.C. §§ 301-392 (1976 & Supp. IV 1980) and the Occupational Safety and Health Act of 1970, as amended (part), 29 U.S.C. §§ 651-678 (1976 & Supp. IV 1980).

Finally, regulatory crime may consist of the creation of private arrangements in violation of legal standards established by statute. Thus, the Sherman Antitrust Act of 1890, as amended, 15 U.S.C. §§ 1-7 (1976) makes the private organization of cartels a crime, and the National Labor Relations Act of 1935, as amended, 29 U.S.C. §§ 151-169 (1976 & Supp. IV 1980) makes certain behavior by union or management officials criminal. Statutes such as the Federal Election Campaign Act of 1971, as amended (part) 2 U.S.C. §§ 431-441, 451-456, 490 a, b, and c (1976 & Supp. IV 1980), which regulates political activity, make certain kinds of political activity or political contributions a crime. Article 240 of the Model Penal Code deals with the criminal offenses of bribery and corrupt influence.

Tax crimes. Tax crimes are violations of the liability or reporting requirements of the tax laws. These acts are made criminal in order to counteract the powerful incentives not to admit tax liabilities or pay taxes owed. They extend to all taxes, for instance, federal income tax, federal customs duties, state sales taxes, and local property taxes.

ALTERNATIVES TO CRIMINALIZATION

The role of the criminal law in the area of economic crime cannot be property assessed without consideration of the alternative enforcement strategies available. A theft of property is in the first instance a matter between two individuals. The law may impose civil liability on the wrongdoer but not make his conduct criminal. Most torts and breaches of contract are handled in this fashion. The individual who drives negligently or breaks a promise may have to pay large damages to those he injures, but he is not subject to criminal punishment.

Civil remedies have many advantages. They are activated by private individuals and do not require significant administrative and investigative resources. The state need only provide (1) a judicial system in which the person harmed can make and prove his claim, and (2) procedures for enforcing the decisions of the judges. Second, if the private parties involved do not feel that a remedy is required, they can decide not to seek it, reducing the possibility that the law will be put in the position of punishing conduct that is not harmful (Landes).

Civil remedies also have limitations. If the injured individual is unable to identify or locate the person who has harmed him, he will be unable to activate the remedial process. The potential gain to the injured individual is only the amount of his harm, which may not be sufficient incentive for him to bring a private action. A person who repeatedly harms others but is only occasionally sued and forced to pay damages will profit from the activity. In the case of large-scale, organized criminal activity, an occasional civil judgment could easily be absorbed as a "cost of doing business."

There is an important intermediate area between the civil and criminal penalties. The incentives for the private civil plaintiff can be strengthened by providing for the recovery of attorney's fees or some amount larger than the damages the plaintiff has suffered. In American law the most prominent example of this enforcement strategy has been the provision in the antitrust laws for private recovery of treble damages. Congress extended this approach to other crimes in the Racketeer Influenced and Corrupt Organizations Act (RICO) of 1970, as amended, 18 U.S.C. §§ 1961-1968 (1976 & Supp. IV 1980) (Title IX of the Organized Crime Control Act of 1970).

Even where there is no private victim of the crime to pursue a civil remedy, statutes can provide for civil fines payable to the government. For example, the penal code of the Federal Republic of Germany makes provision for a class of "regulatory violations" that are enforced by administrative fine (Kadish, p. 448). Taxes can often be more easily collected by suit for the taxes due, fraud penalties, and government levy upon the taxpayer's assets than by invocation of criminal procedures. The SEC can sanction conduct of its

regulates by threatening to revoke or suspend their licenses. These administrative remedies may often be more effective and less difficult to pursue than the criminal alternative.

PROBLEMS OF THE CRIMINAL REMEDY

Complexities of proof. The criminal remedy for economic crime must be administered within the traditional procedural rules of the criminal law, including a high burden of proof. Economic-crime cases present special problems of proof because they often involve many transactions and involved dealings.

Consider the prosecution of an embezzler who with the aid of confederates has created dummy firms to bill his employer for nonexistent supplies, analyzed and rendered ineffective the employer's procedures for verifying the regularity of bills, collected the payments, and diverted them to himself and his confederates. By analyzing the extensive and apparently regular commercial documentation and comparing it to the actual deliveries made to the employer, it would be possible to demonstrate that payments were made for goods not delivered. That proof would suffice in a civil action by the firm for return of the erroneous payments.

To prove a criminal case, the prosecutor would have to show that the defendants were the ones who purposefully manipulated the employer's payment system and submitted the erroneous bills for their own gain. This might require tedious proof of extensive commercial dealing and require the jury to make inferences from unfamiliar material. The defendants could argue that they believed the bills were legitimate and that they were as dismayed as the employer to discover that a mistake had been made.

In an antitrust case, the government might argue that a series of trade meetings occurring over a period of years, when considered together with the pricing and production actions of the industry, show a criminal price-fixing conspiracy. The defendants might argue that the meetings were simply social events bringing together businessmen with similar interests and that the industry's pricing and production actions were dictated by economic forces, such as the price of raw materials and the preferences of customers.

The burden on the prosecutor. The prosecutor will face special problems in economic-crime cases, because he will have to prove complex allegations against a defendant who may be well financed and capable of hiring skilled counsel. Prosecutors' offices, with heavy work loads and limited budgets, may be unable to dedicate sufficient legal talent to a case to analyze and explain effectively to the trial court the significance of a mass of facts. These forces may cause a prosecutor eager for a good conviction record to choose not to pursue economic crime cases vigorously. If an economic-crime prosecution is pursued, the prosecutor has to give up the opportunity to obtain many more convictions in simpler cases. The prosecutor who nonetheless continues to pursue economic crime may find that his staff, after obtaining expertise in cases of this kind, will then depart for private employment, the demand for their talents having been generated by the prosecutor's own program of vigorous enforcement. In the 1970s in the United States, concern about these problems has led to special programs designed to enhance the ability of prosecutors and their staffs to deal with the prosecution of economic crimes (Miller).

The impact on procedural protections. The presence in the criminal justice system of a class of defendants with large resources creates pressures for the curtailment or abrogation of civil liberties. For example, it has been argued that federal judges should be authorized to deny bail for persons charged with large drug transactions, because these persons are so wealthy that they will not hesitate to forfeit any bail that is put up. Yet, a no-bail rule does violence to the principles that a defendant is presumed innocent until proved guilty and that personal freedom should not be lost until after conviction. More generally, procedural protections that on the whole work well where defendants have state-provided counsel or limited private resources, may become insuperable barriers to the conviction of guilty defendants in the hands of defense counsel with unlimited resources. This in turn creates pressures to limit those procedural protections.

Pressures on the definition of criminal conduct. The fact that the criminal remedy is being used creates special but conflicting pressures on the definition of *criminal activity*. On the one hand, notions of criminality carry with them the idea that the activity prohibited must be intentionally wrongful to justify the use of such a severe sanction. Thus, a criminal penalty may import into a regulatory area standards of conscious wrongfulness that warp and disrupt the regulatory purpose. It has been argued, for example, that the prosecutorial focus of the SEC diverts the commission's attention from the need to provide a framework that will support efficient capital markets (Karmel). The fact that the Sherman Antitrust Act is a criminal statute has caused courts to emphasize issues of intent and purpose more than the economic effects of business relationships in constructing the statute.

Conversely, the problems of proof in criminal actions create pressures to reduce the standards of liability in order to make the sanction effective, a pressure that has been particularly apparent in the emergence of modern doctrines of strict criminal liability and criminal liability for corporate or conspiratorial acts.

Strict liability. A rare and unusual form of criminal liability that appears most often in the area of economic regulatory crimes is the imposition of liability on individuals for unanticipated consequences of their acts. Criminal liability is generally imposed for conduct that was "intentional." However, some statutes are construed to impose liability—called "strict" or "absolute" liability—without regard for intent. This is justified on the ground that the imposition of such liability will cause individuals to try harder to avoid liability under the statute by anticipating the consequences of their actions.

The courts have looked askance at the creation of criminal offenses not requiring proof of intent, and have held that the omission of an express intent requirement from a criminal statutes does not mean that the offense is a strict-liability one. In *Morissette v. United States,* 342 U.S. 246 (1952), the United States Supreme Court held that a statute making it a crime to steal government property required proof that the defendant intended the offense. Justice Robert Jackson observed: "The contention that an injury can amount to a crime only when inflicted by intention is no provincial or transient notion. It is as universal and persistent in mature systems of law as belief in freedom of the human will and a consequent ability and duty of the normal individual to choose between good and evil" (250). The Supreme Court followed *Morissette* in *United States v. United States Gypsum Co.*, 438 U.S. 422 (1978) when it held that proof of a criminal offense under the Sherman Antitrust Act required proof of an intent to cause the proscribed harm.

Justice Jackson went on in *Morissette* to note the rise of modern offenses

> The industrial revolution multiplied the number of workmen exposed to injury from increasingly powerful and complex mechanisms, driven by freshly discovered sources of energy, requiring higher precautions by employers. Traffic of velocities, volumes and varieties unheard of came to subject the wayfarer to intolerable casualty risks if owners and drivers were not to observe new cares and uniformities of conduct. Congestion of cities and crowding of quarters called for health and welfare regulations undreamed of in simpler times. Wide distribution of goods became an instrument of wide distribution of harm when those who dispersed food, drink, drugs and even securities, did not comply with reasonable standards of quality, integrity, disclosure and care. Such dangers have engendered increasingly numerous and detailed regulations which heighten the

duties of those in control of particular industries, trades, properties or activities that affect public health, safety or welfare [253-254].

In the United States, strict criminal liability has been imposed under the Federal Food, Drug and Cosmetic Act, 21 U.S.C. § 333(a); *United States v. Dotterweich,* 320 U.S. 277 (1943); *United States v. Park,* 421 U.S. 658 (1975); the so-called Refuse Act of 1899, 33 U.S.C. § 411 (1976); and *United States v. United States Steel Corp.,* 328 F. Supp. 354 (N.D. Inc. 1970), *aff'd,* 482 F.2d 439 (7th Cir. 1973). Both the food and refuse statues are designed to protect large populations from risks to their health and safety. The Supreme Court held, however, that the liability of a corporate officer under the Food, Drug and Cosmetic Act did not extend to actions that it would have been impossible for him to correct (*Park,* 673).

Corporate crime. Many economic crimes are necessarily committed by large and complex economic organizations. Within these organizations, it may be difficult to locate any single individual who is responsible for the combination of acts and omissions that constitute the crime. Yet, it will be clear that the crime has been committed. Strict liability is one response to this problem. Another response has been to impose criminal liability not on an individual but upon the organization or corporation itself. Courts have regularly and with little difficulty accepted the argument that corporations are just as capable of committing crimes as people are.

Courts have commonly imposed criminal liability on corporations by analogy from the master-servant law that makes a corporation civilly liable for the acts of its employees. Under the majority American rule, a corporation is criminally liable for the criminal acts of an employee if the employee commits a crime within the scope of his employment and with the intent to benefit the corporation. Section 2.07 of the Model Penal Code, which has been influential, provides three different ways in which a corporation may be criminally liable for the acts of its employees. The first applies to crimes of intent where no "legislative purpose to impose liability on corporations plainly appears." A corporation can be held liable for these crimes only if the offense was performed, authorized, or recklessly tolerated by the board of directors or a high corporate officer. The second applies to crimes where the legislature intended to impose corporate criminal liability. A corporation is liable for these crimes if the acts fall within the master-servant rules. The third applies to strict-liability crimes where the corporation is liable without regard to whether there was any intent to benefit the corporation (Developments in the Law, pp. 1246-1258).

The sentencing dilemma. The convicted economic criminal presents the court with a serious problem of sentencing policy. He may appear before the court as a man of culture and means who has threatened no one with physical harm. He will profess regret and offer to use his means and talent for the benefit of the community. On the other hand, the potential profits of his criminal activity may have been so high, and the difficulties of detection and successful prosecution so great, that no one would be deterred from pursuing similar opportunities in the future unless very large and severe punishments were imposed. Yet, it may be obvious to the sentencing judge that the man before him is, in a fundamental sense, far less evil than the killer whom the judge has just sent to prison.

In the academic literature, the debate over sentencing has focused on whether a fine or imprisonment offers the best approach to deterrence. It has been argued that because many economic criminals have property, their cases present a particularly propitious area for the imposing of a fine. Simply by making the fine large enough to offset the potential gains from the criminal activity, the crime can be deterred. A fine avoids all the deadweight loss of imprisonment: the direct costs of imprisonment itself and the loss of the defendant's own productive potential (Posner). On the other hand, it has been argued that only by imprisonment, an expression of society's strong disapproval of the defendant's conduct, can the full weight of the criminal law be brought to bear on that conduct (Coffee). To fine the economic criminal but to imprison the pathetic, violent misfit is to condone implicitly the activities of the economic criminal.

The problem of prison administration. The economic criminal who is imprisoned may present special problems for the prison administrator. Without a taste or talent for violence, he is unlikely to attempt escape. With abilities and possibly wealth, he has strong incentives to return to society. Because of the differences between the economic criminal and the rest of the prison population, incarceration may actually threaten his safety and health. These factors create pressures on prison administrators to provide alternative confinement facilities for their "model" prisoners both because such facilities can be provided more cheaply and because they avoid the problems involved in mixing the different populations. Such "country club" prisons are the common abode of convicted economic criminals; the most famous in the United States is the minimum-security prison located at Allentown, Pennsylvania.

The absence or complicity of the victim. In many economic crimes either there will be no identifiable victim or the victim will have actively cooperated in the crime. Laws that prohibit the provision of goods or services are violated with the cooperation of people who want to buy those goods and services, who usually know they are being provided illegally, and who often assist the violator in the perpetration of the crime. The only way that violators can be found and detected may be for investigative agencies to use undercover agents to offer suspects an opportunity to commit the crime. In many fraud cases, the victim is induced into the fraud by appeals to his greed. Only when the fraud turns out badly for him does he become unhappy. A modicum of care and attention would have prevented the crime. Why should a prosecutor use his limited resources to protect those so unwilling to protect themselves?

Even the corporation victimized by management fraud may fail to take essential precautions to prevent abuse of office (Elliott and Willingham). In the Foreign Corrupt Practices Act of 1977 (part), 15 U.S.C. § 78 m (Supp. IV 1980), Congress required publicly held American corporations to maintain a system of internal accounting controls sufficient to provide reasonable assurance that transactions are recorded so that all assets can be accounted for.

The political overtones. Many economic-crime prosecutions have political overtones. This is most dramatically evident in cases brought against incumbent public officials for bribery or abuse of office, but the overtones are heard in almost any substantial prosecution for economic crime. These overtones further complicate the task of the prosecutor, trial court, and prison administrator in seeking to administer the law in a fair and evenhanded way.

Because the number of prosecutions for economic crimes is small in relation to the number of such crimes actually committed—or so it is believed—even if the defendant is indisputably guilty, the further question arises of why this defendant in particular was singled out for investigation and prosecution. Even if the criminal acts have been recorded on videotape, that does not answer the question of what process led the investigative agency to expend substantial resources to target the particular defendants. Was it an impartial process of following investigative leads, or was it a process shaped by other forces? Even if the investigative agency has proceeded impartially, who gave the agency the leads that initiated the inquiry? The agency, claiming the need to protect its investigative sources, is not likely to explain.

Even when the defendant in an economic-crime case is not a political figure, he may be viewed by many as representative of a class of persons. For some, the indicted corporate official may be a symbol of the failures of an entire class, while his fellows may be muttering to themselves, "There, but for the grace of God, go I." To the extent that the defendant in an economic-crime case is viewed as representative of a larger and politically powerful class, the case inevitably takes on political overtones. Public and corporate officials may outwardly decry corruption, but they may be able to muster little real enthusiasm and support for the prosecutor who has made the vigorous investigation and prosecution of economic crime his hallmark. Conversely, so many prosecutors have ridden into high political office on the publicity generated by sensational prosecutions of the rich or powerful that the defendants in such cases can persuasively argue that they have been chosen for persecution simply to advance the career of the prosecutor.

Whatever the facts of a particular case, their overtones make the fair and impartial administration of these criminal laws especially difficult. The prosecutor and judge cannot rely on unanimous social condemnation of the defendant. The social commitment to the criminal law being enforced may be ambivalent. The society that makes the sale and consumption of liquor or drugs a crime but simultaneously supports a large illegal industry cannot be expected to unite in support of vigorous criminal enforcement. The complexity and difficulty of prosecution justifies a large area of prosecutorial discretion. Yet, the existence of that discretion leaves open the suspicion that it is being used for inappropriate ends.

THE VARIABLE-RESPONSE ENFORCEMENT STRATEGY

A pervasive feature of economic crime is that prosecutors do not attempt to pursue a policy of seeking criminal convictions in all cases that come to their attention. Instead, they follow a highly selective enforcement policy in which the decision to prosecute is determined by a number of interacting variables. These include (1) whether or not the victim is complaining; (2) whether or not the victim has been made whole for any loss; (3) the availability and efficacy of civil remedies available to the victim; (4) the extent to which the prosecutor's resources are equal to the complexity of the prosecution and the likely resources of the defense; (5) the degree of social harm the prosecutor thinks is caused by the criminal conduct; and (6) the impact a criminal conviction may have on the efficacy of the government's overall enforcement strategy.

The resulting pattern of variable criminal enforcement is further complicated by the fact that whether or not a violation comes to a prosecutor's attention may be determined by others. In the case of a theft crime such as shoplifting, a prosecutor may learn of violations only if the store chooses to pursue a policy of criminal prosecution rather than one of civil reimbursement. Under statutes with independent administrative enforcement officials, such as the federal securities acts or health and safety inspection laws, the relevant administrative officials make an initial decision whether to pursue violations civilly or to report the conduct to a prosecutor.

The result of these variable enforcement strategies is that people displaying conduct identical under the statute will be differentially treated. Most tax evaders who are caught will reach a civil settlement with the government. A few will be chosen for criminal prosecution, perhaps because their prominence (or perhaps even their political views) makes them effective examples. Prostitution in one part of a town will be ignored, whereas in another it will be dealt with harshly.

Prosecutorial policies of this sort raise obvious problems of fairness for the criminal law, and may also distort the associated civil procedures. A defendant who enters into a civil consent decree to avoid the risks of criminal prosecution may surrender rights or concede administrative jurisdiction that is not supported by the law. A zealous and dedicated enforcement agency such as the SEC can use this process to broaden its statutory powers (Kripke).

These well-known problems associated with economic crimes have led to repeated calls in the literature for de-emphasis of the criminal penalty in economic regulation and for a general reduction in the reach and ambition of the criminal law (Morris and Hawkins; Kadish; Bator). These calls have fallen on deaf legislative ears, and the scope and reach of regulatory crimes have continued to expand.

THE EVOLUTION OF ECONOMIC CRIME

The evolution of economic crime illustrates the quasi-private character of the crime. Criminal penalties for economic crimes seem to emerge only as social experience demonstrates the need for a criminal sanction to reinforce civil duties. Over time, the definition of *criminal theft* has been expanded to include new forms of economically valuable property as they emerge (Hall). Illustrations from the 1970s are the criminalization of trade-secret theft and increased use of the criminal penalties against copyright infringement. The first is a response to the increased value in modern society of technological information, and the second, a response to the ease with which copyrights can be infringed by using modern copying technologies. However, the ambivalence of the legislators in these marginal areas is illustrated by the fact that neither trademark nor patent infringement is criminal.

The elaborate regulatory crimes of the twentieth century are not simply a product of the increased complexity of the modern economy; they also reflect the sophistication and resources of the modern state. When the reach and effectiveness of the King's justice was uncertain at best, it seemed absurd to entrust the protection of private property to the King rather than to the care and attention of its owner. However, the development of modern bureaucratic organizations supported by effective tax systems has made it possible for the state to assume a more ambitious role – to undertake not only to protect private property but to define and defend many more subtle and complex economic expectancies such as safety, health, and freedom from fraud.

ECONOMIC CRIME IN THE SOCIALIST STATE

The discussion of economic crime here has been confined to the practice of such crime in the capitalist state. It should be noted, however, that the problems of economic crime are different in a state where the role of private property is limited. Where there is no private property, there are no private incentives to protect that property. Every offense that interferes with the production and distribution of economic goods is an offense only against the state. Thus, the state must rely exclusively upon its own administrative and criminal process to protect that property. Because state prosecution becomes the first and only line of defense, its vigorous and successful pursuit becomes a matter of far greater social importance. Consequently, in socialist states economic crimes are treated far more harshly than in capitalist states, sometimes even resulting in capital punishment.

CONCLUSION

There is a sharp contrast between the academic writing on economic crime, which tends to call for uniform enforcement of economic-crime statutes and reduction of the scope of criminal liability, and the practice of legislatures and prosecutors, who proscribe broadly and disregard frequently. The system in practice is untidy, but it permits the officials of the criminal justice system to respond in practical ways to the fact that the statutes often reach conduct that should not be criminal, and ensnare individuals who can reasonably be described as innocent. Unfortunately, the discretion thus conferred is also capable of great abuse with little remedy.

The scholars who have grappled with these problems have tried to treat economic crime as a unity. That is probably the ultimate artificiality, for economic crime is as diverse and varied as man's economic activities. Too much of the criminal scholarship in this area discusses the criminal aspect of the problem without attention to the underlying regulatory substance. On the other hand, the scholarship that addresses particular substantive areas, such as antitrust issues, securities regulation, and housing-code enforcement, has tended to ignore the criminal aspect of economic regulation.

Stanford H. Kadish, *Some Observations on the Use of Criminal Sanctions in Enforcing Economic Regulations*, 30 U. CHI. L. REV. 423–449 (1963)*

Those who have had occasion to look for answers to the problems of the use of sanctions, taken to include the whole range of official modes of securing compliance with norms of conduct, have commonly agreed for some time now that there are few to be found. In view of the antiquity of the legal experience, which for the most part has always entailed the use of sanctions of one kind or another, this is a remarkable verdict. Indeed, works written at the turn of the eighteenth century by Jeremy Bentham are still the basic works in the area, a sobering observation which could scarcely be made of more than a handful of subjects of inquiry. In this state of affairs it is not surprising that we are largely ignorant of the impact of the penal sanction, which is only one aspect of the larger problem of sanctions; and still less so that we know little about the use of the penal sanction in an area of relatively recent development, economic regulatory legislation. There are only sectors of a much larger unexplored terrain.

Moreover, unnecessary confusion has become an ally of ignorance in impeding understanding of these areas. Because strong ideological differences separate the proponents and opponents of economic regulation, judgments about the effect of penal sanctions in achieving compliance tend to turn upon judgments about the merits of the substantive regulation. Liberally oriented social scientists, otherwise critical of the case made for the deterrent and vindicatory uses of punishment of ordinary offenders, may be found supporting stern penal enforcement against economic violators. At the same time conservative groups, rarely foes of rigorous punishment for ordinary offenders,

appear less sanguine for the criminal prosecution when punishment of business offenders is debated.

This statement of the undeveloped state of the art is by no means designed as an introduction to an ambitious effort to close the ancient gap in understanding. Quite the contrary, it is meant rather to excuse the modest ambit of these observations. What I would like to accomplish is to outline the special characteristics of economic regulatory legislation relevant to the use of the criminal sanction; to indicate what implications they have for effective use of the criminal law; and to suggest relevant concerns in the use of this sanction beyond the goal of enforcing the specific regulatory norm.

I

The kind of economic regulations whose enforcement through the criminal sanction is the subject of this inquiry may be briefly stated: those which impose restrictions upon the conduct of business as part of a considered economic policy. This includes such laws as price control and rationing laws, antitrust laws and other legislation designed to protect or promote competition or prevent unfair competition, export controls, small loan laws, securities regulations, and, perhaps, some tax laws. Put to one side, therefore, are regulations directly affecting business conduct which are founded on interests other than economic ones; for example, laws regulating the conduct of business in the interest of public safety and general physical welfare. Also to one side are laws directly affecting business conduct by their general applicability; for example, embezzlement, varieties of fraud and related white-collar offenses.

The class of regulations so defined possesses several characteristics that have a direct bearing upon the uses and limits of the criminal sanction as a means of achieving compliance. The first is the very feature suggested as the identifying characteristic of such legislation; that is, the nature of the interest protected. Certainly the use of criminal sanctions to protect interests of an economic character is not a contemporary departure. The extension of the classic larceny offense by courts and legislatures to embrace fraud, embezzlement and similar varieties of misappropriation that threatened newly developing ways of transacting business is a well documented chapter in the history of the criminal law. Indeed the process continues today. But there is an important difference between the traditional and expanded property offenses and the newer economic regulatory offenses – a difference reflecting the shift from an economic order that rested on maximum freedom for the private entrepreneur to one committed to restraints upon that freedom. The traditional property offenses protect private property interests

* Reprinted with permission.

against the acquisitive behavior of others in the furtherance of free private decision. The newer offenses, on the other hand, seek to protect the economic order of the community against harmful use by the individual of his property interest. The central purpose, therefore, is to control private choice, rather than to free it. But the control imposed (and this too has significance) is not total, as it would be in a socialistic system. Private economic self-determination has not been abandoned in favor of a wholly state regulated economy. Indeed, the ideal of free enterprise is maintained, the imposed regulations being regarded as necessary to prevent that ideal from consuming itself. Whether the criminal sanction may safely and effectively be used in the service of implementing the large-scale economic policies underlying regulatory legislation of this kind raises fundamental questions.

A second relevant feature of these laws concerns the nature of the conduct restrained. Since it is not criminal under traditional categories of crime and, apart from the regulatory proscription, closely resembles acceptable aggressive business behavior, the stigma of moral responsibility does not naturally associate itself with the regulated conduct. Moreover, the conduct is engaged in by persons of relatively high social and economic status; since it is motivated by economic considerations, it is calculated and deliberate rather than reactive; it is usually part of a pattern of business conduct rather than episodic in character; and it often involves group action through the corporate form.

The third noteworthy attribute of this legislation is the role provided for the criminal sanction in the total scheme of enforcement. Typically the criminal penalty is only one of a variety of authorized sanctions which may include monetary settlements, private actions (contemporary or penal), injunctions, inspections, licensing, required reporting or others. Its role, therefore, is largely ancillary and takes either or both of two forms. On the one hand, the criminal penalty may serve as a means to insure the functioning of other sanctions, as, for example, penalties for operating without a license, or without prior registration or reporting. On the other hand, the criminal sanction may serve as a separate and supplementary mode of enforcement by directly prohibiting the conduct sought to be prevented, as in the Sherman Act. Furthermore, implicit in the legislative scheme is the conception of the criminal sanction as a last resort to be used selectively and discriminatingly when other sanctions fail. The array of alternative non-penal sanctions appears unmistakably to carry this message. That this is assumed by enforcement authorities is apparent from the relative infrequency of the use of the criminal as

compared to other sanctions, and in the occasional appearance of published criteria of enforcement policy. And in some legislation, of course, the message of selective enforcement is explicit in the law. Finally, the responsibility for investigation, detection and initiating prosecution is often vested in a specialized agency or other body rather than left with the usual institutions for policing and prosecuting criminal violations. Moreover, these bodies such as the Office of Price Administration during the war, or the Securities and Exchange Commission, commonly are not specialized organs of criminal enforcement, but are the agencies broadly charged with administering the legislative scheme.

This statement of the relevant features of the laws under inquiry, in terms of the interest protected, the behavior regulated and the contemplated role of the criminal penalty, is not meant to suggest that these laws are ultimately unique in the problems they raise for criminal enforcement. Apart from the nature of the interest protected, most, if not all, of these characteristics may be found in other areas of the criminal law: upper-class criminality in white-collar crime generally; selectivity in enforcement in the whole range of the criminal law, to a greater or lesser degree; deliberate, patterned conduct for gain engaged in by organizations in many other classes of offenses. And even though the nature of the interest protected is by definition unique, many of the problems it poses, such as making criminal morally neutral behavior, are common to other areas as well. All that is suggested is that if one asks, "What problems are raised for the effective use of the criminal sanction as a mode of achieving compliance in this area?" the beginnings of an answer are to be found in this congeries of characteristics. It remains now to suggest what bearing they have.

II

I propose to deal with the relevance of these characteristics in terms of three major problems: the problem of defining the proscribed conduct, the problem of corporate criminality and the problem of moral neutrality.

A. The Problem of Defining the Proscribed Conduct

The fact that the protected interest is the preferred functioning of the economic system, and entails only partial restriction upon the operation of American business, bears directly upon the task of defining the proscribed behavior with sufficient specificity to meet the requirement of fair notice generally applicable to criminal legislation. Where the criminal sanction is used to police other enforcement devices, as for example, when it becomes criminal to market a security issue without registration or to do business without a license, the standard is met without difficulty. But the requirement of specificity is notably difficult of fulfillment where the crime itself purports to define the substantive economic behavior sought to be avoided. A notable example is the Sherman Act's prohibition of "restraint of trade or commerce" and "illegal monopolization." Only to a small degree, if at all, is the difficulty remediable by better draftsmanship. As Thurman Arnold observed, "antitrust policy touches fields and boundaries which recede as you approach them and disappear each time you try to stake them out." The reason for this arises from several sources. First, the economic policy is itself unclear, constituting largely a vague aspiration for a proper balance among competing economic goals. Second, illegality must turn on judgments that are essentially evaluative in character, rather than upon purely factual determinations. Third, the inevitable development of novel circumstances and arrangements in the dynamic areas under regulation would soon make precise formulations obsolete, even to the limited extent they proved feasible.

A key question is whether what would be an intolerable vagueness in conventional crime is less objectionable here in view of the preventive character of these laws. But deferring this question for the moment, are there alternatives for meeting the difficulty short of eschewing criminal sanctions where the conduct cannot be defined with accepted specificity?

The requirement in an otherwise unconstitutionally vague definition of criminal conduct that the defendant must be shown to have acted willfully or knowingly has sometimes been held to remedy the defect of definition. Thus the Supreme Court found no unfairness in convicting a motor company for failing to reroute their explosive-laden truck "as far as practical, and where feasible" to avoid congested areas, where it was necessary to prove that this was done "knowingly"; or in convicting a taxpayer for attempting to evade taxes by making "unreasonable" deductions for commissions paid to stockholders as compensation for service, where the action was taken "willfully." A requirement that the defendant have intentionally committed the act with a full and correct understanding of the factual circumstances is of no help to a defendant faced with an unclear definition of the conduct forbidden. On the other hand, however vague the line between what is permissible and what is criminal, where the actor is aware that his conduct falls squarely within the forbidden zone he is in no position to complain. "A mind intent upon willful evasion is inconsistent with surprised innocence." Apparently, therefore, it is scienter in this sense, that is, knowledge by the actor that he is violating the law, which is held in these cases to eliminate the vagueness problem. Yet this premise probably affords defenses to a larger group than intended, since a defendant who knew nothing of the existence of the law would be in as good a position as one who did not know that his action came within its terms. If the prosecution must prove that the defendant knew his conduct fell within the terms of the law, it could hardly to so without proof as well that he knew of its existence. A legislature, however, could presumably resolve the semantic impasse by making it a defense that the defendant did not know his acts fell within its terms, or perhaps, more narrowly, that he could not reasonably know it, though not a defense simply that he did not know of the law's existence.

Another approach to mitigating the difficulties of a vague formulation is through administrative choice of cases to prosecute. If the enforcement agency initiates criminal prosecution solely where the meaning of the statute has become acceptably clear through judicial interpretation, the unfairness of the original unclarity may be thought adequately reduced. An example is the announced policy of the Department of Justice to institute criminal prosecutions for Sherman Act violations only where there is a per se violation, such as price fixing, a violation accompanied by a specific intent to restrain competition or monopolize, the use of predatory practices, or where the defendant has before been convicted of a Sherman Act violation. This approach, unlike the legislative requirement of scienter, is of no avail where the vagueness of the statutory formulation renders the law constitutionally unenforceable. It is also dependent upon the existence of means other than criminal prosecutions to develop clarifying interpretation. In the Sherman Act this is provided through the civil suit as a parallel means of enforcing the identical standard of conduct. This, in turn, however, may be a mixed blessing. One of the purposes of looseness and generality in the formulation of the standard is to create a flexibility that will allow judicial interpretation to keep pace with the changes in the character of the area under regulation. Courts may prove understandably reluctant to sustain expansive, although desirable, interpretations where the consequence will be to subject defendants to criminal as well as civil sanctions.

There are several alternatives to civil litigation as a means of producing clarifying interpretation. The most obvious is to delegate to the responsible administrative agency the authority to issue so-called "legislative regulations" in implementation of the statutory scheme. Providing criminal penalties for violation of these regulations then eliminates the vagueness problem to the extent of the clarity of the regulation. There is still, to be sure, a requirement of some specificity in the legislative standard from which the agency derives its authority. But this raises the different, though related, issue of delegation of powers, where requirements of specificity are considerably less than those applicable to criminal statutes. The declaratory order, in which the agency renders an advisory judgment on the legality of a contemplated course of action, is another possibility. This has utility both in providing further clarification of the applicability of regulations and in rendering interpretive guidance of the law when it, rather than a regulation, is the direct source of the prohibition. Section 5 of the Administrative Procedure Act provides a precedent for such an order, although the use authorized therein is considerably more limited than it might be.

Still another alternative is flatly to prohibit certain kinds of activity, except where an administrative agency, interpreting and applying general legislative standards, expressly allows it, as by issuing a license. The criminal penalty may then be imposed for the clearly defined offense of engaging in the activity without authorization. This, of course, is to use the criminal sanction, as previously suggested, as a means of enforcing another, non-criminal sanction. It is readily usable in such narrow areas as marketing securities, or engaging in other particular types of business. It is impractical where the thrust of the prohibition goes to ways of conducting any and all kinds of business, as in the Sherman Act.

B. The Problem of Corporate Criminality

Conduct reached by economic regulatory legislation is typically group conduct often engaged in through the corporate form. This raises the formidable issue of corporate criminality. From the legislative viewpoint, the principal questions are twofold. First, what difficulties beset enforcement agencies in affixing criminal liability upon responsible actors where the principal violator is the corporation? Second, in any event, what are the possibilities of effective enforcement through the imposition of criminal penalties upon the corporation itself?

Fixing criminal liability upon the immediate actors within a corporate structure generally poses no special problem. But the immediate actors may be lower echelon officials or employees who are the tools rather than the responsible originators of the violative conduct. Where the corporation is managed by its owners, the task of identifying the policy formulators is not acute. But where the stock of the corporation is widely held, the organization complex sprawling, and the responsibility spread over a maze of departments and divisions, then, as has recently been shown, there may be conspicuous difficulties in pin-pointing responsibility on the higher echelon policy-making officials. The

source of the difficulty is the conventional requirement that to hold one person criminally liable for the acts of another he must have participated in the acts of the other in some meaningful way, as by directing or encouraging them, aiding in their commission or permitting them to be done by subordinates whom he has power to control. The difficulty is exemplified in the now famous antitrust prosecution of the electrical equipment manufacturers. Here the high policy makers of General Electric and other companies involved escaped personal accountability for a criminal conspiracy of lesser officials that extended over several years to the profit of the corporations, despite the belief of the trial judge and most observers that these higher officials either knew of and condoned these activities or were willfully ignorant of them.

It cannot be known to what extent this legal obstacle to convicting the policy initiators actually reduces the efficacy of the criminal sanction in achieving compliance. Certainly, it would prove more significant in those areas, like antitrust, where giant corporations are the principal targets of the law, than in areas where they are not. But other factors may be more influential in preventing wide scale successful prosecution of individual corporate officials; under the antitrust laws, for example, there have been strikingly few convictions of corporate officials, even of officials of closely held corporations and the lesser officials of large, public corporations.

At all events, one means of reducing the difficulty would be to alter by statute the basis of accountability of corporate directors, officers or agents. An amendment, for example, of the antitrust law was recently proposed which would have changed the present basis of accountability (that such persons "shall have authorized, ordered or done" the acts) to make it suffice that the individual had knowledge or reason to know of the corporate violation and failed to exercise his authority to stop or prevent it. This falls short of outright vicarious liability since accountability is made to turn on fault in not knowing and acting rather than on a relationship simpliciter. Essentially it makes a negligent omission the basis of accountability. Still a standard of accountability resting on precisely how much of the far-flung operations of a nation-wide corporation an official should reasonably be aware of approaches vicarious liability in its indeterminateness, since neither the common experience of the jury nor even specialized experience affords substantial guidance. In effect, it introduces an element of uncertainty concerning accountability into laws that often, like the Sherman Act, are already marked by uncertainty concerning the conduct forbidden.

I defer to a later point the issue of whether such scruples are appropriate in business offenses. To the extent they are, a possible alternative is the legislative formulation of rules and standards of accountability. Where state regulatory laws are involved this might be accomplished through amendment of the corporation laws to fix the lines of accountability in intra-corporate relationships compatibly with the needs of an effective system of regulation. The problem, however, arises principally with national regulatory laws sought to be applied to officials of large interstate corporations. Professor Watkins has long suggested a federal incorporation law to restore responsibility in such corporate structures by eliminating the diverse and confusing lines of accountability under state corporation laws. If, as he suggests, the problem of fixing accountability is due neither to the complexity of business nor to willful attempts to baffle outsiders, but rather to "the absence of uniform standards and rules for delegation of authority in these huge corporations in which nobody appears to know who is responsible for what," there may be no just means for meeting the problem short of his proposal. On the other hand, the complexity of the task and the further inroad into an area of traditional local jurisdiction might not be regarded as worth the cost, since the legal standards of accountability may prove to be only one of several factors, and not necessarily the most crucial, as we will see, militating against enforcement through conviction of corporate officials.

Fixing criminal liability upon the corporation itself has posed fewer legal obstacles in the enforcement of regulatory legislation. The earlier conceptual difficulties of ascribing criminal intent to a fictitious entity have been largely removed by the developing law. And whatever doubt may exist is readily met by expressly providing for corporate liability in the regulatory statute. But the problem of corporate accountability—that is, when the entity is liable for conduct of its agents at various levels of responsibility—is analogous to the problem of holding corporate officials accountable for the acts of lesser agents. It has been resolved more sweepingly in the case of the entity. For acts of its high managerial agents it is by definition accountable since a corporation cannot act by itself. For the acts of its lesser agents the tendency has been, at least in the regulatory offenses, to hold the corporation accountable for the acts of employees within the scope of their employment or while acting as employees. Whether the consequential imposition of vicarious responsibility upon the corporate entity, as well as upon shareholders, is justified raises the question of the deterrent efficacy of convicting and fining the corporate entity.

The case for corporate criminality rests presumably upon the inadequacy of the threat of personal conviction upon the individual actors. As said earlier, difficulties of proof under legal principles of accountability have interfered with effective prosecution of high corporate officials. And the commonly observed jury behavior of convicting the corporate defendant while acquitting the individual defendants, even where proof is apparently strong, further supports the case for the alternative sanction. Moreover, "there are probably cases in which the economic pressures within the corporate body are sufficiently potent to tempt individuals to hazard personal liability for the sake of company gain, especially where the penalties threatened are moderate and where the offense does not involve behavior condemned as highly immoral by the individual's associates." Yet the question remains of the effectiveness of corporate criminality as a supplementary deterrent.

The only two practically available modes of imposing criminal sanctions upon the corporate defendant are through the stigma of conviction and the exaction of a fine. The former, classified by Bentham as the "moral or popular" sanction, operates as he suggested through the adverse reactions to the conviction of persons in the community. Whether there is any substantial moral opprobrium attached to violation of economic regulatory legislation (even where individuals are convicted) I defer until later. Assuming there is, can it be said to have any appreciable significance when directed to a corporate entity? There is no substantial empirical basis for answering this question. It seems unlikely that whatever moral stigma may attach to a convicted corporation would be felt in any effectual way by the corporate individuals, especially in large corporations where responsibility is diffused. On the other hand, the point has been made (though denied as well) that the corporate stigma may operate as a deterrent by impairing the reputation of the corporation in its business operations and hence adversely affecting its economic position. Until there is more to go on one can only guess at the validity of this observation, though there is reason to expect that the impact of the conviction would operate differentially, depending on the size of the corporation, the extent of competition and the dominance of its market position, the degree to which its conviction attracted public notice, and the like.

The exaction of a corporate fine serves in part to give color to the moral stigma of conviction. Insofar as this is its role, its value depends upon the existence and power of the stigma to deter. On the other hand, the use of the corporate fine apart from the stigma of conviction raises no issue peculiar to the criminal sanction, since civil fines afford identical deterrent possibilities. Whether it would prove effective to increase the economic hazard of misconduct by authorizing higher fines than those now commonly authorized depends on such considerations as the general ability of the corporation to recoup its losses through its pricing policy and the likelihood that courts would impose the higher fines. An alternative recently proposed would substitute for the fine a governmental proceeding designed to compel the corporation to disgorge the profits attributable to its violation. These alternatives raise substantial questions concerning sanctions, but not the criminal sanction, strictly speaking.

C. The Problem of Moral Neutrality

Viewed in the large, the characteristic of the conduct typically proscribed by economic regulatory legislation most relevant for the purposes of criminal enforcement is that it is calculated and deliberative and directed to economic gain. It would appear, therefore, to constitute a classic case for the operation of the deterrent strategy. Nonetheless, it is a widely shared view that the strategy has not worked out in fact, that the criminal sanction has not proved a major weapon for achieving compliance. Part of the explanation may be attributable to the difficulties of enforcement suggested above, such as the resistance to vaguely defined standards of criminality, the difficulty of fixing culpability upon high corporate officials, and the muffled and absorbable impact of corporate criminal sanctions. But it is likely that other factors play a more dominant role.

A common explanation of the failure of the criminal sanction is simply that the powerful business interests affected do not want these laws enforced and employ their power and position in American life to block vigorous enforcement. Influence is exercised over the legislatures to keep enforcement staffs impoverished and sanctions safely inefficacious. Enforcement officials, as prospective counsel for business interests, and judges as former counsel, identify with these interests and resist criminal enforcement. Moreover, news media, under the control of these same groups, work to create hostility to these laws and their vigorous enforcement and sympathy for the violators. In short, "those who are responsible for the system of criminal justice are afraid to antagonize businessmen. . . . The most powerful group in medieval society secured relative immunity from punishment by 'benefit of clergy,' and now our most powerful group secures relative immunity by 'benefit of business.'"

It would be dogmatic to assert that influences of this kind do not exist, but it may be doubted that they play a dispositive role. Business surely constitutes a powerful interest group in American life; but the profusion of regulatory legislation over the ardent protests of important economic interests in the past thirty years is some evidence that it is not all-powerful. Opposing forces have been able to marshal considerable public sentiment against a variety of business practices. Moreover, it is perhaps an oversimplification to identify all business as united in monolithic opposition. There is less a single business interest than a substantial variety of business interests. What then, in addition to business propaganda and influence, has accounted for the failure of the criminal sanction? Or, if we must have a villain, how has it been that business, which has not always gotten its way, has been this successful in devitalizing the use of that sanction?

It is a plausible surmise that the explanation is implicated in another feature of the behavior regulated by these laws; namely, that it is not generally regarded as morally reprehensible in the common view, that, indeed, in some measure it is the laws themselves that appear bad, or at least painful necessities, and that the violators by and large turn out to be respectable people in the respectable pursuit of profit. It is not likely that these popular attitudes are wholly products of a public-relations campaign by the affected business community. The springs of the public sentiment reach into the national ethos, producing the values that the man of business himself holds, as well as the attitude of the public toward him and his activities. Typically the conduct prohibited by economic regulatory laws is not immediately distinguishable from modes of business behavior that are not only socially acceptable, but affirmatively desirable in an economy founded upon an ideology (not denied by the regulatory regime itself) of free enterprise and the profit motive. Distinctions there are, of course, between salutary entrepreneurial practices and those which threaten the values of the very regime of economic freedom. And it is possible to reason convincingly that the harms done to the economic order by violations of many of these regulatory laws are of a magnitude that dwarf in significance the lower-class property offenses. But the point is that these perceptions require distinguishing and reasoning processes that are not the normal governors of the passion of moral disapproval, and are not dramatically obvious to a public long conditioned to responding approvingly to the production of profit through business shrewdness, especially in the absence of live and visible victims. Moreover, in some areas, notably the antitrust laws, it is far from clear that there is consensus even by the authors and enforcers of the regulation—the legislators, courts and administrators—on precisely what should be prohibited and what permitted, and the reasons therefor. And as Professor Freund observed, "if a law declares a practice to be criminal, and cannot apply its policy with consistency, its moral effect is necessarily weakened."

The consequences of the absence of sustained public moral resentment for the effective use of the criminal sanction may be briefly stated. The central distinguishing aspect of the criminal sanction appears to be the stigmatization of the morally culpable. At least it tends so to be regarded in the community. Without moral culpability there is in a democratic community an explicable and justifiable reluctance to affix the stigma of blame. This perhaps is the basic explanation, rather than the selfish machinations of business interests, for the reluctance of administrators and prosecutors to invoke the criminal sanction, the reluctance of jurors to find guilt and the reluctance of judges to impose strong penalties. And beyond its effect on enforcement, the absence of moral opprobrium interferes in another more subtle way with achieving compliance. Fear of being caught and punished does not exhaust the deterrent mechanism of the criminal law. It is supplemented by the personal disinclination to act in violation of the law's commands, apart from immediate fear of being punished. One would suppose that especially in the case of those who normally regard themselves as respectable, proper and law-abiding the appeal to act in accordance with conscience is relatively great. But where the violation is not generally regarded as ethically reprehensible, either by the community at large or by the class of businessmen itself, the private appeal to conscience is at its minimum and being convicted and fined may have little more impact than a bad selling season. Are there modes of dealing with these consequences of making morally neutral behavior criminal? A commonly suggested remedy for inadequate enforcement is a campaign of strict enforcement aided by strengthened prosecution staffs, and perhaps more severe penalties. But to the extent that the deficiency in enforcement is attributable to the moral inoffensiveness of the behavior, the major limitation of such a call to arms is that it is addressed to the symptom rather than the cause. How will legislatures be convinced to expend substantial sums for criminal enforcement, or prosecutors to go for the jugular, or courts or juries to cooperate in the face of a fundamental lack of sympathy for the criminal penalty in this area? Enlarged resources for prosecution may well afford staff enthusiasts an opportunity for more vigorous enforcement, but one may doubt that it can achieve more than a minor flurry of enforcement.

An attack on the cause, insofar as moral neutrality is the cause, would presumably require a two-pronged program: one directed at the obstacle of popular nullification; the other at inculcating the sentiment of moral disapproval in the community. Each, of course, would inevitably have an effect upon the other. The former might proceed, not simply by allocating greater enforcement resources, but by arrangements that would reduce the traditional discretionary authority of the various bodies involved in criminal law enforcement. For example, the decision to prosecute might be exclusively centered in the agency responsible for the whole regulatory program; conservative legal interpretation might be dealt with by authorizing agency interpretative regulations which are made relevant in criminal prosecutions; the temporizing of juries might be avoided by eliminating, where possible, jury trials; the judge's sentencing discretion might be curtailed by mandatory minimum penalties. There is, of course, the substantial task of persuading legislatures to abjure the traditional mediating institutions of the criminal law in an area where, the moral factor being largely absent, they might be thought to have their historic and most useful function to perform. But if enacted, one might reasonably suppose that such legal arrangements could result in a somewhat more frequent and rigorous use of the criminal sanction and a heightening of the deterrent effect of the law.

The other prong of the program, the cultivation of the sentiment of moral disapproval, is perhaps closer to the heart of the matter. To some extent the more frequent enforcement and the more stringent punishment of violators may tend to serve this objective as well as its more direct in terrorem purposes, especially where cases are selected for enforcement with this end in view. Whether a governmentally mounted campaign should be employed as well to give widespread publicity to successful convictions and to shape the public conscience in other ways may be questioned from various viewpoints, but it surely would be consistent with the basic strategy of using criminal sanctions in these areas.

How effective a campaign of selected prosecutions and attendant publicity would prove in creating a changed moral climate is problematical. Certainly one can not confidently deny that the spectacle of frequent conviction and severe punishment may play a role in molding the community's attitudes toward the conduct in question. Experience offers uncertain guidance. Tax evasion has a history that provides some support. We have come a considerable distance, though not all the way, from the day when an English judge could observe from the bench, "there is not behind taxing laws, as there is behind laws against crime, an independent moral obligation." The change was accompanied in this country by a gradual tightening of the criminal sanction. In 1924 tax evasion was upgraded from a misdemeanor to a felony and maximum imprisonment raised from one to five years; reforms in 1952 converted the criminal prosecution from a tax recovery device and weapon against the professional racketeer to a means of general deterrence of tax evasion by widespread and selected enforcement against all levels of violators. While the tax evasion prosecution is still something of a special case, the record of successful prosecution has become genuinely impressive and the tax evasion conviction a sanction of some consequence. Experience such as this, however, gives little more than support for the plainly plausible assumption that criminal enforcement may play some part. One can not be sure of the extent to which other factors, not necessarily present in areas other than tax, created the conditions for optimum use of the criminal sanction as a moralizing weapon, or indeed, of the extent to which other influences rather than, or in addition to, the criminal sanction, produced the changed climate. The caution is further indicated (though, of course, not demonstrated) by less successful experiences in attempting to deal through the criminal law with behavior that did not attract any substantial degree of reprobatory unanimity, such as prohibition or gambling. At all events, Mannheim's caveat is a useful one: "It is only in a Soviet state and through a legal system on the lines of the Soviet penal code, which deliberately uses the political weapon of criminal prosecution to shape the economic system according to its ideology, that old traditions of such strength can be comparatively quickly destroyed."

III

I have reserved for last those issues and concerns that arise out of goals other than the effectiveness of the criminal sanction in achieving compliance. Those which most prominently compete for consideration are: first, the sentiment of fundamental fairness – justice, in a word; and second, the retention of the vitality of the criminal law in its traditional sphere of application. They come into play in connection with two aspects of the use of the criminal law to enforce economic regulatory laws; namely, the loosening of minimum requirements for culpability in the cause of enforcement efficiency, and the criminalizing and punishing of behavior that does not generally attract the sentiment of moral reprobation.

A. *Requirements of Culpability*

At several points attention has been called to the obstacles to effective prosecution created by certain conventional requirements of the criminal law; for example, the requirement of specificity in defining the prohibited conduct and the requirement of minimum conditions of accountability in holding persons responsible for the acts of others. Whatever basis these requirements have in the area of traditional crime, may they properly be diluted or dispensed with in the area of economic regulatory crime? The issue is fundamentally the same as that posed by the use of strict criminal liability, though, interestingly enough, this appears to have been much less commonly employed in economic regulation than in those controls on business directed to public health and safety.

The case for the irrelevance of these traditional requirements is reflected in the observation of a trustbuster of an earlier generation: "The rights of the accused which are of the utmost importance where liberty of an individual is in jeopardy, are irrelevant symbols when the real issue is the arrangement under which corporations in industry compete." In essence the concept is that the purpose behind the criminal sanction in this area is not penalization, but regulation. Unlike the area of conventional crime against person and property where criminalization serves to reassure the community, to express condemnation and to set in motion a corrective or restraining regime, as well as to deter proscribed behavior, here the concern is solely with this last factor. "[T]he problem of responsibility is not the general social phenomenon of moral delinquency and guilt, but the practical problem of dealing with physical conditions and social or economic practices that are to be controlled."

A countervailing consideration commonly adduced in discussions of strict liability is equally applicable where culpability requirements are otherwise withdrawn by statutes that do not adequately announce what is prohibited or that impose varieties of vicarious responsibility. Absent these requirements, it cannot be said, except in a strictly formal sense, that the actor made a choice to commit the acts prohibited. Hence, it is said that the law has no deterrent function to perform, offering no lesson to the actor or to other persons, beyond the Pickwickian instruction that even if he does the best he can, or anyone could, to comply with the law he may nonetheless be punished. Yet the argument does not quite persuade. For it may as plausibly be argued that the consequence of dispensing with the requirement of proof of culpability eases the task of the enforcing authorities, rendering successful prosecution more likely and, through discouraging insistence on trial and simplifying the issues when trials are held, enhances the efficiency of prosecution. In a word, certainty of conviction is increased. This may readily exert an added deterrent force upon the actor faced with a choice, since the chances of escaping punishment for a culpable choice, intentional or negligent, are decreased. And even where there is no immediate choice, the effect could sometimes be to influence persons to arrange their affairs to reduce to a minimum the possibilities of accidental violation; in short, to exercise extraordinary care. Further, the persistent use of such laws by legislatures and their strong support by persons charged with their enforcement makes it dogmatic to insist they can not deter in these ways.

Closer, perhaps, to the core of the opposition to dispensing with culpability is the principle that it is morally improper and ultimately unsound and self-defeating to employ penal sanctions with respect to conduct that does not warrant the moral condemnation that is implicit, or that should be implicit, in the concept of a crime. The issue is whether these considerations are adequately dealt with by the contention that laws dispensing with culpability are directed to regulation rather than penalization.

The contention plainly proves too much. If the sole concern is a non-reprobative deterrent threat, then it follows that the sanction should be drastic and certain enough to overcome the motive of economic gain, and not necessarily that the sanction should be criminal. Civil fines, punitive damages, injunctions, profit divestiture programs or other varieties of non-criminal sanctions would thus appear to offer equivalent possibilities of enforcing the regulatory scheme. Indeed, these alternatives might enhance the possibilities, since proof and evidentiary requirements are more onerous in criminal prosecutions than in civil suits. The conclusion appears difficult to resist that insistence on the criminal penalty is attributable to a desire to make use of the unique deterrent mode of the criminal sanction, the stigma of moral blame that it carries. If so, the argument of regulation rather than penalization turns out in the end to be only a temporary diversion that does not escape the need to confront the basic issue: the justice and wisdom of imposing a stigma of moral blame in the absence of blameworthiness in the actor.

So far as the issue of justice is concerned, once having put the moral question the footing becomes unsteady. Is the moral difficulty inconsequential, requiring simply the side-stepping of an otherwise useful symbol that happens to stand in the way of attaining immediately desirable goals? Does it yield to a pragmatic evaluation in terms of an estimate of the soundness of departing from principle to some degree in particular cases in order to attain goals of greater consequence? Does it present an insuperable objection entailing commitment to values of such profundity that compromise is unthinkable? For present purposes it is perhaps enough to put the questions, though three points may be suggested. First, the starkness of the moral issue is to some degree assuaged by regarding laws dispensing with culpability as empowering enforcement officials to use their discretion to select for

prosecution those who have in their judgment acted culpably. Plainly, however, the issue is not escaped since it remains to justify dispensing with the safeguards of trial on this single and crucial issue. Second, the recognition of the moral impasse does not necessarily require agreement that the criminal law *should* use its weapons for the purpose of fixing moral obloquy upon transgressors. It is sufficient that it is broadly characteristic of the way criminal conviction operates in our society. Third, and in consequence, the moral difficulty exists only so long as and to the extent that criminal conviction retains its aura of moral condemnation. The impasse lessens to the extent that the element of blame and punishment is replaced by a conception of the criminal process as a means of social improvement through a program of morally neutral rehabilitation and regulation. (Though such a development has important implications which I mean to return to shortly.)

Concerning the issue of ultimate wisdom, the point frequently made respecting strict liability is equally applicable to the dilution of these aspects of culpability typically at issue in economic regulatory legislation. The dilution is not readily confined within the narrow area for which it was designed, but tends to overflow into the main body of conventional crimes. The distinction between offenses that regulate and those that penalize in the traditional sense proves inadequate to divide the waters. For example, traditional concepts of liability in the main body of criminal law tend to receive a new and diluted form when construed as part of a regulatory statute. Moreover, the habituation of courts and legislatures to crimes dispensing with culpability in the regulatory area may readily dull legislative and judicial sensitivity to the departures from minimum culpability requirements already fixed in the main body of the criminal law. This expansion of criminality without culpability in statutory offenses and convictions, and its spread and solidification in the general criminal law heightens the moral difficulty. As the area expands and deepens it becomes necessary at some point to face the issue as entailing a judgment on the abandonment of principle rather than one of the wisdom of utilitarian compromise for a larger good. Moreover, the risks entailed in depreciating the impact of condemnation in a criminal conviction become greater to the extent that conviction without culpability becomes more common and pervasive. To the extent that the crucial distinguishing factor of the criminal sanction is ''the judgment of community condemnation which accompanies and justifies its imposition,'' and to the extent that this characteristic contributes substantially to its effectiveness in influencing compliance with proscribed norms, the proliferation of convictions without grounds for condemnation tends in the long run to impair the identity of the criminal sanction and its ultimate effectiveness as a preventive sanction, both in the area of economic crimes and in the areas of its traditional application.

B. *The Criminalization of Morally Neutral Conduct*

But let it be assumed that the traditional grounds of culpability have been adhered to so that the defendant can fairly be held accountable for a choice to violate the economic prohibitions. May there be costs, even so, in terms of principle and other goals, in employing the criminal sanction where the violative behavior does not attract in the community the moral disapprobation associated with a criminal conviction? How different and how similar are the considerations involved in dispensing with culpability? The question is the obverse of an aspect of the relation between criminal law and morals which has been much considered – the use of the criminal law to prohibit and condemn behavior that is widely (either actually or formally) viewed as morally reprehensible, where secular interests, in the sense of concerns beyond the immorality of individuals, do not exist. Here the issue is the use of the criminal sanction to prohibit and condemn behavior that threatens secular interests, but that is not regarded as fundamentally and inherently wrong.

The central consequence of diluting or eliminating requirements of culpability is, as suggested, the criminalization and punishment of persons who cannot be said to warrant the condemnation thereby imported. It is this consequence that gives rise to the hard question of principle and practical consequences. In a sense a similar consequence follows from punishing conduct that is not itself blameworthy, even when culpably engaged in: Persons are stigmatized with conviction for conduct not regarded as deserving the moral stigma. The problem of principle, however, is of considerably smaller dimension, since the choice to act in defiance of the criminal prohibition may be regarded as in some measure furnishing an independently adequate ground for condemnation. (Yet it is necessary to add that the ground exists only in cases where the culpability requirements are extended to include knowledge or culpable disregard of the existence of the prohibition, an extension only occasionally made in regulatory legislation.)

The danger of debilitating the moral impact of the criminal conviction and hence decreasing the overall effectiveness of the criminal law can not as readily be put aside. As Professor Henry Hart has noted, "the criminal law always loses face if things are declared to be crimes which people believe they ought to be

free to do, even wilfully." It may be mitigated to a degree by maintaining a proper proportion in the punishment authorized for various offenses in accordance with the moral culpability of the behavior. The limitations of such a strategy are, first, that there is always a strong pressure to raise authorized penalties when violations become widespread or conspicuous, and second, that there is an irreducible minimum in the moral condemnation comported by conviction of crime. Such considerations have led one observer to "decry the trend toward an increasingly undiscriminating employment of this branch of the law, and to repudiate the suggestion that criminal law should be applied more extensively in the areas of ordinary economic relationships."

It may of course be answered that the conviction of violators of laws of this character serves as a means of moral instruction to the community; in short, that the onus of conviction is transferred to the behavior prohibited. That there will be a transference would appear quite likely. But that it should necessarily or generally be expected to involve imparting moral onus to the behavior rather than moral indifference to the conviction is considerably less so. The more widely the criminal conviction is used for this purpose, and the less clear the immorality of the behavior so sanctioned, the more likely would it appear that the criminal conviction will not only fail to attain the immediate purpose of its use but will degenerate in effectiveness for other purposes as well.

There is another cost not paralleled in the dilution of culpability requirements. The behavior under discussion involves restraints upon the free operation of business without at the same time denying commitment to a free enterprise system. The demarcation of the line between the legitimate, indeed the affirmatively desirable, and the illegitimate in business conduct is continually in flux and subject to wide controversy in the community. To say there is no complete consensus on what business decisions should be regulated and what left free of regulation is to say what is minimally true. It would not follow from this that a legislature should abstain from enacting such controls as command a majority. But the appropriateness of the criminal sanction as a means of enforcing the imposed control is another matter. I have already suggested that the criminal remedy in this situation tends to be ineffective and destructive of its overall utility as a sanctioning device. Here the point is different. To the extent it is effective in generating strong moral commitments to the regulatory regime it supports it has the dangerous potential of introducing a rigidification of values too soon, of cutting off the debate, or at least restricting the ease of movement to new positions and a new consensus. This seems to me the wisdom of Professor Allen's caveat that "the function of the criminal law in these areas is not to anticipate but to reflect and implement the consensus already achieved in the community."

A word in conclusion on lines of legislative action. The widescale abandonment of the criminal sanction in those areas where its cost is excessive is as unlikely as it is desirable. Legislative habit and the simple logic of here and now expedience have a compulsion not to be denied by contemplation of long range consequences in areas removed from the immediate target of legislative concern. A more acceptable and hence more fruitful course is the development of means of reducing the costs of the use of the criminal sanction in economic regulations, which do not demand that it be abandoned altogether. If such means exist one would expect they would be found in ways of dealing with the central fact principally responsible for the predicament, the irreducible core of condemnation in a criminal conviction. One possible approach is to institutionalize a system of gradation of convictions, just as systems of grading punishment have long been a part of the law. There is no adequate basis for accomplishing this under present law. The distinction between offenses mala prohibita and male in se carries something of the flavor, but it is an informal rather than an institutionalized distinction and lacks any clear meaning. The felony-misdemeanor distinction has an established statutory basis. However, the categories have largely lost significance in distinguishing degrees of blameworthiness, some misdemeanors embracing crimes of serious moral import, and some felonies embracing relatively minor transgressions. Moreover, there is need for a category of offense carrying considerably less weight than a misdemeanor. The petty offense category which appears in many statutes is essentially a petty misdemeanor, retaining its label as a crime and being punishable with imprisonment. In those cases in which the label has been removed, the substance (that is, provision or imprisonment) has not. The Model Penal Code has attempted to meet the inadequacies of existing law by adding to its three categories of crime (felonies, misdemeanors and petty misdemeanors) a separate non-criminal category designated a "violation" which is punishable only by a sentence of fine (under 500 dollars or any higher amount equal to double the pecuniary gain made by the offender) or civil penalty, and which does not "give rise to any disability or legal disadvantage based on conviction of a criminal offense." The design of law in these areas is not to anticipate but to reflect and implement the consensus already achieved in the community."

A word in conclusion on lines of legislative action. The widescale abandonment of the criminal sanction in those areas where its cost is excessive is as unlikely as it is desirable. Legislative habit and the simple logic of here and now expediency have a compulsion not to be denied by contemplation of long range consequences in areas removed from the immediate target of legislative concern. A more acceptable and hence more fruitful course is the development of means of reducing the costs of the use of the criminal sanction in economic regulations, which do not demand that it be abandoned altogether. If such means exist one would expect they would be found in ways of dealing with the central fact principally responsible for the predicament, the irreducible core of condemnation in a criminal conviction. One possible approach is to institutionalize a system of gradation of convictions, just as systems of grading punishment have long been a part of the law. There is no adequate basis for accomplishing this under present law. The distinction between offenses mala prohibita and mala in se carries something of the flavor, but it is an informal rather than an institutionalized distinction and lacks any clear meaning. The felony-misdemeanor distinction has an established statutory basis. However, the categories have largely lost significance in distinguishing degrees of blameworthiness, some misdemeanors embracing crimes of serious moral import, and some felonies embracing relatively minor transgressions. Moreover, there is need for a category of offense carrying considerably less weight than a misdemeanor. The petty offense category which appears in many statutes is essentially a petty misdemeanor, retaining its label as a crime and being punishable with imprisonment. In those cases in which the label has been removed, the substance (that is, provision for imprisonment) has not. The Model Penal Code has attempted to meet the inadequacies of existing law by adding to its three categories of crime (felonies, misdemeanors and petty misdemeanors) a separate non-criminal category designated a "violation" which is punishable only by a sentence of fine (under 500 dollars or any higher amount equal to double the pecuniary gain made by the offender) or civil penalty, and which does not "give rise to any disability or legal disadvantage based on conviction of a criminal offense." The design of this proposal "reflects the purpose of the Code to employ penal sanctions only with respect to conduct warranting the moral condemnation implicit in the concept of a crime." Since strict liability even for crimes properly so regarded presents the same problem, the same solution is applied by treating crimes committed without culpability as "violations."

While novel in American law, the German law has for some years adopted an approach quite similar to that proposed by the Model Penal Code. Separate from a three-level classification of crimes, properly so called (Straftat), is another category of offense, the "regulatory violation" (Ordnungswidrigkeit). These regulatory violations are not punishable by imprisonment. A fine is the sole available sanction, indeed a fine which bears a special designation (Geldbusse, literally "monetary repentance") as opposed to the penal fine (Geldstrafe, literally "monetary punishment"). These fines are not registered in the punishment registry and are imposed at the first instance by the responsible administrative agency subject to the right of the violator to object and to be tried in the courts.

The feasibility of using the category of regulatory violation for sanctioning economic regulation is, of course, the principal issue. Here the German experience may offer some evidence for decision. Unfortunately there appear to be no empirical studies of the relative effectiveness of its use in Germany. But to judge from the statute books it is the typical non-civil sanction for economic misconduct. All antitrust violations, for example, are regulatory violations, as are violations of other restrictions upon economic behavior such as certain behavior prohibited by the foreign trade law, laws governing the operation of loan banks, laws governing the closing of shops, transportation rate laws and other laws. Particularly suggestive is the strategy used in connection with certain kinds of economic offenses as a means of individualizing the determination of whether a defendant's behavior is to be treated as a crime or a regulatory violation. For violations of certain price control laws, import restrictions and unlawful overcharging, a legislative determination of the appropriate category of the offense is withheld in favor of a judicial determination in each case. The law requires an offense under these laws to be dealt with as a regulatory violation unless the nature either of the conduct or of the defendant warrants dealing with it as a crime. It is a crime when the conduct "by virtue of its scope or consequences is likely to prejudice the goals of the economic system, especially those of market or price regulations"; or when the defendant is a "repeated or professional violator or acts in culpable selfishness or otherwise irresponsibly, and by his conduct shows that he lacks respect for the public interest in the protection of the economic system, especially of the market or price regulations." With all their vagueness these provisions suggest a need in any system that employs a non-criminal category of violation and uses it to deal with economic violations, for a flexible device whereby violations may, with changed public sentiment and in consideration of the extremity of

the circumstances, be raised to the category of crime.

One can hardly say that this approach through a tertium quid is the clear answer to the problems of using criminal sanctions to enforce economic restrictions. There are many imponderables with respect to its effectiveness both as a preventive and as a means of reducing the costs of an indiscriminate use of the criminal sanction. On the side of preventive effectiveness, is the reprobative association of a genuine criminal conviction a needed weapon of enforcement? Would the semi-criminal category of offense convey enough of a sense of wrongness to perform its tasks? Can these laws be enforced efficiently enough without such associations? Is the loss of the power to imprison a substantial loss? Does what is left of the criminal process still provide efficiencies not available in the pure civil remedy? Will the regulatory offense prove politically acceptable to legislators and administrators as an alternative to outright criminalization? On the side of reducing costs, how much will it help that a new label has been created so long as the criminal process is used, or that imprisonment is not available as a sanction, when in fact it is rarely used anyway? And finally, is whatever is lost in effectiveness worth what is gained in other respects? One cannot be dogmatic in answering these questions. But one can, I think, insist that these are the kinds of questions which must be asked about this alternative as well as others if we are to escape the limited options inherited from different days in the use of the criminal sanction.

Harry V. Ball and Lawrence M. Friedman, *The Use of Criminal Sanctions in the Enforcement of Economic Legislation: A Sociological View*, 17 STAN. L. REV. 197–223 (1965)*

Concern over the use of criminal sanctions in the enforcement of business legislation is by no means new. As late as 1961, however, Whiting remarked that "the history of antitrust enforcement to date should not cause undue alarm to the corporate executive." Two recent prosecutions have intensified the

---

discussion and called Whiting's conclusion into question. In *United States v. McDonough Co.* one president and three vice-presidents of several comparatively small garden tool manufacturing firms received ninety-day jail sentences and a fine of $5,000 for deliberate price fixing and market rigging. The defendants entered pleas of *nolo contendere.* The Government felt that a fine would be "a sufficient deterring factor"; the defendants argued against a jail sentence, pointing out that no jail sentence had been imposed in *nolo contendere* cases during the 59-year life of the Sherman Act. The judge ignored both the Government and the defendants. His position was that Congress would not have provided for imprisonment in the original act and retained it thereafter unless that penalty was intended to be used whenever a sentencing court believed jail sentences proper.

In the second and more famous case, the *Electrical Equipment Antitrust Cases,* the Government demanded jail sentences in several instances. Moreover, the prosecutor asked the court to refuse pleas of *nolo contendere* from the individual defendants. The Government argued that acceptance of such pleas "would neither foster respect for the law nor vindicate the public interest" in the light of the fact that the grand jury's indictments "charge violations of rigging and price-fixing as serious as any instances ever charged in the more than half a century life of the Sherman Act." The judge agreed. The sentences imposed included, in addition to fines and probation, seven straight sentences to imprisonment for thirty days and thirty-one suspended sentences for various periods. The court described the defendants' conduct as a "shocking indictment of a vast section of our economy" that "flagrantly mocked the image of the economic system of free enterprise which we profess to the country and destroyed the model which we offer today as a free-world alternative to state control and eventual dictatorship." Later the Attorney General of the United States classified the defendants' conduct as "a serious threat to democracy."

On the other hand, many major newspapers paid little or no attention to the convictions and sentences; some critics of the prosecution saw "ominous overtones" in the fact that men had been sent to jail for "something that has been going on for years as an accepted business practice"; and a convicted president of one of the twenty-nine accused corporations questioned the right of the Government to enact such "regulations," much less to send a person to jail for their violation, and asserted that "price stabilization" was an essential element of "free enterprise."

Perhaps these price-fixing (price-stabilizing) and market-rigging (market-stabilizing) cases are not typical of the broader class of criminal-penal laws regulating business. The defendants knew they were violating the law, they acted in secret collusion, huge sums of money were involved, and the Justice Department strove mightily to equate the conduct in the second case to a fraud against the Government. Quite different are mine-run violations of regulations affecting business, especially those involving strict liability where intentional violation is not an essential element of the crime. At least these may raise more clearly the problem of what Professor Sanford Kadish has called "moral neutrality." The issue is whether severe criminal sanctions ought to be imposed on those who violate the legal but not the moral code. In the view of Kadish and others, a key factor in any discussion of the propriety and effectiveness of the use of criminal sanctions in enforcing business regulations is the relationship between prevailing morality and the norms of the criminal law. Are economic crimes morally wrong? If they are, should men be sent to jail for committing them? Even the price-fixing cases raise the issue, though in a slightly different form.

This essay is an attempt to explore the relationship between popular morality and the use of criminal sanctions in regulating business practices. We shall begin by setting forth some basic distinctions necessary for a sociological analysis of the problem.

First, when we speak of using criminal sanctions, we may be referring to more than one meaning of the term *use.* One may distinguish between (a) *authorization* by the legislature of the employment of criminal sanctions, and (b) their *application* by the administrator. That is, the law may be said to "use" a sanction when a statute authorizes its use; in a second sense, the sanction is "used" only when it is actually applied. Discussing antitrust laws, for example, one might debate whether it is proper to append criminal sanctions for violations of the regulations at all; and even those who concede that it is proper may question whether it is right to unsheathe the sword in particular cases. Thus, those who are distressed because even a small proportion of the implicated officials of the electrical industry were imprisoned are probably opposed to any authorization of criminal sanctions in regulating business affairs; they can hardly argue that these particular offenders merited any special leniency. On the other hand, persons who complain because criminal sanctions are rarely invoked in mine-run antitrust cases and who look upon this as an indication of favoritism to "white-collar criminals" are questioning the administration of the sanctions while conceding – or even urging – the propriety of their authorization. Problems of the legislative authorization of criminal sanctions and problems of the administrative decisions to apply the sanctions ought to be analyzed separately.

Secondly, what do we mean by the term "criminal sanctions"? Statutes aimed at economic regulation often provide multiple, alternative sanctions. Sometimes mandatory sequences of use are prescribed. The sanctions may include cease-and-desist orders (enforced through contempt proceedings), injunctive divestiture proceedings, awards of damages or treble damages, monetary fines or forfeitures (which may or may not involve imprisonment for nonpayment), seizures of goods, revocations of business or occupational licenses, prison sentences, and probation with a threat of fine or imprisonment for the violation of probation. Of these, some classes of fines, direct imprisonment, and probation with threat of fine or imprisonment for the violation of the conditions of probation are generally considered "criminal" sanctions.

However, fines or money forfeitures are widely used also as sanctions in actions formally classified as "civil proceedings." Criminologists generally approve of the use of fines as a sanction for violation of laws punishing deliberate, calculated, antisocial "profit making," because the fine divests the violator of his profits; it is a penalty which plausibly can be said to deter profit-making misconduct. However, this defense of the propriety of the fine fails to distinguish a criminal fine from a civil forfeiture, or from treble damages or other forms of punitive damages, which may also deter. One may, of course, ask whether money penalties are appropriate sanctions against a business organization; and there are other subsidiary questions, *e.g.*, should the state or the victim receive the money? But such questions are irrelevant to a discussion of whether the sanction of a money penalty should be "civil" or "criminal." Therefore, when one asks whether certain conduct should be subject to criminal sanctions, one is not asking whether the conduct should be subject to a money penalty. The civil law "punishes" breaches of contract and torts with damage awards, but no one imagines that money damages here are criminal sanctions. For these reasons we are eliminating the fine or money penalty from our consideration of criminal sanctions. When discussion is directed to the question of the use of "criminal" sanctions, then, the issues raised are essentially these: (a) Must the evidence establish the defendant's guilt beyond a reasonable doubt, and shall the defendant be entitled to all the procedural safeguards of criminal law? (b) Shall the defendant and his conduct be publicly labeled as criminal? (c) Shall the defendant, upon conviction, be subject to imprisonment or conditional probation with the threat of loss of liberty for violation of the conditions?

Finally, what is the meaning in this context of "economic regulations"? Professor Kadish feels there is more than one kind of economic regulation, and limits his discussion of enforcement problems to regulations "which impose restrictions upon the conduct of business as part of a considered economic policy." He would exclude "regulations directly affecting business conduct which are founded on interests other than economic ones; for example, laws regulating the conduct of business in the interest of public safety and general physical welfare." He is concerned with those regulations intended "to protect the economic order of the community against harmful use by the individual of his property interest" and whose "central purpose . . . is to control private choice, rather than free it," in contrast to the "traditional property offenses," intended to "protect private property interests against the acquisitive behavior of others in the furtherance of free private decisions." Thus, he is concerned with violations of "such laws as price control and rationing laws, antitrust laws and other legislation designed to protect or promote competition or prevent unfair competition, export controls, small loan laws, securities regulations, and, perhaps, some tax laws." For such offenses the "nature of the interest protected is by definition unique."

Professor Kadish certainly has the right to specify these types of regulation, and for his purposes they may constitute a unitary category. However, his reasons for isolating them—the uniqueness of the protected interest and their origin as part of a considered economic policy—cannot be defended upon empirical grounds. Let us test some of his examples in the light of his claimed differentiae.

For Professor Kadish, the economic crime *par excellence* is the antitrust violation. The text of the Sherman Antitrust Act reflected legislative awareness of existing common-law doctrine concerning restraint of trade. The enactment of a much-debated federal criminal statute on the subject owed more to political forces and theories operating in the late nineteenth century than it did to economic theory, policy, or ideology. The primary interest involved was and is "the emergence of the modern corporate organization as presenting a problem in the distribution of power," the continuing problem of individual freedom of choice, and the functioning of democratic processes in a society where large corporations had tremendous wealth and power, including political power. The basic problem has been and is "that of the control of the conduct of the business organization rather than a problem of preserving 'competition.'" This was clearly recognized at the time of the enactment of the Sherman Act by proponents and opponents alike. William Graham Sumner, for example, opposed "federal interference" because he was firmly convinced that industrial "bigness" was economically desirable *and* that government was too weak to resist being taken over by a business plutocracy if it sought to interfere with the trusts. Arguably, considered economic policy entered the picture when the courts rejected arguments based on bigness per se and explicitly read the concepts of reasonableness and control into federal antitrust law. "Dissolution is not a penalty but a remedy" to be employed only "if the industry will . . . need it for its protection." Economic policy in its purest form entered the arena not as the primary purpose of the legislation but as an alleviation against its strictness in the face of good faith on the part of the regulated. Much of the vagueness of antitrust regulation must be ascribed not to efforts to restrict business but to efforts to prevent the use of the "political" Sherman act to hamstring productive efficiency.

Laws regulating maximum prices or rents represent the same basic situation. They are necessary to restrict the power of persons to use property in ways contrary to the public interest because some emergency condition has eliminated the freedom of the normal market. The crisis situation is viewed as a general threat to national health, safety, and welfare — even survival. In such a situation extraordinary powers are assumed by the agents of the politically organized community against, for example, "speculative, unwarranted and abnormal increases in rents, exactions of unjust, unreasonable, oppressive rents and rental agreements, overcrowding occupation of uninhabitable dwellings, speculative, manipulative and disruptive practices by landlords of housing accommodations, and other acts and conditions endangering the public health, safety, welfare and morals" of the community while allowing, "at the same time, to landlords, fair and equitable rents." Private housing has, in the legislature's opinion, become vested with a public interest. Where the distribution of power pertinent to the larger interests is not an issue — as in Honolulu during the Korean War where the rents charged workers in company housing were established as part of the collective bargaining agreement between the plantation corporations and the ILWU — the government is likely to adopt a hands-off policy.

The preceding also suggests the difficulty of maintaining Professor Kadish's claimed distinction between "economic" laws which are part of "considered economic policy" and "economic laws" relating to health and physical safety. In which category, for instance, belong the laws limiting the employment or the hours of work of women and children? These were propounded as health laws, to be sure, but another important factor was a considered economic policy giving job preference to male heads of households over the competition of women and children. In general, "considered economic policy" and health and safety factors are inextricably bound together in the history of all types of regulation. For example, occupational licensing and similar laws are curious mixtures of economic policy and health and safety measures. The Wisconsin barber statute makes it unlawful "for any barber to use any instrument or article that has not been disinfected in accordance with . . . sanitary standards"; but the statute makes it equally unlawful to "advertise a definite price for any barbering service by means of displaying a sign containing such prices so that the same is visible to persons outside the barbershop." The two sections of this law are, to be sure, analytically separable; but the whole statute is animated by one spirit, in which an economic aim (protecting barbers from competitors) is mixed with a public-welfare aim (improving sanitary conditions of public barbershops).

In short, Kadish's attempt to distinguish the "economic" from other forms of regulation produces numerous inconsistencies. Thus, a rent-control law directed against unjust rents is viewed by Kadish as referring to morally neutral behavior and as part of a considered economic policy; a tenement house law that requires minimum standards of quality, regardless of the amount of rent, is presumably a health measure. In similar fashion, that part of most rent-control laws which makes it criminal for a landlord to seek to evict an existing tenant under certain circumstances would also be a regulation of morally neutral behavior. But how would Professor Kadish classify an "open occupancy" statute that makes it criminal for a landlord to discriminate on the basis of race in the initial selection of tenants? . . .

. . . Labeling conduct as "criminal" may change the public attitude toward the man who breaks the law as well as the attitudes of those who are themselves tempted to break the law. We shall examine these aftereffects later. For the present, it is enough to note that there is no necessary connection between the label "crime" and public morality; nor between the forces which tend to induce compliance with statutory precepts. Criminal law, particularly as it relates to economic crime, is a set of techniques to be manipulated for social ends.

The history of criminal law is in fact a history of the reasons why techniques of criminal-law enforcement have been brought to bear in particular areas to advance social goals. One factor dictating the use of criminal sanctions has been unduly ignored in most treatments of crime. This is the fact that the cost of enforcing the criminal law is borne by the state and that the initiation of criminal process and its administration are conducted by servants of the state. This is, in fact, a major social distinction between criminal and noncriminal law. To say that breach of contract is not a crime is not a statement about the morality of breach of contract, though we may consider breach of contract highly immoral under certain circumstances. Liability for breach of contract in the twentieth century has been imposed in some situations where the prior law did not impose liability, because of popular feelings that certain kinds of breach of contract are "unfair" (that is, immoral) and should therefore give rise to liability. The use of the concept of "unjust enrichment" affords a good illustration. The noncriminal nature of breach of contract means that the initial decision to "punish" a man who breaches his contract lies in the private sector and is, in fact, the exclusive decision of the man whose contract has been breached. In addition, once the aggrieved party decides to pursue his action in court, he must bear the expenses himself (though he hopes to recover some of them if he wins). He must hire his own lawyer and make arrangements to pay him. The state provides judges and courtrooms as a service; but the state has no interest in whether the plaintiff chooses to terminate his case before judgment, or whether he chooses to levy execution on the goods of the defendant after judgment. The victim of theft, on the other hand, does not hire the state to punish the thief. It is generally true of theft that the state will not prosecute unless a private citizen complains. But there are many areas of criminal law where this is not so. Murder is an obvious example.

We do not suggest that the only difference between criminal law and noncriminal law is that the former has socialized the process of enforcement, but this is an important distinction between the two areas, particularly with respect to economic regulation. Often the morality or immorality of proscribed conduct has little to do with whether the law labels the conduct criminal or leaves enforcement in private hands.

A striking example is usury. In Wisconsin, for example, usury was considered a socially dangerous and immoral practice by most of the population, as far as we can judge, through most of the nineteenth century. It was not, however, a crime. It was discouraged by severe civil penalties under some of the statutes; under one statute, based on a New York model, the usurer was barred from recovering either principal or interest and thus might lose the entire amount of his loan. Common statutory provisions called for treble damages, as in modern antitrust law. Provisions for punitive or multiple damages tend to encourage (and are meant to encourage) private enforcement. But since usury was punished only by civil sanctions, penalties inured to the private citizen who pursued his remedy. He made the choice of suing or not suing, and he saw the matter through the courts.

In 1895 usury was made a crime in Wisconsin, punishable by fine. It would be a rash assumption to say that usury became a crime because in 1895 a heightened sense of the immorality of usury suddenly gripped the public. The true explanation is more subtle. In the Middle West of the 19th century, usury had been primarily a problem of the rate of interest on farm mortgages. By the turn of the century it became preeminently a problem of urban consumption loans. Those who suffered from usury were unable to handle enforcement themselves because of their social and economic status. Loans were small; the borrowers were in large measure landless urban workers, many of them foreign born. By contrast, the farmers in the 1850's and 1860's had had a larger voice in the affairs of the community and had been willing, to judge from court records, to enforce the usury laws. Making usury a crime was thus a legislative judgment that it was best to socialize remedial action, not because of the immorality of usury, but because under existing social conditions civil enforcement had failed.

Lending money at interest is an economic act; and usury is an economic wrong under the law of the American states. The historical development just related demonstrates that the progression from civil to criminal sanctions does not necessarily represent any change in the moral status of the act proscribed. Usury was stamped with immorality both before and after it was made criminal in Wisconsin. It is probably more typical of economic regulatory crimes that the forbidden conduct is not considered "immoral" either before or after the imposition of criminal sanctions. Statute books are filled with economic crimes whose congruence with popular morality is either completely absent or so muted that one need not consider it. Take, for example, the Wisconsin statute which makes it a crime for any publicly supported hospital to "furnish to its inmates or patrons . . . any oleomargarine." Offenders are liable to fine "not to exceed $200 or imprisoned in the county jail not to exceed 6 months, for the first offense"; for subsequent offenses, fines may range up to $500, with imprisonment "not less than 30 days nor more than 6 months." The origins and purposes of the statute are perfectly obvious; but it is dubious to assert that it arose out of popular *morality*; and whether the public brands the purveyor of oleomargarine to patients in public (as opposed to private) hospitals with any special obloquy is even more dubious. Another Wisconsin statute forbids the sale of baking powder unless the label lists the ingredients, is printed "in the English language," with black ink, in type not smaller than eight point, bold-faced, Gothic capitals," and contains "the name and address of the manufacturer of such baking powder, and the words: 'This baking powder is composed of the following ingredients and none other.'" This crime bears the same penalties as the crime of giving oleomargarine to hospital patients. There may be considerable popular revulsion against the selling of poisonous or harmful or deceptive foods; but surely neither before nor after the passage of the act were there any deep well-springs of disgust against selling imported baking powder with a French label in small type-faces, or printed in green ink instead of black. The purpose of the act is regulatory; as in the case of the criminal usury law, administrative considerations probably led to the choice of criminal sanctions. Theoretically, the state could give the buyer of baking powder which did not conform to statutory standards a civil action for damages, or the right to rescind his purchase. This would certainly fail to accomplish the purpose of the statute, since the buyer of a small amount of baking powder would never bother to sue the seller. The individual transactions which form the subject of this legislation are too trivial for civil enforcement to effectuate the state's policy in regard to baking powder. The criminal law is here used as an administrative technique, as a way of socializing the costs of enforcement, which are too great for individuals profitably to bear.

Frequently, however, the general criminal processes will prove too cumbersome and inefficient to attain the state's policy goals. The next step is to vest responsibility for enforcement and administration in an administrative agency. Although mislabeling of baking powder formally remains a crime in Wisconsin, one can be fairly certain that enforcement and policing of baking powder labels (if any) is carried out by the staff of the appropriate executive department or agency, not by the district attorneys of the various counties.

The shift to administrative enforcement takes place partly because criminal sanctions drag with them all the traditional safeguards surrounding the defendant. Proof beyond a reasonable doubt, trial by jury, and other forms of protection are required. The socialization of remedies thus has the dysfunctional result of making large-scale enforcement difficult for reasons irrelevant to the purpose of making the proscribed acts criminal. Thus, transfer to an administrative agency is likely to occur as soon as such an agency is available. The criminal sanctions remain as threats—they are "used" in the sense of being authorized, but no longer "used" in the sense of wholesale application to offenders. . . .

Interactions Between Criminal Law and Business Conduct

Historically, growth in the number of regulatory crimes represents a broadening of the techniques for the enforcement of state policy. Nevertheless, the word "crime" has symbolic meaning for the public, and the criminal law is stained so deeply with notions of morality and immorality, public censure and punishment, that labeling an act criminal often has consequences that go far beyond mere administrative effectiveness. As noted in our discussion of criminal sanctions generally, imprisonment or threat of imprisonment and the public stigma of the criminal process are the real issues about which the discussion of criminal sanctions in regulating business revolves. It is generally accepted today that fear of criminal prosecution is an effective deterrent to businessmen, professional men, and the middle class. It follows that criminal sanctions ought to be highly effective in dealing with economic crimes. Also, noncriminal sanctions are presumably made more effective if the threat of criminal prosecution lurks in the background. The study of rent control in Honolulu already alluded to provides some confirmation. The study found that some landlords wanted to violate legal ceiling rents. However, they did not do so because they were afraid of criminal prosecution. When they found out that under current policy "collusive" violations of ceilings (those agreed upon by both landlord and tenant) were not prosecuted, these landlords tended to enter into just such collusive arrangements.

The very effectiveness of criminal sanctions in restraining the behavior of businessmen accounts in large part for the concern over the use of criminal-penal sanctions in regulating business. Businessmen abhor the idea of being branded a criminal. Society does not particularly care whether murderers and rapists like being branded as criminals; but businessmen, after all, form a large, respectable, and influential class in our society. Therefore, effectiveness of the penal sanction in this case leads to pressure against use of the sanction. The phenomenon is a general one; middle-class persons resent being "treated like a criminal," no matter what legal rule they may violate. But rules acquire legitimacy through being adopted in the regular processes utilized in society for making rules. The legitimacy of rules derives from the use of a standardized process of adoption, as much as or more than from the subject matter with which the rules deal. Americans in general accept the proposition that it is "wrong" to violate the law, even if they feel the law acts unwisely when it prohibits certain conduct. The very fact that a criminal statute has been enacted by the legislature is a powerful factor in making the proscribed conduct illegitimate in the eyes of a potential actor, even when the actor disagrees with the purpose of the law. . . .

LOUIS B. SCHWARTZ AND PAULA R. MARKOWITZ, COMMENT ON REGULATORY OFFENSES, I. Working Papers of the National Commission on Reform of Federal Criminal Laws 403–406, 410–417, 1970)

"Regulatory" Distinguished from Traditional Offenses. —Criminal law has always differentiated between two kinds of punishable behavior. On the one hand, homicide, rape, robbery and the other common law crimes are universally recognized outrages and threats to common security. Common morality forbids such behavior, and there is little possibility of innocent transgression. Commission of offenses of this sort evidences a serious disregard for the rights of other individuals, and identifies the offender as dangerous because of his lack of inhibitions and distorted system of values. Traditionally, offenses of this first type have been designated "mala in se", that is, "evil in themselves", in contrast with the other category of offenses, "malum prohibitum", that is, "bad because forbidden".

The regulatory statutes . . . belong in the "malum prohibitum" class. The behavior is not immediately recognizable as evil or dangerous, and does not necessarily identify the actor as immoral. In a complex modern society, there are hundreds of thousands of legal commands and prohibitions, violation of which may incur criminal liability. The motor vehicle laws offer the best examples: driving over the speed limit or without a license, failure to carry a registration card or a safety inspection certificate, parking in a prohibited zone, passing a stopped school bus, and a host of others. The conduct of businesses is often minutely controlled by statute and by rules and orders issued by administrative agencies. The appendix to this comment contains a sample of Federal regulatory offenses. Included are regulations protecting the safety and comfort of passengers by ship, airplane, rail and motor carriers; food and drug controls; animal inspection and quarantine; prohibitions of rate discrimination, deceptive advertising, and other unfair business practices; license and inspection requirements for various businesses; regulation of packaging and labeling; compulsory maintenance of records and filing of reports.

There are other touchstones by which to distinguish regulatory offenses, in addition to the distinctions between malum in se and malum prohibitum. It is characteristic of regulatory controls that they are prophylactic in purpose; that the standards of behavior are detailed, specific, and subject to change and development, and that special expertise is called for in laying down and modifying the rules.

The prophylactic purpose means that the rules are designed to *prevent* harms from occurring, rather than to punish perpetrators of actual harms. If the forest rules forbid or restrict campfires, it is to cut down even remote possibilities of conflagration. The rule may prevent ten perfectly safe fires in order to avert the possibility of one unsafe fire. It makes no difference what precautions a particular camper takes with his fire. Thus a careful man would feel no impropriety in building his fire if he had no notice that fires were absolutely forbidden. Similarly, in the field of business regulation, a hundred legitimate operators may have to keep elaborate business records to facilitate government enforcement of tax or production controls against the occasional dishonest operator. So, also, rules against conflicts of interest by public servants inhibit many innocent relationships in order to forestall corruption by a few. The fact that prophylactic controls inevitably affect many more law-abiding people than evildoers dictates a policy of relatively low maximum penalties for regulatory offenses.

Detailed, specific, and flexible controls are characteristic of regulatory offenses. That is why many Federal regulatory statutes penalize violation of such rules and orders as may be issued by the administrative agency after enactment of the statute. it is not possible for Congress to provide in advance for all the situations that may arise. Safety in transportation may be threatened in new ways, or new safety devices may be invented; new plant or animal pests may be identified; new devices to evade controls may have to be countered by new reporting or disclosure requirements. Sometimes the characteristic detail and specificity appear in the statute itself. (*See,* for example, the wild life conservation provisions of 18 U.S.C. §§ 41 and 42.)

It is clear from the characteristics of regulatory statutes already discussed that expertise in a particular field is essential to formulate the substantive requirements of these laws, rules, and administrative orders. The necessity for such expertise and for delegation of authority to administrative agencies is therefore an additional indication that we are dealing with material that logically belongs outside the Criminal Code (except for the penal provisions). The Committees of Congress which regularly deal with conservation and the Department of the Interior can then handle the substantive wildlife provisions mentioned above, leaving the criminal provisions to the Judiciary Committees with their dominant concern with the administration of justice.

Two more identifying characteristics of "regulatory" offenses may be noted in concluding this comment. It will often be found that regulations apply to particular groups, *e.g.*, distillers, drug manufacturers, public officials, operators of specified public service facilities rather than to the general public; and that nonpenal sanctions are more effective than penal sanctions for this kind of misbehavior. License suspension, forfeiture of illegal goods, civil penalties, dismissal from employment—these may be more drastic and more appropriate than prosecution. . . . The main defect of existing law of regulatory sanctions is its lack of discrimination between serious and trifling offenses. (*See* the appendix *infra*.) At the end of a long and complicated regulatory statute, the draftsman—he is likely to be expert in the substance of carrier or food and drug law, but inexpert in criminal law—typically adds a section making it a misdemeanor to violate any provision of the law or any rule or order issued thereunder. This not only leaves vast discretion to prosecutors as to whether to treat trivial offenses as criminal; it actually impedes enforcement insofar as trivial offenses have to be handled with the cumbersome formality of substantial prosecutions in the United States District Courts. . . .

APPENDIX

Statute	Subject matter	State of mind	Criminal penalty	Civil penalty
REGULATIONS CONCERNING PASSENGERS AND CARRIER EMPLOYEES				
46 U.S.C. § 452	Carrying too many passengers on vessel		Liable to passengers for amount of passage and $10 for each excessive passenger.	
46 U.S.C. § 153	Accommodations of steerage passengers	Knowingly	$100 and/or 30 days	$250.
46 U.S.C. § 155	Medical care of steerage passengers		$250.	
46 U.S.C. § 156	Sanitary requirements for steerage passengers.		$250.	
42 U.S.C. § 271(b)	Violation of quarantine by vessel, plane		$5,000.	
45 U.S.C. § 63	Railroad employee may not work more than 16 consecutive hours.		$200 to $500.	
42 U.S.C. § 271(a)	Violation of quarantine by passenger on ship or plane.		$1,000 and/or 1 year	
46 U.S.C. § 151	Carrying too many steerage passengers		$50 for each excessive passenger and/or 6 months.	
45 U.S.C. § 66	8 hours shall be a day's work in contract covering railroad employees.		$100 to $1,000 and/or 1 year.	
46 U.S.C. § 154	Food for steerage passengers	Willful	$500 and 6 months	
46 U.S.C. § 156a	Animals must be kept apart from steerage passengers.		$1,000 and 1 year	
SAFETY EQUIPMENT REGULATIONS				
49 U.S.C. § 26(h)	Installation of railroad system		$100 plus $100 each day.	
45 U.S.C. § 18	Equipment of locomotive with safety ash pan		$200.	
45 U.S.C. § 6, 13	Equipment of railroad cars as prescribed		$250.	
45 U.S.C. § 34	Equipment of locomotives as prescribed		$250.	
46 U.S.C. § 481(c)	Equipment of vessel with lifesaving, firefighting devices.		$1,000 owner or operator, $500 master.	
15 U.S.C. § 1212	Equipment of refrigerators with inside handles.		$1,000 and/or 1 year.	

APPENDIX

Statute	Subject matter	State of mind	Criminal penalty	Civil penalty
REGULATIONS FORBIDDING TRAFFICKING IN CERTAIN ITEMS				
15 U.S.C. § 1398	Manufacturing of substandard autos, tires.		$1,000 each; limitation of $4,000 for related series.	
16 U.S.C. § 853	Transportation of black bass and other fish where law prohibits.		$200 and/or 3 months	
21 U.S.C. § 63	Dealing in filled milk		$1,000 and/or 1 year	
21 U.S.C. § 134e	Violation of regulations re animals exposed to disease.	Knowingly	do	
21 U.S.C. § 158	Dealing in harmful, worthless serums, toxins for animals.		do	
21 U.S.C. § 333	Dealing in adulterated food, drug, device, cosmetic.	1. None (good faith exception) 2. Intent to defraud or mislead	1st conviction $1,000 and/or 1 year. Subsequent conviction $10,000 and/or 3 years	
21 U.S.C. §§ 461, 465	Dealing in unwholesome poultry	None (except carrier; Knowledge or reason to know).	1st conviction $3,000 and/or 6 months, 2nd conviction $5,000 and/or 1 year, subsequent conviction $10,000 and/or 2 years.	
15 U.S.C. § 1196	Dealing in flammable fabrics	Willfully (good faith	$5,000 and/or 1 year	
21 U.S.C. § 104	Importation of diseased animals	Knowingly	$5,000 and/or 3 years	Forfeiture of vessel.
21 U.S.C. § 676	Dealing in adulterated meat	1. None (good faith exception)	$1,000 and/or 1 year 2. Intent to defraud; distribution of adulterated meat.	$10,000 and/or 3 years
46 U.S.C. § 481(d)	Manufacturing, sale of defective lifesaving or firefighting equipment.	Willfully and knowingly.		$10,000 and/or 5 years
21 U.S.C. § 122	Import, export of infected livestock, poultry.	Knowing	$100 to $1,000 and/or 1 year	
21 U.S.C. § 127	Unlawful transportation of cattle, poultry from quarantine.	do		
21 U.S.C. § 117	Transportation of diseased livestock, poultry by carrier.	Knowingly	$100 to $5,000 and/or 1 year	

APPENDIX

Statute	Subject matter	State of mind	Criminal penalty	Civil penalty
		UNFAIR TRADE PRACTICES		
49 U.S.C. § 1021(b) and (c).	Discrimination in rates— freight forwarder and person obtaining by any means.	Knowing and willful.	1st conviction $500, subsequent conviction $2,000.	
46 U.S.C. § 815	Discrimination in shipping rates and by false means.	do	$5,000	
49 U.S.C. § 917(b),(c)	Discrimination in water carrier rates; solicitation, acceptance; false claim to obtain.	do	$5,000	
49 U.S.C. § 1472(d)	Air carrier participation in rebate; concessions to obtain lower rates.	do	$100 to $5,000	
49 U.S.C. § 322(c)	Participation in discrimination in motor carrier rates.	do	1st conviction $200 to $500, subsequent conviction $250 to $2,000.	
49 U.S.C. § 10(1),(2) and (3)	Discrimination in railroad rates; false billing to permit obtaining lower rates by false claim (fraud).	do	$5,000 and/or 2 years	
7 U.S.C. § 207	Rates must be filed and published—stockyard dealers.	1. None 2. Willful	$500 and $25 a day.	$1,000 and/or 1 year
46 U.S.C. § 844	Intercoastal shipping rates must be filed and posted.		$1,000 a day.	
49 U.S.C. § 322(h)	Motor carrier rates must be filed		$500 and $250 each day.	
49 U.S.C. § 322(a)	Deviated from filed and posted rates.	Knowing and willful.	1st conviction $100 to $500 each day, subsequent conviction $200 to $500 each day.	
49 U.S.C. § 10(1)	Railroad—unlawful combinations, agreements.	Willfully	$5,000	
7 U.S.C. § 195	Packers and stockyards— monopoly, price fixing.		$500 to $10,000 and/or 6 months to 5 years	
27 U.S.C. § 208	Interlocking directorates— liquor.		$1,000	
49 U.S.C. § 20a(12)	Same—railroad carriers.		$1,000 to $10,000 and/ or 1 to 3 years	
49 U.S.C. § 1(7)	Free transportation— railroad.		$100 to $2,000	
46 U.S.C. § 817(b),(c)	Free transportation for government personnel on American, foreign vessels.	Knowing	$500 to $10,000	
27 U.S.C. § 207	Exclusive outlets, tied house, bribery—liquor.		$1,000	

APPENDIX

Statute	Subject matter	State of mind	Criminal penalty	Civil penalty
45 U.S.C. § 83	Government-aided railroad— failure to afford equal facilities.		$1,000 and minimum 6 months, if jail imposed, no maximum [sic].	$100 to each person plus damages.
49 U.S.C. § 1(20)	Unlawful extension/ abandonment of railroad lines.	Knowing	$5,000 and/or 3 years	
7 U.S.C. § 491	Dumping by commission merchants.		$100 to $3,000 and/or 1 year	
7 U.S.C. § 499c	Commission merchants, misrepresentation, substitution after grading.	1. Not willful	Fees due and $25 a day.	
		2. Willful	$500 and $25 a day.	
46 U.S.C. § 1228	Conflicts of interest, collusion in bidding— subsidized shippers.	Knowing and willful	1. Natural person $10,000 and/or 1 to 5 years; 2. Corporation $25,000.	
7 U.S.C. § 1596	False advertising—seeds.	1. None	$25 to $500.	
		2. Knowingly or gross negligence.	1st conviction $1,000; subsequent conviction $2,000.	
27 U.S.C. § 207	Deceptive advertising— liquor		$1,000	
15 U.S.C. § 1335	Deceptive advertising— cigarettes		$10,000	
21 U.S.C. § 333	Improper false advertising— food, drug, device, cosmetic.	1. None	1st conviction $1,000 and/or 1 year; subsequent conviction $10,000 and/or 3 years.	
		2. Intent to defraud or m[i]slead [sic]	$10,000 and/or 3 years.	

APPENDIX

Statute	Subject matter	State of mind	Criminal penalty	Civil penalty
CONDUCT FORBIDDEN WITHOUT LICENSES, PERMITS				
7 U.S.C. § 499c	Commission merchants require license	1. Not willful		Fees due and $25 a day.
		2. Willful	$500 and $25 a day.	
49 U.S.C. § 1471	Certificate of airworthiness		$1,000.	
27 U.S.C. § 203	Liquor dealer—permit		$1,000	
7 U.S.C. § 135f(a)	Economic poisons (insecticides) must be registered.		$1,000	
7 U.S.C. § 586	Exporting of apples, pears, requires certificate of quality.	Knowingly	$100 to $10,000	
7 U.S.C. § 596	Exporting of grapes, plums requires certificate of quality.	do		
7 U.S.C. § 218a	Poultry dealers—license		$500 and/or 6 months	
42 U.S.C. § 262	Traffic in biologicals (virus, serum, toxin) unlawful unless prepared at licensed establishment.		$500 and/or 1 year	
21 U.S.C. § 158	Toxins for animals must be prepared at licensed est.; importation requires permit.		$1,000 and/or 1 year	
46 U.S.C. § 391(a)7	Vessels carrying inflammable liquid cargo in bulk-permit.	do		
21 U.S.C. § 676	Meat dealers must register	1. None (good faith exception)	$1,000 and/or 1 year	
		2. Intend to defraud	$10,000 and/or 3 years	
21 U.S.C. § 212	Practice of pharmacy in consular districts of China requires license.		$50 to $100 and/or 1 month to 60 days	
21 U.S.C. § 145	Importation of milk and cream—permit	Knowing	$50 to $2,000 and/or 1 year	
21 U.S.C. § 188L	Production and distribution of opium—license.		$2,000 and/or 5 years	
21 U.S.C. § 515(a)	Manufacture of narcotic drugs—license		$10,000 and/or 5 years	

APPENDIX

Statute	Subject matter	State of mind	Criminal penalty	Civil penalty
		INSPECTION REGULATIONS		
15 U.S.C. § 1398	Inspection of auto plants		$1,000 each.	
49 U.S.C. § 20(7)(d)	Railroad land, buildings, equipment		$100 each day.	
49 U.S.C. § 26(h)	Railroad carriers, apparatus		100 and $100 each day.	
46 U.S.C. § 277	Register or license of vessel by revenue officer.	1. None	$100.	
		2. Willful	"Fine" $1,000 and/or 1 year	"Penalty" $1,000.
45 U.S.C. § 34	Locomotives		$250.	
7 U.S.C. § 135f(b)	Examination of economic poisons		1st conviction $500; subsequent convictions $1,000 and/or 1 year.	
7 U.S.C. § 586	Apples, pears for export	Knowingly	$100 to $10,000	
7 U.S.C. § 596	Grapes, plums for export	do		
42 U.S.C. § 262	Establishments preparing biologicals (virus, serum, toxin); of products.		$500 and/or 1 year	
21 U.S.C. § 134e	Animals and carriers to prevent spread of contagion.	Knowingly	$1,000 and/or 1 year	
46 U.S.C. § 391a(7)	Vessels carrying inflammable liquid cargo in bulk.		$1,000 and/or 1 year	
21 U.S.C. § 158	Establishments preparing viruses, serums, toxins for animals; products; imports.		$1,000 and or 1 year	
21 U.S.C. § 676	Meat, meat plants	1. None (good faith exception.	$1,000 and/or 1 year	
		2. Intent to defraud	$10,000 and/or 3 years	
21 U.S.C. § 461	Poultry—premises		1st conviction $3,000 and/or 6 months; 2d conviction $5,000 and/or 1 year; subsequent conviction $10,000 and/or 2 years.	
21 U.S.C. § 145	Imported milk, cream	Knowing	$50 to $2,000 and/or 1 year	
21 U.S.C. § 212	Prescriptions		$50 to $100 and/or 1 month to 60 days	
49 U.S.C. § 1474	Aircraft—ports of entry, clearance, quarantine.	$500 and forfeiture.		
15 U.S.C. § 233	Label apple barrel if not standard size	Knowingly	$1 and costs each barrel.	
21 U.S.C. § 23	Misgrading, misbranding apples	do	do.	

APPENDIX

Statute	Subject matter	State of mind	Criminal penalty	Civil penalty
7 U.S.C. § 1596(b) cf. § 1596(a).	Identification of seeds; alteration forbidden.		$25-$500.	
7 U.S.C. § 135f(b)	Insecticides, identity; poison labels; alteration forbidden.	1st conviction $500; subsequent conviction $1,000 and/or 1 year.		
27 U.S.C. § 207	Liquor—identification; alteration forbidden.		$1,000	
7 U.S.C. § 1595(a) cf. § 1596(b).	Seeds—identification; alteration forbidden.	Knowingly or gross	1st conviction $1,000; negligence or failure to make a reasonable effort to inform.	subsequent conviction $2,000.
15 U.S.C. § 1233	Auto—price; make	1. Willful failure to affix by manufacturer.	$1,000	
		2. Willful alteration by any person.	$1,000 and/or 1 year	
15 U.S.C. § 1335	Cigarettes—caution		$10,000	
21 U.S.C. § 17	Sale of dairy, food products falsely labeled or branded.		$500 to $2,000	
16 U.S.C. § 853	Black bass, fish identification		$200 and/or 3 months	
15 U.S.C. § 1264	Dealing in misbranded hazardous substance; alteration of label forbidden.	1. None	1st conviction $500 and/or 90 days; 2d conviction $3,000 and/or 1 year.	
		2. Intent to defraud, mislead.	$3,000 and/or 1 year.	
42 U.S.C. § 262	Biologicals—identity, license number of manufacturer; alteration; falsity.		$500 and/or 1 year	
21 U.S.C. § 333	Misbranding food, drug, device, cosmetic.	1. None (good faith exception	1st conviction $1,000 and/or 1 year; subsequent conviction $10,000 and/or 3 years.	
		2. Intent to defraud or mislead.	$10,000 and/or 3 years.	
21 U.S.C. § 676	Meat identity; mark of inspection	1. None (good faith exception.	$1,000 and/or 1 year	
		2. Intent to defraud	$10,000 and/or 3 years.	

APPENDIX

Statute	Subject matter	State of mind	Criminal penalty	Civil penalty
21 U.S.C. § 461	Poultry-identity; inspection; false label; counterfeiting inspection mark.	None (except carrier: Know or reason to know).	1st conviction $3,000 and/or 6 months; 2d conviction $5,000 and/or 1 year; subsequent conviction $10,000 and/or 2 years.	
21 U.S.C. § 212	Practice of pharmacy in consular district of China—poison labels.		$50 to $100 and/or 1 month to 60 days	
19 U.S.C. § 467	Importing liquor without stamp		Forfeiture.	
19 U.S.C. § 468	Emptying package of imported liquor without destroying stamp.		do.	
19 U.S.C. § 469	Dealing in empty stamped imported liquor containers.		$200 each forfeiture.	
7 U.S.C. § 499c	Tampering with stamps, commercial merchandise.	1. Not willful	Fees due and $25 a day.	
		2. Willful	$500 and $25 a day.	
15 U.S.C. § 1264	Use of food, drug, cosmetic container for hazardous substances.	1. None	1st conviction $500 and/or 90 days; 2d conviction $3,000 and/or 1 year.	
		2. Intent to defraud, mislead.	$3,000 and/or 1 year.	
21 U.S.C. § 461	Reuse of marked contained (for poultry)	None (except carrier: Know or reason to know).	1st conviction $3,000 and/or 6 months; 2d conviction $5,000 and/or 1 year, subsequent conviction $10,000 and/or 2 years.	
27 U.S.C. § 206	Liquor—bottling and bulk regulations		$5,000 and/or 1 year	Forfeiture.

APPENDIX

Statute	Subject matter	State of mind	Criminal penalty	Civil penalty
		REPORTS AND RECORDS		
49 U.S.C. § 20(7)(c)	Reports by carrier—railroad		$100 each day.	
49 U.S.C. § 20(7)(a)	Failure to keep, submit records by railroad, pipeline carrier.		$500 each day.	
15 U.S.C. § 1398	Failure [to] [sic] make reports; refusal of access to records auto—manufacture.		$1,000 each; limitation of $400,000 for related series.	
7 U.S.C. § 1596	Records required—seed manufacturer	1. None	$25 to $500.	
		2. Knowingly	1st conviction $1,000; subsequent conviction $2,000.	
46 U.S.C. § 309	Failure to report arrival of merchandise by ship to collector.		$50 each day and forfeiture.	
49 U.S.C. § 322(h) (cf. § 322(g) below)	Motor carrier—keep file, records, reports.		$500 and $250 each additional day.	
49 U.S.C. § 26(h)	Accident reports—railroad and pipe (failure of system).		$100 and $100 each day.	
19 U.S.C. § 1460	Failure to report arrival of vessel to customs.		$100 each day and penalty equaling value of unreported merchandise and $500 for each passenger landed and forfeiture.	
45 U.S.C. § 34	Accident reports—railroad	$250.		
45 U.S.C. § 39	Monthly accident reports		$100 each day	
7 U.S.C. § 135f(b)	Access to records; right to copy (insecticide dealers).		1st conviction $500; subsequent conviction $1,000 and/or 1 year.	
49 U.S.C. § 917(d)	Water carrier—make reports, answer questions, falsifications.	Willfully	$5,000	
49 U.S.C. § 1021(d)	Same—freight forwarded	do	$5,000	
49 U.S.C. § 322(g)	Same—motor carrier	do	$5,000	
49 U.S.C. § 1472(e)	Air carrier—make reports, keep records, falsification.	Knowingly and willfully.	$100 to $5,000	
15 U.S.C. § 1264	Access to, copying of records (dealers in hazardous substances).	1. None	1st conviction $500 and/or 90 days; 2nd conviction $3,000 and/or 1 year.	
		2. Intent to defraud, mislead.	$3,000 and/or 1 year.	
46 U.S.C. § 391a(7)	Documents required—ships	$1,000 and/or 1 year		

APPENDIX

Statute	Subject matter	State of mind	Criminal penalty	Civil penalty
21 U.S.C. § 333	Refusal to permit access to or copying records; maintenance of records; making reports — food and drug dealers	1. None	1st conviction $1,000 and/or 1 year; subsequent conviction $10,000 and/or 3 years.	
		2. Intent to defraud or mislead.	$10,000 and/or 3 years.	
21 U.S.C. § 461	Access to, copying records; maintenance — poultry dealers.	None (except carrier; Know or reason to know).	1st conviction $3,000 and/or 6 months; 2d conviction $5,000 and/or 1 year; subsequent conviction $10,000 and/or 2 years.	
49 U.S.C. § 20(7)(b)	Falsification records, reports, accounts — railroad and pipelines.	Knowingly and willfully	$5,000 and/or 2 years	
7 U.S.C. § 221	Failure to keep prescribed records — packers, stockyards, poultry dealers.		$5,000 and/or 3 years	
21 U.S.C. § 515(a)	Keeping of records, reports narcotics		$10,000 and/or 5 years.	
21 U.S.C. § 212	Pharmacy in China — maintenance of prescriptions.		$50 to $100 and/or 1 month to 60 days	
49 U.S.C. § 322(a)	Reports — motor carriers	Knowingly and willfully	1st conviction $100 to $500; subsequent conviction $200 to $500.	
7 U.S.C. § 491	False report about produce by commission merchant.	Knowing and with intent to defraud.	$100 to $3,000 and/or 1 year	
49 U.S.C. § 1472(g)	Refusal to produce papers (or testify) air carrier.		$100 to $5,000 and/or 1 year	

APPENDIX

Statute	Subject matter	State of mind	Criminal penalty	Civil penalty
		IMPROPER DISCLOSURE OF INFORMATION		
49 U.S.C. § 1021(f)	Improper disclosure of information about cargo of freight forwarder.	Knowingly and willfully.	1st conviction $100; subsequent conviction $500.	
7 U.S.C. § 135f(b) and (c).	Of formulae of economic poisons	1. None	1st conviction $500; subsequent conviction $1,000 and/or 1 year.	
		2. Intent to defraud, misuse.	$10,000 and/or 3 years.	
49 U.S.C. § 15, par.(11)	Re cargo of railroad	Knowing	$1,000	
49 U.S.C. § 917(f)	Re cargo of water carrier	Knowing and willful.	$2,000	
15 U.S.C. § 1264	Misuse of confidential information about hazardous substances.	1. None	1st conviction $500 and/ or 90 days; 2d conviction $3,000 and/or 1 year.	
		2. Intent to defraud	$3,000 and/or 1 year	
49 U.S.C. § 20, par (7)(f)	Disclosure of confidential information by agent, accountant, examiner of railroad carrier.	Knowingly and willfully	$500 and/or 6 months	
49 U.S.C. § 322(d)	Same—of motor carrier	do	$500 and/or 6 months	
49 U.S.C. § 917(e)	Same—of water carrier	do	$500 and/or 6 months	
49 U.S.C. § 1021(e)	Same—of freight forwarder	do	$500 and/or 6 months	
21 U.S.C. § 333	Misuse of confidential information—food drugs etc.	1. None		1st conviction $1,000 and/or 1 year; subsequent conviction $10,000 and/or 3 years.
		2. Intent to defraud or mislead.	$10,000 and/or 3 years.	
21 U.S.C. § 461	Misuse of information re poultry	None (except carrier: Know or reason to know).	1st conviction $3,000 and/or 6 months; 2d conviction $5,000 and/or 1 year; subsequent conviction $1,000 and/or 2 years.	

APPENDIX

Statute	Subject matter	State of mind	Criminal penalty	Civil penalty
		FURNISHING OF FALSE INFORMATION OTHER THAN IN LABELS, REPORTS		
7 U.S.C. § 135f(b)	Giving of false guaranty of conformity (insecticides).		1st conviction $500; subsequent conviction $1,000 and/or 1 year.	
15 U.S.C. § 1264	Same—hazardous substances	1. None	1st conviction $500 and/or 90 days; 2d conviction $3,000 and/or 1 year.	
		2. Intent to defraud or mislead.	$3,000 and/or 1 year	
21 U.S.C. § 333	Same—food, drug, etc.	1. None	1st conviction $1,000 and/or 1 year; subsequent conviction $10,000 and/or 3 years.	
		2. Intent to defraud or mislead.	$10,000 and/or 3 years.	
15 U.S.C. § 1196	Same—flammable fabric	Willfully	$5,000 and/or 1 year	
7 U.S.C. § 499c	Commission merchant—make false statement for fraudulent purpose.	1. Not willful	Fees due and $25 a day.	
		2. Willful	$500 and $25 a day.	
21 U.S.C. § 212	Pharmacy in China—fraudulent representation to evade regulations.		$50-100 and/or 1 month-60 days.	
21 U.S.C. § 515(b)	False statement in application for license to manufacture narcotics.	Willful	$2,000 and/or 1 year	
21 U.S.C. § 188L	Same—manufacture opium	Willful	$2,000 and/or 1 year	
49 U.S.C. § 1472(o)	Interference with accident investigation—aircraft-removal of part of plane or property.	Knowingly	$100-$5,000 and/or 1 year	
45 U.S.C. § 60	By threat, order, attempt to prevent furnishing of information on railroad accident.		$1,000 and/or 1 year	
49 U.S.C. § 1472(b)	Forgery of certificates; false marking of aircraft.	Knowingly and willfully.	$1,000 and/or 3 years	
49 U.S.C. § 1472(c)	Interference with air navigation—signals.	Intentional	$5,000 and/or 5 years.	

APPENDIX

Statute	Subject matter	State of mind	Criminal penalty	Civil penalty
RULES PURSUANT TO REGULATIONS				
7 U.S.C. § 608a(4) & (5)	Violation of any order issued under section establishing sugar quotas.	Willful	$100	Sum equaling value of excess at current market price.
49 U.S.C. § 1159(a)	Violation of rules to be made on use of air facilities outside continental United States.	Knowingly and willfully.	$500 and/or 6 months	
49 U.S.C. § 1523	Security regulations affecting aircraft	Knowingly and willfully.	$10,000 and/or 1 year	
50 U.S.C. § 192	National emergency regulations for ships in territorial waters.	None if owner, master, crew; otherwise must have knowledge.	$10,000 and/or 10 years.	Forfeiture of vessel if by person in charge.
46 U.S.C. § 1228	Violation of order, rule, regulation of Federal Maritime Board if no other penalty prescribed.	Knowingly and willfully.	$500 each day	

B. Crime and Tort

John C. Coffee, Jr., *Does "Unlawful" Mean "Criminal"?: Reflections on the Disappearing Tort/Crime Distinction in American Law*, 71 B.U. L. REV. 193–246 (1991)*

My thesis is simple and can be reduced to four assertions. First, the dominant development in substantive federal criminal law over the last decade has been the disappearance of any clearly definable line between civil and criminal law. Second, this blurring of the border between tort and crime predictably will result in injustice, and ultimately will weaken the efficacy of the criminal law as an instrument of social control. Third, to define the proper sphere of the criminal law, one must explain how its purposes and methods differ from those of tort law. Although it is easy to identify distinguishing characteristics of the criminal law – e.g., the greater role of intent in the criminal law, the relative unimportance of actual harm to the victim, the special character of incarceration as a sanction, and the criminal law's greater reliance on public enforcement – none of these is ultimately decisive. Rather, the factor that most distinguishes the criminal law is its operation as a system of moral education and socialization. The criminal law is obeyed not simply because there is a legal threat underlying it, but because the public perceives its norms to be legitimate and deserving of compliance. Far more than tort law, the criminal law is a system for public communication of values. As a result, the criminal law often and necessarily displays a deliberate disdain for the utility of the criminalized conduct to the defendant. Thus, while tort law seeks to balance private benefits and public costs, criminal law does not (or does so only by way of special affirmative defenses), possibly because balancing would undercut the moral rhetoric of the criminal law. Characteristically, tort law prices, while criminal law prohibits.

The fourth and final assertion of this Article is that implementation of the crime/tort distinction is today feasible only at the sentencing stage. Neither legislative action nor constitutional challenge is likely to reverse the encroachment of the criminal law upon areas previously thought civil in character. But, at the sentencing stage, courts can draw a line between the enforcement of norms that were intended to price and those intended to prohibit. Indeed, because a sensible implementation of the crime/tort distinction requires a close retrospective evaluation of the defendant's conduct, sentencing may be the only juncture where the distinction can be feasibly preserved.

None of these assertions can be proven in a dispositive manner; nor will this Article attempt to do so. But, given the plausibility of these assertions, their implications need to be examined and assessed. In particular, the distinction between pricing and prohibiting carries several important implications for the structure of criminal justice. First, it sets boundaries by implying that the criminal law should generally not be used when society is unprepared to disregard the social utility of the defendant's behavior – that is, when it prefers to "price" the behavior in question in order to force internalization of social costs. Thus, more specifically, it suggests that criminal liability for negligence is generally inappropriate. Second, once it is recognized that society generally intends to prohibit behavior through the criminal law, it follows that there cannot be an "optimal" rate of crime that is to be attained by pricing the subject behavior. As a result, Learned Hand's famous rule for determining tort liability does not properly apply to criminal law. Although some economists, most notably Gary Becker,- have advanced such a "pricing" model of the criminal law, the rival view implied by this pricing/prohibiting distinction is that only enforcement costs justify allowing the "optimal" rate of crime to exceed zero – at least with respect to the "true" crimes that society wishes to prohibit, not price. Because society has refused on moral grounds to recognize the legitimacy of the benefit to the defendant in these cases, then by definition the benefits of the crime to the individual can never exceed the costs it imposes on society. Thus, the criminal law threatens the defendant with a much sharper, more discontinuous jump in the costs that the defendant will incur for its violation than does tort law, because the criminal law has little reason to fear overdeterrence (that is, the chilling of socially valuable behavior) within its appropriate domain.

Fundamental as the distinction between pricing and prohibiting misbehavior may be, there are still cases that fall on the borderline. Chief among these is the problem of corporate criminal liability. Essentially, corporate criminal liability (at least as recognized in the United States) is a species of vicarious criminal liability; that is, the principal is held liable for the acts of its agent – even when the principal makes a substantial good faith attempt to monitor the agent and prevent the illegality. Conceptually, vicarious criminal liability for failing to prevent the agent from acting illegally seems a form of behavior that should be

---

* Reprinted with permission of the author.

priced, rather than prohibited. This is because society must make a judgment about the appropriate amount of behavior (i.e., preventive monitoring) to demand and cannot take a simple all-or-nothing position. Once it is conceded that some level of monitoring could be excessive, then the cost to the corporation must be compared to the benefit to society. Essentially, a pricing policy does this, focusing presumably on the gravity of the social harm involved.

This observation does not deny that in other cases corporations might have "intended" the crime (at least to the extent that senior officials encouraged, tolerated, or ratified it). Nonetheless, the point remains that to the extent that the role of corporate criminal liability is to encourage the principal to monitor its agents, the criminal law is inevitably caught up in the problem of pricing. To be sure, the law is not pricing the value of the illegal benefit to the defendant, but rather the cost of preventing the crime to the principal. Still, the analysis is much the same because private costs (i.e., monitoring expenditures) and public benefits (i.e., the deterrent benefits of crime suppression) are subject to a trade-off.

The bottom line is that the criminal law seems to be expanding into a variety of areas where it is infeasible or even irrational to ignore the costs of law compliance. Yet, both Congress and state legislatures have shown little interest in slowing this trend; nor is there much possibility that the Supreme Court will place constitutional limits on crime definition (as Professor Hart had hoped). As a result, the only decision makers who can attempt in a coherent way to determine when the criminal law should price and when it should prohibit are those who make sentencing policy and judgments. Uniquely, the sentencing stage affords a perspective from which nuances too subtle or fact-specific to be defined in advance by legislation can be examined retrospectively and in detail. In the case of the corporation, for example, it becomes possible to consider whether the corporate defendant simply failed to monitor a reckless agent adequately or whether it pressured its agents into criminal misconduct.

The difference between pricing and prohibiting misbehavior involves much more than the question of penalty levels. Ultimately, the law's focus should also shift. From a pricing perspective, the critical determination is the setting of the penalty that brings public and private costs into balance. However, from a prohibitory perspective, the central decision is the framing of the legal standard. As Professor Cooter has shown, once expected penalties are raised to a prohibitory level, individuals become extremely responsive to changes in the legal standard, while under a pricing system, individuals respond to the price, not the legal standard. Thus, this

Article's normative assertion that the criminal law should generally prohibit, not price, requires one to specify carefully the legal terrain within which such a policy is to be pursued. The mere fact that conduct is in violation of a known and valid legal standard is insufficient, because sometimes society may wish only to price such violations. The structure of this Article reflects this concern; Part I essentially argues that the criminal law has been over extended precisely to the extent that it is being applied to behavior that society must necessarily price. Ultimately, pricing is necessary on moral as well as economic grounds when sufficiently clear partitions cannot be erected between the unlawful behavior and closely related lawful behavior to justify a prohibitory policy. Unfortunately, this condition holds true throughout much of the "white collar" criminal context.

Other commentators have started at the same point as this Article, recognizing that the criminal law is not simply a pricing system. Even among "law and economics" scholars, several have recognized at least the plausibility of the position that the benefit to the defendant from criminal behavior should be disallowed in public policy decision making. Yet, they have not followed this idea through clearly as a map of the tort/crime distinction. Correspondingly, our leading criminal law scholars—among them Henry Hart, Sanford Kadish, and Herbert Packer—have periodically warned of the danger of "overcriminalization": namely, excessive reliance on the criminal sanction, particularly with respect to behavior that is not inherently morally culpable. But one cannot meaningfully use the term "overcriminalization" without first defining the boundaries within which the criminal sanction may appropriately be used, and to answer this latter question only by saying that the behavior must be "blameworthy" simply uses an adjective in lieu of a theory.

The prior literature on "overcriminalization" has had a variety of specific targets, depending largely on the particular development that troubled the particular critic. Thus, Herbert Packer was principally concerned with "victimless crimes;" Sanford Kadish, with the use of the criminal sanction to enforce economic regulations; and Henry Hart, with the increased tendency of criminal statutes to impose strict liability or vicarious responsibility. In common, however, all three agreed that a basic "method" distinguished the criminal law. As they saw it, the principal elements of this method were advance legislative specification of the conduct proscribed, strict construction of ambiguous terms, an emphasis on the defendant's state of mind (or "mens rea"), and a close linkage between the criminal law and behavior deemed morally culpable by the general community. They argued that any substantial deviation from that "method" threatened the criminal law's legitimacy. In truth, these standards had not always been faithfully observed, but this Article will argue that the rate of the departures from these norms seems plainly to have accelerated over the last decade.

Three trends, in particular, stand out. First, the federal law of "white collar" crime now seems to be judge-made to an unprecedented degree, with courts deciding on a case-by-case, retrospective basis whether conduct falls within often vaguely defined legislative prohibitions. Second, a trend is evident toward the diminution of the mental element (or "mens rea") in crime, particularly in many regulatory offenses. Third, although the criminal law has long compromised its adherence to the "method" of the criminal law by also recognizing a special category of sub-criminal offenses – often called "public welfare offenses" – in which strict liability could be combined with modest penalties, the last decade has witnessed the unraveling of this uneasy compromise, because the traditional public welfare offenses – now set forth in administrative regulations – have been upgraded to felony status. This Article will refer to this last trend as the "technicalization" of crime and will combine departures from most of the above-described elements that characterize the criminal law's "method."

The upshot of these trends is that the criminal law seems much closer to being used interchangeably with civil remedies. Sometimes, identically phrased statutes are applicable to the same conduct – one authorizing civil penalties, the other authorizing criminal sanctions. More often, the criminal law is extended to reach behavior previously thought only civilly actionable. Either way, this practice of defining the criminal law to reach all civil law violations in a particular field of law in order to gain additional deterrence may distort the underlying legal standard. What needs to be more clearly recognized is the variety of ways in which such distortion can occur. For example, some civil law standards may be aspirational in character (e.g., the rule that attorneys should avoid any "appearance of impropriety"). Other standards may frame prophylactic rules, which prevent the possibility of misconduct, but involve no element of culpability. Some recent writers in the "law and economics" tradition have theorized that society may have a particular "transaction structure" for dealing with different areas of social behavior, sometimes using rules that would trigger only civil liability and at other times using rules whose violation would be criminally prosecuted. Thus, overlaying the criminal law on the civil law may disrupt these transaction structures. Still, provocative as this concept of "transaction structure" is, it has remained an underdeveloped idea, which requires a fuller account of why society should prefer the structure of the civil law over that of the criminal law.

In overview, the two principal claims made by this Article exist in some obvious tension. If true, the first claim – that the criminal law is more a system of socialization than of pricing – makes the second predictable: namely, that the criminal sanction is increasingly being used by regulators as a preferred enforcement tool without regard to the traditional limitations on its use. Almost by definition, a system for socialization will be put to new uses, as authorities attempt to harness its educational power. Thus, the very success of the criminal law as a socializing force implies the erosion of the traditional point at which the tenuous crime/tort distinction had been maintained. Indeed, traditional libertarians – such as Hart, Kadish, and Packer – have been criticized on this ground by sociologists, who have argued that the social standards of blameworthiness necessarily evolve over time along with other social attitudes. These critics have found the "over-criminalization" thesis to be empty of content, because of its failure to recognize the interactive, reciprocal relationship between the content of the criminal law and the public's perception of what conduct is blameworthy. In their view, the public learns what is blameworthy in large part from what is punished.

Undoubtedly, there is some merit in this argument. Obviously, new problems may arise for which the criminal law is the most effective instrument, but which involve behavior not historically considered blameworthy. Modern technology, the growth of an information-based economy, and the rise of the regulatory state make it increasingly difficult to maintain that only the common law's traditional crimes merit the criminal sanction. In fact, historically, the criminal law has never been static or frozen within a common law mold, but has constantly evolved. This has been especially true within the field of "white collar" crime. Even the first modern "white collar" offenses to be criminally prosecuted – price-fixing, tax fraud, securities fraud, and, later, foreign bribery – were "regulatory" crimes in the sense that they had not been traditionally considered blameworthy. In short, the line between malum in se and malum prohibitum has been crossed many times and largely discredited. Today, to rule out worker safety, toxic dumping, or environmental pollution as necessarily beyond the scope of the criminal law requires one to defend an antiquarian definition of blameworthiness.

But where does this leave us? Those following in the footsteps of Hart, Kadish and Packer have a powerful rejoinder: if the criminal law is over used, it will lose its distinctive stigma. While conceding that the criminal law is a system of socialization, they would reply that for precisely that reason it must be used parsimoniously. Once everything wrongful is made criminal, society's ability to reserve special condemnation for some forms of misconduct is either lost or simply reduced to a matter of prosecutorial discretion. Still, valid as this response is, it does not answer fully the criticism that the traditional criminal law scholar's focus on blameworthiness is anachronistic because it freezes the criminal law's necessary evolution, like a fly in amber.

If so, what alternative is left? What substitute bulwark can prevent the criminal law from sprawling over the landscape of the civil law? One answer is to update the notion of blameworthiness, looking not only to historical notions of culpability, but to well-established industry and professional standards whose violation has been associated with culpability within that narrower community. Another answer is to focus on the temporal relationship of the civil and criminal law. At some point, a civil standard can become so deeply rooted and internalized within an industry or professional community that its violation becomes blameworthy, even if it was not originally so. Insider trading may supply such an example, where the norm has long since become internalized within the industry. The relationship of the civil and criminal law here is sequentially interactive: the civil law experiments with a standard, but at some point it may "harden" into a community standard that the criminal law can enforce. At that point, it may be appropriate to prohibit, rather than price, at least if society believes that the defendant's conduct lacks any colorable social utility.

But who makes these determinations? Ideally, the legislature should, but there is little prospect that it will; nor is it properly positioned to compare varying degrees of culpability. Thus, a "second best" answer is a sentencing commission, which in drafting sentencing guidelines should attempt to separate those instances when society should price from those when it should prohibit. Only an administrative agency can both make such determinations on a continuing and provisional basis and also attempt to determine the correct "price" when pricing is appropriate.

A road map of this Article is in order. Part I will advance this Article's positive claim that the line between the civil and criminal law has blurred. Part II will consider the rationales for separating the civil and criminal law, and Part III will address the implementation of a means for preserving the tort/crime distinction.

I. THE BLURRING OF THE BORDER

Three distinct subarguments will be made in this section. First, the criminal sanction has been applied broadly, and sometimes thoughtlessly, to a broad range of essentially civil obligations, some of which were intended as aspirational standards and others which are inherently open-ended and evolving in character. Second, there has also been a retreat from the traditional "method" of the criminal law, as the role of mens rea has been diminished and that of vicarious liability expanded. Third, a transition is evident in the characteristic "white collar" prosecution. Prosecutions increasingly tend to be less for violations of a statutory standard than for failures to comply with administrative regulations. Characteristically, these regulations resemble what an earlier era called "public welfare offenses," but with two differences: (1) substantial criminal sentences are authorized, and (2) the sheer volume of regulations that are now potentially enforceable through criminal prosecution means that the criminal sanction has penetrated much further into everyday life.

A. Criminalizing the Civil Law

Short of a doctrinal treatise or a major empirical study, no article could hope to demonstrate the degree to which the criminal law has encroached upon formerly "civil" areas of the law. What can be done, however, is to illustrate this trend by examining changes in some areas that had seemed quintessentially civil in character. For example, few legal categories seem inherently less "criminal" in character than the civil law applicable to fiduciary duties or to the use of economic duress in negotiations. Yet, both areas have, to an uncertain extent, been subjected to the reach of the criminal law. This section will use these two areas as case studies to illustrate how overlaying the criminal law on the civil law may distort the latter.

1. The Criminalization of Fiduciary Duties

The federal mail and wire fraud statutes supply the most obvious example of the criminal law being overlaid on civil law standards. By the mid-1960s, federal courts had accepted the principle that the term "scheme to defraud" (which is the critical element in both the mail and wire fraud statutes) required neither that there be any pecuniary or property loss to the victim nor that the purpose of the scheme be contrary to state or federal law. Rather, it was sufficient that a victim was defrauded of an "intangible right," such as the duty of public officials to provide "honest and faithful" services. The contours of this "intangible right" theory have always been uncertain, in part because the governing standard was the ineffable principle of "fair play." As several courts said in explaining the boundaries of the intangible rights theory of mail fraud:

Law puts its imprimatur on . . . accepted moral standards and condemns conduct which fails to match the reflection of moral uprightness, of fundamental honesty, fair play and right dealing in the general and business life of members of society. Despite the fulsome prose in these decisions, their underlying facts usually involved bribes or kickbacks, either to public officials or to purchasing agents of private businesses. During the 1970s, however, prosecutors began to exploit the latent potential in the "intangible rights" theory by prosecuting cases that truly involved only a deprivation of such a claimed right. A bizarre series of decisions followed. In United States v. Condolon, the victims were young women, who had been deceived into providing sexual favors for the defendant who had misrepresented his status as a talent scout. In United States v. Lounderman, the victims were defrauded of the intangible right to privacy when defendants tricked the telephone company into revealing their addresses.

Still, the decisions that had the greatest impact were those that seemed to criminalize any knowing failure to disclose a conflict of interest by a person subject to a fiduciary duty. As late as 1976, the Second Circuit in a decision by Judge Henry Friendly suggested that the "intangible rights" doctrine applied only to public officials and not to private fiduciaries. However, at the beginning of the 1980s, the Second Circuit overrode his thoughtful distinction. In United States v. Bronston, it upheld the conviction of a lawyer who secretly represented one client while his law firm represented a rival contender for a public franchise. Bronston was a watershed decision, because no bribes or kickbacks were involved, and the evidence did not demonstrate that the defendant had actually used his fiduciary position to injure the firm's client. After Bronston, all that seemed necessary to support a mail fraud conviction was a knowing and undisclosed breach of a fiduciary standard. These decisions seemingly turned the mail and wire fraud statutes into mandatory disclosure statutes that required all public officials and private fiduciaries to disclose any conflict of interest to which they were subject.

The highwater mark of this theory of liability came in the mid-1980s, when federal prosecutors successfully used it to reach not only self-dealing conduct by corporate officials against the interests of the corporation, but also actions by corporate officials that were intended to benefit the firm, but had not been adequately disclosed to the board or shareholders. In United States v. Siegel and United States v. Weiss, corporate officers who created off-book slush funds in order to facilitate questionable corporate payments were convicted of fraud, even though they did not misappropriate any funds. Indeed, in Weiss, the subordinate had acted pursuant to direct instructions from his superiors to establish the secret fund. In a strong

dissent in Siegel, Judge Ralph Winter observed that this new construction redefined the crime of fraud by judicial fiat: "In effect, a new crime—corporate improprieties—which entails neither fraud nor even a victim, has been created." A long-time professor of corporate law, Judge Winter understood the basic distinction between the duty of loyalty and the duty of care, which the rest of the panel seems to have missed in Siegel and Weiss. In both cases, the defendants may have violated their duty of care, but they did not engage in self-dealing in any form. As a practical matter, they probably faced relatively little prospect of civil liability, because the duty of care has historically not been strictly enforced. The bottom line then is ironic: the criminal law has been cantilevered out beyond the civil law as defendants have been convicted of a federal felony on facts that would have been unlikely to support civil liability in a derivative suit.

This line of cases came to a screeching, but temporary, halt in 1987 when the Supreme Court decided, in McNally v. United States, that the mail fraud statute did not reach schemes to deprive victims of the intangible right of honest services, but only schemes to obtain money or property. For a time, McNally seemed a major obstacle to the continuing growth of a judge-made law of white collar crime. Then, two things happened. First, the Supreme Court announced in Carpenter v. United States that confidential business information could amount to a form of intangible property. Under this theory, it upheld Foster Winans's conviction for using data obtained through his employment as a Wall Street Journal reporter to engage in insider trading. Understandable as this result was, the theory adopted—i.e., that an employee may not use confidential business information acquired during his employment—is extremely open-ended. For example, what happens when an employee changes firms? Arguably, his use of information acquired while working for one employer for the benefit of a subsequent employer might be said to deprive the former of confidential business information. Yet, if this theory is carried even part way to the limits of its logic, then the employee's mobility and, indeed, his own human capital would be substantially restricted. The irony here is that the civil law had always sought to disfavor constraints on employee mobility by declining to enforce covenants not to compete, except to a very limited extent.

Thus, Carpenter may illustrate an occasion on which the extension of the criminal law into a previously civil law domain effects the policy underlying substantive civil law. No longer do employers have only very limited power to restrict their employee's mobility, because the employee's transfer of information incident to a change of employment could trigger criminal liability or, more likely, a civil RICO action. More generally, Carpenter threatened to trivialize McNally by allowing prosecutors simply to relabel what they had indicted, before McNally, as a deprivation of an intangible "right" as a deprivation of intangible "property." To a limited extent, this has in fact happened.

The second post-McNally development was even more important: in 1988, Congress enacted a statutory definition of the critical term, "scheme to defraud." New section 1346 defines this term to include any "scheme or artifice to defraud another of the intangible right of honest services." At a stroke, this language may criminalize any violation of fiduciary duties or the law of agency. The expansion of section 1346 then supplies a paradigm of the criminal law being overlaid unthinkingly on top of the civil law, without serious consideration being given to whether the civil law standard in question should be backed by the special threat of the criminal law.

How have courts and prosecutors responded to this extension of the criminal law's scope? The early evidence is that they have read section 1346 even more broadly than its language would seem to permit, reaching all cases that were within the scope of the pre-McNally case law. In the recent RICO prosecutions of commodities brokers on the Chicago Mercantile Exchange ("CME"), the prosecutors charged the defendants under section 1346 with breaching their duty to maintain the "honest functioning of the marketplace." This view that section 1346 simply supplies a charter for continued judicial lawmaking ignores the counterargument that the statute's language requires that its "intangible right of honest services" be tied down to some definable common law or statutory right. Where do "rights to honest services" come from? Are they discovered by federal judges based on principles of fair play? Or, must they already exist in the common law of the jurisdiction whose law applies to the transaction in question? To date, the only federal courts to face these questions have preferred the expansive view that section 1346 authorizes them to continue to "condemn conduct which fails to match the reflection of moral uprightness, of fundamental honesty, fair play and right dealing in the general and business life of members of society."

What is wrong with such an approach? As a matter of civil law, the short answer is relatively little. Courts constantly create or discover new torts. However, as a matter of criminal law, this approach should be unacceptable, for several reasons. First, in traditional constitutional terms, it denies fair notice, invites arbitrary and discriminatory enforcement, and violates the separation of powers principle that has traditionally denied federal courts the power to make common law crimes.

However, in terms of this Article's concerns, the vocabulary of constitutional law does not adequately express the full dimensions of the problems inherent in broadly criminalizing civil law standards. The basic problem is that tort law standards often display a soft-edged quality that is consistent with their evolutionary and often aspirational character. For example, Cardozo wrote: "A trustee is held to something stricter than the morals of the marketplace. Not honesty alone, but the punctilio of an honor the most sensitive, is then the standard of behavior." And often this should be the standard expected of the fiduciary. But, precisely because such a standard can neither be realized fully nor even be defined with specificity in advance, it should not be criminalized. Aspirational standards imply that there will be shortfalls in performance, and this in turn means that to criminalize such a standard is to ignore the prudential constraint that criminal laws should be capable of even and general enforceability.

Civil standards are sometimes experimental, and on occasion courts retreat from prior high-water marks. Within the corporate context, courts in recent years have announced major new rules of fiduciary duty and have sometimes later retreated from these positions. If one accepts the premise that blameworthiness should be a prerequisite for the justified use of the criminal sanction, it is difficult to reconcile this premise with the idea that new and sometimes novel civil standards could carry criminal penalties. In addition, criminalizing fiduciary duties might halt (or at least retard) this process of lawmaking, as courts would predictably become more conservative in their willingness to announce new duties if they believed severe penalties automatically followed from noncompliance.

The precision with which a legal standard speaks logically depends on the purpose to which the standard will be put. Because the tort law is primarily concerned with compensation and loss allocation, rather than outright deterrence, it has less need to give precise notice of where its strictures begin and end. Phrased more generally, when society's objective is only to "price" behavior, it may be fair to give only an approximate notice of where the point is at which the actor will be asked to internalize the costs it imposes on others. Thus, tort law rules often (and perhaps characteristically) are expressed in fuzzy and indeterminate language (such as the "reasonable person" standard) that does not give rise to "bright line" standards (as the criminal law characteristically requires). Put simply, both tort standards and many ethical rules do not mean to place a clear stop sign in front of the actor, which says "go no further;" rather, they say that if you do go further, your behavior may be costly to you because you must compensate those who are injured by your conduct. In contrast, the criminal law threatens exemplary penalties and so must speak with greater precision. The difference is between saying "Proceed at Your Own Risk" and "Halt."

2. The Hobbs Act

Can it be criminal to breach a contract? On its face, the idea sounds absurd. Holmes's famous statement that the obligation created by a contract was to perform or pay damages seemed to recognize that the payment of damages discharged the obligation. Proponents of the efficient breach theory argue that it is desirable that contracts be breached when the breach will create value. We need not enter this debate, but only note it to understand the significance of this next development: under some recent decisions, a breach of contract could be criminal.

To be sure, no decision has said this squarely, nor is one likely to, but uncertainty already has been created. The source of this uncertainty is a series of recent decisions that read the Hobbs Act to criminalize the extortion of property from a person by placing that person in "fear of economic loss." The Hobbs Act defines extortion as the "obtaining of property from another, with his consent, induced by wrongful use of actual or threatened force, violence, or fear, or under color of official right." The term "fear" has recently been given an expansive judicial interpretation to include actions or threats which place another in fear of economic loss. This so-called economic duress theory has not yet been pushed to the degree that the "intangible rights" theory of mail fraud has, but this may mean only that we are at an earlier moment in the evolution of still another new theory of white collar crime.

Consider then the degree to which much of commercial life could be reached by this theory. Suppose that in the construction industry, a subcontractor is under a fixed-price contract to complete a phase of a skyscraper—for example, the basic plumbing—without which further construction is impossible. It has contracted to complete the job for $5,000,000, but it now demands a price of $10,000,000, because it knows the general contractor faces costly delays if it fails to perform. Not surprisingly, contract law provides a restitutionary remedy for the general contractor if it pays this added amount under the circumstances. But even if this behavior amounts to a form of economic extortion, should it be deemed a felony under the Hobbs Act? No case has yet clearly dealt with such a fact pattern, but the theory of fear of economic loss covers this case just as much as the more common case of the labor leader who, unless given a payoff, will call a strike.

Why should the criminal law not reach such a fact pattern? One reason may be that it is very hard to differentiate the case in which the subcontractor is seeking to extort from the case in which it has truly encountered force majeure or other unexpected difficulties, the cost of which it is entitled to pass on to the general contractor. Too much depends on subjective motivations, because the defendant's actions are equivocal—that is, they could be consistent with either criminality or innocuous behavior. When equivocal conduct is criminalized, defendants may effectively be punished more for their intentions than for their conduct. A second reason may be that contractual breaches, even of this special kind, are endemic and would arguablyoverload the criminal justice system. Again, criminalization would violate the prudential side constraint that the use of the criminal sanction is appropriate only when the norm can be evenly and generally enforced. A third reason is that civil remedies are more likely to be adequate in this context because there is less risk of nondetection. Ultimately, however, there may be an overshadowing reason for declining to criminalize: the behavior in question—i.e., use of economic duress—may have social utility. If so, society should price, rather than prohibit, the behavior in question (through means such as punitive damages).

Some courts have tried to place limits on this economic duress theory of extortion, but these limits do not address the real problem—namely, that sometimes it is legitimate to use economic threats. To determine when it is and when it is not, a court must engage in a retrospective factual evaluation and delicate line drawing, both of which exist in uneasy tension at best with the ideal of fair notice. Once again, the development of this "fear of economic loss" theory of extortion illustrates an idea being expanded to the limits of its logic—and beyond. Again, the piecemeal development of an idea in the classic case-by-case method of the common law proves inappropriate for the criminal law because it creates great uncertainty, leaving few bright lines that individuals may approach safely.

B. The Diminution of Mens Rea

American criminal law scholarship has always placed the issue of mens rea at center stage. Its greatest achievement—the Model Penal Code—creates a presumption that mens rea applies to every material element in the crime, unless the statute clearly indicates otherwise. In Morissette v. United States, the Supreme Court seemed to give such a presumption a quasi-constitutional gloss:

The contention that an injury can amount to a crime only when inflicted by intention is no provincial or transient notion. It is as universal and persistent in mature systems of law as belief in freedom of the human will and a consequent ability and duty of the normal individual to choose between good and evil. A relation between some mental element and punishment for a harmful act is almost as instinctive as the child's familiar exculpatory 'But I didn't mean to'. . . .

More recently, in Liparota v. United States, the Court reaffirmed this presumption, at least with respect to those elements in the crime that establish moral blameworthiness. Simultaneously, however, Liparota acknowledged that an exception to this generalization existed for "public welfare offenses." Reviewing its prior decisions on mens rea, the Court explained that in those cases in which it had upheld the omission of a mental element, the statute "rendered criminal a type of conduct that a reasonable person should know is subject to stringent public regulation and may seriously threaten the community's health or safety."

This language frames a central question: what is the scope of this exception for public welfare offenses? Lower courts have read the Liparota exception as limited to cases in which the risks created by the defendants' conduct "may be presumed to be regulated because of their inherent danger." As an example, the Liparota Court cited United States v. Freed, a case in which the Court upheld a conviction for illegal possession of unregistered hand grenades, notwithstanding the defendant's claim (and the trial court's failure to instruct the jury) that he could be convicted only if he had knowledge that the hand grenades were unregistered. Both Liparota and Freed thus involved defendants who claimed lack of knowledge of the applicable regulations; but Liparota won, and Freed lost. Seemingly, the obvious public safety factor present in Freed was not present in Liparota, which involved only the unauthorized use of food stamps and not a deadly weapon.

If public safety is the deciding test, the possibility arises that many environmental statutes, which commonly require permits before various conduct (e.g., the disposal of waste, the filling-in of wetlands, etc.) may be engaged in, will fall on the strict liability side of the line. Here, the circuit courts of appeal have recently divided. In United States v. Hoflin, the defendant was convicted of aiding and abetting the illegal disposal of hazardous waste in violation of the Resource Conservation Recovery Act (RCRA). What had the defendant done? While Director of Public Works for the town of Ocean Shores, Washington, he had authorized the disposal of leftover road paint by burial on property adjoining the town's sewage treatment plant. After testing, the Environmental Protection Agency ("EPA") determined that the paint fell within the class of hazardous waste for which the EPA requires a disposal permit. Hoflin's defense was that he did not know the town lacked such a permit and that, therefore, the trial judge was required to instruct

the jury that to convict Hoflin it had to find that he knew either that the town lacked the requisite permit or was acting in violation of one. Rejecting this claim, the Ninth Circuit found that the statute need not be read to require knowledge of the lack of a permit.

On a policy level, such a decision can be defended if one reads the burial of excess paint in Hoflin to be conduct equivalent to the possession of hand grenades in Freed. Yet, common sense tells us that the average citizen knows hand grenades are dangerous (and therefore presumptively regulated), but has no similar reaction to disposing of ordinary paint, which the average person has encountered and used much of his or her life. Burying paint becomes "hazardous" only once we apply that label to it, not from ordinary human experience. In short, the presumption that danger-invites-regulation is reasonable in one case, but not in the other.

Ultimately, the only factor truly suggesting "blameworthy" conduct on the defendant's part was the knowledge (or lack thereof) that an EPA permit was lacking. Thus, the mental element that the Hoflin court read out of the statute was the lone connection between "blameworthiness" and the criminal sanction. In contrast, a defendant in possession of a quantity of hand grenades is at least presumptively involved in "blameworthy" conduct simply based on possession. The line between Freed and Liparota then is not simply the presence or absence of a threat to the public safety, but the existence of factors corroborating blameworthiness in one and their absence in the other. Part II will return to the significance of this linkage between some minimal element of blameworthy conduct and the use of criminal sanctions, but the immediate point is that because many regulatory statutes involve conduct creating some threat to the public safety, a theory may be on the verge of judicial acceptance that effectively severs this linkage between blameworthiness and criminal punishment.

C. Vicarious Responsibility

Generally, in American criminal law, individuals are criminally liable only for conduct that: (1) they direct or participate in; (2) they otherwise aid or abet; or (3) with respect to which they conspire. Corporate officers, however, now appear to face an additional form of vicarious liability. In United States v. Park, the Supreme Court upheld the imposition of criminal liability upon "corporate employees who have 'a responsible share in the furtherance of the transaction,'" even when the corporate officer took action to prevent the violation. Lower federal courts have extended this principle to apply, even when it has appeared that subordinate employees had purposely failed to follow the superior's orders or that the officer took significant corrective action that could not be implemented in time because of a labor strike.

Park's "responsible share" theory was announced in the context of a strict liability statute, whose uncompromising harshness the Court actually relaxed marginally by recognizing an "objective impossibility" defense. Both legislation and subsequent decisions seem to be extending Park's standard of vicarious liability both to other "public welfare" statutes and, more questionably, to statutes requiring higher mens rea levels. This expansion of the Park doctrine has particular significance in light of new and proposed "reckless endangerment" statutes. Under one environmental statute, a defendant can receive fifteen years in prison for "knowing endangerment" that creates a risk of "serious bodily injury." Although the mens rea level here of "knowing" is certainly adequate to satisfy traditional civil libertarian concerns, Park's "responsible share" concept broadens the scope of potential defendants so as arguably to make anyone within the corporate hierarchy with power to correct or mitigate the risk liable if they have knowledge of it. Is, for example, a vice president for public relations liable where he or she has knowledge and might conceivably have influenced the chief executive officer to change a practice? Similar liability is possible under an OSHA statute that forbids employers willfully to violate a mandated health or safety standard that causes the death of a worker. Although the statutory focus is on the employer, Park could be read to expand the class of persons liable so as to reach all "responsible" managers within the firm.

In 1990, California actually enacted such a broadly inclusive statute. Under it, both the corporation and any "manager with respect to a product, facility, equipment, process, place of employment or business practice" is criminally liable if the manager has constructive knowledge of "a serious concealed danger" and fails to warn the appropriate regulatory agency and affected employees within fifteen days. The California statute thus combines a negligence level of mens rea with Park's broadened responsibility and then imposes liability essentially for an omission: failing to report the danger and warn employees within an abbreviated time period. Such breadth may shock traditional civil libertarians, but it could be the wave of the future.

D. The "Technicalization" of Crime

Regulatory violations that involve no mental element and pose strict liability have long been known to the criminal law. Nearly sixty years ago, Professor Francis Sayre catalogued the occasions on which legislatures and courts had dispensed with mens rea, naming this special class of criminal prosecutions "public welfare offenses." Tracing the history of such offenses back before the Civil War in the United States and even earlier in England, he found their common denominator to be an attempt to protect the public health and safety by attaching light penalties (usually small fines) to police regulations. Typically, the offenses so criminalized involved the sale of adulterated food or alcohol and narcotics violations where mere possession was deemed sufficient to establish liability. Although Sayre approved of the creation of such a special category of offenses involving no showing of personal culpability, he was emphatic that the doctrine neither should be extended to "true crimes" nor should justify more than de minimus levels of punishment, because "[t]o do so would sap the vitality of the criminal law."

Since the mid-1980s, American law has experienced a little noticed explosion in the use of public welfare offenses. By one estimate, there are over 300,000 federal regulations that may be enforced criminally. Over the last three years, the federal government has prosecuted more than 400 cases involving environmental crimes, resulting in cumulative prison sentences of nearly 300 years. The total fines annually imposed in environmental crime cases rose from $3.6 million in 1987 to over $12 million in 1989. With the advent of sentencing guidelines, prison terms for environmental crime have become both more likely and longer, with the presumptive benchmark for a felony conviction now estimated at two years in prison. Indeed, as Stanley Arkin, one of the most experienced defense counsel in this area, has observed: "Remarkably, the environmental guidelines almost always call for a sentence exceeding the statutory maximum, thereby forcing a court to sentence the offender to the maximum penalty prescribed by the relevant statute."

Obviously, environmental crime is important, and knowing violations – such as falsification of records or willful endangerment – are serious offenses that do not merit leniency. But, the typical environmental offense involves the mishandling of toxic substances, and recent decisions have reduced or eliminated the role of mens rea in these statutes, while also applying Park's doctrine that corporate officers who have a "responsible relation" to the performance of the statutory obligations are liable under them. As a result, the traditional public welfare offense has now been coupled with felony level penalties. While the defendant in Park was only fined, corporate executives in an equivalent position in the future may face years in prison.

This process is only beginning. Although the Environmental Protection Agency has been notably aggressive in referring violations for criminal prosecution, other agencies with similar statutory authority have been much less ready to make criminal referrals. In time, these more hesitant agencies seem likely to respond to public pressure and follow the EPA's lead. Recently, the SEC has begun to make criminal referrals in stock parking cases, which at bottom involve record-keeping and reporting violations having little, if any, relationship to the public health or safety. Exxon has been indicated in connection with the Valdez oil spill for entrusting control of a vessel to a person that it allegedly knew or should have known to have been an alcoholic. Finally, the recent indictment of Eastern Airlines and several of its employees for failure to follow correct maintenance and safety procedures, as required by Federal Aviation Administration regulations, opens a vast horizon of potential criminal prosecutions. As with stock parking prosecutions, the actual behavior involves falsification of the company's own business records. At this point, there are few, if any, federal regulations that could not potentially support a federal criminal prosecution under one theory or another.

In fairness, the federal government's attempt to use criminal sanctions in traditionally civil areas – such as stock parking – has met with some judicial resistance. During the last year, the Second Circuit has reversed several securities fraud convictions in marginal cases, but affirmed others where the evidence of intent was clearer. Still, these decisions lack any clear rationale and tend to depend on specific ad hoc judicial theories that seem in some cases driven by a need to justify reversal on as narrow a ground as possible. Conceivably, the phenomenon of judicial nullification is at work in some of these cases, but such a process is at best an inconsistent, sometime thing.

E. An Initial Summary: The Uncertain Cost/Benefit Calculus

Public concern about a newly perceived social problem – the environment, worker safety, child neglect, etc. – seems to trigger a recurring social response: namely, an almost reflexive resort to criminal prosecution, either through the enactment of new legislation or the use of old standby theories that have great elasticity. Increasingly, criminal liability may be imposed based only on negligence or even on a strict liability basis. The premise appears to be that if a problem is important enough, the partial elimination of mens rea and the use of vicarious responsibility are justified. No doubt, the criminal sanction does provide additional deterrence, but what are the costs of resorting to strict liability and vicarious responsibility as instruments of social control? This will be a theme of Part II, but one aspect of this problem deserves

special mention in view of the apparent escalation of public welfare offenses into felonies.

If the disposal of toxic wastes, securities fraud, the filling-in of wetlands, the failure to conduct aircraft maintenance, and the causing of workplace injuries become crimes that can be regularly indicted on the basis of negligence or less, society as a whole may be made safer, but a substantial population of the American workforce (both at white collar and blue collar levels) becomes potentially entangled with the criminal law. Today, most individuals can plan their affairs so as to avoid any realistic risk of coming within a zone where criminal sanctions might apply to their conduct. Few individuals have reason to fear prosecution for murder, robbery, rape, extortion or any of the other traditional common law crimes. Even the more contemporary, white collar crimes – price fixing, bribery, insider trading, etc. – can be easily avoided by those who wish to minimize their risk of criminal liability. At most, these statutes pose problems for individuals who wish to approach the line but who find that no bright line exists. In contrast, modern industrial society inevitably creates toxic wastes that must be disposed of by someone. Similarly, workplace injuries are, to a degree, inevitable. As a result, some individuals must engage in legitimate professional activities that are regulated by criminal sanctions; to this extent, they become unavoidably "entangled" with the criminal law. That is, they cannot plan their affairs so as to be free from the risk that a retrospective evaluation of their conduct, often under the uncertain standard of negligence, will find that they fell short of the legally mandated standard. Ultimately, if the new trend toward greater use of public welfare offenses continues, it will mean a more pervasive use of the criminal sanction, a use that intrudes further into the mainstream of American life and into the everyday life of its citizens than has ever been attempted before.

Several replies are predictable to this claim that there is a social loss in defining the criminal law so that individuals cannot safely avoid its application. Liberals may claim that the traditionally limited use of the criminal sanction was class-biased and that a more pervasive use of it simply corrects that imbalance. Economists may argue that the affected individuals will only demand a "risk premium" in the labor market and, having received one, cannot later complain when the risk for which they were compensated arises. Others may conclude that the anxiety imposed on such employees, while regrettable, is necessary, because it is small in comparison to the lives saved, injuries averted, and other social benefits realized from generating greater deterrence. This may be true, but the cost/benefit calculus is a complex and indeterminate one that depends upon a comparison of marginal gain (in terms of injuries averted) in comparison to other law enforcement strategies (such as greater use of corporate liability or civil penalties) that have not yet been utilized fully. Moreover, on the cost side of the ledger, one must consider not simply the consequences to those actually prosecuted, but the anxiety created within the potential class of criminal defendants. To the extent that liability is imposed for omissions (i.e., failure to detect and correct dangerous conditions), such fear will affect a broad class of employees, most of whom will never be prosecuted or even threatened with prosecution. In addition, there is a cost to civil libertarian values, because statutes that apply broadly can never be enforced evenly. Hence, some instances of "targeting" or selective prosecutions (based on whatever criteria influence the individual prosecutor) become predictable. These costs would be more tolerable if the conduct involved were inherently blameworthy, but negligence, like death and taxes, is inevitable.

Ultimately, much depends on how we define the purposes of the criminal law. If its purpose is simply to prevent crime, the costs of the broad use of the criminal sanction against corporate managers to deter pollution, negligence-caused injuries, or other social harms may be justified. But if we define the criminal law's purposes more broadly — for example, as to "liberate" society from fear, or to enable the realization of human potential — these broader goals may be seriously compromised by a pervasive use of the criminal sanction against individuals who cannot escape its potential threat. Pursued single-mindedly, a purely negative definition of the criminal law's purposes that asserts that the criminal law's only goal is the prevention of crime ultimately ends up, as Herbert Packer wrote, "creating an environment in which all are safe but none is free."

* * *

III. SEPARATING TORT FROM CRIME: TOWARD IMPLEMENTATION

Part I of this Article argued that the realm of the criminal law is expanding, as behavior that was once considered merely tortious or a regulatory violation is now prosecuted as a crime, often under statutes that provide for significant penalties but give only a diminished role to the defendant's mental awareness of the factors establishing his culpability. The driving force behind this transition is two-fold. First, tortious conduct can impose enormous externalities upon society, and in some of the new areas where the criminal sanction is being used — worker safety, toxic dumping,

securities fraud — existing tort and regulatory remedies are generally believed not to have produced adequate deterrence. Second, use of the criminal sanction is easy to defend on utilitarian grounds. It seems to work and is not significantly more costly than civil prosecutions. In short, public authorities get a bigger bang for the buck.

Part II then argued that this utilitarian justification for expansion of the criminal category threatens to conflict with the educational and socializing role of the criminal law. Still, there is no immutable line between crime and tort. Rather, this Article has suggested that the line depends primarily on whether society is willing to recognize social utility in the value that the criminal derives from the criminal behavior. If it does, the strategy should be to price, rather than to prohibit, in order to minimize the external costs. Conversely, when society wishes to prohibit the behavior, it cannot permit the offender to derive any benefits from the activity without undercutting the educational and socializing impact of the criminal law. Generally, society seeks to prohibit (rather than price) those activities that violate fundamental community standards. Yet, over time, society can and does decide that some activities, which formerly were only priced, should be prohibited. Unlawful toxic dumping seems a clear example of a form of conduct where society's attitude has changed. Once this might have been seen as simply a regulatory matter — a malum prohibitum offense in the language of an earlier era — but today it is more likely to be viewed as behavior that knowingly endangers human life. Community standards have changed, and they will continue to do so.

Admittedly, substantial problems of implementation surround any attempt to operationalize a distinction between pricing and prohibiting. Two stand out: (1) the "real world" continuum of criminal behavior, ranging from the trivial to the egregious, has few, if any, obvious partitions; thus, an abrupt shift from a "pricing" policy of incremental cost increases to a "prohibitory" policy of sharp, discontinuous jumps in penalty levels may seem unjustified; and (2) the competence of juries to judge issues of social utility seems highly questionable. Nonetheless, to shift from pricing to prohibiting without framing some role for the jury as fact-finder might be thought to trivialize the constitutional safeguards surrounding the trial stage.

The most feasible answers to both these problems dovetail. Put simply, the existence or non-existence of criminal intent supplies a traditional jury issue that also furnishes the most practical breakpoint at which to shift from pricing to prohibiting. To illustrate the kind of criminal intent on which the jury should be asked to focus, it is useful to return to a case briefly noted earlier: United States v. Sellers. In Sellers, the court refused to give a jury instruction that required the jury to find that the defendant realized that his disposal of waste substances "could be harmful to others or the environment." To be sure, such a level of mens rea is not constitutionally required, but this focus on harm to others supplies a practical test, readily comprehensible to a jury, for determining when the defendant's conduct knowingly lacks any claim to social utility (and hence should be subject to "sanctions," rather than "prices" in Professor Cooter's terminology). Ideally, criminal legislation might therefore distinguish two grades of the crime of toxic dumping: the higher grade requiring a subjective perception by the defendant of the serious risk of harm to others, and the lower grade not. The former might be "prohibited," and the latter "priced."

Such an approach might be ideal, but it is also constitutionally permissible for the court to engage in this same inquiry at sentencing.

A. The Role of the Sentencing Commission

The line drawing problems in determining whether to price or to prohibit are obviously difficult, both because community standards may properly shift over time and because a retrospective factual examination of the particular case will frequently be necessary to see on which side of the line it should fall. Where does this leave us in terms of policy options? First, it suggests that the line between tort and crime cannot feasibly be constitutionalized. In any event, there is virtually no possibility that the Supreme Court would attempt to draw such a line. Recurrently, the Court has suggested that "a crime is anything which the legislature chooses to say it is." It has upheld strict liability offenses, and has been unwilling even to treat "victimless" crimes involving consensual sexual conduct as beyond the legislature's reach. Only in Lambert v. California did the Court suggest any limits on what the legislature could criminalize, and the more than three decades that have passed since that decision have confirmed Justice Frankfurter's prediction in his dissent that the decision would "turn out to be an isolated deviation from the strong current of precedents—a derelict on the waters of the law." Perhaps it should not be, but the momentum for change seems lacking.

If the courts will not draw a line between tort and crime, the legislature might still be asked to do so. But such an appeal seems even more likely to be unsuccessful. Criminal legislation is enacted for a variety of reasons: sometimes as an ad hoc, often hasty response to a perceived crisis; sometimes as an afterthought; sometimes as a means of dignifying the status of a federal agency so that knowing violations of its administrative rules can be criminally prosecuted.

Whatever the reason, there is usually a constituency that wants criminalization, and seldom one that visibly opposes it. To oppose criminalization usually places an individual legislator in the exposed position of appearing not to consider the subject matter of the statute sufficiently serious to merit serious penalties. Such perceived insensitivity can be politically harmful, if not fatal. More importantly, any attempt to draw statutory lines that better distinguish "true" criminal behavior from merely tortious behavior would involve an effort of heroic complexity, and in all likelihood it would produce problems with which courts would struggle for decades. Not only would the charging and trial stages become more complex, but it is ultimately doubtful that satisfactory lines can be drawn in advance. Too many details matter, and hence a retrospective evaluation is necessary.

Another group that might be appealed to is prosecutors themselves. Prosecutorial guidelines could be adopted seeking to decriminalize negligent or strict liability offenses. Yet, for prosecutors to decide systematically not to prosecute what the legislature has deemed criminal is also a politically dangerous act, one that seems to undermine the legislature's position as the sovereign lawmaker. Thus, although such prosecutorial guidelines and policies would normally be lawful, they would undoubtedly draw criticism from the regulatory bodies whose enforcement powers would thereby be curtailed, as well as from their legislative allies.

In my judgment, this leaves one agency with an incentive to undertake systematically the task of determining when to price and when to prohibit a particular type of misconduct: the United States Sentencing Commission. Established by Congress in 1984 to draft presumptive sentencing guidelines, it cannot avoid this question without shirking its legislatively imposed duty. To be sure, the Commission cannot prevent the prosecution of offenses that do not amount to "true" crimes (under whatever criteria are used to draw that line), but it can ensure that such crimes are treated at sentencing like public welfare offenses. In truth, public welfare offenses have been a subterranean part of our law for over a century, but only in the last decade or so have substantial fines or criminal sentences been imposed for their violation. Recognizing that the world is imperfect and that a doctrinally pure distinction between crimes and torts will never be observed by lawmakers, the Sentencing Commission could still take as its task the implementation of Professor Cooter's distinction between prices and sanctions. Thus, for behavior that society wishes only to tax, fines should be framed so as to force the actor to internalize costs, but for behavior that society wishes to prohibit, a deliberately sharp and discontinuous jump should be structured into the sentencing guidelines.

Not all cases fit this simple dichotomy of pricing versus prohibiting. For example, what should be done when the defendant (typically a corporation or a corporate officer) is placed on notice that it is not in compliance with some legal obligation and then seeks in good faith to bring itself into compliance – but fails? In one case, the president of a corporation that owned an open-air food storage warehouse was convicted for failing to correct a health problem caused by bird infestation, even though he directed the design and construction of an elaborate bird cage that would have adequately protected the facility. Unfortunately, a labor strike prevented the installation of the device, with the result that the problem remained uncorrected when health inspectors next visited the plant. On appeal, the Ninth Circuit affirmed the conviction, rejecting the "objective impossibility" defense established by Park and noted with apparent approval the prosecution's argument that the firm always had the option of shutting down the business until the device was installed. Such a judicial response poses the basic question: does society value the productive capacity of this enterprise during the interim? Arguments can be made on both sides of this question, but the potential social loss from shutting down the firm and laying off its employees may be disproportionate to the harm realistically threatened by the offense. Such a case presents a paradigm of the pricing versus prohibiting dilemma and suggests that sometimes pricing is the more appropriate response.

B. An Agenda for the Sentencing Commission

An appropriate procedure would be to allow consideration of these questions at sentencing. Sentencing guidelines could respond in the following general ways:

1. Strict Liability. In principle, strict liability offenses should not result in incarceration or high financial penalties, unless the prosecution can show at sentencing that the individual acted with at least the minimum level of mens rea that American criminal law defines as "recklessness." Although regulatory authorities maintain with some truth that they prosecute only defendants, who, they believe, acted with actual knowledge, this issue is seldom resolved at trial, at least if the statute dispenses with mens rea toward the element in question. Absent legislation that appropriately frames this issue, it should still be resolved at sentencing (albeit with lesser formality and a lower burden of proof) before punishment above that appropriate for traditional public welfare offenses could be imposed.

2. Fear. Nozick's basic claim – that the criminal law is primarily justified by the noncompensable fear that

some unlawful actions impose on others – deserves explicit recognition in any morally sophisticated system of sentencing. Its role should be that of an aggravating factor. Obviously, such a criteria distinguishes crimes, such as insider trading, from homicide. But what kinds of fear count? Community values probably answer this question and imply that fear of a financial loss is not the same as fear of injury or illness. Note, however, that the fear need not be directly attributable to a personal assault. Toxic dumping crimes, for example, may subject an even larger proportion of the citizenry to fears that they are drinking contaminated water. Similarly, crimes involving concealed exposure of workers to dangerous substances (e.g., asbestos) could fall under this same heading.

3. Industry Standards and Agency Rules. Hart's approach can be faulted as backward-looking and anachronistic because it looks only to traditional moral standards. Perhaps unintentionally, it thus implicitly revives the discredited malum in se versus malum prohibitum distinction. Often, however, the regulatory rules imposed by an agency will have simply codified standards long recognized within an industry or other professional community. Significant departures from these standards may involve the same degree of culpability within that specialized group as departures from prevailing moral standards recognized universally within the larger community. In short, if the conduct would be seen as wholly unjustified by those within the field (who best understand it), it should be prohibited, not priced. Egregious departures from professional norms should not be excused simply because the rules involved were technical. In this light, consider again the pending indictment of Eastern Airlines for failure to conduct adequate maintenance on its planes. The gravity of such a crime can range from the trivial to the very serious. How should a court appraise it? While industry standards are never dispositive, they provide the most useful benchmark for measuring the culpability of such an offense. When well-established industry standards are violated, the court's response should be the same as if the conduct violated fundamental community standards.

4. Corporate Crime. Corporate crime can be distinctive in several respects, but two respects bear special mention here. First, sometimes the corporation has failed to comply with a standard toward which it was making substantial progress, and, second, sometimes (but probably less often) the crime can be the consequence of a "rogue" employee acting contrary to specific instructions or corporate policy. The Y. Hata & Co. case, in which a strike prevented the corporate officer from installing the necessary bird cage around an open-air food storage warehouse, illustrates the first scenario. The court's view that the

business could have been shut down if compliance were otherwise physically impossible seems extreme, because it denies that there is any social value in the continued operation of the plant pending full compliance. While one can easily criticize the court's decision, the more difficult question arrives at sentencing. Having rejected the defense, can the court still consider this same factor as a mitigating factor that reduces the fine? This Article's answer would be yes, at least when thecrime is essentially a public welfare offense that should be priced, not prohibited. This conclusion rests, however, on the defendant's good faith in attempting to correct the problem. Once again, behavior that has social utility should be priced, not prohibited. Deliberate defiance, however, lacks such utility and should be prohibited because it undercuts the socializing role of the criminal law.

The second recurring element in corporate crime is the claim that a "rogue" employee was responsible. Often, this claim is overstated, because the so-called rogue may be responding to subtle (or not so subtle) intra-organization signals and pressures that place profit above law compliance. Indeed, middle managers are often almost fungible, with the result that the corporation can replace those employees who are caught with little harm to itself—if the fine will be modest so long as senior corporate personnel are not implicated. Nonetheless, it cannot be denied that cases arise in which a rogue employee does appear to have frustrated a good faith corporate attempt to comply with the law. In these cases, the corporation's culpability seems low, and a pricing approach would be appropriate, whose intent would be to induce the corporation to install improved monitoring controls.

The problem with this answer is that any corporation can adopt a compliance plan and it may be difficult for the prosecution to prove, except in the most egregious case, that it was cosmetically manipulated. When internal monitoring amounts to a sham, the conclusion seems obvious that it lacks social utility, and a prohibitory approach becomes appropriate. Thus, a sharp, discontinuous jump in corporate penalties is appropriate when there is evidence that senior corporate officials knew of, or "recklessly" tolerated, the criminal behavior or sought to outflank monitoring controls.

But how does one draft guidelines that distinguish "true" from "cosmetic" monitoring? One approach would be to grant a provisional sentencing credit for seemingly adequate monitoring controls, but then treat this credit as a suspended sentence which is forfeited if there is any repetition of the behavior (as evidenced by either subsequent civil or criminal findings during a period of corporate probation). Such an approach takes much of the burden off the court by assuming that cosmetic monitoring will ultimately result in future violations, and the time to be punitive is at that future moment. Above all, corporate recidivism merits prohibition, not pricing.

CONCLUSION

Ultimately, appropriate sentencing policy is a function of one's theory of the criminal law. Those who view the criminal law as a "pricing" system can make a coherent case for their view that Sentencing Commission guidelines for corporate offenders are too high and that courts should reduce the sentences currently imposed on corporations by recognizing any of a variety of offsets or mitigating factors. In contrast, those who believe that the criminal law is intended to prohibit and not price can view high fines with equanimity and argue that if they are too severe corporations have only to obey the law to avoid them.

Although this Article has argued that the criminal law should normally prohibit, and not price, it has also recognized that the expansion of the criminal law into formerly civil areas of law and the increasing departures from the traditional "method" of the criminal law make it difficult to state this policy as an iron rule. An either/or choice is also unnecessary. Rather, pricing is appropriate precisely in those areas where the criminal law has relaxed its usual requirement of mens rea or has abandoned its normal hostility to vicarious responsibility. Clearly, corporate criminal responsibility straddles this line, and thus distinctions must be drawn that the current federal law of corporate criminal liability does not make.

How can these distinctions best be drawn? The sentencing determination today represents the only point in our criminal justice system where it remains feasible to preserve the distinction between "true" crimes and public welfare offenses. To say that this can be done is not to claim that such distinctions are today being drawn or will be in the near future. Procedural reform, clearer sentencing guidelines that are more focused on culpability factors, and numerous other steps would be desirable. Still, if the criminal law is not to be corrupted into simply a utilitarian instrument for administering legal threats, reform at the sentencing stage is the last, best hope.

Kenneth Mann, *Punitive Civil Sanctions: The Middleground Between Criminal and Civil Law,* 101 YALE L.J. 1795–1813, 1844, 1860–1873 (1992)*

INTRODUCTION

When harmed by another member of society, one assumes that two fundamentally different legal responses are at one's disposal-criminal sanctions and civil remedies. This view is reflected in Justice White's majority opinion in Hicks v. Feiock:

> The States have long been able to plan their own procedures around the traditional distinction between civil and criminal remedies. The abandonment of this clear dividing line in favor of a general assessment of the manifold and complex purposes that lie behind a court's action would create novel problems where now there are rarely any-novel problems that could infect many different areas of the law.

At the heart of this statement is the idea that the criminal law is meant to punish, while the civil law is meant to compensate. The criminal and civil law, each with different purposes and procedural rules, constitute paradigms by which legislatures and courts analyze their actions and by which textbooks and scholarly literature structure arguments. These paradigms shape both legal principles and the legal profession with respect to issues such as the specialization of attorneys, the definition of procedural rules, and the division of authority among courts.

Though attractive to the legal mind, however, the bifurcation of legal sanctions into two categories is misleading. In numerous civil cases plaintiffs have sought punitive sanctions against defendants who were charged with serious wrongdoing. Under the False Claims Act, the United States government sought a punitive civil penalty of $130,000 from an individual who filed $535 in false claims; under the Comprehensive Forfeiture Act of 1988, the First Circuit Court of Appeals compelled a man to give up 17.9 acres of property on which a home was situated after police seized 130 marijuana plants on the property; under the Racketeer Influenced and Corrupt Organizations Act (RICO), private plaintiffs filed suit for $10 billion, mostly for punitive damages, against an electrical

power company for fraud in overcharging; under common law tort principles, a woman defrauded by an insurance company received an award of $840,000 in punitive damages, more than four times her actual damage. Although these sanctions did not share the same basis of liability and were not ultimately imposed in all of the cases, each case affirmed the idea of punitive civil sanctions. The purpose of punitive civil sanctions is to punish, even though their procedural setting is civil.

While new criminal laws are appearing with great frequency and criminal sentences are growing more severe, punitive civil sanctions are rapidly expanding, affecting an increasingly large sector of society in cases brought by private parties as well as by the government. These sanctions are sometimes more severely punitive than the parallel criminal sanctions for the same conduct. Punitive civil sanctions are replacing a significant part of the criminal law in critical areas of law enforcement, particularly in white-collar and drug prosecutions, because they carry tremendous punitive power. Furthermore, since they are not constrained by criminal procedure, imposing them is cheaper and more efficient than imposing criminal sanctions. As a result, the jurisprudence of sanctions is experiencing a dramatic shift. With more punishment meted out in civil proceedings, the features distinguishing civil from criminal law become less clear. As civil law becomes more punitive, serious doubt arises about whether conventional civil procedure is suited for an unconventional civil law.

I use the term "middleground" to describe the jurisprudential arena of punitive civil sanctions. The middleground draws on the two basic paradigms that form the doctrinal basis for the entire field of sanctioning law: criminal law and civil law. The paradigms of criminal and civil law stem from longstanding conventions about the essential nature and function of legal sanctions. Within this paradigmatic framework the criminal law is distinguished by its punitive purposes, its high procedural barriers to conviction, its concern with the blameworthiness of the defendant, and its particularly harsh sanctions. In contrast, the civil law is defined as a compensatory scheme, focusing on damage rather than on blameworthiness, and providing less severe sanctions and lower procedural safeguards than the criminal law. The middleground draws on these two basic paradigms to form a hybrid jurisprudence in which the sanction's purpose is punishment, but its procedure is drawn primarily from the civil law.

While the middleground includes both state-invoked and privately invoked proceedings, these punitive sanctions rest on different assumptions. The privately invoked sanction derives from the common law right of

---

* Reprinted by permission of The Yale Law Journal Company and Fred B. Rothman & Company from *The Yale Journal,* Vol. 101, pages 1795-1873.

the jury to award exemplary damages, and is thus doctrinally circumscribed by little other than the concept of discretion uninfluenced by corrupt motive. The state-invoked sanction, on the other hand, is rooted in the sovereign's prerogative and police power, and thus prompts suspicion of state power and questions about the need for special procedural doctrines to protect the citizen from overreach and unreasonableness. This Article focuses mainly on state-imposed punitive civil sanctions-that is, punitive sanctions in which the government, usually an administrative agency, is the moving party. Although the government has long possessed the power to impose sanctions that do not fit into the conventional paradigms of civil and criminal law, the differentiation of legal sanctions into two groups created a false dichotomy even before punitive civil sanctions became commonplace.

The distinction between criminal and civil law has continued to shape the jurisprudence of sanctions, creating a framework for case law and legislative policy. Particularly, given the rapid growth of punitive civil sanctions, one must conclude that either (1) the paradigms have been wrongly defined and have therefore produced an incorrect understanding of the law, or (2) courts and legislatures have wrongly allowed the development of sanctions that do not incorporate the values of the civil and criminal paradigms. These issues have become more pressing because of the controversy surrounding the allegedly growing use of punitive damages in tort and the increasing congressional willingness to allow citizens to act as private attorneys general to bring punitive civil proceedings in the name of the state or in place of the state.

At the same time, Congress has also enlarged existing powers and provided new authority to administrative agencies to punish offenders in civil proceedings. While legislatures and courts have busily created punitive civil sanctions for the state to impose, they have gone to great lengths to avoid labeling them as "punitive" to circumvent the application of criminal-type procedural rules. In many instances, the very motivation for the creation of civil punitive sanctions was to avoid criminal procedural protection.

The growth of state-invoked and privately invoked punitive civil sanctions raises critical questions for current and future sanctions for illegal behavior. When should law enforcement agencies choose criminal sanctions over punitive civil sanctions? What is the role of full-fledged criminal sanctions in a legal system increasingly characterized by punitive civil sanctions? If a process labeled "civil" metes out punitive sanctions, should criminal-type procedural protections apply? How much can the "punitiveness" of sanctions imposed in civil proceedings be increased to strengthen law enforcement tools without turning to the criminal law? Is there a proper place for parallel proceedings-one private and one brought by the state-seeking punitive sanctions against the same person or entity for the same conduct? Should legislation encourage private punitive proceedings to take an increasingly large part of the law of sanctions out of the hands of the state?

Part I details the conventional paradigms of criminal and civil law.

Part II conceptualizes the parameters of the middleground, mainly focusing on state-invoked, punitive civil monetary sanctions. A main theme of this material is the Supreme Court's use of legal fictions in describing punitive civil sanctions to avoid the procedural implications of punitiveness, particularly the creation of high procedural barriers to imposing sanctions. With these fictions, the Court has suppressed the development of distinctive procedural rules for middleground sanctions.

Part III focuses on the reasons behind the accelerating growth of punitive civil sanctions. The causes are complex and include the growing influence of utilitarianism and deterrence theory in the law, the general expansion of law and litigation, the increasing authority of administrative agencies, frustration with the procedural obstacles of the criminal law, and reforms in civil procedure.

Part IV discusses the implications of middleground jurisprudence. First, I suggest increasing both the size and frequency of punitive civil monetary sanctions. This would have the major benefit of decreasing the use of the criminal law, confining it to areas of clearly egregious behavior in which severely punitive civil monetary sanctions are ineffective. Thus, I advocate the shrinking of the criminal law in order to fit it into its proper role in the law of sanctions, next to an expanding arena of punitive civil sanctions.

Second, I add my voice to those who have argued that the procedure with which punitive civil sanctions are imposed fails to properly protect substantive and procedural due process values and that the future use of such sanctions, should they grow in size, may subvert these values if no independent middleground procedure is developed. I expand on this argument by connecting changes in state-invoked punitive civil sanctions to the development of privately invoked sanctions, both of which present the problem of finding a correct procedural form.

I. THE PARADIGMS OF CIVIL AND CRIMINAL LAW

To grasp the significance of the conventional paradigms for the development of the law of sanctions, it is essential to note that early English and American judges and commentators adopted a language fraught with bipolar images of the law of sanctions. They wrote about the "criminal law" and the "civil law" in spite of the fact that middleground sanctions, such as punitive damages in tort, always existed. The law of sanctions theoretically recognized only two paradigms of legal ordering, when in fact the actual sanctioning forms contained a substantial variation of substantive definitions, purposes, remedies, and procedures.

Describing the law of the fourteenth and fifteenth centuries, Holdsworth observed that it was "in this period that the foundations of our present law as to Wrongs criminal and civil [were] laid." The differences apparently became quite well entrenched. In 1776 Lord Mansfield said, "Now there is no distinction better known, than the distinction between civil and criminal law; or between criminal prosecutions and civil actions." Out of this historic division between the two main categories of legal process emerged the deeply ingrained language distinguishing criminal penalties from civil remedies. These terms reflected the development of a dominant ideology, clustering the different traits of legal sanctions together to create important normative focal points in jurisprudence: the criminal and civil law paradigms. Thus, a sanction may be viewed within the criminal law paradigm as a penalty, or within the civil law paradigm as a remedy.

The criminal and civil paradigms attempt to abstract a set of traits from the complex and multifaceted nature of sanctions, in which substantial areas of overlap exist between civil and criminal law. Almost every attribute associated with one paradigm appears in the other. Imprisonment, associated with the criminal process, also exists in the civil arena; civil contempt, for example, is punishable by incarceration. Payment of money, distinctively associated with civil law, takes the form of fines in the criminal law. The paradigms misrepresent the field of actual legal processes because they ignore a large variety of hybrid sanctions. In particular, they fail to identify the central role of punitive civil sanctions in the broader arena of legal sanctions.

In many instances, the correlation of an attribute with its paradigmatic context is an empirically valid reflection of the attribute's primacy in one paradigm rather than the other. In other instances, the paradigmatic co-option of attributes stems from historical conventions that are now eclipsed, and thus the paradigms contradict the actual development of attributes in sanctioning arrangements. This is precisely the case with punitive sanctions, which are paradigmatically associated with the criminal law, but now characterize so much of the civil law that punishment no longer seems a distinctive attribute of the criminal law. The

paradigms continue to be used widely, however, because they seem to capture what legal minds consider distinctive features of the law of sanctions.

In discussing the particular nature of the civil and criminal paradigms, it is assumed that as with every system of sanctions there must be definitions of wrongs, purposes, procedures, and remedies. This part reveals the generic aspect of these dimensions by examining the different characteristics found in the criminal and civil paradigms. The following analysis focuses on criminal law (the statutory law defining public norms) and the common law of torts rather than on contract law (the law of private norms).

A. Subjective vs. Objective Liability and Wrongful vs. Harmful Acts

Any sanctioning system must define the wrongs to which its sanctions may be applied. Two features of prohibited acts are prominent in distinguishing the paradigms: the mental element required and the effect produced.

1. The Mental Element in Prohibited Acts

In paradigmatic criminal law, commission of a wrongful act must be accompanied by a mental element of wrongdoing: mens rea, or subjective liability. This is a distinctive aspect of criminal law deeply rooted in English legal sources and generally not required for imposition of civil liability.

Since the middle of the thirteenth century, English law has emphasized heavily the mental element required in the criminal law. "[Y]our state of mind," said Bracton, "gives meaning to your act, and a crime is not committed unless the intent to injure (nocendi voluntas) intervene, nor is a theft committed except with the intent to steal." The special mental element required in criminal law also runs through much of the American writing on the subject. For example, Bishop stated that "[t]he doctrine which requires an evil intent lies at the foundation of public justice."

While criminal law and civil law are similar in that both require voluntary acts, civil law depends principally on the notion of objective liability, either disregarding the mental element in conduct or requiring only negligence. The civil law imposes a sanction when there is "a failure to live up to an ideal standard of conduct which may be beyond the knowledge or capacity of the individual, and in acts which are normal and usual in the community, and without moral reproach in its eyes." Negligence gradually increased in importance in the law of torts after the seventeenth century.

2. The Effects of Prohibited Acts

A second paradigmatic difference in the key elements of wrongful conduct concerns the effect of the act to which the sanction applies. Within the criminal paradigm, wrongful acts are sanctioned because they are public wrongs, violating a collective rather than an individual interest. The criminal sanction will apply even if no individual interest has suffered direct injury. The paradigmatic civil sanction, on the other hand, applies to conduct that causes actual damage to an individual interest; this is generally a prerequisite to civil liability. Thus, Holdsworth wrote, "a private person cannot sue civilly unless he can show a special grievance, whereas the king can lay the charge generally; a suit by a private person sounds in damages, whereas a suit by the king ends in the punishment of the guilty party." This distinction between private and public injury was prevalent in early Anglo-American law and provided the basis for Blackstone's classification of law. The generalizations accurately describe distinctive correlations between characteristics of wrongs subject to sanctions and the sanctioning paradigm in which they are found. Jerome Hall put the difference this way: "[I]n torts, 'effects' almost invariably include actual damage to some person, whereas in crimes, damage is not essential-instead the notion of a 'social harm,' supplies the requirement there."

B. Purpose: Punishment vs. Compensation

A second generic dimension that distinguishes paradigmatic civil and criminal law is purpose. Purpose defines the reason or motivation for constructing and using a sanctioning system. We are accustomed to saying that the purpose of the criminal law, in its most general sense, is control of antisocial behavior. But, historically, there have been different emphases in defining the purposes of criminal law, particularly with respect to the role of retribution in the criminal system. Retribution is not necessarily derived from or part of a theory of social control, for in the Kantian sense retribution is not justified or explained by any notion of utility. Punishment in the criminal law, then, can be understood as either a retributive and completely nonutilitarian act or as a means to achieve social control.

In modern legal theory the criminal and civil law share the purpose of social control; however, in the conventional paradigms, which predate the modern overlapping of the civil and criminal law, it was inappropriate to label the civil law as an instrument of social control. Before the language of the social sciences infused the law of sanctions, only criminal law was associated with punishment, both as a form of vengeance and as an instrument for protecting the public.

Substantial normative disagreement has long characterized the debate about the primary justification for the criminal sanction. Yet despite the different emphases and the evolution of different philosophies

on this central issue, most would agree that either as a means or an end, punishment is a distinctive, i.e., paradigmatic, characteristic of the criminal law, even though it is not exclusive to it. The convicted defendant and the community understand that the state uses the criminal law to condemn publicly the offender, who experiences shame because of the notoriety of his punishment. Punishment is an overdetermined concept, for while the idea of punishment qua punishment and punishment for deterrence are conceptually distinct, it is difficult to unravel the two when imposing a sanction. Although policy makers and courts may seek primarily to achieve one of the alternative ends of the criminal sanction, the core retributive aspect of the criminal sanction remains. The principal paradigmatic purpose of the criminal law-the reason for invoking criminal law rather than some alternative sanctioning system-is punishment. Basic texts on criminal law and case law readily illustrate this point.

The principal paradigmatic purpose of the civil sanction, on the other hand, is compensation for damage caused. This is borne out in conventional views of the law of torts. As Prosser put it:

> There remains a body of law whch [sic] is directed toward the compensation of individuals, rather than the public, for losses which they have suffered within the scope of their legally recognized interests generally, rather than one interest only, where the law considers that compensation is required. This is the law of torts.

Tort law made compensation for actual damages the essence of its function. "[A] civil satisfaction in damages," said Blackstone, constitutes compensation for a "private wronge"; whereas "a public mischief" is punished "to secure to the public the benefit of society, by preventing or punishing every breach and violation of those laws" and operates through "the terror of punishment or the sword of the public magistrate." Courts and commentators have recurrently characterized civil law in this way.

C. Remedy: Stigma and Incarceration vs. Restitution and Monetary Payments

The third paradigmatic dimension lies in the remedies provided. A remedy is an action taken by an authoritative body-a legislature, a court, or an administrative agency-to enforce compliance with prescribed conduct or to impose a cost for failure to comply. Every system of legal ordering possesses some kind of remedy. In the past, remedies have included burning at the stake, coerced public service, payment of money, and imprisonment. However subdivided, all remedies are used to achieve the purpose of the sanctioning law, whether it be civil or criminal.

Throughout the history of sanctioning law, commentators have argued that the distinctive remedy of the criminal law is imprisonment or the threat thereof. In modern criminal law, the stigma of a criminal sanction has become a special kind of remedy because of its burdensome and sometimes destructive consequences for the individual. Though other remedies in criminal cases, such as fines and probation, may actually be imposed more often than imprisonment, imprisonment and the special stigma associated with convictions are the core remedies used to achieve the purposes of the criminal sanction.

Two paradigmatic remedies exist in civil law, each closely linked to the purpose of the civil law. The first is the court order mandating a return to the status quo ante, so as to make the injured party whole, or enjoining the continuation of injury. The second is the order to pay money as compensation for damage caused. Blackstone succinctly described the remedies of the civil law:

Now, as all wrong may be considered as merely a privation of right [in the civil law], the one natural remedy for every species of wrong is the being put in possession of that right, whereof the party injured is deprived. This may either be effected by a specific delivery or restoration of the subject-matter in dispute to the legal owner; . . . or, where that is not a possible, or at least not an adequate remedy, by making the sufferer a pecuniary satisfaction in damages. . . .

Within the paradigmatic framework, the civil law was meant to provide remedies specifically designed to repair the damage or provide money to enable the victim to obtain the value of the damage caused.

D. Procedure: High vs. Low Certainty and State vs. Private Initiative

Procedure regulates the application of a sanctioning system's remedies. Thus, the capacity of any system of law to mete out sanctions against wrongdoers depends in part on its procedural characteristics. Two elements of procedure are central for distinguishing paradigmatic criminal and civil law: evidentiary rules and the identity of the moving party.

1. Evidentiary Rules

The presentation of information about conduct to a decision maker is a sine qua non of sanctioning. Three fundamental questions about information necessary to the sanctioning process capture the paradigmatic differences in evidentiary rules between civil and common law.

First, what methods may be used to obtain access to information? This question focuses on the rules defining investigatory powers, such as when and where a search may be conducted, and whether an authoritative entity may force witnesses to produce documents or to testify. Paradigmatic criminal procedure allows more intrusion into individual and corporate domains and more compulsion over targets of investigation than does paradigmatic civil procedure. Within the framework of the paradigms, the state has more leverage over targets in the criminal process than does a plaintiff over a defendant in the civil process. This additional leverage is best exemplified in the police powers of search and custodial interrogation, and the prosecutor's power to subpoena witnesses before a grand jury.

Second, what sources of information are admissible in the decision making process? One system of sanctions may, for instance, base its decisions on information provided by the potential subject of the sanction. A different system may prohibit the use of information provided by the subject of the sanction, requiring exclusive reliance on witnesses. Within the paradigms, criminal procedure historically put more limitations on the information available in the decisionmaking process than did civil procedure. The rules of evidence exemplify these differences. The privilege against self-incrimination and the prohibition on character evidence, for instance, are broader in the criminal process than in the civil process.

Third, what level of certainty is required for the imposition of sanctions? Variation in factual certainty is a central concern when comparing sanctioning systems. One system of sanctions may impose remedies on the basis of facts creating a suspicion in the mind of a single person, while another system may require that many members of a judicial body reach unanimous agreement that all exculpatory explanations of any probability are false. Paradigmatic criminal procedure requires more information than paradigmatic civil procedure because it puts a higher value on certainty before imposing sanctions. This is because criminal penalties are thought to be more severe than civil penalties. Paradigmatic criminal procedure requires proof beyond a reasonable doubt; paradigmatic civil procedure requires only a preponderance of evidence. Thus, a plaintiff could win a civil case while the government could lose a criminal case against the same defendant based on the same evidence.

Civil and criminal law answer the foregoing evidentiary questions differently because of the different public interests implicated by wrongful conduct and because of the fear of the intrusive and punitive use of state power. A fundamental principle of due process requires a positive correlation between investigative intrusiveness and severity of sanction on the one hand and stringency of procedural protections on the other. The rules of information control defined here-that is, the rules of evidence-reflect these values. They require special procedural protections for the investigative techniques of the criminal process, restrict the admissibility of evidence in criminal cases, and require greater certainty before allowing the imposition of criminal sanctions. Thus, the different procedural rules in the paradigmatic forms of criminal and civil law reflect distinct attitudes toward the severity of sanctions and due process.

2. The Moving Party

Following the English example, by the twentieth century, the paradigms of civil and criminal law in the United States indicated that the state held the role of moving party in the criminal law, whereas a private party was the moving party in civil law. The paradigms reflect the idea that the state should hold the power to sanction offenders when the purpose of the sanction is punishment. Complementing this idea, private parties control the sanction in paradigmatic civil law, in which the purpose of the sanction is compensation. In this arrangement, the violation of private interest calls for mobilizing action on the part of the private party.

E. A Summary of Principal Paradigmatic Distinctions

The arrangement of the generic dimensions of sanctioning systems defines the normative framework in which much of the jurisprudence of sanctions has developed. The table below summarizes the distinctive key dimensions of civil and criminal law.

Table 1. Summary of the Criminal and Civil Paradigms

	Criminal Paradigm	Civil Paradigm
Moving Party	State	Private Entity
Wrong Defined	Subjective Liability; Violation of Public Norms	Objective Liability; Actual Injury to Private Interests
Procedure	1) High Leverage to Obtain Information	1) Low Leverage to Obtain Information
	2) Restrictive Admissibility of Evidence	2) Inclusive Admissibility of Evidence
	3) High Burden of Proof	3) Low Burden of Proof
Remedy	Imprisonment; Stigma	Money Payment; Injunction
Purpose	Punishment	Restitution; Compensation

The paradigms have shaped our overall understanding of legal sanctions and have often constituted normative measuring sticks for certifying or disapproving new forms of legal sanctions. They continue to inform the legal mind today. However, the paradigmatic criminal process and the paradigmatic civil process accurately describe only part of the empirical arena of sanctioning processes. They fail to capture the special combination of punitive purposes and civil procedural rules that characterizes hybrid sanctions, which occupy a vast middleground between criminal and civil law. The middleground is not sui generis in the sense that it possesses distinctive characteristics found in neither of the paradigms; rather, it mixes the characteristics of these paradigms in new ways. Against the background of strongly perceived conventional paradigms, the middleground represents a truly hybrid sanction.

* * *

III. The Increased Role of Punitive Civil Sanctions Explained

Legislative adoption of punitive civil sanctions-multiple damages, forfeitures, and penalties-grew rapidly during the middle of the century and has continued to expand in recent years. In 1979, Colin Diver found that twenty-seven federal departments and independent agencies enforced 348 civil statutory penalties. Since that time, Congress has added new punitive civil sanctions, increased their size, and made their imposition procedurally easier. Not only are there many new statutes on the books, but administrative agencies also tend to impose sanctions rather than refer cases for criminal prosecution. Several factors have contributed to the rapid development of punitive civil sanctions. These include a changed philosophy of sanctioning, the general expansion of sanctioning, the growth of the administrative state, and reforms in procedural rules.

* * *

IV. Implications of the Growing Role of Punitive Civil Sanctions

The vast growth in punitive civil sanctions has broad implications for future legal sanctioning. A society in which many offenders can be made to pay severe civil penalties has compelling reasons to shrink the criminal law. A newly conceptualized three-paradigm jurisprudence of sanctioning-composed of criminal, punitive, and remedial sanctions-would reserve criminal law for a much smaller proportion of all sanctionable offenses. As the most extreme form of the state's punitive power, the criminal law would be invoked only when necessary to maintain a public threat of severe punishment for those who cause the most harm in the most blameworthy circumstances.

Under the new tripartite structure, the growth of punitive civil sanctions would result in more sanctioning, and consequently more social control, than would occur under a legal regime in which the government could only choose between criminal and compensatory civil sanctions. Under the traditional paradigmatic structure, a broad range of offenses goes entirely unsanctioned. Potential targets of enforcement probably perceive this result as an expression of society's jealousy of freedom of action. In the tripartite structure, therefore, the rise of punitive civil sanctions may bring with it the specter of increasing governmental intrusion into private and corporate life for the purpose of greater social control; while the change in sanctioning capacity has an Orwellian hue, the actual consequences of these developments will depend on how the implementation of these sanctions is checked and controlled.

This Article advocates an expansion in the size and availability of punitive civil monetary sanctions. The jurisprudence of the past suppressed growth in civil monetary sanctions because courts persisted in the fiction of calling them forms of compensation, deterrence, or debt collection, apparently to avoid using procedures drawn from the criminal paradigm. Now that these sanctions have been called punitive and have nonetheless survived constitutional challenge, we have an important opportunity to create a new regime of punitive sanctions. A new paradigm can be established in the middleground between civil and criminal law. This new approach would levy punitive monetary sanctions (but not as punitive as criminal sanctions) in response to behavior that is culpable (but not egregious enough to require criminal sanctions). Severely punitive monetary sanctions would require especially stringent procedures (but not as stringent as criminal procedures).

These changes would reflect the appropriate position of the criminal law in an era in which specialized agencies wield growing prosecutorial responsibilities. As punitive civil sanctions are used with greater frequency to punish and deter wrongdoers, criminal law should become more of a residual sanction. It should continue to reinforce social solidarity around basic values, but routine sanctioning should be achieved through state-invoked punitive civil sanctions, which are capable of a broader reach because of their less serious implications and their less burdensome procedural setting.

A. Administrative Agency Prosecution

The grant of broad punitive powers to administrative agencies has caused most of the state's punitive sanctioning to occur in the context of civil proceedings. But the principal mission of administrative agencies-the regulation of specialized areas of economic and social life-does not require such a grant of power. Administrative agencies have long possessed a wide range of tools: the power to dispense money, to set standards, to bring civil suits seeking cease-and-desist orders or injunctions, to initiate contempt proceedings for violations of such orders or injunctions, to issue licenses, and to order compensation awards, forfeiture, disqualification, and, of course, money penalties. Although each of these sanctions can serve punitive purposes, all but money penalties can also function in a nonpunitive manner. For example, agencies spend money to influence action; they set standards to provide measures of minimally acceptable conduct; they issue injunctions to prevent wrongful conduct; they withhold licenses to exclude unreliable persons from positions of public responsibility; and they forfeit contraband to exclude harmful items from public access.

In assessing the powers of administrative agencies and the role of punishment in regulations, we should recognize that it is possible to confine all punitive power to the office of the criminal prosecutor, which could also be authorized to seek punitive civil penalties as an alternative to criminal penalties; such an approach would be consistent with applying those procedural requirements that proponents of the middleground have sought to avoid. But the movement toward punitive civil sanctions has taken a different direction, transforming not only the law but also the administrative agency, and, at a larger level, the organization of law enforcement. It is no longer correct to say that administrative agencies only regulate action; administrative agencies also prosecute. The multiplication of administrative agencies has further decentralized the power to punish.

B. The Attenuated Role of Criminal Prosecution

The growth of punitive civil sanctions directly affects criminal law. It lessens the need to use the criminal law to sanction wrongs and permits a more flexible response to wrongful conduct. Legislatures can authorize new civil penalties rather than develop criminal sanctions, and enforcement agencies can impose the new punitive civil sanctions, saving litigation costs and avoiding unnecessarily harsh criminal punishment. While the reach of the criminal law has expanded consistently, the availability of punitive civil sanctions has avoided some of the inflation of criminal laws that would otherwise have occurred. In the future, reliance on the criminal law to achieve punitive purposes should be reduced, and increases in the number and size of available civil penalties, the number of agencies that can impose them, and the range of conduct to which they apply should be encouraged.

Criminal law has a distinctive normative role, and it should be reserved for the most damaging wrongs and the most culpable defendants. Middleground jurisprudence presents a special opportunity for reform, permitting the criminal law to be scaled back where it has been overextended-with respect to petty and middle-range crimes, regulatory and administrative offenses, and some of the so-called victimless crimes where the use of criminal sanctions has long been controversial. Punitive civil penalties can both increase sanctioning power and reduce reliance on criminal law for a range of intermediate offenses, particularly those committed by the middle class in the course of their occupations.

C. Relationship Among Criminal, Punitive Civil, and Remedial Sanctions

The recognition of a new paradigm requires an analysis and appreciation of the interrelationship of the various sanctions, and calls for a refined jurisprudence of their substantive scope, their severity, and the procedures for their imposition.

1. Substantive Scope

In a tripartite structure of paradigms, criminal, punitive civil, and remedial sanctions co-exist. Punishment is meted out in the first two categories; the third category includes both compensatory sanctions and other civil sanctions whose aim is prophylactic rather than punitive. Criminal law derives its character from its relation to punitive civil sanctions and remedial sanctions, just as these other sanctions derive meaning in relation to, and as distinguished from, characteristics of the criminal law. The interrelation of these sanctions affects both their substantive scope and their respective procedural contexts.

A logical and normatively coherent system of sanctions should define each paradigm-criminal, punitive civil, and remedial-in relation to the others, with reference to both the purpose and the severity of the wrongful conduct addressed by each. Different sanctions should apply to wrongs of different magnitudes. The universe of wrongs to which punishment applies should be divided so that criminal law is applicable only to the most severe wrongs, while punitive civil sanctions are limited to other wrongs requiring punishment.

The normative structure of legal sanctions has equally important implications for the relationship between criminal and civil punitive sanctions on the one hand and remedial sanctions on the other. Because of the existence of two paradigms of punitive sanctions, a coherent jurisprudence must first distinguish between civil and criminal processes within the field of punitive sanctions. Second, it must differentiate between conduct for which punitive sanctions are fitting and conduct for which they are inappropriate. Limiting the

scope of punitive sanctions for wrongful conduct creates a definitive substantive area of remedial sanctions that is designed to compensate an injured party or to prevent the occurrence of wrongful conduct through nonpunitive measures. These distinctions properly suggest that punitive and remedial sanctions may be applied to the same conduct, the two sanctions serving different purposes.

Within this tripartite framework, legislatures, administrative agencies, and judges will have to perform a critical task. They must formulate guidelines for the seriousness of offenses that rationally allocate wrongs in the substantive areas of each paradigm, and they must systematically divide the universe of wrongs into criminal, punitive civil, and remedial categories. Broad legislative and administrative guidelines should be developed to rank the seriousness of cases for the purpose of distinguishing criminal and civil punitive sanctions. The interpretation of such guidelines give judges a central role in creating the jurisprudence of punitive sanctions.

2. Are Punitive Civil Sanctions Desirable?

Punitive civil sanctions have long been part of the American law of sanctions. After United States v. Halper, it seems likely that, in many areas of public life, government agencies will increasingly obtain independent power to use them. This Article argues that punitive civil sanctions play a central role in protecting society from both underenforcement and overenforcement of the norms that make up the social order.

The middleground prevents underenforcement by providing a punitive sanction for conduct that, within the two-paradigm structure, would be pushed into the remedial paradigm because it is not severe enough to justify a criminal sanction. The middleground also avoids overenforcement by providing a noncriminal punitive sanction for conduct that otherwise would be pushed into the criminal paradigm because its severity makes it unreasonable to impose only a remedial sanction. In this sense, the middleground allows for more proportionate punitive sanctioning. When punitive civil sanctions are available, cases otherwise confined to the conventional paradigms shift into the middleground, increasing overall sanctioning while reducing reliance on both criminal sanctions and merely remedial sanctions. This increased proportionality argues for expanding the use of punitive civil sanctions, but this development will not be justified until the distortion in procedural protections that has developed within middleground jurisprudence is corrected.

3. Parallel State-Invoked Punitive Sanctions

The historic overlap of criminal and punitive civil authority stemmed not only from the advantages deriving from flexible sanctions, but also from the fact that the integrity of decision making processes drew strength from the checks and balances created by the institutional interdependence of agencies and criminal prosecutors; each decision maker knew that another entity was making many of the same assessments. In addition, the government enjoyed extra leverage over potential defendants by being able to pursue two avenues simultaneously. In parallel enforcement proceedings, defendants risked getting one penalty "ratcheted up" if they obtained a good settlement in the other; to avoid this risk, defendants had to deal with both antagonists at once.

To the extent that these dynamics helped law enforcement, the Halper rule will probably make law enforcement more difficult, though fairer for potential defendants. Under Halper, punitive civil sanctions cannot be imposed for conduct that has already been punished by a criminal conviction. It appears that criminal punishment likewise cannot be imposed for conduct for which the government has already obtained punitive civil sanctions. However, the Halper Court implied that simultaneous imposition of criminal and punitive civil sanctions is valid. But barring a decision to seek both sanctions at the same time, law enforcement authorities must decide which sanction to choose. The old system of postponing the decision, or of pursuing both punitive sanctions at the same time without paying attention to which is imposed first, is no longer feasible.

At a minimum, this development implies that prosecutors and administrative agencies must find new ways to coordinate their actions and establish rules binding on both concerning whom to punish and whether to use criminal or civil sanctions. A key question, then, is how to unify decision making between these two players in meting out punitive sanctions.

Preserving the administrative agency's role in making decisions about sanctioning is critical to the rationalization of punitive sanctions. Administrative agencies have special expertise in identifying and assessing violations. They have firsthand experience with potential offenders and with the substantive law over which they have regulatory authority. This expertise provides them with important advantages in understanding the seriousness of a particular violation. Agency specialization can therefore play a key role in distinguishing cases fit for criminal sanctions from those fit only for punitive civil sanctions, particularly when both kinds of sanctions are available.

Without a jurisprudence of severity, the choice between criminal, punitive civil, and remedial sanctions would be arbitrary. Because of their specialized advantage in making the complex distinctions about severity necessary for equal and proportionate treatment

in a unified system of punitive sanctions, administrative agencies should play a significant role in shaping punitive sanctioning policy. Prosecutors should have to consult administrative agencies before bringing criminal prosecutions. By the same token, however, administrative agencies must also consult prosecutors before imposing punitive civil sanctions, lest they foil plans for a subsequent criminal prosecution. Since the same conduct can often be punished with either criminal or civil sanctions, any solution must include joint decision making.

4. Private Punitive Sanctions

Punitive sanctioning in actions brought by private citizens has recently become a more important element of the entire sanctioning scheme, and the Supreme Court has upheld large punitive damages awards against due process challenges. This trend is desirable because the private version of a punitive civil sanction removes the burden of prosecution from the government, thereby allowing the private sector to fund law enforcement. A system that lets private plaintiffs secure punitive sanctions can save the government money and increase the community's total sanctioning power.

Privately sought punitive sanctions are an integral part of the middleground. In Halper and other cases, the Court has relied on the law of punitive tort damages to justify state-invoked punitive civil sanctions, thereby implicitly recognizing the similarities between state and private punitive sanctions. Understandably, then, many of the issues raised by state-invoked punitive civil sanctions also have implications for privately invoked punitive civil sanctions.

Even though the government may no longer seek additional punitive sanctions for conduct that it has already punished, current law does not prohibit parallel state and private punitive sanctions. A more rational way to organize punitive sanctioning would be to prohibit independent private suits for punitive sanctions if the state used or intended to use punitive sanctions on its own. This system would protect citizens from cumulative punishments. This proposal is even more important in view of recent case law, which indicates that some privately invoked punitive monetary sanctions are more severe than state-invoked punitive monetary sanctions. The tripartite structure proceeds on the idea that the severity of a sanction should guide its classification. If money sanctions disproportionate to the damage caused are punitive enough to raise claims of double jeopardy when the government seeks them after securing other punitive sanctions, it is unclear why the situation should be any different when the subsequent action is brought by a private party rather than the government.

Limiting punitive sanctions to a single judgment,

however, would risk suppressing private initiative because it is often uncertain whether private plaintiffs can complete their cases without government intervention. Compensatory payouts to private plaintiffs might solve this problem. The desire for the simultaneous completion of all sanctioning does not justify sacrificing the advantages of private enforcement suits; unity in decision making requires only that the government and a private party not both invoke punitive sanctions for the same conduct. The government should control the decision of whether itself or a private party will initiate such sanctions, but it need not always assume itself the burden of enforcement. Finally, the interrelationship among different sanctions strongly suggests that private suits for punitive sanctions call for special procedural protections similar to those granted in state-initiated punitive civil proceedings. Heightened protections in private suits, indeed, might even induce legislatures and courts to open the way for more such actions seeking punitive sanctions.

5. A New Procedural Middleground?

Present middleground jurisprudence, including Halper, has blurred normative distinctions underlying the old separation between criminal and civil procedure. In American law, the concept of due process held the state to special tests of accuracy and fairness when it sought to punish-that is, to intrude on an unconsenting individual's privacy and autonomy. The various procedural requirements established and protected a hierarchy of values. Current middleground jurisprudence, however, has weakened this special normative task of procedure.

The Boyd line of cases maintained important differences between procedural rules in punitive civil cases and those in strictly remedial cases. But the Supreme Court's later approaches to middleground jurisprudence moved toward a unified (civil) procedure, eliminating most distinctions between the procedures used in punitive civil cases and those used in remedial cases. As a result, individuals subject to punitive sanctions lost significant procedural protections when their cases were diverted from the criminal to the civil process. The expansion of state-invoked punitive civil sanctions now harms many defendants by shifting the balance of procedural advantages.

This Article argues that the procedure followed in deciding whether to impose a sanction should be related to the function of the sanction. This proposition is based on two core norms of American constitutional due process: (1) the more severe the sanction, the more the procedure must protect against the sanctioning of the innocent, and (2) the more it must protect the accused's dignity and privacy. The logical and normative implications of these ideas are that the

criminal sanction should be contingent on the use of the most stringent procedural rules and that punitive civil sanctions do not demand equally strict procedures. As a corollary, procedural rules for punitive civil sanctions should be more stringent than procedural rules for nonpunitive sanctions.

Congress and the Supreme Court have tended to establish due process requirements using a bipolar distinction between criminal and noncriminal cases, for they have created a middleground procedure that provides very few distinctive protections for defendants in punitive civil proceedings. This bipolarity, however, requires closer scrutiny as punitive civil sanctions become more severe. When one considers the function of severely punitive civil sanctions, our society's normative ideas of procedure strongly suggest that such sanctions should be accompanied by procedural rules that offer extra protection against their erroneous imposition.

This point draws strength from the historical centrality of due process in the American adversary system. Should that system allow a person to be deprived of his or her life savings and home in an administrative hearing? Should it permit a potentially bankrupting treble penalty for alleged insider trading in a civil procedural setting with minimal barriers to sanctioning? What about the forfeiture of a person's home for growing marijuana in the backyard? As the availability of civil monetary sanctions increases, so does the possibility that the application of such a sanction will deeply affect the life of a person or corporation. American constitutional law's vision of due process strongly suggests the need for an independent mix of procedural rules for middleground jurisprudence.

CONCLUSION

Two paradigms, criminal and civil law, have long dominated the American law of sanctions. Judges and lawmakers have used these terms to represent sharp and well-defined differences in the nature of the legal process used to redress wrongs. But between these two paradigms there has always been a middleground in which legislatures and courts sought punitive ends through nominally civil proceedings. The history of middleground jurisprudence demonstrates the inadequacy of the bipolar paradigms for governing actual sanctioning policy. While the legal community has always recognized that many sanctions do not fit into either paradigm, it has never developed a systematic jurisprudence to explain the substantive and procedural position of punitive civil sanctions within the field of sanctioning.

Since at least the early nineteenth century, Congress has granted federal administrative agencies the power to impose punitive sanctions in civil procedural settings, first through the initiation of lawsuits in courts and later through purely administrative assessment. As the federal bureaucracy has grown, the power to impose punitive civil sanctions has been extended to more executive offices and independent agencies. At the same time, punitive sanctions have become more severe: what were once penalties of hundreds of dollars are now penalties of hundreds of thousands of dollars.

In Halper, the Court suggested that there is neither any limit on the permissible punitiveness of monetary civil sanctions, nor any special procedural requirements for the imposition of such sanctions. The Court may have intended to sever the relationship between the severity of civil sanctions and procedural protections in civil law, which can only worry those who seek to protect due process values. This procedural erosion calls for the resurrection and extension of a middleground that connects procedural rights with the severity of sanctions.

But the existing framework of punitive civil monetary sanctions must be criticized not only for the inadequate procedural protections it provides for defendants, but also for the inadequate severity of the sanctions allowed. Lawmakers may have resisted increasing the size of money sanctions when they expected that citizens would be protected only by run-of-the-mill procedures. An appropriate procedural setting, however, would permit substantial growth in the size and effectiveness of money sanctions. This development should also correct the currently excessive reach of the criminal law, while concurrently reducing the proportion of cases that escape punitive sanctions altogether because a criminal sanction is inappropriate and a middleground solution is unavailable.

However, a tripartite law of sanctions, with a large middleground of punitive civil sanctions, carries the potential for two serious problems. First, if offenders will be punished where previously they would have been liable only for compensation, we may be creating a draconian regime. The development of appropriate procedural protections should help protect against this evil, but the very existence of a broad range of highly punitive civil sanctions may create dangers that procedural rules can only soften. Protection against overextension must be a primary concern of those who cultivate the middleground.

Second, punitive civil sanctions might carry a socioeconomic bias. By their very nature, punitive civil money sanctions are effective only against those who can pay. Such sanctions therefore will focus on crimes characteristic of the middle and upper classes-typically crimes of fraud, embezzlement, theft by deceit, violation of trust, and drug offenses, along with the whole range of offenses committed by corporations. An enhanced regime of punitive civil sanctions will not be effective against poor people who commit crimes; while the middleground sanctions should help to keep some people out of prison, those who cannot pay will go to prison. This would only exacerbate the existing inequality. Scaling money sanctions to financial resources, so that the sanctions impose roughly equivalent burdens on populations of varying wealth, may somewhat limit this problem. Yet there will always be a bankrupt population for whom the only answer is imprisonment. The need to preserve equality of treatment may thus require the imprisonment of rich people too, even when money sanctions against them would otherwise suffice. This solution would not contradict any of the basic tenets of the middleground, for I have not argued that punitive civil money sanctions should replace prison in every instance in which the defendant can pay. Indeed, society's basic retributive needs will always call for the use of demonstrative public sanctions such as imprisonment against at least some offenders.

Abraham S. Goldstein, *White Collar Crime and Civil Sanctions,* 101 YALE L.J. 1895–1899 (1992)*

In his comprehensive review and assessment of "punitive civil sanctions," Professor Kenneth Mann has shown us that the prosecution of white-collar crime is being transformed. The criminal law is now being used not only to imprison offenders but also to provide the basis for financial remedies, such as forfeiture, profit-fines, and restitution. Probation is being used to impose conditions on businessmen and corporations, making it the functional counterpart of injunctive remedies. And civil damage actions are being brought to supplement criminal cases-sometimes for treble damages or for punitive damages. Either the state or the victims of the offenses, alone or in class actions, may bring these damage actions. There is even talk of allowing private parties once again to initiate certain kinds of criminal prosecutions, in addition to or in lieu of the state.

* Reprinted by permission of The Yale Law Journal Company and Fred B. Rothman & Company from *The Yale Law Journal,* Vol. 101, pages 1895-1897.

The conduct ordinarily described as white-collar crime is under attack in all the ways available to the regulatory state-through criminal, civil, and administrative law. The objective seems to be to achieve the state's regulatory purpose unimpeded by the "technical" limits imposed by criminal law or criminal procedure. This results in the erosion of formal distinctions between "criminal" and "civil" actions. The erosion, by collapsing traditional categories, has created a serious risk that the central role of criminal law in a system of sanctions may be compromised or even lost.

In this Comment, I would like to supplement Professor Mann's observations by describing some of the currents in criminal law, criminology, and public opinion that have brought us to our present situation.

I

The central concepts of what we now regard as a distinctive body of criminal law emerged from cases involving crimes of passion, violence, and theft. These concepts take as their model the genuinely culpable individual who "deserves" to be used for the criminal law's purposes-whose condemnation will assuage retributive impulses, deter potential offenders, reinforce legal norms, and lead to incarceration of the demonstrably dangerous. Much of contemporary scholarly writing embraces this model and treats it as fundamental, as inherent in the very concept of crime. To lack culpability (blameworthiness), it is said, is not to be a criminal at all. The underlying assumptions are that criminal law is less concerned with social control of deviant behavior than with defining who should be used in that effort, and that criminal law is a technique of social control which is to be used sparingly- with a wholesome regard for its stigmatizing power and the extraordinary pains imposed by imprisonment.

This attitude underlies the very important United States Supreme Court opinion, Morissette v. United States. In that case, the Court held that mens rea was required for criminal liability even when the statute creating the crime does not use any of the talismanic words of mens rea, such as malice, intent, knowledge, or recklessness. In effect, the Court said that a legislature must virtually negate the mens rea requirement before it will construe a statute as having imposed strict liability. The Model Penal Code of the American Law Institute (ALI) has largely adopted this position: if the state wishes to punish conduct without a showing of some mens rea, it must call the conduct a violation, not a crime; it may not imprison the offender; and it may impose only de minimis sanctions.

Those who embrace the dominant theory have treated as virtually illegitimate the older lines of cases that reflected an entirely different theory-one that focused more on achieving social control than on assessing personal culpability. This secondary theory is exemplified in the opinions of English and American courts dealing with offenses like bigamy and adultery-older versions of what we now tend to call public welfare offenses. Those opinions reflected a willingness on the part of courts and legislatures to abandon, or at least to limit sharply, a subjective theory of liability when necessary to achieve important social objectives. As Holmes pointed out in his famous essay The Criminal Law, from the beginnings of our criminal law, courts have not hesitated to impose criminal liability on those who are only objectively liable. And that perspective has endured to the present day. Our Supreme Court has upheld the imposition of strict liability, or liability for negligence or vicarious liability, for offenses carrying very heavy prison sentences. Those cases, like the earlier ones, assume that to achieve social control it may be necessary to abandon the mens rea requirement or to keep notions of subjective culpability to a minimum.

The two theories of criminal liability-one emphasizing social control and the other stressing personal culpability-have long been competing for primacy, most conspicuously in the law of traditional crimes. Doctrines based on objective theories of liability (like the felony murder rule or vicarious responsibility) have met fierce criticism. For the most part, the advocates of personal culpability and strict procedures have won the contest. But in doing so, they have tended to carry their critique beyond the traditional crimes to which it had been addressed-the crimes of passion and violence and theft. These crimes are indeed "personal" and are easy targets for a subjective theory. It is less clear that the subjectivist critique has equal application to the new types of crimes. These are usually characterized by vague definitions and by the abandonment or reduction of the mens rea requirement, as legislatures try to respond to the pressures of the Industrial Revolution and the regulatory state. Nevertheless, the academic community and the ALI have tended to describe the law on the books as if it had already accepted the subjective theory of liability across the board.

This apparent consensus has made legislatures, courts, and prosecutors reluctant to use criminal law to achieve the kind of social control that is the raison d'etre of many of the new regulatory crimes. Thus, by narrowing the boundaries of the area that may or should be reached by criminal law, the reformers have created strong pressures on the courts either (1) to stretch criminal law beyond the newly proper ("subjectivist") boundaries, or (2) to avoid the constraints associated with criminal law and criminal procedure by abandoning the criminal law as a regulatory tool. The latter course, abandonment, would obviously be easier if civil measures were available that could do better, and more efficiently, the work of criminal law in the specialized areas associated with white-collar crime.

II

The increasing prominence of civil sanctions also receives support from Edwin Sutherland's influential theory of white-collar crime and from the populist impulses latent in that theory. In his studies of high status individuals who had violated the law, Sutherland counted as crimes events that "were rarely prosecuted in criminal court: they were violations of administrative rules or simply contract cases to be processed, if at all, in civil court." In his view, it was overly technical to act as if crimes do not exist because they have not led to prosecution and conviction. He also believed that the criminal charge was an especially unreliable guide to the nature and extent of crime because white-collar offenders were prosecuted less often and punished less severely than ordinary offenders were. Sutherland's work on white-collar crime provides a direct link to a regulatory approach that locates criminal law alongside the other methods of controlling deviant behavior. A corollary of that approach is that policy makers in complex economic and technological areas must take into account that, for those persons whose conduct they are trying to reach, the fruits of offending outweigh the harm of punishment. From this perspective, the difficulty of effectuating public policy against such offenders makes it necessary to augment the criminal law with a wider range of sanctions and processes.

The connotation of the term "white-collar crime" has had a powerful effect on public attitudes and on the content of criminal law and criminal procedure. The term evokes a highly emotive image of great corporations and those who run them making all of us their victims-overcharging us for our purchases, polluting our environment, and making us less safe so that they may make more money. These are the consummately rational offenders who know what they are doing to us, who are motivated by greed, and who get away with their conniving. In dealing with such offenders, the argument continues, the criminal law is beset with technicalities that sacrifice regulatory objectives on the altar of a pure doctrine of personal culpability. That doctrine may have a place in conventional criminal law where a wide array of sociological and psychological "explanations" for crime exists and where defendants are seen as poor and untutored, often abused by the police, and needing protection from excessive interrogation and arbitrary searches. For such defendants, it may seem appropriate to indulge in doctrines favoring innocence. White-collar offenders, on the other hand, are widely perceived as deserving little or no sympathy because of their status, wealth, and education.

The spotlight that the social science literature and the popular media have focused on alleged favoritism for the affluent has contributed to a reduction in the protections accorded to defendants in cases of white-collar crime. Notions of personal guilt are readily abandoned as negligence, strict liability, and vicarious liability are routinely put to use. Concepts like "enterprise" and "pattern of racketeering activity" are permitted to take their places alongside "conspiracy" as even looser vehicles for imposing group and vicarious liability. The maxim that criminal statutes must be construed strictly is often replaced with a principle of liberal construction in favor of the government. The law of presumptions is stretched to make up for expected difficulties of proof in complex cases. And the courts tolerate an extraordinary measure of vagueness in defining crime. Reducing these protections has provided an incentive to "decriminalize" white-collar offenses- by adding more easily applied and substitutable civil sanctions-not out of sympathy for these offenders but to be "tougher" on them and to regulate their conduct more effectively.

III

What we now have is a helter-skelter cumulation of processes and sanctions. Civil processes and sanctions have emerged that are often more punitive than criminal processes but equally stigmatizing. Yet civil sanctions may bring with them fewer procedural protections than do criminal sanctions: they may be established by a preponderance of evidence, and need not meet the proof beyond a reasonable doubt standard; they may be instituted by private parties without being screened by a public prosecutor serving as surrogate for the public interest; and they may be tried by a judge rather than a jury.

Professor Mann has demonstrated that we are at a critical divide. We who teach and write on criminal law have been so absorbed with traditional crimes that we have slighted a new field that competes directly with the criminal law and threatens to supplant it. The challenge now is to separate out the several strands-to recognize that each civil and criminal remedy is part of a network of sanctions designed to control deviant behavior; to provide screening mechanisms to determine which sanctions should be brought to bear, and by whom, in order to make law enforcement more effective overall; and to create the hybrid procedures uniquely appropriate to each of these hybrid processes. If we do not succeed in meeting this challenge, there is a genuine risk that the stigma and sanctions associated with "crime" will be imposed, in both civil and criminal processes, on persons who are not culpable in any widely accepted sense of that term. If that happens, if offenders who do not match the public image of criminality are too casually found to be criminal, the "crime" label will lose its incremental utility, the moral force of the criminal sanction will be dissipated, and many more people will suffer unjust treatment.

Mary M. Cheh, *Constitutional Limits in Using Civil Remedies to Achieve Criminal Law Objectives: Understanding and Transcending the Criminal-Civil Distinction,* 42 HASTINGS L.J. 1325–1366 (1991)*

I. Introduction

Today, the distinction between criminal and civil law seems to be collapsing across a broad front. Although the separation between criminal and civil cases is a legal creation both imperfect and incomplete, this basic division has been a hallmark of English and American jurisprudence for hundreds of years.

The Constitution, statutes, and the common law all draw fundamental distinctions between criminal proceedings, which emphasize adjudication of guilt or innocence with strict adversarial protections for the accused, and civil proceedings, which emphasize the rights and responsibilities of private parties. We have separate criminal and civil courts, employing different rules of procedure, burdens of proof, rules of discovery, investigatory practices, and modes of punishment. This distinction is cemented in every law student's mind by the division of the law school curriculum into criminal and civil categories.

Now, however, there is a rapidly accelerating tendency for the government to punish antisocial behavior with civil remedies such as injunctions, forfeitures, restitution, and civil fines. Sometimes civil approaches completely supplant criminal prosecutions as certain behavior is "decriminalized," or as offenders are treated as ill instead of guilty. More frequently, civil remedies are blended with or used to supplement criminal sanctions, as evidenced by the widespread use of forfeiture in drug cases.

Many states are using civil law techniques to check domestic violence, drug trafficking, weapons possession, and racial harassment. The federal government,

through the Racketeer Influenced and Corrupt Organizations Act (RICO), is using divestiture and treble damage actions to strike at businesses run by white collar criminals and members of organized crime. The federal government also has reinvigorated the qui tam action, which effectively deputizes private citizens to enforce monetary penalties against persons who have defrauded the government.

The idea of using civil remedies to redress criminal behavior is not new. A criminal who injured or robbed another traditionally faced two potential trials – a criminal prosecution by the government to adjudge her guilty and punish her for the offense, and a civil action by the victim for recompense. Similarly, in the administrative or regulatory sphere, the federal government long has pursued antitrust and securities law violators with civil injunctions as well as criminal complaints. Yet the current phenomenon of civil remedies blending with criminal sanctions never has been more actively or consciously pursued.

Forfeiture is a case in point. The United States Attorney General has declared forfeiture a top priority and even has created the Executive Office of Asset Forfeiture to oversee all aspects of the Justice Department's forfeiture efforts. The federal government's use of forfeiture to seize the proceeds and instruments of crime has grown so spectacularly that in 1989 alone the amounts forfeited – over $600 million worth of currency, cars, planes, boats, and even cattle – are twenty times the amounts forfeited just four years earlier. In the past five years, combined state and federal efforts have stripped more than one billion dollars from drug dealers, and the states are working to adopt a model forfeiture statute that would further expand their power and the opportunities to seize property used in crime.

This melding of civil remedies and criminal penalties portends significant changes in both legal doctrine and the institutions which are charged with applying and enforcing criminal law. When officials take into account the objectives of deterrence, recompense, and retribution, as well as the reality of scarce resources, their range of possible responses to antisocial behavior now includes a full spectrum of criminal and civil remedies. Determining the proper mix of these remedies in order to address a particular problem presents subtle policy questions and requires resolution of conflicting goals. Moreover, efforts to mix and match criminal and civil sanctions, especially in a single proceeding, undoubtedly will require procedural and jurisdictional reforms. Indeed, viewing antisocial behavior as a problem to be met, managed, and resolved by whatever civil or criminal tools promising may trigger a reexamination of how prosecutors' offices are perceived and organized.

This Article primarily focuses on another consequence of the melding of civil and criminal remedies: the pressures brought to bear on individual rights by the proliferation of civil supplements operating in tandem with the criminal law. Police and prosecutors have embraced civil strategies not only because they expand the arsenal of weapons available to reach antisocial behavior, but also because officials believe that civil remedies offer speedy solutions that are unencumbered by the rigorous constitutional protections associated with criminal trials, such as proof beyond a reasonable doubt, trial by jury, and appointment of counsel. A persistent question remains regarding the use of civil remedies to check antisocial behavior: what constitutional limits constrain their use?

One difficulty in ascertaining the appropriate constitutional limitations is determining whether a particular proceeding is criminal or civil. Several protections of the Bill of Rights are expressly limited to "any criminal case" or "all criminal prosecutions," or, conversely, are confined to "suits at common law" or civil cases. Other provisions, though not expressly limited to criminal cases, have been so interpreted by case law.

Commentators have devoted considerable energy to this engaging and nettlesome issue. They frequently recognize that it is extremely difficult to draw principled lines to distinguish between criminal and civil cases. Moreover, attempting to fit all cases neatly into one category or the other, though sometimes necessary and useful, can cause a good deal of mischief. If "criminal case" is defined too broadly, then the cumbersome baggage of criminal procedure will be carried into a wide range of government and private lawsuits. If it is defined too narrowly, then the values that underlie various constitutional provisions will be sacrificed simply because they arise in a proceeding denominated as civil. Perceiving this dilemma, the Supreme Court sometimes has struggled to unravel its doctrine from the tangled embrace of the dichotomy. For example, in deciding what constitutes double punishment under the double jeopardy clause, the Court recently declined to rest its decision on whether the punishments arose in a criminal or civil proceeding. It found that such an approach was too "abstract" and not adequately responsive to the "humane interests" safeguarded by the double jeopardy clause.

This Article examines the constitutional issues presented by the criminal-civil "mix and match" phenomenon by offering and applying a workable test for distinguishing between civil and criminal cases. At the same time, it aspires to confine the importance of that distinction to a limited subset of constitutional problems. Part II surveys the types of civil remedies now used both to complement and to supplement the enforcement of the criminal laws. Part III explores and criticizes various bases for distinguishing between civil and criminal cases, and offers an alternative, narrow test that, with few exceptions, will follow the legislature's label.

More specifically, Part III explains why, in all but two kinds of cases, the legislature's declaration must be the exclusive determinant of whether a proceeding is civil or criminal. A legislative label approach is consistent with much of what the courts have done, and it offers a workable, bright-line test. More fundamentally, it recognizes that criminal proceedings are more than just a means of punishing specific persons; they are officially designated ceremonies of guilt adjudication. As such, they express society's ideology of individual free will and personal responsibility and serve as a reaffirmation of moral rules.

This Article explores and ultimately rejects other means of distinguishing between civil and criminal cases, such as comparing the severity of the sanctions involved, assessing the degree of stigma associated with particular proceedings, or ascertaining whether a proceeding operates to punish. Not only are these approaches inconsistent with precedent and almost impossible to implement in a predictable or principled way, but they also fail to take into account society's vital interest in criminal proceedings.

Part IV of this Article argues that, in any event, the criminal-civil distinction should play only a limited role in preserving constitutional liberties. I argue that, on the constitutional level, the distinction only matters where the issues involve the proper procedures or burdens of proof to apply in a particular case. Thus, for example, the sixth amendment's requirements of a trial by jury and appointment of counsel, and the fifth amendment's due process requirements of proof beyond a reasonable doubt and the presumption of innocence, need only apply in criminal cases. Other constitutional provisions, such as the protections against double jeopardy and excessive fines, as well as freedom from self-incrimination, although traditionally limited to criminal cases, should not be so confined. Indeed, one of the consequences of the recent extension of civil responses to criminal behavior has been the nascent refashioning of constitutional doctrine along these lines.

Part V of this Article observes that, so long as we continue to draw distinctions between civil and criminal cases, there are likely to be unique constitutional harms caused by using both criminal and civil proceedings as parallel means of checking antisocial behavior. That is, if civil and criminal cases, however defined, follow different rules of procedure, burdens of proof, and rules of discovery, the mere prosecution of simultaneous civil and criminal actions may force defendants to compromise constitutional protections in one forum in order to preserve advantages in the other. For example, if a defendant is forced to admit ownership of property in order to resist its forfeiture in a civil proceeding, she may thereby waive her privilege of self-incrimination in a concurrent criminal action.

In Part VI, I show how the unfair and oppressive effects sometimes produced by certain proceedings, despite the fact that they are constitutionally deemed civil, can be checked by a more vigorous judicial application of due process norms. Just as the rise of the "new property" in the 1960s and 1970s led to a recasting of due process and an eclipse of older ideas; so now, the rise of the "new penalties" may trigger a more vigorous application of due process protections.

Finally, the Article concludes with a look at one particular civil remedy, the use of civil protection orders in domestic violence cases. Such orders, now widely available, are obtained in civil proceedings but, like criminal law proscriptions, are enforced with arrest, prosecution, and incarceration. By looking at the use of these orders, we can see how a new understanding of the distinction between criminal and civil cases, including an understanding of when the distinction is and is not constitutionally relevant, permits a more systematic and complete accounting of the constitutional dangers posed by hybrid criminal-civil proceedings.

II. The Interplay of Civil and Criminal Remedies

A criminal justice system seeks to prevent crime, but, failing that, to find and punish offenders. While there always have been a variety of means to pursue these objectives, the traditional criminal justice response has been arrest, prosecution, and incarceration. For a long time, the conscious and systematic blending of criminal and civil remedies as part of a single law enforcement strategy has been pursued primarily by regulatory agencies in fields such as antitrust, securities trading, and customs control.

That generalization is, however, no longer true. Because of the changing nature of crime, the proven inadequacy of conventional law enforcement methods, and the demonstrated success of laws like RICO and the asset forfeiture rules for drug cases, criminal justice officials are energetically pursuing multiple strategies to prevent and punish criminal acts. The following section catalogs the ways that civil remedies can be used to achieve criminal justice goals. And it shows that these instances are not isolated, unrelated phenomena; rather, taken together, they represent a new way of looking at criminal justice issues.

A. How Civil Remedies Complement Criminal Law Objectives

The civil law is rich in remedies. It offers compensatory damages, punitive damages, restitution, specific performance, injunctive relief, constructive trusts, abatement of nuisances, and forfeitures. In the regulatory sphere, the government has adapted all of these remedies as means of enforcing a wide range of rules and regulations. In the criminal justice arena, the same adaptive process is underway.

There are three distinct ways to accomplish this adaptation. First, civil remedies can be incorporated into a criminal proceeding. Forfeiture or restitution, for example, can be prescribed as part of a criminal sentence. Second, the civil remedy can be chosen as an explicit alternative to criminal prosecution. A legislature may consider certain antisocial behavior, such as motor vehicle driving offenses, too petty to be criminal, and yet seek to deter or punish infractions. Or a legislature may consider certain offenses, like racial harassment, too difficult to prove under the strict procedural rules applicable to the criminally accused. It even may believe that some harms, like spousal abuse, are better dealt with as mental health or family law matters. Third, civil remedies may be used as supplements to criminal sanctions. In this case, the government may seek a civil remedy, a criminal penalty, or both. The same activity that forms the basis for a criminal prosecution also serves as the basis for a civil sanction. In other words, the civil remedy is linked directly to the underlying criminal activity. What follows is a brief survey of particular civil remedies and a description of how each is now used to complement enforcement of the criminal law.

B. Varieties of Civil Remedies

(1) Restitution and Recompense

Persons injured by the criminal conduct of others may bring a civil action for damages. In such actions, as in any other form of civil action, the victim must initiate the suit and bear the costs and burdens associated with maintaining and enforcing it. The legal system has responded to the victim's plight by trying to lighten these burdens. The federal government and most states permit courts to require restitution by criminal defendants either as part of their sentences or as a condition of probation. Less formally, the fact that a criminal has made restitution often figures in police and prosecutorial decisions to reduce charges or not to charge at all.

When restitution remedies are incorporated into the criminal justice system, an important question arises: must the amount of restitution be limited to the sum that is the basis of the conviction? State courts and commentators have taken many approaches to this question and have answered it differently. But, whether or not limited in total amount, restitution may take forms other than money damages. For example, courts may order restitutionary relief in the form of a constructive trust on property fraudulently transferred, a reformation of instruments, or the reconveyance of property fraudulently transferred.

A variety of statutes permit the government, like ordinary citizens, to recover the damages and costs it incurs as a result of a criminal act. The government may have "rough compensatory justice" or "remedial recovery" for destruction of government property, losses from fraud or theft of government property, interest and costs associated with collecting back taxes, or damages to public interests such as to the environment. Governmental recovery via restitution, compensation, and remediation, like that of an ordinary citizen, can be effected through a separate lawsuit, or directly incorporated into the criminal justice system.

Sometimes the government's recovery, through compensation or remediation, includes the criminal's gains received as a result of her unlawful conduct. The recovery of such profits and proceeds can be viewed broadly as compensatory, even though there may not be a specific victim beneficiary. The idea is more to deprive the wrong-doer of her ill-gotten gains than it is to restore any particular person to a status quo ante. In some cases, however, the pursuit of proceeds may become so far removed from the underlying wrong that it no longer retains its compensatory nature. Rather it becomes a punitive measure akin to a statutory penalty or fine.

(2) Statutory Fines and Penalties

There exists a variety of statutory regimes that prescribe or prohibit certain conduct and impose monetary penalties or fines for violations. Examples include tax laws, environmental regulations, securities trading statutes, and workplace safety rules.

Sometimes the fine or penalty under these laws takes the form of a double or treble damage award. In other cases, there may be a fine for each day of violation or simply a flat fee for each infraction. Sometimes a private citizen can initiate and litigate the penalty action against the offender, though the government ultimately enforces the penalty.

Civil fines or monetary penalties are used frequently as alternatives to criminal prosecution. If, for example, a legislature decides to decriminalize certain conduct, such as possession of small amounts of marijuana, it may, nevertheless, maintain some punishment to deter such behavior. A schedule of money penalties may seem more appropriate than a misdemeanor prosecution. Or, the regulated conduct may never have been deemed criminal but always have been considered sufficiently undesirable to warrant some form of deterrence. The common system of motor vehicle parking citations and fines presents a good example.

Sometimes the proscribed activity, such as nonpayment of taxes, insider trading, or restraint of trade, is subject to both civil and criminal sanctions. In such cases the civil regime directly supplements the criminal law, and an offender faces two separate systems of sanctions. The linkage between civil and criminal law may be so direct that recovery under the civil law is made dependent upon the plaintiff proving that the defendant committed the criminal act with criminal intent. In a civil RICO suit, for example, a private person may recover treble damages for harms caused by a pattern of racketeering, but only if she can show that the defendant committed certain "predicate" crimes such as murder, arson, or fraud.

Although civil fines and other equivalent monetary penalties—much like liquidated damages—can operate as a form of restitution or recompense, many are meant to punish. They operate as a kind of punitive damages exacted for society's benefit.

(3) Loss of Government Benefits and Privileges

In our modern administrative state the government controls valuable opportunities through its power to confer benefits, employment, and licenses. Ordinarily, the loss of government benefits is not incorporated directly into a criminal proceeding as part of the defendant's sentence. Rather, the loss occurs collaterally. A recipient can lose a benefit or privilege automatically upon conviction of a crime. A conviction also can be used as evidence of lack of "good moral character" or "unfitness" in a later disbarment, license revocation, or disqualification proceeding. For example, three airline pilots recently were convicted under a new federal law that makes it a crime to fly a jetliner while under the influence of alcohol. The convictions followed the pilots' dismissal by the airline and the suspension of their licenses by the Federal Aviation Administration.

There is almost no limit to the creativity of Congress in thinking of ways to sanction participants in government-regulated activities. Consider, for instance, recently proposed amendments to the Federal Food, Drug, and Cosmetic Act. The proposals provide for debarment, civil monetary penalties, and suspension of drug approvals for fraud or corruption occurring in connection with applications to the Food and Drug Administration.

Regulatory sanctions can and often do operate wholly outside of the criminal law. Nevertheless, regulatory enforcement can complement criminal law enforcement in two ways. First, in those areas where antisocial behavior violates both regulatory and criminal law norms, the regulatory sanction can provide an alternative to prosecution, such as where prosecution seems too expensive or presents insurmountable proof problems. Second, even if the government prosecutes, it also may seek regulatory sanctions to remove a criminal offender (and perhaps her associates and her business) from the regulated industry.

(4) Forfeitures

The most popular "new" remedy for law enforcement officials is the very old remedy of forfeiture. Federal and state authorities have seized houses, boats, cars, apartment leaseholds, guns, and even entire businesses, under laws that permit forfeiture of property that is used for or derived from criminal activity.

Currently, the prominent targets for forfeiture are assets used by those who engage in drug trafficking and narcotics use. But the breadth of state and federal forfeiture statutes permits the seizure of property acquired in violation of antitrust laws, property used for illegal gambling, vehicles used in violation of liquor laws, guns or other equipment used unlawfully in national parks, and property smuggled in violation of customs laws. Many states have generalized forfeiture statutes that permit the seizure of virtually any property used as an instrumentality of a crime.

Since forfeiture is the "divestiture without compensation of property used in a manner contrary to the laws of the sovereign," property can be forfeited even if the underlying activity is not defined by law as criminal. Examples of this type of activity include selling adulterated food and importing banned products from disfavored countries. Thus, forfeiture can be used as an alternative to the criminal justice system; indeed, forfeitures are a pervasive mode of regulatory enforcement.

Under both state and federal law, property may be forfeited either as a punishment imposed in a criminal proceeding (criminal forfeiture), or as part of a separate civil proceeding (civil forfeiture). There are important differences between these two types of forfeiture.

Criminal forfeitures are in personam proceedings instituted as part of the criminal case against a defendant. The forfeiture affects only the interests of the defendant in the property. Because criminal forfeiture is a part of the criminal process, all of the rights defendants enjoy in criminal cases, such as proof beyond a reasonable doubt, attend the proceeding. Generally, the property may not be seized until the defendant has been found guilty of the offense and there is a finding of forfeiture by the trier of fact.

A civil forfeiture is an in rem proceeding. It is an action brought against the property, not against any particular person having an interest in the property. Historically, the proceeding was justified by the legal fiction that the property itself was guilty of wrongdoing. In a civil forfeiture action, the government seizes property, often summarily, and persons with an interest in the property must sue to recover it. In order to do so, they may either prove that the property is not subject to forfeiture, or show that, although subject to forfeiture, the property should be returned to the owner because she had no knowledge of its illicit use.

Forfeiture can be divided into three separate categories based on the kind of property seized and the rationale for seizing it. First, there is "contraband": anything prohibited by law from being imported, exported, or even possessed. Forfeiture is allowed because the property itself is "guilty," being a prohibited article in which there may be no traffic. The customs and import laws, for example, are enforced by summary forfeiture both of contraband and of any vehicle in which contraband is transported. Just about anything can be contraband if the legislature so designates it. Some examples are: adulterated and misbranded products, narcotics, counterfeit money, firearms, and cars with falsified identification numbers.

Second, there are "instrumentalities": any property used to produce, store, or transport contraband. This category also includes "any property intended for use in violating the provisions of the internal revenue laws." The definition of instrumentality has been expanded considerably in recent years. Originally intended to reach property that actually was used to commit a crime, it now includes any property having even the most tangential connection to criminal activity, such as real property where a crime was planned. Under this broad definition, the government has gone so far as to seize leaseholds as "instrumentalities."

Third, there are "proceeds" or "profits" derived from illegal activity. This category includes the profits from a business fraudulently obtained, as well as any enterprise or goods in which money from criminal activities has been invested. The idea is to recover the ill-gotten gains of criminal behavior and not permit the criminal to profit from her misconduct. As has been the case with the definitions of "contraband" and "instrumentalities," however, the concept of "profits" or "proceeds," especially in relation to enterprise forfeiture, has been stretched far beyond its original boundaries so that the value of profits or proceeds may exceed the criminal's ill-gotten gains. For example, an entire business enterprise can be forfeited if the defendant has committed crimes in his management or conduct of it.

Civil forfeiture is quick, easy to use, and expansive in scope. It is also highly lucrative. In 1988, for example, Broward County, Florida seized property valued at almost four million dollars. About one fourth of that total was kept by county law enforcement agents for use in their departments. Florida, like many other jurisdictions, permits law enforcement agencies to benefit directly from aggressive forfeiture efforts. These features have made civil forfeiture enormously attractive to law enforcement personnel. However, the harsh effects of forfeiture, particularly on innocent persons, have drawn increasing attention and critical review.

(5) Injunctions and Civil Protection Orders

Despite the seeming variety, many of the recent innovations in using civil proceedings to address criminal or antisocial behavior actually draw upon an ancient and familiar remedy: the injunction. An injunction is a court order that directs a particular defendant to do or to refrain from doing specific acts. The order is enforced through a contempt proceeding. Injunctions take many forms, including: civil protection orders used to protect persons from domestic violence; orders to abate nuisances caused by maintaining premises where illegal activity, such as drug dealing, has occurred; and orders to cease gang activity or interference with another's civil rights. Indeed, many of the "new" law-enforcement schemes are simply modern adaptations of statutes which have been on the books for decades.

Injunctive relief also has been incorporated into criminal proceedings in the form of conditions imposed before a confined person will be released. Judges long have used the imposition of conditions to qualify a criminal defendant's release pending trial and as part of a criminal defendant's sentence of probation. Defendants, on pain of losing their freedom, sometimes are required to undergo drug tests, stay at home after dark, get a job, make restitution to the victim of the crime, or perform community service.

Increasingly, injunctive relief is being used as an alternative or as a supplement to criminal prosecution. For example, some states have enacted statutes that permit abused spouses to seek a court order enjoining further mistreatment. Sometimes an injunction can be sought for activity that alone is not criminal, in which case the regime operates as a remedy apart from the criminal law. Sometimes an order may be sought even though the conduct on which it is based constitutes a crime, such as simple or aggravated assault. In such circumstances, the injunction operates as a supplement to the criminal statutes.

(6) Detention and Civil Commitment

Although we ordinarily associate the loss of physical liberty, through confinement, detention, or jailing with criminal sanctions, such deprivations also may be permitted in what the United States Supreme Court has called "regulatory" contexts. The Court has approved such regulatory measures as pretrial detention, detention during wartime and insurrection, detention of resident aliens pending deportation proceedings, post-arrest detention of juveniles, detention of criminal defendants who are incompetent to stand trial, and the involuntary commitment of mentally ill persons who are a danger to themselves or to others. Although most of these types of confinement last for a relatively short period of time, some, such as the confinement of the mentally ill, can turn out to be life sentences.

The linkage between the involuntary commitment of a person who is mentally ill and the criminal justice system often can be quite close. Some statutes recognize the commission of a criminal act as a predicate for commitment and have even been interpreted to permit committed individuals to be housed in the state penitentiary. Involuntary civil commitment can be used to confine and treat a person who is not competent to stand trial or is found not guilty by reason of insanity. More generally, commitment of the dangerously mentally ill may be the only means of protecting society when proving a criminal case is impossible.

C. The Appeal of Civil Remedies

There are many reasons why legislators and other governmental officials are embracing greater use of civil remedies to respond to criminal or antisocial behavior. Civil remedies can increase the degree of punishment inflicted on a wrongdoer. If the offender faces both a civil and a criminal sanction, the double liability may satisfy a perceived need for greater retribution or enhanced deterrence. In some instances, however, double punishments may not be constitutionally permissible. In that event, a legislature need not rely on parallel civil proceedings to increase punishment. It can simply prescribe a harsher criminal sanction.

The wider use of civil remedies also may increase the incidence of punishment by increasing the likelihood that offenders will be pursued. In general, civil remedies are easier to use, more efficient, and less costly than criminal prosecutions. When authorities can act with a greater potential for success and with less expense and use of resources, there is greater likelihood that they will act. The theory here may be that half a loaf really is better than none. That is, although an offender may not face the full force of the criminal law because a prosecution is too costly or guilt beyond a reasonable doubt cannot be proved, she will still be held accountable in some fashion.

If due process and other constitutional guarantees are refashioned or simply applied more rigorously to civil proceedings, the benefits of greater efficacy and efficiency may be somewhat diminished. And if the government elects to pursue both a criminal and a civil action against an offender, the civil proceeding actually may prove to be inefficient. There is evidence, for example, that Congress expanded the use of criminal forfeiture in drug cases to include property of the defendant "used, or intended to be used, in any manner or part, to commit, or to facilitate the commission of, such violation" precisely because it would be more convenient to avoid holding both a criminal trial and a civil forfeiture proceeding.

Furthermore, certain civil remedies offer opportunities to respond directly to politically active groups, including groups of victims' rights of spousal abuse and racial harassment. The expanded use of the restitution remedy, for example, is a direct response to the victims' rights movement. Of course, civil remedies are not the only way, and may not always be the best way, to provide relief or demonstrate that special efforts are being made on a group's behalf. The criminal justice system can achieve these goals by creating special offices or special prosecution priorities.

The special contributions of civil remedies would seem to lie elsewhere. First, when civil remedies are used as an alternative to criminal remedies, it is possible to reserve a special province for criminal justice and the criminal sanction. Criminal law can focus on serious transgressions and harms involving culpable conduct, not merely negligent or impaired action. Civil remedies are a means to impose strict liability for offenses and to identify behavior as antisocial without invoking the full procedural and moral artillery of a criminal case. The idea is that, to maintain its moral force, the criminal law should address only seriously antisocial behavior and only behavior involving persons who are responsible for their actions.

Second, when civil remedies are used as supplements to the criminal process, they permit the government to take actions and enlist citizen resources that are not generally available to the criminal justice system. In terms of action, remedies such as forfeitures, injunctive relief, and constructive trusts enable the government to reach the systemic supports of criminal activity – the organizations and business that underlie ongoing criminal enterprises. Law enforcement personnel long have recognized that the arrest and prosecution of individuals, even on a massive scale, is often not enough to end political corruption, organized crime, or the operation of illicit businesses. Civil remedies, such as a constructive trust imposed on a corrupt union, offer flexible means of targeting the organizational supports for crime. In fact, some criminal activity only can be addressed through such systemic reform.

In terms of expanding available resources, civil remedies permit the government to enlist and even conscript citizens to prosecute, sue, and shun criminals. Under qui tam statutes, citizens essentially are converted into bounty hunters and paid handsomely, out of the offenders' pockets, to sue those who have defrauded the government. With civil RICO, plaintiffs can reap multiple damage awards if they prove that enterprises are engaged in a pattern of racketeering. RICO plaintiffs thus vindicate the harm done to themselves, and at the same time, they exact heavy financial penalties from transgressors. Moreover, civil forfeiture makes citizens, on pain of losing their property as an instrument or proceed of crime, monitor the behavior of guests in their cars, family members in their homes, or anyone who borrows or leases their property.

Similarly, since the proceeds of crime are subject to forfeiture in the hands of innocent persons who have knowing business dealings with criminals, business people such as lawyers, doctors, or landlords must cease such dealings or run the risk that money earned in an arm's length transaction may be forfeited under a "profits and proceeds" theory. Citizens and businesses also act as monitors when threatened with vicarious liability carrying regulatory penalties such as loss of a license or debarment. Criminal sanctions, focused as they are on culpable individuals, have neither the scope nor the flexibility of civil remedies.

* * *

VI. REINING IN THE ABUSES OF CIVIL PROCEEDINGS – THE PROTECTIONS OF DUE PROCESS OF LAW

At bottom, many of the objections lodged against using civil remedies to complement criminal law enforcement rest on claims of unfairness, irrationality, and government overreaching. Given the narrow definition of what is a criminal proceeding and the inapplicability of certain constitutional procedures to civil proceedings, it is vital that remedies be disciplined by rigorous civil law due process protections.

Unfortunately, perhaps because so much seems settled once a court decides that a particular proceeding is not a criminal one, the courts have not been particularly vigorous in identifying and preventing unfairness in the imposition of civil penalties. Frequently, due process challenges have been turned away in opinions that have a wooden and formulaic cast – the antithesis of the vigilant, flexible, and equitable spirit of due process of law.

In ordinary civil suits, for example, procedural due process requirements are satisfied under the interest balancing approach of Mathews v. Eldridge, which requires notice, an opportunity to be heard, and such other procedures as will ensure an accurate and rational action.

Ordinarily this means a predeprivation hearing, allocation of the evidentiary burden to the moving party, a preponderance standard for the burden of proof, and no right to appointment of counsel. Civil proceedings that work in tandem with the criminal laws, however, include novel remedies: double and treble damage awards, magnificent forfeitures, branding of persons as "racketeers" or "unfit," and summary seizures of property. The enormity of the impact of these "new penalties" calls into question whether the ordinary civil due process formulae adequately fulfill the constitutional promises. The Supreme Court already has demonstrated that, when the stakes are high enough, due process may mean according civil defendants more stringent procedural protections, sometimes even protections akin to those found in criminal cases. Thus, in re Gault, the Court elevated the preponderance standard of proof to that of clear and convincing evidence, and in Lassiter v. Department of Social Services, it stated that appointment of counsel may sometimes be required in civil cases.

Commentators have taken aim at the new penalties, primarily on procedural due process grounds. Civil forfeitures and civil RICO are recurring candidates in calls for recalibrating the civil due process calculus. Commentators have condemned summary ex parte seizures in civil forfeitures, the burden of proof rules applicable in civil RICO suits, and the denial of appointment of counsel in various settings.

Courts have not been sympathetic. For example, they have rejected: raising the burden of proof in civil RICO cases, pleas for appointment of counsel in civil forfeiture, and conflict of interest challenges to victims serving as prosecutors In civil contempt cases.

Perhaps the best candidate for stringent application of due process protections is civil forfeiture. Civil forfeiture has been described aptly as "a farrago of injustices sanctified by tradition." The practices followed in seizing a person's assets frequently fall below even ordinary due process requirements of prior notice, opportunity to be heard, and burden of proof rules. Indeed, in some cases forfeiture may even violate the substantive due process minimum of rationality.

Under certain forfeiture statutes, property that fits within expansively defined categories of contraband or instrumentalities and proceeds of crime may be seized summarily and without notice. Property within these categories is subject to seizure even if the owner is wholly innocent of crime and is without knowledge of the property's illegal use or origin. Although there is usually a requirement that the seizing officer have probable cause to believe that the property is subject to forfeiture, the probable cause determination need not have a judicial imprimatur or be accompanied by the issuance of a warrant. Moreover, once the government has established probable cause to believe property is subject to forfeiture, the burden falls on the

property owner to prove by a preponderance of the evidence that the property is not subject to forfeiture. Although there is usually a requirement of a prompt post-seizure hearing where summary seizure has occurred, lengthy delays often occur. Indeed, if the government is seeking in personam forfeiture from a criminal defendant, an innocent third party may have to wait until the outcome of the criminal case, months or even years later, to be heard on her claim that the forfeiture is wrongful.

The courts have found substantial fault with the application of civil forfeitures in particular cases and have struck down various provisions as unconstitutional. No court, however, has taken the novel and perhaps needed step of viewing civil forfeitures as substantively and procedurally unconstitutional because of their cumulative, aggregate unfairness. Yet it is the overall operation of civil forfeiture that most belies its inequity.

Critique of forfeiture practice is already well-trod ground, but it is instructive to take a look at two particular due process lapses, namely, summary ex parte seizure and the seizure of property of innocent owners.

A. In Rem Summary Seizures

Procedural due process ordinarily contemplates notice and an opportunity to be heard prior to the deprivation of a property interest. Sometimes, however, notice and opportunity to be heard can be postponed until after the seizure is effected. Such a relaxation of the ordinary rule requires an "extraordinary situation" and a "special need for very prompt action." In Fuentes v. Shevin, the Court identified three criteria for the exceptional case:

First, in each case, the seizure has been directly necessary to secure an important governmental or general public interest. Second, there has been a special need for very prompt action. Third, the State has kept strict control over its monopoly of legitimate force: the person initiating the seizure has been a government official responsible for determining under the standards of a narrowly drawn statute, that it was necessary and justified in the particular instance.

In applying these rules to civil forfeitures, the courts have acknowledged that only extraordinary circumstances can justify summary seizures. At the same time, however, they have found that the moveable quality of property subject to forfeiture is an extraordinary circumstance. Thus, statutes permit, and the courts have sanctioned, the summary seizure of moveable goods if there is probable cause to believe that the property is subject to forfeiture, and if there is a procedural mechanism for a prompt post-seizure hearing. The Supreme Court, for example, validated the summary seizure of a yacht under Puerto Rico's drug forfeiture laws by saying that, procedurally speaking, "this case presents an 'extraordinary' situation in which postponement of notice and hearing until after seizure did not deny due process." Further, the Court has noted that "[t]he property seized – as here, a yacht – will often be of a sort that could be removed to another jurisdiction, destroyed, or concealed, if advance warning of confiscation were given."

Courts have questioned, however, whether a seizure of real estate can ever be procedurally proper without first affording the property owner notice and an opportunity to be heard. Not only is real property not readily moved or subject to being dissipated but, where the real property is an individual's home, values of privacy and freedom from governmental intrusion are also at stake. As one court noted, the government's interest In preventing real property from being improperly transferred can be satisfied readily by the filing of a lis pendens along with a restraining order or bond requirement.

A particularly stark example of real property forfeiture, government overreaching, and the need for procedural protection is provided by In Re Application of Kingsley. On the basis of a secret affidavit, Kingsley was dispossessed of his home and all of his personal belongings, including his pets and food. The government alleged, on information and belief, that Kingsley was a veteran cocaine dealer and that all of his property was subject to seizure as proceeds of his criminal business. Despite Kingsley's attempt to challenge the action, the government did not file an application for civil forfeiture and no hearing was held until almost fifty days later. The government did not file a criminal complaint, on which seizure of the house was predicated, until seven months after the original allegations.

B. The Irrationality of Certain Forfeitures as Applied to Innocent Owners

When government action is challenged under substantive due process, the outcome ordinarily depends on whether a court applies a vigorous strict scrutiny standard or an easily satisfied rational basis review. Social and economic legislation that does not interfere with specific "fundamental rights," such as rights to raise children, use contraceptives, or marry and divorce, is judged under the lenient rational basis test. That is, the law is presumed constitutional, and if it rationally serves any permissible police power objective (public health, convenience, morals), it will be upheld. Thus, legislatures, when not acting to affect fundamental rights, constitutionally are permitted to make all rational choices about how society will be ordered. They are free to decide what conduct will be criminal, what activities will be taxed, and what behavior will be regulated.

As a result, there is ordinarily no meaningful substantive due process basis upon which to attack the use of civil remedies to control, sanction, or regulate antisocial behavior. For example, legislatures rationally may conclude that the integrity of the tax system requires monetary fines for late payments, or they rationally may adopt a measure making the possession of dangerous drugs illegal and providing for seizure and forfeiture.

In rare cases, however, a civil remedy might operate so disproportionately or be applied so irrationally that even this substantive due process standard could impose a limit. Forfeiture and some regulatory sanctions may be potential candidates for this restraint.

The Supreme Court consistently has held that forfeiture laws do not violate due process simply because they are made applicable to property interests of innocent owners. This makes sense if the forfeited property is contraband because, by definition, contraband may not be owned or possessed: the nature of the item itself indicates guilt. Forfeitures applied to innocent owners also may be reasonable if the property in question is traceable proceeds of a crime, even if such proceeds now rest in the hands of an unknowing third party. This conclusion can be justified by the argument that, as between the harm to the innocent party and closing off avenues for criminals to launder their gain, a legislature may choose to frustrate the criminal. Moreover, a third party, such as a lawyer, is sometimes in a position to consider whether the property she has received was transferred by a known or suspected criminal. The Supreme Court specifically has rejected arguments that due process prevents the forfeiture of attorneys fees paid by criminals and traceable as proceeds of a RICO violation.

Forfeitures applied to innocent persons whose property is used as an instrumentality of a crime, however, may be irrational under due process analysis. The Supreme Court itself implicitly recognized this prospect in Calero-Toledo v. Pearson Yacht Leasing Co. In that case, the Court upheld the civil forfeiture of a yacht because a single marijuana cigarette was recovered on board. The yacht was being used by tenants under a long term lease and the owner-lessor was innocent of any involvement with or even knowledge of the drugs. The Court stated that laws permitting In rem forfeitures of innocents' property are justified by their "punitive and deterrent purposes." Although presumably there would be no basis to punish the innocent lessor, the Court noted that on the facts of this case "confiscation may have the desirable effect of inducing them to exercise greater care in transferring possession of their property." The lessor in Calero, having offered no evidence as to his degree of care, forfeited the yacht. The significance of Calero lies in the Court's dictum that:

It would be difficult to reject the constitutional claim of an owner . . . who proved not only that he was uninvolved In and unaware of the wrongful activity, but also that he had done all that reasonably could be expected to prevent the proscribed use of his property; for in that circumstance, it would be difficult to conclude that forfeiture served legitimate purposes and was not unduly oppressive.

Although courts have relied on this dictum, Calero's implication that certain extreme and arbitrary forfeitures of property will violate fundamental fairness has had little practical significance. There are two explanations for this fact. First, many statutes permit "innocent" owners to seek remission of their property. Second, and more disappointingly, courts have applied a very narrow meaning to innocence or reasonable care. For example, courts have found lack of reasonable care when a parent loaned the family car to a son who had a minor criminal record. When the son later used the car to transport drugs, the car was forfeited. Forfeiture of "instrumentalities" owned by innocent persons thus retains an air of happenstance and superstition about it—a little like lightning striking.

* * *

VIII. Conclusion

We are in the midst of fundamentally altering the way we approach criminal justice problems. Law enforcement authorities are no longer content to fight crime with the traditional methods of arrest, prosecution, and jailing. They have observed that crimes such as fraud, extortion, and drug dealing are often complex phenomena involving networks of criminals, subtle and complex business transactions, and societal acquiescence or tolerance. In response, law enforcement officials have enlisted civil remedies—particularly asset forfeiture—and have begun to rely on private law suits. Encouraged by their initial success, they have pressed the merger of traditional criminal and civil remedies to reach a broad spectrum of antisocial behavior.

The systematic joinder of criminal and civil remedies presents unusual challenges to a legal system largely built on the idea that the criminal and civil law are separate and distinct. This Article has addressed only one set of issues that must be confronted, namely Bill of Rights limitations on the use of hybrid or multiple remedies. It has had to begin by offering a coherent basis on which to distinguish criminal from civil proceedings because the Constitution itself embodies a separation between the two. But, important as that effort is and may prove to be In the future, this

Article has also sought to show when, constitutionally speaking, the distinction should be ignored.

More work remains to be done. The widespread blending of criminal and civil remedies strains the capacity of our bifurcated procedural systems to accommodate hybrid forms of action. It obscures the boundary line between governmental and private action In applying constitutional and legislative limits on "state action." Moreover, it presses us to consider whether prosecutor's offices formally should be reorganized along problem-solving, regulatory lines. At the moment, law enforcement practices are running ahead of our legal theories and our procedural systems. This Article is just one step toward catching up.

C. White Collar Crime

Edwin H. Sutherland, *White Collar Criminality*, 5 Am. Soc. Rev. 1–12 (1940)

This paper is concerned with crime in relation to business. The economists are well acquainted with business methods but are not accustomed to consider them from the point of view of crime; many sociologists are well acquainted with crime but are not accustomed to consider it as expressed in business. This paper is an attempt to integrate these two bodies of knowledge. More accurately stated, it is a comparison of crime in the upper or white-collar class, composed of respectable or at least respected business and professional men, and crime in the lower class, composed of persons of low socioeconomic status. The comparison is made for the purpose of developing the theories of criminal behavior, not for the purpose of muckraking or of reforming anything except criminology.

The criminal statistics show unequivocally that crime, *as popularly conceived and officially measured,* has a high incidence in the lower class and a low incidence in the upper class; less than two per cent of the persons committed to prisons in a year below to the upper class. These statistics refer to criminals handled by the police, the criminal and juvenile courts, and the prisons, and to such crimes as murder, assault, burglary, robbery, larceny, sex offenses, and drunkenness, but exclude traffic violations.

The criminologists have used the case histories and criminal statistics derived from these agencies of criminal justice as their principal data. From them, they have derived general theories of criminal behavior. These theories are that, since crime is concentrated in the lower class, it is caused by poverty or by personal and social characteristics believed to be associated statistically with poverty, including feeble-mindedness, psychopathic deviations, slum neighborhoods, and "deteriorated" families. This statement, of course, does not do justice to the qualifications and variations in the conventional theories of criminal behavior, but it presents correctly their central tendency.

The thesis of this paper is that the conception and explanations of crime which have just been described are misleading and incorrect, that crime is in fact not closely correlated with poverty or with the psychopathic and sociopathic conditions associated with poverty, and that an adequate explanation of criminal behavior must proceed along quite different lines. The conventional explanations are invalid principally because they are derived from biased samples. The samples are biased in that they have not included vast areas of criminal behavior of persons not in the lower class. One of these neglected areas is the criminal behavior of business and professional men, which will be analyzed in this paper.

The "robber barons" of the latter half of the nineteenth century were white-collar criminals, as almost everyone now agrees. Their attitudes are readily illustrated. Commodore Vanderbilt asked, "You don't suppose you can run a railroad in accordance with the statutes, do you?" A.B. Stickney, a railroad president, said to sixteen other railroad presidents in the home of J.P. Morgan in 1890, "I have the utmost respect for you gentlemen, individually, but as railroad presidents I wouldn't trust you with my watch out of my sight." Charles Francis Adams said, "The difficulty in railroad management . . . lies in the covetousness, want of good faith, and low moral tone of railway managers, in the complete absence of any high standard of commercial honesty."

The present-day white-collar criminals, who are more suave and deceptive than the "robber barons," are represented by Kreuger, Stavisky, Whitney, Mitchell, Foshay, Insull, the Van Sweringens, Musica-Coster, Fall, Sinclair, and many other merchant princes and captains of finance and industry and by a host of lesser followers. Their criminality has been demonstrated again and again in the investigations of land offices, railways, insurance, munitions, banking, public utilities, stock exchanges, the oil industry, real estate, reorganization committees, receiverships, bankruptcies, and politics. Individual cases of such criminality are reported frequently, and in many periods more important crime news may be found on the financial pages of newspapers than on the front pages.

White-collar criminality is found in every occupation, as can be discovered readily in casual conversation with a representative of an occupation by asking him what crooked practices are found in his occupation.

White-collar criminality in business is expressed most frequently in the form of misrepresentation in financial statements of corporations, manipulation in the stock exchange, commercial bribery, bribery of public officials directly or indirectly in order to secure favorable contracts and legislation, misrepresentation in advertising and salesmanship, embezzlement and misapplication of funds, short weights and measures and dishonest grading of commodities, tax frauds, misapplication of funds in receiverships and bankruptcies. These and many others are found in abundance in the business world. They are what Al Capone called "the legitimate rackets."

In the medical profession, which is here used as an example because it probably displays less criminality than some other professions, are found illegal sale of alcohol and narcotics, abortion, illegal services to underworld criminals, fraudulent reports and testimony in accident cases, extreme cases of unnecessary treatment, fake specialists, restriction of competition, and fee-splitting. Fee-splitting is a violation of specific laws in many states and a violation of the conditions of admission to the practice of medicine in all. The physician who participates in fee-splitting tends to send his patients to the surgeon who will give him the largest fee rather than to the surgeon who will do the best work. It has been reported that two thirds of the surgeons in New York City split fees, and that more than half of the physicians in a central western city who answered a questionnaire on this point favored fee-splitting.

These varied types of white-collar crimes in business and the professions consist principally of violation of delegated or implied trust, and many of them can be reduced to two categories: misrepresentation of asset values and duplicity in the manipulation of power. The first is approximately the same as fraud or swindling; the second is similar to the double-cross. The latter is illustrated by the corporation director who, acting on inside information, purchases land which the corporation will need and sells it at a fantastic profit to the corporation. The principle of this duplicity is that the offender holds two antagonistic positions; one of them is a position of trust which is violated, generally by misapplication of funds, in the interest of the other position. A football coach permitted to referee a game in which his own team was playing would illustrate this antagonism of positions. Such situations cannot be completely avoided in a complicated business structure, but many concerns make a practice of assuming such antagonistic functions and of regularly violating a trust thus delegated to them. When compelled by law to make a separation of their functions, they make a nominal separation and continue by subterfuge to maintain the two positions.

An accurate statistical comparison of the crimes of the two classes is not available. The most extensive evidence regarding the nature and prevalence of white-collar criminality is found in the reports of the larger investigations to which reference was made. Because of its scattered character, that evidence is assumed rather than summarized here. A few statements will be presented, as illustrations rather than as proof of the prevalence of this criminality.

The Federal Trade Commission in 1920 reported that commercial bribery was a prevalent and common practice in many industries. In certain chain stores, the net shortage in weights was sufficient to pay 3-4 per cent on the investment in those commodities. Of the cans of ether sold to the Army in 1923-1925, 70 per cent were rejected because of impurities. In Indiana, during the summer of 1934, 40 per cent of the ice-cream samples tested in a routine manner by the Division of Public Health were in violation of law. The Comptroller of the Currency in 1908 reported that violations of law were found in 75 per cent of the banks examined in a three-months' period. Lie-detector tests of all employees in several Chicago banks showed that 20 per cent of them had stolen bank property, and these tests were supported in almost all cases by confessions. A public accountant estimated, in the period prior to the Securities and Exchange Commission, that 80 per cent of the financial statements of corporations were misleading. James M. Beck said, "Diogenes would have been hard put to it to find an honest man in the Wall Street which I knew [in 1916] as a corporation lawyer."

White-collar criminality is generally recognized as fairly prevalent in politics and has been used by some as a rough gauge by which to measure white-collar criminality in business. James A. Farley pointed out that "the standards of conduct are as high among officeholders and politicians as they are in commercial life," and Cermak, while mayor of Chicago, said, "There is less graft in politics than in business." According to John Flynn, "The average politician is the merest amateur in the gentle art of graft, compared with his brother in the field of business." And Walter Lippmann wrote, "Poor as they are, the standards of public life are so much more social than those of business that financiers who enter politics regard themselves as philanthropists."

These statements obviously do not give a precise measurement of the relative criminality of the white-collar class. They do not mean that all businessmen and professional men are criminals, just as the usual theories do not mean that every man in the lower class is a criminal. The statements are adequate evidence, however, that crime is not so highly concentrated in the lower class as the usual statistics indicate, and they refer in many cases to leading corporations in America and are not restricted to quacks, ambulance chasers, bucket-shop operators, dead beats, fly-by-night swindlers, and the like.

The financial cost of white-collar crime is probably several times as great as the financial cost of all the crimes which are customarily included in the "crime problem." An officer of a chain grocery story in one year embezzled $600,000 which was six times as much as the annual losses from five hundred burglaries and robberies of the stores in that chain. Public enemies numbered one to six secured $130,000 by burglary and robbery in 1938, while the sum stolen by Kreuger is estimated at $250,000,000, or nearly two thousand times as much. The *New York Times* in 1931 reported four cases of embezzlement in the United States with a loss of more than a million dollars each and a combined loss of nine million dollars. Although a million-dollar burglary or robbery is practically unheard of, million-dollar embezzlers are small fry among white-collar criminals. The estimated loss of investors in one investment trust from 1929 to 1935 was $580,000,000. This loss was due primarily to the fact that 75 per cent of the values in the portfolio were in securities of affiliated companies, although the firm in question had advertised the importance of diversification in investments and had provided an investment-counseling service. In Chicago, the claim was made six years ago that householders had lost $54,000,000 in two years during the administration of a city sealer who granted immunity from inspection to stores which provided Christmas baskets for his constituents.

The financial loss from white-collar crime, great as it is, is less important than the damage to social relations. White-collar crimes violate trust and therefore create distrust, which lowers social morale and produces social disorganization on a large scale. Other crimes have relatively little effect on social institutions or social organization.

White-collar crime is real crime. It is not ordinarily called crime, and calling it by this name does not make it worse, just as not calling it crime does not make it better. It is called crime here because it is in violation of the criminal law and belongs within the scope of criminology. The crucial question in this analysis is the criterion of violation of the criminal law. Conviction in the criminal court, which is sometimes suggested as the criterion, is not adequate because a large proportion of those who commit crimes are not convicted in criminal courts. This criterion, therefore, needs to be supplemented. When it is supplemented, the criterion of the crimes of one class much be kept consistent in general terms with the criterion of the crimes of the other class. The definition should not be the spirit of the law for white-collar crimes and the letter of the law for other crimes, or in other respects be more liberal for one class than for the other. Since this discussion is concerned with the conventional theories of the criminologists, the criterion of white-collar crime must be justified in terms of the procedures of those criminologists in dealing with other crimes. The criterion of white-collar crimes, as here proposed, supplements convictions in the criminal courts in four respects, in each of which the extension is justified because the criminologists who present the conventional theories of criminal behavior make the same extension in principle.

First, other agencies than the criminal court must be included, for the criminal court is not the only agency which makes official decisions regarding violations of the criminal law. The juvenile court, dealing largely with offenses of the children of the poor, is not in many states under criminal jurisdiction. The criminologists have made much use of case histories and statistics of juvenile delinquents in constructing their theories of criminal behavior. This justifies the inclusion of agencies other than the criminal court which deal with white-collar offenses. The most important of these agencies are the administrative boards, bureaus, or commissions; and much of their work, although certainly not all, consists of cases which are in violation of the criminal law. The Federal Trade Commission ordered several automobile companies to stop advertising their interest rate on installment purchases as 6 per cent, since it was actually 11½ per cent. Also, it filed complaint against *Good Housekeeping,* one of the Hearst publications, charging that its seals led the public to believe that all products bearing those seals had been tested in their laboratories, which was contrary to fact. Each of these involves a charge of dishonesty which might have been tried in a criminal court as fraud. A large proportion of the cases before these boards should be included in the data of the criminologists. Failure to do so is a principal reason for the bias in their samples and for the errors in their generalizations.

Second, for both classes, behavior which would have a reasonable expectancy of conviction if tried in a criminal court of in a substitute agency should be defined as criminal. In this respect, convictability rather than actual conviction should be the criterion of criminality. The criminologists would not hesitate to accept as data the verified case history of a person who was a criminal but had never been convicted. Similarly, it is justifiable to include white-collar criminals who have not been convicted, provided reliable evidence is available. Evidence regarding such cases appears in many civil suits, such as stockholders' suits and patent-infringement suits. These cases, which might have been referred to the criminal court, were referred to the civil court because the injured party was more interested in securing damages than in seeing punishment inflicted. This also happens in embezzlement cases, regarding which surety companies have much evidence. In a short consecutive series of embezzlements known to a surety company, 90 per cent were not prosecuted because prosecution would have interfered with restitution or salvage. The evidence in cases of embezzlement is generally conclusive, and would probably have been sufficient to justify conviction in all the cases in this series.

Third, behavior should be defined as criminal if conviction is avoided merely because of pressure which is brought to bear on the court or substitute agency. Gangsters and racketeers have been relatively immune in many cities because of their pressure on prospective witnesses and public officials; and professional thieves, such as pickpockets and confidence men who do not use strong-arm methods, are even more frequently immune because of their ability to influence police action. The conventional criminologists do not hesitate to include the life histories of such criminals as data, because they understand the generic relation of the pressures to the failure to convict. Similarly, white-collar criminals are relatively immune because of the class bias of the courts and the power of their class to influence the implementation and administration of the law. This class bias not only affects present-day courts but to a much greater degree affected the earlier courts which established the precedents and rules of procedure of the present-day courts. Consequently, it is justifiable to interpret the actual or potential failures of conviction in the light of known facts regarding the pressures brought to bear on the agencies which deal with offenders.

Fourth, persons who are accessory to a crime should be included among white-collar criminals as they are among other criminals. When the Federal Bureau of Investigation deals with a case of kidnapping, it is not content with catching the offenders who carried away the victim; it may arrest and the court may convict twenty-five other persons who assisted by secreting the victim, negotiating the ransom, or putting the ransom money into circulation. On the other hand, the prosecution of white-collar criminals frequently stops with one offender. Political graft almost always involves collusion between politicians and businessmen, but prosecutions are generally limited to the politicians. Judge Manton was found guilty of accepting $664,000 in bribes, but the six or eight important commercial concerns that paid the bribes have not been prosecuted. Pendergast, the late boss of Kansas City, was convicted for failure to report as a part of his income $315,000 received in bribes from insurance companies, but the insurance companies which paid the bribes have not been prosecuted. In an investigation of embezzlement by the president of a bank, at least a dozen other violations of law which were related to this embezzlement and involved most of the other officers of the bank and the officers of the clearinghouse were discovered, but none of the others was prosecuted.

This analysis of the criterion of white-collar criminality results in the conclusion that a description of white-collar criminality in general terms will also be a description of the criminality of the lower class. The crimes of the two classes differ in incidentals rather than essentials. They differ principally in the implementation of the criminal laws which apply to them. The crimes of the lower class are handled by policemen, prosecutors, and judges with penal sanctions in the form of fines, imprisonment, and death. The crimes of the upper class either result in no official action at all or result in suits for damages in civil courts or are handled by inspectors and by administrative boards or commissions with penal sanctions in the form of warnings, orders to cease and desist, occasional rescinding of a license, and in extreme cases with fines or prison sentences. Thus, the white-collar criminals are segregated administratively from other criminals, and largely as a consequence of this are not regarded as real criminals by themselves, by the general public, or by the criminologists.

This difference in the implementation of the criminal law is due chiefly to the disparity in social position of the two kinds of offenders. Judge Woodward, when imposing sentence upon the officials of H.O. Stone and Company (a bankrupt real estate firm in Chicago), who had been convicted in 1933 of the use of the mails to defraud, said to them, "You are men of affairs, of experience, of refinement and culture, of excellent reputation and standing in the business and social world." That statement might be used as a general characterization of white-collar criminals, for they are oriented basically to legitimate and respectable careers. Because of their social status they have a loud voice in determining what goes into the statutes and how the criminal law as it affects themselves is implemented and administered. This may be illustrated from the Pure Food and Drug Law. Between 1879 and 1906, 140 pure food and drug bills were presented in Congress, and all failed because of the importance of the persons who would be affected. It took a highly dramatic performance by Dr. Wiley in 1906 to induce Congress to enact the law. The law, however, did not create a new crime, just as the Federal kidnapping law which grew out of the Lindbergh case did not create a new crime; the Pure Food and Drug Law merely provided a more efficient implementation of a principle which had been formulated previously in state laws. When an amendment to this law, which would have brought within the scope of its agents fraudulent statements made over the radio or in the press, was presented to Congress, the publishers and advertisers organized support and sent a lobby to Washington which successfully fought the amendment principally under the slogans of "freedom of the press" and "dangers of bureaucracy." This proposed amendment, also, would not have created a new crime, for the state laws already prohibited fraudulent statements over the radio or in the press; it would have implemented the law so that it could have been enforced. Finally, the administration has not been able to enforce the law as it has desired because of the pressures by the offenders against the law, sometimes brought to bear through the head of the Department of Agriculture, sometimes through congressmen who threaten cuts in the appropriation, and sometimes by others. A statement made by Daniel Drew describes the criminal law with some accuracy: "Law is like a cobweb; it's made for flies and the smaller kinds of insects, so to speak, but lets the big bumblebees break through. When technicalities of the law stood in my way, I have always been able to brush them aside as easy as anything.' [sic]

The preceding analysis should be regarded neither as an assertion that all efforts to influence legislation and its administration are reprehensible nor as a particularistic interpretation of the criminal law. It means only that the upper class has greater influence in molding the criminal law and its administration to its own interests than does the lower class. The privileged position of white-collar criminals before the law results to a slight extent from bribery and political pressures, but largely from the respect in which such men are held and without special effort on their part. The most powerful group in medieval society secured relative immunity by "benefit of clergy," and now our most powerful groups secure relative immunity by "benefit of business or profession."

In contrast with the power of the white-collar criminals is the weakness of their victims. Consumers, investors, and stockholders are unorganized, lack technical knowledge, and cannot protect themselves. Daniel Drew, after taking a large sum of money by sharp practice from Vanderbilt in the Erie deal, concluded that it was a mistake to take money from a powerful man on the same level as himself and declared that in the future he would confine his efforts to outsiders, scattered all over the country, who wouldn't be able to organize and fight back. White-collar criminality flourishes at points where powerful businessmen and professional men come in contact with persons who are weak. In this respect, it is similar to stealing candy from a baby. Many of the crimes of the lower class, on the other hand, are committed, in the form of burglary and robbery, against persons of wealth and power. Because of this difference in the comparative power of the victims, the white-collar criminals enjoy relative immunity.

Embezzlement is an interesting exception to white-collar criminality in this respect. Embezzlement is usually theft from an employer by an employee, and the employee is less capable of manipulating social and legal forces in his own interest than is the employer. As might have been expected, the laws regarding embezzlement were formulated long before laws for the protection of investors and consumers.

The theory that criminal behavior in general is due either to poverty or to the psychopathic and sociopathic conditions associated with poverty can now be shown to be invalid for three reasons. First, the generalization is based on a biased sample which omits almost entirely the behavior of white-collar criminals. For reasons of convenience and ignorance rather than of principle, criminologists have restricted their data largely to cases dealt with in criminal courts and juvenile courts, and these agencies are used principally for criminals from the lower economic strata. Consequently, the criminologists' data are grossly biased in respect to the economic status of criminals, and the generalization that criminality is closely associated with poverty is not justified.

Second, the generalization is inapplicable to white-collar criminals. With a small number of exceptions, they are not poor, were not reared in slums or badly deteriorated families, and are not feeble-minded or psychopathic. The proposition, derived from the data used by the conventional criminologists, that "the criminal of today was the problem child of yesterday," is seldom true of white-collar criminals. The idea that the causes of criminality are to be found almost exclusively in childhood is also fallacious. Even if poverty is extended to include the economic stresses which afflict business in a period of depression, it is not closely correlated with white-collar criminality. Probably at no time within the last fifty years have white-collar crimes in the field of investments and corporate management been so extensive as during the boom period of the twenties.

Third, the generalization does not explain lower-class criminality. The sociopathic and psychopathic factors which have been emphasized doubtless have something to do with crime causation, but these factors have not been related to a general process which is found both in white-collar criminality and lower-class criminality; therefore, they do not explain the criminality of either class, though they may explain the manner or method of crime – why lower-class criminals commit burglary or robbery rather than crimes involving misrepresentation.

In view of these defects in the conventional theories, a hypothesis that will explain both white-collar criminality and lower-class criminality is needed. For reasons of economy, simplicity, and logic, the hypothesis should apply to both classes, for this will make possible the analysis of causal factors freed from the encumbrances of the administrative devices which have led criminologists astray. Shaw and McKay and others, working exclusively in the field of lower-class crime, have found the conventional theories inadequate to account for variations within the data of lower-class crime and with that difficulty in mind have been working toward an explanation of crime in terms of a more general social process. Such efforts will be greatly aided by the procedure which has been described.

The hypothesis suggested here as a substitute for the conventional theories is that white-collar criminality, just as other systematic criminality, is learned; that it is learned in direct or indirect association with those who already practice criminal behavior; and that those who learn this criminal behavior are segregated from frequent and intimate contacts with law-abiding behavior. Whether a person becomes a criminal or not is determined largely by the comparative frequency and intimacy of his contacts with the two types of behavior. This may be called the process of differential association. It is a genetic explanation both of white-collar criminality and lower-class criminality. Those who become white-collar criminals generally start their careers in good neighborhoods and good homes, graduate from colleges with some idealism, and, with little selection on their part, get into particular business situations in which criminality is practically a folkway, and are inducted into that system of behavior just as into any other folkway. The lower-class criminals generally start their carers in deteriorated neighborhoods and families, find delinquents at hand from whom they acquire the attitudes toward, and techniques of, crime. The essentials of this process are the same for the two classes of criminals.

This is not entirely a process of assimilation, for inventions are frequently made, perhaps more frequently in white-collar crime than in lower-class crime. The inventive geniuses for the lower-class criminals are generally professional criminals, while the inventive geniuses for many kinds of white-collar crime are generally lawyers.

A second general process is social disorganization in the community. Differential association culminates in crime because the community is not organized solidly against that form of behavior. The law is pressing in one direction, and other forces are pressing in the opposite direction. In business, the "rules of the game" conflict with the legal rules. A businessman who wants to obey the law is driven by his competitors to adopt their methods. This is well illustrated by the persistence of commercial bribery in spite of the strenuous efforts of business organizations to eliminate it. Groups and individuals, however, are more concerned with their specialized group or individual interests than with the larger welfare. Consequently it is not possible for the community to present a solid front in opposition to crime. The better business bureaus and crime commissions, composed of professional men and businessmen, attack burglary, robbery, and cheap swindles but overlook the crimes of their own members. The forces which impinge on the lower class are similarly in conflict. Social disorganization affects the two classes in similar ways.

I have presented a brief and general description of white-collar criminality on a framework of argument regarding theories of criminal behavior. That argument, stripped of the description, may be stated in the following propositions:

(1) White-collar criminality is real criminality, being in all cases in violation of the criminal law.

(2) White-collar criminality differs from lower-class criminality principally in an implementation of the criminal law which segregates white-collar criminals administratively from other criminals.

(3) The theories of the criminologists that crime is due to poverty or to psychopathic and sociopathic conditions statistically associated with poverty are invalid for three reasons: first, they are derived from samples which are grossly biased with respect to socioeconomic status; second, they do not apply to white-collar criminals; and third, they do not even explain the criminality of the lower class, since the factors are not related to a general process characteristic of all criminality.

(4) A theory of criminal behavior which will explain both white-collar criminality and lower-class criminality is needed.

(5) An hypothesis of this nature is suggested in terms of differential association and social disorganization.

Stanton Wheeler, *White Collar Crime: History of an Idea*, 4 ENCYCLOPEDIA OF CRIME AND JUSTICE 1652–1656 (1983)*

Crimes committed by persons of respectability have drawn the attention of societies throughout history. In the United States, interest in such phenomena far antedates the first public use of the concept of white-collar crime by Edwin Sutherland. The muckraking tradition at the turn of the century produced may persons who condemned abuse of position for private gain. Sociologists E.A. Ross, in *Sin and Society,* drew attention to "the man who picks pockets with a railway rebate, murders with an adulterant instead of a bludgeon, burglarizes with a 'rake-off' instead of a jimmy, cheats with a company prospectus instead of a deck of cards, or scuttles his town instead of his ship" (p. 7).

The varied misdeeds denoted by Ross give an early hint of both the value of the concept and the difficulties that have plagued its use. The value is essentially social and evocative. It connotes not a particular type of crime or a statutory violation, but a concern for some combination of abuse of trust, authority, status, or position. In a society whose criminal justice system deals mainly with common crimes and common offenders, it bespeaks a concern for the misdeeds of the haves rather than the have-nots, and it raises the specter of class bias in law enforcement. However, its signifying power is precisely its weakness as an analytical tool, for its meaning shifts with changes in the character of society and in the underlying values and interests of the varied scholars and policy makers who invoke it. It is thus a distinctively social, rather than legal, concept, one suffused with vagueness and ambiguity.

THE EVOLUTION OF WHITE-COLLAR CRIME

The legacy of Sutherland. Sutherland's interest in the topic dates at least to the 1920s, although the

---

* "White Collar Crime: History of an Idea" by Stanton Wheeler. Reprinted with permission of Simon & Schuster Macmillan from *Encyclopedia of Crime and Justice,* Sanford H. Kadish, Editor in Chief. Vol. 4, pp. 1652-1656. Copyright © 1983 by The Free Press.

research resulting in his *White Collar Crime* was initiated during the depression years of the 1930s. The first public treatment of the subject occurred when Sutherland titled his presidential address to the American Sociological Society in 1939 "The White Collar Criminal." He was apparently drawn to the topic in his search for a general theory of crime. The usual explanations in his day (and often today) stressed poverty and other pathological social conditions, but, argued Sutherland, these factors could not be a general cause of crime if crimes were also committed by persons of respectability and high social status. In the book-length version of the speech, which appeared a decade later, Sutherland aimed simultaneously to weaken theories depending on the behavior of the deprived and the depraved, and to provide support for his own social-learning approach to crime causation — the theory of differential association.

Sutherland was rather casual in his conceptualization of white-collar crime, at times stressing social status, at times behavior carried out in an occupational role, and at times crime committed by organizations or by individuals acting in organizational capacities. The confusion is reflected in his most frequently cited definition: "White collar crime may be defined approximately as a crime committed by a person of respectability and high social status in the course of his occupation" (p. 9). His book was devoted, however, to the crimes of organizations, not of persons: seventy large corporations and fifteen public utilities. Thus, a firm basis for ambiguity had been laid. Those following Sutherland sometimes focused on persons of high status, sometimes on occupation, and sometimes on corporate bodies. Sutherland's book described the illegalities committed by those corporations, arguing that the corporations share most of the characteristics of professional thieves: their offenses are deliberate and organized, they are often recidivists, and they show disdain for law. Needless to say, with these conclusions the book had a controversial reception. Many in the social sciences hailed it as a landmark, whereas many in law and business attacked it as misleading and distorted. The principal basis for disagreement concerned the underlying concept of crime. The "crimes" of the corporations Sutherland examined were rarely prosecuted in criminal court: they were violations of administrative rules or simply contract cases to be processed, if at all, in civil court. Many in the legal community insisted these were not crimes at all. Sutherland's answer was that businessmen were more able to influence the course of legislation; it was only their greater power (relative to the lower-class criminal) that kept their offenses out of the traditional criminal law.

The battle over definition aside, Sutherland's pioneering work stirred few fires in the two decades after its publication. Detailed studies of particular offenses, such as Donald Cressey's examination of the violation of financial trust, were the exception rather than the rule. Of the triumvirate of status, occupation, and organization that underlay Sutherland's conception, interest tended to turn away from the status dimension itself, and toward those crimes made possible because of the defendant's occupational role (Newman). Some analysts spoke not of white-collar crime but of occupational crime. Offenders studied in these terms were not exclusively of high status. They included retail pharmacists, meat inspectors, and bank tellers. Although a much-publicized case of price-fixing in the electrical industry in 1961 (Geis and Meier) helped sustain an interest in the topic of crimes committed through, and on behalf of, organizations, sustained study of organizational crime did not flower until the next decade. Criminological research and theory continued to concentrate on juvenile delinquency and violent crime.

It is unclear why Sutherland's work generated so little new research or theory, although several reasons are plausible. The massiveness of Sutherland's undertaking, as well as confusion regarding the concept itself, may have played a part. The 1950s and 1960s were not depression decades, and the problems of a younger generation occupied public and governmental attention. It had also proved more convenient, historically, for social scientists to study the weak and deprived, rather than those in more powerful positions. The symbolic and evocative nature of the concept remained, however, awaiting changing conditions for new meaning to be infused into it.

From offender to offense. Social interest in white-collar crime grew rapidly in the 1970s, rivaling the attention street crime had received in the preceding decade. Prosecutors gave it higher priority than in the past. Targets of investigation included individual businessmen, corrupt politicians, and such corporate activities as international business bribery, the manufacture of dangerous products, and environmental pollution. The renewed interest was motivated at least in part by the discovery of corruption and other illegal practices at the highest levels of government, and by a growing sensitivity to dangerous corporate practices. The growth in interest was great enough that it could fairly be labeled a social movement (Katz, 1980).

When the pace of scholarship on white-collar crime also revived, it became evident that the wide range of phenomena suggested by the concept had to be broken down into components. Attention had focused so much on the nature of the offender that actual criminal behavior had gone unexamined. It seemed to make little sense to include under a single rubric as diverse a set of activities as bank embezzlement, land swindles, price-fixing, fraudulent loan applications, and bribery. The first important shift away from the legacy of Sutherland was accomplished by taking the offense itself as the principal object of inquiry. In the first such effort, Herbert Edelhertz proposed to define white-collar crime as "an illegal act or series of illegal acts committed by nonphysical means and by concealment and guile, to obtain money or property, to avoid payment or loss of money or property, or to obtain business or personal advantage" (p. 3). A related shift is to search for behavioral patterns that characterize different *types* of white-collar crime. Susan Shapiro, for example, distinguishes fraud, self-dealing, and regulatory offenses (pp. 20-24), and Mitchell Rothman separates frauds, takings, and collusion.

The impulse that gives rise to typological efforts is the felt need to put order into the enormous range of behaviors at issue. The statutes that define white-collar crime, passed by legislatures for various purposes at various times, are a patchwork. Important as they may be for prosecution, the legal categories are of limited value for analytic purposes. A given statutory offense may include a wide array of actual behaviors; bank embezzlement, for example, may range from a simple theft by a bank teller to a complex fraudulent loan arranged by a trust officer. Essentially the same behavior may be punished under statutes as different as those governing mail and wire fraud, securities fraud, and false claims and statements. Typologies allow one to see some of the similarities between crimes as different as bribery and price-fixing, which share the element of collusive activity.

The underlying assumption of this type of analysis—still to be proved—is that parallels in behavior may suggest parallels in either the causal processes producing such behavior or in the methods of detection and enforcement brought to bear upon them. Such work is likely to be only partially successful until there is greater agreement on the core properties of white-collar crime. To the extent that the legal categories themselves are a function of concerns not reflected in the underlying conduct—a concern, for example, that the conduct be reachable by federal authorities, or that regulatory agencies can police it—typologies that concentrate on underlying conduct may be prematurely dismissive of the important role played by legal categorization itself.

From offense to organization and consequence. A second trend is to emphasize not behavior but its consequences. This trend rediscovers issues that occupied reformers at the turn of the century—a concern for the power of organizations and the harms they commit. From the late nineteenth century on, harms caused by the production and sale of adulterated goods and similar activities were recognized as "strict liability" offenses—criminal acts not requiring proof of a guilty mind. throughout the twentieth century these activities, and many others later recognized to pose a similar threat, came increasingly to be the subject of administrative regulation, which was seen as a wiser and more effective device for protecting the public interest. Regulation expanded as new dangers to health and to life itself were recognized—dangers to individuals posed by the air they breathed, the water they drank, the food and drugs they consumed, the automobiles and other products they used, and the places at which they worked.

Rediscovery of the power of organizations to inflict physical damage as well as economic injury has led some scholars to direct their attention to specifically organizational offenses. The central concern here is those actions taken by the officials or other agents of legitimate organizations that have a serious physical or economic impact on employees, consumers, or the general public (Schrager and Short). A growing number of analysts thus speak of organizations as offenders, of "organizational deviance," and of illegalities committed through the organizational form. This is a response to a society in which organizations increasingly are major actors, and although it reflects experience in the United States, both the concept of white-collar crime and a concern with corporate and governmental offenses are found throughout the world.

The focus on organizational offenses brings with it enduring issues of law and policy. One is the question of the standard by which individual conduct is to be judged. Should organizations' executives be sanctioned for failure to supervise middle-level officials engaged in wrongdoing? Should strict liability be employed, as in some of the earlier public-welfare offenses? How should sanctions be distributed between organization and employees? When the focus is on the corporate body itself, there is the question of how best to protect against harmful corporate practices without stifling organizational innovation and creativity. For example, should unwanted conduct be deterred through increased penalties against the corporation? Or is it more effective to control wrongdoing by reaching inside the organization, either through rules governing production processes and information flow, or rules regarding the composition of the board of directors? The treatment of offenses of organizations remains fraught with complex policy choices (Coffee; Kadish; Stone).

Finally, there is the issue that sparked the original debate over the concept of white-collar crime: Are these offenses administrative rule violations or "real" crimes?

The most complete follow-up study to *White Collar Crime* defines its subject as any act, committed by a corporation, that is punishable by the state, whether through criminal, administrative, or civil law. The title of this study, *Corporate Crime,* while reflecting the shift to the corporate form as a primary focus of inquiry, maintains the view that such conduct be labeled criminal (Clinard and Yeager, p. 16). The corporate sanctions examined, however, are overwhelmingly civil or administrative. Thus, the matter of definition remains controversial some forty years after Sutherland's initial exploration of white-collar crime.

WHITE-COLLAR CRIME
FROM THE ENFORCEMENT PERSPECTIVE

White-collar crime, in either its individual or organizational form, often involves complex paper manipulations and sophisticated cover-up activities. When these traits are combined with the embeddedness of illegalities in organizations, the problems of gathering evidence with respect to motive, intent, and act are compounded. It is often extremely difficult to know who engaged in or authorized the conduct in question, what specific illegality has been committed, or whether there is a crime at all. For these reasons, crucial differences between white-collar crime and common crime appear when one examines how each is detected and prosecuted.

For common crimes, prosecution and defense are typically brought into play only after a crime has occurred and an arrest has been made, but in the case of white-collar crimes, the investigative work of prosecutors and the protective efforts of defense counsel characteristically precede, rather than follow, formal action. Indeed, from an enforcement perspective, white-collar crimes are those detected and investigated by white-collar workers, in contrast to the men in blue who respond to common crimes (Katz, 1979). The first officials to be brought into the case are not police but, more likely, tax agents or employees of a regulatory agency. Defense counsel will be hired when the defendant first becomes aware that he is a target of an investigation – typically, long before an indictment is forthcoming. This means that white-collar crime prosecution and defense often more closely approximate complex civil litigation, with its various strategic moves to gain or shield information from the opposing side, than they do the typical common-crime case. The effect of these differences is to make prosecution of white-collar cases vastly more expensive and time-consuming than that of typical common crimes. With limited resources, prosecutors may find it difficult to justify heavy expenditures for a problematic white-collar investigation when the same resources might be devoted to a number of common-crime cases.

Sentencing of white-collar offenders is also complicated. As in common crime, most cases will be settled by a guilty plea. But sentencing is problematic because the white-collar defendant, although frequently having committed offenses of long duration and great economic magnitude, is more likely to have an exemplary prior record. Judges are torn between the desire to show such offenders leniency because of their past good citizenship, and the desire to show severity because the white-collar offender has abused a position of trust. Thus, at each stage of the criminal justice system, white-collar offenses present a distinctive set of problems for law enforcement officials. For the legal philosopher as well as the policy maker, these differences raise questions of equality of treatment between common-crime and white-collar crime defendants, as well as questions of fundamental fairness in the operation of the criminal justice system. For the researcher, they point to the need to devote detailed attention to the comparative study of the administration of justice in white-collar-crime and common-crime cases.

CONCLUSION

As this review suggests, the concept of white-collar crime is in a state of disarray. Its evolution has been marked by changed in meaning that often preserve, rather than reduce, fundamental ambiguities. The term still denotes crimes of high status to some, while to others it refers to either occupational or organizational illegality. Some concentrate on the nature of the offense; others, on its consequences. The offending conduct appears in a different guise when the enforcement perspective is examined, and analysts still cannot agree whether it should be regarded as criminal.

Given this confusion, the logical solution is to abandon the concept of white-collar crime and develop separate, more neatly bounded areas of inquiry. One body of researchers might devote their attention to the relation of social status to criminality and to sentence disparity; another group, to the use of occupation in the commission of crimes. Still other investigators might study the various layers of formal organizations so as to examine how corporate offenses are conducted, and yet others might focus on regulatory agencies and their enforcement activities.

As neat as this solution might seem, it misses a fundamental point. Ambiguous since its outset, the concept of white-collar crime nevertheless appears to have enormous staying power. Why is it still in use, given its frailties? The suggestion is that the concept reflects deeply felt concerns that make psychological and social sense, even if they present logical ambiguities. The overall crime problem is commonly perceived to center on the lower echelons of society. It is the down-and-out, the unemployed, and the victims of stratification and race prejudice who constitute the bulk of those processed by the criminal justice system. White-collar crime, on the other hand, stands for all the wrongs committed by those in more advantaged positions. The source of the advantage may differ, sometimes reflecting individual status, sometimes occupational role, and sometimes organizational position. The animus that nourishes the concept is often an expression of frustration or outrage at the great imbalance of power between large organizations and their victims. Often, however, it reflects a concern for the weakening of the social fabric created when people in privileged positions destroy trust by committing crimes. Their offenses eat into the life of the community just as surely, if not as visibly, as physical assault. It is this combination of evocative features that keeps the concept of white-collar crime alive despite its flawed logical status.

When the original arguments over the meaning of the concept were at their height, the sociologist Vilhelm Aubert cautioned against efforts to decide on the concept's true meaning. White-collar crime struck him as a phenomenon highly reflective of more pervasive features of the social order. Theoretical interest lies precisely in the varying attitudes regarding such conduct held by persons from different stations in life. This view remains relevant and may well help explain the longevity of the concept. Many middle and upper-class citizens engage in some forms of white-collar illegality while condemning others. Rather than abandoning the concept because of its logical flaws, there is a need to examine its social meaning, as well as the conditions under which the various offenses that are grouped under the "white collar" rubric are committed, detected, and sanctioned.

D. Corporate Crime

EDWIN H. SUTHERLAND, *Crime of Corporations, The Sutherland Papers,* 78–96 (1956)*

About twenty years ago I began to study violations of law by businessmen and have continued the study intermittently to the present day. This study was begun for the purpose of improving the general explanations of criminal behavior. The theories of crime which

*Reprinted with permission from *The Sutherland Papers,* edited by Albert Cohen, Alfred Lindesmith, and Karl Schuessler. Copyright 1956 by Indiana University Press ©.

were then current and which are still current emphasized social and personal pathologies as the causes of crime. The social pathologies included, especially, poverty and the social conditions related to poverty, such as poor housing, lack of organized recreational facilities, the ignorance of parents, and family disorganization. The personal pathology emphasized in the earlier period was feeble-mindedness; the early theory asserted that feeble-mindedness is inherited and is the cause of both poverty and crime. At about the time I started the study of business crimes, the personal pathology which was used to explain crime was shifting from defective intelligence to defective emotions, as represented by concepts such as frustration, the inferiority complex and the Oedipus complex.

These theories that crime is due to social and personal pathologies had considerable support from the fact that a very large proportion of the persons arrested, convicted, and committed to prisons belong to the lower economic class.

In contrast to those theories, my theory was that criminal behavior is learned just as any other behavior is learned, and that personal and social pathologies play no essential part in the causation of crime. I believed that this thesis could be substantiated by a study of the violation of law by businessmen. Businessmen are generally not poor, are not feeble-minded, do not lack organized recreational facilities, and do not suffer from the other social and personal pathologies. If it can be shown that businessmen, without these pathologies, commit many crimes, then such pathologies cannot be used as the explanation of the crimes of other classes. The criminologists who have stated the theories of crimes get their data from personal interviews with criminals in the criminal courts, jails, and prisons, or from criminal statistics based on the facts regarding such criminals. But when businessmen commit crimes, their cases go generally before courts under equity or civil jurisdictions or before quasi-judicial commissions, and seldom before the criminal courts. Consequently, the criminologists do not come into contact with these businessmen and have not included their violations of law within general theories of criminal behavior.

I have used the term white-collar criminal to refer to a person in the upper socioeconomic class who violates the laws designed to regulate his occupation. The term white-collar is used in the sense in which it was used by President Sloan of General Motors, who wrote a book entitled *The Autobiography of a White Collar Worker.* The term is used more generally to refer to the wage-earning class which wears good clothes at work, such as clerks in stores.

I wish to report specifically on a part of my study

of white-collar crimes. I selected the 70 largest industrial and commercial corporations in the United States, not including public utilities and petroleum corporations. I have attempted to collect all the records of violations of law by each of these corporations, so far as these violations have been decided officially by courts and commissions. I have included the laws regarding restraint of trade, misrepresentation in advertising, infringement of patents, copyrights, and trademarks, rebates, unfair labor practices as prohibited by the National Labor Relations Law, financial fraud, violations of war regulations, and a small miscellaneous group of other laws. The records include the life careers of the corporations, which average about 45 years, and the subsidiaries as well as the main corporations. In this search I have been limited by the available records found in a university library, and this is far from complete. I am sure that the number of crimes I shall report on tonight is far smaller than the number actually decided by courts and commissions against these corporations.

This tabulation of the crimes of the 70 largest corporations in the United States gives a total of 980 adverse decisions. Every one of the 70 corporations has a decision against it, and the average number of decisions is 14.0. Of these 70 corporations, 98 percent are recidivists; that is they have two or more adverse decisions. Several states have enacted habitual criminal laws, which define an habitual criminal as a person who has been convicted four times of felonies. If we use this number and do not limit the convictions to felonies, 90 percent of the 70 largest corporations in the United States are habitual criminals. Sixty of the corporations have decisions against them for restraint of trade, 54 for infringements, 44 for unfair labor practices, 27 for misrepresentation in advertising, 26 for rebates, and 43 for miscellaneous offenses.

These decisions have been concentrated in the period since 1932. Approximately 60 per cent of them were made in the ten-year period subsequent to 1932, and only 40 per cent in the forty-year period prior to 1932. One possible explanation of this concentration is that the large corporations are committing more crimes than they did previously. My own belief is that the prosecution of large corporations has been more vigorous during the later period and that the corporations have not appreciably increased in criminality.

Of the 70 large corporations, 30 were either illegal in their origin or began illegal activities immediately after their origin; and 8 additional corporations should probably be added to the 30. That is, approximately half of the 70 corporations were either illegitimate in birth, or were infant and juvenile delinquents, as well as adult criminals.

All of the 980 decisions were decisions that these corporations violated laws. Only 159 of these 980 decisions were made by criminal courts, whereas 425 were made by courts under civil or equity jurisdiction and 361 by commissions. The most important question regarding white-collar crime is whether it is really crime. That is a difficult and somewhat technical question, and I shall not attempt to deal with it tonight since I have published a paper on that question. The general conclusion stated in that paper is that the violations of law which were attested by decisions of equity and civil courts and by administrative commissions are, with very few exceptions, crimes.

The statistics which I have presented are rather dry and may not mean much to the average student who is not a specialist in this field, but the prevalence of white-collar crimes by large corporations can be illustrated more concretely. If you consider the life of a person, you find that from the cradle to the grave he has been using articles which were sold or distributed in violation of the law. The professional criminals use the work "hot" to refer to an article which has been recently stolen. For the purpose of simplicity of statement, I wish to use this word to refer to articles manufactured by corporations, but I shall expand the meaning to include any official record without restricting it to recent times, and shall refer to a class of articles rather than articles manufactured by a particular concern. Using the word in this sense, we can say that a baby is assisted into this world with the aid of "hot" surgical instruments, rubbed with "hot" olive oil, wrapped in a "hot" blanket, weighed on "hot" scales. The father, hearing the good news, runs a "hot" flag up on his flag pole, goes to the golf course and knocks a "hot" golf ball around the course. The baby grows up, surrounded by such articles, and is finally laid to rest in a "hot" casket under a "hot" tombstone.

I now wish to describe in more detail violations of some of the specific laws and shall take first misrepresentation in advertising. Although the Pure Food and Drug Law contains a provision prohibiting misrepresentation on the labels of foods and drugs, the administrators of that law have not published regular reports including the names of the corporations which have been found to be in violation of the law. I shall therefore restrict the discussion to the misrepresentations in advertisements which have been decided on by the Federal Trade Commission.

This is one of the less important white-collar crimes, in comparison with the others. Decisions have been made in 97 cases against 26 of 70 corporations. No decisions were made against 44 of the 70 large corporations under this law. Of these 44 corporations against which no decisions were made, 27 may be classed as non-advertising corporations. That is, they do not advertise for purposes of their sales, although they may advertise for general goodwill or for the goodwill of the newspapers and journals. They sell their products to expert buyers, who cannot be influenced by advertising. It would be a waste of money for U.S. Steel to distribute pamphlets among the expert buyers of its products, claiming that its products were made from the finest ores, or with Bessemer steel imported from England, or to show a picture of a movie star in a Pullman saying, "I always select railroads which use rails made by U.S. Steel, because they are better rails," or a picture of a baseball manager saying, "I feel that my players are safer if they ride the trains on rails made by U.S. Steel, because these rails are safer." If these large corporations which do not advertise for sales purposes are eliminated, approximately 60 per cent of the large corporations which do advertise for sales purposes have decisions against them for misrepresentation in advertising.

These misrepresentations in advertising are not, in most cases, mere technical violations. The Federal Trade Commission each year makes a survey of several hundred thousand advertisements in periodicals and over the radios. From these they select about 50,000 which are questionable, and from these they pick out about 1,500 as patently false, and made adverse decisions against about 1,000 of these each year. Also, in their selection, they tend to concentrate on certain products in one year and other products in other years. About 1941, they concentrated on false advertisements of vitamins and issued desist orders against about 25 firms on this one product. The advertisements of vitamins at that time claimed with practically no qualifications that vitamins would restore vigor, aid digestion, eliminate sterility, prevent miscarriage, increase sex vigor, decrease blood pressure, reduce neuritis, reduce insomnia, stop falling hair, cure hay fever and asthma, cure alcoholism, prevent tooth decay, eliminate pimples, make chickens lay more eggs, and keep the dog in good health.

Misrepresentations fall into three principal classes. First, some advertisements are designed to sell products which are physically dangerous, with the dangers denied, minimized, or unmentioned. Most of these advertisements are in the drug and cosmetic businesses. Only 2 of the 70 large corporations have decisions against them for advertisements of this nature.

Second, some advertisements exaggerate the values of the products, and this is equivalent to giving short weights. An extreme case of advertisements of this nature was a case decided against two hoodlums in Chicago about 1930. They sold at a price of $10 a bottle of medicine to a blind man, with the claim that this would cure his blindness. When analyzed, the medicine was found to consist of two aspirins dissolved in Lake Michigan water. The hoodlums were convicted and sentenced to six months' imprisonment. The advertisements by large corporations are frequently of this class except that they are not so extreme and are not followed by convictions in criminal courts and imprisonment. Garments advertised and sold as silk or wool are almost entirely cotton. Alligator shoes not made from alligator hides, walnut furniture not made from walnut lumber, turtle-oil facial cream not made from turtle-oil, Oriental rugs not made in the Orient, Hudson seal furs not made from the skins of seals are further instances of such misrepresentation. Caskets advertised as rustproof are not rustproof, garments as mothproof when they are not mothproof, garden hose as three-ply when it is only two-ply, and radios as "all-wave reception" that do not receive all waves. Electric pads are advertised with switches for high, medium and low heat, when in fact they have only two degrees of heat. Storage eggs are sold as fresh eggs, old and re-conditioned stoves as new stoves, and worn and re-conditioned hats as new hats. Facial creams sold as skin-foods, corrective of wrinkles, do not feed the skin or correct wrinkles. Some corporations advertise that their tea is made from tender leaves, especially picked for these corporations, when in fact their tea is purchased from lots brought in by importers who sell the same tea to other firms. Cigarettes are advertised as having been made from the finest tobacco, for which the company pays 25 per cent more, but other cigarettes are also made from the "finest tobacco" for which the manufacturers pay 25 per cent more than they do for chewing tobacco.

The third class of misrepresentation overlaps the two preceding and is separated from them principally because certain advertisements do special injury to the competitors rather than to consumers. One mail-order company advertised their furnaces as containing features which no other furnaces contained when in fact the furnaces of competitors contained the same features. Consumers Research Service, which claimed to make impartial and unbiased appraisals of automobiles, was found, in fact, to be receiving payments from an automobile company for reporting that their cars were superior.

I wish to describe a few of the important cases of misrepresentation in advertising. A prominent automobile manufacturer originated the 6 per cent installment purchase plan in 1935. This plan as advertised stated that the interest rate on unpaid balances on cars purchased on the installment plan was only 6 per cent. The Federal Trade Commission, after an investigation, reported that the interest rate was actually in excess of 11 per cent and that the exaggeration in the interest rate was nearly 100 per cent. Before the Commission had ordered the pioneer firm to desist from this misrepresentation, practically all the other large automobile companies adopted the same method of taking money under false pretenses. Again, in 1936, all the important automobile companies were ordered, on two counts, to desist from misrepresentation in advertising their cars. First, they quoted a price which did not include necessary parts and accessories, the price for the car as actually equipped being 10 per cent higher than the advertised price. In addition, they added handling charges independent of transportation costs, which further increased the price required. Second, they advertised a picture of a car which was not the model actually named and priced. Again, in 1941, three of the four principal manufacturers of automobile tires were ordered to desist from misrepresentation in their advertisements of special sales prices on the fourth of July and on Labor Day. These companies advertised prices which were reductions of 20 to 50 per cent from the regular prices. When the Federal Trade Commission investigated, it found that the 20 per cent reduction was actually only an 8 per cent reduction and the 50 per cent reduction only an 18 per cent reduction. In addition, one tire company was found to have engaged in misrepresentation in two respects. First, it advertised that with its tires a car would stop 25 per cent quicker. It did not say 25 per cent quicker than what, but the implication was 25 per cent quicker than with tires of other manufacturers, and this was not true. Second, it made claims for the greater safety of its tires on the basis of the fact that these tires were used in the Indianapolis speedway races, whereas in fact the Speedway tires had been especially constructed, so that there was no assurance that the company's tires for regular passenger cars were safer than other tires.

When the Federal Bureau of Investigation hunts kidnappers, it tries to find everyone who is in any way accessory to the kidnapping. The Federal Trade Commission, similarly, has attempted to some degree to bring into the picture those who are accessory to misrepresentation in advertising. They have, for instance, issued desist orders to many of the advertising agencies, which prepare the advertising campaigns for the manufacturers. Though these desist orders have included many small and unimportant advertising agencies, they have included also the largest and most prominent agencies.

Also, practically all the newspapers and popular journals have participated in dissemination of false advertisements. These include publications which range from the Gannett publications at one extreme to the *Journal of the American Medical Association* at the other. Although the *Journal of the American Medical Association* claims that it does not carry advertisements which have not been checked and found to be true, it has for years carried advertisements of Philip Morris cigarettes. In earlier years the company had claimed that these cigarettes cured irritated throats and in later years claimed that they produced less irritation in the throat than other cigarettes. As proof of their truth, these advertisements cited the opinions and experiments of physicians many, if not all, of whom had received payment for their statements. Competing tobacco companies employed other physicians, who performed experiments and gave testimony which conflicted with the testimony in the Journal of the *American Medical Association*. The Philip Morris Company made a grant of $10,000 to St. Louis University to test these propositions. The Medical School insisted on complete freedom in its methods of testing and in making its report. The report was that no accurate method of testing throat irritation had been devised or of testing the effect of the substances in question, and that conflicting claims of experimenters were all bunk. The Philip Morris Company gave no publicity to that report, but their advertisements continued to appear in the Journal of the *American Medical Association*.

I do not want to take the time to go into similar detail in regard to other types of violations of law, but I shall describe a few incidents involving violations of the National Labor Relations Law. This law was enacted first in 1933 and in more developed form in 1935. It stated that collective bargaining had proved to be a desirable policy and prohibited employers from interfering with the efforts of employees to organize unions for purposes of collective bargaining. A violation of this law was declared to be an unfair labor practice. Decisions have been made against 43 of the 70 large corporations, or 60 per cent, with a total of 149 decisions. Of these 43 corporations, 72 per cent are recidivists or repeaters; 39 used interference, restraint, and coercion, 33 discriminated against union members, 34 organized company unions, 13 used labor spies, and 5 used violence. Violence has been confined largely to the steel and automobile industries. One steel corporation from 1933 to 1937 purchased 143 gas-guns, while the police Department of Chicago purchased in the same years only 13; the steel corporation also purchased 6,714 gas shells and grenades while the Police Department purchased only 757. The corporations customarily argue that they purchase this military equipment merely to protect themselves against the violence of the unions. Doubtless the equipment is used for protective purposes, but it is also used on some occasions for aggression. I wish to report one decision of the National Labor Relations Board concerning the Ford Motor Company. Henry Ford is reported to have said in 1937, "We'll never recognize the United Automobile Workers union or any other union." The Ford Corporation organized a service department, under the supervision of Harry Bennett, an ex-pugilist, and staffed it with 600 members equipped with guns and blackjacks. Frank Murphy, at the time governor of Michigan and previously mayor of Detroit, said, regarding this service department, "Henry Ford employs some of the worst gangsters in our city."

In 1937 the United Automobile Workers Union was attempting to organize the employees in the River Rouge plant of the Ford Motor Company. A public announcement was made that the organizers would distribute literature at this plant at a specified time. Reporters and others gathered in advance. When a reporter asked a guard what they were going to do when the organizers arrived, the guard replied, "We are going to throw them to hell out of here." The organizers arrived, went with their literature up onto an overhead pass into one of the entrances. There they were informed that they were trespassing on private property. According to many witnesses they turned quietly and started away. As they were leaving, they were attacked by the Service staff. They were beaten, knocked down, and kicked. Witnesses described this as a "terrific beating" and as "unbelievably brutal." The beating not only occurred on the overhead pass but was continued into the public highway. One man's back was broken and another's skull fractured. The cameras of reporters, who were taking pictures of the affray, were seized by the guards and the films destroyed. A reporter who was taking a picture from the highway was observed by a guard, who shouted, "Smash that camera." The reporter jumped into the automobile of another reporter, and they were chased by the guards at a speed of eighty miles an hour through the streets of Detroit until they could secure refuge in a police station. According to pre-arranged plans, women organizers arrived later to distribute literature. As they alighted from the streetcar at the entrance to the plant, they were attacked by the guards and pushed back into the cars. One woman was knocked down and kicked. While these assaults were being committed, city policemen were present and did not interfere; the Director of the Service Department was also present.

I wish next to give a few illustrations of embezzlement and violation of trust by officers of corporations. Seiberling organized the Goodyear Rubber Company and was its manager for many years. Because of financial difficulties in the corporation, he lost control of it in 1921. His successors found that Seiberling was short nearly $4,000,000 in his account with the company, that

is, that he had embezzled that amount from the company. The suits which were brought resulted in a settlement by which Seiberling agreed to reimburse the company. He not only did this but also secured credit from Ohio financiers and started the Seiberling rubber company, which has been quite successful.

President Sloan, Mr. Raskob, and other officers of General Motors developed a plan to pay bonuses to the officers and directors of General Motors. Under this plan President Sloan secured a total payment from the corporation of $20,000,000 between 1923 and 1928. When suits were started in later years these excessive payments prior to 1930 were not included in the suits because of the statute of limitations. The court held, however, that these officers had appropriated by fraudulent methods of calculating their bonuses approximately $4,000,000 and ordered them to repay this amount to the corporation.

George Washington Hill and other officers of the American Tobacco Company were criticized and sued for appropriating corporate funds for their enormous salaries and bonuses. One of these suits was to be tried before Judge Manton in the Federal Court in New York City. Shortly before the trial Judge Manton suggested to the attorney for the American Tobacco Company that he needed to borrow $250,000. The attorney mentioned this to the assistant to the president of the American Tobacco Company, who mentioned it to Lord and Thomas, the advertising firm for the company, and Lord and Thomas lent Judge Manton the $250,000. Judge Manton decided the case in favor of the American Tobacco Company. Probably his decision was correct, but he was convicted of receiving a bribe, the attorney for the company was disbarred from practice in federal courts, and the assistant to the president, who made the arrangements, was promoted immediately after the decision to the position of vice-president, where he was entitled to a bonus. In another suit, the American Tobacco Company paid from its own treasury $260,000 to the complainant, and also $320,000 to its law firm, and made other payments to bring the total for fixing this case to approximately a million dollars. A court later ordered the officers, against whom the suit was brought, to reimburse the corporation for these payments.

Finally, I wish to discuss the violation of the antitrust laws. Restraint of trade was prohibited by the Sherman Antitrust Law of 1890 and by several subsequent laws, and also by the laws of most of the states. Decisions that such laws were violated have been made against 60 of the 70 large corporations in 307 cases. Three motion-picture corporations stand at the top of the list for restraint of trade with 22, 21 and 21 decisions, respectively. Thus 86 per cent of the seventy corporations have decisions against them for restraint of trade, and 73 per cent of the corporations with such decisions are recidivists. Although no decisions have been made against the other to corporations, other evidence indicates that probably every one of them has in fact violated these laws. These decisions tend to corroborate the statement made by Walter Lippmann, "Competition has survived only where men have been unable to abolish it." Not law but expediency and practicability have determined the limits of restraint of trade. Big Business does not like competition, and it makes careful arrangements to reduce it and even eliminate it. In certain industries the negotiations among large corporations to avoid competition are very similar to international diplomacy except that they are more successful.

For competition these businessmen have substituted private collectivism. They meet together and determine what the prices shall be and how much shall be produced, and also regulate other aspects of the economic process. This is best illustrated by the trade associations, although it is not limited to them. These trade associations not only fix prices and limit production, but they have set up systems of courts with penalties for violation of their regulations. Their system of justice applies both to their own members, in which case they have a semblance of democracy, and also to non-members, in which case they resemble dictatorship and racketeering. Among 92 trade associations investigated in 1935-39, 28 had facilities for investigating or snooping on their members, 11 had provisions for fining those who violated regulations, and 18 had provisions for boycotting the offenders.

Although businessmen often complain that the antitrust law is so vague that they cannot determine whether they are violating the law or not, a very large proportion of the decisions against these 70 corporations are for making agreements to have uniform prices—that is, not to compete as to prices. This practice is clearly in violation of the antitrust law, and no one at all acquainted with its provisions and with the decisions made under it could have the least doubt that such behavior is illegal. Also, many of the agreements limit production. Businessmen have insisted for at least seventy-five years on limiting production in order to keep prices from falling. Though many people have regarded as ridiculous the agricultural policy of killing little pigs, it is in principle the policy which industrial corporations have been using for many generations, long before it was ever applied in agriculture.

What significance do these violations of the antitrust law have? The economic system, as described by the classical economists, was a system of free competition and laissez faire, or free enterprise, as we call it today. Free competition was the regulator of the economic system. The laws of supply and demand, operating under free competition, determined prices, profits, the flow of capital, the distribution of labor, and other economic phenomena. When profits in an industry were high, other businessmen rushed into that industry in the hope of securing similar profits. This resulted in an increase in the supply of commodities, which produced a reduction in prices, and this in turn reduced profits. Thus, the excessive profits were eliminated, the prices were reduced, and the public had a larger supply of the commodity. Through this regulation by free competition, according to the classical economists, Divine Providence produced the greatest welfare of the entire society. Free competition was to be sure, a harsh regulator. Cut-throat practices were general, and in the achievement of the welfare of the total society weaker establishments were often ruined.

Because free competition regulated the economic system, governmental regulation was unnecessary. The economic system of the classical economists developed primarily because business revolted against the governmental regulations of the feudal period, which were not adapted to the changing conditions of the eighteenth century. Government kept out of business after this system was established, except as it enforced contracts, protected the public against larceny and fraud, and enforced the principles of free competition by the common law prohibition of restraint of trade.

During the last century this economic and political system has changed. The changes have resulted principally from the efforts of businessmen. If the word "subversive" refers to efforts to make fundamental changes in a social system, the business leaders are the most subversive influence in the United States. These business leaders have acted as individuals or in small groups, seeking preferential advantages for themselves. The primary loyalty of the businessman has been to profits, and he has willingly sacrificed the general and abstract principles of free competition and free enterprise in circumstances which promised a pecuniary advantage. Moreover, he has been in a position of power and has been able to secure these preferential advantages. Although businessmen had no intention of modifying the economic and political system, they have produced this result. The restriction of the principle of free competition has been demonstrated by the practically universal policy of restraint of trade among large corporations.

The restriction of free enterprise has also come principally from businessmen. Free enterprise means, of course, freedom from governmental regulation and governmental interference. Although businessmen have been vociferous as to the virtues of free enterprise, and have in general insisted that government keep its hands out of and off business, businessmen above all others have put pressure on the government to interfere in business. They have not done this en masse, but as individuals or as small groups endeavoring to secure advantages for themselves. These efforts of businessmen to expand the governmental regulations of business are numerous and have a wide range. One of the best illustrations is the early and continued pressure of business concerns to secure tariffs to protect them from foreign competition. Many statutes have been enacted as the result of pressure from particular business interests to protect one industry against competition from another, as illustrated by the tax on oleomargarine. Another illustration is the fair trade law of the Federal and state governments, which prohibit retail dealers from cutting prices on trademarked articles. The Federal fair trade law was enacted in 1937. The bill was presented by Senator Tydings, as a rider to a District of Columbia appropriations bill, where it could not be discussed on its merits. The bill was prepared by the law partner of the senator, and this law partner was the attorney for the National Association of Retail Druggists. The bill was supported by many national associations of manufacturers and dealers, who were opposed to the competitive principle and to free enterprise. The bill was opposed by the Department of Justice and the Federal Trade Commission, which have been attempting to preserve the principle of free competition and free enterprise.

In fact, the interests of businessmen have changed, to a considerable extent, from efficiency in production to efficiency in public manipulation, including manipulation of the government for the attainment of preferential advantages. This attention to governmental favors has tended to produce two results: first, it has tended to pauperize business in the sense in which charity tends to pauperize poor people, and second, it has tended to corrupt government. But the most significant result of the violations of the antitrust laws by large business concerns is that these have made our system of free competition and free enterprise unworkable. We no longer have competition as a regulator of economic processes; we have not substituted efficient governmental regulation. We cannot go back to competition. We must go forward to some new system—perhaps communism, perhaps co-operativism, perhaps much more complete governmental regulation than we now have. I don't know what lies ahead of us and am not particularly concerned, but I do know that what was a fairly efficient system has been destroyed by the illegal behavior of Big Business.

Furthermore, the businessmen have practically destroyed our system of patents by the same procedures.

The system of patents was authorized in our Constitution to promote the development of science and the arts. The patent system has become one of the principal methods of promoting monopoly. Not one patent in a hundred pays even the costs of registration. Patents are important for business establishments primarily because they can be used to eliminate or regulate competitors. This is illustrated by the variation in the extent to which corporations apply for patents and bring suits for infringements of patents. In industries such as steel, very few patents are secured, and very few patent-infringement suits initiated, because establishments in this country are protected from competition by the heavy capital investment. On the other hand, in industries such as the chemical industry and the manufacture of electrical equipment, new competitors can start with a very small investment. The large companies protect themselves against competition by taking out patents on every possible modification of procedure, bringing suits on every possible pretext, and granting licenses to use patents only with a highly regimented and bureaucratic control. The patent is important principally because it is a weapon for fighting competitors. This can be seen in the practice of some of the small concerns, where widespread monopoly is not threatened. The Miniature Golf Corporation secured a patent on its vacant-lot recreation and filed scores of suits against anyone who used this method without a paid license from them. The Good Humor Corporation engaged in patent litigation for more than a decade with the Popsicle Company and other manufacturers of ice-cream bars, to determine which firm had invented this contribution to science and the arts. Similarly, the Maiden-form Brassiere Company and the Snug-Fit Foundations, Inc., were before the courts for many years regarding their patented designs, each charging the other with infringement.

The general conclusion from this study of the 70 large corporations is that the ideal businessman and the large corporation are very much like the professional thief.

First, their violations of law are frequent and continued. As stated previously, 97 per cent of the large corporations are recidivists.

Second, illegal behavior by the corporations is much more prevalent than the prosecutions indicate. In other words, only a fraction of the violations of law by a particular corporation result in prosecution, and only a fraction of the corporations which violate the law are prosecuted. In general, a few corporations are prosecuted for behavior which is industry-wide.

Third, the businessman who violates laws regulating business does not lose status among his business associates. I have mentioned President Sloan of General Motors and Seiberling (previously of the Goodyear Rubber Company), and many others could be mentioned who have appropriated the funds of their own corporations fraudulently, and who have not lost status in their own corporations or in the eyes of other businessmen. Leonor F. Loree, chairman of the Kansas City Southern, knowing that his company was about to purchase stock of another railway, went into the market privately and secretly and purchased shares of this stock in advance of his corporation, and then, when the price of the stock increased, sold it at the higher price, making a profit of $150,000. This profit, of course, was made at the expense of the corporation of which he was chairman, and he could make the profit because as an officer he knew the plans of the corporation. The courts, however, determined that this profit was fraudulent, and ordered Mr. Loree to reimburse the corporation for the violation of his trust. Shortly after this decision became generally known, Mr. Loree was elected president of the New York Chamber of Commerce, perhaps in admiration of his cleverness.

Fourth, businessmen feel and express contempt for legislators, bureaucrats, courts, "snoopers," and other governmental officials and for law, as such. In this respect, also, they are akin to the professional thieves, who feel and express contempt for police, prosecutors, and judges. Both professional thieves and corporations feel contempt for government because government interferes with their behavior.

Businessmen, being like professional thieves in these four respects, are participants in organized crime. Their violations of law are not identical and haphazard, but they have definite policies of restraint of trade, of unfair labor practices, of fraud and misrepresentation.

Businessmen differ from professional thieves principally in their greater interest in status and respectability. They think of themselves as honest men, not as criminals, whereas professional thieves, when they speak honestly, admit that they are thieves. The businessman does regard himself as a law-breaker, but he thinks the laws are wrong or at least that they should not restrict him, although they may well restrict others. He does not think of himself as a criminal because he does not conform to the popular stereotype of the criminal. This popular stereotype is always taken from the lower socioeconomic class.

I have attempted to demonstrate that businessmen violate the law with great frequency, using what may be called the methods of organized crime. I have attempted in another place to demonstrate that these violations of law are really crimes. If these conclusions are correct, it is very clear that the criminal behavior of businessmen cannot be explained by poverty, in the usual sense, or by bad housing or lack of recreational facilities or feeble-mindedness or emotional instability. Business leaders are capable, emotionally balanced, and in no sense pathological. We

have no reason to think that General Motors has an inferiority complex or that the Aluminum Company of America has a frustration-aggression complex or that U.S. Steel has an Oedipus complex, or that the Armour Company has a death wish or that the DuPonts desire to return to the womb. The assumption that an offender must have some such pathological distortion of the intellect or the emotions seems to me absurd and if it is absurd regarding the crimes of businessmen, it is equally absurd regarding the crimes of persons in the lower economic class.

MARSHALL B. CLINARD AND PETER C. YEAGER, ILLEGAL CORPORATE BEHAVIOR 14–25, 109–115, 147–148 (1979)*

The extensive nature of law violations by corporations is unquestioned today; it has been widely revealed by many government investigative committees, both state and federal. These investigations have covered banking institutions, stock exchange operations, insurance, railroads, and the large oil, food and drug industries. More recently, investigations have exposed widespread corporate domestic and foreign payoffs and illegal political contributions. Throughout the violations have shown the immense economic and political power, the widespread operations, and the enormous amounts of money involved. . . .

B. Corporate Crime as White Collar Crime: Distinctions

Corporate crime is, of course, white collar crime; but it is of a particular type. As will be explained, corporate crime is actually organizational crime that occurs in the context of complex and varied sets of structured relationships and interrelationships between boards of directors, executives, and managers on the one hand and between parent corporation, corporate divisions and subsidiaries on the other. Such a concept, in terms of crime, has developed rather gradually, and it is only natural that it should often be confused with a broader area of more general crime among the so-called "white collar" groups. The concept of white collar crime was developed to distinguish

---

* Reprinted with permission of Law Enforcement Assistance Administration, United States Department of Justice.

a body of criminal acts that involved monetary offenses not ordinarily associated with criminality. It is distinguished from lower socio-economic crimes in two respects: the nature of the violation and the fact that administrative and civil penalties are far more likely to be used as punishment than criminal penalties. Relatively speaking, it is a rather recent addition to criminological theory.

Most white collar crimes are crimes associated with, and linked to, an individual's occupation. They are acts of individuals, or of small groups of individuals, as for example, a typical business or concern that sells securities. Except for the similarity to some types of business violations, corporate crimes are completely different. Crimes committed by them cannot be likened to those of individuals, even if one regards a giant corporation, in a legal sense, as a "person." As was initially pointed out, they are organizational crimes occurring in the context of extremely complex interrelationships. Corporate conduct "must be enacted by collectivities or aggregates of discrete individuals, it is hardly comparable to the action of a lone individual" (Shapiro, 1976: 14). Here it is the organization, not the occupation, that is of prime importance.

The entity that is called a corporation is completely different from the collection of its management personnel; many corporations are, in fact, huge conglomerates. If occupational crime is to be considered as synonymous with white collar crime a distinction can be made between the crimes of corporate officials which represent corporate crime and those that constitute white collar or occupational crime. Distinctions are based on whether the official is acting for the corporation or for his personal interest and against the corporation. If a policy making corporate executive is acting in the name of the corporation and the individual's decision to violate the law is for the benefit of the corporation, as in price-fixing violations, the violation would constitute corporate crime. If, on the other hand, the corporate official acts against the corporation, as in the case of embezzlement, and financing benefits in a personal way from his official connections with the corporation, his acts would constitute white collar or occupational crime. White collar criminal acts committed for the benefit of a corporate official, therefore, such as embezzlement or corporate funds, etc. are not considered corporate crimes. Doing something for the corporation and for oneself against the corporation can, on occasion, however, coalesce.

C. The Recognition of Corporate Crime

In the field of criminology there has been limited research on white collar crime, and within this area there has been very little research on corporate crime. Sutherland carried out the first empirical study in the field, and his work served to convince criminologists of the importance of doing research in this field. His *White Collar Crime,* published in 1949, dealt with the illegal behavior of 70 of the 200 largest U.S. non-financial corporations (Sutherland, 1949). For 25 years following Sutherland's work, however, there was only limited follow-up research and only minimal study was made on illegal corporate behavior. Relatively few quantitative research articles have appeared, all rather narrow in scope and again dealing largely with antitrust violations. Of significance is this relative lack of research; Sutherland's study remains basically the only broad research on corporate crime, as his *White Collar Crime* should actually have been *Corporate Crime.* It continues, therefore, to be widely cited in spite of its largely obsolete data, the weak methodological procedures, the unsystematic analysis of the data, and Sutherland's failure to use independent variables in data analyses. In addition, this study covered only federal law violations by a small group of large corporations.

For some decades since Sutherland, criminologists paid only lip service to the topic of corporate crime; largely it has been only since the mid-1970s that corporate crime has been incorporated into the criminology discipline and serious studies have been incorporated into the criminology discipline and serious studies have been undertaken. The first basic book to include a chapter on corporate crime appeared in 1973 (Clinard and Quinney, 1973: Chapter 8). Criminology textbooks now conventionally include a chapter or a lengthy discussion on the subject. Corporate crime first appeared as a separate topic covered at a professional society meeting at the 1975 session of the American Society of Criminology; in each subsequent year there has been a section on corporate crime. Similar sections are now included in the meetings of the Society for the Study of Social Problems and those of the American Sociology Association, and articles on corporate crime are appearing more frequently in professional journals.

This increased recognition of corporate crime has largely been a quite natural response to social forces, particularly the growth of public concern for, and knowledge about, corporate wrongdoings. Perhaps a central force in the present and growing interest in crimes in this area of business might be said quite simply to be the dramatic increase in both the role and the impact of the major corporations in contemporary American society. The major corporations are the very central institutions in our society; little wonder then that public and regulatory attention is turning increasingly toward them.

It is possible to identify some of the more specific

social forces in American society which have contributed to what appears to be an almost sudden criminological interest and concern with corporate crime (see Clinard and Yeager, 1978). They include certain highly publicized serious corporate violations, increased recognition of corporate irresponsibility, the growth of the consumer movement, increased environmental concern, reaction to the overconcentration on concern with lower-class crimes and poverty problems, and the influence of conflict analysis and Radical Criminology on Criminology (see Quinney, 1974 and 1977; Chambliss and Seidman 1971; and Taylor, Walton and Young, 1973).

The paucity of research on corporate illegalities has been due to a number of factors. First, an important barrier has been a lack of experience and appropriate training. For criminologists trained in criminal law and accustomed to studying individual offenders, the study of corporate crime has necessitated a significant reorientation – greater familiarity with the concepts and research in the areas of political sociology, complex organizations, administrative law (for example, the regulatory agencies), civil law, and economics. Corporate violations, as well as their control, take place within a complex political and economic environment, and most often they involve administrative and civil sanctions to which criminologists have generally had only limited exposure. State and federal agencies rather than the courts, furthermore, handle most of the enforcement, and criminologists for the most part have had little experience with these agencies. Second, it was generally believed in the past to be difficult to gain access to regulatory agency enforcement data, or to court cases related to corporations. Third, only limited funds have been available for research in this area, while resources have been plentiful for research on ordinary crime, due to the traditional interest in conventional crime, to a lack of concern for research on illegal corporate behavior, and also to the fact that criminologists have felt unable to set up viable research projects. As a result, criminologists have generally taken the easy path and have continued to study conventional crime, or, at best, small-scale consumer frauds. This situation is now changing, particularly in the availability of research funds for studies on white collar and corporate crime. Many of these funds have recently been made available through the Law Enforcement Assistance Administration of the Department of Justice.

D. The Definition of Corporate Crime

The criminal law may be defined as a body of specialized rules of a politically organized society that contain provisions for punishment (probation, fine, imprisonment, and even death) administered in the name of the political state when a violation has been substantiated through judicial or court procedures. In a strictly legal sense, an act is a crime only if the statutes so specify; these statutes; together with the subsequent interpretation of them by the courts, constitute the body of criminal law. This definition applies well to burglary and robbery; corporate crimes, however, cannot be defined and studied in such a limited manner. Our criminal laws represent only a part of a larger body of law; there are in addition administrative and civil laws. Although these laws are not applicable to the ordinary criminal offender, they are for the most part the manner in which corporate violations are handled. Violations of these civil and administrative laws are also subject to punishment by the political state. From the research point of view, then, corporate crime includes any act punished by the state, regardless of whether it is punished under administrative, civil or criminal law (Sutherland, 1945 and 1949; Clinard, 1952; Clinard and Meier, 1979: 168-169).

In the research study of corporate crime, which is the main subject of this report, however, the wide range of seriousness of corporate violations has been recognized. Consequently violations have been ranked as serious, moderate and minor and much of the analyses reflect this distinction. Reporting, such as paperwork, violations and similar violations of administrative law have generally been considered minor violations; other types of violations of administrative law may be considered serious or moderate, depending on the nature of the violation. On the other hand when considering enforcement actions no such distinction can generally be made as to seriousness because, for example, a warning letter, an administrative consent agreement or a court-imposed consent order may actually have involved a serious or moderate violation.

Because of their more recent origin and the considerations of legislative power that both white collar classes and corporate bodies possess they are far less likely to be punished under the criminal law. The criminal sanctions used in criminal law cases are, therefore, not as likely to have been provided as penalties for corporate violations. Penalties provided for the latter violations area far more likely to be exclusively or alternatively civil or administrative. Any definition of crime, therefore, solely in terms of the criminal law is too restrictive for an adequate understanding of behavior like corporate crime; in many cases the regulation of white collar and corporate offenses provides for the criminal law along with alternative sanctions such as civil and administrative actions. Moreover, the criminal law, because of power difficulties in its application, is not as likely to be used. In general business and corporate offenders are "administratively segregated" from conventional offenders in the United States (Sutherland, 1940: 8). Administrative rather than criminal sanctions against corporations are widely used in Great Britain and Canada (Goff and Reasons, 1978). Moreover, civil and criminal cases cannot be distinguished on the basis of the formal burden of proof required. It appears that, if anything, civil courts, in practice, have a more exacting burden of proof than do criminal courts (Pepinsky, 1974: 226). The two categories in actuality do not necessarily differentiate wrongs by seriousness.

The administrative and civil enforcement measures generally used in corporate violations include warning letters, consent agreements or decrees and agreements not to repeat the violation, seizure or recall of commodities, administrative or civil monetary penalties, and court injunctions to refrain from further violations. For the most part corporate lawbreakers are handled by administrative quasi-judicial boards of government regulatory agencies such as the Federal Trade Commission, the National Labor Relations Board and the Food and Drug Administration. These government regulatory agencies may impose an administrative "remedy" or they may ask the civil or criminal courts to do so, as for example to issue an injunction. Although only officers of a corporation can be sent to prison or fined, an action seldom taken, corporate liability is becoming increasingly common under the criminal law. Corporations are also being more often punished by fines, sometimes heavy ones, under the criminal law. A "corporation" cannot, of course, be jailed, so the major penalty of imprisonment, as used to control individual persons (with the exception of corporate officers), is unavailable in the case of corporations.

It is believed by many that violations that lead to administrative or civil penalties are not really crimes. Unless one uses a more inclusive concept of "crime" it is not possible to deal analytically with the different illegal activities that are punished by law according to social class, such as corporate crime. A conviction in the criminal court is not an adequate criterion, since a large proportion of those who commit crimes are not convicted in the criminal courts but through administrative hearings and civil courts (Sutherland, 1940: 5). Sutherland stated that the criterion of the criminal law should be supplemented by other forms of law and in doing so the criteria of the crimes of one class should be kept consistent in general terms with the criterion of other class crimes (Sutherland, 1940: 5).

Even in the broad area of legal proceedings, however, corporate crime is generally treated with an aura of politeness and a respectability rarely afforded, if ever, in cases of ordinary crimes. As alternative penalties to the criminal law are provided, corporations are also seldom referred to as "criminals." Even if violations of the criminal law were involved along with other laws, this study revealed in conversations about corporate crime that enforcement attorneys, as well as corporation counsels, generally refer to the "corporation having a 'problem,'" or "the corporation should bring its 'problem' to the enforcement official." One does not speak of the robber or the burglar as "having a 'problem' with the government."

Even after a consent order or other legal settlement has been reached it is typical for a corporation to deny guilt partly to avoid possible other government actions and private suits. In one settlement of $229,000 for illegal campaign contributions of millions of dollars, which involved "laundering" the money, a Gulf Oil spokesman stated that the company had made the payment settlement "without admitting any corporate liability." He added that it was made to "protect the company against any future claims" regarding the past transfer of political funds from overseas (*The Wall Street Journal*, November 14, 1977). In settling a $4.3 million Saudi Arabian payoff, Hospital Corporation of America stated: "The company believes that its actions with regard to payment of fees was reasonable and appropriate under the circumstances and its actions did not constitute violations of applicable laws." It agreed to terminate this controversy in order to avoid expenses and the inconvenience of protracted litigation (*The Wall Street Journal*, October 27, 1978). After Schlitz Brewing Company had pleaded guilty to kickbacks to retailers and had been fined $761,000 the brewing company said it should not be construed as an admission on the part of the company that it had violated any law or regulation.

E. The Present Study

This particular research represents the first large-scale comprehensive investigation of corporations directly related to their violations of law. It examines the extent and nature of these illegal activities, and examines the data in terms of the corporate structure and the economic setting in which the violations occurred. The study has concentrated on an empirical investigation of the 582 largest publicly owned corporations in the United States: 477 manufacturing, 18 wholesale, 66 retail and 21 service. A major focus has been on manufacturing enterprises. Corporations in banking, insurance, transportation, communication and utilities have been excluded as in Sutherland's 1949 study because of the unusual nature of these businesses (i.e. they are subject to more strict regulation and/or licensing). The annual sales for 1975 of the corporations studied ranged from $300 million to more than $45 billion, with an average sales volume of $1.7 billion for parent firms. Data covered all enforcement actions that could be secured, initiated or imposed by 24 federal agencies during 1975 and 1976. Revealed for the first time ever, therefore, is the wide range of types of corporate violations, as well as actions initiated and imposed by government agencies. Predictions of what types of corporations violate the law have also been attempted through an analysis of data in terms of corporate structure and financial data which are then used to compare with industry-level data. Some of the hypotheses are that unfavorable trends in such areas as sales, profits, and earnings are associated with violations. An analysis is presented of the characteristics of corporations against which limited actions have been initiated with those against which initiated actions have been extensive. Actions of parent corporations have then been compared with their 101 largest subsidiaries, whose 1976 annual sales ranged from $300 million to $7.8 billion, on the hypothesis that pressures from parent corporations to increase profits contribute to the greater violations of the subsidiaries.

The present study is basically similar in approach to that used by Sutherland: both study the largest corporations and attempt to cover a wide range of enforcement actions rather than actions restricted, for example, to antitrust violations as has been done in other studies. Both define corporate "crime" as violations of administrative and civil, as well as criminal, law; they are in accord that research limited to the criminal law violations would give a limited, as well as a false, picture of corporate crime simply because alternative procedures are available, which is not the case with ordinary crime. They both also exclude public utility, transportation, communication, and banking corporations on the ground that they are regulated by commission and that the violations that might occur in these areas are thus restricted both in nature and in extent.

These are the similarities in the studies; the differences are extensive, in fact so extensive that only a few superficial comparisons of the findings are possible. This research is on a far more comprehensive scale; it is much more complex methodologically; and it also attempts to predict economic variables related to violations. Sutherland's methodology was simplistic, with little description even offered of the problems encountered and how they were met. Less than seven paragraphs or four pages were devoted to the description of the data and methodology. Sutherland's contribution was significant, in the final analysis, because he studied empirically and for the first time, the crimes of the giant corporations and because he attempted a theoretical interpretation of their importance and nature, not because of his findings or the rigor of his research. . . .

ENFORCEMENT ACTIONS AGAINST CORPORATIONS

The discussion that follows describes the analysis of enforcement actions or sanctions taken by the federal government against 582 large corporations, including 477 manufacturing, during 1975 and 1976.

A. Diversity of Enforcement Actions

As with corporate violations, the great diversity of enforcement actions necessitated the construction of an extensive four-level code to represent increasing specificity of the sanctions. It followed the same pattern as used with the violations data, information on up to five enforcement actions in a single case was coded. For each of the five enforcement actions, information was gathered as to which case it referred to, whether it was a detail of a single violation or a separate sanction, the status (imposed, proposed or prosecution terminated), whether the corporation had consented to it, the level of enforcement of the sanction (court or administrative and criminal, civil or administrative), and whether it was against the corporation, the officer or both. Several factors complicated the coding scheme: (1) Although the unit of analysis was the violation, sometimes more than one enforcement action was brought in response to a single violation, and (2) While each case could involve multiple sanctions, one enforcement action (for example a consent order) could involve numerous conditions or requirements. The relation of the sanction to the violation was analyzed in order to be certain the case involved multiple sanctions. Repeated follow-up contacts often had to be made with the various agencies in order to ascertain whether an enforcement action was considered a separate sanction or as an aspect of one violation.

Since most of the analyses were intended to focus on the primary sanction (the most severe sanction or in some cases the first one encountered on the data card), a hierarchy was set up to determine, in those instances where multiple sanctions or details were involved, which sanction should be coded as the primary or most important sanction. No attempt was made to determine seriousness of sanction on a case by case basis, as had been done for violations, but an attempt was made to assure that the most severe action would be represented as the primary sanction. Unlike ordinary crime, no precedent existed for ranking sanctions. The following guidelines were followed:

(1) Court imposed sanctions were considered more severe than administrative actions.
(2) Criminal cases took precedence over civil cases, and administrative cases were the least serious.
(3) A sanction that would result in monetary loss to the corporation either by being required to

make amends for the past actions (for example by reimbursing customers or paying back-wages), being required to expend capital (for example, for pollution control equipment) or payment of fines and civil penalties or damages was more serious than a sanction that did not directly affect the corporation's balance sheets.

(4) An action against the corporation was given precedence over one against an officer because of the larger scope of the action.

(5) An imposed sanction was more severe than a proposed sanction regardless of type.

Seven major types of enforcement actions were devised in the code for this research: monetary penalties, orders (unilateral, consent and not elsewhere classified), actions enjoined, nonmonetary penalties against officers, warnings, other san[c]tions [sic] and unspecified detail.

1. *Monetary penalties.* Criminal fines (against both the corporation and officer[s]), damages (double, treble and punitive) and civil penalties against both the corporation and officers fall into this category. The data often did not present the amount of monetary penalty in a concise manner; in some cases the total amount would be specified but if multiple officers or both officers and the corporation were involved, it was impossible to know which portion applied to which officer or to the corporation. At other times, no amount at all was provided.

2. *Orders.* There are three different types of orders, each comprising a separate code Level I, but some of the analyses combine them in one category. Unilateral orders are those imposed directly from the agency or court and do not involve any consent on the part of the corporation. Consent orders (decrees or agreements) involve discussion between the corporation and the agency or court. The corporation agrees to carry out the stipulations of the order, but does not admit guilt. If the conditions are not met, however, the company is in contempt if the order comes from the court. The category of "orders not elsewhere classified" includes those orders for which it was not possible to determine if they were consented to or not. Each of these three code Level I's contained details that were classified as having either a retroactive or a future effect. The retroactive effect means that the action called for is remedial in nature and that it is intended to correct the injury levied by the violation. Although monetary compensation (refunds, credits, replacements, damages, reimbursements) is included in this category, an actual overlay of money is not the only action considered to be remedial in nature. Divestiture, seizure and destruction of products,

cleaning up pollution, corrective advertising and recalls, clearing of employees' records, reinstating discharged employees and setting aside of a union election are retroactive in effect.

Most future effect orders require the corporation to cease and desist from continuing their illegal activities in the future. Requirements to notify both governmental and non-governmental groups, to make capital investments to reduce pollution, to make information available, to modify sales policy, to come into compliance, to take affirmative action and to prevent future violations are all considered to have a future effect—they are not remedial in nature. It should be noted that there are some areas of administrative law where the question of what constitutes a "remedial" order is not definite; for example, the FTC which, like so many agencies, is largely limited by statute and case decisions to issuing orders which have only a "remedial" as opposed to a "punitive" effect, has successfully asserted in court that corrective advertising is a remedy which is essentially "remedial" in nature. If it were unable to carry this legal burden, the remedy would not be allowed by the courts in the absence of a specific statutory grant of authority to the agency. It is with orders that details occur most often; one order may state numerous requirements but it is only one actual order coming from the agency or the court.

3. *Nonmonetary penalties against officers.* This category includes incarceration, suspended sentences, suspension from corporate activity, probation and civil contempt. As with monetary penalties, the length of the sentence and the number of officers involved were at times not clear.

4. *Actions enjoined.* injunctions are issued by the courts; they are used to halt quickly an illegal practice. Violations of Securities and Exchange Act provisions often result in injunctions, as do discriminatory labor practices and illegal economic actions (such as practices that tend to fix and/or raise prices or suppress price competition, allocation schemes and conspiratorial practices), environmental pollution and illegal political contributions. Violations of a consent order can be followed by an injunction, as can distribution of adulterated/contaminated/mislabeled products. Proposed acquisitions can be enjoined, and officers can be enjoined from being officers of any public corporation. Plants can be shut down or production halted quickly by the use of an injunction.

5. *Warnings.* The administratively-imposed enforcement actions are far less severe than a criminal or a civil action, and are often the first step taken by an agency to bring about compliance. The Environmental Protection Agency (EPA) issues Notices of Violation

(NOVs) for air and water pollution, and they are considered to be "details" if they are subsequently followed by an order to cease and desist. Regulatory letters requesting that corrective action be taken are issued by the Food and Drug Administration, and copies of this correspondence were obtained directly from the agency.

Recalls were the most widely used action in cases involving the National Highway Traffic Safety Administration (NHTSA), the Consumer Product Safety Commission (CPSC) and the Food and Drug Administration (FDA). In both the CPSC and the FDA, as is discussed below, it was clear that these actions should be considered enforcement actions, although the company usually initiated the recalls. The decision to consider most "voluntary recalls" as enforcement actions was reached only after careful and lengthy consideration. A basic reason for this decision came from discussions with enforcement personnel of the agency dealing with recalls who indicated that "voluntary recalls" were generally the result of government "arm-twisting," concern for adverse publicity, or possible consumer suits if the recall were ordered by. . . .

6. *Other sanctions.* This category includes those which could not be easily classified in any other category. Those represented were preliminary injunctions, putting the company on probation, requiring a change in management or director structure, debarment from future contracts (facility made ineligible for federal subsidies/contracts/grants), corporation must contribute goods to charity in lieu of a fine, and license suspension.

7. *Unspecified detail.* For some of the violations data the sources used did not provide information on what sanctions had been imposed or proposed.

It was impossible to follow up all enforcement actions taken during 1975 and 1976 to discover whether or not the action was affirmed or dismissed after appeal to an administrative board or court or other change in action. Some enforcement cases may take months or even years beyond the time period of this study to reach a final decision. Actually, most enforcement cases do not appear to be reversed; moreover, there was a degree of balance since those enforcement actions taken in early 1975 were for cases originally brought before this period and some cases in late 1976 would subsequently go to appeal. However, the number of initiated and completed enforcement actions cannot balance out because of pending cases. This situation with corporate cases is no different from ordinary crime. One is simply making a study in a cross-section in time. In most research on ordinary crime, one does not know what was the eventual or final outcome in a study of arrests, prosecutions or convictions. . . .

C. Analysis of Enforcement Actions

The decision to bring an administrative, civil or criminal action in response to a corporate violation is influenced by many legal and extralegal considerations. The government cannot bring a criminal action against each corporation that may deserve such action. Not only is there insufficient prosecutory manpower and time, but the nature of the corporation and the regulatory process make such an action difficult to initiate. Enforcement officials are hard-pressed to penetrate the corporate structure to determine responsibility. With no well-defined patterns with which to work, generally each case must be worked out on an individual basis. in addition, if a criminal case is to be developed adequately, thousands of corpo[r]ate [sic] documents must often be examined and accurate testimony gathered as to the chain of events. Generally, little cooperation can be expected from the corporation. A Presidential Crime Commission has pointed out that complex instances of corporate crime may require a year or more to investigate (President's Commission on Law Enforcement and Administration of Justice, 1967:106). Moreover, regulatory agencies have the power to issue administrative subpoenas for documents that may "reasonably" come under their jurisdiction, but the government is often in the position of not knowing that certain essential materials exist. The government is usually dependent upon the record systems of the corporation and its ability (or willingness) to furnish needed information. Delay, if not avoidance, is common.

From conversations with various federal officials a composite picture can be put together of some of the criteria generally employed in decisions to bring a criminal action, when legally available, against a corporation. These factors include:

(1) The degree of loss to the public
(2) The level of complicity by high corporate managers
(3) Duration of violation
(4) Frequency of the violation by the corporation
(5) Evidence of intent to violate
(6) Evidence of extortion, as in bribery cases
(7) Degree of notoriety engendered by the media
(8) Precedent in law
(9) History of previous serious violations by the corporation
(10) Deterrence potential

(11) The degree of cooperation evinced by the corporation

When these criteria are not sufficiently involved, then civil actions may be undertaken. Civil actions, such as injunctions or damage actions, are particularly useful:

(1) Injunctions: to stop an ongoing, not a past, violation of an extensive nature that would be much delayed if a criminal action or a civil damage action were initiated.

(2) When the violation is recent and likely to be repeated unless an injunction is quickly obtained.

(3) In cases where the statute of limitations for criminal action is running out, a civil damage suit may more rapidly accomplish an objective.

If the above conditions are not fulfilled, then an administrative action becomes more likely.

A total of 1554 federal enforcement actions were imposed against the 582 parent corporations in 1975 and 1976. At least one sanction was imposed against 371 corporations (63.7 percent). Conversely, 211 (36.3 percent) had no actions completed against them. This was an average of 2.7 per corporation, and an average of 4.2 for those corporations with at least one sanction imposed on them. A maximum of 65 enforcement actions were taken against one corporation.

For the 683 corporations (parents and subsidiaries), 4115 (60.8 percent) had at least one enforcement action. One or more sanctions were imposed on 356 (65.7 percent) of the 542 manufacturing corporations and on 59 (41.8 percent) of the 141 non-manufacturing companies. Enforcement actions were taken against 321 (67.3 percent) of the 477 parent manufacturing firms and against 50 (47.6 percent) of the 105 parent non-manufacturing firms. Sanctions were imposed on 35 (53.8 percent) of the 65 subsidiary manufacturing corporations. . . .

D. Summary of Enforcement Actions

Over 60 percent of the corporations in this study had at least one enforcement action completed against them in 1975 and 1976. The average for those with one or more was 4.2 actions. There were twice as many warnings used as compared to any other sanction type, with an average of 3.6 warnings for those corporations with at least one. Monetary penalties and orders were used many times more often than injunctions and, generally, corporations were not subjected to the full force of the legally possible sanctions when they violated the law. Corporate actions that directly harm the economy were more likely to receive the greater penalties, while

those affecting consumer product quality were responded to with the least severe sanctions. Although over 85 percent of all sanctions were administrative in nature, those harming the economy were most likely to receive criminal penalties.

Large corporations received more sanctions than their proportion in the sample would indicate. They had about 70 percent of all sanctions, and tended to be assessed a monetary penalty. Small and medium firms tended to more often receive warnings and orders. The oil refining, motor vehicle and drug industries accounted for approximately 4 out of every 10 sanctions for all cases and for serious and moderate cases as well. They had 3 times more actions than their size in the sample indicates and they had 2.7 times more actions for serious and moderate cases.

Each type of violation has a typical sanction type associated with it, with level of enforcement strongly related to seriousness of violation and violation type. The court or agency nature of the enforcing institution was slightly related to sanction type, and moderately related to whether an order had a retroactive or future effect. Generally, orders by administrative agencies tend to be future in effect and court orders show no preference.

The average time to complete a case was 6.7 months. Civil cases took the longest (two and one-half years) and administrative cases took about 4 months. Serious cases took approximately 1 year and minor cases about 1 month.

Monetary penalties, although at times extremely large, tend to be in the $1000 range. Less than 1 percent were over $1 million, while over 80 percent were for $5000 or less. When those for $5000 or less were removed from consideration, there were still only about one-fifth that were over $100,000. Because of the fact that large corporations are more often assessed a monetary penalty for their minor violations, there is a general negative relationship between corporate size and amount of monetary penalty.

Corporations were most likely to consent to a future effect court order and to a retroactive administrative order. Consent agreements were more likely than unilateral orders to have a retroactive effect. Of the consent agreements, administrative agencies tended to use future effect sanctions, and courts generally did not show a preference.

In terms of repeated sanctions within a two-year period, more than one-third of the parent corporations and more than two-fifths of the parent manufacturing corporations had two or more enforcement actions completed against them. About one-fourth had two or more for serious or moderate violations. Moreover, one out of every six corporations had 5 or more sanctions imposed, and one out of every 13 had 5 or more sanctions in serious or moderate cases.

Irwin Ross, *How Lawless Are Big Companies?*, 102 FORTUNE 56–72 (1980)*

Crime in the executive suites has come to command media attention of a sort formerly reserved for ax murders. An abundance of anecdotal evidence about corrupt practices – commercial bribery, price-rigging schemes, fraud against customers – has led critics of business to charge that far more crime exists than has come to light. Defenders of business, on the other hand, argue that the well-publicized episodes are aberrations, totally untypical of the way corporate America operates. The big cases are often shockers. Bethlehem Steel, for example, was recently fined $325,000 in connection with an elaborate kickback scheme that involved the laundering in Europe of hundreds of thousands of dollars in phony commissions and the return of the cash by courier for distribution as bribes. Such sleazy goings-on by a company as prestigious as Bethlehem indicate that big-business crime hasn't been swept away in a tide of post-Watergate morality. But no single case tells much about the extent of corporate delinquency in America. Hence the compilation by FORTUNE on the accompanying six pages in this book of significant corporate offenders and offenses since 1970.

The guidelines

There is, of course, no standard definition of corporate corruption. Our list is limited to five crimes about whose impropriety few will argue – bribery (including kickbacks and illegal rebates); criminal fraud; illegal political contributions; tax evasion; and criminal antitrust violations. The latter consist entirely of price-fixing and bid-rigging conspiracies and exclude the vaguer and more contentious area of monopolistic practices, which are the subject of civil antitrust suits. Also excluded are Federal Trade Commission complaints that have to do with the ways companies "signal" price changes to competitors.

Of the 1,043 major corporations in the study, 117, or 11%, have been involved in at least one major delinquency in the period covered (see pages 58 to 61). Some companies have been multiple offenders. In all, 188 citations are listed covering 163 separate offenses – 98 antitrust violations; 28 cases of kickbacks, bribery, or illegal rebates; 21 instances of illegal political contributions; 11 cases of fraud; and five cases of tax evasion. This roll call of wrongdoing is limited to domestic cases; the list would have been longer had it included foreign bribes and kickbacks.

A Roster of Wrongdoing

Company	Offense
Allied Chemical	1974 – Fixing prices of dyes. Pleaded nolo contendere.
	1979 – Tax fraud related to paying kickbacks. Nolo plea on some charges.
Amerada Hess	1976 – Fixing prices of gasoline. Convicted after trial. Executive acquitted. Conviction being appealed.
American Airlines	1973 – Illegal campaign contributions of $55,000. Guilty plea
	1975 – CAB charges related to slush fund used for contributions. Settlement.
	1977 – SEC charges related to same. Consent decree.
American Bakeries	1972 – Fixing prices of bread. Nolo plea.
Amer. Beef Packers	1975 – Company and president charged with defrauding a creditor. Both found guilty on some counts.
	1976 – SEC charges related to same matter. Injunction against president.
American Brands	1978 – James B. Beam subsidiary and two executives charged with bribery of state liquor official. All pleaded guilty.
American Can	1976 – Company and executive charged with fixing prices of folding cartons. Nolo pleas by both.
American Cyanamid	1974 – Fixing prices of dyes. Nolo plea.
American Export Ind.	1979 – American Export Lines subsidiary n1 charged with fixing prices of ocean shipping. Nolo plea.
Anheuser-Busch	1977 – SEC charges concerning $2.7 million in payments to customers. Consent decree.
	1978 – Treasury Dept. charges about same matter. Settlement and $750,000 fine.
Archer-Daniels-Midland	1976 – Defrauding grain buyers by short-weighting. Nolo plea.
Arden-Mayfair	1971 – Company and executive charged with fixing prices of dairy products. Nolo pleas.
	1977 – SEC charges related to $4.4 million in rebates and off-book accounts. Consent decree.
	1978 – Price fixing of dairy products. Nolo plea.
Armco	1973-77 – Three cases of fixing prices of steel reinforcing bars. Nolo pleas by company and three executives.
Ashland Oil	1973 – Illegal political contribution of $100,000. Guilty plea.
	1975 – SEC charges about allegedly illegal payments. Consent decree.
	1977 – Fixing prices of resins used to make paint. Nolo plea.
	1980 – Ashland – Warren subsidiary pleaded guilty in three cases involving bid rigging in highway construction. Fined a total of $1.5 million.
Associated Milk Prod.	1974 – Illegal political contributions. Guilty plea.
Beatrice Foods	1974 – Fixing prices of toilet seats. Company and president of Beneke division pleaded nolo.
	1978 – SEC charges about improper accounting for $11.7 million in rebates. Consent decree.
Bethlehem Steel	1973-74 – Two cases of fixing prices of steel reinforcing bars. Company and one employee pleaded nolo; another convicted after trial.
	1980 – Mail fraud related to bribes paid for ship-repair business. Guilty plea.
Boise Cascade	1978 – Fixing prices of corrugated containers. Nolo pleas by company and two plant managers.
Borden	1974 & 1977 – Two cases of fixing prices of dairy products. Company and three executives pleaded nolo.
Borg-Warner	1971 – Fixing prices of plastic pipe fittings. Nolo plea.
Braniff International	1973 – Illegal political contribution of $40,000. Guilty pleas by company and chairman.
	1975 – CAB allegations about contribution. Settlement.
	1976 – SEC charges related to $900,000 slush fund and contributions. Consent decree.

Company	Offense
	1977 – Criminal restraint of trade. Nolo plea.
CPC International	1977 – Fixing prices of industrial sugar. Nolo plea.
Carnation	1971 – Fixing prices of dairy products. Company and executive pleaded nolo.
	1973 – Illegal political contributions of $9,000. Company and chairman pleaded guilty.
	1974 – Fixing prices of dairy products. Nolo pleas by company and general manager.
Carter Hawley Hale	1974 – Bergdorf Goodman subsidiary charged with fixing prices of women's clothing. Company and executive pleaded nolo.
Ceco	1973-77 – Three cases involving fixing prices of steel reinforcing bars. Company and one executive pleaded nolo; another executive convicted after trial.
Celanese	1971 – Fixing prices of plastic pipe fittings. Company pleaded nolo; executive acquitted.
Cenco	1976 – SEC charges related to falsifying inventory. Seven of eight former executives signedconsent decrees.
	1979 – Seven executives indicted on criminal charges of mail fraud related to the same scheme. Three pleaded guilty, three convicted after trial, and one acquitted of fraud charges. Convictions are being appealed.
Champion Intl.	1974 – Bid rigging in purchase of timber from public lands. Company found guilty after trial. Executive acquitted.
	1976 – Fixing prices of folding cartons. Nolo plea.
Chemical New York	1977 – Chemical Bank charged with violations of Bank Secrecy Act in scheme by two branch officials to launder money for alleged narcotics dealer. Officials pleaded guilty to tax charges and company to reduced
Chicago Milwaukee	1976 – SEC allegations of improper use of assets and political contributions. Consent decree.
Combustion Engin.	1973 – Fixing prices of chromite sand. Company and executive pleaded nolo.
Consolidated Foods	1974 – Fixing prices of refined sugar. Nolo plea.
Continental Group	1976 – Fixing prices of paper bags. Company and one executive convicted after trial; two others acquitted. Company fined $750,000.
Cook Industries	1976 – Defrauding grain customers by short-weighting. Company pleaded nolo and five executives pleaded guilty.
Dean Foods	1977 – Price fixing of dairy products. Nolo pleas by company and executive.
Diamond International	1974 – Illegal campaign contributions of $6,000. Company and executive pleaded guilty.
	1974 – Fixing prices of paper labels. Nolo pleas by company and two executives.
	1976 – Fixing prices of folding cartons. Company and seven executives pleaded nolo.
Diversified Industries	1976 – SEC charges related to alleged short-weighting of customers in metal-recovery processes. Consent decree.
Du Pont	1974 – Fixing prices of dyes. Nolo plea.
Equity Funding	1973 – SEC charges relating to $2 billion in fictitious insurance policies. Consent decree.
	1973 – Former chairman and 21 other former executives charged with fraud. All pleaded guilty to some counts.
FMC	1976 – Fixing prices of persulfates. Company and executive pleaded nolo.
Federal Paper Board	1976 – Fixing prices of folding cartons. Company and two executives pleaded nolo.
Federated Dept. Stores	1976 – I. Magnin subsidiary charged with fixing prices of women's clothing. Nolo plea.
Fibreboard	1976 – Fixing prices of folding cartons. Company and executive pleaded nolo.
Firestone	1976 – SEC charges about slush fund and allegedly illegal political contributions of $330,000. Consent decree.

Company	Offense
	1979 – False tax-return charges related to $13 million in set aside income. Guilty plea on some counts.
Flavorland Industries	1979 – Fixing prices of meat. Nolo plea.
Flintkote	1973 – Fixing prices of gypsum board. Company, chairman, and president pleaded nolo.
Franklin New York	1974 – SEC charges against nine executives relating to the bankruptcy of Franklin National Bank. Company and eight executives signed consent decree.
	1975 – Eight former executives and employees of bank charged with fraud. All pleaded guilty.
	1978 – Three other former executives charged with fraud. All convicted after trial.
Fruehauf	1975 – Company, chairman, and vice president charged with criminal tax evasion. All convicted after trial.
GAF	1974 – Fixing prices of dyes. Nolo plea.
GTE	1977 – SEC charges relating to political contributions and payments to local officials. Consent decree.
General Dynamics	1977 – SEC allegations of improper accounting to disguise political contributions. Consent decree.
General Host	1972 – Fixing prices of bread. Nolo plea.
General Tire & Rubber	1976 – SEC charges concerning slush fund and allegedly illegal political contributions. Consent decree.
Genesco	1974 – Fixing prices of women's clothing. Nolo plea.
Gimbel Bros.	1974 & 1976 – Saks & Co. subsidiary charged with two cases of fixing prices of women's clothing. Company and executive pleaded nolo.
B. F. Goodrich	1978 – Tax evasion related to slush fund used for illegal political contributions. Nolo plea by company; charges against an executive dropped.
Goodyear	1973 – Illegal political contribution of $40,000. Company and chairman pleaded guilty.
	1977 – SEC charges concerning slush fund of $500,000 for contributions. Consent decree.
Great Western United	1974 – Great Western Sugar subsidiary charged with fixing prices of refined sugar. Nolo plea.
Greyhound	1974 – Illegal campaign contributions of $16,000. Guilty plea.
Gulf Oil	1973 – Illegal political contributions of $100,000. Company and executive pleaded guilty.
	1975 – SEC charges about $10-million slush fund used for political contributions. Consent decree.
	1977 – Company and two employees charged with giving illegal gifts to an IRS agent. Company pleaded guilty, one employee pleaded nolo, the other convicted after trial.
	1978 – Fixing prices of uranium. Pleaded guilty.
Gulf & Western	1976 – Brown Co. subsidiary charged with fixing prices of folding cartons. Company and two executives pleaded nolo.
Hammermill Paper	1978 – Palmer Paper Co. unit charged with fixing prices of paper products. Company and executive pleaded nolo.
Heublein	1978 – Bribery of state liquor official. Guilty plea.
Hoerner Waldorf	1976 – Fixing prices of folding cartons. Company and four executives pleaded nolo.
	1978 – Fixing prices of corrugated containers. Nolo plea.
ITT	1972 – ITT Continental Baking subsidiary charged with fixing prices of bread. Nolo plea.
Inland Container	1978 – Fixing prices of corrugated containers. Nolo plea by company and executive.

Company	Offense
International Paper	1974 – Fixing prices of paper labels. Company and two executives pleaded nolo.
	1976 – Fixing prices of folding cartons. Company and four executives pleaded nolo.
	1978 – Fixing prices of corrugated containers. Nolo plea. Fined $617,000.
Walter Kidde	1977 – SEC charges against U.S. Lines subsidiary n7 related to $2.5 million in allegedly illegal rebates. Consent decree.
	1978 – Federal Maritime Commission charges related to same. Settlement.
	1979 – U.S. Lines charged with fixing prices of ocean shipping. Nolo plea. Fined $1 million.
Koppers	1979 – Bid rigging in connection with sale of road tar to State of Connecticut. Nolo plea.
LTV	1978 – Agriculture Dept. charges against Wilson Foods subsidiary related to alleged illegal payoffs to customers. Settlement.
Liggett Group	1978 – Paddington Corp. subsidiary charged with bribery of state liquor official. Guilty plea.
Litton Industries	1974 – Fixing prices of paper labels. Convicted after trial.
3M	1973 – Illegal campaign contribution of $30,000. Company and chairman pleaded guilty.
	1975 – SEC charges related to $634,000 slush fund for contributions. Consent decree.
Marcor	1976 – Container Corp. subsidiary charged with fixing prices of folding cartons. Company and eight executives pleaded nolo.
	1978 – Subsidiary charged with fixing prices of corrugated boxes. Company and two executives pleaded nolo.
Martin Marietta	1978 – Martin Marietta Aluminum subsidiary charged with fixing prices of titanium products. Company and executive pleaded nolo.
Mattel	1974 – SEC charges related to false disclosures to influence stock prices. Consent decree.
	1978 – Former president indicted on criminal charges related to same matter. Nolo plea.
J. Ray McDermott	1976 – SEC charges related to slush fund of more than $800,000 used for commercial bribes and illegal political contributions. Consent decree.
	1978 – wire fraud and racketeering charges relating to the bribes and contributions. Guilty plea.
	1978 – Bid rigging and allocation of contracts relating to pipeline and offshore-oil-rig construction. Company, president, and three other executives pleaded nolo. Company fined $1 million.
Mead	1976 – Fixing prices of folding cartons. Company and executive pleaded nolo.
National Distillers	1978 – Bribery of state liquor official. Pleaded guilty.
	1980 – Treasury Dept. allegations of illegal payments to customers. Settlement and $750,000 fine.
Northern Natural Gas	1972 – Mail fraud related to bribery of local officials to obtain right-of-way permits for pipeline construction. Company and one executive pleaded nolo to some counts; charges against another executive dropped.
Northrop	1974 – Illegal campaign contributions of $150,000. Company and two executives pleaded guilty.
	1975 – SEC charges related to slush fund for $500,000 in domestic contributions. Consent decree.
Occidental Petroleum	1974 – Illegal campaign contribution of $54,000. Executive and later the chairman pleaded guilty.
	1977 – SEC charges related to $200,000 slush fund for contributions in the U.S. and abroad. Consent decree.
Olinkraft	1978 – Fixing prices of corrugated containers. Company and one executive pleaded nolo; another executive acquitted.

Company	Offense
Owens-Illinois	1978 – Fixing prices of corrugated containers. Company and one executive pleaded nolo; two others acquitted.
Pan American	1975 – Illegal fare cutting. Nolo plea.
	1977 – Fixing prices of military fares. Nolo plea.
Peavey	1977 – Defrauding grain customers by short-weighting. Nolo plea.
Penn Central	1974 – SEC charges of fraud relating to the bankruptcy of the railroad. Consent decree.
Pepsi Co	1970 – Frito-Lay subsidiary charged with fixing prices of snack food. Nolo plea.
	1977 – Parent company charged with fixing prices of industrial sugar. Nolo plea.
	1979 – Parent company and two executives of Monsieur Henri subsidiary charged with bribing a union official. All pleaded guilty.
Pet	1970 – Fixing prices of snack foods. Nolo plea.
Phillips Petroleum	1973 – Illegal campaign contribution of $100,000. Company and chairman pleaded guilty.
	1975 – SEC charges related to $2.8-million slush fund, a portion of which was allegedly used for domestic illegal political contributions. Consent decree.
	1975 – Fixing prices of gasoline. Nolo plea.
	1976 – Tax evasion related to the slush fund. Guilty plea.
Pittston	1977 – Brink's Inc. subsidiary charged with bid rigging and fixing prices of security services. Company and five executives pleaded nolo. Company fined $625,000.
H. K. Porter	1974 – Fixing prices of steel reinforcing bars. Nolo plea.
Potlatch	1976 – Fixing prices of folding cartons. Company and one executive pleaded nolo; another executive acquitted.
Purolator	1978 – Bid rigging and allocation of markets for security services. Nolo plea.
Rapid-American	1978 – Schenley subsidiary and three executives charged with bribery of a state liquor official. All pleaded guilty.
	1979 – SEC charges against Schenley related to $6 million in allegedly illegal payments to customers. Consent decree.
Reichhold Chemicals	1977 – Fixing prices of resins used to make paints. Company and executive pleaded nolo.
R. J. Reynolds Ind.	1977 – Federal Maritime Commission charges against Sea-Land Services subsidiary relating to illegal payments to customers. Settlement and $4-million fine.
	1978 – SEC suit against Sea-Land related to $25 million in allegedly illegal rebates and political contributions. Consent decree.
	1979 – Fixing prices of ocean shipping. Nolo plea. Fined $1 million.
Rockwell International	1978 – Fixing prices of gas meters. Pleaded guilty.
St. Regis Paper	1976 – Fixing prices of folding cartons. Company and executive pleaded nolo.
F.&M. Schaefer	1978 – Treasury Dept. allegations of $600,000 in illegal rebates to customers. Settlement.
Jos. Schlitz Brewing	1977 – SEC charges related to $3 million in illegal rebates to customers. Consent decree.
	1977 – Fixing prices of beer. Company and executive pleaded nolo.
	1978 – Treasury Dept. allegations of illegal marketing practices and rebates. Consent decree and $750,000 fine.
Joseph E. Seagram	1977 – SEC charges related to over $1 million in allegedly illegal rebates to customers and political contributions. Consent decree.
	1978 – Seagram Distillers, three other subsidiaries, and four executives charged with bribery of a state liquor official. All pleaded guilty.
	1979 – Illegal payments to members of a state liquor-control board. Guilty plea. Fined $1.5 million.
Seatrain Lines	1978 – Payment of illegal rebates and violation of currency regulations. Guilty plea in criminal case and $2.5-million fine paid in Federal Maritime Commission case.

Company	Offense
	1979 – Fixing prices of ocean shipping. Nolo plea.
	1980 – SEC suit related to $14 million in rebates to customers. Consent decree.
Singer	1975 – Illegal campaign contribution of $10,000. Guilty plea.
SuCrest	1977 – Fixing prices of industrial sugar. Nolo plea.
Tenneco	1976 – Packaging Corp. subsidiary charged with fixing prices of folding cartons. Company and four executives pleaded nolo.
	1978 – Mail fraud in connection with bribery of a local official. Guilty plea.
Textron	1978 – Fixing prices of gas meters. Pleaded guilty.
Time Inc.	1976 – Eastex Packaging subsidiary charged with fixing prices of folding cartons. Nolo plea.
Trans World Corp.	1975 – TWA charged with illegal fare cutting. Nolo plea.
	1977 – Fixing prices of military fares. Nolo plea.
Uniroyal	1977 – SEC charges related to allegedly illegal political contributions. Consent decree.
United Brands	1975 – SEC charges related to improper use of funds to pay a $1.2-million bribe to a Honduran official. Consent decree.
	1978 – Wire fraud charges related to the same matter. Guilty plea.
U. S. Steel	1973 – Fixing prices of steel reinforcing bars. Company and an executive pleaded nolo.
Jim Walter	1978 – Knight Paper subsidiary charged with fixing prices of paper products. Company and executive pleaded nolo.
Ward Foods	1972 – Fixing prices of bread. Nolo plea.
	1978 – Fixing prices of meat. Nolo plea.
Weyerhaeuser	1976 – Fixing prices of folding cartons. Company and three executives pleaded nolo.
	1978 – Fixing prices of corrugated boxes. Company pleaded nolo, fined $632,000. Two executives acquitted.
Wheelabrator-Frye	1976 – A. L. Garber subsidiary n13 charged with fixing prices of folding cartons. Nolo plea.
Zale	1977 – SEC charges related to slush fund to reimburse executives for political contributions. Consent decree.

Listed on these pages are the major successful federal cases against big companies since 1970. FORTUNE canvassed the 1,043 companies that appeared at some point during that period on our lists of the 800 largest industrial and non-industrial corporations; 117-11%-turned out to be offenders.

There is no standard definition of corporate corruption. The list is limited to five offenses about whose impropriety there is little argument-bribery (including kickbacks and illegal rebates), criminal fraud, illegal political contributions, tax evasion, and criminal antitrust violations – all undertaken for the benefit of the corporation rather than for personal profit. Not included are crimes directed against the corporation, such as embezzlement. The list excludes bribery, kickbacks, and "questionable" payments made abroad. (The one exception is United Brands' $1.2-million bribe to a Honduran official, because many of the events surrounding it occurred in the U.S.) All the cases resulted either in conviction on criminal charges or in consent decrees (or similar administrative settlements), in which the companies neither affirm nor deny past transgressions but agree not to commit them in the future. Fifty executives from 15 companies went to jail in various of these cases. Fines were levied on most of the convicted companies but aren't listed unless they came to $500,000 or more.

Minor cases of corruption far down the chain of command have been excluded. The standard throughout was corporate responsibility at a high level. In the lists that follow, the dates refer to the year that the indictments or complaints were filed.

All the cases resulted either in conviction on criminal charges or in consent decrees (or similar administrative settlements), in which companies typically neither affirm nor deny past transgressions but agree not to commit them in the future. Many of the defendants were convicted on pleas of nolo contendere (no contest) – tantamount to guilty pleas but often preferred by defendants for both psychological and practical reasons. To unsophisticated ears, a nolo plea does not have the ring of a confession of guilt. A practical benefit in an antitrust case is that the nolo plea cannot be used as automatic evidence of guilt in a civil suit for treble damages.

Eleven percent of major American corporations involved in corrupt practices is a pretty startling figure. It would hardly be as startling, of course, if it referred to businesses of modest size, for which data are lacking. The bribing of purchasing agents by small manufacturers and the skimming of receipts by cash-laden small retail businesses are a commonplace of commercial life.

Our compilation of cases covered a substantial slice of time, to be sure, and management changed in many of these large companies during the period; after a major scandal, the culprits were often sacked and the board of directors took sweeping measures to avoid a recurrence. On the other hand, it is axiomatic that there was more crime than was exposed in public proceedings.

A number of companies have been repeat offenders. Ashland Oil, for example, pleaded guilty to making a $100,000 illegal political contribution. It was also convicted, after a nolo plea, of fixing the price of resins. This year its construction subsidiary pleaded guilty in three cases of rigging bids for highway construction work in Virginia.

Gulf Oil has four entries on the list—two for illegal political contributions, one for bribing an IRS agent, one for fixing the price of uranium. International Paper was convicted three times, after nolo pleas, in major antitrust cases—involving paper labels, folding cartons, and corrugated containers. Eastex Packaging Inc., a subsidiary of Time Inc., the publisher of FORTUNE, was one of 22 other companies convicted in the folding-carton case.

Briefcases full of cash

In the Bethlehem Steel case, the company pleaded guilty to criminal activity over five years, 1972-76, but the government contended that the kickbacks had been going on for a much longer time. The purpose of the scheme was to bribe representatives of ship lines to steer repair work to Bethlehem's seven shipyards or to speed up payment of bills.

Since 1961, according to the indictment, Bethlehem had been using a Swiss company called Office pour le Financement du Commerce et de l'Industrie to launder the kickback money. OFCI was a convenient conduit, for it had a worldwide network of agents who drummed up ship repair business.

Clifford R. Wise, head of Bethlehem's ship-repair sales office in New York, would send payments to OFCI that ostensibly represented sales commissions but actually were levies fraudulently added to customers' bills. After the money entered into OFCI's books (OFCI taking a cut for its cooperation), it was available for recycling back to the U. S. Typically, Wise or his secretary would fly to Switzerland, stuff a briefcase with cash, and return to New York. Over five years, according to the indictment, a million dollars was funneled into the U.S. and two South American countries; on just one day in August 1975, Wise flew $115,000 in cash over to New York. The government traced some $400,000 to kickbacks. What happened to the rest of the money is not altogether clear. Bethlehem is seeking the return of funds it claims Wise embezzled; he denies the charges.

In several celebrated cases, illegal corporate political contributions have also been part of an elaborate pattern of deception that went on for many years. For more than a decade, for example, Gulf Oil used a subsidiary in Nassau to launder funds sent from the U.S., ostensibly to be used to prospect for oil. At least $4.5 million returned to these shores to be distributed as political handouts.

Firestone Tire & Rubber Co., according to the findings of its audit committee, was in the business of doling out illegal political contributions from at least 1960 through 1973. But Firestone's audit committee discovered that the volume of funds" appropriated" for political purposes, as it put it, increased substantially after 1968, when Robert P. Beasley became chief financial officer and overseer of the political slush fund. In 1972, for example, Beasley got Raymond C. Firestone, then the chief executive, to initial a treasury voucher authorizing the transfer of $107,777 in Firestone funds to an outside bank account controlled by Beasley. Top officers of the corporation would make personal political contributions, all apparently quite legal, and be reimbursed in cash by Beasley.

Beasley was simultaneously "appropriating" Firestone funds for his own use—an indication of the sluice gates that are opened once accounting controls are relaxed. In the end, the U. S. Attorney for the Southern District of New York charged him with embezzling $1 million; he pleaded guilty to charges involving nearly half that sum and received a four-year sentence. Firestone was convicted on tax charges relating to $12.6 million in corporate income that Beasley had put in special reserve accounts and failed to report at the proper time.

From one point of view—say that of a librettist for a corporate version of Guys and Dolls—these shenanigans are pretty comic. A moralist, or even an amateur dabbler in corporate sociology, would find them hairraising. What indeed is going on here? Why do some of the largest, most prestigious corporations in America get involved in complex scenarios of illegality that rival the paranoid fantasies of their bitterest critics?

No single answer accounts for the variety of corporate misbehavior. One generalization often invoked plays on the distinction between malum in se – a crime in itself, like the immemorial offenses of the common law – and malum prohibitum – purely statutory crimes that vary with the society. As a celebrated corporate defense counsel recently put it, "These business crimes are perceived by individual actors as victimless. We all grew up in an environment in which we learned that thou shalt not murder, rape, rob, probably not pay off a public official – but not that it was a crime to fix prices."

Most of the economic crimes that fill the lists on the following pages do not bring the social obloquy that attaches to robbery or embezzlement. One chief executive recently boasted to FORTUNE about how he had once rid his company of some executives who had run afoul of the antitrust laws. "That sent the message to the organization," he said. Ten minutes later, however, he expressed dismay about how his statements would look in print. After all, some years had passed; the men were still living in the community; they had made their peace with the company. Would the same solicitude be accorded a bank robber?

The "bottom-line philosophy"

Corrupt practices are certainly not endemic to business, but they do seem endemic to certain situations and certain industries. A persuasive explanation for many violations is economic pressure – the "bottom-line philosophy," as Stanley Sporkin, the SEC's enforcement chief, puts it." In many instances where people are not lining their own pockets you can only explain corporate crime in terms of 'produce or perish.' "

The common practice of running a company through decentralized profit centers, giving each manager his head but holding him strictly accountable for the results, often provides a setting in which the rules can readily be bent. The temptation comes when heightened competition or a recession squeezes margins.

The pressures that led to criminal behavior in the folding-carton industry were exhaustively described in a 1978 article in the Harvard Business Review by Jeffrey Sonnenfeld and Paul L. Lawrence. Price fixing had long been common in the industry because profit margins were tight, competition was intense, and prices were set at a relatively low level in the corporate hierarchy – a consequence of the many kinds and shapes of boxes ordered. Top management had little control over the impulses of salesmen and junior managers to exchange price information, rig bids, and divvy up customers.

The authors quote the self-exculpatory statement of one executive: "We're not vicious enemies in this industry, but rather people in similar binds. I've always thought of myself as an honorable citizen. We didn't do these things for our own behalf . . . [but] for the betterment of the company."

In a similar vein, Irving S. Shapiro, Du Pont's chief executive, attributes antitrust violations to "weak companies" and "weak managements." For years, Shapiro had served as an antitrust lawyer at Du Pont, preaching the gospel of legal compliance to the managers down the line. But he had not long been installed as C.E.O. when the Justice Department, in 1974, hit the company with an indictment charging an antitrust conspiracy by Du Pont's dye group and several competitors.

The scheme began in 1970. Wanting to raise prices, Du Pont's dye people called on the competition and won agreement to a "follow the leader" scheme. The following January, Du Pont announced a 10% price increase; the competition followed suit in February and March. When brought to book, the nine companies involved all pleaded nolo and were fined between $35,000 and $50,000 each. Shapiro says he then laid down the law – he would countenance no further violations. Was the dye group a "weak" – that is, hard pressed – division? Indeed yes, said Shapiro; he got rid of most of it last year at a loss of $64 million. (For a report on a more promising line of business at Du Pont, see page 92).

Rush to the courthouse

Once the Justice Department starts looking into a suspicious pricing pattern, it often has no difficulty making a case. Most price fixers are anything but hardened criminals. It is also true that antitrust enforcement in the U.S. is in general tougher than abroad. By convening a grand jury and sending out subpoenas Justice can touch off what one official calls "a rush to the courthouse" by executives eager to trade testimony for immunity.

Competitive pressures can account for kickbacks and other forms of commercial bribery, but perhaps equally significant are industry custom and structure. In trucking, in construction, and on the docks, the pressure of time seems to be the key element. If goods are delayed in transit, or if construction is held up because of the inability to obtain materials or workers, great financial loss can result. Where bribes are not freely offered, they are often extorted.

Companies in regulated industries sometimes violate the law because of the simple fact of regulation. in the beer and liquor industries, for example, both the federal government and the states prohibit or curtail some normal techniques of salesmanship, such as discounts and rebates. The result: illegal rebates and gifts of merchandise to persuade liquor retailers to promote a company's products.

A thumb on the scales

The great grain-elevator scandal of the mid-Seventies clearly resulted from conditions that were pervasive in the industry in the New Orleans area. Thirteen grain-trading companies, together with several score employees, were convicted of short-changing customers. Continental Grain, for one, was fined $500,000 on 50 counts of filing false export statements. Employees at Continental's elevator at Westwego, Louisiana, had set their scales to register one-twentieth of 1% more than the true weight. The company's lame excuse was that the employees thought they were within their rights because the law required scales to be accurate only within a tolerance of one-tenth of 1%. True enough, but not when they were systematically rigged to shortchange customers.

Simple economic incentives explain much illegal behavior: corruption seems to pay, at least in the near term. In industries like folding cartons or corrugated boxes, where antitrust cases were brought, executives perceived an advantage in maintaining price levels, sharing the market, the keeping marginal firms alive. In such a situation, of course, the customers pay and the whole economy suffers from a measure of inefficiency. When a corporation is caught, the shamefaced executives take a drastically different view of the cost-benefit ratio. Some companies might have been better off in the long run if they had followed the alternative, and legal, strategy of expanding their market share by driving their weaker brethren to the wall.

Except in cases hinging on illegal political contributions – once a way of life in many corporations and rarely investigated or prosecuted prior to Watergate – the chief executive is seldom personally implicated. Typically, even the executives running the guilty subsidiary or division disavow any knowledge of the wrongdoing below. Such was the situation at Bethlehem Steel, which in its public statement of contrition was careful to assert that top management – including the head of the shipbuilding division – had been ignorant of the kickback scheme.

Conspiracy of silence

Particularly when violations are persistent, however, it is hard to escape the cynical conclusion that if the line managers are ignorant, it is often because of an unspoken conspiracy of silence: the boss doesn't pry too vigorously, and his underlings get the impression that he would regard it as a betrayal if they volunteered too much.

A question that FORTUNE's compilation inevitably leaves unanswered is whether corporate corruption was on the increase in the last decade. More wrongdoing was exposed because of the crackdown in the aftermath of Watergate. But there are no data to allow comparisons over time about the extent of corporate lawlessness.

The publicity accorded the business scandals of the Seventies has given some impetus to reform. If the chief executive of a multibillion-dollar corporation cannot policy every corner of his organization, he can establish an appropriate policing program and do much to set the right tone. A number of companies, including some sued for treble damages, have mounted vigorous compliance programs to instruct employees about the dangers of getting too chummy with competitors. But hard-pressed managers will probably still be weighing the risks of detection against the benefits of sharing markets and bribing purchasing agents. It sometimes seems that the only true believers in unfettered competition are professors of economics and business journalists.

Francis T. Cullen, William J. Maakestad and Gray Cavender, Corporate Crime Under Attack 37–40, 50–53 (1987)*

"How lawless are big companies?" asked a 1980 *Fortune* article. *Fortune*'s investigation of legal infractions by 1,043 major corporations revealed an unsettling answer: "A look at the record since 1970 shows that a surprising number of them have been involved in blatant illegalities." Aside from firms whose violations escaped detection by government enforcement officials, fully 11 percent of the businesses in the sample committed at least "one major delinquency," a statistic that *Fortune* termed "pretty startling."

These observations and those offered by other commentators suggest that corporate lawlessness is extensive. But are the crimes of "big companies" costly? Too often, the actual consequences of this type of illegality are concealed from the public. Yet the veil of corporate secrecy is lifted on special occasions, such as the recent scandal at E.F. Hutton and the

---

* Reprinted with permission. Copyright 1987 Anderson Publishing Co.

notorious electrical-equipment conspiracy of the 1950s, and we gain a fuller view of the true costs of crime in the business world. The results of these exposes have generally proved to be disquieting.

The production of the Pinto automobile by the Ford Motor Company presents such an opportunity to look into the corporate world. In the chapters that follow, we will see what happens when the fourth largest corporation in the world markets a product that many allege to be dangerously defective. We will also explore the successes and failures surrounding subsequent attempts to sanction Ford criminally, and then evaluate how this case sheds light on the central controversies involved in the control of corporate lawlessness.

In this chapter we present a general overview of the "corporate crime problem," with emphasis on the ways in which business entities may illegally force financial burdens upon society, damage the social fabric, and physically assault unsuspecting citizens (as some believe was the case in the Ford Pinto incident). We do not intend to paint a uniformly dark picture of all business enterprises; such a picture would weaken credibility by ignoring the complexity and variability of economic undertakings and would suffer the shortcomings of any stereotype. Nonetheless, the customary manner of thinking about crime has often blinded the public to the full dimensions—especially the violent aspects—of America's corporate crime problem. Therefore this chapter will seek to broaden the traditional view of "serious crime" by showing the magnitude of the costs incurred when corporations move beyond prevailing legal boundaries.

Before embarking upon this task, we will set a context for our discussions by considering two issues. First we will explain what we mean when we call corporate behavior "criminal." Then we will examine how corporate illegality (as noted above) frequently remained a secondary concern—particularly before the recent events that brought corporations under attack—when criminologists and other citizens contemplated the problem of crime in America.

CORPORATE CRIME AS WHITE-COLLAR CRIME: DEFINITIONAL ISSUES

In the 1940s, Edwin Sutherland introduced and popularized the concept of "white-collar crime." This idea had the revolutionary effect of sensitizing subsequent students of crime and, ultimately, those outside academic circles to a range of behaviors that had previously escaped careful scrutiny: the illegal activities of the affluent.

Although Sutherland's own research concentrated on the pervasiveness of the unlawful actions of corporations, he proposed a considerably more comprehensive definition of white-collar criminality, which encompassed all offenses "committed by a person of respectability and high social status in the course of his occupation." The very breadth of this definition has been a source of the concept's vitality and ambiguity. The major advantage is that it prompted social commentators to investigate the full range of criminal offenses emanating from the occupations of the rich, including crimes by politicians, crimes by professionals such as physicians, tax cheating, crimes against businesses, such as employee theft or embezzlement, and crimes by corporate organizations themselves. On the other hand, while these various offenses share a common thread—if nothing else, they fall well outside traditional categories of street crime—important qualitative differences exist among them. Thus the use of a catchall term like "white-collar crime" risks obscuring the differences among many of these offenses: for example, the act of a physician who defrauds the government by billing for false Medicaid payments and that of a multimillion-dollar corporation that markets a defective product. Therefore, when analysts speak generally of "white-collar crime," it is not always clear what they have in mind.

In short, Sutherland's selection of the term "white-collar" to demarcate a realm of occupational behavior was not free of limitations. More controversial, however, was his tendency to characterize the occupational transgressions of the upperworld as "crime." The controversy centered around the reality that most of the actions subsumed under Sutherland's concept of white-collar crime are not often defined by the state as criminal. Although important changes are now taking place, criminal sanctions traditionally have been employed only sparingly in the social control of the business, political, and professional deviance of the affluent. Civil courts, where monetary damages can be won, and administrative agencies, which develop and enforce regulations for industry, have been relied upon to control the occupational behavior, particularly the corporate behavior, of those in the upper strata. Critics have thus questioned whether the behavior included in Sutherland's definition can rightly be called "crime."

The most notable criticism, because it was both an early and a forceful critique of Sutherland's view of white-collar criminality, was the 1947 essay by lawyer-sociologist Paul Tappan, titled "Who is the criminal?" Tappan's chief concern was that Sutherland's concept was frequently used to encompass any means of accumulating profits that commentators might see as socially injurious or morally reprehensible, whether or not the conduct violated existing criminal codes. Therefore, whether an act was defined as a "crime" depended less upon the applicability of legal standards than upon the ideology or idiosyncrasies of any given scholar. Not surprisingly, this state of affairs, in Tappan's view, caused the term "white-collar criminality" to lose its conceptual rigor and to "spread into vacuity, wide and handsome." Such confusion meant that it was impossible to demarcate what constituted a "crime" among the occupationally advantaged, a condition that precluded systematic scientific investigation. For Tappan, the only solution was to restrict criminological analysis to that set of behaviors which met the criteria imposed by a narrow, legalistic definition of crime. Being more a lawyer than a sociologist, Tappan concluded, "Only those are criminals who have been adjudicated as such by the courts. Crime is an intentional act in violation of the criminal law (statutory and case law), committed without defense of excuse, and penalized by the state as a felony or misdemeanor."

In reaction to Tappan and similar critics of that time, Sutherland was able to make a persuasive argument for the legitimacy of a broad definition of white-collar crime and for the inclusion of a wide range of business violations within criminology. First, he noted that the failure of criminal sanctions to regulate the behavior of the rich and powerful was largely a reflection of the elite's ability to use their position to avoid exposure to prosecution. "White-collar criminals," he stated, "are relatively immune because of the class bias of the courts and the power of their class to influence the implementation and administration of the law." Thus the absence of criminal convictions among the rich cannot be taken as evidence for the absence of criminality. Second, Sutherland observed that much occupational deviance could ultimately be punished by criminal penalties. In some instances, the exercise of such penalties is contained as a possible option in the legislation proscribing particular business activities (e.g., price fixing); in others, criminal sanctions are available when injunctions to obey the rulings of an administrative agency are ignored. Sutherland included injunctions because such penalties were, by law, "part of the procedure for enforcement"; consequently their use involved "decisions that the corporations committed crimes." In any event, Sutherland proposed that the appropriate criterion for determining the criminality of an act—whether by someone wearing a white collar or by someone unemployed—is its *potential* to be criminally sanctioned. "An unlawful act is not defined as criminal by the fact that it is punished," he asserted, "but by the fact that it is punishable."

Our review of Sutherland's attempt to delineate a new realm of criminality serves as a necessary prelude for understanding what is implied by "corporate crime," a term often used but not always defined in the literature. Corporate crime is conceived most accurately as a form of white-collar crime; it is thus a "crime of the rich" or part of "upperworld criminality." Corporate violations, however, differ from other forms of white-collar illegality. The most distinctive feature of corporate crime is that it is *organizational,* not individualistic. This is not to suggest that corporate acts are not the product of individuals; after all, a corporation cannot do anything but through the acts of its agents. The crucial point, however, is that the individuals involved in corporate criminality are acting in behalf of the organization and not primarily for direct personal gain—although higher corporate profits, including those obtained illegally, may bring executives such personal benefits as promotions, bonuses, and salary increases. Thus an executive who participates in a price-fixing scheme to stabilize a company's market position is committing a corporate offense; an executive who embezzles funds or profits from an insider-trading scheme is not.

Corporate crimes are organizational in another sense as well: the activation of nearly all corporate policies—whether legal or illegal—requires the coordination of diverse elements within a corporation. Thus few violations of the law could be committed without the involvement (though not necessarily the culpability) of many persons within the corporate structure. . . .

THE PREVALENCE OF CORPORATE CRIME

As we noted in introducing this chapter, an investigation by *Fortune* found that 11 percent of a sample of 1,043 companies committed at least "one major delinquency" between 1970 and 1980.

In 1982, *U.S. News and World Report* furnished a similar account in its article, "Corporate Crime: The Untold Story." The reporters discovered that "of America's 500 largest corporations, 115 have been convicted in the last decade of at least one major crime or have paid civil penalties for serious misbehavior." The picture was even bleaker when the conduct of the nation's twenty-five biggest companies was examined. Since 1976, seven had been convicted on criminal charges, and "seven more have been forced into settlements of major non-criminal charges—a total of 56 percent linked to some form of serious misbehavior." On a broader level, the magazine reported that from 1971 to 1980 "2,690 corporations of all sizes were convicted of federal criminal offenses."

Although these figures indicate that corporate illegality is widespread, it appears that they underestimate the true prevalence of lawlessness in the business community. A more detailed search of records and rulings by a team of researchers headed by Marshall B. Clinard and Peter C. Yeager paints an even darker picture. These researchers calculated the number of criminal, civil, and administrative actions either initiated or completed by 25 federal agencies against the 477 largest publicly owned manufacturing corporations in the United States during 1975 and 1976. For these two years alone, they discovered that "approximately three-fifths of the . . . corporations had at least one action initiated against them." When offenses were classified according to seriousness, it was found that one-fourth of the firms "had multiple cases of non-minor violations." Further, some corporations were found to be far worse than others: only 8 percent of the corporations in the sample "accounted for 52 percent of all violations charged in 1975-1976, an average of 23.5 violations per firm."

Clinard and Yeager's data also provide a point of comparison with the earlier research of Edwin Sutherland. As noted, Sutherland's study of 70 corporations over a 45-year period led him to conclude that nearly all corporations recidivate and that most are "habitual criminals." Clinard and Yeager reached a similar conclusion on the basis of the number of actions successfully completed (not simply initiated) against the corporations sampled, the criterion of corporate crime employed by Sutherland. In the two years covered by their study, 44 percent of the companies were repeat offenders. Moreover, "if one could extrapolate the number of sanctions over the average equivalent time period used by Sutherland, the result would far exceed his average of 14 sanctions."

Finally, Clinard and Yeager were careful to observe that their statistics represent "only the tip of the iceberg of total violations." Because they could not obtain access to agency records that detailed all actions taken against corporations, the researchers estimated that their figures may undercount such allegations by as much as one-fourth to one-third. In addition, the figures are based only on actions undertaken by federal agencies, and thus do not include transgressions detected by state and local administrators and investigators. Beyond these considerations, Clinard and Yeager relied on "official statistics" to measure illegal corporate behavior: actions initiated or completed by federal agencies. As noted, official statistics invariably underestimate actual violations because they do not reflect the many cases in which court or enforcement officials do not know that an offense was committed. At present we have no way of learning the exact dimensions of the "hidden delinquency" of corporations. When we realize, however, that major corporate misdeeds (such as price fixing) have continued undetected for a decade or more, we have reason to believe that the "hidden" or "dark" figures of corporate lawlessness are substantial.

In conjunction with Sutherland's *White Collar Crime*, Clinard and Yeager's research remains the most systematic analysis of illegal corporate conduct. Subsequent empirical studies, though more limited in scope, reinforce the view that law and order have yet to be established in the business community.

Some scholars, however, disagree with Clinard and Yeager's conclusions. Favoring a strict legalistic definition of corporate crime rather than the broad definition used by researchers of the Sutherland tradition, Leonard Orland questions whether Clinard and Yeager's study can be used to "support the claim of widespread corporate crime in America." He revives the Tappan-Sutherland debate and chides Clinard and Yeager for trying to assert "that corporate crime is prevalent by pointing to a large number of incidents that have nothing to do with criminal law and even less to do with crime." Instead, he says, the "tabulation of recorded crime should be the starting point for determining the actual extent of crime."

Despite this criticism, Orland does not dispute that corporate crime – even when defined by strict legalistic criteria – is a frequent and troubling occurrence; he reports that for the fiscal years 1976-1979, 574 corporate criminal convictions were obtained in federal courts. He also inspected filings to the Securities Exchange Commission to determine the number of corporations that had reported being involved in "material legal proceedings." Because criminal cases are not automatically "presumed to be material," SEC filings constitute only a "minimal estimate of corporate criminal convictions." Even so, for 1978 alone, "fourteen of the 100 largest industrial corporations disclosed criminal convictions to the SEC."

A more recent study, in the *Academy of Management Journal*, analyzed violations of antitrust laws and the Federal Trade Commission Act by Fortune 500 companies between 1980 and 1984. Corporate illegality was measured by the "total number of instances in which firms were found guilty in litigated cases, were parties to nonlitigated consent decrees, or involved in unsettled cases in which the court found substantial merit to the charges against the cited firms." Even though the researchers investigated only a limited area of corporate conduct, they found that the companies in their sample averaged nearly one violation apiece, and "that the mean for those firms which were involved in some type of illegal activity was three acts."

Recent media reports provide similar evidence of corporate lawlessness. Revelations of misconduct have become so common that, as a *Time* article titled "Crime in the Suites" observes, "the way things are going, *Fortune* may have to publish a 500 Most Wanted List"; according to another *Time* writer, "during 1985 the business pages often looked like the police blotter as investigators uncovered case after case of corporate crime." Newspapers across the nation also voiced concern about the prevalence of corporate brushes with the law. The *New York Times* concluded that "a corporate crime wave appears to be exploding," while the *Peoria Journal Star* ran the headline, "Corporate Crime Was Big Business in 1985." To be sure, talk of a "crime wave" may reflect the increased sensitivity of the media to corporate illegality rather than an escalation in real rates of such misdeeds. Nonetheless, it appears that in the future, the media will suffer no shortage of newsworthy material. "It's not going to stop," comments Robert W. Ogren, head of the fraud section for the Department of Justice. "We have a terrific pipeline of cases," adds Joseph H. Sherick, former chair of the Securities and Exchange Commission.

Some readers might object that the data and news report cited here present an excessively bleak and potentially misleading image of corporate management—that most executives do not violate the law repeatedly, if at all. Although studies suggest that some managers' ethics in economic matters are questionable, we have no reason to believe that executives are any more or less moral than other men and women. We also recognize that of the thousands who make and implement policy in a large corporation, only a few corrupt or harried executives are needed to involve a company in illegal activities. Yet, even though such statements are useful in balancing our view of the corporate manager, two considerations should be kept in mind.

First, readers should be careful not to apply a double standard, even unwittingly, when examining scholarly research on unlawful conduct in the business community. "If a criminologist undertakes a study of mugging or murder," observes one scholar of corporate crime, "no one expects a 'balanced' account which gives due credit to the fact that many muggers are good family men . . . or perhaps generous people who have shown a willingness to help neighbors in trouble." Nonetheless, "criminologists are expected to provide such 'balance' when they study corporate criminals."

Second, an evaluation of corporate lawlessness ultimately is less a matter of individual morality than of organizational consequences. It is not so important to know whether most executives abide by laws and regulations most of the time if the organizational environment produces *a rate of corporate crime that continues to exact huge and unwarranted costs from society*—and nearly every student of corporate illegality agrees that business crime is widespread and enormously costly. Later we will examine the extent of these costs, showing how corporate offenses illegally redistribute wealth, undermine the nation's moral and social fabric, and inflict injury, illness, and death of unsuspecting victims. . . .

Leonard Orland, *Reflections on Corporate Crime: Law in Search of Theory and Scholarship,* 17 AMER. CRIM. L. REV. 501–520 (1980)*

I. INTRODUCTION

"Crime," the late Professor Packer wisely reminded us, "is a sociopolitical artifact, not a natural phenomenon. We can have as much or as little of it as we please, depending on what we choose to count as criminal." Americans in the last hundred years have indiscriminately turned to the criminal law as a primary instrument of social, political, and economic control, and in the process have counted much as criminal. Problems as diverse as sexual immorality, gambling, racial discrimination, and the use of alcohol have been the subject of extensive regulation by criminal statute. The "persons" who were the subject of these efforts at control by criminal law were natural persons, *i.e.*, human beings. But, for more than three quarters of a century, Congress has not hesitated to apply the criminal law to corporations, which are artificial persons. In recent decades, and with increasing frequency, Congress has turned to the criminal law as a major instrument for economic and social control of corporate conduct. Criminal convictions of corporations in the federal courts are now common.

Of course, criminal law cannot always be applied to corporations in the same way that it is applied to individuals. A corporation cannot be incarcerated, although it can be executed; a corporation cannot, in the ordinary course of events, engage in much of the conduct that has been the traditional concern of criminal law. For example, legitimate business corporations have neither the inclination to commit murder, nor the ability to commit a sex offense. However, there is a broad range of corporate conduct that is clearly within the ambit of traditional criminal law. For example, a corporation might well commit perjury, evade taxes, or bribe public officials, all historic concerns of the criminal law, which have traditionally been denominated as "mala in se."

---

* Reprinted with permission of the author.

In the last half-century, Congress has enacted a vast array of penal economic regulatory statutes directed at the corporate enterprise which has resulted in "hundreds of thousands of legal commands and prohibitions, violation of which may include criminal liability." These regulatory statutes, which have traditionally been denominated as "mala prohibita," have been described as a "vast and disorganized set of proscriptions that are used for the job of regulating the mode in which business enterprise . . . is carried on."

Historically, the Supreme Court has given these "regulatory" corporate criminal statutes a prosecution-oriented interpretation. Thus in 1909, when ruling that a corporate entity could itself violate the criminal law, the Supreme Court stated:

> We see no valid objection in law, and every reason in public policy, why the corporation which profits by the transaction . . . shall be held punishable. . . . While the law should have regard to the rights of all, and to those of corporations no less than to those of individuals, it cannot shut its eyes to the fact that the great majority of business transactions in modern times are conducted by these bodies, and particularly that interstate commerce is almost entirely in their hands, and to give them immunity from all punishment because of the old and exploded doctrine that a corporation cannot commit a crime would virtually take away the only means of effectually controlling the subject matter and correcting the abuses aimed at.

Sixty-six years later, in upholding corporate criminal convictions under "regulatory" criminal statutes which imposed affirmative duties to prevent crime on corporate executives, the Court again concluded:

> [I]n providing sanctions which reach and touch the individuals who execute the corporate mission the [Federal Food, Drug, and Cosmetic] Act imposes not only a positive duty to seek out and remedy violations when they occur but also, and primarily, a duty to implement measures that will insure that violations will not occur. The requirements of foresight and vigilance imposed on responsible corporate agents are beyond question demanding, and perhaps onerous, but they are no more stringent than the public has a right to expect of those who voluntarily assume positions of authority in business enterprises. . . . Congress has seen fit to enforce the accountability of responsible corporate agents dealing with products which may

affect the health of consumers by penal sanctions cast in rigorous terms, and the obligation of the courts is to give them effect so long as they do not violate the Constitution.

Despite this extraordinary expansion of the legal concept of corporate crime, both by Congress and by the federal courts, the study of corporate crime remains a curiously neglected area of scholarship. The legal literature is astonishingly thin, and the non-legal literature is hopelessly misguided. Formulation of theories of corporate crime has been impeded by the fragmented nature of legal education and scholarship. Antitrust, securities regulation, corporate taxation, and environmental affairs are highly specialized subjects with separate legal literatures and separate lawyer and student constituencies. Thus, an informed and intelligent analysis of the general problems of corporate criminal justice administration is retarded by the inherent complexity of a field which requires legal sophistication in a broad range of highly technical areas of the law.

A rational study of corporate crime should have a number of objectives: an understanding of the nature of the conduct sought to be regulated by criminal statute, an evaluation of existing statutes which impose criminal sanctions on corporations, a theoretical examination of organizational behavior to develop a better understanding of the forces which produce corporate crime, a tabulation of corporate criminal convictions, from which an informed estimate of the extent of corporate crime can be derived, and an examination of the effectiveness of existing sanctions against corporate crime. Most of these issues have not been explored in the legal literature. Only one issue, the extent of corporate crime, has been the subject of significant organized investigation by criminologists. This essay will evaluate the major criminological studies which have sought to measure corporate crime, and then consider the effectiveness of existing sanctions against corporate crime.

II. THE TASK OF DEFINING AND MEASURING CORPORATE CRIME

It is difficult to address "corporate crime" issues without considering the work of Edwin Sutherland, the criminologist who popularized this expression, as well as the term "white-collar crime," more than twenty-five years ago. It is equally difficult to consider Sutherland without detailing the enormous theoretical and methodological deficiencies of his work. The distinguished English criminologist Nigel Walker recalls that Sutherland was one of a number of "hopelessly perfectionist" sociologists who sought a single explanation—a "grand theory"—for all crime. The concept of a "grand theory" had "the sort of prestige among sociologists of deviance which Grand Opera had in the world of singers." Sutherland's grand theory was "differential association":

> The hypothesis of differential association is that criminal behavior is learned in association with those who define such behavior favorably and in isolation from those who define it unfavorably, and that a person in an appropriate situation engages in such criminal behavior if, and only if, the weight of the favorable definitions exceeds the weight of the unfavorable definition.

Sutherland applied this grand theory of differential association to business-related crimes.

Sutherland's concept of white-collar crime, however, was exceedingly broad. It not only included the traditional non-violent crime categories, such as bribery, embezzlement, and tax fraud, but also certain tortious conduct which the law had never considered criminal, such as false advertising. In addition, Sutherland's concept of white-collar crime enveloped conduct which the law had never even considered tortious, such as unnecessary medical treatment or fee splitting. To Sutherland, this ill-defined melange of illegal, unethical, or deviant conduct constituted white-collar criminality. Under his theory of differential association, Sutherland defined certain acts as criminal if the party performing the act was "respected," "socially accepted and approved," or otherwise emulated. Sutherland's approach, in short, was Marxist: criminality was based primarily upon the socio-economic status of the offender, with the definition of crime extending far beyond accepted legal categories.

A similarly expansive definition of crime appeared in Sutherland's subsequent *Crime of Corporations,* which presented a "tabulation of the crimes of the seventy largest corporations in the United States." Sutherland once again expanded the term crime to encompass not only non-criminal public wrongs, such as unfair labor practices and false advertising, but also such business torts as patent, trademark, or copyright infringement. Applying this sweeping definition of corporate crime, Sutherland found 980 adverse decisions against the seventy largest corporations, with multiple violations by many corporations. To Sutherland, this data established a widespread pattern of corporate criminal recidivism; he concluded that ninety percent of the largest corporations in the United States were habitual criminals. Sutherland did acknowledge that only 159 of the 980 adverse decisions tabulated as corporate crime were handed down by criminal courts, and that the balance were entered by civil courts or by administrative agencies with no criminal

jurisdiction. Nevertheless, to Sutherland, a corporation which had *never* been indicted or criminally convicted, but which had been found, on multiple occasions, to have engaged in an unfair labor practice or trademark or copyright infringement was not only a corporate criminal, but a criminal recidivist.

It is difficult to know how legal scholars should respond to Sutherland's generalizations, which are at war with fundamental principles of law as well as common sense. One takes small solace in Nigel Walker's judgment that "criminologists say some very strange things about causation and explanation" and that deficiencies in criminological scholarship "originate from a failure to think about what is being explained." It is possible, of course, to argue that some corporate misconduct which is treated as a civil wrong *should* be challenged as criminal, and that bias in enforcement is the sole differential. That argument may legitimately apply to areas where existing lines of criminality are blurred, such as antitrust or securities violations and where enforcers have great discretion in deciding whether to proceed criminally or civilly. But it is difficult to move from this quite legitimate perception to Sutherland's method of labeling as criminal whole categories of conduct, such as trademark or copyright infringement, which were never considered to be serious social or moral wrongs.

It is one thing for a theorist to argue that some wrongful conduct of corporations is ignored or erroneously perceived by law enforcers as "tort" when it should have been seen as "crime." It is quite another matter for an empiricist to tabulate adverse adjudications by civil courts and non-criminal administrative agencies and automatically classify these violations as crime, thereby converting a multiple tort offender into a criminal recidivist. The empirical model which results only distorts the legal system that purports to be described.

Despite the massive flaws of this work, Sutherland continues to be cited in the popular literature and revered in the sociological community. Currently, a new generation of criminologists has perpetuated and, to a large extent, expanded Sutherland's errors.

The recent work of Marshall Clinard and his associates is a startling example of a Sutherlandian exercise in misconceived empiricism. Utilizing a quarter of a million dollar grant from the Law Enforcement Assistance Administration, Clinard set out to measure the extent of corporate crime. But, like Sutherland, Clinard employed an expansive definition of crime. Ignoring criticisms of Sutherland's approach, Clinard asserted that since corporate conduct is regulated by a comprehensive body of law, including administrative and civil laws as well as criminal statutes, "corporate crime includes any act punished by the state, regardless of whether it is punished under administrative, civil or criminal law. . . . Any definition of crime, therefore, solely in terms of the criminal law is restrictive for an adequate understanding of behavior like corporate crime. . . ."

Clinard's concept of governmental acts of punishment, which he considers criminal enforcement, encompasses "warning letters, consent agreements or decrees and agreements not to repeat the violation, seizure or recall of commodities, administrative or civil monetary penalties and court injunctions to refrain from further violations." Applying this broad concept of punishment, Clinard found that 1,554 enforcement actions had been imposed upon the 582 largest American corporations. Throughout the study, enforcement actions are referred to interchangeably as violations, sanctions, illegal corporate behavior, and penalties.

The vast bulk of these enforcement actions have very little to do with crime as that term is commonly understood by non-criminologists. This is apparent not only in his defense of his broad definition of corporate crime, but also in his frequent reference to tabulated events in the aggregate as criminal, or as criminal convictions. For example, Clinard describes his book as a "research study of corporate crime" and observes that "corporate crime is combatted by a variety of federal regulatory agencies." In a section entitled "Controlling Corporate Crime," Clinard explicitly refers to the 1,554 tabulated enforcement actions and concludes that his study reveals that "approximately two-thirds of large corporations violated the law, some of them many times."

Similar distortion occurs when Clinard tabulates 1,860 cases initiated against corporations, which are referred to at various points as recorded violations, and illegal behavior, as well as crime. It is claimed that these cases represent "far more significant personal and monetary damage than does ordinary crime." Finding that an average of 4.8 actions were initiated against 300 parent manufacturing corporations that had committed at least one violation, Clinard concludes that "a single instance of illegal corporate behavior, unlike 'garden variety' crime often involves millions of dollars and can affect the lives of thousands of citizens." Here, Clinard's use of the terms "violation" and "crime" would seem to mean actual convictions, or at least, criminal accusations. Yet even here, these violations are in fact no more than a selected sample of formal or informal non-criminal preliminary agency actions.

The result is a study of neither corporate crime nor corporate wrongdoing. Rather, it is a study of federal administrative regulation of large corporations. The Clinard tabulation of violations is nothing more than a collection of discretionary decisions to initiate formal or informal non-criminal agency procedures against a particular corporation for a particular

event; it appears that less than 1% of these "violations" involve accusations of crime as Congress, lawyers, and courts have defined crime. *Illegal Corporate Behavior* is a more fundamentally flawed work than Sutherland's *Corporate Crime*. Clinard's work reflects a deep confusion about corporate behavior, a refusal to respond to the criticisms of Sutherland, pervasive naivete about the nature of federal regulatory control of corporations, and lack of understanding of elementary principles of law. The publication of the Clinard work under the auspices of the Justice Department's National Institute of Law Enforcement and Criminal Justice creates the risk that this misleading study will be utilized to support the argument that corporate crime is widespread. In fact, the data presented lend no support to the claim of widespread corporate crime in America. The Clinard study asserts that corporate crime is prevalent by pointing to a large number of incidents that have nothing to do with criminal law and even less to do with crime.

By failing to isolate the number of recorded criminal accusations and convictions against America's largest corporations, Clinard ignored a significant body of criminology which teaches that tabulation of recorded crime should be the starting point for determining the actual extent of crime. Intelligent analysis of hard data on corporate convictions would then permit an informed estimate of how much "unreported and unsolved crime (the 'dark figure') exists." The prevailing view among criminologists is that the "dark figure" of crime is probably much larger than the figure for reported crime. The contours of this concept of hidden crime have been delineated by two of the giants of western criminology, Sir Leon Radzinowicz and Professor Thorsten Sellin. Professor Radzinowicz points out that "the crimes actually committed and the crimes legally recorded are two fundamentally different phenomena." Professor Sellin adds: "Unfortunately, criminal statistics do not contain information about the criminal conduct that actually occurs. Criminal statistics are based on recorded criminality. . . . This recorded criminality is only a small sample of total criminality, the latter being an unknown quantity." In addition, Sellin indicates that the size of this sample depends on two criteria: the nature of the offense and the intensity of law enforcement.

Application of the Sellin criteria to corporate crime suggests that the gap between recorded and actual corporate crime may be even greater than for other forms of crime. This is because the perceived harm that results from many kinds of corporate crime is diffuse or non-existent and enforcement is often sporadic. In these circumstances Professor Sellin has concluded that the number of reported crimes will be low: "When only the public or the government can be said to be the victim of the offense, violations are rarely reported to the authorities by private citizens, who suffer no direct or immediate injury." Clearly, a fair and informed estimate of the actual extent of corporate crime would require a prior measurement of the number of corporate criminal accusations and convictions.

Reliable and comprehensive data on the actual extent of corporate crime would significantly illuminate our understanding of the appropriate relationship between criminal law and corporate misconduct. However, a major barrier to measurement of the number of corporate convictions is the lack of centralized and readily available data. While publicly-held corporations must report material legal proceedings to the Securities and Exchange Commission (SEC), criminal proceedings (other than environmental offenses) are not presumed to be material, and there is good reason to believe that the totality of reports filed with the SEC does not accurately reflect the total number of criminal convictions of corporations regulated by that agency. It is nonetheless possible to derive some minimal estimate of corporate crime convictions by examination of SEC filings. My own preliminary examination of 1978 filings reveals that fourteen of the 100 largest industrial corporations disclosed criminal convictions to the SEC.

At present, it is not possible to secure centralized corporate crime conviction data from any other reliable source. In fact, the investigative arm of the Justice Department, the Federal Bureau of Investigation (FBI), is a curiously inadequate source of useful data on corporate crime. The Uniform Crime Reports contain *no* information on corporate crime and the FBI maintains *no* records on corporate offenders. As a result, federal prosecutors, pre-sentence investigators, and federal judges have no readily available information by which to evaluate the criminal record of a corporation. In addition, with the present dearth of relevant statistics, social scientists are unable to measure the extent of corporate criminal convictions.

To remedy this critical lack of information, Congress could, but has chosen not to, amend the securities laws to require corporations to report all criminal indictments and convictions. Congress has also not seen fit to require corporations convicted of crime to publicize that fact—a strategy which has been adopted in a number of foreign countries—and has failed to utilize its own investigative power to ascertain the true state of corporate criminality. It is within the present capabilities of both the FBI and Congress to take the necessary steps that would allow researchers to tabulate the true amount of corporate crime. But, until the necessary governmental initiative is taken, empirical studies of the extent of corporate crime will be of limited value, even if the researcher avoids the methodological deficiencies of Clinard. . . .

IV. CONCLUSION

Corporate crime remains an obscure and seriously misunderstood phenomenon. The empirical studies of the extent of corporate crime have done much to confuse the issues; they proceed from a definition of corporate crime that suffers from overinclusiveness, and then erroneously report the existence of rampant corporate criminality. Ultimately, the investigative power of the government, and not the musings of criminologists, should be used to quantify the actual amount of reported corporate crime. These data will permit criminologists to estimate the prevalence of unreported corporate crime; it is likely they will discover that the amount of "hidden" corporate crime is vast, and that true corporate crime is substantially underprosecuted.

Sound legal theory requires an informed factual basis. In the search for a theory of corporate criminal law, one finds that the factual data are meager and existing theoretical work scarce. Yet, some attempt at assessing the existing legal framework should be made. Perhaps this article may provoke some reassessment of legal thought about corporate crime. In an effort to focus on critical areas for future studies, I suggest a number of tentative proposals concerning the nature of corporate crime and corporate criminal justice administration:

1. Current generalizations by criminologists about high corporate crime rates are clearly erroneous, since they are based on a statistical analysis of non-criminal governmental enforcement. However, preliminary data on actual convictions suggest a probability of significant corporate crime rates. Post-Watergate disclosures of corporate misconduct reinforce this suggestion. Researchers should undertake the cumbersome task of longitudinal tabulation of actual corporate crime convictions.

2. Congress has passed hundreds of regulatory criminal statutes directed at corporations, and the Supreme Court has tended to give these statutes a pro-enforcement construction, in some cases eliminating any requirement of *mens rea*. Many of these statutes are not directed at truly wrongful or seriously harmful behavior. These regulatory statutes should be moved from the system of criminal enforcement into a civil regulatory context.

3. Overcriminalization of corporate conduct demeans the seriousness of criminal convictions in the eyes of corporate executives, prosecutors, and judges.

4. There is a range of serious, wrongful corporate conduct which is appropriately subject to criminal sanctions but which is substantially underprosecuted.

5. Sentencing in corporate crime cases is ineffective. Probation is overutilized for executives and underutilized for corporate entities. Present fines have little deterrent value, and incarceration of the truly culpable is unlikely.

6. Even where serious corporate crime is prosecuted successfully, the corporation frequently escapes

substantial punishment and effectively shields culpable executives from harm.

Many of the current problems of corporate criminal law are traceable to the fact that there is no consensus among prosecutors and judges that corporate crime as it is presently defined is truly culpable. That perception may be quite accurate with regard to regulatory offenses, but is inappropriate with respect to truly criminal corporate misconduct. If a criminal bribes, perjures, or evades taxes, it is irrelevant that the wrongdoer is a fictional rather than a natural person. Yet the preliminary evidence appears to indicate that there is less condemnation and weaker sanction when the culprit is a corporation. This bias in the enforcement of criminal law that favors corporate wrongdoers at the expense of individuals results in a serious inequity that offends notions of equal justice, but more importantly suggests the inability of government to control effectively misconduct of large corporations. The practical effect of this governmental inability to control true corporate crime is to augment the power of these already powerful "fictitious persons [who] are taller and richer than the rest of us and have rights that we do not have."

The failures of corporate crime legislation and enforcement are attributable to the casualness of Congress in enacting regulatory statutes with criminal sanctions, to the absence of perspective and determination by federal prosecutors, and to the lack of firmness and imagination of federal courts in imposing sanctions. But these failures are more understandable than the studied failure of successive generations of scholars to confront the central problems of corporate criminal law and its administration.

E. Corporate Criminal Liability

Gerhard O.W. Mueller, *Mens Rea and the Corporation*, 19 U. Pitt. L. Rev. 21–48 (1957)*

Introduction

Many weeds have grown on the acre of jurisprudence which has been allotted to the criminal law. Among these weeds is a hybrid of vicarious liability, absolute liability, an inkling of *mens rea* – though a

---

* Reprinted with permission.

rather degenerated *mens rea* –, a few genes from tort law and a few from the law of business associations. This weed is called *corporate criminal liability (herba responsibilitas corporationis M.,* for those who prefer the botanical term). Nobody bred it, nobody cultivated it, nobody planted it. It just grew. To be quite sure, it has not done much harm; at least nobody has established any harmful results stemming from its mere existence, so that some may well wish to conclude upon its usefulness. Has it done any good? Again, nobody knows, though the farmers of the law have formed many opinions, all resting on rather educated agronomic conjecture.

When a few years back the American Law Institute decided to cultivate the criminal law acre, it was clear that something had to be done about *herba responsibilitas corporationis.* One would think that a dissection of one specimen of the plant for a complete analysis would have been in order. But such was not done, for lack of funds, I suppose. Instead, it was decided to uproot the plants and to re-plant them in an orderly fashion, the tall specimens on the left, the short ones on the right, those with blue blossoms up front, those with red blossoms way in the back, and those with white blossoms in the middle. All specimens of the plant are now assembled on a rather neat little plot, designated section 2.07.

Would it have been better to plow all these herbs under and to forget about them? Only an agronomist of the radical school or a stupid peasant would have resorted to such a crude and unscientific method. At least, the wise agrarian would subject the plant to a thorough inspection first.

Well then, how good and useful for human use and consumption is this one-century-old hybrid plant? Let us begin with the observation that most other peoples do not grow it, do not even permit it to vegetate, certainly do not eat it and most certainly would not swallow it whole. That may be a matter of taste. After all, we do not eat rotten eggs which, as some travelers report, the Chinese cherish, and on the Continent it took the clubs of Frederick's corporals to make the peasants grow our delightful potatoes and to make the burghers eat them.

The reader may permit me now to leave the farm and turn the agrarian discussion into a utilitarian one which can best be continued in the laboratory of human and legal experience.

Our Present Law – The Result of Leaps Without Looks

The present state of law of corporate criminal liability is not complicated. Nor is its brief history at all obscure. From the position that a corporation can not possibly incur criminal liability because, not being a natural person, it can not (1) have a *mens rea,* (2) be indicted nor tried in person—there being no appearance by attorney in the old days—, (3) be punished corporally, and (4) criminal acts of a corporation would be *ultra vires* and thus void, the law has rapidly moved to the stand that a corporation can be guilty of most, if not all, crimes. While some cases took the restrictive position that corporations can not be guilty of crimes which are *inherently human,* such as bigamy, perjury, rape or murder, by ever widening statutory interpretations and analyses the group of these *impossible* crimes has been narrowed constantly. While I can not imagine a case in which a corporation could be found guilty as a principal in the first degree of bigamy, adultery or fornication, it certainly has now been established that a corporation may be guilty of manslaughter. There is no logical reason why a corporation should not equally be able to incur criminal liability for murder, although the weight of the dicta denies this possibility. Why should not a corporation be guilty of murder where, for instance, a corporate resolution sends the corporation's workmen to a dangerous place of work without protection, all officers secreting from these workmen the fact that even a brief exposure to the particular work hazards will be fatal, as was the case int he notorious *Hawk's Nest* venture in West Virginia, where wholesale death was attributable to silicosis? Most corporate prosecutions, however, were for offenses of an economic or regulatory nature, such as illegal sales, violation of employment laws, blue sky laws, anti-trust laws, food and drug laws, road traffic laws, etc.

On the whole, courts have been liberal enough in interpreting penal statutes to include in their coverage corporations together with natural persons. But the nature of the punishment, ordinarily fitted for natural persons only, has provided a most persistent conceptual-technical barrier against corporate liability. In turn, this difficult barrier to expansion of corporate criminal liability was overcome by legislation in a great number of states.

While the law of corporate criminal liability is easy to understand or, for any given jurisdiction, easy to ascertain, the rationale of corporate criminal liability is all but clear. It is safe to say that, for the most part, the law has proceeded without rationale whatsoever—particularly in the area of regulatory and absolute liability offenses. It simply rests on an assumption that such liability is a necessary and useful thing. Where the courts did try to rationalize, especially with respect to *mens rea* offenses,

> "the penal liability of corporations has been based on analogies from private law, *e.g.,* the

fact that corporations can be sued for malicious prosecution. That ground is hazardous, to say the least. The penal liability is also rested on the ground that criminal acts which 'from the very necessity of the case must be performed by human agency * * * in given circumstances become the acts of the company' . . . Haulage Co., Ltd., 30 C.C.A. 31 (1944). Do they become the acts of the company as a matter of fact or as an evaluation that makes sense when applied to human beings? Or are these acts 'imputed to' a fictitious entity in the belief that it is just to do that and that the imposition of such liability has beneficent effects?''

Answers to such embarrassing questions rarely are suggested in the cases, and scientific data is lacking. This is particularly amazing in view of the fact that the wealth of corporate interests could hardly be expended on any more fruitful and profitable economic-legal inquiry.

THE POSITION OF THE MODEL PENAL CODE—ANOTHER LEAP WITHOUT A LOOK

The criminal "liability of corporations, unincorporated associations and persons acting or under duty to act, in their behalf,'' may be found in section 2.07 of the Model Penal Code, Tentative Draft Nos. 4 and 5. The penalties to be imposed upon corporations are stated in section 6.04.

According to its draftsman, "these sections attempt no revolutionary change in the existing law of the subject.'' The Code subjects corporations to criminal liability for all *violations,* within the meaning of section 1.04, Tentative Draft No. 4, Model Penal Code, whether included in the Code or not, and for all other offenses to be specially listed in the Code and all those outside the Code for which it plainly appears that the legislature meant to include corporations. (Subs. 1(a)) Also included are all crimes of omission of duty imposed upon the corporation by law (subs. 1(b)) and all other offenses, the commission of which "was authorized, requested, commanded or performed by the board of directors or by a high managerial agent acting within the scope of his office or employment in behalf of the corporation.'' . . .

During the 1956 debates on the section Professor Glanville Williams, without question the leading English criminal law scholar, appeared as the voice of caution. "It seems to me, he said, "that the judges have not always looked where they are going.'' He called the law which section 2.07 seeks to restate "an example of this kind of juristic logic, of this new-fashion in criminal development being pursued without really looking where you are going.'' Professor Williams stated two examples:

"This corporate liability has been applied to public corporations, so that when an officer of the railway executive was guilty of cruelty to sheep, a stiff fine was imposed on the railroad executive, which presumably may mean that passenger fares tend to go up in order to meet the fine.

And when the Yorkshire Electric Board was guilt of some technical breach of regulation, the Chief Justice imposed a fine I think of $20,000 or $60,000 on the Yorkshire Electric Board, which I suppose means that electric rates go up in Yorkshire more than in other parts of the country."

Professor Williams' examples of public corporations were especially skillfully selected, for in the case of competitive private corporations, *e.g.,* a soap manufacturing company, one could argue that the fine visited upon the corporation will result in actual pecuniary detriment to the corporation in that it puts it into a disadvantageous position competitively, since the soap company can not simply raise the price of a bar of soap in order to recoup the loss it sustained through imposition of a fine. It must consider the market. Without pursuing this thought further at this point, it will be well to make the observation that two points were well taken by Professor Williams:

(1) The law has developed the concept of corporate criminal liability without rhyme or reason, proceeding by a hit and miss method, unsupported by economic or sociological data. Moreover, instances are easily imaginable which completely disprove the popular belief in the efficacy of corporate criminal liability by suggesting its utter futility.

(2) The Model Penal Code section dealing with corporate criminal liability rests on the basis of conjecture, and whatever modification it suggests likewise rests on conjecture and is unsupported by scientific data.

Professor Williams' *caveat,* although that of a most experienced and renowned scholar, likewise does not rest on scientific data, simply because none is available at this time. But the very source of this *caveat* entitles it to weighty consideration. But there is a second *caveat.* This is the experience of other countries, as it was available for consideration, though not utilized, through comparative law research. The comments to section 2.07 do not contain a single word about the civil law in point. Is it not noteworthy that corporate criminal liability has been rejected in practically every civil law country?

CIVIL LAW OF CORPORATE CRIMINAL LIABILITY

Apart from a few temporary and partial exceptions the maxim that *societas delinquere non potest* is still firmly recognized in the civil law. Only the natural person acting for the corporation can incur criminal guilt. Everybody who acts for a corporation knows that he can not escape criminal liability by shifting the blame to the body corporate. Courts can not, as our juries are inclined to do, convict the corporation alone so that the individual defendant may escape punishment. Such a law is deterrence practiced at its best, nay, it is deterrence, whereas the punishment of the body corporate with the possible sub rosa acquittal of the truly responsible individual defendant, and the resulting exaction of a fine from the corporation, *i.e.,* from the ordinarily ignorant and innocent shareholders and consumers of the corporation's products, has no semblance to principles of penal law but simply amounts to the exaction of a contingency tax.

The doctrine *societas delinquere non potest,* although of ancient origin, had been widely ignored in the Europe of the Middle Ages and as late as the 18th Century— when it stood virtually unchallenged in the common law—until Savigny and Feuerbach re-established it firmly in the early 19th Century. Since then it has remained unshaken in practice except for wartime economic legislation of limited applicability which has been retained in a few regulatory statutes to this day. But even in these instances the law rests largely on the original meaning of vicarious liability by ordinarily permitting exculpation of the corporation through a showing of due diligence on the part of the corporation, acting through its shareholders or management.

France:

French law has adhered to the principle of penal immunity of corporate bodies, *personnes morales,* mainly as a matter of principle. The courts reason that corporate criminal liability is irreconcilable with the guilt principle, *i.e.,* the doctrine of *mens rea,* which is the true basis of all criminal law. Consequently, corporate criminal liability would be ineffectual as a deterrent, because deterrence addressed to no mind at all is a hollow phrase. However, in recent years the belief has spread that where ethico-legal considerations of guilt are of minor or no importance at all, namely in the law of penal- economic regulation, it is both consistent with the basic principle of criminal law and utilitarian to subject corporations to criminal liability. *Defense sociale, i.e.,* protection of the public safety and order, has become the slogan justification for, and connotation of, this form of liability. The fear that no other means are available to check the growing activities, lawful as well as unlawful, of corporate bodies, has dictated several important pieces of legislation imposing corporate criminal liability, especially immediately preceding and during World War II. Such corporate crimes concern tax fraud, foreign investment violations and foreign exchange violations.

The latter punishes the corporation for acts done by managerial officers acting within the scope of their employment and in the interest of the corporation. The Price Regulation Law of 1945 provides for termination of the business privilege as punishment against violating corporations and also for the imposition of fines upon both the corporation and its management, as well as for confiscation of the products.

A post-war measure of some significance is an ordinance of May 5, 1945, which decrees confiscation as punishment for publishing establishments which had collaborated with the enemy. A significant clause of this law provides for the compensation of all those shareholders who can establish their personal innocence:

"Toutefois, s'aqissant de societes pourront beneficier d'une indemnisation . . . ceux de ses membres qui n'y aurront exerce, depuis le commission de l'infraction, au cune fonction de direction ou d'administration et qui se, seront opposes ou auront tente de s'opposer a l'exercice de l'activite criminelle de la personne morale ou qui aurront ete dans l'impossibilite absolue de la faire."

This compensation remedy is commonly regarded as a model legislative device for exempting the innocent shareholder from the sweep of corporate criminal liability. In the other few instances where French law utilizes corporate criminal liability an exculpation of the innocent shareholder or even the corporation *quae* management is not used.

These few statutes must be regarded as odd exceptions to the otherwise firmly entrenched rule that corporations can not be subjected to criminal liability. The trend among the writers and legislators, of which I spoke earlier, has definitely been checked by the persistent and conservative stand of the *Cours de Cassation* to the effect that ordinarily corporations are not even criminally liable in the area of regulatory laws, where Anglo-American courts had the least difficulty extending criminal liability to corporations.

In passing it should be mentioned that Belgium law, closely akin to that of neighboring France, is likewise opposed to corporate criminal liability and admits of only few and partial exceptions.

Germany:

The German point of view is not unlike the French. The German Supreme Court has constantly rejected an extension of criminal liability to corporations, except where the legislature has expressly so provided. Current German law knows only two instances of corporate criminal liability. A few older statutes of corporate criminal liability are no longer in force.

The German Internal Revenue Code provides for the assessment of fines and costs against corporations for tax violations committed within the enterprise. The guilt of a natural person need not be ascertained in such cases. This is a coterminous liability of the corporation together with the responsible high managerial agent or officer. It has been explained by the fiscal interest to recover the fine for the violation of a fiscal nature. The Economic Penal Law of 1949 introduced a further instance of corporate criminal liability, which is now embodied in section 5 of the Economic Penal Law of 1954. This section provides:

"If an act for which this law imposes a penalty or fine is committed within any enterprise, a fine up to DM 50,000. – [$12,000. –] may be imposed upon the owner or manager, and if the owner or manager is a body corporate, then upon such body corporate, provided that the owner or manager or his representative has neglected his supervisory duty intentionally or negligently and the violation is a result of such neglect."

This section operates with a presumption of supervisory negligence on the part of the shareholders or management of a corporation, but it provides for exculpation in all cases where the shareholders or managerial agents can establish that the violation (ordinarily price regulation violations) occurred despite the exercise of due care. In such cases the corporation is relieved of criminal liability and only the guilty individual is subjected to punishment. The policy of this law provides an incentive for supervisory diligence. Such an incentive is totally lacking in laws imposing punishment upon the corporation despite the exercise of due care on the part of ownership or management.

These few exceptions to the maxim *societas delinquere non potest* can hardly be said to constitute a repudiation of the maxim. On the whole, German lawyers have found no cause to be dissatisfied with the penal immunity of corporations.

Japan

An eminent Japanese jurist, the late Supreme Court Justice and Professor Hyoichiro Kusano, has assured us recently that "no [Japanese] book treating of criminal law in general acknowledges the capacity of offence of a corporation." However, the Japanese distinguish the moral-tainted "capacity of offence" from the moral-free "penal ability." The practical distinction seems to be roughly that of imputability of orthodox crimes, requiring *mens rea,* the former, and of regulatory offenses, *mala prohibita,* the latter. Thus, Japanese law does not admit of the liability of a corporation for ordinary crimes, but has created a few statutory exceptions, similar to those of French and German law, already discussed.

Under the Law Concerning Violations of Tax Laws or Ordinances, Law No. 52 of 1900, article 1, a corporation may be fined for statutory violations on the part of its representatives, servants or other persons engaged by it and in the course of their employment. This law was patterned after prior ordinances providing for vicarious liability of the master for the acts of his servants.

Another instance is article 12 of the Foreign Exchange Law, Law No. 83 of 1941, which threatens punishment to both the corporation and its acting agent for any statutory violation. It appears that this dual punishment has not met with the approval of most Japanese criminal law scholars. Moreover, vicarious liability is not favored, so that under both laws only the liability of the corporation for the crimes of its managerial agents finds approval. This somewhat inconsistent stand is explained by the hypothesis that corporation and governing body must be treated as identical, since it is the governing body which carries on the corporate business. The fact that the governing body in reality is a group separate and distinct from the group of the owners—shareholders is explained by reasoning that this relation is a monistic one of representation (no vicarious, but only direct liability), rather than one of substitution or surrogation (vicarious liability).

Through this reasoning, as throughout Judge Kusano's article, there speaks a firm belief in the necessity of a *mens rea* for all criminality, including corporate criminality, and a conviction that a belief in the effectiveness of absolute, vicarious and corporate liability for crime is naive. . . .

It would be as naive to conclude upon the futility of corporate criminal liability because the civilians do not have it, as it would be to conclude upon its utility because we have it. The point I wish to make is simply this: We are not dealing with a subject on which the laws of all countries are in agreement. A substantial portion of the world rejects corporate criminal liability after more thought and contemplation than has ever been given to the subject in this country. That is a noteworthy fact. On principle it can make no difference that the U.S.A. have more corporate bodies than, *e.g.*, Germany or France. I doubt whether England has more corporations than Germany, yet, the former operates with corporate criminal liability, the latter without it. Thus, before we leap again, we ought to ascertain the economic effects ensuing from either rule of law and then make our decision. Truly, such an inquiry would require much expenditure of time and money. *Ad hoc*, therefore, the least we can do is to analyze the wholesome rationale of criminal liability of our law in the hope that it may shed some light on the utility or futility of subjecting corporations to criminal liability.

PRINCIPLES OF ANGLO-AMERICAN CRIMINAL LIABILITY

The common law is a creation by individuals for individuals. Organized aggregations of private individuals had little influence on its making. They were neither subjects nor objects of the law to any material extent. In fact, when centuries after the incept the private body corporate made its appearance on the scene, the machinery of the common law was perplexed. The common law of crimes addressed itself just as much to the individual personality as did the common law of private wrongs and rights. As said by Hale:

"Man is naturally endowed with these two great faculties, understanding and liberty of will, and therefore is a subject properly capable of a law properly so called, and consequently obnoxious to guilt and punishment for the violation of that law, which in respect of these two great faculties he hath a capacity to obey: The consent of the will is that, which renders human actions either commendable or culpable; as where there is no law, there is no transgression, so regularly where there is no will to commit an offence, there can be no transgression, or just reason to incur the penalty or sanction of that law instituted for the punishment of crimes or offences."

Hawkins began his TREATISE OF THE PLEAS OF THE CROWN with these words:

"The guilt of offending against any law whatsoever, necessarily supposing a wilfull disobedience, can never justly be imputed to those who are either incapable of understanding it, or of conforming themselves to it."

But it was Coke who phrased the now famous maxim expressive of what always had been the rule of the common law of crimes:

"*Actus non facit reum nisi mens sit rea.*"

It is clear, then, that the common law—as it then was and still is in the restricted sphere of its application—after connecting an individual with a harmful result by the application of ordinary rules of causation, inquires into the *factum* of this individual's responsibility by attempting to establish whether the harm attributable to the individual rested on his conduct. Such conduct can be active or omissive, but in any event, its primary ingredient is the outward appearance of conduct, *i.e.*, the physical movement where the law commanded physical rest, or the physical rest, where the law commanded physical movement. However, the early common law judges were sophisticated enough to perceive that the mere outward appearance of conduct is not indicative of true conduct. The physical movement of an epileptic during a fit is an appearance of conduct, but no true conduct, since conduct is willed by the exercise of the mind. Thus, conduct consists of mental self-direction and physical movement.

But Coke, Hale and Hawkins had more than that in mind when they talked of "guilt," "capacity to obey," "wilfull disobedience" and "*actus reus*" and "*mens rea*." Mental self-direction and physical movement do not tell us whether a defendant meant to be wilfully disobedient, whether he had the capacity to obey, whether his mind was tainted with guilt for an act which in fact amounts to a violation of the legal mandate, whether his mind was evil, etc. The conduct consisting of mental self-direction and physical movement could well be the product of a diseased or otherwise incapacitated mind, in which case no rational law would stamp the offender guilty. Moreover, it would be utterly futile to practice deterrence on such an offender, since the insane or blank mind is not perceptive to threats and does not react rationally to pains. And certainly the threat of punishment for an insane mind can hardly be justified as an inducement to all citizens to practice mental hygiene – even if the potential lunatic knew how to ward off the evil forces which might lead him to insanity which, in turn, might lead him to unlawful conduct. Thus, even where a diseased mind is capable of entertaining mental self-direction – and in many instances a diseased mind may well not be so capable – conduct often falls short of being unlawful, despite technical breach of the law, namely because of a lack of capacity to entertain a *mens rea*.

But even the person not laboring under any of the recognized incapacities may well bring about a proscribed harm without incurring guilt. Conduct attributable to superior force, duress and coercion, while imputable to the defendant by the application of colorless rules of causation, nevertheless will not subject the actor to criminal liability because, although the actor willed the harmful result (in the sense of mental self-direction), there was little, too little, room for choice in his decision. Thus, while the actor willed his conduct, he did not will any wrongdoing. And so where an innocent mistake of fact has induced a defendant to conduct himself in a proscribed manner, the common law judges and lawyers realized that the infliction of punishment upon the actor who acted without moral guilt – not having chosen to do any harm or being ignorant of any harm – would be as inequitable as futile.

Such, in brief, was the state of the common law prior to the date on which the private corporation made its entry into the history of the common law. It was a law nicely adjusted to deal with the individual culprit, both actual and potential. It was a law both just and utilitarian. It was a rational law because it recognized that only the just can also be utilitarian.

The sole objective of the criminal law was and is to promote peaceful existence by coercing the actual or potential wrongdoer to compliance with the set standards of society through the threat or application of sanctions, which are actual deterrent influences acting upon the minds of potential or actual wrongdoers.

The common law of torts, in part – a very small part – has the same objective. But the primary function of tort law is different. It is not to deter, but to compensate. Tort law distributes the loss of a harmful occurrence. The loss must be borne by the person to whom the harmful occurrence is attributable. Causation, thus, is the primary means for imputing liability in tort, while *mens rea* plays only a minor and steadily diminishing role.

> "*Moral culpability is of secondary importance in tort law – immoral conduct is simply one of various ways by which individuals suffer economic damage.* But in penal law . . . the immorality of the actor's conduct is essential – whereas pecuniary damage is entirely irrelevant."

RECONCILING CORPORATE CRIMINAL LIABILITY AND MENS REA

Corporate criminal liability managed to sandwich itself into these juridical doctrines and considerations. Several difficulties had to be overcome. Some of these were procedural and were overcome with comparative ease, as already mentioned. Others were substantive, and some of these have not been overcome to this day. Among these are the two most important (1), the conceptual question whether a corporation can engage in conduct at all, *i.e.*, whether it is capable of mental self-direction and physical movement, and (2), the more difficult question, whether its activities can at all be tainted by moral-legal wrongfulness, *i.e.*, whether it can entertain a *mens rea*. Since *mens rea* presupposes mental self-direction (actually evidenced by physical movement), the answers to the two questions must be identical in part. The second answer is the more difficult since it must embody an ethico-legal element. Preliminarily, suffice it to say that a corporation must of course be able to act (mental self-direction and physical movement), else the whole theory of incorporation would make no sense whatsoever. As soon as the corporation appoints "its" primary agents, the board of directors, "it" acts. When "it" hires "its" operatives, "it" acts. When "it" manufactures, "it" acts, and when "it" ships "its" products to the market, "it" acts again. But the answer is not quite so simple. Since the difficulty of reconciling the imposition of psycho-ethical legal guilt, blameworthiness, upon a brainless, soulless entity with the mandate of our law that all criminal liability must rest on personal conscious wrongdoing has proved to be the more difficult question, and since, if *properly* answered, the answer to this question can also resolve all doubts about the ability of an entity to act at all, I propose to discuss this question next.

The advocates of absolute criminal liability have had no difficulty in imposing criminal liability upon the corporation. He who does not believe in *mens rea* can not find it to be a stumbling block ever. Thus, by ignoring the problem, they have solved it. Most courts, it must be conceded, have not considered the problem at all, but simply have imposed liability upon an *offending* corporation on the authority of previously adjudicated cases, most of which can be traced back to a few ancient English cases of vicarious—but non-corporate—liability for maintaining a nuisance. The growth of corporate criminal liability was fostered by analogies from the law of torts. Many courts simply failed to appreciate any material difference between the two bodies of law. Thus, the question now confronts us squarely: is it possible to reconcile the principle of psycho-ethical guilt with a theory of corporate criminal liability? Yes, upon one well recognized line of reasoning.

If by the threat of a sanction we can coerce the corporate owners, shareholders, to be meticulously careful in the selection and supervision of the managerial agents, *i.e.*, the board of directors, then any imposition of a fine upon the corporation, resulting in loss to the shareholders, is punishment for the shareholders' recklessness or lack of concern. This is entirely consistent with the guilt principle of our criminal law. But this reasoning rests on some mighty big assumptions: (1) that the shareholders, or any individual shareholders, in fact had the power to select and supervise the board of directors, (2) that the breach of the law did not occur despite such meticulous selection and supervision, (3) that the loss through fine is not passed on to the consumer, (4) that the criminal act is in fact the act of a member of the board of directors (within the limits of the recognized rules of accessoryship), etc.

Thus, here we are faced with the first cliff. It is this cliff which we call vicarious liability, *i.e.*, the imposition of the burden of punishment upon a *possibly* innocent person for the criminal act and intent (if any) of one who is appointed, or has assumed to act in behalf of, the legally responsible person. That such vicarious liability may well amount to absolute liability, namely when in fact the shareholder has no power of control, is readily apparent. This could be shrugged off by arguing that

> "[w]hoever becomes active within a political or economic association must be deemed to consent to having this possibility withdrawn or curtailed if the association misuses its position of power,"

as did the German criminal law scholar von Weber. Such a theory, however, does little more than add a legal gamble to the economic gamble which already inheres in most, if not all, stock market ventures of the investing citizen.

To repeat, it is only in cases where the shareholder has a power of control over the board of directors that vicarious criminal liability (for the criminal acts of members of the board), within rules of accessoryship), the most typical form of corporate criminal liability, is consonant with the guilt principle, which is the basis of the common law of crimes.

Assuming that we have successfully circumnavigated the first cliff, *i.e.*, that the typical corporate sanction acts *in terrorem* against nonchalant or careless shareholders, we are swiftly approaching the second cliff. If "the corporation," as an entity apart from its owners (shareholders), commits crimes for which it binds the shareholders, how then does it commit these crimes in the first place? Of whose *actus reus*, of whose *mens rea*, can be talk as corporate? It is noteworthy that the common law has long ceased thinking in terms of vicarious liability every time a corporation is said to breach the law and is convicted. On the fiction of control through the shareholders, we are no longer worried about them and their ultimate loss through the imposition of the fine upon the corporation—for the shareholders really bear the brunt of most corporate convictions. As a matter of convenience and expediency the law thinks of the corporation as the operating concern in terms of a man-like phenomenon. The *corporation* thinks, acts and becomes liable. How does the corporation think and act? Through those uppermost responsible because entrusted by the corporate owners (shareholders) with its management. Logically, therefore, the corporation can become liable only for the acts of shareholder-elected officers, *i.e.*, the board of directors, acting jointly, or the individual members of the board acting separately within their proper spheres. . . .

SUMMARY

(1) The common law has developed the method of imposing criminal liability upon corporations without any evidence of its effectiveness in the promotion of future lawful conduct by corporations.

(2) The reconcilability of corporate criminal liability and the common law principle of liability for ethico-legal wrong-doing has been a matter of conjecture.

(3) The Model Penal Code restates the principles of corporate criminal liability as developed during the last hundred years by the courts and sweepingly extends it to cover all violations by operatives, acting within the scope of their employment and in behalf of the corporation.

(4) In adopting and extending this rule, the Model Penal Code rests on the same conjecture which marks most precedents of corporate criminal liability and is devoid of economic-legal proof of the necessity for such liability.

(5) Law comparison shows that the civil law abhors the concept of corporate criminal liability. In the few instances where it employs the concept, it ordinarily provides for exculpation upon showing of due diligence by the responsible high managerial agent.

(6) Civil law courts and scholars are convinced of the greater effectiveness of imposing personal liability upon the truly responsible individual who acts for the corporate entity.

(7) Corporate liability is a special of vicarious liability, imposing the burden of punishment for the acts of agents upon innocent principles, so that the only widely used form of corporate punishment, fine, will cause economic detriment to innocent shareholders (or consumers). If the utility of corporate criminal liability for the crimes authorized, requested, commanded or performed by the board of directors of individual members thereof is assumed, then

(8) the logical extension of this form of vicarious liability so as to include the acts of other high managerial agents is proper on principle;

(9) such liability, on the analogy of unlawful conduct of natural persons, is in keeping with the *mens rea* principle of the common law, since, by reason and experience, high corporate management is the brain center of the corporation. Such liability could well be effective as a deterrent.

(10) In providing for the exculpation of the corporation through a showing of due diligence to prevent the commission of crime, the Model Penal Code rests on commendable common law principles of *mens rea*.

(11) But in nullifying the exculpation provision whenever "it is inconsistent with the legislative purpose in defining the particular offense" — other than an offense for which absolute liability has already been imposed — the Model Penal Code deviates grossly from principles of utility, deterrence and *mens rea*, permits the imposition of additional absolute liability and invites a judicial development toward abolition of all *mens rea* requirements for corporate crimes.

(12) It is urged that an economic-legal inquiry into the supposed effectiveness of corporate criminal liability be undertaken before the Model Penal Code sanctions its use, and that, in any events, the *mens rea* requirements of the common law be rigidly adhered to.

CONCLUSION

A generation ago, Professor Joseph A. Francis concluded a similar article with these words:

> "Until and unless it is demonstrated that the social good demands that corporations be held responsible for crimes, there is no sound reason for so holding them. The mass of confusing dicta must be cleared away before they are enacted into bad laws. Special instances may demand that the legislature impute crimes to corporations, but the general principles of the law . . . will be our safest guides."

Among these principles are the most important the theory of deterrence which addresses the threat of legal sanction to a guilty or potentially guilty mind, and the theory of *mens rea* without which deterrence is an empty phrase. If it be decided that corporate criminal liability is useful, then we will have no difficulty in imputing the evil (unlawful) act of "a corporation" to the entity *if* its mind was evil, and the corporate mind is that of one, several or all members of the inner circle of management. In the words of another author who spoke a generation ago:

> "It is suggested that *criminal* liability be imposed on those legal persons which are corporations *only for the acts of the human* beings who as primary representatives wield the powers of the groups upon which they are predicated."

It seems that in Britain such admonitions and considerations had some effect upon the legislature, for, our good colleague John Llewellyn Edwards could write about this problem quite recently "that the legislature's increasing accent on personal responsibility portrays a welcome and significant attitude." Response does not come so easily in America. For us, as for Mephistopheles, the word holds true:

"Yu'll have to say it thrice."

Brent Fisse, *Reconstructing Criminal Law: Deterrence, Retribution, Fault and Sanction,* 56 S. Cal. L. Rev. 1141, 1183–1213 (1983)*

CORPORATE FAULT

Is it possible to attribute fault to a corporation on a genuinely corporate yet workable basis? This question has proven to be the blackest hole in the theory of corporate criminal law. If we consider, however, the way in which corporations react to their corporate wrongdoing and how unsatisfactory reactions induce attitudes of resentment in society toward corporations, some headway might be made. . . .

A concept of corporate fault emerges which may be sufficiently corporate and workable to satisfy the theoretical and practical demands of corporate criminal law. Since this concept seeks to reflect attitudes of resentment toward a corporation that fails to react satisfactorily after engaging in unjustified harmdoing or risktaking, it will be called "reactive corporate fault."

A. THEORIES OF CORPORATE *MENS REA*

In virtually all United States jurisdictions, *mens rea* is vicariously attributed to a corporation on the basis of the mental state of an agent acting with intent to benefit the corporation. The reason these jurisdictions do not insist upon genuinely corporate fault is probably that none of the existing concepts of corporate *mens rea* is satisfactory. Three concepts of corporate *mens rea* have been suggested:

1. Managerial *mens rea*: *mens rea* based on the

---

* Fisse, *Reconstructing Corporate Criminal Law: Deterrence, Retribution, Fault, and Sanctions, 56 S. Cal. L. Rev.* 1141-1246 (1983), reprinted with the permission of the *Southern Califormia Law Review.*

mental state of a person acting on behalf of the organization in a senior managerial capacity. This is not a concept of genuinely corporate fault and is usually very difficult to prove.

2. Composite *mens rea*: *mens rea* pieced together from the knowledge of various individuals within an organization. This mental state may be easier to prove but bears no necessary connection with corporate blameworthiness.

3. Strategic *mens rea*: *mens rea* based on express or implied organizational policy. This concept reflects genuinely corporate blameworthiness but only rarely can be proven.

1. *Managerial* Mens Rea

The concept of managerial *mens rea* was entrenched in English law by *Tesco Supermarkets Ltd. v. Nattrass,* a decision of the House of Lords in 1971. In that case, a large supermarket operator was charged with a violation of section 11(2) of the United Kingdom's Trade Descriptions Act of 1968. This section prohibits advertising goods at less than their actual offering price. The central issue was whether Tesco Supermarkets could successfully plead a statutory defense of reasonable precaution and due diligence despite a supermarket manager's negligence. The House of Lords held that fault under the statute was personal, not vicarious, and that the company had not displayed any "personal" lack of reasonable precautions or due diligence. The supermarket manager, said the House of Lords, was not high enough in the corporate hierarchy for his negligence to be identified as that of the company itself.

Tesco Supermarkets was thus a case in which on the facts, the manager's fault was not imputed to the corporation. Nonetheless, the concept of managerial *mens rea* was finally upheld and has since become clearly recognized in Australia, New Zealand, and Canada, as well as in Great Britain. In the United States both the Model Penal Code and the Brown Commission's proposed Federal Criminal Code have adopted as the fault requirement for certain offenses.

The glaring theoretical deficiency of the concept of managerial *mens rea* is that it bears no necessary connection to *corporate* blameworthiness. To establish fault on the part of a *director* or *manager* is not necessarily to establish *corporate* fault. Fault on the part of one aberrant director or manager may exist despite exemplary behavior elsewhere in the organization. The concept of managerial *mens rea* is not a concept of genuinely corporate *mens rea* at all, but a variant form of vicarious responsibility.

Managerial *mens rea* is also unworkable in practice for several reasons. First, the concept is based on a hierarchical view of corporate decision making which is inconsistent with the diffusion of responsibility and delegation of tasks found in large modern corporations. In such corporations, news of an offense may reach top management long after the offense has been committed by someone on a lower level of the hierarchy. This possibility has led several courts to adopt vicarious *mens rea* as the means to ascribe corporate fault. Second, the combination of corporate loyalty, secrecy, and sanctimonious policy directives presents a formidable challenge to any enforcement agency seeking to uncover evidence of managerial *mens rea*. Unless extensive reliance is to be placed on the use of spies, electronic surveillance, and entrapment, these organizational barriers are nearly insurmountable. Third, managerial *mens rea* cannot be clearly defined because decentralization and delegation of tasks often make it impossible to distinguish "managers" — those who make corporate policy — from those who carry it out.

2. *Composite* Mens Rea

A different approach to corporate *mens rea* is to construct a composite *mens rea* from knowledge possessed by various personnel. *United States v. T.I.M.E.-D.C., Inc.* is often cited for the proposition that the collective knowledge of all employees is attributable to the corporation. In that case, the requisite element of knowledge for an offense of unsafe use of a vehicle was composed of two parts — the knowledge of a dispatcher than an unfit driver had driven a company vehicle and the knowledge of corporate officers that the company's stringent new policy about absenteeism generally encouraged unfit drivers to continue working.

Although composite *mens rea* is less susceptible than managerial *mens rea* to evasion due to the diffused nature of corporate decision-making, the concept of composite *mens rea* bears no necessary connection to corporate blameworthiness. The facts of *T.I.M.E.-D.C.* involved a reckless corporate policy, but instances of composite *mens rea* can be readily imagined in which there is no semblance of genuinely corporate *mens rea*. Such a situation arose in *Rex v. Australasian Films Ltd.*, a decision of the High Court of Australia. In this case, a film company was acquitted on charges of fraudulently evading import duty on exhibited films. One employee knew that certain films had been imported and others were aware that they had been shown to the public, but the court refused to treat this collection of discrete items of knowledge as the company's intent to defraud.

This decision seems correct; unlike the situation in *T.I.M.E.-D.C.*, corporate intent in *Australasian Films* existed only in a highly artificial sense. Even if the company had been negligent in having defective internal communications procedures, the statutory offense

at issue required an intent to defraud, not mere negligence. Accordingly, composite *mens rea* is a mechanical concept of mental state that fails to reflect true corporate fault; discrete items of information within an organization do not add up to corporate *mens rea* unless there is an organizational *mens rea* in failing to heed them.

3. *Strategic* Mens Rea

Strategic *mens rea* may be defined as *mens rea* manifested by a corporation through its express or implied policies. This concept is hinted at in a number of cases, including *T.I.M.E.-D.C.*, but has been most clearly expressed by French. He has argued that, through their policies corporations exhibit an intent that is not reducible to the intent of directors, officers, or employees. Thus, although corporations may lack "human" mental capacity," it does not follow that *mens rea* "has no meaning when applied to a corporate defendant."

Although strategic *mens rea* is a genuinely corporate concept of mental state, requiring the prosecution to establish a criminal corporate policy at or before the time that the *actus reus* of an offense is committed would make corporate *mens rea* extremely difficult to prove. Corporations almost never endorse criminal behavior by express policy, and boilerplate anti-crime policy directives may make it very difficult to establish the existence of implied criminal policies. The difficulty of proving strategic *mens rea*, however, may be significantly reduced if the requisite criminal *mens rea* based on corporate policy need not be shown to have existed at or before the time of the *actus reus* of the offense. If the corporate defendant is given a reasonable opportunity to formulate a legal compliance policy after the *actus reus* of an offense is brought to the attention of the policy making officials, the corporation's fault can be assessed on the basis of its present reactions rather than its previously designed formal policy directives. Before pursuing these and other implications, however, the origins of the concept of reactive corporate fault will be outlined.

B. VICARIOUS LIABILITY AND REACTIVE CORPORATE FAULT

1. *Vicarious Liability*

The vicarious attribution of *mens rea* to corporations, an approach upheld by the Supreme Court in the landmark decision, *New York Central & Hudson River Railroad v. United States*, has provided a valued means of avoiding the unworkability of managerial *mens rea*. However, because the concept of vicarious *mens rea* imposes strict responsibility on a corporation for the conduct of an agent, it has also been roundly criticized as unjust. What has gone nearly unnoticed is the role that vicarious liability has played as a pathfinder in the evolution of concepts of corporate fault. As decisions have been made on the basis of vicarious liability theories, courts have gradually reshaped the application of vicarious liability to more adequately reflect true corporate fault. This section shows how this pathfinding approach is pointing toward a new concept: reactive corporate fault.

Vicarious liability in corporate criminal law has evolved from the civil doctrine of *respondeat superior*. This development is often seen as an analogy to tort law that lacks an adequate basis in corporate criminal law policy. Reliance upon the civil analogy of *respondeat superior,* however, is readily understandable. During the formative stages of the modern law of corporate criminal liability, courts and legislators lacked any satisfactory, workable concept of corporate *mens rea*. The course followed was to adopt the civil method of vicarious attribution of intent and to allow ideas of corporate fault to mature with experience.

Traces of a rough concept of corporate fault can be found in several pioneering decisions. For instance, in *People v. Albany & Vermont Railroad*, the Supreme Court of New York maintained:

> It is no answer to say that the act of the corporation is manifested and carried into effect by individuals, and that those persons are always liable to the process of the law, and may be punished, and therefore an injured party has always the means of redress. It is a poor compliment to the law to say that, while the principal is the real offender, though you cannot reach his agent, – his instrument. Besides, the agent may be entirely irresponsible, or comparatively innocent.

One explanation of corporate *mens rea*, quoted by the Supreme Court in *New York Central & Hudson River Railroad v. United States,* expressed the concept of corporate blameworthiness even more clearly:

> Since a corporation acts by its officers and agents their purposes, motives, and intent are just as much those of the corporation as are the things done. If, for example, the invisible, intangible essence of air, which we term a corporation, can level mountains, fill up valleys, lay down iron tracks, and run railroad cars on them, it can intend to do it, and can act therein as well as viciously as virtuously.

Although the notion of corporate blameworthiness had some formative influence in the early development of corporate criminal liability, any attempt to define a specific concept of corporate *mens rea* would have been premature since organizational theory was still in its infancy. The main concern of the courts was not conceptual definition, but pragmatic management of uncertainty. In light of the lack of guidance from organizational theory, vicarious liability had much to offer. It avoided the inevitable narrow applicability of any concept defined in terms of corporate will, while generating feedback to the courts as to the nature of corporate responsibility. This pathfinding role of vicarious liability has continued without any special recognition, case-by-case evolution being an inherent feature of the legal system.

2. Reactive Corporate Fault

The most significant contribution of vicarious liability as a pathfinder in corporate criminal law is the concept of reactive corporate fault, which is latent in corporate sentencing practice today. Vicarious liability has led the courts to take account of *corporate* fault as a factor relevant to mitigation or aggravation of the sentence. The fault stressed under a reactive approach is not merely fault *at the time* of the *actus reus* of the offense, but fault based on the performance of the corporate defendant *in reaction* to the occurrence of the *actus reus* of the offense.

A prime illustration of court assessment of a corporate defendant's reaction to the occurrence of the *actus reus* of an offense is *United States v. Olin Corporation*. Olin Mathieson, a leading firearms manufacturer, pleaded no contest to a charge of conspiring to ship 3200 rifles to South Africa in violation of a trade embargo. The maximum allowable fine was $510,000, but the court ordered a fine of only $45,000 because of the corporation's reactive performance. In light of the disciplinary and other preventive steps taken by Olin, combined with a $500,000 charitable endowment which it created in restitution, Judge Zampano commended the company for its exemplary performance.

As a corporate offender's reactions are emphasized in mitigation of sentence, the focus shifts from the threshold requirement of vicarious liability – acts and mental states of individual agents – to the adequacy of the corporate defendant's reactive program (reflecting acts and policies not necessarily attributable to any individual). Thus, sentencing broadens the horizon of inquiry. As Coffee has observed:

> At sentencing, the court can inquire into developments since the time of the crime and even since the time of the trial: Have new measures been taken to prevent repetition? Have responsible or negligent employees been disciplined or fired? Such a wider angle of vision creates a stronger incentive for the corporation to reform itself. Indeed, by using some well-established circumlocutions, the court could indicate steps

it wishes to see taken, and suggest that it would reduce the financial penalties initially imposed if such measures were taken.

The next step would be to make the reactive program of a corporate defendant an explicit basis of corporate criminal responsibility, rather than merely a factor relevant to sentencing. If the pathfinding role of vicarious liability is thus followed to its natural conclusion, a new concept of—reactive corporate fault—may be seen. Reactive corporate fault may be broadly defined as a corporation's fault in failing to undertake satisfactory preventive or corrective measures in response to the commission of the *actus reus* of an offense by personnel acting on behalf of the organization. This concept, it is argued, is not a legalistic artifice but an expression of ordinary attitudes toward corporate reactive behavior.

C. REACTIVE CORPORATE FAULT AND ATTITUDES TOWARD IRRESPONSIBLE CORPORATE REACTIONS

By using only the time prior to and during the commission of the *actus reus* of an offense to measure the blameworthiness of corporate behavior, previous proposals fail to recognize that reactions to socially harmful acts are a common source of public resentment toward corporations. By contrast, the concept of reactive corporate fault directly reflects our attitudes toward corporations which, having engaged in unjustifiably harmful or risky acts, fail to react in a responsible manner.

Consider the well-known Kepone case, *United States v. Allied Chemical Corporation,* in which Allied Chemical pled no contest to 940 counts of water pollution resulting from the escape of the pesticide Kepone into the waterways of Virginia. Because Allied was convicted under a statute that imposed strict responsibility, fault was relevant only to gravity of sentence. In the opinion of District Judge Merhige, Allied had been at fault at the time of the *actus reus*: "I disagree with the defendant's position that all of this was so innocently done, or inadvertently done. I think it was done because of what it considered to be business necessities, and money took the forefront." Yet it is not clear that the *corporation* intentionally or recklessly committed illegal acts of pollution. A few middle managers may have possessed *mens rea,* but, as we have seen, managerial *mens rea* alone does not indicate genuinely *corporate* blameworthiness.

Suppose, however, that upon proof of the *actus reus* of the pollution offenses charged, the court had required Allied to prepare a compliance report detailing a program of preventive and restitutionary measures which the company proposed to undertake in

response to the violations. Suppose further that the compliance report was unsatisfactory to the court, or bent upon scapegoating rather than reforming. In this situation, public attitudes toward Allied's conduct would focus on its compliance program in response to the prosecution rather than on what it intended at or before the time the *actus reus* was committed. Moreover, if notice were given to the company that its compliance report would be treated as a record of top-level corporate policy, public attitudes would focus on *corporate* intent, rather than on the individual states of mind of one or more middle managers.

If the reactive strategies of corporations represent corporate policy in this way, then unsatisfactory reactive strategies would display strategic *mens rea* and thus, in absence of good excuse, corporate blameworthiness. In other words, if society looks to a corporate defendant to generate a reactive prevention and cure strategy, then an unsatisfactory response would tend to indicate a noncompliant corporate policy and hence arouse attitudes of resentment and blame toward the corporation.

The concept of reactive *mens rea* reflects very sharply the organizational reality of management by exception. An axiom of orthodox management is that routine tasks should be delegated, leaving managers to use their creativity and leadership to the greatest possible corporate advantage. In the normal course of corporate business, top management assumes that compliance with the law is routine. Management typically issues policy directives from time to time, which are implemented by means of standard operating procedures. Only when an "exceptional" event occurs, as when the corporation is alleged to have committed an offense, are questions of compliance referred upwards to managers. For instance, in the Kepone case, there is reason to believe that top managers at Allied Chemical had not even heard of Kepone before the disaster became public news, but, once the problem had surfaced, a program of corrective action was initiated as a matter of high managerial priority.

Although for every criminally proscribed corporate action we may expect a corporate responsive reaction, this Article does not suggest a narrow time frame for assessments of blameworthiness. Reactive and proactive corporate *mens rea* provide alternative bases of corporate blameworthiness, with proactive fault being relevant until the commission of the *actus reus* of an offense, and reactive fault being relevant thereafter. How far the time frame of inquiry should extend in either direction can be debated, but blame *can* be allocated on the basis of both pre and post-*actus reus* corporate policy. Blameworthiness is not governed by an absolute temporal standard, but is relative to the time over which performance is judged.

Some may object that resentful attitudes toward inappropriate corporate reactions are incompatible with a deterministic view of corporate behavior and hence provide a tenuous foundation for the concept of reactive corporate fault. Intriguing as the corporate free will versus determinism debate may be, however, it is premature to take sides. Doubtless corporate behavior can sometimes be so restricted by structural and other forces as to be substantially unfree, but it is far from obvious that free corporate choice is nonexistent. Given this indeterminacy, the only practical course is to accept the possibility of both worlds and explore them as best we can.

The concept of reactive corporate fault is compatible with this pragmatic approach. Although the concept is based on a postulate of corporate free choice, when free choice is diminished, corporate responsibility can be reduced accordingly. Excuses for inadequate corporate reactions need to be recognized; those excuses can include as many deterministic exemptions from responsibility as we desire. Just as duress, insanity, and provocation are deterministic excuses in the context of human behavior, economic duress, malfunctioning communications, and contradictory government regulations could provide deterministic excuses in the context of corporate behavior. This view of determinism may very well be more readily accepted in corporate criminal law than in individual criminal law because our attitudes toward corporate behavior are much less biased by a presumption of free will. In fact, rather than summarily rejecting deterministic excuses for corporations, a number of courts already appear to have recognized them.

D. REACTIVE CORPORATE FAULT AS A LEGAL CONCEPT: TOWARD A WORKABLE PROPOSAL

Given that the concept of reactive corporate fault appears to crystallize our attitudes toward inappropriate responses by corporate violators, it is necessary to consider how the concept might be adopted into the law. A legal framework for the concept of reactive corporate fault would require a legal definition of reactive corporate fault, delineation of categories of substantive offenses to which reactive fault could apply, and specification of reactive duties. Without attempting an extended discussion of these matters, this section outlines a potential legal scheme of reactive fault, and then addresses some practical concerns about it.

1. *A Suggested Framework*
a. *Definition of reactive corporate fault*: As discussed above, reactive corporate fault may be defined broadly as fault on the part of a corporation in failing to take satisfactory preventive or corrective measures in response to the commission of the *actus reus* of an offense by personnel acting on behalf of the organiza-

tion. For legal purposes, reactive corporate fault could be delimited more precisely as follows:

1. A serious offense of reactive noncompliance would require proof of strategic *mens rea* — an express or implied corporate policy of deliberate or reckless noncompliance with a legal duty to undertake preventive or corrective reactive measures;

2. A less serious offense of reactive noncompliance would require a failure to comply with a legally imposed reactive duty, subject to an affirmative defense that the corporation exercised due diligence in attempting to comply.

The required mental element of the more serious offense would be similar to the *mens rea* of criminal contempt, but with corporate intent defined on the previously discussed basis of corporate policy. The less serious offense would follow an analysis similar to that of the corporate due diligence defense advanced in the commentary *Developments in the Law — Corporate Crime*, but the defense would be oriented toward corporate reactive performance. The grading of the offense would be determined by the level of authorized maximum punishment; for example, serious offenses might be defined as those carrying a maximum punishment of at least $100,000 or community service of the same cost.

Note, *Increasing Community Control Over Corporate Crime — A Problem in the Law of Sanctions,* 71 YALE L.J. 280–306 (1961)*

When individuals employ the corporate form in an illegal fashion, the community, acting through its various official agencies, may respond in a variety of ways. It may punish; it may enjoin future illegality; and it may require compensation of the injured. The edict implementing the community response may run directly against the corporate form, and it may run directly against the individuals. In each case the responsible agency should select a response or a set of responses which will most justly and efficiently maximize formalized community values. This Comment attempts to construct an analytical framework

---

* Reprinted by permission of The Yale Law Journal Company and Fred B. Rothman & Company from *The Yale Law Journal*, Vol. 71, pages 280-306.

against which available and proposed community responses to the illegal employment of the corporate form may be evaluated.

The construction of such a framework cannot begin until the concept "corporation" is defined. The corporation is a legal form embodying a complex of relationships. At this level it has much in common with such other abstract legal forms as marriage, property and contract. Because corporation is a term on a very high level of abstraction, it frequently tends to conceal the real actors in a given situation. Many would agree with the following abstract proposition: when corporation X is found guilty of price fixing it should be fined $Y. Reduced to a more meaningful level of analysis, however, such a proposition inevitably conceals a complex of relationships. Corporation X, for example, may be owned by 10,000 shareholders who annually hire officers A, B and C to operate the business for a fixed salary plus a specified share of the profits. If these officers, without the knowledge of the shareholders, conspire with agents of "competing" corporations to fix prices over a five year period; and if at the end of this five year period, the officers retire from their positions; and if corporation X is subsequently found guilty of price fixing, the impact of the fine of $Y would be distributed among the "innocent" stockholders. This example illustrates how differently the equities in a given situation may appear when described at different levels of abstraction. Many who would agree that the "corporation" should be fined, might well be troubled by the punishment of the stockholders. To be sure, facile equation of the corporate form with the policy makers and stockholders may produce little distortion when the small closely held corporation is considered. But such an equation is apt to be highly misleading when applied to the more complex "endocratic" corporation.

Individuals may engage in self serving criminal behavior with differing effects upon the corporate form. an individual may commit a crime which benefits himself at the expense of the corporation (*e.g.*, embezzling corporate funds); he may commit a crime which benefits himself without affecting the corporation (*e.g.*, overstating business expenses on the income tax form); or he may commit a crime which benefits himself and also benefits the corporation (*e.g.*, increasing both corporate profits and his own commission by doing corporate business in violation of Sunday closing laws). Some crimes may, of course, fit into any of these categories, their classification depending on surrounding circumstances. A conspiracy to fix prices, for example, may be engaged in by a sales executive in order to eliminate or reduce the psychological and physical strain of active competition even though he knows that the conspiracy will result in lower profits to the corporation; in such a case the interests of the individual would be "out of harmony" with the interests of the corporation. A price fixing conspiracy may similarly be engaged in, but without discernable effect upon the corporation, if the prices were fixed accurately to reflect competitive prices; in such a case the interests of the individual would be "in neutral harmony" with the interests of the corporation. Finally, a price fixing conspiracy could be engaged in by an individual whose compensation was in some way geared to corporate profits for the specific purpose of increasing such profits by preventing competitive forces from bringing down prices; in such a case the interests of the individual would be in "active harmony" with the interests of the corporation. This Comment will concern itself only with the case of the individual who illegally employs the endocratic corporate form for the *immediate* purpose of increasing corporate, as distinguished from personal, wealth; such conduct shall henceforth be referred to as acquisitive corporate crime.

A PROPOSED HYPOTHESIS

An hypothesis concerning the rate of acquisitive crime among endocratic corporations will now be proposed. This hypothesis does not presume to account for all the variables reflected in a decision to engage in illegal conduct; it simply purports to serve as a conceptual framework against which the administration of sanctions may be evaluated.

> The rate of acquisitive corporate crime engaged in on behalf of any endocratic corporation will a) vary directly with the expectation of net gain to that corporation from the crime, and will b) vary inversely with the certainty and severity of the impact with which the criminal sanction personally falls upon those who formulate corporate policy.

This hypothesis assumes that in many instances the immediate goals of policy makers who engage in corporate crime is the enrichment of the *corporate* treasury. This assumption is not meant to minimize the selfish personal motives of such individuals. For corporate policy formulators generally have direct and important personal interests — both financial and social — in an increase in the profits of the corporation. Greater dividends, salaries, incentive compensation, bonuses, promotions, security and prestige — all of which may flow from increased profits — are frequently the *ultimate* conscious motives behind the decision to employ the corporate form in an illegal fashion. But the *immediate* goal of these formulators — the method chosen to secure these ultimate ends — is an increase of *corporate* profits. To the extent that the enhancement of one's corporate status motivates the conduct of corporate personnel therefore, an increase or decrease in the expectation of enhancing corporate profits should affect the rate of acquisitive corporate crime.

It is additionally assumed that the corporate form—the conduit which initially receives the bounty of the acquisitive crime for ultimate distribution to the policy formulators and others—does not make decisions. Decisions are made for it and through it by a variety of persons at a variety of levels both within and without the corporate hierarchy. These policy formulators presumably can be coerced into refraining from employing the corporate form in an illegal fashion if the personal ends which they seek to achieve by such illegality—increased wealth, security, prestige—are jeopardized by the real threat of punishment.

Punishment, of course, is peculiarly reserved for individuals; it cannot meaningfully be imposed upon a legal form. One may speak of the relative advantages or disadvantages of imposing punishment upon designated individuals rather than upon a designated corporation. But one is generally saying no more than: punishment should be imposed upon individuals A, B and C indirectly or by diffusing it through a given form from which they generally reap certain benefits.

A neat line cannot always be drawn between the diminution of motive (i.e., a decrease in the expectation of illegal profits) and the coercion of formulators (i.e., punishment). It is apparent, for example, that the imposition of severe criminal sanctions upon the corporation will indirectly penalize and thus coerce the policy formulators. The point to be emphasized, however, is that the degree of coercion cannot be measured at its point of contact with the corporate form; it must be measured at its point of contact with the individual policy formulators. The degree of motive diminution, on the other hand, can be measured at its point of contact with the corporate treasury. . . .

Note, *Developments in the Law—Corporate Crime: Regulating Corporate Behavior Through Criminal Sanctions,* 92 HARV. L. REV. 1227, 1229–1311, 1365–1375 (1979)*

I. INTRODUCTION

The twentieth century has witnessed a tremendous explosion in the number and size of corporations, to the point that virtually all economic and much social and

* Reprinted with permission. Copyright © (1979) by The Harvard Law Review Association.

political activity is greatly influenced by corporate behavior. During this same period, and partly as a response, there has been a dramatic increase in the efforts of the federal government to regulate that activity through the creation of multitudinous administrative agencies and volume upon volume of regulatory laws.

While many of the early attempts at regulating corporate behavior included criminal sanctions for enforcing compliance, criminal prosecution was generally employed only as a supplement to the general pattern of civil regulations, a last resort to punish particularly recalcitrant or egregious corporate behavior. During the last decade, however, in areas ranging from tax, securities, and antitrust to the newer fields of environmental control, safety regulation, and the prevention of "corrupt practices," the federal government has come to rely more and more on the deterrent effect of criminal punishment to shape corporate action. It is this recent phenomenon and the problems it has engendered that provide the subject of this Note.

Two themes emerge in the Parts that follow. First are the problems engendered by the use of criminal sanctions in the regulatory field. Foremost among these is that the choice made between criminal and civil sanctions often accords neither with the rationales that have traditionally characterized the criminal law, nor with the specific aims of the regulatory provisions themselves. For example, corporate criminal sanctions sometimes deviate greatly from the general mens rea model of the criminal law, purportedly in the name of increased deterrence. Yet the resulting invocation of the procedural protections afforded criminal defendants renders enforcement more difficult, undermining any deterrent effect. On top of this, the crazy quilt pattern of overlapping, duplicative, and even contradictory civil and criminal regulations diminishes the coherence of regulatory efforts and impedes the achievement of government objectives.

Second, the very involvement of a collective corporate entity in criminal cases is problematic. The difficulty of dealing with this entity as a "person" is particularly acute in the area of criminal law. The artificial and inanimate nature of the corporation renders uncertain the range of constitutional protections which a corporation may invoke when prosecuted. It also opens to question the necessity and utility of employing criminal sanctions directly against corporations themselves in order to regulate their behavior. The inability to imprison a corporation and the questionable effect of a criminal stigma on such an entity often leads to the prosecution of individuals within the corporation, both for their own acts and the acts of others. This focus upon individual defendants, however, serves to heighten the concern engendered by the use of criminal laws which deviate from the traditional mens rea model. Any fair and rational approach to the problem of corporate crime requires that decisions regarding which individuals within a corporation should be punished be made at least partly contingent upon the nature of the sanction and the elements of the crime.

These themes provide the central focus of the following discussion. This Note is not intended to provide an examination of the substantive law which falls under the rubric of corporate crime, but rather to trace out the issues and recurring problems relevant to corporate crime in general. The Note begins with an examination of the rationales which might justify the imposition of criminal sanctions on corporations and the individuals within them for violations of regulatory statutes. Building upon this examination, Part III addresses the problem under present and proposed statutes of determining when to impose criminal liability upon the corporation itself and which individuals within the corporate hierarchy should be held criminally responsible. Once criminal charges are brought, the presence of the corporation and a number of individual defendants, as well as the nature of the evidence in regulatory cases, raises special questions in the area of criminal procedure. Part IV analyzes the protections which a corporate defendant may assert when prosecuted, as well as the difficulties occasioned by the relationship of the individual defendants to the corporation and each other.

The subsequent Parts shift the focus to the procedural and practical problems created by the overlapping pattern of criminal and civil regulatory laws. The administration of both civil and criminal laws by the same government agencies is discussed in Part VI, and the collateral effects which may accompany the criminal prosecutions of a corporate defendant for violations of the regulatory laws are examined in Part VII. Finally, the Note concludes with an evaluation of the present approach to corporate crime and offers a proposal for reform.

II. RATIONALE

A. The Rationale for Regulatory Crimes

Traditionally, criminal sanctions have been justified by one or more of four rationales: rehabilitation, incapacitation, deterrence, and retribution. The first three are often combined in a utilitarian or other consequentialist theory of punishment, according to which punishment is viewed as the means of obtaining certain socially desirable consequences — rehabilitation of the offender, incapacitation of the offender, and deterrence of other would-be offenders. The relationship between punishment and these consequences is an empirical one: it is a question of fact whether punishment

does lead to such results. In contrast, a retributive justification of criminal sanctions appeals to notions of moral culpability or just deserts. Imposing criminal sanctions on a guilty person is justified, not because of the consequences which will result, but because it is morally proper to punish that person.

Consequentialist and retributive theories of punishment are often thought to be incompatible, but this conflict results only if the theories are given certain interpretations. It may be supposed, for example, that each theory is attempting to provide both necessary and sufficient conditions for the application of punishment. A consequentialist theory would then be interpreted to hold that punishment is justified if and only if the ends of punishment — rehabilitation, incapacitation, and deterrence — are attained, while a retributive or just deserts theory would be interpreted to hold that punishment is justified if and only if the offender is morally culpable. Given these interpretations, the two theories will conflict whenever punishment would result in the desired ends but the offender is not morally culpable, or whenever the offender is morally culpable but the punishment would not attain those ends. In the former case, the consequentialist theory would call for punishment while the retributive theory would prohibit it; in the latter case, the situation would be reversed.

The preceding interpretations are not, however, the only possible interpretations of consequentialist and retributive theories of punishment. In fact, it seems unlikely that a consequentialist would view his theory as providing sufficient conditions for punishment. A consequentialist may best be understood as addressing the question, "Why should society have an institution of punishment that inflicts suffering on some of its citizens?" His answer is that the institution has value because it results in such beneficial consequences as rehabilitation, incapacitation, and deterrence. To this extent, then, consequentialism provides a necessary condition for punishment, since punishment will be justified only if these benefits occur. There is no reason, however, to suppose that attaining these beneficial consequences is also a sufficient condition for punishment; the consequentialist may limit the pursuit of these benefits in various ways. Some of these limits may be explained by undesirable consequences which can result from punishment. For example, punishment may not be justified where the expenses of apprehension and conviction are too high or where the presence of criminal sanctions would over-deter by making people excessively cautious. However, an advocate of a consequentialist theory of punishment may also insist on limits for nonconsequentialist reasons; merely holding that punishment is a valuable institution because it prevents crime does not require one to explain all values in consequentialist terms. Thus, a consequentialist may, without contradiction, recognize the retributive requirement of moral culpability as a limit on punishment. Indeed, the view that criminal sanctions seek to serve consequentialist goals but may only be imposed when the offender is morally culpable has been attractive to many commentators.

It is less clear whether moral culpability can justify the imposition of criminal sanctions when the punishment will not result in deterrence, incapacitation, or rehabilitation. One retributive argument for this position is that society is more morally just when the good prosper and the bad suffer—when, in Kant's words, there is a "proportion between welfare and well-doing." The well-recognized difficulties with this position are that it would require punishment for moral offenses which are not socially harmful (or even punishment for bad character); that society generally makes no efforts to distribute benefits and burdens according to moral worth; and that punishing an offender may harm innocent persons who love or depend upon him. These objections, however, do not necessarily mean that moral culpability by itself is never a justification for punishment; they merely imply that moral culpability alone does not always, or perhaps even often, justify punishment. It is difficult to deny that there are situations in which many of us have strong intuitions that a person simply deserves to be punished, but whether there is a moral justification for these intuitions remains an unresolved issue. As a constitutional matter, Supreme Court opinions apparently indicate that a legislature may impose criminal sanctions for retributive reasons alone.

In justifying the imposition of criminal sanctions for illicit corporate activity, commentators most often cite deterrence as the primary rationale. They reason that retribution cannot be a concern of statutes dealing with activities which are not in and of themselves morally wrong; indeed, the activities proscribed may come very close to what is seen as good corporate practice in the competitive business world. Similarly, it is argued, society is not concerned with incapacitating or rehabilitating those who might well be pillars of the community had they not violated a technical economic regulation. Furthermore, while criminals generally do not carefully calculate the probable consequences of their actions and therefore are often not deterred by the threat of punishment, this cannot be said of the corporate criminal. Since corporate activity is normally undertaken in order to reap some economic benefit, corporate decision makers choose courses of action based on a calculation of potential costs and benefits. The calculating criminal is the one best deterred by punitive sanctions. Hence, commentators reason, deterrence plays a more significant role in the area of corporate crime than in other areas of the criminal law.

An examination of the statutes appears to support the conclusion that deterrence is the major goal of corporate criminal sanctions. For example, the securities laws passed during the Great Depression evidence a desire to protect investors by promoting honesty and fairness in corporate securities transactions. In order to achieve this goal, civil and criminal sanctions were designed to regulate the conduct of investors, brokers, and corporate managers. Similarly, health and safety laws and antitrust statutes seek to deter those who, for economic or other reasons, might be tempted to act in a socially harmful manner. Environmental sanctions likewise do not emphasize retribution, rehabilitation, or incapacitation, but rather strive chiefly to ensure clean lakes and skies by making it undesirable to pollute in the first place. As one commentator noted, "[t]he overriding general policy which the environmental prosecutor serves is to stop pollution where it presently exists and to prevent it from continuing or commencing in the future." Thus it seems evident that the basic aim of these statutes is not to punish morally culpable violators, but to deter undesirable conduct regardless of culpability.

The absence of an element of retribution in some areas of corporate crime is substantiated by the existence of strict liability crimes. Although it has been argued that strict criminal liability raises constitutional due process problems, the Supreme Court has apparently indicated that the legislature may establish a strict liability standard for criminal conviction. Despite the deterrent advantages of such a standard, however, legislatures have rarely chosen to adopt it.

Even though deterrence clearly plays a critical role in the justification of corporate criminal sanctions, the argument that retribution cannot be involved is unconvincing. It is not clear that the underlying activity is morally neutral in all cases. For example, while inadvertent leakage from a pollution control facility may be seen as morally blameless, the same would probably not be said of the intentional release of carcinogenic pollutants into a community's drinking water. Furthermore, even when the activity proscribed by law is not in itself morally wrong, the knowing violation of the law may be morally blameworthy. If a statute regulates and structures important social behavior and institutions, there is probably a moral duty to obey that law, at least in a reasonably just society. Thus even in the area of corporate crime, moral culpability could serve as a limitation upon the imposition of criminal penalties. If so, then the theory of corporate criminal liability mirrors the widely accepted view that criminal sanctions, while aimed primarily at deterrence, incapacitation, and rehabilitation, may only be applied when the offender is morally culpable.

It may also be argued that the statutes themselves evidence some retributive limitation upon their deterrent rationale. The requirement contained in many regulators laws that the proscribed conduct be "willful" can be viewed as a legislative effort to ensure some degree of moral culpability before criminal punishment is imposed. However, courts have limited the degree of moral culpability required under the willfulness standard in that they have interpreted it to mean that the act be deliberately wrongful and no more; the actor need not have known that the conduct was illegal. The requirement has been further weakened by judicial willingness to infer the requisite intent from the conduct itself. This may reflect an emphasis on the deterrent rationale of such statutes, since the conviction of defendants who did not know that their act was illegal may help to deter similar conduct in the future by encouraging corporate actors to discover in advance the legal limitations on their behavior.

The legislative requirement of willfulness, however, may not only be intended to constitute a retributive limitation on the system. It may also seek to prevent overdeterrence, a goal which is consistent with a consequentialist rationale. While maximum deterrence would be achieved by a strict liability standard, the extreme cautiousness required by such a standard might be counter-productive in some cases. Intent requirement thus may serve utilitarian ends rather than reflect a role for retribution in corporate criminal law.

Perhaps reflecting the traditional belief that some degree of moral culpability is required before criminal sanctions can be imposed, the courts must in general be convinced that the legislature consciously intended to create a strict liability crime. Where the legislative purpose is vague or uncertain, courts have repeatedly read some form of intent requirement into the law. The Supreme Court's general policy toward strict liability crimes was recently applied specifically to the realm of corporate crime in *United States v. United States Gypsum Co.* In considering the defendants' conviction for interseller price verification in violation of antitrust laws, the Court interpreted the Sherman Act to require intentional misconduct before criminal penalties for price-fixing may be imposed. The Court declared that strict liability crimes are the exception rather than the rule, and found that the availability of civil antitrust alternatives to achieve regulatory ends negated any inference that Congress intended to attain those same

ends through strict criminal liability. The Court seems to have indicated that a statute will not be interpreted to provide criminal liability in the absence of intent if civil sanctions exist to regulate unintentional conduct.

Admittedly, the *Gypsum* holding can be read as a response to the possibility of overdeterrence in the antitrust context, as well as an endorsement of retributive limitations on corporate crime. The Court noted that any strict liability statute in the antitrust area "holds out the distinct possibility of overdeterrence; salutary and procompetitive conduct lying close to the borderline of impermissible conduct might be shunned by businessmen who chose to be excessively cautious in the face of uncertainty regarding possible exposure to criminal punishment for even a good-faith error of judgment." But after setting forth this overdeterrence argument, the Court employed language which suggests retributive limitations on the imposition of corporate criminal sanctions: "The [strict liability] criminal sanctions would be used not to punish conscious and calculated wrongdoing at odds with statutory proscriptions, but instead simply to *regulate* business practices regardless of the intent with which they were undertaken." The *Gypsum* Court thus implied that more than pure deterrence should, and perhaps even must, underlie the application of criminal sanctions; an element of moral culpability must also be present if the use of such sanctions is to "square with the generally accepted functions of the criminal law."

The Court in *Gypsum* did not consider whether a strict criminal liability standard could pass constitutional muster. Rather, the Court distinguished the antitrust area from those contexts in which strict liability had been imposed, such as food and drug laws, on the basis of potential overdeterrence; in the antitrust area "the excessive caution spawned by a regime of strict liability will not necessarily redound to the public's benefit," while "excessive caution on the part of [food and drug] producers is entirely consistent with the legislative purpose." But the language in *Gypsum* which did recognize retributive limitations might be seized by lower courts to overturn existing strict liability interpretations of criminal statutes, and perhaps even to declare such liability unconstitutional.

The current state of the law seems to be that while such strict criminal liability is constitutional, it is heavily disfavored. It is by no means generally accepted that deterrence alone is sufficient to justify regulating corporate activities through criminal sanctions. The common imposition of an intent requirement by the legislature, the tendency of courts to infer such a requirement even when it is not explicitly provided by statute, and the *Gypsum* Court's recognition of a dichotomy between regulatory aims and the criminal law, all indicate the preference for some retributive element in statutes imposing corporate criminal liability. Thus while the primary aim of corporate criminal sanctions is deterrence, there may be some retributive limitations on the pursuit of this goal, and courts as well as legislatures will likely continue to require some blameworthiness on the part of the defendant in the vast majority of cases.

B. Corporate Moral Blameworthiness

There is no single, broadly accepted theory of corporate blameworthiness which justifies the imposition of criminal penalties on corporations. For an individual defendant, the mental state with which he committed the illegal act determines his moral culpability. But mental state has no meaning when applied to a corporate defendant, since an organization possesses no mental state. Three different theories of corporate blameworthiness are reflected in the various systems of corporate criminal liability.

The first theory of corporate blameworthiness considers the corporation morally responsible for the acts and intent of each of its agents. This theory treats a corporation as a principal responsible for the acts of every one of its agents, imputing to the corporation through the theory of agency the mental state of any employee. Under this theory, a corporation is blameworthy even when a single agent commits a crime for the benefit of the corporation. Yet, it is unfair to impute to the corporation the intent of a lone agent without also considering whether conscientious efforts were made by other agents to prevent the crime.

The second moral theory identifies the corporation only with its policy making officials, and so holds the corporation morally responsible only for their acts and intent, but not for those of lower-level employees. This theory distinguishes top officials from other employees on the ground that stockholders, through their elected representatives on the board of directors, have the power to appoint and the opportunity to supervise only high-level executives. Recognizing that criminal sanctions against the corporation often harm stockholders, this theory attempts to implement the just deserts principle that individuals should not be punished for acts they had no power to control. However, in any but small, closely held corporations, the average stockholder wields no actual influence over the decisions of even the highest-placed executives. If this interpretation of the just deserts principle were applied in practice, so that corporate liability was imposed only when stockholders could bring pressures to bear to prevent the crime, corporations would be virtually immune from liability. Moreover, this interpretation

fails to recognize that stockholders take financial risks whenever they invest, and these risks are no more unfair because they derive from illegal, rather than inefficient, managerial conduct. The same risk is imposed on stockholders by any government regulatory program which applies civil sanctions to corporations, or otherwise constrains them in their pursuit of profit. Therefore, the second theory of corporate blameworthiness fails to accord with the realities of the relationship between stockholders and management.

The third theory proposes that a corporation is blameworthy only when its procedures and practices unreasonably fail to prevent corporate criminal violations. More than the two preceding theories, this theory recognizes that generally the criminal acts of a modern corporation result not from the isolated activity of a single agent, but from the complex interactions of many agents in a bureaucratic setting. Illegal conduct by a corporation is the consequence of corporate processes such as standard operating procedures and hierarchical decision making. Therefore, just as an individual's moral blameworthiness depends on his mental processes, corporate moral fault may be said to depend on its internal processes. Thus, under the third theory, a corporation is blameworthy when its practices and procedures are inadequate to protect the public from corporate crimes. Corporate blameworthiness therefore depends not solely on the commission of a crime but on the overall reasonableness of corporate practices and procedures designed to avert injurious regulatory offenses.

III. Standards of Liability

Standards of criminal liability for corporate offenses should be evaluated in light of the dual rationales for regulating corporate conduct through the criminal law—deterrence and just desserts (retribution). These two rationales frequently conflict in practice, so no standard of liability can fully achieve both goals. Standards which require no finding of wrongful intent or carelessness may effective deter illegal behavior but do not comport with the moral principle of just deserts. At the other extreme, standards which require evidence that the crime was committed willfully or knowingly accord with the just deserts principle but make liability easy to evade and difficult to prove, thus providing inadequate deterrents to corporate crime. In designing standards of criminal liability for corporations and for individuals accused of regulatory offenses, the courts and legislatures must attempt to strike an appropriate balance between deterrence and just deserts. Under existing law, both the corporation and its responsible agents can be convicted for the same offense; corporate and individual criminal liability are complementary, not mutually exclusive. Observers differ as to whether existing criminal sanctions against corporations provide a sufficient deterrent to corporate crime, but most agree that with vigorous enforcement and stringent penalties, the threat of criminal liability can spur corporate efforts to detect and prevent illegal activity. The first Section of this Part reviews the existing systems of corporate liability, and, in light of the theories of corporate blameworthiness, elaborates a new system of liability based on the reasonableness of a corporation's overall efforts to comply with the law.

Individual criminal sanctions also deter corporate crime by strengthening employees' incentives to resist corporate pressures to violate the law in the pursuit of increased profits. The threat of a jail sentence in particular induces employees to forego even substantial corporate profits rather than risk individual criminal liability. Fines are less likely than imprisonment to deter, in part because of the possibility of insurance and indemnification; but even if an individual defendant does not personally pay the fine or his legal fees, he still suffers the stigma of a criminal conviction with the ensuing damage to his reputation in the community and his prospects within the corporation. The second Section of this Part applies the two established standards of individual liability, strict liability and specific intent, to the activities of supervisory officials. It then presents a new standard of reckless supervision which attempts to respond to the weak moral grounding of strict liability and the inadequate deterrent provided by specific intent statutes.

A. Corporate Liability

Corporations have been held criminally responsible for strict liability offenses since the mid-nineteenth century, and for crimes of intent since 1909. The systems of corporate criminal liability developed by American courts and commentators carry different degrees of deterrent effectiveness and reflect varying notions of corporate blameworthiness. The doctrine of respondeat superior, which predominates in the federal courts, offers the greatest deterrent strength and adopts the first theory of corporate blameworthiness. The systems proposed in the Model Penal Code, promulgated by the American Law Institute in 1962 and subsequently enacted by several major states, provide different levels of deterrence and incorporate aspects of all three moral theories. These systems will be described and evaluated in terms of their effectiveness in achieving the conflicting goals of deterrence and just deserts, and an alternative system will be proposed which attempts to achieve a more appropriate balance between these goals.

I. Respondeat Superior. – The respondeat superior doctrine of corporate criminal liability, derived from agency principles of tort law, is the common law rule in the federal courts and in most state courts today. The federal criminal code proposed in 1978 also adopts this majority rule. Under the doctrine of respondeat superior, a corporation may be held criminally liable for the acts of any of its agents if an agent (1) commits a crime (2) within the scope of employment (3) with the intent to benefit the corporation.

First, it must be proved that an illegal act was committed by an agent of the corporation, and that the agent acted with the specific intent required by the governing statute. Proving specific intent should be the same for a corporation as for an individual defendant, because under respondeat superior, the intent of the offending agent is imputed directly to the corporation. However, since the corporation is perceived as an aggregation of its agents, it is not necessary to prove that a specific person acted illegally, only that *some* agent of the corporation committed the crime. Thus, proving that a corporate defendant committed the illegal act is in practice substantially easier than an individual prosecution.

Courts have also found the requirement of corporate criminal intent satisfied where no agent's criminal intent has been shown. Corporations have been convicted of crimes requiring knowledge on the basis of the "collective knowledge" of the employees as a group, even though no single employee possessed sufficient information to know that the crime was being committed. For example, in *United States v. T.I.M.E.-D.C., Inc.,* a trucking company was found guilty of knowingly violating an ICC regulation which forbade truckers from driving when ill. One employee, a dispatcher, knew that the driver in question had telephoned to say he could not work, and then changed his mind after learning of the company's new absentee policy. Corporate officers, the court found, knew that the harsh new policy was likely to encourage truckers to drive despite being ill. Through the collective knowledge of the dispatcher and the officers, the corporation was found to have known that the driver was unfit to drive under the ICC regulation.

In addition, there is some evidence that juries attach less importance to the intent requirement for corporate than for individual defendants. In a number of joint trials where the individual defendants were the only conceivable persons involved in the corporate offense, juries have convicted the corporation while acquitting the individual defendants. Since, under respondeat superior, corporate intent is imputed only from individual intent, it is logically inconsistent under that doctrine to find a corporation guilty when no individual agent is found to have had the requisite intent. Federal courts generally have permitted such inconsistent verdicts to stand, although they have complained at times.

Second, to establish corporate liability under the doctrine of respondeat superior, the prosecution must show that the illegal act was committed within the agent's scope of employment. The traditional agency definition limits scope of employment to conduct that is authorized, explicitly or implicitly, by the principal or that is similar or incidental to authorized conduct. However, courts generally find conduct to fall within the scope of employment even if it was specifically forbidden by a superior and occurred despite good faith efforts on the part of the corporation to prevent the crime. Thus, scope of employment in practice means little more than that the act occurred while the offending employee was carrying out a job-related activity. This extension is essential, for if scope of employment were limited to authorized conduct under the doctrine of respondeat superior, a corporation could too easily evade criminal liability. The board of directors, for example, could protect a corporation from liability for the acts of all officers and employees through a simple prohibition of illegal conduct, thus placing such conduct outside the scope of employment.

Third, it must be proved that the agent committed the crime with the intent to benefit the corporation. The corporation may be held criminally liable even if it received no actual benefit from the offense, although the existence or absence of benefit is relevant as evidence of an intent to benefit.

The requirements of scope of employment and intent to benefit the corporation can also be met through ratification. When an employee commits a crime with no intent to benefit the corporation, or while acting outside the scope of his employment, subsequent approval of the act by his supervisor will be sufficient to hold the corporation liable for the employee's criminal act. In a sense, under the doctrine of ratification, a corporation is culpable for approving the criminal act, rather than committing it.

2. The Model Penal Code. — Adopted by the American Law Institute in 1962, the Model Penal Code offers a complex, multifaceted approach which includes three distinct systems of corporate criminal liability. The first system applies to crimes of intent where no "legislative purpose to impose liability on corporations plainly appears"; this includes crimes which are usually committed by individuals, such as mail fraud, larceny, and manslaughter, but does not cover crimes generally involving corporations, such as price-fixing and securities fraud. Under this first system, a corporation can be held liable for a crime committed by an agent only if the offense was performed, authorized, or recklessly tolerated by the board of directors or a high managerial official. As with respondeat superior, the corporation is liable only when a director or managerial official acts "in behalf of the corporation" and "within the scope of his office or employment." But unlike respondeat superior, only the intent of top officials and not that of subordinates is imputed to the corporation. The Model Penal Code defines a "high managerial agent" as an officer or other agent of the corporation "having duties of such responsibility that his conduct may fairly be assumed to represent the policy of the corporation. . . ."

The second system of corporate liability also concerns crimes of intent, but it deals with crimes for which the legislature has plainly intended to impose liability on corporations. Like respondeat superior, this second system holds a corporation criminally responsible for the crime of any agent committed within the scope of employment and with an intent to benefit the corporation. But the draftsmen of the Model Penal Code, believing that the primary purpose of holding corporations accountable for the acts of lower-level employees is to encourage diligent supervision by managerial officials, added an affirmative defense: the corporation can escape liability under the second system by proving by a preponderance of the evidence that the high managerial agent with supervisory responsibility over the subject matter of the offense acted with the "due diligence" to prevent it.

The third system created by the Model Penal Code applies only to strict liability crimes; it assumes a legislative purpose to impose liability on corporations for these crimes "unless the contrary plainly appears." The principles of respondeat superior apply to this system, but since only strict liability crimes are involved, neither evidence of specific intent to commit a crime nor intent to benefit the corporation is required to find corporate liability. The defense of due diligence is not available. Imposing liability on the corporation for strict liability crimes has the effect of punishing stockholders for offenses they could not have prevented, but this is justified, as with any strict liability crime, by the pressing need to prevent the injury caused by the offense.

The Code also sets forth a small category of offenses based on the failure to discharge a "specific duty of affirmative performance" imposed by law on corporations. "Specific duty" refers to narrowly defined tasks set forth by statute or regulation, such as a duty to file a report with an administrative agency; it does not encompass any generally imposed obligations, such as the duty of reasonable care. This standard of corporate liability should be considered a part of the third system, since resting corporate guilt solely on the failure to discharge a specific duty is one form of strict liability.

With both strict liability and duty to act offenses, liability focuses solely on the results of corporate action or inaction; the position in the corporate hierarchy of the person who acted and the intent with which he acted are irrelevant to the determination of liability.

3. Critique. – The doctrine of respondeat superior and the three systems presented in the Model Penal Code must be compared in terms of the dual purposes of the corporate criminal law – deterrence and just deserts. Two factors which affect the degree of deterrence differ substantially among the various systems of corporate criminal liability. The first factor, ease of evasion, reflects the ability of a corporation to benefit from an illegal act by an employee but still not be legally subject to liability for it. The second factor, difficulty of detection and proof, is based on the assumption that the corporate defendant is legally subject to liability, and focuses on the evidentiary burden the prosecution must carry in order to win a conviction.

Corporate criminal liability is most easily evaded under the first Model Penal Code system. This is the only system where liability rests solely on the conduct of top corporate officials. Consequently, liability can be evaded whenever illegal activity occurs without the authorization or reckless toleration of top officials. Since an executive cannot authorize or recklessly tolerate an offense unless he knows about it, a corporation can escape liability under this system as long as high officials remain ignorant of illegal activity. Superiors can preserve their ignorance by conveying to employees the understanding that they do not wish to be told of information which may subject the corporation to liability. Alternatively, they can protect themselves from knowledge – and the corporation from liability – simply by delegating to subordinates full responsibility for those activities which might result in criminal violations. Corporate liability is more difficult to evade under the other three systems, because under each the corporation is responsible for the acts of every agent, nor merely those of high managerial officials. Superiors thus cannot shield the corporation from liability by delegating responsibility or refusing to learn of criminal conduct by subordinates.

The first Model Penal Code system has an additional drawback in that large corporations can more easily evade liability than small ones. Larger, multidivisional organizations generally maintain a layer of top managers who reserve their own energies for policy making, coordination, and program evaluation, and delegate responsibility for day to day operations to middle-level employees. Smaller corporations tend to have fewer layers of authority and less sharp differentiation between managerial and operational roles. Thus, large corporations can more easily evade conviction since the top officials whose conduct would subject the corporation to liability are often too far removed from daily operations to be charged with authorizing or recklessly tolerating criminal activity at lower levels. . . .

4. A Proposal. – A new system of corporate liability based on the reasonableness of the corporation's practices and procedures to avert illegal conduct would better reflect the blameworthiness of the corporation as an entity. Under this new system, a corporation could be held criminally liable, as under respondeat superior, when an agent acting within the scope of employment commits a crime on behalf of the corporation. But the corporation could rebut this presumption of liability by proving by a preponderance of the evidence that it, as an organization, exercised due diligence to prevent the crime. Since the acts of top officials are likely to represent the practices and procedures of the corporation, the involvement of policy making officials in corporate criminal activity should almost always refute a due diligence defense. Effective deterrence can be achieved under this system only if, in order to establish the affirmative defense of due diligence, a corporation must adopt stringent procedures to combat illegal activity. The corporation should be required to demonstrate that it employed two kinds of precautions: first, that the illegal conduct had been clearly and convincingly forbidden, and second, that reasonable safeguards designed to prevent corporate crimes had been developed and implemented, including regular procedures for evaluation, detection, and remedy. Proper evaluation assures on a continuing basis that the safeguards adopted are adequate to prevent violations through such procedures as periodic assessments of price-setting policies. Detection procedures, such as outside audits and regular compliance reports, bring dangerous conditions and ongoing violations to the attention of top management. Adequate remedies include disciplining wrongdoers and insuring prompt repair of conditions conducive to future violations.

A system of liability based on the absence of reasonable efforts to prevent corporate crime would rest criminal responsibility on the blameworthiness of the corporation, yet effectively deter corporate crime. For these reasons, Congress should adopt the due diligence defense for all corporate crimes in its revision of the federal criminal code. Even if Congress merely codifies the now predominant respondeat superior doctrine, federal courts could on their own develop corporate due diligence as an affirmative defense. The traditional criminal law principle that sanctions should rest on blameworthiness justifies courts in providing corporate defendants with the opportunity to establish the absence of blameworthiness by proving the reasonableness of corporate practices and procedures. . . .

Note, *Decision making Models and the Control of Corporate Crime,* 85 YALE L.J., 1091–1129 (1976)*

The complexity of modern corporate decision making tends both to obscure and to diffuse responsibility for corporate actions. Thus, efforts to deter corporate crime have been frustrated by difficulties in identifying the lawbreakers and in determining appropriate grounds for liability. Set against this background of frustration, the recent expressions of concern by Congress, the Department of Justice, and the Supreme Court suggest that legal policy with respect to corporate crime may be entering a period of transformation.

This Note argues that effective legal policy concerning corporate crime must be founded on an understanding of the decision making process underlying corporate action. With this understanding, legal policy makers—legislators, prosecutors, and judges—can impose criminal penalties on those decision makers most capable of preventing corporate lawbreaking. As a result, those who shape the corporate decision making process will be encouraged to do so in a way that enhances the likelihood of law-abiding corporate conduct.

The Note proceeds by analyzing different characterizations of the corporate decision making process and exploring their implications for the development of appropriate legal policy. The analysis is structured by three widely used models of decision making, each of which isolates and illuminates distinctive facets of the decision making process. These models have been most thoroughly and rigorously articulated by Graham Allison in explaining the foreign policies of governments. In this Note the models are employed to elucidate how corporate lawbreaking takes place and how it may be controlled.

I. Shortcomings of Current Federal Law: Entity and Employee Liability for Corporate Crime

The liability of corporate entities and employees for lawbreaking to advance the interest of the corporation is not defined by any one federal statute. Rather, corporate criminal law is a pastiche of regulatory statutes, judicial interpretations of vague legislative mandates, and adaptations of civil liability rules.

Statutory provisions expressly imposing criminal liability on corporate entities are scattered throughout

* Reprinted by permission of The Yale Law Journal Company and Fred B. Rothman & Company from *The Yale Law Journal,* Vol. 85, pages 1091-1129.

the United States Code. Where a statute does not expressly apply to corporations, entity liability may still be authorized. Title 1, § 1 of the United States Code provides that in acts of Congress the words "person" and "whoever" include corporations "unless the context indicates otherwise." Furthermore, the Supreme Court has long held that if the problems the legislature intended to reach through a regulatory statute are as likely to involve corporations as natural persons, the words "any person" in the statute's penal clause can be construed to include corporate entities.

Because of the imprecision of statutory language, the courts rather than Congress have been primarily responsible for delimiting the circumstances under which corporate entities are criminally liable. The judicial consensus is that corporations are liable for acts of employees which constitute or cause criminal offenses if such acts are done on behalf of the entity and are within the scope of the actor's authority. The "employees" for whose acts the corporate entity is penalized are commonly executive or managerial officials, but the status of the lawbreaking employee in the organizational hierarchy is irrelevant to entity liability. Lawbreaking acts "on behalf of" the corporation are those of which the entity was the intended beneficiary: if the employee acted for his own personal benefit or for that of another, the entity is not criminally responsible. However, so long as the entity was the intended beneficiary, it does not matter whether the employee's actions actually had a beneficial effect. The "scope of authority" within which an employee's criminal conduct may become the basis for entity liability is quite broad: courts have rejected corporate defenses that employees acted beyond their official authority and that the unlawful conduct had been specifically forbidden by corporate superiors.

Judicial opinions describing a corporation's criminal liability frequently allude to tort concepts. Building on principles of civil liability, courts have penalized entities for crimes which require willfulness and knowledge as well as for those for which strict liability is imposed, and for conspiracies as well as for substantive offenses. Unfortunately, the tort analogy may be a misleading guide for determining entity liability. Such an analogy overlooks the different policy considerations underlying criminal and civil penalties. In particular, although both criminal and civil law are concerned with deterring undesirable conduct, only the latter is also concerned with compensating injured parties. Under certain circumstances, the compensation rationale for damage awards may dictate entity liability though employee liability may be preferable on deterrence grounds. Thus, the tort analogy does not offer a wholly satisfactory answer to the basic question of when entities should be held criminally responsible.

Problems in defining criminal responsibility also pervade statutory and case law concerning corporate employees. Unquestionably, employees may be criminally liable for corporate offenses in which they have been involved. However, neither Congress nor the courts have stated clearly what status in the organization and what degree of involvement are necessary to sustain individual criminal liability. With the rare exception of a provision declaring specific officials liable for corporate violations, statutes typically authorize criminal sanctions for individuals designated variously as "officers," "directors," "managers," "agents," or "employees." But even provisions that do not mention certain of these individuals may be the basis for imposing liability on them: the Supreme Court has held that if a statute does not expressly include such liability, those who have a "responsible share" in a proscribed transaction on behalf of the corporation are subject to the statutory penalties.

Such a holding, however, begs the critical question, for the courts have failed to delimit precisely the "responsibility" of corporate employees. Of course, criminal liability attaches to the employee who personally performs the forbidden conduct – the worker who intentionally mislabels a drug shipment or the messenger who knowingly delivers corporate payments to a politician. But responsibility in this most literal sense may also be the least meaningful, for focusing sanctions exclusively on corporate underlings may vitiate a statute's deterrent effect. Active participation in a corporate offense may also take the form of directing the lawbreaking conduct of others; where there is evidence of authorization to commit the illegal act, courts have had little difficulty imposing penal sanctions on the superior corporate employees who gave that authorization. Frequently, however, there is no evidence of explicit direction to transgress the law, and the liability issue is whether a corporate employee who assented to, acquiesced in, or failed to halt illegal conduct by others is criminally responsible. In these situations of passive participation, courts usually have approved penal sanctions only when the applicable statute imposed an affirmative managerial duty and the employee charged was a corporate executive.

Despite the web of penal statutes surrounding corporate entities and employees, the capacity of the criminal law to control corporate crime has been widely discounted. The basic problem is that the law is not founded on an understanding of the decision making process that the law must shape in order to deter corporate lawbreaking. This is not to say that legislators, prosecutors, and judges have no conception of how corporate lawbreaking takes place. A legislator drafting a regulatory statute, a prosecutor framing his theory of a case, a trial judge giving jury instructions, or an appellate judge reviewing the admission of evidence – all work with assumptions about how corporate crime occurs and how that occurrence can be deterred most effectively. But legal policy has not been based on a systematic analysis of corporate decision making that sets out the factual patterns and deterrence strategies implied by the various assumptions. As a result, the assumptions of legal policy makers are usually unarticulated and untested, and the actions based on those assumptions are often misguided.

In this regard, models of corporate decision making may prove to be useful conceptual tools. Each model represents a set of consistent assumptions about corporate decision making that legal policy makers can employ to analyze instances or patterns of corporate lawbreaking. Each model associates certain facts with its assumptions, and thereby each can guide legal policy makers to evidence that validates or invalidates those assumptions. Lastly, in accordance with its distinctive characterization of corporate decision making, each model implies that certain deterrence strategies are most likely to be effective. Thus, having systematically determined which characterization is warranted, legal policy makers can select the appropriate strategy to prevent corporate lawbreaking.

The definition of criminal responsibility that emerges from decision making models is a functional one: responsibility lies with whichever corporate decision makers were capable of preventing the corporate offense that occurred. The models imply that the identity of these decision makers varies according to the character of the corporate decision making process. By illuminating that process, the models can benefit legislators trying to fashion statutes to control corporate conduct as well as prosecutors and judges trying to formulate precise theories of liability from general legislative provisions. The result should be legal policy making that more effectively deters corporate crime. First, because the models would make the boundaries of criminal responsibility more intelligible to corporate decision makers, the latter should be encouraged to shape their actions in accordance with the law. Second, because the models would help legal policy makers discern how a corporate violation occurred and which decision makers might have prevented it, the law should represent a more credible threat to potential offenders. Finally, because the sanctions imposed in accordance with the models would be tailored to have maximal impact on the particular offender, convicted corporate lawbreakers should be more effectively induced to prevent subsequent violations. The remainder of this Note constitutes an initial effort to elaborate this argument and to demonstrate the value of decision making models in achieving deterrence of corporate crime.

II. The Models: Rational Actor, Organizational Process, and Bureaucratic Politics

Each of the three decision making models applied in this Note has been employed extensively, with slight variations in terminology and emphasis, by those who study organizations. Nevertheless, the application of these models to corporate criminal law warrants two important caveats. First, the models are not wholly realistic. They do not, and are not intended to, capture the variety and intricacy of corporate decision making. Rather, each serves as a "conceptual lens" which magnifies, highlights, or reveals certain aspects of the decision making process and blurs or neglects others. Second, the models are not exhaustive. Other models, as well as modifications and combinations of the three introduced here, could provide new insights. For the purpose of this Note, however, three models suffice: their different characterizations of corporate decision making demonstrate the utility of models and yield diverse implications for the control of corporate crime.

The Rational Actor Model (Model I) is based on two propositions familiar to economists. The first proposition is that corporate action should be treated as unitary – as if decisions were made by a single-minded actor, the corporate entity. Since the entity itself is the decision maker, the decision making process is activated by corporate problems, framed by corporate alternatives, and guided by corporate values. Model I is not blind to the existence of individuals beneath the corporate facade – even individuals who are occasionally irrational. Rather, the model regards the behavior of corporate employees as sufficiently concerted to justify synthesizing their numerous individual acts into a corporate decision making process that can be characterized as unitary.

The second proposition underlying Model I is that corporate action should be treated as rational – as if the corporate entity chose from among all available options the course of action that would maximize its values. Typical corporate options include choice of personnel, products, and markets. Corporate values may include profit, the single value traditionally posited by neoclassical economic theory, as well as others that have been suggested by observers of corporate behavior.

The Rational Actor Model's conception of unitary, rational decision making differs sharply from the characterization of corporate action provided by the Organizational Process Model (Model II). Instead of the

unitary actor postulated in Model I, Model II conceives of the corporation as a constellation of loosely allied decision making units (e.g., a marketing group, a manufacturing division, a research and development staff), each with primary responsibility for a narrow range of problems. Though all units operate within general corporate guidelines, the complexity and breadth of corporate operations allow each unit to exercise some autonomy in setting priorities, defining problems, processing information, and taking action. At the same time, important operations transcend the jurisdiction of any one unit, so that executive intervention is necessary to coordinate the activity of the decentralized decision makers.

According to Model II, however, an executive works under certain constraints, for the actions of the corporation's decision making units are not rational. Rather, action is determined largely by preexisting organizational routines, and decision making is structured by the problems identified, information gathered, and actions initiated according to these routines.

When a decisionmaking unit perceives a familiar problem, it refers to its standard operating procedures (SOPs) established to cope with the type of problem involved. SOPs are generated in various ways. Some are introduced through oral or written directives which articulate the corporate practices to be followed under stated circumstances by employees filling specified positions in the organization. Others emerge from customary ways of accomplishing certain everyday tasks, with routinization resulting from force of habit rather than specific instruction. According to Model II, most corporate actions (e.g., replying to consumer complaints, maintaining quality control, disposing of waste material) consist simply of subcorporate units following these regularized procedures.

The viability of corporate action based on established procedures depends on the ability of subcorporate units to narrow the range of unexpected problems. Units seek to avoid uncertainty by negotiating with other units and competitors. Negotiation with other units may reduce uncertainty about such matters as primary responsibility for particular corporate tasks or allocation of prospective budget increases. Negotiation with competitors may concern development of product lines, entry into new markets, or lobbying efforts for legislative or executive action.

Despite negotiation, some degree of uncertainty is inescapable; on occasion, unfamiliar or unpredictable problems do arise. When a unit confronts such a problem, it initiates "search" – a sequential canvass for applicable SOPs, beginning with those designed for apparently analogous circumstances. Thus, according to Model II, a corporate action is not tailored to the situation at hand but rather reflects the most appropriate of the available SOPs. The action may be ill-suited if the situation does not conform to a scenario anticipated by the subcorporate unit.

The Bureaucratic Politics Model (Model III) diverges significantly from each of the other models. Corporate action under Model III is neither rational calculus nor routinized procedure but, rather, political resultant. It is the outcome of a bargaining game involving a hierarchy of players and a maze of formal and informal channels through which decisions are shaped and implemented. Each decision can be conceived as a single game, with the identity of the players (*e.g.,* plant manager, marketing specialist, chief lobbyist) dependent both on the issues involved and on the organizational structure.

Since separate individuals with different intentions contribute to the political outcome, actual corporate action may not be the preferred course of any particular player or team. It may be an amalgam of independent decisions, a compromise among the views of several teams or the relatively unalloyed preference of a certain subset of players. Moreover, even if the decision is unanimously supported, the support may stem from dissimilar interpretations of the proposed action. Indeed, the pace and pressures of bureaucratic bargaining make misunderstandings among players common — and often crucial to reaching a consensus. Finally, what is planned may not correspond to what is implemented. The need for vagueness in order to build consensus in the formulation stage may be exploited by subsequent maneuvers in the implementation stage.

During a particular game, a givenplayer's participation may vary considerably. He may be quite active in early stages (*e.g.,* when alternative solutions are being identified) and inactive thereafter; or he may not have an opportunity to start bargaining until the basic course of action has already been set. Individuals who are officially non-participants may in fact be influential on certain matters; on the other hand, those who, according to the organization charts, have authority in a specific area may be circumvented by other players.

Organization charts are not irrelevant under Model III, however. Because of his position, each player holds particular bargaining chips, feels committed to specific projects, remains sensitive to parochial issues, and strives to attain certain corporate and subcorporate objectives. Each player also carries his own "baggage" (*e.g.,* personal goals, stature with and obligations to various extracorporate groups or individuals, and skill in bureaucratic infighting).

Bargaining among players is structured by laws, corporate charters, corporate policies and practices, market forces — in short, by the rules according to which all corporate games are played. These rules collectively establish the positions of the players, the paths of access to these positions, the inherent power of each position, the routes particular decisions must follow from player to player, and the boundaries of acceptable conduct. Thus, although Model III, like Model II, denies the validity of Model I's propositions of unitary and rational decision making, it does so in a different way. First, it emphasizes the multiplicity and parochialism of intracorporate groups and individuals. Second, it stresses the conflict and compromise that underlie corporate action.

This second fact of Model III contradicts Model I rationality in two respects. The *result* of the Model III decision making process is only by coincidence, if at all, the course of action that maximizes the values of the entity as a whole. Furthermore, the Model III *process* itself lacks the qualities of purposefulness and consistency that are basic to Model I decision making. The irrationality of Model III decision making thus is due not to any mental quirks of the decision makers but rather to the organizational system in which they interact.

III. Implications for Legal Policy

Although one of the implications of decision making models is that no single conception of corporate decision making is always adequate, this part of the Note considers each model separately in order to clarify the distinctive insights that each offers. The discussion focuses on the utility of the models for legislators, prosecutors, and judges.

A. The Rational Actor Model

According to the Rational Actor Model, corporate lawbreaking results from the purposeful, consistent acts of the corporate entity. Model I suggests to legal policy makers that the key to controlling corporate crime is to focus on the rational calculus that underlies corporate violations.

Legislators taking a Model I approach would try to influence corporate entity actions by manipulating corporate values and corporate options. Manipulation of corporate values (*e.g.,* the primacy of profits) may be beyond the capacity of law, for the values are likely to be imbedded firmly in the cultural environment of the corporation as well as in the psyche of corporate management. In contrast, manipulation of corporate options seems well within the power of the criminal law. Legislators can criminalize, and therefore penalize, the exercise of certain options. Consequences of illegal options can be made more costly by increasing the penalties associated with them or by increasing the probability that the penalties authorized for an illegal option will actually be imposed. Another means of raising costs is to impose criminal penalties on corporations that choose socially disfavored options unless they engage in resource-consuming activities (*e.g.*, filing reports, obtaining clearances). in sum, the aim of legislative policy under a Model I approach would be to effect the substitution of desirable courses of action for undesirable ones by influencing the corporate calculus.

Model I also provides some guidance as to the types of sanctions which legislators should authorize in order to weight the scales of corporate choice against undesirable actions. Model I argues for imposing sanctions on the corporate entity rather than on employees, for the entity is the decision making unit. The specific sanctions should depend on the specific values that influence the corporation's conduct. Conceivably, legislators confident that all corporations maximize the same value or values could include in every pertinent criminal statute a particular corporate sanction tailored to that universal behavioral norm. For example, if profit maximization were considered the norm, a fine determined by the entity's profitability during the period of the offense could be imposed; or the fine could be set so as to cancel out any profits reaped from the illegal action, perhaps with a suitable multiplier to adjust for the probability of being convicted for the offense. Similar sanctions could be devised for other corporate values, such as sales volume.

Alternatively, entity sanctions could concentrate on intermediate values whose maximization lays the foundation for the attainment of profit or sales targets. For example, the convicted corporation could be prohibited from bidding on government contracts, obtaining government franchises, or otherwise benefiting from government largesse. Likewise, to the extent that public goodwill is an intermediate corporate value, publicizing corporate convictions could be effective.

Any one of these entity sanctions might be authorized by legislators who are confident that the chosen sanction would be optimally effective in controlling the conduct of all corporations. However, if legislators are uncertain as to which corporate values are dominant or believe that they vary among corporations, Model I suggests that statutes provide for a range of entity sanctions from which judges could choose in accordance with their analysis of the particular corporate offender.

From a Model I perspective, then, current federal statutory provisions for corporate penalties are deficient because they generally impose fines whose relation to corporate profits, sales, or other values is unclear. The severity of the sanction should continue to depend on the gravity of the offense, but the form of the sanction should be varied to strike most effectively at the values of the offending corporation. . . .

B. The Organizational Process Model

The Organizational Process Model dissents from the Model I view that corporate actions can be interpreted as the results of unitary, rational decision making by the entity as a whole. Model II's focus on subcorporate units discourages the reliance on entity liability endorses by Model I. But this does not automatically compel advocacy of employee liability. Indeed, Model II suggests that employees have limited capacity to control the decision making process within subcorporate units. Invariably there are disparities between the decisions individuals themselves would make—or do make—and the corporate action that emerges from a system of fragmented power and routinized procedures. Thus, one could contend that Model II argues against placing criminal responsibility on managerial or other employees by attributing to the corporate decision making process qualities which would frustrate even able, law-abiding managers. This interpretation, however, distorts the implications of Model II. For the model's appreciation of the difficulties confronting management does not support immunization of corporate decision makers from individual liability. Rather, it underscores the importance of placing liability for corporate lawbreaking clearly and specifically on those in a position to promulgate and oversee the SOPs of subcorporate units.

Model II implies that corporate violations occur because existing SOPs mandate or allow illegal actions or because no SOPs exist to prevent illegal actions. Therefore, individuals with knowledge of the illegality or inadequacy of SOPs and with authority to correct them can most effectively ensure that corporate lawbreaking does not take place. Depending on the structure of the particular corporation, liability imposed on knowledgeable and authoritative employees could touch several managerial echelons--from top management of the organization through divisional executives to perhaps subdivisional supervisors. To prevent evasion of accountability by lower-level managers denying authority to modify unlawful SOPs and by higher-level managers professing ignorance of violations of SOPs, liability might also attach to those with either knowledge or authority.

Legislation embodying Model II liability principles would impose on individual corporate decision makers an affirmative duty to correct or attempt to correct SOPs they know to be flawed and to ferret out flawed SOPs they have the authority to correct. To encourage the fulfillment of this affirmative duty, statutes might require that corporations file reports about certain activities, thereby forcing a monitoring function on those officials responsible for preparing the reports. Similarly, if regulatory agencies made an explicit practice of notifying particular corporate employees of first violations, they would facilitate successful prosecution of those employees for subsequent SOP offenses. . . .

C. The Bureaucratic Politics Model

The Model III conception of the decision making process implies that responsibility for corporate crime must be defined in terms of the actions of individuals. Unlike Model I, Model III focuses on the interests and influences of individuals, not entities. Unlike Model II, Model III conceives of these individuals as conscious proponents of corporate action rather than as constrained followers of preselected procedures. From this view Model III seems especially favorable to theories of individual liability.

The implications of Model III suggest that criminal liability in the corporate context must be two-pronged if the law is to achieve maximum deterrent effect. One component should be directed at those who participate in lawbreaking, the other at certain decision makers who do not participate. With respect to the former, culpable participation in bargaining games should include acquiescence in an unlawful decision as well as advocacy of it. The guiding principle should be that every corporate decision maker has an affirmative duty to purge a course of action of its illegal aspects before acquiescing in it.

This first component of Model III liability of course applies to high-level corporate officials — those who are most active and influential in making bargains. But Model III also implies that middle-level managers should be liable for illegal corporate actions under certain circumstances. Model III recognizes the leeway granted to those carrying out corporate decisions by reason of the imprecision characteristic of consensual mandates. Therefore, liability should be imposed on those who use illegal means to implement lawful decisions and on those who fail to resist the implementation of unlawful decisions. The conception of corporate action presented by Model III suggests that only by imposing liability at the lower levels of the corporate power structure as well as at the higher levels can corporate lawbreaking be controlled.

The objective of the second component of Model III liability is to ensure that potentially influential players do not insulate themselves from a consensus that, either in formulation or in implementation, is tainted by illegality. The instrument is the imposition of an affirmative duty on such players to ensure the lawfulness of the political resultants emerging from their areas of responsibility. Responsibility need not — indeed, according to Model III, should not — be equated with official authority. Rather, all individuals heavily involved in a particular problem area — regardless of their official status — could be required to report their identity by signing permit applications, regulatory reports, or other required documents. Alternatively, legislators could authorize use of investigative powers to gather sufficient information to discover which corporate decision makers have potential influence in a particular game or class of games.

By enacting statutes embodying these standards of liability, legislators would, in Model III terms, transform the rules of the corporate bargaining game and thereby shape the conduct of corporate decision makers. Model III implies that the most effective sanctions for violating the rules would be those that diminish the influence of lawbreaking players. Such sanctions not only would increase the relative influence of law-abiding players but also would threaten potential lawbreakers with deprivation of status, wealth, and other values that derive from influence. Fines, publicity, incarceration, exclusion from office — all these would reduce, to varying degrees, the influence of the penalized official and indicate that nonparticipation may result in similar penalties. Sanctions against the corporate entity might also be desirable to the extent that they constrain corporate employees. But this seems to be a blunt instrument, for it is unclear which employees would be most penalized by such sanctions. . . .

CONCLUSION

The three models employed in this Note are paradigmatic, not Procrustean. In applying them to actual instances of corporate lawbreaking, the task is not to reduce the infinite gradations of corporate decision making to three inflexible types. Rather, the three models, as well as eclectic alternatives, should be employed to gain insights into the diversity and complexity of the decision making process. The primary insight provided by the models is that the character of corporate decision making varies widely; at every level of legal policy making it must be regarded as an issue of fact. By providing guidance for the discovery and interpretation of facts about corporate decision making, the models make their most valuable contribution.

That contribution has been sketched in preliminary fashion in this Note. By conceptualizing corporate decision making, the models alert legal policy makers to the relevance of particular facts and suggest deterrence strategies consistent with the conceptions supported by the facts. Collectively, the models imply that only under limited circumstances can effective deterrence by achieved by penalizing the corporate entity rather than corporate employees. For most circumstances, the models recommend the creation of affirmative duties for certain individuals to monitor corporate procedures and to participate in corporate bargaining.

If the imposition of liability is rooted in systematic analysis of facts, the concept of criminal responsibility can reflect the variations in corporate decision making without becoming amorphous. By encouraging such systematic analysis, the models can enhance the law's capacity to define criminal responsibility with sufficient clarity to guide both legal policy makers and corporate decisionmakers.

John C. Coffee, Jr., *Corporate Criminal Responsibility*, I. Encyclopedia of Crime and Justice 253–264 (1983)*

Introduction

In the majority of American jurisdictions the corporation is criminally responsible for illegal acts of its agents that are (1) committed within the scope of their employment and (2) intended to benefit the corporation ("Developments in the Law," pp. 1246-1250). This simple black-letter rule represents, however, an uneasy marriage of civil and criminal concepts of responsibility that has long proved troubling to legal scholars. (Comment, 1975; Miller; U.S. National Commission on Reform of Federal Criminal Law). Indeed, although the use of criminal sanction against the corporate entity is now relatively common in American courts, the concept of corporate criminal responsibility is accepted to a far more modest extent in Great Britain, and not at all in civil law jurisdictions (Leigh; Mueller).

The debate over corporate criminal liability has had two distinct levels, conceptual and pragmatic. On the first level, the American common-law rule of corporate liability for an agent's crimes has been criticized both on the ground that it entails an acceptance of vicarious responsibility (that is, the acts of the agent

* "Corporate Criminal Responsibility" by John C. Coffee Jr. Reprinted with permission of Simon & Schuster Macmillan from *Encyclopedia of Crime and Justice*, Sanford H. Kadish, Editor in Chief. Vol. 1, pp. 253-264. Copyright © 1983 by The Free Press.

are imputed to a corporate principal – here, the employer) and because it arguably downgrades the significance of intent and blameworthiness in the criminal law. On the pragmatic level, much skepticism has been expressed about the efficacy of corporate criminal responsibility: Is the corporation an apt or appropriate target for criminal sanctions? Would civil remedies be more effective? Does corporate liability tend to deflect attention from the responsibility of the individual?

Development of corporate criminal liability

The case law. The early English common law denied that a corporation could commit a crime (*Anonymous Case* (No. 935), 88 Eng. Rep. 1518 (K.B. 1701)). Four distinct barriers inhibited judicial recognition of corporate criminal liability. First, until the maturation of the doctrine of *respondeat superior* (the principle that an individual was civilly liable for the acts of his agents) as a concept of tort law in the nineteenth century, a conceptual basis was lacking for the imputation of acts committed by an individual to the corporation (Leigh, pp. 4-5). Second, where specific intent was an element of the crime, it struck early jurists as an obvious contradiction to speak of the corporation as having the requisite mens rea – in effect, to look for a guilty mind in the case of the corporation seemed a search for the ghost in the machine. Third, the doctrine of *ultra vires* posed a further conceptual impediment since until well into the nineteenth century this doctrine limited the corporation's powers to either those expressly authorized by its charter or those necessarily implied by such express powers. Thus, because the charter would formally empower the corporation only to commit lawful acts, the corporation logically lacked any power to commit a crime. Fourth, a corporate prosecution could not be squared with the rigid procedural requirements of the time, which required, for example, that the defendant be personally brought before the court for an arraignment; again, since the corporation was not an individual, it could only appear through its agents or attorneys – a concept that was entirely foreign to the English law, which disfavored criminal prosecution in absentia.

These obstacles, however, did not totally preclude corporate criminal liability. As industrialization began to spread across England in the mid-nineteenth century, the English courts were confronted with violations of law committed by railroads, and they responded by holding that the corporate entity could be prosecuted for a criminal omission (*Regina v. Birmingham & Gloucester Railway*, 114 Eng. Rep. 492 (Q.B. 1842)). Initially, the rationale was narrow: the case of omissions was different, it was held, because no individual agent of the corporation was responsible for the corporation's omission. That is, because only the corporation was under a duty to perform the specific act in question, no individual had violated the law; hence there was no imputation of guilt from agent to principal, and the supposed evil of vicarious responsibility was thus avoided.

Nonetheless, as the tort doctrine of *respondeat superior* became established, this initial category of corporate crimes was soon expanded to include, first, nuisance offenses and, by the end of the nineteenth century, public welfare and similar regulatory offenses generally. In these cases, because specific intent was not an element of the offenses, the problem of defining the corporate mens rea was evaded, and the liability could be rationalized as essentially civil in character. For the most part, American courts followed in the path of their English brethren, and by the end of the nineteenth century it was generally established that the corporation could at least be convicted of those crimes that did not require proof of specific intent as an element of the offense.

With the advent of the twentieth century, however, the paths of American and English courts parted dramatically. American courts responded to the political climate of the Progressive era, both by expanding corporate liability to include mens rea offenses and by making irrelevant the level of the agent within the corporate hierarchy. In contrast, English courts articulated a much narrower "alter ego," or "organ," theory of corporate criminal liability in the case of mens rea offenses, under which only the acts of the most senior corporate officers—who constituted the corporation's "brain"—could, for criminal law purposes, be imputed to the corporate entity.

The landmark American case was the Supreme Court's decision in *New York Central & Hudson River R.R. v. United States,* 212 U.S. 481 (1909), which upheld the constitutionality of the prohibition on the granting of rebates by common carriers in interstate commerce set forth in the Elkins Act of 1903, 49 U.S.C. §§ 41-43 (1976 & Supp. III 1979)(mostly repealed). In the Elkins Act, Congress had specifically provided that acts and omissions of an officer functioning within the scope of his employment were to be deemed those of the corporation employing him. Thus, the Court was faced with a clear legislative intent to impose vicarious liability for a crime that required specific intent. At the same time, the political context of the decision was undoubtedly also clear to the Court: railroad rebates had been a central tactic used by the industrial trusts to acquire monopoly power, and their elimination had been a rallying cry for Progressive era reformers, whose efforts had culminated in the Elkins Act.

Against this historical backdrop, the Court not only accepted the possibility of corporate criminal liability but proclaimed the need for it in emphatic terms. The "public history of the times" showed, the Court wrote, that if only individuals were subject to the criminal law, "many offenses might go unpunished." Seeing "no good reason why corporations may not be held responsible," the Court used the tort law doctrine of *respondeat superior* to justify such a result (*New York Central,* 494-495). This step had significant doctrinal consequences because, by offering this analogy to tort law, the Court opened the door to corporate criminal liability in cases where the legislature had not explicitly intended to impose it.

Although *New York Central* could in principle have been confined to instances where the legislature had found corporate responsibility essential to its regulatory scheme, the tone of the decision invited a more expansive reading. Lower courts were not long in accepting this invitation. Statutes that forbade "any person" to commit an act were soon read to include any corporation, and distinctions were quickly dismissed between "regulatory" crimes, such as the paying of a rebate, and traditional *mala in se* offenses. Indeed, within a decade of the *New York Central* decision, Judge Learned Hand held that a corporation could be convicted of violating the Espionage Act of 1917, ch. 30, title I, § 3,40 Stat. 217– ironically, an offense similar to the crime of treason, which William Blackstone (*476) had said a corporation could not commit (*United States v. Nearing,* 252 F. 223 (S.D.N.Y. 1918)). In so finding, Judge Hand wrote that no distinction should be drawn between the civil and criminal liability of the corporation, each being "merely an imputation to the corporation of the mental condition of its agents" (231).

In marked contrast, English courts during this same period shrank from any acceptance of vicarious criminal liability and instead developed a theory that held the corporation liable only for the acts of its "alter ego," but not for those of its agents generally (Leigh, pp. 91-108). Under this formulation, the corporation's liability was (at least in theory) not vicarious, because the criminal act or intent was not imputed from agent to principal, but rather the corporate entity was in effect defined for criminal law purposes to mean the limited class of its senior officers and directors. This distinction was rationalized through an anthropomorphic analogy: the lower-level agents were seen as merely the corporation's hands, whereas the senior officials were viewed as its "mind," or "will," and hence were the corporation itself. As a result, under the British rule only the acts of senior officials within the corporate hierarchy would be imputed to the corporation when mens rea offenses were involved. Even in the case of statutes that contain a strict liability standard, contemporary English law has permitted the corporation to show as a defense that the act of the agent was against the corporation's policy and hence unauthorized. Conversely, under the prevailing American rule, the corporation can be held criminally liable for the acts of even its lowest subordinates (cf. *Tesco Supermarkets, Ltd. v. Nattrass,* [1972] A.C. 153 and *United States v. George F. Fish, Inc.,* 154 F.2d 798 (2d Cir. 1946)).

Statutory developments. Although the British "alter ego" theory of liability has never been accepted by the federal courts, its influence appears discernible in the American Law Institute's Model Penal Code, which has been substantially adopted by a number of states. The Model Penal Code takes an essentially tripartite approach with respect to corporate criminal liability. First, for those crimes of intent where no "legislative purpose to impose liability on corporations plainly appears" (that is, common-law crimes such as fraud and manslaughter), the Code essentially adopts the British "alter ego" theory by providing that a corporation may be held liable for the criminal acts of an agent only if the offense was performed, authorized, or recklessly tolerated by the board of directors or a high managerial agent (§ 2.07(1)(c)). The critical term *high managerial agent* is broadly defined, however, to mean an officer or other agent "having duties of such responsibility that his conduct may fairly be assumed to represent the policy of the corporation" (§ 2.07(4)(c)). In a comment, the Code indicates that corporate liability would not therefore result from the unauthorized conduct "of a foreman in a large plant or of an insignificant branch manager" (1955, commentary on § 2.07).

In contrast, for crimes of intent where a legislative intent to penalize the corporation is plain, such as price-fixing and securities violations, the 1962 Code expressly accepts the principle of *respondeat superior* and makes the corporation liable for crimes committed by agents acting within the scope of their employment and with an intent to benefit the corporation (§ 2.07(1)(a)). However, in contrast to the federal rule, the Code permits an affirmative defense: the corporation can still avoid liability by proving that a high managerial agent with supervisory responsibility over the subject matter of the offense acted with "due diligence" to prevent it (§ 2.07(5)).

Still a third basic form of criminal liability is recognized by the Model Penal Code if the crime is one of strict liability, that is, if it lacks any requisite element of intent. In such cases, the Code assumes that the legislature intended to hold the corporation liable on a theory of *respondeat superior* "unless the contrary plainly appears" (§ 2.07(2)). Here, the defense of due diligence would not be available. More a liberalized version of the British "alter ego" theory than a statutory expression of the federal rule, the Model Penal Code assumes that the basic purpose of corporate criminal liability is to encourage managerial diligence in supervising corporate obedience to law, rather than to punish or deter corporate violations generally. This premise in turn rests on the belief that the criminal law has no other realistic aim in punishing the corporation and should not impose losses on innocent stockholders for acts that their managerial agents sought reasonably to prevent. Accordingly, by creating an incentive to encourage managerial supervision through its provision of an affirmative defense of "due diligence," the Code seeks to accomplish what it believes can be achieved—increased supervision and oversight within the entity—without imposing the potentially high cost of general deterrence on shareholders.

In overview, British and American federal courts have responded in predictably divergent fashion to the conceptual problems posed by corporate criminal responsibility. More legal realists than formalists, American courts have for the most part rationalized a relaxation of the usual substantive limits on criminal liability, because to do otherwise seemed to threaten important regulatory policies and also to invite a sharp conflict with the legislature. More legal formalists than realists, and never prodded by their legislature, English courts instead constructed an elaborate, if sometimes crudely anthropomorphic, rationale by which to distinguish primary from vicarious corporate liability.

CURRENT STATE OF THE AMERICAN LAW: SOME COMPLEXITIES IN *RESPONDEAT SUPERIOR*

The rule of *respondeat superior* should not be confused with strict liability. The corporation is not liable simply because an agent commits the actus reus of an offense. Rather, three elements must be proved: that an agent (1) has committed a crime (2) while acting within the scope of his authority and (3) with an intent to benefit the corporation. Close questions can arise in each of these areas.

The first of these requirements would seem to imply that the corporation could not be convicted if the agent committing the actus reus lacked the requisite intent. However, federal case law has relaxed this intent requirement in several respects. First, intent may be imputed to the corporation from a person distinct from the one who commits the actus reus, such as a supervisory official who realized the significance of the act. Nor has it been necessary for the prosecutor to identify the actual agent who committed the crime if the prosecutor can show that some person within the corporation must have so acted. Even more significantly, inconsistent verdicts are tolerated under which the corporation is convicted but all conceivable individual agents are acquitted. Finally, some decisions have accepted a theory of "collective knowledge," under which no single individual had the requisite knowledge to satisfy the intent requirement, but various individuals within the organization possessed all the elements of such knowledge collectively (*United States v. T.I.M.E.-D.C., Inc.*, 381 F. Supp. 730 (W.D. Va. 1974)).

Normally, an agent's scope of authority is limited by express instructions from his principal. Yet in the context of corporate criminal prosecutions, the requirement that the agent act within the scope of his authority has also been eroded. Virtually any act engaged in by an employee in a job-related activity will satisfy this requirement ("Developments in the Law," pp. 1249-1250). Obviously, such a result has a strong policy justification, for if express restrictions could negate corporate liability, the board of directors could immunize the corporation simply by adopting formal policies to the effect that employees not fix prices, make materially misleading statements, pollute the air or water, or tolerate unsafe products. In general, good-faith efforts by the corporation to prevent the crime will not constitute a defense in the federal courts. In contrast, English decisions have found discretionary acts by lower-echelon officials to have been beyond the scope of their delegated power, even in the case of strict liability offenses. In *Tesco Supermarkets, Ltd.*, for example, a corporation was not held liable for the ministerial acts of a store manager not authorized by the corporation, even in the case of a strict liability regulatory statute.

Similarly, an intent to benefit the corporation remains a precondition of liability, but the federal courts have downgraded it from an essential element of the crime to merely an evidentiary consideration. No actual benefit need be received by the corporation so long as an intent to benefit it can be reasonably inferred by the fact finder. However, where an employee acts adversely to the corporation's interests but within the scope of his authority, it remains a valid defense for the corporation to assert that its agent was on a frolic and detour. Thus, in *Standard Oil Co. of Texas v. United States*, 307 F.2d 120 (5th Cir. 1962), evidence that employees of one corporation were acting to benefit a rival corporation (which had bribed them) when they violated a regulatory statute was sufficient to exonerate the employer corporation. Even in such cases, however, liability to the employer corporation might result if it was found to have ratified or tolerated the act.

The majority of state courts now subscribe to the federal rules set forth above. Exceptions, of course, exist in those jurisdictions that have enacted the Model Penal Code and in a small number of cases that have accepted corporate good faith and due diligence as a defense. Pending legislation to recodify the Federal Criminal Code also adopts the federal rule intact and would in substance codify it for the first time.

Other special problems with the theory of corporate liability arise where the analogy breaks down between the fictional person of the corporation and real individuals. For example, can a dissolved corporation be prosecuted? Despite the view that the defendant is civilly dead, the answer appears to be in the affirmative (as in *Melrose Distillers, Inc. v. United States*, 369 U.S. 271 (1959)). Similarly, can the corporation be convicted of conspiring with its subsidiaries or with its employees? Here, legal realism appears to be triumphing, and the case law (at least in the antitrust context) has begun to reject the idea of such "bathtub conspiracies," recognizing that the corporation must necessarily act through its agents (as in *Sunkist Growers, Inc. v. Winckler & Smith Citrus Products Co.*, 370 U.S. 19 (1962)). A consensus appears to have developed that any other rule would give undue significance to such fortuitous factors as whether corporate subunits were denominated as subsidiaries or only as unincorporated divisions. However, this same realism has also prevented parent corporations from insulating themselves against criminal liability through the use of subsidiaries. In such instances, the corporate subsidiary can itself be viewed as an agent and its action imputed to the parent corporation, if the subsidiary appears to have been acting to benefit the parent and has little independent reality apart from the parent corporation.

A POLICY APPRAISAL: IS CORPORATE CRIMINAL LIABILITY USEFUL?

"Corporations don't commit crimes; people do." This theme (borrowed, of course, from the opponents of gun control) has been implicit in a substantial body of legal commentary that has criticized the idea of corporate criminal liability. The criticism has had two quite different focal points: (1) the asserted injustice of vicarious criminal liability; and (2) the alleged inefficiency of corporate liability. The following critiques have been repeatedly made. First, with respect to the rationale underlying corporate liability, it has been claimed that:

1. Vicarious liability is appropriate only as a principle of tort law since its justification lies in its allocation of the loss to the party more able to bear it (or at least more deserving of the burden), but it is unrelated to the purposes of retribution,

deterrence, prevention, and rehabilitation that underlie the criminal law (Leigh, p. 15).

2. Vicarious liability is unjust because its burden falls on the innocent rather than the guilty—that is, the penalty is borne by stockholders and others having an interest in the corporation, rather than by the guilty individual (U.S. National Commission, p. 163; Comment, 1975, p. 920).

3. Vicarious liability results in a disparity between businesses conducted in the corporate form and those run as a proprietorship, since the individual proprietor will not be criminally liable for the independent acts of his employees (Leigh, p. 118).

4. Vicarious liability for the corporation may in the future open the door to expanded vicarious criminal liability for individuals as well.

Second, a number of arguments have been advanced to claim that corporate punishment is inefficient or even counterproductive:

1. Corporations are largely undeterrable; fines are ineffective, and only the imprisonment of guilty individuals achieves real deterrence (U.S. National Commission, p. 163; Leigh, pp. 154-155).

2. Prosecution of the corporation may lead courts, juries, and prosecutors to acquit or dismiss charges against individual defendants, and thus corporate liability serves as a shield behind which the truly guilty can hide ("Developments in the Law," pp. 1248-1249).

3. Civil remedies are more flexible and potentially as severe, and they also avoid the constitutional restrictions associated with a criminal prosecution ("Developments in the Law," pp. 1369-1375).

4. No additional deterrence is achieved under the federal rule, since the Model Penal Code's affirmative defense will also give the corporation an incentive to monitor and police its employees (Miller, pp. 66-68).

Although none of these arguments is frivolous, each on closer examination seems seriously overbroad or at least unconfirmed by the relatively slim empirical evidence available. Each will be assessed below, as will the equally debatable arguments for corporate liability.

The debate over rationale. Should vicarious liability be limited to the context of tort law as a device for equitable allocation of losses? This argument has a surface plausibility to the extent that tort and criminal law are thought to have substantially different concerns: the former with compensation, the latter with deterrence. Still, vicarious liability may be more closely related to the goal of deterrence than its critics

concede. Economists have asserted that the most efficient way to deter organizational crime is to focus on the organization, not the individual (Elzinga and Breit, pp. 132-138). Although others have objected to aspects in this analysis (Coffee, 1980), it does seem likely that the organization has a greater capacity than do public authorities to monitor and police its own internal processes. Thus, if it could be deterred, it would in turn more effectively supervise its agents. Indeed, the corporation could undertake preventive measures in advance of any crime's commission, whereas the state is essentially forced to restrain its own hand until afterward because its right to act (at least insofar as the criminal law is concerned) is initiated only by the commission of the crime.

Conversely, in the absence of corporate penalties, the corporation may, consciously or otherwise, encourage noncompliance by its agents and even pressure for it (Coffee, 1981, pp. 413-415). Thus, a twofold answer seems possible to those who object to corporate vicarious criminal liability for criminal acts of an agent: (1) such vicarious liability may well be closely related to the criminal law's chief aim of prevention, both by deterring individual offenders and by encouraging the corporation to install incapacitative monitoring controls; and (2) victim compensation might also be a legitimate goal of the criminal law, both through sentences such as restitution (which the corporation almost uniquely is able to afford) and through the potential collateral estoppel impact of a criminal conviction on civil litigation brought by the victims of the crime.

Still, the argument that the penalty falls on the innocent remains troubling. The traditional answer to this criticism of corporate liability has been that a penalty imposed on the corporation simply eliminates unjust enrichment: since the stockholders indirectly benefited from the crime, they should indirectly bear the penalty (Edgerton, p. 837). This defense of corporate liability seems oversimple, however, because frequently the penalty will greatly exceed the gain (if any) from the crime. Indeed, many economists believe that adequate deterrence can only result if the expected penalty exceeds the expected gain by a margin sufficient to adjust for limited risk of apprehension and conviction. For example, if the expected gain were $1 million and the risk of apprehension were as low as 10 percent, only a penalty of $10 million would in theory remove the incentive to commit the crime.

This observation heightens the dilemma stemming from the fact that innocent parties suffer when the corporation is punished. But ultimately, the claim that corporate criminal liability is unjust because of the injury caused by the overspill of corporate penalties onto nonculpable shareholders proves too much. First, society does not face this issue exclusively in the context of the criminal law. If avoidance of punitive burdens on shareholders is taken as a first principle, it should also require the elimination of punitive damages in tort cases, treble-damage awards in civil antitrust cases, civil penalties, and possibly the very concept of *respondeat superior* as well. Equally important, the loss imposed on shareholders is generally mitigated through "cost spreading." That is, if a penalty of $10 million were imposed on a company having 100,000 shareholders holding its securities on a pro rata basis, the penalty per shareholder would be only $100 apiece—a loss that is considerably less significant than if the corporation had only a few shareholders. In reality, shareholders protect themselves from such risks through diversification of their investment portfolios, so that their exposure to such penalties is minimal. In short, the problem is not that the impact of a corporate penalty is unjustly severe, but rather that it is so negligible (on a per shareholder basis) that it gives shareholders little incentive to seek to hold management accountable.

The argument that corporate vicarious liability creates an unfair disparity between proprietorships and corporations also seems less than compelling. To be sure, the individual proprietor is not normally criminally liable on a vicarious basis for the criminal acts of his agents, but he is subject to incarcerative penalties if the prosecutor can convince a jury that he conspired with such agents. This risk is real, even if he is innocent, since conspiracy may be proved on circumstantial evidence. One suspects that if a disparity exists here, it favors the corporate shareholder, who seldom will be exposed to a threat of incarceration.

Finally, there remains the "open floodgates" argument: will vicarious liability for the corporation lead to similar liability for individuals? This ominous possibility might well have chilled commentators in 1909, immediately after the *New York Central* case, but in the years since that decision, no rush by the legislature to adopt statutes imputing criminal liability from one individual to another has been evident.

In any event, one answer to the "open floodgates" argument may be to redefine corporate criminal responsibility so that it is not truly a species of vicarious criminal liability. At bottom, vicarious liability rests on the imputation of evil intent from one juristic person to another. But such an imputation is not necessary to justify the application of a sanction. Alternatively, one can focus on the negligence or recklessness of the entity in suffering or permitting the act of its agent, and thereby omit the conceptually troublesome fiction of transferring the agent's intent to the entity.

Although this theory—which for the sake of convenience might be called a suretyship rationale—has received little attention from courts, it has been advanced by commentators. One writer has made the interesting suggestion that the corporation should be viewed not as a legal personality but as a "committable common fund" whose "members incur [a] diminished or derivative liability that penalizes them only through their common fund" (Stoljar, p.172). Conceptually, such a rationale avoids personifying the corporation, instead focusing on the granting of the corporate franchise by the state and construing it as having been conditioned upon an obligation to act as surety for defined criminal acts of its agents.

Under this implied-consent theory, the suretyship is a voluntarily accepted responsibility, to which the stockholder consents in return for the grant of the charter. In contrast, the English law's emphasis on culpability involving an "alter ego" of the corporation sees the corporation not as simply an insurer but as itself morally blameworthy. In essence, then, the English law on corporate responsibility is closely tied to a retributive rationale for punishment. Yet only a few commentators (for example, Fisse, "Reconstructing Corporate Criminal Law") see the corporation as a suitable vehicle for retributively motivated punishment, and there is some risk that in imposing retributive punishment on the corporation the law will appear to many to have been blinded by its own fiction. If so, the special moral and educative force that the criminal law possesses may be compromised.

A surety rationale is also potentially broader than the concept of vicarious liability. Under such a theory, the entity could be held liable for suffering an act by another, even though the individual actor would not necessarily be criminally liable. Thus, if the corporation's agent acts without the requisite level of intent—recklessly but not willfully, for example—the corporation cannot today be held liable under a vicarious theory of liability since under such a theory the corporation simply stands in the shoes of its agent, who is not here guilty. Yet it is far from self-evident that the legislature should be denied the power in all cases to so hold the corporation criminally liable; for example, the legislature might wish to hold the corporation more strictly accountable than its agent for tolerating a life-threatening safety hazard to exist, or for suffering an inadequately trained employee to operate a nuclear power plant. These cases can be reached today by making the offense one of strict liability and by enforcing the statute, as a practical matter, only against the corporate principal and not the agent. But a suretyship rationale permits a more formalized distinction between the liability of the individual and that of the entity by creating different standards of culpability for the individual and the entity, thus enabling the legislature to enact substantial deterrent penalties for the entity without permitting incarceration of individuals for behavior that was only negligent.

Similarly, the reach of a vicarious theory of liability may fall short of the surety theory in those cases where the actual actor cannot be identified or where the actor pursues his own ends rather than those of the corporation. For example, sexual harassment of female employees by their male supervisors could be criminalized, but corporate liability would not normally follow under current law since the agent did not act to benefit the entity. Of course, it is possible to legislate the crime of suffering an act by another, either negligently or as a matter of strict liability, but initially it seems anomalous to create a lower threshold of criminal liability for the party who suffers the act by its agent than for the agent who actually commits it. Yet under a surety rationale it is at least comprehensible that society might, in some limited class of cases, wish to impose a higher standard of intent for the accused individual actor than for the entity employing him, in part because the entity is only being held liable as a guarantor but not "punished" in any retributive sense. This argument raises in turn a more basic question: to the extent that a suretyship rationale is legislatively adopted, should its use be confined to civil rather than criminal sanctions?

As a legal theory, a surety rationale would expand to its logical limits the idea, already inherent in the current federal law of vicarious corporate liability, that a person can be blameworthy for suffering an act by his agent. In practice, such a rationale would modify American law by eliminating the need for the act to be in the interests of the corporation or within the agent's real or apparent authority, and it would permit different levels of intent to govern the liability of the agent and the entity. Yet, although such an expansion of criminal liability is probably constitutional (since strict liability statutes have been upheld), it would leave little remaining distinction between civil and criminal concepts of legal responsibility. From either a civil libertarian perspective or from one that seeks to conserve and protect the special educative force of the criminal law as a legal sanction, it can be questioned whether the gains in deterrence generated by such an expansion justify the potential costs that are risked through overuse of society's most powerful (and theatrical) sanction. The corporation is an anomaly in the criminal process, and the requirement that the agent act to benefit the corporation may well help to rationalize that anomaly and help society conceive of the corporation as a "true" offender.

The utility of corporate punishment. Some critics of corporate liability have doubted whether the corporation itself can be deterred. Such an evaluation seems premature, however, given another conclusion which virtually every commentator on the subject has reached: that corporations tend to receive very small fines in relation to their size, their earnings, or even their expected gain from the criminal transaction (Comment, 1975, pp. 921-922; Note, 1961, pp. 285-287). Thus, it is logically difficult to assert simultaneously that corporations are not punished and that they are not deterrable.

But here a problem noted earlier resurfaces: corporate punishment tends to fall on the innocent—not only on stockholders but also on employees (who may be laid off), creditors, the surrounding community, and, of course, the consumer, who may in effect indemnify the corporation if the fine can be passed on as a cost of doing business. Thus, an apparent paradox is reached: the economist's model asserts that only the imposition of severe fines in an amount well in excess of the expected gain will generate adequate deterrence, since it is necessary to compensate for a risk-of-apprehension factor that invariably falls well below 100 percent. But if corporate penalties are escalated in this fashion, the remedy may be worse than the disease, because layoffs, plant closings, and the threatened insolvency of major corporate institutions may be a more adverse result than the financial loss suffered by consumers or the government as a result of price-fixing or tax fraud (Coffee, 1981, pp. 415-422).

This problem suggests the desirability of corporate penalties that minimize "overspill." A number of proposals have been made in this regard: for example, the use of an equity fine levied in common stock would avert corporate insolvency and eliminate injury to nonstockholders, while also threatening a change of corporate control in order to activate management (Coffee, 1981, pp. 427-439). Similarly, a sentence of corporate probation has been recommended as a vehicle for public intervention in the internal decision making of delinquent corporations (Note, 1979). Others have recommended increased use of a publicity sanction and a sentence to render community service (Fisse, 1971, 1981). These proposals suggest that the issue of corporate liability can and should be divorced from that of the optimal form of corporate punishment.

An argument frequently made against corporate liability is that it may interfere with the assignment of individual liability. Here, anecdotal evidence does suggest that juries have sometimes compromised, acquitting all individual defendants while convicting the corporation (Comment, 1975, p. 923). The pervasiveness of this pattern cannot be estimated. Still, public-opinion surveys suggest that many white-collar crimes are no longer viewed as mere "regulatory" or technical violations but are ranked relatively high on a scale of seriousness, and consequently this pattern of jury reluctance to convict individual defendants for white-collar crimes may be a declining phenomenon. In any event, the prosecution always has the option of not prosecuting the corporation – or, at least, of not doing so in the same proceeding. Conversely, corporate liability may make it easier to convict the individual defendants. In any multidefendant prosecution, the interests of the defendants are at least potentially adverse, since each can generally gain concessions by implicating another. The corporation is no exception to this rule and is in a position to provide evidence against individual defendants or to discipline them, in return for leniency for itself. Drafts of the pending federal criminal code have appropriately recognized this by instructing the sentencing court, when levying a fine against the corporation, to consider the degree to which the corporation has undertaken internal disciplinary measures (S. 1722: A bill to codify, revise, and reform title 18 of the United States Code, and for other purposes, § 2202(a)(4), 96th Cong., 1st sess. (1979)). In short, such an invitation to mitigate the fine if the corporation will dismiss or discipline responsible officials makes it desirable from a law enforcement perspective to prosecute the corporation along with the individual defendants.

Still another perspective on the potential utility of corporate criminal liability begins from the much-repeated observation that it is frequently difficult to identify the "true" culprit within a firm. Although the point is undoubtedly correct, its truth may lie less in the ability of the "true" culprit to hid his identity than in the absence of any such "true" offender in a broad range of cases. From a social-science perspective, it is virtually a truism that knowledge may exist collectively within an organization, even though it is not localized within any one individual. This theory proceeds from a view of the corporation as a bureaucratic institution, and from this organizational perspective it is frequently argued that information flows poorly and in a selectively biased fashion within the corporate hierarchy. Lower echelons do not wish to communicate adverse information to those above, and those above filter out information that does not confirm their prior expectations. In addition, upper echelons within the corporation tend increasingly to speak a very different language than those at operating levels – one focused on financial results and unfamiliar with a production or operational vocabulary (Coffee, 1977). Thus it is likely that information will exist at one level of an organization that would alter decisions at another, but no mechanism will necessarily force the transmission of this information to where it is needed. Some federal decisions appear to have responded already

to such considerations by recognizing a "collective knowledge" doctrine, under which the corporation may be held liable even though no single individual had the requisite information (*T.I.M.E.-D.C., Inc.*).

These problems indicate one inadequacy of an exclusive focus on the individual decision-maker; recurrently, it is unlikely that any single individual within the corporate hierarchy will have the requisite intent, and yet the firm as an entity may have knowledge of an unsafe design, a carcinogenic risk, or a dangerous side effect that its products can cause. In this light, the argument for corporate liability rests not only on the evidentiary problems of identifying the "true" culprit but on the organizational reality that there may be no actual individual culprit at all, because of the diffusion of responsibility within the corporate hierarchy. Moreover, an insistence on finding a responsible individual decision-maker might produce a scapegoat system of criminal justice, in which lower-echelon operating officials would probably bear the primary responsibility and risk of exposure.

The foregoing arguments focus on the problem of cognitive failures within the corporation's internal information processing as a justification for corporate liability. An alternative justification proceeds from the motivational failures that also accompany the corporate form. Almost inevitably, there is an incongruence between the interests of the manager and those of the firm as an entity: criminal behavior may be attractive to the pressured or ambitious manager, even if it is not to the corporation. Compounding this problem is the tendency for conflicting signals to issue from the senior levels of the corporate hierarchy to the middle echelons, which tend to be the locus of criminal behavior. Such signals may formally require obedience to law, but they also demand and reward short-term profit maximization. The implicit signal may thus be read by middle-level managers as meaning only "don't get caught." Of course, individual criminal liability may partially countervail this pressure on the middle manager. But even if the severity of the criminal sanction vastly exceeds that of the counter-threats the corporation can make, such as dismissal, demotion, or foregone promotion, the absolute severity of the sanction must be discounted by its probability of imposition (Coffee, 1981). This means that the discounted threat of apprehension and conviction by the state for a criminal offense may be less than that of the strong likelihood of internal discipline or dismissal by the corporation for failure to maximize profits. Thus, the manager faces both public and private sanction, and the latter, although lesser in gravity, tend to be higher in probability, making the outcome uncertain and possibly dependent on the level of risk-aversion of the individual manager.

The alternative of civil remedies. Corporate sanctions may be necessary, but it is far from clear that such sanctions must be criminal in nature. Civil penalties are now utilized by many, if not most, administrative agencies. Moreover, a system of civil penalties offers some obvious advantages to the prosecutor. First, the corporation could not claim the protection of constitutional rights, such as the "reasonable doubt" standard or double jeopardy, that are applicable only to criminal proceedings. Second, the possibility of judicial or jury nullification is reduced because of the lesser stigma. Third, courts of equity traditionally have been more able than criminal courts to fashion flexible and novel forms of relief. Thus, from the standpoint of specific deterrence and incapacitation, some have concluded that civil penalties offer significant advantages over criminal law enforcement in the case of the corporation ("Developments in the Law," pp. 1365-1374).

In this light, what arguments remain for the use of the criminal law as a preferred legislative strategy? Little agreement exists here, but the following arguments deserve consideration. First, the criminal law has long been thought uniquely capable of performing an educative role in defining and reinforcing the boundaries of acceptable conduct. The civil law's quieter, less theatrical character limits its ability to perform this socializing function. Closely allied to this point is the criminal law's ability to stigmatize and employ publicity as a sanction. The highly publicized prosecution of the Ford Motor Company in 1979 for the allegedly unsafe design of the Pinto illustrates this capacity of the criminal process. Second, the criminal law characteristically moves at a faster pace than the civil law. Thus, to the extent that restitution is an authorized sentence, the criminal law can serve as the engine by which to obtain victim compensation more quickly. In addition, because the double jeopardy clause does not preclude a successive civil prosecution after an acquittal in a criminal trial, the prosecutor can in effect obtain a second chance by proceeding first criminally and then civilly.

Third, courts of equity have traditionally been barred from imposing penalties, and although this does not amount to a constitutional barrier, there may linger a reluctance on the part of courts when operating in a civil mode to pursue deterrent objectives. The basic format of the civil enforcement proceeding also has yet to be resolved, and the fairness and reliability of administratively determined civil penalties is a matter of serious dispute.

Finally, joint prosecutions of the corporation and its agents require a criminal forum if the threat of incarceration is to be used to deter individuals. From a law enforcement perspective, such joint trials are desirable both because they are less costly than separate prosecutions and because they permit one prosecutor to pursue the case in an integrated fashion; a separate prosecution, particularly if pursued in a different forum, might require a different prosecutor.

At most, these arguments suggest that corporate prosecutions for truly significant violations might best remain in a criminal courtroom, but they do not deny that corporate prosecutions for many regulatory and strict liability offenses, which today fit awkwardly at best within the criminal process, could be safely transferred to the civil process.

Affirmative defenses. As noted earlier, the Model Penal Code permits the corporation to prove as an affirmative defense that it exercised adequate diligence to supervise its employees (§ 2.07(5)). The underlying premise here, which is shared by British law, is that the function of corporate criminal liability is more to deter criminality by executives and encourage supervision of subordinates than to punish the corporation generally for all misdeeds caused by its agents ("Developments in the Law," p. 1252). Yet it is questionable whether recognition of such a defense advances or frustrates its announced purposes. Without such a defense, the corporation would still have an incentive to monitor and police its employees since, as a practical matter, it will probably be held strictly liable for any offense committed by employees in the course of their work. But by recognizing the defense, one raises the possibility of feigned compliance and thus encourages cosmetic attempts at monitoring. Worse yet, there is the danger that honest efforts at monitoring and compliance will be mistaken by middle-level management as only a cynical attempt to prepare a due-diligence defense in advance.

On a more theoretical level, once such a defense is recognized, the corporation might invest less funds in monitoring and detecting illegal and potentially illegal behavior since, once the minimal standard of diligence is met, the corporation becomes legally immune and has no remaining incentive to prevent criminal acts by its agents, even though further investment might prevent such crime. In theory, the ideal position for the corporation would be to invest just enough to establish the defense but not to prevent those crimes profitable to the corporation. Yet without the defense, the rational corporation would invest in crime prevention by any means (including research or experimentation with new techniques) up to the level at which such expenditures equaled the expected penalty—that is, the likely fine discounted by the likelihood of apprehension and conviction. In short, the absence of the defense creates an incentive to seek new methods of prevention not yet established or required by a due-diligence standard. Ironically, the more diligence is made a defense, the less it is encouraged.

Still, a total refusal to recognize any role for corporate due diligence may seem unjust. Thus, a role might be created for such a defense that would be less likely to result in reduced deterrence. This would be done by reducing the role of due-diligence efforts from an affirmative defense to a sentencing consideration (S. 1722, § 2202(a)(4) so provided in its attempt to recodify the Federal Criminal Code). The legislature could provide that the court shall consider at sentencing any corporate efforts directed at internal reform or at the discipline of employees. In particular, such a step would give the corporation an incentive to seek out guilty individual sin order to reduce its own penalty, whereas otherwise there might exist a desire to avoid such an inquiry for fear of detecting still-undiscovered violations. The threat of individual liability would thus be increased since corporate employees would come to expect that their employer would turn them in if it faced conviction itself.

Making due diligence a sentencing consideration rather than an affirmative defense has other desirable consequences as well. First, it ensures that violation by an agent will result in a corporate conviction, thereby authorizing the court to order restitution to victims and to consider interventionist strategies that might be implemented through a sentence of corporate probation. Second, the conviction would have a res judicata effect on civil litigation brought by injured victims of the crime; such civil liability in turn increases the corporate incentive to monitor. Finally, the court would gain a wider angle of vision in determining the adequacy of corporate monitoring efforts since it could consider developments subsequent to the offense that would be legally irrelevant at trial.

Summary

As noted at the outset, the problem of corporate criminal responsibility has a conceptual and a pragmatic dimension. On the conceptual level, the majority American rule of *respondeat superior* has troubled those who understandably fear vicarious liability and a reduction in the role of intent in the criminal law, but it has evoked little concern on the part of the public. On a theoretical level, a different rationale — the surety rationale — might respond to these concerns by adopting a less fictional justification for punishing the corporation, but such a rationale (focused as it is on suffering an act rather than on vicariously being the actor) fits awkwardly at bets with the public's conception of criminal responsibility.

On a pragmatic level, the lack of empirical scholarship about corporate behavior clouds all efforts to understand the impact of corporate criminal liability, but much of the criticism of the contemporary federal rule seems overstated. To immunize the corporation from criminal liability and to focus only on the individual actor could significantly reduce the deterrent threat underlying the criminal law insofar as (1) the corporation can implicitly threaten its agents with private sanctions (such as dismissal) that have a higher likelihood of being imposed than the state's penalties; (2) no single individual may have acted with sufficient specific intent to justify conviction; and (3) such a step invites the corporation to relax its efforts at monitoring its agents. In addition, corporate liability can potentially serve other purposes, such as victim compensation, and it offers a vehicle for interventionist strategies directed at the corporation that are not realizable through prosecutions of individuals.

Although a focus on the firm, as opposed to the individual actor alone, thus seems prudent, the case for corporate criminal liability is problematic and, as civil enforcement procedures are formalized and enhanced, it may diminish significantly. Ultimately, it must rest either (1) on practical considerations which suggest that the prosecutor obtains tactical advantages or can succeed in imposing greater penalties in a criminal context; or (2) on the greater visibility of the criminal process and the consequent utility of the criminal trial as a means of communicating an essentially moral and educative lesson about the boundaries of acceptable conduct. Neither foundation is today secure, but, correspondingly, adequate alternatives are unproved and largely unauthorized.

Kathleen F. Brickey, *Close Corporations and the Criminal law: On "Mom and Pop" and a Curious Rule,* 71 WASH. U. L.Q. 189 (1993)*

I. INTRODUCTION

* * *

Established principles governing corporate criminal liability apply indiscriminately to all corporations, regardless of size or corporate form. Yet to date, little consideration has been given to the question whether

---

* Reprinted with permission of Washington University Law Quarterly.

the reasons supporting recognition of corporate liability for crime apply with equal force to close corporations. Nor has the question whether the same sentencing rules should apply to close corporations and their publicly held counterparts been addressed. Hence, this Article journeys off the beaten path to explore these intersecting themes.

II. "MOM AND POP"

Cases through which courts fashioned the rule that corporations could be liable for crime viewed such liability as a necessary check on corporate power. In a seminal turn of the century case, the Supreme Court observed that in modern times, corporations conduct "the great majority of business transactions" and that "interstate commerce is almost entirely in their hands." That being true, to adhere to "the old and exploded" notion that corporations are incapable of committing crimes "would virtually take away the only means of effectually controlling" them and of "correcting the abuses" at which the criminal law is aimed. The Massachusetts Supreme Judicial Court more recently voiced concern that if corporations were shielded from criminal liability, they could "inflict widespread public harm" and leave the public with no prospect of redressing the wrong.

Both courts undoubtedly had large publicly traded corporations in mind. One can only wonder whether the courts would have been equally receptive to institutional liability if the prosecutions had been brought against small "mom and pop" corporations. Would the corporate form of doing business have been relevant to the developing liability rule? To address this question, it is necessary to consider these contrasting corporate forms and what "corporateness" really means.

Publicly held corporations are owned by many shareholders. Their ownership and management thus are separate and distinct. Close corporations, in contrast, are privately owned, and their ownership and management usually overlap. The term "close corporation" is variously defined as an organization that has relatively few shareholders, one whose stock is not widely traded in the securities market, or one characterized by substantial identity of ownership and management. The term "closely held" corporation invariably refers to a privately owned corporation that has few or relatively few shareholders. Regardless of which term is used, these corporations will have a relatively small number of shareholders because their stock will not be traded on an exchange or in securities markets.

Although recognition of the distinctive nature of close corporations is largely a twentieth century phenomenon, the importance of this corporate form cannot be overstated. Today, the vast majority of incorporated organizations in this country are closely held, and many are small, family owned businesses.

Do small, closely held corporations "behave more like individuals than organizations?" If so, one might posit that in this context the organizational behavior model is inapt and that applying institutional rules of criminal liability to them thus makes little sense. The strongest case against imposing criminal liability on close corporations can be made where complete or substantial overlap exists between management and ownership. Consider, for example, the corporation whose records were subpoenaed in Braswell v. United States.

After conducting his business as a sole proprietorship for fifteen years, Braswell decided to incorporate. To comply with state corporation law requirements, he appointed three officer/directors. They were, respectively, Braswell, who served as president; Braswell's wife, who was named corporate secretary-treasurer; and Braswell's mother, who was named vice-president. Neither his wife nor his mother had any authority over the business. Thus, in essence, Braswell continued his sole proprietorship, but conducted it in corporate form.

One might argue that in Braswell's setting, imposition of criminal liability on the corporation would be needlessly redundant. One reason that corporate criminal liability is recognized is recognized is the difficulty of identifying individual wrongdoers within the organization. Many modern corporations are large, complex, highly decentralized organizations with multiple layers of bureaucracy. These entities depend on a system of delegation that diffuses responsibility throughout the organization. In consequence, lower echelon employees "often exercise more responsibility in the everyday operations of the corporation" than does corporate management. Indeed, under the collective knowledge doctrine, there need not be a single culpable corporate agent. Hence, fining the corporation becomes an alternative to fining the unidentified or nonexistent wrongdoer.

Even when middle or low-level wrongdoers can be found, there may be other reasons to hold the corporation accountable. Especially in the context of crimes like antitrust violations, the misconduct may be a response to institutional pressures – subtle or overt – to maximize profits. Consider, for example, a purchasing agent whose profit maximization efforts result in an unlawful pricing agreement. He agrees to the unlawful arrangement on behalf of the corporation and for its benefit. If the corporate ethos encourages or tolerates such practices, one might reasonably regard the core of the problem as institutional. To single out the lowly employee whose violation occurred in pursuit of the corporate mission could well be regarded as choosing a convenient scapegoat.

Even if high-level managers consciously seek to foster an environment that encourages practices that cross the line and give rise to criminal liability, it is by no means clear that they will bear their share of the blame. The ease with which wrongdoing can be concealed in an organizational setting is another reason corporate criminal liability is recognized. High-level decisions to risk violating the law will not be recorded in corporate minutes. They will, instead, be shrouded in secrecy. Thus, we recognize institutional liability for crime partly because group action makes it possible to conceal misconduct even at the highest levels of management.

In the context of Braswell's "one man show," these considerations may seem less than compelling. Although Braswell enjoys the advantages of doing business in corporate form, the cast of characters is small. His business has few employees and no bureaucracy. Thus, miscreant agents will be easier to identify, and opportunities for concealment are considerably reduced. One might posit, moreover, that in a small organization like his, the desire for personal gain is more likely to actuate the wrongdoing. Hence, the identified wrongdoer is less likely to be regarded as a scapegoat. The organization may, indeed, be his alter ego.

The premise that close corporations act more like individuals than organizations clearly applies to Braswell's one person corporation. It could apply with equal force to five or ten person corporations, where a small group of people work cooperatively toward a common goal. But as the number of individuals involved in the venture, the complexity of its organization and operations, and the volume of business conducted in its name all increase, the characteristics that made its behavior analogous to individual behavior ultimately disappear.

A look at the one thousand largest privately held companies makes the point. Cargill Inc., the largest close corporation in the country, boasts sales of $42 billion and employs nearly 54,000 workers. United Parcel Service, the fifth largest, has more than $13.5 billion in sales and more than 250,000 employees.

The one hundred largest privately held companies include a litany of household names—corporate providers of goods like Publix Super Markets, Montgomery Ward, Bechtel, Phar-Mor, Hallmark Cards, Levi Strauss, Amway, SC Johnson and Son, Land O'Lakes, Domino's Pizza, Borg-Warner, Ace Hardware, Estee Lauder, and Dow Corning. They include corporate transportation providers like Trans World Airlines and Budget Rent a Car as well. All of the companies in this category have at least $1.5 billion in sales, and half of them employ tens of thousands of workers.

The corporate characteristics these organizations display are not limited to the very largest. The top two hundred privately held companies include corporations like Barnes and Noble, Del Monte Foods, Mack Trucks, Maritz, Gulfstream Aerospace, and GAF. Businesses in this second tier post sales ranging from roughly $900 million to $1.5 billion and employ up to 45,000 people.

Levitz Furniture, Seiko of America, Olan Mills, Hartz Mountain, Goodwill Industries, Bell and Howell, and National Car Rental are corporations among the top 300 privately owned companies. The volume of sales in this tier ranges from $640 to $880 million. A majority of these businesses employ more than 3000 people, and employees of about fifteen percent of them number in the tens of thousands.

The top 400 include well known corporate entities like Timex, Alamo Rent A Car, Sverdrup, Franklin Mint, ComputerLand, and Camelot Music. The volume of sales for this tier ranges from $460 to $540 million. Most of these businesses have more than 2000 employees, and nearly thirty percent employ 5000 or more.

Asplundh Tree Expert, Wickes Lumber Company, and the Bose Corporation are among the top 500. The volume of sales in this tier ranges from $400 to $460 million, and most of these companies employ several thousand employees.

And so it goes down to the thousandth largest privately owned company, Booth Newspapers Inc. Booth has sales of $450 million and employs 2700 persons.

The contrast between these corporations and Braswell's business is as stark as that between night and day. Organizations that employ tens of thousands (or perhaps just thousands) of workers are bound to have layers of bureaucracy characteristic of large publicly held corporations. Far removed from the one, five, ten, or even thirty person firm, these close corporations function much like their large, publicly held counterparts.

Indeed, some of these entities have had prior incarnations as publicly held corporations. During the corporate takeover mania of the 1980s, the "going private" movement rapidly gained momentum. Motivated by the desire to eliminate the trouble and expense of complying with SEC regulations, the need to focus on long-term business strategies rather than quarterly earnings, the determination to avoid hostile takeovers or the like, many publicly traded companies went private—i.e., were acquired by private investment groups or individuals—and thus became close corporations. Instead of being owned by millions or tens of thousands of shareholders, they ordinarily fell into the hands of a single institutional owner—a partnership, management group, corporate subsidiary or the like.

Corporate giants like RJR Nabisco, Beatrice Foods, Safeway, Borg-Warner, Southland Corporation, Macy's, Burlington Industries, and National Gypsum jumped on the going private band wagon. But not all of them stayed private for long. Once the threat of a hostile takeover dissipated, for example, so might the sole or principal reason for going private. Thus, within a few years of going private, some firms like RJR Nabisco and Safeway went public again.

These changes in corporate form did not transform the affected entities into smaller, less complex, or less bureaucratic organizations. Just as Braswell's one man corporation continued to function much like a sole proprietorship, large companies that went private in the 1980s continued to behave, for all intents and purposes, like their publicly held counterparts. Their management and capital structures remained the same. All that changed was the shareholder structure—i.e., a change in ownership.

A rule that would subject the RJR Nabiscos and Safeways of the world to criminal liability before they went private and again after they reestablished public personae—but not in between—would be a startling incongruity. The reasons that support recognition of corporate criminal liability are wholly unrelated to the question of who owns the corporation. They are tied, instead, to the bureaucracy that makes personal accountability less likely. That bureaucracy will exist in large corporations whether they are publicly or closely held.

If the rule of institutional liability should treat Braswell and RJR Nabisco differently, then, it is not because Braswell's corporation is closely held. It is because the behavior of his small business is analogous to individual behavior. There are no layers of bureaucracy to penetrate, and he can monitor his few employees with relative ease—not because he is the owner, but because he is the manager. Thus, for purposes of crafting an appropriate institutional liability rule, the corporate form in which he does business has no significance.

Although it is relatively easy to draw gross distinctions between Braswell and RJR Nabisco, to craft a rule that quantifies those distinctions would be a daunting task. A rule that merely selected a minimum number of managers and/or employees, for example, would likely be arbitrary and oversimplified. One that attempted to detail all of the relevant characteristics that distinguish Braswell and RJR Nabisco, on the other hand, would likely be overly complex.

* * *

IV. CONCLUSION

Recognition of corporate criminal liability by the

courts was an acknowledgment of the growing power corporations have over commerce. Corporate liability for crime provides a check on corporate power. This core concern applies with equal force to close corporations, which constitute an estimated ninety percent or more of incorporated organizations and include within their ranks some of the largest business entities in the country.

Although many small "mom and pop" operations like Braswell's conduct business as closely held corporations, their ownership structure is not germane to the question whether their operations should be subject to the rule of institutional criminal liability. What makes the "corporateness" of these operations qualitatively different is not that they are privately held, but that they are small, uncomplicated organizations in which the owners often actively manage the business. In these organizations, wrongdoers can be identified with relative ease because there is little corporate bureaucracy or hierarchy to cloak their identities or motives.

Whether these corporations should be governed by the institutional liability rule is partly a function of the practical relationship between personal and institutional accountability, and partly of what (or whether) we gain from demanding both. If we do demand both, it makes little sense to disregard the institution's "corporateness" absent strong identity between the convicted owner/manager and the corporation itself.

Pamela H. Bucy, *Corporate Ethos: A Standard for Imposing Corporate Criminal Liability,* 75 MINN. L. REV. 1095–1148, 1182 (1991)*

INTRODUCTION

Responsible social policy mandates that we deter those who victimize society through egregious and dangerous acts. Historically, the criminal law has been the vehicle for such deterrence. Corporations are increasingly significant actors in our economy and, to the extent their actions can victimize society, they too

* Reprinted with permission of the Minnesota Law Review and the author.

should be deterred. For this reason, criminal prosecution of corporations has routinely occurred in American courts for almost a century. Commentators, however, have consistently questioned this use of the criminal law. Moreover, the debate over corporate criminal liability will likely intensify as the government increasingly prosecutes prominent corporate defendants. Two major issues have dominated this debate. One is the failure to identify or prove corporate intent. Traditionally, the criminal law has been reserved for intentional violations of the law. Yet, our prosecutions of corporations have been marked by floundering efforts to identify the intent of intangible, fictional entities. A second issue in the debate concerns sanctions. In addition to proof of intent, a major distinguishing characteristic of the criminal law has been the threat of imprisonment. Critics of corporate criminal liability suggest that because a corporation cannot be imprisoned, the criminal law is not an appropriate vehicle for controlling corporate behavior. Much of the recent scholarship on corporate crime has addressed the sanctioning issue. This Article, however, addresses corporate intent and suggests that a better resolution of this issue would eliminate much of the controversy concerning corporate criminal liability, including the controversy over sanctions.

Scholars have long decried the inability of our current standards of corporate criminal liability to address corporate intent. According to Gerhard O.W. Mueller, "[m]any weeds have grown on the acre of jurisprudence which has been allotted to the criminal law. Among these . . . is corporate criminal liability. . . . Nobody bred it, nobody cultivated it, nobody planted it. It just grew." John Braithwaite is more succinct: "A criminology which remains fixed at the level of individualism is the criminology of a bygone era." Brent Fisse calls the inability to address corporate fault "the blackest hole in the theory of corporate criminal law."

This Article proposes a standard of corporate criminal liability that uses a new conceptual paradigm for identifying and proving corporate intent. This standard assumes that each corporate entity has a distinct and identifiable personality or "ethos." The government can convict a corporation under this standard only if it proves that the corporate ethos encouraged agents of the corporation to commit the criminal act. Central to this approach is the assumption that organizations possess an identity that is independent of specific individuals who control or work for the organization. This corporate identity, or "ethos," results from the dynamic of many individuals working together toward corporate goals. The living cell provides an apt analogy: Just as a living cell has an identity separate from the activities of its constituent molecules, a corporation has an identity separate from its individual agents.

In a sense, this corporate ethos standard takes its cue from notions of intent developed in the context of individual liability. When considering whether an individual should be held criminally liable we ask, did this person commit this act accidentally or purposely. If the individual committed the act purposely, we consider it to be a crime, while if the individual committed the act accidentally, we do not. Similarly, the standard proposed herein imposes criminal liability on a corporation only if the corporation encouraged the criminal conduct at issue. If it did, the criminal conduct is not an accident or the unpredictable act of a maverick employee. Instead, the criminal conduct is predictable and consistent with corporate goals, policies, and ethos. In the context of a fictional entity, this translates into intention.

This proposed standard offers the following four advantages over the current standards of liability. To the extent that historical and current standards of corporate criminal liability allow criminal convictions without proof of the corporation's intent, they encourage the blurring of criminal and civil liability. This blurring dilutes the impact of a criminal conviction, and, ultimately, erodes the power of the criminal law. The theoretical and practical framework of the corporate ethos standard provides a method for identifying and proving the intent of corporate actors. This is its first and major advantage.

The second advantage of the corporate ethos standard is that it distinguishes among diverse corporations. The current standards of corporate criminal liability often treat all corporations alike by imposing criminal liability on corporations for the acts of their individual agents, regardless of the circumstances within a particular corporation. From Bentham on, scholars and practitioners have recognized that a fundamental requirement for any criminal justice system is that the system treat like actors alike and different actors differently. Anyone, from the average person on the street to the most respected scholar in organizational behavior, recognizes that no two corporations are alike. Our criminal justice system should not treat them as if they were.

The third advantage of the corporate ethos standard is that it rewards those corporations that make efforts to educate and motivate their employees to follow the letter and spirit of the law. This encourages responsible corporate behavior. This advantage is in sharp contrast to the Model Penal Code's standard of liability that discourages higher echelon employees from properly supervising lower echelon employees. This advantage also contrasts with the minimal deterrence achieved by imposing criminal liability on individuals within the corporation. Convicting individual agents and employees of a corporation does not stop other corporate employees from committing future criminal acts if sufficient internal corporate pressure to violate the law continues to exist. In such an environment, the agents are cogs in a wheel. Those convicted are simply replaced by others whose original propensity to obey the law is similarly overcome by a corporate ethos that encourages illegal acts. Unless inside or outside forces change the lawless ethos, it will corrupt each generation of corporate agents. The proposed standard of liability addresses this problem by punishing any corporation that establishes a lawless ethos which overcomes its employees' propensity to obey the law.

The last advantage of the corporate ethos standard is that it is practical, workable, and provable, from concrete information already available in grand jury investigations of corporate crime. To ascertain the ethos of a corporation, and to determine if this ethos encouraged the criminal conduct at issue, the fact finder should examine: the corporate hierarchy, the corporate goals and policies, the corporation's historical treatment of prior offenses, the corporation's efforts to educate and monitor employees' compliance with the law, and the corporation's compensation scheme, especially its policy on indemnification of corporate employees. These facts are typically, or easily, examined in any criminal investigation of corporate misdeeds and are subject to proof in a courtroom.

Part I of this Article provides background. It sets forth the current standards of corporate criminal liability and describes their approach to intent. Part I then explains why proof of intent is essential to a criminal justice system, and provides an historical discussion of how American criminal law developed corporate criminal liability without this traditional emphasis on intent. Part II sets forth the corporate ethos standard, listing each of its elements and discussing how to prove each element. After examining the results in different types of cases when using the corporate ethos standard versus the current standards of corporate criminal liability, Part II compares the corporate ethos standard to other proposals for enhancing corporate responsibility. Part III addresses the procedural implications of adopting a standard such as corporate ethos, while Part IV answers potential criticisms of the corporate ethos standard.

* * *

II. THE CORPORATE ETHOS STANDARD OF CORPORATE CRIMINAL LIABILITY

The standard of corporate criminal liability proposed herein focuses on the "ethos" of a corporation and provides as follows: A corporation should be held criminally liable only when its ethos encourages criminal conduct by agents of the corporation. Under this standard, the government must prove, beyond a reasonable doubt, four elements: (1) a corporate ethos (2) that encourages (3) criminal conduct (4) by agents of the corporation.

A. PROVING THE ELEMENTS

1. The Existence of a Corporate Ethos

Aristotle developed the rich concept "ethos" to describe one component of a successful orator. In the third century B.C., the study of rhetoric was so popular in Greece that it dominated the traditional education of young men preparing for public life. Several factors contributed to rhetoric's importance. Most young men aspired to be a politician or statesman, and public speaking was an "indispensable accomplishment" for any politician. In addition, Athens was an "unusually litigious" society, and the law required that every citizen plead his own case in a court of law. In this environment, oratorical skills were necessary, advantageous, and cherished. Some citizens, including Aristotle, were not pleased with this emphasis on rhetoric, believing that young men cultivated "quickness and dexterity" at the expense of sound logic, scientific inquiry, veracity and sincerity. In Aristotle's years as a young adult, Socrates' school of rhetoric was at the height of its popularity. The factitious and vacuous approach that this school fostered apparently so moved Aristotle that he established a rival school of oratory. In his three part work entitled Rhetoric, Aristotle advanced his views on oratory, and distinguished the views of his rivals'. Aristotle argued that the most important ingredient of successful oratory was systematic logic and scientific exposition. He identified three modes of persuasion by which a speaker communicated his logic and exposition. One was the content of the speech. Another was putting the audience in a frame of mind responsive to the arguments made, a mode that required an analysis of the human character, motives, and feelings of the audience. The third mode of persuasion . . . "??" or ethos – "depend[ed]" on the personal character of the speaker." According to one Aristotelean scholar,

This kind of ethos is most important . . . to the success of the speech: for the opinion of any audience as to the credibility of the speaker depends mainly upon the view they take of his intentions and character intellectual and moral; his ability to form a judgment, his integrity and truthfulness and his disposition toward themselves, to one they will listen with attention, respect and favor; another if they look upon him as of the opposite character, they will regard with dislike and impatience and an inclination to disbelief and criticism.

Aristotle's notion of ethos has continued in our modern society. Today, the term refers to the characteristic spirit or prevalent tone of sentiment of a community, institution or system. The historical concept of ethos is appropriate for our consideration of a corporation's characteristic spirit or prevalent tone of sentiment. Aristotle's "ethos" focused on the abstract, intangible character of a speaker that was separate from the substance of the speaker's words. So too, the notion of corporate ethos is the abstract, and intangible, character of a corporation separate from the substance of what it actually does, whether manufacturing, retailing, finance or other activity. And like Aristotle's speakers, each corporation has a distinctive ethos or "characteristic spirit." Superficial things such as the manner of dress and the camaraderie of the employees as well as formal, written goals and policies evidence this ethos. Additionally, a corporation's ethos may be tied to one or a few individuals or it may transcend individuals and even generations.

Scholars and practitioners of organizational theory have long recognized that organizations differ from each other: "It is not true that all big companies are the same – they aren't. . . . Companies develop their own distinctive personality and ethos which is so ingrained, so much a part of them, that the corporate identity expresses itself in their every action."

Much of the voluminous business literature on corporate culture is premised on the notion that organizations have distinctive cultures. For example, one commentator has described the distinct personalities of the world's dominant oil companies as follows: Texaco "with its selfishness and greed cultivates a reputation for meanness and secrecy"; Mobil "is in many ways the most sophisticated of American [oil companies] . . . much concerned with communications and image"; Exxon maintains a "tranquil style." Its headquarters are "silent" and "elegant," its atmosphere "rarefied," Exxon is "full of rhetorics of global responsibilities [and] likes to stress that it serves not only its American shareholders but all the nations where it operates." Shell, "lordly and sedate," demonstrates an "obsessive introversion" and "self containment" – "Shellmen . . . cultivate . . . diplomacy [and]. . . prefer not to talk about anything as squalid as profits."

In their popular work, Corporate Cultures, Deal and Kennedy identify five elements of a company's culture: business environment, values, heroes, rites and rituals, and cultural network. By analyzing these elements, these authors develop four types of corporate cultures: the "Tough-guy, Macho" culture, where stakes are high and feedback is quick (construction and entertainment companies); the "Work hard/ Play hard" culture, where the employees live in a world of small risks – no one sale will make or break a player (real estate and door-to-door sales); the "Bet-Your-Company" culture, where high risk but slow feedback prevails because players often must invest

millions in a project that takes years to develop (capital goods and oil companies); and the "process" culture where the low risk and slow feedback forces employees to focus on how they do something, not what they do (utilities and insurance companies).

Peters and Waterman are two organizational scholars whose work builds on the premise that corporations have distinct cultures. Their study of companies that demonstrated organizational effectiveness and management excellence uncovered eight characteristics of the "excellent company." The "excellent" companies maintain cultures that incorporate certain values, such as a strong recognition and respect for the customer's needs as well as the needs of employees to control their own destiny. Poorer performing companies also often have strong cultures, but dysfunctional ones that usually focus on internal politics rather than on the customer, or on "the numbers" rather than on the product and the people who make and sell it.

Sometimes the culture of a corporation is visible in very specific contexts. Christopher Stone demonstrates this point through a comparison of worker safety records in coal mines owned by traditional coal mining companies and those owned and operated by steel firms. The mining companies experienced an average of 0.78 deaths and 40.61 injuries per million man-hours worked whereas the steel companies experienced an average of 0.36 deaths and 7.50 injuries per million man-hours worked. Stone attributes this tremendous disparity to a difference in culture and values: The coal companies were accustomed to accepting a great loss of life and limbs; the steel companies were not and would not tolerate poor safety performance.

For criminal justice purposes, some of the most interesting work on organizational character has been conducted by sociologists who have examined the commission of corporate crime to determine the characteristics of lawful and unlawful organizations. These scholars suggest that certain social structures and processes internal to an organization encourage unlawful behavior.

Marshall Clinard interviewed sixty-four retired middle management employees of fifty-one Fortune 500 corporations engaged in industrial manufacturing. Clinard focused his study on unethical as well as unlawful behavior. Through his interviews, Clinard found that most of the executives believed that "unethical corporate behavior can usually be traced to internal rather than external forces." The interviewees identified two internal factors as primarily determinative of whether the corporation promoted lawful or unlawful behavior. The first was top management. The interviewees portrayed top management as generally knowledgeable about the unethical or unlawful activity before or after it occurred. Not surprisingly, they therefore deemed top management to be "largely responsible for the unethical or illegal behavior within a corporation." The interviewees also associated the following management characteristics with the law-abiding corporation: an appreciation of applicable government regulations, explicit instructions and enforcement of these regulations, open lines of communication between top and middle management about compliance problems, and stable and respected leadership that came from within the corporate ranks. The second factor identified by the interviewees as influencing a corporation's propensity to comply with the law was the internal pressure on middle management to show a profit and maintain satisfactory employee relations.

Interestingly, the executives thought that these two internal factors contributed more to whether a corporation complied with the law than did the external factors such as a poor financial situation, unfair practices of competitors, or the type of industry. This focus on internal rather than external factors supports the view that an ethos developed within a corporation can encourage, or discourage, criminal conduct by corporate employees.

In Controlling Unlawful Organizational Behavior, Diane Vaughan examines one case study of organizational crime: Revco Inc., which in 1977, pled guilty to submitting false medicaid claims totaling $521,521.12. Drawing on this case study, Vaughan analyzes the relationship between corporate structural factors and unlawful behavior. She concludes that the "[o] rganizational processes . . . create an internal moral and intellectual world" in which individuals within the organization are encouraged to engage in unlawful behavior. These organizational processes include internal education and training, reward mechanisms, and informational processing and recording methods. Vaughan notes that the organizational processes that encourage unlawful behavior "may vary by subunit of an organization, or by position within a subunit and over time."

One can draw several clear conclusions from these works on corporate culture: (1) each corporation is distinctive and draws its uniqueness from a complex combination of formal and informal factors; (2) the formal and informal structure of a corporation can promote, or discourage, violations of the law; and (3) this structure is identifiable, observable, and malleable. In light of such conclusions, a standard of criminal liability that fails to recognize the unique character of corporations or fails to promote law-abiding behavior by such corporations is unjustified.

2. A Corporate Ethos that "Encourages"

To apply this standard of liability, it is not necessary to ascertain the overall and complete ethos of an organization. The corporate ethos standard is concerned only with the ethos relevant to the criminal conduct in question. Thus, a corporation's ethos or "characteristic spirit" toward employees' rights, competitors, research and development, marketing, and the like is relevant only to the extent it sheds light on whether there exists a corporate ethos that encouraged the particular criminal conduct at issue.

Identifying the corporate ethos relevant to the criminal behavior in question will require a resort to circumstantial evidence, as does proof of intent in every criminal case. Although the actual evidence available will always turn on the particular facts of each case, there are certain guides for every fact finder. When the defendant is an individual, the fact finder looks to the statements and actions of the defendant before, during, and after the crime as well as corroboration for and explanations of such statements and actions. From this information, the fact finder assesses the defendant's mens rea for the criminal conduct charged. By comparison, in applying the corporate ethos standard of liability, the fact finder should look to the following types of facts to determine whether a corporate ethos existed which encouraged corporate employees to commit the criminal conduct. If so, the government has proven the corporate mens rea. These facts concern the internal, formal and informal, structure of the corporation.

Two practical points should be borne in mind when applying the following factors. First, as noted, sometimes it may not be possible to determine which individual within an organization actually performed the illegal conduct, much less encouraged it. The corporate ethos test does not require that the government prove which individual is at fault. It does, however, require the government to prove that the criminal conduct was committed by a corporate agent and that a corporate ethos existed that encouraged the criminal conduct. Thus, if the government shows that the criminal conduct occurred in the accounting department, proof of a corporate ethos that encourages criminal conduct in the research and development division is not sufficient; only evidence of such an ethos in the accounting department will suffice. Second, like Aristotle's speakers who were taught to identify and then to control and alter their own character to suit their audience, a corporation can manipulate and control its corporate ethos from within. Accordingly, the fact finder using a corporate ethos standard of liability, like an audience listening to a politician, must determine whether they are observing fact or fiction.

* * *

3. Criminal Conduct

The third element of the corporate ethos standard is whether the ethos encourages criminal conduct. This element is not as simple as it may appear; phrasing this element as "conduct that is determined to be criminal" may be more accurate. The type of offense for which corporations are often prosecuted, white collar crime, necessitates this distinction.

It is apparent that burglary, homicide, and distributing cocaine, for example, are criminal conduct. With white collar crime, however, it is often not apparent that conduct is criminal until after a jury and an appellate court have spoken. The jurisprudence of white collar crime is replete with examples of courts and legislatures struggling to clarify what is, or is not, a crime. For example, in McNally v. United States, the Supreme Court reversed a mail fraud conviction and held that conduct that all of the federal appellate courts had considered mail fraud for forty years, was not. Similarly, in Williams v. United States, the Supreme Court reversed a bank fraud conviction; in so doing, the Court found the relevant conduct was not bank fraud, even though courts had for many years held that such conduct constituted bank fraud. In considering payments made between health care providers, the federal courts of appeal have disagreed over the legality under kick-back statutes of certain long-standing payment practices. The list could go on and on. A criminal defendant may be aided in two ways when the legality of the conduct at issue is not clear. First, a court may agree that the conduct is not a crime and acquit the defendant on that basis. Second, even if the court deems the conduct to be criminal, the fact finders may decide that because the defendant did not know the criminal nature of his act at the time he acted, he did not have the requisite intent to violate the law, and thus acquit the defendant.

The corporate ethos standard of liability allows for this nuance in white collar crimes. Although the facts may clearly show the existence of a corporate ethos that encouraged certain conduct ultimately found to be criminal, the fact finders may appropriately acquit the corporate defendant (just as they may acquit an individual defendant) if they believe it reasonable not to have known that such conduct was criminal. This is one of the ways the intent requirement introduces flexibility into corporate criminal law. Given the ambiguity surrounding what constitutes white collar crime, such flexibility seems especially appropriate for defendants, whether individual or corporate, charged with white collar crimes.

4. By Agents of the Corporation

Historically, before courts would hold a corporation liable, they required that an agent of the corporation acting within the scope of employment and with the intent to benefit the corporation perform the illegal activity. The corporate ethos standard of liability retains only the requirement that an agent of the corporation perform the illegal activity.

Over the years, the "within the scope of employment" requirement has evolved to mean "little more than that the act occurred while the offending employee was carrying out a job related activity." The cases where corporations were held liable even though the corporate employee acted in disregard of specific instructions best demonstrate this minimal interpretation. Commentators who support this broad interpretation argue that it is necessary, since otherwise every corporation could avoid liability by issuing a directive from the board of directors prohibiting all illegal activity. The corporate ethos standard does not disregard the requirement "within the scope of employment;" rather, it is a rigorous application of this requirement. If the ethos of the corporation encouraged the agent to commit the illegal conduct, the agent's acts are within her de facto authority. If the corporate ethos did not encourage her acts, they are outside her authority.

Courts have also interpreted the element "for the benefit of the corporation" almost out of existence. As one court noted, "[t]here have been many cases . . . in which the corporation is criminally liable even though no benefit [to the corporation] has been received in fact." Given current interpretations, all this element now means is that courts cannot hold a corporation liable for the illegal acts of its agents when the corporation is the intended victim of the illegality. Standard Oil Co. v. United States provides an example. Various individuals engaged in a scheme to pump more oil from wells than Texas law allowed. Working with a third party, employees of a Standard subsidiary stole oil from Standard to facilitate the scheme. The United States Court of Appeals for the Fifth Circuit reversed the conviction of Standard and its corporate subsidiary, finding that Standard was the victim of the theft and did not realize a benefit from the illegality.

Even if courts wanted to stringently impose this requirement, it is unclear how they could. It seems impossible to apply literally. For example, if an employee takes bribes for favors to corporate customers, has the corporation benefited? If so, how do courts measure the benefit? Do the disadvantages, such as poor relationships with other customers, a criminal conviction, detrimental publicity, internal dissension, and poor morale, outweigh the benefit?

In conclusion, the corporate ethos standard explicitly retains only the first portion of the traditional requirement that a court can hold a corporation criminally liable only for the conduct of an agent acting within the scope of employment and with the intent to benefit the corporation, namely, that an agent of the corporation perform the criminal act. A corporation should not be liable for every person in the world who might stumble in and use corporate resources to commit a crime. The corporate ethos test does not explicitly include the requirement "within the scope of employment" because simply applying the corporate ethos standard will include this proof. Nor does the corporate ethos standard explicitly require proof that the agent at issue was acting "for the benefit of the corporation." Historically, this requirement has been read into nonexistence with one caveat: Corporate liability cannot result when the corporation itself is the victim of the illegality. This seems to be such an obvious caveat for corporate liability that it needs no emphasizing and certainly does not warrant the currently broad overstatement. Moreover, it is not clear how courts could reasonably apply a "benefit" element. For all of these reasons, the third element of the corporate ethos standard is simply that an agent of the corporation perform the criminal act.

* * *

IV. A RESPONSE TO CRITICS

The corporate ethos standard, like most new proposals for change, will likely draw criticism. This section addresses this potential criticism and explains how these supposed weaknesses are, in some respects, actually strengths. In other respects, the criminal justice system will need to recognize the ramifications of adopting the corporate ethos standard and adjust accordingly.

One likely criticism of the corporate ethos test is that it is not workable. It is, theoretically and practically. Several analogous legal standards that demonstrate courts' effective use of the organizational liability concept already exist.

One analogy is the Pinkerton Rule in conspiracy law. Daniel and Walter Pinkerton were moonshiners in rural Alabama in the 1940s. When Daniel was incarcerated for previous offenses, his brother continued to make the contraband whiskey and failed to pay the applicable taxes. Both Daniel and Walter were thereafter indicted and convicted on conspiracy and tax evasion charges. Both were convicted on the conspiracy charge. Walter was convicted on the substantive tax evasion charges. To Daniel's surprise, so was he even though the alleged tax evasion occurred while Daniel was in jail. On appeal, Daniel argued that he should not be liable for the substantive violations of the tax laws when he clearly could not have committed or even participated in them. The Supreme Court disagreed. It held that because of Daniel's own act of joining the conspiracy and failing to disavow his association with the conspiracy, he became vicariously liable for all substantive offenses that other co-conspirators committed in furtherance of the conspiracy.

Similarly, by a corporation's own act of creating and continuing an ethos that encourages criminal conduct, it becomes liable for the criminal offenses committed by its agents. The corporate ethos standard still employs, of course, vicarious liability since it holds the corporate defendant liable for the acts of others. It is, however, a more fine-tuned form of vicarious liability than the traditional respondeat superior or MPC standards because it alone provides a mechanism for focusing criminal liability only on those corporations that manifest an intent to violate the law.

Another analogy can be found in municipal liability under 42 U.S.C. § 1983, which provides that persons, including fictional persons, who deprive citizens of certain rights are liable to the injured person. In Monell v. New York City Department of Social Services, the Supreme Court held that this section clearly envisions liability of municipal corporations "only where the municipality itself causes the constitutional violation at issue." Section 1983 does not utilize traditional respondeat theory, whereby a municipality can be found liable for an employee's isolated act. Rather, like the corporate ethos standard for corporate criminal liability, it provides a "faultbased analysis for imposing . . . liability." It does so by focusing on the municipal "custom" or "policy" that is the "moving force" of the constitutional deprivation, and imposes liability only if the evidence shows that "some official policy 'causes' an employee to violate another's constitutional rights." Since the Monell decision in 1978, therefore, courts and juries have worked with and applied the notion that a fictional entity can devise a policy that makes it responsible for illegal acts by its employees.

Presumably, commentators will direct the major thrust of their workability criticism at the "ethos" element—namely, that it is not possible to fully, completely, and accurately ascertain a corporate ethos. This is true; it is not possible. But who are we fooling? The criminal law has long imposed a factually impossible burden on the government with its requirement of mens rea. We are accustomed to this burden, however, and so do not easily realize that, truly, direct proof of intent is impossible and we have simply become comfortable with approximations that do not overcome the impossibility of our task. Assume X has been indicted on mail fraud charges for devising a scheme to defraud investors. X's consistent defense is that he never intended to defraud anyone, but his good plans, like many business ventures, simply went awry. Y is indicted for murder. Her consistent defense is that she did not purposely kill the victim; it was an accident. The government will present circumstantial evidence from which fact finders can attempt to infer these defendants' true mental states. In both instances, however, no one – not the grand jury, prosecutor, petit jury, or judge – will ever know what was in X or Y's minds. However, our inability to directly prove intent does not cause us to reject the entire concept, or given sufficient circumstantial evidence, to question whether the fact finders have accurately deduced a person's intent. So it is with corporate ethos. When the government presents sufficient circumstantial evidence, we can and should feel confident in the fact finders' deduction of a corporation's ethos.

Another criticism of the corporate ethos test may be that the government will invade corporate privacy in its search to gather evidence of a corporate ethos that encourages unlawful behavior. In fact, the corporate ethos test would not encourage this invasion of corporate privacy any more than do current standards of liability. In virtually every criminal investigation of corporate misdeeds, the government also investigates the potential criminal liability of corporate officers. To fully investigate this potential individual liability, agents, prosecutors, and the grand jury must delve into the inner machinations of the corporation. Moreover, even when corporate criminal liability (and not individual criminal liability) is the issue and due diligence is allowed as an affirmative defense, the government should fully investigate the inner workings of the corporation for two reasons. The first is to determine if the corporation is indictable. If the corporation will have a strong due diligence defense, it may well be inappropriate for the grand jury to return an indictment. Second, assuming the government will be able to indict the corporation, it will use the investigative resources of the grand jury to gather evidence to overcome any due diligence defense. Thus, criminal investigations of corporate targets have been as broad under current standards as they would be under the corporate ethos test.

A third criticism of the corporate ethos standard may be that using this test will result in fewer criminal prosecutions of corporate defendants. This criticism is probably true, and may appear to be a weakness to those who favor relentless pursuit of miscreant corporations. Upon full reflection, however, critics should see this fact not as a weakness, but as a strength of the standard. Criminal prosecution is only part of the arsenal available to combat corporate misbehavior. Specialized agencies exist to monitor and regulate corporations. An honest appraisal of the limited role that the criminal law should play in regulating corporate misbehavior could help channel additional resources to these agencies. Beyond this, the crucial point of the corporate ethos test is that it will target only the morally culpable corporation for criminal prosecution.

Thus, the corporations indicted will be the "bad" corporations that have demonstrated an intent to violate the law. As such, the exercise of prosecutorial discretion will be more consistent, the sentences rendered will be harsher, and greater deterrence of unlawful behavior will result.

A fourth criticism of the corporate ethos standard – that courts will find it more difficult to administer than current standards of liability – is both a weakness and a strength. In part, the difficulty will stem from unfamiliarity with a new standard of liability. Such difficulty also will stem from the fact that the corporate ethos standard is more fact-sensitive than are the current standards of liability. Assessing the many facets of a corporation's ethos to determine whether it encouraged the particular criminal conduct at issue is a complicated task. Certainly, this inquiry is more complex than simply assessing whether a corporate agent committed the conduct (the traditional respondeat superior test), or whether a high managerial agent performed, authorized, or recklessly tolerated the conduct (the MPC test). In the context of criminal law, however, such sensitivity is a strength, not a weakness. Justice requires the criminal justice system to treat like parties alike. Tests based on crude versions of vicarious liability do not allow for this symmetry. Under the traditional respondeat superior standard of liability, and to a lesser extent, under the MPC standard, it is irrelevant whether a corporation made vigilant efforts to encourage its employees to comply with the spirit as well as the letter of the law, or whether a corporation boldly encouraged its employees to flout the law at every turn. By comparison, the corporate ethos standard of liability strives to distinguish between such corporations, and subjects only the latter to criminal liability.

Another likely criticism and a true weakness in the corporate ethos standard is that by enhancing the efficacy of a particular defense strategy, the corporate ethos standard may encourage executives to falsely incriminate the corporate defendant. Courts can remedy this weakness only by diligent enforcement of sixth amendment rights.

Another valid criticism of the corporate ethos standard is that it addresses only one of the jurisprudential problems concerning corporate criminal liability – intent. The corporate ethos test does not address the issue of what type of conduct the criminal law should focus upon. Murder for hire, kidnapping, rape, and arson for profit are all evil and immoral acts, and most people would agree that public resources and the stigma of the criminal law should be brought to bear on those who commit such acts. Similarly, most people would vehemently oppose legislation that makes criminal the driving of a dirty automobile (however intentionally) or the failure to mow one's grass on a certain schedule (again, however intentionally). We would agree that these trivial matters are unworthy of the resources or power of the criminal law. When the criminal law is turned toward corporate actors, however, the type of conduct appropriate for its attention presents a particularly poignant problem. More so than with individual criminal conduct, the public does not always perceive the conduct for which a corporation is potentially criminally liable as morally bad or evil. Often, the conduct only jeopardizes a particular economic model. Antitrust laws are an example: If corporations willfully engage in certain monopolistic behavior in a market economy, they have committed a crime. By contrast, if business persons in communist economies dare to compete with the government approved monopolies, they have committed a crime. If conduct is truly evil, then surely our perception of it as evil and criminal will not blow with the winds of economic change.

The morally neutral content of many of the criminal statutes that apply to corporations raises a separate jurisprudential problem: How much and how often can the government prosecute corporations for morally neutral behavior (however intentional the behavior), before use of the criminal law becomes inappropriate? An obvious question follows: If the criminal justice system should attempt to reserve the criminal law for morally evil conduct, how are we to decide whether conduct is morally evil?

This Article does not address this morality of conduct controversy beyond noting that when we say the criminal law is to punish only morally culpable behavior we mean two things: that only certain types of conduct should be punished, and then only when such conduct is committed intentionally. These two components are inextricably intertwined. Any progress that this Article makes toward resolving the intent issue is limited until we also resolve the issue of what type of corporate conduct is appropriately subjected to criminal liability.

CONCLUSION

American jurisprudence currently utilizes two general standards for imposing criminal liability on corporations: traditional respondeat superior and the Model Penal Code. The traditional respondeat superior standard holds a corporation liable if any corporate agent committed a criminal offense while acting within the scope of his employment and for the purpose of benefitting the corporation. The MPC standard provides that a corporation is liable if a high managerial agent performed or recklessly authorized the criminal conduct. Both of these standards employ vicarious liability by imputing the intent of an individual corporate agent to the corporation. This Article suggests that proof of intent is too essential to the nature, and power, of the criminal law to employ crude standards of vicarious liability that poorly focus on intent. Just as the notion of intent has evolved in the past, it must continue to evolve if the criminal law is to be used to convict fictional entities.

This Article proposes a new paradigm of corporate intent that builds upon the traditional respondeat superior and MPC standards as well as on criticisms of these approaches. Like both of the current standards, the corporate ethos standard of liability looks to the acts and intent of individuals within the corporation. Like Fisse's notion of reactive corporate fault, the corporate ethos standard looks to the remedial efforts (or lack thereof) that a corporation takes after a first violation. Like the due diligence affirmative defense, the corporate ethos standard considers the corporation's diligence in preventing criminal conduct by its agents. Although all of these factors are relevant under the corporate ethos standard, none is sufficient to determine a corporation's criminal liability. Rather, the fact finder will examine each of these facts, along with a corporation's formal and informal corporate hierarchy, its goals and policies, its compensation scheme, and the education and monitoring it provides for corporate employees. If this examination shows that a corporation whose employees violated the law perpetuated an ethos that encouraged this violation, the corporation is criminally liable for the acts of its agents. If no such ethos exists, the corporation is not criminally liable even though its agents violated the law.

By providing a theoretical and practical framework for identifying and proving corporate intent, the corporate ethos standard of liability offers advantages over our current standards for holding corporations criminally liable. It enhances our ability to distinguish among diverse corporations, and encourages corporations to implement meaningful internal controls that reduce the potential for corporate crime. Further, it compensates for deficiencies in controlling corporate misbehavior through imposing criminal liability on individuals within corporations. Finally, it is practical, workable, and provable from information already available through criminal discovery and trials.

The criminal justice system is a potent vehicle for protecting society and putting lives back on course, but like an old car used to carry too much too far, it will burn out if we force it to do that which it cannot. Accordingly, courts should use the criminal law only for those problems that can benefit from its unique power. Because this power comes from applying the criminal law only to intentional acts, we must respect this limitation in our pursuit of corporate criminal defendants. Historically, however, we have not sought, or proven, corporate intent. As a result, we have done a poor job of policing corporate misdeeds and have squandered the power of the criminal law. The standard of liability proposed in this Article is a conceptual and practical suggestion for remedying this deficiency.

Part II

Punishment

A. White Collar Punishment

Richard A. Posner, *Optimal Sentences For White Collar Criminals,* 17 AM. CRIM. L. REV. 409–418 (1980)*

I have agreed to participate in this symposium because it gives me an opportunity to argue a favorite plank in the economist's platform for reforming the legal system, in a context in which the economic position can be simply but persuasively stated without elaborate argument and evidence. The plank is the substitution, whenever possible, of the fine (or civil penalty) for the prison sentence as the punishment for crime; the appealing context in which to argue the case for such substitution is the punishment of the white collar criminal.

The coiner of the term "white collar crime" defined it "as a crime committed by a person of respectability and high social status in the course of his occupation," but this is not a good definition. The terms "respectability" and "high social status" are ambiguous, and the definition arbitrarily excludes certain white-collar crimes, such as evasion of the personal income tax, which are not committed in the course of one's occupation. More important, it is not an apt definition from the standpoint of sentencing policy, which is the focus of this article.

I shall instead, for reasons that I hope will soon become clear, use the term white-collar crime to refer to the nonviolent crimes typically committed by either (1) well-to-do individuals or (2) associations, such as

* Reprinted by permission of the author and The American Bar Association. © 1980 American Bar Association.

business corporations and labor unions, which are generally "well-to-do" compared to the common criminal. White-collar crime in the sense I use it is illustrated by the criminal offenses created by the securities laws, the labor laws, the antitrust laws, other regulatory statutes, and the income-tax laws. But not every offender under such laws is a white-collar criminal as I use the term. A waitress, for example, could commit a criminal violation of the tax laws by not reporting her tips as income; but because, as we shall see, the affluence of the offender is very important to the correct punishment for the offense, I would not described *her* offense as a white-collar crime. Nor would a murder committed by a wealthy person – or by a criminal gang seeking to monopolize the garbage-collection business of a city, for example – be a white-collar crime; the reason, as again we shall see, is that the proper punishment for a crime of violence raises special questions. To summarize, white-collar crimes are those more likely to be committed by the affluent than by the poor criminal – crimes that involve fraud, monopoly, and breach of faith rather than violence. The white-collar criminal is the affluent perpetrator of those crimes.

The point I wish to argue in this article, an application of the economic analysis of crime and punishment pioneered by Gary Becker, can now be stated simply: the white-collar criminal as I have defined him should be punished only by monetary penalties – by fines (where civil damages or penalties are inadequate or inappropriate) rather than by imprisonment or other "afflictive" punishments (save as they may be necessary to coerce payment of the monetary penalty). In a social cost-benefit analysis of the choice between fining and imprisoning the white-collar criminal, the cost side of the analysis favors fining because, as we shall see, the cost of collecting a fine from one who can pay it (an important qualification) is lower than the cost of imprisonment. On the benefit side, there is no difference in principle between the sanctions.

The fine for a white-collar crime can be set at whatever level imposes the same disutility on the defendant, and thus yield the same deterrence, as the prison sentence that would have been imposed instead. Hence, fining the affluent offender is preferable to imprisoning him from society's standpoint because it is less costly and no less efficacious.

The reason that the fine is the cheaper sanction is that, unlike imprisonment, it is a transfer payment. Because the dollars collected from the criminal as a fine show up on the benefit side of the social ledger, the net social cost is limited to the costs of collecting the fine. A term of imprisonment, on the other hand, yields no comparable social revenue if we disregard the negligible, and nowadays usually zero, output of the prisoner. On the contrary, to the social costs of imprisonment must be added the considerable sums spent on maintaining prisoners. To be sure, for a middle-aged offender, a short prison term might be the deterrent equivalent of a large fine. But it would not follow that the social costs of the short prison term were correspondingly low, because the greater one's income, the greater is the cost of imprisonment in lost earnings. As long as these are earnings in legitimate occupations, their loss is a social cost similar to the cost of the prison guards. The large fine avoids these costs.

I anticipate relatively little disagreement with the proposition that fines are cheaper to society than imprisonment when the offender can pay the fine. I expect great resistance, however, to the proposition that the social *benefits* of punishment are no greater when punishment takes the form of imprisonment than when it takes the form of a fine. It will be argued that there is no money equivalent to the pain of imprisonment, perhaps especially to the affluent, educated, "sensitive" person—the white-collar criminal—that would be within his power to pay. (The offender here is necessarily an individual: a corporation or other "artificial" person cannot, of course, be punished by imprisonment.) But whether this is so depends, in a theoretical analysis, on the gravity of the crime in relation to the probability of apprehension and conviction, and,

in a practical analysis, on the severity of the prison sentences actually imposed for white-collar crimes. As to the first, it is no doubt true that very few people would consider a fine of any size to be as severe a punishment as death, or imprisonment for life, or, perhaps, imprisonment for twenty years. Thus, if these are optimal punishments (putting aside the consideration that imprisonment is more costly to administer), it might indeed be difficult to find a monetary equivalent. Perhaps these are optimal punishments for some white-collar. If so, my proposal to substitute fines for prison for white-collar criminals is in serious difficulty—but only in a rather academic sense. For whatever may be theoretically optimal, white-collar criminals, at least in this country, are not punished by death or long prison terms. Table 1 provides some data on the type and length of sentences for various federal crimes. With the (surprising) exception of securities offenses, the prison sentenced for white-collar crimes—when prison sentences are imposed on the perpetrators of such crime—barely exceed two years. Even this figure greatly exaggerates the actual time served behind bars, which is shortened by parole and time off for good behavior.

Perhaps, as I have suggested, these prison terms are too short given the gravity of the crimes and the difficulty of detecting the. That is a large question that I do not propose to investigate here. I shall instead treat the existing level of imprisonment for white-collar crime as part of the background of the analysis. Given that level, it is highly improbably that there is *no* fine equivalent to a prison sentence in the amount of disutility it imposes on the offender. An individual who has the boldness, the effrontery, to commit a crime—even of the white-collar variety—will have the capacity and inclination to consider realistic trade-offs between 90 days, or even a year or two, in one of the federal system's minimal security prisons and a hefty fine. If he would be deterred by the threat of such a prison sentence, he would be equally deterred by the threat of a $50,000 or $100,000 or $250,000 fine. (And fines could be indexed to prevent inflation from reducing their bite.)

Table 1
Type and Length of Federal Prison Sentences, 1976

Nature of the Offense	Total Def's Sentenced	Number Imprisoned	Average Sentence of Imprisonment (months)	Number Fined Only
Total	40,112	18,478	47.2	3,198
Homicide, total	108	84	125.1	0
Robbery, total	2,286	2,031	134.3	0
Embezzlement, total	1,650	289	22.4	14
Fraud, total	3,691	1,234	22.7	222
Income Tax	1,157	340	15.4	68
Lending Institutions	390	121	18.4	12
Postal	938	404	31.1	37
Securities and Exchange	86	40	45.7	12
Federal Statutes, total	4,208	565	29.7	1,501
Antitrust	175	1	Not shown	137
Food and Drug Act	103	6	Not shown	78
Customs Laws	182	36	19.9	34
Motor Carrier Act	105	0	Not shown	97
Agricultural Acts	459	3.7	20.0	203
Migratory Bird Laws	894	17	Not shown	621
Postal (other than fraud, obscenity, and embezzlement)	1,003	150	7.6	32

It should be noted also that the affluent offender presents interesting opportunities for society to exercise its ingenuity in the collection of fines. For example, a penalty that takes the form of barring the defendant from pursuing his occupation – a penalty frequently used by the SEC in dealing with securities fraud and by state authorities in dealing with misconduct by lawyers – is the equivalent of a fine. The amount of the "fine" is simply the difference between the defendant's future income in the occupation from which he is barred and the income in his best alternative occupation, discounted to present value. This device offers a means of collecting a large fine from an individual who has a large earning capacity but little wealth. An alternative possibility is the collection of a large fine in periodic installments. The availability of these devices enables one to contemplate realistically the possibility of levying very large fines in lieu of the present prison sentences for white-collar crimes.

If it is objected that the schedule of prison-fine equivalences cannot in fact be calculated, there are two replies. The first is that a nice calculation is not required; the prison sentences imposed in white-collar cases – or in any other cases for that matter – are not themselves the product of any nice calculation of the amount of disutility imposed by the sentence on the offender, but are only the roughest of guesses. The second and more interesting reply is that there are in fact methods, imperfect ones to be sure, of empirically tracing out the curve of indifference between fine and imprisonment. One incomplete method would be to calculate directly the costs of imprisonment to the prisoner (primarily in terms of income foregone by him); the other and, I think, more promising method would be to infer statistically the relative deterrent effect of fine and prison. Suppose that in one federal district the average fine for a federal white-collar offense is $1,000 and the average prison term 30 days, and in another district it is $800 and 40 days, and so forth. Then, by comparing the incidence of the offenses across districts, we should be able to infer the rate of exchange at which days in jail translate into dollars of fine with no loss of deterrence. (A study of state white-collar prosecutions, conducted along similar lines, might also be feasible.) Since no such study has been attempted, I cannot evaluate the difficulties it might encounter arising, for example, because the incident of many white-collar crimes (e.g., price-fixing conspiracies) is unknown, or the gravity of the crime may vary across districts or states, which affects the optimal sentence. Such a study might not produce results entitled to great confidence. Nevertheless, supplemented by the intuition that guides judges today in devising fine-prison "packages" to impose on white-collar offenders, such a study should provide a close enough approximation of the actual fine-prison trade-off that we need not fear that by substituting fines for prison sentences in white-collar cases we would be drastically altering the expected punishment cost, and hence the level, of white-collar crime. The substitution could, of course, be made incrementally, one offense at a time, starting with the least important.

Professor Coffee, in his contribution to this sympo-sium, offers three reasons why the threat of imprison-ment is inherently greater than that of a fine. One is that the optimal fine may exceed the offender's ability to pay. While this is certainly possible, it is no reason to prefer imprisonment to fines in cases where offend-ers *can* pay the fines. All I am arguing in this paper is that fines are preferable to imprisonment where the fines are collectible.

Second, Coffee, following Block and Lind, argues that in order to be sure that an offender will pay what-ever fine is levied, he must be threatened with a prison sentence that is more severe than the fine. If there is no different in severity, the offender will be indifferent between the two forms of punishment. This point is correct but does not support Coffee's position. The purpose of imprisonment in Block and Lind's analysis is not to deter the offender but to coerce collection of the fine. The very premise of their proposal is thus the superior economic efficiency of fines to imprison-ment as a method of punishment.

Third, Coffee erects an elaborate argument on Block and Lind's further point that offenders are risk preferrers with regard to imprisonment even if they are risk averters with regard to fines. Coffee compares two probability distributions of punishment having the same mean, one a distribution of prison sentences and the other a distribution of fines, and argues that the latter distribution will be wider (*i.e.* more dispersed) because there is less difference among individuals in the disutility of imprisonment than in the disutility of fines. Coffee argues that, because the offender is a risk preferrer with regard to imprisonment will make imprisonment a less attractive form of punishment than its fine equivalent. Of course, if people are risk averse with regard to fines, as Coffee himself had argued initially in his paper, the greater dispersion of the probability distribution of fines would have a deterrent effect symmetrical to that of the narrower dispersion of the probability distribution of imprison-ment. Yet Coffee retracts his earlier point and argues that offenders will also be risk preferring with regard to the fine distribution, because the opportunities to

conceal assets are greater at the high end of the distri-bution. Therefore, he concludes, the narrower disper-sion of the probability distribution of imprisonment is unequivocally less attractive to offenders.

Every step in Coffee's complicated argument can be questioned, but it is unnecessary to do so because the argument leads nowhere. If it is true, for whatever rea-son, that imprisonment is unpleasant relative to fines – because of a "stigma" effect, or because prison guards are brutal, or because imprisonment interferes with an offender's predilection for taking risks more than fines do – this affects simply the exchange rate between dollars of fine and days of imprisonment and not the choice of which method of punishment to use. If we think that the term of imprisonment for a crime provides the cor-rect amount of deterrence, then in computing the fine equivalent we will want to be sure that we take account of all of the factors that make imprisonment a source of disutility. The fine equivalent is still the cheaper pun-ishment method, however, as long as the fine can be collected from the offender.

I turn now to what seems a separate, but is really the same, objection to substituting fines for imprison-ment in white-collar crimes: namely, that a system in which poor offenders were usually imprisoned and rich offenders usually fined would be a system that discriminated against poor people. This argument is just a variant of the fallacy that imprisonment is inher-ently more punitive than fines. It gains some plausibil-ity only from the ridiculous "rates of exchange" that used to be commonplace in crimes where the criminal had the option of paying a fine or going to jail, a practice that has been invalidated by the Supreme Court under the Equal Protection Clause of the four-teenth amendment. The assumption behind that argu-ment, however, is false. For every prison sentence there is some fine equivalent; if the fine is so large that it cannot be collected, then the offender should be imprisoned. How then are the rich favored under such a system?

A possible answer is that the rich could "buy" more crime under a fine system than under an impris-onment system. Suppose that the expected cost to soci-ety of a crime is $100, the probability of apprehension and conviction is 10 percent, and therefore the fine is set at $1,000 so that expected punishment cost will be equal to the expected social cost. A rich man would not be deterred from committing this crime as long as the expected benefits to him were greater than $1000. But now suppose that instead of a fine of $1000, a prison term of one month is imposed for this crime based on a study which shows that disutility of a month in prison to an average person is $1000. Since the disutility of imprisonment rises with income, this form of punishment will deter the rich man more than the poor one. Stated differently, a nominally uniform prison term has the effect of price discrimination based on income. .

But this is not to say that a system of fines discriminates against the poor. It is rather that a *uniform* prison term discriminates against the rich compared with a *uniform* fine. If we want to discriminate against the rich through a fine system, that is easily done by progressively varying the fine with the offender's income. If we want not to discriminate against the rich through an imprisonment system, we can make the length of the sentence inverse to the offender's income. In either case the choice to discriminate is independent of the form of the punishment.

Professor Coffee is of course not alone in disregarding the "equivalence principle" developed above. It is commonly disregarded both in discussions of punishment for white-collar criminals, and in the assumption that only the threat of imprisonment will deter white-collar crime. For example, a survey of merchants "revealed that they considered imprisonment [for black market violations] a far more effective penalty than any other government action, including fines." Findings like these have led some criminologists to consider imprisonment and fines incommensurable sanctions. Yet in the same analysis we read that a company found to have committed black market violations involving 300,000 pounds of meat in a five-month period received a total fine of $1,500; the profit from the violations seems to have been at least $25,000.

Where fines are trivial, it is natural to suppose that only substantial jail sentences will carry a "stigma" effect which adds to deterrence. Yet even if, improbably, imprisonment produced a stigma effect which no magnitude of fine could duplicate, only the rate of exchange between fine and imprisonment, and not the principle of equivalence, would be affected. The fine equivalent would then be higher than if a fine carried a stigma as well. But, in fact, the presence of stigma is an argument for fines rather than for prison sentences. Most students of the criminal process locate the source of the stigma in the fact of conviction rather than the form of the sentence. The more punishment society obtains simply from the stigmatizing effect of conviction, the smaller the fine that must be imposed to produce the optimal severity of punishment; and the smaller the fine, the less likely it is to exceed the white-collar criminal's ability to pay.

The existence of a stigma of conviction bears on the question, why, if a money sanction is adequate, is criminal punishment necessary at all? Why not rely entirely on money damages, as in a civil action? If the stigma arises either because the action is brought by the state and denominated as criminal, or because the higher standard of proof for criminal cases makes it less likely that a convicted defendant is really innocent, then it would be lost if civil penalties were substituted for criminal fines. Of course, the latter aspect of the stigma effect could be preserved simply by increasing the standard of proof in a civil penalty suit to the criminal level.

I am not entirely happy with this answer, however, and not only because I think the stigma or moral revulsion that attaches to certain conduct does so because of the nature of the conduct rather than the fact that it is labeled criminal or proceeded against by the criminal process. The economic objection to relying on stigma for deterrence is that, like imprisonment, it is more costly to society than the pure fine (or civil penalty) because it does not yield any revenue. (Stigma, unlike a fine, imposes costs on the criminal with no corresponding gain to society.) Hence, it would seem more efficient to drop the criminal label, and any stigma attached to it, and offset any loss in disutility to the criminal by increasing the size of the civil penalty. In that way, the social revenue can be increased with no loss of deterrence.

In fact a good deal of punishment is meted out in civil penalty suits. The example with which I am most familiar is the treble-damage action in antitrust cases, in which two-thirds of every damage award is in effect a fine—often a much higher one than the statutory maximum for a criminal antitrust suit—albeit the fine is paid to the plaintiff rather than to the state. I am inclined to think that the civil penalty is superior to the criminal fine as a method of punishing white-collar criminals. Whether the penalty should be paid to a private plaintiff or to the state, however, should depend on the relative efficiency of private and public enforcement in particular contexts, an issue discussed elsewhere. But I am straying into the question of decriminalization. My subject is the sentencing of white-collar criminals, which assume that some white-collar offenses should, or at least will, continue to be dealt with by the criminal process. If the criminal sanction is to be retained in this area, then, as I have argued in this article, fines should be substituted for prison sentences when the optimal fine is within the power of the offender to pay. In principle, this position could, and I think should, be extended beyond the white-collar domain to include the non-white-collar crimes that the affluent occasionally commit. The problem is that while some of these crimes, such as murder, are so serious that even the affluent cannot pay adequate fines, not all white-collar crimes are less serious than crimes of violence. Nevertheless, the most serious white-collar crimes are probably committed by corporations rather than by individuals. Within this corporate category, the gravity of the offense is probably more or less proportional to the size of the company, so solvency limitations should not preclude the imposition of very large fines for white-collar crime where such fines are optimal.

The reference to corporations brings me to the final point that I want to make in this article. It concerns the case for a different approach to crimes committed by individuals acting as agents for corporations or other associations rather than acting on their own behalf. There is an argument that I have made elsewhere in this antitrust context for confining criminal (or civil-penalty) liability to the corporation, on the theory that if it is liable it will find adequate ways of imposing on its employees the costs to it of violating the law. Of course, this assumes the existence of an adequate set of sanctions, capable of hurting the corporation for its violations of the law. Perhaps this is too quixotic an assumption or aspiration (outside of the antitrust context) to support so radical a proposal. I mention it only to make clear that the adoption of such a proposal would still leave a wide area in which one would want to retain criminal or civil-penalty sanctions for white-collar crime as I have defined it; for not all white-collar crimes are the work of corporations—and in the area of income tax, for example, not most. But wherever and for whatever reason it is decided to retain criminal sanctions for individual white-collar offenders, the movement should be toward the abolition of imprisonment and the substitution of fines—albeit fines more severe than those today meted out to such offenders.

John C. Coffee, Jr., *Corporate Crime and Punishment: A Non-Chicago View of the Economics of Criminal Sanctions,* 17 AM. CRIM. L. REV. 420–439, 449–465, 468–471 (1980)*

Among economists, the tide of academic imperialism has reached full flood. No longer content to focus the tools of their profession on the traditional problems

* Reprinted by permission of the author and The American Bar Association. © 1980 American Bar Association.

of economics, over the last dozen years they have begun to analyze aspects of human behavior not characterized by market transactions. In so doing, economists have applied their central premise that individuals engaged in utility-maximizing behavior to such diverse fields as family planning, political participation, altruism, and crime.

Predictably, the reaction of the academic legal community to these colonizing ambitions has been mixed and perhaps even defensive. Few would deny that the contributions made by the economists have been serious, provocative, and original. But it disquiets many to watch the easy facility with which the economist moves across fields of knowledge to apply his approach and reach policy conclusions that tend to be strikingly inconsistent with those long held within the field. Such omniscience raises doubts. One has a sense approaching that of watching Howard Cosell broadcast on successive nights a boxing match, Monday Night Football, and the World Series; as the speaker moves farther and farther from his field of expertise, thin spots in his knowledge appear, overgeneralizations multiply, and, progressively, the descriptions seem less and less to match the events actually occurring in the arena.

These skeptical comments do not deny that the field of criminal law scholarship has long stood in need of the kind of rigorous cost-benefit examination that the economist can offer. Indeed, this article will attempt to develop an essentially economic analysis of criminal sanctions. But, if the lawyer tends to accept uncritically the traditional assumptions of criminal law, there is a countervailing bias in the economist's approach. Recurrently, there seems to be an unwillingness to acknowledge that the economic approach is essentially an analytic language—hereinafter called "EcoSpeak"—rather than any set of deductively derived policy conclusions. Yet, despite the seeming precision with which this language speaks, those fluent in EcoSpeak have sometimes disagreed diametrically in applying its reasoning to the criminal law. In truth, this should be reassuring, rather than surprising, for it is exactly this latitude within the economic approach that distinguishes it from a cult. In the social sciences, rigid models tend to be short-lived, but perspectives endure. Thus, to argue, as this article will, that no single model can legitimately claim to be *the* economic theory of criminal sanctions is not to condemn the economic approach, but rather to suggest that EcoSpeak has an enduring relevance which transcends the uses to which it has been put by its truest believers.

Modern efforts to develop an economic theory for the optimal use of criminal sanctions essentially began with the work of University of Chicago Professor

Gary Becker. In essence, Becker has propounded a "cost minimization" model that recognizes three general types of costs associated with crime: (1) the social costs that result from the illegal conduct; (2) the punishment costs that result from the imposition of a sanction upon the offender; and (3) the transaction costs to the judicial system that are associated with apprehending and punishing offenders. Whether these are the only costs which should be considered will be examined later, but from this definition of the relevant costs the Becker model can proceed to its basic assertion: an optimal system of criminal justice reduces the aggregate of these costs to a minimum. Inherently, such a model requires trade-offs, because reducing one type of cost (*e.g.*, the cost to the victim) will not reduce the aggregate cost if in so doing another cost component is increased by a more than corresponding margin. From such a perspective focused on getting the "biggest bang for the buck," a number of trade-offs become evident:some forms of criminal sanctions may be more expensive than others; it may be more costly to achieve a high apprehension rate than to punish severely those few who are apprehended; the harmful effects of some crimes may be less than the enforcement costs necessary to deter them. The temptation arises to draw some fairly obvious policy conclusions from the Becker model and proclaim them the fruit of economic reasoning. Indeed, although Professor Becker has surrounded his own conclusions with a number of careful qualifications, his disciples have begun to treat his model as a set of policy prescriptions which are ready for implementation. As so modified, this theory for the optimal use of criminal sanctions—which this article will call the Free Market Model—has three basic tenets, each of which contradicts the conventional wisdom which both criminal lawyers and criminologists have long shared:

1. *The Preferred Form of Sanction*: Fines are seen as the optimal form of criminal sanction, superior to incarceration, because imprisonment wastes both society's resources and the offender's productive capacity. Thus, confinement is a sanction of last resort to be used only when the offender either will not or cannot pay an adequate fine.

2. *The Appropriate Cost-Bearer*: When crimes are committed on behalf of an organization, the organization, rather than the individual who actually engages in the criminal act, should pay the fine. (The assumption here is that the organization will discipline its agent if it is in its interest to do so.) In addition, some economists also argue that this fine should be the exclusive penalty, precluding even the award of civil damages, because the potential availability of

damages creates a "perverse incentive" leading claimants to misrepresent their injuries and to extort settlements.

3. *The Certainty-Severity Trade-Off*: In general, high penalties are favored over more vigorous law enforcement. That is, it is asserted to be more cost efficient to raise the severity of the sanction than the probability of conviction, because society can incarcerate more cheaply than it can apprehend additional offenders.

It is an understatement to call such a model counter-intuitive. More accurately, it is a profound attach on traditional criminal law scholarship, one that almost seems to gain a perverse delight in reversing assumptions that have stood since the times of Bentham and Beccaria. No doubt, the practical lawyer is inclined to respond to such contentions in the manner of Dickens' Mr. Bumble, but the consistent response of the Chicago school to its critics has been that the test of a model is its ability to predict, not the plausibility of its premises.

Cogent as this claim may seem, the present state of empirical knowledge does not permit either side to claim more than fragmentary evidence in its favor. Thus, in the absence of unambiguous data (a situation likely to persist), it is necessary to focus on the internal logic of the Free Market Model. This article will do so partly as a primer, because criminal justice policy planning cannot continue to ignore the possible relevance of economic analysis. The larger objective of this inquiry, however, will be to demonstrate that the Free Market Model is not *the* economic theory of criminal sanctions, but only *an* economic theory. Moreover, it is an economic theory which seems flawed once we introduce both traditional elements of economic analysis (such as uncertainty) and noneconomic factors that are deeply embedded in the structure of our criminal justice system (such as the tendency toward nullification of extreme penalties). These factors, however, can be introduced into a rational-actor model for the "criminal choice" decision. Once this is done, the method of economic analysis seems to lead to policy conclusions quite different from those of the Free Market Model. Dramatic differences emerge from only modest differences in premises. From a starting point only marginally different from that of the Free Market Model, this article will assert that economic analysis tends to support the following propositions:

(1) the threat of incarceration typically will have a greater deterrent value than the threat of a fine;
(2) more deterrence is generated by penalties focused on an individual than on an organization; and
(3) the *certainty* of a sanction is, within the context discussed, more important than its *severity*.

Professor Posner, in his contribution to the Symposium, summarizes this article's arguments in a manner that I believe misrepresents them. To unmuddy the waters thus clouded, several prefatory comments are in order.

First, this article does not assert that monetary equivalents to incarceration cannot exist. Within the sentencing ranges authorized for organizational crime, it is likely that monetary sanctions exist that are even more severe than the typically symbolic sentences of imprisonment which are imposed for such crimes. Actual severity, however, is not synonymous with the notion of a legal threat. This article will suggest that the notion of a legal threat must be developed (at least in the case of the rational potential offender) in terms of a "mean/variance" analysis of the total range of penalties applicable to the offender. From this premise, it will be deduced that: (1) the legal threat inherent in any realistic range of incarcerative penalties will generally exceed that applicable to the range of monetary penalties authorized for the same crime; and (2) the greater threat associated with incarcerative penalties cannot be efficiently offset simply by increasing the severity of authorized monetary penalties.

Second, beyond a simple rebuttal of the Free Market Model, this article attempts to outline the conditions necessary to maintain a mixed system having different forms of criminal sanctions without sacrificing the additional deterrence of incarceration. This essentially involves developing an arbitrage-like mechanism to reduce the disparity in the threat potential of fines and imprisonment. In so doing, it is acknowledged that there are some advantages, such as victim compensation, which fines uniquely offer.

Third, because criminologists are increasingly skeptical of deterrence theories that are not "crime specific," it should be stressed that the model here offered is advanced only within the context of organizational crime. In this context, we can largely discount the traditional reply of the skeptic to the theorist seeking to explain crime: *i.e.*, that crime is a complex, nonrational phenomenon, too deeply rooted in the individual's psychopathology or in sociological forces to be explained by rationalistic criteria. As valid as this generalization may sometimes be, it seems here more an intellectual crutch than a rebuttal. If ever the rational-actor model employed by the economist has predictive power with regard to criminal behavior, it is in the context of organizational crime that its explanatory capacity is greatest. Within this context, the typical offenses (price-fixing, tax fraud, securities, and other regulatory violations) scarcely amount to "crimes of passion," carry relatively little stigma, and are committed by individuals who neither come from deprived backgrounds nor act out of uncontrollable impulses. Far more comprehensible and easily deterred motivations – personal gain and organizational loyalty – appear to supply adequate causal explanations.

The term "organizational crime" is here used in preference to the more widely known phrase of "white-collar crime" because the latter term includes both the individual who commits a crime against an organization (*e.g.*, an embezzler) as well as the individual who commits a crime for an organization (*e.g.*, the price fixer). Important distinctions exist between these two types. It is the second type, the "organizational criminal," who will be the principal object of our study, because his crimes seem more likely to be planned collectively and with fuller consideration of the respective costs and benefits.

I. THE ORGANIZATIONAL CRIMINAL AND BR'ER RABBIT'S BRIAR PATCH: UNCLE REMUS LOOKS AT THE CHOICE OF CRIMINAL SANCTIONS

Debates about the relative merits of fines versus incarceration as criminal sanctions usually involve one side focusing on relative costs and the other on relative benefits. Those favoring greater reliance on fines make the following arguments: (1) fines are cheaper to society, because they do not involve the costs of a prison system; (2) fines can be used to compensate the victim, either through direct restitution or by funding a more generalized victim compensation system, thereby reducing the costs to the victim and easing the burden on civil courts; and (3) fines, which are in essence only transfer payments, do not involve the "dead weight" loss on society that occurs when a productive individual is incarcerated. Although the concept of reduced social productivity may be taken much more seriously by economists than by the legal community, some cases can certainly be posited in which it merits attention (for example, when the sole doctor in a rural town is convicted of Medicaid fraud).

The proponents of incarceration can be equally succinct:

(1) fines will be "passed on" to the organization, either through indemnification payments or covert increases in salary or fringe benefits, thereby undercutting the deterrent effect of the penalty; (2) although fines may provide deterrence, they do not incapacitate the dangerous offender – a point which may seem irrelevant in this area of non-violent crime, but which still may deserve some weight once the statistics on "corporate recidivism" are examined; (3) even if a monetary equivalent to imprisonment exists, courts could never accurately determine the trade-offs and would waste considerable time and resources in the attempt; and (4) reliance on fines is so demonstrably discriminatory against the poor that, even if constitutional, it would exacerbate social antagonisms along predictable class and racial lines.

Overshadowing these arguments, however, is a more fundamental issue:are fines and imprisonment equivalent deterrents? On this issue, a legion of legal commentators have confidently asserted that only the threat of imprisonment can truly deter the businessman. If such assertions could be cited as evidence, the case against fines would be strong indeed. In general, however, little is cited in support of this contention beyond anecdotal experiences and personal beliefs.

Equally dogmatic, the classical economist asserts that for any period of imprisonment there is a monetary equivalent. To the majority of non-economists, this "insight" sounds suspiciously like an *ipse dixit*. But here, the economist is simply carrying the idea of the indifference curve to its logical extreme. An indifference curve does nothing more than plot a series of trade-offs between two goods or outcomes between which the individual has no preference. Thus, an individual can be extremely averse to imprisonment and even highly sensitive to small increases in the length of a sentence; yet a monetary equivalent could exist.

As Diagram A illustrates, only an extraordinarily severe fine could make a wealthy offender prefer confinement, and only enormous decreases in the size of the fine could tempt him to accept small increases in the length of confinement. Nonetheless, the hypothetical individual whose trade-offs are represented by this curve can be said to be "indifferent" among the following outcomes, which are each plotted as a point on the curve: (a) a two million dollar fine and no imprisonment, (b) a one-year sentence and no fine, (c) a $500,000 fine and a six-month sentence, and (d) a one million dollar fine and a three-month sentence. Such an analysis does not deny that there may be periods of imprisonment for which monetary equivalents do not exist, but posits that within some ranges trade-offs are possible. At present, both the authorized and actual sentences of imprisonment applicable to organizational crime are extremely low. Given, for example, that the longest prison

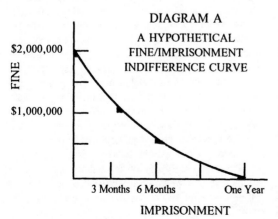

DIAGRAM A
A HYPOTHETICAL FINE/IMPRISONMENT INDIFFERENCE CURVE

FINE

$2,000,000

$1,000,000

3 Months 6 Months   One Year

IMPRISONMENT

sentence actually served by a "white-collar" offender convicted of price-fixing has never exceeded one year, it must be conceded that there is an equally severe monetary penalty for such a sentence, even if one still doubts that there would be a monetary equivalent for, say, a ten-year sentence. Consider, for example, a typical senior executive of a large corporation who is nearing retirement and over a forty-year career has accumulated a substantial estate. If the choice were between a three-month period of confinement and a $500,000 fine, he could well choose the former, because the accumulation of a sizable personal fortune may have been his dominant life goal (both in order to enjoy it during retirement and to pass it on to his heirs).

Little is resolved, however, by conceding that there can be a monetary equivalent to imprisonment. It is still possible to see the sanction of fines as the equivalent of Br'er Rabbit's Briar Patch—*i.e.*, the option which the offender will prefer even though he may protest much to the contrary.

To explain this statement, it is necessary to introduce the concept of the probability dispersion. Put simply, when a potential offender evaluates the risk of his actions, he does not assume that he will receive the average sentence; rather, he must face the possibility that, if convicted, he may receive any sentence within the authorized range. Thus, there is a conceptual flaw in using the indifference curve as the starting point from which to analyze the deterrent effect of different criminal sanctions. The fallacy arises because the indifference curve ignores the uncertainty that the potential offender faces when he analyzes the costs and benefits of criminal behavior. Inevitably, there exists a range of authorized possible penalties for a particular crime (*e.g.*, zero to three years for price fixing). As a result, even if it were true that there existed a monetary equivalent for an incarcerative sentence authorized by the legislature, it does not follow that the probability dispersion for authorized fines would be congruent with that for incarceration. Further, even if the two probability dispersions had the same expected mean value (*i.e.*, weighted average), it would still not necessarily follow that they had equivalent deterrent effects because of an additional factor called "variance" (which is simply a measure of the dispersion of outcomes around the mean).

These two factors—mean value and variance—are the central elements in the approach of standard microeconomic theory to the problem of valuing a probability dispersion. If we assume a rational hypothetical offender, then these elements should also be central to his analysis of the potential cost to him of criminal behavior. Yet, they are ignored by an approach that looks not at the risk the prospective criminal confronts before the commission of a crime, but only examines the ability of the sentencing court to find a monetary penalty that is as severe as the incarcerative sentence it would otherwise impose. In short, any analysis that starts by postulating an indifference curve between specific penalties (*e.g.*, a tariff of specific fines and/or terms of imprisonment) has fallen into the error of looking at the criminal choice decision retrospectively rather than prospectively. What actually confronts the potential offender is not a fixed tariff of penalties, but a fundamental uncertainty as to what the penalty will be within a range of possibilities. It is this dispersion which must be valued in order to determine the deterrent effect of criminal sanctions under a rational-actor model.

This critique of the Free Market Model will become clearer after a more detailed examination of the basic economic theory for decision-making under conditions of uncertainty. Following this primer, this article will turn to the real world structure of the probability dispersions for fines versus imprisonment and, ultimately, to the theoretical context in which the two dispersions have the same mean value. The fundamental premise underlying this inquiry can, however, be simply stated: the deterrent threat of the law comes not from the *specific* sanction that the court imposes, nor even from the *modal* (*i.e.*, most likely) sanction it may impose, but from the *range* of possible penalties it could impose. From this premise, it becomes possible to proceed to two important conclusions: (1) the dispersion associated with incarceration will have a greater mean value, and, therefore, a higher deterrent threat; and (2) the rational offender's attitude toward risk will differ according to the type of sanction that is to be employed, because of the differing marginal utilities between additional increments of incarceration and fines.

C. An Initial Summary and Response to Posner

The argument to this point has been that the threat of incarceration would have a greater deterrent value than the threat of fines even if the authorized ceilings on fines were infinitely high. The collectability boundary implies that the degree to which the offender can be threatened by monetary penalties is necessarily lower than in the case of incarcerative sanctions. This conclusion, as I argue below, is also supported by the difficulty that society would have in compelling payment of a monetary penalty which was in fact more severe than the highest authorized incarcerative penalty. A more severe incarcerative range must be authorized to enforce the imposition of fines, because, in the absence of such a higher threat, the rational offender would simply refuse to pay the fine and

thereby elect imprisonment. No reliance, however, has yet been placed on arguments about the psychology of the offender (*i.e.*, is he a risk averter or preferrer?) because we have been basically dealing with the case in which one dispersion has a higher mean than the other.

In his article, Professor Posner argues that the foregoing argument leads "nowhere" because, even if it were true that the range of incarcerative sanctions applicable to a crime had a higher mean value, the state can simply adjust by changing the rate of exchange between fines and imprisonment. He also claims that this argument means only that some individuals cannot pay an optimal fine, but that it has no implication with respect to those cases in which the offender can pay such a fine. To reply, it is best to start by placing Posner's arguments into a concrete example. Let us assume that a given offender would be indifferent between two fixed sanctions, both of which are adequate to deter him: one year in prison or a fine of $50,000. However, because the crime is punishable not by a fixed penalty, but by a range of potentially applicable penalties (hypothetically: zero to ten years or, alternatively, zero to $250,000), the offender is more deterred by the incarcerative sentencing range, which (we will assume) has a higher expected punishment cost because its ceiling is perceived by him to be considerably higher. Posner's answer to this, I take it, would be to impose whatever higher fine (perhaps $150,000) carried the same threat as the incarcerative sentencing range, even if this results in the imposition of a fine that is more severe, standing apart as a single fixed penalty, than the one-year sentence with which we originally would have been satisfied. Thus, the offender is once again indifferent between the two threats, and, because fines are asserted to have other advantages, they should be preferred.

Logical as this may sound, there are several serious flaws in this analysis. First, there may be no monetary equivalent for the discounted value of the incarcerative threat. For example, under the proposed recodification of the Federal Criminal Code recently reported out by the Senate Judiciary Committee, the maximum terms of imprisonment for Class A, B and C felonies are life, twenty years and ten years, respectively. If the reader's intuition matches my own, he will doubt that there is a monetary equivalent to any of these sentences. Granted that such penalties are seldom imposed, they nonetheless raise the discounted value of the incarcerative threat—particularly if the potential offender is a risk averter (who by definition focuses on the maximum penalty in making the criminal choice). In this sense, incarcerative sentencing ranges provide a kind of "cheap" deterrence by barking more than they bite.

Second, the collectability boundary constitutes an even more serious barrier to the kind of exchange rate adjustments that Posner thinks can offset the greater threat latent in the incarcerative penalty structure. Posner appears to regard the collectability boundary as just another way of saying that some individuals cannot afford to pay the optimal fine. But this is too simple. Almost certainly there are individuals who can afford, but who cannot be compelled, to pay an optimal fine. Because they can hide assets, divert expected income, overstate expenses or hire superior legal talent to resist collection efforts, they can shelter a significant portion of their total wealth from the court. This will result in the court both underestimating the optimal fine (assuming, as I do, that the court will wish to fit the fine to the offender) and granting subsequent motions for a downward modification.

In general, the greater the residual wealth sheltered by the collectability boundary, the weaker will be the deterrent threat of a fine. In part, this is because, whatever the level of authorized fines, the relevant legal threat extends only to this boundary. In contrast, the threat of incarceration for most felonies extends beyond both this boundary and the further point at which monetary equivalents cease to exist. In addition, this boundary accentuates the effect of the declining marginal utility of money because it prevents us from approaching the bottom dollar where the loss will be felt most deeply. If this premise is accepted, then the impact of a fine must be examined in terms not of its absolute size, nor even of its relative size in proportion to the offender's total wealth, but rather of the remainder of the offender's wealth after the fine is imposed. A proportionate fine (e.g., 50% of the offender's existing assets) is thus almost as discriminatory as a flat fine (e.g., $25,000 because it takes the low-or middle-income offender closer to his bottom dollar, and represents for him a subjectively greater sanction. In theory, this could be compensated for by adopting a progressive schedule (e.g., a 70% fine for the wealthier offender, 50% for the middle income, and 25% for the poor). But here the collectability boundary interferes by in effect setting a ceiling on exchange rate adjustments. Indeed, under a system of severe fines, it might even produce regressive taxation because the level of the collectability boundary is arguably higher for the wealthier offender (whose assets tend to be less visible and who can afford the legal costs of resisting collection). Thus, with respect to Posner's article, the irony here is that the concept of the collectability boundary is not just another way of saying that fines do not adequately deter those who cannot pay them; rather, it implies that those most able to pay them will be the least threatened by them.

Still another problem lurks in any attempt to construct a schedule of financial penalties carrying the same deterrent threat as incarceration:as a matter of geometric necessity, any such schedule would have to employ very high mandatory minimum penalties. If there are some incarcerative penalties for which a monetary equivalent does not exist (e.g., 20 years), then the fine schedule would have to start at a higher floor in order to offset this higher ceiling for incarcerative penalties and produce the same mean. For example, while the incarcerative schedule of penalties might start at well below one year and extend to ten years, the lowest financial penalty might have to be the equivalent of three years if both dispersions were to have the same threat. This is the flaw in the assumption that exchange rate adjustments between time and money can be easily made: the result of attaining the same deterrent threat through fines is the loss of flexibility through the adoption of a rigid penalty structure with high mandatory minimum fines. In order to deter wealthy offenders, we would have to provide for minimum fine levels that would deprive them of a significant portion of their assets. This could be achieved either by enacting mandatory fines (e.g., $1,000,000) or by requiring that the fine be equal to a minimum percentage of the offender's assets (e.g., 50%). Either way, the result is a substantially greater burden on the less wealthy offender (given the declining marginal utility of money). Politically, it asks the legislature to create a separate sentencing alternative for only the wealthiest class of offenders. In short, to be assured of the equivalent effectiveness of fines, we would have to focus the penalty structure on what would be a small percentage of offenders. Even then, the risk averter would prefer the fine penalty structure because it would have less variance than that associated with incarceration.

Finally, Professor Posner seems to assume that the state can, at no cost to itself, change the rate of exchange between dollars and time served in prison. In fact, the empirical evidence suggests that the default rate increases with the size of the fine. This default rate is already high enough (apparently around 40% in federal courts) to suggest that very high enforcement costs would be incurred if we were to simultaneously raise and seek to collect the average fine. If the use of fines appears cheaper today, this may be in large part because we do not make a more serious effort to collect them.

A theoretical case remains to be considered: what if the probability dispersion for fines had the same or an even greater mean value than that pertaining to incarceration? Because this could only occur in an unlikely world, one in which the collectability boundary did not exist, a detailed analysis will be deferred.

Suffice it to say that even if the mean values were the same for the two dispersions, the extreme variance which would have to be structured into the fine dispersion to achieve this result would probably make a rational offender prefer being subjected to the exterior fine dispersion over the interior incarceration dispersion. As a probable risk preferrer in this context, he would be more deterred by the incarceration penalty structure, which would have a relatively narrower range (*i.e.*, less variance) in terms of the possible penalties as he subjectively perceived them. If we further extended the dispersion for fines to give it a higher mean value than that for incarceration, we encounter an enforcement problem:the rational offender should not comply unless there is a greater threat (*i.e.*, incarceration held in reserve).

II. THE COSTS OF SANCTIONS

Even if the deterrent benefits of incarceration exceed that of fines, their respective costs still must be weighed. Four distinct topics will be examined in this section: (1) the judicial and transaction costs associated with imposing the appropriate sanction; (2) the feasibility of the Free Market Model's formula of determining the optimal penalty; (2) the "passing on" question — *i.e.*, on whom does the incidence of a financial penalty actually fall; and (4) the issue of demoralization costs — *i.e.*, are there costs beyond those recognized by a cost-minimization model? The answers this article reaches will again find the conventional wisdom more right than wrong.

III. THE INDIVIDUAL OR THE ORGANIZATION: WHO SHOULD BEAR THE COSTS?

A distinctive feature of organizational crime is that it is committed by agents for the primary benefit of a principal. Axiomatically, although the corporation must act through its agents, the profit accrues primarily to the firm and its owners. Thus, the cost of deterring the agent may be less than that of deterring the firm. Not only will the organization incur greater gain from crime than will its agents, but, if there exists no monetary equivalent to a harsh prison sentence, then the organization also faces a lesser deterrent threat.

In terms of a cost-effective strategy, therefore, it seems strange that the Free Market economists agree that the organization should be the cost bearer. It may be revealing that they give substantially different reasons why this should be so. Elzinga and Breit use as their starting point the persistent unwillingness of the federal courts to impose imprisonment on antitrust violators, even in blatant cases of price fixing. They noted that, as of 1976, no such organizational offender appeared to have ever served as much as a year in prison. This pattern has continued even though the

Antitrust Division now regularly submits a sentencing memorandum recommending imprisonment. They attribute this phenomenon to the court's lack of confidence that it has the truly culpable official before it; perhaps, they suggest, the court fears that a subordinate official is "taking the rap" for those higher up.

Here, Elzinga and Breit appear to have overstated their case. Judicial doubts about the true locus of the criminal decision within the organization may play a role in sentencing patterns, but probably not a decisive one. Not only does the experience of Watergate suggest that subordinates do "spill the beans" when facing imprisonment, but judges frequently articulate a variety of plausible reasons to explain their reluctance to imprison executives.

First, judges are understandably concerned about the health and safety of the defendant. To commit middle-aged and physically weak offenders to a closed society in which they are likely to be at the mercy of others who are younger, stronger, and violence-prone is not self-evidently to treat them "equally." It is a strange notion of equality that requires the lion and the lamb to be placed in the same cage. Second, the sentiment exists (however debatable it may be) that the "white-collar" offender has already suffered enough, to a degree not matched by other defendants, because of the greater stigmatization and loss of status incident to his conviction. Third, little consensus exists among judges (or anyone else) on the relative gravity of "white-collar" crimes. Finally, judges inevitably may sympathize with those whose background and community position match their own.

None of these justifications, however, necessarily leads to the conclusion that it is unfair to punish any party other than the firm. In addition, there is some evidence that courts have resisted heavy penalties in the case of the corporate defendant as much as they have resisted the use of incarceration in the case of the individual defendant:the typical fine imposed on corporations for antitrust violations, for example, has been ludicrously low. Thus, the factor of judicial nullification emphasized by Elzinga and Breit cuts both ways.

Professor Posner, using a more traditional economic analysis, argues that because the firm is the decision-maker, it is the firm's utility function, not the individual's, that should be altered. From this perspective, the individual is little more than an anonymous cog within the firm, and if he misbehaves in a manner adverse to the firm, the firm will discipline or fire him.

There are several counter-arguments to this analysis. First, as already noted, it may be less expensive to punish the individual rather than the organization, because the individual's expected benefit is lower. Second, because the corporation is better positioned than the individual to pass along the cost in the form of higher prices, it will be less deterred. Attempts by the state to impose higher penalties against the corporation may also require higher transaction costs, because the corporate defendant may be expected to expend more resources resisting conviction. In contrast, the transaction costs associated with mounting a legal defense are far more significant to the individual defendant, who accordingly has a greater incentive to plea-bargain. Thus, it may be more cost efficient to focus on the individual decision-maker.

Third, there is little evidence that fines in fact trigger any internal disciplinary mechanism within the firm, even if they should do so in theory. In the electrical equipment price fixing conspiracy of the late 1950's, the convicted defendants were eventually obliged to settle civil actions by paying approximately $600 million to the private plaintiffs. Despite criminal trials, congressional investigations, derivative suits, and research by a legion of journalists, no credible evidence was uncovered linking senior executives of any of the major corporations to the conspiracy. On the contrary, the participants were basically middle level managers who hid their involvement from their superiors. According to Professor Posner's theory, the organization is expected in such a situation to discipline the individuals who have exposed it to such an extraordinary loss by firing them. Rarely would there have been greater justification for such an action.

But what in fact happened? Westinghouse "imposed absolutely no disciplinary treatment upon the individuals responsible." General Electric demoted some and asked for the resignation of others, but retained still others who had been convicted. The other corporate conspirators appear to have taken no punitive action against any employees. Even those fired by General Electric were able to find similar positions in other firms. Thus, even in the case when the organization had disciplined the employee, there is reason to doubt that he has suffered a sufficiently significant penalty to deter others from engaging in future frolics and detours. In overview, the loyalty shown by the corporations involved in the electrical equipment conspiracy to their convicted employees was remarkable: most were retained even in the face of derivative suits against their corporation's directors for negligent supervision, and shareholder proxy proposals seeking their dismissal were soundly defeated. Those convicted generally were seen as unfortunate scapegoats who merited special treatment by their companies— in effect, corporate prisoners of war.

This same pattern is reflected in the experience of corporations convicted of offenses growing out of the Watergate investigation. A follow-up survey in 1975 by the *New York Times* found that "most of the 21 business executives who admitted their guilt" to the Special Prosecutor were "still presiding over these companies."

V. CONCLUSION

Among the principal points advanced by this article have been the following:

(1) The threat counts more than the penalty. In order to determine the deterrent effect of a legal sanction in a world of uncertainty, one must consider the entire range of outcomes with which the offender was *threatened,* not simply the penalty *imposed.* As a result, simple exchange rate adjustments between the size of the fine and the length of a prison sentence are not feasible, because, to increase the deterrent threat of the fine as a criminal sanction, one must impose not simply a higher fine in an individual case, but rather one must increase the mean value of the entire probability dispersion for fines.

(2) From this perspective, fines will generally lack the deterrent value of incarceration because the range of the threatened sanction in the case of imprisonment typically exceeds that of fines. This difference is not merely a quirk of existing statutory structures. Rather, a variety of factors prevent us from structuring an equivalent range into the penalty distribution for fines: (a) the collectability boundary; (b) the possibility of evasion, downward modification, or nullification of a severe fine; (c) the constitutional prohibition against increasing the fine once it has been imposed; (d) the tendency of inflation to erode the significance of a statutory maximum fine; and (e) the availability of covert techniques for "passing on" the fine to the organization employing the offender. Only by establishing very high mandatory minimum levels for fines can these factors be even partially offset.

(3) If substantial reliance is to be placed upon fines as a means of deterring organization crime, the predictable result will be higher transaction costs to the judicial system. The offender will have every incentive to evade full payment and to seek reduction or delay whenever installment payments or a percentage-of-income formula is employed. Constant monitoring and contested hearings become unavoidable. Although prisons may be even costlier, these are sunk costs which, given the limited number of white-collar offenders, seem largely discountable in a marginal cost comparison.

(4) The Becker formula for determining the optimal level of the fine, by ascertaining the expected gain to the offender and the probability of conviction, is too elusive to implement. Because neither the expected

gain to the individual offender (who, in the organizational context, is typically an agent to whom only a portion of the crime's benefits flow) nor the frequency of the overall crime (because the victims of white-collar crimes seldom know of their injury) can be reliably estimated, the equation has too many unknowns to be solved.

(5) Criminal justice reforms must take into account the problem of demoralization costs. A system that fines the rich and jails the poor risks the appearance of institutionalizing bias, and its asserted efficiency may depend upon myopic social cost accounting. Thus, to the extent different forms of criminal sanctions are used, some means of seeking equivalence is necessary.

(6) To the extent that fines are used, both high transaction costs to the judicial system and high demoralization costs to society can probably best be avoided by giving the offender a strong incentive to offer a satisfactory fine. Thus, precise guidelines establishing monetary penalties for a given crime should not be promulgated because uncertainty will act to promote equivalence and reduce inequality.

(7) The assertion that the firm rather than the individual should be punished for corporate crime depends for its validity on questionable assumptions about (a) the efficiency of the market for corporate control, (b) the likelihood of an internal disciplinary response within the firm, and (c) the difficulty of re-entry into the employment market for the fired executive. None of these assumptions is confirmed by the available empirical evidence. To the extent that there is a separation between ownership and control within the modern corporation, then the case for focusing on the individual decision-maker is far stronger than the Free Market Economist concedes. To the extent that corporate managers are seeking to maximize their individual positions rather than their shareholder's wealth, then the corporation is far less deterrable than the Free Market Model would lead one to believe. Conversely, non-pecuniary penalties directed at the firm—such as those incorporated in a number of recent SEC consent decrees—may yield deterrent, incapacitative and "rehabilitative" benefits. That is, to the extent that a possible sanction such as a period of corporate probation threatens the managerial autonomy of those controlling the firm, its potential availability may yield a considerable deterrent benefit while very little of its cost is passed through to stockholders, employees and consumers.

(8) Even if the neo-classic assumption that a firm will always profit maximize is accepted, the prospects are not encouraging for achieving adequate corporate deterrence through reliance on penalties aimed solely at the firm. Under such a theory the penalty must be increased to a point which, after discounting it by the likelihood of apprehension, it still exceeds the expected gain. Corporate crime tends to be uniquely concealable and hence apprehension rates may often fall well below 10%. If this occurs, the penalty would have to be tenfold greater than the gain in order to be effective. This would frequently require the imposition of penalties that raise the prospect of bankruptcy and thus face nullification by courts unwilling to injury share-holders or employees. Thus, a rational strategy must focus both on the decision-maker and, in appropriate cases in which corporate behavior has been repeatedly delinquent, on the need for preventive restraints.

In sum, the case for the conventional wisdom is not weak, even when articulated in the language of EcoSpeak. Translated into a policy, this view of the "economic approach" suggests that a short sentence (say three to six months) should be the benchmark norm for most willful organizational crimes. Maximum authorized sentences would have to be longer (perhaps five years), and fines would primarily be used either as a supplementary penalty or in cases where the offered payment clearly represented an appreciable portion of the individual's economic wealth.

On a more general level, it must be concluded that a pure theory of the optimal criminal sanction that is divorced from empirical research is dangerously overextended. This does not necessarily mean that the "economic approach" has only limited applicability to the context of criminal behavior. As a filter through which reality in its confusing detail can be examined and clarified, economic analysis has much to offer. For example, the practical lawyer's long-standing belief that incarceration carries a greater threat than fines becomes more comprehensible when we comparatively evaluate both the actual and possible probability dispersions associated with each. Similarly, the assertion that certainty of punishment is more important than the severity of the sanction can be translated and examined as a statement that offenders tend more to be risk preferrers than risk averters.

But limits on the use of the economic approach need to be clearly recognized when such an analysis is used outside the context of market transactions. First, there are value-laden issues surrounding the premises of a cost-minimization model. Almost certainly, a theory of criminal justice which gives equal weight to the interests of both offender and victim, and which places transaction costs on a parity with both will satisfy few. Thus, the challenging question is what the economic approach can achieve once it either abandons cost minimization as its criterion or accepts some rules of priority by which to rank different categories of costs. This article has suggested that, at least for the present, the economic approach should focus on achieving equivalence between penalties rather than on quantification of the precise penalty.

A second problem with the economic approach is its susceptibility to the danger of over-aggregation. In market transactions, we can be fairly certain that an increase in the price will lower the quantity demanded. This model may have considerable predictive power for criminal sanctions as well (*i.e.*, a significant increase in the penalty will probably reduce the amount of crime, other things being equal), but the dangers of the non-conforming, idiosyncratic case are far greater. For example, as earlier discussed, if the relevant population of potential offenders is composed both of risk averters and risk preferrers, then raising the sanction without also increasing the apprehension rate will leave the latter group largely undeterred. The danger to society from leaving any group of potential offenders systematically undeterred is too great to rely heavily on a theory which, although it has predictive power, refuses to acknowledge the likelihood of non-conforming cases.

A third problem with reliance on economic theory as a tool for the formulation of criminal justice policy is the necessity for incorporating non-economic factors into the equation before it works. This article has explored two such factors: (1) the "risky shift" phenomenon under which collective decisions appear to be made in the face of risks that would have deterred an individual decision-maker; and, (2) the phenomenon of judicial nullification under which courts decline to enforce severe penalties.

This tendency for the "real world" to ignore the script and deviate from the course predicted by the model underscores the dangers of the "Pygmalion syndrome." Named after the mythical Greek sculptor who, having carved the figure of the perfect woman in marble, fell in love with the model and lost interest in other women, this syndrome should remind us that infatuation with models can produce a resulting disinterest in more mundane reality. Models can guide, but they also can blind. Few vested interests are as strong as a previously published theory.

These criticisms do not deny the worth of economic analysis as a tool for the formulation of legal rules, but they suggest the need for the intrepid economist to cease being a solo explorer and take along a guide familiar with the local terrain (such as, here, a criminologist). More a language than a science, EcoSpeak

needs to be supplemented by external premises in order to work well. In the end, our reply to the Free Market Economist, as academic imperialist, must be that of Hamlet to Horatio:

There are more things in Heaven and Earth, Horatio, Than are dreamt of in our philosophy.

Kenneth Mann, Stanton Wheeler and Austin Sarat, *Sentencing the White Collar Offender,* 17 AM. CRIM. L. REV. 479–500 (1980)*

I. INTRODUCTION

How do judges go about deciding the appropriate penalty for a particular crime? Questions of equal justice are raised in any comparison of common crime and white-collar crime sentencing, but it is not obvious what equality of sentencing means when one is dealing with offenders as diverse as the unemployed alcoholic who habitually steals and forges checks, and the businessman who commits a single, massive stock fraud or price-fixing scheme. The wide range of criminal behavior and the great differences in type of injury caused make such comparisons extremely difficult. The problem is exacerbated by the existence of very different types of sanctions, ranging from fines and a variety of conditions of probation, to various forms of imprisonment, for there is no single underlying metric that provides a standard of comparison. Yet this is precisely the problem that judges face: meting out fair sentences when choosing from a wide array of sanctions applied to a wide range of offenses and offenders.

At the level of sentencing policy, the choice among alternative punishments is again an important issue. Should imprisonment be a commonly used sentence for white-collar criminals? A mounting body of theory argues that monetary fines can have a deterrent effect equivalent to that of imprisonment for at least certain classes of offenders, and that since it is less costly for the system (saving money through fines rather than paying it out through costs of confinement) the preferred sanction will nearly always be a fine rather than imprisonment. Where fines may be inappropriate, the

* Reprinted by permission of the author and The American Bar Association. © 1980 American Bar Association.

idea of "alternative sentences"—non-incarcerative sentences other than or in addition to probation—have drawn a great deal of attention.

These matters of sentencing policy for white-collar offenders have gained increased salience in the post-Watergate era, with its sharp focus on the prosecution of white-collar crime. These discussions, however, have proceeded largely in the absence of systematic data from those actually charged with sentencing responsibility, the sentencing judges. In the federal system and in most of our states, it is the judge who must choose among the sentencing alternatives, which usually include fines, imprisonment, and the possibility of special conditions attaching to probation. It is the judge who faces the difficult task of arriving at a particular sanction in each case. If new or modified systems of sanctioning are to be employed, it is the judge who must be convinced of their utility. Furthermore, judges deal in the real world of sentencing, and may face considerations unperceived and unattended by those whose concerns are dictated by current academic theorizing.

It is thus important to examine how judges go about the task of arriving at a particular sentence, and in the process to discern through judges' thinking and actions, the relative role given to imprisonment, fines, and other forms of sanctioning. That is our aim in this article, which reports a portion of results of a study of federal district court judges and their views regarding the sentencing of white-collar offenders. After a brief description of the study, we proceed to report on judges' conceptions of the goals of sentencing in white-collar versus economy crime cases, the distinctive traits of white-collar offenders and offenses that influence the choice of sanction, and the limited role perceived for fines in contrast to other sentences. We conclude by suggesting the need for an enlargement of the scope of sentencing considerations if sentencing policy is to reflect the real world concerns of those who impose sentences.

II. The Study

The core material for this presentation is taken from one section of a broadly focused interview study of judicial attitudes toward sentencing white-collar criminals. The study was conducted over the last two years as part of a larger project on white-collar crime being conducted at Yale Law School with the support of the Law Enforcement Assistance Administration. In the project, two separate though related studies were designed in the sentencing area. The first, part of which will be reported here, is designed to determine how judges approach sentencing in actual white-collar crime cases. The goal is to learn as much as possible about the judges' thinking process concerning sentencing: the considerations used in selecting and weighing information about the offense and the offender, the sentencing alternatives rejected as well as those used, and the standards of comparison and contrast adopted by judges in arriving at what they consider to be fair sentences. The second study, not reported here, is a quantitative analysis of sentences actually imposed on offenders.

We conducted lengthy interviews with fifty-one federal district judges in seven federal districts, including those with the heaviest "white-collar crime" caseloads. Our interview technique was designed to maximize our respondents' attention to the factual detail of cases over which they presided. We aimed at having the judges reveal their individual views of sentencing by leading us through some of their most recent cases. Thus the interviews were open-ended. We were particularly interested in having respondents explain to us why they arrived at one sentence rather than another, why defendants in a multi-defendant case received different sentences, and why a defendant in one white-collar case received a different sentence from a defendant in a similar white-collar case or in a "comparable" non-white-collar case.

In choosing actual rather than hypothetical cases we had the benefit of discrete factual situations from which to draw answers to general questions. While we were equipped with a systematic interview schedule and a strong sense of significant areas to explore, the interview had its own dynamics depending on the judges' particular orientation to the case or cases discussed. We did not hesitate either to interrupt the judges where sentencing inconsistencies appeared, or to adopt an "adversarial" stance when appropriate. Underlying our questions and interaction was a desire to encourage our subjects to confront overly simple generalizations and to explore otherwise unarticulated reasons and motivations for meting out particular sentences. In what follows we have presented a selection of the actual responses so as to let judges, as much as possible, speak for themselves.

III. General Sentencing Goals

To understand why judges choose or decline to choose a sentence of imprisonment when that option is clearly open to them, it is first necessary to understand the purposes judges hope to serve in sentencing decisions. Our interviews indicate that judges' rationale in sentencing white-collar criminals is significantly different from their rationale in sentencing non-white-collar criminals. In non-white-collar cases judges have at least three, if not four, purposes in mind when they impose a sentence—punishment, incapacitation, general deterrence, and occasionally rehabilitation—and they tend to believe that their sentence will serve each purpose, to some extent and however imperfectly. In the white-collar area, in distinction, the sentencing purpose and rationale tends to be undimensional: judges are concerned with general deterrence, deterring other persons in similar positions from engaging in the same or like behavior. They tend not to be concerned at all with rehabilitation or incapacitation and (for reasons explored further below) only minimally with punishment. Here is an illustrative response of one judge who was asked about his purpose for the imposition of a sentence in a particular case of bribery of a public official.

> In a white-collar crime, particularly one like this, I am often dealing with someone who has never been in trouble before, who comes in with a packet of all kinds of positive information on his background, ministers' letters, public officials' letters. The decision is definitely tougher. You are not putting someone away in order to safeguard the rest of the community from physical harm when you are dealing with a white-collar case, so you simply do not put people away as you do when you are dealing with violent crimes. Now, here I would point out another important factor. Prisons are simply not going to rehabilitate white-collar offenders. In fact, they may have the opposite effect, so I'm not concerned about rehabilitation either.

A judge in another district had a similar comment to make when he volunteered his justification for meting out short prison terms in cases of tax and securities fraud:

> In the tax case and in the securities case, I'm looking at deterrence. And this is one of the problems I think, because I don't think you deter very much the bank robber by giving a 20-year sentence to another bank robber. That is a hazard of the trade that they accept. They know they are playing a risky game, and a high stakes game on both sides of the equation. Therefore, I don't think deterrence is that significant in that kind of a crime, but in the other two that I mentioned it is very much so. The income tax case is the one that is most particularly troublesome as far as white-collar crime is concerned, as I say, because every mild sentence that is afforded in an income tax case is an inducement to those who ought to be deterred to go and do likewise.

Another judge, who thinks that prison sentences have only a very small deterrent effect in cases of violent crime, gave one reason why he believes deterrence works in white-collar cases.

> When I was still practicing there were the electrical equipment antitrust cases around 1960 or thereabouts in Philadelphia. They made screaming headlines. A few businessmen went to prison for terms like thirty, sixty, ninety days. I thought those were very sound sentences. And as a private practitioner I was made aware that all of a sudden businessmen were running into our firm wanting to know what the hell were the antitrust laws and how do you obey them. It really had an impact. . . .I literally could see it and feel it.

Evidence of the judges' concern for the impact of a prison sentence in a similar occupational setting is suggested in the following explanation of the sentence in a bank embezzlement:

> Another consideration very important to me is a sentence that would act as a deterrent, a deterrent to this man from ever considering doing something like that again—if perchance he got into a position of trust someway. And a deterrent to others knowing what the punishment was, a deterrent to them if they might be considering conduct like that.

> Q: So that you have in the back of your mind other persons in similar positions who might be tempted to do this kind of thing, is that what you are saying?

> A: Well, I think, let's say that you got around 100,000 bank employees around the country. For them to know that the top of one of the biggest banks got three years for embezzling from the bank, I think that is a deterrent to people in white-collar jobs in the banking industry, or white-collar jobs with big companies in the financial areas.

For almost all of our respondents, general deterrence emerged as the purpose that quite substantially outweighed any other purpose in sentencing white-collar criminals. But what about the role of punishment for its own sake in the sentencing of white-collar offenders? Judges do give much attention to the role of punishment in the whole criminal process, but its role for white-collar offenders *at the time of sentencing* is limited. Most judges share a widespread belief that the suffering experienced by the white-collar person as a result of apprehension, public indictment and conviction, and the collateral disabilities incident to conviction—loss of job, professional licenses, and status in the community—completely satisfies the need to punish the individual. In discussing a case of embezzlement in which a bank manager was sentenced, we asked what effect the defendant's probable loss of employment had on the judge's consideration of sentence. The judge stated that the jail sentence that he did give out would have been longer had the defendant's professional loss not been an almost certain result in the conviction; he implied also that he may not have given any prison sentence had there not been a need for a "deterrent message."

> That loss of position as a bank manager was a huge mitigating factor. But for that I would have sentence him longer . . . it was obvious as night follows day that the minute he pleaded guilty this was all gone, this was all in his past. From now on the only thing he could get is a job as a bookkeeper or maintenance man, or something.
>
> Q: So that is something that you want to take into consideration. . . .
>
> A: Mitigation—you bet. My sentence was less as a result of that fact. That was punishment in itself. I had to take into consideration that he had already been punished.

The reason why deterrence tends to get considerable attention by the time the defendant arrives at the sentencing hearing is indicated by these additional views of our respondents on the punishing impact of the criminal process prior to the imposition of sentence. When asked how he reacted to the apparent public perception that white-collar offenders "get off easy," one judge responded:

> Well, as I said to you earlier, I don't think a sentencing procedure should be very much concerned with what the public's perception would be. If the public perception is bad it is because some writers or journalists stirred up a concept which isn't valid, made the public believe that. Some branch of the public always thinks the rich are getting away with it. The average white-collar defendant in this court is broke by the time sentence is imposed. He has lost his job. All his debts have come due. Most of them are mortgaged to the hilt. He has had to take care of his family obligations, most of which are heavy. Attorney fees in some of these cases are tremendous, fifty, sixty, eighty thousand dollars for cooperating defendants or for defendants who want to cop out. It is not unusual in this district. So some members of the public look at it and think that the rich are getting away with murder. I think those cases are few and far between.

Another judge focused more on the strong impact that the issuance of an indictment has on the offender in cases of white-collar crime.

> There is not doubt about the fact that in most white-collar crimes as such, the return of the indictment is much more traumatic than even the sentence. Pronouncing of the sentence is not as injurious to the person, his relationship to the community, to his family, as the return of the indictment. A loss of credit, a loss of bank credit, a loss of friends, social status, occasionally loss of a wife, members of the family, children around the father, more when they hear that an indictment has been returned and he has been charged than they do after they have gotten used to the idea and he is sentenced for it. There is no question about the fact that that is much more severe on the white-collar criminal than it is on the blue-collar defendant.

The commencement of the criminal process against a defendant also may cause severe damage to an offender's professional standing. One judge emphasized, for instance, that a lawyer was going to lose his practice as a result of a felony conviction. We asked the judge whether he thought that this was comparable to the kind of punishment suffered by a person who is given a prison sentence. He responded:

> Don't you agree? If a man who has gone through three years of law school, and then gone through a bar review course and taken the bar review exam, and has a nice practice, and is making—I think in this case—something like $40,000 a year and suddenly he is disbarred, I would consider that a stiffer punishment than anything I would be likely to impose. I just have gotten through a trial of two young attorneys for perpetrating . . . a fraud, or rather for participating in an attempt to return stolen bonds to the Manufacturers Hanover Trust Company. And those fellows, unless the conviction is reversed, are going to be automatically disbarred, and they are two young fellows in their late 20's or early 30's, just getting started. And their career is shot. And I don't know what in the world I will do by way of sentencing those fellows, but certainly the law which provides for automatic disbarment is a stiffer sentence than any I could think of imposing.

And a third judge summed up this view in this statement:

> Well, you have a person who has a certain status, has surrounded himself with a certain aura, and you strip that aura away and let him stand

naked and in front of his peers, that itself is pretty serious punishment.

We do not wish to overstate the point. These are instances in which the judge concludes that the defendant deserves the additional punishment of a harsh sentence in addition to whatever "punishment" accompanied the process of indictment and conviction. A serious breach of public trust is one example. And there are other seriousness factors – amount of monetary damage, type of victims, length of time that the offense continued prior to conviction, and the nature and degree of cover-up and scheme used in the commission of the crime – that can significantly aggravate the seriousness of crimes in the view of judges. Indeed, such questions of seriousness have a central role in sentencing decisions. But the major theme of a recent study of minor offenders in the lower criminal courts would appear to apply as well to these very different types of offenders: the commencement of the criminal process against a defendant is the punishment. And with the limited role seen for both incapacitation and rehabilitation, only general deterrence remains as a primary sentencing goal.

IV. LIMITING THE ROLE OF GENERAL DETERRENCE

If the primary goal at the time of sentencing is general deterrence, one might expect that judges would frequently use imprisonment as a sanction. It is clear from their own testimony that they believe in the deterrent effect of imprisonment and have no confidence that fines or other non-incarcerative sanctions would be as efficacious. Yet they often do not impose a prison sanction. How do they justify or rationalize this seeming inconsistency?

One factor is implicit from our discussion of punishment. When judges feel an offender has already been punished enough through the process of indictment, trial, and conviction, they find it hard to impose what will be additional punishment for the offender, solely to achieve the aims of deterrence. It is much easier to justify deterrence when the offender also deserves to be punished. Because the deterrent goal of the process is aimed at a public audience while much of the "punishment" suffered by the defendant is incurred prior to sentencing, judges will sometimes give a public incarcerative sentence solely for deterrent purposes. They do not, however, like to do so. Four additional reasons are brought into play to help bring the judge to a lesser sanction than would be called for by the deterrence rationale alone: the judge's perception of a special sensitivity to imprisonment on the part of white-collar offenders, the desire to prevent injury to innocent parties, the facilitation of compensation, and the idea of non-incarcerative

"reparations." Each will be described with illustrative cases from the interviews.

A. SPECIAL SENSITIVITY TO IMPRISONMENT

Most judges we interviewed tend to believe that white-collar defendants are more sensitive to the impact of the prison environment than are non-white-collar defendants. For this reason, they give special consideration to the possibility of not imprisoning the white-collar defendant, even in those instances in which the seriousness of the crime and the need for deterrence would otherwise make it a likely disposition. One judge described a white-collar defendant's special position vis-a-vis the prospect of prison this way:

I think the first sentence to a prison term for a person who up to now has lived and has surrounded himself with a family, that lives in terms of great respectability and community respect and so on, whether one likes to say this or not I think a term of imprisonment for such a person is probably a harsher, more painful sanction than it is for someone who grows up somewhere where people are always in and out of prison. There may be something racist about saying that, but I am saying what I think is true or perhaps need to be laid out on the table and faced. Maybe we have to correct that notion and say that that is the kind of contrast that is constitutionally impermissible, and we won't have it. But I haven't seen the doctrine that tells me that yet. And we still live with this kind of idiotic individualization thing where we are going to send somebody to prison, whether he is white-collar or black-collar, we consider whether he is sick, whether he is old, has a family, all kinds of thinks about him that we believe in a crude way will deliver messages to us about how rough prison is for him as compared with somebody else.

A large number of our respondents felt that prison has a significantly greater impact on white-collar defendants, and that the prison environment has to be compared to the environment from which the defendant comes in order to determine an appropriate sentence. Another judge affirmed the importance of this factor:

There is no getting away from the fact that the type of existence that jail provides is more hard on people who are accustomed to the better existence than it is on people who may not be fed as well in their homes as they are in jail. That is something you really can't articulate. It sounds as though you are penalizing poverty. There is no question that that is a fact. A person who doesn't get three square meals a day, and no possibility of getting it, isn't so seriously hurt by being put in an environment where at lest you are to get three meals a day, regardless of what other disadvantages there are, than one who is in the habit of—he is just deprived of—gets no benefit from it—all deprivation. But you can't articulate that. It sounds condescending—but it has to be a factor. . . . I guess there is not getting away from the fact that the judge empathizes more with a white-collar person whose hardships you can understand, because a lifestyle is more like his or her own, than someone whose lifestyle you really can't understand.

Still another judge made the following statement on the same subject:

A white-collar criminal has more of a fear of going to jail than this syndrome we find in the street crime. And I am not saying that if you cut everyone they don't bleed red blood. A person who commits a robbery or an assault, they don't want to go to jail either. But the white-collar criminal has more to lose by going to jail, reputation in the community, business as well as social community, decent living conditions, just the whole business of being put in a prison with a number on his back demeans this tremendous ego that is always involved in people who are high achievers.

B. Prevention of Injury to Innocent Parties

By not imposing a prison sentence, or by imposing only a short one, judges appear to want to avoid eliminating the contribution to community and family that white-collar offenders make in the normal course of their lives. Again, to exemplify, we can look at the judges' responses. When we asked one judge whether there is anything unique about defendants in cases of white-collar crime that bears on sentencing, he answered:

I don't think the defendants in white-collar cases are any more troublesome to the judge in performing the function, but I think that they have a peculiar characteristic to them which is perhaps more challenging to a judge as to what a proper sentence is. . . . Usually the defendant is one who looks as though he can resume his place, if indeed not just continue on his place, in society, as a valuable and contributing member of society. Almost always he is a husband and a father. Almost always he has children who are in the process of becoming what we like to think children ought to be—well brought up, well educated, nurtured, cared for—usually

he is a member of the kinds of civil organizations in his community who value his services and derive value from his services. . . . As a result you are up against this more difficult problem in degree in so-called white-collar criminals as to whether you are not going to inflict a hurt on society by putting such a person in a prison and making him cease to be a good father and a good husband and a good worker in the community.

This perspective on sentencing white-collar offenders carries with it a distinct view of the relationship of the criminal act to the rest of the personality of the white-collar offender. The crime tends to be seen as a separable part of the offenders' total personality; it is one negative characteristic amidst a cluster of other positive characteristics. Judges told us that this is what they most often learn from presentence reports. In a typical case the defendant is married and has children; he is reported to be a good parent, an employer with dependent employees or a professional person with clients dependent on him; he may be active in his church and a fund raiser for local charities. "He just happened to cheat the IRS out of $30,000 in the last three years," as one judge said.

In looking at this white-collar offender, the judge wants to impose a deterrent sentence, but would like to do it without also punishing the defendant's spouse and children who will lose their source of emotional and financial support, his employees or clients who will lose their employment or professional service, and the general community that will lose an otherwise exemplary citizen. Prevention of these potential losses to the defendant's network of dependents and associates is a significant consideration in sentencing white-collar offenders. In short distinction, the defendant convicted of bank robbery or a simple theft is typically perceived to be without family and work-related dependents. Being less anchored in a social matrix, less damage is done by sending him away.

In pursuing the question of the effect of family circumstances on the sentenced meted out to a white-collar offender, a judge explained his sentence of six months work release given to a defendant who had sold fake automobile franchises to many persons in several states, resulting in a loss of tens of thousands of dollars of his victims' investments:

Now the fellow that we have spent most of our time talking about was the ringleader, really put it together. The next in line was the sales manager, and his conduct was pretty bad too. Not as bad as the leader's, but it was calculated and inexcusable. I learned through the presentence report—he did not testify at trial—that he was a very modest man who had never been in trouble before and who miraculously, in my judgment, having raised four youngsters, is succeeding in helping his four kids go to college. He had completed two college educations and was in the middle of a third one, and another one ticketed for a year, maybe eighteen months. But when I learned this about him, and he did have a job, a good one, a good, solid job down in Atlanta, Georgia, then the whole thing came out. I checked with the Bureau of Prisons and found that the only work release program which was available in Atlanta was no more than six months. If I sentenced him to more than six months, they could not put him in this facility. So I made the reduction.

Another judge brought forth the same view with the following statement:

Whether there are people who are dependent on him or her, whether they are really making a contribution to the people, whether there is going to be an injury to others if I incarcerate him: that has a profound effect on me and when I sense that, I am much more inclined to be lenient. In this particular case, the defendant . . . was pleading guilty to a calculated fraud, which you could tell from his own admissions and from what the indictment was, but you also had evidence of his prior background, you had the report on his family, and all that. My recollection is now, although I've sentenced so many people since then, but I think he was separated from his wife. I don't think there was a problem [in this case] where you are taking somebody out of the home and really inflicting the major punishment on innocent people.

The importance of the impact of a sentence on family members may be extended to employees and the larger community. In a major tax evasion prosecution in which the defendants were convicted of understating their corporate income by hiding ownership interest in a significant sector of their actual business, the judge gave the following explanation for a sentence that required the defendants to report to a local prison facility on weekends only:

If you take these two income tax evaders, if you take them and say, "Okay, you are going to spend three years—I am going to throw the book at you—three years to the custody of the Attorney General," forty people, forty of their employees are out of work. I don't know how many hundreds of kids in the ghetto who

need jobs to rehabilitate themselves, how many of those will go back to crime because they are not working, you see. Fine, give them three years, forget all these other salutory purposes that a light sentence in this case—a work release, staying in their own business and working with a charitable foundation—accomplishes.

Another judge, sentencing a defendant convicted of operating fraudulent businesses in which unsophisticated persons were sold machines that would not perform their advertised functions, decided not to impose a prison sentence. He stated:

I felt a jail-type sentence was not called for because if I had sent the person away there would have been dozens of people who would have lost their jobs completely and would not have had any means of finding new employment. I made it a condition of probation that the defendant make all reasonable efforts to find jobs for persons who had been employed in his business, all of whom were going to lose their livelihood when the company would be liquidated. I therefore reserve the possibility of committing this guy if he didn't comply with this probation condition.

Other judges cited the need for maintaining an individual's professional contribution to his community as a reason for not imposing a prison sentence. In a conviction for Medicaid fraud, a physician was given probation so that he could continue to practice medicine. The judge stated:

I didn't want to send him to jail because I felt that it would deprive him and his family of the livelihood he could make as a doctor and it would deprive the neighborhood of his services. So what I was trying to accomplish was to see that to some extent he could repay society. In this particular case there was a way he could do something of social usefulness. I felt that this was a strong enough reason to overcome whatever good would be done for society by imposing a sentence for general deterrence, which is the only justification that exists for sentences in these cases.

Our interviews disclosed a relatively large number of cases in which judges took into account the unique service that professional persons, particularly doctors, and business persons provide to a community. In some of these cases, judges considered the possibility of a non-prison disposition for the reasons cited above but rejected it because of overriding considerations concerning the seriousness of the particular white-collar crime. In particular, there was a strong feeling among many judges that because business and professional persons are vested with public trust, their offenses require sanctions more severe than those meted out where the violation does not entail a breach of public trust. While we do not intend to discuss this issue in detail here it should be emphasized that the desire to avoid hurting family, business, and community may be outweighed by the judges' belief that persons who breach public trust have to be singled out for exemplary sanctions. One judge described the interplay between these two factors this way:

> So the way I resolve it, and of course why I would give him prison, is because of the trust issue that I talked about. I believe if someone can come in and commit a crime like that (investor fraud) and go out with nothing but probation people would just laugh off the idea that there is any punishment for those types of activity. And so I balance, I give what I think is a moderate sentence (an investment banker is not going to want to serve a year in jail). To me it is enough, yet it isn't a lot, it doesn't keep him out of commission for years and years. He has responsibilities to a family and elderly people and all, and I didn't want to keep him out of commission for a long time. You know, you weigh these imponderables, the good things in his behalf, the need to get him back functioning. Yet he has committed a serious crime involving the trust other people have put in him, and there is the need to vindicate the law in a gentle way. And you come out with a year. There isn't any formula. You could come out differently.

V. FINES

There are strongly divergent views about the role that fines have in cases of white-collar crime within the present statutory framework. We discussed cases where the sentencing judge felt that fines were definitely effective in accomplishing the deterrent aim of sentencing. More generally, however, we found a conspicuous absence of responses by judges that a fine was the appropriate sanction to be imposed on a defendant. Fines clearly had a much more limited role in the view of most of our judges than did prison terms, restitution, or alternative community service. In several cases we were told that fines were imposed but little import was attributed to their impact. Where fines were used in conjunction with another sentence it was generally the other sentence – community service or short prison term – that was thought to have

the intended deterrent effect. Where the fine was used alone, the idea that the commencement of the criminal process against the defendant was the punishment seemed to be more important in the judges' minds than the fine itself. . . .

VI. CONCLUSION

What we have described above is one small portion of a large body of data on the federal judges' experience of the sentencing process. Throughout we have been concerned with *their conceptions* of the process. We have also stressed major themes and the way those themes get expressed, rather than describing the total range of variation. We have not examined here the important of the seriousness of the offense or the culpability of the offender, but factors which may dictate a prison sentence. That variation, and many other matters of sentencing policy, will be addressed in a forthcoming monograph. But certain conclusions seem evident to us from even the partial examination of our date.

We are struck by the fundamental tension many judges feel between the aims of general deterrence on the one hand, and the particular attributes of white-collar offenders on the other. This tension is expressed in a variety of ways, but its central core is suggested in one final quotation from one of our judges:

> The problem is the tension between use of incarceration for its deterrent factor, and the inclination not to use it because it is too excessive given the non-criminal record of the offender. From the individual standpoint there are good arguments against sentencing; from the societal interest of deterring crime there are some good arguments for using the sentence. And that tension is more pronounced with the white-collar criminal who by and large has in my judgment no prior record so that his personal interests are in his favor but the crime he has committed I tend to think, are the ones that are deterred by sentences more so than the bad check guys and the other guys where I don't think there is much deterrent effect by incarceration. So the deterrent effect I think is at its highest, the personal situation rather favorable, and so the tension between those two values is very acute.

In seeking to resolve this conflict many judges appear to look for a compromise: A sentence that will have what they perceive to be a deterrent effect, but without imposing the deprivations that would come from an extended stay in prison. The weekend sentence, the very short jail term, and the relatively frequent use of amended sentences (where a judge imposes a prison term and later reduces it) are evidence of this search for a compromise.

We are also impressed by the extent to which considerations other than the usually discussed aims and purposes of sentencing feed into the judges' decision-making process. These considerations would rarely be thought of as primary aims of sanctioning, but they often appear to play a primary role. In carrying out that task judges seem to develop their own common law standard sentencing. One implicit rule might be formulated as follows: sentence so as to reduce the total social cost of the offense to its victims. This leads to sentences that will facilitate victim compensation and reparations. Another explicit rule would appear to be: sentence so as not to harm innocent parties. This leads to sentences that keep the offender in the home and at work. These and perhaps other implicit principles appear to weigh heavily in the judges' decisions.

The judges, however, rarely formulate these considerations as aims or principles of sentencing. Rather, they arise as practical matters of concern in particular cases. If anything, there would appear to be a predilection against a formulation of abstract sentencing principles, and a strongly felt need to keep the process oriented to the individuals who are most affected by it. This is one reason for their interest in alternative sentences that bring the offender into some relationship with the victim or the community, and for a disposition against thinking in strict cost-benefit terms with regard to fines.

That these concerns seem more evidence in their discussion of white-collar crime than of common crime sentencing may be a result of prominent "empathy" theme in the white-collar cases. The interview responses repeatedly give evidence of the judges' understanding, indeed sympathy, for the person whose position in society may be very much like their own. In places the interviews exude the pain that judges feel in seeing the offender uprooted from his family, humiliated before his friends, and exposed to the degradation of imprisonment. The idea that prison sentences should be avoided so that the offender may continue to make a contribution to the well-being of his community also suggests the special appreciation for the occupational role of white-collar offenders. Whether this empathy plays an active role in the influencing the sentencing decision, or only accompanies decisions based on other considerations' remains an open question.

Finally, there is the question of equity in the sentencing process. It is difficult to define precisely what disparity in sentencing might mean, let alone provide evidence as to whether there is disparity and in what direction it runs. What is clear is that factors intimately related to the defendant's social status do receive weight in the judges' thinking. Sometimes, as in the violation of public trust, the weight goes against the white-collar defendant. But often because of factors — such as the concern for the special sensitivity of such defendants to imprisonment, and the sense of greater loss to family members and to the community if a white-collar person is sent away — they cut in the opposite direction. Questions are also raised by the predisposition to use economic sanctions when the defendant can clearly pay for them — sanctions that are unavailable to the defendant who is poor. These matters raise questions of fundamental fairness in the sentencing process that we do not attempt to analyze here. They would appear to be of paramount concern to those who would fashion a just as well as an efficient sentencing policy.

B. Corporate Punishment

John C. Coffee, Jr., *"No Soul To Damn, No Body To Kick": An Unscandalized Inquiry Into the Problem of Corporate Punishment,* 79 MICH. L. REV. 386–459 (1981)*

Did you ever expect a corporation to have a conscience, when it has no soul to be damned, and no body to be kicked?

Edward, First Baron
Thurlow 1731–1806

The Lord Chancellor of England quoted above was neither the first nor the last judge to experience frustration when faced with a convicted corporation. American sentencing judges are likely to face a similar dilemma with increasing frequency in the near future, for a number of signs indicate that corporate prosecutions will become increasingly commonplace. At first glance, the problem of corporate punishment seems perversely insoluble: moderate fines do not deter, while severe penalties flow through the corporate shell and fall on the relatively blameless. Nonetheless, this Article will submit that there are ways both to focus the incidence of corporate penalties on those most able to prevent repetition

---

* Reprinted with permission of the author and The University of Michigan Law Review.

and to increase the efficiency of corporate punishment without employing *in terrorem* penalties.

This assertion may be greeted with polite indifference since an obvious and simpler alternative to pursuing new forms of corporate penalties is simply to prosecute the individual executive and ignore the corporate entity. The case for such an individual focus to corporate law enforcement is strong, but it is not unqualified. This Article will argue that law enforcement officials cannot afford to ignore either the individual or the firm in choosing their targets, but can realize important economies of scale by simultaneously pursuing both.

Because this Article's arguments are interwoven, a preliminary road map seems advisable. First, Section I will examine three perspectives on corporate punishment and will develop several concepts in terms of which corporate penalties should be evaluated. Although this analysis will suggest several barriers to effective corporate deterrence, Section II will explain why a sensible approach to corporate misbehavior still must punish the firm as well as the individual decision maker. Section III will then evaluate three proposed approaches: (1) the "equity fine," (2) the use of adverse publicity, and (3) the fuller integration of public and private enforcement. In addition, it will consider whether anything is gained by prosecuting the corporation in a criminal, as opposed to civil, proceeding. Finally, Section IV will look beyond remedies designed to increase deterrence to the possibility of incapacitative sanctions. This latter inquiry is promoted by recent judicial decisions and legislative proposals that permit courts to place corporations on probation. Interesting questions are thus presented: Can an organization be rehabilitated? If so, what goals should the sentencing court pursue and what remedies can it realistically implement? . . .

I. Perspectives on Corporate Penalties: Why Sanctions Fall Short

The literature on corporate sanctions sometimes seems to consist of little more than the repeated observation that the fines imposed on convicted corporations have historically been significant. True as this point undoubtedly is, it is also a short-sighted critique. It ignores both the judiciary's reasons for declining to impose more severe penalties and the possibility that a monetary penalty sufficiently high to deter the corporation may be infeasible or undesirable. Once these possibilities are considered, the problem of corporate criminal behavior becomes radically more complex. Three independent, but overlapping perspectives each suggest that monetary penalties directed at the corporations will often prove inadequate to deter illegal behavior. In order, this Article will survey the field from the perspectives of the neo-classical economist, the organization theorist, and the public policy specialist who is concerned that the costs of punishment may exceed the benefits of deterrence.

A. *The Deterrence Trap*

Our first perspective flows directly from the application of the economic theory of deterrence to an empirical premise. Economists generally agree that an actor who contemplates committing a crime will be deterred only if the "expected punishment cost" of a proscribed action exceeds the expected gain. This concept of the expected punishment cost involves more than simply the amount of the penalty. Rather, the expected penalty must be discounted by the likelihood of apprehension and conviction in order to yield the expected punishment cost. For example, if the expected gain were $1 million and the rise of apprehension were 25%, the penalty would have to be raised to $4 million in order to make the expected punishment cost equal the expected gain. One may well question the adequacy of this simple formula when applied to individual defendants, because the stigmatization of a criminal conviction constitutes an additional and severe penalty for the white-collar defendant. But this loss of social status is a less significant consideration for the corporate entity, and we are thus forced to rely largely on monetary sanctions.

The crux of the dilemma arises from the fact that the maximum meaningful fine that can be levied against any corporate offender is necessarily bound by its wealth. Logically, a small corporation is no more threatened by a $5 million fine than by a $500,000 fine if both are beyond its ability to pay. In the case of an individual offender, this wealth ceiling on the deterrent threat of fines causes no serious problem because we can still deter by threat of incarceration. But for the corporation, which has no body to incarcerate, this wealth boundary seems an absolute limit on the reach of deterrent threats directed at it. If the "expected punishment cost" necessary to deter a crime crosses this threshold, adequate deterrence cannot be achieved. For example, if a corporation having $10 million of wealth were faced with an opportunity to gain $1 million through some criminal act or omission, such conduct could not logically be deterred by monetary penalties directed at the corporation *if the risk of apprehension were below 10%*. That is, if the likelihood of apprehension were 8%, the necessary penalty would have to be $12.5 million (*i.e.*, $1 million times 12.5, the reciprocal of 8%). Yet such a fine exceeds the corporation's ability to pay. In short, our ability to deter the corporation may be confounded by our inability to set an adequate punishment cost which does not exceed the corporation's resources.

The importance of this barrier (which this Article will call the "deterrence trap") depends on whether rates of apprehension for corporate crimes are typically low. Although there are exceptions, most corporate crimes seem highly concealable. This is so because, unlike victims of classically under-reported crimes (such as rape or child abuse), victims of many corporate crimes do not necessarily know of their injury. The victim of price-fixing may never learn that he has overpaid; the consumer of an unsafe, toxic, or carcinogenic product typically remains unaware of the hazards to which he has been exposed. Even the government or a fellow competitor may rarely discover the tax fraud or illegal bribe which has cost it a substantial loss in revenues.

The ability to conceal corporate crime has been little noticed by economists, in all likelihood because they have often been preoccupied with the antitrust context. Yet the characteristics of horizontal price-fixing (the classic antitrust violation) make it more subject to eventual exposure than the safety and environmental violations that now especially concern society. At bottom, a price-fixing conspiracy among competitors is a very unstable enterprise because it must extend beyond the individual firm. If one may generalize based on detected price-fixing conspiracies of recent years, they tend to have involved dozens of corporate participants within an industry, and thus many employees are likely to know about the illegal activity, thereby multiplying the likelihood of exposure. More importantly, when a new competitor enters the affected market because of the excessively high prices, the existing conspiracy must either offer the entrant membership in the cartel, or engage in some form of strategic price-cutting to drive it out. Add to this picture, in industries that employ sealed competitive bidding, the tendency for price-fixing conspiracies to produce conspicuously parallel price movements and the odds of eventual exposure rise exponentially in comparison to an illegal activity wholly contained within a single firm. Admittedly, other forms of crime may produce lasting evidence as well; for example, an environmental violation may leave scars lasting for decades. But illegal toxic dumps and industrial rivers tell few tales by which to connect the evidence to a particular actor.

Beyond ease of concealment, legal and behavioral characteristics distinguish price-fixing from other corporate crimes: safety and environmental violations involve questions of judgment which the participants can rationalize without consciously (or at least explicitly) engaging in behavior they know to be illegal. In addition, many, if not most, forms of corporate crime require some element of intent (*i.e.,* "knowingly" or "willfully") which can be exceedingly difficult to prove in the context of prosecuting a white-collar worker for a "regulatory" offense. Although intent is also a prerequisite for a criminal antitrust violation, a price-fixing conspiracy, if detected, speaks for itself. These legal and behavioral differences between antitrust and other violations may affect the expected punishment cost necessary to deter corporate crime. If the individual does to realize he is committing a crime, his perceived risk of apprehension will be very low. Similarly, if intent is difficult to prove in prosecutions for regulatory offenses, the risk of conviction – if not of apprehension – will be lower than in the price-fixing cases. Accordingly, the penalty necessary to deter such illegal activity would rise. Thus, the classic price-fixing conspiracy may not be a representative example of organizational crime.

The final element in the deterrence equation requires little emphasis: corporate misbehavior involves high stakes. A $50,000 bribe may secure a $50 million defense contract, a failure to report a safety or design defect in a product may avert a multi-million dollar recall, and the suppression of evidence showing a newly discovered adverse side effect of a popular drug may save its manufacturer an entire product market. Thus, when all the elements of the equation are combined, it is not unrealistic to predict that cases will arise in which the expected gain may be $10 million or higher, while the likelihood of apprehension is under 10%. If so, a mechanical application of the economist's deterrence formula suggests that only penalties of $100 million or above could raise the "expected punishment cost" to a level in excess of the expected gain. Few corporations, if any, could pay such a fine and any attempt to levy it in installments would require the court to charge very high interest in order to compensate for the time value of money (which implies that a deterred fine is a substantially reduced fine).

B. *The Behavioral Perspective*

An abstract quality surrounds the foregoing economic analysis. Lucid as its logic seems, it ignores the organizational dynamics within the firm and treats the corporation as a "black box" which responds in a wholly amoral fashion to any net difference between expected costs and benefits. Students of organizational decision-making have always rejected this "black box" model of the firm and have been quick to point out that a fundamental incongruence may exist between the aims of the manager and those of the firm. Indeed, this assertion is but a corollary of the famous Berle-Means thesis that control and ownership have been divorced in the modern public corporation. Given this separation, it follows that the "real world" corporation manager may view corporate participation in criminal activities from the standpoint of how to maximize his own ends, rather than those of the firm.

Does the behavioral perspective indicate that corporate misbehavior may be easier to deter than the foregoing economic analysis suggests? Regrettably, the reverse may be the case: for several reasons, the behavioral perspective suggests that it may be extraordinarily difficult to prevent corporate misconduct by punishing only the firm. First, from such a perspective, it seems clear that the individual manager may perceive illegal conduct to be in is interest, even if the potential costs to which it exposes the firm far exceed the potential corporate benefits. For example, the executive vice president who is a candidate for promotion to president may be willing to run risks which are counterproductive to the firm as a whole because he is eager to make a record profit for his division or to hide a prior error of judgment. Correspondingly, the lower echelon executive with a lackluster record may deem it desirable to resort to illegal means to increase profits (or forestall losses) in order to prevent his dismissal or demotion. Others in between these two extremes may haven an interest in incentive compensation or other personal objectives which cause their interests to deviate from those of their firm. Necessarily, the manager acts within a shorter time frame than the firm (if only because in the long run, the manager, unlike his firm, will be dead), and thus may focus more on short-run profit maximization.

Neo-classical economists have always objected to this argument. They have framed a theoretical rebuttal: if properly motivated, the corporation could implement controls adequate to detect and penalize such free-lance activity by its agents. In theory, the firm has the power to reduce the incongruence between the aims of the manager and the firm by using internal sanctions to compel the manager to adopt the firm's ends as his own. In practice, it is debatable whether such a system could be installed since some forms of misconduct may be easily concealed even from the firm. The deterrence trap discussed above also poses a barrier, since if the firm cannot be adequately penalized, it will not vigorously monitor its agents.

In light of this possible rejoinder, it is important to move from theoretical to empirical arguments. The theoreticians of deterrence tend to assume that the actor has perfect knowledge, or at least can calculate with reasonable accuracy the odds of apprehension. In reality, we lack even an approximate estimate of how much white-collar crime occurs or how often it results in conviction. Because an accurate calculation of the cost/benefit calculus which the microeconomic approach utilizes is thus improbable, the critical variable becomes the actor's attitude toward risk. Is he a risk averter or a risk preferrer? Other things being equal, the risk-averter manager tends to be deterred by high penalties even when they are associated with low rates of apprehension, while a risk-preferring manager would look at the same combination of penalties and probabilities and not be deterred. Knowing only that apprehension is a long-shot, the risk preferrer will be likely to chance profitable illegal behavior, even though an apprehension would devastate his career.

Although some theorists have argued that the typical corporate manager is risk averse, some empirical evidence points in the opposite direction. Repeated studies have detected a phenomenon known as the "risky shift": businessmen participating in role-playing experiments have shown a pronounced tendency to make "riskier" decisions when acting in a small group than when acting alone. That is, the degree of risk they are willing to accept increases dramatically when the decision is reached collectively within a small group—exactly the context in which most business decisions are made. Other experiments have found such small groups of businessmen willing to ignore extremely strong evidence of social irresponsibility and legal obstacles when making business decisions involving the introduction of dangerous or unsafe products. These experiments can be read in several ways. They may indicate that businessmen are more risk-preferring (at least, collectively) than the average citizen, or they may imply that businessmen acting in small groups become more optimistic and reduce their estimates of the risks in a given situation from what they would perceive them to be individually. Either way, the result is the same: so long as the odds on apprehension are unknown, but probably low, many businessmen are likely to reach a subjective estimate of the legal risks in a given situation which leads them to accept these risks—even if the average citizen alone would not.

A related and reinforcing perspective on the psychology of the representative business manager is suggested by another central tenet of the organization theorist. While the economist assumes that firms uniformly seek to maximize profits, organization theorists, such as Nobel laureate Herbert Simon, have found the typical manager more likely to engage in what they term "satisficing" behavior. That is, instead of assembling all available information and choosing the best alternative, individuals tend to accept the first alternative presented to them that satisfies the minimum criteria. In short, individuals pursue not optimal solutions, but satisfactory ones; they seek not answers that maximize, but ones that suffice. From this perspective, which assumes that individuals act not on perfect knowledge but rather on random search strategies, it is possible to see why the harried manager finds illegality attractive in many circumstances. Over-worked, overloaded and faced with a maze of sometimes conflicting governmental regulations, the simplest solution which permits him to function is often that of falsification.

Finally, the behavioral perspective highlights one of the most basic causes of misbehavior within organizations: individuals frequently act out of loyalty to a small group within the firm with which they identify. Thus, engineers working on the development of a particular project may develop an intense dedication to it which leads them to suppress negative safety findings. Similarly, a plant manager may falsify environmental data out of fear that the prohibitive costs of bringing the plant into compliance might result in its closing. This pattern is consistent with a considerable body of social science data which suggests that the individual's primary loyalty within any organization is to his immediate work group. Within this group, he will engage in candid disclosure and debate, but he will predictably edit and screen data before submitting them to superiors in order to cast his sub-unit in a favorable light.

From this perspective, the following generalization becomes understandable: the locus of corporate crime is predominantly at the lower to middle management level. Although public interest groups are vocal in their denunciations of "crimes in the suites," in truth the most shocking safety and environmental violations re almost exclusively the product of decisions at lower managerial levels. Senior executives may still bear some causal responsibility, but the chain of causation is remote, and their influence on decisions is only indirect.

To understand this assessment, the multi-divisional and often radically decentralized structure of the modern public corporation must be examined. Increasingly, a central corporate headquarters monitors operationally autonomous divisions, but its review is focused on budgetary matters and strategic planning. Operational control typically remains in the division. Indeed, some economists have compared the central corporate office to a miniature capital market, since its primary function is to allocate funds to profitable divisions and to discipline those which fail to meet targeted profitability goals.

The nature of this disciplinary monitoring by the central office is of particular relevance. Because it is at considerable organizational distance and its attention is focused on the income statement, the central office can avoid responsibility for operational decisions while at the same time holding the division responsible for a failure to meet profit quotas assigned it. Through a variety of penalties and incentives—*i.e.*, salary and fringe benefits, increased or diminished staff and budget, and the threat of dismissal or demotion—the central office in the multi-divisional firm pressures the operating divisions to comply with its goals. Thus, the directive from the top of the organization is to increase profits by fifteen percent, but the means are left to the managerial discretion of the middle manager who is in operational control of the division.

Properly applied, such pressure establishes and enforces accountability without sacrificing the flexibility and adaptiveness that are the virtues of decentralization. However, this structure also permits the central headquarters to insulate itself from responsibility for operational decisions while simultaneously pressuring for quick solutions to often intractable problems. The middle manager is acutely aware that he can easily be replaced; he knows that if he cannot achieve a quick fix, another manager is waiting in the wings, eager to assume operational control over a division. The results of such a structure are predictable: when pressure is intensified, illegal or irresponsible means become attractive to a desperate middle manager who has no recourse against a stern but myopic notion of accountability that looks only to the bottom line of the income statement. Paul Lawrence, a professor of organizational behavior at the Harvard Business School, has summarized this dilemma:

> A certain amount of tension is desirable. But at many companies the pressures to perform are so intense and the goals so unreasonable that some middle managers feel the only way out is to bend the rules, even if it means compromising personal ethics. . . . When a manager feels his job or division's survival is at stake, the corporation's standards of business conduct are apt to be sacrificed.

For the middle-level official the question is not whether the behavior is too risky to be in the interests of the corporation from a cost/benefit standpoint. Rather, it is: which risk is greater—the criminal conviction of the company or his own dismissal for failure to meet targets set by an unsympathetically demanding senior management. Because the conviction of the corporation falls only indirectly on the middle manager, it can seldom exceed the penalty that dismissal or demotion means to him. The middle manager thus faces a very different set of potential costs and benefits from the corporate entity. For example, a given crime may carry with it a forty percent risk of apprehension—presumably too high a level to be very attractive to the corporation. But if compliance with the legal standard subjects the middle manager to a fifty percent chance of dismissal for failure to meet a corporate profit quota, crime may well be attractive to him even if it is anathema to his corporate employer. Caught between Scylla and Charybdis, this middle-level manager will seek short-run survival through concealment, falsification and, when necessary, illegality.

To sum up, in the modern public corporation it is not only ownership and control that are divorced (as Berle and Means recognized long ago), but also strategic decision-making and operational control. In an era of finance capitalism, the manager responsible for operational and production decisions is increasingly separated by organization, language, goals, and experience from the financial manager who today plans and directs the corporation's future. This tends both to insulate the upper echelon executive (who may well desire that the sordid details of "meeting the competition" or "coping with the regulators" not filter up to his attention) and to intensify the pressures on those below by denying them any forum in which to explain the crises they face. This generalization helps to explain both the infrequency with which corporate misconduct can be traced to senior levels and the limited effort made to date within many firms to develop a system of legal auditing which approaches the sophistication of financial auditing.

This portrait is to a degree deliberately overdrawn. Some corporations have developed procedures by which middle managers participate in the shaping of long-term profit goals for their division, and relatively few corporations enforce the notion of accountability so rigidly as to permit no excuse for failure to meet a profit goal. Consider it, then, a portrait of the pathological organization. But to the extent it even approximates the internal dynamics within some firms, such corporations are essentially undeterrable (at least in the short run) by penalties focused only on the firm. In the last analysis, whether we take the economic perspective or the behavioral one, we tend to reach the same conclusion.

C. The Externality Problem

The idea of externalities as applied to the actions of public bodies is probably best illustrated by the common practice of most highway departments in liberally dumping salt on frozen roads. This technique cures their problem of ice-coated roads at a relatively low cost, but it also imposes an "external cost" on landowners and drivers: plants die along the borders of such roadways, and cars rust and deteriorate more quickly because of the effect of the salt on their exteriors. This cost, however, is not borne by the highway department, and thus is externalized in the same sense that a manufacturer traditionally never bore the cost of his pollution that fell on the adjoining landowners downwind.

In this same sense, punishment imposes both external and internal costs. For example, the direct public cost of imprisonment (e.g., the cost of the prison system) is an internal cost which law enforcement authorities must recognize in jailing people. But the welfare cost of sustaining the jailed person's family is likely to be externalized, falling on other agencies and receiving less attention.

The problem of external costs is present in the case of corporate punishment, and comes into focus when we consider the incident of financial penalties imposed on the corporation. As a moment's reflection reveals, the costs of deterrence tend to spill over onto parties who cannot be characterized as culpable. Axiomatically, corporations do not bear the ultimate cost of the fine; put simply, when the corporation catches a cold, someone else sneezes. This overspill of the penalty initially imposed on the corporation has at least four distinct levels, each progressively more serious. First, stockholders bear the penalty in the reduced value of their securities. Second, bondholders and other creditors suffer a diminution in the value of their securities which reflects the increased riskiness of the enterprise. These points have been made many times both in the Model Penal Code, and in the writing of such respected scholars as Francis Allen, Sanford Kadish and Alan Dershowitz. The analysis, however, needs to be carried several steps further: the third level of incident of a severe financial penalty involves parties even less culpable than the stockholders. As a class, the stockholders can at least sometimes be said to have received unjust enrichment from the benefits of the crime; this arguably justifies their indirectly bearing a compensating fine. However, if the fine is severe enough to threaten the solvency of the corporation, the predictable response will be a cost-cutting campaign, involving reductions in the work force through layoffs of lower echelon employees who received no benefit from the earlier crime. Severe financial penalties thus interfere with public goals of full employment and minority recruitment by restricting corporate expansion. In a society willing to bail out a Chrysler to save the jobs of its workers, it would seem perversely inconsistent to punish a Ford for its Pinto by imposing financial sanctions that resulted in plant closings and layoffs. Finally, there is the fourth level of incident of a financial penalty: it may be passed onto the consumer. If the corporation competes in a product market characterized by imperfect competition (a trait of most of the "real world"), then the fine may be recovered from consumers in the form of higher prices. If this happens, the "wicked" corporation not only goes unpunished, but the intended beneficiary of the criminal statute (i.e., the consumer) winds up bearing its penalty. . . .

III. Optimizing Corporate Deterrence From Description to Prescription

The preceding sections have argued that both real and perceived externalities associated with corporate punishment have restrained courts and legislators in authorizing and imposing penalties on a corporation. This Section will argue that it is therefore desirable to find "socially cheaper" methods of punishing the corporation. This notion of social economy does not imply less severe penalties, but rather penalties which minimize both the real and the apparent overspill of the costs of deterrence onto the non-culpable. Concededly, any assertion that there can be "socially cheaper" penalties may seem unintelligible to the neo-classical economist. If one proceeds from the assumption that the "expected punishment cost" must exceed the expected gain before the firm will act to prevent criminal behavior by its agents, then our quandry may be insoluble, at least for crimes having a low risk of apprehension. But from a behavioral perspective, which examines the internal dynamics within the firm, we can identify leverage points where a parsimonious use of penalties directed at the firm may still be effective.

An analogy may help clarify this difference in approach: both the neo-classical economist and the conventional liberal politician seem to have agreed that fines will not work unless they are severe. Under a regime of harsh penalties, the state simply bludgeons the corporation into compliance. Such a strategy reminds one of two giant sumo wrestlers circling each other before the charge: force meets force in a head-on conflict, and innocent parties may get trampled in the ensuing havoc. There is an alternative: to extend this analogy, the judo wrestler relies not on brute force, but rather turns the innocent less subject to injury. Similarly, the behavioral perspective suggests opportunities for controlled uses of force which, like the judo expert, exploit the target's own internal forces and tensions.

George Orwell demonstrates in *1984* that every man has some subconscious fear which society can bring to bear against him. While Orwell's example terrifies us, it can also instruct us as to how society might harness the internal forces within the firm to enhance the deterrent threat of the law. Specifically, to deter corporate crime more effectively, one might sensibly begin by exploring the principal fears and interests of the manager, and then match the consequences of a criminal conviction to them. Several possibilities suggest themselves: (1) much evidence suggests that corporate managers fear a hostile take-over of their firm, which would typically be accomplished through a tender offer; (2) the manager's self-interest is very much identified with the value of the firm's

stock, and stock option, phantom options, stock bonus plans, and other forms of incentive compensation cement such a linkage; (3) the competitive struggle for advancement and promotion within the firm implies that managers identified publicly as having been involved in corporate misconduct will be disadvantaged in their opportunities for advancement (both internally and externally with other firms); (4) there is a general fear within most organizations of loss of autonomy; any intrusion into the sphere in which the manager sees himself as autonomous will be resented and resisted. Penalties that play on these fears and interests may effectively increase deterrence. Finally, private litigation in the form of the derivative suit may evade nullification by transferring costs imposed upon the corporation to the responsible officials (who may view the penalty as substantial because it is a large percentage of their net worth). Thus, the possibilities for efficient integration of civil and criminal enforcement deserve particular attention. How these forces might be harnessed in the aftermath of a criminal conviction of a corporation will be the focus of this Section.

A. *The Equity Fine: Toward a More Focused "Capital Punishment"*

The time has come for a basic policy assertion: when very severe fines need to be imposed on the corporation, they should be imposed not in cash, but in the equity securities of the corporation. The convicted corporation should be required to authorize and issue such number of shares to the state's crime victim compensation fund as would have an expected market value equal to the cash fine necessary to deter illegal activity. The fund should then be able to liquidate the securities in whatever manner maximizes its return. . . .

B. *The Hester Prynne Sanction: Using Adverse Publicity to Trigger Internal Reform*

As Hester Prynne knew, public stigmatization can be a powerful sanction. Although we cannot hand a scarlet letter on the corporation, the criminal process has a unique theatricality which can convey public censure far more effectively than the civil-law process. Recent research also suggests that the threat of stigmatization may be the primary deterrent in the case of middle-class defendants. But can we focus adverse publicity with similar efficacy when it is the corporation that is convicted? If we can, adverse publicity might seem an optimal penalty for corporate misbehavior, because it seems to minimize the externalities associated with other forms of corporate punishment.

Little doubt exists that corporations dislike adverse publicity and that unfavorable publicity emanating from an administrative or judicial source has considerable credibility. From this starting point, commentators have suggested a variety of formal publicity sanctions; for example, Professor Brent Fisse has recommended that the government publish a "corporation journal" which would detail the offenses of convicted organizations. There is a danger, however, that in practice such well-meaning reforms would become so bureaucratized and pedestrian as to have only a negligible impact. A cool-headed appraisal of the limits on adverse publicity as an effective legal sanction for organizations seems necessary. Such an appraisal will serve as a prelude for this Article's suggestion that the focus of adverse publicity as an organizational penalty should be shifted from the corporate entity to the individuals within the firm. Such an approach again harnesses internal forces within the firm so as to reduce the incongruence between the interests of managers and their firm.

A strategy that seeks to deter corporations through adverse publicity aimed at the firm may fail because of the following problems:

First, the government is a relatively poor propagandist. It has trouble being persuasive; rarely is it pithy; never can it speak in the catchy slogans with which Madison Avenue mesmerizes us. At its best, the government sounds like the back pages of the *New York Times* ("good, gray and dull"); at its worst, its idea of communication is exemplified by the *Federal Register*. This soporific quality of governmental prose matters little when it is addressed (as it usually is) to lobbyists, bureaucrats and lawyers. But to be effective, a publicity sanction must make the public pay attention. Those who have had success in reaching the public – *e.g.*, the television networks and the advertising agencies – recognize H.L. Mencken's maxim as an iron law: No one ever lost money underestimating the intelligence of the American public. Such insight may have made Freddie Silverman famous, but in this context it raises an ethical dilemma: publicity requires over-simplification. The message must be simple and catchy – even if a price must be paid in terms of its accuracy. But this price is troubling; it seems indecent for the government to engage directly in so dubious an endeavor as attempting to persuade in the manner of Madison Avenue advertising agencies.

Second, government publicity may be drowned out because the communication channels of our society are already inundated with criticism of corporations. In the language of the communications theorist, there is too much noise in the channels for any message to be heard with clarity. Unkind words about corporations come from a multitude of sources today: Notorieties, editorialists, television commentators, politicians facing election campaigns, etc. The result is that the currency is being devalued. Weak criticism tends to rob accurate censure of its expressive force. The criminal conviction of the corporation should be a unique event, but it loses its special force when the public constantly receives an implicit message that all corporations are corrupt or amoral.

Third, corporations can dilute this sanction through counter-publicity. As recent Mobil Oil advertisements about the energy crisis should remind us, the corporation can fight back – and effectively. In addition, recent Supreme Court decisions uphold-ing the corporation's first amendment right to comment on public issues cloud the constitutional status of any attempt to restrict such corporate rebuttals. In sum, these first three factors require us at least to be tentative in any judgment about the effectiveness of governmental publicity.

Fourth, the efficacy of publicity in cases involving consumer fraud or jeopardy to the public safety does not imply that publicity will be equally effective in dealing with "regulatory" crimes. The public responds with outrage when it learns it has been sole an unsafe product, administered a dangerous drug, or exposed to a carcinogenic environmental hazard, but its reaction may be far less intense when the crime threatens no obvious injury. The muckrakers learned this lesson to their dismay at the start of this century. While an Upton Sinclair or an Ida Tarbell could arouse the public's indignation over the contents of sausage, they were less successful at crystallizing public concern over institutional corruption. Aiming at America's brain, they hit only its belly. To be sure, the recent history of the Watergate scandals and particularly of the illegal corporate payments scandals may lead us to temper this conclusion. The public did show considerable interest in the details of the Lockheed, Gulf Oil and United Brands scandals. But novelty wears off, and companies which subsequently disclosed illegal payments at least as extensive received far less public attention. In any event, there is little evidence that either the public or investors changed their behavior because of these disclosures in any way which prejudiced these corporations. Consumers did not shun Gulf gasoline or United Brands bananas as a result of illegal payments publicity. Those who did suffer were largely producers of capital equipment – such as Lockheed and Northrup – who lost prospective sales to foreign governmental purchasers. Only in these cases did publicity not directly aimed at the quality of the defendant's product produce financial injury to the corporation. But this observation leads to still another, more general problem with publicity as a sanction:

Fifth, if publicity directed against the corporation

is effective, it will produce the same externalities as cash fines. Adverse publicity is something of a cannon; its exact impact cannot be reliably estimated nor is it controllable so that only the guilty are affected. Here, the recent Ford Pinto case supplies a paradigm: although acquitted, Ford's ability to market the Pinto has obviously been impaired. The impact of reduced sales or the termination of a produce line once again falls disproportionately on workers at the bottom of the hierarchy. If we are willing to bear these costs (as sometimes we must), it seems easier to rely on even cash fines in preference to the wholly unpredictable impact of a legal stigma. By no means is this argument a rejection of governmentally mandated publicity as a means of correcting false advertising or of alerting the consumer to potential dangers. But the civil law can also achieve these goals and with less effort and greater precision. Through product recalls, civil orders requiring corrective advertising, and even notices from the producer asking customers to desist from further use of the product, administrative agencies can and have used publicity to protect the consumer. Here the end result is achieved without the extraneous emotion and complexity that follows from attempting to use publicity itself as a form of punishment.

Finally, civil liberties issues surround the use of publicity as a sanction. The criminal process inherently involves adverse publicity, and, to this extent, some element of the punishment precedes the conviction. Publicity begins with the indictment, and an acquittal does not fully undo the damage. In contrast, the quieter, less public character of civil-law adjudication allows us to withhold the impact of adverse publicity until there has been a finding.

Although a corporate defendant may be required to give notice of its convictions to victims, more serious problems emerge when the government itself seeks to broadcast the significance of the conviction outside the courtroom. In the frequent case where the defendant plea bargains and the government in return drops some of the charges in the indictment, it would seem improper for the government to discuss unproved and unadmitted allegations in its publicity efforts. . . .

C. *Integrating Public and Private Enforcement: A Reexamination of the Private Attorney General*

Nullification of criminal penalties may be a fact of life which, like death and taxes, simply must be accepted. Whether this phenomenon is premised on a fear of the adverse social consequences from penalties imposed on the corporation, or whether courts are simply unwilling to impose high penalties which do not compensate the victims of the offense, nullification is an obstacle to adequate deterrence which intelligent

policy planning must find a way to circumvent. But one exception to this problem clearly exists: while courts are reluctant to impose high penalties to punish or deter, they tolerate enormous damages awards to compensate victims. For example, in the famous electrical equipment conspiracy of the 1950s, the largest single fine (levied on General Electric) was $437,500, but approximately $600 million was paid by the defendants to settle private litigation. Comparable, but lower amounts have been paid already in more recent and still unresolved price-fixing cases.

At the risk then of seeming to rediscover the wheel, it is best to start our appraisal of private enforcement by noting that it offers two distinct advantages: (1) private enforcers are able to raise the total penalties exacted from the corporation to a level well in excess of those which either the criminal law or public enforcement generally can levy, and (2) by acting as "private attorneys general," civil plaintiffs multiply society's enforcement resources and thereby increase the probability of detection. This latter theme has been much emphasized, and the private antitrust plaintiff's ability to discover conspiracies and violations which have escaped the attention of public enforcers is frequently glorified as the great virtue of private enforcement. But here, a heretical observation is unavoidable: recent experience confirms the first assertion that private enforcement raises the penalty for illegal activity, but it provides very little evidence to corroborate the second proposition. Indeed, in the antitrust context, the current pattern is almost the reverse of the theory: the private plaintiff is typically a "free rider" who files his civil action in the wake of an indictment brought by the Antitrust Division. It is not uncommon today for the private enforcer to attend the criminal trial and to take copious notes so that evidence uncovered by the government will yield a treble damage recovery for him. In effect, the private enforcer reaps the benefit of the enforcement efforts by public enforcers. In such cases, the actual litigation undertaken by the private enforcers is chiefly internecine: they skirmish among themselves over such procedural issues as the appointment of lead counsel, the size of the settlement, and the allocation of attorney's fees. Nor is this pattern unique to antitrust cases. In the securities law filed, it has been observed that few cases of insider trading have been detected by private plaintiffs; rather, once again, the private plaintiff rides the coattails of the SEC's enforcement staff. . . .

IV. BEYOND DETERRENCE: THE IMPLEMENTATION OF PREVENTIVE RESTRAINTS

Deterrence is an indirect organizational strategy: we raise the costs of an activity in anticipation that the organization will restrain its agents. Frequently, the civil law has relied on a more direct strategy, the injunction, which can be framed to require, rather than simply encourage, internal reform. Only recently have criminal-law scholars begun seriously to consider that the criminal law could also intervene directly by interjecting the court or its agents into the corporation's decision-making processes ion an attempt to remedy dysfunctions that seem causally related to the criminal behavior. The most promising vehicle for such an attempt is the sentence of probation. Traditionally, probation was seen as an elective disposition which the offender had to request or at least accept. Thus, because the corporation would typically prefer to pay the fine as a cost of doing business rather than change the way it actually did business, it might often refuse such a disposition. More recently, however, probation has come to be seen as a disposition which, being as much in society's interest as the offender's, is neither elective nor a temporary holding category, but rather a sentence in its own right. Concomitant with this transition, both the current Senate and House bills to recodify the Federal Criminal Code authorize a probationary disposition for convicted organizations, and the Second Edition of the *American Bar Association's Minimum Standards for Criminal Justice* has endorsed the use of such a sentence in some circumstances. A few cases have also accepted the idea of corporate probation under existing law. . . .

CONCLUSION: TOWARD PUNISHMENT THAT FITS THE CORPORATION

One last question should be addressed: Do all the reforms discussed in this Article necessarily require legislative action? Or can they be at least partially implemented by the judiciary alone? Perhaps surprisingly, courts may be able to achieve them in substantial measure without legislative action. A publicity sanction could, for example, be implemented by placing the corporation on probation. The *nolo contendere* plea is already a discretionary decision given to the court. Although the equity fine is not within the inherent power of the court, there is no necessary obstacle to the court accepting such a fine when offered by the defendant *as the alternative to a higher cash fine.* This scenario is more realistic than it at first sounds. Frequently, a single criminal transaction will either violate multiple criminal statutes or be divisible into numerous counts of the same offense. As a result, a cumulative fine can be levied equal to the maximum fine per count times the number of counts resulting in conviction. Under the pending Senate bill to recodify the Federal Criminal Code, the maximum fine would be $1 million per count. Thus, very high fines

are possible, particularly in environmental cases where the illegal activity often takes place many times over an extended period. As a result, it ironically may be a defendant and not a prosecutor who is the first to ask a sentencing court to consider the possibility of an equity fine. But clearly, the court could prepare the way for such a request by tentatively imposing a high cash fine and then suggesting to defense counsel that it consider developing an alternative formula that would offer equivalent deterrence.

Corporate probation is an area where courts undoubtedly should proceed cautiously, and this Article has intended more to scout the perimeters of that remedy than to recommend it as a mandatory sentence. But in an economy characterized by imperfect competition, organizational slack, and innumerable obstacles that interfere with the expected impact of penalties for corporate misbehavior, direct judicial intervention in certain areas of the firm's decision-making processes will at times be necessary. It is a curious paradox that the civil law is better equipped at present than the criminal law to authorize these interventions. Corporate probation could fill this gap and, at last, offer a punishment that fits the corporation.

The strategies outlined in this Article—the equity fine, adverse publicity, integration of civil and criminal remedies, plea bargaining for restitution, and corporation probation—have a common denominator: like the judo wrestler they use existing forces within the legal environment and the corporation's social system to increase corporate deterrence with a minimum of socially counter-productive results. Unless we follow such a course, the Lord Chancellor's frustrated observation that the corporation has neither a soul to damn nor body to kick may remain an epitaph for society's attempts to control organizational misbehavior.

Barry D. Baysinger, *Organization Theory and the Criminal Liability of Organizations,* 72 B.U. L. REV. 341–376 (1991)*

Policy Preferences and Assumptions

The United States Sentencing Commission's sentencing guidelines for organizational crime appear to

---

* Reprinted with permission of Boston University Law Review.

have been shaped by three fundamental policy preferences. The first is a preference for incrementalism over absolutism in determining the optimal level of organizational crime and formulating strategies to achieve that goal. The second is a preference for imputed over individual liability for the social harm caused by organizational crime. The third is a preference for the imposition of modest economic sanctions on corporations over more extreme penalties. . . .

The Assumption of Effective Managerial Control

The Commission's sentencing strategy outlined above is supposed to operate similarly to a closed hydraulic system. In such a system, fluid pressure is equal everywhere, and any change in pressure that occurs at one point in the system is efficiently, truly and rapidly transmitted by the fluid to all points in the system. In the context of controlling organizational crime, the Commission assumes that the threat of sanctions imposed on the firm's owners, directors and top-level managers will be efficiently, truly and rapidly transmitted to the firm's low-level employees who are most likely to commit economic crimes. Organization theory questions this assumption.

Managers of large, complex organizations have not clearly demonstrated that they have effective control over their employees, even in areas such as product quality, service excellence and innovation. While an entire cottage industry has grown up around the problem of finding effective strategies for changing organizational change and development strategies has been limited.

* * *

This record of frustration suggests that any policy based on the presumption that top-level managers are able to affect the criminal behavior of their subordinates should be subject to the closest scrutiny. The Sentencing Commission may be able to alter the choices facing corporate shareholders, directors and top-level corporate managers. It does not necessarily follow, however, that this will have much immediate effect on the behavior of those individuals within corporations who commit the vast majority of economic crimes. Nor does it appear that corporate compliance programs and the institution of ethical codes of conduct are very effective. Corporate claims that they should be given credit for the existence of such programs at sentencing time should also be scrutinized carefully.

This Article elaborates on the shortcomings in the Guidelines by illustrating some of the difficulties managers confront in trying to change behavior that has become habitual in complex organizations. It does not present, however, a fully developed theory of corporate crime and institutional change. Rather, it is merely a first reaction to the critical assumptions underlying the Commission's sentencing guidelines from the perspective of organization theory. The central theme is caution, not conclusions. No public policy implications are intended in the absence of formal modeling and empirical testing.

The Article synthesizes and applies previous research in organization theory and organizational economics to the problem of understanding (1) how corporate strategy affects the way organizations are structured, (2) how organizational structure affects the development of internal control processes and norms and (3) how different internal control processes and norms affect individual behavior – lawful or otherwise. The Article further examines the relation between corporate diversification strategies and the adoption of internal control processes which tend to focus primarily on quantitative performance criteria, such as accounting profit or return on investment, in the evaluation and reward of individual behavior and outputs. To the extent that lawful activity conflicts with meeting these performance criteria, criminal behavior may ensue. A central theme in the Article is that until the systematic forces generating these criteria change in fundamental ways – until corporations restructure – management's ability to control the criminal acts of their subordinates, through conventional methods of control, will remain ineffective. . . .

I. ORGANIZATION THEORY AND INDIVIDUAL BEHAVIOR

All organized human activity gives rise to two basic and conflicting requirements of organizational effectiveness. One is a drive toward specialization and the division of labor; the other is a drive toward the integration and coordination of specialized tasks to accomplish goals effectively and efficiently. As organizations grow in size and complexity, a variety of coordination and control mechanisms evolve to facilitate communication vertically within the organizational hierarchy and laterally among inter-related and interdependent departments. These mechanisms also maintain control over individuals performing specialized tasks whose private interests do not always coincide with those of the firms' owners. Organizational structure is the sum of the ways managers meet these two requirements for organizational effectiveness. Organization theory is the subdiscipline of management theory which studies how organizational structures evolve adaptively and how these adaptions affect organizational performance.

Understanding the basics of organization theory is important in the present context for two reasons: first, to understand the tools available to managers for controlling the behavior of their subordinates, and second, to understand that organizational structure affects the behavior of individuals in complex organizations in ways which are often beyond the total control of management. These twin themes will be played out repeatedly in this paper and therefore need to be developed early on.

A. Coordination and Information Processing

Management coordinates the activities of specialized individuals and sub-units within complex organizations by a variety of mechanisms. The three primary coordinating mechanisms are informal mutual adjustment among individuals, direct supervision of subordinates and development and enforcement of performance standards through which behavior is coordinated "automatically." Mutual adjustment occurs when specialists communicate among themselves to coordinate their activities without resorting to the chain of command. It is efficient, but is not always as effective as direct supervision. Through direct supervision subordinates' actions are programmed and planned out from above; coordination is achieved when the superior issues orders or instructions to subordinates whose tasks are interrelated. It is less efficient than mutual adjustment, but affords managers more control.

To economize on the loss of control and bureaucratic costs associated with mutual adjustment and direct supervision, organizations often attempt to coordinate the activities of specialists and departments through the enforcement of behavioral and performance standards. Work process standardization coordinates the work of interdependent units or people by specifying the steps in the work process that are appropriate for any given situation. Management formalizes behavior by imposing standing operating instructions, elaborated job descriptions, rules and regulations, and so forth. Output standardization, in contrast, coordinates activities within the organization by specifying performance targets, letting individuals work out strategies for meeting these targets, then rewarding individuals based on their success in meeting those targets.

To economize on the costs of implementing these coordinating mechanisms, managers can turn to less intrusive forms of standardization. For example, the standardization of skills and technical knowledge, through indoctrination and formal training, facilitates coordination among similarly trained individuals, who can respond automatically to contingencies by virtue of their common skills and knowledge. An example of this is two police officers making an arrest. Finally, management can develop standardized norms of proper conduct informally through tradition, history and on-the-job experiences. Where the standardization of norms is successful, the highest-level management can trust subordinates to make decisions and take actions that facilitate coordinated action across diverse specialized tasks and interdependent departments.

The preceding might suggest that organizational dysfunction is due primarily to defects in communication and coordination. This, however, is not the case. Only a naive view of organizations would argue that they are collections of individuals pulling together to achieve common objectives. Were this so, organizational dysfunction would always be attributable to ignorance and poor communication. Organizational design would then simply involve the effective management of information flows to decision points within the organization and the implementation of the coordinating mechanisms outlined above.

In reality, organizations are collections of individuals who attempt to achieve their own personal objectives through their membership in the organization. Inevitably, problems of agency conflict, moral hazard or goal divergence arise and must be regulated through various governance mechanisms. That is, individuals who are well informed about the standards they are to live up to, and who have been subjected to attempts to develop standardized norms, may still act opportunistically, pursuing private goals which conflict with organizational goals. As a result, organization theorists study the development of control strategies within organizations. It is in this area of control that economics and organization theory may be combined to produce a unified theory of organizational behavior.

B. Organizational Economics

Organizational approaches to control benefit from the application of basic microeconomic choice theory to the problem of understanding rational organizational behavior, especially with respect to how that behavior is shaped and controlled. At the risk of promoting economic imperialism, much of management theory and practice reduces to the practical application of axiomatic choice theory to behavior that occurs not in markets, but within the "black box" of the hierarchical organization.

A basic goal of microeconomic theory is to predict how changes in opportunities, such as income and relative prices, affect the choices of rational people. Economists assume that people rationally choose among their opportunities to maximize their utility according to individual preferences. Since the particular opportunity an individual chooses is assumed to be sensitive to both changes in available opportunities or changes in personal preferences, one can promote "desired" behavior either by shaping the individual's opportunities or shaping the individual's preferences.

Shaping opportunities provides economic incentives for "desired" behavior, while shaping preferences increases the individual's psychological inclination to behave in the "desired" manner. Although economists typically assume constance preferences and focus on the relation between choice and opportunities, a basic purpose of management is to influence preferences through leadership and to shape opportunities through control. Moreover, individuals acting within complex organizations have their preferences and opportunities shaped by systemic forces over which neither they nor management have much control. A key issue this Article discusses is how the contest between these uncontrolled systemic forces and management's ability to shape the behavior of their subordinates is affected by organizational growth, complexity and structure.

C. *Shaping Behavior: Leadership and Control*

Recent developments in organization theory recognize two basic strategies for shaping the behavior of individuals within hierarchic systems. These strategies broadly reflect the distinction between shaping preferences and shaping opportunities. The first behavior shaping strategy used in organizations is "managerial leadership." It entails the standardization of professional values and organizational norms in order to shape preferences toward goal-directed behavior. The aim is to minimize the divergence of preferences between subordinates and a firm's owners. The owners and management lead through employee selection, training, indoctrination and socialization.

Through careful selection and subtle or explicit indoctrination, the owner's and management motivate the people acting within the organizations to adopt norms and make decisions in accordance with their preferences. The organization's members are encouraged to cooperate in the achievement of organizational goals in acceptable ways. From the perspective of top management, indoctrination makes people more responsive to the organization's goals so that they can be trusted to make appropriate decisions and take desired actions with minimal direct supervision. They do so because they understand and have internalized the organization's goals and behavioral norms.

Norms are also formed through the action of systemic forces over which managers may have little if any control, such as the effect of intense industry competition on ethical conduct. People adopt such norms of behavior in response to contextual factors such as the organization's history, professional standards, core technology or structure.

The second behavior-shaping mechanism is "management control." It is analogous to the standardization-of-outputs method of coordinating interdependent behavior discussed above. Control strategies attempt to shape individual behavior through a cybernetic process of monitoring and rewarding individual behavior and performance. This mechanism emphasizes information processing and focuses on assessing various aspects of subordinate behavior and evaluating this behavior against the objectives of the organization's top decision makers. Such evaluations of low-level managerial performance can be based either on inferences concerning the qualify of the decision-making process—behavior control, or the measurable outcomes of decision-making processes—outcome control.

Professor Gupta, in his discussion of corporate-division relations, characterizes strategic control in terms of promoting openness between corporate level managers and division managers and in terms of corporate management's willingness to rely on subjective information in evaluating division manager performance. With strategic controls, managers are evaluated on the basis of performance criteria ex post, as well as on the basis of the strategic desirability of their decisions, ex ante. Conversely, under a system of financial controls, the organization evaluates and rewards managers primarily on the basis of their success in meeting impersonal, quantitative performance criteria. Financial data rather than richer forms of information are the media of communication and evaluation under this system. Headquarters personnel set quantitative standards for division managers to achieve, and establish strict penalties for failing to meet the standard.

Employee behavior is often sensitive to whether the organization relies on strategic or financial controls. Organizations are both risk-sharing and work-sharing collectives. Employees risk their employment when they act, and they bear increasing risk as controls become more outcome based. Since the relationship that develops among controls, risk bearing and the propensity toward criminal acts significantly informs this Article's criticism of the Sentencing Guidelines, a major objective of this paper will be to explore this relationship.

II. BEHAVIORAL IMPLICATIONS OF VARIOUS CONTROL STRATEGIES

Large, diversified firms operate in numerous complex and turbulent environments. Team production and environmental uncertainty combine to sever the link between managerial conduct and performance outcomes. Performance outcomes can fall short of projections, but it is often difficult to draw inferences concerning the quality of managerial performance from such shortfalls alone. They may be the result of bad luck, systemic forces beyond management control, managerial incompetence or managerial opportunism. Examples of the last are shirking or otherwise using firm resources for personal benefit at the expense of shareholders. "In other words, good outcomes can occur despite poor efforts and poor outcomes can occur despite good efforts."

An important function of top management in the diversified firm is to monitor the behavior of lower-level managers, assess the causes of poor performances accurately and protect the interests of shareholders by correlating performance with regards. The classic relation in economic theory that "runs from marginal productivity to the distribution of income[,] implicitly assumes the existence of an organization, be it the market or the firm, that allocates rewards to resources in accord with their productivity." If the internal control system of an organization only correlates rewards with the behavior generating outcomes, productivity will be lower. Management will focus on the internal control system in order to reduce employment risk; they will not focus on actual productivity or other objectives. Therefore, it is important that the information processing system, "have, or at least be perceived as having, the power to go beneath the apparent evidence to determine what in fact did happen." This is the purpose of the system of multidivisional or M-form controls that have evolved to govern behavior in the typical multi-product—that is, diversified—American corporation.

When employees are penalized or rewarded for outcomes that are not totally under their control, they bear some of the organization's risk. Rational subordinates, however, usually will be willing to take risks only where the internal control system displays the ability to separate "those outcomes that are due to changes in the condition of the environment from those that result from managerial decision-making." To the extent the system cannot differentiate between the outcomes that managers can and cannot control, employment risks are shifted to division managers, with predictably adverse behavioral consequences. As Professors Fischel and Bradley note: "risky projects can have poor outcomes; if managers are [penalized] whenever decisions that were optimal ex ante turn out poorly ex post, they will tend to avoid risky projects."

The purpose of strategic controls is to prevent this risk-shifting phenomenon. Subordinate managers are willing to make long-term investments and take other risks only if they are confident that they will not be penalized unfairly if those strategic initiatives fail. Unfortunately, strategic controls are costly to implement and maintain. Both corporate and division managers must invest in the preparation and communication of pertinent information. Yet, although such a process

may slow the decision making process, strategic controls pay for themselves in terms of both incentives and risk-bearing. They reduce conflicts of interest between division managers and shareholders by encouraging division managers to take optimal risks, manage for the long run and behave generally in a manner which is consistent with the organization's important objectives.

Financial controls, on the other hand, are relatively easy to implement, even in highly diversified organizations. Financial controls facilitate efficient vertical information processing, but they do not afford division managers the opportunity to articulate the extenuating circumstances which have caused disappointing financial results. Thus, although financial controls provide incentives which deter agency misbehavior, they can have pernicious effects on risk-bearing.

Attempting to draw correct inferences concerning the causes of poor performance outcomes is a tremendous challenge, especially in large, complex organizations. Top echelon managers must keep track of numerous divisions and make important resource allocation and disciplinary decisions; yet, they do not have sufficient information to draw correct inferences about the quality of lower-level managers' decisions. Therefore, financial controls almost inevitably result in errors in evaluating lower management performance.

It is typical, for example, for upper echelon management to attribute poor financial outcomes to mismanagement when they are actually due to investments in cost-saving technology that will take effect only over time. The result, as Professors Luce and Raiffa observe, is too often that "the strategist is evaluated in terms of the outcome of the adopted choice rather than in terms of the strategic desirability of the whole risky situation." Given this, managers, "realizing that outcomes rather than decision processes will be evaluated, are naturally reluctant to expose themselves to high variance undertakings."

The way rational people are controlled in organizations affects not only the intensity of their effort, i.e., their level of opportunism, but the direction of that effort as well—whether they will take appropriate risks. As the next Part shows, an individual may perceive that committing economic crimes in the context of a large, complex organization is an effective way to reduce the risk that she will be penalized for poor performance. Criminal behavior may be encouraged by organizational structure and controls associated with diversification and growth. In such situations, it may be very difficult for top-level management to affect the criminality of their subordinates, regardless of the penalties top-level management might impose.

III. Accomplishing Lawful Ends Through Unlawful Means

This Part describes systemic organizational factors that may influence organizational crime. Organizational crimes are economic; they are not crimes of passion. Individuals typically commit economic crimes with the expectation that they will be made better off in terms of income, status or security by choosing a criminal activity than they would by choosing non-criminal acts. Therefore, organizational crimes are simply the means by which individuals accomplish legitimate organizational objectives to maintain or advance their standing in the firm.

An individual operating within a business organization may have no intention of violating the law to accomplish her business objectives. Yet, when opportunities for organizational crimes arise, the individual will, perhaps implicitly, run through a decision calculus weighing the personal costs and benefits of criminal behavior. Substantial rewards often flow from unlawful acts, thus providing a powerful incentive which is immediate and certain. The costs of taking these opportunities, on the other hand, are uncertain. Moreover, the individual may well believe that budgetary considerations and an unwillingness to impose severe penalties on the garden variety "economic criminal" limit society's ability to reduce this uncertainty.

Individuals who, when outside an organization, would never consider engaging in criminal conduct, might, for a variety of reasons, find such behavior palatable and even necessary within an organizational setting. Economic crimes are typically malum prohibitum, such as regulatory violations, and, consequently, may not be taken very seriously either by individuals in organizations or in the general society. Furthermore, behavioral research demonstrates that business people acting as members of small groups are more optimistic and may develop an indifference to social norms and legal considerations when making business decisions. Additionally, individuals operating at lower levels in corporate hierarchies may be sufficiently uncertain about the current state of the law in such technical areas as resale price maintenance so as to be unaware that their behavior is illegal.

Achieving organizational objectives unlawfully is also tempting because the stakes are often so high. Because of the dollars involved, achieving one's goals through actions one knows are illegal becomes acceptable. To the extent that this criminal behavior leads to bonuses and career advancement, it may become positively desirable. Moreover, if others are trying to perform their tasks legally, unlawful acts provide a competitive advantage to the individual willing to compromise principle or risk detection. Similarly, if others are accomplishing their objectives unlawfully, an individual may conclude that engaging in illegal acts is a minimum requirement for personal survival. In many cases this Hobson's Choice may be resolved through the commission of economic crimes.

Of course, the risks of detection are not zero, and violators of criminal laws are not free of personal risk: individual criminal liability has long existed. Yet, the organizational member may very rationally believe that penalties for organizational crime are light. For example, while it is usually quite easy for prosecutors to establish the collective guilt of a corporation, establishing the guilt of individuals without violating due process is often difficult. As Professor Etzioni observes, "[b]ecause the crimes may involve complex financial transactions over long time periods, it may not be possible to determine exactly which individuals are responsible for what actions."

Additionally, there is a very low probability of being caught after committing an organizational crime. Although the "textbook" deterrence strategy would be to impose heavier individual penalties – jail sentences, for instance – in order to increase the expected cost of unlawful conduct, due to the peculiarities of the criminal justice system, the rational organizational member may discount this threat. It seems highly unlikely that malum prohibitum offenses would be penalized by jail time. Juries may feel that it is "unjust to single out one corporate employee for substantial punishment when the offense resulted from habits common to the organization as a whole." In addition, juries may take the view that individuals commit crimes virtually out of economic necessity and thus, view their commission as understandable, even excusable. Finally, individuals may not have the wherewithal to pay the fines typically imposed to punish malum prohibitum crimes, and thus, they may view such penalties as empty threats. Furthermore, even if they could pay the fines, it seems unlikely that juries would devastate a family simply to impose the economically efficient harm-based penalty on an individual wrongdoer.

Therefore, while personal standards of conduct and the risk of criminal sanctions undoubtedly affect criminal behavior at the margin, a variety of organizational and legal factors provide positive incentives to commit economic crimes. Moreover, when rational individuals compare the costs of government-imposed criminal sanctions against the costs of organization-imposed economic sanctions for failing to meet performance objectives, they may come to the conclusion that violating the law is the more desirable alternative.

That individuals are tempted to commit economic crimes is no mystery, and deterring such criminal behavior may now be seen as a considerable challenge. The purpose of the next Part is to show how, as organizations grow through diversification, they adopt internal governance systems that can decrease perceived employment risks relative to criminal liability and, hence, increase the pressure to engage in unlawful acts.

IV. Corporate Strategy, Structure, and White Collar Crime

This Part synthesizes research in organizational economics and organization theory relevant to the issue of organizational crime. From this synthesis a theory that links corporate diversification strategy and associated internal controls to employment risk and, hence, to differential pressures to commit organizational crimes is developed.

A. *Preliminary Observations on Organizational Dysfunction*

The large corporation represents a very efficient vehicle for raising equity and debt capital at low risk and, hence, reasonable cost. Yet, it would be a mistake to infer that because they dominate other organizational forms that such organizations are perfect. Among the notable drawbacks of large corporations is their inadequate ability to provide incentives for internal innovation or entrepreneurship. As one recent article put it, "go-go small-business culture can't easily be grafted onto a deliberate corporate giant. The practices that make corporations successful – training procedures, personnel policies, hierarchical management structures – are anathema to risk-taking, free-wheeling entrepreneurs."

The problem stems from the fact that in large diversified firms, corporate managers tend to use a return-on-investment (ROI) criterion for evaluating division manager performance. In response, division level managers develop a tendency to meet short-term ROI objectives by reducing expenditures that are critical for long-run organizational efficiency but are not essential to maximum short-run accounting profits. Thus, where meeting accounting profit goals decreases employment risk, subordinate managers will naturally tend to "work on their stats," even at the expense of overall organizational goals.

B. *Strategy, Structure and Internal Controls*

Corporate diversification has emerged as a major economic trend in the United States economy. Large diversified firms currently account for a substantial percentage of the total assets managed by U.S. industrial establishments. The hallmark of M-form organization is the decomposition of centralized strategic and operational decision-making, accompanied by the transfer of decision-making to semi-autonomous divisions. Decomposition and specialization of strategic and operating responsibility conserves the limited information processing capacities of corporate-level managers. Managers in such organizations maintain control over a fairly large number of separate businesses through delegation of day-to-day operating authority to divisional managers. Long-term strategy formulation and coordination of cash flows remains the responsibility of corporate headquarters staff.

Properly implemented systems of internal control can favorably shape the behavior of mid-level and supervisory managers. The diversified M-form, "can be thought of as substituting an administrative relation between an operating division and the firm's stockholders where a market relation had existed previously." As long as these organizations avoid excessive diversification, to the point where "it cannot competently evaluate and allocate funds among the diverse activities in which it is engaged, the substitution of internal organization can have beneficial effects in goal pursuit, monitoring, staffing, and resource allocation." Strategic controls in moderately diversified firms provide lower-level managers with incentives to perform well on the organization's behalf, and promote optimal risk-bearing.

Of course, unbridled diversification resulting in the use of financial controls compromises the beneficial properties of the M-form. Once such reliance on financial control begins, the basic challenge facing top-management is differentiating between poor performance that is due to opportunism and poor performance that is due to strategic long-term investments, factors beyond management control or both. To accomplish this important task, upper-level management institutes internal auditing procedures to detect managerial opportunism or incompetence, and then manipulate the firm's incentive machinery to reward performance that can be traced to management decisions. These tasks are performed by top-level corporate managers and a professional staff at the organization's general office.

Ideally, the general office has access to a body of rich information regarding the true causes of performance outcomes and can distinguish between poor outcomes and poor management. Division managers who, being subordinates in a hierarchical system of internal control, naturally regard internal disclosure of sensitive internal information "as necessary to the integrity of the organization" and thus provide this information. The general office of the M-form thus supplements the financial reports with a "backup internal audit that reviews divisional performance and attempts to attribute effects to the several possible causes." This is strategic performance control in operational terms.

C. *The Degeneration of the Ideal M-form*

Recent developments in organization theory strongly suggest, on both theoretical and empirical grounds, that not all diversified corporations are able to implement systems of strategic performance control successfully. The choice between using financial and strategic controls appears to be informed by the firm's antecedent choice of corporate diversification strategy. As firms diversify from their dominant business activity through mergers, acquisitions and new business development, strategic control degenerates into financial control. Moreover, the general office's limited information processing capacity eventually compromises its ability to attribute effects to the several possible causes.

With increased diversification, "the utility of organizational structure in helping top management to deal with strategic variety may be much more limited than the traditional strategic management literature would have us believe." While organizational structure "can attenuate the *intensity* of strategic variety that corporate-level management must deal with, . . . it cannot substitute for the need to handle strategic variety at the corporate level." That is, as firms diversify, top management's ability to evaluate the performance of ever greater numbers of more diverse divisions and assign rewards in a properly discriminating manner, diminishes.

Operationally, the general office staff must distill the rich information they have gathered to the leanest possible form. They communicate this information to the top management team as data. As an increasing amount of data flows to top management, they eventually lose their ability to maintain the type of open, subjective relationship with low-level managers that strategic control systems require: it simply becomes impractical. As a result, top management focuses almost exclusively on financial results – particularly the net profit for the period and the rate of return on invested capital – since these data are the most accessible through written reports.

This focus on financial data creates a gulf between hierarchic levels and limits division managers' ability to mitigate performance outcomes:

> [i]n an era of finance capitalism, the manager responsible for operational and production decisions is increasingly separated by organization, language, goals, and experience from the financial manager who today plans and directs the corporation's future. This tends both to insulate

the upper echelon executive . . . and to intensify the pressures on those below by denying them any forum in which to explain the crises they face.

These conditions shape the behavior of lower-level managers to favor actions which minimize employment risks. The next section argues that where low-level employees in financially controlled corporations perceive the risks of failing to meet financial objectives to be less than the risks of criminal sanctions for unlawful behavior, such employees may be more prone to accomplish their otherwise legitimate ends through unlawful means, than would their peers in less diversified organizations.

D. *Financial Controls and Organizational Crime*

In the aftermath of the electric-equipment price-fixing conspiracy, General Electric was described as "a very severely managed system of reward and punishment that demanded yearly improvements in earnings, return and market share, applied indiscriminately to all divisions, [and thus] yielded a situation which was – at the very best – conducive to collusion in the oligopolistic and mature electric equipment markets." General Electric was, of course, an M-form organization that had diversified extensively, perhaps to the point where strategic controls had degenerated into financial controls. In this structural setting, the organizational culture may have encouraged low-level managers to accept a norm of expediency to accomplish their objectives, a norm that could rationalize illegal actions in an effort to improve the bottom-line.

Financial controls tend to drive out goals that cannot be readily measured by financial control systems, such as product quality, pride in work and customer service. In effect, "the economic goals drive out the social ones." According to Professor Sutherland, "criminal behavior is learned in association with those who define such behavior favorably and in isolation from those who define it unfavorably. . . . [A] person in an appropriate situation engages in such behavior if, and only if, the weight of the favorable definitions exceeds the weight of the unfavorable definitions." Sutherland attributes favorable definitions of criminal conduct to such cultural factors as excessive competitiveness and urban business practices which tend to be impersonal. Thus, a business person's deviation in the line of duty from social norms condemning criminal behavior may imply little about that person's personal preferences.

An organization's internal control system can subtly shape an individual's opportunities to that organizational crimes are committed virtually out of necessity. A prominent business periodical offers the opinion that unlawful conduct by managers below the level of the top echelon

> is rooted in the short-run focus on profits that has hypnotized so many corporate managements. This year's profits—and even more important, this quarter's—determine the management's actions. The future of the corporation is lost in the shuffle. In the diversified corporation run by financial people who have no feel for the fiber and texture of a business, the bottom line is all that matters. They manage the bottom line to produce a desired number of dollars in profit, and then they order division executives to produce their share or else. The door is opened for shenanigans that the top management doesn't expect and cannot curtail because it doesn't understand the business.

Although perhaps not based on systematic reasoning, this observation clearly suggests a causal relation among corporate strategy, organizational processes and unlawful behavior. More systematic observations have yielded the same conclusion. Professor Ackerman concludes that the financial reporting systems which evolve within large, diversified firms

> may actually inhibit social responsiveness. By focusing on economic performance, even with appropriate safeguards to protect against sacrificing long-term benefits, such a system directs energy and resources to achieving results measured in financial terms. It is the only game in town, so to speak, at least the only one with an official scoreboard.

Additionally, as noted above in Part I, section C, recent advances in organization theory tend to bear these observations out.

In sum, diversification need not lead to M-form controls that encourage unlawful behavior. Yet, when diversification goes too far, strategic M-form controls degenerate into financial controls, and employment risks are shifted from the shareholders, where they belong, to lower level managers. Once this shift occurs, the expected personal consequences to an individual employee of failing to meet performance targets may become less attractive than the expected personal consequences of engaging in criminal activity to meet them. Therefore, as corporations diversify, their cultures undergo a transformation that may unintentionally exacerbate the problem of organizational crime.

This process of essentially rewarding crime is subtle and pervasive and, more to the point, will be very difficult to change through the type of public policy offered by the Commission.

V. A CRITICAL EVALUATION OF THE SENTENCING GUIDELINES

The Commission's sentencing guidelines for organizational crime are based on the belief that top-level corporate managers have the power to shape their employees' criminal behavior. A standard of strict vicarious liability and stiff fines for organizational crime should lead top-level managers to monitor employee behavior more closely—action planning—and to provide incentives to accomplish organizational objectives through lawful means—performance controls. From the perspective of organization theory, however, neither of these options appears very promising.

A. *The Private Deterrence of Organizational Crime*

The hallmark of M-form organization, it will be recalled, is the decomposition of centralize strategic and operational decision-making. The top-echelon managers of such organizations are able to manage a large number of separate businesses by delegating responsibility for day-to-day operations to divisional managers. In so doing top management abdicates direct control over divisional operations. As a result,

> [h]eadquarters managers who are concerned about legal liabilities or the public relations effects of decisions [e.g., unlawful acts], or even ones personally interested in broader social issues, may be tempted to intervene directly in the divisions' decision-making process to ensure proper attention to social matters. But they are discouraged from doing so by [the] . . . strict division of labor: Divisional autonomy requires no meddling by the headquarters in specific business decisions.

Therefore, diversification and the implementation of financial controls not only foster a short-run orientation among lower-level managers, but also reduce top-management's ability to shape the preferences and opportunities of their subordinates.

As top-level managers cannot "meddle" in division affairs without compromising production efficiency, they cannot engage in action planning to regulate criminal behavior, and they cannot manipulate incentives to shape the opportunities of would-be offenders through performance control techniques. Therefore, top-level managers can influence the behavior of their subordinates directly only through the shaping of preferences. Unfortunately, this process of shaping preferences is difficult to manage in simple organizations and may be nearly impossible in large, complex corporations.

B. *Shaping Behavior in Large Organizations: Forrester's Law*

Organizational research demonstrates that the behavior of people operating in complex social systems is shaped by a wide array of forces, some of which corporate policy-makers directly control, and many of which they do not. Moreover, empirical observation has given rise to Forrester's Law, which suggests that complex social systems usually behave counterintuitively; what is plausible often tends to be wrong. If so, the Commission's worse mistake may have been to put faith in the intuitive appeal of the "closed hydraulic system" approach to deterring organizational crime. Others have adopted this inapt faith in intuition.

Policy initiatives that make a straightforward intuitive attempt to control economic opportunities within a complex social system, without giving due deference to powerful social forces shaping individual preferences within those systems, are prone to fail. The United States government, for example, may have discovered Forrester's Law when it tried to force North Vietnam to bargain through carpet bombing. Recent United States attempts to deter the terror tactics of Shi'ite Muslim Fundamentalists in the Middle East through the strategy of retaliation, or imposing civil liability on the Palestinian Liberation Organization for damages borne by U.S. citizens in terror attacks, are likely to suffer the same fate. Closer to home, parental efforts to force their teenage children to stop smoking by suspending driving privileges, and so forth, are often unsuccessful. Despite the intuition that offering a clear economic quid pro quo—by making the sanctions for non-acceptance much greater than the costs of compliance—would effect behavior, in each of these cases the intuition proved false.

A hypothetical can be devised that illustrates Forrester's Law's similar application in large organizations. Suppose a complex government bureaucracy existed whose mission was to arrange for the design, production and operation of a fleet of manned space vehicles which would be loaded with cargo, regularly launched into space by chemical rocket boosters, orbit earth and then return to the ground like an airplane. Within this organization is an operating core of engineers, scientists and astronauts responsible for the safe and efficient operation of the fleet, and administrators responsible for acquiring resources for the core operators and maintaining the system's efficiency as a "going concern". Because of differences in backgrounds, values and pure economic interests, conflicts arise between these organizational elements, and must be resolved politically. Top decision makers sometimes put on their "management" hat and make decisions which

promote fast mission turnaround and intensive use of the fleet: the administrators' interests win out. At other times, they put on their "engineer's" hat and compromise commercial viability and Congressional support by favoring operational proficiency and crew-payload safety: the operating core's interests win out.

SUMMARY AND CONCLUSIONS

This Article offers an organization theory perspective on the control of organizational crime. It relates the incidence of organizational crimes to aspects of organizations that pressure employees and management to focus on short-term financial performance and risk avoidance. The analysis assumes that people commit organizational crimes primarily to avoid employment risks associated with failure to reach organizational objectives through more lawful means. More specifically, the Article develops a theory concerning the relation between organizational crime and diversification strategies that lead to internal controls that emphasize short-term financial results at the expense of longer-term objectives.

The implications of organization theory do not provide much joy to those who favor the "hydraulic approach" to the control of organizational crime. As James Q. Wilson once observed in reference to the problem of predatory street crime, "the proper design of public policies requires a clear and sober understanding of the nature of man and, in particular, of the extent to which that nature can be changed by plan." Planned attempts to change the "nature of man" have proved less than satisfactory; "rehabilitation has not yet been shown to be a promising method for dealing with serious offenders. . . ." The same insights and principles should apply to the control of organizational or white collar crime. The United States Sentencing Commission should, therefore, design its guidelines for sentencing organizations whose employees commit organizational crimes with a "clear and sober understanding" of human nature, and in full recognition of how difficult it is to change human nature "by plan."

Simply transferring the responsibility for controlling criminal behavior to the private sector may not provide the solution. Common experience suggests that the forces resisting change in organizations are typically much stronger than the forces promoting change. Therefore, the Commission's guidelines for organizational crimes will continue to be met by strong resistance in the corporate sector.

This may, however, be as it should be. Simple solutions to complex problems tend to violate Forrester's Law and thus pose the threat of unintended consequences. An example of such unintended consequences might result if the Commission adopted a policy of imposing monetary penalties that were sufficiently onerous to induce programs of corporate restructuring. The Commission would announce the date at which vicarious liability and heavy fines for organizational crime would take effect. Corporate decision makers would be given adequate time to sell enough of their businesses to permit the implementation of strategic controls. Since may view high levels of diversification as socially inefficient, this policy might not only reduce the social costs of crime, but increase productivity and innovation as well. Organization theorists have not, however, firmly established that diversification leads to lower productivity. It may still turn out that organizational crime is an inevitable social cost in advanced industrial economies.

In sum, the United States Sentencing Commission's Sentencing Guidelines for Organizational Crime do not appear—as is their statutory mandate—to "reflect, to the extent practicable, advancement in knowledge of human behavior as it relates to the criminal justice process." Of course, neither do the policy recommendations of some of the Commission's more ardent critics. The Commission and its critics need to abandon simple economic models of organizational behavior and evaluate organizations "as they are."

The Commission would do well to follow the move away from abstraction and simplification effected by other social scientists. These scholars have simply followed the advice of Knight to take "human nature as it is". The same advice would seem to apply at the organizational level of analysis: to formulate public policy that is intended to reach inside organizations and affect behavior where it happens, those formulating policy must take organizations "as they find them."

Leonard Orland, *Corporate Punishment by the U.S. Sentencing Commission,* 4 Fed. Sent. Rep. 50 (1991)*

The Sentencing Commission's Guidelines for Sentencing Organizations will become final on November 1, 1991, absent Congressional intervention. This essay assesses the Commission's product and the process by which it went about its task.

In most civil law countries, organizational sentencing is simply not a problem because corporations are

* Reprinted with permission of the author.

legally incapable of violating the criminal law. The American legal tradition is quite different; corporate criminal liability has been the rule since 1909, when the Supreme Court declared

> We see no valid objection in law and every reason in public policy why the corporation which profits by the transaction . . . shall be held punishable. . . .

Congress has regularly applied the criminal law to corporations for more than a century. In the past decade, there has been a proliferation of federal corporate crime statutes and dramatic expansion of corporate criminal liability. These include statutes in the fields of securities, banking and defense procurement; sentencing provisions for alternative fines based on profit derived from or loss caused by the criminal conduct; criminal and civil forfeiture; injunctions against fraud; restitution and notice to victims of the offense; and probation as an independent sanction rather than as an adjunct to the suspended sentence.

I. THE ORGANIZATIONAL GUIDELINES

In a three year period, the Commission tendered three diverse drafts of Organizational Guidelines. It is extraordinarily difficult to trace the Commission's progress because it gave no explanation for its work. In the version finally sent to Congress, the Commission promulgated four clusters of guidelines and policy statements. The first two-dealing with remedies (restitution, remedial orders, community service and notice to victims, 8B1.1-8B1.4) and special assessments, forfeitures and costs (8E1.1-8E1.3), are for the most part a recapitulation of statutory provisions and do not appear materially to alter the status quo. The last two clusters-guidelines and policy statements for fines (8C1.1-8C2.8), and probation (8D1.1-8D1.5)—are sources of considerable controversy and concern.

A. Base Fines and Multipliers

The centerpiece of the Organizational Guidelines is the provision on fines. Section 8C2.4 instructs the sentencer to consult an "offense level" table which arrays fines in 32 gradations, beginning with $5,000 (level 6 offense) to $72,500,000 (level 38 offense).

The base fine is subject to enhancement or reduction based on the offender's "culpability score" (8C2.5). The higher the "culpability score," the higher the "multiplier" of the base fine. An offender with the highest culpability score (10 or more) will be subject to a minimum doubling multiplier and a maximum quadrupling multiplier. Hence an offender with the highest level offense of 38 could see its $72.5 million base fine doubled to $145 million or quadrupled to $290 million. Factors which increase culpability include involvement in or tolerance of criminal activity by senior personnel (8C2.5(b)), prior history of wrongdoing (8C2.5(c)), and violation of a court order or a condition of probation (8C2.5(d)). The multipliers can also substantially reduce fines. This feature has been the subject of considerable controversy, since a "culpability" score of less than 5 can reduce the fine below the base minimum. An offender with a score of 0 or less receives the benefit of a minimum multiplier of 0.05 and a maximum multiplier of 0.20. Hence an offender with offense level 38 could see its $72.5 million base fine reduced to $3.625 million. Factors which decrease culpability focus on compliance and cooperation, e.g., whether or not the organization has an "effective program to prevent and deter violations of law" and "reports the offense to the appropriate authorities, fully cooperated in the investigation, and clearly demonstrated recognition and affirmative acceptance of responsibility."

B. Organizational Probation

To the human defendant, probation is often preferable to incarceration. To the corporate defendant, probation may be less desirable than a fine since it creates the substantial risk of ongoing supervision of the corporation by a federal court.

In contrast to earlier drafts, the Organizational Guidelines embrace, over objections by the corporate community, enlarged use of the probation sanction. The Commission's 1989 draft confined probation to special circumstances, while the 1990 draft enlarged the circumstances for probation. Continuing this expansion, the provisions submitted to Congress mandate probation in a broad range of cases. These include instances in which the offender did "not have an effective program to prevent and detect violations of law," or "engaged in similar misconduct as determined by a prior criminal adjudication" in the preceding five years, or if probation "is necessary to ensure that changes are made within the organization to reduce the likelihood of future criminal conduct."

II. THREE FUNDAMENTAL QUESTIONS

A rational sentencing commission approaching the problem of corporate crimes and punishment should address three concerns: − "Who" (i.e., what groups of offenders should be the subject of its concern)? − "Why" (i.e., what problems should it seek to remedy)? − "How" (i.e., what structure and form should its sanctions take)?

A. Who: Treating Disparate Organizations Similarly

The Commission adopted a single policy for all organizations, large and small, profit making or not-for-profit, and grouped them with unions, pension funds, governments and political subdivisions. An unincorporated organization, a partnership or trust, a unit of local government and a non-profit organization are treated the same as a large multi-national corporation. This approach raises the concern that by treating unequals equally, the Commission has created inequality. As Professors Heumann and Thomas observe, federal sentencing guidelines are "a 'good thing' if similarly situated defendants receive similar sentences; . . . [they are] a 'bad thing' . . . [if unlimited discretion] is 'replaced' by the equally objectionable disparity of treating different cases as if they were the same."

The potential inequality of treating all organizations alike is exacerbated by the Commission decision to grant substantial sentencing credit for corporate compliance programs which only the largest corporations employ. Functionally, this denies the credit to small corporations, partnerships, pension funds, unions and municipalities, which will be exposed to aggravating multipliers but be unable to benefit from mitigating multipliers. The Commission's uniform treatment of organizations is inconsistent with the Congressional requirement that guidelines consider the size and profitability of the organization. In the Criminal Fine Improvements Act of 1988, Congress directs the sentencer to consider, with regard to all offenders, "the defendant's income, earning capacity, and financial resources." Congress is even more explicit in the case of organizational offenders; it directs the court to consider "the size of the organization. . . ."

The statute also directs the court to consider "whether the defendant can pass on to consumers or other persons the expense of the fine." The guidelines ignore these requirements.

A commission driven to legislate uniformly with respect to all "organizations" should justify that result. The scholarly literature provides no support for a uniform fining policy for all organizations. The Commission ignored this literature and refused to consider the implications of organizational behavior theory on criminal sanctioning policy.

B. Why: The Assumption of Corporate Sanction Disparity

The goal of sentencing equality derives from a documented demonstration of inequality in sentences imposed on individual offenders. However, neither Congress, the Commission nor scholars have empirically demonstrated disparity in the sentencing of corporations, let alone all "organizations."

There is an acknowledged lack of valid empirical studies on patterns of corporate crime convictions and sentences. By rushing to guideline promulgation on a flimsy data base, the Commission bypassed the opportunity to conduct empirical research.

The Organizational Guidelines were promulgated without a Congressional declaration that they were needed. Of greatest concern is a new Draconian fine provision which has no statutory basis-confiscatory fines for what are denominated "criminal purpose organizations": 8C1.1 Determining the Fine-Criminal

Purpose Organizations If, upon consideration of the nature and circumstances of the offense and the history and characteristics of the organization, the court determines that the organization operated primarily for a criminal purpose or primarily by criminal means, the fine shall be set at an amount (subject to the statutory maximum) sufficient to divest the organization of all its net assets. . . . This rule raises substantial constitutional problems of vagueness, due process and cruel and unusual punishment. It will doubtless spawn much litigation.

A parallel concern is the Commission's failure to enlist Congress as a collaborator in the development of integrated probation policy. A major problem is to fashion an adequate remedy for the organizational probation violator. At the initial hearings, I argued that the court might have the power to order officers and directors to be personally bound by the probation order and, in a subsequent violation, to use the coercive contempt power. I noted that under existing law, the sentencing judge lacked clear authority to deal with organizational probation violation and that, ultimately, Congress needed to fashion some method for sanctioning organizational probation violation.

The guidelines include an elliptical policy statement addressing probation violation. Upon a finding of a violation of a condition of probation, the court may extend the term of probation, impose more restrictive conditions of probation, or revoke probation and resentence the organization. The Commission makes no effort to relate this to existing laws or to address the necessity for legislation.

C. How: Process and Politics

At the Commission's initial hearings, given the absence of research on corporate sentencing, several academics (including me) urged the Commission to issue corporate policy statements rather than guidelines, coupled with an explicit acknowledgment of the newness of the problems being addressed. We suggested that the Commission invite district court judges to collaborate with it in developing sound corporate sentencing policy. The Commission rejected this course.

After the implementation of the guidelines, many sentencing judges voiced the same concern-that complicated and hypertechnical guidelines complicated the sentencing process and made it impossible for the sentencing judge to explain, honestly and clearly, the rules which determine the offender's fate.

Those concerns are renewed by the cryptic structure of the organizational guidelines. The basic Fine Guideline, which frames the entire scope of the Organizational Guidelines, reproduced in its entirety, illustrates how the Commission communicates:

8C2.1 Applicability of Fine Guidelines The provisions of 8C2.2 through 8C2.9 apply to

each count for which the applicable guideline offense level is determined under: (a) 2B1.1, 2B1.2, 2B1.3, 2B2.3, 2B4.1, 2B5.3, 2B5.4, 2B6,1; 2C1.1, 2C1.2, 2C1.4, 2C1.6, 2C1.7; 2D1.7, 2D3.1, 2D3.2, 2D3.4; 2E3.1, 2E3.2, 2E3.3, 2E4.1, 2E5.1, 2E5.2, 2E5.3, 2E5.4, 2E5.5, 2E5.6; 2F1.1, 2F5.2; 2G3.1; 2K1.1, 2K1.2, 2K2.1; 2L1.11 2N3.1 2R1.1; 2S1.1, 2S1.2, 2S1.3, 2S1.4; 2T1.1, 2T1.2, 2T1.3, 2T1.4, 2T1.5, 2T1.6, 2T1.7, 2T1.8, 2T1.9, 2T2.1, 2T2.2, 2T3.1. (b) 2E1.1, 2X1.1, 2X2.1, 2X3.1, 2X4.1, with respect to cases in which the offense level for the underlying offense is determined under one of the guideline sections listed in (a) above.

This rule is a puzzle. It addresses a central policy issue—offenses and offense levels to be reached by the Organizational Guidelines. Rather than attempt to classify and grade related offenses by some neutral principle, such as type of harm, a task of formidable complexity, the Commission has incorporated some but not all organizational crimes. The form in which the rule is cast makes it almost impossible to appraise the soundness of the Commission's hidden policy decisions on scope and severity. The Commission attempted a more substantive approach in its July 1988 Discussion Draft of Sentencing Guidelines and Policy Statements for Organizations when it distinguished Government fraud, tax theft, environmental, and food and drug offenses.

The Commission plunged ahead with a broad based fine table and a decreasing multiplier guideline system which places an extraordinary premium on corporate compliance programs. The Commission moved in this direction despite the fact that neither sentencing judges nor the government view compliance programs as significant in determining prosecutorial priorities, liability or sentences. The decreasing multiplier credit plan is premised on the assumption that compliance programs can conform organizational behavior to the law. Organizational theory literature casts doubt on that assumption. From the enforcement perspective, the magnitude of the credits for compliance appears to be inappropriately steep and was opposed by the Justice Department for precisely that reason. On the practical level, the Commission places substantial barriers to the effectiveness of existing corporate compliance programs by conditioning credit on corporate self-reporting of crime to the government. This will make it difficult if not impossible for corporate counsel to secure candid and complete responses from corporate executives with knowledge of wrongdoing who will be understandably reluctant to communicate with counsel if they believe that their inculpating statements

PART II: PUNISHMENT 227

will be turned over to the government. As a matter of public policy, the Commission creates a radical regime of semi-compulsory confession inconsistent with the underlying premises of the American accusatorial system.

The Commission acted without an articulated theoretical or empirical justification, an explicit Congressional mandate or an evolved body of corporate sentencing case law. This suggests that its objective was less to remedy a sentencing problem than to respond to a perceived political need. There is indeed a political reason for acting vigorously against corporate crime-the perspective that a "war" on white collar and corporate crime is needed, given such highly publicized events as the insider trading and defense procurement prosecutions, and the savings and loan debacle. For the Commission to react in this fashion is contrary to its mandate to serve as a buffer between the political pressures on Congress for ever more harsh criminal sanctions and the dispassionate goal of due process and moderation embraced by the federal judiciary.

CONCLUSION

Shortly after passage of the Sentencing Reform Act of 1984, Marvin Frankel and I expressed the hope that the United States Sentencing Commission would emerge as "an agency . . . virtually compelled to think uniquely and connectedly of something genuinely resembling a system," an agency which discharges a "mandate . . . to think of crimes and punishments in relation to each other," and an agency making informed decisions regarding "degrees, purposes, effects and costs of punishment." Unfortunately, the Commission's Organizational Guidelines provide no evidence that these hopes are being realized.

Leonard Orland, *Beyond Organizational Guidelines: Toward a Model Federal Corporate Criminal Code,* 17 WASH. U. L.Q. 357 (1993)*

A rational sentencing system presupposes a rational system of criminal law. While refusing, after years of debate and study, to enact a federal penal code, Congress enacted the Sentencing Reform Act of 1984, which is essentially the sentencing provisions of the draft federal penal code. By putting the sentencing

---

* Reprinted with permission of the author.

cart before the penal horse, Congress functionally isolated the sentencing scheme from an organized system of substantive law and made the Herculean task of organizing a fair guidelines system virtually impossible. Judge (and Commissioner) Steven Breyer has documented the difficulty the United States Sentencing Commission (the "Commission") faced in creating guidelines in a legislative vacuum, without the benefit of a substantive code. Despite the difficulty, all but the harshest of critics of the United States Sentencing Guidelines for organizations (the "Sentencing Guidelines" or the "Guidelines") would have to admit that the Commission made some order out of the chaotic morass of existing federal penal law.

The difficulties that the Commission initially faced with the individual guidelines were relatively minor compared to the problems the Commission encountered several years later when it fashioned guidelines for corporate crime. Here, in addition to a lack of substantive provisions, the Commission encountered an absence of general statutory provisions establishing corporate criminal liability, and a congressional failure to consider systematically corporate aggravants, mitigants, or sanctions. These statutory failures led the Commission to devise corporate sentencing policy which is legislative in nature and resulted in organizational guidelines with virtually no statutory basis. The result is legislation by commission edict.

In the absence of statutory authorization, for example, the Guidelines authorize confiscatory fines for "criminal purpose organizations." Perhaps it is desirable and constitutional to define a "criminal purpose organization" and to confiscate the assets of such an organization when it is convicted of crime, but certainly Congress, not the Commission, should decide. Again, in the absence of a statutory direction to do so, the Commission adopted a single fine policy for all organizations, large and small, profit and not-for-profit, and grouped these organizations with unions, pension funds, governments and political subdivisions. I disagree with Commissioner Nagel's conclusion that the Commission's treatment of fines established a "theoretical foundation of consistency." The Commission not only acted without a statutory mandate, but in the process it "treat[ed] unequals equally," and "created inequality."

Finally, the Guidelines' provisions on fines array thirty-two gradations of fines ranging from $5000 to $72,500,000. The enhancements and reductions in this thirty-two level gradation scheme, in form and function, constitute a series of complicated aggravants and mitigants. The Commission devised this scheme once again acting without statutory support. Perhaps the presence of an effective corporate compliance program should mitigate a sentence, and the involvement of senior management should aggravate a sentence, as the Commission has decided, but Congress should decide these and other policy choices, not the Commission.

In an effort to stimulate discussion on the policy choices that Congress should have (but has not) made concerning corporate crime, and in an effort to underscore how deeply the Guidelines arrogate to the Commission basic policy matters that are more properly within the business of Congress, I propose a Model Federal Corporate Criminal Code (the "Model Code"). This Code is designed to function either independently of, or in conjunction with, a sentencing commission and is based on a number of explicit policy preferences.

1. Scope

As a general rule, in most industrialized nations, corporations are legally incapable of violating the criminal law. The unique American rule of corporate criminal liability has as its theoretical base the notion that large profit-making organizations should not be permitted to profit from wrongdoing with immunity from criminal sanction, and that it is proper to hold the organization liable for what is, after all, organizational behavior. Large publicly held, profit-making corporations fit within this model of organizational liability. Professor Brickey makes a powerful argument that large closely held profit-making corporations also fit the organizational liability model. It is less clear that smaller partnerships, closely held corporations, nonprofit organizations, pension funds, and unions fit the organizational liability model; as a matter of organizational theory, many of these smaller entities behave more like individuals than organizations. For this reason, the Model Penal Code applies only to large corporations, whether publicly or privately held, and utilizes a line of demarcation regarding the meaning of "large" drawn from commonly accepted distinctions in the law of corporate governance.

2. Principles of Corporate Criminal Liability

There is no existing federal statute which establishes general principles of corporate criminal liability. Professor Bucy argues that the current federal case law standard for corporate criminal liability is "not jurisprudentially sound" because it does not "require proof of intent as a prerequisite for corporate criminal liability." I disagree, and the Model Code rests on the belief that the current federal case law standards are sound but would benefit from statutory elaboration. In S.1, and later in S.1437, the Senate articulated a statutory basis for corporate criminal liability that was intended, for the most part, to restate preexisting law. The Model Code adopts these formulations, along with a provision (also derived from S.1437) which creates a new crime of reckless failure to supervise a corporate employee.

3. Elimination of Corporate Probation and Creation of New Presumptive Sanctions

The Sentencing Guidelines reflect multiple failures in the treatment of sanctions, including a failure to consider new corporate intermediate sanctions and a failure to escape preoccupation with fines. Furthermore, reliance on corporate probation, which the courts have addressed with some difficulty and hostility, carries with it the self-evident problem of a lack of effective sanction in the event of corporate probation violation. The Commission has ignored this problem. In the process, the Commission has virtually ignored some of the fresh approaches articulated by the American Bar Association (ABA) in its most recent Standards for Sentencing and Sentencing Alternatives. The Commission has also overlooked the emerging penological literature on the importance of intermediate sanctions in a rational sentencing scheme.

The Model Code proceeds on the assumption that it is preferable and more appropriate to array a range of intermediate sanctions to corporate crime than a simplistic, sharply graded fine grid. Thus, utilizing the ABA Standards, the Model Code proposes that sentencing courts impose mandatory sentences of acknowledgment of wrongdoing and compliance programs and discretionary sentences of community service and notice to victims for all felony convictions of publicly held companies. These sanctions would serve as free-standing judicial orders in a criminal case, independent of probation, and would be fully capable of enforcement by the contempt sanction.

4. Gradation

Congressional failure to enact a federal criminal code has perpetuated an array of federal criminal statutes enacted over the course of a century. These criminal statutes fail to differentiate properly among crimes. The Sentencing Guidelines finesse the problem of gradation by engrafting the gradation of seriousness of individual offenses from the individual guidelines onto the organizational guidelines. The Commission fails to articulate a justification for this problematic approach.

The need for gradation in a criminal code is tied to sanctions. For example, the American Law Institute's Model Penal Code adopted felony categories that relate to the length of prison time—the higher the degree of the felony, the higher the authorized maximum term of imprisonment. In contrast, there is no imprisonment in corporate sanctioning, only fines and probation. The problems with imposing only fines is that their impact is mostly felt by innocent stockholders. The problem with corporate probation is that a court has no effective threat available if a corporation violates a probation order. In part for these reasons, the Model Code eliminates corporate probation and reduces the traditional paramount importance of the fine, characterized by Commissioner Nagel as "the centerpiece of the Sentencing Guidelines structure." This approach reduces the need for Congress to undertake the difficult task of redefining and grading all felonies.

5. Aggravants and Mitigants

The absence of statutory aggravants and mitigants led the Commission to devise its own factors in the Sentencing Guidelines without statutory guidance. This approach is troublesome, not because of the Commission's particular policy choices, but because the Commission was unwilling to recognize that the Guidelines rest on important policy determinations that Congress has not made. The Model Code articulates aggravants and mitigants applicable to corporate conduct in order to focus upon the underlying policy issues and to permit discussion in the broader context of the legitimacy of the corporate aggravation and mitigation scheme. Many of the Model Code's aggravants and mitigants were derived in large part from the Commission's Guidelines.

6. Ancillary Provisions

At the present time, no centralized repository for information on corporate criminal convictions exists. Thus, while corporate conviction records play a critically important role in calculating fine levels under the Commission's Guidelines, probation officers must gather this vital information either from the offender or from public sources. To remedy this problem of a lack of centralized information, the Model Code requires corporations to report criminal convictions to the Securities and Exchange Commission. In addition, the Model Code directs the Federal Bureau of Investigation to maintain centralized criminal records on corporate offenders.

CONCLUSION

Conventional law review scholarship consists of exposition and footnotes not statutory drafts; but I believe that one can best understand the virtues of codification of corporate sanctions by the articulation and examination of a Model Code. This Article presents such a code below, in an effort to "produce some order in an area which has developed in a rather disorderly way, and to state some general principles around which a rational formulation can be constructed." Perhaps the Model Code might also interest Congress and the Clinton administration as they begin to grapple with problems of criminal law reform.

MODEL FEDERAL CORPORATE CRIMINAL CODE

CHAPTER A. GENERAL PROVISIONS

§ 1 Definitions and Applicability

(a) Definition of Corporation: As used herein, "corporation" means an entity created under the corporation laws of a state that as of the record date for its annual shareholders' meeting when the offense occurred had at least $5 million or more of total assets. [Derivation: American Law Institute Principles of Corporate Governance § 1.31-4 (Proposed Final Draft 1992), which, in turn, is derived from Securities Exchange Act § 12(g), Rule 12g-1 under that Act, and Federal Securities Code § 402(a).]

(b) Applicability: This statute is applicable only to the sentencing of corporations, as defined in subsection (a), for crimes classified as felonies under federal law.

§ 2 Liability of a Corporation for Conduct of an Agent

A corporation is criminally liable for an offense if the conduct constituting the offense

(a) is conduct of its agent, and such conduct–

(1) occurs in the performance of matters within the scope of the agent's employment, or within the scope of the agent's actual, implied, or apparent authority, and is intended to benefit the corporation; or

(2) is thereafter ratified or adopted by the corporation; or

(b) involves a failure by the corporation or its agent to discharge a specific duty of conduct imposed on the corporation by law.

[Derivation: S.1437, 95th Cong., 1st Sess. § 402 (1977).]

§ 3 Liability of an Agent for Conduct of a Corporation

(a) Conduct on Behalf of a Corporation: A person is criminally liable for an offense based upon conduct that the person engages in or causes in the name of the corporation or on behalf of a corporation to the same extent as if that person engaged in or caused the conduct in his or her own name or on his or her own behalf.

(b) Omission to Perform a Duty of a Corporation: Whenever a statute, regulation, rule or order issued pursuant thereto imposes a duty upon a corporation, an agent of a corporation having significant responsibility for the subject matter to which the duty relates is criminally liable for an offense based upon an omission to perform the duty, if the person has the state of mind required for the commission of the offense, to the same extent as if the duty were imposed upon him or her directly.

(c) Reckless Failure to Supervise Conduct of a Corporation: A person responsible for supervising particular activities on behalf of a corporation who, by his or her reckless failure to supervise adequately those activities, permits or contributes to the commission of an offense by a corporation, is criminally liable for the offense.

[Derivation: S.1437, 95th Cong., 1st Sess. § 403 (1977).]

CHAPTER B. SENTENCES

§ 4 Authorized Sentences

A corporation found guilty of an offense shall be sentenced, in accordance with the provisions of this statute, to

(a) Acknowledgment;

(b) Compliance Program;

(c) Community Service;

(d) Notice to Victims;

(e) Restitution;

(f) A Fine;

(g) Criminal Forfeiture.

Sentencing courts should give priority to the use of sanctions that have the purpose and effect of promoting the offender's future compliance with the law. Sentencing courts shall impose the sanctions authorized by subsections (a) and (b) in all cases. Sanctions authorized by subsections (a) through (g) are independent and the court may impose any combination of sanctions appropriate to a just disposition of the case. The sentencing court is authorized to retain jurisdiction over the corporation to supervise the corporation's performance of a sanction for the term specified in the sentence.

[Derivation: AMERICAN BAR ASSOCIATION STANDARDS, SENTENCING ALTERNATIVES AND PROCEDURES §§ 18-3.12, 3.13, 3.14, 3.15 (3d ed. 1993).]

§ 5 Acknowledgment

(a) A corporation found guilty of an offense shall be sentenced to an acknowledgment sanction requiring the corporation to give public notice and explanation of the conviction.

(b) The purpose of an acknowledgment sanction is to promote the corporation's future compliance with the law, to inform the public of the circumstances that gave rise to the corporation's criminal behavior and to act as a deterrent to the corporation and others.

(c) The sentencing court, in imposing an acknowledgment sanction, may order communications to the public at large, or to particular classes or persons, of information about the corporation's conviction and such other facts about the offense as appear appropriate to the court.

(d) An acknowledgment sanction may provide that the corporation, at its expense, supply managers, employees of the corporation, or agents hired from outside the corporation to perform the acknowledgment sanction for the period of the sentence.

(e) The term for an acknowledgment sanction shall be not more than six months.

[Derivation: American Bar Association Standards, Sentencing Alternatives and Procedures § 18-3.18 (ACKNOWLEDGMENT SANCTIONS) (3d ed. 1993).]

§ 6 Compliance Program

(a) A corporation found guilty of an offense shall be sentenced to a compliance program.

(b) The purpose of a compliance program is to promote the corporation's future compliance with the law.

(c) A compliance program may require that a corporation cease or modify specified practices or activities that gave rise to the corporation's criminal behavior, including a requirement that the corporation engage in an internal investigation to identify such practices or activities. A compliance program may involve supervision of or change in the management or control of the corporation.

(d) To the extent possible, a compliance program shall not interfere with, or delay the making of legitimate business judgment decisions by the corporation's management, governing board, shareholders or members.

(e) Continuing judicial oversight may be (1) ordered as part of a sentence of a compliance program if the sentencing court finds that the corporation's criminal behavior was serious, repetitive, or facilitated by inadequate internal management, accounting or supervisory controls, or presented a clear and present danger to public health or safety;

(2) effected through the adoption of monitoring, reporting, record keeping or auditing controls designed to increase the corporation's mechanisms for internal accountability, such as an independent audit committee, special counsel, or a separate staff system for a corporation's governing board.

(f) The term for a compliance program sanction shall be not more than two years.

[Derivation: AMERICAN BAR ASSOCIATION STANDARDS, SENTENCING ALTERNATIVES AND PROCEDURES § 18-3.14 (Compliance Programs for Organizations) (3d ed. 1993).]

§ 7 Community Service

(a) A corporation found guilty of an offense may be sentenced to perform specified community service for a public agency or for a private non-profit organization without compensation.

(b) A community service sentence may provide that the corporation, at its own expense, supply managers or employees of the corporation to work for a public agency or for a non-profit organization for the period of the sentence.

(c) The term for a community service sanction shall be not more than two years.

[Derivation: AMERICAN BAR ASSOCIATION STANDARDS, SENTENCING ALTERNATIVES AND PROCEDURES § 18-3.17 (Community Service) (3d ed. 1993); 18 U.S.C. § 2563(b)(13) (1985) (existing law permits "work in community service" as a condition of probation).]

§ 8 Notice to Victims

(a) The court, in imposing a sentence on a corporation found guilty of an offense, may, in cases involving fraud or other intentionally deceptive practices, or in any other case in which the court ascertains the need to notify victims, order that the corporation give reasonable notice and explanation of the conviction, in such form as the court may approve, to victims of the offense. The court may order the offender to give notice by mail, by advertising in designated areas or through designated media, or by other appropriate means. In determining whether to require the corporation to give such notice, the court shall consider the factors set forth in 18 U.S.C. § 3553(a) to the extent that they are applicable, and shall consider the cost involved in giving the notice as it relates to the loss caused by the offense.

(b) The term for a notice to victim sanction shall be not more than six months.

[Derivation: Modification of existing law; this section eliminates current limitations on sanctions in 18 U.S.C. § 2555 (1985) to only "an offense involving fraud or other intentionally deceptive practices" and the $20,000 monetary cap on cost of the notice. It proceeds independently of, but is related to, the acknowledgment sanction specified in § 5 of the Model Code.]

§ 9 Restitution

(a) The court, in imposing a sentence on a corporation that has been found guilty of an offense, may order that the corporation make restitution to the victim of an offense.

[Derivation: Modification of existing law, 18 U.S.C. § 3556 (West Supp.1992). It utilizes the same standard as existing law, but does not impose the sanction as a condition of probation. In addition, it omits the qualifications and limitations on probation currently in 18 U.S.C. § 3563 (1985).]

§ 10 Fines

(a) Fines for Corporations: Except as provided in subsection (b) of this section, a corporation that has been found guilty of an offense may be fined not more than the greater of

(1) the amount specified in the law setting forth the offense; or

(2) the applicable amount under subsection (b) of this section.

(b) Alternative Fine Based on Gain or Loss: If a corporation derives pecuniary gain from the offense, or if the offense results in pecuniary loss to a person other than the corporation, the sentencing court may fine the corporation not more than the greater of twice the gross gain or twice the gross loss.

(c) Factors to be Considered in Imposition of Fine: In determining whether to impose a fine, and the amount, time for payment and method of payment of a fine, the court shall consider, in addition to the factors set forth in section 3553(a) of title 18

(1) the corporation's income, earning capacity, and financial resources;

(2) the burden that the fine will impose upon the corporation relative to the burden that alternative punishments would impose;

(3) any pecuniary loss inflicted upon others as a result of the offense;

(4) whether the court ordered restitution or whether the offender made restitution and the amount of such restitution;

(5) the need to deprive the corporation of illegally obtained gains from the offense;

(6) whether the corporation can pass on to consumers or others the expense of the fine;

(7) the size of the corporation and any measures taken by the corporation to discipline any officer, director, employee or agent of the corporation responsible for the offense and to prevent a recurrence of such an offense.

(d) Fine not to Impair Ability to Make Restitution: If as a result of the conviction, the corporation has the obligation to make restitution to a victim of the offense, the court shall impose a fine or other monetary penalty only to the extent that such a fine or penalty will not impair the ability of the corporation to make restitution.

[Derivation: Modification of 18 U.S.C.A. §§ 3571-3572 (West Supp.1992).]

§ 11 Criminal Forfeiture

The court, in imposing sentence on a corporation that has been found guilty of an offense described in section 1962 of title 18 or in Title III of the Comprehensive Drug Abuse Prevention and Control Act of 1970, may order, in addition to the sentence that is imposed pursuant to the provisions of section 10 of this statute, that the corporation forfeit property to the United States in accordance with the provisions of section 1963 of title 18 or section 413 of the Comprehensive Drug Abuse and Control Act of 1970.

[Derivation: Modification of 18 U.S.C. § 2554 (1985). The Code makes forfeiture discretionary rather than mandatory.]

§ 12 Imposition of Sentence

(a) Mitigating Factors: In sentencing a corporation found guilty of an offense under this statute, the court shall consider, in addition to any other factor specified by law, the following mitigating factors:

(1) Effective Compliance Program: The offense occurred despite an effective program to prevent and detect violation of law unless

(a) a high level manager of the corporation or the culpable unit of the corporation, or a person responsible for the administration or enforcement of a program to prevent and detect violations of law participated in, condoned, or was willfully ignorant of the offense; or

(b) after becoming aware of an offense, the corporation unreasonably delayed reporting the offense to appropriate governmental authorities.

(2) Self-reporting: The corporation, prior to an imminent threat of disclosure or governmental investigation and within a reasonably prompt time after becoming aware of the offense, reported the offense to appropriate governmental authorities and fully cooperated in the investigation.

[Derivation: UNITED STATES SENTENCING COMMISSION, GUIDELINES MANUAL § 8C2.5(f) (1993).]

(b) Aggravating Factors: In sentencing a corporation found guilty of an offense under this statute, the court shall consider, in addition to any other factors specified by law, the following aggravating factors:

(1) Involvement in or Tolerance of Criminal Activity:

(a) a high-level manager of the organization participated in, condoned, or was willfully ignorant of the offense; or

(b) tolerance of the offense by personnel with substantial authority was pervasive in the corporation or the culpable unit of the corporation.

(2) Prior History: The corporation committed any part of the offense

(a) less than ten (10) years after

(i) a criminal adjudication based on similar misconduct; or

(ii) civil or administrative adjudication based on two or more separate instances of similar misconduct; or

(b) less than five (5) years after a criminal conviction.

(3) Violation of an Order: The corporation, in committing the offense, violated a judicial order, injunction, or a condition of probation.

(4) Obstruction of Justice: The corporation willfully obstructed or impeded, attempted to obstruct or impede, or aided, abetted, or encouraged obstruction of justice during the investigation, prosecution, or sentencing of the instant offense, or, with knowledge thereof, failed to take reasonable steps to prevent such obstruction or impedance or attempted obstruction or impedance.

[Derivation: UNITED STATES SENTENCING COMMISSION, GUIDELINES MANUAL § 8C2.5 (1993).]

§ 13 Violation of Court Imposed Sanction

(a) Upon a finding of a violation of

(1) any court-ordered sanction, the court may resentence the corporation;

(2) any sanction ordered under §§ 5, 6, 7 or 8 of this act, the court may invoke contempt of court sanctions

(a) against the corporation; and

(b) after adequate personal notice and service, upon designated notified senior management, officers, or directors of the corporation.

CHAPTER C. ANCILLARY PROVISIONS

§ 14 Self-Reporting of Criminal History and Criminal Convictions to Securities and Exchange Commission

(a) Each corporation required to file annual or quarterly reports with the Securities and Exchange Commission shall file a report with the Securities and Exchange Commission, at such time and in such form as such Commission shall prescribe, disclosing any judgment of conviction or criminal sentence filed in any federal or state court against such corporation since January 1, 1980.

(b) Each corporation required to file annual or quarterly reports with the Securities and Exchange Commission shall include in such report disclosure of any criminal indictment, information, or sentence of conviction filed in any federal or state court in such form as the Securities and Exchange Commission shall prescribe.

(c) All criminal charge or conviction reports received by the Securities and Exchange Commission under subsections (a) and (b) shall be available for public inspection and shall be transmitted by such Commission to the Federal Bureau of Investigation.

§ 15 Maintenance of Corporate Criminal Records by Federal Bureau of Investigation

The Federal Bureau of Investigation shall maintain records of criminal charges and convictions against corporations for use in law enforcement and to facilitate sentencing of corporations by the federal and state courts.

C. Ancillary Sanctions and Collateral Consequences

David J. Fried, *Rationalizing Criminal Forfeiture,* J. CRIM. L. & CRIMINOLOGY 328, 329–352, 357–367, 410–420, 430–436 (1988)*

I. INTRODUCTION AND SUMMARY

Eighteen years have passed since the penalty of criminal forfeiture was reintroduced into American law by the Racketeer Influenced and Corrupt Organizations Act ("RICO") and the Continuing Criminal Enterprises Act ("CCE"). Despite early disagreement, the courts have settled most doubts about the reach of criminal forfeiture in favor of an expansive

* Reprinted by special permission of Northwestern University School of Law, *Journal of Criminal Law and Criminology,* Volume 79, Issue 2, pp. 328-436, (1988).

interpretation by the Comprehensive Forfeiture Act of 1984, ("CFA") which also expanded RICO by adding predicate offenses, by providing for pre-indictment and post-indictment restraining orders on the transfer of property subject to forfeiture free of the procedural barriers erected by some courts, and by codifying the "relation-back" theory of forfeiture, the theory that title to forfeitable property vest in the government from the moment the criminal act is committed, potentially making voidable all later transfers. In addition, Congress has extended the penalty of criminal forfeiture to most federal drug offenses and to trafficking in child pornography.

This endorsement and expansion of criminal forfeiture, which made it possible for the government to seek forfeiture more aggressively and with a greater likelihood of success, has created a scholarly and public uproar. So far commentators have focused on an important but narrow set of issues: the constitutionality and propriety of restraining orders which prevent defendants from paying their attorneys, and the threat of forfeiture of attorney's fees already paid upon conviction. All the circuit courts of appeal which have considered the matter have agreed that Congress intended to authorize such forfeitures and that they do not violate the fifth or sixth amendment rights of defendants.

The focus on attorneys' fees has unfortunately diverted attention from larger and more important questions. Criminal forfeiture is, in effect, the first new punishment for crime since the rise of the penitentiary in the early nineteenth century. Why was so obvious a penalty enacted after being so long overlooked? What is its appropriate relationship to other criminal and civil penalties? To what extent can criminal forfeiture be justified in terms of such traditional objectives of punishment as deterrence and retribution? Finally, should criminal forfeiture be imposed as a penalty for all crimes committed for gain?

The first step in answering these questions is to distinguish the various sorts of property subject to RICO and CCE forfeiture. These are the proceeds or gross receipts of crime, the "instrumentalities of crime," such as property, both real and personal, employed (sometimes very tangentially) in the commission of the offense, and "interests" in a RICO "enterprise" operated through or acquired by a "pattern of racketeering activity." This Article begins by tracing the process of case interpretation and statutory amendment by which the proceeds of crime became a necessary object of forfeiture despite the difficulty of interpreting 1970 RICO to justify such forfeitures. It concludes that such proceeds are in fact the only appropriate object of forfeiture.

The forfeiture of instrumentalities of crime, however, is an inappropriate criminal penalty. Such forfeitures are closely modeled upon existing civil forfeitures. Civil forfeiture is a farrago of injustices sanctified by tradition. Its historical justifications, such as they are, have been left behind by its alarming extension in recent years, and its adoption as a criminal punishment, when its validity has always depended on its status as a civil penalty, is unprincipled. Finally, the Article criticizes enterprise forfeiture as a criminal penalty. Enterprise forfeiture is a central innovation of RICO. It treats the criminal's whole business as proceeds of crime or as an instrumentality thereof, with the aim of separating racketeers from their rackets. Certainly criminals should forfeit legitimate businesses which are themselves the proceeds of crime. This Article argues, however, that it is usually wrong to forfeit a legitimate business because its owner has committed a crime in the course of its operation. Such forfeitures too often result in arbitrary and disproportionate punishments for white-collar offenses. Criminal control of legitimate businesses is a problem best attacked by civil divestiture.

If, however, "enterprise" and "instrumentality" forfeiture are rejected as criminal punishments, leaving only proceeds of crime as an appropriate object of forfeiture, there is no compelling reason to limit criminal forfeiture to RICO and drug offenders. After all, no offender should be permitted to retain his ill-gotten gains. This conclusion is reinforced by the fact that RICO is not, on its face, restricted to the prosecution of activities traditionally associated with organized crime and has not been so limited in practice. The Congressional notion that organized crime has particular characteristics which make criminal forfeiture peculiarly necessary, never well-supported logically or empirically, has all but vanished. Moreover, there are signs that both state legislatures and Congress have come to see the enactment of criminal forfeiture penalties as a popular way of demonstrating toughness on crime and as a method of supplementing appropriations for the administration of criminal justice. Many states have passed RICO statutes, and the Justice Department has officially recommended forfeiture as a new punishment for other crimes. In this climate, the limitation of criminal forfeiture to RICO and drug offenses may well be an anomaly and a potential source of unfairness.

This Article contends that the forfeiture of the profits of crime should be general and mandatory. It is the minimum just penalty, because it ensures that the offender shall not benefit by his wrongdoing. However, criminal forfeiture has more in common with civil restitution than with traditional punishments. Like restitution, it merely restores the *status quo ante* and, thus lacks the expressive quality of traditional punishments which have the capacity to express the moral opprobrium of the community. Therefore other punishments, such as fine and imprisonment, should ordinarily supplement criminal forfeiture.

The penalty of forfeiture of criminal profits is closely related to civil restitution on the one hand and enforceable orders of restitution imposed as part of the sentence on the other. All three are intended to effectuate the principle that criminals should not profit by their crimes. However the existing criminal forfeitures under RICO and CCE largely disregard the fatal inconsistency between restoring the proceeds of crime to the victim and forfeiting them to the state. In fact, under federal law, the proceeds of crime are automatically forfeited to the government upon conviction, whereas the judge may sentence the defendant to make restitution to his victims out of his own funds. Far from having a right to restitution, victims without legal title to forfeited property must petition the Attorney General for a discretionary remission of forfeiture.

Any general forfeiture statute must address these contradictions. The punitive purpose of forfeiture is accomplished when the defendant is deprived of the proceeds of his or her crime; the criminal has no interest in the identity of the recipient. All individual claims against the convicted defendant, whether by victims, attorneys, general creditors, or even dependents, therefore should be prior to those of the state. In particular, the appearance of justice requires an end to the Assets Forfeiture Fund, which gives the United States Attorney and local law enforcement officials with whom he must cooperate a budgetary stake in the vindication of the government's claim to the property. The amount of forfeiture should equal the greater of either the provable proceeds of crime, without any requirement or pretense of tracing, or the provable losses suffered by the victims. All sums collected from the offender, whether as fines or forfeitures, should be allocated in accordance with a scheme of priorities. Perhaps an independent Custodian of Forfeited Property could be appointed to receive, administer and distribute such property. Of course, victims will retain their right to bring civil actions to recover all their losses, less sums actually received.

This approach has the incidental merit of resolving the struggle over attorneys' fees. Attorneys are creditors of the defendant like any other, provided that they are not laundering the proceeds of crime through fraudulent fee arrangements. Indeed, attorneys require a special priority because of their indispensable role in the adversary system. However, it is fundamentally unfair to give an absolute preference to the attorney's claims over those of the defendant's victims, other creditors, and dependents. This Article recommends that the attorney's fee, if derived from the proceeds of the crime, be treated as a voidable preference which must be returned to the Custodian of Forfeited Property upon the defendant's conviction, and then should be distributed to claimants, of whom the attorney is one. The attorney will, however, have a claim prior to those of other creditors for reasonable compensation as determined by the court.

II. THE EVOLUTION OF CRIMINAL FORFEITURE SINCE 1970: JUDICIAL INTERPRETATION AND CONGRESSIONAL REACTION

RICO and CCE forfeiture was, when introduced in 1970, an innovation virtually without precedent in American law. In one important respect it paralleled the nearly forgotten common law penalty of forfeiture of estate and corruption of blood. RICO forfeiture, like forfeiture of estate, was an automatic consequence of conviction for RICO violations rather than a punishment set by the judge and discretionary with him or her within statutory limits. RICO forfeitures are thus in personam, but the 1970 statute simply borrowed the procedures long mandated for in rem customs forfeitures, relegating third party claimants to an administrative petition for remission or mitigation. The original statute made no attempt to answer such vexing questions as when the government's title to forfeited property first attached and how the property might be secured from dissipation or concealment before or after indictment. Perhaps more important, there was great uncertainty about the meaning of fundamental RICO concepts such as "pattern of racketeering" and "RICO enterprise." In the last analysis, this uncertainty derived from the more pervasive uncertainty about the objectives of RICO and whether such objectives could be achieved constitutionally.

There is little point, at this late date, in attempting to establish the true meaning and purpose of the forfeiture provisions in RICO and CCE in their 1970 form. The pre-1984 cases embody two competing methods of resolving the uncertainties about RICO forfeiture. According to what may be called the "strict interpretation," RICO is essentially a measure of economic regulation, an antitrust act intended to prevent the corruption of the free market by the importation of mob tactics financed by the proceeds of illegitimate crime. RICO forfeiture is therefore an instrumental penalty aimed at the establishment of a *cordon sanitaire* between the mob and legitimate businesses by forcing the divestiture of interests in such legitimate businesses acquired, maintained, or fostered by corrupt means. Its effect as punishment is real but incidental to its primary purpose.

The "interpretation," on the other hand, added the forfeiture of proceeds and of substitute assets to the

RICO arsenal. Its proponents did not deny, of course, that RICO provides for "enterprise forfeiture." Rather, they emphasized the independent deterrent value of forfeiture as a means of taking the profit out of crime. They argued that the broader purposes of RICO are not served by treating the profits of organized crime as sacrosanct until such profits are invested or by an insistence upon the necessity of tracing.

The strict interpretation excluding the forfeiture of profits accords better with the legislative history of 1970 RICO and with a careful reading of the text. It is not, however, the more practical interpretation and it has serious, although inchoate, theoretical difficulties. Not surprisingly, the courts have largely rejected it. Attempts to apply the strict interpretation created the impression that RICO was full of loopholes and essentially unworkable. Once corrupt interests in legitimate business were subject to forfeiture, a ban on the forfeiture of profits and proceeds began to look like an arbitrary and unjustified restriction in the war on crime. Congress agreed and ratified the interpretation in the 1984 Comprehensive Forfeitures Act and the 1985 amendments, which authorized the forfeiture of substitute assets.

There is thus a substantial consensus that the central purpose of RICO forfeiture is to deter crime by removing the profit. If this is so, the non-application of *in personam* forfeiture to all economic and white-collar crime begins to look anomalous. It may be useful to trace the process by which this consensus developed from 1970 to the present before taking a broader and more theoretical perspective.

A. THE RE-INTRODUCTION OF IN PERSONAM FORFEITURE: LEGISLATIVE HISTORY AND CONTEMPORARY COMMENT.

The legislative history and contemporary comment about the re-introduction of criminal or *in personam* forfeiture into American law are sketchy. One commentator described RICO as having its "genesis in social science theory," including economic theory, about the nature of organized crime and its deleterious effect on civil society. The remedy was the erection of a wall around organized crime by criminalizing the investment of proceeds from organized crime in legitimate business and providing for the forfeiture of interests so acquired. The proponents of Title IX did not advocate forfeiture as the appropriate measure of punishment but merely as a means to this desired separation. As one commentator stated, "No suggestion appears [in the legislative history] that Congress intended to reach beyond the relevant 'enterprise,' of to forfeit fruits or profits of racketeering except when used to acquire control of an 'enterprise.' Indeed, there is much evidence to the contrary."

The critics of the RICO bill largely aimed their attack at the impossibility of limiting RICO to this laudable purpose, especially in view of the absence and constitutional difficulty of any statutory definition of organized crime, the possibility that unrelated convictions might make up a "pattern of racketeering activity," and the broad reach of the predicate offenses, which included several, such as stock fraud, not typically associated with organized crime. No critic foresaw that RICO would or could be read to require the forfeiture of uninvested criminal proceeds. This possibility may have been overlooked because of the second major criticism of RICO: that it was fundamentally unworkable. No prosecutor, it was said, would take on the additional burden of proving a "pattern" of racketeering activity if he or she could prove the underlying offenses, and the tracing of proceeds was too notoriously difficult to bother with. If these predictions were accurate, there would be little reason for alarm about the potential scope of criminal forfeiture. The critics instead attacked RICO forfeitures as a revival of "forfeiture of estate," and even as a reversal of 18 U.S.C. § 3563, which has prohibited "corruption of blood or any forfeiture of estate" since 1790.

B. RICO FORFEITURES IN PRACTICE: 1970–1984.

The courts endorsed these conclusions by holding that 1970 RICO permitted the forfeiture of substitute assets; then Congress amended RICO to provide explicitly for such forfeitures. But RICO forfeiture has still not been transformed from a method of compelling divestiture of criminal interests in legitimate business into a simple and automatic measure of retribution for specified crimes. The "interpretation" of the statute has not supplanted the "strict interpretation;" it has merely extended the reach of forfeiture. Now that substitute assets in the amount of illegal proceeds are subject to forfeiture, there is less need to trace the proceeds themselves. Attempting to extract the proceeds from third parties may still be easier. Of course, criminals will still try to conceal their assets, but the United States, as a judgment creditor, has the power to rescind any fraudulent conveyances and/or attach assets in the hands of third parties.

The Comprehensive Forfeitures Act of 1984, however, did not, as finally adopted, authorize the forfeiture of substitute assets, although it provided for a substantial equivalent by imposing an optional fine of up to twice the gross profits from the offense. It therefore seemed necessary to provide for restraints upon the transfer of property subject to forfeiture at the earliest possible moment and to reach such property in the hands of others. The 1970 Act, while authorizing such restraints, did not provide any standards or procedures for imposing them, and the courts manifested extreme hesitation in developing such procedures. At least one court held, despite the statutory authorization, that a pre-conviction restraining order was incompatible with the presumption of innocence and a defendant's right not to incriminate himself. The courts also were troubled by the seizure or attachment of the defendant's property upon an ex parte application. The entry of an indictment identifying certain property as subject to forfeiture was no substitute for the immediate adversary hearing required by Rule 65 of the Federal Rules of Civil Procedure and indeed by due process. Finally, most courts held that the United States must show by a preponderance of the evidence that it will be able to establish the guilt of the defendant and the forfeitability of the named property beyond a reasonable doubt.

C. The 1984 Reforms and the Reaction of the Courts.

From a theoretical standpoint, the most remarkable innovation in the Comprehensive Forfeiture Act of 1984 ("CFA") was "relation back," the principle that the government's title to property subject to forfeiture vests at the moment of the crime. Because the criminal cannot pass a title he does not have, the effect of "relation back" is to invalidate transfers made after the crime, with the statutory exception of transfers to "a bona fide purchaser for value . . . who at the time of purchase was reasonably without cause to believe that the property was subject to forfeiture. . . ." This principle, which is essentially without historical precedent, provides a theoretical justification for pre-indictment restraining orders and for the seizure of property in the hands of third-party transferees for value, most notably including both retainers to defense attorneys and fees already paid for services rendered. The statutes specifically authorize such restraining orders and seizures. Congress also provided that restraining orders or injunctions may be entered upon the filing of an indictment or information alleging that the identified property would be subject to forfeiture upon conviction. This was an attempt to forestall the hearings mandated by the courts under 1970 RICO and CCE which tended to become mini-trials on the defendant's guilt of the underlying offense. Congress further denied standing to intervene and the right to commence an independent action to any third party who asserts an interest in property subject to forfeiture, until the defendant has been convicted.

On the whole, the courts have not been friendly to these procedural innovations. . . .

Whatever one may think of these consequences of the CFA as policy, they are a natural development from RICO, which seeks to drive a wedge between organized crime and the rest of society. If the attempts to effectuate this purpose by regulating the activities of criminals have largely failed, the next logical step is to penalize and criminalize dealings with criminals by those who are not otherwise wrongdoers. There is no indication in the legislative history of the CFA that Congress understood that it was imposing a collateral civil forfeiture upon innocent persons dealing with RICO offenders, a fact which should count for little against the clear and unambiguous language of the statute. The Justice Department apparently recognized that it could have such a collateral effect: "[S]ome lawyers may decline to represent a CCE or RICO defendant . . . from the natural caution that anyone might exercise in deciding not to deal with a defendant facing a CCE or RICO charge unless there are reasonable assurances that any money received is from a legitimate source."

To date, however, lawyers are the only non-criminal third parties who have been threatened with this extended civil forfeiture. As a result, every case dealing with the "relation-back" principle of the CFA has turned on the defendant's qualified sixth amendment right to counsel. . . .

III. The Purpose of Criminal Forfeiture

As often occurs in the law, the remarkable development of criminal forfeiture since 1970 has taken place without benefit of much theory. Congress, the courts and the commentators have assumed that criminal forfeiture is a broadly appropriate remedy, although they have not agreed upon the evils at which it is directed. There has been little effort in this country, however, to describe its appropriate role in the battery of available criminal remedies, and still less to define its proper place in the jurisprudence of criminal punishment. The casual justifications scattered throughout the case law and literature have naturally evolved in tandem with the broad evolution from the "strict interpretation" to the "loose interpretation" of RICO and CCE described in the previous section.

This Article endorses the trend toward the extension of forfeiture to additional crimes but rejects a number of the goals ostensibly served by existing forfeiture statutes. Forfeiture as a criminal penalty should be confined to the proceeds of crime narrowly defined, excluding the forfeiture of interests in an enterprise and instrumentalities of crime, which belongs on the civil side only. Within these limits, forfeiture is a uniquely appropriate minimum penalty which should be extended to cover most criminal offenses involving economic gain. Such a minimum penalty would serve to enforce a rough proportionality between crime and punishment and would tend to eliminate the perception that existing punishments are a tariff whose payment entitles the criminal to enjoy his gains in peace. Paradoxically, criminal forfeiture lacks most of the qualities of punishment and more closely resembles a civil penalty. Criminal forfeiture, like civil restitution, only requires the criminal to pay back what he has taken, thus restoring the *status quo ante.* For this reason it carries no particular moral opprobrium. Nor does criminal forfeiture have any special rehabilitative or deterrent value, contrary to some claim. Thus forfeiture must be combined in most cases with fine or imprisonment to punish adequately.

The existing forfeiture statutes, however, did not originate in any theory of punishment, but were an *ad hoc* attack on certain perceived evils. They cannot be generalized in their present form. On the one hand, they aim at a very worth objective: the prevention of the domination of certain businesses and labor unions by organized crime, which uses violent coercion for oligopoly power and plain theft. Congress wanted to accomplish this objective by compelling the forfeiture of the interests of organized criminals in such enterprises as an incident of their criminal convictions. However, Congress could better accomplish this essentially economic objective civilly, as indeed RICO permits, by targeting those industries and unions, few in number, which are in fact controlled by organized crime. Or failing this, the "pattern of racketeering" which may result in enterprise forfeiture should be limited to instances where the use of violence or the threat of violence accompanies the conduct of the business. The hallmark of organized crime activity in legitimate business is precisely they use of violence means to establish a monopoly or cartel. Such an approach would put an end to the imposition of the penalty of enterprise forfeiture under RICO to isolated illegalities committed by ordinary businesspersons.

Similarly, existing forfeiture statutes enlarge traditional *in rem* forfeitures, such as the forfeiture of contraband and the instruments of crime, and make them mandatory punishments for crimes. There is no theoretical justification for this extension. Civil forfeiture is problematic enough from a due process standpoint, particularly when third parties have interests in the property. These problems are aggravated in criminal proceedings, in which third parties have no standing to intervene.

In an attempt to justify these tentative conclusions, it is helpful to classify and review the explicit and implicit justifications for criminal forfeiture advanced to date. These are, beginning with the least plausible:

(1) The utility of criminal forfeiture as a means of financingincreased law enforcement efforts and making such efforts atlease partially self-supporting;

(2) The deterrent effect of criminal forfeiture against hardened offenders who regard the threat of imprisonment with equanimity as merely a cost of doing business;

(3) The general deterrent effect of the possibility of disproportionate penalties; such as the loss of one's entire business, for relatively small offenses;

(4) The usefulness of criminal forfeiture as a means of disrupting the organizational continuity of racketeering by separating racketeers from legitimate businesses which they have corrupted;

(5) The retributive advantages of the forfeiture of criminal profits as a penalty which is and is seen to be precisely tailored to the offense.

All these justifications except number five are fatally flawed. The use of forfeiture as a source of government revenue places serious institutional temptations in the way of prosecutors and exacerbates the conflict between the government and innocent third parties such as victims, persons claiming a property interest, creditors and dependents. Criminal forfeiture is an insignificant deterrent against racketeers and is not much more effective against ordinary white-collar criminals. Draconian forfeitures of cars, houses, stock, salaries, and businesses as penalties for petty or first offenses are presumably more effective deterrents. Such criminal forfeitures have been established by analogy with existing civil forfeitures. Such civil forfeitures are mostly wrong in principle while often unjust in practice, and they are not improved by their transmigration. Finally, the separation of racketeers from their corrupt businesses is best pursued as a distinct goal through carefully limited civil actions, and not as an incident of criminal conviction.

A. "A HUGE BUSINESS FOR THE FEDERAL GOVERNMENT:" FORFEITURE AS PRIVATEERING.

No one really knows, of course, how much organized crime earns from illegal gambling, loansharking, drug dealing, and other activities. It seems that no one has even attempted to estimate the take from all the predicate offenses for which a RICO indictment would lie. It is probably safe to assume that the gross receipts, in a four trillion dollar economy, are not less than $200 billion or five percent, largely untaxed, and they could run far higher. Much of this money is earned by the sale of illicit goods and services to willing buyers who are knowing participants in a criminal transaction, so that there is no identifiable owner or victim with a prior claim.

It is not surprising, therefore, that there has been a tendency to view forfeiture as a method of expropriating some of this wealth for the benefit of the government and specifically for the benefit of law enforcement agencies. Forfeitures, especially administrative civil forfeitures, can become a source of fast cars, boats and planes for undercover and interdiction efforts, and of cash to supplement appropriations, to pay rewards to informants, and to finance drug buys. A share in the booty can be used to reward cooperation from other federal agencies and local law enforcers, and the promise of a share may induce such cooperation. As a result, struggles for turf may be intensified as additional agencies seek statutory authorization for a share. The dollar value of forfeited property becomes a convenient way to measure the success of enforcement efforts in general and to distinguish between the performance of individual officers. Finally, other agencies, more remotely connected to law enforcement, have begun to argue that they are entitled to a share for such purposes as drug education and rehabilitation programs, claiming that such an application of forfeited funds is a form of restitution to the victims of "victimless" crime and a means of drying up the market by cutting demand.

This process has been in full swing for about a decade, and it seems likely that an appetite for forfeited assets and a growing dependence upon them in an age of budgetary cutbacks and deficits has helped drive the substantive changes previously discussed. The 1981 Report of the Comptroller General on the failure of asset forfeiture to limit drug trafficking tended to measure the success of RICO forfeiture by the dollar value of property criminally forfeited. The Comptroller General justified his proposal to subject criminal proceeds and substitute assets to forfeiture simply as a means to "increase the amount of assets subject to forfeiture," without any appeal to theoretical considerations. The substantive expansion of civil forfeiture during this period and its administrative simplification have been still more significant factors in increasing the take. The CFA in 1984 created the Assets Forfeiture Fund to collect, administer, and distribute the proceeds of both civil and criminal forfeitures. The principal purpose of the Fund was to enable the Justice Department and the Customs Bureau to defray incidental costs of forfeiture such as the repair, storage and sale of forfeited property. Congress has amended the statutory provisions governing the Fund to increase the number of agencies entitled to share in the spoils and the objects for which they may be paid out.

Potentially more significant, however, is the removal of the interim ceiling on the sums retained in the Assets Forfeiture Fund and Customs Forfeiture Fund from year to year after all authorized payments. Originally all sums in the Assets Forfeiture Fun in excess of $5 million were to be deposited in the general fund of the Treasury each year. Congress has now followed the recommendation of the President's Commission on Organized Crime and removed the ceiling. The change will make up to $500 million in unappropriated funds, not derived from general revenues, available for criminal law enforcement. The Commission sought to have all such funds derived from drug forfeitures devoted exclusively to anti-drug programs; this proposal has not been implemented.

These are, on the whole, disquieting trends. There is an abiding contradiction in the United States between public concern about the inroads of crime, which ebbs and flows, and the public unwillingness to finance law enforcement at appropriate levels, which is more or less constant. Of course each wave of concern leaves a high water mark in the United States Code in the form of new crimes, so that the gap between the tasks with which the Justice Department is entrusted and its resources tends to widen over time. This gap should not be filled, however, by making the Justice Department dependent on forfeited assets. The prosecutor's charging decisions may be distorted by considerations of the most profitable course. Even the appearance of such distortion is intolerable. Similarly, the conflict between the federal government and third party claimants to forfeited assets should not be exacerbated by giving the Justice Department an institutional stake in defeating private claims. Finally, the "privatization" of the funding of law enforcement is a retrograde step reminiscent of the payment of naval officers in the eighteenth century largely out of the proceeds of the sale of captured ships. It is late in the day to begin issuing letters of marque to United States Attorneys.

B. Forfeiture as Specific Deterrent: The Heroic Fallacy

Forfeiture, like any penalty or punishment, deters criminals from repeating their offenses and deters the law abiding from taking up a career of crime. "Specific deterrence" is a name which has been given to the first of these effects, the discouragement of recidivism; the name "general deterrence" has been applied to the second, the discouragement of crime in general by the exemplary effect of punishment.

The courts, legislative committees and presidential commissions have periodically advanced the idea that criminal forfeiture is an effective specific deterrent — perhaps more effective than imprisonment. The notion is that there is a subset of hardened criminals, particularly participants in organized crime, who view crime as a business and make rational calculations of profit and loss. Such criminals, supported by the ethos of their profession, supposedly regard the threat and fact of imprisonment as a "cost of doing business." They are willing to pay this price if, upon release, they may freely enjoy the fruits of their crimes. Therefore, they will only be deterred by the forfeiture of their profits. This idea was particularly popular when the fines available as punishment for hugely profitable felonies were disproportionately small.

The idea that criminal forfeiture is efficacious as a specific deterrent is probably a fallacy even when limited to the paradigmatic "organized criminal," the Mafioso soldier or capo. It is more fallacious when applied to white collar criminals like corrupt public officials and those who corrupt them. Still less will it help to justify a generalization of criminal forfeiture beyond the limits of RICO and drug offenses. It may nonetheless serve as a starting point for an exploration of the relationship between criminal forfeiture and theories of punishment. . . .

IV. THE FORFEITURE OF PROFITS AS THE USUAL PENALTY FOR CRIME

This Article has traced how criminal forfeiture was first revived as a means of reversing the infiltration of racketeers into legitimate business. Because the profits of crime, especially the very great profits realized by the sale of narcotics, facilitate such infiltration, such profits became forfeit through a process of statutory construction and amendment. This Article has shown, however, that forfeiture of profits, originally an afterthought, is in fact the only form of criminal forfeiture which is justifiable in theory and practice. The proof thus far has proceeded by exclusion. The Article has demonstrated the impropriety of the forfeiture of derivative contraband and of interests in a legitimate enterprise as a criminal punishment in the large majority of cases. It has also shown the folly of expecting criminal forfeiture to do too much: to deter offenders who are not deterred by the fear of exposure, trial and imprisonment; to strip defendants in advance of trial of the means with which they may defend themselves; to deprive them of the proceeds of crimes with which they have not been charged; and to stop all relationships of friendship and commerce between criminals and others.

In contrast, the forfeiture of profits from all crimes committed for the sake of economic gain seems to effectuate the old common law principle that no one may benefit by his or her own wrong. Such forfeitures would seem to be an ideal minimum penalty, because they are necessarily proportional to the severity of the offense, they restore the status *quo ante* as far as

possible, and they assure, in conjunction with appropriate fines, that the criminal will not find his loot waiting for him when he leaves prison. If the amount of profit can be determined with even rough accuracy, it should be taken from the defendant's available property without the necessity of tracing. Of course, the defendant should still forfeit any assets which are in fact traceable to crime, although they may have appreciated since their acquisition.

Finally, whatever property is extracted from the defendant, whether under the rubric of forfeiture, fine or restitution, must be made available to his victims, creditors, including defense counsel, and even to a certain extent to is innocent dependents. This may seem inconsistent with punishment and deterrence, because the defendant will to some degree realize real and psychic benefit from such a distribution of his property. As previously shown, however, the forfeiture of profits is not a punishment and even under the present state of affairs is not a very effective deterrent. The limited benefit to the defendant may be offset by other punishments, chiefly imprisonment, while the state must in fairness carry out its purpose of punishing him or her with as little cost to the victims and innocent bystanders as possible.

Far from being revolutionary, this proposal is an attempt to rationalize existing trends, which from several distinct starting points are converging upon the surrender of criminal gains as an indispensable minimum penalty. These trends include: the rise of white-collar crime, or to be more precise the criminalization of administrative violations and civil wrongs, making crime far more profitable than ever before; a concomitant increased interest in restitution as a supplementary penalty; a new concern for "victim's rights," commonly defined to include the right of state compensation for immediate injuries; and the extraordinary triumph since about 1970 of "just deserts" as the only broadly accepted justification for punishment, supplanting a long-lived liberal consensus that punishment must be tailored to the circumstances of the offender and not the offense.

These trends are of course interrelated. White-collar criminals often inflict substantial quantifiable injury, usually have funds available for restitution, and are not in need of or are not good candidates for rehabilitative punishment. More broadly, however, each of these trends is symptomatic of the breakup of the public/private distinction. The tripartite division between criminal offenses, which are punishable by the state, civil wrongs, which are actionable by private persons, and sins, which are left in a liberal regime mostly to God, has broken down, as snorting cocaine and trading on inside information come to be defined as equally

serious offenses against public order. As this has occurred, however, the interest of the state in punishing
the offender has come more and more pointedly into
conflict with the interests of his victims in compensation.
Under these circumstances, it is no longer satisfying to
repeat bromides about the impropriety of using the criminal justice system to collect private obligations. A new
system is needed which harmonizes these conflicting
interests as far as possible.

A. THE GROWTH OF RESTITUTION AS A CRIMINAL PENALTY

The idea that criminals should compensate those
whom they have injured was, of course, dominant during the long centuries during which criminal law had
no existence as an entity distinguishable from tort law.
However, the developed common law included rules
which barred the victims of criminal offenses from civil
recovery or at least made such recovery unavailing.

The American common law courts rejected these
rules, adopting restitution not as a punishment, but only
as a condition of probation or as part of an informal
settlement. In recent years, however, many writers have
advocated enforceable orders of restitution as the primary punishment for crime. Restitution, they claim is
retributive, because the penalty is precisely equivalent
to the gravity of the offense measured by the harm done.
It rehabilitates, because the offender is forced to confront
and make good the damage he had done to an identifiable
human being. For most crimes, and indeed all non-
violent crime, it is thus far superior to imprisonment,
given the harm that prisons do to prisoners and to society
at great public expense. Finally, its advocates argue
openly that in a criminal system where punishment is
based upon restitution there is no place for so-called
"victimless" crimes, those without an identifiable victim
or quantifiable injury.

These arguments are generally made in a liberal
and reformist spirit, and have in fact often been criticized as utopian. At least in tone, they seem difficult
to reconcile with the theory of "just deserts." Restitution as an authorized criminal punishment has made
its greatest gains, however, on both the state and federal levels during just that period, roughly since 1970,
during which the retributivists were routing the utili-
tarians and social scientists from the field. In fact, retri-
butivism is perfectly consistent with restitution. Retributivists mean to make the offender give up the unfair
advantage he or she has obtained over his or her fellows
by crime, an emphasis which is supposed to distinguish
retribution from retaliation. Restitution is a natural way
of effecting this result. However, because criminal restitution has been widely adopted as a punishment during
the heyday of "just deserts" with its emphasis on deter-
minate sentencing, it has not received the primary role
desired by its most ardent advocates.

Until the passage of the Victim and Witness Protection Act in 1982, Congress had not authorized the
federal courts to impose an order of restitution as part
of a sentence, but only as a condition of probation.
The restitution provisions of the Act, read together
with the Sentencing Reform Act of 1984, go a long
way toward making restitution the usual punishment
whenever the victim suffered a quantifiable injury. A
fine, public service work, or sentence of restitution is
now mandatory when a defendant is placed on probation. The payment of restitution takes precedence over
the payment of any fine. The courts must give reasons
whenever they refuse to order restitution. Most significantly, whereas restitution as a condition of probation
may be limited to "actual damages or loss caused by
the offense for which conviction was had," a defendant may be sentenced to make restitution to a victim
of [his] . . . offense." The courts have interpreted this
difference to authorize sentences, but not probation
orders, requiring restitution of the full losses of the
victims, although such losses exceed those charged in
the indictment and indeed are not attributable to the
counts upon which the defendant was convicted.

B. THE CONFLICT BETWEEN RESTITUTION AND FORFEITURE

The proceeds of crime cannot simultaneously be
forfeited to the government and remain available to
satisfy either an order of restitution or the victim's
civil claim for damages. This conflict between the
government and the victim, to the extent it arises, is
now resolved in an *ad hoc* manner, generally through
administrative remission in favor of the victim/claim-
ant. However, forfeiture of the proceeds of crime cannot become a general penalty for economic wrongdoing without reforms that grant legal standing and explicit priority over the government to victims who
claim restitution whenever forfeiture will interfere
with their ability to collect. . . .

D. THE REPLACEMENT OF CRIMINAL FORFEITURES BY PROCEEDS FINES

Criminal forfeitures under RICO and CCE are mandatory in that they are removed from the discretion of
judges and are not dependent on findings of fact. Substantial and automatic punishment for serious crime, independent of the vagaries of individual judgment and
free from considerations of rehabilitation, has a powerful
appeal, but the complete separation of criminal forfeiture
from the traditional sentencing process and the dual role
of the jury in determining guilt and fixing the punishment
of criminal forfeiture give rise to serious problems of
due process. One might guess that when Congress originally reintroduced criminal forfeiture it deliberately
wished to take punishment out of the hands of judges,
perhaps seeing them as unduly lenient to organized

crime. Congress was also motivated by the inadequate and even nominal fines then available under federal law. However, since RICO and CCE were adopted, Congress has significantly toughened criminal punishments, constrained judicial discretion in sentencing, and abolished parole.

At the same time, as already described, the evolution of RICO and CCE have made the forfeiture of criminal proceeds a central remedy. A further convergence has occurred between RICO/CCE and the penalties for other crimes. Congress has prescribed a fine equal to up to twice the criminal proceeds as an alternative fine for RICO and CCE offenses. It has also prescribed a similar alternative fine as a transitional punishment for all crimes involving pecuniary harm to the victim or benefit to the perpetrator. The question arises, therefore, whether there remains any justification for retaining the forfeiture of criminal proceeds as an independent remedy in RICO and CCE. Is its function adequately performed by very large fines, in conjunction with restitution? Should the criminal justice system replace forfeiture with a mandatory general fine equal to criminal proceeds?

Fines, which by general agreement were both too small and too rarely imposed, have been increased to a maximum for each count of $250,000 if the offender is an individual, $500,000 if the offender is an organization. In 1986, Congress enacted maximum fines of up to $8 million for a recidivist drug dealer and $20 million for an organization. At such levels fines may in many cases be equivalent, or nearly so, to the forfeiture of proceeds, without the evidentiary difficulties of tracing or a showing of inability to trace. It remains to be seen how far the federal courts will employ their new authority. A fine, a sentence of restitution, or community service work is now mandatory, however, when a defendant is placed on probation. Fines have also been made far more readily collectible by the Criminal Fine Enforcement Act of 1984. As the courts gain experience with reformed sentencing, prosecutors may come to see real advantages in asking for high fines rather than forfeiture even in RICO and CCE cases.

The fact that criminal forfeiture is mandatory in those cases in which it is a prescribed penalty is distinct from the fact that its imposition is a jury function. The statute could ensure that the defendant would be deprived of his or her criminal profits through a mandatory fine, without involving the jury in determining the amount. There is no hint in the legislative history, however, that the draftsmen considered such a fine. Rather, they seem to have assumed that a special jury verdict is constitutionally necessary for the forfeiture of the defendant's interests in an enterprise either criminally acquired or criminally maintained and operated. The facts underlying such a forfeiture, involving the manner in which the offense was carried out, are perhaps too closely intertwined with the offense for fair determination at a post-conviction sentencing hearing.

Once, however, the courts had decided that 1970 RICO did authorize the forfeiture of proceeds, Congress recognized the utility of imposing a fine measured by the amount of criminal proceeds. Such fine of up to twice the proceeds is an optional substitute for other fines, but it could as easily be mandatory after a special hearing to determine the amount of proceeds. Is a jury determination of such amount, which does not go to the defendant's guilty or innocence, constitutionally required? Under the Sentencing Reform Act, the judge will in many cases determine the amount of the victim's loss or the defendant's gain in a sentencing hearing, because such amount is relevant in fixing the amount of the fine and must be determined before the judge enters a sentence of restitution. The new requirement that the court shall "state in open court the reasons . . . for the particular sentence" and the availability of appellate review seem to remove all due process objections to "proceeds fines." The constitutional question may be resolved in the near future, because such fines are already prescribed by federal law in some instances.

Thus far it appears that very little turns on the distinction between proceeds fines and proceeds forfeitures. There is, however, one important procedural difference: the possibility under current law of attaching a defendant's assets or enjoining him or her from transferring them before trial and even before indictment. The government's right to do this is obviously a consequence of conceptualizing forfeiture as the recapture of property which the government already has title, in other words the "relation-back" fiction. It seems difficult to imagine the government asserting such a right with respect to something called a "fine." By definition a fine is a punishment imposed after conviction. Intuitively, the government cannot have title to the funds needed to pay a fine even before indictment. However, the availability of pre-trial restraining orders need not and should not depend on making the jury the finder of fact with respect to the amount of proceeds and calling the resultant penalty a "forfeiture," if it is desirable for other reasons to lodge this function with the judge at a post-conviction hearing. The due process difficulties with pre-trial restraining orders were considered earlier; in this connection it suffices to say that they are far less objectionable if the funds are being sequestered ultimately to satisfy the claims of victims, defense counsel, and creditors rather than to remove the funds permanently from their reach.

The above argument presupposes, of course, that the government will hold the fruits of a mandatory proceeds fine, no less than the fruits of a mandatory forfeiture, subject to the prior claims of victims and creditors. It is customary, however, to think of a fine as a penalty paid to the government as the representative of a wronged society. Once again the only difficulty is definitional. However, formal categories should not prevent the just modification of the system of criminal penalties.

V. CONCLUSION

Criminal forfeiture re-entered American law in a manner characteristic of legal innovations. Its inventors saw criminal forfeiture as a remedy for a peculiar problem: the infiltration of legitimate business by organized crime. They did not foresee its revolutionary implications. It was entangled at its birth in procedures drawn from the inappropriate model of civil forfeiture. A principle of universal appeal and applicability has quickly emerged to justify criminal forfeiture: wrongdoers shall not profit from their crimes. This principle, once recognized, demanded that forfeiture should be extended to criminal proceeds without a requirement of tracing, and so it was, but only in the context of RICO and drug offenses. There is no principled reason, however, for confining the remedy of proceeds forfeiture to this context. It should be extended to all crimes committed for gain as a mandatory minimum penalty.

The forfeiture of interests in a RICO enterprise and of instrumentalities of crime appears to be a grave error. It leads to capricious and disproportionate punishments and is capable of dangerously discriminatory application. Even when particular interest forfeitures are not constitutionally disproportionate, it is wrong for the criminal justice system to surrender control over the determination of punishment, replacing legislative penalties graded in accordance with the seriousness of the offense with penalties fixed by accidents of circumstance. Any added deterrent effect attributable to such penalties is purchased at too high a price. Forfeitures should be generalized, but they should not be made to do work appropriately reserved for traditional punishments such as fine and imprisonment.

The imposition of criminal penalties always and inevitably injures the innocent friends, associates and creditors of the guilty defendant, and even his victims, because their interests are not identical with those of society or of the state. The existing system of criminal forfeitures tends to magnify these effects. At best, it largely ignores the legitimate competing interests of such third parties, relegating them to administrative remission available not as a matter of right but of grace. Attorney fee forfeiture is only a special instance of this general problem, which requires general rules of priority. Defense attorneys should not have priority over victims, but should have priority over other creditors of the defendant to the extent of a reasonable fee for the services

performed. "Reasonableness" in this context must take into account the special complexities of criminal defense under such statutes as RICO. The courts must not limit defense lawyers to the notoriously inadequate statutory fees paid to appointed counsel.

The crisis in criminal forfeiture is, of course, related to larger trends in the development of criminal law, especially federal criminal law. Legislators multiply crimes and multiply punishments for such crimes. They scarcely ever repeal criminal statutes once enacted; they rarely make punishments less severe. At the same time, wrongdoing in the semi-official and wholly private spheres, relegated in the classic liberal state to the civil law or left entirely unregulated, is criminalized by statutes of broad scope and uncertain limits. Since government resources devoted to enforcement do not expand in step, prosecution, always an inherently selective business, becomes more selective over time. The likelihood of discrimination and persecution increases, or, at least, the appearance of discrimination, which is almost as bad.

The existing system of forfeitures exacerbates this problem. It has an odor of state self-interest about it, if not, indeed, of statism. The forfeiture of criminal proceeds for the government's benefit at the expense of victims and creditors makes the state a metaphorical partner in crime. The forfeiture of a car for the purchase of ten dollars' worth of drugs or of a private school for the filing of a false report about class enrollments shocks the conscience. The substantive content of the criminal law and its prescribed punishments are a civil liberties issue just as are the form of criminal procedure. The limitation of criminal forfeiture to its proper place advocated in this Article is intended not only to rationalize the system of criminal penalties but to make it more just.

Pamela H. Bucy, *Indemnification of Corporate Executives Who Have Been Convicted of Crimes: An Assessment and Proposal,* 24 IND. L. REV. (1991)*

Payments to indemnify corporate executives convicted of crimes, though ostensibly forbidden by state incorporation codes and Directors and Officers (D&O)

* Reprinted with permission. Copyright 1994, The Trustees of Indiana University.

Liability Insurance policies, can actually occur routinely, and quietly. This system of corporate indemnification is both excessive and overly restrictive – excessive because corporations' ability to fully indemnify executives convicted of criminal offenses is potentially unlimited, yet overly restrictive because executives who perform in good faith and are virtually vindicated by criminal proceedings have no statutory right to reimbursement. This odd result exists, in part, because indemnification developed in the context of civil liability and was extended to the criminal arena simply by tacking a few words about criminal liability onto existing indemnification statutes. Unfortunately, this extension was unaccompanied by a thorough analysis of the practicalities and unique policy concerns of the criminal law.

If convicted, it is likely that corporate executives will be assessed fines and penalties. They will undoubtedly incur attorneys fees for their unsuccessful defense. If acquitted or if the charges are dismissed, the executive will not be assessed fines or penalties but will have incurred attorneys fees. Currently, there are two major avenues through which corporate executives may seek reimbursement for these costs. The first is from the corporation, which receives power to indemnify its executives from state incorporation statutes or from internal sources such as bylaws or contracts. The second avenue is the D&O insurer. Executives turn to a D&O insurer when their corporation is either unwilling to indemnify, as in the case of a hostile take-over, or is unable to indemnify, as in the case of insolvency.

Part One of this Article addresses the first avenue and surveys the full panoply of opportunities corporations have to willingly, even eagerly, indemnify corporate executives who have been convicted of crimes. This survey also covers the few odd occasions when deserving executives have no rights to indemnification. Part Two describes the additional reimbursement opportunities presented by D&O insurance which, as noted, is an executive's surrogate for indemnification when the corporation is unwilling or unable to indemnify. Part Three provides a summary and assessment of indemnification and D&O insurance, suggesting that our current approach poorly serves the public interest. Appendix A contains a proposed indemnification statute that better accommodates the public interest while also preserving the important, and needed, protection indemnification should provide.

I. INDEMNIFICATION BY THE CORPORATION

A. OVERVIEW

Corporations are empowered to indemnify their directors and officers through four possible sources:

statutes in force in the jurisdiction of incorporation, bylaws, corporate resolutions, or contracts negotiated with individual directors.

As part of its incorporation statute, each state has enacted provisions dealing with indemnification of corporate executives for costs associated with their corporate duties. Currently, the most influential statutes are the Delaware statute and the 1984 Revised Model Business Corporation Act (RMBCA).

The first indemnification statute was passed by New York in 1941 in response to New York Dock Co., Inc. v. McCollom, decided two years earlier. In New York Dock, the New York court of appeals held that a corporation did not have the power to pay the expenses of directors sued in a derivative suit who had successfully defended themselves on the merits. This decision was contrary to the generally accepted common law view that corporations had power to reimburse successful executives. Alarmed over this decision, business interests quickly rallied state legislatures to pass statutes empowering corporations to indemnify executives who incurred legal liability in the exercise of their corporate duties. As new generations of indemnification statutes developed, more sophisticated features were added such as mandatory indemnification for the successful executive; indemnification for costs incurred in ERISA, criminal, administrative, and legislative actions; indemnification for threatened actions that never culminated in actual "claims" but which may have generated attorney fees; and, indemnification for costs incurred in compromise settlements.

Since the mid-1980's, the trend in the states has been to statutorily expand the power of corporations to indemnify their executives. Whereas the most dramatic expansion has been with regard to shareholder derivative lawsuits, the expansion of exclusivity and advancement of expense provisions directly affects executives who face criminal liability.

Virtually all indemnification statutes follow the same general pattern: they require corporations to indemnify directors in some instances but permit indemnification in other instances as long as certain standards of conduct are met. All of the statutes set forth a procedure for authorizing indemnification and indicate whether the statute is the exclusive mechanism for providing indemnification.

Thirty statutes are purely nonexclusive, and thus allow corporations to indemnify executives in circumstances other than those set forth in the statute. No statutes are truly exclusive but two, those of Minnesota and North Dakota, come close. Although these statutes give corporations the authority to limit the indemnification provided in the statute, they do not allow corporations to expand indemnification rights beyond those set forth in the statute. A few statutes present a hybrid approach on the exclusivity issue. Nine of the statutes professing to be nonexclusive appear to place some restrictions on indemnification made outside the statute. Another nine statutes, following the RMBCA, prohibit indemnification that is "not consistent with" the provisions of the statute.

Virtually all of the statutes address two additional issues, advancement of attorneys fees and purchase of D&O insurance. All statutes, except Vermont's, specifically allow corporations to advance funds to pay attorneys fees as those fees are incurred, rather than after judgment. Every state indemnification statute, except Vermont's, specifically authorizes corporations to procure D&O liability insurance without regard to whether the corporation has the power to indemnify.

In states where the indemnification statute is nonexclusive, corporations may pass bylaws or corporate resolutions or negotiate contracts with individual executives allowing indemnification. These bylaws, resolutions or contracts may allow indemnification beyond that permitted in the statute. Bylaws and corporate resolutions tend to favor corporate executives. Most seek to expand the benefits of indemnification to directors and officers in "new and unexpected ways." As might be imagined, ad hoc agreements negotiated between corporations and individual executives allow for the broadest discretion to negotiate terms of full indemnification. To date, the only requirement imposed by the courts on such contracts is that new and independent consideration must support the agreement. Courts have liberally construed what suffices as "new and independent" consideration.

B. THE INDEMNIFICATION STATUTES

1. Mandatory Indemnification

All but six state incorporation statutes make indemnification mandatory when an executive has been successful in defending against criminal charges, but these statutes differ in their description of "success." California's statute requires that the executive must be "successful on the merits." Twenty-eight state statutes require that the executive be "successful on the merits or otherwise," while fifteen statutes require that the executive be "wholly successful on the merits or otherwise."

* * *

2. Permissive Indemnification

For those executives who have been convicted on criminal charges and do not qualify for mandatory indemnification, indemnification may still be available if these executives can qualify for permissive indemnification. There are potentially eight different provisions in the various incorporation statutes that determine whether a corporation is permitted to indemnify a convicted executive. Although no incorporation statute directly permits reimbursement for criminal fines, penalties, or attorneys fees incurred in the unsuccessful defense of the criminal charges, the combination of these provisions makes it quite possible for a corporation to indemnify convicted executives. The following five provisions are included in almost every state's incorporation statute: (1) a standard for permissive indemnification (2) a procedure for authorizing indemnification, (3) a provision addressing the exclusivity of the statutory standards, (4) a statement regarding the authority to advance expenses, and (5) a statement of the significance to be accorded a conviction or plea of nolo contendere. Additionally, the following three provisions are variously included in some state incorporation statutes: (1) power given a court to indemnify executives who have not met the statutory standards for indemnification, (2) shareholder disclosure requirements, and (3) miscellaneous restrictions.

* * *

C. SUMMARY OF INDEMNIFICATION BY CORPORATIONS

A corporation is empowered to indemnify its executives through the incorporation statute of the state where it is incorporated. Although the statutes vary in their definitions of "success," all statutes require that corporations indemnify executives who have been successful in defending the charges against them. Depending upon the definition of "success," executives convicted in part may qualify for mandatory indemnification. Incorporation statutes also permit corporations to indemnity executives who have not successfully defended themselves on the criminal charges if the executives qualify for "permissive" indemnification. Convicted executives can easily qualify for permissive indemnification under most incorporation statutes despite their convictions because of trends in criminal law regarding proof of mens rea; the standards that must be met to qualify for permissive indemnification; the procedure for determining whether an executive has met these standards; the explicitly insignificant relevance attributed to a criminal conviction by most statutes; and, the secrecy in which indemnification may be granted.

Moreover, even if the convicted executive fails to qualify for permissive indemnification, she may still receive indemnification through a variety of statutory avenues that dispense with the need for compliance with the permissive standards. Twenty states allow a court to order indemnification even if the permissive standards have not been met. Forty-eight states allow corporations to disregard the statutory standards for indemnification to some extent, if not altogether, and order indemnification pursuant to bylaws, resolutions or privately negotiated contracts. Lastly, forty-nine statutes explicitly allow advances of litigation costs. These advances may result in defacto indemnification to a convicted corporate executive who is ultimately found to be incapable of meeting statutory standards. There are no meaningful requirements for a preliminary assessment of eligibility for indemnification before the advance is made, and there is no meaningful mechanism to enforce repayment of advances if the executive is later found to be utterly incapable of meeting the permissive standards.

The only limit on indemnification legitimately made through the above avenues is a review by the courts to determine if the indemnification frustrates public policy. However, because the courts review only a fraction of indemnification awards, and because they erratically interpret and apply principles of public policy, this is an unpredictable and ineffectual limit on improper indemnification.

Despite this seemingly good news for the convicted executive, she may still have cause for concern. A corporation's willingness to indemnify its executives depends upon the corporation's economic stability and leadership. The corporation with few or no assets cannot indemnify anyone. And, if the officials charged with authorizing indemnification are hostile to the executive seeking indemnification, or determine that the executive has failed to meet necessary standards, there is little chance indemnification, statutory or otherwise, will be paid by the corporation. For this reason many executives turn to D&O liability insurance for reimbursement. It is less likely, however, that the convicted executive will fare well with D&O insurers.

II. D&O INSURANCE FOR CONVICTED EXECUTIVES

A. OVERVIEW

D&O insurance has expanded tremendously since the first two policies were sold in 1962. Currently, every state incorporation code, except that of Vermont, specifically authorizes corporations to purchase D&O insurance even allowing coverage of costs not indemnifiable by the corporation. The Delaware code, followed by forty-eight states, provides . . . that "[a] corporation shall have the power to purchase and maintain insurance on behalf of any [corporate executive] . . . whether or not the corporation would have the power to indemnify him against such liability under the provisions of this section."

D&O insurance provides coverage for losses arising from wrongful acts committed by directors and officers, and in some cases, by other employees. A "wrongful act" includes "any actual or alleged error or misstatement or misleading statement or act or omission or neglect or breach of duty by the [insureds] . . . claimed against them solely by reason of their being [executives] of the company." Losses covered include "damages, judgments, settlement and costs, charges and expenses, incurred in the defense of actions, suits or proceedings and appeals".

* * *

B. D&O COVERAGE FOR THE CONVICTED EXECUTIVE

Compared to corporate indemnification, D&O insurance provides less of an opportunity for convicted executives to receive reimbursement for costs associated with criminal liability. Historically, insurance coverage has not been available for deliberate and willful acts. The definition of "loss" in most D&O policies grows out of this history. These policies specifically provide that the "loss" covered by the policies "shall not include fines or penalties imposed by the law or matters which may be deemed uninsurable under the law pursuant to which this policy shall be construed." This definition would seem to exclude insurance coverage for any costs incurred by a convicted executive. Some commentators, however, have suggested that this definition does not exclude coverage for criminal or other intentional acts. They rely on the phrase, "matters which are uninsurable under the law pursuant to which this policy shall be construed." In some jurisdictions, the law pursuant to which an insurance policy is construed allows insurance coverage of intentional or even criminal misconduct. In these jurisdictions the definition of loss, by explicitly incorporating this applicable law, may extend to intentional or criminal misconduct.

* * *

III. SUMMARY, ASSESSMENT AND PROPOSAL

A. SUMMARY

Assume a corporate executive becomes the target of grand jury investigation or is indicted. During the investigation, pretrial negotiations, and trial if one occurs, the executive incurs hundreds of thousands of dollars in attorneys fees. Although there may not yet be a judgment that would indicate whether or not the executive qualifies for indemnification from the relevant corporation or reimbursement from the applicable D&O insurer, it is likely that the executive will seek an advance to cover these attorneys fees. If the executive seeks the advance from the corporation and meets statutory criteria (virtually pro forma) he will receive the advance without posting security or proving an ability to repay if he is ultimately found ineligible for indemnification. If the executive seeks an advance from the D&O

insurer, or if the corporation seeks coverage for amounts it advanced to the executive, the law is unclear and the policy language and the jurisdiction will determine whether coverage is available.

If the grand jury does not return charges against the executive or if the executive is acquitted on all charges, he will be entitled to mandatory indemnification from the corporation for all attorneys fees and other costs. The corporation should then be able to collect the amount it indemnified its executive from its D&O insurer. If the executive's corporate employer is unable or unwilling to indemnify, the executive should be able to recover directly from the D&O insurer for the attorneys fees and other costs he paid. If the executives secures a pretrial dismissal on procedural grounds of some of the charges, and seeks indemnification from the corporation, he is entitled to mandatory pro-rata indemnification for the dismissed charges only if the applicable indemnification statute requires reimbursement when one is "successful on the merits or otherwise."

If the executive negotiates a plea agreement and secures a dismissal of some of the charges in return for a plea of guilty to other charges, he is not entitled to mandatory reimbursement if the applicable statute requires that one be "wholly successful." He is entitled to any mandatory pro-rata reimbursement for the dismissed charges if the applicable law requires only that one be "successful."

If the executive has been partially successful on the criminal charges, (i.e. through pretrial motions to dismiss charges or a plea agreement dismissing some of the charges), but this measure of success is insufficient to qualify for mandatory indemnification, the executive may still receive indemnification by qualifying under statutory standards for permissive indemnification. Similarly, the executive who has been convicted on all criminal charges may receive indemnification by qualifying under these permissive standards. Through the interplay of applicable principles of corporate, criminal and insurance law, a convicted executive may well qualify under these permissive standards. However, even if the executive cannot qualify under the permissive standards, he may still receive indemnification under the incorporation statutes of the twenty states that allow a court to order indemnification even if the permissive standards are not met. Also, an executive who is ultimately unable to meet the permissive standards may receive defacto indemnification in forty-nine states by receiving an advance of attorneys fees with no repayment required or, in some cases, even requested. In the forty-eight states governed by a nonexclusive or quasi-nonexclusive incorporation statute, the executive may obtain indemnification from the corporation even if he fails to meet the statutory standards as long as corporate bylaws, resolutions, or a negotiated contract allow indemnification. The only hurdle the convicted corporate executive must overcome in receiving indemnification through any of these routes is principles of public policy enforced by the courts. However, because of the small likelihood that an indemnification award will be reviewed by a court, and because courts erratically apply these principles of public policy, this is an unlikely impediment.

If the convicted executive attempts to collect from the insurer for his fines, penalties and defense costs, or if the corporation attempts to collect from the insurer for amounts it indemnified the convicted executive, coverage is uncertain. D&O policies purport to exclude coverage of claims arising from criminal liability. However, because of ambiguity in the policy definitions and exclusions, and because some policies grant coverage equal to a corporation's power to indemnify, such claims may be covered.

B. ASSESSMENT AND PROPOSAL

Having surveyed this land of riches for convicted executives, the merits of such reimbursement must be evaluated. There are legitimate business reasons why corporations and insurers should be allowed to reimburse executives for costs these executives incur due to liability arising from their corporate duties. It is probably true, and it is certainly the perception, that corporate executives may be exposed to greater risks of liability than are most of us. With increasingly creative plaintiffs, a financial market riddled with scandals, and courts rendering unpredictable verdicts, these risks may even be rising. In today's business environment, some degree of indemnification is undoubtedly necessary to attract and retain talented and capable executives. Moreover, executives cannot be burdened with layers of bureaucracy installed solely to protect them against frivolous lawsuits. The fear of litigation cannot be allowed to cripple our innovative executives who can, and should, be able to act quickly and intuitively before promising business opportunities vanish. To the extent indemnification and D&O insurance provide this freedom, they should be encouraged. However, reimbursement to convicted executives is a different matter. It should not be allowed to continue unchecked because we fail to acknowledge its true girth or because we fail to comprehend the unique policy interests it tramples.

An analogy may help demonstrate why indemnification to convicted executives should not be allowed. We would not be concerned if the family of a convicted bank robber paid the expenses of his defense and the fine imposed upon him. Indeed, most of us would probably approve of such familial support at a time of stress and need. The difference between our bank robber and the corporate executive, however, is in who is paying and the threat such payment poses to our legal system. If the bank robber's "family" was a gang that recruited individuals to be bank robbers and to share their ill-gotten gains with the organization, reimbursement of fines, penalties and expenses by the gang after a gang-member's conviction would strengthen this organization's influence on its remaining members. It is not difficult to see that if an organization is able, by money, to partially neutralize the sanctions of society, the organization's values have a better chance of superseding those of society. When the members of the organization see payments to their fallen comrade, they cannot help but believe that wealth and status within the organization are worth the risks (now neutralized, at least somewhat, by money) of robbing banks. The analogy of a gang of bank robbers to a corporation is faulty in two respects, both of which provide further insight as to why we should not indemnify convicted executives. First, robbing banks is clearly a crime and it would take alot of indoctrination to overcome society's stigma of it as criminal. Often, however, corporate crime is not clearly criminal; it is "puffing" a little too much about the value of assets, or speculating too optimistically about profits, or compromising on technical regulations to meet a deadline. Corporate crime is also "hidden within an organization" and, because it may take the independent acts of many people to actually complete the criminal conduct, its criminal character is often subtle. Since corporate crime is not as obvious of a crime as is bank robbery and does not fit our traditional notion of a crime, it is also not as hard to convince otherwise respectable people to engage in it. In short, a corporate organization has a better chance of instilling its values in its members than does a bank-robbing gang.

The second flaw in our analogy to bank robbers is the respective impact on society of bank robbers and corporate criminals. Bank robbers are not good for any of us, but their immediate damage is confined to a particular bank and its employees or customers. Their long term harm to the security of our savings system is dwarfed, however, by the harm caused by white collar crime. Whether we are talking about our savings system, political infrastructure, environment, health care system, defense industry, or pension system, the damage caused by white collar crime debilitates the foundation of our society. Because of this impact, there is a greater societal need to control our many corporations than our few bank-robbing gangs.

There can be no question that because of the increasingly significant role corporations assume in modern society, it is essential that they encourage lawful, rather than unlawful, behavior. They have the power to do either. To examine this, all one has to do is turn to the wealth of business literature on corporate culture which examines how a particular corporate environment can encourage, or discourage, behavior. For criminal justice purposes, some of the most interesting work on corporate culture has been conducted by sociologists who have examined the commission of corporate crime to determine the characteristics of lawful and unlawful organizations. These scholars suggest that certain social structures and processes internal to an organization encourage unlawful behavior.

For example, in a study of sixty-four retired, middle management employees of Fortune 500 corporations, Marshall Clinard found that these executives consistently identified corporate internal structure (versus outside market forces) as primarily determinative of whether a corporation was lawful or unlawful. One such internal factor was top management's attitude toward applicable laws and regulations. Top management who encouraged law abiding behavior were described as respectful of applicable government regulations, encouraging of their enforcement, and effective in monitoring their compliance by employees. Another significant internal factor was the pressure placed on middle management to show a profit. Companies that encouraged unlawful behavior communicated to their employees that compromises in following the law were permitted if necessary to meet the profit goal. Indemnification of executives convicted of violating the law cannot help but communicate this.

Diane Vaughan's study of Revco Inc. is especially interesting as a case study of organizational crime. In 1977, Revco Inc., a pharmaceutical retailer, pled guilty to submitting over $500,000 in false Medicaid claims. Drawing upon this case study Vaughan focuses, in part, on the relationship between corporate structural factors and unlawful behavior. She concludes that the "organizational processes . . . create an internal moral and intellectual world" in which "individuals within the organization are encouraged to engage in unlawful behavior." These organizational processes include reward mechanisms, internal education and training, and informational processing and recording methods.

In short, there is no question that the formal and informal structure of a corporation can encourage or discourage violations of the law. Indemnification by a corporation or reimbursement by an D&O insurer to an executive who has been convicted of crimes is part of this structure. By paying a convicted corporate executive for fines, penalties and costs incurred in his criminal case, and often by doing so after explicitly finding that this executive acted in good faith and had no reason to believe his conduct was unlawful, corporations and insurers are sending a message to corporate executives. They are telling these employees that pursuit of corporate goals justifies breaking the law and that they will reward those who do so. Moreover, this indemnification separates corporate executives from other criminal defendants. With someone else paying their litigation expenses and fines or penalties, corporate executives do not feel the pain or stigma of a criminal verdict and sentence as do other criminal defendants. Thus, indemnification and insurance not only contribute to a corporate culture that encourages corporate crime but also perpetuate two levels of justice.

When one examines the historical evolution of indemnification and D&O insurance, one can see how their potential for encouraging corporate crime was overlooked. These methods of reimbursement developed in the context of civil law, the traditional objective of which is reimbursement to a victim by the party causing the injury. Indemnification and insurance further this goal because they assist the party found liable in paying the judgment to the victim. Notably, even when indemnification does not further this goal, as when the civil defendant has sufficient assets to pay the judgment, indemnification still does not detract from it.

By comparison, the major objective of criminal liability is deterrence. Our criminal justice system is based upon the belief that by public condemnation, sufficiently harsh penalties and loss of privileges, a defendant and all others who observe his conviction and sentence will be discouraged from engaging in the proscribed behavior. Indemnification and D&O insurance never serve this goal of deterrence; rather, they allow a private party (either a corporation or an insurer) to neutralize, if not defeat it.

While this proffered explanation may help explain our current practice of indemnifying convicted executives, it cannot justify it. We cannot continue to ignore the very different impact indemnification and D&O insurance have in the civil and criminal arenas. Reimbursement through indemnification and D&O insurance to convicted executives should not be allowed. Indemnification statutes should be amended so that they directly and plainly exclude indemnification to any convicted executive. The non-exclusivity provision in these statutes should also be amended so that corporations cannot circumvent such a prohibition by indemnifying convicted executives through bylaws, resolutions, or contracts. To the extent that the definition of "loss" or the dishonesty exclusion in D&O policies obligates insurers to reimburse convicted executives or corporations that have indemnified convicted executives, these polices should be redrafted to clearly exclude such coverage.

Advances of fees to executives who are targets of a criminal investigation or who have been charged but not yet acquitted or convicted, presents a more complex question than does that posed by reimbursement to convicted executives for fines and penalties. Currently every state incorporation code, except that of Vermont, gives corporations the power to advance attorneys fees before there has been a judgment.

* * *

Whether a corporation will initiate or be able to recover an advance of funds paid to its executive, is a different matter. A corporation may not seek recovery of advances despite the egregiousness of the executive's actions because the remaining corporate executives are loyal to their convicted colleague or her family. More cynically, these executives may fear that their colleague will start pointing fingers at them unless she feels beholden to them, which she may if the corporation allows her to keep the funds advanced. For whatever reason, if the corporation is unwilling to seek recovery, there is a smorgasbord of loopholes by which the corporate executives may legally justify not doing so.

Even if the corporation decides to seek recovery of the funds advanced, however, it may be unable to find assets available. Perhaps anticipating a guilty verdict, wealthy executives may secret their assets or legally transfer title in them. Or, it is possible that during the years it may have taken the criminal case to run its course, the executive's wealth has been dissipated through over-leveraging or other financial misfortunes. This brings us back to the ineffectual nature of the "undertaking to repay" requirement. Without security, this undertaking to repay is worthless and confers defacto indemnification to executives who may have egregiously and blatantly committed crimes.

Sorting out the merits of allowing advances of attorneys fees is now easier. It is not only fair and equitable, but probably necessary to attract quality individuals, that these advances be available to corporate executives. This consideration is more powerful than the one typically suggested, that advances are necessary to encourage and facilitate a vigorous defense. Granted, a few executives may be able to wage a more vigorous defense if an advance is available but given the assets, personality, and reputation at stake of most executives, this rationale is relatively insignificant. On the other hand, the opportunity to influence an indicted or targeted executive's decisions in the criminal case is probably the main reason insurers and corporations prefer to make advances. Given the hazards this influence poses to potential civil plaintiffs, and perhaps even to the executive herself, however, this reason militates against advances, at least from a public policy point of view. Lastly, the protections against imprudent advances already in the incorporation statutes cannot serve as an argument in favor of allowing advances because these protections are inadequate.

The previous proposal, that incorporation statutes be amended to categorically disallow indemnification to a convicted executive, should encourage a corporation to seek recovery of funds it advanced to an executive who now stands convicted of crimes. If this change is made, there would be no loopholes through which a corporation could dodge its obligation to seek recovery of advances. The ability to actually recover the monies advanced presents a separate problem, however. Before they are given an advance, which is in effect an interest-free loan, executives should be required to commit to a meaningful undertaking to repay; in other words, they should have to post security. There should also be mechanisms for exempting those executives who truly are unable to post security, but need advances. Qualifying for this exemption could be handled in several possible ways, such as a blanket exemption for all outside directors representing charitable or consumer groups, or an exemption granted by a court after an ex parte review of the executive's financial statement.

Requiring security in all but appropriate exceptions recognizes the importance of providing corporate executives with advances to pay attorneys fees without doing so at the expense of the public interest. With the requirement of security the corporate executive is assured of sufficient money to hire able counsel, while shareholders are assured that they will not be left with the bill for the attorneys fees if the executive is ultimately convicted. More importantly, the public is assured that the goals and integrity of the criminal justice system cannot be flouted by private parties.

The last proposal for change pertains to the standards for mandatory indemnification in state incorporation statutes. Unlike the other avenues for reimbursement to convicted executives discussed herein, the statutory standards for mandatory indemnification are too restrictive. By failing to account for the practicalities of the criminal justice system, these standards can lead to bizarre and unfair results. Use of the "wholly successful" and "successful on the merits or otherwise" standards, while perhaps well-intentioned, delegate decisions with tremendous personal and policy ramifications to the unbridled discretion of one prosecutor. Because of the "wholly successful" language, executives who have been vindicated on serious and substantial charges but convicted on minor charges are not entitled to mandatory indemnification pro-rated to cover the charges on which they were

successful. Because of the "successful on the merits or otherwise" language, executives who have secured a dismissal of criminal charges on procedural grounds but reek of bad faith and illegal intentions are entitled to full indemnification. A better approach to mandatory indemnification would be to require that the court before whom the criminal proceeding is pending determine whether the interests of justice are served by allowing indemnification to the executive who has been successful, in whole or part, on the criminal charges. Because the condition precedent to the court's exercise of such power is some form of success by the executive on at least some of the criminal charges, the court's discretion is considerably limited. Because the only court eligible to make this determination is the court before whom the criminal matter is pending, there is little danger of the manipulation and duplication posed by the provision in some statutes that allows courts other than the one familiar with proceedings to authorize indemnification.

* * *

IV. CONCLUSION

Because of the interplay of incorporation statutes, criminal law, and insurance law, corporations have broad discretion to indemnify their corporate executives who have been convicted of crimes. Because of ambiguity in D&O insurance policies and the courts' erratic application of principles of public policy, it is possible that insurers will be held liable for costs incurred by a convicted executive. One cannot assume that corporations or insurers will protest strongly about this. Corporate executives often want to indemnify their convicted colleagues. Moreover, due to the potential collateral estoppel effect of an executive's conviction on the future civil liability of the corporation, on other corporate executives and on the D&O insurer, these sources may be quite willing to indemnify the convicted corporate executive. Lost in the shuffle is the public's interest in fairness and the deterrence of corporate crime.

The compensatory goal of civil liability is well served by indemnification. This is the context in which corporate indemnification and D&O insurance developed and most commonly exists. With little analysis of public policy concerns, however, these sources of reimbursement have been extended to the criminal arena whose goal of deterrence is undercut by reimbursement to a convicted executive. Modifications in incorporation statutes and D&O insurance policies such as those suggested herein are needed to insure that indemnification continues to serve the appropriate needs for which it was designed, yet not frustrate the goals and integrity of our criminal justice system.

Part III
Crimes

A. Federal White Collar Crimes

RICHARD W. BECKLER AND MAURY S. EPNER, *Principal White Collar Crimes,* BUSINESS CRIMES: A GUIDE FOR CORPORATE AND DEFENSE COUNSEL 1–63 (Jeffrey Glekel, ed.) (1982)*

The federal white collar crimes discussed here may be divided into two groups: particular classes of conduct, such as fraud or the making of false or misleading statements, and broad classes of generally violent or dangerous behavior, otherwise the object of purely local attention. In both instances, such acts are federal crimes because they either affect or are in some way furthered by an instrumentality of the interstate system.

Certain statutes explicitly punish attempts and conspiracies to violate their substantive provisions; others do not. Those in the latter category may nonetheless be the objects of conspiracy prosecution under the general federal conspiracy statute. A single transaction may thus subject a defendant to prosecution not only for the substantive offense itself but for the separate crime of conspiracy. Indeed, a defendant involved in but one transaction may be subject to prosecution under two or more separate substantive provisions, in addition to conspiracy.

Mail and Wire Fraud

The mail fraud statute generally prohibits anyone from using, or causing to be used, the mails in connection with any intended or actual fraud. The wire fraud

* Reprinted with permission of the author and the Practising Law Institute, New York, New York 1982.

statute is virtually identical. It prohibits anyone from using, or causing to be used, in interstate or foreign commerce any form of radio, television, or wire communication in connection with any intended or actual fraud. The elements of the offenses are: (1) a scheme to defraud; (2) specific intent to defraud; and (3) use of at least one of the instrumentalities (mail, telephone, etc.) in furtherance of the scheme.

The statutes forbid anyone from devising or intending to devise a scheme to defraud. As such, one person, acting alone, is capable of violating either statute. For this reason, where the scheme involves two or more individuals, conspiracy may also be charged.

The statutes do not define "scheme or artifice to defraud." Even so, courts examining particular schemes have construed the statutes broadly. All that is required of a particular scheme is that it be "reasonably" calculated to deceive persons of ordinary prudence and comprehension.

Traditional schemes, of course, violate the statutes. Thus, where government officials or corporate employees accept bribes, they are subject to prosecution. Unconventional frauds are also prohibited. In *United States v. Keane,* for instance, a Chicago alderman was convicted under the fraud statute because he used information unavailable to the public for his own benefit. He thus defrauded his constituents by breaching a fiduciary duty, namely, the obligation to use confidential information for the public good rather than personal gain. Similarly, frauds that do not involve money or other property, or even breaches of fiduciary duty, are prohibited by the fraud statutes. Recent schemes to seduce women or obtain confidential information have been prosecuted under the mail and wire fraud statutes.

It has been clearly established that a defendant need not be successful in his fraudulent endeavor to violate the statutes. Once the prosecution demonstrates that a defendant employs the mails or some means of interstate wire communication for the purpose of executing a fraudulent scheme, the success or failure of the scheme is irrelevant.

INTENT

Although success is not an element of the offense, contemplation of harm to one's putative victims *is* required. That is, in order to be guilty of mail or wire fraud, a defendant's scheme must be one *designed* to defraud. For this reason, at least one court has held that false representations alone (without actual or intended harm) simply do not violate the mail or wire fraud statutes.

In *United States v. Regent Office Supply Co.*, the defendant was in the business of selling stationery supplies by telephone, and some of the defendant's sales persons made false representations to customers in order to secure sales. Some sales agents represented themselves as doctors, claiming that they had unwanted stationery they were willing to sell. Other imaginative sales agents claimed to have friends who had recently died, and had received immediately before their deaths large orders of stationery, which now, of course, they would be unable to use (and were consequently available for resale).

In *Regent,* the prosecution failed to allege any actual or intended harm to any customer because no purchaser received other or less than what he paid for. Thus, despite the defendant's bizarre conduct, the court was unwilling, absent some showing of actual or intended harm, to elevate such conduct to the level of fraud.

What is necessary under the fraud statutes, then, is not merely knowledge (or reckless disregard) of the falsity of one's representation. The defendant's intention to injure another to his own advantage by withholding or misrepresenting material facts must also be shown. This, however, is all that must be intended by the defendant. It is unimportant that the defendant did not intend, in purposefully engaging in some fraudulent scheme, to employ one or more of the jurisdictional means of communication, so long as some involvement of such means is demonstrated and was reasonably foreseeable.

USE OF MAILS OR WIRES

While the use of one or more of the jurisdictional means need not be intended by the defendant as part of his scheme, it is necessary that such use further the execution of some fraud. In other words, there must be some connection or nexus between the alleged use of the mails or wire communications and the fraudulent scheme.

This requirement may be expressed as a matter of timing. When the entire use of one or more of the jurisdictional means occurs before the scheme is formulated, or subsequent to its completion, this use is insufficient for the purposes of the statutes. Thus, where defendant made unauthorized credit card purchases, the subsequent lawful mailing of invoices was held insufficient for the purposes of the mail fraud statute. Likewise, where the treasurer of a charity lawfully received contributions through the mail but wrongfully converted a portion of those contributions to his own use, or where certain members of a local school board embezzled a portion of the district's tax revenues, previously billed and collected by mail, all use of the mails occurred prior to the execution of the fraud. For this reason, there were insufficient connections between the wholly proper uses of the jurisdictional means and the wrongful acts that followed them.

Provided a sufficient nexus may be demonstrated, however, it is not also necessary that the defendant himself use the jurisdictional means; it is enough that he "causes" use. Thus, in *United States v. Calvert* the defendant was convicted of defrauding an insurance company under the mail fraud statute, although the only mailing alleged was between a local insurance agent and the agent's home office. *Calvert* also suggests that it is not necessary, for the purposes of the statutes, that any fraudulent representation itself be transmitted, only that use or transmission be "for the purpose of executing" a fraudulent scheme.

The two statutes differ in one important respect. Under the mail fraud statute, any mailing, interstate or intrastate, is sufficient to trigger a violation; under the wire fraud statute only an interstate transmission is sufficient. For the purposes of section 1343, however, the interstate character of such a transmission may be purely technical and completely unintended by the defendant. In *United States v. Davila,* because Western Union transmissions between two small Texas cities were routed through West Virginia (all Western Union transmissions are so routed), defendant's use was deemed of sufficient interstate character to satisfy the requirement of section 1343.

Finally, where a fraudulent scheme involves more than one participant, a single use of the jurisdictional means by any one of the participants is sufficient to render all of them liable, provided each is a knowing participant and use of the mails or wires could reasonably be foreseen. . . .

False Statements

It is a federal crime knowingly and willfully to make a false statement or material omission, or an intentional or reckless misrepresentation, in any matter within the jurisdiction of a federal agency or department.

Two statutes that outlaw the making of false statements are of special interest with regard to white collar criminal activity: the general federal statute, and the statute prohibiting false entries associated with any federally chartered banks. The elements of the two offenses are substantially the same: (1) any statement or entry that (2) is made to one who is protected by the statutes, (3) is false, (4) is material, and (5) was so intended by the maker, is prohibited.

STATEMENT OR ENTRY

One may not make any false or fraudulent statement, representation, writing, or document under section 1001, nor may any person make a false entry in a book, report, or statement of any bank under section 1005. For section 1001 purposes, the "statement" may be written or oral, and need not be made under oath. Formality is dispensed with as well under section 1005, where to constitute an "entry," a falsity need not appear in any formal financial record. Indeed, the "entry" need not even be a writing; a material omission is sufficient for section 1005 purposes.

STATEMENT OR ENTRY MUST BE MADE TO ONE PROTECTED BY THE STATUTES

Under section 1001, a false statement made "in any matter within the jurisdiction of any department or agency of the United States" is prohibited. In section 1005, a broad class of banks and bank-related officials (including federal agency officials) are protected from false entries. The class of protected parties in section 1005 is explicit. The same cannot be said for section 1001. It is unclear from the face of the statute what falls within the jurisdiction of any agency or department of the federal government and, indeed, just what constitutes an "agency" or "department" for the purposes of the statute.

For example, one who volunteers false information to the FBI may be prosecuted under section 1001, because that statute is "couched in very broad terms to encompass [a] variety of deceptive practices," and the term "agency" must "be given a broad, nontechnical meaning." Consistent with this is *United States v. Matanky,* where the court held that making false statements to a private contractor, working on behalf of a federal agency, violates section 1001. In *Matanky,* a doctor submitted false medicare payment vouchers to private insurance carriers and was convicted under section 1001.

This breadth of application is further reflected in the fact that wherever there is some statutory basis for an agency's request for information, false statements made pursuant to such requests are actionable under section 1001, even if the statutory basis is subsequently repealed. As broadly as it is read, however, section 1001 does not cover false statements made concerning matters within the jurisdiction of a federal district court, or statements made before grand juries. The appropriate remedy for false statements in these contexts is a perjury prosecution.

Another exception to the otherwise broad scope of section 1001 relates to false statements made in connection with federal criminal investigations. Where a defendant's statement amounts to an exculpatory "no," he generally will not be punished under section 1001. One reason for this is the fifth amendment policy against self-incrimination; another is that the purpose of section 1001 (and presumably section 1005 as well) is to assure that government programs are administered without interference.

False statements made in civil actions also are excluded from the coverage of section 1001. In *United States v. D'Amato,* the court not only presumed that section 1001 does not apply to statements in private civil actions, but also held that section 1001 will not punish the making of a false statement where the United States is a party. Once again, perjury is committed in such a context; absent evidence of any fraud upon the United States or any deception upon a regulatory or investigative agency, section 1001 does not apply.

STATEMENT MUST BE "FALSE"

Requiring that statements or entries be "false" in order to come within the terms of sections 1001 and 1005 would seem to establish a clear and simple standard for determining violations. Such, however, is not the case. For example, material omissions as well as false statements are explicitly prohibited by section 1001. Moreover, while section 1005 prohibits only false entries by its terms, it has also been construed to include material omissions. Both statutes thus prohibit both affirmatively false statements and omissions that deceive; both, in other words, encompass two distinct offenses, with separate elements necessary to prove each. For this reason, if the prosecution charges a defendant with a false statement, but then proves the elements of an omission, the indictment must be dismissed as duplicitous.

An additional pitfall may await the prosecution. False entries made with "intent to injure or defraud" are proscribed by section 1005. Suppose, however, that a defendant, while committing fraud or other illegal act, enters his unlawful transaction in the bank's records but does so *accurately.* Surely the defendant has acted "with intent to injure or defraud," but has he also made a *false* entry and thus violated section 1005? Two cases, presenting similar factual situations, rendered opposing answers.

In *United States v. Erickson,* defendants arranged a complex scheme to make a substantial loss suffered by their bank. The arrangement called for the bank to sell some of its securities at inflated prices and permit defendants to record the transactions as profitable. The *quid pro quo* for this required that the bank later repurchase these same securities, again at inflated prices. The bank's record *accurately* reflected defendants' machinations, and they were charged with violating section 1005. The court, however, dismissed the indictment, observing that "entries recording fictitious transactions or inaccurately recording actual transactions are false within the meaning of section 1005, [but] an entry recording an actual transaction . . . exactly as it occurred is not a false entry."

Similar facts were presented in *United States v. Gleason*. In that case, in order to conceal a loss, defendants arranged for their bank to enter into contracts for future delivery of foreign exchange at inflated rates. In fact, the transactions took place, and as such were accurately reflected in the bank's records. This, however, did not immunize the defendants from prosecution under section 1005. Despite the reality of the transactions, the court held that "the profit shown on the record of the foreign exchange transaction was known by the defendants to be false and fictitious, concocted for the very purpose of distorting the financial statement. The result was a violation of . . . § 1005."

MATERIALITY

Section 1005 prohibits the making of false entries. Nowhere, however, does it explicitly require that such false entries be material, although such a requirement makes sense, at least in cases where section 1005 is extended to include an implied prohibition against omissions. In those cases, requiring that omissions be material assures that the coverage of section 1005 is consistent with the explicit terms of section 1001.

Section 1001 explicitly creates two offenses: the making of false statements and the concealment of material facts. Yet despite section 1001's explicit use of the word "material" to describe only one of the two offenses contained therein, the prevailing view is that materiality is an essential element of both under section 1001.

A statement is material if it has a natural tendency to influence, or is capable of influencing, a decision required to be made by an agency in the exercise of a governmental function–if it is capable of inducing action or reliance by an agency of the federal government in a determination required to be made.

INTENT

Whoever "knowingly and willfully" makes a false statement or omits a material fact violates section 1001. Whoever makes a false entry "with intent to injure or defraud" violates section 1005. The phraseology differs, but the requirement is the same: a misrepresentation, to violate section 1001, must be intentional or reckless. A false entry, to be punished under section 1005, cannot be the result of mere negligence; it, too, must be intentional or reckless. . . .

Perjury

A person who willfully and knowingly makes an absolutely false statement that is material to proceedings in which he is under oath, and is by law required to speak the truth, may be prosecuted for perjury.

Any discussion of prospective criminal charges in a white collar investigation must include mention of the perjury statutes, 18 U.S.C. sections 1621 and 1623. For example, the government will often be unable to prosecute the substantive fraud case successfully, but will be able to proceed to trial on indictments alleging perjury committed by one or more of the defendants during the course of the investigation.

The tactical question of whether or not to allow your client to be interviewed or to testify in the grand jury is discussed later in this book. This section will deal only with aspects of the perjury offense itself.

18 U.S.C. SECTION 1621

The elements of perjury in 18 U.S.C. section 1621 are: (1) that the defendant be under oath and, pursuant to federal law, be required to speak the truth; (2) that he willfully make a false statement; (3) that the statement be material to the proceedings; (4) that the defendant have knowledge of its falsity; and (5) that the statement be made before a competent tribunal, officer, or person.

It should be emphasized that perjury cases are often the most difficult to prosecute successfully. The questions which elicit the perjurious answer must be clear and unequivocal; and if there is any reason to doubt the absolute falsity of the answer when considered in terms of the question, courts will often lean in favor of defendants in their rulings. Thus, the defendant's statements will be considered in light of his whole testimony, not in isolation. And in general, the alleged perjurious statement must be one of fact, not of opinion or belief. Statements that are merely nonresponsive, even if intentionally misleading, do not constitute perjury when they are not absolutely false.

Moreover, under what is known as the "two-witness rule," the falsity of the testimony in question must be proved by the sworn testimony of at least one witness, and the testimony as to falsity of that witness must be corroborated by the testimony of a second witness or by other evidence.

18 U.S.C. SECTION 1623

The essential elements of perjury in 18 U.S.C. section 1623 are the same as those in section 1621, *except* that the conviction under section 1623 does not require a showing of willfulness. In addition, the "two-witness" rule does not apply to prosecutions under section 1623. Section 1623 requires a lesser burden of quantitative proof than does section 1621 and has thus not only facilitated perjury prosecutions but also enhanced the reliability of testimony in proceedings before federal courts and grand juries.

Section 1623 employs a "carrot and stick" approach. Incorporated into it, but not into section 1621, is the doctrine of recantation, which affords perjurers a qualified opportunity to recant and thereby avoid prosecution. Recantation is a bar to a perjury prosecution unless the prior false declaration has substantially affected the proceeding or it has become manifest that its falsity has been or will be exposed. The purpose of providing an opportunity for a perjurer to correct his false statement voluntarily is to induce the witness to give truthful testimony and, again, to enhance the reliability of evidence in the proceedings.

Currency Transport

Any person who willfully and knowingly fails to report the transport or receipt of over $5,000 in cash or bearer paper into or out of the United States is subject to criminal penalties and may be required to forfeit all the instruments of money transported or received.

Federal law requires that any person who knowingly transports "monetary instruments" in excess of $5,000 into the United States from abroad, or out of the United States, must report such activity to the Secretary of the Treasury. The "willful" failure to do so is criminally punishable. The willful failure to report, or the making of material misstatements or omissions in such reports, also subjects one to the forfeiture, in a separate civil proceeding, of his unreported money. To obtain a criminal conviction, however, the government must establish each of the following elements: (1) the defendant willfully violated the requirement that one who knows (2) he is transporting monetary instruments (3) in excess of $5,000 on any one occasion (4) must report the same.

INTENT

Section 1101 requires that anyone who *knowingly* transports more than $5,000 must report this fact. The *willful* failure to do so is punishable. The prosecution must therefore prove not only that a defendant actually knew of the reporting requirement imposed by section 1101, but that he specifically intended not to abide by it. It follows that where a court fails to instruct the jury that ignorance of the reporting requirement is a defense, any subsequent conviction must be reversed.

Naturally, if a defendant has notice of the reporting requirement, the defense of ignorance is unavailable. With this in mind, at least one court has held that where, at the conclusion of an international flight, a defendant was provided with a form asking whether he was carrying more than $5,000 and stating that, if so, he must file an additional report, defendant had sufficient notice of the reporting requirement. Where no such form is distributed, however, a defendant's statement that he is "aware" of United States currency laws is in and of itself insufficient proof that defendant knew of the section 1101 reporting requirement.

TRANSPORTING "MONETARY INSTRUMENTS"

One must report to the Secretary of the Treasury whenever he "transports or causes to be transported monetary instruments" and the transport is either from any place within the United States to someplace abroad, or vice versa. One must also report when he receives within the United States monetary instruments that have been sent from abroad.

The term "monetary instrument" is carefully yet broadly defined in the statute and in supporting Treasury regulations. What constitutes transport, however, is more strictly construed. The statute forbids transport "from any place within the United States to or through any place outside" it. If, for example, this is read to include those defendants who do no more than prepare to board airplanes, carrying unreported sums in excess of $5,000, then the statute might be interpreted to punish *attempts*, in addition to actual transports of unreported sums. In *United States v. Gomez-Londono,* however, the court refused to go so far, holding instead that the statute does not punish attempts.

Such a holding evokes concern in some quarters because it is believed to render the statute unenforceable. The presumption is that if the statute does not punish attempts, one does not violate it until he physically takes leave of the United States, at which time he is beyond the territorial jurisdiction of federal law enforcement officials. This, however, need not be the case. As the *Gomez-Londono* court observed:

> nothing would have prevented the officers from delaying their intervention until [defendant] had been tendered and had filled out a false [f]orm . . . and had then surrendered his passage coupon, had received his boarding pass, and was ready to board, or had taken his place in the aircraft.

The essence of the offense is the willful failure to *report* one's transport of more than $5,000; by no means is it the transport itself. Thus, because one cannot willfully fail to do something before the opportunity to do it arises, one cannot willfully fail to report one's transport until it has occurred or is in the process of occurring.

The same reasoning applies to those who transport "*to* any place within the United States from or through any place outside the United States. . . ." In fact, if anything, such cases should result in the statute's being even more strictly construed. After all, punishing someone for failure to report currency transports *into* the United States hardly presents the sort of danger to the proper functioning of law enforcement that failing to report transports *out* of the country threatens. By entering the United States, one *submits* to its territorial jurisdiction; by no means does one threaten to escape it. For this reason, at least one court has held that a defendant lacked sufficient intent to violate section 1101 where the government alleged no more than that she failed to volunteer the fact that she was transporting cash *into* the United States in excess of $5,000.

REPORT REQUIREMENT

Section 1101 requires that any person who transports, causes to be transported, or receives monetary instruments in excess of $5,000 must report this fact. The statute proscribes only the willful failure to report the transport or receipt of such sums; it does not punish the transport or receipt itself. For this reason, requiring such a report cannot constitute self-incrimination in violation of the fifth amendment, because there is nothing criminal about merely transporting or receiving large amounts of money. Neither does the report requirement constitute an unlawful search in violation of the fourth amendment.

PENALTIES

The willful failure to report one's transport or receipt, standing by itself, may be punished with a fine of up to $1,000, imprisonment for up to one year, or both. Where such willful failure to report is accompanied by other culpable behavior, however, the penalties increase dramatically. One who willfully fails to report and does so "in furtherance of the commission of any other violation of Federal Law" or "as part of a pattern of illegal activity involving transactions exceeding $100,000 in any twelve-month period" subjects himself to a fine of up to $500,000, imprisonment of up to five years, or both.

Apparently, the first aggravating circumstance mentioned above requires that the violation of federal law, furthered by defendant's willful failure to report, be outside the ambit of the Currency and Foreign Transactions Reporting Act. For example, section 1059(1) would apply to the willful failure to report the transport of money outside the United States with the intent to purchase cocaine. The second aggravating circumstance – the existence of a pattern of illegal activity – apparently need not be unconnected to the failure to report. This is by no means clear, however,

because while Congress expressly defined "pattern" for the purposes of the Racketeer Influence and Corrupt Organizations Act (RICO), it provided no such definition in the Currency Reporting Act. What is a pattern for the purposes of section 1059(2), then, remains unsettled.

It is clear that when one fails to report his transport, or in reporting make a material misstatement or omission, section 1102 authorizes the government to seize the entire transport and, if it wishes, to institute civil forfeiture proceedings in addition to or in lieu of the imposition of criminal penalties. Because the proceeding is a civil one, the government, in order to prevail, need only demonstrate by a preponderance of evidence that the defendant willfully failed to report or, in reporting, willfully misstated or omitted material facts. Moreover, if forfeiture is sought in addition to and after the imposition of some criminal penalty, the defendant is estopped from denying his willful behavior if he pleaded guilty in the earlier criminal proceeding. The Secretary of the Treasury has the absolute discretion, however, to remit any forfeiture in whole or in part.

Securities Law Violations

The anti-fraud provisions of federal securities law impose criminal penalties on persons who willfully engage in fraudulent schemes in connection with an offer, purchase, or sale of any security, if an interstate instrumentality has been used, even incidentally, in furtherance of the scheme.

The Securities Act of 1933 and the Securities Exchange Act of 1934 comprehensively regulate the securities industry. Each act contains an anti-fraud provision, of interest to white-collar criminal attorneys because the sections are subject to criminal enforcement. Securities-related fraud is made criminal by virtue of provisions in each of the acts which generally outlaw the willful violation of almost all sections of the respective acts.

SECURITIES FRAUD

The anti-fraud provisions contained in the 1933 and 1934 Acts are virtually identical. When enforced criminally, both prohibit any person from intentionally making untrue statements of material fact, omitting to state material facts, or otherwise engaging in any fraudulent practice in the offer or sale (1933 Act) or in connection with the purchase or sale (1934 Act) of securities, by means of any instrumentality of interstate commerce, including the mails.

Intent

Section 24 of the 1933 Act prohibits the willful violation of any statutory provision, or rule or regulation promulgated thereunder. Section 32 of the 1934 Act prohibits the same, with two exceptions. First, with respect to false statements made in documents required by the Act to be filed with the Securities and Exchange Commission, one must act both "willfully and knowingly" to be liable for prosecution. Second, if one who violates a rule or regulation promulgated under the 1934 Act can establish that he had "no knowledge" of the particular rule, he may escape imprisonment.

The Supreme Court has observed that " 'willful' is a word of many meanings, its construction often being influenced by its context." Judge Friendly, in *United States v. Dixon*, examined the context in which the term appears in the 1934 Act and concluded: that willfulness does not require specific intent to disregard or disobey a law (rather, this seems to be what "knowingly" means); that willfulness does not require knowledge of the particular rule violated (thus the exception noted above); and that it *does* require some realization on a defendant's part that he is performing a wrongful act. In short, willfulness seems to combine the requirements of general intent (one intends the consequences of his acts) with motive (one's act is consciously wrongful). Presumably, the meaning of willful is similarly limited in the 1933 Act.

False Statements, Omissions, and Fraud

The anti-fraud provisions of the securities laws are read broadly to prohibit all schemes designed to deceive and harm persons of ordinary prudence. Thus, in committing a fraud, a defendant need not seek to obtain money or other property to come within the prohibitions of section 10(b) and Rule 10b-5, as long as such fraud is "in connection with" the offer, purchase, or sale of a security.

One violates the anti-fraud provisions by making an untrue statement of material fact, or omitting to state a material fact, when such misstatement or omission occurs in connection with the offer, purchase, or sale of a security.

In the case of *TSC Industries, Inc. v. Northway, Inc.*, the Supreme Court was called upon to settle the meaning of materiality in connection with a proxy statement required to be filed with the SEC pursuant to the 1934 Act. In *TSC* the Court rejected a standard that would prohibit misstatements or omissions for any fact a reasonable shareholder *might* consider important, and opted instead for the more certain "*would* consider important" standard. As articulated by the Court, "[a]n omitted fact is material if there is a substantial likelihood that a reasonable shareholder would consider it important. . . ."

Because the standard looks to what a reasonable shareholder would regard as important, rather than what an expert, piecing together esoteric facts into a mosaic, might treat as important, the anti-fraud provisions presumably do not require sophisticated analysts to disclose data they have, by virtue of their expertise, rendered material.

Although material misstatements and omissions are explicitly included within the terms of the anti-fraud provisions, no such mention is made of *silence*. It does not fall within either of the first two classes of behavior outlawed in the anti-fraud provisions: it is neither a "device, scheme, or artifice to defraud", nor by its very nature can it be an "untrue statement" or an "omission to state a material fact in order to make [other] statements made . . . not misleading. . . ."

Even so, mere silence has supported a number of civil plaintiffs. The theory under which such plaintiffs have recovered is that silence, where defendant has a *duty* to speak, constitutes a "practice which operates . . . as a deceit" and for this reason violates the anti-fraud provisions. Clearly, the securities laws themselves impose no such affirmative duty; rather, the duty to speak arises out of certain fiduciary relationships. Thus, corporate insiders have been held to have violated the anti-fraud provisions when they neither abstained from trading nor disclosed material inside information, as have brokers operating on behalf of their clients. Where one is duty-bound to speak, silence may constitute fraud.

Fraud Must Be "In Connection with" an Offer, Purchase, or Sale

All persons are prohibited by the anti-fraud statutes from employing any scheme to defraud, making false statements or omissions of material fact, or engaging in any practice that operates as a fraud or deceit, when such acts occur in or in connection with the offer, purchase, or sale of any security. Section 17(a) of the 1933 Act prohibits such activity in the offer or sale of securities; Rule 10b-5 of the 1934 Act does so in connection with the purchase or sale of securities. Practically speaking, however, the distinction between "in" and "in connection with" is without significance. In either case, the connection between the proscribed behavior and some securities transaction does not require that the victim be an offeree, purchaser, or seller. In *United States v. Naftalin* the defendant was convicted under section 17(a) when he defrauded a securities *broker*.

The requirement that a fraudulent act be in or in connection with an offer, purchase, or sale means only that there *be* some transaction to which a civil plaintiff or the government (in either a civil enforcement or criminal context) is able to point. Yet even this requirement is broadly construed. For the purposes of section 17(a), a sale includes a pledge of stock as collateral for a loan, upon default of such loan. Likewise, a merger of two securities-issuing entities, which results in the issuance of new shares or an exchange of merged company shares for merging company shares, is a "sale" for the purposes of section 10(b) and Rule 10b-5.

What Is a Security?

The anti-fraud statutes forbid any fraudulent activity in, or in connection with, transactions involving securities. To be sure, the term security is defined quite broadly in the 1933 Act. Even so, the meaning of the term for the purposes of the anti-fraud statutes is not without its ambiguities.

Part ownership of a citrus grove, for example, constitutes ownership of a security, because the owners invest money in a common enterprise managed by others, with the intention of profiting therefrom. An interest held in a pension fund, however, is not a security, even though one or more of the definitions of security in the 1933 Act could arguably be read to include such an interest. One neither invests in a pension fund nor profits from it. Moreover, receipt of pension benefits is in no way the result of risk-taking on the recipient's part; rather, he qualifies for such benefits simply by working a sufficient length of time. In non-traditional situations, then, whether some interest may be characterized as a security requires a factual inquiry, guided by the principle of economic reality.

Use of an Interstate Instrumentality

To become operative, the anti-fraud statutes require that the defendant, in engaging in his securities-related fraud, use either the mails or some other means of interstate transportation or communication. In addition, Rule 10b-5 is violated when a defendant uses any facility of any national securities exchange in conducting his fraud.

As with other federal criminal statutes, the jurisdictional means requirement in the securities fraud statutes is satisfied rather easily. Thus, even where some use of an interstate means may be described as incidental, it is sufficient for the purposes of the anti-fraud statutes if it is somehow employed in furtherance of the scheme. Moreover, use of an interstate means (the telephone) has been held sufficient even where such use occurred entirely within a single state. Finally, the defendant need not specifically intend to use any interstate means of transportation or communication, provided there is in fact some use.

OTHER CRIMINAL VIOLATIONS

Both the 1933 and 1934 Acts contain provisions making the intentional violation of any section of either act a crime. The 1933 Act focuses for the most part on new issues of securities, requiring that they be registered and that any offering be preceded or accompanied by a prospectus. Any willful violation of the intricate registration and prospectus requirements of sections 5 and 10 of the act will thus subject a broad class of individuals to criminal liability. Those susceptible to prosecution include issuers, underwriters, and dealers—categories of persons that, for the purposes of the 1933 Act, are defined somewhat more expansively than might otherwise be expected.

The 1934 Act, on the other hand, is concerned for the most part with secondary trading in securities. Market manipulation is thus regulated under the 1934 Act, meaning that trading in some security for the purpose of influencing its price, or creating a false impression of market interest, is prohibited. Credit is also regulated under the statute where it is to be used in connection with securities transactions. The 1934 Act also contains its own registration and reporting requirements. The "willful" violation of these sections is a criminal offense, although the making of false statements in registration materials or reports is criminal only if made willfully and knowingly.

Mention should also be made of the anti-fraud provisions of section 49 of the Investment Company Act of 1940 and section 217 of the Investment Advisers Act of 1940, 15 U.S.C. sections 80a-48 and 80b-17, respectively. Those provisions make the willful violation of the acts, or of any regulations promulgated pursuant to them, a federal offense. . . .

The Hobbs and Travel Acts

The Hobbs and Travel Acts make it a federal crime to obstruct or impede interstate commerce through robbery or extortion or related offenses, and to travel in or use a facility of interstate commerce in connection with the commission of a purely local crime. Thus, the two acts bring federal involvement to areas of criminal activity previously left entirely to local law enforcement.

THE HOBBS ACT

The Hobbs Act generally prohibits anyone from obstructing or delaying commerce by means of robbery or extortion. The act also prohibits attempts or conspiracies to engage in the same behavior, as well as the commission or threat of physical violence in furtherance of such behavior. To sustain conviction under the Act, the prosecution must prove an obstruction, delay, or effect on interstate commerce by means of robbery or extortion (or any attempt or conspiracy to rob or extort) or actual or threatened physical violence.

Impact on Interstate Commerce

For the purposes of the Hobbs Act, the effect on interstate commerce of the unlawful behavior need only be minimal. For instance, in *United States v. DeMet* defendants were police officers convicted of extorting from the owner of a neighborhood tavern. Because the bar purchased beer directly from an out-of-state brewery, an effect on interstate commerce sufficient for the purposes of the act was demonstrated, even though there was no connection whatsoever between the extortion and beer purchases.

It is highly unlikely that the defendants in *DeMet* intended or even realized that they were affecting interstate commerce. Such a lack of intent is of no significance in such cases as long as the prosecution proves an intent to rob or extort and demonstrates that the natural effect of such intent is an impact on interstate commerce.

Extortion or Robbery

The Hobbs Act requires that an impact on interstate commerce be the result of actual, attempted, or planned robbery or extortion. Robbery and extortion both are defined in the act. Even so, until the Supreme Court decided *United States v. Culbert,* there was some question whether the Hobbs Act applied to all robberies with the requisite interstate impact, or was limited to those arising out of racketeering activity. In *Culbert,* the Court held that the act applies to any robbery because the language of the statute, together with its legislative history, permits no other interpretation. Despite the breadth of robbery coverage, however, most prosecutorial attention under the Hobbs Act is directed at extortion (which presumably is subject to the same broad coverage as *Culbert* held applies to robbery prosecutions). The elements of the extortion offense are wrongful use of either actual or threatened force, violence, or fear, or, wrongful use of one's official position, either of which results in the taking of some property by the extortionist.

Force, violence, or fear. The fear instilled in the victim need not be fear of physical injury, or even injury to tangible property. Fear of harm to one's purely economic interests, such as the viability of one's business, is sufficient for Hobbs Act purposes. Moreover, provided the victim's fear is reasonable, it is not even necessary that such fear be induced by the defendant as long as he exploits it. Thus, in *United States v. Crowley,* defendant police officers violated the Hobbs Act when they preyed upon a businessman's fear of continuing vandalism. By promising to respond quickly to requests for police protection only if paid regularly by the victim, the defendants exploited an existing fear and so violated the act.

Wrongful use of official position. Suppose, in *Crowley,* that the police officers had neither created nor exploited any fear in their victim. Suppose they had simply accepted periodic payments. The Hobbs Act defines extortion to include "the obtaining of property from another, with his consent, induced . . . under color of official right." This means that it is not necessary for one in an official position to threaten force or violence, or induce or exploit fear, in order to commit an act of extortion for the purposes of the Hobbs Act. One may simply abuse one's official position. Yet an offense of this nature, without the sort of coercion that accompanies the standard case of extortion, begins to look suspiciously like bribery, which is not explicitly within the terms of the Hobbs Act. This is of no significance to a number of courts, which have held that bribery and extortion, at least for the purposes of the Hobbs Act, are not mutually exclusive.

Property. The Hobbs Act requires that an extortionist obtain property. Classic cases under the act involve money—protection payments or kickbacks—but the term "property" has, for the purposes of the act, been given a reading far more expansive than that. In *United States. v. Tropiano,* the right to solicit business in a particular geographical area was held to constitute "property."

The act, however, requires more. Not only must a victim be coerced into parting with his property; such property must also be obtained by the defendant. In *Tropiano,* both the defendant and his victim were in the trash removal business. Whatever business the defendant forced his victim to forego became, by default, the defendant's own business. Tropiano thus obtained property.

THE TRAVEL ACT

The Hobbs Act forbids the commission of two offenses, usually the objects of local attention, where the *effects* of such activity spill beyond a single state's borders. The Travel Act, on the other hand, requires no such effect on interstate commerce. Instead, it prohibits anyone from traveling in, or using any facility of, interstate or foreign commerce with the intent to perform certain acts. Those acts include distributing the proceeds of unlawful activity, committing crimes of violence in furtherance of unlawful activity, and promoting or facilitating the promotion of unlawful activity.

The essence of a Travel Act violation, then, is the commission of a purely *local* crime, but with an ancillary interstate component. The elements of a violation are thus: (1) travel or use of a facility with (2) the intent thereafter to (3) distribute the proceeds of, commit a crime of violence in furtherance of, or promote or facilitate the promotion of, unlawful activity.

Travel or Use of a Facility
in Interstate Commerce

The act requires "travel . . . in interstate or foreign commerce or use [of] any facility in interstate or foreign commerce." But how much travel or use is required to satisfy the act? The Hobbs Act, for example, requires no more than a *de minimis* impact on interstate commerce, because what begins as a purely local criminal act is *transformed*, by virtue of its impact, into an interstate offense. No such impact is required by the Travel Act, and thus no transformation occurs. What begins as a local offense *remains* local; it is only when there is *associated with* those acts some interstate travel, or the use of some interstate facility, that federal involvement even becomes possible. For this reason, more than simply a de minimis involvement with interstate travel or an interstate facility is required under the act.

Such involvement, moreover, must immediately precede the overt acts (such as "distributing the proceeds of unlawful activity") required by the act. The statute prohibits traveling in or using a facility of interstate commerce with intent to engage in one or more specified overt acts, "*and thereafter* perform[ing] or attempt[ing] to perform" such acts. Where a defendant first engages in one or more of the prohibited overt activities, and only then travels in or uses a facility of interstate commerce, he does not violate the Travel Act.

Intent

The statute prohibits travel in or use of a facility of interstate commerce with intent to perform one of three overt acts. What it requires, then, is an intention on the part of the defendant to commit one of the acts, rather than an intent to travel interstate, or to use an interstate facility. Thus, if *somebody* connected with the scheme either travels interstate or uses an interstate facility, it is unimportant that the defendant himself was unaware of this.

Overt Acts in Furtherance of "Unlawful Activity"

The Travel Act defines "unlawful activity" to include two distinct classes of criminal behavior: "business enterprises" involving gambling, liquor, narcotics, and prostitution; and extortion, bribery, and arson. To establish an offense of the first type, namely, one involving a business enterprise, the government must allege a "continuous course of conduct." No single act involving gambling, liquor, narcotics, or prostitution will suffice, nor will "sporadic, casual involvement" in such activity. A single act of extortion, bribery, or arson, however, *is* sufficient for the purposes of the statute.

In order to qualify as unlawful activity for the purposes of the Travel Act, however, these two classes of behavior must be "in violation of the laws of the state in which they are committed or of the United States." Suppose, then, conduct that constitutes bribery in State A is not proscribed in State B. Two different defendants might commit the same act, one in

State A and the other in State B, and while prosecution under the Travel Act could proceed for the first defendant, no federal offense could be established for the second (unless the act in question also violated some independent federal statute).

What constitutes a violation of the Travel Act varies from state to state. Yet this was apparently Congress' intent, for it sought "to add a second layer of enforcement supplementing what it found to be inadequate state authority and state enforcement."

The Racketeer Influenced and Corrupt Organizations Act

The Racketeer Influenced and Corrupt Organizations Act (RICO) prohibits the use of income derived from racketeering activity or the collection of unlawful debts to acquire an interest in any otherwise legitimate interstate enterprise.

RICO generally prohibits anyone from combining racketeering activity with involvement in any enterprise engaging in or affecting interstate commerce. The Act also prohibits conspiracies directed at such behavior. More specifically, anyone who either engages in "a pattern of racketeering activity" or collects an "unlawful debt" is prohibited from using income so derived to acquire an interest in any enterprise engaged in or affecting interstate commerce, directly acquiring such an enterprise, or participating in such an enterprise's affairs through his racketeering or debt-collecting activity. The essential elements of the RICO offense are commission of a predicate offense (either engaging in a pattern of racketeering activity or collecting an unlawful debt), and involvement with an interstate enterprise.

Punishment for violations of RICO is severe and is designed to deter the involvement of racketeers in otherwise legitimate businesses. In addition to stiff fines and jail sentences (section 1963(a) provides for fines of up to $25,000 and imprisonment up to twenty years), RICO provides that business interests acquired through one's racketeering activity shall be forfeited upon conviction. This forfeiture provision thus assures that once a convicted racketeer is removed from his tainted business enterprise another will not simply replace him and perpetuate the corruption.

COMMISSION OF A PREDICATE OFFENSE

Pattern of Racketeering

RICO defines this pattern to mean the commission of two or more of the enumerated offenses. The definition of "racketeering activity" says nothing, however, of any need for the defendant previously to have been convicted of committing such predicate offenses. Thus, the defendant may be charged in the same indictment with committing the predicate offenses and with violating RICO as a distinct and independent count. Thus, also, the expiration of a state statute of limitations will not prevent a predicate state offense from being included as an element in a RICO prosecution. Nor, for that matter, will *acquittal* on state criminal charges defeat a subsequent RICO prosecution.

In *United States v. Frumento,* the court reasoned that RICO prohibits racketeering; the act does not federalize state crimes. Thus, while the federal crime of racketeering is defined with reference to state law and to a long list of federal offenses, it is in no way *dependent upon* any particular prior criminal conviction. If the government establishes all the elements of a RICO offense, including the commission of at least two predicate offenses, it is immaterial whether one or both of these offenses have been the subject of a prior proceeding.

The definition of racketeering activity also does not indicate the degree of interrelatedness, if any, required of the predicate offenses. The reason such an issue arises at all is the concern of some courts that, without any implied requirement of interrelatedness, the statute would be impermissibly vague, that a defendant committing a second predicate offense completely unrelated to his first would have no notice that this second criminal act also transformed him, for the purposes of RICO, into a racketeer. By reading an interrelatedness requirement into the definition of racketeering activity, however, one eliminates the notice problem.

Moreover, given the sort of organized criminal activity Congress sought to reach with RICO, reading into it a "requirement that the racketeering acts must have been connected with each other by some common scheme, plan or motive so as to constitute a pattern" seems consistent with such intent. This does not mean, however, that the predicate criminal acts themselves must be *similar*. The interrelatedness requirement is satisfied if the criminal acts are tied by a common plan, or are somehow "related to the affairs of [an] enterprise."

Unlawful Debt

No interrelatedness questions are raised where a RICO defendant, through the collection of an unlawful debt, involves himself in the affairs of some interstate enterprise. With unlawful debts, a single act is sufficient to set in motion a RICO prosecution. Even so, an "unlawful debt" is defined to mean one incurred both in connection with the *business* of unlawful gambling or the *business* of lending money usuriously. Thus, while for the purposes of RICO only one unlawful debt must be established, such a debt does not become "unlawful" unless it arises in connection with

an entire business devoted to creating such indebtedness.

INTERSTATE ENTERPRISE

To fall within the prohibition of RICO, a putative defendant must not only engage in a pattern of racketeering activity or collect an unlawful debt; he must, furthermore, be involved with an "enterprise engaged in or affecting interstate or foreign commerce." Simply committing the sort of predicate offenses set forth in RICO does not make one a racketeer. Only by corrupting some enterprise tied to interstate commerce does the racketeer commit an abuse of the type RICO was designed to eradicate.

The Nature of the Enterprise

RICO defines enterprise to include not only formal, legal entities, but also informally structured organizations. This broad definition is designed to prohibit the corruption of legitimate commerce in whatever form it takes.

Despite the breadth accorded the term enterprise, RICO fails to establish whether this broad reading applies only to *lawful* enterprises, or whether enterprise may also include *unlawful* entities. Until recently, it had been argued in some quarters that to include *unlawful* entities within the term enterprise would make redundant the dual requirements of a pattern of racketeering activity in addition to an enterprise.

The Supreme Court, in *United States v. Turkette,* recently rejected this analysis, holding instead that a RICO enterprise need not be engaged in otherwise lawful conduct to fall within the statutory proscription. In so holding, the Court reasoned that the statutory definition of enterprise is not limited on its face to those that are otherwise lawful. Moreover, the Court argued, such a holding does not make the enterprise requirement superfluous. To convict under RICO, the government still must prove that some entity, some enterprise, is engaging in a pattern of racketeering activity. While proof of the separate elements "may in particular cases coalesce, proof of one does not necessarily establish the other."

The definition of enterprise in the statute also fails to clarify whether public, as well as private, entities are included. At least two courts have held that enterprise includes a municipal police department, reasoning that the definition contains no language to suggest a more restrictive reading. One other court has held that a Governor's office is an enterprise, arguing that the term must include public entities because at least two of RICO's predicate offenses—bribery under certain state laws and extortion under color of law—can *only* be committed by public employees. To include such offenses, the argument goes, yet exclude the possibility that any perpetrators of such offenses could be prosecuted under the act, would make no sense. At least one court, however, has held that a Governor cannot violate RICO in his role as a public servant because the *state* is not an enterprise for purposes of the statute.

The Nexus Requirement

Section 1962(c) of RICO prohibits any person associated with an interstate enterprise from participating in any way in such enterprise's affairs "through a pattern of racketeering activity or collection of an unlawful debt." Arguably, this means that one who commits the predicate offenses also violates RICO when all that is demonstrated is that he is somehow connected to an interstate enterprise. No court, however, has been willing to go quite so far. Indeed, a number of courts have done just the opposite, holding that there must be some connection or nexus between commission of the predicate offenses and the very conduct of the enterprise. There is no consensus on the extent of such a connection.

To illustrate, some courts look intently at each word in the statute, reasoning that if the word through is to have any significance ("it shall be unlawful for any person . . . to . . . participate . . . in the conduct of [an] enterprise's affairs *through* a pattern of racketeering activity"), then it should be given its dictionary meaning: "by means of, by reason of."

Where the government is then unable or unwilling to demonstrate a defendant's participation in an enterprise by means of some pattern of racketeering activity, as was the case in *United States v. Nerone,* there can be no conviction under section 1962(c).

Similarly, where an employee in an interstate enterprise simply lends money to his fellow employees at usurious rates, he does not for this reason alone violate section 1962(c). Without some demonstration that his job-related conduct is connected with his unlawful activity, he may not be treated as a racketeer for section 1962(c) purposes.

In *United States v. Field,* the court, while recognizing the need for some connection between the defendant's racketeering activity and his conduct in the enterprise in question, did not require nearly so extensive a nexus as courts like that in *Nerone* did. In *Field,* the defendant, an official in the Longshoremen's union, simply received illegal payments from a company that employed longshoremen. This was sufficient, the court held, for the purposes of section 1962(c), because that section "nowhere requires proof regarding the advancement of the union's affairs by the defendant's activities, or proof that the union itself is corrupt, or proof that the union authorized the defendant to do" what he did. In contrast, the *Nerone* court reversed the defendant's conviction because the government did not "show that gambling revenues were used by or in any way channeled into the corporation."

An Enterprise in or Affecting Interstate or Foreign Commerce

The enterprise mentioned in RICO must be one engaged in or affecting interstate or foreign commerce. That the *enterprise* must be one in or affecting interstate commerce, however, does not also mean that the defendant's conduct—his debt—must have such an effect. Once a court is satisfied that the enterprise is sufficiently tied to interstate commerce, "the magnitude and effect of [the defendant's] conduct are irrelevant."

CONSPIRACY

RICO contains its own conspiracy prohibition, which differs from the general federal conspiracy statute, 18 U.S.C. section 371, in one important respect. While section 371 requires agreement on one or more particular offenses, a RICO conspiracy requires agreement to engage in a pattern of racketeering activity or in the collection of an unlawful debt. A RICO conspiracy is thus simultaneously easier and more difficult to establish than is a section 371 conspiracy.

On the one hand, the agreement necessary for a RICO conspiracy, unlike that under section 371, is not an agreement to commit particular offenses such as arson or extortion. The conspirators need only agree to combine for the purpose of engaging in racketeering activity. In other words, it is irrelevant for the purposes of section 1962(d) that each defendant participates in different or even unrelated crimes. There need be no consensus on particular offenses, as long as an agreement to engage in *racketeering,* as defined in the statute, is demonstrated. For this reason, difficult questions of whether the conspiracy should be characterized as a chain or a wheel do not plague the prosecution.

On the other hand, unlike a section 371 conspiracy, which requires agreement only as to the commission of a single criminal act, a RICO conspiracy requires that the government establish that defendants agreed to confederate so as to engage in a *pattern* of racketeering activity. In other words, there must be an agreement to commit *two* or more predicate offenses. Even so, the RICO conspiracy does share with section 371 conspiracies the requirement that while all defendants know of the essential nature of the conspiracy, all need not be aware of each of its details.

Conspiracy

To be guilty of conspiracy under federal law, two or more persons must agree to commit an offense against the United States or defraud the United States or any of its agencies and at least one such person must perform some act in furtherance of the conspiracy.

When a defendant is found guilty of participating in a continuing conspiracy, he may also be held responsible for substantive offenses committed by a co-conspirator in furtherance of the conspiracy, even though he does not participate in the substantive offenses themselves or have any actual knowledge of them. Thus, as long as "the partnership in crime" continues, the partners act for each other in carrying it forward. The criminal intent to do the act is established by the formation of the conspiracy and the overt act of one partner within the scope of the conspiracy is attributable to all.

A defendant may not be liable for a substantive offense under this doctrine, however, unless he was a member of the conspiracy at the time the offense was committed. Thus, for example, a conviction for aiding in the preparation of false tax returns was reversed where the evidence was insufficient to establish beyond a reasonable doubt that the defendant was a party to the conspiracy at the time of the transaction at issue.

AGREEMENT AMONG TWO OR MORE PERSONS

"The gist of the offense of conspiracy . . . is agreement among the conspirators to commit an offense. . . ." Thus, if one simply performs an act that happens to further the object of a conspiracy, without also being in agreement with those who so conspire, he is not guilty of conspiracy. One's mere presence among conspirators or association with them is also insufficient to establish guilt under section 371. Conspiracy requires agreement; it does not require that any agreement be formal. As long as some agreement may be inferred, the statute forbids it. Of course, one does not agree to commit some offense without knowledge that he so agrees. For this reason, one cannot conspire to commit a substantive offense without at least that degree of intent necessary to commit the offense itself. Once there is agreement to commit a particular offense, however, it is immaterial that the conspirators stand little or no chance of succeeding in their endeavor.

OBJECT OF THE AGREEMENT

Two or more persons must agree either to violate a federal criminal statute or to defraud the United States or any of its agencies. The fraud in question here is not limited to common law fraud; the statute reaches every conspiracy to impair, obstruct, or defeat any lawful function of the government. For this reason, a fraud need not result in the government's suffering property or pecuniary loss in order to violate section 371.

THE OVERT ACT

Violation of the conspiracy statute requires that at least one of the conspirators perform some act demonstrating the existence of an agreement. This act need not be criminal. It need only be in furtherance of the conspiracy. Indeed, a simple phone call will do. The overt act itself may be insignificant. Requiring it is designed to do no more than evidence the existence of a conspiracy. It follows, then, that any such act renders all co-conspirators subject to prosecution, regardless of whether they themselves so act. . . .

Aiding and Abetting

It should also be noted that, in any federal prosecution, even if a person is not convicted for the substantive offense, he may be found guilty of aiding and abetting under 18 U.S.C. section 2 and punished as a principal. Thus, the guilt of a defendant may be established without proof that the accused personally committed every act constituting the offense charged, as long as the defendant willfully participated in the commission of that offense. Willful participation is knowing and voluntary assistance in the crime as something the defendant specifically wants to bring about.

The Supreme Court has held that a defendant may be convicted of aiding and abetting another individual in the commission of a crime, even though the other person has been acquitted of the offense. Even if the government's theory in a case is that the defendant was the principal actor in the commission of an offense, the jury may be given "aider-abettor" instructions.

Obstruction of Justice

A conviction may be obtained for obstruction of justice whenever a defendant endeavors to influence, intimidate, or injure another person in connection with federal court proceedings or criminal investigations, regardless of his success.

Any discussion concerning white collar criminal statutes should include some treatment of the two criminal statutes prohibiting the obstruction of justice and the obstruction of criminal investigations. Those two sections are intended both to prevent miscarriages of justice in cases pending in a federal court and to protect witnesses, jurors, and others in those cases from injury, intimidation, and undue influence. Section 1510 extends the protections of section 1503 beyond pending proceedings to include the criminal investigations conducted prior to those proceedings.

The obstruction of justice offenses apply to any endeavors or efforts on the part of the defendant; he need not have been successful in obstructing justice or in preventing the transmission of information during an investigation. The two statutes have been held to prohibit offenses such as seeking to procure another to kill or injure a witness, furnishing the witness with false testimony to be given before the grand jury, asking another person to speak to a judge about a case, and destroying corporate records with knowledge that they are being sought by a grand jury. A conviction may be had under section 1510 even if the prohibited conduct occurs after the investigation has been completed. Furthermore, section 1510 applies to retaliatory assaults as well as to assaults intended to discourage persons from providing information to criminal investigators.

Other Federal Criminal Statutes

This discussion has focused on the most commonly encountered federal white collar crimes. Many other federal statutes include provisions for criminal liability and deserve brief mention.

For example, criminal sanctions are provided in the Wheeler-Lea Amendment to the Federal Trade Commission Act for advertising that is false, deceptive, unfair, or materially misleading with respect to food, drugs, or cosmetics. Criminal penalties may also be imposed for the adulteration or misbranding of foods and drugs, regardless of one's good faith or ignorance of the law.

One may be convicted for willfully violating the Fair Labor Standards Act, which regulates wages, hours, and child labor. The Labor Management Relations Act prohibits the making of payments to employee representatives or union officers. One may be held criminally liable under section 17(e) of the Occupational Safety and Health Act if one's willful violation results in the death of an employee.

A number of federal environmental statutes forbid "knowing" violations of their terms. These include the Federal Insecticide, Fungicide and Rodenticide Act; the Toxic Substances Control Act; the Endangered Species Act; the Marine Protection Act (ocean dumping); as well as the recently enacted Comprehensive Environmental Response, Compensation, and Liability Act (better known as "Superfund"), which punishes those who fail to report the release of hazardous substances.

Certain violations of the federal antitrust laws, such as the Sherman Antitrust Act; the Clayton Act; and the Robinson-Patman Act, regulating price discrimination, may result in criminal prosecution.

Finally, one may be convicted for willfully violating the Foreign Corrupt Practices Act, especially in connection with a currency transport prosecution.

Ninth Annual Survey of White Collar Crimes, 31 AM. CRIM. L. REV. 403 (1994)*

ANTITRUST VIOLATIONS

Section 1 of the Sherman Act ("Act") provides for criminal sanctions against any person "who shall make any contract or engage in any combination or conspiracy" in restraint of interstate commerce. The Act, which is the primary federal antitrust provision, applies to both criminal and civil offenses, but does not distinguish between them. Although Congress intentionally left the task of distinguishing between civil and criminal offenses to the judiciary, the Act includes a number of common law terms to assist the courts in their task. The lack of a clear legislative pronouncement of their meaning has resulted in the development of a federal common law. The Supreme Court has characterized the Sherman Act as a "charter of freedom [with a] generality and adaptability comparable to that found desirable in constitutional provisions."

I. ELEMENTS OF THE OFFENSE

A civil plaintiff must establish three elements to prove a violation of section 1 of the Sherman Act: (1) two or more entities formed a combination or conspiracy; (2) the combination or conspiracy (potentially) produces an unreasonable restraint of trade or commerce; and (3) the restrained trade or commerce is interstate in nature. In a criminal antitrust prosecution under section 1 of the Sherman Act, the government must prove an additional element: that the defendants intended to restrain commerce and acted "with knowledge of [the] probable consequences" of their actions.

A. Conspiracy

Under section 1 of the Sherman Act, a conspiracy

---

* Reprinted with permission of the publisher, American Criminal Law Review. © 1994 Georgetown University.

"must comprise an agreement, understanding or meeting of the minds between at least two competitors, for the purpose of or with the effect of unreasonably restraining trade." The contractual form and the ultimate success of the venture are immaterial as long as the agreement is formed.

B. Restraint of Trade

The Supreme Court has noted that the term "restraint of trade" "refers not to a particular list of agreements, but to a particular economic consequence, which may be produced by quite different sorts of agreements in varying times and circumstances." Such consequences include elimination of competition, creation of monopoly, artificial maintenance of prices, and interference with the free play of market forces.

In determining whether a given activity constitutes an illegal restraint of trade, courts have employed two distinct analytical approaches. First is the "per se" rule announced by the Supreme Court in *United States v. Socony-Vacuum Oil Co.* Application of this rule has been limited to activities which have no legitimate justification and lack any redeeming competitive purpose: price-fixing, division of markets, group boycotts, and tying arrangements are examples. Under "per se" scrutiny, any activity in restraint of trade is held to be illegal. Courts presume anti-competitive effects and the defendant's intent to produce such effects. The government need only prove the existence of an unlawful agreement.

The second approach, the "rule-of-reason" standard applies to activities which have not been labeled "clearly anti-competitive" under the Sherman Act. Under the rule-of-reason, courts analyze the anti-competitive effects of the agreement to determine if the activity poses an "unreasonable" restraint on free trade. Courts may also take into account the possibility that some arguably anti-competitive practices may actually increase economic efficiency and competitiveness and therefore not constitute a violation. The Supreme Court affirmed that there is a presumption favoring the rule-of-reason standard over per se analysis: a "departure from that standard must be justified by demonstrable economic effect. . . ."

C. Interstate Nexus

To establish jurisdiction under the Sherman Act, the government must allege and prove a sufficient connection between the defendant's illegal activities and interstate commerce. The historical expansion of congressional power under the Commerce Clause has resulted in the expanded reach of the Sherman Act. "Purely local" trade practices are exempt from the Sherman Act only if they are not in the flow of interstate commerce and have no significant impact on that flow. Temporary pauses in the flow of interstate commerce do not terminate the interstate nexus for the purposes of the interstate commerce requirement.

Courts have split between two distinct tests in determining whether the interstate commerce requirement has been met: the "in the flow of interstate commerce" test, and the "effect on interstate commerce" test.

Under the "in the flow of commerce" standard, the government must prove that the challenged activity: (1) involves a "substantial volume of interstate commerce;" and (2) "is an essential, integral part of the transaction and is inseparable from its interstate aspects." The Eleventh Circuit, however, has held that jurisdiction under the "in flow of commerce" theory is not established where the defendant's customer's activities were in the flow of interstate commerce, but the defendant's activities were not.

The "effect on commerce" test primarily applies to interstate activity. Under this analysis the government must prove that "(1) a substantial amount of interstate commerce was involved, and (2) the challenged activity [does not have an] 'insubstantial effect' on interstate commerce." According to one commentator, this "practical effects" test comes "so close to covering virtually every restraint that the judicial formulae covering proof of jurisdiction seem mainly to complicate, confuse and lengthen antitrust litigation without affecting the outcome."

Lower courts have applied conflicting interpretations of the Supreme Court's holding in *McLain v. Real Estate Board of New Orleans,* wherein the Court articulated the effect-on-commerce test. The point of controversy in *McLain* is whether the interstate nexus applies to the specific challenged activity, or to the defendant. The Ninth Circuit adopted the latter (broader) approach in *Western Waste Service Systems v. Universal Waste Control.* The court held that as long as the defendant's business activities have an interstate impact, the antitrust violation alleged need not have affected interstate commerce. Conversely, the Tenth Circuit expressed a narrower view in *Crane v. Intermountain Health Care, Inc.* The *Crane* court found that the proper focus after *McLain* continues to be on the nexus between interstate commerce and the challenged activity, not on the defendant's general or overall business.

D. Intent

In *United States v. United States Gypsum Co.,* the Supreme Court held that a section 1 criminal prosecution generally requires proof of the defendant's intent, rather than "constru[ing] the Sherman Act as mandating a regime of strict-liability criminal offenses." The Court emphasized that proof of "the perpetrator's knowledge of the anticipated consequences is a sufficient predicate for a finding of criminal intent." Proof of criminal intent requires either direct evidence or an inference drawn from evidence. A mere presumption of intent is usually inconclusive, especially in cases involving acts which have not been deemed inherently anti-competitive.

Gypsum involved an exchange of price information that the Court found illustrative of the "gray zone of socially acceptable and economically justifiable business conduct." The Court distinguished such activity from that which is per se illegal based upon its unquestionably anti-competitive effect. Since per se illegalities do not require any showing of *mens rea*, the lower courts have applied the intent requirements from *Gypsum* only in rule-of-reason cases. Consequently, the Department of Justice Manual provides that proof of the existence of a price-fixing or bid-rigging arrangement is customarily sufficient to establish intent.

An additional controversy surrounding the Court's decision in *Gypsum* has arisen over proper jury instructions under the rule-of-reason standard. The Court held that the requirement of intent for rule-of-reason cases should not be presumed as a matter of law, but rather is a permissible inference based on the existence of an agreement with potential anti-competitive effects. Therefore, in cases in which the per se nature of the alleged conduct is uncertain, the Antitrust Division of the Department of Justice should first present evidence of anti-competitive effects and then ask for jury instructions that explain the *Gypsum* knowledge standard for proving intent. . . .

COMPUTER-RELATED CRIMES

I. INTRODUCTION

A. Defining Computer Crime

The rapid emergence of computer technologies has spawned a variety of new criminal behaviors and an explosion in specialized legislation to combat them. The field of "computer crime" has evolved so quickly that it has evaded a solid definition. While computer crime includes traditional crimes committed with a computer, the term also encompasses offenses against intellectual property and other crimes which do not fall within traditional criminal statutes. The diversity of computer-related offenses thus demands a broad definition. The Department of Justice defines computer crime as "any violations of criminal law that involve a knowledge of computer technology for their perpetration, investigation, or prosecution."

Estimates of the extent of computer crime vary. Many experts value losses due to computer crime in the hundreds of millions and even billions of dollars.

Computer crime legislation attempts to respond to the problems of both old and new crimes committed with new technology. Some efforts have closed loopholes in existing statutes; other statutes function as independent computer crime chapters.

This article tracks recent developments in computer-related criminal law and legal literature, including an analysis of federal computer crime legislation and enforcement, and state and international approaches.

B. Types of Computer-Related Offenses

There is no "typical" computer-related crime. However, it is possible to classify computer-related crimes by considering the role the computer plays in a particular crime.

First, a computer may be the "object" of a crime, meaning the computer itself is targeted. Theft of computer processor time and computerized services are included in this category.

Second, the computer may be the "subject" of a crime. In these cases, the computer is the physical site of a crime, or is the source of or reason for unique forms of assets lost. The use of "viruses" and "logic bombs" fit into this category. These crimes present novel legal problems because of the intangible nature of the electronic information which is the object of the crime.

Third, a computer may be an "instrument" used as a means of committing traditional crimes such as theft, fraud, embezzlement, or trespass, albeit in a more complex manner. For example, a computer might be used to scan telephone codes automatically in order to make unauthorized use of a telephone system.

There are just as many motivations as there are types of computer-related crimes. Computer criminals can be teenage "hackers", disgruntled employees, mischievous technicians, or international terrorists.

II. FEDERAL APPROACHES

A. Federal Criminal Code

Until 1984, computer crimes were prosecuted under a wide variety of sections of the federal criminal code. Due to the unique aspects of computer-related crime, this approach proved to be inadequate. Since the first federal statute specifically aimed at computer crime was passed in 1984, the volume of such legislation has expanded greatly to meet the challenge of more types of computer-related crime. This section will examine the major federal statutes directed at computer-related crimes, and some of their practical shortcomings.

1. Computer Fraud and Abuse Act

In 1984, Congress passed the Counterfeit Access Device and Computer Fraud and Abuse Act ("1984 Act"). Critics quickly complained that the 1984 Act was ambiguous and too narrow in scope to provide adequate protection against computer-related offenses. In 1986, Congress amended the 1984 Act with the Computer Fraud and Abuse Act ("1986 Act"), in an attempt to strengthen and clarify the 1984 Act.

The 1986 Act is directed at unauthorized intentional access to federal interest computers. The statute proscribes six classifications of illegal activities. It prohibits unauthorized access of a computer: (1) to obtain information relating to national defense or foreign relations; (2) to obtain information in a financial record of a financial institution or consumer reporting agency; and (3) to manipulate information on a computer that would affect the United States government's operation of the computer. It also prohibits: (4) access to a "federal interest computer" without or in excess of authorization and with intent to defraud or obtain anything of value; and (5) intentional access of a "federal interest computer," without authorization, and thereby altering, damaging, or destroying information, or preventing "authorized use" of the computer. The access must either cause an aggregate loss of $1,000 during a one year period, or actually or potentially modify or impair medical examination, diagnosis, treatment, or care. Finally, the 1986 Act prohibits: (6) "knowingly," and with intent to defraud, trafficking in passwords which either would permit unauthorized access to a government computer, or affect interstate or foreign commerce.

An attempt to commit an offense is punished as a violation regardless of its ultimate success. The 1986 Act gives the United States Secret Service, and any other agency, authority to investigate offenses.

The 1986 Act defines "computer," "federal interest computer," and "exceeding authorized access," as well as "financial institution," and "financial record." Significant statutory language, however, remains undefined by both the statute and the limited case law, including "access," "unauthorized," and "affects the use."

2. Other Statutes

Other statutes have been useful in prosecuting computer-related crimes that do not fall under the Computer Fraud and Abuse Act. Such offenses may range from theft of computer software to unauthorized access of a computer system without causing damage.

Any person who unlawfully copies and distributes software may be subject to punishment for criminal copyright infringement. The criminal copyright infringement statute has three elements: (1) infringement of a copyright; (2) done willfully; (3) for commercial advantage or private financial gain. The first element of copyright infringement may be satisfied by the mere unauthorized copying of computer software, but the second and third element are often more difficult to prove.

The National Stolen Property Act prohibits the transportation in interstate commerce of "any goods, wares, securities or money" valued at $5,000 or more and known to be stolen or fraudulently obtained. This statute has been applied to various computer-related crimes, including fraudulent computerized transfer of funds. There are no cases deciding whether computer software stored on a disk or tape constitutes "goods" or "wares" under the National Stolen Property Act, but courts have broadly interpreted "goods" and "wares" to include similar types of scientific materials embodied in a physical form, which may be analogous to software stored on a disk or tape. While the Tenth Circuit has held that computer programs are not "goods" and "wares" if the programs were solely in an intangible form, the same court distinguished between the theft of tangible hardware covered by the terms "goods" and "wares" in the National Stolen Property Act.

The federal mail and wire fraud statutes, prohibit using interstate wire communications and mails to further a fraudulent scheme to obtain money or property. These statutes would seem to readily apply to "any computer-aided theft involving the use of interstate wire, the mails or a federally insured bank." Furthermore, any attempt to obtain an unauthorized copy of a computer program in an intangible form would seem to be covered by the mail and wire fraud statutes.

The Electronic Communications Privacy Act of 1986 ("ECPA") updated the federal law pertaining to wire and electronic communications interception to prohibit unauthorized interception of computer communications. Additionally, it created a new offense of obtaining, altering, or preventing authorized access to data stored electronically in a facility through intentional, unauthorized access of the facility. The ECPA was intended to prevent hackers from intercepting computer communications by: (1) expanding privacy protection to individuals; and (2) expanding the number of crimes that can be investigated through electronic surveillance methods. The offense created by section 2701 seems to provide additional deterrence to hacking, although there have been no successful prosecutions under the statute.

I. WORKER SAFETY

A. Occupational Safety and Health Act

Due to the trend of increasing employment deaths

and injuries in the late 1960s, Congress enacted the Occupational Safety and Health Act to ensure worker safety. OSHA includes a general duty clause which requires employers to furnish their employees with a hazard-free working environment. In addition, the statute requires employers to comply with specific occupational safety and health promulgated by the Secretary of Labor.

1. Elements of the Offense

There are three main components of the general duty clause of OSHA relating to its violation: (1) the violation must have been committed by an "employer"; (2) a civil violation must meet certain specified criteria; and (3) in order to apply criminal sanctions, certain criteria are mandated.

a. Employer

Until recently, "employers" under the OSHA definition have been limited to corporations as entities. Under this reasoning prison sentences could only be imposed upon sole proprietors since corporations cannot be jailed. Because it has now been settled that officers qualify as employers in other criminal contexts, in more recent OSHA cases, corporate officers as employers have been criminally sanctioned under this broader definition. Furthermore, recent OSHA cases establish that an employee cannot be subjected to criminal liability as an aider and abettor of the corporate employer's criminal violation of OSHA. However, the potential liability of a third party or an employee acting in some other capacity who aids and abets his employer remains a live issue.

b. Civil violation

To establish a serious civil violation of OSHA's general duty clause, the Secretary of Labor must prove that: (1) the employer failed to render its workplace free of a hazard; (2) the hazard was "recognized"; (3) the hazard caused or was likely to cause death or serious physical harm; and (4) the hazard was preventable.

c. Criminal violation

Criminal sanctions may be applied where an employer's willful violation causes the death of an employee. A willful violation for OSHA purposes is one involving voluntary action, done either with an intentional disregard of, or plain indifference to, the statutory requirements. Criminal penalties may also be imposed for giving advance warning of unannounced safety inspections and for making false representations in a document filed pursuant to the statute.

2. Preemption

In 1992, the Supreme Court held that state regulation of occupational safety and health issues for which a federal standard is in effect and which have not been approved by the Secretary of Labor is preempted and that such state regulation consequently conflicts with the full purposes and objectives of OSHA. States may, however, regulate worker safety if a state plan is approved by the Secretary of labor. Twenty-three states and two territories have received the Secretary's approval for their plans.

3. Penalties

To enforce OSHA's worker safety mandate, Congress provided for the possibility of both civil and criminal penalties. Employers who willfully or repeatedly violate the general duty clause or any specific OSHA standard may be assessed a civil penalty of not more than $70,000 for each violation, but not less than $5,000 for each willful violation. Citations for serious violations as well as those determined not to be of a serious nature may earn a civil penalty of up to $7,000 for each violation.

The imposition of civil sanctions is limited, however, and rarely have criminal fines been used to punish employers. To date, only one employer has been imprisoned, although home confinement and time in halfway houses have occasionally been imposed. Due to the small number of OSHA cases prosecuted by the Department of Justice, and because of the minimal civil fines levied upon employers coupled with the increasing use of settlements rather than prosecution, OSHA has drawn criticism for its limited deterrent effect on employers. One commentator has suggested that some employers may be more effectively prosecuted under the "knowing endangerment" provisions of the "Clean Water Act" and the Resource Conservation and Recovery Act than under OSHA.

B. Federal Mine Safety and Health Act

The Federal Mine Safety and Health Act, like OSHA, protects worker health and safety through a combination of civil, criminal, and administrative enforcement mechanisms. An operator of a mine in which a safety or health violation is found is civilly liable without a showing of fault and is criminally liable if the violation is wilful.

FMSHA also imposes civil and criminal liability on corporate officers, directors, and agents of a corporate operator who knowingly authorize, order, or carry out a violation. An agent of a noncorporate operator is not subject to any penalties under FMSHA. Although the Mine Safety and Health Administration has a more vigorous criminal enforcement program than OSHA, few criminal prosecutions have been brought under FMSHA.

C. State Criminal Law

1. Effectiveness of State Criminal Law

Although states are preempted by OSHA from regulating workplace safety, the application of all state criminal sanctions against employers is not invalidated. State courts have held that state penal laws applied in a workplace context are not preempted by OSHA, and employers have been prosecuted for homicide under state criminal statutes. . . .

FALSE CLAIMS

. . . In 1863, as a result of increasingly widespread procurement fraud in Civil War defense contracts, Congress enacted the first False Claims Act. In so doing, Congress sought to protect both government funds and property from fraudulent claims. Today, most False Claims litigation involves alleged violations of either section 287 of Title 18 of the United States Code, imposing criminal liability on individuals making false claims, or sections 3729 through 3733 of Title 31 of the United States Code, which impose civil liability on such individuals. The 1986 amendments to the False Claims Act have blurred the dividing line meant to separate criminal false claims, as governed by Title 18, and civil false claims, as governed by Title 31. Accordingly, this article, while principally focusing in 18 U.S.C., § 287, also discusses relevant developments and applications of sections 3729 through 3733 of Title 31, specifically, qui tam litigation and double jeopardy implications.

Under section 287 it is illegal to present a false, fictitious or fraudulent claim to the federal government. The courts have construed section 287 broadly, enabling the government to use it in prosecuting a wide array of false claims, including fraudulent federal tax refunds, Medicare and Medicaid fraud, Social Security fraud, government contract impropriety, fraudulent claims concerning unperformed services under government programs, and numerous other fraudulent claims submitted to the federal government. Prosecutors may simultaneously bring both section 287 charges and section 1001 false statement charges under the civil false claims statutes.

I. ELEMENTS OF THE OFFENSE

To establish a section 287 violation, the prosecution must show that: (1) a defendant presented a claim against the United States or any agency or department of the United States; (2) the claim was false, fictitious, or fraudulent; and (3) the defendant knew his claim was false, fictitious, or fraudulent.

A. Presentation of a Claim

Both the legislature and courts have defined the terms "presentation", "claim" and "department of agency" broadly. Although section 287 does not explicitly define the term "claim", the language in its civil liability companion, section 3729 of Title 31, states that any request or demand for money or property from the United States can constitute a claim. However, a direct demand for federal funds is not required to constitute a claim; indirect demands are also sufficient to establish a section 287 violation. . . .

Both the Eighth and Tenth Circuits have held that ignorance of federal involvement in a program or project is not a defense to a section 287 violation, when the defendant's intent was to present a false claim. The Fifth Circuit, while following the rule that a mistake of law is not an adequate defense, recognizes good faith reliance on a third party's actions as an appropriate defense to a section 287 charge. The Ninth Circuit has held that the knowledge necessary to sustain a section 287 conviction could be imputed to a tax protestor who counseled taxpayers on how to file false tax returns. In this case, the defense argued that the government failed to allege and prove that the taxpayers actually submitting the false returns knew that they were false. Nevertheless, the court held that the taxpayers' knowledge was irrelevant because the defendant tax protestor knew that his advice violated the tax laws.

II. LEGISLATIVE AMENDMENTS

In response to increasing fraud against the federal government in the early 1980's and inadequate enforcement procedures, Congress passed the False Claims Amendments Act of 1986, which instituted major reforms with respect to both the civil and criminal law. With the amended legislation, Congress attempted to enhance the government's ability to recover losses sustained as a result of fraud by modernizing enforcement mechanisms, increasing recoverable damages, and encouraging private individuals to come forward with information of government fraud.

One change brought about by the 1986 amendments was the elimination of the option of imposing either a fine or a prison sentence in the event of a criminal false claim conviction. The statute now mandates both a fine and imprisonment for all convictions. While the maximum prison sentence remains five years, the maximum fine has been linked to the general penalty provisions of Title 18. Thus, a criminal defendant may face fines of up to one million dollars for each false claim charge.

Another change effected by the 1986 amendments governs the admissibility of criminal pleas in subsequent civil actions. Rule 11(e)(6) of the Federal Rules of Criminal Procedure provides that a *nolo contendere* plea shall have no collateral estoppel effect in related civil proceedings. The amended Act, however, prevents a criminal defendant who had entered a *nolo contendere* plea from denying liability in a later civil false claims action.

A third modification in the 1986 amendments was specific incorporation of "reverse false claims" into the definition of false claims. A claim filed to avoid or decrease a payment to the government is now actionable under the amended statute.

Finally, the 1986 amendments expanded prosecutorial discovery powers. The amendments authorize the Justice Department to issue civil investigative demands ("CIDs") for information relating to a False Claims Act investigation prior to the initiation of litigation. A CID may require the production of documents, written answers to interrogatories and/or oral testimony. While the statute specifically applies to civil actions, it also allows disclosure of evidence gathered under a CID to other authorized officers of the Department of Justice. In effect, this facilitates information gathering prior to indictment.

The 103rd Congress is currently considering a set of housekeeping amendments which would clarify certain provisions of the False Claims Act mostly by facilitating suits initiated by qui tam plaintiffs. One proposed Senate bill provides that the 1986 amendments made by the False Claims Act "shall apply to cases filed on or after the date of the enactment of such Act." This, in effect, would make the False Claims Amendments Act of 1986 retroactive. The bill would also allow whistle blowers, who have collected evidence in the public record "which is not being pursued by the United States in an open and active fraud investigation," to bring suit. Finally, the bill would allow government employees to file suits as qui tam plaintiffs.

III. QUI TAM LITIGATION

Section 3730 of Title 31, which was designed to encourage private enforcement of false claims actions, authorizes a citizen to bring a civil action for a violation of section 3729 on behalf of the United States. Amendments to these "qui tam" provisions of section 3730 have further enhanced individual involvement in initiating false claims actions. Under the previous version of the statute, the qui tam plaintiff initiating the suit played a detached role in litigating the case. Section 3730(c) now provides qui tam plaintiffs, in a case where the Government takes control, a more direct role in protecting their financial stake. Subsection (c)(1) enables a qui tam plaintiff, upon request, to receive copies of all the filed pleadings and deposition transcripts. The qui tam plaintiff may also formally object to any motions to dismiss or any proposed settlements between the Government and the defendant. The amendments also increased the amount qui tam plaintiffs may recover. The qui tam plaintiff's share was increased from no more than 10% to no more than 25% of the government recovery in cases where the government intervenes. A similar increase from no more than 25% to no more than 30% in the qui tam plaintiff's share of the recovery was also included in the amendments when the government does not proceed with the action. Since defendants may be liable for treble damages under the civil false claims statute, the potential recovery for a qui tam plaintiff can be considerable.

The number of qui tam lawsuits has been rapidly increasing in recent years. Approximately 600 qui tam cases have been filed in the seven years since the amendments, as compared to twenty in the ten years prior to the amendments. As a result of this increase, the government has recovered upwards of $500 million.

The great majority of qui tam lawsuits are filed against defense contractors, including prominent government contractors like Northrop, Rockwell, Unisys, Honeywell and United Technologies Corporation. In July 1992, the government recovered $55 million in a settlement with Bicoastal Corporation; $8.7 million of that amount went to qui tam plaintiffs for their role in initiating the lawsuit. Less than a month after the Bicoastal settlement, the government recovered another $59.5 million in the settlement of a qui tam lawsuit against General Electric Co. . . .

FEDERAL FOOD AND DRUG ACT VIOLATIONS

In 1938 pursuant to its constitutional authority to regulate interstate commerce, Congress enacted the Federal Food, Drug and Cosmetic Act ("FDCA" or "Act"). The primary goal of this legislation is to protect the health and safety of the public by preventing deleterious, adulterated or misbranded articles from entering interstate commerce. Those who violate its provisions are subject to criminal penalties, injunctions, and seizure of adulterated or misbranded goods.

I. ELEMENTS OF THE OFFENSE

The Food and Drug Administration ("FDA") and the courts impose broad standards of criminal liability for violations of the FDCA. In *United States v. Dotterweich*, the Supreme Court established a standard of strict liability for violations of the Act's provisions by holding that proof of the defendant's intent to commit a violation was not required to obtain a conviction.

In the majority opinion, Justice Frankfurter reasoned that the goal towards which the FDCA was aimed, protection of the public health and safety, demanded a standard that "dispenses with the conventional requirement for criminal conduct—awareness of some wrongdoing." In an attempt to define the limits of this assertion, the Court held that a finding of corporate guilt would extend only to those individuals who had a "responsible share in the furtherance of the transaction which the statute outlaws."

Many later courts have applied the *Dotterweich* strict liability standard in cases involving criminal penalties under federal regulations. However, a number of courts encountered difficulties in defining the *Dotterweich* phrase "responsible relation" as it applied to the scope of criminal liability under the FDCA. The Supreme Court resolved this confusion in *United States v. Park*. In *Park*, the Court limited the *Dotterweich* "responsible relation" standard by requiring that the government establish a prima facie case showing that the defendant failed to act on authority which could have prevented or corrected the violation.

Despite the *Park* clarification, lower courts and commentators continue to struggle to determine the appropriate scope of strict liability with respect to corporate officers. The confusion results from the *Park* Court's statement that although the Act's strict liability standard "requires the highest standard of foresight and vigilance, [the criminal aspect of the Act] does not require that which is objectively impossible." This limitation of *Dotterweich* holding provides the foundation for a defense of impossibility.

Despite the confusion surrounding its scope, strict criminal liability continues to be the standard in prosecutions under the FDCA. The courts do, however, consider the extent of the executive's responsibility and authority over the events which contributed to the violation. Where an individual is in a position of power or authority which would allow him to prevent, detect, or correct violations of the Act, the individual will be held strictly liable for failing to act on that authority.

FINANCIAL INSTITUTIONS FRAUD

This article reviews three methods by which the federal government may take action in cases involving financial institutions. The first section discusses federal prosecutions of financial institutions fraud under section 1344 of Title 18 of the Untied States Code, the basic provision under which such crimes are charged. The second section explores the framework by which the federal government brings claims against officers, directors and third party fiduciaries who fraudulently manage defunct financial institutions. Specifically, this section discusses the application of the doctrine of "adverse domination," which has been used to toll the statute of limitations provided by the Financial Institutions Reform, Recovery and Enforcement Act ("FIRREA"). The final section discusses the role of the Bank Secrecy Act ("BSA") in preventing deceptive financial transactions. In particular, this section focuses on methods of preventing individuals from deliberately "structuring" transactions in

order to evade the BSA's reporting requirements.

I. BANK FRAUD: SECTION 1344

This section addresses federal prosecutions of bank fraud under 18 U.S.C. § 1344 ("Bank Fraud Statute"). Crimes which constitute bank fraud under section 1344 require that the perpetrator engage in a scheme to defraud a financial institution of its own assets or assets within its control.

A. Potential Scope

Although broadly written, section 1344 does not reach all crimes relating to banks. Money laundering and bribery of bank officials fall outside its scope. Similarly, section 1344 does not protect a bank customer defrauded of funds legally withdrawn from an account if those funds were no longer under the "custody or control" of a financial institution when the fraud occurred. Because section 1344 requires that the intended victim be a bank, it does not apply to fraud committed by a bank on its customers.

Recent developments further suggest that Congress did not intend section 1344 to cover every kind of banking crime. Although the original version of section 1344 defined a financial institution as a "federally chartered or insured financial institution," the original version also contained a catch-all provision suggesting a broader interpretation of "financial institution." The definitional subsection of the original section 1344 was eliminated in the 1989 amendments to section 1344 contained in FIRREA. The government now uses FIRREA's definition of financial institution. Although the difference in definitions is largely due to the dissolution of the Savings and Loan Insurance Corporation, FIRREA's version does not include a catch-all provision, suggesting a limitation on the application of section 1344. . . .

The "complete" domination doctrine maintains that if an "informed stockholder or director could have induced the corporation to sue," then there was no adverse domination. The category of likely informers has been extended to informed, non-wrongdoing employees in the Ninth Circuit. If the defendant can expand the group of individuals who have a responsibility to bring a suit, then the likelihood of proving adverse domination under the "complete" domination theory is diminished.

In other jurisdictions, stockholders are under no duty to use "due diligence" in uncovering wrongdoing on the part of directors and officers because a fiduciary relationship exists between members of the Board and stockholders. Thus, a defendant's ability to argue that the stockholders could or should have discovered the wrongdoing is not a defense in some jurisdictions against the application of the adverse domination doctrine. Quite simply, stockholders do not havҿ access to knowledge or information necessary to bring a suit against directors and officers.

The doctrine of adverse domination has the potential to expand the sphere of defendants liable for recovery beyond culpable directors, officers and third parties who had a fiduciary duty with the defunct institution.

III. THE BANK SECRECY ACT

A. Purpose

Congress enacted the Bank Secrecy Act ("BSA") in 1970 out of concern that financial institutions were playing an increasingly extensive role in the laundering of unreported income or illegally obtained funds. The express purpose of the BSA is to "require the maintenance of records, and the making of certain reports, which have a high degree of usefulness in criminal, tax, or regulatory investigations or proceedings." Reports documenting the movement of large volumes of currency by way of deposit, transfer, or exchange, is one way of discovering the concealment and disguise of currency. As a result these reports assist in the enforcement of federal tax and criminal laws and regulations.

B. Reporting Requirements

The Bank Secrecy Act authorizes the Secretary of the Treasury to prescribe regulations setting forth reporting and record keeping requirements for domestic financial institutions of transactions for the payment, receipt or transfer of U.S. currency or coins. The principal report promulgated by the Treasury Secretary is the Currency Transaction Report ("CTR"). Under 31 U.S.C. § 103.22(a)(1), each financial institution "shall file a report of each deposit, withdrawal, exchange of currency or other payment or transfer, by, through, or to such financial institution which involves a transaction in currency of more than $10,000.

In 1987, Congress determined to end the purposeful circumvention of the CTR reporting requirement, amended the Bank Secrecy Act with 31 U.S.C. § 5324 to prohibit the "structuring" of transactions for the purposeful evasion of the CTR reporting requirement. These anti-structuring measures have not gone untested. Indeed, recent Bank Secrecy Act cases have primarily involved interpretations of the anti-structuring statute. This section now examines two primary controversies involving section 5324 of the Bank Secrecy Act.

C. Mens Rea

The mens rea requirement for section 5324(3) is met when the prosecution establishes a person has "willfully" violated section 5324. Two interpretations of this mens rea requirement have emerged.

Almost all courts have held that the willfulness requirement in the context of section 5324 is met where the defendant: (1) knew that the bank was legally obligated to report transactions exceeding $10,000; and (2) intended to deprive the government of information to which it is entitled. Under this analysis, the government need not prove that the defendant was aware of the illegality of structuring currency transactions under section 5324.

The legislative history of section 5324 indicates that Congress, "only intended to require proof that the defendant structured a currency transaction in order to prevent the financial institution from filing a currency transaction report." In enacting section 5234 no modification was made to the traditional meaning of "willfulness." Before section 5324 was enacted, " 'willful' generally meant no more than that the person charged with the duty knew what he was doing. It did not mean that, in addition, he must suppose that he is breaking the law." The enactment of section 5324 did not usher in a new definition of willful. Unlike other violations of the act the anti-structuring statute does not require the government to prove an intent to break the law because "structuring is not the kind of activity that an ordinary person would engage in innocently." Individuals who inadvertently divide a currency transaction in excess of $10,000 into smaller transactions would not be subject to structuring liability since proof beyond a reasonable doubt is required that the purpose of the structured aspect of a currency exchange was to evade the reporting requirements.

The First Circuit rejected the approach that willfulness is satisfied by intent for the purposes of the anti-structuring act. In an en banc decision, the court established its rule that the willfulness requirement of the anti-structuring statute is met by, "either the violation of a known legal duty or reckless disregard of the law."

MAIL AND WIRE FRAUD

Although the federal mail fraud statute has been subject to different interpretations in recent years, it remains as powerful a tool for federal prosecutors as it has been since its enactment in 1872. The statute provides:

> Whoever, having devised or intending to devise any scheme or artifice to defraud, or for obtaining money or property by means of false or fraudulent pretenses, representations or promises . . . for the purpose of executing such a scheme or artifice or attempting to do so [uses or causes the mails to be used] . . . shall be fined not more than $1,000 or imprisoned not

more than five years or both. If the violation affects a financial institution, such person shall be fined not more than $1,000,000 or imprisoned not more than 30 years, or both.

The federal wire fraud statute, enacted in 1952, contains nearly identical language and prohibits fraudulent schemes that make use of interstate television, radio, or wire communications. These two statutes have been applied to "cover not only the full range of consumer frauds, stock frauds, land frauds, bank frauds, insurance frauds, and commodity frauds, but [also] . . . such areas as blackmail, counterfeiting, election fraud and bribery." In areas in which legislatures have been slow to act, they have "frequently represented the sole instrument of justice that could be wielded against the ever-innovative practitioners of deceit."

This article focuses on the mail fraud statute, which has been utilized more frequently than its companion. Because the mail and wire fraud statutes are similar, court decisions addressing the character and scope of one statute are generally applicable to the other. The following sections outline the elements of mail fraud, address interpretations of and changes in the elements brought about by Supreme Court rulings and Congressional action, and examine the available defenses against charges of mail and wire fraud.

I. ELEMENTS OF THE OFFENSE

To prove mail fraud under section 1341 the government must show: (1) a scheme to defraud; (2) committed with intent to defraud; and (3) use of the mails to further the fraudulent scheme. The government is not required to prove that the scheme to defraud was successful. It need only prove that a scheme existed in which use of the mails was reasonably foreseeable and that an actual mailing occurred in furtherance of the scheme. Each use of the mails constitutes a separate offense, thus, each mailing can constitute a separate count in an indictment.

A. Scheme to Defraud

Determining what constitutes a "scheme or artifice to defraud" is essential to applying the statute. Prior to 1988, the Circuit Courts were inconsistent in their determination of what constituted such a scheme. Many courts applied a broad definition and found fraud where the defendant's conduct strayed from a standard of "moral uprightedness, of fundamental honesty, fair play and right dealing in the general business life of members of society." Other courts interpreted the phrase narrowly to include only those schemes aimed at obtaining tangible property ("traditional funds"). Still other courts extended the meaning

of the phrase to include schemes involving deprivation of intangible rights.

In 1988, Congress clarified these discrepancies with its addition of section 1346 to Title 18 of the United States Code. This amendment firmly established that deprivation of intangible rights fell within the reach of the mail and wire fraud statutes. This was passed in response to the Supreme Court's ruling in *McNally v. United States,* which excluded those schemes that deprived victims of intangible nonproperty rights. The amendment essentially restores the law to its pre-*McNally* status.

Although current application of the mail fraud statute allows prosecution for the deprivation of intangible property or non-property rights, there remains some uncertainty as to exactly which intangibles may be protected by the statute. At least one circuit court has held that a federal court may look to the state law of its jurisdiction to determine if an interest is "property" for purposes of the statute.

1. Traditional Frauds

Traditional frauds are those activities "intended to defraud individuals of money or other tangible property interests . . . [and] involve calculated efforts to use misrepresentations or other deceptive practices to induce the innocent or unwary to give up some tangible interest." These types of schemes involve "some sort of fraudulent misrepresentations or omissions reasonably calculated to deceive persons of ordinary prudence and comprehension." Examples of traditional fraudulent schemes prosecuted under Section 1341 include false insurance claims, fraudulent investment schemes, misrepresentations in the sale of used automobiles, false application forms for loans, fraudulent loan marketing schemes, check kiting schemes, false advertising, and various bribery and kickback schemes.

2. Frauds Involving Intangible Rights

Frauds involving deprivation of "intangible rights" may also be prosecuted under the mail and wire fraud statutes. The term "intangible rights" encompasses both property and non-property rights. Unlike traditional frauds which may arise regardless of the relationship between the defendant and the victim, frauds related to intangible rights stem from a fiduciary relationship between the defendant and the defrauded party or entity.

Intangible rights cases involving non-property rights are premised on the theory that a fiduciary who fails to disclose material information to his principal deprives him of a right to honest and faithful services. The mail fraud statute has thus been used to prosecute cases of voter fraud and public corruption involving bribes and kickbacks. Anyone who bribes a public official or offers a kickback is also subject to prosecution for depriving the citizenry of its right to honest services by inducing a public fiduciary to breach his duty to the public.

Breaches of fiduciary duty between employers and employees can also form the basis of a violation of the mail fraud statute. The Second Circuit, however, has ruled that only those breaches constituting "concealment by a fiduciary of material information which he is under a duty to disclose to another under circumstances where the non-disclosure could or does result in harm to the other" are actionable. In cases where this test is applied to convict corporate officials, the courts have often found that the fiduciary has concealed material information about the breach of his fiduciary duty from his employer, and that the fiduciary's concealment of this information was potentially harmful to the employer.

In applying this "material information" test, other circuits have ruled that monetary loss is not required for conviction—that the loss of economic information is sufficient. Other courts, including the District of Columbia Circuit, have utilized a slightly different test focusing on the foreseeability of the harm. The inquiry is whether the employee could reasonably foresee that nondisclosure of information would cause the employer harm. Although the mail fraud statute does not require actual harm to the victim, the D.C. Circuit requires that the defendant at least have contemplated that harm would probably result.

There is some debate in the Circuit Courts about whether tangible rights can be violated if they are not premised upon fiduciary duty. For example, the majority of circuit courts have held that permits, licenses and certificates are not the "property" of the government for purposes of prosecuting schemes to fraudulently acquire such papers. However, a few courts have found that state issued licenses constitute property, due to the states' regulatory interests and the accompanying rights which are bestowed on the holders.

B. Intent to Defraud

To establish liability for mail fraud, the government must prove that the defendant intended to defraud another person of property or services. "Intent" means that the defendant must have knowledge of the scheme to defraud. The behavior of the target of the scheme is irrelevant to determining the defendant's intent. If a conspiracy to defraud is established, each participant in the scheme can be held liable for mailings made by the other participants, even if a formal conspiracy is not charged in the indictment. It is not necessary for the government to establish that a particular defendant either devised the scheme or participated in every aspect of the scheme.

In determining whether in fact a defendant intended to defraud, courts draw a distinction between false representation and "puffery." Puffery is mere exaggeration that heightens the attractiveness of a product, but does not go so far as to constitute fraudulent activity. On the other hand, reckless disregard for the truth of statements can constitute fraudulent activity. Intentional concealment of information known to be pertinent to proper decision making is another basis for establishing a fraudulent scheme. However, mere deceit without accompanying intent to harm will not suffice to establish a scheme to defraud.

The government may establish that the defendant had the requisite intent to defraud through either direct or circumstantial evidence. Evidence of attempts by the defendant to conceal certain activities may be probative of intent. Additionally, as in other crimes that require proof of intent, evidence of prior offenses is admissible absent substantial prejudice. Intent to defraud does not have to be listed as a separate element in the jury instructions.

C. Mailing in Furtherance of a Scheme

The final requirement for conviction under Section 1341 is use of the mails to further a fraudulent scheme. This "in furtherance" requirement has been interpreted and applied broadly. It is satisfied when the government proves the defendant acted "with knowledge that . . . use of the mails [would] follow in the ordinary course of business, or where he could reasonably foresee that . . . use of the mail would result. It is not necessary to prove the accused . . . actually intended the mail to be used." If the defendant is charged with wire fraud, the government must prove only that it was reasonably foreseeable that a wire communication would occur. It is not necessary to prove that it was reasonably foreseeable that the wire communication would be interstate.

It is not necessary that the mailings be "an essential part of the scheme," and the mailings do not have to be made or received by the defendant. Nor do the mailings themselves have to be fraudulent. Furthermore, the precise details of the mailing need not be established; it is sufficient to show that use of the mails is part of the sender's regular business practice.

There are some limitations on the "in furtherance" requirement, however. For example, mailings which occur after the scheme is completed cannot form the basis of a mail fraud count. The Supreme Court reversed the conviction of a defendant charged with mail fraud relating to the use of a stolen credit card. The

Court found that the scheme ended once the defendant used the credit card to pay for a motel room, and therefore, the mailings between the vendor and the bank which had issued the credit card could not be charged as part of the defendant's fraudulent scheme.

Mailings are also not properly charged under the statute if they aid in the detection of the scheme rather the [sic] than the furthering of it. However, mailings which postpone the detection of the scheme are properly charged under the statute even if the defendant has already received the benefit of the fraud. An example of this type of mailing would be a "lulling" letter mailed to the victim of a fraudulent investment, that seeks to quell his concerns and give him a false sense of security. The proper inquiry is whether the mailings occurred before the defendant's scheme reached its fruition. Mailings that are routine and would be made even in the absence of the fraudulent scheme are not chargeable, and thus, constitute another limitation on the statute's reach. The seminal case is *Parr v. United States*. In *Parr*, the defendants were commissioners of a school tax board who misappropriated funds for their personal use. The mailings charged were tax assessments paid by residents of the community of the school board. The Court found that since the taxes would have been assessed absent the fraudulent scheme, these mailings could not constitute mai! fraud. However, routine business mailings that would not be mailed but for the existence of a fraudulent scheme are chargeable. Therefore, in the elaborate check kiting scheme set up by the defendant in *United States v. Freitag*, the mailings of printed checks and monthly statements to the defendant's checking account, established specifically to perpetrate the fraud, were properly charged under the statute.

The government may use either direct or circumstantial evidence to prove use of the mails. Introduction of the envelope in which the mailing was made is strong direct evidence of use of the mails. Testimony of office practices as to use of the mails is, in some cases, sufficient circumstantial evidence to establish the mailing. The Seventh Circuit has held that circumstantial evidence, such as testimony regarding office practice, will be allowed if it eliminates all reasonable doubt that the mails were in fact used. However, use of the mails will not be established where evidence exists that shows both public mailings and private mailing services (e.g., Federal Express) were used in the office.

Money Laundering

Money laundering is the process by which one conceals the existence, illegal source, or illegal application of income, and disguises that income to make it appear legitimate. Laundering "dirty money" has become a lucrative and sophisticated business in the United States and is an indispensable element of organized crime's activities. Without the ability to move and hide its enormous wealth through laundering techniques, large scale criminal activity could operate only at a small fraction of current levels, and with far less flexibility.

In recognition of this phenomenon, Congress passed the Money Laundering Control Act of 1986 (the "Act"), holding criminally liable any individual who conducts a monetary transaction knowing or with reason to know that the funds involved were derived from unlawful activity. Unlike earlier unsuccessful efforts to control the movement of illegal income through financial institution reporting requirements, the statute is aimed at "the lifeblood of organized crime" itself—the act of converting funds derived from illegal activities into a spendable or consumable form.

I. Background

The Money Laundering Control Act of 1986 defines and prohibits for the first time a category of activity known as "money laundering." The Act not only reaches the proceeds of conduct characteristic of organized crime such as narcotics trafficking, Racketeer Influenced and Corrupt Organizations Act (RICO) predicates, or certain state offenses, but also encompasses many additional criminal offenses ranging from espionage, to trading with the enemy, to tax evasion.

Although the proceeds of crime historically have been subject to seizure by warrant for use as evidence, the Act makes criminal proceeds perpetually illegal. Long after the criminal offence which generated the proceeds has come to an end, those who conduct prohibited financial transactions or transportation of the funds engage in criminal conduct independent of the income-producing original crime. The concept is to bar all "monetary transactions" in "criminally derived property." The Act does not limit itself to transactions conducted through financial institutions, but appears to reach a broad variety of routine commercial transactions which affect commerce.

II. Overview of the Statutes

A. Section 1956

Section 1956(a) contains ten separate crimes, distinguished by the particular defendant's knowledge and intent, divided into three broad categories. The first subsection of section 1956 prohibits knowing involvement in a wide range of transactions dealing with the proceeds of criminal activity, either (1) with the intent to promote unlawful activity or (2) with the knowledge that the transaction is designed either to conceal some aspect of the funds, such as its ownership, control, or source, or to avoid the currency transactions reporting requirements. Another subsection of section 1956 prohibits the transportation of monetary instruments in foreign commerce with the same intent or knowledge requirements, and the third subsection authorizes the use of government sting operations to expose criminal activity under this section.

1. Transaction Money Laundering

The first category of crimes contained in section 1956 may be referred to as transaction money laundering because the prohibited action is the conducting of a financial transaction. The four offenses contained in this subsection result when an individual conducts or attempts to conduct a financial transaction with "dirty" money. The four potential crimes are: (1) conducting a financial transaction with the intent to promote specified unlawful activities; (2) conducting a financial transaction with the intent to engage in 26 U.S.C. section 7201 or section 7206 tax evasion violations; (3) conducting a financial transaction designed to conceal or disguise; and (4) conducting a financial transaction designed to avoid a state or federal reporting requirement.

The elements of category one crimes are: (1) knowledge that the party involved represents the proceeds of some form of unlawful activity; (2) the property does in fact involve the proceeds of a specified unlawful activity; (3) conducting or attempting to conduct a financial transaction; and (4) requisite intent for the specific crime charged.

Simply stated, section 1956(a)(1) concerns a person who has dirty money, but who is unsure how the money is dirty. Therefore, to be culpable under this section of the statute, the defendant must engage in a transaction with the intent to promote specified unlawful activity, to commit certain tax offenses, to conceal or disguise, or to avoid a reporting requirement.

2. Transportation Money Laundering

Category two of section 1956 contains three separate crimes relating to the transportation of dirty money. The three crimes are: (1) transportation of a monetary instrument into or out of the United States with the intent to promote the carrying on of a specified unlawful activity; (2) transportation of a monetary instrument into or out of the United States knowing it represents the proceeds of some form of unlawful activity, and the transportation is designed to conceal or disguise such proceeds; and (3) transportation of a monetary instrument into or out of the United States knowing it represents the proceeds of some form of unlawful activity, and the transportation is designed to avoid a state or federal transaction reporting requirement. Unlike the crime specified in section

1956(a)(1)(A)(ii), there is no crime resulting from tax evasion in category two.

Section 1956(a)(2)(B) provides for the case of a transportation sting operation. Pursuant to the Crime Control Act of 1990, the knowledge that the monetary instrument or funds involved in the transportation represent the proceeds of some form of unlawful activity "may be established by proof that a law enforcement officer represented [such] as true, and the defendant's subsequent statements or actions indicate that the defendant believed such representations to be true."

3. Sting Operations

Category three was added by the Anti-Drug Abuse Act of 1988. It deals with government sting operations generally, where a financial transaction is conducted with property represented by a law enforcement officer to be the proceeds of specified unlawful activity, or property used to conduct or facilitate the conduct of specified unlawful activity. This section therefore provides for the uses of informants.

The standards of intent which define the category three crimes are the same as those specified for category two crimes. As in category two, there is no crime resulting from tax evasion in category three. Category three creates the following potential crimes from sting operations: (1) conducting a financial transaction involving sting money, with the intent to promote specified unlawful activity; (2) conducting a financial transaction involving sting money, with the intent to conceal or disguise; and (3) conducting a financial transaction involving sting money, with the intent to avoid a state or federal transaction reporting requirement.

B. Section 1957

Section 1957 specifies only one potential crime, as compared to the ten crimes found in section 1956. This section provides for the punishment of "[w]hoever . . . knowingly engages or attempts to engage in a monetary transaction in criminally derived property that is of value greater than $10,000 and is derived from specified unlawful activity." The statute does not require that the recipient exchange or launder the funds, that he have knowledge that the funds were proceeds of a specified unlawful activity, nor that he have any intent to further or conceal such an activity. Thus, section 1957 has a much broader reach than section 1956 because of the seemingly "innocent" acts or commercial transactions which it criminalizes.

The intent of Congress in enacting section 1957 was to dissuade people from conducting even ordinary commercial transactions with people suspected to be involved in criminal activity. Not surprisingly, then, the absence of a criminal intent requirement for a crime under section 1957 has led many commentators to criticize the statute for its breadth.

III. ELEMENTS OF THE OFFENSE

There are five key elements which are used to determine the criminality of an act under 18 U.S.C. sections 1956 and 1957. Those elements are knowledge, the existence of a specified unlawful activity, financial transactions, proceeds and intent.

A. Knowledge

Knowledge is a requisite element for all of the crimes established by the Money Laundering Control Act, although the exact type of knowledge required varies for different offenses. Both sections 1956 and 1957 require that the property or money in question is the proceeds of a specified unlawful activity. Section 1957 imposes a knowledge requirement that the offender "knowingly engages or attempts to engage in a monetary transaction in criminally divided property." Thus, to be prosecuted under section 1957, a person need not know from what specific activity the property was derived. The only requisite knowledge is the knowledge that the money is the result of some form of criminal conduct.

Section 1956 has a somewhat more restricted knowledge requirement. Under section 1956, the offender must have knowledge "that the property involved in a financial transaction represents the proceeds of some form of unlawful activity." Section 1956(c)(1) further clarifies the knowledge requirement by stating that "some form of unlawful activity" means some form of felonious conduct. Thus, under section 1956, the offender must at least have specific enough knowledge to know that the property is the proceed of a felony. However, section 1956(c)(1) also makes it clear that the offender need not know the specific criminal activity from which the proceeds are the result.

Section 1956 contains a secondary knowledge requirement which is related to the defendant's intent. Sections 1956(a)(1)(B) and (a)(2)(B) require that one takes action knowing that the transaction or transportation is designed to conceal information about the proceeds of specified criminal activity, or knowing that it is intended to avoid a transaction reporting requirement under state or federal law. In this second requirement, the knowledge specified is that of the person who designed the transaction, but if the designer and the defendant are two different people, the defendant can still be found to have the requisite knowledge of what the transaction was designed to do.

Determining how knowledge may be proven and at what point a person has attained the requisite knowledge has presented problems for the courts. Most circuits have allowed the use of circumstantial evidence to prove knowledge.

1. Willful Blindness

The knowledge requirement in both sections 1956 and 1957 is for actual knowledge, rather than a lesser standard of "should have known" or "reckless disregard." However, the actual knowledge requirement is "softened somewhat" because it can be met by showing "willful blindness." Although the final drafts of sections 1956 and 1957 do not specifically address the issue, it has generally been assumed that Congress intended to include willful blindness in their definition of knowledge. Consequently, the willful blindness standard has been upheld by the courts. Additionally, it has been held that the willful blindness doctrine is limited only by whether the jury could reasonably find willful blindness.

2. Constitutional Vagueness

Under section 1956, it is unclear at what point a citizen may be deemed to have gained sufficient knowledge about his dealings with someone to "know" that the person's funds were obtained from some unlawful activity. Consequently, several challenges have been made that the statute is unconstitutionally vague. This claim, however, has been rejected by every court to which it has been presented.

B. Specified Unlawful Activity

Sections 1956 and 1957 both criminalize only those transactions that actually involve the proceeds of a "specified unlawful activity." Section 1956(c)(7) contains a laundry list of crimes that constitute specified unlawful activities. For the purposes of section 1957, "the term 'specified unlawful activity' has the meaning given that term in section 1956. . . ." One court explains: "So long as the cash is represented to have come from any of the [listed illegal] activities, a defendant is guilty of the substantive offense of money laundering."

The Money Laundering Control Act was originally intended to combat the movement of money derived from drug-related offenses, but the extensive list of activities that constitute specified unlawful activities has allowed the statutes to be used to prosecute a number of cases of non-drug-related money laundering. Even though the proceeds of some unconventional activities may form the basis of indictment under this statute, the sentencing guidelines acknowledge the congressional intent to punish narcotics trafficking by punishing money laundering by persons involved in drug-related activities more harshly.

1. Pleading with Particularity

The Department of Justice has recognized that differences in terminology in the predicate offense statutes are critical to the proper pleading of section 1956 charges. The Department of Justice's manual on section 1956 cautions against departures from the statutory language:

> In the context of prosecutions predicated upon narcotic[s] trafficking, it is important to remember that the term "specified unlawful activity" is based upon RICO predicate offenses. . . . Thus, it would seem that the drug must be a "narcotic or dangerous drug" to form the basis of a Section 1956 or Section 1957(a) or (b)(1) violations.

Subsection 1956(c)(7) also defines the term "specified unlawful activity" in terms of specific acts or activities which constitute discrete offenses. The use of such terminology should dictate that the government plead more than broad, generic categories of criminal activity. For example, merely pleading that defendants violated certain criminal statutes would appear to be insufficient because it would not provide notice of any specific acts or activities constituting an indictable offense or offenses under federal law. In practice, however, the courts have not required a high level of particularity in the pleadings in response to defendants who have challenged the particularity with which the specified unlawful activity must be alleged in the indictment.

2. Double Jeopardy

A possible defense to the statutory requirement of a predicate specified unlawful activity is that of double jeopardy. In *United States V. Edgmon,* the defendant challenged his conviction for money laundering on the grounds that the conviction violated the Double Jeopardy Clause of the Fifth Amendment. He contended that his conviction for both conversion and money laundering constituted multiple punishments for the same offense. His argument was based on the fact that the crime of conversion was a necessary element of the money laundering offense.

The court rejected Edgmon's argument, saying that his money laundering conviction was not a violation of double jeopardy because "Congress appears to have intended the money laundering statute to be a separate crime distinct from the underlying offense that generated the money to be laundered."

The Senate report and the statute itself indicate that Congress intended simply to add a new criminal offense to punish activity that was not previously punished criminally: the post-crime hiding of the ill-gotten gains. Congress directed the money laundering provisions at conduct that follows in time the underlying crime rather than to afford an alternative means of punishing the prior specified unlawful activity. The *Edgmon* court concluded: "Congress enacted the money laundering statute to provide a punishment in addition to other punishment rather than instead of other punishment. We find that Congress intended money laundering and the 'specified unlawful activity' to be separate offenses separately punishable." Courts are in general agreement on this point.

C. Financial Transaction

The foundation of, and jurisdictional predicate for, a section 1956 violation is that a "financial transaction" occur. The definition of the term is not limited to banking or other financial institutions. Read broadly, virtually any exchange of money between two persons constitutes a financial transaction subject to criminal prosecution under section 1956, provided only that the transaction affects interstate commerce and is conducted with the intent to conceal or disguise property believed to be the proceeds of an illegal activity.

The legislative history of section 1956 demonstrates that Congress did not view every transfer or delivery of property as a financial transaction. Still, the term "financial transaction" has been interpreted broadly. Transactions that have qualified as financial transactions within the meaning of the statute include transferring title to a truck; the sale of automobiles; writing a check, either for cash or to a vendor who has provided services, or in conjunction with a payroll check laundering scheme; mailing of drug proceeds; transferring cashier's checks; making a payment with a money order; and transporting cash from one state to another. Even an attempt to launder money has been held sufficient to constitute a financial transaction.

Some movements of funds have managed to escape being considered financial transactions under the statute. One court cautioned against turning "the money laundering statute into a money spending statute" by defining the term financial transaction too broadly. Situations in which courts have found that the defendants' activities do not constitute financial transactions within the meaning of the statute include: placing cash proceeds in a safety deposit box at a bank, storing money in a shoe box, and transactions where the requisite intent to conceal the source of the proceeds was lacking.

1. Multiple Transactions

A potential problem of construction is posed by the term "financial transaction." Sophisticated money laundering schemes may employ many financial and non-financial institutions in various jurisdictions and countries. Criminal proceeds may thus pass through many entities before reaching their final destination. Each separate transfer or deposit should constitute a separate and discrete indictable offense, so long as each such transaction affected interstate or foreign commerce.

Defendants have argued multiplicity in cases where the defendant has been charged with a separate offense for each transaction in a money laundering scheme. Courts have held that it is not multiplicitous to charge a defendant for each discrete transaction in the unlawful proceeds, as long as the individual transactions may somehow be separately identified. One court explained that "[i]t is the individual acts of money laundering which are prohibited under section [1956] (a)(1)(B)(I), and not the course of action which those individual acts may constitute."

2. Interstate Commerce

For a violation of section 1956, the transaction involved must "affect[ ] interstate . . . commerce" or involve a financial institution "which is engaged in, or the activities of which affect, interstate or foreign commerce in any way or degree." The purpose of this requirement is to confer federal jurisdiction over these cases. Congress recognized that a clear interstate nexus was required to obtain federal jurisdiction: "Thus, for example, the use of proceeds of unlawful activity to purchase a residence would be covered if any of the materials could be shown to have come from out of State." The requirement has been interpreted to require only a "minimal effect" on interstate commerce to confer federal jurisdiction. Some examples of transactions determined to be sufficient to confer federal jurisdiction include: purchase of a car; investment in construction of a shopping mall; a transaction involving funds on deposit at a federally insured financial institution; a transaction involving a check or money order; and drug purchases.

Although the commerce clause is a broad jurisdictional basis for both sections of the Act, it is not without limits. Under section 1956 the government must show that the financial transaction itself affected interstate commerce. The government could not, for example, rely upon the fact that the criminal activity which generated the proceeds involved in the transaction had an effect on commerce. While the interstate commerce requirement would be met where financial institutions were involved or where interstate or foreign transfers occurred, the simple interstate, physical transfer of cash would appear to be insufficient.

D. Proceeds

Section 1956 prohibits conducting transactions that involve the "proceeds of specified unlawful activity." The statute does not define the term "proceeds," and thus invites a wide range of interpretation. The primary issue is whether "proceeds" can be something other than money. In section 1957, Congress prohibited certain transactions involving "criminally derived property," rather than "proceeds." Yet, "criminally derived property" is broadly defined in terms of proceeds: "any property constituting, or derived from, proceeds obtained from a criminal offense." If the two statutes are read together, the phrase "derived from" in section 1957 may suggest that the term "proceeds" in section 1956 has a limited meaning.

However, the accepted definition of "proceeds" seems to include more than just money. In *United Stats v. Werber*, the court adopted the common law understanding of proceeds. The court concluded that the words, as used in section 1956(a)(1), can include property other than money or cash equivalents, even if that property has not been purchased with the money derived from unlawful activity.

In response to constitutional challenges, several courts have held that neglecting to define the term proceeds does not render section 1956 void for vagueness. In reaching this conclusion, the courts applied the void-for-vagueness test set forth in *Kolender v. Lawson*: "The void for vagueness doctrine requires that a penal statute define the criminal offense with sufficient definiteness that ordinary people can understand what conduct is prohibited and in a manner that does not encourage arbitrary and discriminatory enforcement." Challenges based upon the vagueness of other portions of section 1956 have failed as well.

1. Tracing

The government need not trace proceeds involved in a money laundering scheme back to a particular offense. The government may present evidence that tends to show that transactions in which the defendant was engaged are typical of transactions designed to conceal the source of illegal proceeds. While such evidence may be considered insufficient to convict the defendant standing along, the jury may draw an inference from this and other circumstantial evidence to conclude that the proceeds could have only been derived from an illegal source.

Tracing is not required when the illegal funds are commingled in a bank account with legitimate funds. One court found that although Congress did not specify what proportion of the financial transaction must involve illegal proceeds, the use of the word "involves" demonstrates that Congress intended to reach transactions where illegal funds are commingled with legitimate funds.

2. Sting Operations

The Department of Justice initially cautioned against using sting operations to enforce section 1956. As a result of complaints by Department of Justice representatives, amendments were proposed to section 1956 as part of the Money Laundering Improvements Act of 1988. Section 1956(a)(3) now permits conviction where the defendants believed the money was, in fact, the product of specified unlawful activity, despite the fact that, in reality, no illegal proceeds were involved.

E. *Intent*

The intent requirement is a necessary element of a money laundering conviction under section 1956, and the specific intent is determinative of the crime with which a suspect will be charged. Intent is a very fact-specific inquiry, and is often closely related to the second knowledge requirement. Courts have repeatedly cautioned against combining in practice intent requirements that are separate in the statute. Some courts have suggested that the government advise the district court and defense counsel whether it is proceeding under the former, the latter, or both, and that the jury be charged accordingly. Still, the fact that the government has imposed an additional burden on itself by trying to prove both requirements will not generally warrant a reversal.

Transportation sting operations, governed by section 1956(a)(2)(B) of the statute, present a unique challenge to courts in their formulation of the requisite intent to support a criminal action. In the context of a transportation sting, the defendant's criminal intent must be corroborated by the government. Courts, in construing this intent, have adopted a standard which enables law enforcement officials to be effective as undercover agents without violating the mens rea required by the statute. In dealing with the potential transportation money launderer, the undercover agent is not required to alert the suspect to the illegal source of the funds. It is enough to satisfy the requirement of mens rea that the defendant "believe" the funds have been derived from an illegal source (because in reality they have not) rather than "know" as the statute on its face provides. The intent requirement for sting operations generally, (found in section 1956(a)(3) of the statute) is the same as that in subsections (a)(1)(B)(I) and (a)(2)(B)(I).

When all of the other elements of a section 1956 offense are satisfied, a court may look to whether the transaction was a "typical laundering transaction" as evidence of the defendant's criminal intent. Where it is not a "typical transaction," a court is less likely to find that the defendant acted with the intent to conceal or disguise such a transaction. Some courts, however, have limited the scope of this analysis.

A final issue that has been raised in reference to the intent requirements of section 1956 is that of transferred intent. Although defendants have attempted to attack section 1956 as unconstitutionally vague for incorporating an element of transferred intent, courts have uniformly rejected this analysis.

RACKETEER INFLUENCED AND CORRUPT ORGANIZATIONS

The Racketeer Influenced and Corrupt Organizations Act ("RICO"), enacted as Title IX of the Organized Crime Control Act of 1970, is designed to combat criminal organization. It prohibits "any person" from: (a) using income received from a pattern of racketeering activity or through collection of an unlawful debt to acquire an interest in an enterprise affecting interstate commerce; (b) acquiring or maintaining through a pattern of racketeering activity or through collection of an unlawful debt an interest in an enterprise affecting interstate commerce; (c) conducting or participating in the conduct of, through a pattern of racketeering activity or through collection of an unlawful debt, the affairs of an enterprise affecting interstate commerce; or (d) conspiring to participate in any of these activities. According to the statute's legislative history, RICO's purpose is to remove organized crime from the legitimate business community. RICO has become an effective weapon against racketeering primarily because it provides criminal and civil sanctions for violations of existing state and federal statutes.

I. BASIC CONCEPTS

A. *Criminal Actions*

Section 1963 provides criminal sanctions for violations of section 1962 that often, but not always, exceed those that could be imposed for two violations of the incorporated offenses. In addition, the statute authorizes forfeiture of any interest the defendant acquired by virtue of the RICO violation, and authorizes courts to enter restraining orders prior to conviction to prevent the transfer of potentially forfeitable property. Because Congress has mandated that the statute be construed liberally, because RICO does not require any mens rea beyond that necessary for the predicate acts, and because RICO provides for severe sanctions beyond those available for the predicate acts, it has become a favorite tool of prosecutors. Moreover, a substantial proportion of crimes prosecuted under RICO have been "white collar" crimes.

B. *Civil Actions*

In addition to civil actions, RICO permits private plaintiffs and the government to seek redress in a civil action. Under section 1964, the Attorney General, or "any person injured in his business or property by reason of a violation of section 1962" may bring a civil action in either state or federal court for redress. Private plaintiffs have successfully exercised this right. RICO provides equitable relief through divestiture of the defendant's interest in the enterprise, restrictions on future activities or investments, and dissolution or reorganization of the enterprise. RICO suits may also be brought as class actions under Rule 23 of the Federal Rules of Civil procedure.

In recent years, the number of private litigants bringing civil RICO actions against "legitimate businesses" involving "ordinary commercial disputes" has increased. The scope of civil RICO litigation has expanded, for example, to include suits involving competitive injury, securities regulations, banking, and injury to business or property.

C. *Liberal Construction*

Congress has mandated that RICO "be liberally construed to effectuate its remedial purposes." In the past, some courts have read the statute as narrowly limited to "organized criminals." These courts discouraged RICO actions arising out of "garden variety" commercial disputes or fraud. However, in *Sedima, S.P.R.L. v. Imrex Co.*, the Supreme Court attempted to halt this trend by concluding that RICO applies to legitimate businesses. The Court in *Sedima* also relied on the liberal construction clause in holding that a civil RICO plaintiff need not allege any additional "racketeering injury" beyond the injury caused by the predicate acts themselves. The Court candidly acknowledged that its ruling would deprive "legitimate businesses" of the judicially-created protections developed to shield such businesses from a statute clearly not aimed at such businesses, but the Court stressed that its holding was dictated by the language of the statute as written and that "correction" of "this defect . . . must lie with Congress."

While the Supreme Court has reaffirmed its reliance on RICO's "liberal construction" clause, it has acknowledged the clause is not without limits. Congress, however, has failed to enact restrictions, and other courts have followed the Supreme Court's liberal lead. . . .

SECURITIES FRAUD

Seven statutes regulate securities transactions. Congress has promulgated other statutes to deal with specific types of substantive fraud. Congress passed the most important of these, the Securities Act of 1933 ("1933 Act") and the Securities Exchange Act of 1934 ("1934 Act"), in the aftermath of the great stock market crash of 1929. Their purpose is to ensure vigorous market competition by mandating full and fair disclosure of all material information in the market place. This article focuses primarily on section 17(a) of the 1933 Act, section 10(b) of the 1934 Act, and Rule 10b-5 promulgated under the 1934 Act. Section I outlines the elements of securities fraud by describing the various activities considered to be substantive frauds under the securities laws. Due to the frequent overlap of civil and criminal bodies of law in securities regulation, this Article incorporates a review of the law in the civil area, in addition to exploring securities fraud as a white collar crime.

I. ELEMENTS OF THE OFFENSE

Although both the 1933 Act and the 1934 Act provide for various types of criminal prosecutions, the section employed most frequently in criminal prosecutions for fraud in the purchase or sale of securities is section 10(b) of the 1934 Act and Rule 10b-5 promulgated thereunder.

To maintain a securities fraud case of action, three elements must be proven: (1) a scheme or artifice to defraud, a material misrepresentation or omission, or a fraudulent act, practice, or course of business; (2) "in connection with the purchase or sale of a security" or "in the offer or sale of a security"; and (3) employing the use of interstate commerce or the mails to allow prosecution of the violation under federal jurisdiction. In addition, each area of substantive fraud has its own necessary elements for establishing a cause of action.

A. *Substantive Fraud*

1. *Material Omissions and Misrepresentations*

Material misrepresentation and omissions give rise to the most common type of securities fraud action. Rule 10b-5 proscribes any and all such false statements as long as they are made in connection with the purchase or sale of securities. In order to recover under the 1934 Act, four elements must be established: (1) the defendant misstated or omitted a material fact; (2) which was made with scienter; (3) on which the plaintiff reasonably relied: and (4) which proximately caused the plaintiff's injury.

a. *Misstatements and Omissions*

In recent years, the Securities and Exchange Commission ("SEC") and the Department of Justice have vigorously prosecuted makers of misrepresentations and omissions in securities filings.

The Fifth Circuit has upheld the conviction of a businessman involved in a scheme to inappropriately use corporate funds to cover loan payments used to expedite the sale of a company, and has found a land developer liable for failing to disclose material facts regarding his property in connection with a bond of-fering. The Seventh Circuit has found a stock pur-chaser liable for falsely denying his intention to make a tender offer. Other circuit court decisions have found defendants liable for misrepresentations and omissions in projections if those projections failed to suggest reliability, were not sufficiently cautious in tone, were not made in good faith, or were not founded on sound factual or historic bases. Lower courts have found liability in cases involving omis-sions and misrepresentations in connection with the sale of real estate limited partnerships, misstatements regarding a stock purchaser's true speculative inten-tions, and nondisclosure of a corporation's economic condition. Lower courts in the Seventh Circuit have followed the Eighth, Ninth and Eleventh Circuits anal-yses in attaching a duty to disclose on public account-ing firms if they know or recklessly fail to know of an ongoing fraud.

b. Materiality

Merely demonstrating an omission or misstatement is insufficient to prove securities fraud unless the infor-mation is material. In *TSC Industries, Inc. v. Northway, Inc.*, the Supreme Court devised a standard for determin-ing materiality which requires the court to use discretion and dismiss the action "[o]nly when the disclosures or omissions are so clearly unimportant that reasonable minds could not differ should the ultimate issue of mate-riality be decided as a matter of law."

In *TSC Industries*, the respondent investors claimed that certain statements made in TSC Indus-tries' proxy statement were false and misleading. The Court formulated a standard under which information is deemed material if it would be significant to the person relying on it in his or her investment decision. The Court stated that this materiality standard:

> contemplate[s] . . . a showing of a substantial likelihood that, under all the circumstances, the omitted fact would have assumed actual signifi-cance in the deliberations of the shareholder. Put another way, there must be a substantial likelihood that the disclosure of the omitted fact would have been viewed by the reasonable in-vestor as having significantly altered the "total mix" of information made available.

While *TSC Industries* made it clear that not all omissions or misrepresentations will be viewed as fraudulent, the Court did not decide the issue of whether prospective information, such as predictions of anticipated profits, could be material. Case law in the area of forward-looking statements has held that "[p]rojections and general expressions of optimism may be actionable under the federal securities laws."

In *Basic, Inc. v. Levinson*, the Supreme Court rec-ognized the potential materiality of prospective infor-mation regarding preliminary merger negotiations. Discussions of a possible merger began between Basic and Combustion Engineering in late 1976. Basic made three public statements in the period between 1977 and 1978 denying that it was engaged in such negotiations. When a merger agreement ultimately was reached in late 1978, former Basic shareholders, who had sold their stock between the date of Basic's first denial of corporate developments and the suspension of trading in late 1978, brought a class action suit against Basic and its board of directors. They alleged that Basic had issued materially false or misleading statements in violation of section 10(b) of the 1934 Act and Rule 10b-5.

After adopting the *TSC Industries* standard of materi-ality for cases arising under Rule 10b-5, the Supreme Court held that a finding of materiality based on contin-gent or speculative information or events depends "upon a balancing of both the indicated probability that the event will occur and the anticipated magnitude of the event in light of the totality of the company activity." The materiality of particular merger discussions is, therefore, a question of fact to be assessed in light of "indicia of interest in the transaction at the highest cor-porate levels." Thus, a plaintiff must show that the state-ments were misleading as to a material fact in order to succeed on a Rule 10b-5 claim. "It is not enough that a statement is false or incomplete, if the misrepresented fact is otherwise insignificant." An omitted fact is mate-rial if there is a substantial likelihood that the investor would consider it important in making an investment decision.

c. Scienter

After establishing the existence of a material omis-sion or misrepresentation, it becomes necessary, in proving a violation of the 1934 Act, to demonstrate that the defendant made the omission or misrepresen-tation with scienter. The idea of reckless scienter, as opposed to negligence, in securities fraud cases was enunciated by the Supreme Court in *Ernst & Ernst v. Hochfelder*. In *In re American Continental Corp./ Lincoln Savings and Loan Sec. Litig.*, the Ninth Cir-cuit adopted the prevalent standard for reckless scien-ter as an extreme departure from ordinary care which presents a danger for misleading buyers or sellers of which the actors must have been aware. In denying Touche Ross and Co.'s motions to dismiss, the *Ameri-can Continental Corp.* court found that certain evi-dence, such as knowledge acquired from Lincoln's directors, and knowledge of public skepticism about American Continental Corp. bore on the element of reckless scienter.

d. Reliance

In *List v. Fashion Park, Inc.*, the Second Circuit articulated a test for reliance which requires a showing that the plaintiff would have acted differently if the truth was made known.

Subsequent decisions have created two exceptions to this rule. The first is found in *Affiliated Ute Citizens of Utah v. United States*, where a rebuttable presumption of reliance is created if the defendant fails to disclose a material fact. The second exception, first enunciated by the Ninth Circuit in *Blackie v. Barrack*, is based on a "fraud on the market" theory and expands the scope of *Affiliated Ute* to cover material misrepresentations that adversely affect the market price of stock traded in efficient markets.

The United States Supreme Court first adopted the fraud on the market theory in *Basic, Inc. v. Levinson* when it applied the theory to a material public misrepresentation. According to *Basic*, the plaintiff must prove five elements before invoking a presumption of reliance. Plaintiff must allege and prove: (1) that the defendant made public misrepresentations; (2) that the misrepresentations were material; (3) that the shares were traded on an efficient market; (4) that the misrepresentations would induce a reasonable, relying investor to misjudge the value of the shares; and (5) that the plaintiff traded the shares between the time the misrepresentations were made and the time the truth was revealed.

The statute of limitations period for Section 10(b) actions is a combination of a one-year period after discovery of the violations and a three-year period in which to discover the violations to be applied retroactively to all pending litigation. This prompted Congress to pass Section 476 of the Federal Deposit Insurance Corporation Improvement Act of 1991 which amends Section 27A of the 1934 Act and reestablishes pre-*Lampf* limitations for cases pending on the date *Lampf* was decided. Section 27(A)(b) allowed for actions dismissed under *Lampf*'s retroactivity rule to be reinstated within sixty days of December 19, 1991.

2. Insider Trading

Insider trading regulations prohibit the use of material, nonpublic information in the purchase and sale of securities. SEC enforcement actions and the Insider Trading Sanctions Act of 1984 ("ITSA") have expanded the scope of insider trading liability. However, no legislative definition of insider trading exists. Commentators claim that the lack of a clear definition of "insider trading" causes inefficient enforcement under ITSA. The purpose of ITSA is to authorize the SEC to seek civil penalties equal to treble the profit gained, or loss avoided, from the insider's illegal trading. In particular, ITSA made it unlawful to purchase or sell a security while in possession of material nonpublic information.

Initially, liability for illegal trading fell only upon "corporate insiders," such as majority stockholders or corporate officers. Since the Supreme Court decided *Chiarella v. United States*, courts have extended liability to various fiduciary relationships. Unlike corporate insiders, non-traditional insiders do not face prosecution under section 10(b) of the 1934 Act for possessing material nonpublic information. In *Dirks v. SEC*, the Supreme Court held that a broker-dealer was not liable for disclosure of information to a third party unless he expected some personal gain.

Criminal defendants have challenged the criminalization of insider trading under Section 10(b) and Rule 10b-5. The defendants have based their claims on the absence of language in the legislative history of Section 10(b) and Rule 10-5 concerning insider trading, and the fact that Congress did not criminalize short swing trading by insiders in Section 16(b), but merely imposed strict liability. Addressing such a challenge, one district court rejected defendant's claim stating that an exception was not carved out by Section 16(b) because it does not apply to the same conduct. Section 16(b) requires no showing of fraud while Section 10(b) and Rule 10-5 solely cover fraud.

The cases following *Chiarella* may be divided into two categories. The first group of cases focuses on a traditional duty to disclose. The Ninth Circuit delineated five factors to consider in determining whether a duty to disclose exists. These are: "(1) the relationship of the parties; (2) relative access to the information; (3) the benefit defendant derives from the relationship; (4) the defendant's awareness that the plaintiff was relying upon the relationship in making his investment decision; and (5) the defendant's activity in initiating the transaction." The defendant's duty to disclose or abstain from trading arises from a fiduciary relationship.

The second group of cases is based on the controversial "misappropriation theory," adopted by the Second, Third, Seventh, and Ninth Circuits. The misappropriation theory originated in Chief Justice Burger's dissenting opinion in *Chiarella*. The Chief Justice distinguished between information obtained through "hard work, careful analysis, and astute forecasting" and that obtained through an illegal act. From this distinction, a body of case law has developed in which individuals with no fiduciary relationship with either the issuer of securities or buyers and sellers in the marketplace are nonetheless liable under Rule 10b-5 as if they were insiders.

The Supreme Court gave support to the misappropriation theory in *Dirks v. SEC*. Footnote fourteen of the decision states that the duty to disclose or abstain could attach to persons who might not traditionally be considered corporate "insiders" but who have temporary access to the same "inside" information. Such "temporary insiders" could include underwriters, consultants, lawyers, or accountants. Courts have held that the principal of a securities firm and financial consultants may also qualify as "temporary insiders."

Generally, courts have applied the misappropriation theory where an individual breaches a fiduciary duty to an employer or to beneficiaries of the employer's business. In *Rothberg v. Rosenbloom*, the Third Circuit applied the misappropriation theory to corporate insiders who purchased stock of an acquisition target. The court held the insiders liable for violations of Rule 10b-5 because an "insider on either side of [a] proposed transaction violates the insider trading rule when he uses insider information in violation of the fiduciary owed to the corporation." To date, the Second Circuit has only applied the misappropriation theory to fiduciary relationships in employment settings.

One year after *Chiarella* was decided, the Second Circuit, in *United States v. Newman*, upheld a Rule 10b-5 charge against an investment bank employee who traded on valuable information he received as a result of his employment. In *Newman*, the court held that the defendant breached a duty to his employer by injuring the reputation of the investment banking firm as a trustworthy repository of clients' confidential information. Under this rationale, the court found sufficient evidence to sustain the Rule 10b-5 charge.

The Second Circuit has expanded the misappropriation theory to include other fiduciary relationships. In *SEC v. Materia*, the Court found that a financial printer who traded on the basis of material, non-public information discovered in tender offer documents had committed securities fraud. Specifically, the court held that the defendant violated a fiduciary duty to the tender offeror. The Second Circuit also found a breach of fiduciary duty by a newspaper columnist in *United States v. Carpenter*. Columnist R. Foster Winans passed on prepublication information about stocks he intended to feature in the *Wall Street Journal*'s "Heard on the Street," a column which predicted the success or failure of particular stocks. In this celebrated case, the court decided that the misappropriation theory encompassed Winans' breach of confidentiality and that application of the theory furthered "the purposes and policies underlying Section 10(b) and Rule 10b-5."

In the wake of the *Carpenter* decision, Congress passed the Insider Trading and Securities Fraud Enforcement Act of 1988 ("ITSFEA"). Although Congress still has not promulgated a definition of insider trading, ITSFEA has substantially enhanced the SEC's ability to combat insider trading. The SEC is now permitted to seek civil penalties against employers who "knew or recklessly disregarded the fact" that a controlled person was likely to engage in insider trading "and failed to take appropriate steps to prevent such act or acts." The civil penalties are the greater of $1,000,000, or three times the profit gained or loss avoided because of the violation. The maximum criminal penalties are a $1,000,000 fine ($2,500,000 for corporations) and/or ten years imprisonment. In addition, the legislative history of ITSFEA endorses the misappropriation theory, stating that it "should be encompassed within Section 10(b) and Rule 10b-5."

When found liable under Rule 10b-5, defendants may seek contribution to alleviate the penalties assigned. In *Musick, Peeler & Garrett, et al. v. Employers Insurance of Wassau, et al.*, the Supreme Court has recently held that defendants have a right to seek contribution as a matter of federal law.

An additional change made by ITSFEA is a uniform five year limitation period for private actions brought by contemporaneous traders under new section 20A of the 1934 Act. ITSFEA imposed a five year limitation period in section 21A(d)(5) for SEC actions seeking civil penalties for insider trading. The limitations period enunciated in *Lampf, Pleva, Lipkind, Prupis & Petigrow v. Gilbertson* applies to Rule 10b-5 actions and is a one-and-three year structure. The Supreme Court rejected the argument finding that the five year limitation period of ITSFEA was the most analogous limitation period for Rule 10b-5 claims.

The case law since *Carpenter* has utilized the misappropriation theory even though the Court was evenly divided on the issue in that case. One example is *SEC v. Clark*, in which the court stated that "the misappropriation theory is the appropriate standard to determine whether . . . [the defendant] had a duty to disclose . . . or refrain from trading." Misappropriation theory was further expanded in *SEC v. Musella* to cover remote tippees who had never known the identity of the original tipper.

The misappropriation theory has expanded the class of defendants well beyond traditional insiders. For example, one court has imposed liability under Rule 10b-5 upon a partner of a law firm for trading based on confidential client information. Another court, in *United States v. Willis*, imposed liability upon a psychiatrist who traded on information received during a counseling session. In *Willis*, Joan Weill, wife of Sanford Weill, the former chief executive officer of Shearson Loeb Rhoads, told Willis that her husband received a commitment to invest one billion dollars in Bank America. Willis then bought stock in the company based on the information and passed the tip to several other customers. The court found Willis liable under Rule 10b-5 by applying the misappropriation theory.

Where there is no existing duty to disclose, courts have refrained from finding liability when an individual simply remains silent about undisclosed, material facts. The Fourth Circuit in *Schatz v. Rosenberg* stated, "Silence, absent a duty to disclose, does not violate section 10(b) and Rule 10b-5." In that case, defendant purchased an interest in plaintiffs' company using promissory notes that misrepresented his financial condition. Plaintiffs argued that defendant's lawyers violated a duty to disclose under the federal securities laws. However, the court found that defendant's lawyers were not liable under section 10(b).

In *Lorenz v. CSX Corp.*, the Third Circuit held that there was no duty of disclosure between a corporation and its debenture-holders. Unlike shareholders, debenture holders and a corporation share a contractual, and not a fiduciary, relationship. The court found no liability under section 10(b) for nondisclosure since the corporate defendant did not breach any terms of the indenture.

During the past several years while the courts were fashioning different theories of securities fraud, both the SEC and Congress created new provisions for the prosecution of insider trading. In direct response to the Supreme Court's holding in *Chiarella*, the SEC promulgated Rule 14e-3 to prevent insider trading in the area of tender offers. This rule prohibits anyone with nonpublic information concerning a tender offer from trading on that information if the trader knows or should know the source is the offeror or subject of the tender offer. The rule also makes it unlawful to "tip" information about a tender offer. Notwithstanding the relatively clear language of Rule 14e-3, it has not been completely effective as a means of eliminating insider trading because it applies only to tender offers.

Although the misappropriation theory and Rule 14e-3 broaden the scope of who might be a potential defendant, treatment of family interactions as fiduciary relationships is still subject to debate. The Second Circuit did not extend the misappropriation theory to nontraditional fiduciary relationships. The Sixth Circuit similarly does not impose a fiduciary duty on family relationships.

Other courts expand the misappropriation theory to cover cases where information was obtained through family relationships and the evidence was mainly circumstantial. In *SEC v. Hellberg*, a jury found the father of a corporate insider guilty of insider trading. *SEC v. Saul* provides a similar illustration. The defendant, the son of a chairman of a target corporation and the tender offeror, was charged with passing information to a friend who traded on the information, knowing that the son breached a duty to his father.

3. Parking

Another growing area in the prosecution of securities fraud is "parking." Loosely defined, parking is "the sale of securities subject to an agreement or understanding that they will be repurchased by the seller at a later time" without shifting the economic risk to the buyer. A court will typically consider five factors in determining whether or not the parties have entered into a parking arrangement: (1) whether the trading of securities was settled in the ordinary course of business; (2) whether there were restrictions on resale of the securities; (3) which party bore the risk of loss; (4) whether the sales were made at market price; and (5) whether there was an "arms-length" transaction.

Although the focus on parking has increased dramatically since the Wall Street insider trading scandal in 1988, the offense is not new. The Second Circuit considered parking in *United States v. Corr*, which involved criminal prosecution of a broker-dealer for conspiracy to violate the securities laws. In the past, parking cases have focused on the use of parking to avoid net capital and margin rules, and the beneficial ownership reporting requirements of section 13(d) of the 1934 Act.

SEC v. Bilzerian illustrates the potential for violations of the margin rules and recording requirements through parking. Defendant Bilzerian allegedly entered into a secret parking arrangement with an employee of Jefferies & Company ("Jefferies"). Pursuant to the arrangement, Jefferies acquired and held securities of Cluett Peabody & Company, Inc. ("Cluett") for Bilzerian's benefit. Bilzerian allegedly acquired the Cluett stock for the purpose of obtaining greenmail from Cluett or to induce Cluett to enter into a "White Knight" arrangement. The complaint alleged that by entering into the accumulation scheme, Bilzerian aided and abetted Jefferies's violation of the margin rules that govern the amount of credit a broker-dealer may extent to each customer. The SEC further alleged that Bilzerian, in engaging in parking arrangements with Jefferies to establish fraudulent tax losses in connection with the common stock of Armco Inc. and H.H. Robertson Co., aided and abetted Jefferies' violations of the margin and books and records rules.

In *SEC v. Kidder, Peabody & Co.*, the SEC argued that a corporation avoided minimum net capital requirements of Rule 15c-1 through parking. Defendant Kidder, Peabody entered into a consent of final judgment in an action alleging that it effected "non-bonafide purchases of" (that is, parked) securities from

Seemala Corporation, the broker-dealer entity controlled by Ivan Boesky. As a result, Seemala allegedly avoided the minimum net capital requirements. The transaction was characterized as non-bona fide because Seemala agreed to "buy back the same securities ['sold' at a particular time and] receive all profits or sustain all losses." Further, Kidder, Peabody was to receive unusually high commissions for the accommodation. Kidder, Peabody was also charged with violating the margin rules by engaging in the parking arrangement, and allegedly extending credit to Seemala in an amount greater than fifty percent of the fair market value of those shares.

Courts have also found liability where defendants failed to comply with disclosure requirements under section 13(d) of the 1934 Act and Rule 13d-1, promulgated thereunder.

Numerous penalties are available when a defendant is convicted in a parking scheme. Violators can be enjoined from further violations of section 13(d) and Rule 13d-1, and be "disgorged" of all profits received in the parking scheme.

4. Broker-Dealer Fraud

The prosecution of broker-dealers has been considered in the previous sections on misrepresentations and omissions, insider trading, and parking. As professionals in the securities market, broker-dealers' exposure to fraud actions is necessarily greater than that of other participants in the market. Broker-dealers are subject to stricter controls by virtue of their being in the field—the so-called "shingle theory." The shingle theory first arose out of SEC administrative enforcement proceedings in *Duker v. Duker*. In *Duker*, the Commission recognized that

> [i]nherent in the relationship between a dealer and his customer is the vital representation that the customer will be dealt with fairly and in accordance with the standard of the profession. It is neither fair dealing, nor in accordance with such standards, to exploit trust and ignorance for profit far higher than might be realized from an informed customer.

This broad standard for liability was approved by the Second Circuit four years later in *Charles Hughes & Co. v. SEC*.

In the context of Rule 10b-5, the shingle theory allows a presumption that a broker represents that his recommendations to buy or sell have an adequate basis, and that a particular security is suitable for the investor. Under this theory, the broker will be liable for knowingly and recklessly engaging in excessive trading in customers' accounts, for accepting funds when he is insolvent, and for manipulating the market.

When a securities broker excessively "buys and sells securities without regard to the customer's investment objectives in order to generate commissions," that broker has engaged in "churning." Churning is a deceptive act which is specifically outlawed by section 10(b) of the 1934 Act and actionable under Rule 10b-5. Churning violates Rule 10b-5 where it operates as a scheme to defraud. The main elements comprising a churning offense are (1) that the broker exercised control over the trading in the account; (2) that the amount of trading was excessive in light of the character of the account, and, when action is brought under Rule 10b-5; (3) the broker must act with intent to defraud or with willful and reckless disregard for the investor's interests (scienter).

In order to sustain a cause of action for churning, the investor must prove that a fiduciary relationship existed-by proving, as a matter of fact, either that the broker had control of the account, or that the account in question was discretionary. In the case of a non-discretionary account, the investor must prove that the investor has "usurped control over a technically non-discretionary account." A broker-dealer accused of churning may have a defense if it can be shown that the customer consented to the trading. The burden of proof is on the investor to show that she did not have the opportunity to consent or that she did not possess the experience, sophistication or "requisite skill" with the market needed to meaningfully consent. The fact that a customer received trade confirmations may be evidence of consent, but it is not dispositive. The difficulty arises because the customer has placed her trust in the broker; the customer essentially has consented to the broker's exercise of expertise. Some factors considered by the court are: whether the client is young, old or naive regarding financial matters; if the broker received prior approval of customer; and the investor's educational level.

One developing area in the regulation of churning is the standard by which "excessiveness" is determined. Excessiveness of trading must be determine in the light of character and objectives of the account and owner. One factor of churning is a high turn-over rate on the account. One problem with turnover rate, despite its easy calculation, is that courts are not always sure what to do with the number once it is calculated. The plaintiff has the burden of setting forth the facts with particularity in the pleadings to demonstrate excessive trading; the plaintiff must specifically plead what factors were compared when arriving at the conclusion that trading was excessive. Another indicator of churning is the ratio of the broker's commission to the size of the account. The most important factor is whether it can be proven that the broker engaged in heavy trading for the express purpose of making a profit without any regard for the customer – that is, that the broker acted with scienter.

Prior to the Supreme Court's decision in *Ernst & Ernst v. Hochfelder,* proof of churning did not require a showing that the broker acted with any fraudulent intent. By definition, churning is a scheme to defraud. The *Hochfelder* decision, however, made scienter a necessary element of all actions under Rule 10b-5. A person acts with scienter when she acts knowingly or willfully to commit the fraud. In a churning claim, it is sufficient to prove that the defendant acted with reckless disregard for the interests of the customer. Fraud by conduct is a violation of Rule 10b-5(a) and (c) and is analogous to a churning claim. Noting the similarity between churning and unsuitability claims, the Tenth Circuit employed churning elements in its formulation of the elements for an unsuitability cause of action: (1) the broker recommended (or, in the case of a discretionary account, purchased) securities which are unsuitable in light of the investor's objectives; (2) the broker recommended or purchased the securities with an intent to defraud or with reckless disregard for the investor's interests; and (3) the broker exercised control over the investor's account.

TAX EVASION

I. I.R.C. SECTION 7201

Violations of the United States Internal Revenue Code ("IRC") are prosecuted under an array of criminal tax statutes. The "capstone of [this] system of sanctions" is the felony provision of 26 U.S.C. § 7201, which provides for a maximum penalty of $100,000 and/or a prison term of five years for a willful attempt to defeat any tax obligation.

A. *Elements of the Offense*

In order to prove a section 7201 offense, the government must prove three elements: (1) the existence of a tax deficiency; (2) an affirmative act constituting an evasion or attempted evasion of the tax; and (3) willfulness. The government bears the burden of proving each element beyond a reasonable doubt. Once a prima facie case is established, however, the burden shifts to the taxpayer, and "the taxpayer 'remains quiet at his peril.'"

1. *Existence of a Tax Deficiency*

Generally, for a defendant to be convicted under section 7201, the amount of tax deficiency must be "substantial." The term "substantial" refers to the "amount of the tax evaded" and not to the amount of income unreported; thus, the government cannot secure a conviction by transferring its proof of a taxpayer's willful failure to pay an insubstantial deficiency to apply to that same taxpayer's inadvertent failure to pay a substantial deficiency.

The existence of a deficiency may be shown by several methods using either direct or circumstantial evidence. The most accurate means of proving a deficiency is the "specific item" method in which the taxpayer's books and records are used as direct proof of taxable transactions. However, "[p]roof of unreported taxable income by direct means is extremely difficult and often impossible." Therefore, the government usually relies on circumstantial evidence to establish the existence of unreported taxable income. Three methods are used: net worth, cash expenditures, and bank deposits. These circumstantial methods do not require the government to prove either the exact amount of the deficiency or its source. The government may choose to prosecute under any single theory of proof or a combination method, including a combination of circumstantial and direct proofs.

The "net worth" prosecution is the most common method of establishing tax evasion. In it,

> the Government, having concluded that the taxpayer's records are inadequate as a basis for determining income tax liability, attempts to establish an "opening net worth" or total net value of the taxpayer's assets at the beginning of a given year. It then proves increases in the taxpayer's net worth for each succeeding year during the period under examination and calculates the difference between the adjusted net values of the taxpayer's assets at the beginning and end of each of the years involved. The taxpayer's nondeductible expenditures, including living expenses, are added to these increases, and if the resulting figure for any year is substantially greater than the taxable income reported by the taxpayer for that year, the Government claims the excess represents unreported taxable income.

It is essential that the government's analysis establish the taxpayer's opening net worth with "reasonable certainty," although it is not necessary to establish with certainty the opening net worth for each of the subsequent years under investigation. The government must also demonstrate that it has conducted a thorough investigation and has negated reasonable alternative sources of nontaxable income. Clear charges and formal instructions outlining the range of permissible inferences both for and against the accused are required.

The "cash expenditures" method is a "simple variant of the 'net worth method'" and requires a showing that the taxpayer's expenditures were derived from taxable income which exceeded the taxpayer's reported income. The government must demonstrate either a "likely source of the unreported income or that it has negated all reasonable nontaxable sources of income." Unlike the net worth method, the cash expenditures method does not require preparation of a formal net worth statement for the period under investigation.

Similar jury instructions are required for both the net worth and the cash expenditures methods.

Finally, under the "bank deposits" method, all non-taxable deposits and amounts deposited in prior years are excluded from the analysis of whether there is a tax deficiency for the year of the tax return being investigated. "[T]he jury is entitled to infer that the difference between the balance of deposited items and reported income constitutes unreported income." As with the cash expenditures method, the government need not prepare a formal net worth statement but must demonstrate that it conducted a full investigation into sources of income. Formal jury instructions on the scope of proper inferences are required.

2. Affirmative Act Constitution Evasion

The Supreme Court has interpreted the second element of section 7201 offenses to require a "positive attempt to evade . . . or defeat" any tax rather than merely "passive neglect." Thus an affirmative act to evade tax must be a commission, rather than an omission. The United States Supreme Court stated that the "Affirmative act" language should be construed broadly to include, *inter alia*: filing false returns, keeping a double set of books, making false entries or alterations, making false invoices or documents, destroying books or records, concealing assets or covering up sources of income, avoiding making records usually kept for transactions or conduct where the likely effect would be to mislead or to conceal.

3. Willfulness

To prove willfulness under section 7201, the government must make "a showing of specific wrongful intent to avoid a known legal duty." The government must demonstrate more than carelessness on the part of the defendant, but it does not necessarily need to show bad faith. The defendant's belief regarding the applicability of a legal duty is a question of fact. Consequently, even an objectively unreasonable misunderstanding of the law negates a finding of willfulness if the jury believes it.

Willfulness is inferred from both the surrounding circumstances and the defendant's affirmative acts of evasion, and "proof of willfulness is usually accomplished by means of circumstantial evidence." When applied, this inference often leads to a blurring of the distinction between willfulness and affirmative acts.

II. I.R.C. Section 7202

Internal Revenue Code Section 7202, which criminalizes both the willful failure to collect taxes and the willful failure to account truthfully for and pay over taxes, is invoked less frequently than the other criminal provisions of Title 26. Prosecutions for conduct punishable under section 7202 are frequently brought under the parallel civil provision, 26 U.S.C. § 6672 because the civil statute has a less stringent willfulness requirement than the criminal provision.

A. Willful Failure to Collect Tax

The crime of willful failure to collect or pay over a tax requires proof of three elements: (1) a legal duty to collect, account for, and pay over a tax; (2) a failure to collect that tax; and (3) willfulness. Prosecutions for willful failure to collect a tax are relatively infrequent because most employers are conscientious about withholding the statutorily required amounts from employees wages, but are merely negligent in paying over such amounts to the government.

B. Willful Failure to Account For and Pay Over Tax

The crime of willful failure to truthfully account for and pay over a tax has four elements: (1) a legal duty to collect, account for, and pay over tax; (2) a failure to truthfully account for that tax; (3) a failure to pay over that tax; and (4) willfulness. Failure to truthfully account for and pay over a tax is a separate offense from the crime of failure to collect a tax. The crime is committed when a company withholds taxes from employees' paychecks but does not account for and does not pay over the withheld amount to the government at the end of the quarter.

The typical situation where section 7202 is violated occurs when an employer uses funds withheld for tax purposes to pay other bills or to enable his company to continue in operation, and later the employer's hope that he will be able to repay the funds at the end of the quarter does not materialize. If an employer seeks protection from its creditors, including the Internal Revenue Services, by declaring bankruptcy, the tax liability against the responsible officers will remain.

C. Elements of the Offense

1. Duty to Collect and Withhold

The legal duty to collect, account for and pay over taxes is consistent for both felonies of section 7202. Sections 3102(a) and 3402(a) require, respectively, that an employer deduct from wages paid to an employee the employee's share of Federal Insurance Contributions Act ("FICA") taxes and the applicable withholding tax on the wages, so that "the amount retained as taxes never leaves the employer's possession." The withheld sums are commonly referred to as "trust fund taxes" because section 7501 requires the employer to keep these withheld amounts in a "special fund in trust for the United States." The employer is treated as trustee of these funds, bearing the responsibility of transmitting to the Internal Revenue Service the taxes that are owed by his employees. An agreement between the employer and employees that the employees will pay "their own FICA and withholding taxes does not affect the employer's statutory obligation." Once net wages are paid to the employee, the taxes withheld are credited to the employee regardless of whether the employer actually pays them to the government, and the employee is not liable for any additional payment.

There is no general requirement that the employer separate the withheld sums from the rest of his funds until the payment of taxes is made to the Treasury. Because the employer is required to collect taxes from each payment of wages but is required to pay these taxes only quarterly, there is a strong temptation for unethical employers to use such funds for business or personal purposes. To prevent illegal use of withheld funds by an employer, the Internal Revenue Service can order the withholder to open a special bank account into which the withholder must deposit all "collected" taxes within two days after collection. An employer is unlikely to use these trust funds to maintain his business because of the severe liability imposed by section 6672 as well as the severity of a felony conviction under section 7202.

All elements of employment compensation are included in the definition of wages. An employer who withholds the proper amount from paychecks disbursed to employees, but does not account for or withhold the proper amount from a secondary element of the employees' compensation may be found guilty of a violation of section 7202.

Determination of a legal duty under section 7202 turns upon whether a person qualifies as an employer. Standing alone, the fact that one has withheld taxes from, and paid the appropriate federal taxes on the earnings of workers does not necessarily justify the inference of an employer-employee relationship. The existence of an employer-employee relationship is determined primarily by examining whether "the person for whom the work is done has the right to control the manner and method of performing the work, as well as the result to be accomplished." It is not necessary that the employer actually exercise this control; he simply must have the right to do so.

Once an employer-employee relationship has been established, it is necessary to determine who within a given corporation, is the person responsible for compliance with section 7202. The Internal Revenue Code and the Treasury Regulations defining the duties of IRS agents do not provide a clear definition of a "responsible person" for purposes of section 7202. A

corporation's by-laws, the ability of a person to sign checks on a corporate bank account or to sign a corporate tax return, or the ability to control the corporation's financial affairs may identify a "responsible person" within the corporation.

An individual corporation may contain more than one responsible person, but the existence of other responsible persons within the corporation does not relieve any other party of individual duty. A person who is no longer employed by a company at the end of the quarter when the taxes are due is not immunized from responsibility. However, courts have exonerated otherwise responsible persons in some cases because of serious neglect by the government in pursuing the employer.

2. Failure to Collect Tax

An employer is subject to prosecution for a violation of section 7202 if he failed to collect taxes as required by a relevant section of the Internal Revenue Code.

3. Failure to Truthfully Account for Tax

Two conflicting views exist as to whether both failure to pay over the tax and failure to account for the tax are required to violate section 7202. One court has held that if a party who has a legal duty to pay over a tax fails to do so, but has accounted for the tax, the party may not be convicted under section 7202. Thus, if a responsible person files truthful returns setting forth the amounts owed, there can be no felony conviction under section 7202.

The government takes a contrary position, maintaining that the duty to account for and the duty to pay over constitute an "inseparable dual obligation" which, when violated in any respect, warrants prosecution under section 7202.

4. Failure to Pay Over

Once the employer has failed to pay over taxes, a subsequent payment of the taxes does not negate the violation, but the subsequent payment or intention to pay is relevant to the issue of willfulness.

5. Willfulness

To establish a violation of section 7202, the government must prove that the responsible person acted willfully. The meaning of "willful" in section 7202 overlaps with the definition found in the other criminal penalty provisions of Title 26, and requires a "voluntary, intentional violation of a known legal duty." Section 7202 requires that both the failure to truthfully account for and the failure to pay over the tax be willful.

III. I.R.C. Section 7203

Persons who have willfully failed to file their returns, supply information or pay their taxes may be prosecuted for a misdemeanor under section 7203 of Title 26. The government must prove beyond a reasonable doubt that a defendant willfully attempted to defeat or evade taxes.

A. *Elements of the Offense*

In order to establish a section 7203 offense, the government has the burden of proving four elements: (1) the defendant was required to file a return; (2) the defendant had knowledge of this requirement; (3) the defendant failed to file a return; and (4) the failure to file the return was willful.

1. *Requirement to File a Return*

A person who earns income must report and pay taxes on the taxable income. When determining whether a person is obliged to file an individual tax return for a particular year, only true income may be considered.

2. *Knowledge of Requirement*

Within the context of section 7203, a "knowing" failure is one which is voluntary and purposeful, and is not caused by mistake, inadvertence, or another innocent reason." Knowledge may be established by evidence of a letter from the IRS to the defendant which indicates that the IRS has not yet received a tax return for the tax year in question.

Evidence of previously-filed proper tax returns gives rise to an inference that a defendant has knowledge of a legal duty to file a proper tax return. Evidence of a taxpayer's subsequent filing of tax returns may also be used to establish knowledge of the requirement to file.

3. *Failure to File a Return*

The mere act of filing a return is not sufficient to avoid prosecution under section 7203. The failure to provide any information, or the act of providing insufficient information on an income tax return is equivalent to the failure to file a return.

4. *Willfulness*

To show "willfulness," the government must establish that the defendant's action was deliberate, intentional, and without justifiable excuse or, as otherwise stated, a voluntary, intentional violation of a known duty.

Courts are divided as to whether a showing of "bad purpose" or "evil motive" is required by the government to show "willfulness." Some courts have held that in the context of this section, "willfully" means a showing of bad faith or evil motive. Other courts have found that evil motive is not required for conviction under section 7203. Therefore, a good faith misunderstanding of the law may not be sufficient to establish a violation of this section. This mistake must be subjectively reasonable to be a defense.

However, neither a good faith disagreement with the goals and policies of the law, nor a good faith purpose of protecting United States' policies will negate willfulness. Similarly, an intent to report income and pay taxes in the future may not negate the willfulness requirement, nor will a defendant's good faith belief that he is not a "person" within the meaning of the statute.

The misdemeanor offense of failing to pay taxes when due and the felony offense of willfully attempting to evade or defeat taxes are distinguishable. To establish the felony offense, some affirmative action in addition to the willful omission must be proved. Therefore, a misdemeanor under section 7203 could be elevated to a section 7201 felony by a prior, concomitant or subsequent false statement.

IV. I.R.C. SECTION 7206

Internal Revenue Code Section 7206 enlarges the arsenal available to federal prosecutors to combat violations of federal tax regulations. There are two principal criminal provisions of section 7206: section 7206(1), the "tax perjury" statute, and section 7206(2), the "aiding and assisting" statute.

A. *Section 7206(1): Tax Perjury*

1. *Elements of the Offense*

The government must prove four elements to convict a taxpayer of violating section 7206(1): (1) the taxpayer made and signed a false return or document; (2) the document contained a written and signed declaration that it was completed under penalty of perjury; (3) the return or document contained a material falsehood; and (4) the false statement was willfully made. To some degree, section 7206(1) parallels the general perjury statute, but it is less stringent in application.

a. *Signing a false return or document*

To prove this element, the government must show a false document was made and subscribed by the taxpayer. The taxpayer's "subscription" is essential to a prosecution under section 7206(1) because it establishes the swearing element necessary for a perjury charge. The taxpayer's signed name on a form establishes prima facie evidence the taxpayer himself signed the document. The taxpayer, however, is given the opportunity to rebut this presumption. While the courts on the one hand, have defined "making" and "subscribing" broadly with regard to third parties, on the other hand, they have construed these terms narrowly by not considering a document to be subscribed until it is filed with the IRS.

For venue purposes, a document can be considered "made" or "subscribed" in any district where an act occurred which contributed to the crime. Making false statements to IRS agents while in a particular district has been considered constructive subscription allowing venue in that district.

b. Penalty of perjury

The tax document must contain a declaration, made under penalty of perjury, declaring that subscription has been made. Current income tax filing forms, such as Form 1040, contain the requisite perjury statement, but a declaration is typically missing from supporting and corollary documents. Such documents are considered "verified by" the declaration contained on the main form. A taxpayer faces an uphill battle in claiming a particular document is unencumbered by a perjury declaration.

c. Falsity as to a material matter

The false information in the document must pertain to a material matter. Generally, a material matter includes a mis-statement regarding the amount of any income tax figure or an improper identification of a source of income. The materiality question bears no relation to the monetary amount involved. The court determines the materiality question as a matter of law.

d. Willfulness

Willfulness in the section 7206 context requires a voluntary, intentional violation of a known legal duty. The government is not required to prove that a defendant had intent to act with evil purpose or to evade taxes.

Willfulness can be established by circumstantial evidence demonstrating the defendant knew of the duty he violated. As a result, willfulness may be inferred from the mere existence of unreported or misreported tax information.

B. Conspiracy

Philip E. Johnson, *The Unnecessary Crime of Conspiracy*, 61 CAL. L. REV. 1137–1164, 1188 (1973)*

The literature on the subject of criminal conspiracy reflects a sort of rough consensus. Conspiracy, it is

---

* © 1973 by California Law Review Inc. Reprinted from California Law Review, Vol. 61, No. 5, (Sept. 1973), pp. 1137-1188, by permission.

generally said, is a necessary doctrine in some respects, but also one that is overbroad and invites abuse. Conspiracy has been thought to be necessary for one or both of two reasons. First, it is said that a separate offense of conspiracy is useful to supplement the generally restrictive law of attempts. Plotters who are arrested before they can carry out their dangerous schemes may be convicted of conspiracy even though they did not go far enough towards completion of their criminal plan to be guilty of attempt. Second, conspiracy is said to be a vital legal weapon in the prosecution of "organized crime," however defined. As Mr. Justice Jackson put it, "the basic conspiracy principle has some place in modern criminal law, because to unite, back of a criminal purpose, the strength, opportunities and resources of many is obviously more dangerous and more difficult to police than the efforts of a lone wrongdoer." To deal with such dangerous criminal combinations the government must have the benefit of special legal doctrines which make conviction easier and punishment more severe.

The overbreadth of conspiracy and its potential for abuse have been extensively discussed in the literature. One principal theme of criticism, best illustrated by Mr. Justice Jackson's opinion in *Krulewitch v. United States*, emphasizes the difficulties which the ordinary criminal defendant may face when charged with conspiracy. The advantages which conspiracy provides the prosecution are seen as disadvantages for the defendant so serious that they may lead to unfair punishment unfairly determined. Critics taking this approach typically propose to trim conspiracy doctrine just enough to provide protection for defense interests without disturbing those rules deemed genuinely important for effective law enforcement. The leading reform proposal of this type is the conspiracy section of the American Law Institute's Model Penal Code, some of whose reforms were incorporated in the proposed Federal Criminal Code now before the Senate Subcommittee on Criminal Laws and Procedures of the United States.

The other major line of criticism stresses the dangers that conspiracy law raised for first amendment freedoms. Prosecutions of political dissidents, including labor organizers, Communist Party leaders, and contemporary radicals, typically have been conspiracy prosecutions. The law of conspiracy is intended, after all, to make it easier to impose criminal punishment on members of groups that plot forbidden activity. Insofar as it accomplishes this end, it unavoidably increases the likelihood that persons will be punished for what they say rather than for what they do, or for associating with others who are found culpable. Critics who are alarmed at the resulting threat to freedom of speech and freedom of association typically have proposed new constitutional doctrines derived from the first amendment to curtail the use of conspiracy charges in cases having some "political" element.

Unfortunately, the proposals for legislative or constitutional reforms of conspiracy law are inadequate. It will not do simply to reform conspiracy legislatively by removing its most widely deplored overextensions, or to reform it judicially by engrafting new doctrines derived from the first amendment. Such measures are appropriate for improving a doctrine that is basically sound, but in need of some adjustment at the edges. The law of criminal conspiracy is not basically sound. It should be abolished, not reformed.

The central fault of conspiracy law and the reason why any limited reform is bound to be inadequate can be briefly stated. What conspiracy adds to the law is simply confusion, and the confusion is inherent in the nature of the doctrine. The confusion stems from the fact that conspiracy is not only a substantive inchoate crime in itself, but the touchstone for invoking several independent procedural and substantive doctrines. We ask whether a defendant agreed with another person to commit a crime initially for the purpose of determining whether he may be convicted of the offense of conspiracy even when the crime itself has not yet been committed. If the answer to that question is in the affirmative, however, we find that we have also answered a number of other questions that would otherwise have to be considered independently. Where there is evidence of conspiracy, the defendant may be tried jointly with his criminal partners and possibly with many other persons whom he has never met or seen, the joint trial may be held in a place he may never have visited, and hearsay statements of other alleged members of the conspiracy may be used to prove his guilt. Furthermore, a defendant who is found guilty of conspiracy is subject to enhanced punishment and may also be found guilty of any crime committed in furtherance of the conspiracy, whether or not he knew about the crime or aided in its commission.

Each of these issues involves a separate substantive or procedural area of the criminal law of considerable importance and complexity. The essential vice of conspiracy is that it inevitably distracts the courts from the policy questions or balancing of interests that ought to govern the decision of specific legal issues and leads them instead to decide those issues by reference to the conceptual framework of conspiracy. Instead of asking whether public policy or the interests of the parties requires a particular holding, the courts are led instead to consider whether the theory of conspiracy is broad enough to permit it. What is wrong with conspiracy, in other words, is much more basic than the overbreadth of a few rules. The problem is not with particular results, but with the use of a single abstract concept to decide numerous questions that deserve separate consideration in light of the various interests and policies they involve.

Although it is true that the confusion that conspiracy introduces into the law has an overall tendency to benefit the prosecution, sometimes it has the opposite effect. Occasionally, use of a conspiracy charge converts a relatively simple case into a monstrosity of conceptual complexity, giving the defense substantial grounds for an appeal. Furthermore, eliminating the substantive crime of conspiracy would not necessarily require the elimination of all the procedural rules that are now associated with it: at most it would require only that the rules be reconsidered on their own merits. In fact, many of these procedural rules are even now applicable in all criminal cases, whether conspiracy is charged or not.

The pages that follow will discuss the many roles of conspiracy in the criminal law and will argue that each of the problems with which conspiracy purports to deal could better be resolved by reference to other doctrines and principles. Conspiracy became the monster it now is by a process of judicial improvisation. Whatever may have been the justification for this patchwork process, the problems it meant to remedy can now be resolved by more specific doctrines with a firmer basis in policy. Hence it is particularly disappointing that the proposed Federal Criminal Code, like its predecessor the Model Penal Code, retains a general conspiracy doctrine. Both codes make an attempt at reform, but one may doubt whether these efforts will accomplish very much. The reforms touch mainly upon matters that are of little importance, while the major sources of abuse are left untouched. Moreover, the history of conspiracy to date, which is one of almost constant expansion, gives little reason to hope that any partial retrenchment will be lasting.

An analysis of conspiracy divides naturally into two parts: conspiracy as a set of substantive rules, and conspiracy as a set of procedural rules. The procedural rules associated with conspiracy doctrine are probably more important as a practical matter, although they purport to be no more than adjuncts to the substantive rules. Most of the theoretical discussion of conspiracy and most of the attempts to defend the doctrine, however, center upon the substantive rules.

The following discussion will concern itself primarily with federal law, although the arguments are equally relevant to questions of state law. Conspiracy prosecutions are especially prevalent in the federal courts, and most of the leading appellate cases are federal cases. In addition, the complete revision of the Federal Criminal Code now in progress offers an unusual opportunity to reappraise a basic doctrine that is no longer either necessary or desirable.

I.
THE SUBSTANTIVE DOCTRINES OF CONSPIRACY

The existing law of conspiracy contains several distinct substantive doctrines. Conspiracy is an inchoate crime, supplementing the law of attempt where more than one person is involved in plotting or preparing a crime. One is guilty of conspiring to commit a particular crime if, with the intention or purpose of furthering its commission, he agrees with some other person to commit it. Some jurisdictions require in addition that one or more of the conspirators have performed some overt act in furtherance of the criminal agreement, but this additional requirement adds little. Practically any act will do, including seemingly innocent conduct that carries the conspiracy no closer to accomplishing its object than the agreement itself. Moreover, an act by one alleged conspirator suffices for all.

Conspiracy is also a device for expanding the substantive criminal law and for enhancing punishment. In theory, at least, the object of a conspiracy need not be a crime: it is criminal to conspire to commit a civil wrong, or to do anything else that is immoral or dangerous to the public health and safety. Even where the object of the agreement is criminal, the penalty for conspiracy may be higher than the penalty for the completed crime; for instance in some jurisdictions conspiracy to commit a misdemeanor is a felony. Furthermore, if conspirators actually carry out the crime they agree to commit, they may be convicted and sentenced for both the conspiracy and for the substantive crime. All these rules are said to be based on the theory that combinations of wrongdoers are more dangerous than individual offenders. Hence, the argument goes, wrongful conduct by such combinations should be criminally punished even when the same acts would be excused if performed by an individual; likewise, group criminal conduct calls for enhanced punishment.

Finally, conspiracy provides a means of expanding the law of complicity in crime. It is difficult to convict leaders of organized crime because they direct the affairs of the organization from a distance, carefully avoiding direct involvement in the specific acts of unlawful betting, drug selling, or the like from which they derive their income. If their power to direct the entire enterprise can be proved, however, they can be convicted of conspiring to violate the gambling or drug laws without proof that they participated directly in placing bets or selling drugs. Furthermore, each participant in a conspiracy is criminally liable for all the crimes committed by any of the participants in furtherance of the common enterprise, even if he would not otherwise be liable as an accessory. Conspiracy thus permits any member of a large-scale organization to be punished for all the crimes committed by its members.

One rarely sees a defense of existing conspiracy law as it has just been described. For example, no informed body of opinion today supports the rule that a conspiracy may be criminally punishable even if its object is only a civil wrong, or some other form of conduct that would not be criminal if undertaken by an individual. Arguably, some conduct which does not threaten the interests of society when a lone individual engages in it should nevertheless be prohibited when carried on by a group. Indeed, certain forbidden acts, such as agreement by competitors to fix prices, by definition require concerted action. It hardly follows, however, that courts should have the authority to declare concerted activity criminal whenever they find it immoral, wrongful, or violative of some principle of tort or contract law. It seems impossible to reconcile such discretionary criminal liability with the constitutional prohibition against overly broad or vague criminal statutes. Constitutional problems aside, there is simply no need for a modern, comprehensive penal code to place such broad legislative authority in the courts. The legislature can easily enact more specific statutes stating the types of concerted activity to be held criminal.

In federal law, this "unlawful purpose" doctrine has been implemented in the offense of "conspiracy to defraud the United States." The courts have held that agreements to defraud the government are punishable even when the particular method of fraud contemplated by the conspirators would not have been criminal if committed by a single person. This offense evolved through judicial improvisation in a period when there were few specific federal statutes aimed at fraudulent practices. Today, when there are too many specific prohibitions rather than too few, it is plainly obsolete. The proposed Federal Criminal Code accordingly punishes only agreements to commit or to cause the commission of crimes.

Statutes which punish conspiracy to commit a misdemeanor as a felony, or otherwise punish the agreement to commit a crime more severely than the crime itself, are probably also obsolete. The theory underlying such statutes is the "group danger" rationale: that persons who combine to commit petty crimes are more dangerous than those who commit them individually. The individual prostitute or bettor certainly poses less of a threat to the interests of society than the organizer of a gambling or prostitution business, but a general conspiracy doctrine is an inexcusably clumsy way to provide increased punishment for the latter. Conspiracy makes the individual prostitute or bettor just as much a felon as the professional manager, since both agree to commit the offense in questions. Moreover, one does not have to be involved in any continuing criminal activity to be a conspirator. Two boys planning to joyride in an automobile are just as much conspirators as two organized crime chieftains managing a large-scale gambling operation. One would expect any modern penal code revision to relate the penalty for conspiracy directly to the penalty for the most serious substantive offense contemplated in the agreement, and to provide in specific sections for increased penalties for persons who organize or direct minor crimes on a continuing basis.

In other respects the substantive rules of conspiracy cannot be so easily dismissed. Conspiracy retains great vitality today as a device for establishing one defendant's complicity in the crimes of another, as a means to obtain enhanced penalties through consecutive sentencing, as an alternative to prosecution for the specific substantive offenses committed by the conspirators, and as an inchoate or preparatory crime. Yet each of these roles of conspiracy could well be abolished without adversely affecting any legitimate law enforcement interests, and with a net gain in the clarity and simplicity of the criminal law.

A. *Conspiracy as a Rule of Complicity*

One who enters into a conspiratorial relationship is liable for every reasonably foreseeable crime committed by every other member of the conspiracy in furtherance of its objectives, whether or not he knew of the crimes or aided in their commission. The Model Penal Code rejected this rule, leaving one conspirator's responsibility for the criminal conduct of another to its general provision on complicity. Early drafts of the proposed Federal Criminal Code took the same position, but the most current draft provides specifically that "a person may be convicted of an offense based upon the conduct of another person when . . . the offense charged was committed in furtherance of a criminal conspiracy and was a reasonably foreseeable consequence of it."

At first glance, the conspiracy-complicity rule seems to add little to the law of complicity or accessorial liability. No one would question that all the persons who plot together to commit a crime are guilty of the crime if one or more of them commits it. Some authorities limit the accomplice's liability to those crimes of the principal which he intended to assist or encourage. Many other authorities, however, have indulged in the legal fiction that one intends the natural and probable consequences of his acts, and thus have

held the accomplice for the crimes of the principal which he should have foreseen but perhaps did not. In any case, the felony murder doctrine imposes liability for unintended consequences in the most common situations: every member of a robbery or burglary gang is liable for any killing committed by any member in the course of the robbery or burglary.

The difficulty lies not in the conspiracy-complicity rule itself, but in the tendency of courts to regard a conspiracy as an ongoing business relationship of indefinite scope and duration, and to consider the conspirators, as one dissenting opinion put it, as "general partners in crime." For example, the defendant in *Anderson v. Superior Court* referred several pregnant women to an abortionist and received a portion of his fees. For this the court held her to have entered into a conspiracy with him to commit abortions generally, and to be liable for subsequent abortions in which she played no part. In the famous cases of *United States v. Bruno*, the circuit court of appeals ruled that a single, immense conspiracy to distribute narcotics included smugglers, middlemen, and retail sellers operating in two different parts of the country. Although the defendants were charged only with conspiracy, in theory the holding implied that each smuggler was guilty of every retail sale and each retailer of every act of smuggling, a pyramiding of liability that seems to be justified by no conceivable penological principle.

The fundamental conceptual error that leads to such absurd results, however, is not the conspiracy-complicity rule itself but rather the assumption that all the major and minor participants in a criminal enterprise are guilty of the same conspiracy. Once it is established that all participants conspired generally to further all the crimes of the organization, it is not surprising that they each should be held responsible for all of the crimes actually committed in furtherance of that agreement. Reforms which would abolish the conspiracy-complicity rule without also abandoning the principle that all participants in a conspiracy are guilty of the same crime of conspiracy are basically inconsistent. The discussion of *People v. Luciano* in the Model Penal Code commentary exemplifies this inconsistency:

> Luciano and others were convicted of sixty-two counts of compulsory prostitution, each count involving a specific instance of placing a girl in a house of prostitution, receiving money for so doing or receiving money for the earnings of a prostitute, acts proved to have been done pursuant to a combination to control commercialized vice in New York City. The liability was properly imposed with respect to these defendants, who directed and controlled the combination; they commanded, encouraged and

aided the commission of numberless specific crimes. But would so extensive a liability be just for each of the prostitutes or runners involved in the plan? . . . A court would and should hold that they all are parties to a single, large, conspiracy; this is itself, and ought to be, a crime. But it is one crime. Law would lose all sense of proportion if in virtue of that one crime, each were held accountable for thousands of offenses that he did not influence at all.

But if each prostitute and runner is a party to a "single, large, conspiracy," why should each not also be liable for the individual crimes which that conspiracy existed to further? Extended liability of this sort flows from the basic absurdity of considering each of the pawns to be conspiring with the king to play the chess game.

The Model Penal Code commentary does not refer in the passage quoted to the "unilateral" theory of conspiracy adopted by the Code, but such a theory could have been used to limit the liability of the minor participants in the *Luciano* conspiracy. The Code defines conspiracy in terms of one person agreeing with another, rather than two or more persons entering into an agreement. This semantic change was intended, among other things, to make it possible to find each of the members of a criminal enterprise guilty of a different conspiracy, depending upon what he *individually* agreed to do. For example, a court might find that the individual prostitutes conspired with Luciano only to commit their acts of prostitution, but that Luciano conspired with all of them to operate the entire business. On the facts of the *Bruno* case, a court might find that the smugglers conspired to commit the retail sales but the retail sellers did not conspire to commit the smuggling. On the other hand, it might very well find that all the parties in the chain of distribution conspired to operate the entire chain, just as it could under the old, "bilateral" or "multilateral" definition of conspiracy. All that would be necessary to justify such a finding is evidence that the parties were aware of the scope of the operation and intended to assist the business as a whole. The approving citation of *Blumenthal v. United States* by the Model Penal Code commentary indicates that such a purpose might not be difficult to find. In *Blumenthal*, a salesman who agreed to sell illegally part of a lot of whiskey was held to have conspired to sell the whole lot because "he knew the lot to be sold was larger and thus that he was aiding in a larger plan."

The proposed Federal Criminal Code does not adopt the unilateral approach of the Model Penal Code. Instead, it defines the act of conspiring as agreeing "to enter into a relationship" having criminal objectives, thus emphasizing the overall relationship and its objectives rather than the separate culpability of each member.

The difference in the wording of the two codes is of doubtful significance because the unilateral theory is unreliable as a means of limiting the scope of conspiratorial liability. A far better way to determine the scope of one individual's liability for the conduct of another would be to abandon conspiracy altogether, with its notions of business enterprises and general partnerships, and look instead to the policies underlying the specific criminal prohibitions at issue. Of course, smugglers of narcotics necessarily foster and encourage retail sales of the narcotics which they smuggle, but Congress must have been aware of this truism when it set the penalty for narcotics smuggling. Of course, each prostitute contributed to the financial health of the Luciano empire, and each seller of part of a carload of whiskey contributed to the sale of the whole lot. But these elementary propositions of business economics have nothing to do with criminal culpability. Absent the confusing concepts that conspiracy introduces, the courts probably would not even consider holding each participant for the crimes of the entire enterprise.

The outrageous extensions of criminal liability inferrable from such cases as *Luciano*, *Bruno* and *Blumenthal* only rarely raise practical problems. In none of those cases were minor participants actually sentenced for every misdeed associated with the enterprise; the courts found single large conspiracies in order to legitimate joinder of offenses and offenders under the procedural rules of conspiracy, an issue discussed in Part II of this Article. Even in a case such an *Anderson v. Superior Court*, where liability for substantive offenses was directly at issue, one would like to think that the sentencing judge did not carry the appellate court's theory to its logical conclusion by imposing consecutive sentences for every abortion. But it is no defense of an absurd doctrine to suggest that sensible judges are likely to disregard it in practice.

B. *Conspiracy and Cumulative Punishment*

At common law, conspiracy, like attempt, was said to "merge" into the completed substantive offense so that conspirators could be convicted either of agreeing to commit a crime or of committing it, but not of both. The modern rule is otherwise. Because collective criminal action is thought to create a greater public danger than individual crime, the Supreme Court held in *Callanan v. United States* that conspirators may be convicted and sentenced consecutively for both the crime and the agreement to commit it.

The *Callanan* rule is subject to the same objections as the rule which makes conspiracy to commit a misdemeanor a felony. Undoubtedly some criminal combinations are more dangerous than individual criminals, but it takes more than agreement between two persons to create a dangerous combination. The Supreme Court undoubtedly had organized professional criminals in mind when it invoked the group danger rationale to support consecutive sentencing in the *Callanan* case, but its rule is equally applicable to two boys who agree to steal a car.

A legislature revising its penal code today can choose among more discriminating means of providing enhanced punishment for particularly dangerous offenders. Early drafts of the proposed Federal Criminal Code included a specific offense of "Organized Crime Leadership," which punished those who direct or finance "criminal syndicates" or who aid such syndicates in certain specified ways. Providing enhanced punishment in this manner gives the defendant the benefit of a jury trial on the question of whether his own criminal conduct was a part of organized crime. The latest drafts of the Code have dropped the discrete offense of organized crime leadership, providing instead that a sentencing judge may impose "upper-range imprisonment" for any crime upon persons whom he finds to be "dangerous special offenders." This category includes, among other offenders, those who commit a felony "in furtherance of a conspiracy with three or more other co-conspirators to engage in a pattern of criminal conduct," if they "initiate, organize, plan, finance, direct, manage, or supervise all or part of such conspiracy or conduct or give or receive a bribe or use force as all or part of such conduct." Leaving this issue to the sentencing process means that the defendant's participation in organized crime may be proved by hearsay evidence and without the safeguards or burdens of a jury trial. The sentencing provisions of the Model Penal Code also provide for extended terms of imprisonment for persistent offenders, multiple offenders, dangerous mentally abnormal offenders, and "professional criminals."

Sentencing provisions of this type do away with the need to allow cumulative punishment for conspiracy and a substantive offense, or even the need to allow any consecutive sentencing at all. When the legislature provides unusually long terms of imprisonment for professional criminals, and takes pains to define that term carefully, it makes nonsense of the whole arrangement to allow the same or greater punishment to be imposed through consecutive sentencing upon a small-time robber who holds up two or three gas stations before he is caught, or upon two small-time robbers who agree to hold up one gas station and do it. Yet the most current draft of the proposed Federal Criminal Code would do just that. It explicitly authorizes consecutive sentences that exceed the maximum "upper-range" punishment for any of the individual crimes, in addition to permitting consecutive punishment for the conspiracy and the completed crime. The drafters of the Code included new sentencing provisions that make conspiracy and consecutive sentencing obsolete as a means of enhancing punishment, but it seems that they could not bear to throw the old tools away.

C. Conspiracy as an Alternative to Prosecution for the Substantive Crime

When a prosecutor does not desire cumulative punishment, he may still charge a defendant with conspiracy as an alternative to prosecution for the substantive offense. He may do so in order to take advantage of the procedural rules associated with conspiracy, the subject of Part II of this Article. He may also, however, feel that the very generality and vagueness of the concept of conspiracy make a conspiracy conviction easier to obtain than a conviction for complicity in substantive offenses.

Where the prosecution is of organized criminals of the traditional variety, this advantage seems more apparent than real. It is true that the leaders of large gambling or narcotics enterprises are careful to keep their distance from the individual criminal acts of their employees, so that it may be easier to prove their connection with the overall enterprise than their direct participation in any specific criminal act. Once a defendant is shown to be the leader of a criminal enterprise, however, any rational view of the law of complicity would hold him guilty of the narcotics sales or gambling transactions committed under his general supervision, however indirect his participation may have been. Moreover, once it is established that a particular defendant is one of the leaders of a continuing commercial criminal operation, there are inevitably specific criminal acts with which he may be charged. In fact, many of the greatest triumphs of organized crime prosecution have been achieved without the use of a conspiracy charge.

A vague charge of agreement to commit crime, not directly tied to a specific criminal conduct, seems most useful to the prosecution in quite another type of case: the political conspiracy. The leaders of a revolutionary political party, or even of a movement involving some degree of civil disobedience, are frequently believed to approve or encourage criminal activity, although the Government may be unsure of exactly what they have done that is illegal. The famous prosecution of Dr. Benjamin Spock and four other opponents of the military draft provides a classic example of this type of case. Spock, Coffin, Goodman and Ferber were convicted of a single conspiracy whose alleged objectives were to counsel and aid other persons to refuse or evade their military obligations, to destroy or discard their draft cards in violation of Selective Service Regulations, and to "unlawfully, willfully and knowingly hinder and interfere, by any means, with the administration of the Universal Military Training and Service Act." The Government's evidence showed that Spock participated in drafting a statement entitled "A Call to Resist Illegitimate Authority," which Coffin and Goodman signed. Goodman published his own statement as well, which like the "Call" could be interpreted as exhorting and encouraging others to refuse to obey the Selective Service Law and Regulations, and he participated with Spock and Coffin at a press conference to publicize the "Call." Ferber organized a "draft card burning and turn-in" in Boston at about the same time (thus establishing venue in Boston for the trial), and brought the turned-in cards to a subsequent demonstration in Washington, D.C., in which all four of the convicted defendants participated. On this occasion more cards were collected, and an unsuccessful attempt was made to present all the cards to the Attorney General.

The Government could have charged the defendants with separate violations of the Selective Service Act for their participation in each statement and demonstration, but it did not. Had it done so, more than one trial would have been necessary, but the issues would have been relatively clear. By charging a general conspiracy to interfere with the draft, and by using the defendants' specific actions primarily as evidence of an underlying agreement to further draft resistance, the Government attempted to make the whole something more than the sum of its parts. It refused to specify what evidence it relied on to establish the requisite illegal purpose, and apparently shifted its position whenever the defendants concentrated their fire on any single element in the evidence. Commenting on the difficulty that so vague a charge must have created for the defendants and for the jury, the court of appeals noted only that "the government's vacillation about which part of the evidence it relied upon cannot, without some special showing, be taken to have prejudiced the defendants. On the contrary, the government is entitled to rely on whatever agreement is shown by the evidence." As a result, the jury may have convicted the defendants of the conspiracy without agreeing on what it was that they agreed to do.

The confusion that the prosecution introduced into the trial by charging conspiracy worked to its disadvantage on appeal. Although the majority found that the "Call" counseled unlawful draft resistance, and that Spock was instrumental in both drafting and promoting it, it concluded that he should have been acquitted because his *other* statements did not explicitly endorse illegal as well as legal methods of draft resistance. The majority also directed Ferber's acquittal because he was not a party to the "Call" or to the press conference that the majority regarded as establishing the agreement. Yet, of all the convicted defendants, Ferber seems to have been most deeply involved in illegal conduct as opposed to speech; to quote the majority's own words, "[h]is activities were limited to assisting in the burning and surrender of draft cards." As one knowledgeable commentator observed, such obscure distinctions among defendants are only to be expected in view of the cloudy doctrines that the court felt it had to apply.

The *Spock* case is a good example of the morass the prosecution creates when it charges a defendant with conspiring to adhere to a vaguely criminal scheme rather than with committing specified criminal acts. Of course, this type of charge is beneficial to the prosecution when the defendant seems to have a general disposition towards unlawful behavior but has not done anything specifically wrong. It is also useful when other persons have committed acts that are clearly criminal, but the defendant's responsibility for those acts is unsubstantiated.

A familiar feature of the current political scene is the demonstration or march in which some participants destroy property, resist arrest, or commit other unlawful acts. After the demonstration, law enforcement officials may wish to prosecute its organizers or prominent spokesmen, who themselves may have engaged in no disruptive activity, on the theory that they plotted and encouraged the destructive acts of others. Because incitement-to-riot statutes reach only explicit incitement of immediate violence, some prosecutors have found a conspiracy theory more promising as a means of convicting organizers or speech makers who can be proved to have advocated or encouraged lawbreaking only from a distance or in a vague or ambiguous manner.

It is not my purpose here to add to the literature on the ever-fascinating question of the scope of first amendment protection for those who advocate violence or other criminal behavior, or who lead demonstrations which involve unlawful behavior. My point is rather that wherever one chooses to strike the balance between the values of public order and free political expression, a prosecution for conspiracy has an inherent tendency to confuse the issues. A statute which penalizes advocacy of violence at a demonstration or organizing a disruptive demonstration unmistakably emphasizes first amendment issues. It also evidences a clear legislative choice that can be measured against first amendment standards. When a general conspiracy statute is used to achieve essentially the same result, the prosecutor rather than the legislature makes the initial decision on where first amendment protection ends and criminal activity begins. Moreover, the use of advocacy as circumstantial evidence of an underlying criminal agreement, rather than as the criminal act itself, obscures the fact that it is speech that is being punished. This consideration explains why some judges and commentators feel that special rules should be derived from the first amendment to restrain the use of conspiracy in cases involving political advocacy. But surely it would be better to abolish conspiracy altogether, unless it fills some other important and legitimate function, rather than to add complex restraints to an already complex doctrine.

D. *Conspiracy as an Inchoate Crime*

Conspiracy is also an inchoate or preparatory crime, permitting the punishment of persons who agree to commit a crime even if they never carry out their scheme or are apprehended before achieving their objective. It is in this role that the crime of conspiracy has been most strongly defended. Indeed, almost the only justification offered by the drafters of the Model Penal Code and the proposed Federal Criminal Code for retaining the offense was the need to punish groups which engage in preparatory conduct which cannot be reached by the law of attempt.

The Model Penal Code commentary offers perhaps the most carefully stated justification for a doctrine of conspiracy that "reaches further back into preparatory conduct than attempt":

> *First*: The act of agreeing with another to commit, like the act of soliciting, is concrete and unambiguous; it does not present the infinite degrees and variations possible in the general category of attempts. The danger that truly equivocal behavior may be misinterpreted as preparation to commit a crime is minimized; purpose must be relatively firm before the commitment involved in agreement is assumed.
>
> *Second*: If the agreement was to aid another to commit a crime or it otherwise encouraged its commission, it would establish complicity in the commission of the substantive offense. . . . It would be anomalous to hold that conduct which would suffice to establish criminality, if something else is done by someone else, is insufficient if the crime is never consummated. This is a

reason, to be sure, which covers less than all the cases of conspiracy, but that it covers many is the point.

> *Third*: In the course of preparation to commit a crime, the act of combining with another is significant both psychologically and practically, the former since it crosses a clear threshold in arousing expectations, the latter since it increases the likelihood that the offense will be committed. Sharing lends fortitude to purpose. The actor knows, moreover, that the future is no longer governed by his will alone; others may complete what he has had a hand in starting, even if he has a change of heart.

Unfortunately, this entire argument is based on an unsound premise. The commentary seems to be justifying the Code's conspiracy provision not as a supplement to its own attempt section (which is substantially identical to the attempt section of the proposed Federal Criminal Code), but as a supplement to the traditional law of attempt which the Model Penal Code rejected.

One of the most important traditional limitations upon attempt prosecutions has been the proximity doctrine, which requires that one go beyond "mere preparation" and come somewhere near success in order to be guilty of attempting to commit a crime. The proximity doctrine seems to have originated in 1855 in the famous English cases of *Regina v. John Eagleton*. Eagleton was a baker who contracted with the guardians of his parish to provide loaves of bread of a certain weight for the "out-door poor." He delivered the loaves directly to the paupers, and received in return from them tickets which he turned in to an officer of the board of guardians. Upon receiving the tickets, the officer credited Eagleton in his account book with the amount due, but the guardians did not actually make payment until some future date specified in the contract. After Eagleton had turned in a number of tickets but before any payment was made, the guardians discovered that he had been delivering underweight loaves, and they caused him to be prosecuted for attempting to obtain money by false promises. Until they actually made full payment in cash, the guardians retained a right to deduct from the total sum any damages for breach of contract. Eagleton's counsel argued to the Court of Criminal Appeal that this reservation made the fact of ultimate payment so contingent or speculative that his client could not be convicted of attempt. Writing for a unanimous court, Baron Parke admitted that the judges had "great doubt on this part of the case," but concluded that the conviction for attempt was proper because the defendant had performed the last act on his part that was necessary to obtain the money. If there had remained anything further for him to do, "as the making out a further account or producing the vouchers to the Board," then his actions would not have been "sufficiently proximate" to the completed crime.

The "last act" rule of the *Eagleton* case never became the law of England, although some authorities have supposed otherwise. Later in the same year, the same court cited *Eagleton* in upholding the conviction for attempted counterfeiting of a man who had obtained dies engraved for manufacturing Peruvian coins, although he had not made any coins or even obtained all the necessary supplies. Since that time, the courts of several nations have spent innumerable hours trying to specify how one can determine when a defendant's actions have gone beyond "mere preparation" and become "sufficiently proximate" to the completed act for conviction of attempt, with the result that considerable confusion has been added to the original uncertainty. The Model Penal Code commentary discerned six formulations in the case law, and proposed a seventh itself. Less important than the various formulations are the results that obtained in some famous cases. An English court held that a jeweler who faked a robbery for the purpose of defrauding his insurer was not guilty of attempting to obtain money by false pretenses, because he had not yet filed a claim. A New York court held that a gang of armed robbers who were apprehended as they drove around the city in search of a particular payroll clerk they intended to rob were not guilty of attempted robbery because they had not yet found the clerk. A California court reversed the conviction for attempted theft of a swindler who tried to induce his victim to withdraw his money from the bank in the course of a "bunco" scheme known as the "Jamaica switch." Because the victim luckily met his wife in the bank and did not withdraw his savings, the swindler's acts amounted only to preparation.

As these cases show, the proximity approach does not consider the dangerousness of the defendant but only how close he came to completing the particular crime. A person carrying a bomb into a public building with the intent to set it off is plainly very dangerous to the community even if by chance he is apprehended before lighting the fuse. The confidence trickster whose scheme is detected before the victim is ready to hand over the money is probably a professional thief. A doctrine that leads to the acquittal of such persons is justifiable only if one views the criminal law to be dominated by the goals of retribution and deterrence. The community's desire for punishment is weaker when the potential criminal does not succeed, or nearly succeed, in completing his crime and inflicting harm upon an identifiable victim. Punishment

for attempts is also relatively unimportant in deterring crime, because the would-be criminal ordinarily expects to succeed and is deterred, if at all, by the punishment for success.

Although retribution and deterrence are by no means irrelevant to modern criminal law, today we tend to emphasize the restraint or rehabilitation of dangerous individuals. We see the primary task of law enforcement as the identification and isolation or supervision of those persons who are likely to offend repeatedly unless rehabilitated or at least safely locked away. With this change in emphasis have come discretionary and indeterminate sentences, probation and parole systems, rehabilitative prison programs and a wider law of attempts. The law is conservative enough not to discard the old rules everywhere, but modern statutory reform proposals such as the Model Penal Code have increasingly taken the view that the crucial issue is the clarity and strength of the defendant's criminal purpose rather than the proximity of his actions to the completed crime.

Pursued to its logical conclusion, the modern approach would permit the conviction of anyone shown to have had a firm intention to commit a crime, whether or not he had taken any steps towards its commission. The limiting factor, however, is our reluctance to put so much trust in either the omniscience or the benevolence of those who administer the law. It is difficult to determine what someone intends to do before he does it, or at least prepares to do it. Even when an individual has plainly said what he intends to do, there remains the question of how serious or definite his intent is. Many of us at some time contemplate or even talk about committing a crime without ever doing anything to carry out the design. But if we refrain from criminal conduct (including conduct that encourages others to commit crime), we are not dangerous, and the deterrent purposes of the criminal law are fully satisfied.

For this reason the modern codes retain the requirement that a defendant go beyond merely planning or contemplating a crime before he can be convicted of an attempt. He must engage in conduct that is a sufficiently substantial step towards completion of the crime to indicate his firm criminal intent, and to identify him as a dangerous individual who would probably have gone on to complete the crime if his design had not been frustrated. Thus, although the modern formulations of attempt law retain conduct as an element of attempt, they relegate it to a lesser, evidentiary role: the defendant's actions must confirm his intent to commit a criminal act. For instance, the Model Penal Code imposes liability for attempt on anyone who, acting with the culpability required by the definition of a particular crime, purposely commits a "substantial step in a course of conduct planned to culminate in his commission of the crime." The crucial term "substantial step" is defined only negatively: a step is not substantial "unless it is strongly corroborative of the actor's criminal purpose." The Code also provides a list of recurring types of preparatory conduct that the trier of fact may find to be a substantial step "if strongly corroborative of the actor's criminal purpose." These include lying in wait for the contemplated victim, reconnoitering the place contemplated for commission of the crime, possession of materials designed for use in the crime, and soliciting an innocent agent to commit the crime. Although the Code does not make the point explicitly, one is led to the conclusion that any form of preparatory conduct is a "substantial step" if it adequately confirms the existence of the actor's criminal purpose. Proximity to success is no longer the crucial issue. The possibility that the actor might change his mind and not complete the crime is dealt with in an affirmative defense of renunciation.

Against the background of a law of attempt dominated by the proximity approach, an independent inchoate crime of conspiracy made sense. Although the defendants in the New York and California cases described previously could not be convicted under traditional attempt law, they could each have been convicted of conspiracy because they worked with confederates and performed an "overt act" in furtherance of the criminal design. Each of these defendants, however, could also be convicted of attempt under the Model Penal Code or proposed Federal Criminal Code attempt sections. These sections are also adequate to reach the leader of organized crime who hires a professional killer to murder the government's chief witness in an upcoming trial, the example given in the *Working Papers* of the National Commission on Reform of Federal Criminal Laws to justify the need for an independent inchoate crime of conspiracy. If any doubt remains, a provision could simply be added which includes agreement with another person to commit a crime among the enumerated types of conduct which the trier of fact may find to be a substantial step if strongly corroborative of the actor's criminal purpose.

Under the conspiracy sections of the Model Penal Code and proposed Federal Criminal Code, however, the act of agreement is the forbidden conduct whether or not it strongly corroborates the existence of a criminal purpose. In justifying this per se rule, the Model Penal Code commentary relied heavily on the argument, quoted previously, that the act of agreeing is so decisive and concrete a step towards the commission of a crime that it ought always to be regarded as a "substantial step." Whether this point is sense or nonsense depends upon how restrictively one defines the term "agreement." Hiring a professional killer to commit murder is an agreement, and surely few would doubt that it is a substantial step toward accomplishing the killing. But the language of the conspiracy sections of both the Model Penal Code and proposed Federal Criminal Code is broad enough to reach conduct far less dangerous or deserving of punishment than letting a contract for murder. As the Model Penal Code commentary concedes, one may be liable for agreeing with another that *he* should commit a particular crime, although this agreement might be insufficient to establish complicity in the completed offense. Furthermore, neither code would change the well-established rule that the agreement may be tacit or implied as well as express, and that it may be proved by circumstantial evidence. In short, the term "agreement" may connote anything from firm commitment to engage in criminal activity oneself to reluctant approval of a criminal plot to be carried out entirely by others. To be sure, the Model Penal Code also requires that one enter into the agreement with the purpose of promoting or facilitating the crime, but the existence of that purpose need not be substantiated by any conduct beyond the express or implied agreement and performance in some cases of a single overt act by any party to it. This point is of particular importance in conspiracy cases involving political activity or agitation. Members of radical societies may be likely to discuss or even to begin to plan criminal activities that they have no serious intention of carrying through.

In summary, insofar as conspiracy adds anything to the attempt provisions of the reform codes under discussion, it adds only overly broad criminal liability. Like its use in every other area of the substantive criminal law, the use of an independent crime of conspiracy to punish inchoate crimes turns out to be unnecessary. Yet the effect of conspiracy is not limited to the substantive law. Conspiracy is unique among criminal offenses in that conspiracy law incorporates a number of procedural rules that are of great consequence. What remains to be considered is whether these rules are in themselves desirable, and if so, how they might be reformulated if a legislature decided to abolish the substantive law of conspiracy.

CONCLUSION

Conspiracy gives the courts a means of deciding difficult questions without thinking about them. The basic objection to the doctrine is not simply that many of its specific rules are bad, but rather that all of them are ill-considered. The first step towards improving a rule of law is to consider the policies it serves. The specific rules of conspiracy, however, are derived more from the logic of an abstract concept than from any realistic assessment of the needs of law enforcement or the legitimate interests of criminal defendants. We need to reconsider the problem of group crime without being distracted by the abstractions that the concept of conspiracy always seems to introduce.

The current revision of the Federal Criminal Code should have resulted in a reassessment of the usefulness of conspiracy as an independent crime, but it has not. The *Working Papers* of the National Commission on Reform of Federal Criminal Laws suggest that the authors of the initial drafts of the proposed Federal Criminal Code wanted to retain conspiracy only as a inchoate offense similar to attempt, but none of the subsequently published drafts of the Code reflect such a limitation. In any case, given the tendency of conspiracy doctrine to expand into new areas of the law, it is doubtful whether any attempt to retain the doctrine in only a limited role can succeed for very long.

Abolition of conspiracy is not an idea whose time has come, because law enforcement interests erroneously regard the doctrine as vital weapon against organized crime and because critics of conspiracy have attacked it piecemeal rather than in its entirety. This Article is therefore addressed more to the law reformers of the future than to those of the present, and its aim is not so much to settle an argument as to start one.

Abraham S. Goldstein, *Conspiracy to Defraud the United States,* 68 YALE L.J. 405–463 (1959)*

It has long been our boast that we class as crimes only those acts that are recognizably dangerous to the community. Never, the maxim has it, do we punish an evil intent alone. Though much of contemporary theory would strip "act" of any significance beyond that of "muscular contraction" and would focus instead upon the state of mind of the accused, the traditional conception of "act" continues its hold upon the imagination of men and upon legal doctrine. It expresses today, as it did three centuries ago, the feeling that the individual thinking evil thoughts must be protected from a state

* Reprinted by permission of the author, The Yale Law Journal Company and Fred B. Rothman & Company from *The Yale Law Journal,* Vol. 68, pages 405-463.

which may class him as a threat to its security. Rooted in skepticism about the ability either to know what passes through the minds of men or to predict whether anti-social behavior will follow from anti-social thoughts, the act requirement serves a number of closely-related objectives: it seeks to assure that the evil intent of the man branded a criminal has been expressed in a manner signifying harm to society; that there is no longer any substantial likelihood that he will be deterred by the threat of sanction; and that there has been an identifiable occurrence so that multiple prosecution and punishment may be minimized.

More than any other important crime, conspiracy impinges on the act requirement. It does so in ways significantly different from the other inchoate crimes. The law of attempts, for example, searches for the point at which criminal intent has proceeded beyond "preparatory" action and has reached the "commencement of the consummation" of the crime. The law of solicitations may substitute for this careful plotting of the line between intent and act a context which indicates the probability that aggressive statement will be transformed into harmful action. In contrast, conspiracy doctrine comes closest to making a state of mind the occasion for preventive action against those who threaten society but who have come nowhere near carrying out the threat. No effort is made to find the point at which criminal intent is transformed into the beginnings of action dangerous to the community. Instead, the mystique of numbers, of combination, becomes the measure of danger. Even when a statute requires an overt act "to effect the object of the conspiracy," as in federal law, it may be a completely innocent one which indicates little or nothing of the kind of injury to society which the conspiracy seeks to bring about. The agreement to accomplish the prohibited purpose furnishes, without more, the basis for criminal liability.

If the prohibited purpose is clearly set forth in the conspiracy statutes, the difficulties are solely those involved in applying the concept of an agreement. When, however, unlawful purpose is vaguely stated, the contours of "conspiracy" become ever more vague, and the dividing line between intent, now designated "purpose," and act, now termed "agreement," tends to disappear. Added to the problems inherent in a concept created to deal with potential anti-social action are new ones which arise when it is not at all clear what kind of anti-social action is threatened.

The federal conspiracy statute brings the problem into sharp relief. Though it purports to specify the purposes which transform mere agreements into crime—prohibiting conspiracy either "to commit any offense against the United States, or to defraud the United States, or any agency thereof in any manner or for any purpose'' – it introduces through the phrase ''defraud the United States'' a concept every bit as shadowy as common law conspiracy. In combination, ''conspiracy'' and ''defraud'' have assumed such broad and imprecise proportions as to trench not only on the act requirement but also on the standards of fair trial and on constitutional prohibitions against vagueness and double jeopardy. Yet the difficulties of ''conspiracy to defraud the United States'' have gone virtually unrecognized by commentators and courts. The federal cases leave the impression that the large problems of defining the crime have long been resolved, with only procedural and tactical minutiae remaining for discussion. Nothing could be further from the truth. An examination first of ''conspiracy'' and then of ''defraud the United States'' will demonstrate their peculiar susceptibility to a kind of tactical manipulation which shields from view very real infringements of basic values of our criminal law.

Conspiracy Examined

''Conspiracy'' has been a favorite of prosecutors for centuries. The reasons for its popularity lies partly in history, partly in the increased punishment potential afforded by its status as a separate crime. Most potent of all, however, has been the tactical advantage it brings to the prosecutor. By charging ''conspiracy,'' he can reach persons who might escape conviction if they were proceeded against separately or if they were charged with accomplished harm to the community. It is in this realm of trial tactics that ''agreement'' and ''unlawful purpose'' affect each other most.

The Dynamics of Conspiracy

The agreement represents the actualization of the intent contemplated by the act-intent maxim. It is the ''act'' which expresses in concrete form the threat to society of an intent shared by two or more persons. Vicarious liability is imputed and hearsay admitted, statute of limitations tolled and venue attained – all by virtue of the terms of that agreement.

Yet, ''agreement'' is almost as much a theoretical construct as the ''intent'' it is supposed to carry over the threshold from fancy to fact. Indeed, in most cases, it is proved by the very same evidence from which intent will be inferred. Thus, instead of anchoring intangible intent to a tangible act, the law of conspiracy makes intent an appendage of the equally intangible agreement. By pouring the same proof into the mold of ''agreement'' and by calling that ''agreement'' an ''act'' – passive thought it may be – courts foster the already elaborate illusion that conspiracy reaches actual, not potential, harm.

The illusory quality of agreement is increased by the fact that it, like intent, must inevitably be based upon assumptions about what people acting in certain ways must have had in mind. It is ordinarily fashioned by a jury out of bits and pieces of circumstantial evidence, usually styled ''overt acts,'' offered to prove that two or more persons are (or were) pursuing a given unlawful purpose. The sensation that the proof consists of little more than ''bits and pieces'' is, of course, intensified by the fact that acts and statements of each of several defendants are being offered into evidence as imputable to each of the other defendants. And overshadowing the entire proceeding is the uneasy feeling that the evidence may be taking the form cast for it in the indictment quite as much because the parties are seated together in the courtroom as defendants in a common trial as because they did, in fact, agree. This is not to say that words of caution are not uttered by judge to jury. Indeed, conspiracy cases are among the rare instances in which trial judges ask juries to be mindful of the vagaries of the process in which they are participating.

More important, however, jurors are also told that the existence of a conspiracy may be inferred from the unfolding of events over an extended period of time and that, though evidence like unexplained meetings of defendants is insufficient in and of itself, such evidence must be used if the crime is ever to be discovered. Judicial folklore is also shared. Conspirators, juries are advised, do not shout their plans from the roof-tops. Nor do they cast them in written form or announce them in the presence of witnesses. The net effect of such commentary is to free juries from the automatic compliance with ''law'' which instructions ordinarily demand and to invite a ''guilty'' verdict on less evidence than might otherwise be required.

This relaxation of standards of proof tends also to affect the criteria of relevance used by the trial judge to determine the admissibility of items of circumstantial evidence. Since it is he and his fellow judges who have impressed conspiracy with a clandestine air, it is not surprising to find the judge allowing considerable latitude in proof-making to those who would discover secretive plotting. Although this latitude is supposedly kept within bounds by the allegations of the indictment, the limitation is illusory. Rules which permit the crime to be charged in little more than the language of the statute, under which amplification by way of bill of particulars is grudgingly granted and which allow proof of acts evidencing the agreement other than those set forth in the indictment tend, in ultimate effect, to make the criterion of relevance applied by the judge as broad or as narrow as the statutory definition of the crime.

The criterion of relevance in a trial for conspiracy to murder or to rob or to effectuate any other crime having a relatively fixed content is not substantially different from that which prevails in the trial of the substantive offense. When, however, the object of the conspiracy is virtually indefinable, as is the case with "conspiracy to defraud the United States," defense counsel is placed in the unenviable position of not knowing what the defendant is supposed to have agreed to do. As a result, he is handicapped in making intelligent objections to the fragments of evidence offered by the prosecutor as bases from which the agreement may be inferred. And the trial judge is unable to deal intelligently with objections, when made. The trial becomes a vehicle for constant shaping and forming of the crime, through colloquies among court and counsel, as each new item of evidence is offered by the prosecution to fill out an agreement whose scope will be unknown until the entire process is completed. Expanding and contracting at each stage of the proceedings is the agreement itself, its nature, at all times, the sole criterion of the relevance of each of the items of evidence offered to prove that it exists at all.

The Group Danger Rationale

That a crime marked by so little procedural and evidentiary rigor would prove a favorite of prosecutors was to be expected. It was, of course, unlikely that so gross a justification as expediency would be offered for treating conspiracy as a crime punishable separately from, and in addition to, the sanction which could be imposed for accomplishment of the unlawful purpose. A more elaborate rationale was fashioned, principally in the cases which refused to hold that conspiracy merged in the completed conduct which was its object. Building on the assumption that a group is more to be feared than individuals acting separately, courts concluded that a plan by two or more persons to commit crime brings with it an increased likelihood that: the participants will reinforce each other's determination to carry out the criminal object; the object will be successfully attained; the extent of the injury to society will be large; those who commit it will escape detection; and the group's planning will have a long-term educative effect on its members, with schooling in crime the result. The potency of some or all of these theories is attested by the fact that conduct is occasionally classed as criminal when planned by two which would not be a crime even if accomplished by one. "Conspiracy to defraud the United States" is the outstanding example, for federal law knows no substantive crime of "defrauding the United States."

Though these assumed dangers from conspiracy have a romantically individualistic ring, they have never been verified empirically. It is hardly likely that a search for such verification would end in support of Holdsworth's suggestion that combination alone is *inherently* dangerous. This view is immediately refuted by reference to our own society, which is grounded in organization and agreement. More likely, empirical investigation would disclose that there is as much reason to believe that a large number of participants will increase the prospect that the plan will be leaked as that it will be kept secret; or that the persons involved will share their uncertainties and dissuade each other as that each will stiffen the others' determination. Most probably, however, the factors ordinarily mentioned as warranting the crime of conspiracy would be found to add to the danger to be expected from a group in certain situations and not in others; the goals of the group and the personalities of its members would make any generalization unsafe and hence require some other explanation for treating conspiracy as a separate crime in all cases.

What does seem to lie at the root of conspiracy's continued independent status is the degree of deliberateness of anti-social tendency it seems to evidence. Since conspiracy ordinarily involves deliberate plotting to commit a crime at some time in the future, it requires a staying power of criminal bent greater than that needed for the kind of intent which virtually coincides with the criminal act. Like assault with a dangerous weapon, conspiracy might therefore be described as a crime of aggravation. Here, however, the group is the instrument which marks the unlawful purpose as one more deliberately entertained and more likely to be accomplished. The distinction between the two cases is that, in assault, the aggravating factor is given content on a case-by-case basis. Not all weapons are "dangerous" and not all juries will find even weapons which appear dangerous to be so. Under conspiracy law, on the other hand, all groups are conclusively presumed to render the proscribed object more attainable, the criminal intent more firmly held and the consequent imposition of additional punishment justifiable. Ordinarily, no effort is made to determine from the facts of each case or class of case the essential issue of whether society has more to fear from the plan of two than from the deed of one.

"*DEFRAUD THE UNITED STATES*"

The federal crime of conspiracy depends for its meaning not upon the common-law development of that concept but upon the unlawful purposes specified in the conspiracy statute itself. The agreement must contemplate *either* the commission of "any offense against the United States" *or* the defrauding of the

United States "in any manner or for any purpose." Since the first of these classes of unlawful objects incorporates by reference every statutory "offense," it follows that all frauds which have been made substantive offenses can be reached under the language of the first half of the statute. What, then, is left to the second half? At first blush, it could be said to reach all "offenses" which involve frauds against the United States. To read the statute in such a fashion, however, would be to attribute to Congress an intention to select for special mention that which was already embraced by the first part of the statute. The history of conspiracy teaches that Congress undoubtedly had something else in mind.

Conspiracy originated in the thirteenth century as a crime punishing conduct equivalent to that now reached by the action for malicious prosecution. By the early seventeenth century, under the aegis of Star Chamber, it had become a generalized inchoate crime encompassing the malicious agreement alone, even if its object had not been attained. Less than a century later, the judges of the King's Bench had extended the conspiracy concept to make criminal all agreements which had crimes as their objects. And by the early eighteenth century, conspiracy came to be used as a means of punishing "all confederacies whatsoever, wrongfully to prejudice a third person." The ease with which so vaguely defined a crime could be used to punish persons agreeing to do that which would not be criminal, even if accomplished by an individual, led to attempts to narrow it. The result was Lord Denman's now famous definition of conspiracy as an agreement "to do an unlawful act, or a lawful act by unlawful means." But "unlawful" proved little better as a guide than the formulation preceding it. To the extent that "unlawful act or . . . means" were not defined as conduct independently made criminal by statute, these words left to the judges a tremendous range of crime-creating power. And that power was enthusiastically exercised. The law of conspiracy became an economic and political weapon, used against a rising labor movement and against groups threatening the *status quo* in many other areas of society.

By the middle of the nineteenth century, enough cases had been decided to permit classification of conspiracy in terms of the kinds of objects which made criminal agreements to attain them. In addition to the substantive crimes, at least a half-dozen recognized objects had crystallized which were not criminal in an individual. Among these, fraud was probably the best known.

It was at this stage in the development of conspiracy law that the federal conspiracy statute was enacted. Congressional limitation of the classes of unlawful objects under that statute to two—"offense" and "defraud"—would seem, therefore, to have signified an intention to discard all but fraud from among the noncriminal objects and thereby to make somewhat more precise a concept which had already been plagued by entirely too much expansibility.

A detailed examination of the cases dealing with "defraud the United States" will reveal that the effort did not prove successful. The phrase has had no fixed meaning. Instead, it has acquired a series of meanings—some supplanting prior ones, others existing concurrently.

The Legislative Setting

The end of the Civil War brought with it insistent demands for relief from the tax burden which Congress had imposed on what was still an immature economy. But the need for large revenues persisted. One obvious means of meeting this need and at the same time giving heed to the resentment was to collect more efficiently that which was already taxable. Since excise taxes on whiskey were designed to supply the greatest part of the federal revenue and since payment of these taxes was being evaded regularly, congressional attention turned to the techniques of avoidance then flourishing. Chief among them were bribes to government distillery inspectors, false entries on documents required to be submitted to the Government in connection with excise taxes and false markings on whiskey cases.

The first legislative attempt to deal with the problem culminated in a statute aimed at the corruptible government inspectors stationed at the distilleries. In 1866, Congress made it a crime for these inspectors to conspire with distillery proprietors or with anyone else "to defraud the United States of the revenue or tax arising from distilled spirits," or, "with intent to defraud the United States of such revenue or tax," to make "any false or fraudulent entry, certificate or return."

Before any opportunity arose to measure the impact of the 1866 statute, the continuing clamor for even greater repression of the tax violator impelled Congress, in 1867, to pass "An Act to amend existing Laws relating to Internal Revenue and for other Purposes"—a thirty-four-section statute which plugged loop-holes in the tax laws and, in addition, created a number of new tax offenses. The conspiracy provision, section 30, was added to the House bill by the Senate. Not a single explanatory reference to it appears in the entire body of hearings and reports. All that can be said with certainty about section 30, then, is that it was enacted at a time and in a setting which strongly suggest that it was aimed at conspiracies either to commit offenses against the internal revenue or to defraud the United States of internal revenue.

CATEGORIZING THE CASES

Thus far, detailed consideration has been given to the conceptual evolution of the phrase "defraud the United States." It is somewhat unclear – because so much of the trial process is lost to all but the participants – whether the cases have in fact rested upon as broad an application of that phrase as judicial interpretations would seem to allow. Nevertheless, the reported decisions lend themselves to some meaningful generalizations. The cases fall into six categories.

1. Agreements to interfere with the administration of official duties, initiated by corrupt officials themselves, or by others corrupting government officials so that they will act for their personal gain and against the interests of the United States. Though false statements may incidentally be involved, the main thrust is bribery or a similar device used to corrupt.

2. Agreements to use practices recognized as frauds at common law, such as false statements or impersonations, by persons dealing with the Government in arm's-length business relationships, in order to obtain money, property, contracts or benefits provided by law.

3. Agreements to steal or "convert" money or property of the Government or its instrumentality.

4. Agreements to defeat the administration of justice in the federal courts or in administrative agencies, either through bribery, perjured testimony or the obtaining of bail by false statements.

5. Agreements to deprive the Government of taxes or customs duties – by means of false tax returns or by smuggling or secreting goods or by mislabeling them so that taxable items appear to be nontaxable.

6. Agreements to defraud by interfering with a lawful function of government, usually in ways similar to those set out above, but where the charge is cast principally in terms of "interference" or "obstruction."

The pattern of conduct which emerges from these six categories and from the hundred-odd opinions they represent involves, in almost every case, an agreement to violate some statute creating a substantive crime or a noncriminal "offense." The bribery, graft and concealment which characterize many of the cases in the first and fourth categories are now reached by statutes specifically directed at the objectionable conduct in question. The false statements and false claims which pervade the second category violate the substantive criminal statutes which punish perjury or false statements made to agencies of the United States or the presentation of false claims to them, though falsehood is not always treated as the gist of conspiracy. The third category clearly mirrors the law of theft.

The fourth category simply identifies the false statements and bribes in the first two categories with the institutions involved in the administration of justice. Each of them – bribery, perjury and the use of falsehood to obtain a bail bond – is now specifically made criminal by statute. The same is true of the fifth category, which is now blanketed by specific crimes dealing with the evasion of taxes or with smuggling, or by statutes which clearly brand certain defined conduct as an "offense" carrying a penalty.

The sixth category, whose outlines are traced by *Haas* and *Hammerschmidt*, is, of course, the one which has caused the greatest difficulty. But here, too, close analysis reveals that virtually all of the cases decided within it fit also into one or more of the five other categories. The interferences with government punished in these cases ordinarily involves false statements or claims, bribes or violations of obligations imposed by statute – either criminal or noncriminal.

If the means ordinarily used to defraud the Government are separately prohibited by statute, then each of them would appear to be an "offense." Why, then, are they not prosecuted under the first half of the conspiracy statute, which reaches conspiracy to commit "any offense" against the United States? As already suggested, the reasons lie partly in history, partly in faulty analysis and partly in tactical considerations.

When the statute was first adopted in 1867, the federal criminal code was in a primitive state. It contained only a handful of substantive crimes, and experience with them was limited. For a long time, for example, the reach of the false-statement and false-claims statutes was not at all clear. Laws dealing specifically with various types of frauds, such as those on the mail or on the revenue, or with particular methods of obstructing justice, was not enacted until later. And the detailed network of statutes designed to reach the corruptible government official had not yet come into existence. With the activities of the federal government fast outstripping the ability of Congress to fashion criminal statutes to guard federal processes, it was hardly unexpected that federal prosecutors would search for an appropriate catch-all category into which they could fit such conduct as they (and perhaps the prevailing mores) deemed to be deserving of punishment. The impact of such pressure upon words of seemingly settled meaning has already been traced.

But times have changed. The problem today is not one of gaps in the criminal code but of overlapping offense categories which multiply the sanctions that can be imposed for a single course of anti-social conduct. The gaps have been filled and filled again, through enactment of specific criminal statutes. This open-end crime remains on the books nevertheless, and not only as the vestigial remnant of another day. Quite the contrary. Contours molded by almost a century of decision are not so easily lost. The vigor of "conspiracy to defraud the United States," at least as measured quantitatively, continues unabated. But where its primary function once was to reach conduct not covered elsewhere in the criminal code, it now serves its original purpose in very limited fashion. Its main significance today is in the field of tactics. Given the choice, a prosecutor will invariably choose to proceed under the statute which affords him the maximum flexibility in framing his charge and presenting his proof. The addition to the conspiracy count (already described as the prosecutor's "darling") of the loosely-defined concept of fraud makes conspiracy "to defraud the United States" peculiarly attractive to the prosecutor and particularly subversive of principles deeply rooted in our criminal law.

THE PROBLEM OF VAGUENESS

All the evils against which the "void for vagueness" doctrine is said to guard exist in "conspiracy to defraud the United States" as interpreted by the Supreme Court. The phrase certainly has no meaning which can be understood by "men of common intelligence." Surprisingly, however, the Court has never passed on the constitutionality of the crime, although it came close in *Gradwell*. The one court of appeals discussion of the problem is hardly satisfactory. The court found the requirement of definition satisfied by the statute's use "of words [which have a] settled meaning or which indicate offense well known to and defined by the common law." But, as already demonstrated, were a man of "common intelligence" to search long and hard for the "settled meaning," he would discover that neither "conspiracy" nor "defraud" possess it. The only "settled" aspect of the words is that they were known and used at common law—but always as concepts which had within them growth principles as dynamic as the standard of care in torts.

The circuit court's opinion points to the paradox of treating words of "settled meaning" as general exceptions to the rule that the constitutionality of a criminal statute depends upon its meaningfulness to the man of "common intelligence." The very body of law from which the ideal of definition is allegedly drawn—the Anglo-American common law of crimes— is itself the end result of a process of retroactive creation of crime by the judiciary to meet the needs of a society in transition, by expanding old categories and creating new ones. Concepts born of such a process may, of course, be as specifically defined as those

fashioned by a legislature. Unfortunately, however, the "settled meaning" exception assumes specificity even when none exists. Words known to the common law are automatically treated as precise and known to all. This is the case with "defraud the United States." Yet the phrase, as interpreted by the Supreme Court, is too vague to be understood by the man of "common intelligence." It should undoubtedly be held unconstitutional.

That it will be, however, is highly unlikely. Although they agree on the proper formula for decision, the "vagueness" cases have exhibited such diverse results that they cannot be expected to provide very much assistance. No federal statute has been held invalid on vagueness grounds in recent times. Even the state statutes which have met this fate have involved obvious first amendment questions or have embodied avowed catch-all categories unshielded by terms of "settled meaning." Probably no more can be expected from the vagueness argument than that it will exert some leverage towards the framing of doctrines designed to narrow the reach of the statute.

The influence of the vagueness argument will ultimately depend, of course, upon whether there is any contemporary justification for an elastic concept of conspiracy to defraud the Government. Many concededly vague crimes at the lower end of the criminal law spectrum—vagrancy, disorderly conduct and loitering, for example—have on occasion been rationalized as essential catch-all devices enabling police and prosecutor to operate in a twilight zone—both by cloaking with legality otherwise illegal arrests on suspicion, and by reaching anti-social conduct which cannot be fitted into existing criminal categories. A similar rationale for vagueness is sometimes announced for both conspiracy and fraud. It is said, for example, that the man who will use deceit, craft or trickery is the man who will take a precise statement of what he may not do as an invitation to press hard upon the borders of legality. Fraud statutes must, therefore, be vague if they are to serve their function in a criminal code.

Whatever the merits of facilitating civil recoveries for fraudulent schemes, it hardly seems defensible to frame legislation carrying a possible five-year sentence so that persons are invited to rely on its permissions as well as its prohibitions and then, after that reliance, to decide that they have come too close. Such an approach is the very negation of a fundamental tenet of criminal law in the western world: that no one be punished for conduct which has not been legislatively defined and classed as a crime in advance of its commission. The notice-giving function reflected in this doctrine traces to several sources, some of which spring from the struggle for legislative supremacy and the faith in democracy implicit in that struggle.

But perhaps the most important source is the definition of crime as encompassing *mens rea*. That concept represents the historic attempt of the criminal law to ensure that the offender is possessed of a state of mind which makes him deserving of blame and, hence, punishment. Whether this state of mind is found in intent or in some form of negligence, it depends upon the ability of the offender to anticipate the range of consequences likely to follow from action and to guard against, or refrain from, behavior likely to produce those consequences. The underlying assumption is utilitarian: that men are capable of choosing between alternative courses of conduct and that, in a significant number of cases, the threat of punishment will cause them to choose the lawful rather than the prohibited course.

Underlying this assumption is a second and perhaps more questionable assumption – that all men know the law (for, if they do not know it, how can they be deterred?). Thus far, knowledge has been imputed under what is, in essence, a doctrine of constructive notice. The denial of ignorance of law as a defense rests upon the premise that the state has discharged its obligation by drafting a clearly defined statute reasonably available to those who would heed its warning. Opportunity for knowledge, and the attendant ability to make a reasoned choice, exist and need only be utilized.

Statutes cast in terms meaningful to men of "common intelligence" quite obviously discharge the notice-giving function assigned to them. The same is true of most crimes defined by words of "settled meaning." Those words ordinarily refer to conduct so clearly and so long condemned by the mores that reasonable men have come to know its outlines comparatively well. But what of conduct falling within terms of supposedly "settled meaning" but not clearly prohibited by the mores? Or prohibited by the mores of one subgroup within a culture but not of another? Or, indeed, conduct permitted by the mores? Quite obviously, as society becomes more complex and as criminal statute proliferate to include "white collar crimes" and "public welfare offenses," the likelihood that potential offenders actually know what is criminal and what is not – merely because they live in society – becomes increasingly remote.

One can only surmise, of course, how many persons about to engage in conduct at or beyond the periphery of what is permissible are deterred from doing so by the threat of penalties contained in criminal statutes. It is quite reasonable to assume, however, that the further away the conduct is from violence, the more rational (and the more deterrable) is the offender to be dealt with. Certainly, those who agree to defraud are likely to be such men. Though it is possible that they will take precise definition as an invitation to evade, it is equally possible that adequate notice of the nature of the prohibited conduct will deter them from pursuing it. Whatever the precise balance between these views, our system of criminal law is built upon the faith that men are rational and that a vaguely drawn statute will not give the potential offender his last clear chance to refrain from criminal conduct.

Precise definition serves other, equally important, ends. Nothing teaches better than the evolution of "defraud" the extent to which such a phrase invests police and prosecutor with a license to interfere with freedom of action in ways unanticipated by the legislature. Definition tends, therefore, to keep the power of arrest and of indictment within bounds and thereby to minimize discriminatory application of the criminal law. It also helps prevent tactical considerations from unduly influencing the trial process – something particularly likely to occur in a conspiracy trial – by furnishing standards to which prosecution and defense may look in preparing a case for trial; by affording the trial judge a manageable criterion for determining the relevance of evidence; and by permitting meaningful instructions to be given to the jury.

There is still another reason for precise definition, one even more peculiarly associated with the intricacies of the conspiracy prosecution. Because conspiracy is a crime which may continue over a long period of time, each new act pursuant to the original agreement extending its life, it affords the over-zealous prosecutor a unique invitation to by-pass prohibitions against double jeopardy. By the simple expedient of assigning different beginning dates to parts of what is really one conspiracy and attaching different sets of overt acts to each of these parts, he may create the illusion that is discrete which is, in law, continuous. The defendant is then faced with the almost impossible burden of demonstrating that the events, in fact, flow from a single agreement. Conspiracy to defraud the United States, built as it is upon circumstantial evidence and dependent for its meaning upon a vaguely defined object, lends itself to this type of problem, and to another as well. Even when no great multiplicity of acts or objects is involved, the imprecision of "defraud" enables the prosecutor to argue with ease that much of the evidence he offers to prove an "offense" (a false statement or bribe, for example,) is also admissible to prove "defraud." Facts viewed against the latter standard always appear to disclose a plan that is somewhat different from that revealed under the former.

Since that difference will probably satisfy the prevailing "same evidence" test of double jeopardy, the constitutional safeguard is likely to prove unavailing as a bar to subsequent indictments or to cumulative sentences.

CONCLUSION

When all the cases have been read, two words, seemingly rich in legal significance, are shown to have done more to unsettle the meaning of the federal conspiracy statute than if completely new language had been used. The breadth of the concept of common-law conspiracy has conditioned the judiciary to tolerate a looseness of interpretation which essentially allows the fact situation to shape the crime. This result has been facilitated by the fact that "defraud" is itself a word which, though possessed of an "ordinary" meaning, has had that meaning obscured and eventually superseded by an unprecedented degree of judicial expansion. The total picture is even more complex because, whatever the resultant of the conspiracy and defraud vectors may be, it is shielded from view by the notion that words known to the common law are possessed of a "settled meaning." Here, the use of such words functions at one and the same time to impart vagueness and yet to satisfy the constitutional test for the definition of crime.

"Conspiracy to defraud the United States" has evolved in several stages. First, it was a crime reaching only agreements to use falsehood to induce action by the Government which would cause it a loss of money or property. It expanded to include an agreed-upon falsehood which might disadvantage the Government in any way whatever, and ultimately covered virtually any impairment of the Government's operating efficiency. The end to be gained having thus been obscured, it remained only for the means to be made equally shadowy. This was accomplished in the cases which viewed any dishonest act, including concealment, as the measure of an interference with the Government. Suspiciously unethical conduct, the failure to disclose even that which Congress had never required to be disclosed, became the raw material from which criminal liability was fashioned.

As a result of these interpretations, the federal conspiracy statute has become another governmental weapon in the eternal conflict between authority and the individual. By making unclear the line between what is permitted and what is prohibited, by conceiving the statute's reach to be as broad as that of an expanding government, present doctrine places within the power of police and prosecutor an instrument for intruding upon every man. The instrument is all the more dangerous because it wears the garb of conspiracy, with all the tactical and evidentiary benefits that

that doctrine implies. Imprecise definition and procedural advantages combine to make it virtually certain that a charge of conspiracy to defraud the United States will get to the jury—where a showing of suspicious behavior by the sort of people who ought to know better and who least appeal to that body's occasional empathy for those who commit crimes of passion and violence, is very likely to produce conviction.

The main point of this Article might well have been that the crime of conspiracy to defraud the United States has outlived its usefulness and that Congress should repeal it. Repeal is particularly indicated because this is no longer a time when anti-social conduct so outstrips the available criminal categories that a catch-all crime is essential in order to deter persons, particularly at the federal level, from approaching the outer limits of criminality. Indeed, today's detailed federal criminal code reaches so broad a range of anti-social conduct and in such over-lapping fashion that multiplicity of categories covering the same conduct, not sparseness of categories, is the central problem. Furthermore, Congress presently sits in almost continuous session, ready to act on recommendations for criminal legislation from the multitude of federal agencies dealing with all aspects of our national life. The rapidity with which curative legislation can be enacted makes it unlikely that many persons will long escape prosecution for conduct deemed offensive to societal norms.

Nevertheless, repeal of this statute in the near future is unlikely. For those who look upon crime as something to be fought with all the vigor of war, a statute like this one meets a real need. Perhaps this is because the war against crime, like all wars, engenders a flabbiness of principle, a watering down of procedural proprieties. The actors in the unfortunate drama are regularly called upon to respond to conflicting conceptions of what ought to be. The prosecutor who believes fervently in the rule of law seems willing to have it relaxed through the use of devices which shield from him and from his peers the fact that he is doing so. The judge who would not admit to a theory of the judicial process as little more than the manipulation of concepts permits "traditional" doctrines to prevent him from cutting through to the hearts of the problems they veil. And defense counsel, as much a victim as the others in the battle between form and substance, finds it virtually impossible to discover the appropriate referents that will enable him to act out his role.

It will take every bit as much ingenuity to find a way out of the maze as it took unconcern with the larger values of the criminal law and with the usual bounds of statutory definition to enter it. Doctrines must be reshaped with bold strokes and within a much larger frame than has hitherto characterized analysis in this branch of federal criminal law. Until this is done, ''conspiracy to defraud the United States'' will remain on the books as a Kafkaesque crime, unknown and unknowable except in terms of the facts of each case—and even then, not until the verdict has been handed down.

C. RICO

Pamela H. Bucy and Steven T. Marshall, *An Overview of RICO,* 51 ALA. LAW. 283 (1990)*

RICO, Racketeer-Influenced and Corrupt Organizations, is a prosecutor's powerhouse and civil plaintiff's dream. It is also a statute of ''daunting complexity.'' Passed in 1970 as part of a major crime fighting bill, RICO's stated goal is to protect the public from ''parties who conduct organizations affecting interstate commerce through a pattern of criminal activity.'' This article provides a general overview of RICO.

The statute has been extended to cover a wide range of conduct: organized crime, white collar crime, even Croatian terrorists, and abortion clinic protestors. The United States Supreme Court has not been sympathetic when RICO defendants have argued that this broad application exceeds the intended scope of RICO, stating: ''RICO is to be read broadly. This is the lesson not only of Congress' self-consciously expansive language and overall approach . . . but also of its express admonition that RICO is 'to be liberally construed to effectuate its remedial purposes.''' Since 1970, over 20 states have passed statutes similar to the federal RICO statute. In 1988 a ''mini-RICO'' statute was signed into law in Alabama. This statute simply expands the type of property already forfeitable in connection with controlled substance offenses; it contains none of the other major features of the federal RICO statute.

One of RICO's unique features is that it provides both criminal and civil causes of action for a violation of its provisions. Thus, the United States Department of Justice can seek a criminal indictment or file a civil

complaint alleging RICO violations. At the same time, private parties can file a complaint alleging the same RICO violations. RICO has become renown, in part, because of the stiff sanctions it provides: mandatory forfeiture for a criminal violation, in addition to possible imprisonment and fines, treble damages and attorney fees for a civil violation.

The RICO statute is organized very logically. Section 1961 sets forth definitions. Section 1962 lists the four types of conduct that constitute a RICO violation. Section 1963 sets forth the criminal penalties; section 1964 sets forth the civil penalties. Sections 1965 through 1968 provide housekeeping details. Section 1965 deals with venue and process. Section 1966 provides for expedition of certain civil RICO actions brought by the government. Section 1967 gives a court the discretion to close civil proceedings to the public. Section 1968 gives the Attorney General the authority to issue civil investigative demands for documents in certain circumstances.

There are four types of conduct prohibited by RICO. The gist of all four is using a business to commit crime. Whether the case is civil or criminal, the plaintiff must prove that the defendant committed at least one of these types of conduct. Before discussing the prohibited conduct, it is necessary to review three of the major RICO definitions.

The first significant definition is ''racketeering activity.'' Section 1961(1) defines ''racketeering activity'' as committing any one of specifically listed crimes, often referred to as ''predicate acts.'' The crimes listed in 1961(1) include certain state felony offenses (murder, kidnapping, gambling, arson, robbery, bribery, extortion, obscenity or narcotics) and approximately 55 federal felony offenses. The federal offenses include those typically thought of as ''racketeering'' offenses, i.e., the Hobbs Act (interfering with interstate commerce through violence or the threat of violence), distribution of illegal narcotics, bribery, extortion, gambling, prostitution. Also included as ''racketeering activity'' are many white collar crimes: mail fraud, wire fraud, labor union and pension fraud, money laundering, and securities fraud.

One does not commit a RICO offense simply by committing one ''racketeering activity,'' rather, one must engage in a ''pattern of racketeering activity.'' ''Pattern of racketeering activity'' is defined in Section 1961(5) as ''at least two acts of racketeering activity within a ten-year time period.'' The federal courts have struggled with this minimal definition. In 1986 the United States Court of Appeals for the Eighth Circuit gave a narrow interpretation to ''pattern,'' holding that two counts (i.e., two mailings) in a mail fraud scheme were so closely related to each other that they constituted only one ''racketeering activity''

* Reprinted with permission of the author and The Alabama Lawyer. Copyright © Alabama State Bar—*Alabama Laywer,* Montgomery, AL; Vol. 51 - 1990.

and not a "pattern" of racketeering activity. Almost every other federal court of appeals had rejected this narrow interpretation when the Supreme Court also rejected it in a recent decision, H.J. Inc. v. Northwestern Bell Telephone Co.

The Supreme Court attempted to clarify the pattern requirement, but as Justice Scalia observed, the Court's effort provides meager guidance. After examining the legislative history, the Court stated that "the term 'pattern' itself requires the showing of a relationship between the predicates . . . and of 'the threat of continuing activity.'" Addressing first the "relationship" prong of this definition, the Court stated that a relationship exists between acts of racketeering activity if the acts have "same or similar purposes, results, participants, victims, or methods of commission." "Threat of continuity," according to the Court, is both a closed-and open-ended concept. "A party alleging a RICO violation may demonstrate continuity over a closed period by proving a series of related predicates extending over a substantial period of time." But, when a RICO action is "brought before continuity can be established in this way, . . . liability depends on whether the threat of continuity is demonstrated." Such an open-ended threat can be explicit or implicit. An implicit threat could be shown with evidence "that the predicate acts or offenses are part of an ongoing entity's regular way of doing business."

The Court's application of the "pattern" requirement to the facts of H.J. Inc. is somewhat illustrative of this requirement. The plaintiffs in this case were customers of one of the RICO defendants, Northwestern Bell Telephone Company. Bringing a class action suit that included state claims based upon statutory and common law, the plaintiffs alleged that various officers and employees of Northwestern Bell, as well as members of the state utilities commission, engaged in a pattern of racketeering activity (bribery) causing telephone rates to rise. Applying the newly clarified "pattern" definition, the Supreme Court reversed the district court's dismissal of the RICO complaint, noting that the plaintiffs may be able to prove that the alleged predicate acts constituted a "pattern of racketeering activity." Relationship between the predicate acts could possibly be shown if the alleged acts of bribery "are said to be related by a common purpose, [that is] to influence the Utilities Commissioners in . . . order to win approval of unfairly and unreasonably high rates for Northwestern Bell." Threat of continuity, the Court noted, may be satisfied with proof that the bribery "occurred with some frequency over at least a 6-year period", or alternatively, by a showing that the bribes were "a regular way of conducting" either the business of Northwestern Bell or the utilities commission.

Although the Supreme Court's clarification of this element may be meager guidance, at the moment it is the best RICO plaintiffs have. Suffice it to say that hereafter RICO plaintiffs should be sure they can prove a "pattern of racketeering activity" by showing a sufficient "relationship" between the specific acts of "racketeering activity" they have alleged and a sufficient "threat of continuity" (be it the "closed-ended" or "open-ended" version) between such acts. The third significant definition in RICO is "enterprise." Simply engaging in a "pattern of racketeering activity" will not constitute a RICO offense. The statute forbids engaging in a pattern of racketeering only insofar as an enterprise is involved. Section 1961(4) defines enterprise broadly as "any individual, partnership, corporation, association, or other legal entity, and any union or group of individuals associated in fact although not a legal entity." Sections 1962(a)-(d) add that the enterprise "must affect interstate or foreign commerce." This commerce requirement is minimal and easily met.

To prove the existence of an enterprise, the RICO plaintiff must first prove that there exists some type of "ongoing organization, formal or informal." Evidence of just enough organization among individuals to carry out the predicate acts could suffice to meet this burden. The RICO plaintiff must also prove that the various associates in this on-going organization "function as a continuing unit." This "continuity" can be shown by evidence of the commission of the same type of acts where the jobs to be performed remain the same (even if the people performing these jobs change).

Courts also have required clear proof of nexus between the pattern of racketeering activity and the enterprise. In the United States Court of Appeals for the Eleventh Circuit, this nexus is shown by "proof that the facilities and services of the enterprise were regularly and repeatedly utilized to make possible the racketeering activity." It is not necessary to go further and prove that the racketeering activities had "an effect upon the common, everyday affairs of the enterprise."

The United States Court of Appeals for the Eighth Circuit imposes another requirement in proving the existence of an enterprise. It holds that the proof of the enterprise must be distinct and separate from the proof of the pattern of racketeering activity. Other federal courts of appeals, including the United States Court of Appeals for the Eleventh Circuit, reject this position and hold that the same evidence can suffice to prove the existence of the enterprise and the pattern of racketeering activity "as long as the proof offered is sufficient to satisfy both elements." U.S. v. Mazzei, a criminal RICO action brought against individuals, including members of the Boston College basketball team, for a "point shaving" scheme helps demonstrate the practical significance of this distinction. In this case, the government used the same evidence (point shaving and gambling) to prove the existence of the enterprise (a group of individuals associated to engage in a point shaving/gambling scheme) and to prove that predicate acts were committed (gambling). The United States Court of Appeals for the Second Circuit ruled that using the same evidence to prove both components was not a problem but recognized that a contrary holding likely would result using the Eighth Circuit's position.

Although both the United States Courts of Appeals for the Fifth and Third circuits have applied the Eighth Circuit's requirement of distinct proof, it is not clear how stringently they do so. The United States Court of Appeals for the Fifth Circuit hinted that if continuity is proven in the evidence of the pattern of racketeering activity, this same proof could suffice to demonstrate the existence of an enterprise. Given the Supreme Court's subsequent holding in H.J. Inc. that proof of a pattern of racketeering activity must include proof of continuity, the Fifth Circuit's view may now more closely align with that of the Eleventh Circuit. In the Third Circuit's seminal opinion, United States v. Riccobene, the finding of "distinct evidence" to prove the "enterprise" after the pattern had been proven was so broad that such evidence will be present in virtually every case. In Riccobene the Third Circuit found that the enterprise "served [as] a clearinghouse and [provided] a coordination function above and beyond that necessary to carry out any single one of the racketeering activities charged against individual defendants." Evidence of this function was held to be distinct from the evidence of the predicate acts. Common sense tells us that when more than one actor is involved, such "coordination" will always be necessary to commit any acts, including RICO predicate acts.

To summarize these definitions: a RICO offense can occur only when there is a pattern of racketeering activity affecting an enterprise. "Racketeering activity" is easily determined by referring to the list of offenses in 1961(1). The Supreme Court's recent explanation in H.J. Inc. of "relationship" and "continuity" should be used to assess whether a "pattern of racketeering activity" exists. Depending on which federal court of appeals one is in, the following issues must be resolved to determine if a RICO "enterprise" has been shown to exist: presence of an "ongoing organization" which "function[s] as a continuing unit"; sufficient showing of the nexus between the enterprise and the pattern of racketeering activity;

and, proof of the enterprise that is distinct from the proof of the pattern of racketeering activity. Once these definitional hurdles are met, one can move on to determine if conduct has occurred that is prohibited by RICO.

The four types of conduct prohibited by RICO are set forth in four subsections of 1962. Section 1962(a) makes it unlawful for any person to "use or invest" any income derived from a pattern of racketeering activity in an enterprise. United States v. Zang provides an example of a 1962(a) offense. Zang and Porter were partners who owned oil refining and related businesses. They falsified information about the oil they were processing, used the mails to do so and were found to have committed the racketeering activity of mail fraud. A 1962(a) violation occurred because Zang and Porter ("persons") funneled the profits they made from their mail fraud scheme ("pattern of racketeering activity") into one of the businesses ("enterprise") they owned. The portion of this business attributable to the ill-gotten profits was forfeitable property under RICO.

Section 1962(b) makes it unlawful for any person to acquire or maintain control of any enterprise through a pattern of racketeering activity. United States v. Local 560 Int'l Brotherhood of Teamsters provides an example of a 1962(b) action. The United States brought a civil RICO action against 12 individuals, Local 560 of the International Brotherhood of Teamsters, and Local 560's Welfare Fund and Severance Pay Plan. A Section 1962(b) violation occurred because the individuals ("persons") acquired an interest in and control of Local 560 ("enterprise") through extortion and murder ("pattern of racketeering activity").

Section 1962(c) makes it unlawful for any person "employed by or associated with any enterprise" to conduct the affairs of the enterprise through a pattern of racketeering activity. Section 1962(c) offenses are the most common. One study of all reported RICO cases through 1985 showed that 92 percent of the cases charged a violation of 1962(c), or a conspiracy to violate 1962(c). Bennett v. Berg provides an example of a 1962(c) action. Residents of a retirement community filed a civil complaint against numerous individuals and corporations alleging that because of the defendants' fraud, the retirement community was on the verge of bankruptcy and the residents faced the loss of the services they had paid for and been promised. The complaint alleged violations of 1962(c), asserting that some of the defendants ("persons") conducted the affairs of the retirement community ("enterprise") through mail and wire fraud ("pattern of racketeering activity").

Section 1962(d) makes it unlawful for any person to conspire to do any of the acts in 1962(a)-(c) The usual elements of conspiracy must be proven to prevail on a 1962(d) action: the defendants agreed to commit at least one type of RICO conduct as specified in 1962(a)(b) or (c), and at least one conspirator committed at least one overt act in furtherance of the conspiracy. A RICO conspiracy requires proof of an agreement to violate substantive RICO provisions. The RICO plaintiff does not have to prove that each defendant also agreed to personally commit the predicate acts that make up the "pattern of racketeering activity," but the plaintiff must prove that each defendant personally agreed to the commission by someone of the predicate acts. By the same token, proof only that a defendant agreed to the commission of the predicate acts without further proof of an agreement to violate a substantive RICO offense is inadequate to prove a RICO conspiracy.

The following example may help demonstrate what proof is necessary to establish a 1962(d) RICO conspiracy. If a plaintiff proves that the defendants agreed to collect insurance proceeds from the arson of several businesses and that one defendant committed one overt act in furtherance of this insurance fraud, the plaintiff may have proven a conspiracy to commit mail fraud (assuming the insurance claim was mailed). However, unless the plaintiff also proves an agreement to use or invest the ill-gotten insurance proceeds in an enterprise, (a 1962(a) action), or to acquire or maintain control of one enterprise through the insurance fraud, (a 1962(b) action), or to conduct the affairs of an enterprise through the insurance fraud, (a 1962(c) action), no RICO conspiracy has been proven.

If, as one court stated, the RICO statute is "constructed on the model of a treasure hunt," Sections 1963 and 1964 are the treasure. Section 1963 sets forth the criminal penalties. A criminal conviction subjects the RICO defendant to a possible sentence of imprisonment of 20 years, substantial fines, and forfeiture of "any interest . . . acquired or maintained" in violation of RICO. Most of section 1963 deals with the forfeiture penalty. The government is given broad power to seek restraining orders or performance bonds "to preserve the availability of the property subject to forfeiture." In unusual cases, such orders or bonds may be obtained before indictment, ex parte and without notice. Section 1963 also sets forth the procedure a bonafide purchaser of property subject to forfeiture should follow to secure her rights to her property.

Section 1964 addresses standing for civil plaintiffs and civil penalties. It confers standing to bring a civil RICO action on "any person injured in his business or property by reason of a violation of 1962" and sets forth the damages recoverable: "threefold the damages [sustained] and the cost of the suit, including a reasonable attorney's fee."

Standing for the civil plaintiff

In order to maintain a civil action, it is not necessary for a plaintiff to demonstrate that the defendant has been criminally convicted under the RICO statute. Rather, the appropriate standing inquiry focuses upon the injury that has been suffered and its relationship to the defendant's RICO violation.

The courts have encountered difficulty on establishing the parameters of the injury requirement necessary to gain standing. The United States Court of Appeals for the Eighth Circuit has construed injury broadly, granting standing to plaintiffs who were not the targets of the racketeering activity and only suffered "indirect" injury. The courts of appeal for the Second, Fifth and Seventh circuits have granted standing only to those plaintiffs who suffer a "direct" injury arising from the RICO predicate acts.

The Court of Appeals for the Eleventh Circuit, while setting forth an analysis which shuns the indirect/direct injury label, seemingly adopts a view of section 1964(c) consistent with the latter approach. In O'Malley v. O'Neill, the court proffered a three-part test for standing whereby a plaintiff must show: "(1) a violation of 1967; (2) injury to business or property; and (3) that the violation caused the injury." If there is only a "tenuous" relationship between the harm and the RICO violation, the proximate causation requirement is not satisfied, under this Eleventh Circuit test, and standing will be denied. The court stated that it was unwilling to grant standing absent a "strong link" between the defendant's commission of the predicate acts and the plaintiff's alleged injury.

Pleading the criminal or civil RICO cause of action

Generally, a RICO complaint must allege "(1) conduct (2) of an enterprise (3) through a pattern (4) of racketeering activity." These four requirements, while seemingly straightforward, have given rise to a vast amount of litigation concerning motions to dismiss for inadequate pleading. Each allegation is itself a term of art and embodies its own requirements of particularity. For this reason, a comprehensive discussion of all RICO pleading issues is beyond the scope of this overview, but several recurring issues deserve brief discussion.

One issue which numerous courts have addressed is whether a complaint that alleges a fraud offense as a predicate act complies with the requirements of Rule 9(b) of the Federal Rules of Civil Procedure (FRCP). In

Durham v. Business Management Associates, the United States Court of Appeals for the Eleventh Circuit, in examining the sufficiency of mail fraud allegation in a RICO complaint, held that "allegations of date, time, or place satisfy the Rule 9(b) requirement that the circumstances of the alleged fraud must be pleaded with particularity." However, the court cautioned that the particularity requirement does not abrogate the concept of notice pleading embodied in FRCP 8.

A second pleading issue that arises in 1962(c) RICO actions is whether the enterprise can also be the "person" committing the crime. Every federal court of appeals, except the Eleventh Circuit, has said no. These courts hold that for purposes of 1962(c), the enterprise whose affairs are conducted through a pattern of racketeering activity cannot also be the "person" charged. Where the enterprise is the "deep pocket," this rule may reduce the chances for collecting on any judgment obtained. When this is not a problem, this rule is not a difficult one to comply with and would rarely impede charging a 1962(c) action. In almost every RICO action the "persons" charged will include principals of the relevant enterprise. To comply with this rule of pleading, the RICO plaintiff should simply delete the enterprise from the list of persons otherwise charged.

A related pleading question is whether the "enterprise" can be named as a "person" committing 1962(a) offenses. The Supreme Court has not addressed this issue, but the federal courts of appeals have held that this restriction does not apply in 1962(a) actions. In reaching this conclusion, these courts focus primarily on the difference in the language in 1962(a) and (c). Because the pertinent language in 1962(b) is identical to that in 1962(a), it is also doubtful that this pleading nuance would apply in 1962(b) actions.

Double jeopardy

Generally, the Double Jeopardy Clause of the fifth amendment protects a defendant from a second prosecution for the same offense (after an acquittal or conviction) and from multiple punishments for the same offense. Several criminal RICO defendants have asserted that a criminal RICO prosecution after a former trial for a violation of the predicate acts abridges the protections of the Double Jeopardy Clause.

Courts have rejected this "successive prosecution" argument, holding that Congress intended separate convictions for both the RICO offense and the underlying predicate acts. Similarly, courts have rejected RICO defendants' arguments that punishment for both the individual predicate acts and the RICO offense violates the cumulative punishment protection of the fifth amendment. These decisions hold that Congress intended to permit cumulative punishment for substantive RICO violations and the predicate crimes, and thus, found no fifth amendment violation.

While the Double Jeopardy Clause provides little protection to a criminal RICO defendant, its prohibition against multiple punishments may provide some relief to some civil RICO defendants. A recent United States Supreme Court decision may allow the Double Jeopardy Clause to limit the recovery sought against a civil RICO defendant when the action is brought by the government. In United States v. Halper, a former medical service manager, who was previously convicted for violating the criminal false claims act, was sued by the government under the civil false claims act. The defendant, conceding liability under the civil statute, contended that the severity of the additional penalties under the remedial provisions of the civil act violated the multiple punishment protection of the Double Jeopardy Clause. The Supreme Court agreed that, under certain circumstances, such a fifth amendment violation could occur. The Court stated, "[The] Government may not criminally prosecute a defendant, impose a criminal penalty upon him, and then bring a separate civil action based on the same conduct and receive a judgment that is not rationally related to the goal of making the Government whole." Thus, after this decision, a civil RICO defendant may successfully argue that the remedy sought by the government in the civil action is excessive and has no relation to making the government whole. However, the Court in Halper made clear that its decision did not apply when the civil action was brought by a private plaintiff.

Forfeiture

In carrying out the order of forfeiture against the defendant, issues arise as to the effect of the forfeiture order upon private parties not convicted of a RICO violation.

The RICO statute provides following procedure for rights of bonafide purchasers of property subject to RICO forfeiture. Subsequent to the entry of the order of forfeiture, the United States must publish notice of the order in such a manner as directed by the Attorney General and, if practicable, provide notice to any person known to have an interest in the property subject to forfeiture. Within 30 days of the final publication of this notice, any person asserting a legal interest in the property must petition the court for a hearing. The petition must state the (1) nature and extent of the party's right, title, or interest in the property, (2) the time and circumstances of the party's acquisition of the right, title, or interest in the property, (3) any additional facts supporting the petition, and (4) the relief desired. Thereafter, the court shall, if practicable, hear the petition within 30 days of filing.

At the forfeiture hearing, the court alone will make a determination of the issues presented. In making the decision, the court will consider testimony presented by the petitioning party as well as any relevant portions of the record of the criminal case. In order to prevail, the petitioning party must convince the court by a preponderance of the evidence that (1) he has a legal right, title, or interest in the property which vested in the petitioner or was superior to any right, title, or interest of the defendant at the time the criminal acts which gave rise to forfeiture took place, or (2) that he was a bonafide purchaser who at the time of purchase did not reasonably believe the property was subject to forfeiture. If the private party can demonstrate either that legal title existed prior to the criminal acts or that he is a bonafide purchaser, the court thereafter may amend the order of forfeiture and require the government to relinquish its interest in the particular property at issue.

In determining the scope of the order of forfeiture, another issue that has arisen is whether funds intended for use as attorney's fees are subject to forfeiture. In United States v. Mansanto, the Supreme Court addressed this issue and held that a district court can freeze assets in the defendant's possession even when the defendant seeks to use those assets to retain an attorney.

Burden of proof

Section 1964 is silent as to the burden of proof which a civil plaintiff bears in proving the elements of RICO. The Supreme Court has hinted, but not firmly established, what is the necessary evidentiary standard. However, following the Court's suggestion, the circuit courts are in accord that the predicate acts must be proven by a preponderance of the evidence.

Conclusion

RICO is a complex statute but it provides advantages for both criminal and civil plaintiffs. As the criminal plaintiff, the government can join together disparate crimes in one indictment, including crimes over which it otherwise has no jurisdiction. More significantly, however, the government obtains the defendant's property through the forfeiture penalty. With this penalty, the government can hit criminals where it hurts: in their pocketbooks. The civil plaintiff, meanwhile, gains immediate federal jurisdiction, and if successful, automatic treble damages for what is often "garden variety" fraud otherwise litigated in the state courts with only the possibility of punitive damages.

There are hazards with RICO, however. Overuse of RICO by both criminal and civil plaintiffs has seriously jeopardized the statute's future. During the past five years increasingly aggressive efforts have been made in Congress to curtail RICO's provisions by restricting the predicate acts for which treble damages are available. For the civil plaintiff, another hazard exists. The courts have been increasingly willing to impose sanctions on parties bringing inappropriate RICO actions.

Applied correctly and in appropriate situations, RICO serves as a valuable weapon to both prosecutors and civil plaintiffs. RICO litigants should be advised, however, that the statute's future is uncertain and the consequences of its improper use are potentially severe.

Gerard E. Lynch, *RICO: The Crime of Being a Criminal, Parts I, II, III and IV,* 87 COL. L. REV. 661, 680 (1987)*, 87 COL. L. REV. 920 (1987)**

One of the most controversial statutes in the federal criminal code is that entitled "Racketeer-Influenced and Corrupt Organizations," known familiarly by its acronym, RICO. Passed in 1970 as title IX of the Organized Crime Control Act of 1970, RICO has attracted much attention because of its draconian penalties, including innovative forfeiture provisions; its broad draftsmanship, which has left it open to a wide range of applications, not all of which were foreseen or intended by the Congress that enacted it; and the sometimes dramatic prosecutions that have been brought in its name.

RICO's complexity has attracted several efforts to unscramble the many issues of interpretation it poses. The potency of its sanctions and the procedural advantages it bestows on prosecutors have drawn polemics of praise and criticism from practitioners and scholars with ties to law enforcement or defense practice. Yet there has been little discussion of the fundamental questions RICO poses concerning some of our basic assumptions about criminal law and procedure.

One reason for this lack of discussion may be that the uses of RICO that most starkly raise the issues I have in mind were not contemplated in the congressional debates about the statute and have become more clearly dominant with the passage of time. Congress viewed RICO principally as a tool for attacking the

* This article originally appeared at 87 Colum. L. Rev. 661 (1987). Reprinted by permission.

** This article originally appeared at 87 Colum. L. Rev. 920 (1987). Reprinted by permission.

specific problem of infiltration of legitimate business by organized criminal syndicates. As such, RICO has hardly been a dramatic success. Few notable RICO prosecutions have dealt directly with this sort of criminal activity.

Instead, prosecutors have seized on the virtually unlimited sweep of the language of RICO to bring a wide variety of different prosecutions in the form of RICO indictments. All but ignoring those subsections of RICO that directly prohibit the act of infiltrating legitimate business by investment of illicit profits or by illegitimate tactics, prosecutors have relied principally on the expansive prohibition of the operation of an enterprise through a pattern of racketeering activity to strike at those – whether or not they fit any ordinary definition of "racketeer" or "organized criminal" – who commit crimes in conducting the affairs of businesses, labor unions, and government offices.

More importantly, a large proportion of RICO prosecutions, and the greatest number of the most visible ones, have been directed at the operations of illegitimate criminal enterprises themselves. Through an expansive (though quite literal) interpretation of section 1962(c), prosecutors have moved directly against "organized crime" itself, in both the narrow and broad senses of the term. In cases of this sort, defendants have been tried for engaging with others in series of crimes having looser connections than have traditionally been permitted even in conspiracy prosecutions. Although particular "predicate acts" must be proven, such prosecutions tend to focus not on the defendant's particular anti-social acts, but on whether an examination of broad stretches of the defendant's criminal career and those of his associates reveals that he has associated himself with a criminal combine. Necessarily, RICO prosecutions put before the jury charges that a particular defendant engaged in not just one but several, often very loosely related, crimes, and frequently also present an equally ill-assorted set of charges against codefendants.

These creative uses of the statute present a number of interesting questions. First, how did a statute originally conceived to serve a particular, relatively narrow purpose come to be drafted and interpreted as an all-purpose prosecutorial tool? Part I of this Article suggests that the answer is to be found in the practical and theoretical deficiencies of the original RICO idea, and in a legislative dynamic by which the problems of draftsmanship caused by those deficiencies were solved by repeated expansion of the statutory coverage. Second, what in fact have prosecutors done with such a flexible instrument? Part II argues that, given a weapon that could be used against virtually any kind of criminal behavior, prosecutors have responded by using RICO in a few identifiable patterns, which correspond to what law enforcement officials apparently believe to be substantive and procedural gaps in the federal criminal code.

Part III addresses what I believe is the most innovative and questionable feature of RICO, its use as an expanded conspiracy statute to prosecute members of criminal enterprises for an assortment of criminal offenses. That part of the Article asks whether the statute represents a departure from traditional models of criminal law and procedure, and whether the model it adopts should be perpetuated. Part III concludes that this use of RICO represents a continuation and expansion of trends visible in federal conspiracy law that move away from a traditional concentration on assessing conduct in specific transactions and toward the presentation of broader patterns of conduct and association in criminal proceedings. It is argued that such RICO prosecutions should not be understood simply as illegitimate departures from accepted norms. Rather, the prosecutorial and judicial expansion of RICO is a product of the greater knowledge of the nature of organized criminal activities that results from modern investigatory methods.

Overall, the Article concludes that the principal uses of RICO have been appropriate and valuable, but that its major benefits can be captured by a series of specific amendments to the federal criminal code, obviating the need for a statute that sweeps under one heading, with a single penalty structure, everything from illegal dice games to business fraud to terrorism and murder. More tentatively, the Article concludes that to the extent that RICO is not fully consistent with our traditional notions of what constitutes a crime, such inconsistency does not automatically discredit the statute, but rather constitutes reason to reexamine those notions. Part IV summarizes these conclusions and makes specific suggestions for statutory reform.

I. THE STRANGE EVOLUTION OF RICO

A. The Uses of History

There are several reasons for constructing a detailed account of the history of RICO's legislative development and judicial interpretation. First, the legislative history of the statute has been a source of controversy. Though careful commentators have concluded that Congress intended RICO as a specific response to the problem of criminal infiltration of legitimate enterprises, courts, including the Supreme Court of the United States, and at least one highly influential commentator have found in the legislative history much broader purposes and have used their findings to justify sweeping interpretations of the statute. Since the latter view, which has had considerable influence on the development of the law, is wrong, and the commentators who criticize it have presented their conclusions in rather summary form, a careful review of the evidence is necessary to set the record straight.

Second, the story of how RICO came to be what it is has implications for our assessment of the statute. Prior readings of the legislative history have addressed the subject as an aid to interpretation of the statute's proper application in controversial cases. Those controversies have mostly been settled by judicial decision; moreover, legislative amendments in 1984 either specifically or by implication ratified the expansive judicial interpretations, whether or not those decisions accurately reflected the original legislative intent.

But an accurate reading of the legislative history, and of the judicial reaction to that history, has significance beyond the answers to specific issues of interpretation. The radically contingent nature of the drafting, adoption, and interpretation of RICO tells us something about the way in which important concepts enter our law. The history of RICO, moreover, should make us eager to reassess its utility and fairness. If, as I argue below, the broad consequences of RICO are essentially by-products of a failed legislative effort to address a highly specific problem, it becomes all the more urgent to ask whether those consequences are desirable in their own right. At the same time, an understanding that the most significant current uses of RICO were undertaken by prosecutors and legitimated by courts virtually in the teeth of a narrow legislative purpose should give us a healthy respect for the power of the forces motivating those uses.

Third, an examination of this history is instructive about how both the legislature and the judiciary respond to crime. RICO is only the most recent initiative in a long process of federal action against organized criminal activity. As Professor Bradley has shown, the federal role in prosecuting organized crime has consistently expanded for over 100 years, fueled by the political popularity of anything that can be marketed as part of a crusade against a shadowy and threatening enemy. The history of RICO confirms that when pressure to produce crime legislation is present, drafting choices tend to be made in an expansionist direction, and careful consideration of the precise scope of proposed legislation is rare. In the case of RICO, the vagueness of early proposals to address the infiltration of legitimate business was avoided not by refinement of the original concepts, still less by serious debate about whether the effort was worthwhile, but instead by expanding the concept until it was virtually all-encompassing.

The judiciary is under equally severe pressure to expand the reach of criminal statutes. Even assuming that judges, unlike legislatures, are immune to the effects of public clamor to do something about crime (not necessarily an accurate assumption), the internal pressure on judges to affirm convictions for serious crimes must be enormous. In the area of criminal procedure, the Warren Court developed a series of doctrines that emphasized the importance of defending certain principles even at the cost of reversing an occasional conviction. But substantive criminal law too often has been treated in the federal courts as a matter of "mere" statutory interpretation. Without a firm body of constitutional principles to rely on, the tendency to stretch the scope of criminal statutes to the breaking point to accommodate prosecutions has met little resistance.

Finally, and not least, the story of RICO is a good story, which deserves telling for its own sake. Today, RICO is, among other things, the federal government's principal statutory weapon against organized crime. And yet, the whole thing began with a study commission identifying a problem to which it didn't think a new substantive crime was the solution.

B. The President's Crime Commission

The legislative history of RICO begins with the report of the President's Commission on Law Enforcement and Administration of Justice (the Katzenbach Commission) in 1967. Belying the conventional wisdom about presidential commissions and blue ribbon panels, the recommendations of the Katzenbach Commission were highly fruitful in producing significant legislation (if not in controlling crime). Many of the Commission's recommendations for federal legislation were adopted.

The Organized Crime Control Act of 1970, of which RICO was a part, was largely based directly on the Commission's recommendations. Its findings about organized crime are therefore important to understanding the history of RICO. The three aspects of the report most particularly relevant to RICO are its understanding of what organized crime is, its emphasis on the danger of organized crime's infiltration of legitimate institutions, and its recommendations for dealing with the problem.

In defining organized crime, the Commission wavered between two ideas. Dominating the report is the Commission's apparent acceptance of the idea of a single nationwide crime syndicate. The opening paragraph of the chapter, citing the Kefauver Committee's report as support, stresses the image of a highly structured, unitary organization: "Organized crime is a society that seeks to operate outside the control of the American people and their governments. It involves thousands of criminals, working within structures as complex as those of any large corporation, subject to laws more rigidly enforced than those of legitimate governments."

This perception of organized crime is not invariant in the report, however. In describing organized crime's activities, the Commission on several occasions refers loosely to "[c]riminal groups" or to "[o]rganized criminal groups" in ways that suggest a focus on multiple local organizations, not necessarily unified under a single hierarchy. Indeed, the Commission acknowledged that "[s]ome law enforcement officials define organized crime as those groups engaged in gambling, or narcotics pushing, or loansharking, or with illegal business or labor interests."

But the Commission itself rejected this definitional "focus exclusively on the crime instead of on the organization," preferring instead to define "organized crime" as a single invisible empire, analogous to a criminal corporation or cartel, indeed to a private government. The Commission made quite clear that when it referred to "organized crime," it was talking about an entity with particular members, a defined hierarchy, and even an official name:

Today the core of organized crime in the United States consists of 24 groups operating as criminal cartels in large cities across the Nation. Their membership is exclusively Italian, they are in frequent communication with each other, and their smooth functioning is ensured by a national body of overseers. . . . FBI intelligence indicates that the organization as a whole has changed its name from the Mafia to La Cosa Nostra.

While the Commission's picture of a single enemy monolith is perhaps overdrawn, the existence and influence of the traditional Mafia was hardly a fantasy. But the definitional issue lurking in the report is important. As we will see, this tension between the idea of a single Mafia and that of multifarious local syndicates as the target of "organized crime" control would surface again in the drafting and interpretation of the RICO statute.

The second aspect of the Commission's report that is relevant to the development of RICO is its discussion of organized crime's activities. Part of the subject can be dealt with briefly, for the litany of crimes is familiar: gambling ("the greatest source of revenue for organized crime"), loansharking, narcotics (at the importation and largest wholesale levels), and, to a "small and declining" extent, prostitution and bootlegging. But the Commission gives equal prominence to another aspect of organized crime, less familiar from the days of Elliot Ness: the infiltration of legitimate business.

Once again, this theme is apparent at the very outset of the chapter. Its second paragraph summarizes the later discussion:

The core of organized crime activity is the supplying of illegal goods and services—gambling, loan sharking, narcotics, and other forms of vice—to countless numbers of citizen customers. But organized crime is also extensively and deeply involved in legitimate business and in labor unions. Here it employs illegitimate methods—monopolization, terrorism, extortion, tax evasion—to drive out of control lawful ownership and leadership and to exact illegal profits from the public.

The Commission's fuller discussion of the problem of organized crime's involvement in legitimate business and labor treats issues that would later become significant to the RICO statute. The Commission gave special prominence to this problem by giving it essentially the same space and weight in its report as the more traditional problem of the specifically criminal activities of organized crime. This provided the impetus for the legislative proposals that would evolve into RICO. The Commission's discussion of the harm to the public of such infiltration is important to understanding the rationale for prohibiting the infiltration: "Criminal cartels can undermine free competition" through unfair tactics like price cutting financed by tax evasion and cash reserves from illegal business, labor corruption, and violent coercion of suppliers and customers. Moreover, acquisition of legitimate enterprises gives organized criminals the opportunity to engage in new types of ("white collar") crime, such as bankruptcy fraud. Finally, the Commission's analysis of how organized crime acquires legitimate business interests would be critical in constituting the specific prohibitions of RICO.

The third aspect of the Commission's report that bears on the development of RICO is its recommendations. Particularly in light of the fact that the Commission's recommendations with respect to organized crime formed the core of the act of which RICO is a part, it is noteworthy that RICO itself did not flow directly from a Commission recommendation.

The Commission's recommendations were generally concerned with providing new investigative tools for law enforcement, rather than with reform of the substantive criminal law. This emphasis is reflected in a major study prepared for the Commission by G. Robert Blakey, a scholar and law enforcement expert later to become the draftsman and a principal exponent of RICO. Professor Blakey explicitly concluded that "[e]xisting substantive criminal theory is adequate to deal with organized criminal activity." This was so because prosecutors already had at their disposal a powerful and appropriate tool in statutes penalizing conspiracy, and "there is no question that existing conspiracy theory is equal to the challenge of organized crime." The difficulty, rather, was in the inadequacy of investigative devices. Professor Blakey's analysis appears to have persuaded the Commission; its legislative recommendations followed his conclusions in most respects.

Conspicuous by its absence from the Commission's recommendations is anything like RICO. The Commission proposed neither legislation criminalizing the involvement in organized criminal activity as such, nor a statute outlawing organized crime penetration of legitimate business or labor enterprises. Indeed, the Commission advocated the creation of no new crimes at all.

With respect to the particular issue of organized criminal infiltration into legitimate business, which the Commission did so much to publicize as a problem area, the Commission's recommendations were notably cautious. In keeping with its conclusion that existing substantive criminal law was sufficient to deal with organized crime's activities, the Commission recommended no innovations in the penal code. Rather, it saw the infiltration problem as one that could be dealt with most effectively through enforcement of existing civil and regulatory machinery against the illegal tactics of organized criminals in operating legitimate businesses. At least in formulating its recommendations, the Commission appears to have understood the principal danger of organized criminal involvement in legitimate enterprises to be that racketeers would be more likely than other businessmen to engage in unethical or illegal business practices. Strict enforcement of regulations prohibiting such practices, coupled with intensive investigative efforts to uncover them in businesses believed to be operated by organized criminals, were recommended as the tools best suited to countering the problem.

In summary, the report of the Katzenbach Commission is significant in the legislative history of the Organized Crime Control Act of 1970, because so many of the provisions of the act find their origins in recommendations of that body and, in particular, in the analysis performed by its task force on organized crime. Three aspects of the Commission's response to organized crime are particularly notable. First, despite occasional recognition of the diffuse nature of "organized criminal groups," the Commission clearly conceived of organized crime as a single entity and directed its primary attention toward a single target: the Italian syndicate it believed controlled organized crime throughout the United States. Second, the Commission saw as a prime aspect of the threat posed by this syndicate its increasing tendency to involve itself in legitimate business and union activities. Finally, while the Commission's conception of the menace of organized crime is significant in understanding the thinking of those who drafted the RICO statute, the Commission itself did not recommend enactment of anything resembling RICO.

C. The Congressional Response

Perhaps encouraged by the impending 1968 election season, in which public perceptions of increased crime and civil disorder would play a significant role, members of Congress were quick to introduce a variety of anti-crime bills, including many that were specifically responsive to the Commission's recommendations. Included in the flurry of legislative activity were two bills introduced by Senator Roman Hruska that are generally considered ancestors of RICO. One of these bills, S. 2048, would have amended the Sherman Antitrust Act to prohibit the investment or use in one line of business of intentionally unreported income from another line of business. The second bill, S. 2049, created new civil and criminal penalties for the investment of income derived from various specified criminal activities in a business affecting interstate commerce.

No action was taken on the bills. No doubt reflecting the priorities of the election campaign, Congress deferred action on most of the organized crime aspects of the pending bills and Commission recommendations, turning first to actions that could be packaged under the election-year title of the "Omnibus Crime Control and Safe Streets Act of 1968." Although neither of the Hruska bills became law, several features of his suggestions are relevant to the evolution of RICO.

The first noteworthy aspect of Senator Hruska's proposals is their purpose. The Senator introduced his package of proposals with a lengthy speech concerning the "cancerous growth of organized crime in this country." Like the Katzenbach Commission, Senator Hruska adopted the view that organized crime constituted "a tightly knit and strictly disciplined criminal cartel," known as La Cosa Nostra. Even more than the Commission, however, Senator Hruska devoted his principal attention not to the primary illegal activities of the syndicate, but to its penetration into legitimate business. Thus, RICO's earliest ancestor was explicitly tied to the purpose of combatting organized crime infiltration into legitimate fields of business.

It is also worth noting, however, that even this early draft of what would one day grow to be RICO went well beyond this purpose. Nothing in either bill purported to define organized crime, or to limit the bills' scope to actions of the criminal cartel whose activities had called it forth. Thus, S. 2048 applied to anyone who invested deliberately unreported income, regardless of the source of the income or the criminal status of the investor. The language of the bill covered a restaurateur who skimmed cash from his restaurant to invest in a hotel venture as much as the racketeer who used his narcotics profits for the same purpose, even though Senator Hruska was explicit that the "evil to be curbed is the unfair competitive advantage inherent in the large amount of illicit income available to organized crime." Similarly, S. 2049, the more direct ancestor of RICO, applied, despite Senator Hruska's primary concern for the monolithic "Mafia," to anyone who invested income derived from designated criminal activities in a legitimate business, whether or not the investor was a member or affiliate of La Cosa Nostra. The only purported connection between the bill and the Mafia was that the specified crimes were "especially those criminal activities engaged in by members of organized crime families" – although clearly by other, disorganized criminals as well.

Senator Hruska's proposals went beyond the Katzenbach Commission's recommendations in proposing a direct legislative attack on the infiltration problem identified by the Commission, while the Commission itself believed that existing criminal, civil, and regulatory regimes were sufficient to combat the criminal consequences of infiltration. Moreover, Senator Hruska's bills went beyond the specific problem he identified: the bills would have penalized intrusion into legitimate business of criminal capital other than that identified with "organized crime" as he himself understood that term, and indeed, extended even to investments of what would not generally be regarded as criminal proceeds at all. But nothing in the Hruska package contemplated further substantive criminal law reforms to increase the penalties or scope of laws prohibiting either the pre-infiltration racketeering acts that generated the income used to penetrate the legitimate business or the post-infiltration criminal activities in which the racketeer was expected to involve the infiltrated entity.

In any event, the legislative war on organized crime had to wait for the next Congress. Early in that Congress, Senator John L. McClellan introduced a major bill containing most of the organized crime recommendations of the Katzenbach Commission. Senator McClellan supported the bill with a lengthy speech about the evils of organized crime and the legislative steps needed to combat them. The speech, like the bill it supported, was taken largely from themes sounded by the Task Force Report on Organized Crime. Like the Commission, Senator McClellan saw the unitary structure of La Cosa Nostra as "epitomiz[ing], if it does not exhaust, the concept of organized crime." Like the Commission, he gave prominent place to the evils of organized crime's infiltration of legitimate businesses and labor organizations, and its corruption of government activities. And like the Commission, Senator McClellan took the view that of all the factors inhibiting the law enforcement response to organized crime, the single

most important was the procedural and evidentiary difficulty of making cases. Accordingly, his anticrime package included a variety of proposals in the areas of evidence and criminal procedure, most derived from the Commission's recommendations, but suggested no need for changes in the substantive law of crimes. . . .

But Senator Hruska had not given up. He offered a new bill, combining his previous proposals into a coordinated whole, detached from the antitrust laws. This bill, identified as the "Criminal Activities Profits Act," would have made it a crime to invest any income derived from any of several enumerated federal offenses, or any intentionally unreported income, in any business enterprise affecting interstate commerce.

In introducing the bill, Senator Hruska made plain that it was "aimed specifically at racketeer infiltration of legitimate business." Senator Hruska placed his greatest emphasis on the harm that organized criminals could do once entrenched in ordinary businesses. Racketeers, he feared, would use illegitimate tactics to secure monopoly power, with attendant anticompetitive damage to the economy. In addition, racketeer-run businesses would be expected both to utilize "all the techniques of violence and intimidation" for which racketeers are renowned and to turn their criminal talents to the white collar business crimes of embezzlement and consumer fraud. Unlike the Katzenbach Commission or Senator McClellan, however, Senator Hruska would not have dealt with these ills by giving law enforcement agencies additional investigatory tools to uncover and prove crimes committed by racketeers, be they committed before the infiltration that produced the capital or after it through and for the benefit of the penetrated business. Instead, like its immediate predecessors, the bill directly prohibited the entry of criminal money into the legitimate economy.

Following hearings on the various anti-organized crime proposals, Senators Hruska and McClellan joined forces to introduce a more radical revision of the Hruska bill, which was now restyled the "Corrupt Organizations Act of 1969." While the bill was amended in numerous relatively minor respects as it passed through the Senate and House Judiciary Committees, in its essentials the Corrupt Organizations Act was all but identical to the final version of S. 1861 that was enacted into law as title IX of the Organized Crime Control Act of 1970.

A proper understanding of the goals of S. 1861, therefore, is particularly important in understanding the goals of RICO. Fortunately, upon introducing the bill, Senator McClellan made its purposes emphatically clear:

The problem, simply stated, is that organized

crime is increasingly taking over organizations in our country, presenting an intolerable increase in deterioration of our Nation's standards. Efforts to dislodge them so far have been of little avail. To aid in the pressing need to remove organized crime from legitimate organizations in our country, I have thus formulated this bill. . . . This bill is designed to attack the infiltration of legitimate business repeatedly outlined by investigations of various congressional committees and the President's Crime Commission.

The bill proposed to remove the "cancer" of organized crime penetration from the economy "by direct attack, by forcible removal and prevention of return." This "most direct route to accomplish" the goal of "remov[ing] organized crime influences from legitimate organizations" was the exclusion of the racketeer from the infiltrated enterprise: "If an organization is acquired or run by the proscribed method, then the persons involved are removed from the organization." Again citing the antitrust precedent, Senator McClellan went on to note that the goal of these measures was the protection of the public against parties engaging in certain types of businesses after they have shown that they are likely to run the organization in a manner detrimental to the public interest. In [this] spirit, . . . this provision . . . is based upon [the] judgment that parties who conduct organizations affecting interstate commerce through a pattern of criminal activity are acting contrary to the public interest. To protect the public they must be prohibited from continuing to engage in this type of business in any capacity.

This emphasis on infiltration of legitimate organizations remained as the bill made its way through the legislative process. Both the Senate and House committee reports accompanying the final versions of the Organized Crime Control Act state that the purpose of RICO is "the elimination of the infiltration of organized crime and racketeering into legitimate organizations operating in interstate commerce."

The purpose of the revised bill was thus exactly the same as that of Senator Hruska's 1967 proposals. It is worth emphasizing this continuity of intention in such detail because it has not always been recognized by proponents of a broad interpretation of RICO. For example, Blakey and Gettings assert that "[w]hile RICO had its origins in previous attempts to curtail organized crime infiltration into legitimate business, S. 1861, when redrafted and introduced, had a broader purpose; it was directed at all forms of 'enterprise criminality.' It represented the rest of the Crime Commission's integrated package." This assertion of a broadening of purpose is supported by no reference to any statement of the bill's purpose by any of its supporters. As the above detailed discussion of the origins of RICO shows, it could not be, since both parts of the quoted assertion are simply wrong.

First, no public description of the purpose of S. 1861 contained any indication whatever that the previous narrow understanding of the goals of the Hruska bills had been altered. To the contrary, Senator McClellan repeatedly emphasized the same purposes for S. 1861 as Senator Hruska had set out for its precursors: a "direct attack" on the penetration of legitimate organizations by organized crime. Second, as we have seen, the Katzenbach Commission's "integrated package" of proposals to strengthen law enforcement against organized crime included no recommendation for any substantive criminal law changes, either directed narrowly against infiltration of legitimate business or broadly against "enterprise criminality."

Elsewhere, Blakey and Gettings draw support for their view that the purpose of the Corrupt Organizations Act differed from that of its predecessors from a variety of sources. First, they argue that because title IX as eventually enacted was called "Racketeer Influenced (legitimate) and Corrupt (illegitimate) Organizations," the title of the Act reflects an expansion to include all forms of "enterprise" criminality. The claim is, to say the least, strained. As Blakey and Gettings themselves acknowledge, the word "corrupt" is "ambiguous: a 'corrupt organization' could be . . . either the mob itself or a union taken over by it." Their claim that the title of the Act was "therefore" changed from "Corrupt Organizations" to "Racketeer Influenced and Corrupt Organizations" for the purpose of "clarifying the ambiguity and drawing the crucial distinction explicitly" is unpersuasive. The claim that the change in title reflects a change in purpose is decisively rebutted by the fact that the original "Corrupt Organizations Act" uses the two terms interchangeably.

Second, Blakey and Gettings note that the Organized Crime Control Act itself contains a broad statement of its purpose " 'to seek the eradication of organized crime in the United States by strengthening the legal tools in the evidence gathering process, by establishing new penal prohibitions, and by providing enhanced sanctions and new remedies to deal with the unlawful actions of those engaged in organized crime.' " While the particular language of this statement can perhaps be written off as describing the entire Act, and not merely the RICO provisions of title IX, Blakey and Gettings correctly point out that S. 1861 itself contained a similar statement of purpose to "eradicate the baneful influence of organized crime in the United States" and "to arrest and reverse the growth of organized crime in the United States, its infiltration of legitimate organizations, and its interference with interstate and foreign commerce."

This argument too is unpersuasive, however. Obviously, the purpose of all of the provisions then under consideration was to "eradicate" organized crime; this hardly suggests that each particular aspect of the package should be read to penalize all actions committed by anyone associated with "organized crime" in its broadest definition. As Senator McClellan pointed out in introducing S. 1861, RICO was not intended to accomplish the "eradication" of organized crime by itself.

Blakey and Gettings are correct that "[n]owhere in the legislative history does it say that the legislative history was exhaustive or that this purpose [to deal with the infiltration of legitimate business] was the only purpose." But granting the absence of any such improbable disclaimer, it remains the case that nowhere in the legislative history is there even a glimmer of an indication that RICO or any of its predecessors was intended to impose additional criminal sanctions on racketeering acts that did not involve infiltration into legitimate business.

Blakey and Gettings are correct in one respect. If it cannot be documented that any member of Congress understood the bill in this way, the actual language of the Corrupt Organizations Act, and of RICO, its enacted successor, does indeed go far beyond its announced purpose. An examination of the structure of the statute will show that while the fundamental prohibitions of RICO still clearly reflect the purposes motivating Senators McClellan and Hruska in introducing it, the logic of expansion pushed the actual language of the statute much further.

D. The Structure of the Statute

As reintroduced by Senator McClellan, and as currently codified in title 18 of the United States Code, RICO is a statute of daunting complexity, comprising eight separate lengthy sections. But the length and complexity of the statute helps to mask a certain simplicity in the structure of the criminal prohibitions imposed.

The core of the statute, 18 U.S.C. § 1962, creates four new crimes. Under section 1962(a), it is a crime for any person to "use or invest" any income he has derived "from a pattern of racketeering activity or through collection of an unlawful debt" to establish, operate, or acquire an interest in "any enterprise" engaged in or affecting interstate commerce. Section 1962(b) prohibits acquiring or maintaining an interest in, or control of, any such enterprise "through a pattern of racketeering activity or through collection of an unlawful debt." Subsection (c) of section 1962 makes it a crime for any person "employed by or associated with any enterprise" in or affecting commerce "to conduct or participate, directly or indirectly, in the conduct of such enterprise's affairs

through a pattern of racketeering activity or collection of unlawful debt." Finally, section 1962(d) prohibits conspiracies to violate the other three prohibitions.

This structure is neatly designed to deal with the congressional concern with organized criminal infiltration of legitimate business. Section 1962(a) prohibits acquisition of an interest in a legitimate business by the investment of "dirty money" derived from racketeering; section 1962(b) prohibits acquisition of such an interest by means of racketeering acts (as, for example, by extortion or loan-sharking); and section 1962(c) prohibits the operation of a legitimate business (however acquired) by means of unlawful racketeering behavior.

Indeed, the structure of these prohibitions corresponds perfectly to the analysis of organized criminal infiltration of legitimate enterprises presented by Senator McClellan in his speech on organized crime originally introducing S. 30. Thus, Senator McClellan commented that:

Control of business concerns has been acquired by the subrosa investment of profits acquired from illegal ventures [prohibited by section 1962(a)], accepting business interests in payment of gambling or loan shark debts [prohibited by section 1962(b)'s "unlawful debt" language, as defined in section 1961(6)], but, most often, by using various forms of extortion [prohibited by section 1962(b)'s "pattern of racketeering" language, which would outlaw acquiring a business through, inter alia, extortion, under the definition in sections 1961(1)(A) and (B)].

After takeover, the Senator went on, the organized criminal would secure further illicit profits by such means as arson frauds, bankruptcy frauds, and restraints on trade enforced through "techniques of violence and intimidation." Conducting the affairs of an enterprise through such a pattern of racketeering activity is prohibited by section 1962(c).

Certain expansions of the coverage of RICO beyond the "Criminal Activities Profits Act" earlier proposed by Senator Hruska should be obvious. First, although the prohibition against investment of unreported income as such has been dropped, the prohibition of direct infiltration of legitimate business has been considerably expanded. Penetration of a business through extortion and loansharking, as well as through investment of criminal profits, was prohibited, thus striking at all means of infiltration earlier identified by the Katzenbach Commission and Senator McClellan.

Second, in accord with Justice Department criticisms of the bill, section 1962(c) was added, thus providing the means to prosecute not only the act of infiltration, but also the conduct of the affairs of the enterprise through racketeering that could be expected to follow such penetration. While still serving the goal of attacking organized crime's involvement in legitimate business, section 1962(c) takes a different approach to the problem, prohibiting not the act of infiltration itself, but the criminal activities committed by the infiltrated racketeers.

Third, unlike Senator Hruska's bills, which were limited to investment of dirty money in "business enterprises," the RICO bill broadly defined "enterprise" to include "any individual, partnership, corporation, association, or other legal entity, and any union or group of individuals associated in fact although not a legal entity." This expansion clearly broadened the range of activities to be protected against infiltration beyond businesses to include labor unions and government bodies as well, both of which had been identified by Senator McClellan as victims of organized crime penetration "[c]losely paralleling its takeover of legitimate businesses."

Finally, S. 1861 substantially increased the criminal penalties applicable to violators.

In the process of broadening its assault on infiltration, the drafters of the Corrupt Organizations Act also retained and expanded those aspects of the earlier bills that swept beyond that particular problem. RICO continued to make no attempt to define organized crime, either as the monolithic Italian-American conspiracy most often discussed by the Katzenbach Commission and Senators McClellan and Hruska or in the more general sense of structured criminal syndicates or organizations of any kind. Instead, the new bill, like the old, implicitly defined organized crime by what it did rather than by what it was, by listing a variety of crimes to which the prohibitions of the act applied. Like earlier federal statutes enacted out of concern about organized crime, RICO thus makes no attempt to define its target and limit its applicability to organized crime.

Broadening the bill's prohibitions beyond organized crime, however defined, expanded its coverage beyond the "infiltration" problem the bill was supposed to address. The broadening effect of this decision, moreover, was multiplied by other innovations in the newly expanded bill. Since the Hruska proposals dealt only with the investment of profits from criminal activities, defining species of crimes instead of species of criminals as the source of prohibited investments constituted a limited and reasonable expansion of coverage: keeping criminals out of legitimate businesses is desirable whether the infiltrators are officially "made" members of the Mafia, or more localized gamblers or drug dealers. But the new section 1962(c) prohibited as well the conduct of a business through the specified criminal means. As this prohibition applied to anyone who "participate[s], directly or indirectly, in the conduct of [an] enterprise's affairs,"

and not merely to infiltrating gangsters, the dramatic criminal penalties now made available covered ordinary businessmen gone astray as well as career criminals.

Even this expansion would have been modest had the list of activities selected as "typical of organized crime" remained limited to such blue-collar offenses as drug dealing, gambling, and crimes of violence. But the Hruska bill already had included bankruptcy fraud and bribery of federal officials, and Senator McClellan's original Corrupt Organizations Act had added additional white-collar offenses such as embezzlement from union, welfare and pension funds, and interstate transportation of property stolen or taken by fraud. Most critically, the Senate Committee added to the final version of RICO violations of federal laws involving mail and wire fraud, and securities fraud. Without question, these amendments included offenses that infiltrating racketeers would be likely to commit, but the effect of the changes was that any corporate executive who conducted the affairs of his business "through a pattern of" fraud (i.e., by at least two fraudulent acts related in some unexplained fashion within ten years) would violate RICO. In short, the combination of expansions of coverage had the effect-apparently unintended—of drastically increasing the potential penalties facing many "white collar" criminals.

An even more dramatic expansion of the potential coverage of RICO appears when the language of the statute is given an only slightly more creative reading. The logic of the reading is smooth and simple: (1) it is a crime for anyone associated with any "enterprise" to conduct the affairs of that enterprise through a "pattern of racketeering activity"; (2) an "enterprise" includes "any . . . group of individuals associated in fact," a description that manifestly describes an organized crime syndicate; (3) a "pattern of racketeering activity" includes the commission of (almost any) two crimes; (4) therefore, the statute criminalizes not merely, say, the operation of a Mafia-infiltrated carting company through a pattern of extortion, but also the operation of a Mafia "family" itself, for what is a criminal syndicate but a "group of individuals associated in fact" who conduct their affairs "through a pattern of racketeering"? By this logic, RICO could be read as imposing drastic sanctions not only on the infiltration of legitimate business by organized criminals and on the operation of legitimate business in a criminal manner by anyone at all, but also on the operation of organized crime itself. And indeed, since the statute's working definition of organized crime is found only in the expansive definitions of "enterprise" and "pattern of racketeering," the statute so read would apply not only to La Cosa Nostra, but to any group of individuals banded together into an "associat[ion] in fact" to commit any of the wide range of crimes defined by section 1961(1) as "typical of organized crime."

E. The Logic of Expansion

What accounts for the continual expansion of the language of RICO to the point that the statute as enacted is protean in form and pervasive in coverage? The basic structure of the statute and the pronouncements of its supporters all support the view that the statute was initially designed to strike a blow at organized crime by criminalizing the infiltration of legitimate business by members of a nationwide criminal syndicate, and that its principal supporters in Congress never understood the statute to encompass other aspects of the organized crime problem. Nevertheless, the statute that emerged clearly goes beyond the prohibition of the act of infiltration itself and equally clearly includes more than the actions of a monolithic "Cosa Nostra." Moreover, the statute can be read without serious distortion of its language to escalate dramatically the sanctions available against business fraud and against organized criminal activity in the loosest possible sense, neither of which have any necessary relation to the infiltration problem that was all that overtly concerned the Congress. What happened?

The expansion of the coverage of the statute was driven by fundamental definitional and criminological difficulties with the project on which Congress had embarked. The original insight behind RICO—Senator Hruska's notion that it was desirable to mount a "direct attack" against the infiltration of legitimate business by organized crime—was at least plagued by definitional problems and at worst totally misguided. The effort to solve the inherent problems of the approach and salvage a useful law enforcement tool was the engine that drove the expansionist draftsmanship of RICO.

1. Defining Organized Crime. — The first definitional hurdle was faced, and solved in an expansionist direction, at the very outset. If the goal is to prohibit the penetration of legitimate business by organized crime, we must know what we mean by organized crime. Defining organized crime, however, turns out to be a slippery business, from a sociological as well as from a legal point of view. The first reaction of the ordinary citizen is to conjure up visions of "the Mafia" or "La Cosa Nostra"—a formalized, hierarchical secret society, a corporation of crime—whose central members are all but invariably Italian, or more particularly Sicilian. As we have seen, this popular image is not confined to the person in the street; the same understanding of organized crime pervaded the thinking of the President's Crime Commission and the congressional sponsors of the precursors of RICO.

But this understanding of organized crime would not do as a juridical concept in the definition of a crime. Putting aside possible constitutional problems under the bill of attainder clause, the idea that criminal prohibitions should apply generally is deeply imbedded in our traditions. Congress obviously would recoil at a law criminalizing certain actions when performed by members of a specific, named organization that could be performed without penalty by other citizens—even if that organization could be satisfactorily defined and even putting aside the further constitutional and political dubiousness of including ethnic classifications in the definition.

In any event, a definition focused on a single entity, even if one could be devised, would not be desirable. The Mafia may not be a mythical entity, but it is hardly coextensive with syndicate crime in the United States. If professional criminal elements, organized into structured, businesslike units characterized by division of labor and hierarchical organization, are moving into legitimate businesses around the country where they can be expected to continue to utilize unlawful tactics in pursuit of profit, the appropriate law enforcement response does not turn on whether a particular syndicate is affiliated with the largest nationwide organization of its kind. Granted that the devisers of RICO took some inspiration from the antitrust laws, the goal of Congress was obviously not to further competition in the criminal sector of the economy by breaking up Crime, Inc., into smaller, more efficient units.

But what of a definition of "organized crime" that tries to capture the general features of criminal syndicates that make them "organized"? This is a more promising approach, though it too presents problems of definition and proof. Exactly what elements of structure, organization, or activity differentiate a "syndicate" from a mere "gang"? How loose an association of criminals should count? How large or small must it be? Many criminals have accomplices in particular crimes, and, like the business or social associates of individuals in legitimate pursuits, those accomplices are likely to be drawn from a limited and recurring circle of acquaintances. Do these loose affinity groups constitute "organized crime"? When we say "organized crime," we clearly mean the criminal equivalents of General Motors and the University of Chicago Faculty of Law, but do we also mean the underworld counterparts of the Vienna Circle and the Critical Legal Studies Movement? And if not, how do we differentiate more from less highly organized groups in a zone of activity not given to formalized relationships?

The definitional problems here, though real, may not be insoluble. But once again, one may seriously question whether there is any point to solving them, at least if the goal is to criminalize infiltration into legitimate business. Does it really make sense to hold that a hit man or a narcotics dealer who uses his ill-gotten gains to acquire a garbage collection business, or uses strong-arm tactics to take over such a business, is more of a menace if he is associated with a relatively formal criminal organization than if he were simply a somewhat disorganized free lance? Perhaps an argument is available that a member of a functioning criminal organization is more likely to continue in his dishonest ways once ensconced in a legitimate trade, while a relatively casual criminal might use infiltration as a painless route to a straight occupation. Still, Congress can be forgiven for concluding that the distinction was not worth making in a prohibitory statute.

Rather than attempting to define even a broad concept of organized crime in terms of its structural characteristics, Congress' solution, which was reached in the very first of Senator Hruska's proposed bills and never departed from, was to define the problem functionally. Organized crime is as organized crime does. In other words, anyone who performed the criminal acts considered typical of organized crime would be treated the same as the Mafia capo. Of course, the list of crimes typical of organized crime rapidly became a long and diverse list, for is it not a defining characteristic of organized crime that it would do just about anything for a profit?

From such puzzling about the concept of organized crime was born the "pattern of racketeering." Any criminal can be a racketeer, regardless of his involvement in a criminal syndicate, if he commits a "pattern of racketeering acts." The logic of defining crimes in general terms, and the difficulty of defining organized crime structurally, led inexorably to the conclusion that anyone who attempts to acquire a foothold in a legitimate business through violence or usury, or by investing the proceeds of criminal activities, should be subject to the same penalties.

2. Defining Legitimate Business. – Similar problems pushed back the frontiers of the area to be protected against "infiltration." Legal concepts like corporations or partnerships were inadequate to the definitional task. Criminals could, and the studies available to Congress showed that they sometimes did, penetrate not only legal entities officially capable of divided ownership, but also unincorporated businesses nominally owned by a sole proprietor, acquiring covert interests in the profits of such businesses through their muscle or capital. Indeed, "business" itself was too narrow a term. What about labor unions, to take only the most obvious example? Or charitable or social organizations? Or trade associations (the prototypical vehicle for the operation of a "racket")? Or even governmental agencies or offices? The definitional construct had to encompass all of these. Here, Congress' answer was the "enterprise" – a nicely vague and encompassing term that could cover just about anything, and was defined so that it did.

Thus, the technical difficulties of defining key concepts in the conduct Congress sought to attack forced the realization that a fairly broad range of conduct not necessarily included in the catch-phrase description of the evil to be prevented by the statute should be brought within its prohibition. But the core conceptual problem of the approach Congress had chosen would not appear until Congress set about defining what it meant by "infiltration."

3. Defining Infiltration. – Here, too, there was a technical problem, though one that was rather easily solved, again in an expansionist direction. Senator Hruska's original proposals prohibited only the financial penetration of a legitimate business by criminal elements through the investment of the proceeds of criminal conduct. As ultimately enacted, RICO also prohibited acquisition of legitimate businesses through racketeering means such as extortion or loansharking.

This expansion, though simple and logical, marks a subtle change in focus. If the financial penetration model had already, in Senator Hruska's formulation, made its peace with a broadened concept of "racketeer" that did not specifically require that the infiltrator be an agent of "organized crime," at least it retained the idea of the infiltrator as a character previously identifiable as a criminal. That is, in order to have acquired tainted funds to invest in an ordinary business, the infiltrator must have already engaged in a pattern of defined criminal conduct. The image was thus maintained of two separate spheres, the legitimate and the criminal, that meet only when an alien being from the underworld breaches the wall between them by "infiltrating" or "penetrating" the world of legitimate activity.

One needs no prior involvement in criminal activity, however, to violate section 1962(b): anyone who acquires an interest in a business through a pattern of violence or usury is ipso facto a racketeer. Thus, one who was not previously part of the criminal sphere becomes a racketeer by the same act by which he infiltrates the straight business world. There is, of course, nothing peculiar about punishing such conduct, but the change highlights the oddity of "infiltration" as a defining concept in a criminal statute: what is offensive about the violation of section 1962(b) is the conduct of extorting a business interest from a victim, not some metaphorical corruption of the business enterprise that comes about by its invasion by a "racketeer."

The change thus reflects a broader problem inherent in the basic idea of a law prohibiting the "infiltration" of legitimate enterprises by criminals. Putting aside for a moment the acquisition of a business interest through direct criminal action, the act of acquisition is morally neutral, or even beneficial—"black money" is fungible with the ordinary green stuff with respect to its economic function as a source of capital for socially productive businesses. The harm to society is not in the act of infiltration—the investment of criminal proceeds—but in the acts of racketeering that precede and follow it. Society is injured by the narcotics and gambling businesses that are the source of criminals' profits, not by the use of those profits to buy a laundry; any harmful result of the latter comes not directly from the investment itself, but from the predicted operation of the laundry by criminal means.

Of course, this does not pose a critical problem in criminal law theory. Acts not intrinsically harmful in themselves, when committed with a criminal intent, may be punished as attempts. More to the point, specific acts that threaten future harm may be criminalized without the showing of any intent beyond the intent to commit the "preparatory" act itself, as, for example, with statutes prohibiting possession of weapons.

Prohibition of the morally neutral act of investing under circumstances suggesting that the investment may lead to future social harms is thus not conceptually difficult. Such legislation may have its costs: for example, the possibility that legitimate investments might lead criminals to retire from active commission of crimes is foregone. But if Congress concludes, as apparently it did, that criminals entering legitimate businesses corrupt the straight world rather than straightening themselves out, no reason of principle prevents it from prohibiting the act that brings the criminal closer to the accomplishment of his goal, even at the expense of preventing those who would perform the same act for innocent purposes. Section 1962(a) of RICO, in effect, could be construed as a kind of inchoate crime.

The expedience of such a course is another question entirely. The whole point of punishing possession of burglar tools is that it is easier to prove than attempted burglary. Such advantages might well be desirable in prosecuting organized crime figures, who are often difficult to convict. But the RICO infiltration offense is not easier to prove than the charges already available. In order to prove a violation of section 1962(a), the prosecutor still has to prove the underlying racketeering acts that constituted the source of the proceeds or the means of acquiring the enterprise. Since these are by definition already crimes, and constitute the principal socially harmful conduct committed by the defendant, RICO has not made it any easier

(procedural and remedial considerations aside) to prove the case; it has eliminated no element necessary to convict on the underlying charges. On the contrary, it has added an additional element: the use of the proceeds from racketeering to invest in a legitimate enterprise. That element is hardly a trivial one. Even if the underlying illegitimate activities could be proved, it may well be extremely difficult, and it usually will be burdensome, to prove that the funds used to acquire the interest were indeed drawn from the profits of the defendant's racketeering activities, rather than from other sources.

Cases brought under section 1962(b) do not present the same problem. Where the government can prove that an interest in a legitimate enterprise is the fruit of an extortion or the collection of an illegal debt, casting the offense as a violation of section 1962(b) imposes little or no additional burden on the prosecution. Indeed, in most cases the shape of the prosecution's case will not be affected at all. The prosecution will need to show that the victim parted with some property in order to prove most predicate crimes of this category. Even where an equally severe offense not requiring such proof is available, the prosecutor for tactical reasons will generally prefer to prove the loss to the victim, if such a loss actually occurred. It thus imposes no additional burden on the prosecutor, where the proceeds of the crime consist of an interest in an enterprise rather than mere cash, to punish separately the infiltration aspect of the crime.

On the other hand, one may seriously question how helpful this additional weapon is to prosecutors. Acquiring a business through the commission of a crime is, tautologically, a crime already. And those crimes that will most commonly be the means of infiltration are already provided with ample penalties. If section 1962(a) seems too cumbersome a tool to be useful to law enforcement, section 1962(b) appears merely redundant.

4. Defining Pattern of Racketeering. – Prohibiting acts of infiltration per se thus proves to add few useful legal weapons against it. Section 1962(c) represents a possible response to the futility of subsections (a) and (b). If the principal harm to be feared from infiltration is the consequent likelihood that the business will be run in a criminal fashion, and especially if it is difficult to see exactly how to prohibit infiltration in a way that makes it easier for law enforcement to stop it, why not go to the heart of the matter and make it a separate offense, more serious than the underlying crimes themselves, to operate an enterprise in the way racketeers can be expected to: through a pattern of criminal acts?

This step requires no revolution in criminal law theory: sentence-enhancing statutes are common, as are statutes that, in form or substance, create higher degrees of offenses where additional social harms are present. But what precisely is the aggravating circumstance in section 1962(c)? In the case of infiltration, the additional aggravating factor might be thought to be the presence of the racketeer. An ordinary business fraud is bad enough, but a fraud committed by an organized criminal who acquired the business in the first place only so as to commit such frauds is arguably something worse. But there are definitional and conceptual difficulties with this approach. The structure of RICO reflects a decision that it is too difficult and constitutionally problematic to define racketeers other than by their acts. Moreover, section 1962(b) assumes that prior racketeering acts are not necessarily required: if under section 1962(b) one can become a racketeer by acting like one in the acquisition of a business, why cannot one become a racketeer by acting like one in the operation of a business?

Finally, it is by no means clear that, in the context of a "legitimate" enterprise, "being a racketeer" is really an aggravating factor. If the principal danger of racketeers in business is that they will create a social harm by conducting the business in a distinctly criminal way, it is difficult to understand why anyone who conducts a business in such a socially harmful way should not be equally accountable. And so the operation of a legitimate enterprise by criminal means becomes a logical target of RICO, whether or not the perpetrators are infiltrating racketeers.

But if a prior record of racketeering is not the distinguishing aggravating factor in section 1962(c), only the "corruption" of an enterprise is left to distinguish the violation of that statute, with its severe penalties, from the mere commission of predicate offenses. In the abstract, putting the resources of a corporation or a union behind a criminal act, or distorting a legitimate economic institution, may plausibly be thought to aggravate the intrinsic harm or wrongfulness of a particular criminal act. In practical operation, however, it is difficult to isolate this factor. Many RICO predicate crimes can only be committed in the context of an economic enterprise: the claim that a securities fraud or Taft-Hartley violation is worse if it implicates the resources of an economic enterprise is meaningless. Nor is it easy to define the "corruption" of a legitimate organization. News media accounts frequently describe a RICO count as charging that "the defendants in effect converted the [named legitimate enterprise] into a criminal enterprise," but the sense of pervasive corruption this implies is only rarely accurate and is certainly not required by a statute that permits a "pattern of racketeering" to be found in as few as two predicate criminal acts regardless of the size of the enterprise. The addition of section 1962(c) to the statute, then, expands the coverage of the statute to the point that the infiltration idea, and with it any specific harm that can be identified with crime in the context of a legitimate enterprise, totally evaporates.

The logic of expansion has now become fairly clear: the intrinsic illogic of attempting to punish infiltration itself, combined with the difficulties of defining "organized crime," inevitably resulted in a statute that punishes anyone who acts in the way that organized criminals are thought to act when they have infiltrated the legitimate world—by corrupting legitimate institutions to criminal ends. And since corruption of an enterprise from within is no easier to define than infiltration from without, the statute is left punishing anyone who commits more than one crime within the context of a legitimate enterprise, with only the shakiest justification for treating such crime as distinct from or more serious than crime that occurs outside such an enterprise.

Combined with the expansive definition of "enterprise" already discussed, however, the statute can be read to break down even this distinction, by providing enhanced punishment for anyone who acts like an organized criminal—by committing crimes. For, as already noted, an "enterprise" does not need to be a legitimate institution at all. At least if the statutory definition is taken literally, the RICO statute is violated if a "group of individuals associated in fact"—say, the James gang—runs its enterprise not by criminal means that distort its legitimate ends, but by the very crimes that are the object of the association in the first place. As we are about to see, the courts have interpreted RICO very literally indeed.

F. RICO in the Courts: The Expansion Continues

The goal of curbing organized crime's penetration into legitimate sectors of society thus resulted, through the combination of a congressional choice to attack the problem by direct prohibition and the difficulties of drafting a statute that would effectively make such an attack, in a very broadly drafted bill that was capable of being applied to a remarkable range of conduct. But the breadth of potential coverage would not necessarily be determinative. The new law would have to be applied by prosecutors and judges. How they responded to the bill's language would determine its ultimate scope. While they initially responded cautiously, within a few years it would become clear that RICO would have all the reach that its language suggested.

* * *

G. The Consolidation of RICO: Russello and the 1984 Amendments

The Supreme Court's decision in Russello v.

United States may represent the culmination of the judicial acceptance of prosecutors' efforts to transform RICO from a weapon against organized crime infiltration of legitimate business into a statute proscribing criminal organizations generally. Russello, like Turkette, involved an arson-for-hire ring. The arsonists were convicted of RICO violations, among other crimes, and, in addition to fines and prison sentences, various forfeitures were ordered. The issue before the Supreme Court was whether the profits earned by one of the arsonists were subject to forfeiture as part of the RICO judgment.

Though the issue has since been clearly resolved by statute, under RICO as it stood in 1983 the forfeiture was highly dubious. The forfeiture section provided that any person convicted of violating RICO shall forfeit to the United States "any interest he has acquired or maintained in violation of" RICO. Russello argued, in support of a narrow construction, that money or profits acquired through criminal conduct could not constitute an "interest" within the meaning of this provision because an "'[i]nterest,' by definition, includes of necessity an interest in something." In other words, Russello claimed that an interest, as opposed to profits or proceeds, meant an interest in the enterprise itself.

This interpretation, plausible if not necessarily compelling on its face, becomes highly persuasive when the statutory language is considered against the original purpose of RICO and the intended relation of its innovative civil and forfeiture remedies to those purposes. From its earliest precursors, the idea of RICO was to attack organized crime penetration of legitimate enterprises, not only by criminalizing the act of infiltration, but also (indeed especially) by providing remedies in addition to ordinary criminal sanctions in order to remove racketeers from the businesses they had entered. The proponents of RICO, in fact, made much of this feature of the Act. Senator McClellan, for example, in responding to critics of RICO who complained that the statute would do little more than add additional penalties for acts that already were illegal, answered that RICO was intended to do more than just deter undesirable actions by the use of criminal punishment:

[T]he committee ignores the fact that [RICO] adds to the existing criminal penalties of fine and imprisonment the further criminal penalty of forfeiture. Criminal forfeiture under [RICO] serves not only to punish, deter, incapacitate and so on—it serves directly to remove the corrupting influence from the channels of commerce.

Similarly, in introducing S. 1861, the immediate predecessor of the enacted version of RICO and the first version to contain the forfeiture provision, Senator McClellan linked the familiar "cancer" analogy specifically to organized crime's invasion of the body of the legitimate economy, and stressed the surgical effects of forfeiture in removing the racketeer from the infiltrated enterprise: "If an organization is acquired or run by the proscribed racketeering method, then the persons involved are removed from the organization." Examples of such references to the forfeiture provisions can be multiplied.

The close connection between the forfeiture remedy of RICO and the goal of extruding the racketeer from infiltrated legitimate organizations is further emphasized by the parallel forfeiture provisions of the narcotics "kingpin" or "continuing criminal enterprise" statute, enacted essentially contemporaneously with RICO. That statute contained forfeiture language substantially identical to that of section 1963, except for the explicit addition of "profits" as a forfeitable item. The contrast is easily explained. The point of the forfeiture provisions of the narcotics statute is to take the profit out of drug dealing by making the financial penalty commensurate with the profits available from the crime. Since narcotics dealers will rarely operate the sort of "enterprise" in which it is possible to have a legal "interest" or "claim," the way to accomplish this is to forfeit the proceeds of the crime. In RICO, on the other hand, the point of the forfeiture is primarily to remove the "cancerous" corrupting influence from the legitimate enterprise it has invaded. Forfeiture of the profits the racketeer has earned from his crimes does not itself directly address this problem; what must be taken from the racketeer is that which gives him control of the enterprise: the interest he has acquired with those profits.

Despite these strong indications that the term "interest" had been understood by Congress to have a limited meaning, the Supreme Court unanimously rejected Russello's arguments. Although the Court made a number of rather inconclusive arguments from the structure and language of the statute, the critical policy argument that dictated the Court's conclusion is simple and powerful:

We note that the RICO statute's definition of the term "enterprise" in § 1961(4) encompasses both legal entities and illegitimate associations-in-fact. See United States v. Turkette, 452 U.S., at 580-593. Forfeiture of an interest in an illegitimate association-in-fact ordinarily would be of little use because an association of that kind rarely has identifiable assets; instead, proceeds or profits usually are distributed immediately. Thus, construing § 1963(a)(1) to reach only interests in an enterprise would blunt the effectiveness of the provision in combating illegitimate enterprises, and would mean that "[w]hole areas of organized criminal activity would be placed beyond" the reach of the statute. United States v. Turkette, 452 U.S., at 589.

In other words, if the forfeiture remedy is to have any value in illegitimate enterprise cases, an interpretation keyed to the statute's original purpose (which did not reach such enterprises) is unacceptable. Having reached beyond the original purpose of RICO in Turkette, the Supreme Court was virtually compelled to adapt the forfeiture provisions to its expanded substantive reach. By the time Russello was decided, the use of RICO for a direct attack, not on infiltration of legitimate enterprises but on the criminal activities of the syndicates themselves, had become well enough established to govern the interpretation of other portions of the statute.

Whether or not Russello conformed to the understanding of the members of Congress who voted for the Organized Crime Control Act of 1970, it was well in keeping with the spirit of Congress in the 1980s. In the Comprehensive Crime Control Act of 1984, Congress revisited RICO for the first time since its enactment in 1970, expressly adopting the Russello holding and considerably elaborating the forfeiture provisions.

In two major respects, the 1984 forfeiture provisions represent an implicit endorsement of the use of RICO against illegitimate associations. The first, of course, is the codification of Russello. As we have just seen, the forfeiture of the profits of racketeering activity is valuable precisely because it provides serious financial sanctions for RICO prosecutions in the Elliott-Turkette mold. At least implicitly, the congressional endorsement of Russello suggests congressional satisfaction with this branch of the RICO case law.

The second change bears a more complicated relation to the original purposes of RICO. The 1984 amendments provide that the property interest of the United States in assets forfeitable under the statute vests not when the forfeiture is ordered, but rather "upon the commission of the act giving rise to forfeiture under this section." Since the assets thus became government property immediately upon commission of the RICO violation, it follows that the assets cannot be validly transferred by the violator, and the statute accordingly provides that [a]ny such property that is subsequently transferred to a person other than the defendant may be the subject of a special verdict of forfeiture and thereafter shall be ordered forfeited to the United States, unless the transferee establishes . . . that he is a bona fide purchaser for value . . . who was reasonably without cause to believe that the property was subject to forfeiture. . . .

This provision completely divorces the forfeiture remedy from its original function of removing infiltrating racketeers from legitimate enterprises. Under RICO as originally enacted, if the Godfather extorted an interest in a garbage carting business, he could be convicted of violating section 1962(b), and his interest in the business would be forfeited, the forfeiture serving, as we have seen, to remove the corrupting influence of the organized criminal. If, however, the Godfather had sold the business to a bona fide purchaser before the indictment had been brought, he would no longer have any interest in the enterprise to be forfeited. This would not defeat or evade the purposes of RICO. So long as the sale was an actual bona fide transfer, the purpose of RICO had been accomplished, the racketeer having been removed from the infiltrated business.

Under the new provision for forfeitures relating back to the date of the violation, however, since the Godfather's interest in the business would have been forfeited ab initio, if the transferee had reason to know of the Godfather's mode of acquiring the business, the business could be forfeited from the transferee. This sort of forfeiture could well serve to deter legitimate businesspeople from dealing with racketeers, but it is far removed from the kind of divestiture of infiltrated assets contemplated by the sponsors of the original RICO provisions. The "relation back" provisions, like the express provision for forfeiture of the proceeds of racketeering activity and of property "derived from" such proceeds, will likely prove most useful in broadening the scope of forfeiture available in cases brought against illicit enterprises under section 1962(c), where both doctrines will sharply limit criminals' ability to avoid forfeiture by hiding or transferring the proceeds of their criminal activities.

While it may be dangerous to draw authoritative conclusions about the legislators' attitudes toward the body of RICO law developed by the courts over a decade and a half from such haphazardly drafted legislation, it would appear obvious that Congress is reasonably satisfied with what prosecutors and courts have made of RICO. Despite commentators' criticisms of judicial interpretations of RICO and specific recommendations for revision of the statute from the American Bar Association, Congress was content to leave RICO's substantive provisions where it found them. Moreover, the tinkering that Congress did do with the forfeiture provisions makes sense only on the assumption that if Congress had at one time conceived of RICO only as a weapon against organized criminal infiltration of legitimate business, by 1984 it no longer did. If RICO has evolved into something different from what Congress intended at its creation, it is difficult to escape the conclusion that Congress has looked at what has evolved, and pronounced it good.

II. RICO'S PRESENT ECOLOGICAL NICHE

A. RICO, Federalism, and Legality

From this survey of RICO's history, it can readily be seen that, as currently interpreted, RICO is capable of exceptionally broad application. If virtually any criminal federation can be a RICO enterprise, and almost any two criminal acts can be a pattern of racketeering activity, then potential RICO liability exists whenever more than one person engages in more than one crime. Over a wide domain of actors and conduct, RICO has swallowed the penal code. Two significant criticisms of this comprehensive scope can be made.

1. Federalism. – Within the context of our federal system, RICO can be criticized as a major and unjustified expansion of the federal role in law enforcement. RICO, after all, has not only swallowed the federal penal code, but by its incorporation of a wide variety of state crimes as predicate acts, it has also swallowed large chunks of the state penal codes.

I do not find the expansion of federal jurisdiction per se especially troubling. This is not the place for a definitive discussion of the proper role of the federal government in crime control, still less of the proper role of the states as independent sovereignties in today's world. Nevertheless, one may question whether the federalism issue presents a fundamental philosophical problem, or merely a question of the efficient allocation of resources and responsibilities in a rather unwieldy system of overlapping jurisdictions. Over-federalization of law enforcement does not appear to be a pressing political concern, nor is it apparent that prosecution of RICO offenses by federal officials threatens either the rights of individual defendants or the remaining sovereignty of the states.

I note two reservations about my general equanimity concerning expanded federal involvement in law enforcement. First, whatever one's view of the appropriate degree or scope of the federal role in law enforcement, all can agree that the division of responsibility between the states and the federal government should be organized on some rational principle, with the areas of federal involvement specifically defined, rather than permitting discretionary federal intervention into a broad range of local crimes whenever prosecutors choose to intervene. But given the essentially universal quality of RICO's coverage, the latter situation is exactly what has developed. RICO does not extend federal jurisdiction to specific areas of particular federal concern or competence; it creates federal jurisdiction over broad reaches of criminal conduct, characterized only by loose concepts of concerted and repeated activity and minimal subject matter limitations. Prosecutorial judgment and prosecutorial interest are the true determinants of federal involvement.

Second, states do have a strong interest in determining, by their definitions of offenses and ordering of penalties, the relative seriousness and importance of different crimes. Many states have made serious attempts to do this, through reform of their penal codes along the lines suggested by the Model Penal Code, and by recent efforts to control sentencing discretion through rational guidelines. RICO substantially subverts this process by incorporating the substance of state prohibitions without recognizing any of the sentencing or degree gradations present in state offenses, and subjecting violators to a single, severe maximum sentence and (pending the completion of efforts to create federal sentencing guidelines) unrestricted judicial sentencing discretion.

2. Legality. – Another major criticism of RICO's breadth presents an issue not unique to federal systems, but rather general to any system of criminal justice. One of the organizing principles of the criminal law is that criminal prohibitions must comport with the principle of legality. This principle requires, among other things, that in order to be acceptable, penal legislation must describe with some precision the conduct it proscribes and the consequences that may flow from conviction for such conduct.

Although the broad scope of RICO has been seen by some as offending this principle, the courts have not been particularly receptive to challenges to RICO along these lines. The argument that RICO is unconstitutionally vague has been uniformly rejected, and on reasoning that is not unappealing. After all, courts have reminded us that, unlike the imprecise loitering statutes that have been found unconstitutionally vague by various courts, RICO does not require citizens to guess at their peril what kinds of conduct they must avoid to conduct their affairs in accordance with law. Since RICO merely imposes additional liability on those who, under certain conditions, commit particular other offenses, all one needs to do to stay out of trouble is to avoid committing murder, mail fraud, narcotics violations, and other predicate acts. Assuming the statutes defining these crimes are not unconstitutionally vague in their own right, RICO provides adequate notice of the prohibited conduct. As one court put it, RICO "may be broad, but it is not vague."

But this answer dodges important problems. It is not clear that the values of legality for guidance of the citizen are adequately served by a scheme in which prohibitions are clearly stated, but unexpectedly severe penalties can be imposed. Without a reasonably clear statement of the penalties that attach to a particular offense, the citizen planning her activities is not really given full notice of what behavior society truly expects from her. The intensity of society's demand, as expressed in the available punishment, is relevant to the actor's understanding of her responsibilities. In some respects, at least, the Constitution protects a citizen's justified expectation that conduct is only punishable to a particular extent in the same way as her expectation that conduct is lawful: a law raising penalties after the fact is void as an ex post facto law just as much as one that criminalizes conduct legal when committed.

Furthermore, the legality principle is not limited to the requirement that the citizen be given fair notice of what conduct to avoid; it also demands that officials be given reasonably clear instructions concerning how violators should be treated. As the Supreme Court recognized in Papachristou, vague statutes are unacceptable not only because they fail to provide fair notice to the citizen of the prohibited conduct, but also because they permit discriminatory or erratic enforcement, since police, prosecutors and courts have little to go on in determining whether to sanction particular acts. Indeed, the Court has recently suggested that controlling the discretion of law enforcement officers is the more important reason for invalidating vague statutes.

This concern is plainly applicable to RICO. The presumably careful and deliberate attachment of penalties to particular offense categories is effectively undermined if a prosecutor is empowered to increase those penalties dramatically by transforming ordinary offenses into RICO violations simply by the invocation of verbal formulae.

A simple example will clarify the point. A businessman who conceives a fraudulent scheme and mails a single letter in furtherance of it commits mail fraud, a felony punishable by five years' imprisonment and, until recently, by a fine of $1000. Mailing a similar letter to a second victim constitutes a separate offense, bringing the total sentence exposure to ten years and $2000. If, as is not unlikely, the swindler has an associate who can be described as a co-conspirator, he has committed a third felony, raising the potential punishment to fifteen years and a fine of $12,000. Under RICO, however, our protagonist has now also conducted the affairs of his business enterprise through a pattern of racketeering activity and has conspired to do so, exposing himself to the possibility of a forty-year sentence, a $50,000 fine, and most importantly, forfeiture of his entire business. Nothing in the statute imposes any limits or standards to govern prosecutorial discretion in determining whether to invoke the additional sanctions. Thus, the prosecuting authority has the unrestricted power to increase dramatically the stakes in a given case, for any reason that seems appropriate to it.

The judicial response to vagueness challenges to RICO thus points up a weakness in existing vagueness theory. Although the vagueness doctrine aims to provide both fair notice to citizens bound by the law and meaningful constraints on the discretion of the officials who must execute it, the two goals are not always well served by the same strategies. As RICO shows, a statute may be clear enough in informing citizens of the conduct they must avoid, but at the same time be so encompassing as to increase rather than decrease the discretion provided to officials. Indeed, the two goals occasionally conflict, for as we have seen, the effort to avoid vagueness and imprecision in the core concepts of "infiltration" and "organized crime" to a considerable extent account for the extraordinary breadth of the statute's coverage.

Vesting this sort of enhancement power in prosecutors is not exactly unprecedented. Various recidivist and dangerous special offender statutes, for example, permit prosecutors to choose whether to invoke procedures that would increase the defendant's sentence exposure. These statutes, however, affect only limited types of offenders and require that the prosecutor, if the increased penalty is to be exacted, make some particular showing to demonstrate that the defendant in the case at hand falls within the defined category. RICO contains no such limitations. Because it is triggered by a wide variety of crimes, and because the preconditions for its invocation are present in a wide range of cases, its availability is far less limited than that of typical special offender or recidivist statutes. Moreover, no substantial additional element needs to be proven beyond the commission of the predicate offenses, in most instances, for the prosecutor to make the enhanced sentence stick. Finally, the mandatory character of the forfeiture aspect of the RICO sanction places greater sentencing power in the hands of the prosecutor, in a way that special offender provisions without mandatory minimum sentences do not.

Even taking these distinguishing factors into account, however, the extent to which RICO constitutes an expansion of prosecutorial power should not be exaggerated. While in some situations RICO radically increases available penalties without requiring proof of any substantial fact beyond the commission of the underlying criminal acts, this will not inevitably be so. In the typical illegitimate enterprise case, for example, the predicate acts may be offenses such as murder, arson, extortion, or narcotics trafficking, which carry substantial penalties of their own. In such cases, the additional impact of the forfeiture remedy may be slight. And in such a case (unlike the typical business crime case) the requirement that the crimes be committed in furtherance of a particular enterprise presents at least some additional hurdle to the prosecutor, who must show something (albeit something rather nebulous) beyond the mere commission of the crimes themselves.

Moreover, the wide discretion of the prosecutor to broaden or narrow the sentence exposure of the defendant by the selection of charges from a host of overlapping potential charges is characteristic of our system of justice, rather than a departure from it. A single act may violate a number of criminal statutes, and the double jeopardy clause provides only minimal protection against imposition of multiple consecutive sentences. In a mail fraud case more typical than the example used earlier, the schemers may have mailed not two but two-hundred letters, and made as many interstate telephone calls. In such a case, the prosecutor has discretion to seek an indictment charging either a handful or a host of counts, thus either limiting the range of possible sentences to an uncomfortably narrow scope of judicial discretion or broadening it to unrealistic excess without any more legal restraint than guides the RICO determination.

Thus, it would be unduly naive to consider the prosecutorial discretion permitted by RICO a departure from faithfully honored principles of predictability and legality. But while RICO does not create a previously unimagined potential for abuse, a measured concern for the impact of RICO on the principle of legality is wholly appropriate. Few would argue that the enormous range of charging options made available to prosecutors constitutes one of the glories of our criminal justice system; a substantial addition to this armory is cause for concern.

Moreover, RICO presents an extreme case of discretionary charge enhancement. The potential to select from among a wide range of potential charges in describing a particular criminal incident is ordinarily a byproduct of a legitimate legislative purpose to cover a diversity of antisocial conduct with precisely defined statutes. It is precisely because the legislature has been careful to define with particularity each individual act that it regards as an appropriate subject for punishment if committed in isolation that the prosecutor has such wide discretion when numerous legislative enactments are violated at the same time. Similarly, recidivist statutes respond to an understandable desire on the part of legislatures to insist that prior criminal conduct be given substantial weight in judicial sentencing decisions. Here, the prosecutor's power is enhanced, because he retains the power to dispense with the invocation of this particular sanction, even where it literally applies, in cases where it is fair to forego its use.

RICO, on the other hand, is so much broader than other criminal statutes that the discretion it confers may be seen as different in kind. Although it purports simply to define a new crime—which a defendant might or might not commit in conjunction with other crimes and which the prosecutor could then, like other charges, invoke or not in his discretion—the crime thus defined is so far-reaching that the commission of more than one crime will usually trigger availability of RICO automatically. And while even this is not entirely unprecedented, the disparity of scale between the RICO sanctions and those of at least some of its predicate acts suggests that the prosecutor's ability unilaterally to declare a crime major or minor has been dramatically increased.

We may well be willing to live with this result. Despite academic criticism, there is little pressure for substantial reform of the broad charging discretion characteristic of our system and little indication that the discretion is being routinely or seriously abused. Any definition of a new crime increases the discretionary power of prosecutors, and the byproduct of increased prosecutorial power may be acceptable (subject to any system-wide effort to control that discretion) if the ability to punish the conduct thus proscribed is valuable to society. But an offense definition that smudges the entire effort to provide clear definitions of conduct subject to clearly defined sanctions should bear a heavy burden of justification. If the conduct reached by RICO can be subjected to appropriate sanctions by more carefully drawn statutes, then it would be desirable to replace the broad and shapeless statute with the narrow and precise laws that would serve its legitimate purposes without endangering the legality principle.

B. The Uses of RICO

In order to determine whether RICO performs a necessary function, we must first discern what functions it does perform. Examination of the uses to which RICO has been put should accomplish two things. First, it should tell us whether RICO is serving some law enforcement purpose that otherwise could not effectively be served. If it were true, as Professor Bradley has maintained, that "RICO has virtually never been used in a case which was not reachable by other statutes, federal or state, which were on the books prior to its passage," then presumably the statute should be repealed altogether. Second, if categories of cases can be identified in which RICO has served a valuable purpose, by permitting desirable prosecutions that would not otherwise be possible, an examination of such categories might reveal weaknesses or gaps in the present structure of federal criminal law. If possible, it would clearly be desirable to fill such gaps with specific legislation, rather than leaving RICO as a general tool to bring any prosecution that the Justice Department thinks is desirable but that does not fit under any other heading.

An examination of the uses of RICO will also answer several other questions: Has RICO been effective in dealing with the organized crime infiltration of legitimate business and labor organizations that Congress was particularly concerned with in passing the statute? Have prosecutors used the law principally as a weapon against organized crime, or has it been used more widely against broader categories of offenses? How extensively have prosecutors used RICO against white collar crime? Only after such questions as these have been answered will it be possible to decide whether the principal uses of the statute have proved valuable and legitimate responses to criminal conduct not adequately covered by other criminal statutes, and if so, whether more limited additions to the penal code can fill the gaps.

To answer these questions, I surveyed all reported criminal RICO cases decided in the courts of appeals through 1985. The survey yielded an enormous number of cases. From the first reported appellate decision involving the statute in 1974 to the end of 1985, federal appellate courts had handed down reported opinions in cases arising out of nearly 250 indictments containing RICO counts. For 236 of these indictments, enough detail concerning the underlying facts of the criminal transactions and the structure of the indictments was provided in the opinions (or in district court opinions or in related cases) that the opinions could be studied with a view to determining use patterns of the criminal provisions of RICO.

Of course, the reported cases cannot answer many legitimate and important questions about the use of RICO. For example, it is likely that the dramatically enhanced sanctions available through the use of RICO give prosecutors an extra card to play in plea negotiations. Defense attorneys representing subjects in white collar investigations may not uncommonly hear prosecutors mention that a RICO indictment is being considered, and this information may affect their calculations concerning the wisdom of cooperating with investigators rather than maintaining professions of innocence. In some cases, indictments including RICO counts may be handed up and later settled by acceptance of pleas to lesser charges in return for the dismissal of the RICO charges. A study only of litigated cases cannot reveal the extent of this practice.

While it would surely be interesting to know more about the effect of RICO on plea bargaining, that is not the purpose of this study. What I am seeking to discover is whether RICO is currently being used to deal with categories of criminal behavior that are difficult to prosecute under previous legislation. To the extent that the availability of discretionarily enhanced sentences is actually being used by prosecutors to induce guilty pleas, this is simply a concrete manifestation of the dangers of such an unfocused statute already discussed in the last section. Such dangers, we have already concluded, place a burden on those who support RICO to identify the benefits it offers.

What sorts of cases, then, are being brought under RICO?

1. Infiltration of Legitimate Business. – RICO has been a nearly total failure as a weapon against the kind of activity that led Congress to enact it.

* * *

2. An Overview of the Cases. – What sorts of cases, then, are being brought under RICO? Has RICO served legitimate law enforcement purposes that cannot be served by more narrowly drawn statutes? That RICO has not solved the problem its sponsors were principally concerned about does not mean it has no legitimate uses.

Of the 236 RICO indictments discussed in the sample reported appellate cases, 228 of them appear to have charged either substantive violations of section 1962(c) or conspiracies to commit such violations. The most striking feature of these cases is the diversity of the criminal conduct they involve: labor racketeering, terrorism, gambling, narcotics, arson, business fraud, political corruption, prostitution, murder, and copyright violations. As we have seen already, the range of conduct that can be penalized under RICO is broad indeed, and the cases that have actually been brought fully reflect that potential.

* * *

6. Some Conclusions. – None of the uses of RICO encountered so far is radical or revolutionary in any sense. In each instance, the underlying predicate acts are familiar crimes, usually sufficiently closely related to each other that they could have been tried as part of the same indictment under conventional procedural rules; the "enterprise," whether business entity, government agency, or labor union, provides the setting for the crimes, or serves to symbolize its victim or ultimate beneficiary, but does not ultimately affect the nature of the proof offered. The trial of the RICO indictment differs in no significant respect – save perhaps for the offering of evidence relating to a possible forfeiture verdict – from a trial of a hypothetical indictment charging only the predicate acts themselves.

Of course, this does not mean that the RICO indictment serves no purpose, or that the criminals involved could easily have been brought to book had RICO never been enacted. In each area so far examined, federal prosecutors would have reasonable grounds for arguing that if RICO had not been available, under the existing federal criminal code a federal prosecution would have been difficult or impossible, or would have resulted (assuming conviction) in penalties not commensurate with the gravity of the offenses charged. The prosecutions that have been undertaken raise legitimate questions of federal law enforcement policy: Should local governmental corruption be subject to federal prosecutorial jurisdiction? What is the appropriate sentencing structure for business frauds or labor corruption? RICO hardly represents a considered response to these questions and may not provide the correct answers, but the use of RICO has not presented significant problems of unfairness. The adaptation of RICO to these functions by prosecutors and courts cannot be considered an "abuse" of the statute.

Nevertheless, if RICO's use were limited to these areas, it would be rather easily expendable. Given the failure of RICO to accomplish much towards its original goal of directly penalizing organized crime infiltration of legitimate business, the danger presented by a statute that vests so much additional power (whether or not exercised responsibly) in prosecutors and sentencing judges to escalate the potential or actual sanctions for criminal conduct puts too much strain on fundamental principles of legality to be justified by the covert solution of a handful of weaknesses in the federal penal law. The ease with which these gaps could be filled by straightforward legislation directly addressed to each problem, some of which has already begun to be passed, would certainly counsel the repeal of RICO and its replacement with a handful of modest jurisdictional and sentencing reforms.

But these have not in fact been the only uses of RICO; indeed, for essentially the reasons outlined, they do not seem to be the most significant ones. Numerically the largest category of cases in the survey, arguably the most important in terms of the law enforcement benefits obtained, and by far the most important in terms of the challenge it presents to conventional theories of substantive criminal law and criminal procedure, consists of the cases in which RICO has been used not against the criminal infiltration or utilization of a legitimate enterprise, but as a device for a direct assault against illegitimate syndicates or criminal organizations themselves. These cases are so important that they deserve a separate section all to themselves.

D. Mail Fraud

Jed S. Rakoff, The Federal Mail Fraud Statute (Part I), 18 Duq.L.Rev. 771-822 (1980)*

I. INTRODUCTION

To federal prosecutors of white collar crime, the

---

* Reprinted with permission.

mail fraud statute is our Stradivarius, our Colt 45, our Louisville Slugger, our Cuisinard—and our true love. We may flirt with RICO, show off with 10b-5, and call the conspiracy law "darling," but we always come home to the virtues of 18 U.S.C. § 1341, with its simplicity, adaptability, and comfortable familiarity. It understands us and, like many a foolish spouse, we like to think we understand it. To ask us to explain it or deal with its problems, however, is quite another matter; but this article will undertake to try.

The mail fraud statute reads in pertinent part as follows:

Whoever, having devised or intending to devise any scheme or artifice to defraud, or for obtaining money or property by means of false or fraudulent pretenses, representations, or promises . . . for the purpose of executing such scheme or artifice or attempting so to do, places in any post office or authorized depository for mail matter, any matter or thing whatever to be sent or delivered by the Postal Service, or takes or receives therefrom, any such matter or thing, or knowingly causes to be delivered by mail according to the direction thereon . . . any such matter or thing, shall be fined not more than $1,000 or imprisoned not more than five years, or both.

First enacted in 1872, the mail fraud statute, together with its lineal descendant, the wire fraud statute, has been characterized as the "first line of defense" against virtually every new area of fraud to develop in the United States in the past century. Its applications, too numerous to catalog, cover not only the full range of consumer frauds, stock frauds, land frauds, bank frauds, insurance frauds, and commodity frauds, but have extended even to such areas as blackmail, counterfeiting, election fraud, and bribery. In many of these and other areas, where legislatures have sometimes been slow to enact specific prohibitory legislation, the mail fraud statute has frequently represented the sole instrument of justice that could be wielded against the ever-innovative practitioners of deceit.

During the past century, both Congress and the Supreme Court have repeatedly placed their stamps of approval on expansive use of the mail fraud statute. Indeed, each of the five legislative revisions of the statute has served to enlarge its coverage. And while over the past decade Congress has had under consideration wholesale revision of the federal criminal code, until this past year each of the proposed new criminal codes provided for full retention and, in some instances, modest expansion of the crimes of mail fraud and wire fraud.

Recently, however, the successful use of the mail and wire fraud statutes to prosecute "official corruption" cases against such prominent public figures as Judge Kerner and Governor Mandel, and to prosecute certain corporations for bribing foreign officials has provoked outcries from some quarters against what is termed an "unprecedented" expansion of mail fraud and wire fraud jurisdiction. Concomitantly, the House subcommittee on criminal justice has been persuaded to reject the slight expansion of mail fraud and wire fraud jurisdiction contained in the latest Senate version of the proposed criminal code, in favor of a version that would substantially curtail existing mail fraud and wire fraud jurisdiction, reducing it to limits that are arguably the narrowest in its entire history. In response, even some commentators normally at odds with the Department of Justice have warned that the primary effect of such curtailment would be to inhibit the effective prosecution of white collar crime.

On the familiar assumption that in order to understand the present and shape the future it is necessary to study the past, this article seeks to place these current controversies in perspective by tracing the historical development of the mail fraud statute in the context of the overall growth of federal criminal law. Such an examination locates the source of both the unusual characteristics and current problems associated with the modern mail fraud statute in the persistence to this day of constructions given to the original mail fraud statute by some of the very earliest courts called upon to interpret its provisions.

II. THE UNUSUAL CHARACTERISTICS OF THE MAIL FRAUD STATUTE

In its formal characteristics, the federal mail fraud statute, together with those few later statutes that have copied its format, is very unusual and perhaps unique among federal criminal laws. Aside from purely regulatory offenses (MALUM PROHIBITUM), most federal criminal laws — at least those applicable to what are otherwise state crimes — describe a simple structure of two elements. The first or "substantive" element consists of the prohibited criminal conduct, either reprehensible on its fact (e.g., assault, murder, rape) or made so by some reprehensible intent (e.g., carrying a gun with intent to commit murder, or taking money from a bank with intent to steal). The second or "jurisdictional" element consists of some, often wholly incidental, confection between the prohibited conduct and an area of federal power or involvement sufficient to warrant the exercise of federal sovereignty over the prosecution of the crime. For example, to be guilty of violating the federal assault statute, (i) one must have assaulted a person who (ii) happens to be a federal officer. Similarly, to be guilty of federal bank

theft, (i) one acting with intent to steal the money must have taken $100 or more from a bank which (ii) happens to be federally organized or federally insured. In fact, the mere potential for interference with federal interests can, in appropriate circumstances, provide warrant for federal intervention. Thus, for example, a conspiracy to assault a person who happens to be a federal agent is punishable as a federal crime regardless of whether the conspirators knew the person was a federal agent and regardless of whether the assault was actually carried out. As it happens, while Congress might have chosen to limit its exercise of jurisdiction over what otherwise are "state" crimes to those situations where the defendants actually intended to interfere with some matter of federal concern, in fact where Congress has entered this field its usual practice has been to extend its jurisdictional prerogative to all such instances where the criminal conduct itself affects (or is likely to affect) some federal preserve, regardless of the defendant's intention and regardless of whether the conduct that constitutes the federal effect is itself reprehensible.

At first glance it might be thought that the mail fraud statute fits neatly into the format described above, for it likewise consists of two elements: reprehensible activity in the form of devising a scheme to defraud, and federal jurisdiction in the form of a use of the mails. On closer examination, however, neither of these elements quite accords with the general formula. The first element of federal mail fraud — devising a scheme to defraud — is not itself conduct at all (although it may be made manifest by conduct), but is simply a plan, intention, or state of mind, insufficient in itself to give rise to any kind of criminal sanctions. Accordingly, if the second element of federal mail fraud — using the mails — were nothing more than a bare jurisdictional act, having only an incidental relation to the criminal activity described in the first element and no relation whatever to the actor's intent, it is doubtful whether the statute would state a crime (at least in any ordinary sense), since it would not be addressed to any conduct that was both overt and reprehensible. To rectify this deficiency, the language of the mail fraud statute, and the cases construing it, require that the particular mailing charged as the second element of the crime be "sufficiently closely related" to the scheme-to-defraud charged as the first element of the crime as to be fairly held to be "for the purpose of executing it; and further, that such use of the mails in execution of the scheme be "reasonably foreseeable" to someone in the defendant's position.

These added connections between the two elements of federal mail fraud are rather akin to the traditional requirements in a civil tort action that the ultimate injury be proximately caused by the defendant's acts and/or be a reasonably foreseeable result of the defendant's acts. But although such requirements help to define a notion of "fault" sufficient to impose civil liability for damages, they are rarely to be found in criminal statutes, which typically require as a prerequisite to imposing criminal sanctions that the defendant have actual knowledge of the commission of the injurious or forbidden act and that he not only cause but also actually intend its commission. Thus, the appearance of the "civil" requirements of proximate causation and, especially, reasonable foreseeability in the federal criminal mail fraud statute is, at the least, surprising. Moreover, whereas in tort law the requirements of proximate causation and reasonable foreseeability serve to link the defendant with the ultimate injurious act for which he is being held responsible, in the case of the federal mail fraud statute such requirements serve to link the defendant with merely an act of mailing—an act that may be perfectly innocent in itself and that, even in terms of the overall scheme that it is said to further, may be an act of minute consequence.

In some of these unusual characteristics, the federal mail fraud statute, while different from the great majority of federal criminal statutes, bears more than a passing resemblance to the federal conspiracy statute. For example, under the federal conspiracy statute, conduct otherwise unpunishable because it is too inchoate, such a plotting to commit a federal crime, becomes criminal when the conspirators willfully cause an "overt act" to be taken in furtherance of the plot and to effect its objectives, even if some of the conspirators lack actual knowledge of the overt act (provided the act is reasonably foreseeable) and even if the overt act is innocent in itself and of minimal consequence in furthering the plot. Still, the analogy between the mail fraud statute and the conspiracy statute is far from perfect. Obviously, it requires a minimum of two persons to commit the crime of conspiracy, while one person alone can commit the crime of mail fraud; consequently, while the crime of mail fraud can (at least in theory) transpire almost entirely in the mind of the defendant and never manifest itself beyond the causing of the single use of the mails, the crime of conspiracy, requiring as it does the equivalent of a partnership agreement between the two conspirators, must manifest itself by at least such overt activity as is necessary for such "partners in crime" to formulate and mutually reach such an agreement. Furthermore, while it is well established that (in the conceptualistic language favored by some courts) the "essence" of a conspiracy charge is the agreement between two or more persons to commit an evil act, it

is equally well settled that the "gist" of the mail fraud violation is not the evil scheme, but the use of the mails. Therefore, while a single conspiracy gives rise to only a single criminal count regardless of the number of alleged overt acts, each use of the mails that occurs in furtherance of a single mail fraud scheme will support a separate and independently punishable count of mail fraud.

In short, the format of the mail fraud statute in comparison with that of most other federal criminal statutes is idiosyncratic. Moreover, the oddity of its design has had numerous repercussions on its interpretation and application. For example, it has led courts, as noted, to describe the element of mailing as the "gist," "essence," "gravamen," and "substance" of the crime of mail fraud, even though it is obvious that the prime concern of those who commit mail fraud, those who legislate against it, those who prosecute it, and those who judge it, is the fraud and not the mailing. In turn, this legal "fiction" that the mailing is the "gist" of the crime of mail fraud has led to a number of unusual practical consequences.

First, it results in each separate use of the mails constituting a separate crime. Consequently, the number of counts of mail fraud with which a defendant may be charged turns not on the scope or duration of the fraud, the number of victims, the amount of damage, or any other factor relating to the moral culpability of the perpetrator or the social damage inflicted by his fraud, but rather depends on the sheer happenstance of how many times the mails have been used in executing the fraud. Another practical result is that fugitive swindlers can sometimes successfully resist extradition for fraud on the ground that the charges against them, which are typically lodged under the mail and wire fraud statutes, do not state a charge of "fraud," for which extradition will commonly lie, but rather state only a charge of "misuse of the mails," for which extradition often will not lie. Finally, a subtle but highly significant effect of conceiving federal mail fraud as a crime the "gist" of which is the misuse of the mails is that such a conception makes it easier for courts to avoid the issue of whether there exist substantive limitations—imposed by the Constitution, legislative intent, or public policy—on the kinds of frauds appropriate for federal prosecution under this statute. When such questions have been raised in mail fraud cases, many courts have simply reasoned that the questions are inappropriate because the concern of the statute is not with prosecuting fraud per se but with keeping the mails free of taint and misuse. The practical effect of this approach has been to enable the courts to avoid manacling the statute with the kind of substantive limitations that commonly render state fraud statutes ineffectual and that, when judicially created, frequently reflect nothing more than a court's social and economic biases. Ironically, then, the seemingly narrow and artificial view that courts have taken of the function of the mail fraud statute — to protect the mails from misuse — has in practice provided the statute with a flexibility, breadth of coverage, and effectiveness unmatched by most of the other federal criminal laws.

It may be argued, however, that the idiosyncracies of design and interpretation that make the mail fraud statute so effective in combatting fraud likewise render it more liable to irrational, unpredictable or extreme applications and hence, to abuse. While until recently, remarkably few claims of this kind have been leveled against the mail fraud statute over the more-than-a-century of its existence, some potential for abuse undoubtedly inheres in any criminal statute drawn in terms sufficiently broad to preclude easy evasion; and Congress and the courts are likely to remain forever engaged in seeking the ideal balance between "overly broad" and "overly narrow." To the extent, however, that a substantial element of outright irrationality creeps into the design or interpretation of a criminal statute, an added and more deep-seated difficulty arises: by becoming unfathomable, even to initiates, it ultimately ceases to command any moral force. Consequently, any effort to amend, supplant, or perfect the present mail fraud statute should begin with the question of whether the effectiveness of the statute can still be saved while eliminating its seemingly irrational aspects. To answer this question, it seems best to examine the historical development of the mail fraud statute, since careful attention to the long history of this statute is likely to reveal those qualities central to the statute's effectiveness, as opposed to those aspects that are merely vestigial remains of bygone controversies.

III. THE GENESIS OF THE ORIGINAL MAIL FRAUD STATUTE

The original federal mail fraud statute was enacted on June 8, 1872 as part of a 327-section omnibus act chiefly intended to revise and recodify the various laws relating to the post office. Unlike most of the other sections of the act, however, the mail fraud section, section 301, had no obvious precursor. In view of the novelty and breadth of this section, it is surprising that it generated no congressional debate or other legislative history explaining its origins and purpose. Looking at the broader context, however, the mail fraud statute was not unlike a host of federal legislation (both criminal and civil) enacted in the Reconstruction Period immediately following the Civil War, that extended federal authority to areas previously reserved to the states. Two impulses,

in particular, seem likely to have generated such legislation as the mail fraud statute. One was the growth of a national economy, evident even before the Civil War but greatly accelerating after the war, and a concomitant growth in large-scale swindles, get-rich-quick schemes, and financial frauds. With the increase in such crimes, it "soon became apparent that rudimentary criminal codes, conceived for rural societies and confined by state lines and local considerations, could not cope with those who saw manifold opportunities for gain in the new activities." Thus, there existed a perceived need for federal intervention to dispel wide-spread fraud.

This need was coupled with a perception of enlarged and dynamic federal power, hugely enhanced by both the exigencies of fighting a Civil War and by the fervor with which Reconstruction Republicans set about the legislative remodeling of the northern and southern states alike. One result was that, although Reconstruction statutes were passed in response to specific ills and grievances, they tended to be drawn in sweeping language appropriate to the federal government's new-found sense of power. This was particularly true where earlier, more specific legislation proved unable to cope in any coherent fashion with the multitude of upheavals and dislocations that immediately followed the end of the Civil War.

Prior to the Civil War, it was widely believed that Congress' power over the mails did not constitutionally extend to power over the contents of material placed in the mails, including the power to prohibit the mailing of objectionable material. Indeed, one of the early congressional battles between North and South and between nationalists and regionalists was fought on this very issue when, in 1835, President Jackson proposed a bill to prohibit the mailing of "incendiary publications" in the southern states. The proposal was referred to a Senate committee, which concluded that the federal government had no such power, although the states did have that power. Although a number of senators doubted that even the states possessed such power, almost all agreed that the power of Congress over the mails did not extend that far.

With northern nationalism triumphant after the Civil War, the prevailing view on this issue underwent a rapid change, at least among the so-called "radical Republicans" who dominated Congress immediately after the war. A distinction was to be made between the *power* to prohibit the use of the mails to further illicit enterprises and the *means* by which that power was exercised. The mere fact that Congress was forbidden to employ such means as opening sealed letters did not mean that Congress lacked the power to prosecute those who were discovered, through legitimate means of detection, to have used the federal mails for illicit purposes. Accordingly, in 1868 Congress took a first small step toward prohibiting such "illicit" uses of the mails by enacting the so-called "lottery law," which made it unlawful to mail any letters or circulars "concerning [illegal] lotteries, so-called gift concerts, or other similar enterprises offering prizes of any kind on any pretext whatever." This first step did not provoke much opposition, possibly because it was strongly supported by active church and civil "reform" groups, which had already succeeded in convincing numerous states to outlaw lotteries and other common forms of gambling, and possibly because in a period of much economic turmoil and distress, fraudulent lotteries were a common swindle, much dependent on the mails for their success.

In 1872, before there had been time to bring many prosecutions under the new lottery law or to litigate its constitutionality, Congress, as part of its general revision of the postal laws, took three steps that incalculably increased its exercise of criminal jurisdiction based upon the use of the mails. The first step was to criminalize the mailing of any "obscene . . . vulgar or indecent" book, pamphlet, picture, print, or publication, as well as any envelope or postal card on which was written or printed any "scurrilous epithets" or "disloyal devices." The second step was to broaden the lottery law to prohibit the mailing of any letters or circulars concerning lotteries "or concerning schemes devised and intended to deceive and defraud the public for the purpose of obtaining money under false pretenses." Finally, Congress created the mail fraud statute, with its general prohibition against using the mails for the purpose of effectuating "any scheme or artifice to defraud."

Although the historical context in which the mail fraud statute was promulgated thus suggests that Congress intended it be given a broad construction and application, it seems unwise to rest much weight on this conclusion in the absence of more specific legislative history. Perhaps the safest course is to abandon any further search for evidence of legislative intent in the limited historical record surrounding the genesis of the mail fraud statute and to focus instead upon the wording of the statute itself. As originally enacted, the mail fraud statute read as follows:

> That if any person having devised or intending to devise any scheme or artifice to defraud, to be effected by either opening or intending to open correspondence or communication with any other person (whether resident within or outside the United States), by means of the post-office establishment of the United States, or by inciting such other person to open communication with the person so devising or intending,

shall, in and for executing such scheme or artifice (or attempting so to do), place any letter or packet in any post-office of the United States, or take or receive any therefrom, such person, so misusing the post-office establishment, shall be guilty of a misdemeanor, and shall be punished with a fine of not more than five hundred dollars, with or without such imprisonment, as the court shall direct, not exceeding eighteen calendar months. The indictment, information or complaint may severally charge offenses to the number of three when committed within the same six calendar months; but the court thereupon shall give a single sentence, and shall proportion the punishment especially to the degree in which the abuse of the post-office establishment enters as an instrument into such fraudulent scheme and device.

On its face, the wording of the statute explains in large part how the courts came to attribute to the crime of mail fraud many of the qualities that, when viewed in light of the statute's very different present-day wording, seem so peculiar. Specifically, the concept that the "gist" or "essence" of the crime of mail fraud is the misuse of the mails – a concept that, when parroted by present-day courts, seems no better than a legal fiction – looks rather more reasonable in terms of the wording of the original statute. The title of the statute was "Penalty for Misusing the Post-Office Establishment," and the misuse at which it was purportedly directed was the mailing of a letter in execution of such fraudulent scheme as is intended to be effectuated by means of the mails. As noted by the Supreme Court in construing the original mail fraud statute, the "constituents" of the offense were not only the two elements of the present-day statute, but three elements:

> (1) That the persons charged must have devised a scheme or artifice to defraud. (2) That they must have intended to effect this scheme, by opening or intending to open correspondence with some other person through the post office establishment, or by inciting such other person to open communication with them. (3) And that, in carrying out such scheme, such person must have either deposited a letter or packet in the post office, or taken or received one therefrom.

The second element (absent from the present statute) – the intention to effectuate the scheme through a significant reliance on the use of the mails – served not only to bridge the two other elements but also to unify the statute and make it an organic whole, the apparent function of which was to deter the actual and intentional misuse of the mails in furtherance of a truly *mail*-fraud scheme. In addition, the express emphasis on misuse of the mails carried over to the penalty provisions of the original mail fraud statute, which directed the sentencing court to "proportion the punishment especially to the degree in which the abuse of the post-office establishment enters as an instrument into such fraudulent scheme and device." Thus, the punishment was to be based not so much on the degree of the fraud as on the degree of misuse of the mails. Taken together, then, the language of the original mail fraud statute seemed to indicate that Congress' central concern was the misuse of the federal mail facilities.

Yet, it may be that the language of the original statute protests too much its concern with misuse of the mails. To take one small example, at one point, the statute, having already described the conduct constituting the crime, goes on to characterize that conduct as "misusing the post office establishment." In substantive or operational terms, this interjection is utterly superfluous, and any attempt to apply to it the standard rule of statutory construction that every word of a statute should be given effect would be an exercise in futility, because it has no effect of its own. Perhaps it should be dismissed as sloppy draftsmanship; but an alternative explanation for the inclusion of this phrase is that the draftsmen hoped that by stoutly declaring that the proscribed conduct constituted interference with a federal area, otherwise skeptical arbiters would construe it accordingly. A more important example supporting this same interpretation is the penalty provision of the statute, which requires that the punishment be proportioned to "the degree in which the abuse of the post office establishment enters as an instrument into such fraudulent scheme." The only plausible reason for including such an ambiguous, abstract and amoral provision, which would appear to be wholly unamenable to principled application and unlikely ever to be given effect, was to demonstrate a concern with "abuse" of the mails, and thus to make it less likely that the statute would be struck down as an unconstitutional extension of federal jurisdiction over ordinary fraud.

In sum, while the "mail-emphasizing" language of the original mail fraud statute seemed ostensibly to evidence a congressional preoccupation with misuse of the mails and with prosecuting only those fraudulent schemes that in essential respects involved such misuse, an alternative explanation was that Congress was concerned with "dressing up" a statute actually directed at the broadscale prosecution of all kinds of fraud in such a way as to preserve it from judicial override, and to that end, the brave, bold words of the statute announcing

its applicability to "any scheme or artifice to defraud" were circumscribed by those qualifications, limitations and self-characterizations thought necessary to have the statute's constitutionality.

IV. The Effects of *Ex Parte Jackson* on the Interpretation of the Mail Fraud Statute

Ironically, before there was time to test the effectiveness of the "mail-emphasizing" language in preserving the constitutionality of the mail fraud statute, the issue was settled in a different context and in a manner that rendered the mail-emphasizing language extraneous to this putative purpose. In 1877, a unanimous Supreme Court, in *Ex parte Jackson,* upheld the constitutionality of the lottery law with language so broad as to leave no doubt as to the constitutionality of the mail fraud statute as well. Speaking through Justice Field, the Court ruled that "[t]he power possessed by Congress embraces the regulation of the entire postal system of the country. The right to designate what shall be carried necessarily involves the right to determine what shall be excluded." From that premise, it followed that Congress was entirely free "to prescribe regulations as to what shall constitute mail matter" and that the sole limitation on such regulations would derive "from the necessity of enforcing them consistently with rights reserved to the People." In practice, this meant that although postal agents could not, in enforcing the lottery law, open sealed letters without a fourth amendment warrant, they were free to obtain evidence of violation of the statute in numerous other ways, "as from the parties receiving the letters or packages, or from agents depositing them in the post office, or others cognizant of the facts." Once having thus obtained such evidence, the federal government was free to prosecute those who had misused the mails.

In terms of effect on the development of the mail fraud statute, *Jackson* could not have been more significant in fostering an affirmative view of the propriety of expansive federal jurisdiction in this area of criminal law. By broadly affirming the right of Congress to criminally prosecute those who utilized the mails for a purpose – operating lotteries – that was otherwise at most a state crime and beyond Congress' control, *Ex parte Jackson* freed the lower courts from having to address the mail fraud statute's constitutionality, and from possibly being required to "save" the statute by some narrow construction of its scope. Indeed, after the *Jackson* decision, the constitutionality of the mail fraud statute was raised in only one reported decision during the remainder of the nineteenth century, and there the issue was quickly disposed of by reference to *Jackson.* Moreover, any ambiguity that might have remained as to the applicability of *Ex parte Jackson* to the question whether

Congress could constitutionally prosecute what were otherwise state crimes if they happened to involve use of the mails was quickly resolved by the reading given to *Jackson* by the Supreme Court itself. Thus, for example, in *In re Rapier,* where the constitutionality of the lottery law was once again challenged, this time on the express ground that the prosecution of illegal lotteries was reserved to the states and was not reasonably related to any federal postal function, a unanimous Court held that *Ex parte Jackson* was decisive of the question because that decision established "that mail facilities are not required to be furnished for [wrongful] purpose[s]" and that it was "not necessary that Congress should have the power to deal with crime or immorality within the States in order to maintain that it possesses the power to forbid the use of the mails in aid of the perpetration of crime or immorality."

VIII. The 1889 Amendment to the Mail Fraud Statute

After protracted delay, both Congress and the Supreme Court ultimately opted for the broad constructionist approach. In hindsight, this choice may appear to have been "inevitable," given such broad social forces as the increasing growth of a national economy and the increasing prevalence of nationwide fraud schemes that local governmental authorities were unable to control, the discrediting of regional authority and the expansion of federal political power as the result of the Civil War and its aftermath; the large increase of graft, corruption, and governmental fraud, and the strong reformist reaction to it; the alliance between the federal government and established business, for whose benefit some early fraud prosecutors appear to have been brought; and the absence of any well defined social or moral interest in leaving fraud prosecution the exclusive domain of the states. . . .

IX. The 1909 Revision of the Mail Fraud Statute

In 1909, Congress again intervened, and this time eliminated language from the statute in a manner that was clear in both intent and effect. Specifically, Congress amended the mail fraud statute by eliminating the mail-emphasizing language. Gone was the language characterizing the conduct of a person who committed the offense as "misusing the post-office establishment." Gone was the bizarre penalty provision by which courts were required to "proportion the punishment especially to the degree in which the abuse of the post-office establishment enters as an instrument into such fraudulent scheme and device." Most significantly, gone was the entire second element of the crime—the requirement that

the scheme to defraud, as devised by the defendant, be intended to be effected through use of the mails, an element that, even on the broad constructionist view, required proof beyond a reasonable doubt that the defendant intended not only to defraud but also to misuse the mails.

Bereft of these and other mail-emphasizing provisions, the statute ceased to afford any genuine support for the arguments developed by the strict constructionists over the previous thirty-seven years. With the very mention of mailing now reduced to the bare third element—the requirement that in execution of the scheme to defraud there occur at least one mailing—no court could seriously argue that the language of the statute dictated the substantive limitation of the statue's coverage to mail-dependent schemes, or the schemes whose very "essence" was the use of the mails. Moreover, it no longer made sense to say that the statute aimed to deter the abuse of the mail system, because the defendant no longer had to intend any use of the mails whatsoever; the minimal use of the mails that would trigger the statute could, within broad limits, be an incidental or even accidental accompaniment of the defendant's fraudulent scheme. Finally, even beyond the fact that the new wording of the statute would no longer support, wither logically or functionally, the old strict constructionist interpretations, Congress' elimination from the statute of nearly every vestige of the language upon which the strict constructions had based their constructions could itself be interpreted only as a flat rejection of the strict constructionist approach.

If there remained any lingering doubt as to the purpose, effect or propriety of the 1909 amendment, it was promptly dispelled by the Supreme Court in *United States v. Young.* In that case, a unanimous Court overruled an attempt to read into the new statute some of the limitations imposed under the predecessor statute, holding that the elements of mail fraud under the new statute consist of "(a) a scheme devised or intended to be devised to defraud, or for obtaining money or property by means of false pretenses, and (b) for the purpose of executing such scheme or attempting to do so, the placing of any letter in any post office of the United State to be sent or delivered by the Post Office Establishment." On its face, the Court's opinion in *Young*: all that is required for conviction under the new statute is what its bare language specifies. All the constructions, whether "broad" or "strict," built like sandcastles upon the infirmities of the language of the prior statute, come tumbling down now that the supporting language has been washed away.

Thus, for a short time, the new mail fraud statute, as construed in decision such as *Young,* was held to be a simple and unqualified extension of federal jurisdiction over any and all schemes to defraud that involved an act of mailing. That is to say, the mailing requirement functioned as nothing more than a simple "jurisdictional element" plus "overt act" – the conduct minimally necessary to permit the exercise of federal sovereignty and to distinguish the crime of mail fraud from one of pure intent. This left only the question of whether the newly amended mail fraud statute would withstand challenges that it was unconstitutional. Although the Supreme Court's previous decisions in *Ex parte Jackson* and *In re Rapier* seemed strongly to suggest that the new statute was constitutional, the Court expressly settled the issue in *Badders v. United States*. The primary argument advanced by the defendant in *Badders* was that the new, stripped-down mail fraud statute was "beyond the power of Congress as applied to what may be a mere incident of a fraudulent scheme that itself is outside the jurisdiction of Congress to deal with. A unanimous Supreme Court, speaking through Justice Holmes, ruled this contention was so frivolous as to "need no extended answer." In the Court's view, since the "overt act of putting a letter into the post office of the United State is a matter that Congress may regulate," it followed that Congress has the power to "forbid any such acts done in furtherance of a scheme that it regards as contrary to public policy, whether it can forbid the scheme or not."

Badders should have marked the end of the virtual obsession with the mailing aspects of the crime that had plagued the approaches taken by both broad and strict constructionists under the earlier versions of the mail fraud statute. Unfortunately, lower federal courts were unable entirely to shake clear of the approaches to the mail fraud statute that had developed over the prior forth years and had been engrained in extensive case law. For example, to those courts that desired to give the statute a broad application, there was great advantage in following the old "broad constructionist" approach and declaring that the "gist" of the offense was in the misuse of the mails, for it seemed to follow that one did not have to inquire too deeply into the nature and scope of the schemes to defraud or into whether they were appropriate or intended subjects of federal criminal concern. Rather, any objections along those lines could be dismissed with a reference to a long line of pre-1909 decisions declaring that Congress' sole concern was that the mails not be used for any bad purpose; and since, under *Badders*, this was all the Constitution required, there was no basis, according to those courts, for imposing any limitations on what kinds of bad purposes might give rise to prosecution under the statute so long as they in any way included an aspect of fraud, which was to be defined as broadly as possible.

Thus, for example, in *United States v. States*, where the defendants were convicted under the mail fraud statute of stuffing ballot boxes in a state primary election, the Court of Appeals for the Eighth Circuit, citing such old broad constructionist decisions as *Durland* and *Horman*, had no difficulty in concluding that the defendants' conduct fell within the statute, simply because "the definition of fraud in the [the mail fraud statute] is to be broadly and liberally construed to further the purpose of the statute; namely, to prohibit the misuse of the mails." The truth, however, is that at least since the 1909 amendment, the sole genuine purpose of the mail fraud statute has been to prosecute fraud and the mailing has served primarily as a basis for involving federal jurisdiction. But by blindly reiterating the old mail-emphasizing concepts developed under the original mail fraud statute, courts such as the one in *States* have succeeded in avoiding the real questions underlying most of the "controversial" prosecutions brought under the present mail fraud statute, including the precise definition of "scheme to defraud" and the delineation of the substantive limitations, if any, that may exist as to the kinds of schemes to defraud reached under the statute.

The continued vitality in modern decisions of the old "broad constructionist" notion that the "gist" of the offense is the misuse of the mails leads to illogical results, such as making the number of counts dependent upon the number of mailings, and deflects judicial analysis from the true issues. Even more troubling, however, is the persistence of the old "strict constructionist" approach, attempting to limit the substantive scope of the statute in terms of the use of the mails. It appears that some modern courts, seeking to limit the mail fraud statute's scope but unwilling to undertake the formidable task of directly determining whether there are any substantive limitations that may be imposed (as a matter of public policy or otherwise) on the term "scheme to defraud," have sometimes looked to the other terms of the statute as a source of potential limits on its scope. Although the wholesale removal of the mail-emphasizing language from the statute in the 1909 revision has left courts of this persuasion with very little to work with, they have attempted to impose what few limitations they can upon the statute by giving a strict reading to the remaining requirement that the mailing be for the "purpose" of executing the scheme to defraud. Actually, however, there is no reason to believe that Congress intended this term to mean anything more than that the mailing partake of the same relationship to the scheme to defraud as an overt act does to a conspiracy; *i.e.*, that it be a step – however slight, unnecessary or innocent in itself—toward the execution of the criminal design. If Congress had intended to suggest some closer relationship between the mailing and the scheme to defraud, it would have simply retained the old second element of the original mail fraud statute or something close to it, since it was at just such relationships that the old second element aimed. Nonetheless, the appearance in the revised statute of the term "purpose" opened a tiny loophole through which courts so inclined could try to thread some of the old strict constructionist interpretations, and in doing so those courts helped to impose on the statute still further idiosyncracies, such as that the mailing be a "reasonably foreseeable" consequence of the intended scheme to defraud.

X. Some Preliminary Conclusions

Whatever limitations may yet be imposed on the form, scope or substance of the mail fraud statute, it is time for courts of all persuasions to realize the point of the 1909 amendment by doing away with all references to the mailing as the "gist" of the crime of mail fraud, by refraining from reading back into the statute such unsupported and inappropriate requirements as the mailing be a reasonably foreseeable consequence of the intended scheme, and, in general, by ceasing to regard the mailing requirement as anything more than a simple overt act and bare jurisdictional element. The language of the two new versions of the mail fraud statute presently pending before Congress as part of the two current proposals for a revised criminal code would both admit of such a change. Indeed, they appear to go a step further by reducing the required mailing to being solely a jurisdictional act, with the requirement of an overt act being met by any conduct in furtherance of the fraud, whether it be the mailing or any other act. The language of the existing mail fraud statute would not support this further step; but there is nothing in the language of the present statute that prevents courts from viewing the mailing requirement in the very limited way that the 1909 amendment intended—as an overt act and jurisdictional act, and nothing more. Since it appears, at least as of this writing, that passage of a revised criminal code will once again be deferred, courts should not wait for Congress to correct judicial errors but should abandon the restrictive limitations which the courts themselves have constructed upon the simple requirement of a mailing. If in so doing it becomes manifest that the scope of the mail fraud statute is too great, either in requiring only a very minimal amount of reprehensible conduct to trigger its application or in extending its application to an immensely broad and as yet ill-defined spectrum of intentions and activities, so much the better, for such problems, if they in fact exist, can then be addressed directly, rather than indirectly, haphazardly, and irrationally as in the past.

John C. Coffee, Jr., Hush!: The Criminal Status of Confidential Information After McNally *and* Carpenter *and the Enduring Problem of Overcriminalization,* 26 Am. Crim. L. Rev. 121–154 (1988)*

Each of the last three decades has witnessed an intense public reaction to a distinctive type of "white collar" crime. In the early 1960's, public attention was riveted by the Electrical Equipment conspiracy and the image of senior corporate executives of major firms meeting clandestinely to fix prices. In the mid-1970's, the focus shifted to corporate bribery, as the media ran daily stories regarding questionable payments abroad and illegal political contributions at home. The representative white collar crime of the 1980's is undoubtedly "insider trading." The archetype of this new kind of criminal in the public's mind is Ivan Boesky (or perhaps his fictional counterpart, Gordon Gekko, from the movie *Wall Street*).

In response to each of these scandals, there has been much moralizing, some legislation, and ultimately a few academic voices expressing concern that the legislative response was hasty and overbroad. The phrase "overcriminalization" first entered the lexicon of the criminal law with respect to morals legislation in the late 1950's, but in the wake of the 1960's price-fixing scandals it was extended to apply to economic crimes as well. In particular, Professors Herbert Packer of Stanford and Sanford Kadish of Berkeley suggested that there were unnoticed and significant costs in using the criminal law to enforce economic regulations. They warned that over-reliance on the criminal law would erode its moral authority, misallocate its enforcement resources, and invite discriminatory and selective prosecutions. All these dangers were greatest, they claimed, when the regulated behavior was not generally recognized as immoral by the public at large. The "illegal payments" crisis of the 1970's spawned the Foreign Corrupt Practices

---

* Reprinted with permission.

Act, and another debate ensued about the role of the law in regulating corporate governance.

The current insider trading revelations have yet to result in legislation, but have, however, produced a Supreme Court decision, *Carpenter v. United States,* that exhibits all the characteristics of an overbroad, moralistic legislative response. In *Carpenter,* the Court held unanimously that an employee who leaks to third parties confidential business information belonging to his employer embezzles property in violation of the federal mail and wire fraud statutes, even though the employer suffers no apparent economic injury as a result. At bottom, *Carpenter* rests on an analogy that broadly characterizes the unauthorized communication of trade secrets as equivalent to the crime of embezzlement.

As will be argued, this view of "confidential information" as a form of property covered by the laws against larceny is (a) historically unsound, (b) inconsistent with most statutory law dealing with the subject of trade secrets, and (c) capable of trivializing the Court's decision only months earlier in *McNally v. United States,* which clearly sought to cut back on the amoeba-like growth of the mail and wire fraud statutes. More important than all these considerations, however, is the fact that *Carpenter's* logic has the potential to alter significantly the relationship between employers and employees across the landscape of American business life.

More than any other theory that the Court could have chosen to address the evil of insider trading, *Carpenter's* doctrinal invention—the idea that divulging confidential information of one's employer amounts to embezzlement—has the ability to chill employee mobility and increase the social control that employers have over employees. To see this, consider the case of an employee whose position may be legally indistinguishable from that of Foster Winans, the principal defendant in *Carpenter,* but in which the equities are very different: a broker at a major securities firm is fired because of low sales volume and told that, pursuant to the firm's long-standing policy, he may not take with him any list or address book listing his clients, as such information is a trade secret belonging to the firm. As a practical matter, if this broker cannot contact his former clients, he is unemployable with other firms and forfeits valuable "human capital" that he may have developed over a career. Nevertheless, it is clear as a civil law matter that customer lists are confidential trade secrets. To criminalize this civil law rule then effectively arms the employer with a weapon that the legislature never intended to grant it by importing a covenant not to compete, which would ordinarily be unenforceable, into the employment contract.

Why, then, has there been relatively little commentary or outcry with regard to this aspect of *Carpenter?* The probable answer is that insider trading has long been the exclusive province of the corporate and securities bar, within which there is a broad consensus that the conduct of Foster Winans was egregious and rightfully branded as criminal. This author shares those views and entertains no doubt about the need for a criminal prohibition on insider trading. However, the point that has largely escaped the corporate bar's attention is that the *Carpenter* theory of liability vastly transcends the context of insider trading and covers all forms of confidential business information, including, it seems, any release of such information in violation of the fiduciary obligations established by the law of agency. It is as if the Supreme Court, faced with a narrow legal problem in the law of insider trading that could have been covered with a legal handkerchief, chose instead to drape a football field-sized blanket over it. The question thus posed, however, is whether (or to what extent) we wish to criminalize the law of agency.

At this point, we come full circle back to the topic of overcriminalization and its relevance to "economic" or "regulatory" crimes. This theme was first seriously examined by academics in the wake of the antitrust scandals of the early 1960's, but it now stands in serious need of re-examination in light of the current insider trading controversy. Indeed, the concept of "overcriminalization" is far from a neutral one. Those academics who in the 1960's questioned the utility of the criminal law as a mechanism for enforcing economic regulations were sharply attacked by others who argued that the criminal law both reflects and shapes a society's morality. These critics argued in essence that the public learns what is criminal from what is prosecuted. If so, this interactive relationship between the criminal law and public morality means that both law and morality shape each other. Thus, placing the sphere of economic regulation off limits to the criminal law might both produce a class-biased body of law and deny regulators one of the most effective weapons for reshaping society's consciousness. Much in the recent insider trading scandals reinforces this view of the educational power of the criminal law, as the public's perception of insider trading as truly criminal behavior appears to have intensified in the wake of the Boesky revelations.

Clearly then, both sides in this debate can make persuasive arguments for their position. This implies that we should focus more closely on identifying the root evil that lies in over-criminalization. To do so, this Article will seek to use our recent experience with insider trading and the criminal law's response as a prism through which to examine the issue of overcriminalization in sharper relief. The Article proceeds in three steps. First, Part I examines in mere detail both *Carpenter* and the modern law on mail and wire fraud, as it has been reshaped by, and following, *McNally v. United States*. Part II then searches for restraining principles by which to limit the further expansion of the *Carpenter* theory of liability before it reaches the full limits of its dubious logic. Finally, Part III returns to the topic of overcriminalization and the enduring issue of the degree to which the criminal law should overlap with our public morality. It suggests at least a partial rationale for the widely shared belief that there are some forms of misconduct that should be subject to civil, but not criminal, sanctions.

I. Phoenix From the Ashes:
The Death and Rebirth of Intangible
Interests as a Basis for Criminal Liability

To understand *Carpenter's* significance, one must begin with the law of mail and wire fraud as it had evolved prior to June, 1987. In both the public and private fiduciary context, the theory had become widely accepted that any undisclosed breach of the duty of loyalty deprived an employer (or other beneficiary) of its right to an employee's "honest and faithful" services. At its high water mark, this doctrine had permitted the conviction of corporate employees who had established slush funds (in one case following the express instructions of their superiors) to facilitate off-the-books payments, even though there was no evidence of diversion or personal benefit. The mere existence of undisclosed "corporate improprieties" was held sufficient to support criminal liability, even in the absence of a true conflict of interest. As a result, the mail and wire fraud statutes had been effectively transformed from simple prohibitions on fraud into statutes that mandated the public disclosure of all material conflicts of interest and created the new crime of engaging in corporate "improprieties."

In the public fiduciary context, even individuals who did not hold public office but who had *de facto* control over governmental decisions (such as party bosses) were convicted of mail or wire fraud, where they had engineered the appointment of others to office, based on undisclosed political considerations. Although bribes or kickbacks were present in many (but not all) of theses cases, the rationale of these cases required no such payment, but only that there be some conduct motivated by an undisclosed conflict of interest.

This expansion of the mail and wire fraud statutes came, however, to a screeching halt in June, 1987, when the Supreme Court found in *McNally v. United States* that both statutes covered only deprivations of money or property and thus could not reach an alleged scheme to deprive citizens of their asserted rights to the honest and faithful services of their governmental officials. Factually, *McNally* was indistinguishable from several earlier cases that had been successfully prosecuted: public and political officials in Kentucky, including the Chairman of the State Democratic Party, had devised a scheme under which one insurance brokerage agency would continue to purchase specified kinds of insurance for the state in return for its agreement to kickback a percentage of its commissions to other agencies designated by the defendants, including one in which one of them held a hidden interest. No financial loss to the state was alleged from this scheme. Because the critical language in 18 U.S.C. Section 1341 refers to "a scheme or artifice to defraud, or for obtaining money or property by means of false or fraudulent pretenses, representations or promises," the prosecution obviously felt that this disjunctive phrasing made it unnecessary to allege any property loss; the first clause seemed to imply that there could be some "schemes to defraud" that were *not* for the purpose of "obtaining money or property." A seven-justice majority disagreed, however, finding both the legislative history of Section 1341 and the common meaning of the words "to defraud" required that the defendant wrong another "in his property rights."

The *McNally* opinion is dry, technical, and largely focused on the sparse legislative history of Section 1341. Only when one reaches the dissent does one learn that, in rejecting the intangible rights theory, the majority was departing from a rule that all the lower courts that had construed Section 1341 had "uniformly and consistently" followed.

The *McNally* decision seemed then to vindicate— implicitly, but never explicitly—the view that several commentators and some dissenting judges had begun to articulate in the early 1980's: that the "intangible rights" doctrine had resulted in a serious overextension of the criminal law, one that left no meaningful line between the civil law of fiduciary duties and the criminal law of fraud. Because the term "fiduciary" essentially implies only a relationship based on trust and confidence (rather than one based on a market exchange), an interpretation that criminalizes all undisclosed fiduciary breaches seemingly gave the mail and wire fraud statues a nearly universal scope.

Yet, if the *McNally* Court intended to limit the reach of the mail and wire fraud statutes out of a civil libertarian concern about overcriminalization, it did a remarkably half-baked job. The problem is that a broadly expansive definition can be given to the elusive concept of "property." Indeed, Justice Stevens' dissent vividly illustrates just how plastic the concept is, because in a subversively clever footnote he points out that, under standard agency law principles, the principal is entitled to anything that the agent receives as a result of the latter's violation of a duty of loyalty. In short, the ill-gotten gain is the property of the principal. Thus, if an agent receives a bribe, the principal, being entitled to this amount, can be said to have been defrauded by the agent's failure to disclose and surrender it. So viewed, the property loss requirement in *McNally* nearly evaporates, shrinking from a bulwark against prosecutorial overzealousness to simply a pleading rule. In effect, the mail and wire fraud statutes become a Federal Anti-Kickback Act, and even the defendants in *McNally* could presumably be convicted on a reframed indictment.

Within months after *McNally* was decided, several circuits had adopted Justice Stevens' reasoning, convicting employees who received kickbacks without any showing of an economic loss. For example, in *United States v. Runnels,* it seems unlikely that there was any economic loss caused by the agent's misbehavior. A union official took kickbacks from law firms to whom he referred workmen's compensation cases brought to him by his union members. Because the fees that the law firms would receive were set by a state agency, it is doubtful that the agent's gain came at the union members' expense. Yet because there was a fiduciary breach in this situation, the Sixth Circuit upheld the conviction on the ground that the kickbacks belonged under agency law to either the union or its members. In another Fifth Circuit case, the conviction of an employee who took a bribe was upheld, even though the court acknowledged that his corporate employer had suffered no tangible economic loss, but rather had only suffered an injury to its reputation and goodwill.

Actually, Justice Stevens' theory of property reaches well beyond the case where the agent or employee receives a bribe. As he explains it, his theory would reach any act of disloyalty on the ground that there is a failure of consideration: "When a person is paid a salary for his loyal services, any breach of that loyalty would appear to carry with it some loss of money to the employer—who is not getting what he paid for. The problem with this expansive theory is not its logic, but its overbreadth. Under it, an employee who calls in sick in order to go to a ball game has seemingly defrauded his employer of the value of his services for that day (and thereby comes within the statute's reach if the call is made over an interstate telephone line). Similarly, an employee in a supermarket who receives a five dollar tip for reserving a choice cut of meat for a customer has defrauded the employer out of its property interest in this tip, even though

there is no economic loss because the supermarket would not raise its price.

Such examples reveal a fundamental problem with these statutes: unlike many other federal criminal statutes, they include no concept of a de minimis violation. All that keeps a trivial act of disloyalty from being deemed a federal felony is the tender mercy of the federal prosecutor—who sometimes has his own reasons to pursue small or technical violations. In addition, these examples underscore the separation of powers and federalism issues in an expansionist judicial approach to defining criminal liability. The courts, and not the legislature, have made the judgment to expand these statutes, and they have done so in situations where it is doubtful that the Congress would want the federal criminal law to apply, as in either of the foregoing cases. Moreover, rarely, if ever, has federal law stretched a concept —here, the nature of the property subject to theft—in a manner so completely in conflict with the narrower and more careful development of the same concept at the state level. Yet, the justification for such an expansive federal approach—that the mails or interstate wires were used—is largely fictional.

Today, footnote ten of Justice Stevens' dissent hovers, like Banquo's ghost, over the contemporary law of mail fraud, and few conclusions can be expressed that are not subject to the uncertainty that it creates. Already, there is a split among the circuits as to whether to accept its theory that any bribe "defrauds" the employer. Justice Stevens' road map for nullifying *McNally's* property loss requirement is, however, only one of two routes to this end. The other was supplied by a unanimous Court later that same year. Having established the property loss requirement as a prerequisite of mail fraud in June, 1987, the Court waited only until December, 1987, to inflate its concept of property in *Carpenter* in a manner that trivializes *McNally* by making it likely that a property loss will be found in most cases when an employee acts based on a conflict of interest.

In *Carpenter,* the Court took two important doctrinal steps. First, it recognized that there can be intangible forms of property, of which a victim may be defrauded. This seems an obvious conclusion, as one can imagine many valuable forms of intangible property: for example, patents, copyrights, contract rights, etc. Second, it found that one form of intangible property, confidential business information, is embezzled whenever an employee reveals it to others so as to deprive the employer of exclusive possession.

In contrast to this unremarkable first step, the second step is extraordinary, because it eliminates any need for a showing of actual or intended economic injury to the employer. Such a holding was essential to the outcome in *Carpenter,* because the conduct of the principal defendant, Foster Winans, probably involved at most a reputational injury to his employer, *The Wall Street Journal.* As the reporter who wrote the *Journal's* widely followed "Heard on the Street" column, Winans revealed in advance the generic contents of his columns to co-conspirators who traded profitably on the small, but predictable, market reactions its publication caused. This conduct, however, caused no economic injury to the *Journal,* both because it had no interest in these securities and because the information was not revealed to any of its competitors who could publish it. Although the defendants argued that "they did not interfere with the *Journal's* use of the information [and] did not publicize it and deprive the *Journal* of the first public use of it," the Court refused to be limited by an requirement of economic injury. Instead, it adopted a property rights analysis:

> It is sufficient that the *Journal* has been deprived of its right to exclusive use of the information, for exclusivity is an important aspect of confidential business information and most private property for that matter. . . . The concept of "fraud" includes the act of embezzlement, which is the "fraudulent appropriation" to one's own use of the money or goods entrusted to one's care by another.

Taken literally, this is a wildly over-inclusive theory. Under it, a reporter who tells a spouse or a friend the contents of his next day's column deprives the employer of its exclusive use, even though the friend has no interest, and does not trade, in the securities so recommended. As will be discussed below, it also rests on a flawed understanding of the crime of embezzlement and a general ignorance of attempts to deal with the problem of trade secrets both in the common law and statutory law.

However, the immediate question is why the Court reached this novel result, given the distaste it showed in *McNally* for creative expansion of penal statutes. My answer is that it probably saw greater problems with the SEC's "misappropriation theory" of insider trading under Rule 10b-5, as applied to Winan's situation, and sought to sidestep them by turning to mail fraud.

There were two basic weaknesses in the misappropriation theory as it was extended to the unique case of Foster Winans. First, Winans had not received material, non-public information from any of the companies he had interviewed, rather his only alleged "inside" information related to the timing and contents of a newspaper article that was based entirely on publicly

available information. If Winans' relatively weak recommendation was material, so might be the similar recommendation of any securities analyst. Second, the *Journal* itself did not trade and hence could not have maintained a private action for damages against Winans under Rule 10b-5. Nor could injured investors who had traded successfully sue under the Rule because Winans did not owe them any fiduciary duty.

In short, something may have seemed amiss to at least some of the Justices with a theory of liability founded on Rule 10b-5 that asserted Winans had defrauded someone, but recognized no one as an injured victim entitled to sue. More generally, the Court may have viewed the real dispute as simply one between an employer and employee and thus too remote from the securities markets to justify stretching Rule 10b-5 to protect an employer's interest in maintaining the confidentiality of proprietary information. Although a better theory might have been pleaded under Rule 10b-5 that could have justified imposing criminal liability with less sophistry, under the misappropriation theory it is difficult to explain how the *Journal,* as the putative victim, has experienced securities fraud.

Yet the upshot of the Court's decision to rely on mail fraud is clear: having buried the "intangible rights" theory in June, the Court resurrected an "intangible property" theory in December. One suspects that today a creative prosecutor will be able to find intangible property that has been "embezzled" in many of the same contexts where he had formerly found an "intangible right" that had been violated. Of course, the tendency for hard cases to make bad law is not a new phenomenon. Nonetheless, to understand how significant a departure *Carpenter* is from the prior criminal law applicable to trade secrets, this section will examine (a) the prior case law, (b) modern statutory developments, and (c) some applications of *Carpenter* and *McNally* that are virtually certain to arise in future cases.

A. *Information as Property: The Prior Case Law*

On a few occasions in the past, mail and wire fraud statutes have been used to prosecute cases where what was involved was essentially the theft of trade secrets. An illustrative example is *Abbott v. United States,* in which the defendant, an oil investor, was convicted of using the mails to defraud by mailing payments to an oil company employee who supplied defendant with illicit copies of geophysical maps. In *United States v. Newman,* the Second Circuit upheld a conviction both on mail fraud and securities fraud counts where a group of young investment bankers traded on their advance knowledge of takeover targets gained from their firm's clients.

What distinguishes these cases from *Carpenter*? In *Abbott,* the economic harm is clear, and in *Newman,* the Second Circuit emphasized that insider trading before the announcement of a tender offer raised the premium that the bidder must pay. Accordingly, the fiduciary breach increased the bidder's total acquisition cost. Thus, even before *McNally,* courts in this area did not rely on the fiduciary breach alone in upholding convictions involving trade secrets, but rather stressed the existence of some actual economic harm. *Carpenter,* makes a unique and dubious contribution to the law in appearing to hold there can be a property loss without an economic loss. To be sure, the law of fraud would be satisfied with proof of a potential loss (because mail and wire fraud are inchoate crimes), but not even a potential economic loss was asserted in *Carpenter.*

The *Carpenter* decision is also a marked departure from prior law in its casual assertion that depriving the owner of exclusive possession of information amounts to an embezzlement. The history of embezzlement and the law of theft is long and tortuous, but one historical fact is clear beyond serious argument: intangibles could not be stolen or embezzled. Rather, theft offenses had to involve tangible personal property. Despite the obvious importance of information in today's high-tech, post-industrial economy, the modern cases prior to *Carpenter* seem to have faithfully abided by this rule. In *Commonwealth v. Engleman,* an important 1957 decision of the Massachusetts Supreme Court, defendants had been convicted by the trial court for conspiring to steal trade secrets used in the construction of jewelry boxes. The Massachusetts Supreme Court reversed these convictions, ruling that trade secrets could not be the subject of larceny, either at common law or under the Massachusetts statute. In general, state prosecutions involving the conversion of trade secrets have been rare and have usually been based on (1) specific tangible documents that were removed, (2) commercial bribery statutes, or (3) special statutes primarily aimed at the protection of computer data. Thus, prior to *Carpenter,* the transfer of confidential information was not viewed as within the scope of the criminal law, unless a bribe or some theft of tangible property that memorialized the trade secret was involved.

At the federal level, convictions for conduct that essentially involved the theft of trade secrets have occasionally been obtained under the National Stolen Property Act, but the court has always found some tangible item that was transported across a state line and in which the trade secret was physically contained. Nor was this a fortuitous fact. In *United States v. Bottone,* the Second Circuit explicitly acknowledged the need for a transported physical object to support a theft conviction under the Act:

> Where no tangible objects were ever taken or transported, a court would be hard-pressed to conclude that 'goods' had been stolen and transported within the meaning of [19 U.S.C. Sec. 2311]; the statute would presumably not extend in the case where a carefully guarded secret was memorized, carried away in the recesses of a thievish mind and placed in writing only after [state lines] had been crossed.

Besides the rule that the crime of theft applied only to tangible personal property, the common law also imposed the additional requirements that there be a "caption" and an "asportation" – namely, a physical seizure and carrying away of objects. Far from abandoning this ancient rule, the Supreme Court reaffirmed it in 1985 by interpreting the National Stolen Property Act "clearly to contemplate a physical identity between the items unlawfully obtained and those eventually transported, and hence some prior *physical taking of the subject goods.*" In short, copying of a trade secret (either by photographic reproduction or by duplicating computer software) did not automatically amount to theft, at least for the purposes of the federal criminal law. Today, these rules may seem out-of-date relics, but in their time they served the understandable purpose of assuring that the criminal law would be applied only in situations where the actor would unquestionably know that he was behaving in a criminal fashion.

B. *Statutory Developments*

Although the use of the criminal law to protect trade secrets and technology has a long history, it is sufficient for present purposes to note that most states have moved only modestly and marginally over the last thirty-odd years to modify the common law's rules as they applied to intangible property. Typically, state legislatures either recognized trade secrets as "property" in their larceny statues or enacted special statutes aimed exclusively at protecting trade secrets or preventing computer fraud. The common denominator in these statutes is the extreme care with which they define narrowly the kinds of information whose theft was criminalized. Because the locus of Foster Winans' misconduct was New York, it is particularly relevant to look at the New York statutory pattern. Under New York law, trade secrets or confidential information amount to "property" for purposes of the law of theft only when they constitute "secret scientific material." This term is defined by Section 155.00(6) of the New York Penal Law to mean:

> a sample, culture, micro-organism, specimen,

record, recording, document, drawing or any other article, material, device or substance which constitutes, represents, evidences, reflects, or records a scientific or technical process, invention or formula, or any part or phase thereof, and which is not, and is not intended to be, available to anyone other than the person or persons rightfully in possession thereof or selected persons having access thereto with his or their consent, and when it accords or any accord such rightful possessors an advantage over competitors or other persons who do not have knowledge or the benefit thereof.

Under this definition, which requires cumulatively that the information (1) have a scientific character, (2) have been kept secret, and (3) confer a commercial advantage, it seems beyond argument that the contents of Foster Winans' columns would not qualify. Moreover, at worst, theft of secret scientific information can result in no more than a class E felony.

In 1979, the Commissioners on Uniform State Laws adopted the Uniform Trade Secrets Act, which at least fifteen states have now enacted. Although the definition of trade secret in this statute is quite broad, no criminal penalties are authorized by it. Instead, the Act relies upon injunctions and damages suits for its enforcement. Federal law – at least prior to *Carpenter* – also lacked a generally applicable criminal provision relating to trade secrets.

Thus, *Carpenter* has criminalized an area that was only previously subject to criminal penalties in a few cases involving (a) clear economic injury to the employer, (b) the theft of accompanying tangible objects, or (c) the theft either of specially defined types of information (for example, government property or computer software), or under specially defined circumstances. Indeed, the scope of *Carpenter* is not even limited to trade secrets, which the common law and some statutory law has defined, but applies generally to the vaguer category of all confidential business information.

C. The New Property: Some Applications

The fact that neither the common law of theft nor recent statutory developments have ever stated a principle as broad and unqualified as *Carpenter's* off-handed assertion that the disclosure of confidential business information amounts to embezzlement does not prove that such a rule is undesirable. After all, what is wrong with such a rule in a high-tech economy where service industries account for an increasing share of our gross national product? The answer emerges when we look at some fact patterns where the *Carpenter* principle may soon be applied. Let us begin with two examples recently culled from the *New York Times'* business page:

First, following the 1987 acquisition of the brokerage firm E.F. Hutton by Shearson Lehman Brothers, other brokerage firms sought to lure away Hutton's most successful brokers. Dean Witter Reynolds hired some eighty-two Hutton brokers, and this raid resulted in litigation brought by Shearson and Hutton to prevent Dean Witter from using any confidential information it thereby obtained. For present purposes, the litigation between the two firms is less interesting than the way it may be restyled in the future after *Carpenter*. If we assume for the moment that customer lists are confidential business information, brokers at E.F. Hutton in the future could be sued (or simply threatened with suit) for converting this information by denying Hutton its exclusive use. A private action could be brought based both on common law principles for breach of fiduciary duty and on RICO (using mail and wire fraud as the predicate felonies). If there is doubt as to whom the property actually belonged (that is, the broker or the former firm), counsel for the firm will predictably learn over time to rewrite their employee's manuals to make it clear that the firm owns all customer lists and any other data about the customer's financial resources, investment preferences or financial goals. The manual might then add that all copies, extracts or other records based on such data belonged to the employer and must be physically surrendered by the employee on the termination of his or her employment. Effective as these techniques may be for the employer, consider the social desirability of their impact on both the employee and the customer, immobilizing, as they do, the former and often denying to the latter the services of his former agent.

A more recent and more publicized example involved the mass defections from Lord, Geller, Federico & Einstein, a subsidiary of a major British advertising conglomerate. The defectors, including six top executives of Lord, Geller and a total of thirty employees, left to form their own firm, Lord, Einstein & Partners. The mass move, which appears to have been a response to an abrupt change in the corporate culture following the acquisition of Lord, Geller by the British firm, resulted in litigation that led to a New York State court enjoining the departing partners from taking any steps to solicit clients or personnel from their former firm.

If one assumes (as the state court apparently did) that such a mass decision could not have occurred without some coordination and planning (much of it no doubt covertly hidden from the parent firm), then again it follows that this conduct amounted to an undisclosed fiduciary breach. Moreover, to the extent that confidential data about the agency's principal customer (here, IBM) and its marketing plans, advertising philosophy, and other preferences moved to the new firm, it is again possible to argue that *Carpenter's* simple theory that any deprivation of the employer's exclusive entitlement to confidential business information amounts to embezzlement applies as much to this example as to Winans' conduct in releasing the contents of his press columns. Indeed, in both the foregoing cases, the likely financial loss to the employer is greater than was the predictable loss (if any) to *The Wall Street Journal*.

Both the foregoing illustrations underscore the possibility that *Carpenter* will effect a significant reallocation of social control between employer and employee in favor of the former. The danger that this balance will shift is most acute in service industries, such as law, investment banking, medicine, advertising and other consulting businesses. Where previously these same disputes resulted in civil litigation, today there is the prospect of treble damages litigation (under RICO) and criminal indictments. In fact, the potential for private RICO litigation to expand the content of the mail fraud statute by creating precedents that will automatically be carried over to criminal contexts is without precedent and potentially dangerous. Courts will be adopting rules of law in situations where they intend only to shift losses and assign damages, and these same holdings will subject others to a potential loss of liberty. Finally, even if indictments are unlikely in employer/employee disputes, an employer's threat to invoke the criminal law may still have a chilling, if not visible, impact.

The point here is not just that civil wrongs are being casually converted into criminal offenses, but that the equivalent of a covenant not to compete is being created by operation of law. Because the law today favors competition, such covenants are disfavored and generally enforceable only if they have a brief duration and limited scope. However, if *Carpenter's* logic is taken to mean that, in order to avoid potential entanglement with the criminal law, the employee cannot use his former customer lists or must desist from using any particularized knowledge about his customers that he gained in his former employment, then *Carpenter* has given the employer a very powerful weapon to stifle competition, one that does not even require that the employee sign a binding covenant.

A third illustration raises an even darker prospect: what would happen to the whistle blower under *Carpenter*? Suppose a corporate employee reveals to the press that internal corporate studies show some serious environmental consequence of a specific corporate activity. However noble the motive for this employee's conduct, good motives do not excuse embezzlement. Under *Carpenter's* logic, the employee is arguably in the same position as if he stole corporate funds to aid a worthy cause.

Alternatively, a governmental employee could conceivably be prosecuted for leaking confidential information to the press—a result that would convert the mail and wire fraud statute into an Official Secrets Act. Much controversy has surrounded the government's use of an espionage statute to prosecute Samuel Morison, a government employee who gave copies of photographs taken by reconnaissance satellite to a British military journal, *Jane's Defense Weekly*. Ironically, few have noticed that *Carpenter* converts the mail and wire fraud statutes into a far more potent and potentially universally applicable weapon by which the government can deter its employees from leaking information.

To prevent this overbroad result, *Carpenter* should be restricted so as to apply only to trade secrets having "independent economic value" (in the words of the Uniform Trade Secrets Act). However, *Carpenter* does not use the phrase "trade secret" (which has a limiting common law gloss), but instead employs the far more nebulous term "confidential information." The only limiting phrases used by the Court in *Carpenter* with respect to the scope of the covered information were that the "confidential information be acquired or compiled by the corporation in the course and conduct of its business" and that "[t]he confidential information was generated from the business and the business had a right to decide how to use it prior to disclosing it to the public." In contrast, the law on trade secrets has generally required that the information have independent economic value or confer some commercial advantage and that the employer has taken reasonable efforts to maintain its confidentiality. One post-*Carpenter* Second Circuit decision has relaxed even the requirement that the confidential information belong to the employer.

Other examples could be posed. Yet, the central dilemma raised by *Carpenter* follows from the next three premises:

(1) most adult Americans are employees;
(2) most possess some form of confidential information about their employer; and
(3) most will at some point in their careers change employers.

Do all departing employees potentially face entanglement with the federal criminal law? Even if actual prosecutions will be few, the threat of criminal indictments and treble damage actions under RICO will still have a chilling effect.

D. What Remains of McNally?

In principle, *Carpenter*, follows *McNally* in recognizing that a mere conflict of interest is "too ethereal" a basis upon which to rest criminal liability. This suggests that a majority of the Court does not accept

Justice Stevens' position, in footnote ten of his *McNally* dissent. Still, few conflicts of interest are so uncomplicated as clearly to fall within this "ethereal" exception. Consider, for example, the Second Circuit's earlier decision in *United States v. Bronston,* where the defendant, an attorney, had continued to serve his own personal client after his law firm had begun to represent a rival contender for the same franchise. Presumably, this naked conflict would be insufficient today to support a conviction after *McNally.* However, if the prosecutor could allege that the defendant had passed some information about the rival contender's plans or strategies to his own client, then this case would probably still fall within *Carpenter's* reach. A more problematic case is *United States v. Condolon,* where the defendant seduced a number of young women on the false promise of placing them in films or modeling and was convicted of defrauding them of their intangible rights to privacy. Today, given that intangible property rights are recognized after *Carpenter,* the issue would seem to be whether sexual favors fail within this category. Who knows? This uncertainty underscores the discretion thus accorded the federal judiciary to decide what is criminal.

In another well known pre-*McNally* case, employees of a collection agency were convicted for tricking a telephone company into revealing the addresses of defaulting customers whom they wanted to reach. The prosecution's successful theory then was that the defendants defrauded these customers of their intangible right to privacy. Clearly such a theory is dead after *McNally,* but an alternative theory that might work would be that these defendants stole information from the telephone company. To be sure, the information—street addresses—had little or no economic value to the telephone company, but it was nevertheless "confidential information" and clearly the property of the company. If *Carpenter* truly meant to dismiss any requirement of economic loss, then prosecutors need only say to themselves "Goodbye, intangible rights; hello, intangible property," and proceed with business as usual. To illustrate the overbreadth of this theory, consider this hypothetical: several employees in an industrial shop work after hours to build themselves a sailboat out of scrap lumber (which, while superfluous, had not been abandoned). There is no economic loss here, but there is a property loss, and hence the statute would seem to apply.

Few cases are necessarily reversed by *McNally,* at least outside the context of public officials. The one major exception to this generalization are schemes to defraud a government agency, either in order to obtain some form of license or approval or to avoid making a required filing. With some consistency, courts appear to be holding that the government is not deprived of a property right that falls within the ambit of the mail and wire fraud statues under these circumstances. However, theses cases may well be reached by other statutes, such as the Hobbs Act, the Travel Act, or under the theory that there was a conspiracy to defraud the United States. In addition, whenever there is a bribe paid to a governmental official, Justice Stevens' view that the agent is defrauding the principal of the amount of the bribe could arguably be applied to reach even this case.

In the run-of-the mill kickback case, *Carpenter* may even have overruled a defense that was available before *McNally.* Decisions in the Fifth Circuit had apparently held that where there was a kickback paid by a buyer or seller, but the transaction occurred at an established market price, then the absence of loss to the other party implied that it had not been defrauded. Yet, to the extent that courts adopt Justice Stevens' theory that the principal has a property interest in any bribe the agent receives, this defense is now cut off. Several recent cases appear to have adopted just this analysis in upholding convictions for mail or wire fraud. . . .

IV. CONCLUSION

Old wine has been poured into new bottles. The pre-*McNally* doctrine of intangible rights has died only to be reborn as a theory of intangible property in *Carpenter.* Whatever the intent of the *McNally* Court and whatever the language in *Carpenter* about not criminalizing those conflicts that are "too ethereal" to merit the criminal sanction, the theory that confidential information is just another form of property, which disclosure to a third party "embezzles" by depriving the employer of exclusive possession, raises the prospect of overcriminalization far more forcefully than did any of the prior "white collar" crime controversies of the 1960's and 1970's. In particular, *Carpenter's* apparent assertion that there can be a property loss without an economic loss is one that a legislature may be entitled to make (because political accountability can excuse illogical reasoning), but which seems unprincipled for a court to adopt.

Unless constrained, the mail and wire fraud statutes could soon amount to a Federal Trade Secrets Act, with criminal prohibitions more sweeping than any state has yet enacted. Worse yet, these statutes could even evolve into an Official Secrets Act which could threaten any governmental employee who leaks information. All this has been accomplished by a Court that normally gives great deference to the legislature and federalism, but which in *Carpenter* speaks as if there is a federal common law of trade secrets.

Ultimately, the most serious problem with *Carpenter's* equation of the law of agency with the law of fraud is not simply that it is judicial legislation, but that it amounts to one-sided legislation. Both employees and employers can behave opportunistically and "cheat" the other with respect to trade secrets and confidential information. An employee could steal a trade secret to which he has no conceivable entitlement (for example, the secret formula for Coca-Cola), while the employer may deprive the employee of what the economist calls his "human capital" by restricting his mobility. The former kind of opportunism is covered by the criminal law, but the latter is not.

If *Carpenter's* logic suggests that the employer will now gain further leverage by which to restrict the employee, this is probably a predictable consequence of criminalizing the law of agency frames its rules, that body of law, when examined in its historical setting, looks suspiciously like a class-biased product of a pre-industrial, aristocratic society. Indeed, the very language of the law of agency—with its symptomatic references to master and servant—reminds us that it was shaped by courts that in fact wanted masters to remain masters and servants to remain servants. This inherent bias in the law of agency has not had significant consequences for commercial law, both because agency law principles may be more honored in the breach than in the observance and because it is generally possible to contract out of its rules. However, criminalizing agency law through the use of mail and wire fraud statutes makes this body of law more mandatory and forces us to reexamine whether contemporary labor relations should actually be governed by agency law's one-sided favoritism for the employer. Should the creative employee who himself creates the confidential information necessarily be regarded as a mere "servant" and all ownership interest in this intellectual property be given automatically to the employer, or should employer and employee be regarded as joint venturers? The irony in Foster Winans' position is that he was convicted for embezzling information that he alone created; that is, prior to the publication of his column, the *Wall Street Journal's* trade secrets typically existed only in his mind. His case is thus very different from the employee who seeks to acquire secret formulas created by others in order to sell them to the firm's rivals, but the law of agency recognizes no distinction between these two cases.

Arguably, no tears should be shed for Mr. Winans because he should have known his conduct violated the federal securities laws. Still, the logic of his case could similarly support the conviction of a salesperson who departs one firm (or is fired by it), taking his customer lists in order to solicit old customers from a rival firm. Such a result may seem extreme, and

courts may resist it. Nonetheless, it illustrates the greatest deficiency with judicial legislation of the type that *Carpenter* exemplifies: legislation is never neutral. Because the legislature is politically accountable, it is entitled to favor one coalition of interests over another, but this is an activity that courts should avoid. To a degree that is till uncertain, *Carpenter* shifts power and social control to employers and away from employees. That it does so unthinkingly and out of devotion to the black letter law of agency does not excuse the result.

E. Securities Fraud

Matthews, *Criminal Prosecution Under the Federal Securities Law and Related Statutes*, 39 GEO. WASH. L. REV. 901 (1971)*

The Federal Securities Statutes and Their Respective Criminal Provisions

In addition to the 1933 and 1934 Acts, the federal securities laws encompass the Investment Company Act of 1940, the Investment Advisers Act of 1940, the Trust Indenture Act of 1939 and the Public Utility Holding Company Act of 1935. Since its creation in 1934, the SEC has had primary responsibility for the administration and enforcement of all the federal securities laws. Pursuant to the statutes, the SEC has jurisdiction to investigate possible violations of the securities laws, which may result in the institution and litigation of formal administrative, civil or criminal enforcement actions. While the Commission staff itself conducts all such administrative and civil litigation, the Department of Justice has sole jurisdiction over the conduct of criminal prosecutions. Thus the 1933 and 1934 Acts each contain a provision authorizing the Commission to transmit evidence of any violations "to the Attorney General who may, in his discretion, institute the necessary criminal proceedings . . . ," and the other Acts contain similar provisions. In practice, local United States Attorneys, actively assisted by SEC staff members at each stage of the proceedings,

---

* Reprinted with permission of *The George Washington Law Review* © 1971.

present SEC criminal cases to grand juries, draft indictments, conduct the trials, and brief and argue appeals.

The respective statutes generally do not contain specific designations indicating when the commission of a proscribed act or the failure to perform a required act will constitute a criminal offense. Rather, each of the statutes contains a deceptively labeled "Penalties" provision that, with one exception, has three operative sections: first, a general proscription making willful violation of any substantive provision of the statue or any rule or regulation promulgated thereunder a crime; second, a specific proscription making certain willful false filings pursuant to the statute a crime; and third, a section prescribing maximum penalties to be imposed upon conviction.

The overwhelming number of SEC criminal cases have been, and probably will continue to be, brought under sections 24 of the 1933 Act and 32(a) of the 1934 Act. Consequently, the distinctions between the two provisions are important.

Section 24 of the 1933 Act states:

Any person who willfully violates any of the provisions of this subchapter, or the rules and regulations promulgated by the Commission under authority thereof, or any person who willfully, in a registration statement filed under this subchapter, makes any untrue statement of a material fact . . . required to be stated therein or necessary to make the statements therein not misleading, shall upon conviction be fined not more than $5,000 or imprisoned not more than five years, or both.

Section 32(a) of the 1934 Act provides:

Any person who willfully violates any provision of this chapter, or any rule or regulation thereunder the violation of which is made unlawful or the observance of which is required under the terms of this chapter, or any person who willfully and knowingly makes, or causes to be made, any statement in any application, report of document required to be filed under this chapter or any rule or regulation thereunder or any undertaking contained in a registration statement as provided in subsection (d) of section [15] of this title, which statement was false or misleading with respect to any material fact, shall upon conviction be fined not more than $10,000, or imprisoned not more than two years, or both, except that when such person is an exchange, a fine not exceeding $500,000 may be imposed; but no person shall be subject

to imprisonment under this section for the violation of any rule or regulation if he proves that he had no knowledge of such rule or regulation.

Both provisions require a willful violation of one of the substantive provisions of the respective Acts or any rule or regulation promulgated thereunder in order to constitute a crime, which by virtue of the penalties clauses is prima facie a felony. Section 32(a) of the 1934 Act, however, contains an important mitigation concept which provides that a term of imprisonment cannot be imposed for a rule violation if the transgressor can prove that he had no knowledge of the rule. The consequence of this mitigation concept is that criminal violations of the 1934 Act may be either felonies or misdemeanors, whereas criminal violations of the 1933 Act are always felonies. Furthermore, the express false filing provision in section 24 of the 1933 Act relates only to a "registration statement," and a violation constitutes a crime only if done "willfully." The similar provision in section 32(a) of the 1934 Act encompasses "any application, report or document required to be filed" as well as "any undertaking contained in a registration statement" pursuant to section 15(d) of the 1934 Act, and constitutes a crime if done "willfully and knowingly." Although section 24 expressly includes material *omissions* as well as affirmative misrepresentations in filings, section 32(a) literally refers to only "false or misleading" *statements.* It appears, however, that a material omission will render an affirmative statement "misleading," and if made "willfully and knowingly," will constitute a crime under sections 32(a).

As a result of these distinctions, prosecutions of particularly blatant and egregious violations which could come within the purview of either statute, (*i.e.,* willful, false and fraudulent oral statements of material facts made to induce a purchase of securities), will usually be brought under the 1933 Act. Thus, a convicted defendant will be subjected to a more severe maximum sentence, and the defense of "no knowledge" of the applicable 1934 Act rule, with consequent treatment as a misdemeanor, becomes unavailable.

Crimes Prosecuted Under the 1933 and 1934 Acts

The principal crime prosecuted under the 1933 Act, and in fact the predominant crime charged under the federal securities laws, is a violation of section 17(a) – fraud in the sale of securities. Criminal charges are brought somewhat less frequently for violations of section 5 of the 1933 Act – failure to register of the sale of securities. Filing a false registration statement or an amendment thereto is sometimes prosecuted under the 1933 Act pursuant to section 24. In two instances, criminal prosecutions under the "antitouting" provisions of section 17(b) of the 1933 Act have been pursued. Although willful violations of sections 6(a) and 23 constitute crimes, apparently no prosecutions have been brought under either section.

Under the 1934 Act, fraud in the *purchase* or sale of securities is sometimes prosecuted as a criminal violation of section 10(b), and rule 10b-5 thereunder. Manipulation violations regarding both listed and unlisted securities have been prosecuted, as well as violations of the credit and "short selling" provisions. Other 1934 Act crimes that occasionally have been prosecuted include the failure to file required reports; the hindering, obstruction and delaying of the filing of required reports; the filing of false reports; and the use of false reports in communicating with prospective investors or existing shareholders. These included: annual reports on form 10K or financial statements accompanying annual reports; current reports on form 8K; proxy statements; broker-dealer annual financial statements; broker-dealer subordinated loan agreements; "insider" ownership reports; broker-dealer registration statements on form B-D; and broker-dealer books and records. Finally, many fraudulent or deceptive broker-dealer practices, in addition to those indicated above, have been prosecuted under the 1934 Act or rules promulgated thereunder: *e.g.*, failure to disclose control of an issuer; failure to disclose illegal "free-riding;" "churning;" and illegal hypothecation of customers' securities.

In addition to direct prosecutions for substantive violations, the Commission has maintained an active program of bringing criminal contempt prosecutions for violation of civil injunctions issued by federal district courts, which are generally obtained to halt further violations of sections 5 and 17(a) of the 1933 Act. Furthermore the Commission often initiates enforcement proceedings in federal district court in an attempt to obtain compliance with administrative subpoenas utilized by its staff in conducting investigations. Failure to obey a court order directing compliance with an SEC subpoena is punishable as contempt. A direct misdemeanor prosecution under section 21(c) for failure to comply with a subpoena issued under the 1934 Act has been pursued on at least three occasions.

Although SEC criminal cases, like SEC civil actions, are litigated in the federal district courts, criminal defendants have an absolute right to a jury trial while civil injunctive actions are tried solely to a judge. An SEC criminal contempt case may be tried before a judge alone, but a jury trial is required if the court desires to impose a sentence greater than six months.

Pursuant to the doctrine of pendent jurisdiction, federal courts in private civil actions under the federal securities laws may also adjudicate claims under applicable state Blue Sky Laws. There is no comparable doctrine applicable to criminal cases; criminal violations of state securities statutes are tried separately by state authorities in state courts. Under its Cooperative Enforcement Program, however, the Commission often refers the results of its investigations to state authorities, and staff members occasionally assist in litigating state criminal securities law cases.

Related Criminal Provisions

Prior to the passage of the 1933 Act, most criminal prosecutions for fraudulent securities transactions were brought under the Federal Mail Fraud Statute. Even after enactment of the various federal securities laws, indictments have not been limited to securities law crimes. Thus defendants are often additionally charged with mail fraud, wire fraud, conspiracy "to commit an offense against the United States," violation of the federal false statements statute, and perjury or subornation of perjury. Virtually every indictment in an SEC case alleges a violation of the federal "aiding and abetting" statute, as well as the substantive crime charged. In some instances, allegations of obstruction of justice, interstate transportation of stolen or counterfeit property, conspiracy "to defraud the United States or any agency thereof [SEC]," and larceny after trust have been included.

The Genesis of an SEC Criminal Case

Unlike the Internal Revenue Service, the SEC does not utilize special agents whose assignments are limited solely to criminal investigations. The attorneys, accountants, and investigators on the staff of the Commission who have investigatory responsibilities are principally fact-finders. Ordinarily, at the commencement of an investigation, they are unaware if any statutory violations have actually occurred, or, if satisfactory evidence is uncovered, what type of formal or informal enforcement action (if any) will ultimately be taken. Often two or more enforcement remedies will be pursued simultaneously. . . . The recommendations of the OCRSP are simultaneously reviewed by the Associate Director (Enforcement) of the Division of Trading and Markets and by the Commission's General Counsel. If they agree that criminal action is appropriate, the recommendation is forwarded to the Commission for consideration. Should a majority of the Commissioners approve, the report and underlying evidence will be referred to the Department of Justice with a formal recommendation for criminal prosecution. When prosecution for mail fraud is recommended, a copy of the report may simultaneously be sent to the Chief Postal Inspector.

Members of the securities law Bar, as well as SEC staff members, often raise questions regarding what specific policy guidelines, if any, are followed by the enforcement staff of the Commission in determining whether to recommend criminal prosecution in a particular case. The answer is indefinite, for there exist no formal or informal written guidelines to aid the staff in making a decision. As a practical matter, the decision to pursue criminal prosecution is based principally upon the combined visceral reactions of five staff members—the staff attorney in charge of the investigation, the Regional Administrator of the local SEC field office involved (or the appropriate Assistant Director when the investigation is being conducted from Washington), the Assistant Director (OCRSP), Associate Director (Enforcement and the Director of the Division of Trading and Markets.

It appears that three factors are generally given substantial weight in reaching a decision to bring criminal charges: first, whether the prospective defendants have a reputation in the investment community or within the "walls of the SEC" as chronic violators, who through the years have repeatedly appeared as defendants, co-conspirators respondents, or "fringe" participants in fraudulent securities promotions; second, whether the case involves a particularly egregious, or currently "fashionable," promotional scheme; and third, whether the case involves the corruption or attempted corruption of an SEC staff member or other government agent.

For approximately 25 years, when the Commission authorized criminal referral of a case, its staff would send copies of the report simultaneously to the Criminal Division of the Department of Justice and the local United States Attorney in the district where jurisdiction and venue were appropriate. In the view of this writer, this simultaneous referral had two distinct advantages: first, the local United States Attorney's Office could immediately commence a grand jury inquiry and thereby obviate the natural delay otherwise occasioned by a mandatory prior review by the Criminal Division of the Department of Justice; second, the enforcement staff of the Commission could make the initial choice as to which United States Attorney should prosecute a particular case when jurisdiction and venue were available in more than one district.

In the past, the Criminal Fraud Section of the Department of Justice's Criminal Division has been responsible for coordinating all SEC, as well as other agency—developed criminal prosecutions. Although SEC cases have constituted a substantial part of the Fraud Section's workload for the past decade or more, until recently, a separate Securities Unit was never formally created within that Section. Nevertheless, with direct liaison between the Chief of the Fraud Section and the Chief of OCRSP, and with similar relationships at the local level, the Commission and the Department of Justice have established a successful working relationship that has been equaled by few other joint arrangements in federal law enforcement.

Approximately one year ago, the Department of Justice modified the existing SEC criminal referral procedure described above. The procedure now requires the SEC to transmit Criminal Reference Reports and prosecutory recommendations only to the Criminal Division of the Justice Department in Washington, D.C. If the Justice Department decides to prosecute, it then decides which local United States Attorney will be asked to handle the case and what recommendations will be followed. Shortly after this new policy was instituted, the Attorney General announced the creation of a new Securities Unit within the Fraud Section at the Justice Department which will have responsibility for supervision and coordination of all SEC criminal prosecutions.

In recent years, the Commission has not experienced dissatisfaction in working with the Department of Justice. As long as the fears of some skeptics do not become fact—*i.e.*, that recent changes in SEC criminal referral procedures together with the formal establishment of a Securities Unit are part of an aftermath of the now infamous "Nixon letter" to the securities industry, designed to moderate vigorous enforcement of the criminal provisions of the federal securities laws—the Commission's persistent efforts against white-collar crime should continue. Whether the close relationship between the SEC staff, the Department of Justice, and local United States Attorneys will continue, and more importantly, whether the enforcement of the criminal provisions of the federal securities laws will remain as one of the more successful aspects of the Government's drive against white-collar crime, are questions that remain to be answered. Presumably, the changes were made to increase the success of the Commission's criminal enforcement program.

Use of the Jurisdictional Facilities

The constitutional bases of all the federal securities statutes is the use of interstate facilities or the mails. The particular "jurisdictional means" relied upon most frequently in SEC criminal cases are: (1) the mails; (2) an interstate telephone call or other interstate wire facility; and (3) the facilities of a national stock exchange.

Use of the Mails. The most traditionally pleaded jurisdictional basis for a criminal violation of the securities laws is the confirmation of sale mailed by a broker-dealer or other seller to the purchaser. In a broker-to-broker sale, the purchasing broker's reconfirmation to the selling broker will be sufficient. Other mailings occasionally relied upon are delivery of a stock certificate or other security interest, a market letter, progress report, or other literature describing a security being offered or sold, the mailing of a buyer's check to the seller or the mailing of the purchaser's check by the seller's bank for clearance, the mailing of annual reports or proxy solicitation materials to shareholders, or returning the proxy to the issuer, and the mailing of filings, such as a registration statement or an annual report on form 10-K, to the SEC or a stock exchange.

With regard to fraud charges, in determining whether a particular mailing provides sufficient jurisdiction, the differences between a securities fraud offense and a mail fraud charge should be noted. Essentially, the mail fraud statute outlaws use of the mails for the purpose of executing a scheme to defraud. Consequently, the mailing must be a central part of, and not merely incidental to the scheme. The securities fraud statute, however, is designed to outlaw fraudulent schemes in the sale of securities, and *any* use of the mails to this end, even though incidental or collateral, will confer jurisdiction. . . .

Interstate Telephone calls or Other Interstate Wire Facilities. Whether utilized as the jurisdictional basis for securities fraud or wire fraud, the placing of an interstate telephone call or the sending of an interstate telegram, telex, cablegram or other wire transmission is often pleaded in indictments in SEC criminal cases. Thus, in *United States v. Crosby,* an interstate telephone call was alleged as the jurisdictional basis for one of the wire fraud offenses. In *United States v. Abrams,* use of other interstate wire facilities constituted the jurisdictional basis for several of the section 5 counts upon which the defendants were convicted.

Section 17(a) Charges: "Schemes to Defraud"

As stated previously, the most frequent criminal charge in SEC cases is an allegation of willful violation of the anti-fraud provisions of section 17(a) of the 1933 Act. That section is quite similar to the Federal Mail Fraud Statute, which had been successfully utilized in criminally prosecuting persons for fraudulent securities transactions prior to the passage of the 1933 Act. Section 17(a) makes it unlawful in the offer or sale of securities:

(1) to employ any device, scheme, or artifice to defraud, or

(2) to obtain money or property by means of any untrue statement of a material fact or any omission to state a material fact necessary in order to make the statements made, in the light of the circumstances under which they were made, not misleading, or

(3) to engage in any transaction, practice,

or course of business which operates or would operate as a fraud or deceit upon the purchaser.

It is important to note that by virtue of the express provision of section 17(c), section 17(a) may be violated even though the securities are exempt from the registration requirements of section 5 of the Act.

It is not necessary to prove each of the elements of common law fraud or deceit to obtain a criminal conviction under section 17(a). Consequently, a *defrauded* purchaser need not be located, since the Government does not have to establish that a victim actually was deceived, suffered actual loss, or otherwise relied upon the defendant's conduct. A mere offer made in a fraudulent manner violates the statute. In virtually every case, nevertheless, a defrauded investor who has relied upon the defendant's conduct and has suffered actual losses will testify to the alleged offense. The three subsections of section 17(a) each proscribe distinct types of conduct which are susceptible to different modes of proof. With regard to subsection (1) – the employment of a "device, scheme, or artifice to defraud" – it is often erroneously assumed that, similar to a conspiracy, joint action by at least two persons is needed to constitute a "scheme." Under both the securities and mail fraud statutes, however, a scheme to defraud does not require the participation of more than one person. Furthermore, the fact that the scheme would not have deceived persons of ordinary intelligence is no defense. The statute protects the gullible as well as the sophisticated investor since the securities laws "were enacted for the very purpose of protecting those who lack business acumen."

Subsection (2) – misrepresentation or omission of a material fact – encompasses "half-truths" as well as outright falsehoods. It applies to statements made with a "reckless indifference" as to their truth or falsity, even though a defendant did not have actual knowledge of the falsity of his statements. "Materiality" will apparently be determined by the test laid down by the Second Circuit *SEC v. Texas Gulf Sulphur,* an injunctive action under the rule 10b-5 involving fraud in the purchase rather than the sale of securities:

> The basic test of materiality is whether a *reasonable* man would attach importance . . . in determining his choice of action in the transaction in question. . . . This, of course, encompasses any fact . . . which in reasonable and objective contemplation *might* affect the value of the corporation's stock or securities. . . .

Thus, material facts include not only information disclosing the earnings and distributions of a company but also those facts which affect the probable future of the company and those which may affect the desire of investors to buy, sell, or hold the company's securities.

Early in the administration of the 1933 and 1934 Acts, courts rejected the argument that the concept of "materiality" is too vague and indefinite to meet the requisite constitutional standards in criminal cases. False promises or opinions, particularly those involving the present or future value of a security, as well as false statements of existing facts, are clearly proscribed by the statute, and mere "puffing" can constitute fraud in the criminal context. Furthermore while "good faith" is a defense to a section 17(a) criminal charge, the defendant's belief in the eventual prosperity of the issuer, or the fact that his primary purpose is to engender ultimate profits for everyone will not excuse false representations or material omissions, whether made knowingly or recklessly.

The language of subsection (3) — any transaction, practice, or course of business that operates or would operate as a fraud or deceit — similar to that of subsection (1). It appears, however, that a single isolated, fraudulent or deceitful act would violate subsection (3) even though it did not evidence "some connotation of planning and pattern necessary to constitute a 'scheme.'" Moreover, a major difference between the three subsections is that the scope of admissible evidence would appear to be much wider under subsections (1) and (3) than under subsection (2).

Although each subsection constitutes a separate offense, all three are usually included in a singe section 17(a) count. In rejection claims that such counts are defective due to "duplicity," courts have held that "[i]t is well established that where a statute denounced two or more separate and distinct acts, things or transactions as an offense they may be charged in the same count conjunctively and the indictment is not bad for duplicity." This does not mean that a defendant could be subjected to three separate convictions based on one section 17(a) count. Rather, the Government may prove the single sections 17(a) crime by complying with any one of three slightly different modes of proof.

Unlike some comparable state statutes, intent is an essential element of a section 17(a) offense. Furthermore, it should be noted that sections 17(a) only proscribes fraud in the offer or sale of securities; to prosecute fraud in connection with the purchase of securities, section 10(b) of the 1934 Act, and rule 10b-5 thereunder, must be utilized.

Liability of a Principal for Crimes of His Salesmen or Other Agents Particularly in "boiler room" type cases, the responsibility of a principal of a broker-dealer firm for the criminal acts of his salesmen agents may be a crucial issue in a section 17(a) prosecution. To constitute a section 17(a) crime, it is not necessary

for a defendant himself actually to make the misrepresentation or sale to an investor. Any participant in a scheme to defraud, or "aider and abettor" of the seller, will be criminally liable for all crimes perpetrated pursuant to the scheme or committed by the person he is aiding and abetting.

Convictions of principals of broker-dealer firms or other establishments selling securities to the public have been upheld where the principals employed, trained, instructed, and supervised the salesmen, established sales programs regarding particular stock issues, or supervised the preparation and dissemination of fraudulent sales literature. The classic statement in this regard was made by Judge Learned Hand in *Van Riper v. United States,* a mail fraud case involving a "boiler room" securities promotion: "Men do not set up a business of such a kind . . . employing cheats as their active assistants, and keep aloof and ignorant of the means by which the profits are made." Moreover, a broker-dealer principal or sales manager cannot escape criminal liability by claiming ignorance of the falsity of the statements made to investors. The principal has an affirmative obligation to reasonably investigate the accuracy of the representations both he and his salesmen make to the public.

Section 5 Offenses

The 1933 Act is primarily a disclosure statute. The philosophy underlying its passage was not that the federal government should pass upon the merits of a security being sold, but rather that prospective investors should be provided with adequate information about the security and its issuer to reach an informed investment decision. Consequently, the thrust of the 1933 Act is contained in the registration provision in section 5, which makes it unlawful to sell securities or offer them for sale through use of the jurisdictional facilities unless a registration statement is in effect with respect to those securities.

Section 5 has apparently been considered a technical provision, and it has thus been thought by some, that failure to register would probably not result in criminal prosecution. *United States v. Wolfson* (Continental Enterprises) should dispel such reasoning. Contrary to popular belief, Wolfson was not the first person to be criminally prosecuted solely for violation of section 5. As early as 1936, an indictment based solely upon this section was returned in Plymouth Consolidated Gold Mines, and prior to that case, at least two additional indictments charging section 5 violations had been returned.

It would appear that the Government could establish a prima facie criminal violation of section 5 by proving: (1) that the defendant sold securities by use of jurisdictional facilities; (2) that no registration statement filed with the SEC was effective; and (3) that the defendant acted "willfully." Despite the general rule in criminal cases that the Government need not disprove statutory exemptions – although it may be required to affirmatively rebut statutory exceptions contained in a general provision defining an offense – in some section 5 cases involving unregistered sales by individuals, courts have required the Government to disprove certain alleged exemptions. The Second Circuit often requires the Government to affirmatively prove that an "underwriter" was involved in the alleged illegal sales, *i.e.*, disprove section 4(1) exemption.

Proof of Fraud. The primary issue in a criminal prosecution under section 5 is whether particular sales of securities should have been registered with the SEC. It would, therefore, seem that fraudulent acts would not be relevant. Yet, the fact that a defendant is motivated not to register the securities by a desire to conceal his fraudulent activities from the Commission or from investors, is relevant in establishing the element of willfulness in a section 5 prosecution.

In *United States v. Abrams,* a prosecution under section 5, the trial court had admitted evidence that defendants had made misrepresentations to their business associates in causing the stock to be issued, set up "dummy" accounts through which the stock was distributed, told one acquaintance they were manipulating the price of the stock, and had written letters to an attorney, describing some of their corporate machinations as "the worst kind of robbery this side of heaven, insofar as the . . . stockholders are concerned." In holding the foregoing evidence relevant to the section 5 charges on the issue of intent and willfulness, the court of appeals stated:

> It was relevant for the government to show that the failure to field a registration statement was motivated by the desire . . . to conceal . . . fraudulent activities . . . It was pertinent to show that these activities could not have withstood scrutiny by the SEC and that Abrams and Albert must have known that they could never have obtained registration of the Automatic stock by the SEC and therefore they had a motive for concealing their activities and the true condition of Automatic. We have so held when the fraud itself is at issue in counts in the case . . . It is no less relevant on motivation where the fraudulent activities, if revealed, could prevent SEC registration.

Thus, proof of selfish motive and unlawful intent is relevant to the crime of selling unregistered securities in violation of section 5, which, as a result, cannot be treated merely as a technical violation.

Conspiracy Charges

Although the practice has often been criticized, conspiracy charges continue to be employed by prosecutors in securities criminal cases to join multiple defendants and otherwise unconnected offenses arising out of an overall scheme to defraud. One of its principal merits in the eyes of a prosecutor is the useful exception that a conspiracy charge often provides to the hearsay rule at trial: Declarations of co-conspirator made in furtherance of the conspiracy are admissible against all persons who by independent evidence are proven to be a member of the conspiracy.

Criminal Contempt Prosecutions

One of the SEC's principal enforcement tools is an injunctive action against persons found to be in violation of the securities laws. If a person so enjoined continues to violate the statutes, the Commission may pursue a criminal contempt action based upon violation of the injunctive decree.

SEC criminal contempt prosecutions differ significantly from normal SEC criminal prosecutions. Since under rule 42(b) of the Federal Rules of Criminal Procedure a court can appoint SEC staff attorneys to prosecute criminal contempt cases based upon "SEC injunctions," the Commission does not merely refer its recommendation to the Department of Justice in this situation. Rather, the Commission usually invites the Justice Department, through the appropriate local United States Attorney's Office, to join in the filing of an application for an order to show cause why a particular person should not be held in criminal contempt for violating an injunction.

Willfulness and Knowledge

As noted earlier a person must willfully violate a provision of the 1933 Act to be guilty of a crime. Under the 1934 Act, the Government must show either a willful violation of a substantive provision of the Act or that the defendant "willfully and knowingly" caused a false report or statement to be filed. If the crime consists of a rule violation, it will be punishable only as a misdemeanor if the defendant proves that he had no knowledge of the rule. While confusion persists concerning the meanings of "willfully" and "knowingly," it is clear that the two terms have different meanings. Knowledge connotes more consciousness of guilt than willfulness; a "person can willfully violate an SEC rule even if he does not know of its existence."

There is nothing unusual in our system of jurisprudence in holding that a person's willful act constitutes a criminal violation even though the person claims he was unaware of the statute or rule. Competent persons are presumed to know the law pertaining to their conduct and are charged with a duty to obey it. Ignorance of the law, generally will not be a valid defense in a criminal case. "The word 'willful' even in criminal statutes, means no more than that the other person charged with the duty knows what he is doing. It does not mean that, in addition, he must suppose that he is breaking the law." The term "willful" means only that the act was done deliberately, as opposed to accidentally.

The "willfulness" and "knowledge" requirements of the 1933 and 1934 Acts have not been interpreted uniformly. Courts have wrestled with the criminal intent problem in several contexts: (1) in section 5 cases, where intent to defraud is not an element of the offense, and where reliance upon advice of counsel is often interposed as an alleged defense; (2) in fraud prosecutions, usually charging section 17(a) offenses; (3) in criminal contempt cases alleging violations of previously issued court injunctions; (4) in cases involving false filing with the SEC pursuant to either the 1933 or 1934 Acts, where, depending on the statutory provision relied upon, sometimes only willfulness, and other times both willfulness and knowledge, must be proven; and (5) in cases involving rule violations, usually either rule 10b-5 or other rules promulgated under section 10(b) of the 1934 Act, particularly with respect to the "no-knowledge" mitigation concept in section 32(a) of the 1934 Act. Finally, regardless of which statutory provision is relied upon, the elements of a "good faith" defense and the manner of proof in such a defense must be considered.

Section 17(a) Cases: Material Misstatements and Omissions—Schemes to Defraud

In a section 17(a) criminal prosecution, the Government must prove specific intent to defraud, or scienter. This does not, however, require establishing by direct evidence that the defendant had actual knowledge of the material misrepresentation or omission, or of the scheme. Circumstantial evidence may be sufficient to sustain a criminal conviction. Scienter may thus be inferred solely from the conduct of defendant.

While proof of "good faith" is a defense to a section 17(a) fraud charge, honest belief in the ultimate success of the venture will not justify false statements made in connection with the sale of securities. Reckless disregard or indifference as to whether the statements made are true, can constitute sufficient "willfulness" to sustain a section 17(a) conviction, even absent proof that the defendant had actual knowledge of the falsity of the statements. It is important to note that a defendant is entitled to have his alleged "good faith" defense "squarely presented to the jury" either in the trial

judge's instructions to the jury or otherwise.

Criminal Contempt Cases

The "willfulness" requirement for criminal contempt may not be identical to that necessary under the substantive provisions of the 1933 and 1934 Acts. As a practical matter, however, courts utilize the tests of willfulness discussed above in criminal contempt cases.

Donald C. Langevoort, The Insider Trading Sanctions Act of 1984 and Its Effect on Existing Law, 37 Vand. L. Rev. 1273 (1985)*

I. Introduction

The Insider Trading Sanctions Act of 1984 is, on its face, a simple piece of legislation. At the urging of the Securities and Exchange Commission (SEC), Congress added section 21(d)(2) to the Securities Exchange Act of 1934 to give the SEC the authority to seek civil penalties against persons who violate the prohibition against 'insider trading' of up to three times the profits made or losses avoided by the trader.

But this recent legislation means much more than the addition of a new form of remedy. True, the legislative history makes quite clear that Congress did not intend the new law to address, in any direct fashion, the substantive elements of a violation of rule 10b-5 as it applies to insider trading. A familiar canon of statutory construction, however, is that when a statute fails to change the prevailing judicial construction of some prior enacted provision, that failure constitutes an implied endorsement of judicial interpretation, at least to the extent that Congress was aware of the construction and there was a natural opportunity for revision. That maxim applies to the 1984 Act, a fortiori. Congress hardly could be expected to enhance so considerably the enforcement capacity of the SEC when it was dissatisfied with the substantive grounds on which the Commission could bring its actions. Indeed, the legislative history shows that the drafters demonstrated a substantial familiarity with the prevailing law, actively considered addressing that law, but determined not to do so.

In two recent cases, Chiarella v. United States and Dirks v. SEC, the Supreme Court imposed a confining

---

* Reprinted with permission of *Vanderbilt Law Review* © Vanderbilt Law Review 1985.

doctrinal structure on the prevailing law of insider trading – a structure that can be justified, if at all, as a way of promoting greater orderliness in this subject area. The most interesting aspect of the new legislation is that while the drafters formally accepted this restrictive approach, at the same time they strongly expressed an intention that the legal doctrine of insider trading restrictions be inventive and result oriented – flexible enough to reach a wide range of abuses. This legislative schizophrenia will, no doubt, further complicate and convolute the evolution of insider trading theory. This Commentary will consider the new remedy and the effect of its adoption.

II. THE SECTION 21(d)(2) REMEDY

A. Background

In recent years, insider trading enforcement has become the most visible of the SEC's programmatic efforts – achieving a level of emphasis in the present SEC similar to that of pursuit of foreign bribery, corporate slushfunds, and dishonest management in the mid and late 1970's. Notwithstanding an increasing level of academic controversy over the very propriety of insider trading prohibitions, aggressive enforcement in this area has had bipartisan political support within the SEC, and as the new Act illustrates, bipartisan support in Congress as well. Economic theory has fallen to the simple reality that a crusade for 'fair play' in the marketplace has undeniable political appeal.

How best to deter insider trading, however, has been a problem. Until recently, criminal prosecutions were relatively rare – there was no comparable enforcement commitment at the Department of Justice. SEC civil actions were common, but courts effectively limited relief to disgorgement of profits and an injunction against future violations. In light of the difficulty of catching insiders who trade in the first place, these SEC civil actions were not seen as an effective deterrent. The only other form of deterrence was the class action based private remedies for damages – an uncertain mechanism in any event. Class actions did, at least, provide an in terrorem possibility for a period following the Second Circuit's decision in Shapiro v. Merrill Lynch, Pierce, Fenner & Smith, Inc., apparently giving standing to sue for injury suffered by virtue of nondisclosure to everyone in the marketplace who sold between the time the insider bought (or bought, if the insider sold) and the time of disclosure of the relevant information. That holding raised the possibility of damages awards far in excess of the defendant's gains.

Two events in 1979 and 1980 focused the SEC's attention on the need for a superior enforcement mechanism. One was the SEC's deliberations over the American Law Institute's proposed Federal Securities Code. The drafters of the Code had retained the Shapiro approach regarding standing, but had limited class recovery, effectively, to the amount of profits made or losses avoided by the trader – eliminating the in terrorem effect. Altering the damages provision was a high priority of the SEC staff in discussions with the drafters concerning possible SEC support for the Code; the staff proposed a 'multiple of disgorgement' – three times the profits realized by the inside trader – as a preferable approach. Notwithstanding objections that such a measure would be purely punitive and out of sync with the Code's generally compensatory approach to damages, the staff and drafters compromised on a proposal that gave courts discretion to award the plaintiff class 150% of profits realized or losses avoided. In September 1980 the SEC endorsed the Code, subject to this altered damage provision and a number of other changes. The other event, also in 1980, was the Second Circuit's decision in Elkind v. Liggett & Myers, Inc., which essentially followed the original Code approach of simple disgorgement, and incorporated it into the current law. The SEC petitioned for rehearing, raising the same concerns about deterrence that it had raised with the Code's drafters and suggesting a similar type of remedy. The Second Circuit denied rehearing, and the in terrorem effect was, for the present, gone.

Thus, by the end of 1980, the SEC had both focused on the lack of deterrence problem and developed a proposed solution. With the step-up in efforts against insider trading leading to greater public attention – later followed by a substantial increase in political interest when two Reagan Administration officials became the subjects of insider trading allegations – the SEC sensed the opportunity to seek congressional enhancement of its powers and the new form of deterrence.

In September 1982 the SEC submitted a draft legislative proposal that would allow it to seek up to three times profits made or losses avoided as a civil penalty, and would increase the maximum criminal penalty for all securities law violations from $10,000 to $100,000. The House of Representatives held committee hearings in April 1983 on the resulting bill, H.R. 559. The House passed the bill, without objection, on September 19, 1983. The Senate acted more slowly. Senator D'Amato of New York, the chairman of the Senate securities subcommittee, wished to address a number of additional issues, including the definition of insider trading. He held hearings in April 1984, with most of the discussion directed at how to define the prohibited act. On June 29, 1984, the Senate discharged the committee from further consideration of H.R. 559. The text of a companion bill, S. 910, which incorporated most of the substance of the House bill but added some important new items, became the operative proposal that the Senate then passed by voice vote. On July 25 the House accepted all of the Senate amendments, eliminating the need for a joint conference. Notwithstanding last minute objections to the legislation by the Office of Management and Budget, the President signed the legislation on August 10, 1984.

B. The Civil Penalty

Section 21(d)(2) permits a court, in an action brought by the SEC, to impose a civil penalty of up to three times the trading gains, or losses avoided, on traders and tippers upon finding a violation of rule 10b-5 or any other provision or rule under the Securities Exchange Act that prohibits insider trading. This penalty is paid into the United States Treasury. The legislative history states: 'Payment of a civil penalty by any person does not extinguish the liability of any other person. . . . The Commission may, in its discretion, seek a penalty from any or all persons covered by this provision.' That is to say, if X tips Y some inside information allowing Y to profit by $50,000, X and Y each may have to pay up to $150,000.

The new Act does not set guidelines for the exercise of the court's discretion in determining the amount of the penalty. In proposing the legislation, the SEC stated only that the amount should be determined 'in light of the facts and circumstances.' Presumably, the issue will be resolved, much the way it is resolved in other criminal and civil fine contexts, by taking due account of the financial resources of the defendant, the degree of culpability and sophistication of the defendant, and related common factors. Based on the strong legislative expression of the need for deterrence and the difficulty of detection of criminal infractions, it is appropriate—at least insofar as the sophisticated trader is concerned—to treat the 300% civil penalty figure as the rule, not the exception.

The legislation applies 'whenever it shall appear to the SEC that any person has violated any provision of this title or the rules or regulations thereunder by purchasing or selling a security while in possession of material nonpublic information.' Therefore, a violation of any anti-fraud provision of the Securities Exchange Act, principally rules 10b-5 and 14e-3, could give rise to the penalty insofar as trading on the basis of material nonpublic information is concerned. The new penalty, however, applies only to trading 'on or through the facilities of a national securities exchange or from or through a broker or dealer' and 'not as part of a public offering by an issuer of securities.' The SEC placed this restriction in the law to

emphasize that the Act's purpose is protecting the integrity of the impersonal markets; alternative remedial mechanisms and protections are more readily available and effective when buying or selling is face-to-face or in connection with a public offering. Thus, the need for additional deterrence is not as compelling.

To measure profits gained or losses avoided, the court must calculate the difference between the purchase or sale price and the trading price within 'a reasonable period after public dissemination of the nonpublic information.' In arriving at this formulation, the drafters specifically chose not to measure profit by the difference between the defendant's purchase and sale prices. Thus, if an insider buys at five, watches as the stock goes up to ten shortly after public disclosure and sells six months after disclosure at fifteen, the gain per share is five, not ten. On the other hand, if six months later, when the sale takes place, the price has gone back to five, so that there is no actual profit at all, there is still a paper profit of five on which to base the penalty. As to what constitutes a 'reasonable period,' there is a good deal of case law discussing the determination of when the information can be expected to be reflected in the market price. For the most widely traded issuers—those having highly liquid, efficient markets—the price may reflect the information in a matter of hours, if not minutes. In addition to the size of the issuer, a court should take into account the nature of the information. Some new data, such as increased earnings projections or dividends, can be evaluated extremely rapidly; other more subjective types of disclosures may take more time to digest intelligently. A useful presumption is the average trading price the day after disclosure, which could then be adjusted if the nature of the issuer, the market, or the information so requires.

Another important point about the penalty is that it may be collected in addition to any other remedies directed against the wrongdoer. The SEC, therefore, could obtain both disgorgement of profits and treble profits as a penalty—for all practical purposes, a quadruple profits sanction. In the above illustration, when the wrongful profit is five dollars per share, the insider may have to pay five dollars as disgorgement and fifteen dollars as a penalty, for a total of twenty dollars a share. A court should not reduce the civil penalty simply because disgorgement also has been granted; these remedies, according to the legislative history, are cumulative and serve entirely different purposes.

The legislative history refers to the availability of private rights of action against insider trading in two contexts. First, because of questions as to standing and the disgorgement measure, participants in the hearing noted the inadequacy of the private remedy as an effective deterrent. Second, some of the drafters implicitly assumed the availability of the private action in describing the alternative remedies available to the SEC. According to the House Report, for instance, a court might place the disgorged funds in an escrow account to be used to compensate those harmed by the insider trading.

Logically, the measure of damages in a private action should not be affected by the existence of a section 21(d)(2) penalty. Elkind is a functionally sensible decision – the open-market abstain or disclose requirement is simply a way of preventing unjust enrichment, and hence the most sound remedy is disgorgement – although the Elkind damage measure does beg some conceptual problems. The only forceful argument against disgorgement has been its inadequacy as a deterrent, an argument that substantially loses its force as a result of the Act's passage. One would expect Elkind, therefore, to become more firmly established as the prevailing approach.

C. Secondary Liability

A politically sensitive issue during consideration of the penalty provision was the degree to which courts should impose penalty liability on persons other than actual traders or tippers. In dealing with these questions, the drafters have touched on some important issues that extend beyond the insider trading context.

1. Controlling Person Liability

Section 21(d)(2)(B) states that 'section 20(a) of this title shall not apply to an action brought under this paragraph.' Section 20(a) imposes joint and several liability on certain controlling persons for damages assessed on their agents or functionaries. The intent of this exemptive sentence is to assure, for example, that an investment banking firm that employs a person who trades for his own account based on inside information, or tips others, does not automatically become liable as a 'deep pocket' for the penalty. The firm may, of course, still face section 20(a) liability in an appropriate SEC or private action for its employee's disgorgement obligations, but the firm does not have to pay the penalty.

Subsection (B) also states that 'no person shall be liable under this paragraph solely by reason of employing another person who is liable under this paragraph.' This sentence is by no means redundant. The SEC's view, endorsed by a majority of courts, is that, quite apart from section 20(a), the common-law doctrine of respondeat superior makes employers and other principals liable for the acts of their employees and agents done in the course of employment and designed for the employer's benefit. This sentence,

therefore, is designed to assure that the SEC does not use the respondeat superior theory of secondary liability to circumvent the limitation on section 20(a). The addition of this sentence raises two points. First, it represents an explicit statutory recognition of the respondeat superior theory, and should finally resolve what had been a split between the circuits as to whether that common-law doctrine remained available. Second, by focusing closely on 'employment,' the statutory phrasing technically leaves open other relationships that might give rise to common-law derivative liability. For example, could a law firm be liable for a penalty when one of its partners tips or trades? If the intent of the provision is to hold only actual tippers and traders liable for the penalty as the legislative history indicates, then the answer should be no.

2. Principal Liability

The most interesting interpretive question under the 1984 Act arises when an employee trades for the account of his employer while either he or someone else in the firm possesses inside information. Is the firm then liable? Obviously, if the board of directors or senior management both possess the information and direct or authorize an employee to trade on the company's behalf, the company itself is the principal violator and should be liable for the penalty. The result is less obvious when only a junior employee knows the information – for example, a trader in a firm's arbitrage department who has received a tip about an impending tender offer and trades on the firm's behalf. Early in the legislative history, the SEC indicated that it could seek a penalty against the firm in such an instance, although the circumstances might be such that a penalty substantially less than treble profits would be appropriate. Other portions of the legislative history suggest that imposing firm liability based on a junior employee's actions may be the proper approach. For example, the legislative history expresses the need to prevent multiservice firms from facing penalty liability when one branch of the firm possesses material nonpublic information about a company and, without any communication, another branch buys or sells stock of the company for the firm's account – the 'Chinese Wall' problem. The Senate version of the bill had a statutory exemption from secondary liability for multiservice broker-dealers in such instances. The exemption was dropped at the last minute, but only on the expectation that the SEC would act to provide protection for such firms administratively, presumably through rule making similar to that found in rule 14e-3. If a firm is not liable unless one or more members of the senior management both know the information and direct or authorize the trading, then the 'Chinese Wall' problem would rarely, if ever, arise. Continuing concern over this issue, therefore, suggests that at least some of the drafters believed that a firm could face liability even though its upper level management was not simultaneously aware of the information and involved in the trade.

Other parts of the legislative history, however, indicate that firm liability should not be predicated on a junior employee's unguided actions. In describing the situations in which corporate liability is appropriate, the House Report implies that direction by senior management is crucial to liability. Moreover, one of the bill's sponsors clearly stated that '[i]f an investment adviser to an investment company, without the company's knowledge or approval, directs trades on behalf of the investment company while in possession of material nonpublic information, the investment company and consequently its shareholders should not be subject to the triple penalty.' By analogy, neither should the employer firm's shareholders, and on balance, this is the more sensible approach. The only deterrence-type justification for imposing penalty liability on a firm is that it may cause employers to take stronger steps to assure that their junior level employees do not trade on its behalf while possessing confidential information. While this watchfulness might be helpful, the legislative history shows no desire to extend liability to that level of 'fault.' To the contrary, the new Act itself specifically exempts employer liability based simply on failure to supervise. The only difference is that the firm has benefited from the illegality, but this is remedied by making the firm disgorge the improper profits. From a policy perspective, a firm should face liability for treble profits only if some or all of its senior management knew of the inside information and either caused or knowingly permitted the trade to take place for its own account.

3. Aiding and Abetting

The first sentence of section 21(d)(2)(B) states that no person shall be subject to civil penalty 'solely because that person aided and abetted a transaction covered by such paragraph in a manner other than by communicating material nonpublic information.' The intent of this sentence is clearly to assure that only tippers and traders, and not such persons as brokers who execute the unlawful trades, are subject to the penalty. The drafters expressed the view that other remedies, particularly administrative proceedings under section 15(b), provide sufficient deterrence to broker misconduct. Nonetheless, in explaining this exemption, the House Report gratuitously noted that '[t]he Committee endorses the judicial application of the concept of aiding and abetting liability to achieve

the remedial purposes of the securities laws,' and cited two Second Circuit cases with approval. Plaintiffs certainly will try to use this language to support the expansive use of aiding and abetting liability in cases having nothing to do with insider trading.

III. UNLAWFUL TRADING

A. Background

The foregoing discussion shows that the Insider Trading Sanctions Act itself, while raising some interesting interpretive issues, is not difficult to understand. More intriguing is the Act's spillover effect on the issue of what constitutes unlawful trading. As was observed earlier, the Act is to some extent a ratification of current insider trading doctrine. This is not to say that each and every previously decided case is approved of, but rather that the bill's drafters believed that the prevailing law in general provides an acceptable structure to carry out the objective of deterring abusive trading. Again, Congress would not have effectively quadrupled the penalties for insider trading had they been wholly dissatisfied with the underlying approach to the imposition of liability.

As submitted, the SEC draft bill carefully avoided defining insider trading. In a subsequent letter to House subcommittee Chairman Wirth, the Commission said that '[t]he flexibility which is gained by basing the imposition of the penalty on existing case law avoids the problems of freezing into law either a definition which is too broad, or too narrow to deal with newly emerging issues.'

The House Report concurred, stating that the law 'is sufficiently well-developed at this time to provide adequate guidance' and that:

[t]he legal principles governing the majority of insider trading cases are well-established and widely-known. . . . Recent action by the Commission and the courts has clarified the legal principles governing the smaller number of cases that involve trading on information that originates from sources other than the company – for example, information about a future tender offer.

On the Senate side, subcommittee Chairman D'Amato was not as convinced. In the course of the April 1984 hearings, he expressed the view that certain aspects of liability were highly uncertain and could result in a variety of abusive practices remaining unpunished. Senator D'Amato drafted a provision that would penalize a trader 'if he employs the [material nonpublic] information in violation of his own fiduciary or contractual obligations, or if to his knowledge the information is imparted to him in violation of the fiduciary or contractual obligations of the person imparting such information to him.' This proposal provoked a substantial amount of controversy, and many influential persons submitted alternative proposals, leading the SEC's general counsel to comment that drafting a substantive prohibition was becoming one of Washington's leading 'cottage industries.' Recognizing that the inability to agree on either the need for a specific prohibition or how it should be drafted was the single remaining roadblock to the bill's passage, Senator D'Amato dropped the effort in June in order to assure prompt enactment.

B. The Basic Prohibition: Insiders

The legislative history of the Act demonstrates that the drafters accepted the fiduciary duty basis for the obligation to abstain or disclose, established in Chiarella and reaffirmed in Dirks, as the starting point for analysis. In other words, a person must refrain from trading on inside information if he owes a fiduciary duty of disclosure to the class of marketplace traders who are disadvantaged by not knowing those facts. A person owes a fiduciary duty to investors in the securities of the issuer if he is a fiduciary of the issuer. Corporate directors, officers, and employees are the most obvious class of corporate fiduciaries, but as the Dirks case points out, there is a category of 'temporary' insiders that includes attorneys, accountants, underwriters, and other agents, who owe common-law fiduciary obligations of loyalty and care to the issuer during the course of the relationship.

The post-Chiarella case that tests the outer limits of the concept of fiduciary liability is SEC v. Lund. In Lund the district court held that the defendant became a 'temporary insider' of the issuer because the issuer's president, who was the defendant's friend and long time business associate, called the defendant, informed him of a lucrative joint venture that the issuer was planning, and asked the defendant if his company might be interested in a capital investment in the project. No corporate investment was made, but the defendant did purchase shares of the issuer on the basis of the disclosed information. The court held that the defendant became a temporary insider because the venture information had been made available to him 'solely for corporate purposes,' with the implication that it was to be kept confidential.

The Lund decision is largely inconsistent with the recent Dirks case. In Dirks, the Supreme Court explicitly rejected the notion that fiduciary responsibility can arise simply from the receipt of confidential information, absent either some manifestation of assent by the outsider to some fiduciary obligations or participation in a breach of fiduciary duty creating tippee status. Neither assent nor breach was present in Lund. Though well-intended, Lund's fiduciary duty holding is essentially contrary to a 1980 Second Circuit state law decision, Walton v. Morgan Stanley & Co., a

case cited with apparent approval in Dirks.

The above criticism notwithstanding, Lund is one of two cases cited explicitly in the House Report to support its conclusion that the current law is adequate to deal with basic 'outsider trading' abuses. There is no real indication that the drafters of the report were aware of the tenuous temporary fiduciary relationship basis for Lund. Nevertheless, the inclusion of the Lund citation gives some support to the argument of some of the Act's drafters that fiduciary responsibility should in some cases 'run with the information.' This use of Lund is a good illustration of a basic theme in the legislative history. While technically accepting the highly restrictive Chiarella-Dirks framework, the drafters' approach in discussing the substantive issues of liability seemingly eschews conceptualism – the legislative objective is to come down hard on any trading, as in Lund, that is inconsistent with basic notions of honesty and fair play. More important is deterring those who profit from the 'theft' of information, not establishing a neat scheme for explaining coherently why such thefts violate the securities laws. One gets the sense that had the present Congress gone forward with a comprehensive definition of unlawful trading, it would not have chosen to follow the Supreme Court's restrictive approach that forces the sort of manipulation found in Lund.

C. While in Possession of

The language and legislative history of the Act appear to clarify one substantive issue that has arisen from time to time over the last few years. Section 21(d)(2) states that the civil penalty can be imposed on those who violate a rule or statutory provision barring trading 'while in possession of' material nonpublic information. Commentators have questioned whether liability exists only when it can be shown that the information was the reason for the trading or whether it might be a defense if the insider can show that he would have traded anyway, with or without the information. The 1984 Act's new statutory language suggests that the answer is no, that possession of the information, not motivation, is controlling. Further, a discussion in the course of the House hearings suggests that the drafters were aware of precisely what they were doing.

D. Trading in Options

One substantive change that the Act explicitly creates is found in new section 20(d), which makes it unlawful to trade in options and other derivative instruments while in possession of material nonpublic information, whenever trading the underlying security would be unlawful. While prior to the 1984 Act, the issue was not totally resolved, a number of courts had held that because an option holder is not owed any fiduciary obligation by the corporation or its insiders per se, the abstain or disclose rule is inapplicable to options trading. This finding, of course, potentially allowed a major loophole in the law, for profits can be made as easily trading in options as in stocks. Legislative revision was thus sensible, although revision in the 1984 Act raises the same Chiarella-Dirks anomaly noted above. If we assume, as courts have, that option holders are not beneficiaries of any disclosure obligation as a matter of the law of fiduciary duty, the statutory change is effectively a statement that the disclosure obligation should exist, in some cases at least, absent any preexisting fiduciary duty. This extension is contrary to the Chiarella-Dirks rule that a preexisting duty is necessary, showing once again that while the drafters were prepared to recognize and ratify the Supreme Court's approach in construing current law, they believed that from a policy standpoint it can result in too narrow a prohibition.

E. Tippers and Tippees

In Chiarella, the Supreme Court was forced to explain why, if a preexisting fiduciary relationship is necessary to invoke the abstain or disclose rule, tippees could ever be liable under that theory. The Court explained by stating that '[t]he tippee's obligation has been viewed as arising from his role as a participant after the fact in the insider's breach of a fiduciary duty.' Apparently then, a breach of fiduciary duty by an insider is a necessary precondition to tippee liability.

The Dirks case further explored this issue. In Dirks, an investment analyst was visited by two corporate insiders of a company that was fraudulently concealing its true condition. The insiders wanted the analyst to help them expose the misconduct. He did, but not before tipping his clients to sell their shares in that company. The Court's decision rigorously adhered to the fiduciary duty approach, holding that since the insiders had breached no duty to the company in trying to expose the fraud, the analyst had no derivative duty to disclose the information to other investors. The fact that the analyst's clients profited vis-a-vis the rest of the market from access to information directly from inside the company was not enough. Whether or not one agrees with this holding, it was predictable in light of the Court's Chiarella construct. What is more significant about the decision is that the Court, going beyond the missing duty element and discussing extensively the scienter issue for tippee liability, added a new element to the law. Not only must there now be proof of a breach of fiduciary duty by the insider, but there also must be a showing that the tippee 'knew or should have known of the breach,' and to establish this element, the plaintiff must prove that the tippee was on notice that the insider would benefit personally from the tip.

This benefit requirement is a curious and largely unnecessary wrinkle; if there is one clear understanding in the common law of fiduciary responsibility, it is that an intent to benefit is not a necessary element. Moreover, the Court's approach to what constitutes a benefit is so broad that it makes the limitation extremely subjective and largely illusory. For example, the Court suggested that a tip designed to enhance the insider's reputation would be one for personal benefit. More surprisingly, the Court indicated that a 'gift' of confidential information would violate the rule because it resembles 'trading by the insider himself followed by a gift of the profits to the recipient.' To define personal benefit to include the warm glow arising from 'charitable' giving reduces the concept to an absurdity.

The personal benefit prong developed in Dirks has had its effect. In SEC v. Switzer, a corporate insider, attending a track meet, mentioned to his wife that there might be a liquidation of his company. This remark was 'inadvertently overheard' by University of Oklahoma football coach Barry Switzer, who thereupon bought shares of the company. The district court concluded: first, that the insider breached no duty in mentioning the information to his wife; and second, that even had there been a breach, it was not manifestly for an improper purpose. The first of these conclusions is not obvious – talking freely about a highly sensitive corporate matter at a track meet certainly can be a violation of the duty of care owed by a fiduciary. Still, the result is consistent with the strict logic of Chiarella and Dirks, for it is difficult to see that Switzer was actually a participant or co-venturer in the breach. Using this approach, the courts are saying that there is nothing wrong with a true outsider 'getting lucky.'

Dirks was decided just before the House Committee acted on the insider trading legislation, and caused the committee some concern. The committee determined, however, that 'if the Dirks decision is properly and narrowly construed by the courts, the SEC's insider trading program will not be adversely affected.' The House Committee did request the SEC to report periodically with an analysis of the case's effect. This legislative history should encourage courts to find that the benefit test presumptively is met whenever information is conveyed knowingly to an outsider without apparent business justification.

Even a narrow construction of the Dirks approach leaves open one important problem. Imagine that a financial analyst or newspaper reporter has arranged a meeting with a corporate executive to discuss various investment related matters. During the conversation, the executive releases some previously confidential information, in an effort to publicize it. May the analyst or reporter trade prior to 'effective dissemination'? Following Dirks strictly, there was no apparent fiduciary breach by the executive because the release of the information was for a valid business purpose. The answer, however, is not so clear. Conceivably, in the analyst case at least, a court might find it improper for the executive to have disseminated the information 'selectively,' rather than at a press conference, thereby favoring one group of shareholders, through their agent, over others. This improper disclosure would satisfy the first prong of the Chiarella-Dirks test by establishing a breach of fiduciary duty. If the selective disclosure appears to have been for the executive's reputational or other benefit, the second prong of the test would be met as well. Such a holding would require an insider to act with loyalty and care not only with respect to the reasons for communicating sensitive information but in the method of communication as well. One should note, however, a statement by the House drafters that '[w]e anticipate that the courts . . . will be mindful of the necessity, in light of the substantial penalties herein imposed, to avoid unduly inhibiting traders from generating and acting upon valid research information of the sort upon which efficient markets necessarily depend.' Given the difficulty, if not impossibility, of distinguishing clearly between basic research efforts and eliciting useful information, courts may be tempted to treat this legislative language as providing a safe harbor for analysts. Such a restrictive approach would be unfortunate, for one hardly can imagine a more vivid example of 'unfair play' in the marketplace than the analyst/reporter example given above.

F. Misappropriation

One of the more indirectly significant aspects of the Chiarella decision was its failure to reject, and concurring comments from Justice Stevens seemingly in support of, the 'misappropriation' theory of insider trading liability. The misappropriation theory, which holds that converting confidential information for personal trading gain operates as a fraud on the source of the information—usually the trader's employer—was adopted quickly by the SEC as part of its enforcement program, and received a prompt judicial stamp of approval by the Second Circuit in United States v. Newman. The misappropriation theory has become the primary vehicle for reaching nontraditional trading cases, those that are neither clear cut insider or tippee cases, nor proscribed explicitly by rule 14e-3.

There are two serious conceptual problems with this theory, both concerning consistency with the Supreme Court's 1977 decision in Santa Fe Industries v. Green. The lesser difficulty is figuring out how merely using confidential information as the basis for trading is actually deceptive, rather than merely a breach of fiduciary duty—a requirement established by Santa Fe. The more substantial problem is determining how a doctrine whose functional effect is to safeguard an employer's 'confidentiality' interest fits within the 'zone of interests' of the securities laws.

The legislative history of the 1948 Act evidences that the drafters were quite familiar with the misappropriation theory. The House Report cited Newman, for example, in support of its conclusion that the current law deals adequately with basic outsider trading abuses. The SEC repeatedly espoused the theory for illustrative purposes in its statements and in House testimony for enhanced enforcement powers. The Senate gave the misappropriation theory even more detailed consideration. Senator D'Amato raised questions about the viability of the misappropriation approach under current law, and justified his effort to include a definition of unlawful trading, which in many respects would simply have been a codification of the theory, by arguing the need to ensure that misappropriators are punished. The SEC agreed that the theory was not solid law absent affirmative endorsement by the Supreme Court, but nonetheless resisted by effort to define unlawful trading, feeling 'not dissatisfied,' at least, with the use of the theory. Although Senator D'Amato's decision to drop the definition was an attempt to expedite passage of the legislation, there is no evidence that he was convinced that a definition would either be unwise or unnecessary, his floor statement referred in approving terms to the misappropriation approach.

Unquestionably, the legislative history reflects a congressional endorsement of the misappropriation theory, whatever its doctrinal uncertainty. There is repeated evidence from both sides of Congress that the principal drafters considered trading on 'stolen' information an abuse that ought to be remedied. Had there been a consensus that the current law does not reach such trading, clearly Congress would have attempted to cure the defect. Their failure to recognize a pressing need for a new definition of unlawful trading strongly suggests a 'congressional intent' in favor of the misappropriation theory's validity as a general matter.

Simply recognizing the congressional ratification of the misappropriation theory, however, does not provide specific guidance for its application. First, what constitutes a 'misappropriation'? Under Santa Fe, there must be deception for a cause of action under section 10(b). In Newman, there was plain evidence of an active scheme by defendants to prevent detection—among other things, the use of secret foreign bank accounts. The court found this scheme, coupled with the harm the defendants caused by 'sullying the reputations' of their investment bank employers sufficient to establish fraud within the meaning of rule 10b-5. Subsequent misappropriation cases have not been even that analytical, imposing liability for little more than trading on information when it seems clear that the trader's employer or client would object to such use. This type of 'deception,' of course, is close to a simple breach of fiduciary duty. Nonetheless, the Act's legislative history evidences that the latter situation is precisely what the drafters believed should be covered by the insider trading laws, the 'theft' of information. One suspects that this may be one more example of a congressional judgment that calls into question the wisdom of the Supreme Court's strict literalism.

The second conceptual issue is how can the breach of an employer's confidentiality interest be considered 'in connection with the purchase or sale' of securities. From a standpoint of conceptual neatness, a statutory provision that prohibits fraud and deception in connection with a purchase or sale of securities should require a showing that the person allegedly defrauded was engaged in some investment related activity in order to establish liability. In Newman, there was a reasonable connection between the interests of defendants' employers and their clients, who needed confidentiality in order to assure the success of their merger related stock purchase program, and the objectives of the securities laws. The court's reasoning, however, was far broader, essentially finding that the 'in connection with' requirement was satisfied by defendants' own trading, and thus moving the focus completely away from the defrauded parties' interests. Once this step is taken a court may give a wide scope to the misappropriation theory, for by definition there always will be trading by the defendant. This doctrinal invention formed the basis of the recent action against a Wall Street Journal reporter, who purportedly joined with some associates in a scheme of trading based on prepublication information in the Journal's 'Heard on the Street' column. The SEC's complaint alleged that the reporter misappropriated this information 'for his own direct and indirect personal benefit in breach of a duty to the Journal.' If one were to ask the Journal why it felt aggrieved by the reporter's actions, it likely would respond that its journalistic integrity, largely a reputational interest, was threatened. An injury to reputation is harm, of course, but is it really the kind of harm the securities laws were designed to protect against?

The short response to all these conceptual difficulties is that the misappropriation theory may be an ill-fitting invention, but the result it achieves – imposing a measure of fair play in the markets that was lost in the doctrinal rigidity of Chiarella's abstain or disclose approach – accords with the investor confidence building intent of the securities laws generally. To the drafters of the Act, this goal seemed far more important than conceptual consistency. Indeed, the Journal case was cited a number of times in the legislative history as an example of the type of abuse that must be penalized.

IV. CONCLUSION

The legislative history of the Act shows that its principal drafters regarded those who trade on material confidential information as 'thieves,' deserving substantial penalties. The adoption of the Act is an expression that the existing laws should be used aggressively to curb the misuse of information. Unfortunately, such a result-oriented direction fits uncomfortably within the confining conceptual structure for rule 10b-5 built in recent years by the Supreme Court. Lower courts therefore must flesh out the law of insider trading based on inconsistent mandates, which will make the future path of the law both unpredictable and interesting.

Harvey L. Pitt and Karl A. Groskaufmanis, *A Tale of Two Instruments: Insider Trading in Non-Equity Securities*, 49 Bus. Law 187 (1993)*

INTRODUCTION

Not too long ago, conventional wisdom held that insider trading regulation was limited to the equity markets. The wisdom was reflected in a best-selling 1989 portrait of a bond trader's apprenticeship:

Drexel's research department, because of its close relationship with companies, was privy to raw inside corporate data that somehow never found its way to Salomon Brothers. When Milken trades junk bonds he has inside information. Now it is quite illegal to trade in stocks on inside information, as former Drexel client Ivan Boesky has ably demonstrated. But there is no such law regarding bonds (who, when the law was written, ever imagined that one day there would be so many bonds that behaved like stock?).

This conclusion garners some support in securities law commentary. The Securities & Exchange Commission (SEC or Commission) and federal courts face a quandary in applying the insider trading ban outside the familiar realm of the equity markets. The proscription on the use of material, nonpublic information in the trading of securities has been grounded on generic anti-fraud provisions of the federal securities laws. In

---

* Copyright 1993 American Bar Association Business Lawyer, Reprinted by permission.

Chiarella v. United States, the United States Supreme Court concluded that trading on the basis of market-sensitive information can only be "fraud" when the traders owe a fiduciary duty to disclose such information to those opposite them in the marketplace. The requirement of a fiduciary link fits poorly outside the equity markets. An options investor purchases a contract granting the right to purchase or sell the securities of a particular issuer. The issuer and its insiders had no part in that contract; they owe no duty to this investor. Similarly, a debt holder is a creditor; thus investors' rights are defined by contract. In theory, insider trading prosecution should stall in the non-equity markets.

In practice, there exists a tale of two instruments. Options trading has been the subject of a litany of SEC enforcement actions asserting insider trading violations. The courts and Congress addressed and, to some extent, resolved the problems posed by the absence of a fiduciary link. Although trading in debt securities produced only a trickle of cases to date, the dramatic changes in American debt markets created an intense interest in bringing such cases. In the debt context, however, the Commission lacks the express legislative authority it was granted to address options trading.

This legislative shortcoming makes it more difficult to bring such cases. Alternative theories crafted by the courts and SEC rule 14e-3 allow the SEC to address most purported violations. Viewed in the broadest light, however, none of these theories provides a viable weapon against trading by the issuer of debt securities. As prosecution of insider trading in debt securities becomes a priority, the SEC, market participants, and ultimately, the courts will have to consider how to transpose concepts that evolved in the equity markets to the fast-changing world of debt securities.

A Brief History of Insider Trading Regulation

Congress never was particularly specific about its intent when it crafted section 10(b) of the Securities Exchange Act of 1934 (Exchange Act). This section generally forbids the use of "any manipulative or deceptive device or contrivance" in the purchase or sale of a security in violation of Commission rules. Section 10(b) was intended to be a catch-all provision, vesting the Commission with flexibility to respond to new forms of manipulation or fraudulent conduct.

The Exchange Act's legislative history provides sparse detail about this provision. Securities law folklore suggests that rule 10b-5 was adopted under section 10(b) in response to a generic insider trading problem. In 1942, the SEC's regional office in Boston received a report that one company's president was understating the company's prospects in order to acquire its shares at a discount. The Commission's Staff

was asked whether the SEC had any recourse on behalf of the selling shareholders. Even before this episode, the absence of an explicit remedy for sellers of securities concerned the Commission; the SEC lobbied Congress unsuccessfully to expand section 17(a) of the Securities Act of 1933 (Securities Act) to proscribe fraud in the purchase of securities. The Commission's Staff responded to the 1942 query by crafting a general rule which melded the language of sections 10(b) and 17(a). The rule was approved promptly by the Commission; the sole comment was from Commissioner Sumner Pike who asked rhetorically, "Well, we are against fraud, aren't we?" The Commission's release accompanying the new rule indicated that it "closes a loophole in the protections against fraud administered by the Commission by prohibiting individuals or companies from buying securities if they engage in fraud in their purchase."

The Commission formally articulated the insider trading ban two decades later in 1961 in In re Cady, Roberts & Co. Cady, Roberts was a "tippee" case: broker Robert M. Gintel learned from a director of Curtiss-Wright Corporation in November 1959 that the company's dividend would be reduced. Gintel promptly sold shares of Curtiss-Wright. SEC Chairman William Cary started the seminal discourse by observing that sections 17(a) and 10(b), and rule 10b-5 are "aimed at reaching misleading or deceptive activities, whether or not they are precisely and technically sufficient to sustain a common law action for fraud and deceit." Officers, directors, and shareholders—and those who effectively stood in the same position—were subject to a "special obligation" for two reasons: first, they were given access to information for a corporate purpose and not for the personal benefit of anyone and, second, there is an "inherent unfairness" in allowing one party to take advantage of such information knowing it is unavailable to others in the market. Given this imbalance, such insiders must either disclose the material, nonpublic information or refrain from trading. Seven years later, in a case involving trading by corporate insiders in advance of an announcement heralding a major ore discovery, a full panel of the United States Court of Appeals for the Second Circuit affirmed the disclose or abstain requirement.

In 1980, the United States Supreme Court muddied the picture when it finally addressed to whom federal regulators could extend this obligation. Chiarella v. United States involved Vincent Chiarella, a financial printshop employee who, despite his employer's use of safeguards, deduced the identity of tender offer targets. When he traded profitably on such information, Chiarella became the first target of a criminal insider trading action. A divided Supreme Court reversed his conviction.

"Section 10(b) is aptly described as a catchall provision," Justice Powell observed, "but what it catches must be fraud." At common law, the failure to disclose material information prior to the consummation of a transaction is fraudulent only if the party is under an obligation to speak. Such an obligation arises only "when one party has information 'that the other [party] is entitled to know because of a fiduciary or other similar relation of trust and confidence between them.'" A fiduciary relationship exists, for example, between the shareholders of a corporation and the corporate insiders. No such relationship existed between Chiarella and the shareholders of the target companies. He was neither their agent nor their fiduciary, nor was he a person in whom they placed their trust and confidence. "[Chiarella] was, in fact, a complete stranger who dealt with the sellers only through impersonal market transactions."

A rigid application of Chiarella would have decimated the Commission's insider trading program. As even a casual reader of the financial press is aware, the Commission scored impressive settlements with "outsiders" who, like Chiarella, traded on nonpublic information about pending corporate takeovers but had no formal relationship with the companies whose shares they traded. Anthony Materia was one such defendant. Materia was uniquely suited to cite Chiarella in his defense; his fact pattern was the mirror image of Chiarella. Materia also was a financial printshop employee who divined the identity of tender offer targets and converted this information into trading profits. He was tripped up, however, by evolving securities law standards; in 1984, the Second Circuit affirmed a trial court's order that Materia disgorge nearly $100,000 in illicit profits and the Supreme Court proved wholly disinterested in coming to his rescue.

The difference in Materia was the Second Circuit's adoption of the misappropriation theory. The genesis of that doctrine was found in then Chief Justice Burger's dissenting observation in Chiarella that the defendant "working literally in the shadows of the warning signs in the printshop, misappropriated—stole to put it bluntly—valuable nonpublic information entrusted to him in the utmost confidence." The Second Circuit emphasized that "one who misappropriates nonpublic information in breach of a fiduciary duty and trades on that information to his own advantage violates Section 10(b) and Rule 10b-5." The fiduciary duty which was breached ran not from Materia to the shareholders but to his employer. In cases involving outsiders like Chiarella and Materia, the misappropriation theory allows prosecutors to reconcile the realities of the marketplace with the requirements of common law fraud.

REGULATION OF INSIDER TRADING IN THE OPTIONS MARKET

BACKGROUND

An option is a right. The seller (or writer) grants this right to the buyer in exchange for payment of a premium. A call option gives the buyer the right to buy (or call) a set number of shares of a specific company from the option writer at a predetermined purchase price at any time up to and including the strike date. A put option is the mirror image; it grants the buyer the right to sell (or put) a set number of a particular company's shares at a set selling price at any time up to and including the strike date.

The seventeenth-century Dutch tulip bulb market provides an historical footnote to the evolution of modern options trading. At that time, tulip bulb growers could command steep prices for their product. To ensure a minimum price in a volatile marketplace, growers purchased put options on their crops. If the price of bulbs declined below the price specified in the contract, the grower could deliver his crop to the option seller for the contracted price. The options sellers banked on the belief that ever-increasing tulip bulb prices would provide them with a steady stream of premiums for options which never were exercised. As the frenzy reached its peak, average citizens mortgaged homes and sold businesses to raise money to trade bulbs. Inevitably, the tulip bulb market collapsed. The speculators could not deliver on their options, plunging the Dutch economy into a debt crisis.

Prior to 1973, options trading was an esoteric field relegated to a handful of market professionals. Options contracts were sold in the over-the-counter (OTC) market dominated by about thirty firms that belonged to the Put and Call Broker and Dealers Association. Each options contract—its time span, premium, strike price—was the product of negotiations between the buyer and seller. Once crafted, there was a limited secondary market for these options. The handful of options dealers purchased small advertisements in financial newspapers hawking those options available for trading. As a result, most conventional options were held by the original parties until they were exercised or they expired.

Options trading was revolutionized in 1973 by the opening of the Chicago Board Options Exchange (CBOE). The Chicago Board of Trade (CBOT) developed the Chicago-based CBOE in an effort to diversify beyond the then-ailing futures industry. The CBOE replaced individually-negotiated contracts with options in which the expiration dates and exercise prices were standardized. At any given time, the options market offers four expiration dates—the Saturday following the third Friday in the expiration month. Strike prices for options to purchase or sell a security are set at intervals of 2½, 5, or 10 points. The CBOE provided an auction market in which these standardized instruments could be traded. Finally, the Options Clearing Corporation (OCC), a company now jointly owned by several options exchanges (but originally owned by the CBOE), safeguards against the risk of nonperformance. The OCC acts as an intermediary, serving as the writer as far as the buyer is concerned and the effective buyer as far as the seller is concerned. If a buyer exercises an option, the OCC randomly assigns a writer who has not closed its position. At its present pace, stock option volume is expected to total 125 million contracts in 1993.

The organized options markets have evolved and flourished despite a legacy of mistrust in the United States and Britain. Two nagging concerns have endured. The first is that a highly speculative market was made available to unwary individual investors. One primer on the stock market states as "an elementary but easily ignored truth" that "[m]ost individual investors lose money trying to trade options in attempts to beat the market." Moreover, some critics contend that the emergence of options markets is evidence that capital formation is being displaced by casinos. Renowned money manager Peter Lynch contends that "[i]n the multibillion-dollar futures and options market, not a bit of the money is put to constructive use. It doesn't finance anything. . . ." Although proponents of the options market can point to studies demonstrating the options market's role in improving liquidity and stability in the underlying security's price, this complaint continues to have a visceral appeal.

SEC ENFORCEMENT ACTIONS AND THE FIDUCIARY QUANDARY

For speculative investors, options provide a means to leverage gains. This leverage can spell spectacular gains for those trading on inside information. Every options investment is rooted in the "hope that the market moves by a certain time above or below a particular price." Investors who purloin privileged information enter the options market with more than mere hopes. When the confidential information involves a corporate takeover, the options market offers staggering profits. Indeed, the options market is quick to reflect any takeover rumors.

The Commission soon identified the risk that this market posed for abuse of confidential information; the SEC's 1979 study on the options market noted that "[t]he leverage offered by options, which permits substantial percentage gains on a small capital investment, and the existence of a liquid market for options have created new opportunities for profitable options trading based on non-public market information."

Similarly, the legislative report accompanying the Insider Trading Sanctions Act of 1984 (ITSA) noted that "the purchase of options permits the violator to obtain far larger illegal profits than would be possible through purchases of the same dollar amount of common stock." By their very operation, the options markets provide a forum ideally suited to insider trading.

The SEC's enforcement program has borne out that observation from the start. In its seminal Texas Gulf Sulphur decision, the Second Circuit determined that the sudden purchase of short-term call options by corporate officers inexperienced in such trading was evidence of the misuse of material, nonpublic information. Since then, options trading figured in a plethora of the Commission's civil actions involving insider trading allegations. These enforcement actions demonstrated the profitability options offer when betting on a "sure thing." In one case, for example, the SEC alleged that the tippees of a convicted insider trader parlayed an investment of $8483.25 in call options on Colt Industries securities into a profit of $437,972. Media accounts indicated that the burgeoning options markets became the venue of choice for insider traders.

The problem for securities regulators was whether this options trading could be characterized as fraud as required by Chiarella. That decision made it clear that trading on the basis of material, nonpublic information, without more, would not violate the federal securities laws. In order to be fraud, there must be a duty to speak emanating from a fiduciary relationship. Yet there is no fiduciary duty between an issuer or its insiders and an option holder. The security—the option—was issued not by the company but by the OCC. The options contract vests the purchaser not with an ownership stake in the company but with a right to purchase or sell shares until some later date.

A loophole for insider trading—if it did exist—would fly in the face of the Exchange Act's express statutory language. Section 10(b) and rule 10b-5 proscribe fraudulent conduct in the purchase or sale of "any security." The Exchange Act defines the term security to include "any put, call, straddle, option, or privilege on any security. . . ." "Common sense dictates," the Commission asserted in a 1985 amicus curiae brief, "that if insider trading in stocks was prohibited in order to prevent the corporate insider from reaping secret profits, then insider trading in options—designed to capture the same secret profits— must also have been prohibited." Any other result, in the words of one commentator, would "make a mockery of Rule 10b-5."

Congress agreed. Whether or not this potential loophole existed, it was plugged when ITSA amended section 20(d) of the Exchange Act. The amendment of the House bill in the Senate, made late in the legislative process, made explicit that when the insider trading ban is applicable to a transaction in the underlying security, it also extends to a purchase or sale of a "put, call, straddle, option, or privilege." Introducing the amendment, Senator Alfonse D'Amato emphasized that a corporate officer violating the insider trading ban in the market for derivative securities should be subject to the same penalties that would attach to the misuse of confidential information in the stock market. "The misuse of material nonpublic information in the derivative markets threatens the integrity of, and public confidence in, the Nation's securities markets in the same manner as any other abuse of confidential information." Similarly, a discussion in the House demonstrates that legislators intended to forestall the possibility of a loophole for insider trading in options.

The limited legislative history on this amendment makes no mention of Chiarella. This is ironic because Congress completely overlooked the fiduciary requirement mandated by Chiarella. As a result, the legal ramifications of the anomaly were addressed not in the context of SEC enforcement actions but in private civil suits.

* * *

REGULATION OF INSIDER TRADING IN DEBT SECURITIES

INTRODUCTION

At first glance, it would seem implausible that insider trading principles which are well established in the equity markets would not apply to trading in debt securities. After all, section 10(b) of the Exchange Act and rule 10b-5 proscribe fraudulent conduct in connection with the purchase or sale of "any security." And, the Exchange Act's definition of the term security includes "any note, . . . bond, [or] debenture." Moreover, in other contexts, the courts recognized rule 10b-5 actions stemming from transactions involving debt securities. Finally, insider trading cases involving equity securities have ensnared not only traditional market professionals, but also a psychiatrist and a newspaper reporter using information obtained in the course of their professional occupations. Given that far-reaching success, it might seem incongruous to some that a portfolio manager—or an issuer—could trade debt securities with impunity on the basis of his or her knowledge of material, nonpublic information about the issuer.

The Commission had not addressed the paradox—if it is a paradox—that arises out of the relationship between issuers and investors in debt securities. That relationship is one of contract, and does not square well with the common law fraud notions on which

insider trading regulation has been based. Until recently, the SEC had not confronted the issue because these markets offered a relatively limited opportunity for the misuse of material, nonpublic information. In both the corporate and government markets, this has started to change. Congress, the Commission, and the lower courts have stretched classic fraud principles in order to extend the insider trading ban to corporate "outsiders" and "outside" (or market) information. Although these innovations might allow the Commission to address most debt insider trading scenarios, clearly one could escape redress—trading by an issuer of bonds on the basis of material, nonpublic information. The SEC may have no recourse for an issuer's trading in its own bonds—activity the SEC would deem violative had it occurred in connection with equity securities. The paradox exists because the prevailing notion of debt securities expressly rules out the fiduciary relationship that gives rise to a duty to abstain or disclose. Much has changed in the market for corporate debt. These changes fueled a reassessment of those core principles and the potential for insider trading actions involving debt securities.

INSIDER TRADING AND CORPORATE DEBT SECURITIES

A bond is defined as "a long-term, secured, three-party obligation . . . to pay a fixed sum at a time certain, in other words, a debt instrument." The term normally extends more than a decade; the costs of issuing debt securities dictate such long-term maturity. The bond may be secured by mortgages, assignments of revenues, guarantees, or pledges of security or collateral. The three parties are the issuer, the purchaser, and the corporate bond trustee. This trustee "usually contracts with the issuer to serve as the grantee of the mortgage or security interest . . . for the benefit of the bondholders as a group, and performs a variety of other functions for the protection and benefit of the bondholders and for the convenience of the issuer."

A debenture is a type of bond. Typically "a debenture is issued pursuant to a trust indenture but is not secured by a mortgage or other collateral." A note, usually a two-party instrument, normally is secured and held by one individual or a small number of individuals. As a practical matter, corporate bonds and debentures are grouped together in discussions about the "bond market."

Traditionally, corporate bonds were viewed as instruments sufficiently secure for widows and orphans. In 1971, the American Bar Foundation identified "[t]he most obvious and important characteristic of long-term debt financing" as the fact that "the holder ordinarily has not bargained for and does not expect any substantial gain in the value of the security to compensate for the risk of loss." In this market, there was less of a pressing need to maintain the close watch on an issuer which is required when holding a company's stock. The market for suitably-rated corporate debt became a familiar haven for institutional investors.

The vast market for corporate debt has changed in a way that makes it far more susceptible to the misuse of material, nonpublic information. The development of the high-yield or junk bond market revised traditional conceptions about corporate debt. Junk bonds are high yielding bonds rated below investment grade. Standard and Poor's rates these bonds either BB + or less; Moody's rates them Baa or below. Before 1977, this market consisted entirely of "fallen angels" – the bonds of companies that once earned investment grade ratings but fell on harder times. In 1977, the market was transformed by new issues of corporate debt with subinvestment grade ratings. In an effort to entice investors to these "junk" offerings, issuers offered a premium over investment grade bonds. In the 1980s, this $9-billion market grew to $200 billion (spurred by $145 billion in offerings initially rated below investment grade). By the end of the decade, the junk market accounted for one-quarter of newly-issued corporate debt.

The growth of this market was fueled by Drexel, Burnham, Lambert's Michael Milken. He observed that investment in the corporate debt markets often reflected a herd instinct; investors stuck solely to investment grade securities. This market typically concentrated on a company's historical performance. A congressional report noted that "[t]he rating agencies have always emphasized size, historical record, industry position and ratio analysis. However, qualitative considerations such as management's ability, its vision of the future, and its attitude towards public security holders may be more important." Junk bonds required an investor to look at the company to determine whether this upstart or this fallen angel had the means to endure and meet the payments. Milken also tapped demand for debt financing in the vast majority of public companies which had no access to the traditional long-term debt market. Drexel provided the means for this market to function by issuing the lion's share of these bonds and nurturing a secondary market to ensure their on-going liquidity.

One result was a security which in many ways resembled common stock. One congressional witness characterized the bonds as "equity in drag." While a triple A rating would sell an investment grade issue, a C rating required an extensive pitch about the issuer. Like equity securities, junk bonds were valued with an eye on the company's fundamentals, as much as prevailing interest rates. Drexel observed that:

[t]he values of all high-grade or government bonds in a portfolio will decline when interest rates rise. The values of high-yield bonds, on the other hand, are somewhat less sensitive to

changes in the interest rate because they respond to changes in the financial outlooks of the individual underlying companies.

These securities also traded like equities – both in volume and volatility. Moreover, trading patterns in junk bonds reflected the economic cycle in a manner comparable to stocks. These similarities prompted some commentators to question whether the interest paid on junk bonds should be eligible for deductibility in a manner comparable to more traditional forms of corporate debt. "In short, junk bonds behave much more like equity, or shares, than old-fashioned corporate bonds."

Throughout the late 1980s, Drexel and Milken were targets in the most extensive government enforcement action in the history of securities regulation. In a 1988 complaint, the Commission alleged four separate instances of insider trading activity, and a panoply of other securities law offenses. It was likely the specter of vast forfeiture available to the government under the Racketeer Influenced Corrupt Organizations Act (RICO) that prompted Drexel to settle with the government in late 1988. The cost was steep: a $650 million settlement and a vast restructuring of Drexel's operations.

RICO's potent force became prominent in the March 1989 indictment of Milken, his brother Lowell, and Bruce Newberg. Paralleling the Commission's complaint, the criminal case added the demand for a RICO forfeiture of $1.8 billion. About one year later, Milken entered a guilty plea to counts that did not involve insider trading allegations and agreed to pay a $600-million fine. A downturn in business and the shriveling of its capital sources caused Drexel to seek bankruptcy protection on February 13, 1990. Federal Judge Kimba Wood provided the tale with its surprising epitaph – a ten year jail sentence for Milken. These developments undermined severely the market for junk bonds. With Drexel's demise, a primary market-maker became unavailable for thousands of junk bond issues. Regulatory distaste for junk bonds drove out other market participants. The Financial Institution Reform Recovery Enforcement Act (FIRREA), introduced in 1989, required savings institutions to divest themselves of their junk bond holdings by 1994. The collapse of Executive Life stiffened the resolve of state insurance regulators to limit investment by such institutions in high-yield securities.

The junk bond market has rebounded – and matured – since then. A revival of high-yield offerings in late 1991 accelerated to a record $37 billion in 1992, spurred by low interest rates, declining default rates, and an infusion of investor funds into junk bond mutual funds. New public offerings of corporate junk bonds could soar to $45 billion in 1993. At the same time, the National Association of Securities Dealers is developing a "Fixed Income Pricing System," an electronic network which will provide hourly price quotations and improve surveillance in the junk bond market.

* * *

THE PROSECUTION OF INSIDER TRADING CASES INVOLVING CORPORATE DEBT SECURITIES

Overview

If debt relationships are marked by an absence of fiduciary obligations, there exists a compelling question as to what extent—if any—the Commission can prosecute the misuse of material, nonpublic information in the debt markets after Chiarella. Whatever the theoretical difficulties, the Commission and the Justice Department initiated a handful of actions involving insider trading in debt instruments—before and after Chiarella. These cases involve almost no discussion, much less a resolution, of the legal issues that will arise in any sustained effort to prosecute insider trading in the debt markets.

* * *

THE QUANDARY CONFRONTING ENFORCEMENT ACTIONS IN CORPORATE DEBT SECURITIES

If the Commission heeds calls for closer scrutiny of trading in the debt markets, the government may have to confront the inadequacy of its statutory tools. The SEC's Staff concedes that there are "analytic differences" when insider trading principles are transposed to the market for corporate debt securities. Nonetheless, Commission lawyers insist that they have the means to bring such cases. SEC Chairman Breeden expressed confidence that "there are several theories, under both classic insider trading and the misappropriation doctrines, to address insider trading abuses in the markets for debt securities." Indeed, developed insider trading doctrines such as the misappropriation theory, the "temporary insider" concept, and rule 14e-3 provide the government with potent tools to address insider trading abuses, wherever they arise. A survey of these options reveals two ironies. The first is that regardless of the breadth with which courts have applied these principles, none appears to address the purchase or sale of debt securities by the issuer on the basis of material, nonpublic information. The second irony lies in the Commission's rejection of a solution to that paradox.

* * *

The Legislative Fix

This overview suggests that the prosecutorial tools crafted by the government in equity insider trading cases, in most instances, will allow the SEC to address comparable abuses in the debt markets. Nonetheless, an analysis of the existing theories of insider trading liability suggests that an issuer can trade its own debt securities with impunity on the basis of material, nonpublic information in its possession. Putting aside legal niceties, this would seem to be a particularly egregious violation. This is not trading on information purloined by some corporate advisor with whom the investors have no contact. The trading in this instance would be directed by the very officers in whom debt investors placed their faith.

The irony of this quandary is the Commission's rejection of a solution. Former Chairman Breeden advised Senator Riegle that "until the applicable theories have been adequately tested in the courts, I believe a legislative response would be premature." At least one existing legislative response would resolve the Commission's quandary. The Insider Trading Proscriptions Act of 1987—passed up by Congress in favor of ITSFEA— would have extended expressly the insider trading ban to debt securities. The legislation proposed amending section 20(d) of the Exchange Act to make clear that insider trading activity in debt securities would violate federal securities laws. It is ironic that the Commission rejects the same "fix" that it embraced in 1984 to address trading in options.

CONCLUSION: RETHINKING THE REGULATION OF DEBT SECURITIES

The market for debt securities often has been an "after thought" in the federal scheme of securities regulation. The intense scrutiny currently devoted to the misuse of material, nonpublic information in the debt markets is representative of the reforms currently being considered for these markets. For example, there will be increased pressure for more complete disclosure by the issuers of such securities. The markets are becoming more responsive to these pressures. Investors are pressuring issuers to contractually guarantee periodic disclosure. The Municipal Securities Rulemaking Board is developing an electronic library to offset a longstanding paucity of information about municipal issuers. In the wake of the treasury auction scandal of 1991, there remains legislative interest in substantial reforms of the market for government securities.

For the foreseeable future, a robust debate will continue over the proper legal relationship between an issuer and investors in debt securities. Participants in these markets, however, are not waiting to see whether a qualified fiduciary relationship is embraced by the courts or the historical contractual notions prevail. Institutions that trade debt securities are turning to Chinese Wall procedures championed in the Federated proceeding to guard against potential liability. When such procedures are impractical, traders of debt securities increasingly are mindful that the misuse of material, nonpublic information may involve many of the regulatory risks common to the equity markets.

As a matter of legal theory, issuers are not subject to the same level of legal risk. As a matter of prudence, however, issuers considering a repurchase program for their debt securities should weigh seven rules of thumb—at least until the laws are clarified.

First, if an issuer proceeds to repurchase its own debt securities without advance disclosure of that intention, a certain amount of risk must be assumed. Put another way, disclosure of the program, with all the attendant possibilities after the program has been completed (such as offering a premium for any outstanding debentures) is the safest, but most unrewarding (from a fiscal perspective) way to approach such a repurchase program.

Second, issuers should consider dividing a repurchase program into separate phases, offering generic disclosure of the possibilities attendant to subsequent phases. An announcement that debentures are being repurchased, at a time when further steps have not been resolved definitively, may enable an issuer to escape fiduciary liability by noting that the issuer has not concluded what, if any, additional steps it might undertake after the completion of its repurchase program. Debenture holders should be aware that the issuer might (i) not repurchase any further debentures, creating a less favorable trading market for those debentures that remain outstanding after the repurchases are completed, and (ii) repurchase any remaining debentures at a subsequent time, on different terms that might be taken to avoid a situation in which subsequent steps, in fact, have been planned but are not disclosed in any public statement by the issuer announcing its repurchase program.

Third, issuers planning a repurchase program without any additional disclosure should satisfy themselves that they have not made any previous public statements respecting their debentures, or the issuer's intentions regarding those debentures, that might now require clarification or amendment. Because debenture repurchase transactions can be highly visible transactions, issuers who plan to adopt an aggressive posture to their right to repurchase without disclosure should be satisfied nonetheless that no debenture holder can claim to have been misled by a prior statement suggesting a contrary intent on the issuer's part. Affirmative misrepresentation cases tend to secure greater sympathy from jurists than do nondisclosure cases.

Fourth, issuers experiencing serious financial difficulties should refrain from a debenture repurchase program in the absence of advance disclosure. Because some courts imposed an enhanced duty to bondholders on insolvent companies (and their officers and directors), a repurchase program should not be undertaken by any corporation that is in financial distress. For those companies, the risk that liability will be imposed outweighs any business advantages that might otherwise inure from an undisclosed repurchase program.

Fifth, care should be taken to review the terms of the indentures under which the debt securities to be repurchased first were issued. Some indentures contain provisions that expand common law and statutory obligations running from an issuer to its creditors. No repurchase program should commence in the absence of a careful review of the relevant indenture provisions to satisfy the issuer that it is not under some enhanced disclosure obligation.

Sixth, issuers planning a debt repurchase program should review the statutory and common law of the state of their incorporation. Some states, like Delaware, are fairly clear in their view that fiduciary duties do not run from a corporation to its debt holders. Other states may be less clear in their treatment of this issue.

Finally, issuers should limit their undisclosed debt repurchase programs to straight debt securities. Courts examining the relationship between issuers and their convertible debentureholders, for example, have come to differing conclusions as to whether a fiduciary relationship exists between them due to the equity component of the securities. Given the uncertainties in this developing area of the law, prudence might well dictate that issuers avoid unannounced repurchased programs for debt instruments of that nature.

The SEC's Enforcement Division has not accepted Michael Lewis' analysis, outlined in the introduction, that "there is no [insider trading] law regarding bonds." Neither issuers nor market participants have any interest in providing the "test case" that establishes the outer parameters of the Commission's jurisdiction on this issue.

F. Antitrust

Harry First, Criminal Antitrust Enforcement 1–13 (1991)*

History

For many years critics of antitrust policy have argued that the antitrust laws were not being adequately enforced on the criminal side. The Sherman Act, passed in 1890, prohibits in broad language "contracts, combinations, and agreements in restraint of

---

* Reprinted with permission of the author.

trade'' as well as ''monopolization''. Violation of the statute has been a crime since its enactment. Nevertheless, criminal enforcement had traditionally been weak. In the first half-century of the Sherman Act there were only 173 criminal prosecutions, less than 3.5 criminal cases per year.

Although historically there have been few criminal prosecutions, early enforcement efforts did show a willingness to pursue important corporations through the criminal process. Four years after the Sherman Act was passed there were proposals for criminal prosecution of the ''Tobacco Trust'' and, in 1906, the government did prosecute officers of an American Tobacco Company subsidiary for an attempt to monopolize trade. In 1912 thirty executives and employees of the National Cash Register Company (the pioneer in the cash register business, with ninety-five percent of the market) were prosecuted criminally for creating a monopoly. As late as 1940 the Government was still willing to use criminal enforcement to proceed against monopoly.

These efforts notwithstanding, by the 1950s one could fairly say that criminal enforcement was not only infrequent but was also carefully constrained. The 1955 report of the Attorney General's National Committee to Study the Antitrust Laws wrote that then-current enforcement criteria ''insure[d] that criminal action will be limited to outright price fixing, boycotts, racketeering and the like when such misdeeds occur in areas where antitrust coverage is well settled.''

As the 1960s began, criminal enforcement criteria did not change, but the Government did catch some substantial corporate violators. Twenty-nine electrical equipment manufacturers, including the General Electric Company, plus a number of their executives, were prosecuted for a long-standing conspiracy to rig bids and fix prices on the sale of heavy electrical generating equipment. This major criminal prosecution against a Fortune 500 corporation attracted national media attention, including a famous Life Magazine cover showing the convicted executives (seven were sentenced to all of thirty days in jail) grasping the bars of their cells. Perhaps as importantly, the convictions opened up the era of private antitrust treble-damage actions. In the ''follow on'' cases subsequently brought, substantial monetary relief was obtained by the victims of the price-fixing conspiracy, notably government entities that had purchased equipment through what they had thought was a system of competitive bidding. This one-two punch seemed like just the sort of deterrence Congress had ordered in 1890.

Although the 1960s brought some increase in attention to criminal prosecutions, other antitrust problems moved to center stage. The government showed itself more willing to challenge mergers, and the courts readily agreed with the government's position. By the end of the 1960s, the government had embarked on a broad and ambitious civil enforcement agenda, which included an attack on anti-competitive government regulation, litigation against conglomerate mergers, and monopolization litigation against IBM. Criminal prosecutions continued, but the sights were lowered. The potato-chip industry (one target of criminal prosecution) was not on quite the same level as the electrical equipment manufacturing industry.

The 1970s were characterized by a convergence of two somewhat conflicting trends. First, the courts became less generous towards the government's position in antitrust cases. In 1974 the government suffered its first loss in a merger case in the Supreme Court since 1948, while doctrinal developments (often occurring in the context of private civil litigation) showed that the courts had become far less willing to condemn alleged anti-competitive agreements as per se illegal. At the same time, government enforcers began to respond to the persistent criticism that inadequate attention had been paid to criminal enforcement. Between 1970 and 1975 criminal prosecutions increased by more than fifty percent over the previous five years.

This increased attention to the criminal side received legislative impetus in 1974 when Congress amended the Sherman Act, making a violation a felony rather than a misdemeanor and increasing the penalties substantially. Corporate fines jumped from a maximum of $50,000 to $1 million; prison time, from one year to three. In 1976 the head of the Antitrust Division in the Ford Administration appeared personally in court to argue for imprisonment of corporate executives in a criminal prosecution. And in 1977 the Antitrust Division issued its own ''Guidelines for Sentencing Recommendations in Felony Cases Under the Sherman Act,'' which called for substantially longer prison terms than judges generally imposed even under the newly enhanced statute.

Both trends accelerated in the 1980s. Criminal prosecutions reached new highs while civil enforcement declined to a virtual vanishing point. In 1980, the last year of the Carter Administration, fifty-five criminal prosecutions were brought (nearly double the previous year); in 1984, there were 100 criminal prosecutions; in 1988 there were eighty-seven. By contrast, in the entire last four years of the Reagan Administration only forty-three civil cases were filed. Fully eighty-seven percent of government enforcement was now criminal litigation, a dramatic reversal of previous patterns.

By the end of the Reagan years, criminal prosecution had thus become the "top priority" of the Antitrust Division and the head of the Division was pointing out that the Reagan Administration had mounted "the most vigorous criminal enforcement program in the history of the Antitrust Division." His statistics were impressive. More criminal cases had been brought in the eight years of the Reagan Administration than in the first sixty-four years of the Sherman Act, and more than in the preceding twenty-four.

What had been unheeded criticism for so many years thus became conventional wisdom. The head of the Antitrust Division in the Bush Administration has termed criminal prosecution "our number-one enforcement policy," and a 1989 study of the Antitrust Division by the American Bar Association approved the Division's criminal enforcement program. Congress helped out as well. The Sentencing Reform Act of 1984, coupled with the Criminal Fine Improvements Act of 1987, raised criminal fines against individual defendants in antitrust cases, from $100,000 to $250,000, and created a new possible maximum fine both for individuals and corporations of twice the gain or loss caused by the violation. In 1990 Congress enacted a further increase in fines, to $350,000 for individuals and $10 million for corporations.

CURRENT CRITICISM

Current policy has not lacked for critics. One group, attacking from the left, argues that the government's enforcement policy represents no more than a variation on an old failure. The old failure is the unwillingness to take on major corporate interests; the variation is that the Reagan Administration directed antitrust enforcement resources away from civil challenges against a variety of anti-competitive practices and into criminal litigation against small companies involved in very localized markets.

There is empirical support for this criticism. The Reagan Administration's tolerance of merger activity (particularly large-firm mergers) is no secret. But with regard to non-merger enforcement too, a 1989 study reveals how government efforts declined in terms of cases brought against "large" corporations (defined as companies on the Fortune 500 list). Between 1973 and 1980 the Antitrust Division initiated fifty-eight cases against Fortune 500 companies. Forty-two of these cases dealt with price-fixing, customer allocation, or territorial division, the types of restraints that have generally been the focus of criminal prosecution. By contrast, from 1981 to 1988, there were only nine non-merger cases brought against large corporations, eight of which involved price-fixing or customer allocation. Enforcement involving large corporations had thus declined by eighty-five percent.

That the focus of case selection shifted away from large companies to smaller fry is further borne out by examining the kinds of industries that have been the target of criminal prosecution. For example, a list of criminal cases brought in 1987, compiled by the former head of the Antitrust Division to demonstrate that criminal prosecution had been vigorous under the Reagan Administration, shows the following: twenty cases brought against electrical contractors, eighteen against antiques auction pools, thirteen against highway contractors, six against motion picture exhibitors for "split" agreements, five against soft drink bottlers, five against waste haulers, three against harbor dredgers, three against moving and storage companies, and three against bakery companies.

There is another side to the charge that government has focused only on small fry. This criticism does not question the overall aim of the Reagan Administration's antitrust enforcement policy, which took the view that economic theories and values are the sole guide for antitrust enforcement. Rather, the critics argue that criminal enforcement has been indiscriminate in its targets, often prosecuting cartels that are ineffective, in the sense of having no adverse economic effect. According to this view, enforcement should be directed not at cartel behavior – price-fixing or bid-rigging agreements – but should look for impact, pursuing only those cartels that economic theory would indicate are likely to be (or those that actually have been) successful in raising prices.

Empirical support for the argument that the government has for the most part prosecuted ineffective cartels comes from a 1988 study, done by three economists, of civil treble-damage cases that follow on government criminal prosecutions. The authors argue that private buyers will file follow-on suits if they have suffered ascertainable damages from the cartel's activity. Thus "such claims are an excellent measure of the success of the collusive agreement prosecuted by the Justice Department." Examining 117 criminal cases filed between 1972 and 1979, the authors found that only about one-half resulted in follow-on civil suits, despite the fact that all but three of the cases resulted in convictions. They also found, in comparing the cases in which follow-on suits were filed with those in which they were not, that stiffer criminal penalties had been imposed in the follow-on group, a larger volume of commerce had been involved, the conspiracies in the follow-on cases were of longer duration, and the markets in the follow-on cases contained relatively fewer firms. To the authors, this indicated that follow-on suits had been filed in cases where economic theory would predict that collusion might be successful, and had not been filed in cases where collusion was ineffective. The authors comment: "Competition, rather than DOJ litigators, effectively defeated much of the price-fixing activity that did not give rise to subsequent civil suits." Their conclusion is clear. The Justice Department should stop wasting its resources on what it "frequently" does "prosecuting firms that have little chance to successfully fix prices."

Studies demonstrating the ineffectiveness of those cartels that have been prosecuted come as no surprise to a second group of critics, the critics of the right. These critics have generally been skeptical about the wisdom of most antitrust enforcement efforts and are not particularly sanguine about the ability of cartels to achieve their goals of restricting output and raising price. They stress the difficulties faced in successfully organizing and running any cartel, let alone cartels which must be run in the context of a legal regime that provides no remedies for enforcement of their rules and offers the prospect of jail if the cartel is detected. They believe that economic theory teaches that cartels with numerous participants in markets with low entry barriers are particularly unlikely to be successful. As for firms in highly concentrated industries with high entry barriers, theory indicates that over collusion is unnecessary, for these firms need not engage in direct communication to exercise their market power and raise price.

To the critics of the right, criminal antitrust enforcement has been an intellectual blind spot, the only area of antitrust enforcement in which economic criteria for case selection have not been employed. The theme of the right, however, is not so much that the Division should redirect its resources to better civil or criminal cases. (This is the theme of the left.) Rather, the theme of the right is that there really are not very many good cases to bring at all. It is the no-fry theme: non-enforcement is preferable to useless and wasteful (or potentially harmful) enforcement.

A Criminal Law Perspective

Lacking in the debate over proper criminal antitrust enforcement policy has been any criminal law perspective. This is nothing new. Criminal remedies were included in the Sherman Act without particular explanation. To the extent that there has been much thought given to their existence, criminalization has been justified by a presumption of deterrence. Deterrence, however, sweeps too broadly as a guide to enforcement; no doubt we would like to deter every antitrust violation, but we are not about to bring every antitrust case as a criminal matter.

To infuse enforcement policy with a criminal law perspective requires two steps: 1) some appreciation

of the different outlooks of the criminal law and of civil antitrust policy; and 2) some tentative theory to explain why a violation of the antitrust laws should be considered a crime.

Criminal law and civil antitrust policy differ by more than remedy. The criminal law is focused on bad conduct and its core concern is victimization. Criminal law tends to be fact-bound, individual oriented, and court-based. Its reference point is the past. Civil antitrust policy, by contrast, is focused on how the economy should be structured and run. Its core concern is economic welfare and its reference point is the future. Civil antitrust policy therefore tends to be more theory based, group oriented, and regulatory in its approach.

Critics of criminal enforcement policy often view criminal enforcement through the lens of civil antitrust policy. From such a perspective, there is no need for enforcement efforts against behavior that is unlikely to cause "too much" harm in the future. This could be true about a firm that monopolizes a market, if future entry is considered easy. It could also be true about a cartel that tries to set price but is doomed to failure. Such "self-correcting practices" are not worthy of antitrust enforcement. It is no wonder that these critics are disappointed in the criminal enforcement they see.

Government enforcers, however, have also not seen that the criminal law requires a different perspective for case selection from that which fits normal civil antitrust policy. For example, Charles Rule, former head of the Antitrust Division, wrote:

> When clearly defined classes of conduct are unambiguously anti-competitive, the Department brings all available penalties to bear. . . . Price fixing, bid rigging, and naked territorial allocation are among the classes of naked horizontal agreements that produce no significant efficiencies, yet invariably restrict output, raise prices above cost, and unambiguously harm consumer welfare.

This statement puts case selection into the fashionable economic jargon of today, but it mostly fails to connect with the criminal law. The criminal law is not primarily concerned with inefficient behavior, or output restrictions. "Moral culpability should remain the essence of criminal liability," Jerome Hall wrote more than forty years ago. We have not thought it immoral to act inefficiently; wastefulness is not a crime.

If we need to find a moral culpability basis for criminal antitrust enforcement, theft law is a good place to start. Theft law (including its later-developed branches of misrepresentation and wrongful conversion) punishes those who go outside the normal transaction structure to obtain wealth. Theft is punished in part because it transfers wealth involuntarily, in the sense that the victim would not willingly have given over the goods or money had the transaction occurred in accordance with the usual market rules. By analogy, those antitrust violations where victims suffer involuntary wealth transfers in breach of market transaction rules could be considered akin to theft, and criminally punishable.

For some antitrust violations, however, it may not be clear that there has been a transfer of wealth from an identifiable victim to the defendants, even though it is clear that the defendants have breached market transaction rules (and prevent market control by private parties) (for example, by rigged bids). The desire to protect market transaction rule is a core concern of the antitrust laws; the impersonal market, not the government and not private groups of competitors, is to regulate economic transactions. Indeed, this has led courts in the past to state that a mere tampering with price, whether the parties had the power to control price or not, is a criminal violation.

Is it legitimate to criminalize antitrust violations where the defendants have breached market transaction rules, but the economic harm is unclear? There are arguments in favor of such an approach. Certainly, the criminal law has not always required an identifiable victim as a condition of criminalization. It is sometimes enough that there be some identifiable risk of harm; endangerment statutes are a good example. Conduct such as bid-rigging or price-fixing does pose such a risk of harm, even without an identifiable victim. Justice Stevens, for example, has analogized rules against price-fixing to prohibitions on speeding. For both, there is a sufficient chance of harm to warrant illegality: "[Even] a small conspirator may be able to impede competition over some period of time. . . . and inflict real injury upon particular consumers or competitors." In addition, such conduct may be thought of as harmful because rigging the market, rather than following the rules, breaches trust. Commentators since Sutherland have noted that a breach of trust is often the hallmark of white collar criminal offenses.

On the other hand, allowing criminal antitrust enforcement to float free of a demonstrated wealth transfer runs the risk of sweeping too broadly. Overbreadth here implicates both criminal law concerns and the concerns of antitrust policy. Courts have rightly been hesitant to use the criminal law to protect interests that are "too ethereal", the criminal law net should not be cast so wide. And in the antitrust area, courts have been concerned that overbroad criminal law enforcement could have the effect of dampening legitimate, aggressive, competitive behavior.

What is needed is a mechanism to integrate these criminal law perspectives with the fundamental purposes of the antitrust laws, to retain the anchor of victim harm without foregoing our desire to protect our system of market transaction rules and without denigrating the trust-breaching aspect of antitrust violations. An appropriate mechanism would be the use of presumptions. Under current antitrust doctrine, there is no need to prove any harm in the kinds of cases now being prosecuted criminally. Price-fixing and bid-rigging are "per se" offenses; the conduct is illegal in and of itself. A concern for victimization makes it appropriate, however, to modify the application of this rule in criminal cases (even though the black letter law articulation of the per se rule came in a criminal case). This could be done by continuing the presumption that price-fixing and bid-rigging are harmful, but then allowing defendants to produce evidence to rebut the presumption of economic harm in the particular case being prosecuted. Once sufficient evidence of lack of economic harm had been introduced, the government would then bear the ultimate burden of proving economic injury beyond a reasonable doubt. This shifting in the burden of proof would emphasize that the core criminal focus should be on victimization and would recognize the inappropriateness of using the criminal sanction in cases where there is affirmative proof, unrebutted by the government, that no one was harmed.

Although this retreat from per se liability would be a change in the law, it is not as substantial as it might sound. First, the question of harm will not be raised as a defense to every prosecution. For tactical reasons, defendants often choose to forego putting on a defense case, particularly where the defendant will not take the stand to testify. Second, there is a growing understanding that our per se rules are really rules of presumptions and relevance rather than standards of legality. Even in cases that could be characterized as falling into the per se category, courts in civil cases have been increasingly willing to consider justifications to rebut inferences of anti-competitive conduct. If we are willing to look at relevant rebuttal evidence in civil cases, should we not be willing to do the same in criminal cases where liberty is at stake? Third, this approach might actually improve government enforcement. Not only would it require the government to anticipate the issue, leading to better case selection, but it would also make the government's presentation to the jury more effective. Jurors, unschooled in the wisdom of Pareto optimality and welfare economics, might want to know where the harm is. It may be that the government's legal advantage in never having to show the jury becomes a tactical disadvantage, leaving jurors wondering why they should send the defendants to prison for conduct that is not demonstrably harmful.

EVALUATING CURRENT CRIMINAL ANTITRUST ENFORCEMENT POLICY

A criminal law perspective thus provides criminal law policy criteria for case selection: victim harm (through wealth transfer) and breach of trust. A criminal law perspective also provides a checking mechanism to integrate criminal law policy and antitrust policy: instead of a per se rule on liability, the use of presumptions and burden shifting around the issue of harm. With a criminal law perspective, past harms are not "forgiven" because they were slight or are unlikely to recur. On the other hand, cases are not prosecuted criminally where the concern is over more speculative economic harm in the future. In such a case civil enforcement is the appropriate mechanism.

There are two ways in which this criminal law perspective helps in the debate over proper criminal antitrust enforcement policy. First, the proposed case selection criteria can be used to evaluate past prosecutions. Second, a criminal law perspective is useful in assessing institutional resource allocation.

In terms of case selection, the proposed criteria indicate that it is wrong to criticize criminal antitrust enforcement for choosing so-called "small" targets. If an antitrust violation results in an involuntary wealth transfer, prosecution is appropriate whether or not the defendant corporation was on the Fortune 500 list. Even if a case involves the smallest of the small (a highway or electrical contractor who rigged one bid), the appropriate question to ask would be—small in comparison to what? If the comparison is to the universe of economic or white collar crime, even "small" antitrust offenders are of the first rank. In a 1988 study of white collar crime and criminals, for example, antitrust offenses occupy "a very clear and distinctive position" in three measures of victimization: number of victims, amount taken ($100,000 being the high victimization level), and scope (statewide or wider). And no wonder, when most white collar criminal prosecutions are, in the authors' words, "banal and undramatic", ranging from tax prosecutions of employers who fail to withhold taxes, to the bribery prosecution of low-level VA housing inspector, to the prosecution of a federal employee for filing a travel voucher inflated by $204.

It may be that many of the criminal antitrust prosecutions of the Reagan Administration were similarly banal (the antitrust equivalent of the convenience store hold-up). On the other hand, the study of follow-on litigation mentioned earlier (whatever its methodological flaws) does raise concern about whether there really were many victims in the cases brought during this period. Government criminal prosecutions have a prospecting function, much as claims by gold miners or oil drillers, signaling plaintiffs' counsel and victims that there is a significant possibility of monetary recovery. If a substantial percentage of the alleged victims of these antitrust conspiracies are not bringing suit, we need to look more closely at the reasons. Perhaps institutional or legal barriers explain the inactivity, but one cannot totally dismiss the conclusion that inappropriate cases were chosen for criminal prosecution.

The other aspect of the small-fry criticism is that there are bigger fish to fry and the government should be doing so. It is, of course, difficult to know beforehand whether in fact there are bigger fish to fry, either in Fortune 500 terms or in terms of economic impact. Some have argued that larger fry are not being prosecuted because they are not, in fact, violating the law; and they are not violating the law because deterrence is working. The message of the Reagan Administration's prosecutorial policy and the courts' willingness to impose more severe criminal penalties (including prison) have combined to convince well-counseled "major companies" that it does not pay to violate the statute.

This argument is doubtful, even on a theoretical level. Managers of large corporations are surely much more likely to believe their eyes than their ears. Tell managers what you want, if they see no prosecutions in their industries (they are just going after road pavers and movie theatre exhibitors, after all), the deterrence message must be much less effective. Further, in a period of underenforcement of the antitrust laws, both public and private, accompanied by more aggressive competition in many industrial sectors, the conditions are improved for tempting corporate managers into collusive agreements. It is difficult to believe, for example, that since deregulation, firms in the airline and trucking industry have never tried to reconstruct the good old days through meetings and agreements on price. It is also difficult to believe that some of our favorite antitrust recidivist industries, such as the paper industry, have finally learned their lessons and are sinning no more. And it would not be surprising to discover that some of the foreign companies that have targeted U.S. markets had entered into collusive agreements; Thurman Arnold found as much between 1939 and 1945, when the Justice Department brought fifty-two proceedings against international cartels, involving 105 products and 165 firms.

A criminal law perspective, however, also suggests criticisms of current enforcement beyond the size of the defendants, or the effectiveness of the cartel being prosecuted. Most of the criminal cases brought by the government have involved seller agreements among horizontal competitors, where there is wide agreement as to at least the potential for increasing price. The government, however, has also prosecuted some buyer agreements, specifically, motion picture split agreements and auction pools. The proper enforcement approach in these cases is less clear. Auction pools do seem to have wealth transfer effects (from the seller to the pool of buyers), plus the aspect of abuse of trust, thereby meeting the suggested criteria for case selection. The motion picture exhibitor split agreements, however, may have uncertain effects on wealth transfer. Indeed, these cases should be good candidates for the "no harm" defense, a result which seems to be consistent with some of the civil case law on motion picture splits.

On the other hand, a criminal law perspective also suggests that enforcement would be proper outside the area of horizontal cartel behavior. One candidate would be resale price maintenance, where a manufacturer forbids its retailers to cut prices. When engaged in with no pro-competitive justification, this conduct raises prices above what the market would set, meeting the suggested criteria of an involuntary wealth transfer and a breach of market rules.

Finally, a criminal law perspective highlights significant issues in the allocation of enforcement resources. For example, although it may be appropriate to prosecute small-fry, this does not mean that the Antitrust Division of the Department of Justice needs to be the prosecutor. Indeed, those who make the small-fry argument may very well have misstated the problem. The problem with case selection is not that small-fry are being improperly prosecuted. It is that scarce federal antitrust investigative and prosecutorial resources are being misallocated to prosecute them.

This misallocation has a high opportunity cost in terms of antitrust enforcement, diverting resources from other kinds of violations and other types of violators. Criminal enforcement has tended to focus on what has been called "garden-variety" antitrust, that is, naked collusive agreements dealing with price-fixing (and its cousin bid-rigging) and customer allocation. Not only are these the clearest antitrust violations from anyone's perspective, but they are also the ones for which defendants have the most notice that criminal prosecution could occur. An emphasis on criminal enforcement encourages antitrust prosecutors to look for these cases. It may very well discourage investigation into practices where only civil relief would be appropriate (or whether it appears initially that only civil relief would be appropriate). With criminal enforcement as a primary mission, whole areas of antitrust (exclusionary practices, distribution restraints, information gathering and exchange) are readily overlooked.

One solution is to have "less substantial" criminal price-fixing and bid-rigging cases prosecuted by generalist criminal prosecutors, whether from the U.S. Attorney's Office or by State Attorneys General under state law. This allocation of resources would not only free up antitrust resources, but would also recognize some institutional comparative advantages between the Justice Department's Antitrust Division and traditional criminal enforcement agencies. Indeed, a failure to recognize this advantage may be a significant cost of not thinking about criminal antitrust enforcement from a criminal law perspective.

Lawyers attracted to antitrust law are not likely to be hard-nosed criminal prosecutors. Antitrust and criminal law are not generally thought of as a combination, like love and marriage or crime and punishment. Antitrust lawyers, instead, have a perverse fascination with the antitrust laws, and often seem oblivious to other parts of the U.S. Code. Why, for example, are the Mail and Wire Fraud statutes so infrequently used in antitrust prosecutions, when virtually every rigged bidding case involves fraudulent non-collusion affidavits? Why do the drafters of antitrust indictments love to plead one long-running conspiracy when they could prosecute the defendants on fifty counts for each bid rigged? Or why do antitrust investigators not make more use of wire taps and other methods for information gathering beyond granting immunity to low-level employees?

The comparative advantage of the more traditional criminal enforcement agencies shows up when one examines data on outcomes in federal criminal prosecutions. As might be expected, for both antitrust and non-antitrust federal criminal prosecutions, more defendants plead out than go to trial. But more antitrust defendants go to trial than do defendants in almost any other type of federal criminal prosecution. For example, in the ten year period 1980 through 1989, nearly one-quarter of all antitrust defendants stood trial; only fourteen percent of all other federal criminal defendants did so. This greater willingness of antitrust defendants to go to trial may very well reflect the fact that acquittal rates for antitrust cases are also significantly higher than for any other area of federal criminal prosecution. For the same ten-year period, the antitrust acquittal rate was approximately 60 percent. For all other federal criminal prosecutions, it was about 20 percent. And a comparison of antitrust acquittal rates with those in other areas that involve complex economic crimes (such as securities fraud and lending institution fraud), shows that anti-trust prosecutors are the least effective in court.

CONCLUSION

The 1980s were an extraordinary period for criminal antitrust enforcement. Although in some ways it is difficult to fault the government for seriously pursuing criminal penalties, this pursuit has also shown how little has been given to the separate issues of criminal antitrust law. Proper case selection criteria, integrating antitrust and criminal law policy, need to be articulated. Thought must be given to which antitrust cases can be better handled by other criminal enforcement agencies. Attention must be paid to fitting criminal antitrust enforcement within the larger program of antitrust enforcement so that resources are properly used.

Attention to these issues will not only pay dividends in terms of more effective antitrust enforcement. Focus on antitrust as crime forces us to think again about the core goals of our anti-trust laws. In our second century of debate over the relationship between individual enterprise and freedom, and corporate power and the State, the recognition that prison is the proper remedy for some violations of the antitrust laws reminds us again of the fundamental place these laws occupy in our regulation of these relationships and our allocation of freedom and power.

George E. Garvey, *The Sherman Act and Vicious Will*, 29 CATH. U. L. REV. 389–426 (1980)*

I. INTRODUCTION

The Sherman Act, which addresses the problems of economic power and its abuses, is unique in several significant respects. First, the Act's proscriptions are unusually vague. Congress specifically intended that the substance of the Act be developed over time by the judiciary. Second, the Act sets forth a multi-pronged enforcement procedure. Violations may give rise to criminal prosecutions, to private civil actions for treble damages, to private and governmental actions in equity, or to governmental damage suits.

---

* Reprinted with permission of Catholic University Law Review. ©1980 Catholic University Law Review.

Pursuant to its legislative mandate, the courts have developed a "common law" of antitrust by constantly defining and refining the substance of the Sherman Act. The substantive "refinement" producing the most dramatic reaction was the Supreme Court's pronouncement in *Standard Oil Co. v. United States* that only unreasonable restraints of trade violate section 1 of the Act. The vagaries of this "rule of reason" have been partially resolved through judicial creation of the per se rule. But these two rules have been in constant tension and the Supreme Court has never successfully articulated the scope of either rule nor defined their relationship to each other. Antitrust courts have experienced similar difficulties attempting to establish a rational standard or standards to distinguish between legal "monopoly" and illegal "monopolization."

Despite active judicial development of substantive antitrust law, the courts have historically failed to distinguish between those activities that may result in civil liability and those that may lead to criminal conviction. Until recently, a violation of the Sherman Act warranting the issuance of an injunction or an award of civil damages was, without more, a criminal violation.

In *United States v. United States Gypsum Co.*, however, the Supreme Court acknowledged that, even in the context of the Sherman Act, the appeal of a criminal conviction involves different considerations than an appeal of a civil judgment. The Court implicitly recognized that the substance of criminal antitrust violations must be developed under the principles of criminal law rather than civil antitrust precedent alone. The Court held, therefore, that intent is an essential element of a criminal violation of the Sherman Act.

The *Gypsum* decision, in a manner characteristic of the Burger Court's approach to antitrust, is explicitly narrow. It addressed the specific facts before the Court with frequent disclaimers about legal implications beyond those facts. The principles articulated in *Gypsum*, however, should impact on related, though factually different cases.

Since the Supreme Court decided *Gypsum*, several courts of appeals have had an opportunity to apply its principles. Their decisions raise significant issues about the standard adopted by the *Gypsum* Court. The claims of the various defendants and the judicial reactions to those claims have questioned the applicability of the single degree of culpability accepted by the Court in *Gypsum*—knowledge—without regard to the nature of the offense. In particular, defendants convicted under the new felony provisions have contended that a higher standard of culpability should be required because of the increased penalties. Most significantly, however, subsequent decisions appear to be carving out an exception to the *Gypsum* rule that intent is an essential element of a criminal Sherman Act conviction when per se violations are involved. Such an exception is inconsistent with *Gypsum* as well as with the criminal jurisprudential traditions that *Gypsum* reaffirmed.

This article will evaluate the intent issue in several steps. First, *Gypsum* and its progeny will be examined to place the issue in context. Next, the article will consider the status of and reasons for a requisite mental element for criminal condemnation. Emphasis will be placed on the common law development of strict criminal liability. The focus will then shift to the evolution of strict liability in the Supreme Court. Against this background, the Sherman Act's criminal provisions will be analyzed to see if they may be appropriately considered strict liability offenses under common law or federal judicial precedent. Finally, the factors used by the appellate courts to distinguish their cases from *Gypsum* will be reviewed to determine whether they justify a different result.

II. GYPSUM AND ITS PROGENY

A. United States v. United States Gypsum Co.

Gypsum was the first case in which the Supreme Court found that the substance of a Sherman Act offense depends on the nature of the proceeding as well as the defendant's activities. Because of the seminal nature of the opinion, its reasoning must be analyzed carefully to appreciate its implications.

The defendants were manufacturers of gypsum board, a product used in the construction of interior walls and ceilings. After a lengthy grand jury investigation, the defendants were indicted for allegedly conspiring to fix prices, terms and conditions of sales, and handling methods for gypsum board in violation of section 1 of the Sherman Act. The government's case was based primarily upon evidence of widespread price verification between the defendants. The Supreme Court synopsized the prosecution as follows:

> The focus of the Government's price-fixing case at trial was inter-seller price verification — that is, the practice allegedly followed by the gypsum board manufacturers of telephoning a competing producer to determine the price currently being offered on gypsum board to a specific customer.

In response, the defendants attempted to show that all price verification contacts "were for the purposes of complying with the Robinson-Patman Act and preventing customer fraud. They argued that their motivation brought their behavior within a "controlling circumstances" exception to Sherman Act liability. If the issue of liability was put to the jury, the defendants wanted the factual question about their purpose to be resolved. Nevertheless, the trial court's jury instructions, as interpreted by the Supreme Court, considered the defendants' purpose to be irrelevant if the effect of the pricing communications was to fix prices:

> [T]he law presumes that a person intends the necessary and natural consequences of his acts. Therefore, if the effect of the exchange of pricing information was to raise, fix, maintain and stabilize prices, then the parties to them are presumed, as a matter of law, to have intended that result.

Upon this instruction, the jury found each defendant guilty.

The United States Court of Appeals for the Third Circuit reversed, holding that the purpose for price verification activities could create a "controlling circumstance" and provide an affirmative defense to a Sherman Act charge. The court did not distinguish between civil and criminal antitrust litigation. It relied solely on civil precedent in ruling that a good faith attempt to avoid Robinson-Patman Act liability is a "controlling circumstance."

Although the Supreme Court affirmed, its decision was not based on the purported conflict between the Robinson-Patman and Sherman Acts. The Court found instead that the criminal nature of the proceedings added an element to the offense that is not present in civil litigation:

> [W]e hold that defendant's state of mind or intent is an element of a criminal antitrust offense which must be established by evidence and inference drawn therefrom and cannot be taken from the trier of facts through reliance on a legal presumption of wrongful intent from proof of an effect on prices.

Consistent with its growing interest in substantive criminal law, the Court showed a marked aversion to strict criminal liability. Relying primarily on *Morissette v. United States* and the Model Penal Code, it determined that "intent generally remains an indispensable element of a criminal offense" and that strict liability offenses enjoy a "generally disfavored status."

Writing for the majority, Chief Justice Burger enumerated several reasons for the Court's refusal to apply strict liability to Sherman Act criminal offenses. First, in contrast with traditional criminal statutes, "[t]he Sherman Act . . . does not, in clear and categorical terms, precisely identify the conduct which it proscribed." Although Congress intended the federal courts to give substance to the Act's prohibitions, judicial elaboration has provided only "open-ended and fact-specific standards like the 'rule of reason.'" Moreover, the courts have traditionally interpreted the Act with a generality inappropriate for a criminal law.

The Court was also persuaded by the announced policy of the Antitrust Division of the Department of Justice and of a special National Committee to Study the Antitrust Laws that criminal prosecution should be reserved for those who intentionally or willfully violate the law. Finally, the Court feared the possibility of "overdeterrence." If businessmen are threatened with criminal conviction for seemingly legitimate conduct that is found, regardless of intent, to have an undesirable effect on competition, they may forego "salutary and pro-competitive conduct."

Having found intent an essential element of a criminal antitrust violation, the Court determined the nature of the requisite intent. Guided by the Model Penal Code's classifications for culpability—purpose, knowledge, recklessness, and negligence—the Court determined that knowledge was sufficient for conviction: "[W]e conclude that action undertaken with knowledge of its probable consequences and having the requisite anti-competitive effects can be a sufficient predicate for a finding of criminal liability under the antitrust laws."

The scope of this holding was limited in three important respects. First, the Court followed the Model Penal Code and explained that the issue of culpability relates to each separate material element of the offense. *Gypsum* determined that knowledge of anti-competitive effects is sufficient to convict for the "restraint of trade" element, but it did not decide what degree of culpability is necessary for finding agreement or conspiracy. It was concerned solely with "the more traditional intent to effectuate the objects of the conspiracy."

Second, *Gypsum*'s "knowledge" criterion concerns only completed conduct. Knowledge is an adequate predicate for criminal conviction under section 1 only when anti-competitive effects are established. The Court suggested that a "purpose" to achieve the illegal result must be shown in order to convict when the proscribed result has not been realized.

Finally, *Gypsum* does not eliminate the "controlling circumstances" defense. Fear of incurring Robinson-Patman liability, however, is not a "controlling circumstance" when the method used (price verification) will, to the defendant's knowledge, stabilize prices. Although stating it as a negative, the Court acknowledged the continued validity of the exception: "A defendant's purpose in engaging in the proscribed conduct will not insulate him from liability unless it is deemed of sufficient merit to justify a general exception to the Sherman Act's proscriptions."

The holding of *Gypsum* concerning intent may be summarized as follows: intent is an essential element of a criminal Sherman Act violation and must be established by the government to obtain a conviction. If anti-competitive effects are shown, the intent element necessary to establish a restraint of trade is satisfied by proving that the defendants had knowledge of the probable anti-competitive consequences of the challenged conduct. Even if the requisite agreement, knowledge, and effect are established, a defendant may affirmatively defend by proving the existence of "controlling circumstances."

B. Recent Application of Gypsum

Since *Gypsum,* three courts of appeals have addressed the intent issue in the context of criminal Sherman Act prosecutions. Two circuits have held or implied that the Court's opinion in *Gypsum* does not require proof of intent when the purported violation is per se illegal under established case law.

In *United States v. Foley,* the United States Court of Appeals for the Fourth Circuit upheld the convictions of several Maryland real estate brokerage firms and their executives for conspiring to fix commission rates on sales of residential property. The jury had been instructed that "defendants must have known their agreement, if effectuated, would have an effect on prices; that they knowingly joined a conspiracy whose purpose was to fix prices; and that in joining they intended to further that purpose." The defendants claimed they were entitled to an instruction requiring the jury to find that they had "specifically intended" to restrain trade. In their view, the necessary degree of culpability had to be greater than that adopted in *Gypsum* because they were charged under the new felony provisions. The court held, however, that such specificity is not required on either statutory or constitutional grounds, even with the more serious penalties.

In *United States v. Brighton Building & Maintenance Co.,* the United States Court of Appeals for the Seventh Circuit reached a similar conclusion. The defendants were convicted of rigging bids for highway construction projects in Illinois. As in *Foley,* the defendants claimed it was error not to instruct the jury that a conviction could result only if the defendant specifically intended to restrain trade. The court disagreed and found sufficient an instruction that required a knowing agreement to rig bids and intentional assistance in achieving that goal.

The court bolstered its opinion by noting that bid rigging is a per se violation of the Sherman Act, while the price verifications in *Gypsum* were not. It did "not read *Gypsum* as indicating that once defendants are proved to have intentionally made an agreement which is unlawful per se, there must be an instruction that the defendants cannot be convicted unless they are found to have intended to restrain trade or commerce." This dictum raises an issue distinct from that present in *Gypsum*. The Court in *Gypsum* held that a presumption of intent could not be predicated on an anti-competitive effect. There is, however, a subtle distinction between a presumption that the accused knew or intended the result and a presumption that conduct identified as per se illegal is unreasonable. The latter relates to the conduct itself; the former relates to the actor's state of mind. These issues are not the same, and to the extent that *Brighton Building* infers that intent may be presumed because the activity is per se unreasonable, it is inconsistent with *Gypsum*.

United States v. Gillen, however, is the most disturbing of the post-*Gypsum* decisions. In sustaining a conviction for price-fixing, the United States Court of Appeals for the Third Circuit concluded that the intent element required in *Gypsum* applied only to borderline violations:

> The conduct at issue in *Gypsum* concededly was of such a nature as to warrant a further inquiry into intent. The Supreme Court's concern with those who unwittingly violate antitrust laws has no place here. . . . The act of agreeing to fix prices is in itself illegal; the criminal act is the agreement.

Although the court postulated that proof of intent was not required in a price-fixing case, it explained that if intent must be shown, it could be presumed from the agreement:

> [T]he intent requirement[s] will always be met in a case involving a price-fixing conspiracy. . . . Here, where [defendants'] actions were nothing less than price-fixing, the violators cannot be heard to argue that they did not know that their meetings and discussions of price would result in an unreasonable restraint of trade.

The Third Circuit developed this limitation on the *Gypsum* knowledge standard more fully in *United States v. Continental Group, Inc.* After reaffirming that knowledge of anti-competitive effects does not have to be proven in per se cases, the court held that knowingly entering into an agreement to engage in conduct that is per se illegal is sufficient to support a criminal conviction. The *Gypsum* Court, however, did not address the standard of intent required to satisfy the combination element of a Sherman Act violation. Its decision concerned only the intent to achieve the proscribed restraint of trade.

The post-*Gypsum* opinions raise several common issues. For example, the defendants reintroduced the nebulous principle of "specific intent." This concept was avoided in *Gypsum* because the Court adopted the more comprehensible definitions in the Model Penal Code. Regardless of the appropriate standard of culpability, the law would be less perplexing if courts consistently applied the Code's terminology. Concepts such as "criminal intent," "specific intent," "mens rea," or "scienter" may be significant on a philosophical level because they all indicate that an evil state of mind is an essential aspect of criminality. Applying such general notions to fact-specific cases, however, often tends to confuse rather than clarify the inquiry into intent because "[t]he mens rea differs from crime to crime."

Another issue in the post-*Gypsum* cases was whether conviction under the 1974 felony statute required a heightened degree of intent or culpability because of the greater potential penalty and stigma. *Gypsum* involved misdemeanor convictions, and the defendants argued that something more than "knowledge" should be required under the new law. This argument has sound support in criminal jurisprudence but was summarily rejected by each court.

Finally, and most importantly, *Gillen, Brighton Building,* and *Continental Group* intimated that even proof of knowledge was not required if the alleged conduct is per se illegal under the Sherman Act. The requisite intent may be presumed to exist when the defendant's conduct amounted to a per se violation. The Third Circuit in particular appears to opt for strict criminal liability. Its opinions suggest two reasons supporting this variance from the holding in *Gypsum*. First, since the law regarding per se offenses is well established, the defendants were not acting in the unclear realm of the rule of reason. Second, per se offenses involve egregious behavior. The latter reason — that the seriousness of the offense justifies a lowered standard of culpability — is contrary to basic principles of criminal law. . . .

CONCLUSION

Gypsum was a sound and reasoned statement of law. While the Court's knowledge standard may be subject to criticism, the real wisdom of its opinion lies in its ordering of priorities. The Court implicitly established that when there is a conflict between antitrust precedents and significant principles of criminal law, the latter will prevail.

Criminal law, substantive as well as procedural, defines a fundamental aspect of the relationship between citizen and state in a democratic society. It determines when the state may deprive an individual of freedom or property, not for resolving a private dispute between citizens, but for punishing and ultimately shaping individual behavior. The serious implications to an accused of conviction plus the obvious danger of governmental abuse make it essential that fundamental principles of substantive criminal law be preserved. The requirement that only the morally culpable be punished as criminal is a persistent principle that the Court honored in *Gypsum*.

The antitrust laws, however, are also significant to a society that orders its economy through the discipline of a competitive market. Fortunately, there is no real conflict between the antitrust goals and the criminal law's principle that only the morally culpable be punished. Requiring criminal intent does not threaten the efficacy of the Sherman Act. Violators may be enjoined and compelled to pay civil damages regardless of their intent. *Gypsum* merely holds, consistent with criminal law tradition, that the most drastic sanction is available only for those who have a criminal intent.

The post-*Gypsum* cases have relied only on antitrust precedents and have ignored the required synthesis of antitrust and criminal law. The courts should have determined if the existence of a per se violation justified the elimination of the fundament precept of criminal intent. When viewed from the perspective of criminal jurisprudence, per se civil violations of the Sherman Act are not properly subject to strict criminal liability.

The post-*Gypsum* decisions also suggest difficulties in the uniform application of the Supreme Court's standard of culpability. This problem is a manifestation of a persistent antitrust dilemma. Antitrust cases are extraordinarily fact oriented and nuanced, and judicial attempts to make application of the Sherman Act more certain have never succeeded. Thus, while the courts were in error when they completely dispensed with the intent requirement, their implicit finding that a uniform standard is inappropriate may be sound.

If the Supreme Court wishes to apply a single standard regardless of the circumstances of a specific case or the type of violation, it should reconsider the knowledge standard adopted in *Gypsum*. Business activities run the gamut from clearly illegal conduct to conduct which enjoys a strong presumption of legality (per se legal). Strong arguments can be made that violations in the latter category should be the basis for a criminal conviction only upon a showing of specific intent in its broadest sense, that is, an intent to violate the law. Additionally, borderline restraints judged by a classic rule of reason analysis should require a "purposeful" standard, especially if the activity has clearly legal as well as possible illegal aspects. If a variable standard is unacceptable, the purposeful criterion would be less likely to do an injustice to alleged antitrust violators than the knowledge standard applied in *Gypsum*.

The Supreme Court decided in *Gypsum* that intent is a necessary element of a criminal Sherman Act prosecution. The decision was a significant departure from the prior judicial approach to criminal antitrust suits because the propriety of the lower courts' rulings was judged by the standards of criminal law. Future courts should continue to develop the substantive and procedural content of the criminal applications of the Sherman Act so that it is consistent with the principles of criminal jurisprudence. Under these principles, the clarity and gravity of per se offenses do not justify an exception to the general rule that intent is an essential element of a crime.

G. Tax Fraud

Steven Duke, *Economic Crime: Tax Offenses*, 2 ENCYCLOPEDIA OF CRIME AND JUSTICE 683–688 (1983)*

TAX OFFENSES

Dimensions of the problem. The United States government collects approximately $500 billion annually in various taxes. More than half of this sum is received in the form of individual income taxes, another 15 percent in corporate income taxes, and about one-fourth in employment taxes. Although income and employment taxes are withheld on wages, the withheld amounts must be refunded if they exceed an individual's tax liability. Thus, in the main, the receipt of tax revenue by the government depends on the filing by taxpayers of tax returns that acknowledge the obligation. This is referred to as a "self-assessment" system, in contrast to systems that rely on gross income or gross receipts withheld or collected by government agents at the source.

The Internal Revenue Service, the branch of the Treasury Department in charge of tax administration, receives approximately 150 million tax returns annually. Apart from verification of mathematical computations, not more than 2 percent of the returns are

* "Economic Crime: Tax Offenses" by Steven Duke. Reprinted with permission of Simon & Schuster Macmillan from *Encyclopedia of Crime and Justice*, Sanford H. Kadish, Editor in Chief. Vol. 2 pp. 683-688. Copyright ©1983 by The Free Press.

actually "examined," that is, checked, at least to some degree, in order to verify the matters reported. Hence, tax evasion, especially income-tax evasion, is in many cases a very low-risk, high-profit economic crime.

The American system of "voluntary" self-assessment of taxes is widely regarded throughout the world as a marvel of compliance and efficiency. In many Latin American and some European countries, tax evasion is rampant; little effort is made at enforcement, and criminal punishment is rare. In the United States, on the other hand, the traditional official stance of the government has been that tax evasion is uncommon (Long, pp. 389, 397-398). In the late 1970s, the official line came under attack by the popular press, which asserted that compliance was rapidly deteriorating ("How Tax Cheaters Get Away with Billions," p. 102). Such claims persisted into the 1980s (Maital, p. 74).

A study of taxpayer compliance released in August 1979 was the IRS's first effort to measure unreported income. It tended to support press assertions about noncompliance. This study of 1976 returns estimated that from 6 percent to 8 percent of reportable individual income went unreported. In those categories where no tax was withheld, compliance was much lower: only 60 percent to 64 percent of self-employment income was reported, and only 50 percent to 65 percent of rents and royalties. Of income from illegal sources (principally drugs and gambling), the study estimated that only 10 percent to 15 percent was reported; the rest $25 billion to $35 billion, went untaxed (U.S. Department of Treasury, 1979, pp. 8, 17, 133). Based on that study and on follow-ups, the IRS in 1982 estimated that nearly $100 billion in taxes was not being paid. Thus, the government was collecting only about four dollars in five of tax revenues (Wiener, p. 43).

Role of criminal sanctions. The relative importance of criminal sanctions and levels of enforcement in promoting tax compliance in the American system is problematic. Virtually all agree, however, that some criminal sanctions and some enforcement are essential. The limited function of criminal penalties is demonstrated by the statistics: never, since the income tax was enacted in 1913, have as many as 2,500 taxpayers been charged with tax crimes in a single year. In 1979, the number was 1,820 (U.S. Department of the Treasury, 1980, p. 20). The average number over the previous thirty years was well under 1,000 per year (Duke, pp. 35-36, 70-71). Thus, only about 1 tax return in 75,000 ever became the subject of a criminal prosecution.

Criminal prosecutions perform a limited, if vital, role in tax enforcement, for myriad reasons. Many noncriminal monetary sanctions are available that can be assessed and collected administratively, with much less cost to the government, and can directly produce additional revenue. The most extreme civil sanction is applicable to persons required to collect and pay over taxes, for example, an employer required to withhold taxes from an employee's wages: the penalty for willful noncompliance is 100 percent of the tax (I.R.C. § 6672 (1982). Anyone else whose underpayment in whole or in part is "due to fraud" may be compelled to pay a penalty of 50 percent of the underpayment (§ 6653(b)). One who fails to file a return without reasonable cause can be penalized up to 25 percent of the tax due (§ 6651(a)(1)). All these penalties are in addition to the tax and interest thereon.

The civil penalties are not in lieu of criminal penalties. Both can be imposed on the same taxpayer for the same conduct (*Helvering v. Mitchell*, 303 U.S. 391 (1938). Indeed, if a tax-payer is successfully prosecuted for a tax offense, civil penalties are routinely imposed thereafter, and the taxpayer is estopped to contest any issue, such as fraud, found against him in the criminal prosecution (*Moore v. United States*, 360 F.2d 353 (4th Cir. 1965)). Civil penalties are assessed in thousands of cases every year, and over a billion dollars in penalties are collected (U.S. Department of the Treasury, 1980, p. 67). In addition to civil monetary penalties, the IRS has numerous devices to make noncompliance costly, including embarrassing, time-consuming audits, arbitrary assessments, and liens on bank accounts and other property.

The essential contributions of the criminal sanctions to tax compliance are probably as follows, in order of importance:

1. Like all other criminal sanctions, the criminal penalty ceremonializes and solidifies the community's sense of the immorality of proscribed conduct and affirms the morality of compliance.
2. The risk of a criminal sanction is a potent factor in the calculus of many prospective tax evaders, especially since they are often of relatively high status and have much to lose by the stigma of prosecution, conviction, and imprisonment.
3. The implicit threat of criminal sanctions provides powerful leverage to the government in its negotiations with taxpayers over claimed delinquencies; it facilitates investigations and contributes to compromise.

The criteria employed to select targets for criminal tax prosecution are—beyond vague generalities—protected by governmental secrecy. Moreover, no single agency of government makes the decisions or develops the criteria. Most recommendations for criminal tax prosecution originate in the IRS. But after passing through several filters in the IRS hierarchy, a recommendation for prosecution is turned over to the Justice Department for further scrutiny. A recommendation that survives the central review function in the Justice Department is then transmitted to the United States attorney in the appropriate federal district. There, it undergoes further review before being submitted to a grand jury (Duke, p. 57; Chommie, p. 107). In 1979, the Criminal Investigation Division of the IRS proposed more than 3,000 prosecutions. The Office of Chief Counsel of the IRS declined prosecution in 376 cases, the Justice Department declined in 424, and United States attorneys declined an another 425; only about 1,800 survived (U.S. Department of the Treasury, 1980, p. 35).

More significant than the criteria employed to screen cases for prosecution are those used to select returns for audit, since only if a return is among the 2 percent or fewer that are audited is there a serious possibility of prosecution. (It is, however, possible that a criminal investigation by another branch of the government will incidentally disclose tax evasion, in which even tax charges may be added to other charges.) The criteria for audit are also substantially secret. They are arrived at primarily, however, by an intensive audit of 50,000 scientifically and randomly selected individual tax returns every three years. Levels and trends in taxpayer compliance are then measured, and a computerized scoring formula is developed that is applied to every tax return ("Income Taxes," p. 46). Guidelines thus created — for example, relationships between reported income and business or charitable deductions — are employed to screen new returns for analysis and possible audit.

Criteria for selecting returns for audit, and for prosecution of apparent tax evaders, are difficult to formulate because of the immense complexity of the criminogenics of tax evasion and the uncertain role of criminal sanctions in influencing these causes. Among the more important correlates with tax compliance or evasion (in addition to the threat or deterrent effect of sanctions) are, probably, the following:

1. Taxpayer attitudes toward the federal government. Is it "wasting too much money"? Is it spending money on the wrong things? Is it becoming "too big"? Is it "strangling business" and "killing initiative"? Is it "taking away cherished freedoms"? The rhetoric of much political discourse on such themes does not promote a desire to pay taxes. Indeed, some of its extreme forms assert that tax evasion is a patriotic duty.

2. Taxpayer perceptions of the fairness of relative tax burdens. Middle-income taxpayers are responsible for the bulk of income-tax revenues. Their sense of moral obligation will deteriorate if they perceive that others receive such tax advantages as "write-offs," "tax shelters," "loopholes," deductions, credits, and exemptions which are unfair; that the "rich" or "the corporations" or "the politicians" are taxed at rates that are too low; or that other taxpayers, by virtue of having clever accountants and lawyers or improper influence, are obtaining some other unfair advantage.

3. Taxpayer attitudes about the IRS. If taxpayers have acquired resentments toward the IRS, based either on personal experience or on what they have heard or read about "high-handed," "cutthroat," or "illegal" tactics, or even if they have sought IRS assistance and were rebuffed or disappointed, their resentment is likely to affect their sense of obligation to pay taxes.

4. Taxpayer perceptions of the prevailing norms of compliance and evasion. If a taxpayer believes that most others whose circumstances are similar to his are reporting and paying what they owe, he is more likely to do so, for two reasons: (1) he feels more morally obliged to do so (Fried); and (2) he feels that if he cheats he is more likely to be detected and punished because his behavior will be more aberrant.

5. Burdens of compliance. The more burdensome it is, financially, to surrender the taxes one owes, the greater the temptation to evade. Thus, tax evasion may be expected to increase with growth in overall tax burdens or with reductions in disposable income. When taxes are substantially withheld, as they are from wages, the financial burden is not felt as severely as when the taxpayer actually has a choice to make, and pays only such taxes as he feels obliged to pay — as on income from self-employment. Similarly, as tax law becomes more complicated (it is now virtually incomprehensible), the financial, intellectual, and psychic burdens of compliance may contribute to evasion.

6. Fears by taxpayers that compliance will be prejudicial to other interests. A taxpayer who earns his living unlawfully will be tempted to risk tax evasion rather than reporting the source of his illegal income and opening himself to other criminal punishment or loss of livelihood. A normally law-abiding taxpayer who has stolen or embezzled money will be deterred from reporting it. A taxpayer who anticipates a bitter divorce action may "hide" part of his income from his spouse by omitting it from his tax returns. A taxpayer whose income may be entirely lawful may omit information, or evade tax, because he fears that disclosure on his tax return may be embarrassing.

The effect that criminal prosecution can have on

many of the aforementioned variables is minimal. Patterns of prosecution may also reduce one cause of tax evasion only to exacerbate another. For example, undue emphasis on the prosecution of drug dealers or gamblers may convey a message to ordinary taxpayers that they have nothing to fear as long as they stay away from drugs or racetracks. It may also suggest that tax evasion is more common or flagrant than it would otherwise appear to be (Schwartz and Orleans, pp. 274, 276). A stepped-up program of criminal prosecution of "ordinary" taxpayers may produce resentments against the IRS in the populace at large, adversely affecting not only tax compliance but also the willingness of juries to convict. If too great a proportion of politicians or public figures is included among the criminal targets, taxpayers may perceive that tax sanctions are being employed as political weapons. This may produce resentments, as well as perceptions that one can commit tax evasion with relative impunity, provided one maintains a low public profile.

On the other hand, prosecution of prominent people – politicians, entertainers, and gangsters – can provide enormous free publicity for the enforcement program, conveying the message that tax evaders are vigorously prosecuted, no matter how powerful they may be or how high their social position. The publicity value of one such prosecution may be the equivalent of hundreds of prosecutions of rank-and-file taxpayers.

Further compounding the difficulties of decision-makers in selecting targets for prosecution is the fact that producing tax compliance is not – and never has been – the sole objective of criminal tax enforcement. Throughout most of the twentieth century, criminal tax enforcement has been employed not merely for raising revenue but, as one commissioner of internal revenue put it, for "rooting out of our society certain undesirables" (Duke, p. 74). Tax prosecutions were a potent weapon in the government's arsenal during Prohibition – the aim was not to collect revenue but to prevent the unlawful production and sale of liquor – and they continue to be a powerful tool in the war against organized crime and corrupt politicians (Long, pp. 406-410; Chommie, pp. 98-116; Irey; Surface, pp. 15, 120-137).

Sometimes tax sanctions have been employed merely to harass or embarrass persons who were viewed as a threat to the administration. President Richard Nixon, for example, had an "enemies list" of scholars, politicians, political organizations, and reporters whom he directed the IRS to investigate (Lukas, pp. 22-26; White, pp. 151-153).

When limited resources are employed for purposes other than maximizing revenue, tax compliance will suffer. But beyond that, interlarded with and compounding problems of assessing the pragmatic effects of enforcement decisions on tax compliance and non-tax behavior (such as illegal activities), are some moral and legal issues. It is at least a plausible philosophical position to assert that in selecting targets for audit or sanctions the use of any criteria other than those related to tax compliance is morally wrong. Some even assert that it is immoral to place emphasis on taxpayers who earn their incomes illegally (Freedman, pp. 1030, 1034). It is also arguable that, despite its potent publicity value, no weight should legitimately be given to the public prominence of a taxpayer, because to do so is to punish the taxpayer for the activities that produced the prominence. Often, those actions – political activities and the exercise of the rights of freedom of speech and of the press – are constitutionally protected, and to take them into account may chill or burden the constitutionally protected activity. Taxpayers who have been singled out for investigation or prosecution because of their profession (*United States v. Swanson*, 509 F.2d 1205, 1208 (8th Cir. 1975)), their public prominence (*United States v. Peskin*, 527 F.2d 71, 86 (7th Cir. 1975)), or their tax protests (*United States v. Scott*, 521 F.2d 1188, 1195 (9th Cir. 1975); *United States v. Ojala*, 544 F.2d 940, 943 (8th Cir. 1976)) have failed in their challenges to the prosecutions. This does not resolve the moral issues, however, nor finally close the door to similar legal challenges (cf *Lenske v. United States*, 383 F.2d 20, 27 (9th Cir. 1967) and *United States v. Steele*, 461 F.2d 1148 (9th Cir. 1972)).

As with most other modes of human behavior, little is actually known, in a scientific sense, about the variables affecting tax compliance, or the role of criminal sanctions in shaping or controlling those variables. A number of experiments have been conducted that have produced suggestive hypotheses (Schwartz and Orleans; Maital). It is impossible, however, to draw any firm or refined conclusions from experimental studies that do not involve actual taxpayers, actual tax returns, and sophisticated controls. Only the IRS is in a position to engage in meaningful manipulation and measurement of variables, and the task, even for that agency, is monumental.

Major tax offenses. The most serious offender against federal revenue is one who "willfully attempts in any manner to evade or defeat any tax . . . or the payment thereof" (I.R.C. § 7201 (1982)). This crime carries a maximum penalty of five years in prison and a $10,000 fine. To commit the offense, one must engage in an act constituting an "attempt," must do so "willfully" (that is, intending thereby to "evade or defeat" assessment or payment of a federal tax), and must actually have an unsatisfied tax obligation

(*Sansone v. United States*, 380 U.S. 343 (1965)). Unlike most other criminal offenses, attempted tax evasion requires knowledge of the law. One cannot commit the offense unless he believes that he is legally obliged to pay a tax and that his "attempt" will evade or defeat that tax. Thus, it is not attempted tax evasion to omit taxable income from a return or to take an unlawful deduction if the taxpayer was unaware that his act was contrary to the tax law (Duke, pp. 4-5; *United States v. Garber*, 607 F.2d 92 (5th Cir. 1979)).

One "evades or defeats" a "tax or payment thereof" if he merely delays beyond the due date that assessment or payment of the tax. Hence, it is no defense that the taxpayer who willfully filed a false income-tax return intended thereby merely to delay payment and, when his finances improved, to file a correct return and pay the tax. The offense is complete when the false return is filed. (*Sansone*).

Another novel feature of the tax crime is that it preserves to some extent the now largely discarded defense of factual impossibility. Since an actual tax deficiency is an element of the crime, it is a defense that the accused, although he believed he was evading his taxes, was mistaken. If a taxpayer omits income from his return and, years later, even after he is indicted, discovers an offsetting deduction, he is not guilty of the offense (cf. *Willingham v. United States*, 289 F.2d 283 (5th Cir. 1961)).

The typical method of "attempting" tax evasion is the filing of a false tax return. However, one who files a correct return but fails to pay all the tax due thereon, or who fails to file a required return, may commit the offense if he has engaged in any affirmative act "the likely effect of which would be to mislead or conceal" his income or assets, and if "tax evasion plays any part in such conduct" (*Spies v. United States*, 317 U.S. 492 (1943)). Thus, if a taxpayer, aware of an outstanding tax obligation and desiring thereby to "evade or defeat" it, lies to the IRS about his income or assets, he commits the offense (*United States v. Beacon Brass Co.*, 344 U.S. 43 (1952)). The crime may also be committed by "keeping a double set of books, making false entries or alterations or false invoices or documents, destruction of books or records, concealment of assets," or any other deceptive conduct (*Spies*, 499).

Ordinarily, a taxpayer who engages in a series of fraudulent acts, such as filing a false return, submitting false records to the IRS when audited, and lying repeatedly about income, assets, or both, will be charged with only one offense of attempt for each year's tax obligation that he has tried to evade. All of the affirmative acts will be regarded as integrated steps in a single attempt. In one case, however, a taxpayer was held to have committed two separate attempts to evade the same year's tax. He first filed a false return, for which he was convicted and sent to prison. After his release, he attempted to evade payment of the still-outstanding tax obligation by concealing assets. He was again convicted and was returned to prison, the court concluding that he had first, by the false return, attempted to evade payment of the tax (*Cohen v. United States*, 297 F.2d 760 (9th Cir. 1962)). The implications of this decision for more common patterns of tax evasion are unclear, and the rationale is rarely advanced.

A number of lesser felonies can be committed by one whose conduct lacks all the elements of attempted tax evasion. Sections 7206 and 7207 of the Internal Revenue Code punish as felonies the presentation to the IRS of materially false returns or other documents. A general section of the federal criminal code (18 U.S.C. § 1001 (1976)) also reaches such documents, as well as false oral statements (*United States v. McCue*, 301 F.2d 452 (2d Cir. 1962)). It is unnecessary under any of these provisions that the offender actually have a tax deficiency. Nor must the false statement be made with intent to "evade or defeat" a tax or payment thereof (Balter, §§ 11.03, 11.04). Willful failure to file a required tax return or willful failure to pay a tax, in the absence of deceptive conduct, is a misdemeanor only, punishable by imprisonment up to one year and a fine of $10,000 (I.R.C. § 7203 (1982); *Alessi v. United States*, 628 F.2d 1133 (2d Cir. 1980)). It is often argued that willful failure to file a return, that is, failure to file with knowledge of the obligation to do so, is as serious and flagrant an offense as attempts to evade, and ought to be elevated to felony status. However, many non-filers cannot easily be equated with tax evaders. Their mental states often include elements of ignorance, pathological passivity, and even serious mental illness. To treat their intentional omissions as the equivalent, in all cases, of a calculated act designed to deceive and to evade assessment of one's tax obligations would conflict with fundamental distinctions in the criminal law between commissions and omissions (*Spies*).

Sentencing. The sentencing of persons convicted of federal tax offenses is a matter of perpetual controversy and disquieting disparity (Long, pp. 401-406). The IRS and the Department of Justice traditionally take the position that all persons convicted of such offenses should receive at least a substantial jail or prison sentence in order to deter tax evasion and to signify the seriousness of the dereliction (*Heidrich v. United States*, 373 F.2d 540 (5th Cir. 1967)). Many tax evaders, however, are otherwise law-abiding and pose no threat of recidivism. The prosecution and conviction themselves are degrading and traumatic. Accordingly, judges who are not comfortable with a general-deterrent justification for sentencing often impose probationary sentences (Andenaes, pp. 129-148).

Steven Duke, *Prosecutions for Attempts to Evade Income Tax: A Discordant View of a Procedural Hybrid,* 76 YALE L.J. 1–76 (1966)*

Legal proscriptions have proliferated at a Parkinsonian rate during the twentieth century, along with the officials who enforce them. Administrative agencies have assumed much of the prosecutor's prerogative of selecting targets for sanctions. Courts and juries, along with the prosecutor, have surrendered discretion to the agencies, as fact finding, law application, and law determination have all become part of the administrative process.

Administrative expertise supposedly justifies this radical redistribution of power. Efficient use of enforcement resources, skillful selection of sanctions, and deft location of areas of noncompliance are all advantages claimed for deference to the administrator. To the ardent proponent of administrative discretion, judicial review seems a senseless interference with bureaucratic routine, or at best a superfluous ratification.

The Supreme Court has been the bellwether in this process of transferring competence from court to administrator where the sanction is a civil one. Neither the Supreme Court nor Congress, however, has been willing explicitly to advance the same arguments in justification of a reallocation of authority where the sanction is "criminal." Indeed, recent trends in the criminal process have been in the opposite direction—making judge and jury more effective checks on the power of police and prosecutor. Yet the extent to which the Supreme Court has rejected the values of administrative deference in the criminal process can easily be exaggerated. There are still substantial segments of the process which have barely been touched by the Court's epochal decisions. In areas where there is no capital punishment, where the typical target has at least average intellectual and financial resources, and where the investigative officials are narrowly specialized and obviously expert—where, in short, the

only major difference from the typical agency decision to invoke a sanction is that the sanction is criminal, the Court has seemed singularly unconcerned about preserving the trial as a potent vehicle of administrative control. The clearest example of this is the tax evasion prosecution.

Trends in tax prosecution have for at least two decades been continuously running against the main currents in criminal procedure. By subtle doctrinal manipulation, the courts confer more and more discretion on invoking officials and reduce the roles of judge and jury. The judge's role is limited by his abdication of responsibility to define the offense and to determine the sufficiency of evidence. The jury's function is restricted by a procedural panoply which prevents a full and fair test of the Government's proofs.

The main support for a different court of doctrinal development in tax prosecutions than in criminal procedure generally is the fact that civil and criminal sanctions apply to the same conduct and are invoked by the same officials. Tax agents act in a dual capacity, making their investigations ambiguous and creating powerful pressures for self-incrimination. Courts frequently confer procedural advantages upon the Government, and deny them to the accused, by labeling the problem as one of "civil" or "criminal" procedure, as the context requires. A tax prosecution is a procedural hybrid. '

I. The Definition of the Offense

Vagueness of definition, a standard source of administrative discretion, is a significant feature of criminal tax sanctions. Section 7201 of the Internal Revenue Code authorizes infliction of five years in prison, a $10,000 fine and costs of prosecution upon "any person who willfully attempts in any manner to evade or defeat any tax . . . or the payment thereof." Courts agree that there can be no conviction under this statute unless the defendant failed to pay all the income tax that was due. It is not enough that the taxpayer made false entries in his return and thought he was cheating; his efforts must actually have produced a deficiency. Many courts go further and require that the deficiency be "substantial," though underpayment of a few hundred dollars has been held sufficient.

Besides having underpaid his taxes, the defendant must have engaged in some affirmative act, the "likely effect of which would be to mislead or conceal." The usual affirmative act of attempted tax evasion is the filing of a false income tax return. A taxpayer may be convicted of attempting to evade payment of taxes even though he filed no return, however, or even if he filed a correct return but failed to pay his full tax, if there is evidence of some act of deception such as

* Reprinted by permission of The Yale Law Journal Company and Fred B. Rothman & Company from *The Yale Law Journal,* Vol. 76, pages 1-76.

a false statement to revenue agents, willful falsification or destruction of books and records, or any other act of concealment or subterfuge.

The affirmative act is an offense if accompanied by "willfulness." This means, first, that at the time of the act the taxpayer knew he had a tax deficiency. His knowledge of the tax law and of the contents of his return are therefore elements of willfulness. Second, the affirmative act must have been motivated, at least in part, by a desire to defeat the Government in its efforts to collect the tax deficiency. Third, the state of mind accompanying the act must have included a "bad purpose" or "evil motive."

With an Internal Revenue Code of more than a half a million words strung together in sentences and clauses of unsurpassed complexity, supported by policies often both vague and contradictory, it is not unusual for a taxpayer to have an honest doubt about the treatment of a particular item – whether it is ordinary income or capital gain, exempt or taxable, subject to special credits and allowances, deductible in full or in part, a business expense or a personal one. Thus whether or not the taxpayer was aware of the falsity of his return is often, potentially at least, an issue of consequence, apart from the question of whether there was a deficiency. The proper tax treatment will sometimes be sufficiently uncertain to justify letting the jury determine not only what the defendant thought was the tax law governing a particular item, but what it really was. For example, if an increase in wealth is claimed to have been an exempt gift, the question of taxability is "basically one of fact" to be decided by the jury drawing upon its "experience with the wellsprings of human conduct." Herein lies a quagmire.

Whether the taxpayer is aware at the time he files the return of the proper tax treatment of an item will always be a matter of degree. He may be virtually certain that his handling of an item in the return is legally false, may appraise the probabilities of falsity at about 50-50, or may think there is little likelihood that an omitted item is income or a deducted item is non-deductible. The courts have not even suggested what degree of awareness constitutes "willfulness."

The question is further clouded by uncertainty as to what the taxpayer must have been rather sure of in order for him to have known his return was false. He is charged with making a prediction of his own obligations and failing to comply with the obligations as he perceived them. The prediction is apparently of hypothetical attitudes of decision-makers: what they would decide about the item if they knew about it. But who are the relevant decision-makers? Is a taxpayer's return willfully false if he omits as income an item which he believes the local agents would regard as taxable, but which he thinks a court would hold non-taxable? Or which he believes would be held a question for a jury? The courts have furnished no answers.

The taxpayer's knowledge of the facts treated in his return is also often a matter of degree. He may have remained ignorant of the contents of the return or of his books and records in order to avoid learning the truth, or because he was indifferent to the possibilities of error, or simply because he placed faith in his accountant.

Finally, even if the taxpayer knowingly filed a false return, he may not always have done so with a "bad purpose or evil motive." One who intentionally understates his obligations by a relatively small amount is not guilty of a felony, for the understatement must be "substantial." The meaning of "substantial," however, is far from clear.

Millions of taxpayers are arguably guilty of attempting to evade tax, and most of them are arguably innocent too. Yet the courts contribute little in deciding guilt or innocence or in assisting the jury in doing so. As the law stands, almost anyone with income above the subsistence level is a potential criminal defendant.

The Role of the Hunch in Disposing of Issues

A tax evasion case may involve the following issues: (1) Was there a tax deficiency? (2) Was it substantial? (3) Did the taxpayer know that his return included the deduction or excluded the income which produced the deficiency? (4) Did he know that the item in question was not taxable in the manner in which it was treated in his return? (5) Did he, if he filed a return which he knew to be false, do so with an "evil motive and bad purpose?" Or, did he, if he filed a correct return or filed no return at all, engage in "an affirmative act the likely effect of which was to mislead or conceal" income or assets from the IRS and thereby to avoid payment of his taxes? The jury has the predominant role in giving concrete meaning to these concepts and, in order legitimately to convict, must resolve all of the issues against the defendant.

It will usually be impossible for the taxpayer at trial to present a plausible defense on each of the above issues. For several reasons, he will have to select one or two and virtually to concede the others. A stance on one issue may logically preclude a defense on another – defending in the alternative may be lawful yet tactically ruinous. Often a narrowed focus can gather persuasive power from the concession of other points. Moreover, a broad defensive posture may appear, because of its breadth, to be suspect in toto. Finally, a defense which disputes every element of the prosecution's case risks confusing the trier of fact with the result that the cogency of the Government's case on some issues may inadvertently transfuse weaker points. Thus while a defendant may theoretically put the Government to its proof on every issue, he will virtually always make a serious tactical blunder if he in fact strenuously contests every point.

The less defendant knows about the Government's case, the more he must rely on hunches in deciding which issues to press, and the larger the risk that he will tacitly concede the truth of the frailest fragment of the Government's case. The less the defense knows about the Government's proof and strategies, therefore, and the later in the process that the knowledge is acquired, the greater the risk of convicting the innocent.

II. The Prosecution's Burden of Proof

By defining burdens of proof and allocating duties to produce evidence, the courts can greatly affect the risks of error attributable to pretrial ignorance of the evidence and strategies of the opposition. If the defendant appears unduly hampered by ignorance, the burden on the Government to make a prima facie case can be increased so that the cogency of its proof may virtually eliminate risks to defendant resulting from erroneous strategic or investigatory decisions.

If, on the other hand, the Government is thought to be inordinately disadvantaged in pre-trial preparations, the prosecution's burdens can be relaxed. It may be excused from presenting evidence on certain issues until defendant comes forward. Thus, the Government may be required only to adduce evidence of a deficiency, with the question of willfulness tacitly treated as a matter of defense. This adjustment can be rationalized to conform to the principle that the prosecution bears the burden on every element of the offense simply by saying that evidence of a deficiency is, in effect, evidence on every issue; it alone supports an inference of willfulness. A court may go further and hold that even evidence of an explanation for the deficiency, such as mistake of law or ignorance of the contents of the return, does not keep the case from getting to the jury—it merely presents a question of credibility.

The Government's traditional obligation to prove every element of the offense "beyond a reasonable doubt" is one of the most nebulous and pliant responsibilities in the trial process. It means what the courts make it mean. Some seem to think it has virtually nothing to do with the judge's role in controlling the jury, or with what the Government must prove to support a conviction when judicially reviewed, but is merely a precatory admonition to the jury. Others construe it as a significant limitation on the power of a jury to convict. But the latter meaning seems seldom to be given to the concept in tax fraud prosecutions.

The prevailing practice of most courts seems to reflect the belief that the prosecution is unduly disadvantaged in trial preparation, that there is little need for the judge to evaluate the evidence independently, and that the jury may safely be trusted to sift the innocent from the guilty with tolerable accuracy. Thus the government is able to get its case to the jury with a minimum of evidence and the jury is given broad discretion to convict or acquit.

Methods of Proof

A. Specific Items Proof

A large part of the prosecution's proof in virtually every tax evasion case is circumstantial. Sometimes the deficiency can be proved by direct evidence, but the other elements of the offense will almost always be inferred indirectly. Thus, if the Government can show by direct evidence that the return was false, the facts that the defendant filed the return, knew that it was false, and intended to evade his tax obligations will all normally be inferred from the nature of the understatement (its size and character may be such that it would probably not have been over-looked), defendant's experience in tax and business affairs (implying that he knew the proper tax treatment of the item in question), his signature on the return and the fact that it was received in the mail by the IRS (suggesting that he knew the contents of the return and mailed it). Ordinarily, therefore, when the Government can show by business records or direct testimony that a substantial portion of the defendant's gross income was omitted from the return, it has made a prima facie case. It is up to the defendant to adduce evidence of mistake, ignorance, or honest motives.

Tax evasion is not usually proved by the defendant's own records alone, however. A tax evader will frequently fail to keep records which clearly show his evasion or will keep such records out of Government hands. Thus, while the taxpayer's records will often be used, they will usually have to be supplemented with other evidence. When the defendant's records are inadequate, there are two basic methods of proving directly the falsity of the return. The first is by the testimony of an "inside witness"—defendant's bookkeeper, secretary, or former spouse—who testifies that the defendant salted away some income before it was recorded in the books, or that he padded his deductions. The second method is to use witnesses who had transactions with the defendant which do not jibe with the transactions reported in the return. Thus, if a witness testifies that he paid the defendant a salary or a bribe, and his tax return includes only "capital gains" and "business income," there is evidence of unreported income. Likewise, a claimed deduction can be shown false by the testimony of the person to whom it was supposedly paid. This method is hampered by the typically vague entries in a tax return. Specific sources of income, or recipients of deducted expenses, are seldom detailed in the return itself. Usually, there are merely general headings like "business income" or "travel and entertainment expense." In such cases, testimony by an individual that he paid the defendant a sum of money, or that he was not paid any money by the taxpayer, will prove little unless buttressed by records or admissions of the defendant which detail the vague entries in the return. If the defendant's records are not available, a deficiency might be proved by gathering together enough such persons to collectively account for more than the income reported. But this would often require the location and production of dozens, sometimes hundreds, of witnesses. Rarely have only a few individuals been the source of more income than can be encompassed under some broad category in the taxpayer's return. Careful evaders, therefore, can often make detection and proof of guilt very difficult if they cheat in secret and make entries in the return which are nebulous enough to cover almost any items provable by the prosecution.

B. Circumstantial Proof of Deficiencies

Since testimonial proof of the falsity of specific items in the return is often cumbersome and costly, if not impossible, the Government had to develop techniques of proving every element of the case circumstantially. These techniques were first used against racketeers in the 30's. With judicial benediction, they produced convictions at a very high rate. Since then, the Government has come to rely on indirect evidence to prove the deficiency in the typical tax prosecution. As the Supreme Court noted in 1954, indirect methods "have evolved from the final volley to the first shot in the Government's battle for revenue."

The methods employed usually fall into one of three major patterns, each of which has its standardized procedures, thoroughly tested and approved in the courts. Each method permits the proof of unreported income with relatively few important witnesses. And the key witnesses do not need coaxing, nor is there any danger that they will appear in court with impoverished memories, because they are usually internal revenue agents. Each method can also be used without reliance on the defendant's books and records. The essence of each technique is to reconstruct certain changes in the indicia of a taxpayer's economic condition which imply that he had more taxable income than he reported. Since all that is required for the crime is a willfully false return which results in a substantial deficiency, it is unnecessary to prove whether the deficiency resulted from improper deductions or understatements of gross income.

1. The Net Worth Method

The most frequently employed technique of reconstructing taxable income indirectly is the "net worth method." Its basic premise is that most increases in net worth are attributable to taxable income and, as the Supreme Court put it, "when this is not true the taxpayer is in a position to explain the discrepancy." The Government offers evidence of the taxpayer's net worth at the end of the tax year in questions, subtracting from this figure his net worth at the beginning of the year, and adding to the difference (the increment in net worth) his non-deductible expenditures. The result is ostensibly the taxable income for the year. If this figure substantially exceeds the taxable income reported on the return, the jury is asked to infer that the return was willfully falsified by the defendant.

Most net worth increases are probably attributable to taxable income. Accretions to net worth frequently are, however, the result of gifts, inheritances, life insurance proceeds and other non-taxable sources. Thus, there is a danger of error whenever a jury must speculate on the character of a particular increase.

But there is a more serious risk: that the evidence of a net worth increase is false or that the claimed increase indicated is a gross exaggeration. Since wealth may be owned in myriad forms and locations, few people other than the owner or members of his family are likely to know where all of it is kept. When the Government agents in a typical net-worth investigation canvass local banks, property records and stock brokers in a search for assets, they have not thereby excluded the real possibility that the taxpayer has assets elsewhere or under another name. Similarly, even the most resourceful agent may miscalculate net worth by overlooking the existence of liabilities.

Another risk is that non-deductible living expenses, which are added to the net worth increment to determine taxable income, may be exaggerated. The Government's evidence of expenditures is often a mere estimate supported by proof of specific expenditures on luxuries or large items such as homes, cars and fur coats. And taxpayers seldom keep accurate records of their personal expenditures since they have little incentive to do so.

In sum, evidence of a net worth increase as a basis for inferring a deficiency requires all of the following inferences:

1. The items included in the computation of beginning net worth are correct, and do not exclude any assets owned by the accused on that date nor overstate his liabilities;

2. The estimate of taxpayer's non-deductible expenditures is not larger than the actual expenditures;

3. The calculation of net worth at the end of the period does not exaggerate the taxpayer's assets and includes all of his debts;

4. The increase in net worth indicated by the computations was not the result of an exempt gift, and inheritance, life insurance proceeds, or other non-taxable accession to wealth.

If any one of these assumptions or inferences is wrong, the ultimate inference of unreported income is pro tanto also wrong.

2. The Expenditures Method

Evidence that a taxpayer spent considerably more money on non-deductible items during a given period than he reported as income indicates that he (1) lived in part off capital, or, (2) borrowed more money than he paid back during the period, or, (3) had non-taxable accessions to wealth, or (4) under-reported his income. The first three possibilities, consistent with a correct return, probably occur in the aggregate at least as frequently as the fourth. Consequently, evidence that a taxpayer lived beyond his reported income will probably not alone support a conviction. When the Government relies on the expenditures methods, it apparently always lubricates it with something else – typically a beginning net worth too small to account for the expenditures, which excludes the possibility that the taxpayer lived off accumulated capital. When employed in connection with evidence of beginning net worth, therefore, expenditures evidence is merely a variation of the net worth method. Proof of the ending net worth may be dispensed with because the expenditures during the period exceeded assets available at the beginning of the period plus reported income. If the beginning net worth and the expenditures evidence is correct, the taxpayer acquired wealth during the period which was not reported on his tax returns as income. He may have acquired it from loans, gifts, inheritances, tax exempt income or it may have come from taxable sources. The relative duties of the Government and the taxpayer to identify the sources, discussed hereafter, are the same as for the net worth method.

3. The Bank Deposit Method

The major premise employed in this method is that deposits to bank accounts are frequently gross income of the holder of the account, and when they are not, he can explain what they are. If a taxpayer reported $10,000 taxable income, consisting of $12,000 gross income less $2,000 in deductions, the Government may offer evidence obtained from his bank that $20,000 was deposited in his account during the year. The inference advanced is that defendant had $20,000

of gross income, rather than the $12,000 reported. To get from there to the ultimate inference that he understated his taxable income by $10,000, the prosecution is aided by a presumption that the taxpayer claimed all the deductions to which he was entitled, even though he underreported his gross income. Note, however, that at least the following contingencies must be excluded before reaching the ultimate conclusion: (1) the excess money which was deposited to defendant's account might have belonged to someone else; (2) the money could have been the proceeds of a loan, a gift, a sale of property, an inheritance, or exempt income such as life insurance proceeds, damages, or insurance payments for personal injuries; (3) the excess deposits might have been withdrawn previously from a bank account; (4) the money might have been acquired before the prosecution year and held for some time in cash before being deposited; (5) defendant might have understated his deductions as well as his gross receipts. If any of these possibilities is wrongly rejected, the inference that taxpayer under-reported his taxable income by $10,000 is false.

There are palpably so many exceptions to the assumption that bank deposits constitute income that any inference to that effect, drawn from bank deposit evidence alone, is extremely weak. It is strengthened somewhat if the evidence shows regular, periodic deposits rather than a few large sums, yet regularity of deposits is probably not a condition of using the method.

When combined with evidence of a beginning net worth too small to account for the deposits, then bank deposit evidence is also merely a variation of the net worth method. The inference is that defendant had a flow of incoming cash which did not come from prior accumulations and which exceeded reported income. The bank deposit method, however, does not require the use of a beginning net worth. Apparently, if the Government shows that defendant had a business which could produce substantial cash receipts and that he made deposits of such receipts in his accounts, it can make a prima facie case with bank deposit evidence alone, leaving it to the defendant to adduce proof that the deposits did not come from income, and leaving it to the jury to decide whether his proof is sufficient.

4. Mixed Methods

The prosecution may prove its case with any of the foregoing three methods, or it may employ two or three simultaneously, or combine parts of one method with parts of another. Moreover, the three indirect methods outlined above represent merely the three techniques commonly employed to construct a case. There is virtually no limit to the kinds of evidence which can be woven into a circumstantial web.

Defendant's Admissions – The Bedplate of the Typical Case

Revenue agents who suspect fraud usually attempt to build the basis for a net worth case by asking the taxpayer during the investigation for a net worth statement showing changes for each of several years, and including annual non-deductible expenditures. They often get what they ask for. One reason is that the IRS will frequently not consider an offer of compromise without a net worth statement. Thus, if the taxpayer wants to settle a deficiency without criminal prosecution, the price may include not only back taxes and penalties but a detailed net worth statement. Yet negotiations for compromise, even acceptance of a compromise of civil liability, does not preclude a criminal prosecution nor make the statements obtained in such negotiations inadmissible.

Frequently, of course, taxpayers will not be so cooperative as to provide a written net worth statement which reveals substantial disparities between net worth accretions and reported income. The IRS may attempt to get one orally, however, and often succeeds. In *Vloutis v. United States,* for example, the IRS agents had defendant, "an elderly man who reads and writes with difficulty, if at all," come with his bookkeeper to the IRS office, where defendant was put under oath and asked 131 questions. Among the 131 was, "How much, Mr. Vloutis, was your net worth at December 31, 1941?" (This was more than four and one-half years later, August 16, 1946.) At first, defendant said, "I don't recall, I don't remember." Later, when the question was repeated, he said, "I must have had about $40,000 or $50,000 at the time." The statement was used to establish his beginning net worth. . . .

The Investigative Process

The taxpayer's Fifth Amendment rights are nullified in yet another way: the Government is permitted to treat its investigation as a civil matter until its files are full, and to keep the taxpayer unaware of the transmutation of the case from civil to criminal.

The IRS audits three to four million tax returns per year, and from this mass selects approximately 1000 taxpayers whom it recommends to the Justice Department for criminal prosecution. The initial audit is ordinarily performed by a regular Internal Revenue Agent who may write to the taxpayer and request that he come in and explain questioned items or permit the agent to come to his home or office. (Sometimes, however, the agent appears without advance notice.) At this point the audit is usually regarded as a routine civil audit and fraud is not suspected. After the revenue agent makes a preliminary investigation, however, he may scent fraud and call in a special agent from the Intelligence Division, whose job is to investigate criminal fraud suspects. Sometimes, of course, fraud will be anticipated at the outset and a special agent assigned immediately. Even then, a revenue agent may be used in tandem with the special agent to develop the civil aspects of the case and also to continue working with the taxpayer in an attempt to get information before he learns that he is a criminal suspect.

At any state of the investigative process prior to the assignment of a special agent, the revenue agent has virtually unreviewable discretion to close the criminal aspects of the case by suggesting a simple deficiency and thus eliminating almost all possibility that the taxpayer will be prosecuted for evading during the years covered by the audit. Once a special agent is in the case, he also has abundant power over the continuance of the case into further phases of the criminal process. Less than $3/10$ of 1% of all returns audited are carried beyond the routine audit and civil deficiency stage, and even after a special agent is assigned, the chances are about 7 in 8 that prosecution will not be recommended.

During the early phases of an investigation, its character as a civil or criminal case will be ambiguous. The revenue agent calling upon a taxpayer to examine his books is not analogous to the policeman who raps on the door. Since more than 99% of audits which reveal deficiencies are never treated as criminal cases, the probability is high in virtually any case that the main purpose of the audit is, and its ultimate conclusion will be, non-criminal. Moreover, the existence of the criminal sanction, the dread with which most taxpayers regard involvement in criminal proceedings, the vagueness of the crime, and the enormous discretion of the investigator, make noncooperation by an audited taxpayer in most cases an inordinately foolish decision. The civil aspects of an audit also point toward cooperation. The return of almost any taxpayer contains items upon which an obdurate agent can assert a deficiency which is both difficult and costly for the taxpayer to resist. Non-cooperation may be very expensive.

An audit, therefore, usually occurs in an atmosphere which invites the taxpayer to negotiate and compromise. He will usually produce records, give statements, make explanations, tender excuses – often only vaguely aware of their relevance to an ultimate tax prosecution. If prosecution results, however, his statements will be extremely helpful to the Government in narrowing the issues in the case and easing its burden of proof. . . .

Conclusion

Administrative discretion pervades the tax prosecution from commencement of the audit to appellate review. The values behind deference to the administrator in civil cases are well served in criminal tax prosecutions. At every step in the process, basic safeguards and Fifth Amendment rights are subtly sliced away beneath a cloak of conceptualism. The Government is permitted, with its audit procedures and its administrative summons, to gather information from the taxpayer which may be used to convict him of crime. Right up to indictment, its civil-criminal investigation is treated as purely civil. Yet when the taxpayer who is a potential criminal defendant seeks civil discovery in a civil case, discovery is denied because he may use the information in defending the criminal charge. Thus, whether the civil or criminal aspects of the ambiguous pre-trial process predominate depends on which characterization disadvantages the taxpayer. Moreover, if the prosecution at the trial meets what is no more than a civil burden of proof, the taxpayer must establish his innocence. Yet he is denied the means of doing so which he would have if he were truly involved in a civil case. He is not granted significantly more pre-trial disclosure than other criminal defendants.

If increased recognition of criminal safeguards seriously threatened to curtail tax compliance, the burden might be heavy on one who urges even-handed treatment of tax and other criminal defendants. But there is neither evidence nor plausible argument that this is so. Since not one audit in a thousand results in criminal prosecution, revenue agents could be required to adequately warn a taxpayer and to refrain from using the summons to gain evidence for a criminal case without affecting any but a fraction of the confrontations between agent and taxpayer. The investigative process could continue virtually as before, yet taxpayers would not be convicted of crime on evidence obtained from them involuntarily. There is, moreover, no cause to believe that tightening the Government's burden of proof in the criminal case, and liberalizing pre-trial disclosure, would signally interfere with normal tax administration. It would merely make it more costly to convict the guilty and more difficult to convict the innocent. The price seems right.

Jeffrey A. Dubin, Michael A. Graetz, and Louis L. Wilde, *The Changing Face of Tax Enforcement,* 1978–1988, 43 Tax Law. 893 (1990)*

I. INTRODUCTION

Published reports of the so-called "tax-gap," the

---

amount of under-reported federal income taxes, now estimated to have been $83-$94 billion in 1987, and of taxes due but uncollected, now estimated to have been $61-$72 billion in 1987, have raised questions about the administration of the federal tax system. In some quarters, these reports have simply led to calls for more funding for the Service. We, however, regard the current public focus on the Service as creating an opportunity for serious discussion of tax administration, a subject long ignored in both scholarly and professional literature.

We propose here to examine three aspects of tax administration that are widely thought to play a particularly critical role in tax enforcement: the examination (or audit) function, information reporting, and the criminal enforcement process. A major shift in tax enforcement policy has occurred during the last decade. Greater reliance has been placed on information reporting; on the other hand, fewer people have been audited or criminally prosecuted for tax violations, but those who have been so treated have been punished more severely. These shifts in enforcement policy raise important questions of both the efficacy and the fairness of the tax administrative process.

Before detailing our findings regarding these aspects of enforcement policy, however, we shall provide a brief overview of the Service's budgets during the past decade. We shall then turn to a more detailed examination of the Service's audit and criminal investigation functions, including a presentation of data concerning penalties. Since we have a substantial amount of information to present, we have accepted the old saw about saving many words through pictures, and generally have tried to summarize our data in graphs. Finally, we offer some conclusions and suggestions for further research.

II. AN OVERVIEW OF THE SERVICE'S BUDGET

A. The Budget in General

The Service is an extremely large administrative agency; as of 1988, it had a budget of more than $5 billion and almost 115,000 employees. Even adjusted for inflation, the operating costs of the Service have increased significantly during the past ten years – by about 40%. In contrast, costs as a percentage of revenues have remained relatively constant over a very long period of time, amounting in 1987 to about 55 cents per $100 of taxes net of refunds, the same as in 1960. In 1988, this figure increased by about 10% to 60 cents net of refunds. Inflation adjusted costs per return filed present a similar pattern, while real net tax collections per capita increased by about 16% during the past decade. Table 1 summarizes the costs of administering the federal tax system for selected years since 1970.

Table 1: IRS Collections, Costs, Employees, Returns Filed and U.S. Population: Selected Years, 1970–88

	Operating Cost ($ Billions)	Gross Collections ($ Billions)	Cost Per $100 Gross Collections	Refunds ($ Billions)	Net Collections ($ Billions)	Cost Per $100 Net Collections	Employees[1]	Real Cost[2] Per Emp ($)	Returns Filed (Millions)	Real Cost Per Return Filed	Pop (Millions)	Real Cost Per Capita ($)	Real net Collections Per Capita ($)
1970	.886	195.722	.45	16.188	179.534	.49	68,683	30,719	113.08	18.65	204.88	10.29	2086.40
1975	1.585	293.823	.54	32.209	261.614	.61	82,339	32,455	125.12	21.35	213.56	12.51	2065.79
1980	2.281	519.375	.44	54.009	465.366	.49	87,464	30,428	143.45	18.55	228.23	11.66	2379.25
1981	2.465	606.799	.41	63.303	543.496	.45	86,156	30,442	166.52	15.75	230.61	11.37	2507.21
1982	2.626	632.341	.42	75.202	557.139	.47	82,857	31,697	170.37	15.39	232.96	11.27	2391.56
1983	2.969	627.247	.47	79.761	547.486	.54	83,605	34,173	171.17	16.69	235.23	12.14	2240.08
1984	3.279	680.475	.46	85.872	594.603	.55	87,635	34,742	172.51	17.64	237.45	12.82	2325.09
1985	3.601	742.872	.48	86.322	656.550	.55	92,254	36,136	178.22	18.17	239.71	13.90	2469.73
1986	3.842	782.252	.49	94.425	687.827	.56	95,880	35,118	188.02	17.90	242.00	13.91	2551.62
1987	4.366	886.391	.49	96.969	789.422	.55	102,188	36,360	193.16	19.23	244.20	15.21	2746.54
1988	5.069	935.107	.54	94.480	840.627	.60	114,873	36,372	194.30	21.50	245.81	17.10	2818.61

Source: Annual Reports of the Commissioner of Internal Revenue, 1970-1988.

1. Figures after 1982 not strictly comparable with prior years due to change in method of accounting for realized posisions per requirement of the Office of Personnel Management.

2. Adjusted by GNP implicit price deflator, 1982 = 100.

Recent years have produced substantial growth in Service personnel. The method of calculating the number of employees changed between 1982 and 1983, making comparisons before and after that date difficult, but it is significant that the total number of personnel grew by nearly 32,000 employees between 1983 and 1988, from 83,605 to 114,873, amounting to an increase of more than 35%. On the other hand, with the exception of 1988, the costs of collecting $100 of taxes net of refunds was virtually flat during this period and total returns filed grew only from $171 million to $194 million, about 13½. . .

B. Budget Allocations

During the past decade, the allocation of the Service's resources has shifted significantly. While "returns processing and computer services" have increased from about one-quarter to more than one-third of the Service's budget, almost all other activities have suffered a decline in budgetary share. The only other activity that has grown significantly is "appeals," up from 2.6% in 1978 to 4.8% in 1988. "Taxpayer service" is down from 8.25% in 1978 to 6.55% in 1988 (up from 5.7% in 1987) and "technical rulings and enforcement litigation" is down from 3.3% in 1978 to 1.4% in 1988. Of particular importance, the share of the Service's budget devoted to "examinations" (audits) declined from 34.4% in 1978 to 27.8% in 1988.

Table 2 details the allocations of the Service's budget for the years 1978 through 1988 and shows changes in budget categories in real dollars and as a percent of total costs during that period. . . .

Table 2: IRS Cost by Activity, 1978–88
*(thousands of $)

	1978	1979	1980	1981	1982	1983	1984	1985	1986	1987	1988	% Δ 1978-88 Real Dollars	Percent of Total Cost¹ 1978–1988		Δ Percent of Total Costs¹ 1978–1988
(1) Executive Direction Management Services, Internal Audit & Security	59,891	65,961	70,156	79,427	78,218	128,080	98,160	104,945	89,475	90,693	88,151	-.20	3.05	1.75	-1.30
(2) Returns Processing Computer Service	507,384	535,33	574,179	611,308	650,255	681,802	890,343	1,048,470	1,247,482	1,421,112	1,721,665	17.28	25.85	34.19	8.34
(3) Collection	258,302	208,613	297,947	349,410	410,177	529,416	604,149	613,527	606,498	660,659	799,814	7.27	13.16	15.88	2.72
(4) Taxpayer Service	161,906	197,612	203,687	218,153	206,584	232,660	148,293	169,874	208,212	249,606	329,597	1.15	8.25	6.55	-1.70
(5) Examination	675,253	719,568	779,637	834,416	889,631	958,925	1,025,611	1,114,845	1,139,501	1,204,179	1,399,341	5.27	34.41	27.78	-6.63
(6) Employee Plans & Exempt Organizations	62,247	64,144	66,963	65,126	71,315	80,039	90,431	94,398	99,031	104,980	120,988	.32	3.17	2.40	-.77
(7) Tax Fraud Investigation	121,182	130,185	140,631	153,927	172,176	172,619	204,135	219,951	221,304	245,370	261,585	1.15	6.18	5.19	-.99
(8) Appeals	50,939	50,525	59,750	68,935	67,991	121,332	150,391	167,263	162,639	189,694	241,890	3.10	2.60	4.80	2.20
(9) Technical Rulings & Enforcement Litigation	65,025	72,225	77,889	82,866	79,991	63,653	67,554	67,670	67,841	66,388	72,510	-.7	3.31	1.44	-1.87
Total Cost (000's)	1,962,129	2,116,166	2,280,839	2,465,469	2,626,338	2,968,526	3,279,067	3,600,953	3,841,983	4,365,816	5,035,541	34.52			

Source: Annual Reports of the Commissioner of Internal Revenue, 1978-1988.

1. Does not total 100% due to miscellaneous costs.

. . . These shifts in budget allocations are revealing even at a glance. For example, they foretell significant reductions in audit levels, which we detail in Section III below, and demonstrate increasing Service reliance on computer processing, thereby making clear the necessity for the Service to become and remain technologically up-to-date. Although the budget share devoted to appeals still accounts for a relatively small amount of the overall Service Budget, its increase suggests a fruitful avenue for further inquiry; we shall refrain here from offering speculation about the causes of this change.

This division of the Service's overall budget, however, tells only a part of the story. In fact, it sometimes conceals as well as reveals. The proportion of the Service's budget devoted to criminal investigation, for example, has altered only slightly during the past decade, but the criminal investigation process has changed substantially. We shall tell this part of the story in Section V below.

Let us now examine the enforcement process in greater detail. We shall begin with audits.

III. THE DECLINE IN AUDITS AS AN ENFORCEMENT WEAPON

A. Individual Audit Rates

Audits, which – withholding aside – historically have been the Service's principal tax enforcement weapon, have declined significantly over the past two decades. . . . The total audit coverage of individuals has shown a steady decline during the past decade from an audit rate of about 2% in 1978 to 1% in 1988. If one goes back further in time, the decline is even more precipitous; audit coverage exceeded 6% in 1965. . . .

When the audit coverage data is disaggregated by income bracket, an even more dramatic picture emerges. Direct decade-long comparisons are not possible because, beginning in 1981, the Service began classifying individuals for statistical purposes based on total positive income rather than taxable income. Nevertheless, a dramatic decline in coverage is undisputable. The audit rate for nonbusiness returns with gross income of $50,000 or more dropped from almost 8% in 1981 to 2⅓% in 1988. The audit rate of nonbusiness returns with taxable income in excess of $50,000 had been over 10% in 1978. The audit rate for business returns with total positive income in excess of $25,000 dropped from 4⅔% in 1981 to about 2¼% in 1988. In 1978, the audit rate for business returns with more than $25,000 of taxable income had been over 7%.

Audit coverage of Subchapter S corporations and partnerships shows a similar but less precipitous long-term decline. . . . The Service uses a variety of mechanisms in an attempt to increase audit effectiveness. The most important of these is the Taxpayer Compliance Measurement Program (TCMP), which is a series of special audits that the Service conducts about every three years. For individuals, these audits randomly select about 50,000 taxpayers and are quite comprehensive. The data collected from these special audits are analyzed using a statistical technique known as discriminant function analysis (DIF). The process of the analysis is one of the best kept secrets in government, but the goal is to identify the characteristics of returns that are likely to yield additional revenue if audited. The higher the DIF score associated with a return, the more likely that an audit of the return will yield additional revenue above a threshold amount. The primary use of DIF scores is to select returns for routine audits. These routine audits are considerably less detailed than TCMP audits and typically focus on a fairly narrow range of return items.

There is some evidence that these efforts have been effective. For all individuals, the "no change" rate in 1988 was 14%, down from an historic rate of about 25%. This seems to confirm the Service's claim that it has improved its ability to select those returns for audit which are most likely to result in change, although the no change rates still ranged from 10% to 22%.

At the same time, the Service recognizes that the no-change rate is not the only relevant measure of audit efficiency. For example, the Service's estimate of voluntary compliance for noncorporate businesses is about 15% lower than that for individuals without business income. Even though voluntary compliance is estimated to be lower for noncorporate businesses, marginal yield-to-cost ratios (additional tax and penalty from examinations compared to examination costs) are also lower. This is in part due to a relatively higher audit coverage, but another possible explanation is unreported business income which is difficult to detect by audit.

B. Information Reports and CP2000s

At least for some taxpayers, the Service has compensated for the decline in audit coverage by matching tax return information with information from third parties (e.g., employers and payers of interest and dividend income). Whenever the discrepancy between the self-reported tax return information and the information reported by third parties is above a certain threshold, an automatic notice that taxes are due is sent to taxpayers. The notices – CP2000s – are also used to inform taxpayers that additional taxes are due for certain other reasons, such as mathematical errors. The number of both information returns and CP2000s has increased dramatically in the past decade. . . . The total number of information reports per tax return filed increased from around 6 in 1978 to over 9 in 1985 (the latest year for which this data is available), while non-W2 forms by themselves increased from 3.5 to 6. Overall, the number of information reports received by the Service increased from about 600 million in 1980 – covering 16 types of income – to about one billion in 1988 – covering 29 types of income and one deduction (home mortgage interest). The pattern is less clear in the case of CP2000s . . ., although the rate of issuance of CP2000s ultimately increased to 3.58% in 1988, a level that some observers regard as compensating for the decline in individual audit rates. Needless to say, information matching and audits are far from perfect substitutes.

C. Corporate Audits

The process for auditing corporations is quite different from that for auditing individuals. Most large corporations are audited regularly, and audit rates are quite high for corporations with over $1 million in assets. The marginal yield-to-cost ratios, however, are about the same as the individuals', except for the largest corporations. The estimated marginal yield-to-cost ratio for the very largest corporations (with over $100 million of assets), for example, is too high to measure meaningfully.

The Commissioner's 1988 annual report, however, does show significant declines from the prior year's audit coverage of corporations with assets between $50 million and $250 million, a category that recently has produced about $7 of assessments at the margin for each dollar of examination costs. Overall, the number of corporations audited has decreased from 147,340 in 1977 to 38,076 in 1988.

Because there are far more small corporations than large corporations, . . . the audit coverage of total corporations is best regarded as depicting the audit rate of small corporations. Here the audit rate has declined from 8% in 1978 to 1⅓% in 1988. . . .

D. Yield vs. Costs

As with individuals, therefore, a significant decline in the audit coverage of corporations has occurred during the past decade. In both cases, it seems clear that opportunities for productive audits remain. In 1988, the total recommended additional tax and penalties from examinations exceeded $18.5 billion for an average $13.72 yield for each dollar of examination cost. Since the audit process is designed to select first returns with the highest potential yield, marginal yield-to-cost ratios are, of course, lower. These marginal yield-to-cost ratios have ranged recently from about $3 in the least productive individual audit categories to about $7 in the highest. Corporate marginal yield-to-cost ratios have been about the same as for individuals (except, as noted earlier, for the largest corporations).

These yield-to-cost ratios reflect recommended additions to taxes and penalties. The amounts actually collected are apparently lower. These figures also include only direct Service costs and do not take into account the often quite substantial costs that tax-payers incur when they are audited. On the other hand, the marginal yield-to-cost estimates do not include the general deterrence effects of audits. Our own estimates suggest that these revenues may be significant, perhaps as high as 5 to 1 for the ratio of indirect to direct revenues for individual returns.

IV. The Increased Role of Civil Penalties

While the available data are inexact and specific estimates should, therefore, be viewed cautiously, the pattern of increasing civil penalties during the 1980s is indisputable. New and larger penalties enacted during recent years have dramatically increased the gross and net amounts of penalties assessed for both individuals and corporations. Admittedly rough data contained in the Report of the Commissioner's Task Force on Penalties suggest that for individuals, the total net amount of penalties (assessments minus abatements) increased from less than $1 billion in 1978 to more than $6 billion in 1988 ($10.9 billion in penalties assessed minus $4.8 billion of penalties abated). Non-fraud understatement penalties, negligence penalties, and fraud penalties for individuals increased from just over $40 million in 1978 to nearly $400 million in 1988. The amount of penalties assessed under section 6661 for substantial understatements of tax rose from $1.75 million in 1985 to $114.5 million in 1988. As an average amount of penalty per individual return examined, this represents an increase from about $22 to $375.

For corporations, net penalties increased from less than $18 million to $118 million and the average amount of penalty per return examined increased from $120 to $3,100 during the same period. For example, in 1986, net corporate penalties totaled about $49 million ($35 million in 1987) and the average amount of penalty per return examined was about $835 ($795 in 1987).

For individuals, the proportion representing fraud penalties has decreased dramatically, as we would expect due to the enactment of many new nonfraud, nonnegligence penalties. In 1978, for example, fraud penalties accounted for nearly 80% of individual penalties; by 1988 this relationship had reversed, with fraud penalties accounting for only one-quarter of the total. The pattern is not so dramatic for corporations. In 1978, fraud penalties accounted for nearly 90% of the total; in 1988, 62.5%; and in the more typical year of 1986, just under one-half of total corporate penalties were due to fraud.

The relationship of these penalties to the total of additional taxes and penalties due to examinations has also increased substantially. Graph 10 presents rough estimates of the pattern of average penalty rates assessed by examinations for individuals, during the period of 1979 to 1988. It shows an average penalty rate of about 2% in 1979 and 14% in 1988.

Graph 10: Average Net Penalty Rates, Individuals, 1979–88

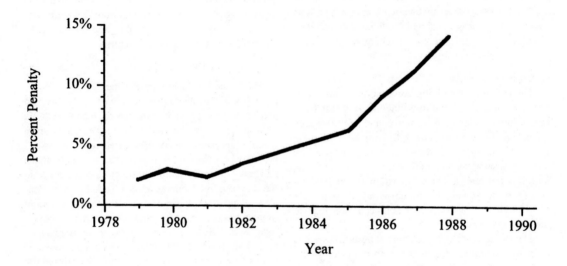

Similar computations for corporations suggest that penalty assessments are playing a far less significant role. In 1988, corporate penalties accounted for about $118 million of the total $11.7 billion of additional taxes and penalties assessed, or about 1% of the total. The comparable numbers for 1987 are $35 million in penalties compared to $10.6 billion total additional taxes and penalties, or 0.3%. A penalty rate computation similar to that performed above for individuals produces average corporate penalty rates of 1% for 1988, 0.45% for 1986, and 0.3% for 1980.

A few general observations may be useful. First, the direct revenue impact of penalties, particularly of the more controversial nonnegligence, nonfraud penalties is not large, although it is significantly larger as a proportion of additional taxes and penalties collected for individuals than for corporations. Direct penalty collections, of course, are not an estimate of the revenue effect of penalties because they ignore the effect of the penalties' existence on the amount of tax reported.

Second, the number of penalties assessed and abated has grown significantly in the past decade, from about 17 million in 1978 to more than 30 million in 1988. Employment tax penalties account for a significant proportion of the increase, having risen from 7.3 million in 1978 to 12.6 million in 1988. Failures to pay penalties have also increased substantially, from nearly 7½ million assessed in 1978 to 14¾ million in 1988.

In sum, enforcement, especially for individuals, seems now to involve a combination of fewer audits with more frequent and significant penalties imposed on audited taxpayers. Along with the recent disallowance of interest deductions on tax understatements, the expected costs to those taxpayers who are audited have increased significantly. In addition, the increase in the Service's budget allocation for appeals seems to imply, at a minimum, that being audited has become both a more elaborate and more costly enterprise for taxpayers. Of course, to the extent that information matching has replaced simple audits, taxpayers avoid the costs of an audit.

V. THE CHANGING FACE OF CRIMINAL TAX ENFORCEMENT

Let us begin this section of this essay with a group photograph. What do the following people have in common? Al Capone, former gangster; William Campbell, a United States judge for forty-eight years who had previously been involved in the prosecution of Al Capone; Mickey Cohen, former gangster; Robert B. Anderson, former Secretary of the Treasury; Joseph D. Nunan, Jr., former Commissioner of Internal Revenue; Dave Beck, former president of the Teamsters Union; Chuck Berry, rock and roll star; Albert Nippon, fashion designer; Mario Biaggi, former congressman and, as of 1989, the most decorated New York City policeman; Spiro Agnew, former Vice-President of the United States; Dana Kirk, former basketball coach at Memphis State University; Robert Huttenbach, former Chancellor at the University of California at Santa Barbara; Victor Posner, millionaire industrialist; Harry Reems, co-star of the porn classic "Deep Throat"; Leona Helmsley, the "Queen" of the Helmsley Hotel chain; Moses Annenberg, founder of TV Guide; and Pete Rose, former baseball player and manager. Such a list might go on and on. What the foregoing group of people have in common is a conviction for a tax crime.

In a sense, where criminal tax enforcement is concerned, there is nothing new under the sun. The foregoing list deliberately spans more than five decades of criminal tax enforcement, a process which has long been characterized by prosecutions of highly visible individuals who have violated only the tax laws as well as prosecutions for tax crimes of persons also engaged in non-tax criminal activity. Indeed, the violation of criminal tax statutes has long been a natural and frequently inevitable handmaiden of the commission of many non-tax crimes.

Recent statutory changes in federal criminal law, however, have multiplied the potential federal criminal violations that may now accompany what historically would have been solely state crimes. The most important of these are RICO (the Racketeer Influenced and Corrupt Organizations statute), the Continuing Criminal Enterprise provisions, the Bank Secrecy Act, the money laundering prohibitions, the Comprehensive Forfeiture Act and other federal drug offense legislation.

The financial investigation skills of the Service's special agents can and does serve an important function in detecting and successfully prosecuting non-tax federal financial crimes, most notably violations of the Bank Secrecy Act and money laundering statutes. Thus, it is no surprise that recent years have witnessed a significant shift of the Service's law enforcement resources in the direction of developing cases against narcotics dealers and other criminals. What is surprising, however, is that this predominantly non-tax law enforcement effort may be of sufficient magnitude to raise questions concerning the continuing ability of the Service at current budget levels to use criminal enforcement adequately to fulfill its primary mission of assuring maximum compliance with federal tax laws.

Although the share of the Service's budget devoted to criminal enforcement has remained relatively constant throughout the past decade, at about 5¾% of the total budget, the increasing role of the Service in enforcing non-tax federal crimes, perhaps in combination with the declining audit rate, has changed the sources of the Service's criminal prosecutions. Far fewer cases now originate with examination. The use of grand juries in tax enforcement has increased dramatically. In addition, the criminal enforcement story shares an important feature in common with the civil enforcement facts we have just presented: those who are caught are likely to face stiffer penalties, in this case prison sentences.

If one begins by attempting to develop a "criminal enforcement" rate, analogous to an "audit rate," two very different pictures emerge. . . . The past decade has witnessed a sharp drop, a drop of about two-thirds, in the criminal investigation rate, the number of criminal investigations started as a percentage of returns filed. Because of the corresponding drop in the audit rate during this same time period (as described in Section II, above), however, the number of criminal investigations as a percentage of returns examined does not reflect this same trend. . . .

If one regards prosecutions or convictions, however, as better measures of the effectiveness of the criminal enforcement effort, the pattern is much more positive. . . . Both the prosecution rate (the number of indictments and information as a percentage of returns filed) and the conviction rate (the number of convictions as a percentage of returns filed) show a steady increase in recent years, and the data with regard to prosecutions and convictions as percentages of returns examined are also more encouraging. . . .

But the selection of cases for criminal investigation that more frequently lead to prosecution and conviction cannot be attributed solely to the Service's criminal investigation division. Although the entire Service's criminal enforcement program has as its goal improving voluntary compliance with the tax laws, many tax convictions result from the Service's participation in law enforcement efforts directed principally at non-tax criminal activity, most significantly involving drugs, money laundering or organized crime. The Service historically has classified cases as falling into either the General Enforcement Program ("GEP"), the category of cases in which violations of the criminal tax statutes are principally at issue, or the Special Enforcement Program ("SEP"), which includes cases in which a non-tax crime is typically coupled with a tax crime. Graph 15 depicts the share of total criminal enforcement cases accounted for by the SEP cases during the period of 1979 to 1988. As that graph shows, by the late 1980s, SEP cases began to approach one-half of the Service's criminal enforcement activity.

Graph 15: Trend of SEP Investigations as a Percent of Total Investigations (GEP plus SEP), 1979–88

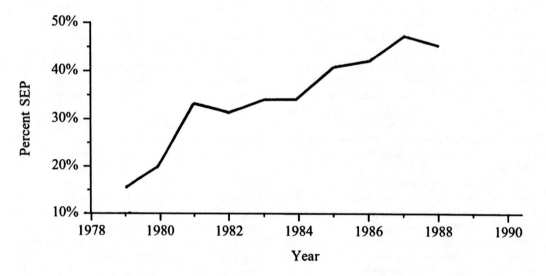

"[The General Enforcement Program] encompasses all criminal enforcement activities of the Criminal Investigation Division except those included in the special enforcement program discussed in IRM 9153. The identification and investigation of income tax evasion cases of substance with prosecution potential is a primary objective. The program also provides for balanced coverage as to types of violations, as well as geographic locations and economic and vocational status of violators as considered necessary to stimulate voluntary compliance.". . . .

The targets of SEP investigations typically are selected by law enforcement agencies other than the Service. . . . These cases are more productive than GEP cases, both in terms of prosecutions and convictions. In 1988, for example, the ratio of indictments to investigations started was 64% in the SEP program compared to less than 51% in the GEP program. The ratio of convictions to investigations started shows a similar pattern (58% versus 46% in 1988).

The recent emphasis by the Service on SEP cases, perhaps in combination with the decline in audit rates, has resulted in a very different pattern of sources for the Service's criminal prosecutions than traditionally has been the case. In particular, there has been a striking decrease in the share of criminal tax cases developed through the examination process. . . . This is true for both the percentage of criminal investigations started through audits, which has declined from 30% in 1979 to less than 20% in 1988, and the corresponding percentage of prosecutions, which has declined from nearly 30% to 14% during the same period.

Not only has the nature of criminal tax cases changed over the past decade, but the pattern of punishment for those convicted of tax crimes has also changed significantly. As in the case of civil penalties, persons convicted of tax crimes can expect greater punishment. The likelihood that a person convicted of tax crime will serve a prison sentence has increased significantly. . . . In 1988, almost 64% of those convicted of tax crimes were sentenced to prison, compared to 42% in 1979 (down from 48% in 1978).

VI. CONCLUSION

Both the audit rate and the rate of criminal prosecutions of tax violators (who have not been engaged in non-tax criminal activity) have declined substantially over the past decade. In an apparent effort to maintain deterrence, however, those audited or convicted of a tax crime have suffered increased penalties.

These trends raise a number of important questions. Foremost is the question of the overall effect of these changes on tax compliance. Our own empirical work suggests that the decline in audit rates has been quite costly to the federal government. The increased reliance on third-party information reporting as an enforcement device does not affect the same categories of taxpayers nor does it identify the same types of tax understatements as do audits.

Moreover, the policy of fewer investigations coupled with harsher penalties of those investigated raises issues of both horizontal and vertical equity. When widespread noncompliance is combated through stiffer penalties on fewer offenders, issues of fundamental fairness are raised. The penalty reform legislation enacted in late 1989 reflects concern with the Service's increasing reliance on civil penalties during the 1980s.

With regard to criminal tax enforcement, it is not clear to what extent the trends reported in Part V of this Article reflect deliberate changes in the Service's criminal enforcement policies. Moreover, to date, there is neither theoretical nor empirical scholarship to provide guidance about the effect of these changes on tax compliance. The data, however, suggest that such questions are worth asking.

While the kinds of financial skills located in the Service's criminal investigation division, to be sure, have an important, perhaps even crucial, role to play in this nation's drug enforcement effort, we must be vigilant to ensure that the tax compliance function of the Service's criminal process is not shortchanged as a result. The increased use of grand juries in the Service's investigations also raises significant questions. Even in the absence of a sound theoretical or empirical grounding, one cannot help but wonder whether even highly publicized drug enforcement by the Service has a tax compliance deterrent effect as powerful as that of pure enforcement cases. Empirical work addressed to this question is feasible and should be undertaken.

H. Money Laundering

John K. Villa, *A Critical Look at Bank Secrecy Enforcement and the Money Laundering Statutes,* 37 CATH. U. L. REV. 487 (1988)*

By pleading guilty to a series of Bank Secrecy Act (BSA) offenses in February of 1985, the Bank of Boston heralded a new chapter in the enforcement of the BSA against federally insured financial institutions. This era is characterized by the realization that federal law enforcement authorities can obtain unexpectedly large volumes of information about currency movements by aggressively enforcing the BSA against financial institutions and their officers and employees. While this approach is unquestionably effective in the short run, it succeeds at the expense of damaging the close relationship that has historically existed between financial institutions and federal law enforcement authorities.

There are several reasons for the government's new approach to BSA enforcement. First, the flood of Currency Transaction Reports (CTR's) that followed the Bank of Boston prosecution revealed that the threat of criminal charges, or merely of being publicly identified with money laundering, was a surprisingly potent motivation for financial institutions. Second, public concern over this nation's drug problem, heightened by the deaths of several prominent athletes, gave legislators greater license to take harsh action against anyone identified with money laundering—an activity that many associate with drug dealers. Third, financial institutions failed to comply strictly with the BSA prior to February 1985 and were, therefore, vulnerable to legitimate criticism.

Nevertheless, the perception by some in the government that the financial services industry blithely ignored the BSA prior to 1985, and that harsh penalties are, therefore, required to motivate compliance,

---

* Reprinted with permission of the *Catholic University Law Review.* ©1988 The Catholic University Law Review.

is inaccurate. In fact, the industry performed precisely as regulated industries historically have acted: the industry reflected the priorities of its regulators, most of whom had little interest in the BSA because it has minimal impact on the principal supervisory goal of preserving the safety and soundness of the financial institutions. Once the regulators emphasized compliance with the BSA, financial institutions quickly followed suit.

In light of that experience, there is no warrant for concluding that harsh penalties and criminal charges based upon 'flagrant organizational indifference' are necessary to motivate the financial services industry. Such an approach may actually be counter-productive because it fails to distinguish between deliberate intent to violate the law and indifference to legal requirements, thus, disregarding notions of 'proportionality' or 'just desserts' that have long been basic to our jurisprudence. Unfortunately, the momentum of current initiatives shows no sign of abating. Unless the government takes steps to reverse the adversarial posture that it has adopted toward financial institutions, the long-term relationship between the government and the banking industry will continue to decline, to the detriment of all.

This Article will chronicle the significant points in Bank Secrecy Act enforcement and will analyze the roles that Congress, the Department of the Treasury (Treasury), and the Department of Justice (Justice Department) have played in this process. The major issues that appear on the horizon will then be surveyed, focusing principally on the new laundering statutes.

I. THE EVOLUTION AND ENFORCEMENT OF THE BANK SECRECY ACT AND THE ENACTMENT OF THE MONEY LAUNDERING STATUTES

A. The Bank Secrecy Act

The federal law now commonly referred to as the BSA was enacted in 1970 as part of the Bank Records and Foreign Transaction Act (BRFTA). As explained in its declaration of purpose, the BRFTA was a response to rising congressional concern over the use of foreign banks to 'launder' the proceeds of illegal activity and to evade federal income taxes. Title I of the BRFTA, which imposes record keeping requirements on financial institutions, has now been assimilated into the text of title 12 of the United States Code, which imposes regulatory duties on federally insured financial institutions. Title II of the BRFTA, originally referred to as the Currency and Foreign Transactions Reporting Act, has survived in chapter 53, title 31 of the United States Code. The provisions of title II are now commonly referred to as the BSA.

The BSA was controversial because it infringed on the traditionally confidential relationship between the bank and the customer. Probably for this reason, the Secretary of the Treasury, who is charged with enforcing the BSA, promulgated regulations which pointedly did not exercise the full scope of his statutory authority. In particular, the regulations did not require that individuals file CTR's regarding their own currency transactions, although the statute would have permitted it. Instead, the regulations required only that financial institutions file CTR's for their customers' transactions.

This self-restraint did not insulate the BSA from attack; in the six years following its passage, it was challenged twice in the United States Supreme Court. In California Bankers Association v. Schultz and United States v. Miller, the Court upheld the major provisions of the BSA. Had it not been for the Secretary's voluntary limitations on the reach of the regulations, however, there is reason to believe that the BSA would have been held unconstitutional as infringing upon the customers' privilege against self-incrimination.

B. Early Enforcement Efforts

Although the California Bankers Association and Miller decisions dispelled the cloud that had obscured the BSA since its enactment, very little enforcement activity occurred prior to the early 1980's. Until that time, prosecutions under the BSA were generally limited to charges against individuals who transported monetary instruments into or out of the United States without reporting them on a Report of International Transportation of Currency (known as CMIR).

Beginning in the early 1980's, however, federal prosecutors became increasingly aware of the volume of cash related to illegal drug transactions that was flowing into the banking system, particularly through financial institutions in the southeastern United States. They responded with a federal law enforcement task force known as 'Operation Greenback,' which targeted large-scale money laundering for drug sellers and resulted in a significant number of prosecutions, including several involving financial institutions. The publicity resulting from Operation Greenback prompted other federal prosecutors to utilize the BSA. Still, only a trickle of cases for failure to file CTR's was brought between 1982 and 1984; the statute was still regarded as one to be used against customers who circumvented the CTR filing requirements by paying off bank employees or by using false names.

In 1984, the newly appointed President's Commission on Organized Crime held a series of sensational hearings at which financial institutions were roundly accused of engaging in money laundering. The hearings resulted in the Interim Report to the President and the Attorney General. The report contained a number of recommendations for statutory changes. The Commission's proposals included an increase in the civil and criminal penalties imposed for BSA violations and proposed legislation that was the precursor to the current statutory prohibition of the laundering of monetary instruments.

Almost simultaneously, Congress revisited the BSA when, as part of the Comprehensive Crime Control Act of 1984, it raised the civil money penalties for BSA offenses from $1,000 to $10,000 for each violation. Because the BSA was still viewed as a weapon against drug dealers, however, this statutory change was largely ignored by the financial services industry.

The turning point in BSA enforcement occurred with the guilty plea of the Bank of Boston in February 1985. The spectacle of a major, well-respected bank pleading guilty to criminal charges generated remarkable media attention and was the subject of highly publicized congressional hearings. Although many in the banking community, both in and out of government, privately stated that they felt that the Bank of Boston had been unfairly held up to public ridicule, it was impossible publicly to come to the defense of an institution that had pled guilty to criminal offenses.

Many financial institutions reacted to the Bank of Boston case by directing internal auditors to review BSA compliance. All too often those auditors discovered that compliance with the BSA had been haphazard at best and that a significant number of transactions had not been reported on CTR's. In most cases, the cause of reporting failures was that financial institutions historically viewed the BSA as directed toward large, suspicious cash transactions. They devoted little attention to the transactions of established customers that might also require reporting.

To their dismay, financial institutions also found a confusing body of regulations governing CTR filing requirements. In broad terms, the regulations required filing of CTR's for all cash transactions exceeding $10,000 by non-exempt customers. The Treasury regulations, however, apparently drew irrational distinctions between the types of customers who were eligible for exemption by the financial institution and those who were not. Erroneous advice by federal officials contributed to the problems. Customs officers, bank examiners, and even federal prosecutors reviewed exempt lists that were riddled with obviously ineligible customers, yet they voiced no objection. In addition, there was confusion over the relationship between the filing requirements of the CMIR, which requires information about international transportation of currency or monetary instruments, and those of the CTR. Many financial institutions incorrectly assumed that due to similarities between the two forms, they would not be required to file a CTR if they filed the CMIR.

Fearing that they would be the next prosecutorial target for their filing failures, financial institutions began a massive campaign to comply with the BSA and filed a virtual flood of CTR's. Some of the financial institutions that discovered significant filing failures approached the Treasury to disclose their mistakes and to resolve the problem in hopes of avoiding a criminal investigation. The Treasury publicly settled with several dozen banks and announced more than a dozen civil money penalty settlements that exceeded $100,000. Other institutions that disclosed significant filing failures reportedly have not been fined.

Although there are good arguments that civil money penalties should not be imposed where the failure to file had been a mere oversight or the result of a misunderstanding, shock waves from the Bank of Boston case apparently convinced many financial institutions to forego that defense and settle rather than to take the risk that they would be prosecuted or even sued to enforce a civil money penalty assessment. Most financial institutions, being particularly cognizant of their public image, concluded they could not risk the stigma of being charged with a violation that smacked of money laundering.

After a substantial amount of media attention, the publicity surrounding the civil money penalty settlements peaked in late 1985. References to money laundering in press accounts of these increasingly routine settlements have gradually receded and have now vanished.

C. The Money Laundering Provisions

Congress returned to the issues of the BSA and money laundering in the Anti-Drug Abuse Act of 1986, which includes subtitle H of title I, referred to as the Money Laundering Control Act of 1986 (MLCA). The MLCA contains amendments to the BSA and two new laundering statutes. The BSA amendments give the Treasury much greater negotiating leverage in civil settlement cases by increasing the maximum civil penalty for each violation to the greater of $25,000, or the amount of the transaction, while not exceeding $100,000. In addition, Congress enacted a new penalty for 'negligent' violations, permitting up to a maximum of $500 per violation.

The MLCA also added a new section to the BSA, which is known as the 'antistructuring statute.' Section 5324(1) and (2) of the antistructuring statute prohibit an individual from causing a financial institution either to fail to file a required report or to file a false report. Congress presumably intended these provisions to address the growing body of cases which have held that because the regulations promulgated under the BSA do not impose a duty on individuals to inform the bank of a reportable transaction, such a duty cannot be imposed in a criminal prosecution without violating the fair warning requirements of the due process clause of the fifth amendment.

The most controversial portion of section 5324 of the antistructuring statute is subsection (3) which prohibits the 'structuring' of transactions to evade reporting requirements, although the act of 'structuring' is left undefined. It appears that the prohibition against structuring was intended to criminalize the division of a single quantity of cash which exceeds the exempt limit into two or more unreportable sums for deposit in different institutions. If that is, in fact, the statute's objective, it goes considerably beyond the bounds of most criminal statutes.

Although it is not yet generally recognized, the statutory changes which will have the greatest impact on financial institutions are the MLCA's two new laundering statutes. Broadly speaking, section 1956 of title 18 of the United States Code prohibits knowing involvement in a wide range of transactions involving the proceeds of criminal activity either (1) with the intent to promote unlawful activity or (2) with the knowledge that the transaction is designed either to conceal some aspect of the funds, such as its ownership, control, or source, or to avoid the currency transaction reporting requirements. Another subsection of section 1956 prohibits the transportation of monetary instruments in foreign commerce with the same intent or knowledge. Section 1957 of title 18 of the United States Code prohibits knowingly engaging in virtually any typical banking transaction involving a financial institution in 'criminally derived property' with a value exceeding $10,000. The penalty for violation of section 1956 is a fine of $500,000 or twice the value of the monetary instrument or funds involved in the transaction or transportation, whichever is greater, and/or imprisonment for not more than twenty years. The penalty for violation of section 1957 is a fine of not more than twice the criminally derived property involved and/or prisonment of not more than ten years.

Although both statutes leave crucial terms undefined—including, most significantly, the concept of 'proceeds'—their thrust is quite clear. These statutes, for the first time, make it a crime to do business with or conduct financial transactions for any person who derives his monies from certain specified unlawful activities. The reach of section 1956 is restricted to some extent by the fact that violation of the statute requires intent to promote the illegal activity or knowledge of an illegal purpose for the transaction by another person. By contrast, mere knowledge of the illegal source of the funds establishes a violation of section 1957. Thus, section 1957 leaves financial institutions subject to prosecution for conducting routine transactions in the accounts of tainted customers.

D. The Bank of New England Case

The most significant recent event concerning the BSA occurred in United States v. Bank of New England, N.A., where the Bank of New England was convicted of committing thirty-one felonies arising out of its failure to file CTRs. Over a period of more than a year, a customer of the bank, James McDonough, withdrew more than $10,000 in cash from a single account at one branch of the bank on numerous occasions. On each occasion, McDonough presented multiple checks to a single bank teller and received in return a lump sum of cash in excess of $10,000. The jury acquitted McDonough as well as two bank tellers who were indicted along with the bank. The bank was convicted, however, and fined a total of $1.24 million.

The BSA provision under which the Bank of New England was convicted imposes criminal penalties on one who 'willfully violat[es]' the CTR filing requirement. Courts interpreting this standard have held that the government must prove the highest level of scienter, or specific intent, imposed by our criminal law. In particular, 'the defendant [must] have actually known of the currency reporting requirement and have voluntarily and intentionally violated that known legal duty in order to be convicted of the crime.'

In Bank of New England, the trial court gave controversial instructions on the issues of corporate 'knowledge' and corporate 'willfulness.' The trial court instructed the jury that the bank could be found to have the requisite specific intent even in the absence of classic respondeat superior liability where an employee, acting within the scope of his duties and for his master's benefit, intentionally violates the law. The jury was told that in order to determine the knowledge of 'the bank as an institution,' it could 'sum' up the knowledge of its separate employees. If the 'sum' of that collective knowledge constituted knowledge of the applicable facts and law, the bank could be deemed to have knowledge of its duties. Furthermore, the bank could be guilty of a willful violation of those duties if it exhibited 'flagrant organizational indifference' to the reporting requirements. Thus, the trial court's instructions permitted a collective entity to be found guilty of a serious federal felony requiring specific intent in the absence of any individual employee, officer, or agent having the requisite intent.

On review of the bank's conviction, the United States Court of Appeals for the First Circuit upheld these instructions. The court reasoned that 'the knowledge obtained by corporate employees acting within the scope of their employment is imputed to the corporation.' According to the court, corporations divide aspects of particular duties and operations into smaller components and the 'aggregate of these components constitutes the corporation's knowledge of a particular operation.' Moreover, the First Circuit held that the corporate 'indifference' standard reflected in the instructions was appropriate because, with respect to federal regulatory statutes, the courts have defined willfulness as "a disregard for the governing statute and an indifference to its requirements." The Supreme Court declined to review the First Circuit's decision.

Contrary to the implications of the First Circuit's opinion, the jury instructions in Bank of New England reflect a significant expansion of traditional principles of corporate criminal liability. Neither the BSA itself nor previous court decisions support the imposition of criminal liability for a specific intent crime based on the collective knowledge of corporate employees. More fundamentally, equating 'willfulness' with 'flagrant organizational indifference' represents an erosion of the level of scienter that is prescribed by the BSA. The cases on which the First Circuit relied arose in the context of 'public safety' regulations, such as those governing railroads and trucking, for which the courts have traditionally imposed a lower standard of criminal intent than in specific intent crimes such as tax evasion. The latter category of offenses has always been understood as involving moral turpitude and, accordingly, some kind of 'evil motive is a constituent element of the crime.' Indeed, when holding that the willfulness standard for 'public safety' violations can be met by mere indifference or negligence, the courts have been careful to emphasize that more is required under statutes where 'willfully' is . . . used to mean with evil purpose, criminal intent or the like.' Applying standards developed primarily in civil, public safety cases to the specific intent crimes arising out of failures to file CTR's poses a substantially enhanced risk of criminal liability for financial institutions genuinely attempting to comply with the BSA.

II. Congress, the Treasury, and the Justice Department

A. Recent Legislative Changes

The BSA, as well as the more recent laundering statutes, implicitly reflect a congressional judgment that law enforcement goals can be achieved more effectively by severely punishing federally regulated financial institutions than by developing cooperative programs with the banking industry. The wisdom of this approach is open to serious question because financial institutions historically have been close allies with the law enforcement community, and have cooperated with federal law enforcement authorities almost to a fault. Moreover, in its headlong rush to be tough on the banks, Congress adopted legislative changes

that have created insoluble problems for financial institutions without any corresponding benefit to law enforcement interests.

A case in point is section 1957 of title 18 of the United States Code. Before analyzing the flaws in the statute, it is worth observing that the statute presents a clear departure from traditional concepts of criminal behavior. Although the criminal law has long forbidden the receipt of stolen goods, it has not generally prohibited a person from doing business with or for another simply because unlawful conduct served as the source of the funds for the transaction. One has the right to sell his house to a gangster as freely as to a clergyman as long as the parties perform the transaction at arm's length with no intent to assist the gangster in the commission of a crime.

Section 1957, by contrast, reflects a new approach and one that seems likely to exact unanticipated social costs. One who suspects a person of offering stolen goods for sale may protect himself by merely declining to purchase the suspect goods. The social cost of declining that purchase is minimal. If, on the other hand, it is a crime to do any business at all with one who deals in the proceeds of illegal activity, then those who are merely suspected of crimes will find that they cannot engage in everyday commerce; fearing criminal liability, no one will risk dealing with them. The impact on the suspected individual can be severe because no knowledgeable person will transact business with him, yet there may be no means by which the suspected individual can clear himself. The social cost of imposing such a stigma on individuals – especially those who have not been convicted of, let alone charged with, any crime – should present grave civil liberties concerns even for the most ardent law-and-order legislator. It is disappointing to find that Congress did not seriously debate these important issues at the time it enacted section 1957.

Putting to one side the serious policy questions presented by section 1957, the statute itself is riddled with ambiguities that present enormous problems for financial institutions. As bank officers confront these ambiguities, they may well choose to read the statute broadly – thus minimizing their own risk of criminal prosecution – which would cause the statute to have an even greater impact than Congress expected. A direct result of loose draftsmanship will, therefore, cause the denial of financial services to some innocent customers by justifiably cautious bankers.

Section 1957 prohibits conducting transactions that involve 'criminally derived property.' Yet, neither section 1957 nor section 1956 define these 'proceeds' concepts, thus, inviting a wide range of interpretation. Do the statutes only apply to the direct fruits of illegal activity or do they also apply to the products of those fruits which are reinvested and thereby change form? If $25,000 in illegal proceeds are placed into a bank account containing $75,000 in legal monies, does every check subsequently written on that account consist of 25% illegal proceeds? If a bank lends a customer $50,000 and subsequently learns that an unlawful activity created his source of funds, can it accept repayment of the loan? If an individual has legal and illegal sources of income, can a bank transact any business with him without fear of prosecution?

Even with adequate definition of the key statutory terms, there is little chance that financial institutions could apply them accurately. Financial institutions are ill-equipped to decide whether a particular customer obtains his funds from illegal sources. It typically takes a trained federal prosecutor, using experienced investigators and the unparalleled power of a federal grand jury, months or even years to identify criminal activity. An experienced banker applying an unintelligible statute like section 1957 has little hope of making a correct decision while a customer transaction is pending. If the financial institution incorrectly decides to terminate business activities with the suspected customer, a major civil lawsuit is inevitable.

The impossible choices that face many financial institutions demonstrate that Congress has simply dropped the problem in the lap of the financial services industry and walked away. None of the options are attractive, but some financial institutions will ultimately decide that unless a customer clearly and openly engages in illegal activity, they will not terminate business contacts with him. While this may be a realistic solution, it is not a happy one. It means that many financial institutions will, for the first time, knowingly operate on the fringe of the criminal law.

The problems in interpreting and applying section 1957 have not been generally recognized because the statute is new and there are no reported section 1957 prosecutions. Prosecution of a major bank or senior bank officer for violating section 1957 undoubtedly will create a furor similar to that which followed the Bank of Boston case. At that point, financial institutions will realize, for the first time, that there are no ready solutions to the difficulties posed by these new statutes.

B. Treasury Department Initiatives

Given the political realities, the flaws in the BSA prior to October 1986, and an apparent shortage of staff, the Treasury has made a creditable effort to reconcile legitimate law enforcement goals with the maintenance of a constructive relationship with the financial services industry. Two criticisms can be leveled at the Treasury. First, the CTR regulations in section 103 of title 31 of the Code of Federal Regulations are unnecessarily confusing. Second, the Treasury has not adequately encouraged financial institutions to voluntarily disclose their CTR violations. The first problem results from the Treasury's failure to direct adequate resources to this issue in the years preceding 1985. The second problem probably results from a lack of resources, an unwieldy statutory scheme, and an adverse political climate.

The regulations governing CTR filing reporting requirements historically have drawn apparently irrational distinctions between the types of customers that financial institutions can exempt. For example, if the goal is to detect criminal activity, then there is no apparent reason to allow financial institutions to exempt bars, restaurants, and race tracks from CTR reporting requirements and, at the same time, prohibit financial institutions from exempting churches, schools, and hospitals. The line which the Treasury drew was to permit financial institutions to exempt businesses that customarily dealt in large amounts of cash regardless of the potential for abuse. An equally reasonable and perhaps more sensible rule might have been to permit financial institutions to exempt businesses that traditionally had little risk of criminal activity. Even accepting the Treasury's distinction, however, it was difficult to justify permitting financial institutions to exempt a retail seller of goods but not a provider of services.

Most financial institutions would probably prefer fewer, but clearer, exemptions to more liberal exemption criteria that are difficult to interpret and apply. The Treasury's rules fail to meet that goal and have contributed considerably to the confusion over BSA compliance. While the current regulations are improving, they have many questions unanswered.

Another source of confusion is the fact that the filing requirements for CTR's and CMIR's are inconsistent. In some instances, financial institutions that filed one form have been fined for not filing the other, despite the fact that they contain the same basic information and that the Treasury records the information from both of them in the same data bank. Some financial institutions that have unwittingly violated these provisions have therefore been assessed civil money penalties in situations where the information loss to the government was minimal.

A second criticism of the Treasury is that it devotes too much of its available resources to extracting civil money penalties from financial institutions who come forward and voluntarily disclose past BSA violations. While there does not appear to be any public information regarding the total amount of resources devoted to the voluntary disclosure cases, the Treasury's small staff—in what is now known as the Office of Financial Enforcement—seems to devote much of its time to the voluntary disclosure cases. At the same time, the Treasury rarely disturbs the vast majority of financial institutions that do not voluntarily disclose past BSA violations. This strategy has the unfortunate effect of punishing the good corporate citizens who come forward while ignoring the financial institutions that elect not to disclose their past violations. It is difficult to conceive of a more counter-productive approach to a regulatory scheme that must, after all, rely upon voluntary compliance to be effective.

There are probably several reasons for the Treasury's approach. The first, and probably most significant, is that there are so few Treasury personnel and so many voluntary disclosure cases, often involving relatively large financial institutions, that the Treasury has no resources to pursue the non-volunteers. An important second reason is that the Treasury once lacked the statutory authority to compel financial institutions to disclose BSA violations. This omission was corrected in the MLCA in 1986, yet the Treasury still has not fully exercised its authority. The third, and more debatable reason for aggressively pursuing those financial institutions that voluntarily disclose, is that congressional overseers are anxious to see a tough enforcement posture by the Treasury against the largest banks, which are the institutions that typically make voluntary disclosures. Thus, even though a 'get tough' approach is remarkably shortsighted in the overall regulatory strategy, Congress seems to favor it and it appears to have influenced the Treasury's actions, especially in the year following the Bank of Boston prosecution.

A review of the Treasury's enforcement of the BSA reveals that it has performed reasonably well under very difficult circumstances, including insufficient staff, a poorly drafted statute (until the MLCA), and unenlightened congressional oversight. By avoiding unnecessary bank bashing, the Treasury has managed to retain credibility with the financial services industry as a responsible regulator. One must, however, conclude that to the extent that the Treasury had hoped for an effective voluntary disclosure program which would have encouraged financial institutions to come forward with past violations, it has failed. Without any incentive to do so, most financial institutions have simply avoided conducting historical reviews, or if they have performed them, they have not submitted them to the Treasury. While the threat of future sanctions has encouraged most institutions to achieve a high level of current compliance, the dubious benefits of voluntary disclosure of past errors to the Treasury have not been great enough to induce such disclosures.

C. Justice Department Activities

Criminal prosecutions under the BSA have, with a small number of significant exceptions, been unremarkable. In large part, the Justice Department has prosecuted bankers or customers for engaging in flagrant and intentional violations of the BSA by failing to file CTR's or filing false CTR's with the intent to mislead the government. The small number of more important prosecutions have been brought against major banks whose criminal liability results from some theory of 'organizational indifference' to the BSA. The first such significant prosecution appears to have been against the Bank of Boston, followed more recently by Bank of New England.

The conviction of the Bank of New England may have produced one of the most important modern decisions on the issue of corporate criminal liability. If taken to its limits, the decision undoubtedly could lead to scores of indictments of federally insured financial institutions for BSA violations, as well as for violations of the new laundering statutes. Bank of New England gives the Justice Department a significant new weapon against financial institutions. Under the 'flagrant organizational indifference' standard, vast numbers of financial institutions are subject to prosecution for lack of BSA compliance prior to the Bank of Boston prosecution in February 1985, which jolted their compliance officers to life. Even more chilling for financial institutions is the prospect of the Justice Department applying the 'collective knowledge' concept in section 1957 prosecutions to convict financial institutions of laundering violations when neither the financial institution nor any of its employees or officers had any criminal culpability whatsoever.

Any critique of the Justice Department's enforcement of the BSA and the laundering statutes should be deferred until it becomes clear how these powerful new tools will be used. If these theories are used against morally neutral conduct—and they clearly have that potential—then it will erode the industry's respect for the processes of administering justice. As Professor Packer has observed, the application of criminal sanctions to morally neutral behavior has the effect of decriminalizing the criminal law and subtly changing people's attitude toward criminality. While this concept is typically applied to criminal activity by individuals, it also applies to corporate behavior. If financial institutions perceive that the government is arbitrarily prosecuting banks for violating statutes which the banks are attempting to obey, then some banks will for the first time divert effort from attempting to obey the law to attempting to escape detection of the inevitable violations. The short term gains from an aggressive use of these tools will not outweigh the long term damage between those financial institutions and federal law enforcement.

III. CURRENT ENFORCEMENT PROBLEMS

The first round of BSA enforcement has concluded with fears of prosecution that have brought the financial services industry into substantial compliance. The question for the future is whether the relationship between the financial services industry and federal law enforcement authorities will continue to be strained or will begin to improve. To answer that question, one must consider the important issues that will arise in the next several years under the BSA and the new laundering statutes.

The first issue is whether Congress will amend section 1957 of title 18 of the United States Code, so that the financial services community will have some notion of the statute's reach. Because of the severe penalties for violations of the statute and the fact that it embodies a relatively new concept in our criminal law, it would be extraordinarily painful for the government to define critical elements of the statute through criminal prosecutions. Even if the prosecutions that are ultimately brought interpret the statute reasonably, the statute's reach will not be clear for a number of years, if ever. In the interim, financial institutions that attempt good faith compliance with this provision will inevitably err on both sides: those that construe the statute too narrowly will become the target of grand jury investigations and possibly prosecuted, while those who construe it too broadly will be sued by customers with whom they unjustifiably refuse to do business. Financial institutions should not be forced to run that gauntlet; the statute should be clarified. The second issue is whether the government—specifically the Justice Department—will develop a 'safe harbor' concept for section 1957. Even if the statute is amended to address its ambiguities, a financial institution that merely suspects a customer of engaging in criminal activity has difficult choices. It can continue to do business with the customer and expose itself, and its individual officers and employees, to criminal liability for violating section 1957 if the customer is ultimately shown to have engaged in illegal activity and the suspicious incidents are deemed sufficient to give the bank knowledge of his activities (which always seems easier in hindsight). Alternatively, the bank can refuse to conduct business with the customer, running the risk that the customer was innocent, or at least cannot be proven guilty, and will sue.

Mr. Rusch is correct in observing that a financial institution that identifies a customer involved in conducting a suspicious transaction may report that fact to the government on a criminal referral form, and if the referral falls within certain guidelines specified in the Right to Financial Privacy Act, the financial institution cannot be held liable for making the referral or for failing to inform the customer of it. This is good as far as it goes. The real question, however, is whether federal law provides protection for the financial institution that decides not to continue doing business with this suspicious customer in order to protect itself and its personnel from criminal prosecution under sections 1956 and 1957. Evidently, there is no protection. In a case arising in Maine prior to the effective date of these statutes, a bank learned this lesson the hard way when it abruptly terminated its relationships with a customer after being told, incorrectly, by a federal agent that its customer was an underworld figure. The customer sued and recovered a $12.5 million verdict against the bank.

One would think that if the financial institution were in doubt and filed a criminal referral on the customer, it would have advanced law enforcement goals and should, therefore, be relieved of the threat of prosecution even if it continued to do business with that customer. That is not the case. In fact, a prosecutor might use the making of a referral against the financial institution as an admission to show that it knew of the possibility that the customer engaged in illegal activities. This will discourage referrals. Because the possibility of a civil suit against the bank often seems more likely than prosecution for a laundering violation, the bank will probably decide to continue doing business with a current customer unless the evidence of illegal activity is very strong. If it continues to do business, then it may also decide against filing a criminal referral to avoid later being charged with knowledge of criminal activity. The result is that the likelihood of a referral declines and, consequently, the government is deprived of significant law enforcement information.

A more rational solution would be to adopt a safe harbor rule providing that if a bank files a reasonable and good faith referral on a customer, then it will not be prosecuted for further dealings of the same kind with that customer. This would encourage the prompt submission of referrals and allow the financial institutions to believe that law enforcement authorities are working with them rather than against them.

The third issue will be the extent to which the Justice Department uses the 'flagrant organizational indifference' and 'collective knowledge' standards from the Bank of New England decision. These concepts could be used to prosecute many financial institutions for their total ignorance of the BSA prior to February 1985, yet no useful purpose would be served at this point by such prosecutions. Similarly, the financial services industry has totally failed to appreciate the dangers inherent in section 1957 in the year after it was enacted and might therefore be vulnerable to the same 'indifference' theory of prosecution in the future.

IV. CONCLUSION

No thoughtful commentator can look at the Bank Secrecy Act and laundering statutes without concluding that they will continue to present unique policy questions for Congress, the Justice Department and the Treasury. The ultimate verdict on whether these powerful statutes are used properly, and effectively, will depend upon whether those charged with drafting and administering these laws carefully define their long-term goals and enlist the help of the financial services industry to achieve those goals.

Sarah N. Welling, *Smurfs, Money Laundering and the Federal Criminal Law: The Crime of Structuring Transactions,* 41 FLA. L. REV. 287 (1989)*

I. INTRODUCTION

In 1970, Congress adopted a statute requiring financial institutions to report cash transactions over $10,000 to the government. Failure to report was a crime. In 1987, Congress made it a crime to structure financial transactions to evade this reporting law. Thus, for example, if Joe arranges his banking so the cash transactions are below $10,000 in order to avoid reporting, Joe commits a federal crime. What brought Congress to this point? Should we be alarmed at the extent of governmental intrusion into the arrangement of our financial affairs, or is the intrusion warranted? This article answers these questions and tells a good story as well.

The story begins with money laundering. Part II provides background on money laundering and describes the government's opening salvo against laundering, a statute requiring financial institutions to report cash transactions over $10,000 to the government. To skirt this law, launderers began to conduct

* Reprinted with the permission of the Florida Law Review. Copyright 1989.

multiple cash transactions just below the $10,000 reporting threshold. The army of persons who scurried from bank to bank to accomplish these transactions became known as "smurfs" because, like their little blue cartoon namesakes, they were pandemic. Smurfs thrived when the 1970 reporting law encountered trouble in the courts. The government's response to this new species was to adopt a new criminal provision, the 1987 anti-smurfing statute.

Congress adopted the anti-smurfing statute quickly and without careful analysis. The legislative history includes examples of problems with the reporting law and descriptions of cases the government lost. Yet the history contains little analysis of the elements of this new crime, and no analysis of its basic theory, constitutionality, interaction with other reporting laws, or its relationship to federal criminal law as a whole. The lack of analysis results from several factors. Congress was in a hurry to plug the loopholes in the reporting statute to halt the drain of laundered money. Congress resented the insolence of money launderers, particularly the smurfs who flooded the banks with multiple transactions for $9900, thereby avoiding the reporting requirement. Finally, the anti-smurfing statute was upstaged, but not obviated, by legislation making money laundering per se a crime.

This article takes a thorough look at the anti-smurfing statute. Following this introduction, part II presents the setting that facilitated the emergence of smurfs. Part III examines the statute itself, including its basic theory, elements, constitutionality, unit of prosecution, and practical operation. Part IV examines how this new crime fits into federal criminal law as a whole. The article concludes that on balance, the reduction in privacy that the anti-smurfing statute effects is warranted by the harm money laundering and the drug trade cause.

II. THE SETTING: CREATING AN ENVIRONMENT CONDUCIVE TO SMURFS

A. Some Background on Money Laundering

Money laundering begins with dirty money. Money can get dirty in two ways. One way is through tax evasion; people make money legally, but they make more than they report to the government. Money also gets dirty through illegal generation. Common techniques include drug sales, gambling, and bribery. Once money is dirty, it must be converted into an apparently legitimate form, or "laundered" before it can be invested or spent. "'Money laundering' is the process by which one conceals the existence, illegal source, or illegal application of income, and then disguises that income to make it appear legitimate."

Laundering has several goals. One is to hide or

sanitize the property so the tax collector does not get it. This aspect of the laundering process has been chronicled in detail. Another goal is to convert the cash into a physically manageable and inconspicuous form. That form often is a postal money order or cashier's check, but it also could be gold, stamps, or any form of property. The importance of converting cash into a manageable physical form is illustrated by the case of Anthony Castelbuono. Castelbuono somewhat conspicuously brought $1,187,450 in small bills to a casino. The cash had an estimated volume of 5.75 cubic feet and weighed 280 pounds.

Whatever its goal, money laundering is harmful. Underground money absorbs no portion of the tax burden. More importantly, laundering is harmful because it allows the underlying criminal activity to thrive. Drug sales, gambling, or other crimes that generate cash are pointless if the cash cannot be invested or spent. Without laundering, the risk/reward ratio for the underlying crime is unattractive. Thus, success of the criminal venture depends on laundering. Efficient laundering renders the underlying crime lucrative, and therefore perpetuates it.

Money laundering has become a major concern recently because of the thriving drug trade. Laundering is required only if large amounts of cash are involved, because smaller amounts of dirty cash can be absorbed inconspicuously into a criminal's lifestyle. Huge amounts of cash require attention to disposal, and the drug trade currently generates such huge amounts. For example, in August 1988, five-thousand pounds of cocaine were seized in New York; the estimated street value was $355 million. Had this cocaine reached the streets, that $355 million would exist originally as cash. To put that cash to its best use, it would have to be laundered.

Aside from combating these measurable harms, putting a halt to money laundering also is emotionally appealing. The existence of laundering schemes indicates that some people get rich unfairly because they pay no taxes. Furthermore, the people who need laundering schemes often get rich because they sell drugs in the United States. Drug money laundering is especially unsavory on an intuitive level, considering the source of the cash that drives it.

B. The Original Reporting Statute

The government's first attack on money laundering was indirect. In 1970, Congress passed the Currency and Foreign Transactions Reporting Act ("the Act") as Title II of the Bank Secrecy Act. The Act imposes reporting requirements for certain financial transactions. One statute provides that when a domestic financial institution is involved in a currency transaction under circumstances prescribed by regulation, the bank must file a report with the government. The regulations require that banks report each transaction in currency exceeding $10,000. Failure to report can result in civil and criminal penalties.

The stated purpose of the Act is to generate reports with a "high degree of usefulness in criminal, tax, or regulatory investigations." Congress recognized that criminals deal in cash. Thus, large cash transactions are suspect; they are often a clue to underlying criminal activity. As Congressman McKinney said, "What legitimate business in the United States of America today transfers money in cash?" Cash is the only practical medium in some businesses, and those are recognized in statutory exceptions. Usually, though, large cash transactions are indeed suspect. Moreover, cash is riskier than other types of paper due to the possibility of loss or theft. The willingness to accept the higher risk makes large cash transactions even more suspect. Thus, Congress concluded that reports of large currency transactions would be valuable in ferreting out crime.

The reporting statute and regulations take an indirect approach in that they only require information. Large cash transactions are not illegal, but they must be reported. Failure to report such transactions, however, is criminal. Once the bank files the report, people are free to deal in cash without constraints.

The bank reporting law attacks laundering by alerting the government to the process at its earliest point, the initial cash transactions. As the laundering process continues, the transactions become byzantine and more difficult to trace. The initial cash transactions are a vulnerable point because large amounts of cash are difficult to obscure. From the government's perspective, the cash transactions are an attractive target because they occur early in the laundering process and are conspicuous.

C. Problems with the Statute and the Judicial Response

The Act and regulations became effective in 1971. In the early years banks largely ignored the reporting law. United States attorneys apparently ignored the law as well, because few criminal cases were reported before the late 1970s. At that time, appellate case law began to develop, and the early cases upheld the prosecutions. Beginning in 1985, however, the cases revealed two distinct problems with the law.

One problem was that the regulations imposed the duty to report cash transactions over $10,000 only on banks. The question arose whether bank customers also had a duty to report these cash transactions. Some courts found that customers did have such a duty, and could therefore be held criminally liable for failure to file a report. These courts reasoned that customers were accomplices of the banks. Other courts refused to hold customers liable for failure to file a report on the basis that the regulations did not explicitly impose such a duty. Criminal liability therefore would be unconstitutional because the laws were too vague to provide fair notice. These courts often reasoned that while the enabling legislation granted the Secretary of the Treasury authority to require "any . . . participant" to file reports, the Secretary's regulations required only that "financial institutions" do so. Thus, the courts concluded, although he had the power, the Secretary specifically had chosen not to require reports from individuals.

Another problem with the reporting law was that the regulations imposed a duty to report only if the cash transaction exceeded $10,000. Assume that Joe, a smurf, is in charge of converting cash drug profits into cashier's checks. To do his job well, he does some research and finds that he can avoid the reporting requirement by manipulating cash transactions so none exceeds $10,000. The cases began to reveal such schemes. The number of variables involved in financial transactions allowed smurfs like Joe endless opportunities for manipulation. The variables included the number of banks, the number of branch offices of a particular bank, the number of teller stations at one branch office, the number of instruments purchased, the number of accounts at a particular bank, the time period during which the transactions were conducted, and the number of persons doing the transactions. Manipulating these variables to keep each transaction under $10,000 required manpower. The armies of lower level operatives who appeared in banks became known as smurfs. As they scurried from bank to bank executing transactions just under the $10,000 reporting limit, they seemed to be everywhere, much like the little blue cartoon characters.

These schemes exploited the lack of any aggregation requirement in the statutes or regulations that defined a $10,000 transaction. The instructions on the back of the reporting form provided for aggregation, but whether these instructions could serve as the basis for criminal prosecution was uncertain at best. Some courts specifically found the instructions to be nonbinding.

The judicial response to the smurfs' use of multiple transactions to avoid filing a report was mixed. In some limited circumstances, courts were willing to collapse the transactions and aggregate the amounts to reach $10,000, thus rendering the defendant liable for failure to file. Generally, though, courts refused to aggregate transactionsand declared the defendants' conduct noncriminal. These courts reasoned that no language in the statute or regulations imposed a duty to aggregate transactions. A criminal conviction therefore would be unconstitutional because nothing clearly warned the defendant that the conduct was criminal. The courts that refused to find defendants liable often stated that it was

for Congress or the Executive to declare conduct criminal, not the courts. Noting further that a Comptroller General's report had identified this aggregation loophole, the courts relied on the Secretary's subsequent inaction to conclude that the Secretary knew of the problem but apparently had chosen not to cure it.

Disagreement on the issues of customer liability and aggregation of transactions caused a split in the circuits. The two issues raised distinct questions. Sometimes a case would present just one of these issues, but frequently they were intertwined. When that happened, courts generally failed to distinguish the issues. The law grew into confused disarray.

D. Governmental Response to Misadventure in the Courts

The government responded to these problems. The Secretary of the Treasury amended the regulations, and Congress passed a new criminal statute.

1. Revised Regulations to Address Aggregation

The Secretary amended the regulations of the bank reporting law to deal with the aggregation question. First, a new regulation clarified the status of branch banks. The old regulations did not specifically address this issue, but the definitions of "bank" and "financial institution" suggested that each branch was a separate entity. Thus, transactions conducted at multiple branches of one institution would not be aggregated. Despite the language in these definitions, the courts concluded that transactions occurring at different branches of one institution should be combined. The new regulation modified the definition of financial institution to reflect the courts' conclusion. This modification codified the cases and left the law essentially unchanged.

The Secretary also adopted a regulation that codified the aggregation instructions on the back of the reporting form. As noted above, the reporting form included aggregation instructions, but the force of these instructions was unclear and the courts were reluctant to rely on them as the basis of a criminal prosecution. This uncertainty has been cured now that the instructions are embodied in a regulation. The new regulation provides: "Multiple currency transactions shall be treated as a single transaction if the financial institution has knowledge that they are by or on behalf of any person and result in either cash in or cash out totaling more than $10,000 during any one business day."

This regulation requires that three conditions exist before multiple transactions are treated as one. The transactions must be "by or on behalf of any person," the transactions must amount to over $10,000 cash in or cash out in a single day, and the bank must have knowledge of both these conditions. If any one of these conditions fails, then multiple transactions are not treated as a single transaction. Assuming that each individual transaction is for less than $10,000, the bank has no duty to report.

This regulation raises several questions, some of which are resolved in the comments accompanying the amendments. For example, the comments indicate that only total cash in or cash out must be aggregated. If $8000 and then $4000 are deposited in one account, the transactions must be aggregated, but if $8000 is deposited and then $4000 is withdrawn, aggregation is not required. Another question the regulation does not explicitly address is whether deposits one person makes to multiple accounts, or deposits multiple people make to a single account, must be combined into a single transaction. The comments indicate that in these situations, the presence of a single person or single account means that transactions involving that person or account must be combined and treated as a single transaction.

Other questions the regulation raises are not addressed in the comments. One such question is the meaning of the requirement that the transaction be "by or on behalf of any person." The regulations define "person" as broadly as possible. This language is literally meaningless because one cannot possibly conjure up a transaction that is not "by or on behalf of any person." The drafters probably meant to refer to transactions by or on behalf of a person or any single person, but were wary of limiting the regulation in this way. To have any meaning, the regulation should be interpreted to mean by or on behalf of a person.

Another question is whether multiple transactions must be treated as one if all three conditions are met, but the cash in or cash out is transferred at different banks. The government's position is that a bank is under no duty to aggregate transactions conducted at different banks, even if the bank has knowledge of the other transactions. The regulation as originally proposed would have captured this situation and required aggregation, but the Secretary rejected that regulation, at least temporarily, in favor of the one adopted.

The amended regulations leave some options open to the ambitious launderer. For example, Joe can manipulate time by limiting his cash transactions to $10,000 or less each day. This is an unattractive option, however, because the laundering process will be too slow for the volume of cash that many drug organizations generate. Another option, assuming Joe uses only a single bank, is to use multiple accounts and multiple agents to limit the bank's knowledge of the relationship between multiple transactions. If the bank lacks such knowledge, it has no duty to treat multiple transactions as single. Finally, Joe can use multiple banks during a single day because the regulations do not require aggregation of transactions conducted at different banks. So long as the transaction at each bank does not exceed $10,000, the bank has no reporting obligation.

2. Recognizing a New Crime

Because launderers still could avoid the aggregation regulations in these ways, the regulations were an incomplete solution to the holes in the reporting law. Thus Congress enacted a new statute, which provides that no person shall for the purpose of evading the reporting requirements (1) cause a financial institution to fail to file a required report; (2) cause a financial institution to file a required report with an omission or misstatement; or (3) structure any transaction with one or more financial institutions. Sanctions for violating this statute include forfeiture, civil penalties, and criminal sanctions of up to $250,000 in fines, five years in prison, or both. The statute is officially titled "Structuring transactions to evade reporting requirement prohibited." Unofficially, the statute should be called the "anti-smurfing statute," in honor of the smurfs who prompted it.

III. THE ANTI-SMURFING STATUTE

A. Elements and Theory of the Offense

1. Clause (1)

Clause (1) takes conduct previously defined as criminal, failure of a bank to file a report, and extends liability to any person who causes that failure. This amounts to an accomplice liability provision tailored to the specific crime of failing to file a report. Federal law includes a general accomplice liability statute, but the courts have disagreed on its applicability to non-reporting. Congress responded to this disagreement by adopting this particularized accomplice liability provision.

This provision of clause (1) is obsolete today. Assume Joe goes to Bank A at ten o'clock, one o'clock, and three o'clock. Each time he buys a $4000 cashier's check with cash. To find Joe in violation of clause (1), Bank A must have a duty to file a report, and must fail to do so. Under the regulations, Bank A has a duty to file only if it knows that multiple transactions for one person total cash in or cash out over $10,000 in one day. If Bank A meets these criteria, i.e., it knows of Joe's three transactions, how could Joe "cause" its failure to file?

The explanation for this anomaly is historical. Congress drafted and adopted clause (1) of the anti-smurfing statute before the Secretary of the Treasury revised the regulations to impose the aggregation requirement. Because clause (1) was designed to impose liability on customers, the bank's knowledge was irrelevant. Under the revised regulation, however, if the bank is ignorant of one person's multiple transactions in one day, it has no duty to combine the transactions and therefore no duty to file a report. Joe's three trips, of course, caused the bank's ignorance and its consequent lack of duty to file. Even so, Joe cannot be held liable for causing failure to perform an act that the bank had no duty to perform.

Clause (1) also contains an attempt provision. Federal law includes no general attempt statute, but instead incorporates attempt language in individual statutes. When Congress defines a new crime, it routinely includes attempt language. The attempt language of clause (1) still is vital under the regulations because it encompasses situations in which a customer attempts to mislead a bank, but the bank discovers the attempt and files a report. For example, assume Joe goes to Bank B at two o'clock and pays $9000 cash for a cashier's check, then returns at four o'clock and does the same. To avoid a report, Joe uses false identification on the four o'clock trip. Bank B discovers that Joe accomplished both transactions and files a report. Under clause (1), the government can charge Joe with attempting to cause Bank B to fail to file.

2. Clause (2)

Clause (2) makes it a crime to cause a bank to file a report containing a material omission or misstatement. In this situation, the bank is aware of the cash transaction over $10,000. The bank reporting law already defines making any misstatement in a report as a crime. Clause (2) of the anti-smurfing statute extends liability to those who cause misstatements. Clause (2) also imposes criminal liability for causing a material omission in a report, conduct the bank reporting law does not reach.

Another criminal statute, 18 U.S.C. § 1001, affects the same conduct. Causing the filing of a bank report with an omission may be criminal under section 1001, and causing the filing of a false report is always criminal under section 1001. Therefore, clause (2) of the anti-smurfing statute defines new criminal conduct in some omission fact patterns. In most cases, however, its impact is to impose another layer of liability to conduct already deemed criminal under other laws.

In addition, like clause (1), clause (2) prohibits attempts to cause incomplete or false filings. This attempt language defines new criminal conduct.

3. Clause (3)

Clause (3) defines an entirely new crime. Clause (3) makes it illegal to structure any transaction with one or more banks for the purpose of evading the reporting requirement. This clause addresses both problems the original bank reporting statute raised: customer liability and manipulation of transactions.

Clause (3) establishes customer liability by imposing liability on anyone who assists or attempts to assist in structuring a transaction. Yet the crux of clause (3) relates to manipulation; it closes the loopholes remaining under the revised regulations.

As noted above, launderers have three methods available under the revised regulations to avoid aggregation and the duty to report. Clause (3) covers each of these. First, the crime of structuring is not limited to transactions accomplished in a particular time period. Thus, transactions that would avoid aggregation under the regulations because $10,000 or less was transferred during one day would still qualify as structured transactions under clause (3). Second, because the crime of structuring does not depend on the bank's knowledge, using multiple agents and multiple accounts to keep the bank in the dark on the total transactions would not defeat liability under clause (3). Third, the crime of structuring includes transactions accomplished at "one or more domestic financial institutions," so conducting the transactions at multiple banks will not avoid liability. This clause is independent of the aggregation regulation, thus it prohibits all structuring regardless of whether the bank has a duty to file a report.

The mens rea required for the crime of structuring is two-tiered. Conviction of any crime under the reporting laws requires willfulness. In addition, the anti-smurfing statute requires that the defendant act for the purpose of evading the bank reporting law. The combination of these two mens reas, each of which is rigorous alone, makes the mens rea element even more difficult to prove.

The conduct element is defined less precisely. It is illegal to "structure" a "transaction." The regulations define the term "transaction in currency" as a physical transfer of currency. The definition of "structure" is more complicated. The statute contains no explicit definition, and the popular definition is not helpful, so legislative intent is relevant. The legislative history reveals no explicit congressional statement of intent concerning the meaning of the term "structure." But the legislative history does include an example of structuring, and the testimony of the government drafters reveals what they intended by the term. In the drafters' view, "structuring" is "breaking up a single currency transaction of more than $10,000 into separate smaller transactions in order not to trigger the [report] filing requirements." This definition is bolstered by the courts' use of the term in this way in cases decided prior to the anti-smurfing statute. These definitions render the conduct element precisely congruous with the mens rea requirement.

Defining a criminal offense based on the structure of one's finances suggests an analogy to tax law. If

Joe can legitimately structure his finances to avoid paying taxes, is it not correspondingly legitimate to structure finances to avoid reporting cash transactions? The answer is no. The courts recognized that this analogy was faulty but failed to identify the reason. The analogy fails because the two acts, structuring finances to avoid paying taxes and structuring finances to avoid filing reports, have different purposes. When he structures to avoid taxes, Joe saves money but still provides information to the government. In contrast, when Joe structures to avoid the bank reporting law, he denies the government information. The statutory use of the term "evade" rather than "avoid" expresses the congressional conclusion that any reason to resist reporting is illegitimate and therefore an evasion. While one might legitimately avoid taxes, there exists no concept of legitimate avoidance of the reporting requirement.

The anti-smurfing statute is based implicitly on the judgment that resistance to reporting cash transactions is even more suspect than the large cash transactions themselves. This judgment is reasonable because no legitimate reason exists to resist reporting large cash transactions. The time it takes Joe to provide the bank with the information for the report is negligible, and it will not cost him any money when the bank files a report.

Joe might object to the bank filing a report on the basis that the report invades his privacy, and that it is a scary situation indeed when the government is entitled to collect information (unrelated to taxes) on financial arrangements. Perhaps Joe is averse to the government knowing about his transactions. When balanced against the threat to society that the drug trade and money laundering pose, however, the threat to Joe's privacy is not compelling. The reduction in privacy is minimal. This country has a tradition of protecting individual privacy from governmental interference, but in view of the documented dangers of drugs and laundering, laws that protect individual privacy at all costs have become a luxury. The anti-smurfing statute results in less than perfect individual privacy, but the harms of drugs and laundering warrant the minimal reduction. Congress in effect made this judgment when it defined structuring to evade the reporting law as a crime.

Beyond inconvenience and privacy, Joe may have another reason for resisting the reporting requirement. Joe may need to hide other criminal activity. This reason is patently illegitimate and is one the law should neither recognize nor endorse.

B. Knowledge of Illegality

The anti-smurfing statute applies only when the defendant acts for the purpose of evading the bank reporting requirement. Assume Joe goes to the bank five days in a row and each day pays $9000 in cash for a cashier's check. If Joe is unaware of the bank reporting law, he is not smurfing because he does not have the required motive to evade the bank reporting law. Joe is smurfing, however, if he is aware of the bank reporting law and structures his transactions to avoid a report. A smurfing conviction is impossible unless the defendant knows of the bank reporting law.

A separate question is whether a smurfing conviction is possible without knowledge of the anti-smurfing law as well. What happens if Joe knows of the bank reporting law and structures his transactions to avoid reporting, but is unaware that such structuring is itself a crime? In other words, is knowledge of illegality an element of smurfing, thus making ignorance of the anti-smurfing law a defense? Some defendants have recently asserted that ignorance of the law is in fact a defense.

The express terms of the anti-smurfing statute do not require knowledge of the law, so the question of whether knowledge of illegality is an element will be left to the courts. In United States v. Balint and United States v. Freed, the statutes prohibited selling narcotics and possessing unregistered hand grenades, respectively. Because the materials regulated were physically dangerous, the Supreme Court declined to infer knowledge of illegality as an element and thus concluded that ignorance of the law was no defense. Likewise, in United States v. International Minerals & Chemical Corp., the Court concluded that knowledge of the statute prohibiting shipping acid without proper documentation was not an element of the crime. The International Minerals Court reasoned that the maxim that ignorance of the law is no excuse was so ensconced in our criminal law that it trumps ambiguous congressional statements. Moreover, because acid is inherently dangerous, the probability of regulation was so great that knowledge of the law could be presumed. The Court's mention of the second basis undermines the first, and indicates the Court's ambivalence toward the maxim that ignorance of the law is no excuse.

That ambivalence culminated in United States v. Liparota, in which the Court held that ignorance of the law was a defense to the crime of unauthorized acquisition of food stamps. The anti-smurfing statute is more analogous to the statute construed in Liparota than those in Balint and Freed because the items the statutes regulate in the former, structured cash transactions and unauthorized food stamps, pose no physical danger. Many of the bases for the Liparota decision also apply to the anti-smurfing statute. The Liparota Court did not rely on congressional intent in construing the food stamp statute because it characterized the statutory language as ambiguous and the legislative history as silent. Likewise, the language and legislative history of the anti-smurfing statute both are silent on knowledge of illegality. The Liparota Court applied the rule of lenity and concluded that because the ambit of the statute was unclear, the defendant should get the benefit. Because the coverage of the anti-smurfing statute is unclear in the same way as the statute at issue in Liparota, the rule of lenity would have the same impact on the anti-smurfing statute. Thus Liparota would likely control the courts' interpretation of the anti-smurfing statute.

Yet one of the rationales of Liparota has questionable impact on the anti-smurfing statute. The Liparota Court held that requiring knowledge of illegality was appropriate in order to avoid criminalizing a broad range of innocent conduct. Applying this reasoning to the anti-smurfing statute, can structuring cash transactions to avoid a reporting law be characterized as innocent conduct?

Structuring cash transactions to avoid reporting might be construed as innocent. One reason is that people may feel that their experience with tax law informs them that structuring cash transactions is acceptable conduct. Although the tax law analogy is defective for reasons discussed above, courts should not expect this level of analysis from the typical bank customer. Another reason that structuring cash transactions might be innocent conduct is that this country historically has protected individual privacy from governmental intrusion. Arranging cash transactions to avoid a report to the government would strike many people as acceptable conduct, or at least noncriminal. At any rate, structuring cash transactions seems as likely to be deemed "innocent" as the conduct in Liparota, in which the defendant furtively bought food stamps that were stamped "nontransferable" at a substantial discount.

On the other hand, structuring cash transactions to avoid reporting to the government arguably is not innocent. To treat smurfing as innocent requires a narrow definition of innocence, one related only to the defendant's ignorance of this particular statute. Smurfs know of the bank reporting law and purposely evade it. As noted above, the only reason to avoid the reporting law is to hide other crime. Smurfing cannot be isolated from the laundering process, nor can it be isolated from the underlying crime that generates the cash. To define smurfing as innocent conduct demands both that we ignore the impetus for smurfing and adopt a compartmentalized definition of innocence. The law need not be limited to a fictional, counterintuitive definition of innocence. Smurfs are not necessarily innocent, even if they are unaware of the anti-smurfing statute.

The implications of Liparota for the anti-smurfing statute are mixed. Other factors are relevant in analyzing whether ignorance of the law should be a defense

to the anti-smurfing statute. Inferring knowledge of illegality can be helpful to limit arbitrary enforcement. If a statute is written broadly so that many violate it, the police freely may pursue the most blameworthy violators. Yet wide application allows police so much discretion that they may decide whom to arrest based on factors besides the violation of a statute. If a statute encourages arbitrary enforcement, then ignorance should be a defense. It would ensure that the law apply only to blameworthy people, and would limit police discretion by narrowing the wide net that such a law creates.

The anti-smurfing statute, however, does not encourage arbitrary enforcement. The statutory language defining the conduct of smurfing (to structure a transaction) is broad, but the mens rea requires a purposeful evasion of the bank reporting law. This mens rea limits the number of persons who violate the anti-smurfing statute and limits police discretion as well.

Another relevant question in determining whether ignorance should be a defense is the likelihood that the defendant had notice that the conduct was illegal. If nothing in the situation a statute addresses would alert a person to possible illegality, then ignorance should be a defense. Several factors illuminate the likelihood of notice. If the proscribed conduct is malum in se because it involves possible physical harm or has moral overtones, then the likelihood of notice is high. Smurfing involves no physical harm. As for moral overtones, smurfing is not as obviously immoral as fraud or statutory rape, but an effort to avoid the bank reporting law is not morally pure either. Smurfing arises only in the wake of an effort to evade another law. Although smurfing is morally ambiguous, Joe's intuition about criminal law should cause him at least to question its legality.

Other circumstances are relevant to the likelihood of the defendant's notice. One factor is how pervasively the field is regulated. Defendants generally have knowledge of the law if they deal with a highly regulated substance like alcohol. Regulation of cash transactions is not as pervasive. No state laws regulate cash transactions, and the only relevant federal laws are the ones this article describes. Nonetheless, a smurf by definition knows of the bank reporting law, although he may be ignorant of the anti-smurfing law. Because smurfs are aware of at least one law regulating cash transactions, the relatively limited extent of regulation does not indicate that smurfs' knowledge of the anti-smurfing law is less likely.

The specialized nature of smurfing also bears on the likelihood of the defendant's knowledge. A person dealing in an unusual substance like dangerous chemicals or toxic waste is more likely familiar with the law than a person dealing in pencils, dental floss, or paper clips. Cash transactions are not specialized activities, although extremely large transactions subdivided into smaller increments are more unusual. Even so, the basic commodity of the anti-smurfing law is cash transactions, which are difficult to put in the specialized category with acid and toxic waste.

Some factors affecting the likelihood of notice are unique to the anti-smurfing statute. Assume Joe sets out to convert $500,000 in cash into cashier's checks. Joe learns that the law requires banks to report cash transactions over $10,000 to the government, and he learns that reports can be avoided by simply keeping each transaction under $10,000. As a practical matter, Joe should question whether such easy evasion is too good to be true. The obviousness of the loophole should cause Joe to question its legitimacy, and alert him that he is acting in an area of questionable legality. Moreover, the Treasury Department is considering specific measures to provide notice of the law to bank customers. If any of these proposals is implemented, the likelihood that Joe will have knowledge of the law will be high.

The final issue in analyzing whether ignorance of the law should be a defense is whether ignorance of the law is itself blameworthy. If a reasonable person would be on notice of the possibility of criminal liability, then that person should investigate; continuing ignorance of the law is blameworthy in that situation. With regard to the anti-smurfing statute, the blameworthiness of ignorance is fairly clear. Smurfing is morally ambiguous enough that a defendant might not be certain the conduct is criminal. Yet the factors discussed above relating to the likelihood of knowledge indicate that smurfs should be alerted at least to the potential of liability. Once on notice of potential liability, smurfs reasonably may be expected to investigate the law. Smurfs know they are evading the reporting law. They obviously have researched the scope of the law, and know how to avoid it. Because smurfs are sophisticated enough to investigate the bank reporting law, it is reasonable to impose on them a duty to investigate related laws. If smurfs remain ignorant of the anti-smurfing statute, their ignorance is blameworthy and should not be a defense.

In summary, various factors indicate that ignorance of the law should not be a defense to the anti-smurfing statute. Admittedly, dealing in cash transactions is not a specialized activity. Structuring finances to avoid reporting to the government may seem acceptable in view of the tax avoidance analogy and the American tradition of privacy. Nevertheless, an ignorance defense is unnecessary to limit arbitrary enforcement. The likelihood is high that smurfs have notice that their conduct is questionable. Smurfs know of the bank reporting law, so they are aware that laws exist regulating cash transactions. Their effort to evade the bank reporting law

also has moral overtones; it only can be deemed innocent by adopting an extremely narrow definition of innocence. Practically, evasion of the bank reporting law is so easy, a smurf should wonder whether it is too good to be true. Once on notice that smurfing may be questionable, continuing ignorance of the law is blameworthy because smurfs have a duty to research the law as they did when they investigated the bank reporting law. On balance, ignorance of the anti-smurfing law should not be a defense to smurfing. Nonetheless, excessively cautious courts may establish it as a defense. The innocence and immorality of smurfing are ambiguous, and Liparota, . . . indicates that the Supreme Court is receptive to the defense. At a minimum, courts may fall back on the rule of lenity to establish ignorance as a defense. If the courts infer knowledge of illegality as an element of the offense, they should not require actual knowledge. Rather, the government should be able to establish mens rea by showing that the defendant should have known the law. This latter option, really a mens rea of negligence, is preferable to actual knowledge. The Court has suggested that this alternative is constitutionally acceptable. More importantly, requiring proof of actual knowledge would exceed the legitimate boundaries of ignorance as a defense. As discussed above, Joe has good reason to be on notice that smurfing is questionable, thus he should have a duty to investigate the law. In this context, Joe's lack of actual knowledge is due only to his negligence. Joe should not be allowed to assert his own negligence as a defense. And, as a practical matter, requiring the government to prove actual knowledge of the law would make prosecution for smurfing impossible in most cases.

The mens rea of negligence is a compromise between the alternatives that knowledge of illegality is irrelevant and that knowledge of illegality must be actual. Once the Treasury Department implements measures ensuring that bank customers are informed of the anti-smurfing law, the combination of these measures with the "should have known" standard for knowledge of illegality will eliminate the defense of ignorance of the law.

* * *

V. CONCLUSION

The anti-smurfing statute resulted from two determined forces converging: the incredibly lucrative drug trade in the United States, and the relentless effort of Congress to halt money laundering and contain the underlying drug trade.

The reporting law scheme was the government's first attack on money laundering. A central part of this scheme is the bank reporting law. When the bankers, prosecutors, and Joes of the world began to notice it, this legislation had an unpredicted consequence – the birth of smurfs. The bank reporting law experienced considerable difficulty in the courts. Soon the case law blossomed into gaudy disarray, and smurfs only occasionally were threatened. Congress quickly adopted the anti-smurfing statute.

The implicit message of the anti-smurfing statute is that no legitimate reason exists to keep large cash transactions secret. The very existence of the transactions is suspect; the bank reporting law acknowledges this. The anti-smurfing statute establishes that avoidance of the reporting law is unjustified. Reporting involves little time and negligible costs. The reports impose slightly on privacy, but weighed against the magnitude of damage that drugs and money laundering cause in our country, the reduction in privacy that the anti-smurfing statute causes is warranted. The only other reason to resist these reports is to hide other crime, either in generating the cash or in tax fraud. This objection to reporting is entitled to no weight and is accorded none.

One of the difficulties of curbing manipulation of the bank reporting law is drafting a law that is broad enough to be effective yet limited enough to avoid abuse. The anti-smurfing statute includes several guarantees against abuse. The mens rea requirement directs the government to prove the defendant acted with the motive of evading the bank reporting law. Smurfing is not totally innocent conduct, so criminal liability should not catch our friend Joe by surprise. Even so, under Liparota, the courts may infer knowledge of illegality as an element and thereby protect even further against abuse. Besides the integral role of mens rea, the anti-smurfing statute should be interpreted to incorporate other controls on abuse. First, the unit of prosecution should be defined to avoid undue proliferation of counts. Second, courts should define the relationship between the anti-smurfing statute and other federal crimes to allow multiple punishment with section 1001 and conspiracy, but not with the bank reporting law. Adopting these positions minimizes the danger of abuse.

The efficacy of the anti-smurfing statute in stemming the tide of laundered dollars is hard to predict. Investigation will be difficult because smurfs easily can obscure structured transactions. Prosecution also will be difficult, primarily because the government must prove the defendant's motive to evade the reporting law, although as a practical matter, this burden may shift to the defendant. Regardless of its efficacy, the adoption of a new crime also has symbolic importance in that it formally expresses society's condemnation of that conduct. Nonetheless, the symbolic importance of a crime is a not a sufficient justification for its existence. The law must confront reality; it cannot lapse into an intricate but irrelevant set of rules to be treated contemptuously and avoided as if in a cartoon. The anti-smurfing statute is a positive step to avoid that result.

I. Homicide

Kathleen F. Brickey, *Death in the Workplace: Corporate Liability for Criminal Homicide,* 2 NOTRE DAME J.L. ETHICS & PUB. POL'Y 753–790 (1987)*

INTRODUCTION

On June 14, 1985, a Cook County Illinois trial judge announced criminal homicide verdicts that sent shock waves through the nation's business community. Concluding an eight week nationally publicized bench trial, Circuit Judge Ronald Banks pronounced the Film Recovery Systems Corporation guilty of involuntary manslaughter and three of its officers guilty of murder in connection with the death of Stefan Golab, an undocumented Polish immigrant who succumbed to cyanide fumes while working at the firm's silver-reclamation plant.

Until these verdicts attracted our collective attention, the concept of corporate homicide prosecutions seemed anomalous. More curious still, the conviction of corporate executives for *murder* in connection with a work-related death was thought to be unprecedented. Extraordinary as they seemed, however, these verdicts signaled the development of similar trends elsewhere in the country and presaged announcements that district attorneys in Los Angeles and in Milwaukee county planned to investigate every workplace death occurring within their respective jurisdictions for possible criminal violations.

These developments have created a predictable set of concerns. Pursuit of aggressive prosecutorial policies may mean, for example, that every bad business judgment has potential criminal repercussions. If that is true, or perceived to be true, we must ask whether management can function effectively in that environment. Those who say it cannot argue that to subject companies and their managers to criminal liability on the basis of day-to-day business decisions would have "devastating effects" on the manner in which American business enterprises are conducted. This and other pragmatic concerns – among which are counted the

---

* Reprinted with permission of the author.

dangers sometimes inherent in the workplace—are making management wary.

These developments have also created concern that local law enforcement agencies are intruding into a domain in which Congress has delegated primary (and perhaps exclusive) jurisdiction to federal regulatory agencies. In the view of some, comprehensive federal statutes that address the problem of workplace hazards should preempt application of conventional state criminal statutes to sanction employers for creating or tolerating unsafe work environments. Businesses that operate nation-wide, the argument runs, should be governed by a single cohesive, civil and criminal regulatory scheme instead of an incoherent patchwork of federal, state and local regulations.

But perhaps the most perplexing problem confronting the business community is that of identifying a comprehensible rule of law under which corporations and their officers are held criminally responsible for workplace deaths and injuries. The Film Recovery Systems indictments charged that Mr. Golab was a victim of criminal homicide. But where is the instrumentality of death that felled him? There is, after all, no smoking gun or blood-stained weapon to incriminate these managers or the enterprise they controlled. And assuming there were, who would have wielded it? Who confronted this man and ended his life?

These issues are compelling, for we will rarely identify a corporate agent who has committed a direct act of aggression against the dead or injured worker. We are speaking, instead, of liability predicated as much upon what corporate officers neglect to do as it is upon their affirmative conduct. Thus, an underlying duty to act must be found, and it is here—in the source, nature and scope of that duty—that we gain insights into the governing rule of law. It is here that we find the conceptual basis for treating workplace "accidents" as assaults, batteries and homicides under the substantive law of crimes.

I. THE FILM RECOVERY SYSTEMS CASE—A PARADIGM

The allegation in the Film Recovery case is, at bottom, a charge that the company and its managers exposed Mr. Golab to work-place hazards that caused his untimely demise. The specific hazard was hydrogen cyanide gas, the byproduct of a cyanide solution used to recover silver from exposed x-ray film. Film Recovery Systems employees were exposed to the fumes directly while working around open cyanide vats and to ambient gas that hovered elsewhere in the plant as well.

On February 10. 1983, Stefan Golab left his post at a vat after complaining of nausea and dizziness. By the time he could reach the adjacent lunchroom, he had begun to shake and foam at the mouth. By the time his co-workers could carry him outside, his heart had stopped beating. By the time paramedics could transport him to a hospital, he was dead. That death is the paradigmatic homicide.

A. *The Manslaughter Charge Against FRS*

If we are to rely on reported case law as an historical measure of the frequency with which prosecutors have charged corporations with criminal homicide, we must conclude that these prosecutions were indeed anomalies. Corporate homicide prosecutions appear throughout this century as relatively isolated phenomena, only a few of which were inspired by industrial accidents.

The relative rarity of these prosecutions reflects in part the difficulty of convincing courts that juristic persons are proper homicide defendants. For despite the settled rule that corporations are capable of committing intentional torts, many courts have been reluctant to hold corporations capable of committing crimes with elements of personal violence or an evil state of mind.

Prosecutors in corporate homicide cases have encountered definitional obstacles as well. In jurisdictions where the common-law or statutory definition of criminal homicide was the killing of one human being *by another,* for example, most courts found that the "another"—i.e., the slayer—must be a member of the same class as the victim—i.e., a human being.

A few early cases permitted prosecutions to proceed, however, either because the court disagreed that the common-law definition was so restrictive as to require a human slayer or on the ground that under a statute making owners of vessels amendable to prosecution for manslaughter, a corporation clearly could be an "owner."

More recently amended penal codes have decreased the number of obstacles to corporate homicide prosecutions by omitting the troublesome "by another" element, by including corporations in the definition of "person," or by creating a comprehensive statutory scheme of corporate criminal liability in general.

Considering our paradigm within this framework, the Film Recovery Systems indictment could not, in all probability, have been maintained prior to a 1961 revision of the Illinois Criminal Code. Before that revision, Illinois courts had severely restricted corporate criminal liability to liability for misdemeanors for which a fine was an authorized punishment. Since corporate prosecutions for felonies and for offenses only punishable by death or imprisonment thus were precluded, the Illinois rule effectively shielded corporations from criminal homicide prosecutions.

Even without these judicially imposed general limitations on corporate criminal liability, the Illinois homicide statutes themselves would have posed formidable obstacles for corporate prosecutions. For while they defined murder and manslaughter as "the unlawful killing of a human being" without reference to the classification of the slayer, the only authorized punishment for these crimes was death or imprisonment—penalties obviously ill-suited for corporate defendants. Thus, it is by no means clear that corporations could have incurred criminal homicide liability under those statutes unless the issues of guilt and amenability to punishment could somehow be severed. While theoretically possible, that opposition was foreclosed by an Illinois criminal code provision requiring that all offenses defined by the code "shall be prosecuted and on conviction punished as by this act is prescribed, and not otherwise."

The Revised Illinois Criminal Code diminishes the theoretical barriers to corporate homicide prosecutions in several important respects. Film Recovery Systems was indicted under a statute that provides "[a] *person* who unintentionally kills an *individual* without lawful justification commits involuntary manslaughter" if the death-producing acts are performed recklessly and are likely to cause death or great bodily harm. The term "person" includes "an individual, public or private corporation, government, partnership, or unincorporated association." Although the term "individual" is not defined by statute, the clear implication is that "individual" denotes only natural persons while "person" denotes both natural and juristic persons. A literal reading of the revised code would thus permit an involuntary manslaughter prosecution against a corporate person to go forward, and Comments published in the code suggest that the Revision Committee did indeed contemplate that corporations might be liable for manslaughter in Illinois.

B. *The Murder Charge against FRS Executives*

It has long been recognized that corporate officers and agents who engage in criminal conduct during the course of their employment are personally accountable for their misdeeds. As early as the beginning of the eighteenth century—well before the common law worked through the theoretical barriers to prosecuting corporate entities—Chief Justice Holt observed in a dictum that "[a] corporation is not indictable but the particular members of it are." By the middle of the next century, the amenability of corporate agents to criminal prosecution for offenses committed on behalf of the corporation was a point on which there could be "no doubt."

But these judges were not speaking of murder. For the most part they were seeking to redress the creation of a public nuisance, the operation of a corporate enterprise without a proper license or without paying required taxes, the pursuit of unauthorized business activities, violation of regulatory statutes and the like. In Film Recovery Systems, on the other hand, the former president, the plant manager and the foreman of the company were prosecuted for killing an employee.

Notwithstanding the relatively greater frequency of purely regulatory prosecutions against corporate officers, as early as the beginning of this century managing officers of a steamship company were indicted under a federal manslaughter statute for failure to provide operable emergency equipment on a vessel that caught fire and sank, killing 900 people aboard. Prosecutions initiated under conventional manslaughter laws sporadically followed thereafter.

Thus, to the extent that the Film Recovery Systems prosecution sought to hold the managers criminally responsible for a death they caused during the course of their employment, the case against the officers—like that against the corporation itself—is unusual but not pioneering. To the extent that the charge against the Film Recovery Systems officers was murder—as opposed to manslaughter—no one could recall a single precedent for the prosecution.

II. BREACH OF DUTY

The indictment in the Film Recovery Systems case did not alleged that any of the defendants physically assaulted Mr. Golab. The fault in this case—if fault there may be—lies in their conduct of the enterprise and their failure to act where action was called for. The fault, therefore, is a derogation of duty. But breach of a duty will trigger liability only if the obligation is imposed by common law or statute. Breach of a moral duty alone does not suffice. Thus we must seek the nature and source of the duty that triggered this extraordinary criminal prosecution.

Common-law duties often arise by virtue of special personal or contractual relationships. Duties based on jural relationships such as parent and child or husband and wife are personal obligations owed by one to the other. Duties arising from contractual relationships, on the other hand, may be obligations that run either to the public or to particular individuals for whose benefit the contract has been made, including one's servants.

In the past, a master's contractual duties to rescue a seaman who falls overboard and to provide a stricken servant emergency medical care have provided foundations for criminal homicide charges. Liability imposed under these theories is limited, however, in that it arises only when the employer fails to respond to an emergency that renders the servant helpless.

To be sure, Stefan Golab's rapidly deteriorating condition utterly disabled him. But when the emergency arose, paramedics were quickly called to the scene. Thus, the indictment did not fault the defendants for neglecting to *respond* to the emergency. It faulted instead their failure to *prevent* the emergency from arising at all.

The indictment charged that the defendants failed to advise Mr. Golab of the nature and dangers of the chemicals used in the plant or to instruct him in the proper handling of the deadly poisons; that they failed to provide safety and first-aid equipment and health-monitoring systems; and that they failed to provide for proper storage, detoxification and disposition of cyanide used in the ordinary course of the company's business. These allegations are clearly based upon omissions to act. The indictment, however, failed to specify what legal duty would make these omissions actionable.

A. *Common-Law and Statutory Duties*

In our effort to define the defendants' duty toward Mr. Golab, we will rarely discover the source of the duty articulated in the reported criminal case law. It is found, instead, in the established body of agency and tort law that defines the limits of a master's obligation to protect his employees from workplace hazards.

Employers have a common-law duty to exercise ordinary care to provide a reasonably safe workplace in which their employees may perform their day-to-day tasks. Employees, in turn, are entitled to assume the employer's proper discharge of his obligation to them. To fulfill his duty the employer must inspect his business premises and equipment as often as is reasonably necessary, repair or alter dangerously defective conditions, and see that rules promulgated to insure workers' safety are enforced.

The duty to provide a safe workplace is "personal, continuous and non-delegable." Liability for fulfilling this implied-in-contract obligation cannot, therefore, be discharged by simply entrusting responsibility for its performance to another. The employer remains liable whether the person who acts in his stead performs the assigned function poorly or not at all.

It does not follow, however, that employers are insurers of their employees' safety or that they are liable for injuries caused by obvious and ordinary hazards known to the employees or merely incident to the business itself. Employers may satisfy the duty to provide a safe workplace by making reasonable efforts to avoid exposing their employees to risks greater than those normally incident to the employment and by warning workers of special risks and dangerous conditions.

As is true in a number of other jurisdictions, moreover, the Illinois legislature has imposed on employers a statutory duty to protect their employees from workplace hazards. The Illinois Health and Safety Act requires every employer "to provide reasonable protection to the lives, health and safety [of employees] and to furnish [them] employment and a place of employment which are free from recognized hazards that are causing or are likely to cause [them] death or serious physical harm.

It thus appears that the Film Recovery Systems indictment could well have premises liability either upon breach of a common-law contractual duty developed under master-servant law to protect workers from enhanced workplace hazards associated with an increasingly industrialized economy, or upon breach of a statutory duty to safeguard those same interests.

III. Culpability

Although the Film Recovery Systems indictment faulted the defendants for failing to discharge a duty to provide a reasonably safe workplace, we must recognize that we are speaking of a duty imposed by civil – not criminal – law, and that not every breach of a civil duty constitutes a crime. Indeed, common experience tells us that violation of a civil duty not to injury normally leads to tort liability or to statutory compensation for the injury under workman's compensation laws. The prosecutor customarily plays no role in this scheme of liability.

It is necessary, then, to establish a base line to differentiate civil and criminal wrongs. As part of that process, we must redirect our thinking momentarily and consider the role of omissions in the criminal law. Criminal liability is based upon conduct. Although some offenses are defined in terms of an omission to act, most definitions assume the commission of affirmative acts. The Illinois homicide statutes, for example, define homicide as the unlawful killing of a human being, and the act of killing usually consists of observable assaultive conduct. An omission to perform a legally required act, however, may also kill – as, for example, a parent's withholding of food and sustenance from an infant.

Thus, proof of an omission to act is proof of but one element – the conduct element – of a crime. Whether the conduct actually constitutes a crime depends in turn on the presence or absence of each of the other constituent elements of the offense – as, for example, causation.

As in the case of wrongful death liability in tort, criminal homicide liability requires a causal relationship between the conduct and the forbidden result. The conduct must not only be capable of killing, it must actually cause a death. But assuming for the moment that our defendants' failure to provide a safe workplace caused Mr. Golab's death—as Judge Banks was convinced that it did—what makes one unintentional loss of life a wrongful death under the civil law and another a criminal homicide? And why were Film Recovery Systems' officers charged with so serious a crime as murder?

The answer lies in the role of the mental element in criminal liability. To constitute a crime, prohibited conduct must be accompanied by a culpable mental state. Whereas a plaintiff suing in tort need only prove negligence (failure to exercise ordinary care) and one seeking recovery under workmen's compensation law is relieves of proving any fault at all, the state is not similarly situated in a criminal homicide prosecution. For in addition to proving the defendant's conduct bore a causal relationship to the death, the state must also establish mens rea, a blameworthy state of mind.

Film Recovery Systems and its managers were charged with different degrees of homicide—involuntary manslaughter and murder—that are distinguished from one another only by the required state of mind. Involuntary manslaughter consists of recklessly causing the death of another. To act recklessly in this context is to act with conscious disregard of a substantial and unjustifiable risk that the conduct will cause death. To be reckless, the actor's disregard of the risk must constitute a gross deviation from the standard of care a reasonable person would observe under the circumstances.

Manslaughter is augmented to murder when the conduct is accompanied by a more blameworthy state of mind. Murder, under Illinois law, consists of death-producing conduct that is accompanied by intent to do great bodily harm, by knowledge that the conduct will cause death, or by knowledge that the conduct creates a strong probability of death or great bodily harm. The prosecution did not proceed, then, on the theory that the corporate managers carelessly disregarded an insignificant risk. It proceeded instead on the theory that these men knew it was likely that workers exposed to conditions existing at the plant would be killed or seriously injured. That is, indeed, a serious accusation.

And what evidence warrants such harsh accusations against them? Let us examine the circumstances that led to their prosecution.

The Employees: At any given time approximately 30 workers were employed to man the cyanide vats. Most were Hispanic or Polish immigrants and most, if not all, were undocumented and non-English speaking. In the prosecutor's view, this hiring practice was inspired by the belief that the immigrants would be reluctant to complain about conditions at the plant, partly because

of their inability to understand English and partly out of fear that their illegal status would be exposed.

Stefan Golab, an undocumented Polish immigrant who spoke no English, had worked at the Film Recovery Systems plant for about two and a half months.

Plant Conditions: The workers mixed dry sodium cyanide with water to produce a cyanide solution in which used film chips were immersed as part of the silver recovery process. The cyanide solution was stored in open vats which gave off noxious fumes that caused burning in the eyes and throat, difficult breathing, dizziness, and nausea. These symptoms were common not only among employees who were regularly exposed to the fumes, but to occasional visitors to the plant as well.

Notwithstanding that no emission-control devices were installed over the vats and that the plant was poorly ventilated, the level of cyanide gas in the plant was not monitored. The workers commonly complained about inadequate ventilation and some—including Golab himself—had asked to be transferred to another plant to escape the sickening fumes. It was later determined that the level of cyanide in the air exceeded permissible federal standards.

The workers' daily routines included mixing cyanide granules with water, stirring film chips in the solution with long rakes, removing cyanide saturated chips from the vats, and cleaning the tanks in preparation for the next batch. Yet few safety precautions were evident. Flimsy paper masks and cloth gloves were about all that protected these workers from the deadly substance around which they worked, and their cloth gloves became saturated with cyanide. As a result of direct contact with the solution, some workers suffered chemical burns and partial loss of eyesight.

According to the product label, cyanide can be fatal in three different ways: (1) ingestion; (2) absorption into the skin; and (3) inhalation of hydrogen cyanide gas. The workers were not told, however, what the chemical was, how hazardous it could be, or what precautions should be taken when working with it. Instead, a sign with the word "poison" written in English and in Spanish was posted without further explanation. Mr. Golab spoke neither English nor Spanish.

Causation: Stefan Golab died of acute cyanide toxicity. The cyanide level found in his blood was twice the lethal dose.

Mr. Golab's co-workers, former FRS employees, insurance and government inspectors, and police officers who investigated the incident on the day Golab died testified that conditions at the plant were unbearable. According to the investigating officers, a "yellowish haze" that hovered over the area where Golab had been working was abrasive to their eyes and throats and made them feel nauseous. The symptoms they described are classical effects of exposure to high levels of hydrogen cyanide gas.

Culpability: The three individual defendants who were convicted knew that cyanide was regularly used at the plant and that cyanide could be fatal. All of them knew of the workers' complaints about conditions at the plant and the physical symptoms they routinely endured.

Yet the defendants failed to disclose to the workers what they themselves knew about hazards in the plant. Some trial testimony suggests, moreover, that they may have actively concealed the nature and extent of the danger as well. A bookkeeper, for example, testified she had been instructed not to use the word "cyanide" in the presence of plant workers and not to linger in the part of the plant where the fumes were heaviest. Another witness testified that he had observed the removal of skull and crossbones symbols from vats containing the deadly poison, and yet another that he had been told to lie to safety inspectors after Mr. Golab died.

Upon evidence such as this Judge Banks concluded that the individual defendants operated the silver-reclamation plant in a manner they knew created a strong probability of death or great bodily harm and upon which he judged them guilty of murder.

And what of the corporation? Upon what state of the evidence was Film Recovery Systems found guilty of involuntary manslaughter? The indictment alleged that the company authorized and performed acts of commission and omission through the individual defendants acting in their managerial capacities. Under Illinois law, a corporation may be held criminally liable for acts of its board of directors or high managerial agents—i.e., corporate officers and other agents who have comparable authority either to formulate corporate policy or to supervise subordinate employees in a managerial capacity—acting within the scope of their employment.

The corporate prosecution, then, proceeded on the theory that the president, vice-president and plant foreman caused Mr. Golab's death while acting within the scope of their authority as managers of the firm. Judge Banks concluded that the corporation recklessly tolerated mismanagement of its affairs by allowing its officers and managers to conduct its business in a manner that led to the death of one employee and to the injury of numerous others. That, in his view, amply supported the verdict of guilt.

Each of the defendants was, in addition, convicted of fourteen counts of reckless conduct for recklessly injuring or endangering other employees by failing to disclose the identity and properties of the cyanide products in the plant and failing to take appropriate measures to assure their safety.

IV. ALTERNATIVE APPROACHES

And where is the wisdom in all of this? Let us examine the consequences of entrusting resolution of the Film Recovery Systems problem to local law enforcement agencies. Three corporate officers, each convicted of murder and fourteen counts of reckless conduct, have been fined and sentenced to serve twenty-four years in prison for mismanaging the firm. A defunct corporation, convicted of involuntary manslaughter and fourteen counts of reckless conduct, has been sentenced to pay a fine. To achieve these results, it was necessary to rely upon a novel application of state penal laws to deal with what is at bottom a tragic industrial accident.

There are, of course, alternative approaches, principal among them the federal Occupational Safety and Health Act (OSHA). Congress enacted OSHA in 1970 to respond to a "worsening trend" in the safety record of American industry. With this legislation, Congress strove to remedy not just problems indigenous to particular industries but to respond, instead, to a problem of urgent national concern. More Americans were being killed on the job than had been killed in the Vietnam war.

To promote OSHA's goal of providing all American workers "safe and healthful working conditions," Congress authorized the Secretary of Labor to set mandatory safety and health standards for businesses that affect interstate commerce and encouraged other initiatives to reduce occupational deaths, injuries, and illnesses.

OSHA's scheme of liability derives from the imposition of two duties upon employers. The first is a general duty to furnish employees "employment and a place of employment which are free from recognized hazards that are causing or are likely to cause death or serious physical harm." The second is a duty to comply with specific occupational safety and health rules promulgated by the Secretary of Labor. Violation of either of these duties is punishable by a civil fine that may be imposed administratively, and willful violation of a specific rule or regulation is punishable as a crime when the violation results in an employee's death.

OSHA's regulatory scheme seems well tailored to our paradigm. The regulations, for example, require employers to instruct employees in the safe and proper handling of poisonous or toxic materials used in the workplace; to advise them of potential hazards and of personal protective measures needed to avoid injury; to provide appropriate first aid services and medical attention; to provide personal protective equipment for employees exposed to hazardous conditions; to classify the hazard potential of open surface tanks like the cyanide vats and to ventilate the tanks to a degree that eliminates the hazard to workers.

Since OSHA directly addresses a host of technical industrial health and safety issues upon which our homicide verdicts of necessity are based, we must inquire whether it would make better sense to fit the Film Recovery Systems case into this model of liability and view OSHA as the appropriate—and perhaps exclusive—mechanism through which employers are penalized for workplace deaths and injuries. Although that prospect has simplicity and logic to recommend it, closer scrutiny undermines its initial appeal.

First, the civil enforcement scheme is relatively weak. The Act is directed primarily toward prevention of work-related injuries and illnesses. Although an employer may be cited and fined for violations that have yet to produce a single injury, a principal purpose of these citations is abatement of the unsafe condition or practice. Imposition of a monetary penalty is purely discretionary unless the violation is designated as "serious," and the maximum civil penalty for serious violations is $1,000. Thus the civil penalty structure has no *in terrorem* deterrent value, especially where correction of the violation would be more costly than the penalty.

The limited compliance incentives the Act provides are further undercut by budgetary and staffing constraints. OSHA has so few inspectors that it is able to inspect only a small fraction of covered workplaces annually. And under a Reagan administration policy initiated in 1981, OSHA field agents could inspect only businesses whose injury rates exceeded the national average, as determined by examination of employer-maintained injury records.

That policy effectively prevented an OSHA inspector, who visited the Film Recovery Systems office *before* Golab died, from entering the plant to observe the offending conditions. Although workers later testified that they wee sent home for days at a time to rest rather than receiving treatment for signs of poisoning, the company records reflected little time lost due to work-related injury or illness. In consequence, the inspector could not inspect a plant that had become or was about to become "a huge gas chamber" that was "totally unsafe."

The results of the few inspections that actually do occur scarcely reflect an aggressive enforcement policy. In fiscal year 1983, for example, the average penalty assessed for serious violations—that is, violations that create a probability of death or serious physical harm—was less than $200. And because the Commission may take into consideration the appropriateness of any particular penalty in light of the size of the business and other related factors, the penalty ultimately imposed may result from a compromise that does not accurately reflect the true gravity of the violation. Indeed, recent policy changes encourage "settlement" of citations by eliminating or reducing financial penalties in exchange for the employer's promise to abate the hazardous condition and comply with the law.

Considering these factors in tandem, a three-year study of OSHA conducted by the congressional Office of Technology Assessment concluded that "given the low probability of inspections and the relatively low penalty rates, the incentive for complying with OSHA standards before an OSHA inspection occurs is actually quite low." Thus, the nature and enforcement history of the civil compliance scheme suggest that it is an unreliable tool for protecting worker health and safety.

OSHA's criminal enforcement mechanism has proven no more effective. For a number of possible reasons, only seven criminal OSHA prosecutions were instituted during the first twelve years the statute was in effect. One obvious disincentive to proceeding under OSHA's criminal provision is that for first time offenders, the maximum fine for willful criminal violations is the same as the maximum fine for willful civil violations. Thus, when the employer is a corporation or other entity that cannot suffer imprisonment, the Commission may perceive little or no immediate value in referring the matter to the Justice Department for criminal prosecution. Unless the conduct of an employer who is an individual—as opposed to an entity—is so egregious that imprisonment seems an appropriate sanction to pursue, OSHA provides little incentive to follow the criminal enforcement route.

Whether Congress meant to extend liability beyond the corporate employer to the corporation's responsible officers and agents is not entirely clear, moreover. The term "employer" is defined to mean "a person engaged in a business affecting commerce who has employees." Although a number of individual agents have been cited for civil and criminal OSHA violations court have, on occasion, cast doubt on the question whether individual corporate agents are employers within the contemplation of this definition. Thus, it remains uncertain whether OSHA's scheme of liability ascribes personal fault to individual business managers, except in the case of a sole proprietor who had not the foresight to do business in corporate form.

To conclude under these circumstances (as one judge seems to have done) that OSHA preempts the use of state laws to penalize employers who act in disregard of their employees' safety would create an obvious enforcement void. But laying aside policy considerations for the moment, the preemption argument fairly misses the mark. Since Congress specifically provided that

OSHA shall not be construed to supersede or affect employers' common-law or statutory duties and liabilities relating to work-related employee deaths and injuries, it is difficult to construct a credible argument that Congress nonetheless intended to preclude the use of state penal statutes to punish employers who recklessly kill and injure in the workplace.

V. COMPETING POLICIES

A decision to permit imposition of criminal liability in a case like this inevitably requires the balancing of competing policy considerations. Corporate enterprises like Film Recovery Systems are engaged in legitimate commercial activity, and if local prosecutors are to second-guess reasoned business judgments, we must recognize the risk that adverse consequences may follow. It may be unwise to permit a jury to speculate about management's knowledge of the probability of death or injury, for example, for once the untoward result has occurred the jury acts with the benefit of hindsight. Managers who would otherwise choose to assume an active role in making the workplace safer may therefore feel a need to insulate themselves from learning too much lest they become subject to criminal prosecution for making an erroneous business judgment.

Despite its facial appeal as a means of limiting liability, remaining ignorant of crucial facts is at best a dubious solution for management's dilemma. Under the willful blindness/conscious avoidance doctrine—which is well established in other contexts—deliberate ignorance of the truth may serve as a substitute for positive knowledge. One who deliberately closes his eyes to the obvious may be charged with knowledge of that which he ought to have seen, so guilty knowledge may be inferred when others in the actor's situation would have known facts he has consciously avoided discovering himself. The willful blindness/conscious avoidance standard thus may prevent corporate management "from circumventing criminal sanctions merely by deliberately closing [their] eyes to the obvious risk that [they are] engaging in unlawful conduct."

But lines of corporate authority are often blurred. Corporations are, after all, organized and managed by committees and boards, and this fact of organization life makes more difficult the task of tracing where responsibility ultimately should lie. To ascribe personal blame to a few select individuals when responsibility is collective raises the disquieting spectre that one who has neither authority nor control over an offending hazard may be held to account for failing to prevent or abate it. The unfairness inherent in that prospect suggests compelling grounds for declining to pierce the corporate veil.

The law is not so illogical, however, as to punish one for failing to accomplish that which is beyond his power to achieve. The duty must, therefore, coalesce with the capacity to act, and one cannot act upon that over which he wields no control. Thus, a corporate officer's inaction constitutes a criminal omission only if he has some degree of affirmative control—albeit indirect—over the critical operation.

But even assuming a degree of control, what about the danger that may be inherent in the workplace? Consider a construction site, for example. There is at least a substantial risk (if not a probability) that one of the construction workers at a high-rise building site will be killed or seriously injured on the job, and that risk is clearly known and understood by the construction company's management. Does it therefore follow that the managers are forever in peril of criminal prosecution for the foreseen (or at least foreseeable) death or injury when it occurs?

The answer, of course, is no. As a general matter, employees are deemed to assume the ordinary risks inherent in the nature of their work. When the market functions as we expect it to, they will have taken the risks into consideration when they arrange their compensation. The construction workers with whose fate we are concerned are paid to assume commensurately greater risks, and their employers presumably have an interest in protecting them from injury.

But if the picture portrayed by the prosecution in the Film Recovery Systems case is reasonably accurate, the market can fail miserably. For rather than discovering that the hazards were accounted for in the employees' compensation arrangement, we find the situation at Film Recovery Systems portrayed as the exploitation of unskilled workers who urgently needed gainful employment. Laboring under what they knew were unbearable conditions, they were both helpless to complain and unable to appreciate the lethal nature of the hazard to which they were routinely exposed.

If the prosecution's evidence is to be believed, moreover, Film Recovery Systems' management concealed the danger even after Mr. Golab died. One co-worker who continued to work at the plant testified that he was not informed that Golab had died. He was told, instead, that Golab was recovering and that the workers "shouldn't worry about it." And according to an OSHA inspector who visited the plant after Golab died, the company president even then expressed his desire not to overemphasize plant hazards for fear of scaring the workers away.

But working with cyanide—like doing high-rise construction work—will always pose risks, and the risks are incurred at the behest of enterprises engaged in socially useful pursuits. Taking risks – perhaps even substantial risks – may be necessary to encourage socially productive activity. At what point, then, do we say the employer's risk taking becomes a criminal matter?

The line of demarcation between acceptable and unacceptable risks obviously cannot be drawn solely with reference to the degree of risk involved. It must accommodate, instead, both the utility and morality of risk-taking under a given set of circumstances. Thus, to ascribe criminal culpability requires more than a finding that a risk is substantial. It must be both substantial and *unjustified*.

To expose one's employees to known risks would be warranted, for example, if the risks are inherent in the nature of the work and reasonable precautions have been taken to minimize them. Thus, the construction company management would be justified in having a properly trained and equipped welder work on the twentieth floor of a steel superstructure, provided that permanent or temporary flooring, guardrails, safety nets, safety lines, or other appropriate safety devices were in place. In stark contrast, to expose one's employees to concealed risks when few – if any – precautions have been taken, would be manifestly unjustifiable.

Management's decision to proceed in either case inevitably affects the bottom line, of course. At some point management must make a calculated cost-benefit judgment about profitability, and one can only draw unfavorable inferences from the Film Recovery Systems trial. One worker testified, for example, that the only response to his complaints about inadequate plant ventilation was "no money." Yet when silver prices were climbing, the company grossed $13-20 million annually and capitalized on the favorable market by expanding its operation.

As this expansion occurred, a worker's compensation insurance inspector noted that the converted warehouse contained too many vats. But business is business. To meet market demands for the reclaimed silver, the number of cyanide vats more than doubled. In the meantime, management offices were moved to newly acquired space in an adjacent building. And as of the date of Stefan Golab's death, not a soul would claim – or even acknowledge – responsibility for plant operations or conditions.

CONCLUSION

If only one lesson were to be drawn from this unfortunate state of affairs it would be this: issues of workplace safety must transcend profit maximization. We cannot allow management to follow the line of least resistance by foregoing – on economic grounds –

a course of action that would make a workplace safe while at the same time pursuing – on pragmatic grounds – a course of action that masks the seriousness of the hazards in order to minimize their workers' concerns. The law should not permit them "to make so unsociable a gamble."

Suppose, however, – as his lawyer insists – that the rise of the president of this enterprise represents the "epitome of the American dream." These were not, after all, wealthy captains of industry. They began a modest business that became, in the end, a casualty of a declining market and its own management style. Is it appropriate to invoke the threat of criminal prosecution as a barrier to market entry for the inexperienced, and perhaps the unwise?

The answer may be yes. Every year the introduction of toxic substances and other hazardous products and processes into the work environment becomes increasingly commonplace. As the dangers inherent in the workplace increase, one might posit, so should the entrepreneurial stakes be raised. Inexperience and undercapitalization are, after all, inadequate to justify industrial Russian roulette. Thus, threatened use of criminal prosecution in cases like this may discourage the proliferation of irresponsible businesses in industries where they threaten the most harm.

That purpose need not be singular, however. For even though some would suggest that this episode could not have occurred in a normal corporate environment, we are left to wonder why that is true. Can we forget so quickly the many dead or dying asbestos workers whose claims still languish in the courts, for example? We cannot dismiss out of hand the charge that known dangers to those workers were concealed or minimized by the asbestos industry for a considerable period of years. Nor can we dismiss out of hand the charge that consumer product manufacturers likewise make – at least on occasion – cost benefit decisions that exalt profit over life and limb, that calculate the economics of anticipated wrongful death claims resulting from a known and correctable hazard and then offset against that cost the economics of preventing the deaths.

Perhaps, then, it is not inappropriate that the criminal justice system should play a role in the regulatory process when management crosses the line. It may play a particularly effective role at that, for the prosecutor has at his disposal the coercive investigatory powers of the state. His investigation, moreover, is immune from the automatic stays in bankruptcy proceedings that permit witnesses and claimants to die and evidence to grow stale before the truth can be found and the blameworthy judged accountable. Perhaps, upon reflection, the criminal justice system will prove to be a highly desirable regulatory alternative because of the swiftness and sureness of its response.

Note, *Getting Away With Murder: Federal OSHA Preemption of State Criminal Prosecutions for Industrial Accidents,* 101 HARV. L. REV. 535 (1987)*

Stephan Golab, a 59-year-old illegal immigrant from Poland, worked for a year stirring tanks of sodium cyanide at the Film Recovery Services plant in Elk Grove, Illinois. On February 10, 1983, Golab became dizzy from the cyanide fumes, went into convulsions, and died. The federal Occupational Safety and Health Administration (OSHA) inspected the plant after the accident and fined the company $4855 for twenty safety violations but later halved the penalty.

The State's Attorney for Cook County took stronger action, filing criminal charges against the company and its officials. Three officials were convicted of murder and fourteen counts of reckless conduct and were sentenced to twenty-five years in prison. The company was also convicted of manslaughter and reckless conduct and fined $24,000.

These convictions have spurred prosecutors in several other states to bring similar criminal charges against corporations and corporate officials for egregious conduct causing employee injuries and fatalities. Ironically, employers, who staunchly opposed the creation of a national agency to enforce safety in the workplace, now seek to use OSHA as a shield against such prosecutions. The Film Recovery officials and other defendant employers, as well as business trade associations, claim that the Occupational Safety and Health Act of 1970 (OSH Act), the statute that established OSHA, preempts state efforts to prosecute employers for workplace accidents.

The first state courts to consider the issue have reached different conclusions. This year, in State v. Sabine Consolidated, Inc., a county court judge in Austin, Texas rejected a preemption claim by a construction company official charged with criminal negligence in the deaths of two workers killed when the

walls of a trench caved in. Several months later, however, in People v. Chicago Magnet Wire Corp., an intermediate appeals court in Illinois found that the OSH Act does preempt state criminal prosecutions, and dismissed indictments for aggravated battery and reckless conduct against officials at a Chicago manufacturing firm. The Illinois court ruled that unless a state receives prior approval from OSHA to administer its own workplace health and safety program, the state cannot prosecute employers for workplace injuries. Both the Texas and Illinois rulings are on appeal, as is the Film Recovery case. As other prosecutions progress, defendants are certain to raise the issue in other state courts as well.

This Note explores the issue of federal preemption of state criminal prosecutions for industrial injuries and fatalities. Part I outlines the basic framework of the OSH Act and the provisions relating to the federal-state relationship. Part II examines the language, structure, and legislative history of the Act in light of preemption doctrine and considers policy and fairness issues. The Note argues that the OSH Act does not preempt state criminal prosecutions. The express preemption language in the Act was not meant to cover such prosecutions, nor is preemption implied. Moreover, state prosecutions do not conflict with the Act, but rather complement it. To turn the OSH Act into a shield to protect employers rather than workers would completely undermine Congress' intent.

I. THE OSH ACT

The declared purpose of the OSH Act is 'to assure so far as possible every working man and woman in the Nation safe and healthful working conditions and to preserve our human resources.' Congress enacted the legislation in response to what appeared to be an epidemic of industrial injuries and deaths. A bipartisan consensus developed in Congress that existing state regulations were but "a sneeze in a hurricane" and that federal action was needed.

The Act established a regulatory program designed primarily to prevent injuries, not to assess penalties for injuries already suffered. Congress gave the Secretary of Labor the power to promulgate health and safety standards for workplaces and established OSHA to enforce those standards through routine inspections and investigations. The Act not only requires employers to comply with specific OSHA standards but also imposes a general duty on employers to provide a workplace 'free from recognized hazards that are causing or are likely to cause death or serious physical harm.'

The enforcement scheme provides for both civil and criminal sanctions. Violators of OSHA standards or of the general duty clause may face civil penalties

---

of up to $1000 for 'serious' violations and up to $10,000 for 'willful' or repeated violations. The statute also provides for criminal fines and up to six months imprisonment, but only for willful violations that cause an employee death. In practice, OSHA has only rarely employed the available criminal sanctions.

Section 18 of the Act addresses the federal-state relationship. Section 18(a) provides that '[n]othing in this chapter shall prevent any State agency or court from asserting jurisdiction under State law over any occupational safety or health issue with respect to which no [OSHA] standard is in effect.' Section 18(b) provides that any state 'which, at any time, desires to assume responsibility for development and the enforcement therein of occupational safety and health standards relating to any . . . issue with respect to which a Federal standard has been promulgated . . . shall submit a State plan for the development of such standards and their enforcement.' Such plans will be approved, the statute provides, only if the Secretary of Labor certifies that the state standards are 'at least as effective' as federal standards and that the state will devote adequate resources to the administration and enforcement of the standards. The Secretary has no statutory authority to reject state standards as too strict. States can and occasionally do adopt more stringent standards and enforcement schemes than OSHA's.

The OSH Act also includes a saving clause, section 4(b)(4), which seems in tension with the apparently preemptive language of section 18. Section 4(b)(4) provides:

Nothing in [the Act] shall be construed to supersede or in any manner affect any workmen's compensation law or to enlarge or diminish or affect in any other manner the common law or statutory rights, duties, or liabilities of employers and employees under any law with respect to injuries, diseases, or death of employees arising out of, or in the course of, employment.

From its inception, OSHA has been the target of tremendous criticism. Advocates of strong workplace safety regulation have found the agency too weak, and employers have complained of costly and unnecessary bureaucratic intervention. The Reagan administration has expressly tried to change OSHA's approach. It sought, unsuccessfully, to require cost-benefit justification for all OSHA standards. The administration also sought a shift from an adversarial enforcement strategy to one of consultation and cooperation with employers. Union officials, members of Congress, and others have roundly complained that the administration is taking the teeth out of OSHA and gutting its enforcement efforts. The recent spate of criminal charges filed by local prosecutors against employers for industrial injuries and deaths has come partly in response to the success of the Film Recovery prosecution, but also in large measure as a direct response to the perceived relaxation of enforcement by OSHA.

II. The OSH Act and Federal Preemption Principles

Federal law may preempt action by states in three general ways. First, Congress can preempt expressly by stating explicitly that any state law within a given field shall be superseded by federal law. Second, preemption is implied if Congress evidences an intent to occupy a given field, leaving no room for state regulation. Third, state law is preempted if it conflicts with federal law.

In all three situations, congressional intent is the 'ultimate touch-stone' for deciding whether a specific state action is preempted by federal law. As the Supreme Court has stated, there is always a presumption that 'the historic police powers of the States were not to be superseded by the Federal Act unless that was the clear and manifest purpose of Congress.'

This presumption 'provides assurance that 'the federal-state balance' will not be disturbed unintentionally by Congress or unnecessarily by the courts,' and it is particularly strong in cases involving state laws and regulations that lie within the traditional purview of state police power, such as health and safety and crime.

A. Express Preemption

The first argument litigants have made in support of OSHA preemption is that section 18 of the Act expressly preempts state criminal prosecutions for injuries caused by hazards regulated by OSHA. Proponents of this argument interpret section 18(a) as precluding states from asserting jurisdiction over any issue for which a federal standard has been promulgated, unless the state obtains OSHA approval to enforce its own state plan under section 18(b).

Although some cases and certain OSHA regulations arguably support this interpretation of the Act, which would preempt all assertions of state jurisdiction when a federal standard is in effect, such a reading gives broader preemptive power to section 18 than the language of the Act suggests. Section 18(a) preserves state jurisdiction over issues for which no federal standard has been adopted; it does not say that states have no authority when a federal standard has been adopted. Section 18(b), not section 18(a), supplies the applicable rule when a federal standard has been adopted: if a state wants to develop and enforce its own standards relating to issues for which a federal standard is in effect, it must gain OSHA approval of a state enforcement program.

* * *

Besides the Chicago Magnet Wire court, only one court has interpreted section 18 as preempting state law other than standards. Although a few courts have framed their decisions in language suggesting a broader reading of section 18, standards have been at issue in every other case in which courts have preempted state laws under section 18. Chicago Magnet Wire appears to be the only case—not only under the OSH Act, but under any federal regulatory law—in which federal regulation has been held to preempt state enforcement of general criminal statutes governing reckless and intentional conduct that threatens public safety.

OSHA itself has interpreted the Act as not preempting enforcement of state and local fire prevention laws in workplaces, even if the state does not have an approved plan. The United States Court of Appeals for the Third Circuit has said that OSHA standards govern only occupational safety and health issues and 'do not preempt state laws that regulate other concerns.' Similarly, general criminal laws touch on broader community concerns than mere violation of regulatory standards; criminal law stigmatizes blameworthy conduct. The common features of these two different types of 'regulation' should not obscure their essential differences, and the fact that section 18 preempts one does not mean it preempts the other.

Given the presumption against preemption, courts should not interpret either section 18(a), which does not address the situation in which there are OSHA standards, or section 18(b), which addresses only standards, as implying that Congress intended to preempt criminal laws. Moreover, reading section 18 broadly to preempt general criminal laws would conflict with section 4(b)(4), which states that 'nothing in this Act shall be construed to . . . enlarge or diminish or affect in any other manner the common law or statutory rights, duties, or liabilities of employers . . . under any law with respect to injuries, diseases, or death of employees.'

Even without this explicit saving clause, the preemption of state criminal prosecutions would directly contravene the Act's express purpose of 'assur[ing] so far as possible every working man and woman in the Nation safe and healthful working conditions.'

B. Occupying the Field

The Supreme Court has frequently stated that Congress may demonstrate its intent to occupy a field of regulation by the comprehensiveness of its legislation. The Chicago Magnet Wire court relied on a combination of this doctrine and the express preemption argument discussed in the previous section to find that state criminal prosecutions were preempted. The structure and legislative history of the Act, however,

do not support such an interpretation. Although OSHA regulations are complex and extensive, they reflect the complexity of the subject matter, not an intent by Congress to make safety and health regulation an exclusively federal concern.

* * *

C. Conflict Preemption

The third possible ground for preemption would arise if state criminal prosecutions conflicted with either the administration of the OSH Act or its goals and purposes. The first test of conflict preemption is whether it is impossible to comply with both the state and the federal law—in other words, whether compliance with one standard requires violation of the other. Under this test, state criminal prosecutions would virtually never be preempted. The OSH Act and state criminal laws would conflict only if OSHA required a specific practice that the state prohibited, or vice-versa.

The second test of conflict preemption is whether state criminal prosecutions 'stand[s] as an obstacle to the accomplishment and execution of the full purposes and objectives of Congress.' Under this test, the federal interest may be one expressly articulated by statute or it may be implicit in the nature of the statute or the subject matter being regulated. The three factors that generally signal an implicit need for exclusive federal superintendence are a tradition of federal dominance of the subject matter, a need for national uniformity, and a statutory scheme that involves a careful balancing of interests.

The language, structure, and history of the OSH Act demonstrate that neither the express goals of the Act nor any of these implicit factors weigh in favor of preempting state criminal prosecutions. Prosecutions of employers whose workers are killed or maimed do not conflict with the Act's explicit goal of 'assur[ing] so far as possible every working man and woman in the Nation safe and healthful working conditions.' Far from conflicting with this goal, state criminal prosecutions advance it. Nor do state criminal prosecutions intrude on an area of traditional national control. To the contrary, the police power and control over violent crime are quintessentially the functions of state governments.

* * *

D. Policy and Fairness Issues

Rather than conflict with the OSH Act, state criminal prosecutions effectively complement it. Under the OSH Act, the federal government serves a function that states were unable to perform effectively on their own: developing and enforcing minimum health and safety standards. Through criminal prosecutions, the states retain authority over what they do best: punishing particularly egregious conduct and protecting their citizens against criminally negligent, reckless, or willful conduct. Federal statutes should not be interpreted so rigidly as to 'prevent States from undertaking supplementary efforts toward [the] very same end.'

Additionally, state criminal prosecutions may serve as a useful check against implementation failure, particularly in light of the unavailability of a private right of action under the OSH Act and the Supreme Court's general reluctance to allow citizen suits to compel agency action. State criminal investigations and prosecutions may also help OSHA itself by bringing the agency's attention to hazards it had not sufficiently recognized. Thus, if OSHA, through lack of enforcement or lax standard setting, fails to protect workers adequately, state criminal laws provide a backup mechanism by which injurious activity can be punished, without the drawbacks of private rights of action or rights to compel agency action.

Even if it did not offend the goals of the OSH Act, a state criminal prosecution might nonetheless conflict with fundamental fairness if the state prosecuted a company that was in full compliance with applicable OSHA standards. The company would have a strong argument that it had no knowledge that its conduct was illegal. Moreover, from a policy perspective, if OSHA standards are set at optimal levels, stricter requirements under state criminal law could deter useful, productive employer activity. These considerations suggest caution in the use of state criminal sanctions.

As a practical matter, however, prosecutions in such cases are unlikely, precisely because compliance with OSHA standards would be strong evidence against a charge of reckless or intentional harm. Also, it would not be unfair to prosecute those companies that fully complied with OSHA rules but that were fully aware that hazards in their workplaces were seriously injuring substantial numbers of their workers or exposing them to an unreasonably high risk. The OSH Act itself allows for civil fines in such situations under the general duty clause, but up to a maximum of only $10,000. To provide more deterrence, such employers should also be subject to penalties under state criminal laws if their conduct is particularly egregious and causes serious or fatal injury. Given its unalloyed pro-safety aim, the OSH Act provides no statutory basis for preempting a state's decision to impose tougher limits or stiffer penalties on its employers than those imposed by OSHA or by other states.

III. Conclusion

Preemption doctrine does not justify using the OSH Act to block state criminal prosecutions for workplace injuries and deaths. The express preemption provisions of the Act do not extend to state criminal laws, the Act was not intended to occupy the field of health and safety protection for workers, and there is no conflict between state prosecutions in that field and the purposes and administration of the OSH Act. To interpret the OSH Act as preempting state criminal prosecutions would flatly contradict the Act's purpose.

The OSH Act established a federal scheme to accomplish what the states seemed unable or unwilling to do on their own: create effective standards to prevent accidents and diseases in the workplace. Congress intended to fill a gap in the existing state-by-state regulatory framework, not to replace it with a narrower framework. A system of OSHA regulation supplemented by state criminal prosecutions thus provides an appropriate range of governmental responses to dangerous employer practices. In practice, state criminal prosecutions are likely to play only a limited role in the overall enforcement scheme. They no doubt will confront the same problems that stymied state enforcement schemes before OSHA: the difficulty of overcoming the procedural barriers and higher burden of proof under criminal statutes, and the economic pressure to police industry less vigorously than competing states. State criminal prosecutions, therefore, are by no means a substitute for a strong and effective OSHA. They do, however, provide a useful supplement to ensure that workers are more adequately protected and that particularly egregious employer conduct does not go unpunished.

Michael B. Metzger, *Corporate Criminal Liability for Defective Products: Politics, Problems and Prospects,* 73 Geo. L.J. 1 (1984)*

Introduction

The idea of the corporation—the attribution of many of the legal characteristics of a human being to a legal fiction—has been described as "one of the most potent concepts in history." Corporations have been incredibly productive, forming the backbone of the most successful

---

* Reprinted with permission of the publisher, The Georgetown Law Journal © 1984 Georgetown University.

economic system in history. Indeed, the prevalence of large, special-purpose organizations like corporations is one of the hallmarks of the modern world. Yet the benefits corporations have brought have not been without cost. As corporations have grown to become the central actors on our national economic stage, so, too, has our concern with regaining some effective measure of control over their activities.

The large, publicly held corporation has been described as soulless, often corrupt, and possessed of inordinate and unjustifiable power. It has a far greater capacity to do harm than does an individual wrongdoer and frequently acts in ways inimical to the public good. The suspicion has arisen that these powerful organizations are effectively beyond the control of any one individual. It has long been an article of faith for most commentators that the separation of ownership and control which typifies most large corporations precludes effective shareholder control over management. There is reason to doubt whether even managers are capable of fully controlling the large organizations that are officially in their charge. Likewise the law, which was developed with individual wrongdoers in mind, has not responded adequately to the particular problems associated with controlling organizational behavior.

In this century the criminal law has been increasingly used to achieve an acceptable level of corporate control. Perhaps the logical culmination of this trend was the indictment of Ford Motor Company on a charge of reckless homicide for the deaths of three Indiana girls in the fiery crash of a 1973 Pinto. The event was heralded as a historic first, sure to be followed by a series of similar prosecutions. Ford ultimately won the case, and the ensuing years have not ushered in a new era of corporate criminal liability for defective products. It seems likely, however, that this will not be the last attempt to hold a manufacturer criminally responsible for the harm caused by its defective product.

Yet in many instances criminal sanctions have been ineffective, whether applied to corporations or to their employees. Although we know very little about how corporations make decisions or how corporations would respond to the various sanctions that are available or have been proposed, our relative ignorance has not dissuaded some commentators from urging increased application of criminal sanctions to corporate conduct. The proposals, most of them controversial and all of uncertain impact, range from the relatively straightforward, like dispensing with proof of *mens rea* as a required element of criminal liability and increasing the penalties incident to conviction, to the novel, like employing innovative individual and corporate sentencing procedures and restructuring corporations in various ways.

The continued concern with deterring certain particularly offensive manufacturer conduct is evidenced by the increasing frequency and amount of punitive damages awards in products liability cases; this despite the statutory "counterrevolution" in products liability laws aimed at retreating from some of the perceived excesses of products liability suits. Proponents of increased corporate criminal sanctions, however, argue that only the criminal law affords the heightened levels of deterrence and punishment necessary to dissuade manufacturers from knowingly or recklessly marketing defective products. Civil suits may not produce the socially desired level of deterrence because manufacturers may not have to bear the full costs associated with knowingly marketing a defective product. Criminal prosecutions may increase the likelihood of civil suits and thus enhance the probability that manufacturers will bear a greater share of the costs associated with their activities. The punitive damages awarded in civil suit have been widely criticized for their unfortunate tendency to punish the innocent as well as the guilty. While the huge criminal fines advocated by some commentators plainly have a similar potential, there are less expensive, and perhaps more efficacious, ways of criminally punishing corporate entities. Extending the criminal sanction into the realm of products liability would also be consistent with the tendency toward increased reliance on the criminal law as a corporate control device. Finally, perhaps certain kinds of manufacturer misconduct merit the "social and moral condemnation" that only the imposition of criminal sanctions can achieve.

It therefore seems likely that those who occupy policy making positions in our society—be they legislators, judges, or prosecutors—will soon be confronted with demands that criminal sanctions be applied to certain kinds of manufacturer misconduct relating to defective products. Whether such a step is socially desirable—that is, whether the net social benefits of imposing criminal products liability sanctions outweigh the net social costs—is by no means obvious. To make an informed decision requires the answers to many questions: What is the nature of the criminal sanction? In what circumstances and to what kinds of offenders is it best employed? What success have previous efforts at controlling corporate behavior with criminal sanctions enjoyed? Are noncriminal devices to achieve the same objectives available? If not, can criminal sanctions be used more effectively to control corporate behavior? If we decide to employ criminal sanctions in this instance, should they be imposed upon corporations, their employees, or both?

The answers to these and a host of subsidiary questions are fraught with controversy. Moreover, the answers do not depend just upon our knowledge of the nature of the criminal sanction and our experience with it as a means of corporate control. We must also seek a better understanding of the corporation. How are corporate decisions made? More specifically, why might a corporation knowingly or recklessly market a defective product, or continue to market a product once its defective nature has become manifest? Who is really "responsible" for such decisions? The answers to these questions can go a long way toward illuminating both the sources of many of our perceived failures at achieving effective corporate control and the paths we must follow to enhance such control.

What follows explores these and other questions relevant to the issue of criminal products liability. The spirit of the exercise is one of an initial exercise in cartography: an attempt to chart a crude map whose details must be filled out by subsequent exploration. . . .

III. Punitive Damages in Products Liability Cases

The punitive damages concept has ancient lineage, although it gained acceptance in common-law jurisdictions only in the eighteenth century. The essential purpose of punitive damages has remained unchanged: "to punish flagrant wrongdoers and to deter them and others from engaging in flagrant conduct in the future." Punitive damages thus are appropriate only where the defendant's conduct evinces a degree of moral culpability significantly beyond that of ordinary negligence. Yet despite the relatively long tenure of punitive damages in our legal system, their application has fostered "a history of stormy controversy" which has resurfaced with vigor over the appropriateness of punitive damages in products liability cases.

Proponents of punitive damages in products liability cases argue that punitive damages are necessary to deter manufacturers from knowingly marketing defective products, to punish those who do so, and to compensate fully the victims of manufacturer misconduct. In the absence of punitive damages, proponents argue, "many manufacturers may be tempted to maximize profits by marketing products known to be defective and to absorb resulting injury claims as a cost of doing business." That is, to the extent that manufacturers operate as rational profit-maximizers, they may perceive that the profits of marketing defective products exceed the costs of paying only compensatory damages to those injured. For, as rational manufacturers well know, "only a fraction [of those injured by a defective product] will be able to identify the

defect as the cause of their injuries, fewer still will sue and . . . even fewer will have the stamina and wherewithal to prosecute to judgment a difficult and expensive lawsuit." Likewise, the vagaries of litigation insure that some valid claims will be defeated. Compensatory damages therefore will not force manufacturers to bear the full social costs of marketing a defective product. The availability of punitive damages, though, arguably makes manufacturers more willing to correct defects, because punitive damages furnish additional incentives for private plaintiffs to uncover and prove manufacturer misconduct. The availability of punitive damages thereby increases both the likelihood that the manufacturer will be identified and punished, and the probable severity of the punishment.

Where deterrence has failed, punitive damages, like criminal penalties, can provide both punishment and revenge and so serve both utilitarian and retributive ends. Punitive damages proponents also argue that punitive damages can serve compensatory ends by reducing substantially the burden of attorney's fees and other expenses of litigation for which recovery is not allowed. Finally, one commentator has argued that the potential award of punitive damages may encourage more manufacturers to settle out of court because the availability of punitive damages so dramatically enhances the risks of litigation. These alleged advantages have led some observers to conclude that punitive damages offer the best available legal advice for controlling reprehensible manufacturer misconduct.

Punitive damages remain less than ideal for controlling undesirable corporate behavior. Proponents of punitive damages tend to assume a rational-actor/profit-maximization model of corporate behavior. They assume that a corporation will respond optimally to prevent actions for which liability could be imposed, or, failing that, will respond to punishment in a rational fashion designed to prevent a recurrence of the behavior. Yet even rational-actor organizations may have difficulty weighing the potential liability risks of marketing a defective product against the economic benefits to be reaped from doing so. The effect that the threat or imposition of punitive damages liability would have on an organization that fails to conform to the rational-actor model is even more problematic. Punitive damages impose no direct burdens on the managers who make corporate decisions, and the lack of congruence between the interests of managers and of their corporate employers may mean that individual managers have incentives to take risks that are not in the best interests of their organizations.

Punitive damages awards of sufficient size would perhaps provoke power responses even from nonrational organizations, but awards of that size would only heighten the risk of overdeterrence. Also, the "private attorney general" aspect of punitive damages which is lauded by its supporters carries the same risks of distortion of proof and incoherent legal evolution which accompany private treble damages for criminal violations. Finally, if we wish to continue to rely on monetary penalties to control undesirable corporate behavior, something is to be said for criminal fines, which inure to the public treasury rather than to private plaintiffs. Opponents of punitive damages in products liability cases have long argued that the criminal law is the proper mechanism for controlling the aggravated corporate misconduct for which punitive damages awards are appropriate. One court, however, has asserted that punitive damages are necessary because government safety standards and the criminal law do not adequately protect consumers from defective products. Certainly punitive damages are sufficiently problematic to be discarded if criminal penalties could be tailored to provide an equal or enhanced level of prevention at a lower social cost. Any such conclusion, however, must rest on an understanding of the operation of the criminal sanction in the corporate context. . . .

THE DESIRED DIMENSIONS OF CRIMINAL PRODUCTS LIABILITY

Courts could employ existing criminal statutes, assuming these were properly worded or sympathetically interpreted, to assess criminal penalties in the manufacturing context. Reckless conduct that causes the death of a human being supports an involuntary-manslaughter or reckless-homicide prosecution in most states. And while most states require more than ordinary tort negligence for manslaughter, a few states have defined manslaughter as negligently causing the death of another. Products that produce nonfatal injuries could also give rise to criminal liability, because reckless or negligent conduct that causes bodily harm supports a battery indictment in most jurisdictions. Indeed, actual harm is not always a necessary predicate to corporate criminal liability, since some jurisdictions have passed "endangerment" statutes which make criminal the reckless creation of a risk of harm to others and which could arguably be used against manufacturers of products that embody such a risk.

Using traditional criminal statutes appears less than desirable, however. The most obvious problem is the *ex post facto* application of traditional criminal statutes in a new context. Certainly it is questionable whether legislatures ever intended criminal statutes to apply in the manufacturing context. Doing so arguably contravenes basic criminal-law principles of *nullem crimen sine lege* and *nulla poena sine lege*. Novel application

of broadly worded, traditional statutes would afford prosecutors undue discretion in deciding which cases to prosecute. A traditional statute provides no express guidance about how to resolve the many difficult issues of, *inter alia,* manufacturing costs, technological feasibility, and safety choices inherent in product-related cases, and would create the risk of "lawless" verdicts based on jury antipathy. The jury might also find it difficult to apply traditional criminal-law terms like "reckless" or "negligent" to new situations. Defendants would have little or no guidance concerning courses of conduct that would minimize their chances of future liability. A further difficulty is that general criminal statutes furnish no guidance on whether compliance with federal regulatory standards should provide a defense against liability. There are significant due process concerns about the ability of the state to punish a manufacturer for conduct that has conformed to such standards.

Product-related prosecutions under existing criminal statutes also raise disturbing problems of multiple punishment similar to those encountered in civil cases. Although multiple prosecutions for the "same offense" violate the fifth amendment's double jeopardy clause, multiple prosecutions for similar product-related offenses appear to be possible.

Individuals within the corporate hierarchy could thus conceivably face multiple indictments for one allegedly wrong product decision. Manufacturers exposed to multiple prosecutions would face the prospect of multiple cash, or perhaps equity, fines, or the daunting prospect of several courts ordering disparate internal structural reforms under judicially imposed restructuring.

It seems obvious that criminal statutes drafted expressly for regulating the products area are required. What should such statutes look like? The first question concerns what kinds of product-related behavior ought to be made criminal. Our previous inquiries indicate that only behavior considered appropriate for punitive damages—concealing known dangers associated with a product, grossly deficient product-testing or quality-control procedures, knowing violation of legislative or administrative product-safety standards, failure to warn customers about or to reduce non-obvious dangers, and failure to warn consumers about or to take steps to remedy product dangers discovered after a product has been marketed—evidences sufficient culpability to merit the criminal sanction.

Whether we should also require that the proscribed behavior produce some tangible harm before criminal liability attaches is a more difficult question. Certainly a statute could be drafted imposing liability when the conduct creates a risk of death or serious bodily injury. Moral culpability, and hence the need to deter, rehabilitate, or punish the offender, does not vary with the degree of harm the behavior actually produces. Making criminal "dangerous" behavior in the absence of harm has been criticized on moral grounds as "cowardice," however. On utilitarian grounds, it appears that the public will more readily accept corporate criminality if the harms resulting therefrom resemble those resulting from traditional criminal behavior. The desire for retribution probably increases with the magnitude of the harm associated with the wrongdoer's conduct, and therefore restricting liability to conduct involving serious harm is likely to assure greater prosecutorial interest and to enhance the possibilities of a stern reaction by judges and juries. Also, limiting corporate criminal liability to conduct that causes serious harm can minimize the potential for multiple prosecutions that endangerment statutes would pose. Finally, given the nature of the product risks at issue and the large number of persons exposed thereto, it is unlikely that a manufacturer will fortuitously avoid punishment because the product failed to produce sufficient harm. Good reasons therefore exist to suggest that at least initial excursions into the uncharted realm of criminal product liability be confined to making criminal behavior that has produced demonstrable and serious harm.

Another issue in criminal products liability is the level of intent required for liability. Difficulties of proof have led to suggestions that some form of strict or vicarious liability may be necessary to achieve adequate deterrence. Both strict liability and vicarious liability represent dramatic departures from the criminal law's traditional insistence of proof of personal culpability.

Vicarious liability has most commonly been applied in public-welfare offenses. Public-welfare statutes are distinguishable from ordinary criminal statutes in several respects: they regulate behavior that is essentially noncriminal and impose criminal sanctions as an adjunct to other noncriminal enforcement; they involve conduct that merits little or no moral approbation and for which only light penalties are imposed; and they tend to impose vicarious liability or liability for omissions. Although the Supreme Court has recently acknowledged that strict liability offenses "do not invariably offend constitutional requirements," it has also observed that such offenses possess "a generally disfavored status."

Dispensing with proof of individual culpability has encountered significant resistance from the commentators as well as the courts. The idea that difficulties of proof justify imposing personal liability without proof of personal fault has been labeled "the most desperate and uncertain justification . . . which could possibly be made." Nor has there been universal acceptance of the idea that the need for deterrence, standing alone, is a sufficient justification for dispensing with proof of individual culpability. In any event, critics convincingly argue that making morally neutral conduct criminal will not necessarily enhance deterrence. The greater procedural protections afforded criminal defendants and the higher burden of proof that the state must bear make enforcement and conviction more difficult to achieve under criminal law than under civil. In addition, making morally neutral conduct criminal dilutes the moral impact of the criminal sanction, with a consequent loss of deterrent force. Certainly juries and courts are unlikely to impose meaningful sanctions on defendants whose behavior fails to demonstrate significant culpability. Linking liability to culpability may also maximize deterrence because potential defendants are then aware that they are committing an offense. Thus, despite the difficult burdens of proof, neither prevention nor retribution appear to be adequately served by dispensing with proof of culpability as a prerequisite for liability.

Requiring culpability does not necessarily mean requiring proof that a particular defendant actually authorized, commanded, or acquiesced in a violation, however. Some observers have attempted to bridge the gap between strict and vicarious liability and more traditional bases of criminal liability by suggesting that an affirmative duty to supervise be imposed on corporate officers who could then be held criminally responsible for negligent or reckless supervision. Such liability is arguably not vicarious because the defendant is being punished not for the acts of employees, but rather for the defendant's own breach of duty. Even advocates of such liability, however, are chary of attaching significant sanctions to supervisory offenses, given the minimal degree of culpability involved. Indeed, others have questions whether such offenses involve culpability sufficient to assure the regular imposition of penalties severe enough to provide credible deterrence. Prudence, therefore, seems to dictate that individual criminal liability for defective products be premised upon the defendant's reckless or knowing behavior which directly contributed to the proscribed harm. Requiring such a high level of culpability may often mean that there are no individuals within the corporate hierarchy who can be indicted. In a great many cases, however, the wrongful conduct will not be attributable to individuals who are so clearly blameworthy as to merit a criminal sanction.

Assuming that proof of culpability is required, Professor Owen's flagrant-indifference standard is as appropriate to corporate criminal liability as it is to punitive damages. This objective test could be applied to corporations in the criminal context on the basis of the collective knowledge of their employees.

Numerous other culpability issues unique to the product-manufacturing context should be addressed by any well-considered criminal products liability statute. For example, unless the statute expressly addresses the issue of cost-benefit analysis by manufacturers, there is every reason to suppose that evidence of this activity will be introduced to prove manufacturer culpability. A statute should provide that a manufacturer's use of cost-benefit analysis, standing alone, is not a basis for liability. Only when the manufacturer's analysis or the conclusions drawn therefrom are so distorted as to evidence a "flagrant indifference to public safety" should liability be imposed.

Likewise, a statute should explicitly address the effect, if any, of a product's compliance with applicable administrative or legislative standards. At a minimum, compliance with standards should create a defense to liability, unless the prosecution can prove that the defendant knew or should have known that the standard was grossly inadequate.

In a related vein, a criminal products liability statute should address the issue of good-faith corporate efforts to prevent violations. Although the weight of authority rejects a general "due diligence" defense to corporate criminal liability, the arguments in favor of such a defense are fairly convincing. A primary justification for imposing criminal liability is to encourage diligent corporate supervisory efforts aimed at avoiding violations. Imposing liability in the face of such efforts not only seems unfair, but also may undermine deterrence by discouraging corporate compliance efforts and diminishing the stigma of a criminal conviction. This judicial reluctance may be due to a fear that harm-causing corporations could easily avoid all liability under a good-faith defense. Such fears are probably inappropriate in the products liability context, however, because manufacturers who successfully put on a good-faith defense against criminal liability are likely to be held strictly liable for compensatory damages in civil suits. While we may not want to punish such manufacturers further by imposing criminal fines, however, repeated instances of otherwise culpable product decisions despite apparent good-faith efforts to the contrary may give rise to the inference that intra-firm bureaucratic flaws are at work which may be amenable to amelioration by judicial intervention. A past history of similar problems should militate against exculpation via a good-faith defense. Finally, if a good-faith defense is adopted, some considerations should be given to the role of a process standard in conscious-design cases.

A criminal products liability statute should also expressly address the disturbing potential for multiple prosecutions. While the prospect of multiple prosecutions for each distinct harm resulting from behavior traditionally adjudged as criminal may not be offensive, the prospect of multiple prosecutions, whether of individuals or of their corporate employers, for behavior that may amount only to serious errors of judgment is considerably more daunting. Many states, however, are unlikely to eschew exercising their sovereign right to prosecute conduct that is actionable under state law merely because a defendant has already been convicted for the same act in another jurisdiction. Thus it would be desirable that Congress preempt state efforts by enacting a federal criminal products liability statute.

Finally, if the criminal sanction is to intrude into the realm of products liability we must also address the relationship between criminal and civil products liability. This involves looking at not only the effect that criminal liability should have on the availability of punitive damages, but also at the offensive collateral estoppel effect that a criminal conviction should have in subsequent civil cases where compensatory damages are at issue. Although in the past the courts have rarely given criminal judgments collateral estoppel effect in subsequent civil suits, "a rapidly growing number" of courts are now willing to do so. This development may have a potentially dramatic impact on products liability cases. The criminal conviction of a manufacturer based on a defective design, for example, could trigger a multitude of civil suits. Plaintiffs' chances of recovery in these suits would be significantly enhanced if they were freed from the challenging task of proving that the product was defectively designed. Thus a single criminal conviction could "trigger millions of dollars of [civil] liability."

There are good reasons to give to criminal convictions stemming from trials collateral estoppel effect in subsequent civil litigation. Defendants in criminal trials receive procedural protections beyond those afforded to civil litigants and therefore cannot readily question either the adequacy of their opportunity to litigate the issues or the reliability of the resultant determination. Also, criminal defendants normally have sufficient incentives to mount a vigorous defense to the charges against them. A conviction under a well-drafted criminal products liability statute would likely be more useful to civil plaintiffs in subsequent civil suits than would a conviction under a general criminal statute: A plaintiff could prove with relative ease that critical issues like defectiveness of design were necessarily decided against the defendant in a trial brought under a criminal products liability statute. Giving collateral estoppel effect to criminal convictions may encourage civil suits by plaintiffs who otherwise would not have pursued a remedy, and may facilitate recovery by some plaintiffs who might otherwise have been denied recovery. Collateral estoppel could thus significantly augment the deterrent potential of criminal statutes and further reduce the need for punitive damages.

Although recent developments have made it easier for plaintiffs to use collateral estoppel offensively in civil contexts, however, there apparently exists "a growing judicial reluctance to apply collateral estoppel in products liability cases. This trend probably results both from troubling aspects of collateral estoppel in general and from special problems inherent in its application to products liability. First, offensive, nonmutual collateral estoppel may encourage some plaintiffs to bring suits that otherwise would not have been brought, while encouraging others to delay filing suit rather than to intervene in existing suits. Thus the judicial-economy rationale often used to support collateral estoppel does not necessarily justify offensive collateral estoppel. A more grave consideration is that giving a prior judgment offensive collateral estoppel effect in future cases involving the same product design" could result in a single jury, sitting in review of certain limited facts, [entering] a verdict which would establish safety standards for a given product for the entire country. Yet given the complex nature of products liability issues, there may be a particularly great risk that the first jury verdict was erroneous. For these reasons it is probably desirable that judgments under a criminal products liability statute not be given offensive, nonmutual collateral estoppel effect in subsequent civil litigation.

CONCLUSION

To conclude our examination of the policies and problems related to criminal liability for defective products we must return to some of the questions raised earlier. Policy makers who adopt a utilitarian view of the criminal sanction must first decide whether we need an additional measure of prevention beyond that now afforded by compensatory damages awards, regulatory action, and the negative publicity attendant thereto. This decision is essentially not amendable to conclusive resolution on any objective basis.

Policymakers animated by retributionist leanings must ask whether manufacturer behavior manifest in the product context demonstrates sufficient moral culpability to merit the application of the criminal sanction. On this point, the results seem mixed: While some product-related behavior manifests a degree of moral culpability

sufficiently akin to traditional notions of criminality to merit punishment for its own sake, a large number of product-related decisions result from bureaucratic behavior and intra-organizational structural deficiencies and thus reside outside the bounds of criminality as conventionally conceived.

Policymakers who opt for enhanced levels of punishment, whether for deterrence or for retribution, should probably question the relative efficiency of the various means available for providing such punishment. Both punitive damages and the criminal sanction, the two most prominent means of punishing corporations, are less efficient than is desirable, due to our misconceptions concerning the nature of the behavior they seek to regulate. The criminal sanction, properly informed by an understanding of the nature of organizational behavior, appears to offer the best hope for enhancing prevention at a lower social cost, however. Criminal sanctions can directly reach the managers who formulate corporate policy. When applied to corporate entities, criminal sanctions in the form of judicially mandated restructuring offer hope for corporate rehabilitation while largely avoiding the spillover effects of punitive damages.

Applying the criminal sanction to product-related behavior also entails costs, both known and unknown. The most obvious of these is the diversion of scarce law-enforcement resources away from the tasks to which they are already devoted. A less obvious cost is overdeterrence or other counterproductive behavior that will reduce economic efficiency. In addition, utilizing novel sanction approaches will undoubtedly produce new enforcement dilemmas and behavioral responses whose costs will become apparent only with increased experience.

If our policymakers conclude that the deficiencies of the present products liability system are sufficiently great as to justify the risks associated with imposing criminal sanctions on manufacturers, they must recognize that the unique problems presented by criminal products liability require special criminal products liability statutes. In particular, criminal statutes must address the question of multiple criminal liability for multiple harms associated with a single product line or product-related decision, the possible defenses of compliance with regulatory standards or of general good-faith efforts, and the inter-relationship between criminal and civil liability. A proper statute would include sanctions for both corporate entities and their employees. Finally, a well-drafted statute would make criminal only behavior that manifests a significant level of moral culpability.

Ultimately, the question of gaining enhanced control over corporate behavior in the products-manufacturing context is a small part of the much larger social question of how to gain more effective control over the large organizations that dominate the nation's economy. Our currently primitive understanding of organizational behavior limits our ability to engage successfully in organizational control. The degree of success attained here and elsewhere depends largely upon our ability to extend the horizons of our knowledge in this critical area of human behavior.